CURRENT
BIOGRAPHY
YEARBOOK
1974

CURRENT BIOGRAPHY YEARBOOK

1974

EDITOR

CHARLES MORITZ

ASSOCIATE EDITORS

EVELYN LOHR
HENRY SLOAN
KIERAN DUGAN
JUDITH GRAHAM

NEW YORK

THE H. W. WILSON COMPANY

THIRTY-FIFTH ANNUAL CUMULATION—1974

PRINTED IN THE UNITED STATES OF AMERICA

Copyright © 1974, 1975
by
THE H. W. WILSON COMPANY

International Standard Book. No. (0-8242-0551-0)

Library of Congress Catalog Card No. (40-27432)

PREFACE

The aim of CURRENT BIOGRAPHY YEARBOOK 1974, like that of the preceding volumes in this series of annual dictionaries of contemporary biography, now in its fourth decade of publication, is to provide the reference librarian, the student, or any researcher with brief, objective, accurate, and well-documented biographical articles about living leaders in all fields of human accomplishment the world over.

CURRENT BIOGRAPHY YEARBOOK 1974 carries on the policy of including new and updated biographical sketches that supersede earlier, outdated articles. Sketches have been made as accurate and objective as possible through careful researching by CURRENT BIOGRAPHY writers in newspapers, magazines, authoritative reference books, and news releases of both government and private agencies. Immediately after they are published in the eleven monthly issues, articles are submitted to biographees to give them an opportunity to suggest corrections in time for CURRENT BIOGRAPHY YEARBOOK. To take account of major changes in the careers of biographees, sketches have also been revised before they are included in the yearbook. With the exception of occasional interviews, the questionnaire filled out by the biographee remains the main source of direct information.

In the back of the volume under *Organizations* can be found the names of men and women who head organizations. Persons who are not professional authors but who have written books are listed under *Nonfiction* or *Literature* in addition to their vocational fields. The annual bestowal of Nobel Prizes and other significant awards has added articles about their winners to the volume.

The pages immediately following contain: *Explanations; Key to Reference Abbreviations; Key to Pronunciation;* and *Key to Abbreviations.* The indexes at the end of the volume are *Biographical References; Periodicals and Newspapers Consulted; Classification by Profession;* and *Cumulated Index, 1971-1974.* The 1940-1950 index can be found in the 1950 yearbook; the 1951-1960 index, in the 1960 yearbook, and the 1961-1970 index, in the 1970 yearbook. The three decennial indexes are cumulated in CURRENT BIOGRAPHY CUMULATED INDEX 1940-1970.

For their assistance in preparing CURRENT BIOGRAPHY YEARBOOK 1974, I should like to thank the associate editors and Dorothy McEntee, editorial assistant.

Charles Moritz

Explanations

Authorities for biographees' full names, with some exceptions, are the bibliographical publications of The Wilson Company. When a biographee prefers a certain name form, that is indicated in the heading of the article: for example, Niemöller, (Friedrich Gustav Emil) Martin means that he is usually referred to as Martin Niemöller. When a professional name is used in the heading, as for example, Anne Bancroft, the real name (in this case Annemarie Italiano) appears in the article itself.

The heading of each article includes the pronunciation of the name if it is unusual, date of birth (if obtainable), and occupation. The article is supplemented by a list of references to sources of biographical information, in two alphabets: (1) newspapers and periodicals and (2) books. (See the section *Biographical References*, found in the rear of this volume.)

Key to Reference Abbreviations

Reference to newspapers and periodicals are listed in abbreviated form; for example, "Sat Eve Post 217:14 S 30 '44 por" means *Saturday Evening Post*, volume 217, page 14, September 30, 1944, with portrait. (For full names, see the section *Periodicals and Newspapers Consulted*, found in the rear of this volume.)

January—Ja	July—Jl	Journal—J
February—F	August—Ag	Magazine—Mag
March—Mr	September—S	Monthly—Mo
April—Ap	October—O	Weekly—W
May—My	November—N	Portrait—por
June—Je	December—D	Review—R

KEY TO PRONUNCIATION

ā āle
â câre
a add
ä ärm

ē ēve
e end

g go

ī ice
i ill

к German ch as in *ich* (iк)

N Not pronounced, but indicates the nasal tone of the preceding vowel, as in the French *bon* (bôN).

ō ōld
ô ôrb
o odd
oi oil
o͞o o͞oze
o͝o fo͝ot
ou out

th *then*
th thin

ū cūbe
û ûrn; French eu, as in *jeu* (zhû), German ö, oe, as in *schön* (shûn), *Goethe* (gû'te)
u tub

ü Pronounced approximately as ē, with rounded lips: French u, as in *menu* (mə-nü); German ü, as in *grün*

ə the schwa, an unstressed vowel representing the sound that is spelled
  a as in sofa
  e as in fitted
  i as in edible
  o as in melon
  u as in circus

zh azure

′ = main accent

″ = secondary accent

AAAA	Amateur Athletic Association of America	**EEC**	European Economic Community
		ERP	European Recovery Program
A.A.U.	Amateur Athletic Union	**ESA**	Economic Stabilization Administration
ABA	American Bar Association		
ABC	American Broadcasting Company	**FAO**	Food and Agriculture Organization
ACA	Americans for Constitutional Action	**FBI**	Federal Bureau of Investigation
A.C.L.U.	American Civil Liberties Union	**FCC**	Federal Communications Commission
ADA	Americans for Democratic Action	**FEPC**	Fair Employment Practice Committee
AEC	Atomic Energy Commission	**FHA**	Federal Housing Administration
AEF	American Expeditionary Force	**FOA**	Foreign Operations Administration
AFL	American Federation of Labor	**FPC**	Federal Power Commission
AFL-CIO	American Federation of Labor and Congress of Industrial Organizations	**FSA**	Federal Security Agency
		FTC	Federal Trade Commission
ALA	American Library Association		
AMA	American Medical Association	**GATT**	General Agreement on Tariffs and Trade
A.P.	Associated Press		
ASCAP	American Society of Composers, Authors and Publishers	**G.B.E.**	Knight or Dame, Grand Cross Order of the British Empire
ASNE	American Society of Newspaper Editors	**G.C.B.**	Knight Grand Cross of the Bath
		G.O.P.	Grand Old Party
B.A.	Bachelor of Arts	**H.M.**	His Majesty; Her Majesty
BBC	British Broadcasting Corporation	**HUD**	Housing and Urban Development
B.D.	Bachelor of Divinity		
B.L.S.	Bachelor of Library Science	**IBM**	International Business Machine Corporation
B.S.	Bachelor of Science		
		ICBM	Intercontinental Ballistic Missile
CAA	Civil Aeronautics Administration	**ICC**	Interstate Commerce Commission
CAB	Civil Aeronautics Board	**I.C.F.T.U.**	International Confederation of Free Trade Unions
C.B.	Companion of the Bath		
C.B.E.	Commander of (the Order of) the British Empire	**IGY**	International Geophysical Year
		I.L.A.	International Longshoremen's Association
CBS	Columbia Broadcasting System		
C.E.	Civil Engineer	**I.L.G.W.U.**	International Ladies' Garment Workers' Union
CEA	Council of Economic Advisers		
C.E.D.	Committee for Economic Development	**I.L.O.**	International Labor Organization
		INS	International News Service
CENTO	Central Treaty Organization	**IRO**	International Refugee Organization
CIA	Central Intelligence Agency		
CIO	Congress of Industrial Organizations	**J.D.**	Doctor of Jurisprudence
C.M.G.	Companion of (the Order of) St. Michael and St. George		
		K.B.E.	Knight of (the Order of) the British Empire
Com.	Commodore		
CORE	Congress of Racial Equality	**K.C.**	King's Counsel
		K.C.B.	Knight Commander of the Bath
D.A.R.	Daughters of the American Revolution		
D.C.L.	Doctor of Civil Law	**L.H.D.**	Doctor of Humanities
D.D.	Doctor of Divinity	**Litt.D.**	Doctor of Letters
D.Eng.	Doctor of Engineering	**LL.B.**	Bachelor of Laws
DEW	Distant Early Warning Line	**LL.D.**	Doctor of Laws
D.F.C.	Distinguished Flying Cross		
D.J.	Doctor of Jurisprudence	**M.A.**	Master of Arts
D.Lit.	Doctor of Literature	**M.B.A.**	Master of Business Administration
D.Mus.	Doctor of Music	**MBS**	Mutual Broadcasting System
DP	Displaced Person	**M.C.E.**	Master of Civil Engineering
D.Pol.Sc.	Doctor of Political Science	**M.D.**	Doctor of Medicine
D.Sc.	Doctor of Science	**M.E.**	Master of Engineering
D.S.C.	Distinguished Service Cross	**METO**	Middle East Treaty Organization
D.S.M.	Distinguished Service Medal	**MGM**	Metro-Goldwyn-Mayer
D.S.O.	Distinguished Service Order	**M.Lit.**	Master of Literature
		M.P.	Member of Parliament
ECA	Economic Cooperation Administration	**M.P.P.D.A.**	Motion Picture Producers and Distributors of America
ECOSOC	Economic and Social Council		
EDC	Economic Defense Community	**MRP**	Mouvement Républicain Populaire

MSA	Mutual Security Agency
M.Sc.	Master of Science
Msgr.	Monsignor, Monseigneur
NAACP	National Association for the Advancement of Colored People
NAB	National Association of Broadcasters
NAM	National Association of Manufacturers
NASA	National Aeronautics and Space Administration
NATO	North Atlantic Treaty Organization
NBC	National Broadcasting Company
NEA	National Education Association
NLRB	National Labor Relations Board
N.M.U.	National Maritime Union
NRA	National Recovery Administration
NRPB	National Resources Planning Board
NYA	National Youth Administration
O.A.S.	Organization of American States
O.B.E.	Officer of (the Order of) the British Empire
OCD	Office of Civilian Defense
OEEC	Organization for European Economic Cooperation
OPA	Office of Price Administration
OPEC	Organization of Petroleum Exporting Countries
OPM	Office of Production Management
OWI	Office of War Information
P.E.N.	Poets, Playwrights, Editors, Essayists and Novelists (International Association)
Ph.B.	Bachelor of Philosophy
Ph.D.	Doctor of Philosophy
PWA	Public Works Administration
Q.C.	Queen's Counsel
RAF	Royal Air Force
RCA	Radio Corporation of America
REA	Rural Electrification Administration
RFC	Reconstruction Finance Corporation
RKO	Radio-Keith-Orpheum
ROTC	Reserve Officers' Training Corps
SAC	Strategic Air Command
SALT	Strategic Arms Limitation Talks
S.J.	Society of Jesus
SCAP	Supreme Command for the Allied Powers
SEATO	Southeast Asia Treaty Organization
SEC	Securities and Exchange Commission
SHAEF	Supreme Headquarters, Allied Expeditionary Force
SHAPE	Supreme Headquarters, Allied Powers Europe
S.J.D.	Doctor of Juridical Science
SLA	Special Libraries Association
S.T.B.	Bachelor of Sacred Theology
S.T.D.	Doctor of Sacred Theology
TVA	Tennessee Valley Authority
T.W.U.A.	Textile Workers Union of America
UAR	United Arab Republic
U.A.W.	United Automobile, Aircraft, and Agricultural Implement Workers of America
UMT	Universal Military Training
U.M.W.A.	United Mine Workers of America
U.N.	United Nations
UNESCO	United Nations Educational, Scientific, and Cultural Organization
UNICEF	United Nations Children's Fund
UNRRA	United Nations Relief and Rehabilitation Administration
U.P.I.	United Press and International News Service
USO	United Service Organizations
U.S.S.R.	Union of Soviet Socialist Republics
U.S.W.A.	United Steel Workers of America
VA	Veterans Administration
V.F.W.	Veterans of Foreign Wars
W.F.T.U.	World Federation of Trade Unions
WHO	World Health Organization
WMC	War Manpower Commission
WPA	Work Projects Administration
WPB	War Production Board
YMCA	Young Men's Christian Association
YMHA	Young Men's Hebrew Association
YWCA	Young Women's Christian Association

CURRENT BIOGRAPHY
YEARBOOK
1974

ALEXANDER, DONALD C(RICHTON)

May 22, 1921- United States government
official
Address: b. Internal Revenue Service, 1111
Constitution Ave., N.W., Washington, D.C.
20224; h. 4100 Cathedral Ave., N.W., Washington, D.C. 20016

The United States Internal Revenue Service has
the awesome job of collecting more than $230
billion a year from some 117,000,000 taxpayers.
When Donald C. Alexander, a former tax attorney,
replaced Johnnie M. Walters as commissioner of
internal revenue in May 1973, he planned to
concentrate on improving the effectiveness of the
IRS in carrying out that task. The Watergate
scandal, which ultimately led to the resignation
of President Richard Nixon in August 1974, altered his plans, however, since it subjected the
service to charges that tax audits had been used
as weapons against opponents of the Nixon administration and that the former President's tax
returns had not been properly examined. Alexander has thus been forced to devote first priority to maintaining public confidence in his
agency.

Established by act of Congress in 1862, the
Internal Revenue Service is a branch of the
United States Department of the Treasury. It
administers and enforces the internal revenue laws,
except those concerned with alcohol, tobacco,
and firearms, which were placed under jurisdiction of a separate bureau in 1972. Its nationwide
policies and programs are developed by its national headquarters organization in Washington,
D.C. and administered by seven regional commissioners through some 1,200 field offices throughout the United States. In addition to its basic
functions of determining, assessing, and collecting
internal revenues and other taxes, it also provides
information and assistance to taxpayers, and it
helps to enforce the President's programs for
achieving stabilization of the economy.

Donald Crichton Alexander was born on May
22, 1921, in Pine Bluff, Arkansas, to William
Crichton Alexander, a cotton grower, and Ella
Temple (Fox) Alexander. He has a sister Judy,
who is married to William T. Seawell, board
chairman and president of Pan American World
Airways. Alexander majored in English at Yale
University but expected to follow his father's
occupation. His senior thesis on cotton farming
received a Patterson Prize and was published as

DONALD C. ALEXANDER

Arkansas Plantation, 1920-42 (Yale Univ. Press,
1943). After obtaining his B.A. degree with honors from Yale in 1942, he served for three years
in the United States Army and saw combat duty
in southern France. He received the Silver Star
and Bronze Star before being discharged with
the rank of major in 1945.

Alexander's interest in law as a profession
stemmed from a chance association with a local
attorney at the time of his graduation from college. Impressed by the financial rewards of legal
work and disheartened by low cotton prices, he
entered Harvard Law School after leaving the
Army, served as an editor of the *Harvard Law
Review*, and graduated *magna cum laude* with
an LL.B. degree in 1948. A course in tax law
that he had taken at Harvard eventually persuaded him to specialize in that field. "I decided
I liked jigsaw puzzles," he explained to Andy
Soltis in an interview for the New York *Post*
(December 29, 1973). "Poring through something like Section 341-B of the [Internal Revenue]
Code and coming out at the end of it actually
knowing what it says is an intellectual achievement that does give you a feeling of pride."

In 1948 Alexander became an associate in
Covington & Burling, a leading Washington, D.C.
law firm, of which the late Dean Acheson had
been a member for a number of years. In 1954
he moved to Cincinnati, Ohio to join Taft, Stet-
tinius & Hollister—the late Senator Robert A.
Taft's law firm—and in 1956 he became a partner.

He left there in 1966 to accept a partnership in another Cincinnati law firm, Dinsmore, Shohl, Coates & Deupree, with which he remained until 1972. Concurrently he served as a member of an advisory group to the Commissioner of Internal Revenue in 1969-70 and as a consultant to the Treasury Department from 1970 to 1972. He was also on the advisory boards of the New York University Tax Institute from 1970 to 1972, Tax Management, Inc., from 1968 to 1973, and the University of California Tax-Exempt Organizations Institute in 1972-73. During his years in law practice, Alexander acquired a reputation as one of the foremost experts on estate and gift taxation in the United States.

On March 19, 1973 President Nixon announced his nomination of Alexander as commissioner of internal revenue to succeed Johnnie M. Walters, who had held the post since August 6, 1971. According to the Washington *Post* (March 20, 1973), strong opposition from the AFL-CIO had previously led the White House to abandon the planned nomination of George Webster, a Washington tax attorney. Confirmed by the Senate on May 17, Alexander formally assumed office on May 29, 1973 after the IRS had completed an audit of his tax returns and found a slight deficiency.

Alexander came to his new job with ideas for improving compliance and taxpayer service, two acknowledged weak points in the federal tax collection system. Although IRS manpower had climbed to over 70,000 in 1973, it had not been able to keep pace with the growing burdens presented by a larger number of returns, increasingly complicated tax laws and regulations, and a higher personal income for the average American, which made tax returns more complex. In addition, significant numbers of service personnel were diverted to help enforce federal wage and price controls under Phase II of Nixon's economic program in 1971-72. Those factors contributed to a decline in the rate of returns audited from 5.8 percent in 1962 to 1.9 percent in 1972 and the shelving of some 1,100 cases of alleged fraud in one twelve-month period. And more and more Americans were complaining about the quality of taxpayer services.

Before Alexander had time to turn to those problems, the IRS had to defend itself against allegations of involvement in the Watergate scandal. Testifying before the Senate Watergate Committee in June 1973, John W. Dean 3d, President Nixon's former counsel, charged that the White House had tried to have the service harass 575 political "enemies" through tax audits. Dean also alleged that supporters of the administration had received favorable treatment in IRS proceedings and that Nixon had told him in September 1972 that after the election the administration would "get people into these agencies who would be responsive to the White House requirements."

While the Congressional Joint Committee on Internal Revenue Taxation opened an investigation into Dean's charges, Alexander launched his own inquiry, "to satisfy ourselves," as he told Eileen Shanahan in an interview for the New York *Times* (July 16, 1973), "that we have the agency we think we had in the past and we darned well are going to have in the future." He explained that his new priority was "maintaining public confidence" in the IRS and added that "politics has no part in the tax system." If the White House picked him to hound political enemies of the administration, he told Timothy D. Schellhardt of the *Wall Street Journal* (June 28, 1973), "then they selected the wrong man."

In November 1973 Alexander announced that his inquiry had shown that the IRS has not been used to harass enemies or benefit friends of the administration, either in his term of office or in his predecessor's. The joint committee's report confirmed those findings in December and noted that the IRS, with the assent of Secretary of the Treasury George P. Shultz, had resisted all White House attempts to force a general audit of "enemy" returns. In July 1974 Alexander assured a subcommittee of the Senate Judiciary Committee that "no political pressure has been brought upon me to start an audit, stop an audit . . . or affect any audit or other process in any way." He added that he would resist and refuse any such request and would consider reporting it to the Justice Department.

In addition, Alexander launched a program of positive action to counter charges of politicization. At a press conference on August 1, 1973 he asserted that political parties and committees would no longer be immune from taxation of such income as capital gains realized from the sale of stocks and other property received as campaign contributions. Such a policy would affect the Republicans more than the Democrats, since they were the chief beneficiaries of that type of contribution. A few days later, the IRS announced that it was disbanding its special services staff, organized in 1969 to monitor "extremist" groups and their leaders. "The IRS will continue to pay close attention to tax rebels," Alexander declared, "but political or social views, 'extremist' or otherwise, are irrelevant to taxation."

In response to a recommendation by Common Cause, the IRS provided space on page one of the 1973 income tax return form for taxpayers to allocate one dollar of their taxes to political candidates. He also moved to give citizen lobbies a voice in IRS policy-making by appointing a representative of Tax Analysts & Advocates, a public interest law firm, to an unpaid twelve-member advisory panel composed of lawyers, educators, and accountants. He told Eileen Shanahan that representatives of such "liberal-left" organizations may not have the same views as the corporate tax lawyers and establishment professors who had made up earlier panels and added, "Some of my best friends are 'enemies.'"

Alexander's agency again became the center of political controversy in the spring of 1974. President Nixon in 1970 had claimed a deduction of some $428,000, to be spread over several years, for the gift of his Vice-Presidential papers to the government. That deduction was not challenged when his returns for 1971 and 1972 were audited in the spring of 1973. Charges of impropriety led to new investigations by both the IRS and the Joint Committee on Internal Revenue Taxation. Both disallowed the deduction and reported in early April 1974 that Nixon owed more than $432,000 in back taxes, which the President agreed to pay.

Appearing on the CBS television program *Face the Nation* on April 7, 1974, Alexander admitted that the IRS had not done as thorough an audit of Nixon's return as it should have in 1973. He pointed out, however, that his predecessors had accepted Presidential tax returns at face value and "in that respect we are breaking new ground." While denying that a fraud penalty had been assessed against Nixon, he declined to answer on grounds of confidentiality when asked whether a negligence penalty had been included in the assessment. Seymour M. Hersh reported, however, in the New York *Times* (April 11, 1974) that Alexander had asked the special Watergate prosecutor to investigate a possible criminal conspiracy among persons who prepared the Nixon returns.

An advocate of more stringent penalties for tax evaders, Alexander has pointed out that the IRS had no part in the Justice Department's bargain with Spiro T. Agnew that led to his resignation as Vice-President in October 1973 and his plea of "no contest" to tax evasion charges. The IRS has instituted civil action to recover Agnew's unpaid taxes. In the fall of 1974, in connection with Senate confirmation hearings on President Gerald Ford's nomination of Nelson A. Rockefeller for the Vice-Presidency, the IRS conducted a five-year audit of the former New York State governor's tax returns. In the settlement reached between Rockefeller and the IRS it was revealed that he had underpaid his federal taxes for the period from 1969 through 1973 by 21 percent.

Despite his enforced preoccupation with politically related problems, Alexander has been able to devote attention to improving the basic functions of his agency. The audit rate turned upward in 1973 for the first time in a decade and was expected to exceed 2 percent in 1974. The computer selection of returns for audit has improved to the point that for fiscal 1974 the average audit was expected to produce an estimated $1,078 in additional revenue, as compared with $431 in 1969. With the help of more agents Alexander has set a 5 percent audit rate as his long range goal but insists that quality comes before quantity. "If we get into setting productivity quotas," he told an interviewer for *Business Week* (September 1, 1973), "then implicitly we will be setting quotas, and I won't do that."

To alleviate the problems of the small taxpayer, the IRS simplified and shortened income tax forms and instructions for 1973, and the agency's toll-free telephone network was extended to handle taxpayers' inquiries. Audit notices now include the name and telephone number of an IRS agent since, as Alexander told the *Business Week* interviewer, "You just can't communicate with a computer." The service had been criticized for holding private tax rulings confidential, but Alexander reversed that policy in July 1974 so that future rulings could be made available to the public in accordance with the Freedom of Information Act. At the same time, he has asked Congress to tighten the law permitting White House access to private tax returns, so that future abuses might be prevented.

About one-half of all taxpayers must pay for professional help in preparing their returns, and some of that assistance has been substandard or unscrupulous. Alexander aims to meet that problem by providing more trained IRS personnel to advise taxpayers and by seeking Congressional legislation to fine and enjoin tax preparers who are unethical or incompetent. He recognizes, however, that much of the problem stems from the Internal Revenue Code itself. As he told an interviewer for *Nation's Business* (February 1974), "I would like to see a law that people can understand and apply to their own situations without the need for outside guidance in most cases."

Donald C. Alexander was married on October 9, 1946 to Margaret Louise Savage of Clarksville, Tennessee, whom he met at the officers' club of Camp Campbell, Kentucky, during World War II. They have two sons, Robert C. and James M. Alexander, who both followed their father to Yale and Harvard. A slim, wiry man, Alexander retains strong traces of his Arkansas drawl. His seven-day, eighty-hour workweek has prompted his wife to describe him as a "workaholic." When he has time for recreation, he enjoys watching football and playing tennis. A member of the District of Columbia bar since 1949, Alexander was chairman of the American Bar Association's section of taxation in 1967-68, and he is a past member of the advisory group to the federal estate and gift tax project of the American Law Institute. He is the author of more than twenty-five articles on federal tax law.

Writing in the *Wall Street Journal* of January 24, 1974, Timothy D. Schellhardt took cognizance of reports that Alexander often displays a "hot temper" and "aggressiveness" and that he left his first two law firms because of personality clashes with other attorneys. Schellhardt added, however, that virtually all of the commissioner's professional colleagues consider him brilliant. As quoted in *Business Week* (September 1, 1973), Harvard law professor Stanley S. Surrey, a Treasury Department official in the Kennedy and Johnson administrations, called Alexander "the thinking man's Republican," and Schellhardt cited one prominent Washington tax attorney's view of Alexander as "perhaps the brightest commissioner in decades."

References

N Y Post p22 D 29 '73 por
U S News 75:28 S 17 '73 por
Wall St J p 1+ Ja 24 '74 por
Who's Who in America, 1974-75

ALMIRANTE, GIORGIO

June 27, 1914- Italian political leader and
member of Parliament
Address: b. Palazzo Montecitorio, Rome, Italy;
h. Via Livorno 20, Rome, Italy

A half century after Benito Mussolini staged his
march on Rome in 1922, marking the beginning
of more than two decades of Fascist rule in Italy,
his spiritual heir, the neo-Fascist leader Giorgio
Almirante, has emerged as a force to be reckoned
with on the Italian political scene. A former journalist and teacher, Almirante served as an official
of Mussolini's short-lived Italian Social Republic
in the final months of World War II and was one
of the founders of the neo-Fascist Movimento
Sociale Italiano (MSI) in 1946. His program of
"law and order," suppression of Communism, and
a modified version of Mussolini's corporate state
struck a responsive chord among the 3,000,000
Italians who, weary of chronic political instability, industrial strife, and corruption, cast their
votes for the MSI in the 1972 parliamentary elections. Although Almirante sees little prospect that
his movement, with less than 10 percent of the
seats in the Italian Parliament, could attain national power in the foreseeable future, he believes
that it can exercise a profound influence on government policy. To that end, he has tried to give
the MSI a more respectable image by purging it
of extremist elements and reconstituting it in early
1973 as the more broadly based National Right
Wing.

A member of a Sicilian family of actors that
had been associated with the theatre for three
generations, Giorgio Almirante was born in Sal-
somaggiore, near Parma, in northern Italy on June
27, 1914 to Mario and Rita (Armaroli) Almirante.
IIis surname suggests that he is of Spanish ancestry. His father had been a member of the
first company to perform Luigi Pirandello's *Six
Characters in Search of an Author* and was also
a motion picture director. During his school years,
Almirante was consistently at the head of his
class. From the age of nine he was a member of
the Fascist youth movement, becoming first a
balilla and later an *avanguardista*. At the University of Rome he was active in the Fascist student
organization and served as literary and film critic
of its magazine. As a student he tried his hand
as a playwright and novelist, but with little success. He also worked as an unpaid apprentice
journalist for *Il Tevere*, Rome's most ardently
Fascist daily. After obtaining his doctorate of
letters with honors from the university at the age
of twenty-three he joined the newspaper's regular staff, and the following year he became editor.

During World War II, Almirante took part in
the North African campaign as an infantry officer
in the Italian army and won the Cross of Valor.
At the same time he continued to work for *Il
Tevere* as a war correspondent. After the retreat
of Italian forces to Benghazi, Almirante returned
to his newspaper office in Rome. With Mussolini's
fall from power in July 1943 and the takeover of

Il Tevere by anti-Fascists, Almirante went back
into the army until September, when the King of
Italy concluded an armistice with the Allies and
the Italian army was disbanded. Not long after
that, Almirante joined militia forces loyal to Mussolini, who had established his Italian Social Republic at Salò under the auspices of German occupation forces then in control of northern Italy.
Helped by a friend who was a member of Mussolini's Cabinet, Almirante obtained a post in the
new government. According to some sources,
Almirante was merely a minor functionary in the
Salò regime; others maintain that he was its
"youngest minister" and was "responsible for
propaganda." Almirante himself said in an interview with Mary Simons in *Intellectual Digest*
(May 1972) that he and Il Duce were "very
close" during the final period of Fascist rule. He
asserted that Mussolini had been driven into Hitler's arms by the Allies against his will and was
defeated by events that were "bigger than he was."

In the same interview, Almirante looked back
upon the Fascist era with nostalgia. "I remained
a Fascist until the very end," he recalled. "They
were important years for me, years in which a
man becomes a man. . . . I remember that period
of Fascism with the same affection one feels toward a woman one loves. . . . I fully shared the
idea of Fascism. . . . But after the war I found
myself in a different world, a world I did not
know, the world of democracy." After the collapse of the Italian Social Republic and the brutal
death of Mussolini at the hands of Italian par-
tisans in April 1945, Almirante made his way
across northern Italy to Turin, where he stayed
for a time with a Jewish anarchist friend whom
he had helped during the war. "Then I spent
eighteen months eating hard-boiled eggs and
sleeping in railway stations and parks," he recalled in an interview that was quoted by Melton
S. Davis in the New York *Times Magazine* (June
6, 1971). "Using forged papers and the name
Giorgio Alloni, I sold soap from door to door."
At various times, Almirante also worked as a messenger, a shoe salesman, and a postal employee.

An amnesty for lesser Fascists that was proclaimed in September 1946 by the Communist
party leader Palmiro Togliatti, who served as
Minister of Justice in Italy's first postwar coalition government, enabled Almirante to resume his
own identity. He returned to Rome, where he
found a job as a teacher of Italian literature in
a secondary school. A few weeks later, disregard-
ing a promise he had made to his father that he
would steer clear of politics, he founded a small
political club that became the nucleus of the
Movimento Sociale Italiano, which was formally
founded by Almirante and seven others in December 1946. Its manifesto was based on the program
of Mussolini's Salò republic, and its inspiration
came from former Fascist dignitaries who were
compelled at the time to remain incognito. Almirante, whose oratorical skill led some old-
time Fascists to see in him a reincarnation of
Mussolini, was elected the new party's secretary
general and also became editor of its newspaper.

Under Almirante's skillful management, the MSI soon began to pick up support. In its first political campaign, for the election of Rome's city council, in September 1947, the party managed to elect three council members despite efforts of opponents to stifle its speakers. In the national elections of April 1948—Italy's first under its new republican constitution—the MSI won some 500,-000 votes and six seats in the Chamber of Deputies, including that of Almirante, who continues to represent the Rome constituency from which he was first elected at that time. Despite its early electoral successes, however, the MSI continued to be considered a political pariah, and its leaders were occasionally arrested for intemperate statements and actions. Almirante himself was once sentenced to a year of house arrest because of his zealous defense of Fascism, and although he was later acquitted on appeal, he was forced to relinquish his teaching position.

In 1950 Almirante, whose stance was at the time considered too militant by many of his fellow party members, was replaced as secretary general of the MSI but continued to work behind the scenes and in Parliament to strengthen the party. It was partly because of his efforts that the MSI, after taking a nationalist position in Italy's dispute with Yugoslavia over Trieste, tripled its voting strength in 1953, electing twenty-nine Deputies and nine Senators. In 1954 his longtime rival, Arturo Michelini, became secretary general and turned the MSI into a "party of nostalgia" and moderation, over the protests of Almirante, who favored a hardline approach of opposition to the established order, even if it meant moving underground. "The MSI is a Fascist party which fights in the streets for the honor of Fascism," Almirante wrote in the party newspaper in January 1958, proudly recalling his own role as a member of Mussolini's Black Brigades. In 1963 he founded a militant splinter group called "Renewal," but was unable to mold it into a viable organization.

After Michelini's death in June 1969, Almirante was again elected secretary general of the MSI and began to revitalize the party, which had become ideologically weakened and had lost votes and numerical strength. (Its parliamentary representation had decreased from twenty-seven Deputies and fifteen Senators in 1963 to twenty-four Deputies and eleven Senators in the 1968 elections.) He streamlined its organization; beefed up its student movement; adopted a militant line to bring back into the fold some of the extremists who had broken with the party; promoted an aggressive campaign against leftist trade unions; and capitalized on discord, wherever it occurred. The MSI and related groups played a major role in the regional unrest that erupted in Reggio Calabria in 1970, and they claimed credit for causing the cancellation of Yugoslav President Tito's planned visit to Rome in December of that year.

By the spring of 1971, the MSI, with a voting strength estimated at about 1,800,000, had—in addition to its twenty-four members in the Cham-

GIORGIO ALMIRANTE

ber of Deputies and eleven Senators—forty-six regional deputies, 142 provisional councillors, 2,479 municipal councilmen, thirty-two local mayors, a self-defense corps of some 200,000 volunteers, and a labor organization, the Italian Confederation of National Labor Syndicates, which claimed about 1,000,000 out of a labor force of some 20,000,000.

In the provincial and municipal elections held in June 1971 in Rome, Sicily, and southern Italy, involving about one fifth of the national electorate, the MSI scored what has been described as the largest shift in votes in twenty-three years. It captured 13.9 percent of the vote, as compared with the 5.2 percent it received in the municipal elections of the previous year. In Sicily alone, its share of the vote was 16.3 percent. The MSI gain, which had come largely at the expense of Premier Emilio Colombo's Christian Democrats, was seen as resulting from a "law and order backlash" against social unrest and political instability. According to a description of the election campaign in Newsweek (June 28, 1971), Almirante, "calling for 'national pacification,' . . . successfully managed to make the MSI seem all things to all men. In the strife-racked cities, the neo-Fascists attacked the unions and the demonstrators; in land-conscious Sicily they told voters that public housing would take away their property; in Rome they appealed to the thousands of civil servants with visions of the power that the bureaucracy enjoyed in Mussolini's days. And continually, Almirante implored the electorate to block the government's steady slip to the left." Almirante was less successful in trying to gain recruits among Italian workers abroad, and in November 1971 his efforts to proselytize brought him into conflict with West German and Belgian authorities.

Having become convinced that the MSI could prosper with a policy of moderation, Almirante tried to invest it with an image of respectability. Under his guidance the party now espoused parliamentary methods, eschewed Fascist slogans and symbols, rejected violence except in self-defense, disowned such extremists as the conspirator Prince Junio Valerio Borghese, and negotiated with the small Italian Democratic party of Monarchical Unity for the possible unification of the forces of the right. When in January 1972 Premier Emilio Colombo's center-left coalition government collapsed, Almirante's MSI claimed the credit for having forced the Christian Democrats to break with their leftist coalition partners.

Unable to form a viable government, President Giovanni Leone dissolved Parliament in February and called for new elections on May 7, 1972, a full year before the existing five-year legislative term was due to expire. Although during the campaign Socialist election posters tried to equate Almirante with Hitler, the MSI leader continued to refurbish his image of respectability by making an impressive showing in his many appearances at public meetings and on television. Adopting an "ecumenical approach," the MSI addressed its election appeal for "authority with liberty" to the middle classes, businessmen, professionals, young people, and nonunionized workers and sponsored rallies for the *maggioranza silenziosa* (silent majority). In the elections the MSI, together with its monarchist allies, received 8.6 percent of the 37,000,000 votes cast and elected fifty-six of the 630 Deputies and twenty-six of the 322 Senators, thus displacing the Liberals as Italy's fourth-largest party.

At its four-day national convention, attended by 1,500 delegates in Rome in January 1973, the MSI formally changed its name to National Right Wing, appealed to public opinion for its acceptance as a responsible political movement, and reelected Almirante as the party's secretary general. Despite his claims to respectability, however, the Chamber of Deputies decided on May 24, 1973, by a vote of 485 to fifty-nine, to strip Almirante of his parliamentary immunity. The Deputies based their action on a speech that Almirante had delivered in June 1972, in which he declared that in the event of a non-functioning government "the national right wing has the duty to create a climate of solidarity around the armed forces and the forces of order, enabling them to do their duty in defense of freedom against all subversion." Ironically, his name was included, along with those of prominent leftists and liberals, on a "death list" discovered in November 1973, naming 1,617 Italians marked for assassination by Fascist extremists.

To remedy Italy's ills, Almirante proposes first of all a "well-organized anti-Communist front" and secondly a revised constitution that would change the existing "quantitative democracy" to a "qualitative democracy," bearing some resemblance to the Fascist corporate state. "From *election*, we must pass instead to *selection* of a legislative assembly in which labor, production, moral and cultural categories are represented," he told Melton S. Davis (New York *Times Magazine*, June 6, 1971). In place of totalitarian dictatorship, which he regards as an "outmoded concept," Almirante prefers a "presidential republic" similar to that established by Charles de Gaulle in France. Almirante, whose foreign policy is first and foremost anti-Communist, supports the United States, NATO, and Italy's armed forces; sympathizes with the government of Spain; and is pro-Israel because of Soviet alignment with the Arab states. A "practising Roman Catholic" who, as he told Melton S. Davis, "also believes in the evil eye," Almirante deplores the increasing tendency of priests to become politicians. While he agrees with the church in its opposition to Italy's liberal divorce law, he differs with its doctrines in that he would permit abortion and birth control. Almirante is the author of *Il movimento sociale Italiano* (1958) and of the two-volume *Processo al parlamento* (1968), and coauthor of *Repubblica sociale italiano; storia* (1959).

Giorgio Almirante is legally separated from his first wife and was married a second time, to the former Raffaela Stramandinoli, according to a report in the New York *Times* (October 23, 1971). He has four grown children who share his political views, and he is a grandfather. A slender man with a high forehead and a receding hairline, Almirante, according to Melton S. Davis, "exudes an air of mildness. Gray-streaked hair and pale, gray-green eyes heighten the impression. . . . With his trim gray mustache and the well-cut double-breasted suit, he could be an English gentleman. . . . Witty, literate, and lucid, Almirante charms crowds [but] . . . beneath the urbane exterior is a core of cold determination. In rare, off-guard moments his eyes narrow, his jaw hardens and he seems to be turning from lamb into lion." His voice, according to Mary Simons, "combines the melody of a priest at high mass and the syrup of a Latin lover." In 1971 Almirante delivered a nine-and-a-quarter-hour speech, the longest ever given in the Italian Parliament. Noted for his physical courage, in 1966 he took part in one of the last sword duels to be fought in Italy. A nonsmoker, he rarely indulges in alcoholic beverages other than wine and hardly ever attends the theatre, motion pictures, or nightclubs. Although he is in good physical condition he engages in no physical exercise other than walking. According to C. L. Sulzberger of the New York *Times* (July 22, 1971), Almirante "has no strange gods, swearing only by Gianbattista Vico and Giovanni Gentile, without whom no one can understand Italian politics, and (as a former literature professor) by Dante, Pirandello, and Verga." His favorite political figure, he told John Cornwell of the *Guardian* (June 20, 1973), is Winston Churchill.

References

Guardian p14 Je 20 '73 por
Intellectual Digest 2:21+ My '72 pors
N Y Times Mag p27+ Je 6 '71 pors
Time 101:37+ Je 11 '73 por

Chi è? (1961)
Panorama Biografico degli Italiani d'Oggi (1956)
Who's Who in Italy, 1957-58

ALTMAN, ROBERT

Feb. 20, 1925- Film director
Address: b. c/o United Artists, 729 7th Ave.,
New York 10019

ROBERT ALTMAN

Offbeat, visually arresting, and unorthodox, the
films of Robert Altman are probably the most
consistently interesting to come out of the United
States in recent years. A former television writer,
director, and producer, Altman was propelled to
fame in 1970 with his second major film,
*M*A*S*H*, an outrageously funny, blood-soaked
antiwar comedy that became one of the biggest
commercial successes in motion picture history,
and it helped to make him something of a cult
figure among the young. Since then his films have
included *Brewster McCloud* (1970), a bizarre
fantasy about a young man who tries to fly in
the Houston Astrodome; *McCabe and Mrs. Miller* (1971), an unromantic look at how the West
was won; *The Long Goodbye* (1973), a satire on
Hollywood and detective movies, in which he
drastically overhauled and updated Raymond
Chandler's classic mystery novel with the same
title; *Thieves Like Us* (1974); and *California
Split* (1974).

Robert Altman was born in Kansas City, Missouri on February 20, 1925. On his mother's side
he is descended from American settlers who
crossed the Atlantic on the Mayflower. His father
was one of the most successful life-insurance
salesmen in the world and an inveterate gambler. "I learned a lot about losing from him,"
Altman told Aljean Harmetz of the New York
Times Magazine (June 20, 1971). "That losing
is an identity; that you can be a good loser and
a bad winner; that none of it—gambling, money,
winning or losing—has any real value; . . . that
it's simply a way of killing time, like crossword
puzzles."

Reared as a Roman Catholic, Altman was educated in Jesuit schools, but he abandoned Catholicism around the time he joined the United
States Army in 1943. During World War II he
was a bomber pilot, flying forty-six missions over
Borneo and the Dutch East Indies. It never occurred to him that he was killing people, Altman told Aljean Harmetz, adding that he doubts
that it would then have bothered him if it had.

After his discharge from the Army in 1947,
Altman attended the University of Missouri for
a time and then began making industrial films
for the Calvin Company in Kansas City. It was
with Calvin that he learned his trade as a writer,
producer, photographer, director, set designer,
and film editor. During the 1950's Altman made
two unsuccessful attempts to break into the
Hollywood film industry, but each time he returned to Kansas City. Then, in 1957, he persuaded United Artists to release a low-budget
film he had written, produced, and directed entitled *The Delinquents*. When it was exhibited
in New York City, an anonymous critic for the
New York *Post* rated it as "fair" on his movie
meter, conceding that the film was able "to gen-

erate interest" because it dealt "with youthful
violence in ways that make you want to join in
and give advice." He added that the film was
"bracketed fore-and-aft with pious pronuncia-
mentoes on the subject of juvenile problems and
parental understanding, thereby completing a
perfect example of sensationalism providing no
answers to a distorted presentation."

With some sixty-five industrial films and documentaries to his credit, Altman was hired by
Warner Brothers to coproduce (with George W.
George) and direct an elegiac biographical documentary called *The James Dean Story* (1957),
in which the young Hollywood actor's life was
reviewed by means of photographs, film clips,
interviews, and a poetic, though somewhat florid,
commentary. Reviewers were generally enthusiastic about its authenticity, earnestness, simplicity, and successful avoidance of the maudlin and
sensational.

For the next several years Altman worked on
over 300 hours of television programs as writer,
producer, or director. Among the shows that he
helped to create were *Roaring Twenties, Bonanza,
Bus Stop, Combat, Suspense Theatre, Kraft
Theatre,* and the pilots for *The Gallant Men* and
The Long Hot Summer. Because of his unconventional approach to television formulas, Altman
found himself fired with regularity. As he explained to Aljean Harmetz, "Because the star of
Combat, Vic Morrow, couldn't be killed off, I'd
take an actor, establish him as an important
character in one segment, use him three or four
times more, and then kill him early in the next
script, offscreen, in a way that had nothing to do
with the plot. That was unorthodox. It made them
nervous. I used to get fired for it."

In the mid-1960's Altman quit television, even
though he was making $125,000 a year, because
he did not want to become "one of those hundreds of creative people who have just died in
television." He was mostly out of work for the
next few years, except for a stint as the director
of a film melodrama called *Countdown* (Warner

Brothers-Seven Arts, 1968). He was fired after that job by Jack Warner in 1966, and when the film was finally released, it gathered such acid reviews as that by Howard Thompson (New York *Times,* May 2, 1968). "Say one thing for 'Countdown,' a limp space-flight drama that landed at neighborhood theaters yesterday," Thompson told his readers. "It makes the moon seem just as dull as Mother Earth." He found most of the film to be only a stultifying and cliché-ridden prologue to the climactic space ride and took Altman to task for his "listless direction."

Aside from that ill-starred episode with *Countdown,* Altman's first chance to direct a major film was *That Cold Day in the Park* (Commonwealth United, 1969), Canada's 1969 entry in the Cannes Film Festival. A drama about a psychotic thirty-two-year-old virgin who becomes obsessed with a young man of twenty, the film starred Sandy Dennis and was shot in the cold rainy winter of Vancouver, British Columbia. Disturbed by the way it tottered between being a serious study of loneliness and a standard thriller, most critics panned *That Cold Day in the Park.* The movie was also a box-office failure.

After completing *That Cold Day in the Park,* Altman was asked by Twentieth Century-Fox to direct a war service comedy based on a novel by a combat surgeon, who wrote under the pseudonym of Richard Hooker. The project had already been turned down by fourteen other directors. Altman took over the orphaned script and created *M*A*S*H,* which earned nearly $30,000,000 for Twentieth Century-Fox and became one of the dozen biggest box-office successes of all time.

Ostensibly set during the Korean War but with obvious reference to Vietnam, *M*A*S*H* portrays life behind the lines at a Mobile Army Surgical Hospital, whose acronym gives the film its title. Like other films of its genre, *M*A*S*H* treats the off-duty antics and pranks of Army personnel, in this instance the doctors and nurses of the hospital. But unlike other service comedies, Altman's film shows with savage realism the revoltingly bloody business of patching and mending the mangled bodies flown in from the battle front. As a result, the film becomes a dark comedy showing the way in which its heroes (Donald Sutherland and Elliott Gould), two young surgeons drafted into service, retain their sanity through sex and attacks on Army bureaucracy.

As Pauline Kael wrote in the *New Yorker* (January 24, 1970), "The surgery room looks insane and is presented as insane, but as the insanity in which we must preserve the values of sanity and function as sane men. . . . The heroes are always on the side of decency and sanity—that's why they're contemptuous of the bureaucracy. They are heroes *because* they're competent and sane and gallant, and in this insane situation their gallantry takes the form of scabrous comedy." Miss Kael called *M*A*S*H* "the best American war comedy since sound came in," and most critics agreed. The film was accorded many honors, including the grand prize at the 1970 Cannes Film Festival, the election as the best film of 1970 by the National Society of Film Critics, and six nominations for Academy Awards, among them for best director and best film.

Altman's next venture was *Brewster McCloud* (MGM, 1970), a satirical fantasy about a young man who wants to fly and is helped by a kind of sexy fairy godmother (Sally Kellerman) whose assistance apparently includes murdering several people and strewing their bodies with bird droppings. Most of the film was shot in the Houston Astrodome. Critics parted company on *Brewster McCloud.* Several, including Judith Crist and Andrew Sarris, included it on their lists of Best Films of 1970; others, like Pauline Kael and Stanley Kauffmann, dismissed it as silly. Although the film's success at the box office was modest at best, it has since emerged as a cult film whose devotees watch it again and again.

With *McCabe and Mrs. Miller* (Warner Brothers, 1971) Altman turned his attention to the venerable American film genre of the western. Set in 1902 in a frontier mining town near the Canadian border, it graphs the rise and fall of McCabe (Warren Beatty), a small-time gambler who prospers by setting up a flourishing bordello with the help and partnership of an opium-smoking whore from Seattle named Mrs. Miller (Julie Christie), with whom he becomes romantically involved. Ultimately, while Mrs. Miller loses herself in opium dreams, McCabe is gunned down by killers hired by a big company that wants to take over the brothel.

"I got interested in the project [of *McCabe and Mrs. Miller*] because I don't like westerns and don't believe in them," Altman told Frank Rich of the *Guardian* (February 16, 1972). "So I pictured a story with every western cliché in it. . . . But why have a straight narrative line when everybody knows the story? I decided to take advantage of what the audience already knows and just illustrate a heroic ballad. Yes, these events took place, but not in the way you've been told. I wanted to look at it through a different window, you might say, but I still wanted to keep the poetry of the ballad." To enhance the idea of the movie as an old story retold, Altman treated the color film with special processes to make it look as old and faded as family photographs long hidden away in an album in the attic.

At the initial screening of *McCabe and Mrs. Miller,* a defective print was used that blurred the sound. Since, like Orson Welles, Altman had used overlapping dialogue—as he does in all his films because it resembles the way people really talk—conversation on the film was already hard to follow and the print made it inaudible. Critics who viewed the film at the preview lambasted it, but the *New Yorker's* Pauline Kael, who saw a corrected print at a later showing, wrote a glowing review in which she called it "a beautiful pipe dream of a movie—a fleeting, almost diaphanous vision of what frontier life might have been." So impressed with the film was she that she launched a campaign to save it from the oblivion to which its initial reviews threatened to abandon it. Many reviewers saw the movie again, and changed their appraisals. "Seen more clearly and heard more distinctly [on second viewing]," wrote Donald J. Mayerson of *Cue* (October 2, 1971), for example, "the film emerges as one of the screen's most unusual and haunting Westerns . . . a sad, funny, gentle, and vicious visual poem which utilizes the talents of Warren Beatty and Julie Christie to their fullest."

Although *McCabe and Mrs. Miller* ended up a critical triumph, it fared less well at the box office. Even less popular with the public was *Images* (Columbia, 1972), a modern Gothic horror tale written by Altman and filmed by him with British backing in Ireland. A study of the mental breakdown of a schizophrenic young woman, the film drew widely ranging estimations from critics, ranging from Howard Thompson's (New York *Times*, October 9, 1972) dismissal of it as a "clanging, pretentious, tricked-up exercise" to Richard Schickel's (*Life*, September 29, 1972) tribute as "a complex, carefully worked out, intricate work . . . the most sophisticated dramatic study of a serious case of mental illness I can recall." For her portrayal of the young psychotic, Susannah York was named best actress at the 1972 Cannes Film Festival.

Like *McCabe and Mrs. Miller*, *The Long Goodbye* got off to a bad start. Based on Raymond Chandler's 1953 detective novel of the same name, *The Long Goodbye* retains Chandler's Los Angeles setting but updates it to the present. Altman's version of Chandler's cynical but high-principled detective, Philip Marlowe—who was made famous by Humphrey Bogart in *The Big Sleep*—is played by Elliott Gould, whose Marlow stumblingly tries to be a 1940's tough guy in a world of altered values. The film had its première in Los Angeles early in 1973 and then went on to play a number of other American cities. Everywhere it was accompanied by such a chorus of boos from critics who considered it a travesty of Chandler's novel and his celebrated detective hero that United Artists withdrew the film from circulation to ponder the reasons for the hostile reaction. Six months later the film was launched again, this time with a New York première and a new advertising campaign that played down Chandler and described the movie as a satire. The film received ecstatic reviews from Pauline Kael and Vincent Canby.

In early 1974 United Artists released Altman's *Thieves Like Us*, a saga of Depression era outlaws starring Keith Carradine and Shelley Duvall. Among the many critics who praised the film was Pauline Kael of the *New Yorker* (February 4, 1974), who called *Thieves Like Us* "the closest to flawless of Altman's films—a masterpiece." Critical reviews of Altman's *California Split*, a tale of compulsive gamblers which was released during the summer of 1974 by Columbia Pictures, were also generally favorable.

Convinced that "moviemaking is a collaborative art," Altman is the antithesis of the stereotyped autocratic Hollywood director. Visitors have described his sets as anarchic. He lets his movies develop as he films them, always taking into consideration suggestions from his cast and crew. Regarding the script as little more than a useful tool in selling the project to a studio, he rewrites as he goes along and encourages his actors to improvise rather than to use written dialogue.

A large man with curly black and gray hair and a beard, Robert Altman was described by Frank Rich of the *Guardian* as looking "not unlike a frenetic latter-day Papa Hemingway." After observing him during the filming of *McCabe and Mrs. Miller*, Aljean Harmetz characterized him as a man of great personal magnetism and charm, who has the stamina and energy to film all day and outdrink his cast at night. Altman has been married three times. By his first wife, whom he married after World War II, he has a daughter, Christine. After his first divorce, around 1951, he married a second time. From that union he has two sons, Michael, who wrote the lyrics for *M*A*S*H*'s theme song, "Suicide is Painless," and Stephen. Altman now lives with his third wife, Kathryn, and their two children, Robert and Matthew, a mulatto child whom they have adopted.

His current projects include directing "Long Division," a film based on a novel by Ann Richardson Roiphe. "It's no fun for me to go and do the same picture over and over again," Altman told Bruce Cook of the *National Observer* (August 16, 1971). "I find I have to do something different every time. I go to a new place or learn about a period in history, and I'm awed. I feel I have to pass my awe on to other people. That's where the fun is for me."

References

Guardian p12 F 16 '72 por
N Y Times Mag p11 Je 20 '71 pors
International Motion Picture Almanac (1973)

AMALRIK, ANDREI (ALEKSEYEVICH) (ä-mäl' rik)

May 12, 1938- Soviet writer; historian
Address: b. c/o Harcourt Brace Jovanovich, Inc., 757 3d Ave., New York 10017; h. Magadan City, Magadan Region, U.S.S.R.

The versatile writer and historian Andrei Amalrik is among the Soviet intellectuals who have preferred to risk harassment, repeated imprisonment, and exile rather than compromise their convictions. By 1965 his maverick outlook had become anathema to the present regime, which exiled him to a primitive collective farm in Siberia. There he began work on two books, *Involuntary Journey to Siberia* and *Will the Soviet Union Survive Until 1984?*, astute and moving criticisms of Soviet foreign and domestic policy written in a sternly objective style. One of the most courageous of the Soviet dissidents, Amalrik is also one of the most enigmatic, for though a brilliant political thinker, he is a thoroughly apolitical man who protests injustice on purely moral grounds and,

ANDREI AMALRIK

unlike his fellow dissidents, is decidedly pessimistic about the prospects for change in his country. The British journalist and critic Edward Crankshaw characterized him in the London *Observer* (November 29, 1970) as a "rare and absolute dissenter," one who would be anywhere "a one-man protest movement, standing for nothing at all but his own personal perception of the truth *in toto* and in detail."

In his account of his exile Amalrik dwells with obvious pride on the many rebels and heretics who contributed to his family heritage. The most immediate influences on him appear to have been his father and an uncle, utter nonconformists who paid dearly for their outspoken criticism of Stalin. Amalrik was born in Moscow on May 12, 1938 at the height of the purges, in an atmosphere that became even more harrowing with the German invasion in 1941. The war and its aftermath figure among his earliest memories: the hysteria of a crowd being herded into a Moscow subway during an air-raid; the kerosene-lighted freight train in which he and his mother were evacuated to the steppe town of Orenburg until 1943; the sense of despair that gripped people after the war when, instead of going ahead with long-awaited changes, the country reverted to Stalinism. Those images were reinforced by the plight of his father, a gifted historian, who despite his service in the battle of Stalingrad, where he was severely wounded, was stigmatized for his anti-Stalinist views and permanently barred from a university career.

Undaunted by the burden of a congenital heart ailment, Amalrik developed into a pugnacious boy who enjoyed playing truant and was suspended from school many times. During his ninth year of school he was permanently expelled and obliged to take his exams externally. Yet, by the time he entered Moscow University in 1959 he had become a serious student who showed exceptional promise as a historian. In 1963, however, he submitted a dissertation on old Russian history that concluded that Scandinavians and Byzantine

Greeks had contributed more to the formation of Russia than ancient Slavs, a viewpoint that was politically unacceptable. Told that his dissertation would be approved if he were to revise his conclusions, Amalrik refused, aware that in doing so, he forfeited not only his degree but the right to any job commensurate with his ability. His assertion of intellectual freedom also resulted in his first clash with the KGB (Committee on State Security, or the secret police), for in his eagerness to solicit the opinion of a Danish scholar with whom he had been corresponding, Amalrik asked the Danish Embassy to forward his manuscript. The request was unconventional enough to arouse the suspicions of embassy officials who alerted the Soviet Ministry of Foreign Affairs, and the KGB, in turn, warned Amalrik against further attempts to send his work abroad.

After his expulsion from the university in 1963, Amalrik worked at various temporary jobs—from postman and technical translator to timekeeper at sports events—that left him time to care for his father, who had been partially paralyzed by a stroke in 1961 (the year his mother died). For the next two years he led a fairly independent life, seemingly indifferent to pressures to conform. He wrote plays, which he considered his "real job"; promoted the work of avant-garde painters such as Anatoly Zverev and Dmitri Plavinsky, who cannot exhibit in the U.S.S.R.; and openly met foreigners who shared his interests. Those activities, unconventional though not illegal, were duly recorded by the KGB, which kept him under constant surveillance and arrested him in May 1965, shortly after he had arranged for the visiting conductor Igor Markevich to sponsor an exhibit of Zverev's paintings in Paris.

While Amalrik was under preliminary investigation, his apartment was searched; his plays were confiscated, as was his art collection, mostly works by Zverev, who had also illustrated the plays; and he was charged with "producing, harboring, and disseminating pornographic works." Shortly afterward he was released, presumably because literary experts for the Union of Writers were unable to define pornography. Apparently, the authorities were merely biding their time until they could indict him on a charge of parasitism, in accordance with the "parasite" decree originally issued to clear the cities of vagrants and alcoholics and later used to dispose of troublesome intellectuals. On May 28, 1965, after a brief interval of freedom, Amalrik was rearrested on that charge and sentenced to two and a half years of forced labor as a cowherd on a collective farm in Guryevka, a bleak Siberian village in the Tomsk region.

Amalrik has provided a meticulously detailed and detached account of his interrogation, trial, and exile in *Involuntary Journey to Siberia* (Harcourt, 1970), on which he began work in 1966. Throughout the book he sustains the dual consciousness of participant and observer, offering a rare glimpse of what Max Hayward, the British translator and critic, has called "a totalitarian structure in decline . . . the first such spectacle in history." In describing the events that led up to his exile, Amalrik illustrates the degree to which daily life in his society partakes of the absurd. Unaware that Amalrik's real crime is not parasitism but his nonconformist plays and other activities, a police officer searches his apartment, finds the plays, and asks why he had not made an issue of them, since they were work of a sort and recognition could not be had overnight. While he is awaiting trial, Amalrik is repeatedly questioned by psychiatrists about his admiration for Dostoevsky, as though that were the clue to his behavior. In the trial itself he is convicted of parasitism even though the judge never discusses the charge but deals exclusively with the plays. Amalrik is sentenced to hard labor, for which prison doctors have declared him unfit.

Involuntary Journey to Siberia contains some haunting portraits of the people who regularly shuttle from jail to exile: alcoholics, prostitutes, vagrants, religious dissidents, poets, and painters. But its most original feature is Amalrik's unsparing analysis of provincial Russia, of a demoralized, ignorant, and apathetic peasantry. Here he explodes the intelligentsia's myth about the "people" as the source of the nation's spiritual regeneration. He shows how the enforced collectivization of the 1930's robbed the peasants of their attachment to the land, leaving them uprooted, alienated, and even more deprived than migrant workers in other countries because they have no freedom of movement. They, like the political prisoners sent to work with them, are merely putting in time. Amalrik concludes that for all practical purposes, the kolkhoz system is based on forced labor and the peasants are "totally without rights."

While in exile, Amalrik learned that his father was critically ill and petitioned for a leave to visit him, but by the time he had overcome bureaucratic delays and made the trip home, his father was dead. His unhappy stay in Moscow had one great consolation in that he persuaded Gyuzel Makudinova, a Tatar painter whom he had met only three times before, to marry him and share his exile. On October 12, 1965 they set off for Siberia, a trip laden, as he recalls, with "sombre overtones of death, deportation, and complete uncertainty about [their] future." They lived together for about five months, until his wife was obliged to return to Moscow in order not to forfeit their residence permit in the city. On July 8, 1966 Amalrik's sentence was suddenly reversed by the Russian Supreme Court, which decreed that as the only living relative of an invalid, he was not guilty of parasitism. By that time he had served nearly half his sentence and the invalid in question was dead.

During the next four years Amalrik and his wife lived poorly in Moscow, but were relatively unhampered by authorities. She earned some money painting portraits of foreign diplomats, journalists, and their children. Until 1968, at least, when the KGB resumed their harassment, Amalrik was permitted to write articles on theatre and the arts for minor Soviet publications. They rented a small, sunless room in a communal apartment, sharing the kitchen, bath, and telephone with eleven other people, some of whom were hired to spy on them. Yet despite the watchful eyes of neighbors and the microphones hidden in their apartment, those cramped quarters, brightened by the paintings of Amalrik's wife and other unorthodox artists, gave him the "inner freedom" he craved. Here he and his wife entertained friends, Russians and foreigners, freely discussing their common interests and lowering their voices only to muffle the names of friends they wished to protect. In public, too, Amalrik showed no willingness to compromise, no sign that sixteen months of exile or the threat of future arrests could intimidate him. He pursued a consistent if somewhat idiosyncratic form of dissent, baffling the authorities and, at times, fellow dissidents in the Soviet Union, whose hatred of the system he shares but not their optimism. Although never one to sign collective protests, when other dissidents were on trial, he would regularly appear outside the courtroom to lend moral support. His anarchic temperament was further revealed by the solitary demonstration he and his wife staged against the British Embassy in Moscow in 1968 to protest Britain's support of the federal Nigerian government's war against Biafra.

Amalrik's protests have not been aimed strictly at governments or government officials. In 1969 he addressed a sharp rebuke to Anatoly Kuznetsov, the Soviet writer who fled to England that year by pretending to collaborate with the KGB. Published in the winter and spring 1969 issues of *Survey*, the British journal on Soviet and East European affairs, the letter charged Kuznetsov with cowardice and willingness to compromise himself for the sake of "external freedom." Although Amalrik conceded that no man should make moral choices for another, he added, "Nonetheless, I do reproach you, not because I want to condemn you personally but because I want to condemn the philosophy of impotence and self-justification which runs through all you have said and written in the West. 'I was given no choice,' you seem to be saying, and this sounds like a justification not only for yourself, but for the whole of the Soviet creative intelligentsia, or at least the liberal part of it to which you belong. . . .'"

The nature of Amalrik's disagreement with the courageous Soviet dissidents who constitute the "Democratic Movement" became clear with the publication of his provocative historical essay *Will the Soviet Union Survive Until 1984?* (Harper, 1970). Here he offers a grim prognosis of a society that, as he sees it, consists of three antagonistic groups: a moribund bureaucratic elite, too inflexible to introduce the reforms crucial to its own survival; a middle-class desirous of change but bent on preserving its own privileges; and, at bottom, a peasant-proletarian mass seething with resentment. All three groups share a vast inertia. Contrary to liberal opinion in the U.S.S.R. and the West, Amalrik regards the apparent liberalization since Stalin's death not as a sign of the regime's renewal but its growing decrepitude. Détente and increased cultural contacts may ultimately produce "a socialism with bare knees," he believes, "but not likely one with a human face." He diverges most from other dissidents in his view of the lower classes, upon which the success of the Democratic Movement depends. The peasants, he insists, are no longer guided by the Christian ethic, which "has been driven out of the popular consciousness." They are ruled by fear, the same fear that on the national level manifests itself in increased militarism and Great Russian nationalism. Given the hostility of both the masses and the suppressed nationality groups, Amalrik predicts, the present Soviet government will pursue a policy of foreign expansion and provoke a war with China that will ultimately tear the nation apart. His apocalyptic vision is rendered with the passion of an Old Testament prophet that, as the critic Alan Pryce-Jones remarked in a review for *Newsday* (July 24, 1970), makes Amalrik's work an "intensely Russian book, a cry from the heart rather than a critique or a program, the warning of a latter-day Ezekiel."

Ironically, Amalrik's decision to authorize publication of his works abroad so as to challenge the constitutionality of a Soviet law that makes such criticism of the state a criminal offense, led some Western journalists to believe he was a KGB agent. The six months of freedom Amalrik enjoyed after his books appeared seemingly lent credence to these rumors. They were dispelled once and for all with Amalrik's arrest in May 1970. Accused of "disseminating falsehoods derogatory to the Soviet state," he was tried in the remote town of Sverdlovsk on November 12, 1970. The prosecution's case against him was based on five documents: Amalrik's letter to Kuznetsov, his two books, and two TV interviews he and other dissidents had with the CBS correspondent William Cole (one of which was broadcast in the United States in July 1970). In his final statement to the court Amalrik declared, "To sentence ideas to criminal punishment, whether they be true or false, seems to me to be a crime in itself. . . . I have nothing to ask of this court." Those remarks allegedly prompted the judge to insist on a three-year term in an intensive labor camp rather than one with a less severe regimen. En route to the Siberian camp Amalrik fell ill with meningitis and recovered against odds in a prison hospital in Novosibirsk. The Soviet government, besieged with appeals, exempted him from hard labor but insisted he serve his full sentence.

As the translator Daniel Weissbort observed in his introduction to a collection of Amalrik's plays, *Nose! Nose? No-se!* (Harcourt, 1973), "Amalrik has had the perhaps unenviable opportunity of knowing that for the true artist, art and life are indissolubly linked." Predictably, Amalrik, who admires Eugène Ionesco and Samuel Beckett, has a keen sense of the absurd, which he uses to great advantage in some of his plays, illustrating the confusion and emptiness of life, and the impoverishment of language in a totalitarian regime. His characters tend to wrangle endlessly in a kind of "No-Speak" riddled with clichés and meaningless slogans. The six published plays are uneven in quality. One entitled "East-West: A Dialogue in Suzdal," which ranges from farce through political satire to passages of great lyric tenderness, was exceedingly well-reviewed after a performance in London in January 1972. The critic Alfred Friendly summed up his impression in the Washington *Post* (January 6, 1972), "That Amalrik is a playwright and a competent one, besides being a brilliant, devastating, and incredibly courageous social and political critic, is a new discovery."

Shortly before Amalrik's sentence was to expire on May 21, 1973, the Harvard University Russian Research Center and George Washington University invited him to lecture and to work in historical research. While these invitations were on their way, Amalrik was detained in camp, charged, as in 1970, with disseminating anti-Soviet propaganda (this time among prison inmates), and resentenced on July 17, 1973 to three additional years in camp. Despite worldwide protest and a 117-day hunger strike that Amalrik staged, Soviet authorities remained adamant. When, by November 1973, his health had become precarious, they commuted his sentence to exile, making it retroactive to May. His term is due to expire early in 1975, because under Soviet law time in prison counts three times that in exile. The government showed further clemency by allowing him to settle and hold a job in Magadan City, a port town with adequate medical facilities and a sizable population. His wife has joined him there and, according to recent reports, the couple have found a congenial community among the former exiles who have chosen to remain in Siberia.

References

N Y Times p8 D 24 '69 por
N Y Times Mag p12+ Jl 29 '73 por
Time 102:33+ Ag 6 '73 por
Washington Post B p5 Ag 2 '70 por; A p14 Je 9 '73
Amalrik, Andrei. Involuntary Journey to Siberia (1970)

ANGELOU, MAYA (an′jə-lō)

Apr. 4, 1928-   Writer; entertainer
Address: b. c/o Gerard W. Purcell Associates, Ltd., 133 5th Ave., New York 10003

A few years ago Maya Angelou gave a series of lectures at the University of California at Los Angeles entitled "The Negro Contribution to American Culture." As a woman of many gifts —an author, actress, singer, dancer, songwriter, teacher, and editor—she herself has added liberally to that contribution. She has written two volumes of autobiography, including the best-selling *I Know Why the Caged Bird Sings*, in addition to plays, short stories, poetry, and TV documentaries, and has performed in Broadway and Off-Broadway plays. In the film industry, especially, through her work in scriptwriting and directing, she has been a groundbreaker for black women.

"I speak to the black experience," she once explained, "but I am always talking about the human condition—about what we can endure, dream, fail at and still survive."

Maya Angelou was born Marguerite Johnson on April 4, 1928 in St. Louis, Missouri. Her father, Bailey Johnson, was a doorman and later a Naval dietician. Her mother, Vivian (Baxter) Johnson, an exceptionally resourceful woman, worked over the years as a card dealer, realtor, beautician, registered nurse, and, eventually, a merchant seaman. She has one brother, Bailey, who gave her the name Maya. The family lived for a time in Long Beach, California, but when Maya was three and her brother was four, their divorced parents sent them by train to Stamps, Arkansas to live with their paternal grandmother, Ann Henderson. The children, supervised by Uncle Willie, helped their grandmother in her shop, the only black general store in the thoroughly segregated town. Despite the grim realities of life for blacks in the South and the absence of her parents, Maya Angelou's childhood was rich in tradition and affection, especially through her association with the local church. She once told Jane Julianelli in an interview for *Harper's Bazaar* (November 1972), "One would say of my life—born loser—had to be: from a broken family, raped at eight, unwed mother at sixteen. . . . It's a fact but it's not the truth. In the black community, however bad it looks, there's a lot of love and so much humor."

Except for a year when, at about the age of seven, she lived with her mother in St. Louis, Maya Angelou remained in Stamps until she graduated with honors from Lafayette County Training School in 1940. She and her brother then went to San Francisco, to the home of her mother, who had recently remarried. At fourteen she won a two-year scholarship to the California Labor School. Through persistence and determination she became the first black female fare collector with the San Francisco streetcar company. Reading *The Well of Loneliness* contributed to her adolescent confusion regarding her sexual identity, and she confronted her fear through a brief affair with a neighbor's boy. Shortly after graduating from Mission High School at sixteen, she gave birth to a son, Guy, in the summer of 1944. When interviewed by Ric Ballad for *Viva* (March 1974), she said, "I'm often asked, 'Why did you end the book [*I Know Why the Caged Bird Sings*] with the birth of your illegitimate son?' And I tell them I wanted to end it on a happy note. It was the best thing that ever happened to me." Among the experiences that she seems to prefer to forget was her first marriage, to a man of Greek origin named Angelou, which was dissolved about 1952.

While still in her teens Maya Angelou attended evening courses in dance and drama in San Francisco. Later, with the help of a scholarship she studied dance with Pearl Primus in New York and then returned to San Francisco to try, without success, to form her own dance troupe. In the 1950's she became a nightclub performer.

MAYA ANGELOU

Specializing in calypso songs and dances, she appeared at the Purple Onion in San Francisco, Mr. Kelly's in Chicago, and the Blue Angel and the Village Vanguard in New York, among many other clubs. She also sang and danced in *Porgy and Bess* on a twenty-two-country tour of Europe and Africa during 1954 and 1955. That widely acclaimed State Department-sponsored production of the Gershwin musical proved to be one of the more effective measures in an effort to counteract growing Communist influence and distrust of America overseas. Between engagements of *Porgy and Bess*, Miss Angelou taught modern dance at the Rome Opera House and the Habimah Theatre in Tel Aviv.

After the tour Maya Angelou returned to the nightclub circuit in the United States. In collaboration with Godfrey Cambridge she wrote, produced, and performed in a revue, *Cabaret for Freedom*, which was presented at New York's Village Gate. She also appeared with Cambridge in Jean Genet's play *The Blacks*, which opened at the St. Mark's Playhouse on May 4, 1961 to much praise, confusion, and outrage. In the all-black cast she had the role of the Queen, a white-masked black reigning over and judging those beneath, the feared and victimized black minority, who turn on their oppressors at the end of the play in a frenzy of hate. *The Blacks* won the Obie award in 1961 for the best Off-Broadway play, American or foreign, and ran for 1,272 performances before closing on May 24, 1964. Miss Angelou had dropped out of the cast much earlier but rejoined the company in the late summer of 1964 to act in the festivals of Venice and Berlin.

While earning her living as a performer, Miss Angelou had acquired a growing interest in social causes, including civil rights. At the urging of Bayard Rustin she served in 1960-61 as Northern coordinator for the Rev. Dr. Martin Luther King's Southern Christian Leadership Conference, a post carrying heavy fund-raising responsibilities. In late 1961 she went to Africa, where for about a year she worked as associate editor of the

Arab Observer, an English-language newsweekly in Cairo, Egypt. Then, moving on to Ghana, she wrote free-lance articles for the *Ghanian Times* and for the Ghanian Broadcasting Corporation in Accra. She was also feature editor of the *African Review* in Accra and a teacher and assistant administrator at the School of Music and Drama at the University of Ghana. In an article for the New York *Times* (April 16, 1972) she wrote, "For Africa to me . . . is more than a glamorous fact. It is a historical truth. No man can know where he is going unless he knows exactly where he has been and exactly how he arrived at his present place." During her stay on that continent she was reportedly married to an African political leader, whose name she has not disclosed.

Maya Angelou's life in the United States, after several years in Africa, seemed more productive and varied than ever before. Joining the Theatre of Being in Hollywood in 1966, she performed in Jean Anouilh's *Medea,* under the direction of Frank Silvera. She wrote and produced a ten-part television series on Africanisms in American life. She also wrote many songs, some of which have been recorded by B. B. King; a book of poems, "The True Believers," in collaboration with Abbey Lincoln; a collection of short stories, "All Day Long"; and two plays, "The Least of These" and "The Clawing Within." In the fall of 1970 Miss Angelou spent several weeks at the University of Kansas in Lawrence as writer in residence.

The idea for writing her autobiography came about during a dinner conversation with friends, among them James Baldwin and Jules Feiffer. *I Know Why the Caged Bird Sings* (Random, 1970) was an immediate critical and commercial success. It is the story of Maya Angelou's life up to the age of sixteen, her experiences in Arkansas, Missouri, and California. Christopher Lehmann-Haupt of the New York *Times* (February 25, 1970) called it "a carefully wrought, simultaneously touching and comic memoir . . . [whose] beauty is not in the story but in the telling." Impressed by the "intensity and life" of the book, Robert A. Gross commented in *Newsweek* (March 2, 1970) on its "rich, dazzling images," but praised it as much more than "a tour de force of language." *Gather Together in My Name* (Random, 1974) continued the story of Maya Angelou's life over four more years. In it, as she explained in an interview with Sheila Weller for *Intellectual Digest* (June 1973), she tried to recount the story not only of the Maya Angelou who escaped a world of poverty and prostitution and the very precipice of drug addiction but also of "the woman who *didn't* escape," who "wrestles" still "with demons."

Just Give Me a Cool Drink of Water 'Fore I Diiie (Random, 1971) is a collection of thirty-nine of Miss Angelou's poems, which mix everyday language with a more conventionally poetic vocabulary. They are divided into two parts: one group intimate in tone, dealing with the gentler emotions; the other at times quite acerbic and militant in its treatment of racial confrontation.

Discussing black writers and white critics on a National Educational Television interview with Bill Moyers on November 21, 1973, Miss Angelou said, "Quite often there are allusions made in black American writing, there are rhythms set in the writing and counter-rhythms that mean a great deal to blacks. A white American can come in and he will hear, he will understand, hopefully, the gist. And that's what one is talking about. The other is sort of 'in' talk."

To fill what she sees as a need for the real character of the American black woman to be explored in films, Maya Angelou wrote the screenplay for *Georgia, Georgia* (Cinerama, 1972), the first original script by a black woman to be produced. The movie, which starred Diana Sands, concerns a black singer, touring Sweden, whose strong attraction to white society contrasts sharply with the attitude of her companion, an angry and embittered black woman. Some critics were dissatisfied with Stig Björkman's direction of the film, and a few thought the generally powerful script faltered now and then. "Despite these faults," Arthur Cooper asserted in *Newsweek* (April 3, 1972), "'Georgia' is admirable for the honesty with which it tries to get a psychic fix on the contemporary black woman." Miss Angelou also wrote the script and music for the screen version of *I Know Why the Caged Bird Sings.* When the film is released, she will be credited as its director, thus adding another first to her list.

Around the time that New York moviegoers saw *Georgia, Georgia,* television audiences heard Miss Angelou as the narrator of "The Slave Coast," part three of the four-part series *Black African Heritage,* photographed by Eliot Elisofon and presented on WCBS-TV in the spring of 1972. She made her Broadway debut in a two-character play, *Look Away,* as the confidante and former dressmaker of Mary Todd Lincoln, portrayed by Geraldine Page. *Look Away* opened at the Playhouse Theatre on January 7, 1973 and closed the same night. Although not enthusiastic about the play itself, several New York critics described Miss Angelou's performance as "excellent." Then, drawing on another of her talents, in early 1974 she wrote an adaptation of Sophocles' *Ajax* for the Mark Taper Forum in Los Angeles.

In a lecture at Yale University in 1970 and in press and TV interviews Maya Angelou has talked about the mythical black woman and about the position of the black woman in both black and white societies. "The black American female has nursed a nation of strangers—literally. And has remained compassionate," she said in the *Intellectual Digest* interview. "This, to me, is survival. She is strong. And she is inclusive, as opposed to exclusive. She has included all the rest of humanity in her life and has often been excluded from their lives. I'm very impressed with her." When asked about women's liberation, Miss Angelou has replied that she supports that movement but believes it is almost superfluous for black women. The very nature of the white man's society has had paradoxical results for the black woman, to whom, unlike the black man, work has always been available. While the white woman has been held back by such a society, the black woman in terms of her social and economic position as well as her familial one has evolved into a person of fortitude and self-reliance.

Maya Angelou is a six-foot tall, imposing woman of a graceful, elegant bearing and a gracious though sometimes formal manner. Helen Dudar of the New York *Post* (December 26, 1970) observed that she conveys "pride without arrogance, self-esteem without smugness." Her hair is cropped short and she dresses in the African style. Having concluded "with delight" that her ancestral roots were in the Ewe tribe of West Africa, she told Miss Dudar, "I have the height and the body and the color and the gap in my teeth."

In December 1973 Miss Angelou married Paul Du Feu, the former husband of Germaine Greer. She has a small house in Berkeley, California with a backyard where she grows scallions and onions in her spare time. Her son, Guy Johnson, who became the first black executive with Western Airlines, also lives in Berkeley and is now intent on a literary career. When Miss Angelou is writing, she becomes totally absorbed, sometimes spending sixteen hours a day in seclusion. Many of her friends, including Alex Haley and Jessica Mitford, are also authors. In addition to English, Miss Angelou speaks French, Spanish, Italian, Arabic, and West African Fanti. She stands politically left of center, believing in social change for the betterment of those who have not shared fully in the American dream. In *I Know Why the Caged Bird Sings* she suggested, "It may be enough . . . to have it said that we [black people] survive in exact relationship to the dedication of our poets."

References

Harp Baz 106:124 N '72 por
Intellectual Digest 3:11+ Je '73 pors
N Y Post p21 D 26 '70 por; p77 N 5 '71 por
N Y Times p28 Mr 24 '72 por
Newsday A p3 Ap 17 '70 por
Viva 1:63+ Mr '74

Angelou, Maya. I Know Why the Caged Bird Sings (1970); Gather Together in My Name (1974)
One Thousand Successful Blacks (1973)

ARIAS NAVARRO, CARLOS

Dec. 11, 1908- Premier of Spain
Address: b. Presidencia del Gobierno, Paseo de la Castellana 3, Madrid 1, Spain; h. "La Chiripa," Paradores 4, El Plantío (Casa Quemada), Madrid, Spain

When Admiral Luis Carrero Blanco fell victim to an assassin's bomb in December 1973, after serving barely six months as Premier of Spain with the title of President of the Government, the aging

CARLOS ARIAS NAVARRO

chief of state, Generalíssimo Francisco Franco, made the logical choice of Carlos Arias Navarro as his successor. The new Premier, who took office in January 1974, has a record of dedicated public service dating back to the last years of Alfonso XIII's reign. Under the Franco regime he served successively as civil governor in three provinces, as director-general of security, as mayor of Madrid, and as Minister of the Interior, displaying an unflinching loyalty to the Caudillo in all those posts. Although considered a tough advocate of law and order, Arias Navarro has also given some hope to those who would like to see some progress made towards liberalization and representative government in Spain. The Premier is also charged with the task of facilitating the transfer of power to Prince Juan Carlos de Borbón under a restored monarchy, when Franco finally exits from the scene.

Carlos Arias Navarro was born on December 11, 1908 in a modest apartment on Madrid's Calle del Humilladero, in a teeming lower middle-class neighborhood near the center of the capital, to Ángel and Nieves (Navarro) Arias, who had four other sons and a daughter. An employee of the Madrid stockyards, Ángel Arias died when Carlos was five; the widow, following the Spanish custom, dressed her orphaned children in mourning despite their youth. Two brothers and a sister (now Mrs. Maria Luisa de García Badell, a widow), survive.

The family later moved to the nearby Calle de Toledo, where Carlos and his sister were taught to read and write by Antonio de Miguel, now a noted octogenarian economist and journalist, before they entered school. Arias Navarro studied with the Escolapio Fathers, a Spanish teaching order founded by St. Joseph Calasanz, and obtained his *bachiller* diploma—the equivalent of a high school certificate—at the age of thirteen.

Not without difficulties, all five of the Arias Navarro brothers managed to attend college. Carlos obtained his *Licenciatura* in law, and later a doctorate, at the old Central University of Madrid. In 1929, before reaching his twenty-first birthday, he won top rating in the civil service exam for the Justice Ministry's corps of technical experts and was assigned to the general directorate concerned with the registration of property and other notarial matters.

In the early 1930's Arias Navarro fulfilled his military obligations by serving with the second railway regiment in Madrid. In 1933, two years after the establishment of the Spanish Republic, he passed a civil service examination qualifying him to serve with the Attorney General's department and was assigned to the office of the public prosecutor in the *audiencia*, or provincial high court, of Málaga. It was in that coastal Andalusian province that he was caught up in the Civil War, which erupted in the summer of 1936. Because of his allegiance to Franco he was imprisoned in Málaga by Republican authorities until Falangist forces took the city. He then joined the insurgent army and was assigned as a prosecutor to the military judicial corps, with the honorary rank of captain. Later he entered the air force judicial staff at the head of the candidate exam list. In 1942 he passed the difficult civil service test for notary public, a post of considerable prestige and responsibility in Latin countries. (It was not, however, until nearly three decades later, while he was serving as mayor of Madrid, that Arias Navarro was finally sworn in as a notary public.)

While serving as public prosecutor in the Madrid district court in 1944, Arias Navarro was given his first political appointment, as civil governor of the province of León. At the same time he became provincial head of the National Movement, or Falange, Spain's only legal political organization. Discussing with the writer and dramatist Alfonso Paso his perennial lack of gusto for politics, Arias confessed that he at first resisted the León appointment because he sincerely believed that he was unprepared and unqualified for a political job. Once he accepted, however, he succeeded in restoring law and order to a vast, largely mountainous region still harassed occasionally by roving partisan guerrillas. During his five years as governor of León he also served for a time as president of the León Industrial Bank.

About 1949 Arias Navarro was appointed civil governor of Santa Cruz de Tenerife in the Canary Islands. Several years later he was sent to Pamplona to serve as governor of the province of Navarre. During his two years in that post he devoted much of his effort to the improvement of housing, education, medical care, and the general welfare. General Camilo Alonso Vega, then Minister of the Interior, who was known as a strict law enforcement official, chose Arias Navarro in June 1957 as director-general of security, a post that made him the nation's top law-enforcement officer. During the nearly eight years that he occupied that post he acquired a reputation for toughness in dealing with criminals and with enemies of the Franco regime.

His appointment, in February 1965, as mayor of Madrid, ushered in a fruitful period of municipal management that lasted more than eight years. During that time he earned a reputation as Madrid's finest mayor since the late eighteenth century, when King Carlos III launched a program of civic improvement and beautification that won the Bourbon monarch the lasting gratitude of the capital's inhabitants. Having inherited from his predecessor, the Count of Mayalde, an unwieldy metropolis of nearly 3,000,000 that was fast outgrowing its boundaries, Arias Navarro tried to resolve its many problems. He ordered the construction of badly needed housing and of schools to provide new classroom space for some 100,000 pupils. New roads were paved, traffic lights were installed, and overpasses were constructed on major thoroughfares. Sanitation and fire-fighting services were improved, and a women's corps was added to the municipal police force. To ensure efficiency, Arias Navarro used to show up unannounced on the sites of public works projects.

To beautify Madrid, Arias Navarro inaugurated fifteen new parks, thus giving *Madrileños* nearly 4,000,000 square meters of additional green space for their recreation. The former Cuartel de la Montaña, a barracks in ruins since the Civil War, was converted into a handsome park featuring an authentic Egyptian temple. Carlos Arias Navarro added a sizeable annex to the permanent dimensions of the Casa de Campo, a large forest preserve on the edge of Madrid, embellishing it with an amusement park and a modern zoo.

As mayor of Madrid, Arias Navarro proved such an untiring worker that the lights of his office in the seventeenth-century city hall were often seen burning until 10 P.M. He once declared that what he mainly demands of his associates and subordinates is a capacity for work and that he cannot brook idleness on the part of others. His success in the thankless job led Franco to appoint him to a second term in February 1971. During his first term, in the fall of 1967, he was also elected a deputy to the Cortes Españolas—Spain's limited parliament—as a representative of the Madrid city council. Not long after that he became a member of the Council of the Realm, Spain's highest consultative assembly, consisting of seventeen representatives of corporate bodies and official institutions.

In June 1973 Franco divested himself of some of the burdens of his office by designating his longtime aide and adviser Admiral Luis Carrero Blanco as President of the Government, or Premier. In the new Cabinet, Arias Navarro, whose name had been on the "eligible" list for a ministerial appointment for a decade, was given the sensitive portfolio of Minister of the Interior. As such, he was responsible for the post office and telecommunications, local administration on the provincial and municipal levels, health and welfare, and perhaps more importantly, the police and internal security.

Shortly before he was appointed to the Ministry of the Interior, Arias Navarro said, as quoted in *Ya* (December 30, 1973): "I have no political ambitions. . . . I'm prepared to accept what I'm told," and added that his ambition had been satisfied when he received his first public job.

Earlier he had indicated that once he finished his second term as mayor of Madrid he would withdraw to the peace and quiet of private life. Following his appointment to the Cabinet post, he declared, according to the New York *Times* (December 31, 1973): "My dedication to the post that has now been entrusted to me will always be governed by the thought of serving our leader with fidelity, with respectful affection, and inalterable admiration."

But Arias Navarro served as Minister of the Interior for barely six months. As a result of the bomb that propelled Carrero Blanco's car over a church wall in Madrid on December 20, 1973, killing the Premier as he was returning from Mass, the Cabinet was automatically dissolved under the terms of Spain's Organic Law. In accordance with that law, after several days of consultation, the Council of the Realm submitted to Franco a list of three candidates for Premier, but Franco overruled the council, which was embroiled in a power struggle between its rightist and moderate factions. Bypassing its three candidates, all of them reportedly military men, he selected Arias Navarro, whom he had long regarded as a trusted friend, and who, like Carrero Blanco, had no personal political ambitions and was not committed to any political faction. Arias Navarro enjoyed the confidence of the moderate senior military officers, whose restraining influence had prevented any severe repressive measures after the assassination of Carrero Blanco. At the same time, his anti-Communist record and commitment to law and order made him acceptable to ultrarightists.

Contrary to predictions that he would make few Cabinet changes, Arias Navarro—who was sworn in on January 2, 1974—demonstrated his independence by thoroughly reshuffling the government. To the nineteen-member Cabinet he appointed eleven new ministers. One of the most significant effects of those changes was the end of the marked influence of Opus Dei, a controversial Roman Catholic laymen's organization of technocrats. Among the Cabinet members ousted in the shakeup was the Opus Dei leader, Foreign Minister Laureano López Rodó, who was replaced by Pedro Cortina, a career diplomat. The new Cabinet appointees were, for the most part, conservative professionals associated with the Falange and, like the Premier, uninvolved in factional politics. In their turn his ministers appointed like-minded officials to their departments.

Nevertheless, the Cabinet changes did not signal a swing to the right and in fact encouraged those who advocated greater democratization. In his speech of January 4, 1974 the Premier declared that the government would "make use of all its authority . . . to defend the common good and maintain an order in whose framework Spaniards can develop their rights and liberties"; would "give great importance to the development of political participation" in view of "the proved civic maturity of the people"; and would promote "better living standards . . . , especially for the working classes."

Prospects for liberalization appeared enhanced by Arias Navarro's eighty-minute televised speech to the Cortes on February 12, 1974, in which he promised to establish the institutional means to enable Spain's 34,000,000 inhabitants to participate more fully in the nation's political and economic life. He outlined proposed legislation to provide for popular election of mayors and other local officials; to allow "political associations" within the framework of the National Movement (as distinct from political parties, which remain illegal); to allow labor and management to form separate organizations within the official syndicates, thus giving labor greater bargaining power; and to make the Cortes more representative by barring government officials—then constituting more than one-third of the 561 deputies—from serving. With regard to foreign policy, the Premier reaffirmed his country's friendship with the United States, called for cordial relations with Portugal, Latin America, and the Arab countries, and expressed the hope that Spain could become part of the European Common Market.

The "spirit of February 12," as the euphoric mood engendered by the Premier's speech was called, received some implementation in the spring and summer of 1974, when the government initiated action to establish political associations and introduced a court reform measure. Some steps were also taken to ease censorship in the arts and the mass media. On the other hand, the abrupt dismissal, in June 1974, of Lieutenant General Manuel Díez Alegría, a political moderate, as chief of the high general staff, was viewed as a setback for the liberals, and in a speech he delivered in Barcelona that month, Arias Navarro made a special effort to reassure hardline conservatives.

Meanwhile, Arias Navarro cracked down on Basque nationalists, who were believed responsible for Carrero Blanco's assassination. That brought his government into confrontation with the increasingly liberal Roman Catholic hierarchy and touched off what has been called the worst church-state crisis since the Civil War. In February 1974 Arias Navarro ordered the house arrest of the bishop of Bilbao, Antonio Anoveros Ataun, claiming that the bishop's call for "just freedom" for the Basque people constituted an attack on national unity. The Premier's later effort, in March, to exile the bishop, almost led to a break in relations between Spain and the Vatican and to an abrogation of the 1953 Concordat. Since the bishop won the solid backing of the Spanish church hierarchy as well as the support of the chairman of the Council of the Realm, Rodrigo de Valcarcel, and of the wife of Generalíssimo Franco, the government had to drop its effort to exile Bishop Anoveros. The outcome was regarded as a major political defeat for Arias Navarro.

In accordance with Article 11 of Spain's Organic State Law, on July 19, 1974 Premier Arias Navarro formally notified the Cortes that Prince Juan Carlos de Borbón was assuming the interim functions of chief of state during the grave illness of Generalissimo Franco. On the same day the Premier witnessed the first official act by the Prince, the signing of the joint Spanish-American declaration of principles concerning mutual defense, which was simultaneously signed in San Clemente, California by President Richard Nixon. The Premier's crucial role in the ultimate transferral of power to Prince Juan Carlos as Franco's successor is expected to be the real test of his political acumen. When Franco resumed the reins of state in September 1974, Arias Navarro asserted in a press interview that, in contradiction to rumors, the activities of his government during the forty-five-day absence of Franco from power had the full backing of the general.

Carlos Arias Navarro and María Luz del Valle Menéndez, a member of a prominent León family, were married in Madrid in October 1956. The Premier and his wife live about nine miles north of the center of Madrid in a suburban villa called "La Chiripa." Although they have no children of their own they maintain a close relationship with their many nieces and nephews. Their summer holidays are usually spent on Spain's north coast at the town of Salinas in Asturias, where Arias Navarro fishes with local cronies. A Breton spaniel named Chirri presides over the family's five dogs, who are occasional companions on their master's hunting and fishing expeditions.

A man who cherishes his memories, Arias Navarro treasures the many mementos of the past in his family archives. His extensive library includes a number of books about Madrid, as well as detective stories by Agatha Christie and Georges Simenon, and works by José Ortega y Gasset, Manuel Azaña, and Benito Pérez Galdós. An aficionado of the *corrida* who favors the classical style of matador Antonio Bienvenida, Arias Navarro is said to be responsible for many of the reforms in the code of bullfighting regulations. He enjoys listening to regional folk music and has a reputation among friends as a gourmet, a shrewd card player, and a witty conversationalist. The Spanish Premier has been decorated with the grand crosses of Civil and of Military Merit, Isabel la Católica, and San Raimundo de Peñafort by his own country, and he holds the rank of knight commander in the orders of Alfonso X el Sabio, Cisneros, and the Yoke and Arrows. He also has decorations from Belgium, Argentina, Thailand, Portugal, and Jordan as well as the Order of Malta, and he is a chevalier of the French Légion d'honneur.

References

ABC (Madrid) p13+ D 30 '73 pors
Blanco y Negro (Madrid) p20+ Ja 5 '74 pors
Christian Sci Mon p3 D 31 '73
N Y Times p3 D 31 '73 por
Newsweek 83:50 F 25 '74
Time 103:23 Ja 14 '74
Wall St J p38 Ja 8 '74
Ya (Madrid) p1+ D 30 '73 pors
Diccionario Biográfico Español Contemporáneo (1970)

BAKER, HOWARD (HENRY, JR.)

Nov. 15, 1925-   United States Senator from Tennessee; lawyer
Address: b. 3311 Dirksen Senate Office Building, Washington, D.C. 20510; h. Huntsville, Tenn. 37756

The ranking Republican on the former Senate Select Committee on Presidential Campaign Activities, Senator Howard Baker was one of the few men who stood to benefit from the Watergate scandal. First elected to the Senate in 1966, the hard-working, productive legislator devoted most of his energies to representing his basically conservative constituents until the Watergate hearings catapulted him to national fame.

During the summer of 1973 Americans who followed the hearings on the alleged illegal campaign tactics employed by the Committee to Reelect the President (CREEP) were impressed by the Senator's sincerity, integrity, and impartiality. While other committee members established facts, Baker tried, in his words, to "identify the forces that caused this to happen." Appearing on ABC-TV's *Issues and Answers* on December 30, 1973, he urged President Richard Nixon to "justify or at least explain some of the conduct that appears otherwise unexplainable." In Baker's view, "There must be a balance at some point . . . on whether the requirements of national security are greater than the requirements of domestic tranquility."

Of traditional mountain Republican ancestry, Howard Henry Baker Jr., the only son born to Howard Henry and Dora (Ladd) Baker, was born on November 15, 1925 in Huntsville, Tennessee, a tiny hill town in the Cumberland Mountains. Both lines of his family were active in politics. His paternal grandfather was a judge; his maternal grandmother succeeded her husband as sheriff; his father, an attorney, was reelected six times to the House of Representatives from the state's Second Congressional District; and his stepmother, Irene Bailey Baker, completed her husband's term when he died in office in 1964. Exhibiting the family aptitude for political debate, Howard Baker won first place in a public speaking contest at the age of eleven. In spite of his precocity, he was viewed by his peers as a "regular" youngster.

After attending public elementary schools in Huntsville, Baker entered the McCallie School, a military academy in Chattanooga. On graduating in 1943, he volunteered for the United States Navy's V-12 program to study electrical engineering, first at the University of the South in Sewanee, Tennessee, then at Tulane University in New Orleans, Louisiana. A brief tour of duty on a PT boat in the South Pacific interrupted his academic career. After his discharge with the rank of lieutenant (j.g.) in 1946, Baker completed his education at the University of Tennessee, where he obtained his LL.B. degree in 1949. "I intended to finish engineering school," he insisted to Myra MacPherson in an interview for the Washington *Post* (June 24, 1973), "but the line was too long on registration day. The line for law school wasn't, so I ended up there. I'm ashamed to admit it, but it's true." While at the University of Tennessee he was president of the student body and was honored by being included in *Who's Who Among Students in American Universities and Colleges.*

Joining the staff of Baker, Worthington, Crossley & Stansberry, the Knoxville-based law firm founded by his grandfather in 1885, Howard Baker acquired a reputation as an able attorney. A cunning cross-examiner, he often obtained relatively light sentences for his clients—a talent that earned him the nickname "Old Two-to-Ten." The citizens of Scott County used to pack the county courthouse to hear his skillfully argued defenses. Equally adept at corporate law, he represented four major coal companies in a legal action against the United Mine Workers and collected a $1,000,000 settlement.

A shrewd businessman, Baker with several of his associates purchased a controlling interest in the First National Bank of Oneida, Tennessee and transformed that moribund institution into a dynamic, highly profitable operation. He was quick to recognize the industrial and recreational possibilities of the Payne-Baker tract—a rolling, 40,000-acre stretch of wilderness rich in timber, coal, and natural gas, partly owned by the Baker family. He formed a partnership with William Swain, an old friend, and John W. Rollins, a corporation executive, and the three men bought the tract for $2,000,000. Recent estimates indicate that the value of the property has more than doubled. Baker resigned his position as chairman of the board of the First National Bank of Oneida and president of the Colonial Natural Gas Company of Wytheville, Virginia when he was elected to the Senate.

Although he was assured election to the Congressional seat held by his father until the older man's death in 1964, Howard Baker decided instead to run for a Senate post that had been vacant since the death of Senator Estes Kefauver in August 1963. Despite the opposition of his wife, the former Joy Dirksen, and his father-in-law, Illinois Senator Everett Dirksen, Baker was determined to "break out of the East Tennessee [Republican] beachhead" in the traditionally Democratic state, as he explained to Christopher Lydon in an interview for the New York *Times Magazine* (September 30, 1973). He carefully avoided identification with Senator Barry M. Goldwater's Presidential drive and campaigned on a conservative platform that promised to restrict federal interference in local education and in the enforcement of recently enacted civil rights legislation. Baker lost the special election to liberal Congressman Ross Bass by 50,000 votes, but he amassed a larger vote total than any Republican in the state's history.

After serving the two years of Kefauver's unexpired term, Bass lost the Democratic Senatorial primary to Tennessee Governor Frank G. Clement. In the Republican contest, Baker easily defeated

HOWARD BAKER

his more conservative opponent Kenneth Roberts, a Goldwater Republican. Taking a more moderate stance than he had in 1964, Baker earned the endorsement of several influential Democratic newspapers that disapproved of Governor Clement's administrative policies. With campaign assistance from Richard M. Nixon, who stumped the state in his behalf, Baker defeated Clement by a plurality of nearly 100,000 votes to become the first popularly elected Republican Senator in the state's history. His support of such liberal legislation as fair housing laws, winning the approval of 65 percent of the youth vote and 35 percent of the black vote, cut heavily into the traditionally Democratic constituency. Baker was returned to the Senate in 1972, defeating Democratic Representative Ray Blanton by more than 276,000 votes.

Senator Baker's voting record, rated at zero percent in 1972 by the Americans for Democratic Action and at 70 percent overall by the conservative Americans for Constitutional Action, supports his contention that he is a "moderate to moderate conservative" voter. In domestic affairs, for example, he opposed the reduction of the oil depletion allowance, voted against no-fault automobile insurance, and approved the ill-fated Supreme Court nominations of Clement F. Haynesworth Jr. and G. Harrold Carswell. He has consistently supported financial aid to higher education, but, on the other hand, secured Senate passage of a Constitutional amendment permitting voluntary prayer in the public schools and opposed busing as "a grievous piece of mischief." Notwithstanding his backing of bills to improve and strengthen law enforcement, including the controversial "no-knock" entry provision of the omnibus "District of Columbia crime bill," Baker has opposed tough gun control legislation. "You've got to listen to the beating drums," he explained to Myra MacPherson. "There are some things simply impossible for me to do politically—such as voting for gun control legislation—as long as I am representing Tennessee."

Baker's legislative efforts, however, have not always taken a conservative direction. In his first major floor fight in 1967 freshman Senator Baker locked horns with his father-in-law, Senate Minority Leader Dirksen, who was trying to delay compliance with the Supreme Court's "one-man, one-vote" ruling on Congressional reapportionment. To drum up support for his bill banning at-large elections in states with more than one Representative, Baker circulated a study among Senators showing that redistricted areas were more likely to elect Republicans than Democrats. The following year, in an attempt to improve the Republican party's civil rights record, Baker persuaded Dirksen, a longtime opponent of open housing legislation, to initiate a compromise bill exempting certain categories of privately owned homes. Defending the final bill in a Senate debate, Baker said he had "agonized" over the language of the amendment: "This amendment originates from me, the junior Senator from Tennessee, who is not taking a popular position from a political standpoint." To insure the participation of all citizens in the democratic process, Baker supported the Equal Rights Amendment and the extension of the vote to eighteen-year-olds and called for the abolition of the Electoral College and for the direct election of Presidents. On other domestic issues, he sponsored the use of highway trust funds to improve mass transit, urged a more equitable tax structure, and served as the chief Senate sponsor of revenue sharing, a measure he introduced in his first floor speech as a freshman legislator in 1967.

Assigned to the Senate subcommittee on air and water pollution as a freshman legislator, the Senator introduced a number of significant environmental protection bills, such as the Clean Air Act of 1970, the Coal Strip Mine Control Act of 1971, and the Water Pollution Control Act Amendments of 1972. Baker, who was the floor manager of a resolution establishing a Joint Committee on the Environment, drafted legislation to create a National Environmental Center and several regional research laboratories. He is a leading advocate of increased research into atomic power as a clean, low-cost alternative to fossil fuels. In recognition of his work, President Nixon asked Baker to chair the Secretary of State's advisory committee for the first United Nations Conference on the Human Environment in 1972. On the other hand, Baker approved funding for the supersonic transport plane, argued in favor of the underground nuclear test on Amchitka Island, and voted for the Alaska pipeline. In authorizing the pipeline, he suggested that the project be protected against environmentalists' court actions. In mid-1973 Baker's environmental voting record was rated at 54 percent by the League of Conservation Voters.

To maintain "a sound defense posture," Senator Baker has regularly upheld Pentagon budget requests. Although he endorsed the arms limitation agreement between the United States and the Soviet Union, he approved additional funding for the anti-ballistic missile system, since he views

the deployment of the ABM as a deterrent to the development of offensive weapons and the "first glimmer of disarmament." A supporter of President Nixon's policy in Indochina, Senator Baker has publicly praised the President's "candor and honesty . . . with respect to Southeast Asia." On the Senate floor, he voted against major "end-the-war" bills, including the Hatfield-McGovern and Cooper-Church amendments. In June 1973 Baker made a major break with Presidential policy when he approved a compromise bill that forbade the expenditure of public funds to continue American military action in Southeast Asia beyond August 15, 1973. Originally opposed to the Senate's repeated attempts to limit executive war powers, Baker reversed his position and on November 7, 1973 joined the majority of his colleagues in voting to override Nixon's veto of the War Powers Bill.

Since his election Baker has repeatedly urged his colleagues to abolish the entrenched seniority system to give freshman legislators a greater voice in Senate leadership. Following Senator Dirksen's death in 1969, Baker announced his candidacy for the post of Minority Leader. Originally backed by a coalition of young liberals, he eventually emerged as the conservative candidate in the three-way race with Senator Hugh Scott and Roman L. Hruska. He lost to Scott by five votes. When, two years later Baker again challenged Scott in a Senate Republican caucus, Scott retained his position, although his margin was smaller than anticipated.

When the Senate unanimously voted to establish a bipartisan committee to investigate alleged wrongdoing during the Presidential campaign in 1972, Baker directed a Republican attempt to guarantee equal committee representation for his party. At the insistence of Minority Leader Scott, he accepted the post of ranking Republican on the committee, after having been named to the committee by every Republican polled by Scott. Following his nomination on February 16, 1973, Baker told newsmen that although the assignment had "its peril," he could not "in good conscience" refuse. Aware that his twenty-year friendship with President Nixon had prompted some critics to accuse him of being "Nixon's man" on the committee, he was determined to pursue a nonpartisan course. In a statement at the opening session of the hearings on May 17, 1973 he commended the "complete unanimity" and the "integrity and fairness" of the committee members and their professional staffs. "This is not in any way a partisan undertaking," he assured the American public. "It is a bipartisan search for the unvarnished truth."

Concentrating on the motives of the men involved in the Watergate break-in and cover-up, Senator Baker patiently but persistently questioned each witness. "I'm not trying to establish the moral culpability but trying to find out what causes a man to do this, so that we can write legislation to keep it from happening again," he explained, as quoted in the July 9, 1973 issue of *Time* magazine. Despite the gravity of the charges, the good-natured Baker could not resist playfully needling Runyonesque CREEP "bagman," Anthony Ulasewicz. As the nationally televised hearings continued into the summer, Baker's skill, charm, and telegenic appearance brought him national attention second only to that received by the colorful committee chairman, Senator Sam Ervin.

According to a Louis Harris survey, taken in mid-July, 57 percent of the American people rated Baker's committee performance as "good" or "excellent," while only 13 percent measured it as "only fair" or "poor," and his public success prompted speculation of a Baker Presidential drive in 1976. To test Baker's vote-getting potential, pollster Harris, in a separate survey conducted in July 1973, paired Baker with Senator Edward M. Kennedy, a leading contender for the Democratic nomination. Baker turned out to be the choice of 74 percent of the Republicans and 51 percent of the independents polled by Harris, and he narrowly defeated Kennedy, 45 to 44 percent. When questioned about his Presidential ambitions by John S. Lang in an interview for a New York Post profile (June 30, 1973), Baker remained noncommittal: "One, I don't have to think seriously about it for the moment. Two, it would be a disservice to the duties I'm trying to perform. Three, I don't think I'd like to be President. . . . But four, I would not be afraid to be President."

A small, compact, boyishly handsome, and impeccably groomed man, Howard Baker Jr. stands five feet seven inches tall, weighs 155 pounds, and has dark-brown hair and green eyes. For recreation, he plays tennis, golfs, pilots a small plane, and rides his trail bike through the backwoods of Tennessee. He maintains fully equipped darkrooms in both his homes and has had a number of well-received one-man photography exhibits in several Southern cities and one fifty-photo exhibit in Washington, D.C. In 1974 he was working on a collection of biographical profiles and a political novel, both to be published by Doubleday & Company. The Senator and his wife, the former Joy Dirksen, whom he married on December 22, 1951, divide their time between a rented Tudor-style house in northwest Washington, D.C., and their sprawling Huntsville estate overlooking the New River. The couple has two children: Darek Dirksen and Cynthia. Affable, articulate, and, according to one correspondent, "deceptively old-shoe," Baker admitted to Myra MacPherson that he often "hides behind words" in his public appearances. In private, he continued, he "isn't the activist, likes to contemplate, escapes to the photo darkroom. . . . The public person never goes down there."

References

N Y Times Mag p11+ S 30 '73 por
Nat Observer p6 Je 16 '73 por
Newsday p1 Jl 29 '73 por
Douth, George. Leaders in Profile (1972)
Who's Who in America, 1972-73
Who's Who in American Politics, 1973-74

BALL, WILLIAM

Apr. 29, 1931- Theatre director; producer
Address: c/o American Conservatory Theatre, 450 Geary St., San Francisco, Calif. 94102

The American Conservatory Theatre, the most lively and productive regional repertory company in the United States, has for its general director William Ball. Founded in Pittsburgh by Ball in 1965, the American Conservatory Theatre has since 1967 made its home in San Francisco, where it has developed a repertory ranging from *King Lear* to *Charley's Aunt*. After beginning his theatrical career as an actor during the 1950's, Ball became recognized as one of New York's most promising young directors. His directing credits included *Ivanov, Under Milk Wood*, and *Six Characters in Search of an Author* Off Broadway, *Tartuffe* with the Lincoln Center Repertory Company, several operas with the New York City Opera Company, and productions at Shakespeare festivals across the United States. Among the plays that he has directed with the American Conservatory Theatre are *Tiny Alice*, and *Cyrano de Bergerac*.

William Ball was born in Chicago, Illinois on April 29, 1931, the son of Russell and Catherine (Gormaly) Ball. After graduating from the Iona (New York) Preparatory School in 1948, he attended Fordham University in the Bronx, New York, where he appeared in student productions of *Uncle Vanya, Candide*, and *Hamlet*. During summer vacations he toured with Margaret Webster's Shakespeare company as assistant designer and as an actor in minor roles.

In 1950 Ball transferred to the drama school of the Carnegie Institute of Technology in Pittsburgh. While a student there he appeared at the Pittsburgh Playhouse as Richard in *Ah, Wilderness!* (1952) and with the Pittsburgh Symphony as Puck in *A Midsummer Night's Dream* and as the Devil in *L'Histoire du Soldat* (1954). His summers from 1950 through 1953 were spent with the Oregon Shakespeare Festival in Ashland, portraying Mark Antony in *Julius Caesar*, Feste in *Twelfth Night*, Lorenzo in *The Merchant of Venice*, Ariel in *The Tempest*, and Claudio in *Much Ado About Nothing*. During the summer of 1954 he acted with the Antioch Shakespeare Festival in Yellow Springs, Ohio, the home of Antioch College, where his roles included Romeo in *Romeo and Juliet*, Trinculo in *The Tempest*, and Puck in *A Midsummer Night's Dream*. He also directed a production there of *As You Like It*. After receiving a B.A. degree in acting and scenic design from Carnegie Institute of Technology in 1953, Ball spent a year in England and on the Continent studying repertory theatre on a Fulbright scholarship. In 1955 he obtained an M.A. degree in directing from Carnegie Tech.

During the summer of 1955 Ball appeared with the San Diego Shakespeare Festival as Hamlet, and that fall he began a one-year NBC/RCA Directors fellowship awarded by the Carnegie Institute. In 1955-56 he also appeared with the

WILLIAM BALL

Group 20 Players in Wellesley, Massachusetts, taking the role of the Lion in *Androcles and the Lion,* of Gonzales in *The Tempest,* and the Witch in *Faust.* At Antioch College in the summer of 1956 he staged *Twelfth Night.*

Off Broadway in New York, Ball played Acaste in Richard Wilbur's version of Molière's *The Misanthrope* (1956), the voice of Rosencrantz in Siobhan McKenna's experimental *Hamlet* (1957), Nicholas Devise in *The Lady's Not for Burning* (1957), and Mr. Horner in *The Country Wife* (1957). After a summer touring with *Visit to a Small Planet,* in which he played Conrad, Ball spent the 1957-58 season with the Arena Stage players in Washington, D.C., appearing as Dubedat in *The Doctor's Dilemma.* He also was the stage manager for another Shavian enterprise, the Broadway production of *Back to Methuselah,* which opened in March 1958.

Ball made his New York debut as a director with his staging of Chekhov's little-known play *Ivanov,* which opened at the Renata Theatre on October 7, 1958. "Poignant and comic, *Ivanov* is an achievement of the first order," wrote Brooks Atkinson of the New York *Times* (October 19, 1958), and the production won Ball the Village Voice Obie and the Vernon Rice award as the best Off-Broadway director of 1958. Over the next few years he staged *Once More, With Feeling* in Houston, *The Devil's Disciple* with the Actor's Workshop in San Francisco, *A Month in the Country* for the Arena Stage in Washington, *Henry IV, Part 1* and *Part 2* (in which he played Hal, Prince of Wales), *Julius Caesar, The Merchant of Venice* and *Twelfth Night* for the San Diego Shakespeare Festival, and *The Tempest* for the American Shakespeare Festival in Stratford, Connecticut. For the New York City Opera he mounted several productions, including *Così fan Tutte, The Inspector General,* Benjamin Britten's *A Midsummer Night's Dream, Don Giovanni,* and *Porgy and Bess.*

Under what Walter Kerr of the New York *Herald Tribune* (April 9, 1961) called "William Ball's superbly inflected direction," a revival of Dylan Thomas' verse narrative *Under Milk Wood* opened at the Circle-in-the-Square on March 29, 1961, and won for its director a special Lola D'Annunzio citation for contribution to the Off Broadway theatre. Two years later, on March 7, 1963, Ball achieved another Off-Broadway success with his production of Pirandello's *Six Characters in Search of an Author* at the Martinique. "William Ball deserves full marks for his imaginative direction," Howard Taubman wrote in the New York *Times* on March 11. ". . . The essential theatricality of the play is conveyed without sacrifice of its human values." Ball, who also staged the play in London that June, received the 1963 D'Annunzio award for his Off-Broadway production of the enigmatic Luigi Pirandello masterwork.

After making his debut at Stratford, Canada in July 1964 with a staging of Gilbert and Sullivan's *Yeomen of the Guard,* Ball finished the libretto for an opera based on Turgenev's *A Month in the Country,* on which he had been collaborating with the American composer Lee Hoiby. The project was commissioned by the Ford Foundation. When, under the title of *Natalia Petrovna,* it had its world première at the New York City Center in October 1964, it received only mixed reviews. Alan Rich and Harold C. Schonberg, for example, felt that the libretto failed to transmute the Turgenev drama into operatic terms and that the characters had become one-dimensional, although Louis Biancolli pronounced the opera the work of a "perfect librettist." All the critics agreed in their praise of Ball's staging. "The presentation . . . was one of the City Opera's best," wrote Schonberg in the New York *Times* (October 9, 1964). "Mr. Ball directed it with a sure sense of the stage."

With the Lincoln Center Repertory Company, then housed in barracks-like temporary quarters at the ANTA Washington Square Theatre, Ball introduced to New York audiences in January 1965 the Richard Wilbur translation of *Tartuffe,* Molière's farcical satire on hypocrisy. For his fast-paced direction of the play Ball was nominated for an Antoinette Perry award. Soon afterward he left for Pittsburgh, where with $115,000 from the Rockefeller Foundation and additional funding from the Pittsburgh Playhouse Association and the Carnegie Institute of Technology, he established a noncommercial repertory company called the American Conservatory Theatre.

Ball envisioned his American Conservatory Theatre as an experimental and educational resource for both actors and directors. In a twenty-five page manifesto he declared that he wanted to create a theatre that would "uninhibit the actor" and give him the freedom "to assert himself wildly" and to perform with a "flamboyant, dashing style." Convinced that the Method was stunting the growth of gifted actors, Ball wanted in his company to explore other styles of acting. "[The Method] has completely dominated our theatre," he told Cecil Smith of the Los Angeles *Times* (Washington *Post,* November 14, 1965).

"Not that it does not have certain validity, but it is all on one stratum. It is all introspective.... It says I am what I am. I have to teach the actor to want. To reach out for something large. I want to awaken courage in them. Give them the vitality to be individualists."

An impressive array of New York actors, including Barbara Barrie, Hal Holbrook, Michael O'Sullivan, and Sada Thompson, were lured to Pittsburgh by William Ball. The American Conservatory Theatre opened its first season in July 1965 at the two theatres in the Pittsburgh Playhouse and in six months presented ten productions, among them *Tartuffe, Six Characters, Tiny Alice, The Rose Tattoo, Uncle Vanya*, and *Death of a Salesman*. As Jerry Tallmer of the New York *Post* (December 7, 1965) wrote, "Pittsburgh Pennsylvania . . . is never going to be the same again. . . . The town has exploded into life, passion, partisanship and, above all, burning interest in and attendance at the shows Ball has been creating."

Despite the success of the American Conservatory Theatre's first season in Pittsburgh, the repertory company found itself without a home in December 1965, when William Ball, the Pittsburgh Playhouse, and Carnegie Tech were unable to agree on the terms of a contract for the next year. Although its future was in doubt, the company remained active, beginning a four-week season at the University of Michigan in Ann Arbor in January 1966. For a March 13, 1966 presentation of the National Educational Television network Ball directed *Under Milk Wood* with Rene Auberjonois, Sada Thompson, and other American Conservatory Theatre performers. In March of that year the Rockefeller Foundation granted Ball $160,000 for the next fifteen months, and the American Conservatory Theatre settled down in New York City to train and rehearse. That summer the group filled engagements at the Westport (Connecticut) Country Playhouse, the Stanford University summer festival near San Francisco, and the Ravinia festival, outside Chicago.

So well received was the American Conservatory Theatre at Ravinia and Stanford that both San Francisco and Chicago made bids to secure the actors as a permanent resident company. It was finally agreed that the two cities would each get the acting group for six months of the year, and late in 1966 the American Conservatory Theatre moved to San Francisco to prepare for its first season, which began in January 1967. Operating simultaneously at two theatres, the 1,500-seat Geary and the 640-seat Marine Memorial, formerly the home of the defunct Actors' Workshop, the American Conservatory Theatre presented sixteen plays, many of them new productions, during their initial twenty-two week season. "The company seems incredibly alive," Richard L. Coe reported to the readers of the Washington *Post* (April 16, 1967), after watching the San Francisco company perform *Death of a Salesman, Charley's Aunt*, and *Man and Superman*. "Players react with their whole selves and the results are scenes galvanized with vitality. . . .

This brings back to the living stage a quality of vitality that long has been snuffed out in the naturalistic drama's psychological introspection."

The American Conservatory Theatre created a mood of unprecedented cultural excitement in San Francisco, as evidenced by the subscription list of 12,000 names that it amassed during its first year, over twice the number of subscribers that the Actors' Workshop had been able to muster at its peak. Nonetheless the 160-member company ended its first West Coast season with a deficit of $245,000, precipitating another of its periodic financial crises. The amount was eventually raised by its San Francisco sponsoring organization, the California Theatre Foundation, but within a few months the group encountered another crisis, when Chicago cancelled its American Conservatory Theatre season, scheduled for the spring of 1968, because of lack of money. In September 1967 the California Theatre Foundation announced its commitment to raise $2,300,000 through box office sales, local contributions, and grants from foundations, to keep the company as a year-round resident of San Francisco. Although the American Conservatory Theatre has run up some staggering deficits since then ($900,000 in 1973), which have prompted frantic fund-raising drives, the support of the California Theatre Foundation has not wavered. The continuing enthusiasm of the people of San Francisco is reflected in the company's enviable record of house occupancy, which in 1973 averaged 90 percent of capacity at all performances. In mid-1974 the Ford Foundation made a grant of $2 million to the American Conservatory Theatre.

The first theatre company in the United States to combine performing with a training conservatory, the American Conservatory Theatre requires that everybody in its performing company study in its school, which is also open to students. Classes are taught by members of the company or by specialists, and include such varied subjects as laughing technique, theatre games, rhetoric, yoga, audience perception, commedia dell'arte, vaudeville, mimicry, transactional psychology, karate, and flamenco. One specialist teaches nothing but a technique called the Alexander method, which helps the actor to gain greater control of his body and its movement.

The American Conservatory Theatre offers its audiences the largest and broadest range of repertory of any company in the United States. In a typical San Francisco season it premières at least one play each month, in addition to rotating performances of the other plays in its repertory. Among the dozens of plays that the company has presented in San Francisco are Fernando Arrabal's *The Architect and the Emperor of Assyria* (United States première); John Guare's *The House of Blue Leaves;* Jason Miller's *That Championship Season;* Charles Dyer's *Staircase;* Jules Feiffer's *Little Murders;* revivals of *Beyond the Fringe, Arsenic and Old Lace*, and *Our Town;* and works by new playwrights such as Jerome Kilty, Anna Marie Barlow, and Joseph Landon. It has also performed a full complement of modern classics like *The*

Seagull, *The Devil's Disciple,* and *A Long Day's Journey Into Night.* It presented the latter in two simultaneous productions with different casts, directors, and interpretations. The plays that have been directed by Ball himself include *King Lear, Hamlet, The American Dream, Cyrano de Bergerac, The Crucible,* and *Rosencrantz and Guildenstern Are Dead.*

In addition to their regular performances at the Geary and Marine Memorial theatres, the American Conservatory Theatre sponsors advanced student productions, a children's theatre, and tours of its smaller and more portable productions to cities and campuses all over California. The company has filled engagements in several major American cities including New York, where it performed during the autumn of 1969 at the ANTA Theatre. In New York it presented three of its most successful productions, *Tiny Alice* and Chekhov's *Three Sisters,* both directed by Ball, and Feydeau's *A Flea in Her Ear,* staged by Gower Champion. Some New York critics were disappointed with the shows, finding the staging gimmicky and the acting below par. Ball apparently took the reception philosophically. "Of course New York is a test," he told Lewis Funke of the New York *Times* (September 29, 1969), "But it isn't the only one. . . . We know that the work we do is not perfect. It isn't meant to be. There are always improvements to be made. Our goal is not popular success. Our goal is human endeavor." Two years later some American Conservatory Theatre players returned to New York, as part of a nationwide tour, with a radically new version of *Hamlet,* directed by Ball, in which Dame Judith Anderson played the melancholy prince of Elsinore.

"I dislike being too closely scrutinized," William Ball told Meryle Secrest of the Washington *Post* (October 25, 1969), who wrote that the director's "reputation of flamboyant eccentricity is a deliberate invention, designed to keep the world at bay." Slender and round-headed, with dark blond hair that is receding, he affected the appearance of a Spanish Don during his early years in San Francisco by wearing a black, flat-brimmed Cordovan hat. Ball has been described as a restless and volatile man with an intense love of the theatre and boundless energy. He demands seemingly impossible amounts of work from himself and those in his company, but everyone seems to thrive on the high-pressure atmosphere. "He keeps the company on the edge of hysteria," one admiring actress told a *Newsweek* reporter (November 20, 1967), "and he himself works on maximum adrenalin."

References

Newsweek 70:118+ N 20 '67 por
Washington Post G p2 N 14 '65
Biographical Encyclopaedia and Who's Who of the American Theatre (1966)
International Who's Who, 1973-74
Who's Who in America, 1972-73
Who's Who in the Theatre (1972)
Who's Who in the West, 1972-73

BEAME, ABRAHAM D(AVID)

Mar. 19, 1906- Mayor of the City of New York
Address: b. Office of the Mayor, City Hall, New York 10007; h. Gracie Mansion, New York 10028

As the 104th mayor of the City of New York, Abraham D. Beame occupies what his predecessor, John V. Lindsay, has called "the second-toughest job" in the United States. New York, the nation's largest and most complex metropolis, suffers from a multitude of social and economic problems, among them crime, racial tension, a dwindling tax base resulting in large part from the flight of business and middle-class residents to the suburbs, and the rapidly escalating need for increasingly expensive municipal services. The major tasks that the mayor faces, in conjunction with the City Council and the Board of Estimate, are setting priorities, raising funds, and equitably distributing those funds among the city's diverse agencies and interest groups. For such responsibilities Beame is admirably suited, having served for a decade as the city's budget director and for two terms as its comptroller.

A veteran of the regular Democratic party organization of Brooklyn, Beame is the first Jew to occupy New York City's highest office. Although he lacks the glamour and flamboyant style of Lindsay, many observers believe that he shows promise of being an effective mayor. "He may have limited vision," Professor Harold Savitch of New York University has said, as quoted in the *Wall Street Journal* (April 23, 1974), "but he can deliver."

Abraham David Beame is of Polish-Jewish origin. His parents, Philip and Esther (Goldfarb) Birnbaum, operated a small restaurant in Warsaw until early 1906, when they had to flee Poland, then under Russian domination, because the Czarist police were about to arrest his father for his association with the revolutionary socialist underground. His father traveled directly to the United States, while his mother moved to the home of a sister-in-law in the East End of London, England, where Abraham was born. The date of his birth, according to an official source, is March 19, 1906. (Most other sources give his birthday as March 20.) Three months later, the family was reunited in New York City, where the name Birnbaum was changed to Beame. With his sister and two brothers, Abe Beame grew up in Manhattan. In their cold-water apartment in a Stanton Street tenement on Manhattan's Lower East Side, the Beames lived in modest circumstances. For a while Philip Beame again ran a restaurant. He then took a job in a stationery factory, where he eventually became foreman in the paper-cutting department. Esther Beame died in 1912. Later Philip Beame remarried and had a son and a daughter by his second wife.

As a small child Abe Beame helped out in the family restaurant and earned pocket money by knocking on doors to wake up neighborhood residents in time for work. His precocious talent for pinochle playing made him something of a celebrity in his neighborhood, where he was known as "Spunky" because of a toughness belied by his diminutive size. He received his primary education at Public School 160 and his secondary education at the High School of Commerce. While in high school he worked an eight-hour evening shift at the factory where his father was employed. On weekends he took part in basketball, boxing, and amateur theatricals at the University Settlement House on Eldridge Street, a social center noted for its many prominent habitués.

Admitting that "it might sound corny," Beame told Richard Montague, one of the writers of a series of articles about him that appeared in the New York *Post* in October 1965, that he was inspired as a boy by the Horatio Alger books, which "preached honesty and good citizenship." On occasion he accompanied his father to Socialist meetings to hear such luminaries of the labor movement as Eugene V. Debs and Morris Hillquit, but the exposure to socialism did not seem to have any profound effect on him.

Completing high school in three and one-half years, Beame graduated at the head of his class and was its only member to score 100 percent in the New York State Regents bookkeeping exam. He entered the evening session at New York's City College as an accounting major, registering at both the uptown and downtown campuses in order to be able to take twice the number of courses officially permitted to night students. While working a full day shift at the paper factory, he completed the curriculum in four years, graduating *cum laude* with a B.B.A. degree in 1928.

On graduating, Beame founded a small accounting firm in partnership with his longtime friend Bernard Greidinger, who is now its sole head. Operating from a desk in the office of a more established concern at 1440 Broadway, the firm of Beame & Greidinger experienced more than the usual growing pains during the early years of the great Depression. To make ends meet, the partners, licensed as certified public accountants in 1930, also became teachers. Specializing in accounting and commercial law, Beame taught for a semester or two at Tilden High School in Brooklyn, then transferred to Richmond Hill High School in Queens, where he remained until 1946. In 1944-1945 he also taught accounting and auditing in the evening session at Rutgers University in New Jersey.

Concurrently, Abe Beame took an active part in local politics in the Crown Heights section of Brooklyn, then a solidly middle-class community, where he had moved in 1928. With Nathan R. Sobel, who later became a justice of the New York State Supreme Court, and others, he helped found the Haddingway Democratic Club to support the 1930 candidacy of Herbert H. Lehman for lieutenant governor. The Haddingway Club was one of six satellite units of the powerful

ABRAHAM D. BEAME

Madison Democratic Club, under the aegis of "Uncle John" McCooey and, after his death in 1934, of Irwin D. Steingut. Beame worked diligently as an election-district captain, and he soon began to attract attention with his success in bringing out his voters almost unanimously for the Democratic party in every election.

After Lehman was elected governor, in 1932, he appointed Beame, on Sobel's recommendation, to an unpaid commission studying the state's taxation program. Afterwards, however, Beame turned down other proffered political appointments, insisting he did not want just any political job, but one in which he could really apply his professional ability. During the early 1940's, however, he did agree to serve as legislative representative for the Joint Committee of Teachers Organizations, a predecessor of the United Federation of Teachers.

The opportunity Beame was awaiting finally came in 1946, during the mayoral administration of William O'Dwyer, who appointed him assistant director of the bureau of the budget at a salary of $9,500 a year. In that post Abe Beame set up a pioneering management-efficiency program, which in 1948 reportedly saved the city some $40,000,000. On March 1, 1952 Mayor Vincent Impellitteri named Beame budget director, considered the most important appointive office in the municipal government, with responsibility for preparing the annual expense budget for each fiscal year. Despite differences with Impellitteri and with Robert F. Wagner, who became mayor in 1954, Beame remained budget director until 1961. He also continued to serve as a district captain, and in 1956, 1960, and 1964 he was a delegate to the Democratic National Convention.

When, in 1961, the Brooklyn Democratic organization reneged on a promise to make him the party's candidate for the borough presidency, Beame accepted an invitation from Wagner, then campaigning for a third term on an "anti-machine" platform, to run with him for the post of city comptroller. The Wagner team was victorious in the November election, with Beame running ahead of Wagner and City Council president-elect Paul R. Screvane by more than 120,000 votes.

As comptroller, New York City's second most powerful official, Beame headed the Department of Finance, was empowered to make policy recommendations and to cast four of the twenty-two votes on the Board of Estimate, and controlled the city employees' pension fund as well as the capital and expense budgets. He won widespread respect for his quiet competence and his conservative approach to monetary matters. Soon after the election he ended his differences with party regulars by coming to the support of Brooklyn boss Stanley Steingut, the son and successor of his old mentor Irwin Steingut, when Wagner attempted to unseat him.

In September 1965 Beame became the Democratic candidate for mayor, after winning 44 percent of the vote in a hard-fought primary election that pitted him against William F. Ryan, Paul O'Dwyer, and front-running Paul Screvane, who was backed by Wagner. In the November election, Beame ran against fusion (Republican-Liberal) candidate John V. Lindsay, then at the height of his appeal, and Conservative William F. Buckley. During the campaign, Beame called for restoration of "fiscal integrity" to the city; referred to "shameful deals" between the Wagner administration and Albany; and called the recent imposition of a 5 percent sales tax "an infamous act." Although he was a member of the Democratic party's anti-Wagner faction, he had to bear the brunt of criticism aimed at Wagner. Furthermore, he was identified as a dull, conventional organization politician in contrast to Lindsay, who was seen as fresh, creative, and glamorous. Not surprisingly, he was defeated by Lindsay by a vote of 1,149,106 to 1,046,699.

Returning to private life, Beame founded Abraham D. Beame Associates and became a financial consultant to industry. From 1966 to 1969 he was also chairman of the finance committee of the American Bank & Trust Company and board chairman of the Arrow Lock Corporation. Aware that a return to public service would involve a sharp reduction in his personal income, Beame decided nevertheless to run again in 1969 as the Democratic candidate for comptroller, a post then paying $40,000 a year. In the three-way mayoral race that November, Lindsay, running as a Liberal-Independent, won election to a second term by a slight plurality of 42 percent. Although Beame had waited until late in the campaign to enter the race for comptroller and failed to garner the support of county Democratic leaders, he won a resounding victory in the November election, running far ahead of Lindsay.

During his second term as comptroller, Beame introduced reforms in dealing with pension funds and the municipal debt and conducted a study on means of improving the city's credit rating. He also issued reports on narcotics control, hospital care, housing, and day care centers. He spoke out in behalf of continued free tuition and open enrollment in the City University system and advocated greater consumer representation in government. As the city's ranking elected Democrat, Beame became a focal point for the growing opposition to Lindsay, whom many New Yorkers held responsible for the city's chronic social, economic, and political problems.

Beame decided in February 1973 to try again for the mayoralty, aware that his age made it likely that this would be his last opportunity to seek elective office. The fight for the 1973 Democratic mayoral nomination was something of a free-for-all, with as many as ten contenders appearing on the scene, among them Lindsay, who had switched parties, and Wagner, who briefly attempted a comeback. By the time of the primary election, on June 4, the field had narrowed down to four, with Beame facing Congressmen Herman Badillo and Mario Biaggi, and Assemblyman Albert Blumenthal. With 34 percent of the total vote, Beame received a plurality in the primary, but since 40 percent was needed to secure the nomination, he had to face Badillo, his closest competitor, in a run-off contest on June 26. After a run-off campaign in which Badillo charged Beame with exploiting the fears of the white middle class and Beame suggested that Badillo was polarizing the city with his strong appeals to blacks and Puerto Ricans, Beame defeated Badillo by a two-to-one margin.

In the November election Beame again faced two of his primary opponents—Biaggi, who had received the Conservative party nomination, and Blumenthal, the Liberal party candidate—in addition to Republican State Senator John J. Marchi. Although he had the backing of most of the city's regular Democratic organizations and was considered a sure winner by leading political observers, he took no chances. In his cautious but energetic campaign he presented himself as an experienced administrator and money manager and a realistic, down-to-earth middle-of-the-roader who appreciated traditional virtues and values. He promised to hold the line on the city budget, to discontinue some of Lindsay's experimental ventures, to keep transit fares at the 35-cent level, and to curb crime by expanding and upgrading the police force and reforming the court system. Beame addressed his appeal in particular to groups that felt ill-served by Lindsay—union members, businessmen, small homeowners, white ethnics, senior citizens, and residents of the four "outer" boroughs. He succeeded in obtaining the support of the greater part of the city's 2,000,000-strong Jewish community, which had never before united behind a Jewish candidate. On November 6, 1973 he won a landslide victory, receiving 955,388 votes against Marchi's 275,362, Blumenthal's 263,604, and Biaggi's 189,185.

Sworn into office in City Hall Plaza on January 1, 1974, Beame expressed disdain for "quick and easy solutions" and "glib slogans" and called for a "rebirth of faith in our city and confidence in our city government." During his first few months in office, Beame concentrated on making appointments and reorganizing his staff. Scaling down the Office of Neighborhood Government and the "superagencies" created by the Lindsay administration, he gave greater authority to the city's commissioners and began to replace Lindsay's "bright young managers," with career civil servants and professionals. As a response to criticism that he was neglecting the city's racial minorities, he appointed airline executive Paul Gibson Jr. to one of the three deputy mayor posts, making him the first black to serve in the top levels of the city administration. Through his efforts to improve the city's relations with organized labor, Beame succeeded in averting a threatened transit workers' strike. On visits to Washington, D.C. and Albany, he established cordial relations with President Richard Nixon and New York Governor Malcolm Wilson with the hope of obtaining necessary increases in federal and state aid. On May 15, 1974 Beame presented his $11.1 billion "austerity" budget for 1974-75. It provided, among other things, for cutbacks in low-priority programs, elimination of thousands of staff positions, a $528,000,000 ten-year bond issue, higher real estate taxes, and an increase from 7 to 8 percent in the unpopular sales tax, in order to overcome a threatened $1.5 billion gap between income and expenditures.

A past trustee of B'nai B'rith and of the Federation of Jewish Philanthropies, Beame has also served on the board of the National Conference of Christians and Jews, and he holds a number of organizational Man of the Year honors. He was awarded the Townsend Harris Medal in 1957 and was given a citation from the Citizens Budget Commission in 1958. From Greece he has received the rank of knight commander of the Order of St. Dennis of Zante.

Abraham D. Beame was married on February 18, 1928 to Mary Ingerman, whom he had met over a game of checkers at the University Settlement House seven years earlier. They have two sons: Edmond M. Beame, an associate professor of history at McMaster University in Hamilton, Ontario, and Bernard ("Buddy") W. Beame, a free-lance film producer who managed his father's 1973 campaign and now serves on his staff; and five grandchildren. Abe Beame, a silver-haired man five feet two inches tall, regularly works an eighteen-hour day. In the little time he has for recreation, he enjoys playing gin rummy, watching television, walking on the beach, and reading mystery stories or political biographies. The Beames' social activities are usually limited to visits with relatives and old friends. Before moving to Gracie Mansion, New York City's official mayoral residence, they maintained a three-room apartment in Brooklyn and a summer home at Belle Harbor in the Rockaways.

According to Helen Dudar, writing in the New York *Post* (November 10, 1973), "Beame is bereft of small talk. He does not drink spirits and eats without enthusiasm. In many ways, his social attitudes suggest a statelier and more innocent time. Small children naked on a beach offend his sen-

sibilities. He has abandoned movie-going—once a beloved entertainment—out of distaste for the candor of modern filmmakers. His younger son, Buddy, says that the strongest term he ever heard Abe Beame apply to anyone, a word reserved for incompetent motorists, was "jackass." According to *Time* (November 19, 1973), Beame once briefly stated his ambition as mayor as follows: "I would like to be like [Fiorello H.] LaGuardia without the frills."

References

N Y Post p12 N 10 '73 por
N Y Times p58 N 7 '73
N Y Times Mag p38+ N 18 '73 pors
New York 6:44+ Ap 9 '73 pors
Times of Israel p19+ My '74 por
Who's Who in America, 1972-73

BERTOLUCCI, BERNARDO (ber-tō-lōō'chē)

Mar. 16, 1940- Motion picture director; scenarist
Address: Via del Babuino 51, Rome, Italy

Italian director Bernardo Bertolucci, a master of the language of film, created an international sensation with his frankly erotic film *Last Tango in Paris* (1972), about the ill-fated romance of a middle-aged American man and a young French girl. Although hailed as a "landmark in movie history" by *New Yorker* critic Pauline Kael, that motion picture was roundly condemned by critics and other moralists who objected to the explicit sexual scenes between Marlon Brando and Maria Schneider. A film maker since the age of twenty-one, Bertolucci has to his credit such triumphs as *Before the Revolution* (1964) and *The Conformist* (1970), and he has been acclaimed for his brilliant imagery, his sense of drama, and his profound psychological insights. Writing in the *International Film Guide 1972*, Peter Cowie called Bertolucci "the finest Italian director of his generation" and "a humanist and sensualist" who has "triumphantly ventured beyond the mass of young directors for whom the cinema is merely a political platform."

A native of Parma, in northern Italy, Bernardo Bertolucci was born on March 16, 1940, the older of the two sons of Attilio Bertolucci, a poet, anthologist, film critic, and teacher of art history. His mother, Ninetta, who is of Italian-Irish parentage (her mother's maiden name was Mulligan), was born in Australia, where her father, a political radical, had found asylum. Bernardo's brother, Giuseppe, has begun to follow in his footsteps as a poet and film maker.

The Bertoluccis lived in the rural outskirts of Parma until the early 1950's, when the father's work took him to Rome. "It was a golden childhood," Bertolucci told Charles Michener of *Newsweek* (February 12, 1973). "A big, comfortable house, servants, understanding parents, and a pursuit of intellectualism." His father's poetry was

BERNARDO BERTOLUCCI

an early inspiration to him. "He made us aware
of reality, its ugliness and its beauty," he recalled for Sidney Fields of the New York *Daily
News* (February 5, 1973). Among the literary
influences that shaped his outlook, Bertolucci has
cited the American authors Ernest Hemingway,
F. Scott Fitzgerald, Dashiell Hammett, and Raymond Chandler. His interest in motion pictures
was aroused by the screenings—sometimes as many
as four in one day—to which he went regularly
with his father.

By the time Bertolucci was twelve he had
published several poems in periodicals. At fifteen,
having obtained a sixteen millimeter camera, he
made two short films about children (his brother
and two cousins) in the country. *In cerca del
mistero* (In Search of Mystery), a collection of
his poems evoking memories of a rural childhood
and reflecting influences of Dylan Thomas and
Emily Dickinson, was published in 1962 by Lon-
ganesi in Milan and won the Premio Viareggio,
one of Italy's top literary awards.

As a student of literature at the University of
Rome, Bertolucci made the acquaintance of the
writer and novice film maker Pier Paolo Pasolini,
a friend of his father. Pasolini engaged him as an
assistant director for his first film production,
Accatone (1961), a grim, realistic picture about
Rome's underworld that received favorable notices
from reviewers. The experience convinced him
that he should, as he told Joseph Gelmis of
Newsday (February 11, 1973), turn to "cinema
as the true poetic language." Determined to make
his career as a film director, he left the University of Rome in 1962 without graduating. On
visits to the Cinémathèque Française in Paris,
he studied the techniques of such film makers
as François Truffaut and Jean-Luc Godard.

Bertolucci's first independent project as a director was *La commare seca* (*The Grim Reaper*,
1962), based on a story by Pasolini, who wrote
the original scenario. On the recommendation
of producer Antonio Cervi, who furnished the

funds for its $90,000 budget, Pasolini assigned
the direction of the film to Bertolucci, who revised the script considerably and filmed it on
location in Rome. A mystery thriller about the
murder of a prostitute on the banks of the Tiber,
the film also concerns an adolescent's awakening
to the realities of life. Although the film received
only mixed reviews at the 1962 Venice Film
Festival and was not a financial success, it brought
Bertolucci recognition as a promising young director. A reviewer for the *Guardian* (November
9, 1962) observed that "Bertolucci seems . . .
to have started his career as a film maker at a
point which many directors might reach only in
maturity."

With his next motion picture, *Prima della rivo-
luzione* (*Before the Revolution*, Iride Cinemato-
grafica, 1964), for which he wrote the script in
collaboration with Gianni Amico, Bertolucci's international reputation as a serious film maker
was assured. Vaguely inspired by Stendhal's novel
The Charterhouse of Parma, the film derived its
title from Talleyrand's statement: "Only those who
lived before the revolution know how sweet life
can be." Its young protagonist, Fabrizio (Fran-
cesco Barilli), tries in vain to divest himself of
his patrician background, flirts with Marxist ideology and revolutionary politics, has an unhappy
love affair with his attractive young aunt (Adriana
Asti), and finally settles down to a humdrum life
and marriage. As Charles Michener noted in
Newsweek, the film "displayed many of the Bertolucci hallmarks: an eclecticism that combined
the sweeping, fluid visual style of old masters
like John Ford and Max Ophuls with the broken
montage of Godard; frank homages to other directors; a nostalgic, uneasy sense of history; and
a dance scene."

Before the Revolution won the young critics
award at the 1964 Cannes Film Festival, and
with a few exceptions it was acclaimed by critics,
some of whom compared Bertolucci with the
young Orson Welles. After viewing it at the New
York Film Festival, Eugene Archer wrote in the
New York *Times* (September 25, 1964): "Bertolucci . . . has managed to assimilate a high degree
of filmic and literary erudition into a distinctly
personal visual approach. . . . Here is a new
talent of outstanding promise." The picture was
released to United States audiences by New Yorker Films in mid-1965.

Despite its critical success, *Before the Revolution* failed to live up to expectations commercially, and for several years Bertolucci had difficulty in obtaining financial backing for his film
projects. During 1965 and 1966 he was commissioned by an Italian oil company in Iran to direct,
as well as write the script and commentary for,
a three-part documentary film on petroleum entitled *La via del petrolio*. In 1967 Bertolucci
worked with Julian Beck and his Living Theatre
on "Agony," a dramatic sketch about death and
apathy, in the film *Love and Rage*; and on "Il
fico infruttuoso" (The Infertile Fig Tree) in
Vangelo 70 (Gospel 70), a portmanteau film that
included contributions by Pasolini and Godard.

He also collaborated on the script of the Hollywood film *Once Upon a Time in the West* (Paramount, 1969), starring Henry Fonda.

For his next full-length feature film, *Partner* (Red Film, 1968), a loose adaptation of Dostoyevsky's novel *The Double*, Bertolucci again collaborated with Amico on the scenario. Described in *Newsweek* (February 12, 1973) as a "brilliantly original study of schizophrenia and youthful disaffection," the film centers upon Jacob (Pierre Clémenti), a shy and politically diffident young drama teacher, whose radical and violent alter ego seeks to transform his theories about the theatre into direct political action. Although some reviewers found the production interesting, most critical comment was unfavorable. Bertolucci himself later repudiated *Partner* as "sadomasochism." It was "sadistic against the public and masochistic against me, because the public hated me," he told Joseph Gelmis in the *Newsday* interview. In the spring of 1969 Bertolucci lectured at the Museum of Modern Art in New York City on the occasion of a retrospective showing of his films.

It was Bertolucci's sense of social justice and his aversion to the corruption prevailing in Italian society rather than any commitment to orthodox Marxist doctrine that caused him to join the Italian Communist party in the late 1960's. Formerly convinced that "with a film you could make a revolution," he later rejected that notion and criticized the continuing effort of his former idol, Jean-Luc Godard, to mix film making with politics as "hybrid and unsatisfactory." The only clearly political films he has made are documentaries he filmed for the Communist party in the early 1970's, including one about conditions in Italian hospitals. Of perhaps greater significance than his political orientation was Bertolucci's decision, at the age of twenty-eight, to undergo psychoanalysis. The experience made him more meditative, and while diminishing his interest in political dynamics it gave him more insight into the individual mind.

In collaboration with Marilu Parolini and Edoardo De Gregorio, Bertolucci wrote the script for *La strategia del ragno* (*The Spider's Stratagem,* 1970), which he directed for Radio Televisione Italiana. The television film, adapted from the short story "Theme of the Traitor and the Hero" by the Argentine author Jorge Luis Borges, was later given theatrical distribution. Judith Crist in *New York* magazine (January 8, 1973) called it Bertolucci's "simplest and most glowing work." It deals with the visit of a young man, Athos Magnani Jr., to the Po valley town where his father, a local anti-Fascist hero, was believed to have been murdered by followers of Mussolini some thirty years earlier. At the urging of the father's mistress (played by Alida Valli), Athos tries to track down the killers and, in the words of David Sterritt (*Christian Science Monitor,* February 16, 1973), "becomes entangled in an eccentric web of intrigues, memories, and labyrinthine past associations." As the story unfolds, Athos (played by Giulio Brogli, who also portrays the father) finds that his father had actually betrayed an anti-Mussolini plot engineered by his friends and had helped to plot his own assassination as an act of atonement and to keep alive the image of the anti-fascist resistance. In the end, Athos concludes that historical truth is irrelevant, that myth becomes reality, and that the past had best remain buried. Shown at the 1970 New York and London film festivals, *The Spider's Stratagem* was released for general distribution in the United States early in 1973. In reviewing the film, critics praised Bertolucci's imaginative craftsmanship, his sense of spectacle, and his insights into human frailties.

With his poignant psychological drama of the Fascist era *Il conformista* (*The Conformist,* 1970), Bertolucci attained full maturity as a director. Filmed with a relatively modest budget (by Hollywood standards) of $750,000, it was produced jointly by Mars Film in Rome, Marianne Productions in Paris, and Maran Film in Munich, with Paramount backing. Bertolucci wrote the screenplay without collaborators, freely adapting it from a novel of the same title by his friend Alberto Moravia. But whereas Moravia had presented a straightforward exposé of fascism, Bertolucci did not attempt an economic or social analysis, confining himself to psychological investigation. The film's protagonist, Marcello (Jean-Louis Trintignant), a young civil servant from a decadent upper middle-class family, tries to overcome the guilt and shame of a traumatic boyhood homosexual encounter and seeks "normalcy" by marrying a simple-minded bourgeois girl (Stefania Sandrelli) and becoming a loyal functionary of the fascist state. On his honeymoon trip he volunteers for the mission of setting up one of his former professors, now an anti-fascist exile in Paris, and the professor's sensuous young wife (Dominique Sanda) for assassination. After the fall of Mussolini, Marcello, still obsessed with conformity, denounces his former comrades to gain a place for himself with the winning side.

In the United States, where it was shown at the 1970 New York Film Festival and released by Paramount in 1971, it won for Bertolucci the National Film Critics best director award and earned him a nomination for an Oscar. Although some questioned Bertolucci's tendency to equate sexual deviation and political extremism, critics chorused their praises of the imaginative style—"so rich, poetic, and baroque," as Vincent Canby (New York *Times,* September 19, 1970) described it—with which he was able to recreate the mood of decadence of the 1930's. "His films just seem to flow, as if the life he photographs had not been set up for the camera but were all there and he were moving in and out of it at will," Pauline Kael wrote in the *New Yorker* (March 27, 1971).

Explaining his motives for making *Ultimo tango a Parigi* (*Last Tango in Paris,* 1972), for which he wrote the script in cooperation with Franco Arcalli, Bertolucci told Mel Gussow (New York *Times,* February 2, 1973): "I wanted to do a film on the present. All my previous films in a sense were in the past. The erotic act is what is most present in today's life." A joint French-Italian venture, produced by Alberto Grimaldi and distributed by United Artists, *Last Tango in Paris* was filmed on a $1,100,000 budget. It was intended by Bertolucci not as an erotic film, but as "a film *about* eroticism." Its hero Paul, a world-weary middle-aged expatriate American in Paris, trying to overcome the shock of his wife's suicide, establishes an impersonal and purely sexual affair with Jeanne, a liberated young Parisienne. Eventually the anonymous affair proves unsatisfactory, and in the end Jeanne kills Paul while trying to resist his drunken advances. Originally Bertolucci had planned to assign the two leading roles to Jean-Louis Trintignant and Dominique Sanda, but they were both unavailable. Approached by Marlon Brando, Bertolucci established a strong emotional bond with the veteran film star and cast him in the role of Paul, shaping the film to fit Brando's unique personality. For the part of Jeanne, Bertolucci, after interviewing scores of actresses, decided on Maria Schneider, a daughter of French actor Daniel Gelin, and a newcomer to motion pictures.

The world première of *Last Tango in Paris* at the 1972 New York Film Festival was termed by Pauline Kael in the *New Yorker* (October 28, 1972) a major breakthrough in the history of motion pictures, comparable to what the première of Stravinsky's *Le Sacre du Printemps* in 1913 represented in the history of music. The months preceding the release of the X-rated film to the American public were attended by a publicity campaign, encouraged by the distributors and highlighted by a cover story in *Time* magazine (January 22, 1973), emphasizing its erotic aspects. In France the picture encountered no serious censorship problems and became a major hit. In Italy it was banned by a Rome judge in December 1972, and Bertolucci, Brando, Miss Schneider, and producer Grimaldi were indicted by a Bologna court in January 1973 on charges of promoting obscenity. The charges were overturned, and the ban on the film was lifted the following month.

When *Last Tango in Paris* opened in theatres in New York in February 1973, with advance ticket sales of $75,000, reviews were mixed, although most critics were impressed by Bertolucci's direction and, in particular, by Brando's acting. Some, objecting to the explicit (although simulated) sex, the nudity, and the salty dialogue, dismissed it as pornographic; others objected not so much to the sex as to the violence; still others called the film an exercise in male chauvinism—a charge that Bertolucci has emphatically denied. *Last Tango in Paris* earned Bertolucci France's Raoul Levy Prize and Italy's Silver Ribbon.

Bertolucci has reportedly suspended plans to make a film based on Dashiell Hammett's 1929 detective thriller *Red Harvest*. He has been working on a motion picture with the tentative title "1900," tracing the parallel lives of two Italians born at the turn of the century, one a landowner and the other a peasant, against a background of seven decades of Italian history.

Eclectic in his approach to moviemaking, Bertolucci takes what he needs from literature, art, nature, and society, and he tries to get the best possible effect from light, color, scenery, and the special talents of his performers. One recurring element in his films is the dance, which has become his cinematic trademark. The lesbian tango performed by Dominique Sanda and Stefania Sandrelli in *The Conformist*, and the climactic dance hall scene in *Last Tango in Paris*, are among the most memorable episodes of his films. According to Vincent Canby (New York *Times*, April 11, 1971), "Bertolucci is something of a ham. . . . He exults in big scenes . . . , in dramatic changes of tempo, in reversals and repetitions, making one aware not only of the effects he is achieving, but also of the fun he's having in achieving them."

Bernardo Bertolucci has remained a bachelor, although he has been romantically involved with several women, including Adriana Asti, who starred in *Before the Revolution*. In 1972 he ended a five-year conjugal relationship with Maria Paola Maino, who designed the sets for *Last Tango in Paris*. Six feet one inch tall and of husky build, Bertolucci is, according to Sally Quinn of the Washington *Post* (February 16, 1973), "handsome in a rugged way, with more Teddy bear appeal than sex appeal" and has "a nice sense of humor." Somewhat camera shy, he once turned down a leading role in Vittorio De Sica's *The Garden of the Finzi-Continis*. He enjoys visiting art galleries and reading literary classics and detective stories. His small Rome apartment is filled with books and records. A baptized Roman Catholic, he left the church while still in his teens. "Like most Communist intellectuals in Europe, I am condemned to be divided," he told Guy Flatley of the New York *Times* (February 11, 1973). "I have a split personality, and the real contradiction within me is that I cannot quite synchronize my heart and my brain."

References

Guardian p10 Mr 14 '73 por
N Y Post p15 F 3 '73 por
N Y Times p20 F 2 '73 por; II p1+ F 11 '73 por
Gelmis, Joseph. The Film Director as Superstar (1970)
International Film Guide, 1972
International Who's Who, 1973-74

BIRMINGHAM, STEPHEN

May 28, 1932 (?)- Author
Address: 158 Lafayette Circle, Cincinnati, Ohio 45220

The fancies and foibles of America's social establishment have been the recurrent concerns of Stephen Birmingham, whose urbane and facile fiction and social histories have probed "Society" and focused on those subtle but overriding distinctions that determine caste and rank—who "belongs," and who does not. A prolific writer, with twelve titles to his credit since the publication of his first novel in 1958, Birmingham is best known for his nonfiction, including *Our Crowd* (1967), an account of the rise of the great German-Jewish families of New York City; *The Right People* (1968), an informal series of essays on contemporary society figures; and *The Grandees* (1971), a history of America's Sephardic Jewish aristocracy. A former protégé of John P. Marquand, to whom he is often compared, Birmingham wrote a biography of the celebrated novelist and social commentator entitled *The Late John Marquand* (1972).

Like Marquand, Stephen Birmingham is particularly concerned with the nuances of social difference in the Northeast, the area of his origin. He was born in Hartford, Connecticut and raised in nearby Andover. His parents are the late Thomas J. Birmingham, a lawyer of Irish Catholic extraction, and Editha (Gardner) Birmingham, a Protestant who is half Irish. Birmingham's birthday is May 28; various sources place the year of his birth between 1929 and 1932. He has one sister, Susan Birmingham Losee.

Although Birmingham has recalled that his parents had little interest in society, they nonetheless sent him to a socially prestigious preparatory school, the Hotchkiss School in Lakeville, Connecticut. There he learned the good manners that accompany good breeding and won the school's poetry prize with fifty poems. After graduating from Hotchkiss, he attended Williams College in Williamstown, Massachusetts. During his college years he edited the college humor magazine, worked in summer stock at the Lake George Playhouse in New York, and attended an endless round of debutante parties ranging from Boston to Philadelphia. A major in English, Birmingham was elected to membership in Phi Beta Kappa and graduated from Williams College with a Bachelor of Arts degree in the early 1950's.

After college, Birmingham moved to New York City, where he got a job as an advertising copywriter for Gimbel's department store. During his spare time he attended fashionable parties. "Sort of having gone to the 'right schools,'" he explained to Bob Abel of the *National Observer* (October 7, 1968), "I was on the [social] lists when I came to New York." His life in New York was interrupted by the draft, however, and he was inducted into the United States Army, serving in California as a public information officer for the Signal Corps. After he was discharged with the rank of sergeant he returned to New York and Gimbel's, but he soon left the mammoth department store for a job writing copy for the advertising agency of Doherty, Clifford, Steers and Shenfield. Among his accounts were the *Ladies' Home Journal,* for which he invented the now classic slogan, "Never Underestimate the Power of a Woman," and White Horse Scotch, which he sold to the public with the slogan, "Let White Horse Whisky carry you smoothly through the evening."

STEPHEN BIRMINGHAM

For nearly fifteen years Birmingham stayed with the advertising agency, doing his own writing after hours. He began getting his articles and short stories published in mass circulation magazines around 1957, and by 1960 his pieces had appeared in *McCall's, Good Housekeeping,* the *Saturday Evening Post, Holiday, Cosmopolitan, Life,* and *Redbook.* After Birmingham published his first novel in 1958 he began slowly to phase himself out of the advertising business, at first working only four days a week, then three, and finally only one day a week as a consultant. He finally quit in 1967 when *Our Crowd* turned out to be a best seller.

Birmingham's first novel, *Young Mr. Keefe,* was published in 1958 by Little, Brown after it was recommended to the publisher by John P. Marquand, who had read it at the house of his literary agent, who also worked for the younger author. The agent arranged for the two men to meet, and until Marquand's death in 1960 they continued to get together often, going over Birmingham's next two novels and discussing the themes of wealth and society that absorbed them both. *Young Mr. Keefe* concerns two young married couples and their marital and emotional difficulties. Although it is set in California, three of its four principal characters are transplants from the kind of wealthy New England society that Birmingham and Marquand knew so well. The novel was generally praised for its polish, construction, and style, but few critics took it more seriously than the Kirkus service reviewer (December 15, 1957) who called it "a personable form of light entertainment."

The central character of Birmingham's second novel, *Barbara Greer* (Little, Brown, 1959), for which he reportedly sold the movie rights, is the daughter of a wealthy New England family who, unhappy in her marriage, contemplates an affair with her brother-in-law. When he dies in an accident on his way to a rendezvous with her, she is jolted into a self-awareness that revitalizes her marriage. Finding the story permeated with "an air of Marquandian rue," John K. Hutchens of the New York *Herald Tribune* (August 4, 1959) wrote, "With a detail or two of dress or decoration, [Birmingham] can indicate the subtleties of class distinction, and make of the cocktail hour a tribal rite among the well-to-do." His third novel, *The Towers of Love* (Little, Brown, 1961), was, in the opinion of some critics, a candidate for publication in the slick women's magazines. John C. Pine, who reviewed it for *Library Journal* (October 1, 1961), dismissed it as "sheer tutti frutti," and predicted that it would "end up in many rental collections and feel right at home."

Set mainly on the West Indian Island of St. Thomas, *Those Harper Women* (McGraw-Hill, 1964) is about a wealthy family struggling to maintain a united front in the face of a journalist's exposé of its financial machinations. Calling it the author's "most subtle and ambitious novel to date," William Barrett wrote in the *Atlantic Monthly* (August 1964) after reading *Those Harper Women*, "With each novel, Stephen Birmingham carves a surer place for himself among the more accomplished of our younger writers." Some other critics, however, found the characters trite, including Thomas Wheeler of the New York *Times Book Review* (June 21, 1964) who wrote, "Mr. Birmingham knows how to bring the world of the rich into focus . . . [but] the difficult theme of capitalism redeemed awaits a more fortunate writer, one who can show it in truly meaningful action."

Fast Start, Fast Finish (New American Library, 1966), Birmingham's fifth novel, deals with a Californian who forsakes the hypertensive ambiance of West Coast advertising to settle down with his family in Westchester County, New York, where he takes up a new career as a painter. There he witnesses the gradual disintegration of his family. Although most critics conceded that Birmingham's motives in writing the novel were unimpeachable, they reviewed the novel unfavorably. Webster Schott, for example, in the New York *Times Book Review* (May 22, 1966), while admitting that Birmingham's characters came alive, had the feeling that the novel was marking time because it amplified "the usual—tired marriage, weak partners, victimized kids, money madness—to a din of hopelessness."

Birmingham first got the idea for the book that later became *Our Crowd: The Great Jewish Families of New York* (Harper, 1967), when he went to school with boys from the New York Loeb and Lehman families. "At one point there was one whole block on 70th St.—70th to 71st with adjoining gardens—where there were eleven families of Lehmans and the twelfth house was their lawyer," the author recalled for Jerry Tallmer of the New York *Post* (December 18, 1973). *Our Crowd*, to which Birmingham devoted two years of research and writing, is a social history of those entrepreneurial German Jews, the "Ashkenazim," who immigrated to the United States before the Civil War, settled in New York City, and succeeded in establishing the great banking fortunes that became the foundations of a new

aristocracy. The book traces the development of the clannish society they formed and the difficulties of the second generation in adapting to the rigorous, often puritanical, standards laid down by the founding fathers. *Our Crowd* so incensed at least one of the families discussed in it, the Warburgs, that they reportedly threatened the publishers with a law suit.

Saul Maloff of *Newsweek* (June 19, 1967) summed up critical response to *Our Crowd* when he called it a "sprightly, delightfully gossipy social history," but to some critics the book had little value beyond those qualities. Mordecai Richler of the *Guardian* (April 26, 1968), for example, complained, "[Birmingham] is glossy and entertaining, but that's all. Such rich material calls for a tougher-minded chronicler. Say, Galbraith or Arthur Schlesinger." On the other hand, David Cort wrote in the New York *Times Book Review* (July 2, 1967), "[Although] some trace of the sycophancy which the very rich require and can enforce is evident . . . , future American histories will have to take into account Mr. Birmingham's financial and social history and imposing cast of characters." *Our Crowd* enjoyed a long stay on the best-seller lists, for much of the time as number one among nonfiction titles.

On the heels of *Our Crowd*'s success Birmingham brought out another best seller, *The Right People* (Little, Brown, 1968), a chatty survey of America's white, Anglo-Saxon social establishment, based on a collection of articles on "Society" and its institutions that Birmingham had written over the past decade for *Holiday* magazine. "To those who say Society is dead, Birmingham offers proof that it is alive and well in Newport, Boston, Philadelphia, and New York," wrote Paul D. Zimmerman of *Newsweek* (April 22, 1968). "Many of his judgments are open to dispute, but, right or wrong, he takes the smallest social difference seriously." Shortly after the publication of *The Right People*, Birmingham published *Heart Troubles* (Harper, 1968), a collection of short stories, most of which had previously appeared in women's magazines.

The Grandees (Harper, 1971) exhibited his continued fascination with America's Jewish aristocracy. A history of American Sephardic Jews, whose ancestors arrived in New York in 1654 in the course of their long wanderings after their expulsion from fifteenth-century Spain, the book traces the financial and social rise of that small and tightly knit community, which considers itself the aristocracy of American Jewry. Although some reviewers criticized the best seller as gossipy and ridden with trivia, others shared the opinion of Allen Churchill, who wrote in the *Saturday Review* (March 20, 1971), "Those who relished *Our Crowd* will find *The Grandees* a more serious work. . . . There may be less bounce here, but Mr. Birmingham has written a straightforward, engrossing, and rewarding book about a group that added subtle flavoring to the American melting pot."

In *The Late John Marquand* (Lippincott, 1972), Birmingham explored the literary career and tangled private life of his former mentor, the author of the extraordinarily successful *The Late George Apley* and other novels about the manners and mores of the "old line" elite. Although a sympathetic biography, the book was written without the cooperation of Marquand's five children and without access to some of his correspondence at the Harvard libraries. The *New Republic* (June 17, 1972) reviewer patronized it as "an easy, entertaining, secondhand book," but other critics were more admiring, including Victor Howes of the *Christian Science Monitor* (June 21, 1972), who called Birmingham "the ideal chronicler of Marquand's life-in-fiction."

Largely an extension of *The Right People, The Right Places* (Little, Brown, 1973) provides a tongue-in-cheek catalogue of the areas favored by today's social aristocracy. Birmingham's latest book is *Real Lace: America's Irish Rich* (Harper, 1973), in which he tells the story of the "F.I.F.'s," or "First Irish Families." He devotes one chapter to the nation's most prominent Irish family, the Kennedys, who, ironically, have always been considered parvenus by the First Irish Families. At present Birmingham is at work on a biography of the late Samuel Goldwyn, the Metro-Goldwyn-Mayer tycoon.

"With his waving, dark hair graying temperamentally in random patches," Andrea Chambers wrote of Stephen Birmingham in the *Christian Science Monitor* (July 13, 1972), "he strikes one as a figure spanning two eras. At one minute he is an elegant hero from a nineteenth-century novel; the next, a highly urbane, contemporary author, often bemused at the social frills and foibles of which he writes." Brown-eyed and brown-haired, Birmingham is six foot one and weighs a trim 158 pounds. Since the early 1950's he has been married to the former Janet Tillson, who is a lecturer on literature, cooking, and housewifely concerns. They have three children, Mark, Harriet, and Carey. The Birminghams, who own a large, Colonial frame house in Rye, New York, recently moved to Ohio, where Stephen Birmingham is a writer-in-residence at the University of Cincinnati. Birmingham does not consider himself especially athletic, but he does ski and enjoys spending the summers around his swimming pool. He is a Democrat and Episcopalian, and his clubs are the Coffee House in New York and Les Ambassadeurs in London. Birmingham thoroughly relishes his role as the Boswell of the social establishment. As he told Susan Braudy of *New York* (May 13, 1968), "I get a kick out of being there, watching, *dégagé*, detached. It's fear that holds these people together. They are afraid people want something from them. They define themselves by exclusion, by erecting walls to keep people out."

References

Christian Sci Mon p15 Jl 13 '72 por
N Y Post p37 D 18 '73 por
Nat Observer p23 O 7 '68 por
New York 1:58+ My 13 '68 por
Who's Who in America, 1972-73

BLAKE, EUBIE

Feb. 7, 1883- Pianist; composer
Address: 284-A Stuyvesant Ave., Brooklyn, N.Y. 11221

Ragtime, a strictly American form of music that sets syncopated melody against an accompaniment in regular two-four time, was created almost exclusively by blacks. One of its greatest exponents is Eubie Blake, whose more than three-quarters of a century of performing and composing have made him a legend in the history of ragtime and in show business. Starting as a teen-age pianist in a bordello, he moved on through yesterday's vaudeville, nightclubs, and musical comedy to today's media of television, concerts, jazz festivals, and recordings. Although he is now past the age of ninety, his skill as a performer remains undiminished as he delights new audiences and critics with his own old songs in the current resurgence of ragtime.

Eubie Blake was born James Hubert Blake in Baltimore, Maryland on February 7, 1883, the eleventh child, and the only one to survive infancy, of John Sumner Blake and Emily (Johnson) Blake, both of whom had been born slaves. His father was a stevedore; his mother, a domestic. Hubie, whose name was later shortened to Eubie, displayed musical talent at the age of six by suddenly playing an organ in a department store. His surprised mother sent him to a neighbor for piano lessons, and for the next six years he studied classical music. At around twelve, he first heard ragtime and quickly learned to play it by ear. Although his deeply religious mother would not allow ragtime to be played at home, he gained great popularity by performing it on the school organ, until his formal education ended in the eighth grade with his expulsion for fighting over a girl.

When Blake was fifteen, an older friend got him a job as a pianist in a bordello. His weekly salary was $3 for seven nights, but Blake received from $10 to $15 a night in tips. His mother, discovering where he worked, strongly disapproved, but his father, who earned only $9 a week, overcame her objections. Eubie continued at Aggie Shelton's place for the next three years. In 1899, at sixteen, he composed his first piece of music, "Sounds of Africa," but since he did not know how to write scores, the rag was not transcribed until some time later and was not published until after 1919, when Witmark brought it out as the "Charleston Rag." During off hours from Aggie's bordello he played at Cockie Lewis' saloon, where a traveling seller of horse medicine heard him and hired him to play the melodeon and to perform a buck dance, a type of tap dance. His show business debut was made with Dr. Frazier's Medicine Show on July 4, 1901 in Fairfield, Pennsylvania. Later, in the troupe of a touring musical *In Old Kentucky*, he saw New York for the first time when the show played the Academy of Music for two weeks in 1902. Back in Baltimore in 1903, Blake worked at

EUBIE BLAKE

Greenfields and then Annie Gilley's, the last bordello he was to play. He filled several other brief engagements in his home city before taking a more or less steady job in 1907 at Baltimore's newly built Goldfield Hotel, where he performed until 1910. During summers, from 1908 to 1914, he played in Atlantic City. In October 1914 his first published piano composition, "Chevy Chase," was brought out by Joseph W. Stern. Not a typical rag, it was stage music without lyrics and indicated the direction in which he was moving—toward musical comedy.

Hired to play at Riverview Park in Baltimore for the summer with Joe Porter's Serenaders, Blake met Noble Sissle on opening night, May 15, 1915, and quickly discovered that the band's vocalist was also a lyricist. The two performers joined forces and wrote their first song, "It's All Your Fault," which Sophie Tucker, who was playing Baltimore, bought for her vaudeville act. In September Sissle went to New York, where he later joined James Reese Europe's Society Orchestra, the first black group to play consistently in the wealthy society mansions of New York, Newport, and Palm Beach. At Sissle's persuasion Europe hired Blake in the spring of 1916. In addition to working in Europe's orchestra, the team again began writing songs and during the summer of 1916 played at the special parties of Europe's top society clients as singer and pianist. Blake continued as a society pianist until May 1919, when Europe was murdered by a temporarily insane drummer. Europe's agents then teamed Sissle and Blake as a vaudeville act, "The Dixie Duo," and after a tryout in Bridgeport, moved them into the Harlem Opera House. Bookers for the powerful Keith vaudeville circuit saw them and, impressed, signed them to open the following week in New York's top vaudeville house, the Palace, where they stopped every show. They were then sent on a long and successful tour of the Keith circuit.

A NAACP benefit in Philadelphia in the summer of 1920 brought them together with another Negro vaudeville team—Aubrey Lyles and Flournoy Miller, who had prepared the book for a musical comedy. Sissle and Blake agreed to write the lyrics and music. When the two teams met again in New York in early 1921, they set to work. Despite great financial difficulties, Shuffle Along, with book by Lyles and Miller, lyrics by Sissle, and music by Blake, opened on May 23, 1921 at New York's 63rd Street Theater, where it electrified Broadway and made theatrical history. The first black show produced in more than a decade, it not only broke the color barrier, but in style and form set the pattern for future Broadway musicals. It ran for 504 performances, a record in those days. Three road companies toured over the next two years, also breaking the color barriers at many previously all-white theatres. In addition to writing the music and leading the orchestra, Blake starred in the show along with Sissle, Lyles, and Miller. Toward the end of the musical, he joined Sissle on stage and they repeated the act that had made them popular in vaudeville. Among the performers connected with the show who went on to become famous were Hall Johnson, William Grant Still, Paul Robeson, and Josephine Baker.

One of the surprise song hits of Shuffle Along was "I'm Just Wild About Harry," which Blake had originally written as a waltz and then changed to a fox-trot. In 1948 President Harry S. Truman made it his campaign song. Another of Blake's enduring songs, "You Were Meant For Me," caught the attention of the producer André Charlot during a rehearsal held by the composer. Charlot bought it for his 1923 show, London Calling, whose stars, Gertrude Lawrence and Noel Coward, singing together for the first time on stage, introduced it to British audiences. It became a hit in America, too, when Miss Lawrence and Jack Buchanan sang it on Broadway in Charlot's Revue of 1924.

Planning to do a second show with Lyles and Miller, Blake was disappointed to discover they had signed with George White. He and Sissle took Shuffle Along back on the road in August 1923 and, attracting even larger audiences than had the original road company, soon earned enough money to buy Lyles and Miller's rights to the musical, paying them $9,000 each. In 1923 Blake also wrote a dozen songs for the musical Elsie. He then turned to a show of his own, with Sissle writing the lyrics as well as collaborating the book with Lou Payton. In Bamville opened at the Lyceum Theatre in Rochester, New York on March 10, 1924, less than two months after the final closing of Shuffle Along. With its title changed to The Chocolate Dandies, it opened at the Colonial Theatre in New York on September 1, 1924. Although Blake still feels its score is the best he ever wrote, the revue was so expensive to stage that it had lost $60,000 by the time it closed on May 15, 1925.

The vaudevillians Sissle and Blake, having revived their act in theatres showing full-length silent movies, were offered a European tour. They sailed on the USS Olympic in September 1925 to spend eight months playing in England, Scotland, and France. Observing their reception in London, Charles B. Cochran asked them to write the lyrics and music for his revue of 1926. But Blake was eager to return home. After a short time back in the United States, Sissle left for Europe without him, thus bringing about the only break in the team's long association. Teaming with Henry Creamer in 1927, Blake wrote music for floor shows. In the 1928-29 season, with the singer Broadway Jones and a cast of eleven, he took *Shuffle Along, Jr.* on a coast-to-coast tour, playing the Keith-Albee-Orpheum vaudeville circuit. The following season he and Jones starred in the Fanchon and Marco stage show, playing the Balaban and Katz circuit. He also contributed songs to the *Folies Bergères* at the Gansevoort Theater and to the Broadway show *Hot Rhythm* in 1930. Between seasons he played in wealthy society homes in Florida.

In partnership with lyricist Andy Razaf, Blake wrote the musical numbers for Lew Leslie's *Blackbirds of 1930*, which featured one of his best-known songs, "Memories of You," and another, "You're Lucky To Me," sung by Ethel Waters. With Blake leading the orchestra, *Blackbirds* opened at the Majestic Theater in Brooklyn on September 1, 1930 to rave reviews. However, producer Leslie made so many inept changes in the production that when it reached Broadway on October 22, 1930, it lasted for only sixty-two performances. Blake turned again to performing in vaudeville and hotels and made several Warner Brothers musical shorts, among them "Pie, Pie Blackbirds." He also conducted the Broadway musical *Singin' the Blues* in 1931.

After Blake's reunion with Sissle in 1932, the team wrote *Shuffle Along of 1933*, but because of the Depression the show ran for only fifteen performances in New York. Then with a new version shortened to fit on the bill with motion pictures, they started a cross-country tour, but it proved unsuccessful. In the mid-30's Blake worked with Razaf writing floor shows. He then turned to writing musical shows with Joshua Milton Reddie, one of which *Swing It,* was presented by the WPA in 1937. After America's entry into World War II in 1941, Blake became a conductor of USO shows and toured Army camps and hospitals.

In about 1946, at the beginning of a long period of semiretirement, Blake enrolled at New York University to study the difficult Schillinger system of composition, a four-year course that he completed in two and a half years to graduate at the age of sixty-six. He then spent many hours writing down in that system the old songs he had committed to memory. Besides writing new music, especially waltzes, a favorite tempo of his, he practised for an average of three hours a day on the piano. He worked for some time on the musical *Shuffle Along of 1952.* But in trying to update the show, its producers used songs from other composers and disregarded the qualities that had made the original show a hit. On opening night in New York on May 8, 1952, it was panned by the critics, and it ran for only four performances.

When, in the 1960's, interest in ragtime revived, Eubie Blake was one of its few surviving pioneers. Since few of his recordings were still available, Columbia Records brought out in 1969 a two-record album, *The Eighty-Six Years of Eubie Blake,* with Blake playing thirty rags, marches, and blues, most of which he had composed. Suddenly, Eubie Blake was in demand again. He began teaching music at Yale, New York, and other universities and appeared as a frequent guest on television. In June 1969 he played at the New Orleans Jazz Festival and in 1970 gave a forty-five-minute concert at Rutgers University. During 1971 he played the Maple Leaf Club in Los Angeles in March, the annual ragtime festival on the showboat SS *Goldenrod* in St. Louis in June, the Newport and Southern California festivals in July, and a ragtime club in Toronto in October. Among his appearances the following year was a March 1, 1972 concert for Town Hall's weekly *5:45 Interlude,* at which he attracted the largest audience since the series began the previous January.

On December 3, 1972, two months before reaching the age of ninety, Blake gave an hour-and-forty-five-minute concert at Alice Tully Hall in New York. John S. Wilson reported in the *New York Times* (December 5, 1972), "He was just remarkable, regardless of age. . . . He played with unabashed assurance and unfailing precision, his unusually long, thin fingers rolling across the keyboard with the agility that could scarcely have been greater when he was cutting down other pianists at the Bucket of Blood in Atlantic City 70 years ago. His singing voice was sure and firm with no quavers or hesitations. . . . When he took his bows, he ran—literally, ran—back and forth to the wings. And he had to take a lot of bows."

Along with other ragtime performers Blake took part in a concert at Philharmonic Hall in New York in mid-January 1973. The reviewers for *Variety* (January 17, 1973), not favorably impressed with entertainers of the evening, singled out Blake as an exception: "During his second-half stint, he played with his usual verve, once again showing that dynamism need not flag at age 89." In the spring three new albums: *Eubie Blake, Featuring Ivan Harold Browning, Eubie Blake; Rags to Classics,* and *Eubie Blake and His Friends Edith Wilson and Ivan Harold Browning,* were issued by Blake's own company, which he had formed in 1972. In addition, he supervised the reissue of *Eubie Blake: Blues and Rags* and *Eubie Blake: 1921,* put out by Biograph, and containing twenty-two of the piano rolls he cut between 1917 and 1921. Another reissue, *Sissle and Blake: Early Rare Recordings,* was presented by his own record firm. In May 1973, on his first plane trip, he flew to Buffalo to cut piano rolls for the ORS Music Rolls Company. Also during that year he played at the Molde Jazz Festival in Norway, the Newport-New York Jazz Festival at Carnegie Hall, and with the Boston Pops Orchestra for "Old Timers Night," which was televised.

Other television programs on which Blake has been seen are the *Johnny Carson Show*, the *Mike Douglas Show*, and *Black Omnibus* with James Earl Jones. On the CBS-TV program *Black Arts* on December 2, 1972 he gave a twenty-minute preview of his Alice Tully Hall concert. He played his own music in a one-hour show presented on WTOP-TV in Washington D.C. in late March 1974. Describing Blake during the four-hour rehearsal, Phil Casey wrote in the Washington *Post* (March 29, 1974), "He remained calm, unperturbed, happy and serene.... He plays with power and joy, laughing, humming, singing, talking to himself and the piano." Earnings of up to $2,500 a performance, plus royalties of over $15,-000 a year from his 315 compositions, assure Blake that he will see no more lean years in his continuing career. Secure in his comeback, he told Pamela Hollie of the *Wall Street Journal* (October 23, 1973), "I'll keep performing until one day when I'm on stage, the man upstairs says nine, 10—you're out."

Eubie Blake is a small, dapper, bald-headed man, who wears a thin moustache, and weighs 125 pounds. He has extremely long and slim fingers, which account in part for his remarkable style and touch, because each hand can span twelve piano keys as compared to the usual span of nine or ten of other pianists. Though quite spry onstage, he is not so agile offstage, as he suffers from an arthritic back. He also has a slight problem with hearing in his left ear. He takes vitamins daily, continues to compose and practise the piano, sleeps for only a few hours, but likes to rise late in the morning. He eats very little, preferring 7-Up, tea, cigars, and the cigarettes he has been smoking since the age of six. On July 29, 1908 he married his schoolgirl sweetheart, Avis Lee, who died in 1939. While touring for the USO in 1945, he met Marion Grant, a former dancer, whom he married in December of that year. The couple moved into the nine-room house that had been her family home in the Bedford-Stuyvesant section of Brooklyn, where they still live. Among his honors are membership in the Songwriters' Hall of Fame, degrees from universities, the Ellington Medal awarded by Yale, and the keys to the city of Baltimore. He has also had theatres named after him. President Richard Nixon proclaimed February 14, 1973 as "Eubie Blake Day." Noting that his wife, who is his manager, has a difficult time keeping up with his busy schedule, he admits he has one further ambition, to write the music for a movie.

References

Ebony 28:94+ Jl '73 pors
N Y Daily News p73 O 31 '73 por
N Y Times p33 D 1 '72 por
New Yorker 49:96 Jl '73
Time 100:97 D 18 '72 por
Washington Post E p3 Ag 12 '72 por
Blesh, Rudi. Eight Lives in Jazz (1971)
Kimball, Robert, and Bolcom, William. Reminiscing with Sissle and Blake (1973)

BLATTY, WILLIAM PETER

Jan. 7, 1928- Novelist; scenarist
Address: b. W. W. Norton & Co., Inc., 55 5th Ave., New York 10003

Amid the current resurgence of interest in the occult, William Peter Blatty's *The Exorcist*, a story of demonic possession, has scored a phenomenal success as both novel and film. The book, published in 1971, is nearing the ten million mark in sales, and the motion picture, released in 1973, is among the biggest money-makers in cinema history. The movie generated controversy among critics, clergymen, and letters-to-the-editor writers and sent psychologists, sociologists, and journalists into tireless explanations of the public's fascination with it.

Plagued from its inception by internal squabbles, unaccountable accidents, shooting delays, and interminable legal and theological problems, *The Exorcist* also failed to win its anticipated quota of major awards from the Academy of Motion Picture Arts and Sciences in 1974. Nominated for ten Oscars, it garnered only two, those for best achievement in sound and best screenplay based on a work in another medium. Attributing the slight to "backlash," a disappointed Blatty remarked, as quoted in the Washington *Post* (April 4, 1974), "I guess they [the members of the Academy] don't want confrontation; they want opium. . . . The Academy likes . . . I can't tell what the Academy likes anymore."

Born in New York City on January 7, 1928, William Peter Blatty is the fifth and youngest child of Peter and Mary (Mouakad) Blatty, both Lebanese immigrants. When Blatty was six his parents separated. He was raised by his broken-English-speaking mother, an illiterate but enterprising woman who intimidated landlords, social workers, public utility companies, and the collection agents of New York City department stores with her artfully crazy ways. She earned her living by peddling homemade quince jelly in front of the Plaza Hotel and on Park Avenue, where she would dart in and out of traffic, selling jars of jelly to startled motorists. "She was indomitable," Blatty told Martha MacGregor in an interview for the New York *Post* (September 1, 1973). "My feeling was that if she couldn't come through with some kind of evidence of survival it couldn't be done."

In the mid-1930's the Blattys moved to Brooklyn, where William attended Brooklyn Prep, a Jesuit school for wealthy boys, on a scholarship. He began writing short stories and essays as a diversion and submitted several of his best efforts for publication. One article, "A Day at Coney Island," was eventually published by, as he recalls, "something called *Dental News*." After graduating from high school, he was awarded a scholarship to study at Georgetown University in Washington, D.C. During his junior year at Georgetown he read a Washington *Post* account of the alleged exorcism of a fourteen-year-old boy by a Jesuit priest. The case struck Blatty, at times a doubting Catholic, as "the corroboration—though not proof—of the life of the spirit," and, with the encouragement of Father Thomas Birmingham, he selected demonic possession as his topic for the senior oratorical contest. He received his B.A. degree in 1950.

Unable to find a teaching position in the Washington area, Blatty sold Electrolux vacuum cleaners door-to-door and drove a beer truck for the Gunther Brewing Company before enlisting in the United States Air Force in 1951. Upon the completion of several months' training at officer's candidate and psychological warfare schools he was assigned to an aerial resupply and communications wing, where he directed psychological warfare policy. After the war he earned an M.A. degree in English literature at George Washington University, in 1954. He was later granted his doctoral degree by the same university.

From 1955 to 1957 Blatty worked for the United States Information Agency. Stationed in Beirut, Lebanon, he edited the *News Review*, a weekly magazine popularizing "the American way of life" which was distributed to all Middle Eastern USIA posts. To augment his income he contributed several humorous articles to the *Saturday Evening Post* and collaborated with James J. Cullen to write *Ulysses and the Cyclops; a Tale From Homer's Odyssey* (Microclassics Press, 1956). His second book, *Which Way to Mecca, Jack?*, (Bernard Geis, 1960), recounted his misadventures as a USIA official. In the New York *Herald Tribune* (November 27, 1960), Hal Lehrman recommended the book "as a guide to the diplomatically perplexed and as a rich lode of yoks, guffaws, and bubbling merriment."

Blatty directed publicity for the University of Southern California at Los Angeles in 1957 and 1958 and public relations for Loyola University in Los Angeles in 1959 and 1960. An amusing conversationalist, he often appeared on Jack Paar's *Tonight* show in the early 1960's. Impressed by his facile story-telling, a motion picture producer commissioned him to write a film script for Danny Kaye. The film, *The Man From the Diner's Club* (Columbia, 1963), opened to generally mediocre reviews in April 1963. In the New York *Herald Tribune* (April 18, 1963), Judith Crist severely criticized the "contrived plot" of the "mechanized screenplay."

Among his other early film credits were *A Shot in the Dark* (United Artists, 1966), a commercially successful farce starring Peter Sellers as the bumbling Inspector Clouseau; *What Did You Do In the War, Daddy?* (United Artists, 1966), a poorly reviewed World War II comedy; *Gunn* (Paramount, 1967), a routine melodrama based on the defunct television private eye series *Peter Gunn*; and *Darling Lili* (Paramount, 1970), a light-hearted musical spoof on the international-intrigue genre featuring Julie Andrews as an English music hall performer who spied for the Germans during World War I.

Considerable notoriety accompanied the publication of his third book, *John Goldfarb, Please

WILLIAM PETER BLATTY

Come Home!* (Doubleday, 1963). A seemingly innocuous novel, it described the attempts of a captured American U-2 pilot to coach a feckless squad of indifferent "Fawzi Arabians" to a revengeful victory over the mighty Notre Dame football team. (The ruler of the mythical oil sheikdom had been offended when his ninety-eight-pound son was cut from the university's varsity roster.) A projected film version of the book so infuriated Notre Dame's trustees that they sought an injunction banning both the book and the film on the grounds that they did "immeasureable damage" to the school's reputation. The injunction was upheld by New York State Supreme Court Justice Henry Clay Greenberg, who ruled in December 1964 that the film had misappropriated the name of Notre Dame in a "clear case of commercial piracy."

Blatty protested that he had no intention of discrediting the university and merely wanted to use its name to achieve the incongruity he felt was essential to the humor of his story. In February 1965 an appellate court unanimously reversed Justice Greenberg's ban and the film, starring Shirley MacLaine as an American journalist and Peter Ustinov as King Fawz, was quickly released by Twentieth Century-Fox. Most major critics agreed with Justice Greenberg's decision that the script was "ugly, vulgar, and tawdry." Bosley Crowther of the New York *Times* (March 25, 1965) dismissed it as "an absolute tangle of gimmicks and jimcracky threads of plot."

The ill-fated *John Goldfarb* was followed by *I, Billy Shakespeare!* (Doubleday, 1965), a satire about six tape-recorded seances with the ghost of the Bard, and the novel *Twinkle, Twinkle, Killer Kane!* (Doubleday, 1967). The commercial failure of both books, the disagreeable, and in his opinion, unwarranted changes in his scripts, and his mother's sudden death in 1967 left Blatty artistically and personally distraught. To escape his problems, Blatty rented a cabin near Lake Tahoe, California, where he completed the draft of a new novel, *The Exorcist*.

Intrigued by the idea of "disembodied intelligences," Blatty had been informally investigating cases of alleged demonic possession for more than twenty years. His research convinced him that most of these cases were the result of mental instability. A "hard core," however, remained inexplicable scientifically, confirming his belief in the existence of demonic forces. In *The Exorcist*, he dramatized the tenacity of such forces as they transform Regan, the ingenuous, charming twelve-year-old daughter of a movie star, into a bizarre creature who speaks a number of foreign languages, exerts supernatural energy, knows the unknowable, and performs fiendish tricks. Like the victim in the Maryland case, on which Blatty relied for documentation, Regan fails to respond to medical or psychiatric treatment and is cured only after Catholic priests reluctantly perform the rite of exorcism.

"I had no plot when I sat down to write it," Blatty recalled to Kenneth Turan in an interview for the Washington *Post's Potomac* magazine (December 17, 1972). "I had mountains of research but no plot whatsoever. At the beginning I was just pleased simply to write a book that was not a humorous novel for a change. . . . I really believe, however, that my unconscious . . . knew the whole story and was divulging it to me a little at a time."

Regarded by many critics as little more than a skillfully wrought horror story, the book, published by Harper & Row in 1971, compiled a phenomenal sales record. By February 1974 *The Exorcist*, which was on the New York *Times's* best-seller list for fifty-five weeks, had sold more than 9,000,000 copies and been translated into a dozen languages. Analyzing the book's impact on the public for the *Guardian* (February 16, 1972), Thomas Wiseman noted that Blatty's "rather cleverly contrived piece of high commercial writing" tapped "a very primitive terror of the adult world in showing childhood as an unknown quantity. . . . The fear of the malign child in the womb (a future Hitler) must be a universal dread."

After selling the film rights of *The Exorcist* to Warner Brothers in 1971, Blatty, acting as both scriptwriter and producer, hired William Friedkin, the Academy Award-winning director of *The French Connection* to direct the film. The author insisted on absolute control over the production of the motion picture. "Too often the producer or the director or the actor or his wife will commit more obscenities of change upon a script than Launce's dog wrought upon a gentlewoman's farthingale in *Two Gentlemen of Verona*" he explained, as quoted in *New York* magazine (January 21, 1974).

Working closely together, Blatty and Friedkin chose for their cast Max von Sydow, Ellen Burstyn, Jason Miller, Lee J. Cobb, and thirteen-year-old Linda Blair, who was selected to portray the bedeviled child. With a $10,000,000 budget, they did location shooting in Nineveh, Iraq, and Washington, D.C., acquired a Georgetown brownstone for the main set, and devised ingenious special effects to simulate the chilling atmosphere and action of the novel.

Released on December 26, 1973, *The Exorcist* attracted record-breaking crowds and grossed about $2,000,000 a month during its initial run. Not even the most adverse reports about spectators vomiting, fainting, or being hospitalized after seeing the film deterred the public, which, according to one incredulous reviewer, seemed to be "possessed" by *The Exorcist*. In Washington, D.C. some officials were so exercised about the film's more unpalatable scenes that capital police intervened to enforce a locally imposed "X" rating. The Motion Picture Association of America's Review Board, which had assigned the film an "R" rating, continued to stand by its original decision in the face of increasing criticism and civic action from angry citizens.

The critics' reactions to the film were decidedly mixed. Joseph Gelmis, writing in *Newsday* (December 27, 1973), praised "Friedkin's total control of his audience's nervous system." He "creates the experience of evil and sustains it for two hours." Archer Winsten, in his New York *Post* review (December 27, 1973), concurred, observing that "the weight of on-rushing events . . . , of shock piled on shock . . . , of sensible people torn from their rational moorings" was so persuasive that one inevitably was "swept along." Judith Crist, on the other hand, regarded *The Exorcist* as a "half-successful film." Writing in *New York* (January 21, 1974), Miss Crist commended Friedkin for his "exquisite directorial touches" and for his "stunning series of special effects" but chided Blatty for having "cut the caring out" in adapting his book to the screen. "We are never told of the complex guilts within the actress's household that make the possession of the child, rather than of an adult, more than an exploitative turn of the screw. And as a result we miss the compassionate sense of relation to individuals, an empathetic experience." In two devastating attacks, published in the New York *Times* on December 27, 1973 and on January 13, 1974, Vincent Canby dismissed *The Exorcist* as "a chunk of elegant occultist claptrap" that "treats diabolism with the kind of dumb piety movie makers once lavished on the stories of saints." Disturbed by the film's popular appeal, he devoted his second piece to an analysis of the manner in which *The Exorcist*'s creators "[exploited] cruelties and our fascination with them." According to Pauline Kael in the *New Yorker* (January 7, 1974), the film was "tiresomely moralistic." One disgusted critic was led to comment that he thought it nothing more than an "elaborate freak show."

Replying to negative criticism, Blatty told an interviewer for *People* magazine (March 4, 1974): "[Those reviewers] belong to a very small, elitist set . . . who have been trapped so long in the squirrel cage of their egos that the world of reality outside their cage is a blur. They neither reap nor sow nor perform any useful social function." He viewed the film as "an apostolic work" and argued that it had a decidedly cathartic

century. With the technology of the new agricultural revolution, however, which had been developed and was being disseminated largely under FAO auspices, it was hoped that the world would gain a reprieve during which it could develop effective forms of population control.

On such a note of hope and challenge, Boerma began his tenure at FAO with a major reorganization aimed at better efficiency in evaluating the food problem. In 1969 he released a report called the Indicative World Plan for Agricultural Development. The result of several years of study, the plan provides a broad blueprint for the way in which the developing nations can bridge the gap between food and population by 1985. The plan would cost a staggering $85 billion in financing over a fifteen-year period, most of which would have to be provided by the developed nations. The Indicative World Plan singles out five key objectives. In the first place, the new high-yield rice and wheat crops must be further developed. Secondly, wastage of foods after harvesting (currently running at about 10 percent) must be reduced. Thirdly, to reduce protein deficiency and provide for the changing dietary habits that come with prosperity, more meat products, chiefly quick-yield chicken and pork, must be produced. Fourthly, because demand for imports tends to outstrip money from exports in developing nations, an emphasis should be put on "selective expansion" of agricultural products suitable for foreign trade. Finally, to counter perhaps the worst problem, that of agricultural unemployment, which brings social unrest and political instability as well as human misery, the report urges that developing countries try to provide jobs by building up industries tied to local agriculture.

In June 1970 Boerma called a World Food Congress in the Hague to which 1,500 delegates from over 100 countries were invited to offer advice on the implementation of the Indicative World Plan. At the conference Boerma stressed the grave problem of unemployment that would affect developing countries as their populations rise and their agriculture changes from subsistence farming to more modern and more efficient methods. He also called attention to the continuing problems of malnutrition, lack of proper education, and a "compelling need for urgent measures to check the rate of population growth." Pointing out that the annual FAO budget equals the cost of just one nuclear submarine, Boerma urged that the delegates "tell people that their own future peace and prosperity may be imperiled by what is happening to the poor and in the poor lands today." By the end of the two-week Congress, FAO had received suggestions from eight commissions that were formed to discuss various aspects of the World Indicative Plan.

Droughts, floods, and other natural disasters blighted the promise of the Green Revolution during the early 1970's. In FAO's 1973 annual report Boerma announced that for the first time in twenty years the world was almost entirely dependent on a single season's weather for its basic food supplies. The surplus stocks of grain that had provided some margin of safety in previous years had been largely bought up by the Soviet Union, after its massive 1972 crop failure, and world food production had actually declined in 1972 for the first time since World War II. To prevent the reoccurrence of such a situation, Boerma proposed that a concept of minimal "world food security" be endorsed internationally. Under his plan governments would regularly consult on needs and supplies, voluntary guidelines would be established to coordinate national stock policies, and "vulnerable" countries would be helped to maintain their stocks, even if they lacked the money to buy them.

At an urgent one-day meeting called in Rome by Boerma in September 1973 to discuss the danger of a world grain shortage, the FAO director general warned delegates from the world's major grain exporting nations that the developing countries must obtain minimally essential grain imports if they were to escape serious political and social instability and possible starvation. Although the consensus of opinion at the meeting was that 1973 grain exports would be adequate to meet demand, the problem of how poor nations could pay inflated wheat prices remained unsettled. By 1973 the price of wheat had trebled to a record of over $200 a ton.

The area of the world most severely hit by natural disaster in recent years is the sub-Sahara region of French-speaking West Africa, which has been afflicted for several years with one of the worst droughts since Biblical times. In 1973 FAO estimated that about 6,000,000 of the region's 25,000,000 people were in danger of dying from starvation. Many were saved by an FAO-sponsored international food distribution plan that year, but thousands of others died from starvation and disease. Drought conditions in the sub-Sahara had worsened by early 1974, according to Boerma, and pledges of aid for 1974 had fallen far short of need.

Addeke H. Boerma makes his home in a villa outside Rome, where he gardens and tends his fruit trees and rose bushes. He was married in 1953 to Dinah Johnston, formerly of Belfast, Northern Ireland, who was at the time his assistant at FAO headquarters in Rome. They have two daughters, Maureen and Pauline. By a previous marriage Boerma has three other daughters. A tall, bulky man with broad features, rosy cheeks, and pale blue eyes, Boerma has been described as an unaffected, approachable man, who enjoys such amenities as French wines, dry martinis, large cigars, and thick Dutch pea soup served with sliced sausage and croutons. For relaxation he attends Italian operas and plays the piano. As befits his international position, Boerma is an accomplished linguist who, in addition to his native Flemish, speaks English, French, German, and Italian. Among the honorary titles that have been bestowed on the U.N. official are Knight in the Order of the Dutch Lion, the highest civil order in the Netherlands, and Commander in the Order of Leopold II of Belgium.

References

N Y Times p17 S 6 '62 por
International Who's Who, 1973-74
Who's Who in the World, 1971-72

BONO, CHER *See* Cher

BONO, SONNY

Feb. 16, 1935- Singer; songwriter; television entertainer
Address: b. c/o ABC Television Network, 1330 Avenue of the Americas, New York 10019

To the millions of viewers who watched *The Sonny and Cher Comedy Hour* every Wednesday evening over CBS-TV, Sonny Bono appeared to be a good-natured bumbler who was perennially outwitted by his glamorous and sharp-tongued wife, Cher. In reality, he is a canny showman who managed to transform the husband and wife team from a youth-oriented rock duo of the mid-1960's into two of the most popular nightclub and television entertainers in the business. A songwriter before he teamed up with Cher in 1964, Sonny Bono has composed most of the couple's hit songs, including "I Got You, Babe," "The Beat Goes On," and "United We Stand." He also branched out into filmmaking with two largely unnoticed works, a rock film entitled *Good Times*, in which he costarred with Cher, and the nonmusical drama *Chastity*, which he wrote and produced for her. An amicable separation early in 1974 ended the Bonos' partnership and brought about the cancellation of their successful TV variety show that fall. Bono went on to appear in his own ABC-TV variety show, *The Sonny Comedy Revue*, which had its première in the autumn of 1974.

The son of Santo and Jean Bono, Sonny Bono was born Salvatore Bono in Detroit, Michigan on February 16, 1935. During his years as a rock star with Cher, he pretended to be about five years younger than his real age, but, he told Earl Wilson in the New York *Post* (June 19, 1971), "I'm thirty-six now. . . . I was twenty-seven for three years, then we decided it was nonsense to count off years, so now we have the comfort of honesty." His parents were impoverished immigrants from Sicily, who often had not even enough money to feed their family. When Sonny was seven years old, the Bonos moved to Los Angeles. His parents were eventually divorced, a traumatic event that Sonny many years later recalled in a hit song entitled, "You'd Better Sit Down Kids."

A poor student, Sonny dropped out of high school and took a job as a delivery boy in a grocery store. By that time he had begun writing songs, including "Koko Joe," which became a minor hit for the Righteous Brothers in 1964. While trying to peddle his songs to recording companies, he worked as a waiter, construction worker, butcher's helper, and truck driver. After a stint as an artist and repertoire man with Specialty Records, where he worked with Sam Cooke and Little Richard, Bono started his own record company. When it failed, he became a record promoter.

Eventually Bono went to work for Philles Records, where he was associated with Phil Spector. At Philles he obtained a virtually complete education in songmaking, writing songs ("You Bug Me, Baby," "Needles and Pins"); singing background music for groups like the Ronettes, the Crystals, and the Righteous Brothers; assisting at recording sessions; learning about sound engineering; contributing arranging ideas; and helping to edit tapes.

While working with Spector, Bono met Cherilyn LaPiere, a sloe-eyed and exotically beautiful teenager who was trying to launch a show business career. Within a year, on October 27, 1964, they were married in Tijuana, Mexico. "As a producer, I thought Cher was a natural star immediately. She was a real generator for me," Sonny recalled in an interview with Digby Diehl of the New York *Times* (July 9, 1967). The pair sang backgrounds together at Philles for a while, and Sonny became convinced that with Cher's robust voice and his songs they could become stars. (He admits that his own voice is at best mediocre.)

When the Bonos made their first appearances and their first recording ("The Letter") they were somewhat archly billed as Caesar and Cleo, but they soon decided to use their own nicknames. As Sonny and Cher they made a couple of moderately successful recordings ("Baby, Don't Go," "Just You"), before striking it big in June 1965 with "I Got You, Babe," which Sonny had written as an expression of their feelings about each other.

After "I Got You, Babe" the hits followed one after the other, including "Laugh At Me," recorded by Sonny alone; "Bang Bang"; "What Now, My Love"; "All I Really Want to Do"; and Sonny's most recorded song, "The Beat Goes On," which has become one of the classics of early rock music. By the end of 1967 Sonny and Cher had sold over 40,000,000 discs worldwide.

Looking back on that period, Bono told Arnold Shaw of *BMI* magazine (April 1972), "It was too demanding. Getting a hit record constantly was on my mind. It gave you three more months of survival as a star. It was almost like a probationary period. When the three months were up, the panic was on. I had to get to the piano and come up with another hit."

During that frenetic period, from mid-1965 until about mid-1967, Sonny and Cher reigned as rock's favorite couple, flouting the adult world's conventions with their mod clothes and lifestyle. Their image at that time is perhaps best captured in the film, *Good Times* (Columbia, 1967), in which they play themselves, an affluent, happily married pair of singing stars ambling through what one critic called "a kooky elaboration of their hit record, 'I Got You, Babe.'" The film, for which Sonny wrote the score and conducted the orchestra as well as acted, in general won admiration from members of the press, including Richard F. Shepard of the New York *Times* (August 3, 1967), who wrote: "They are an ingratiating couple, he long-haired and comic in a way that recalls a touch of Harpo Marx and the Three Stooges. She is long-haired and attractive and robustly voiced, fine for the songs, which are bright and brassy."

By the time that *Good Times* was released, however, Sonny and Cher were finding that their mix of puppy love and music with a simple, easy beat was out of fashion, having been displaced by a more decadent taste for drugs and acid rock. In a desperate gamble to regain their popularity, Sonny wrote and produced in 1968 a film for his wife about a teen-age girl who runs away from home and hitch-hikes around the Southwest into Mexico. He put every penny he could raise into the film, even mortgaging his house. "I was defensive and mad," Sonny explained to Henry Ehrlich of *Good Housekeeping* (May 1972). "I wanted to be a part of show business, and they wouldn't have me. So I invested everything I had—emotionally and financially—in that movie. I was trying to say, 'We're solid entertainers. You've got to accept us.'" When *Chastity* was released by American International in 1969 it failed to impress either the public or the critics, who dismissed it as a shallow and pretentious youth exploitation film. Sonny reportedly lost $500,000 on the venture, although eventual distribution of the film recouped much of his losses.

By 1969 the Bonos were broke, but Sonny promised his wife that within five years he would have them at the top again. As it turned out, it took them only three years, since they were astute enough to perform in nightclubs, to develop a more stable and enduring adult audience. "The biggest mistake a performer makes is to try to stay a teen-ager," Sonny told Earl Wilson (New York *Post*, June 19, 1971). "Young kids have a new idol every year. Someone will always take your place next year."

In nightclubs Sonny and Cher developed the act that later became familiar to their television audiences in the 1970's. It consisted of songs—their old hits, current pop-rock songs, and standards—and witty repartee, often off-color, fashioned in the time-honored context of the war-of-the-sexes that has served many husband and wife acts in show business. Sonny, who was given to monologues that obviously bored Cher, suffered the brunt of put-downs that usually centered on his Italian ancestry, his mother, his short stature, or his limited vocal endowments. He tried to counter with barbs about her daring costumes and her pencil-thin figure, but he was always outclassed in the put-down contest by his wife. Through it all the couple managed to convey the impression that they really loved each other and were only indulging in a game of pretense.

Their success in nightclubs led to television appearances and, in the summer of 1971, to a six-week Sunday night series of one-hour shows on CBS. Sonny devised the basic format of *The Sonny and Cher Comedy Hour* that summer, a

SONNY BONO

combination of elaborately costumed and produced song numbers, repartee between the stars, and comedy skits with guest performers. The formula proved so successful that CBS put the show on its permanent roster beginning in the winter season of 1971-72, where it stayed until mid-1974. When the Bonos were not taping their television shows, they continued to appear before sold-out nightclub and concert audiences.

Not all critics were impressed with Sonny and Cher's charms. *Newsday* television critic Robert Christgau complained (May 8, 1973), for example, that they had become "established. . . as the symbols of nouveau-hip marriage. Their definition of their own union . . . [was] equal parts rancor, schmaltz, and conspicuous consumption." But the public apparently agreed with Tom Shales of the Washington *Post* (September 5, 1973), who wrote after seeing them at the Shady Grove Music Fair, "The Sonny and Cher show is a socko, Las Vegassy, blam-blam, clickety-click, super-professional spectacular. And it's funny."

In recent years Sonny and Cher's song hits have included "United We Stand," "You'd Better Sit Down, Kids," and "A Cowboy's Work is Never Done." The albums that they made together include *The Two of Us, Look At Us, In Case You're In Love, Sonny and Cher,* and *Best,* all on the Atco label. By himself Sonny did a record entitled *Inner Views* (Atco). He produced most of the song albums made by the couple, including Cher's *Bittersweet White Light* (MCA, 1973).

The Bonos shunned Hollywood social life, preferring to live quietly but luxuriously with their daughter Chastity, named for their 1969 film, in the large Mediterranean-style house in Bel Air that they purchased from Tony Curtis a few years ago. Sonny reportedly managed to maintain the couple's extravagant lifestyle (expensive cars, jewels, furs, and servants) even when they had little money. On February 19, 1974 Sonny Bono filed a court petition requesting a legal separation from his wife. By a previous marriage he has a teen-age daughter, Christine.

Sonny Bono is about five feet six inches tall, weighs 140 pounds, and has brown hair and brown eyes. A nondrinker, he has given up smoking cigarettes and opposes the use of drugs. "I went through the whole drug bit too before I met Cher," he told James Bawden of the Toronto *Globe and Mail* (September 11, 1971). His concern about drugs led him to urge at the 1968 Democratic National Convention a plank calling for a youth commission. Like Cher, Sonny is a nonpractising Roman Catholic. Among Bono's philanthropies are the Junior Braille Institute, the county general hospital, and the cerebral palsy society. Sonny Bono has expressed an ambition to devote more time in the future to producing, directing, and acting in films.

References

BMI p9 Ap '72 por
Good H 174:105 + My '72 pors
N Y Sunday News mag p6 My 21 '67 pors
N Y Times II p5 Jl 9 '67 por
Toronto Globe and Mail p23 S 11 '71 por
Who's Who in America, 1972-73

BORG, BJÖRN

June 6, 1956- Tennis player
Address: b. c/o Professional Registration Committee, West Side Tennis Club, Forest Hills, N.Y. 11375; h. Södertälje, Sweden

With the exception of Garbo and the Bergmans, few Swedes are better known internationally than tennis player Björn Borg, the darling of the teenyboppers on the pro circuit. The youngest player ever to do so, the golden-haired Borg rose to world-class status in 1973, when he was seventeen. He earned $62,500 that year and more than $100,000 in 1974, when he won the Italian and French titles and was runner-up to Don Newcombe in the World Championship Tennis tour. Because of the cool he maintains on the court, Borg is nicknamed "the Iceman" by his compatriots. But he has a blazing style, which enhances his deadly forehand and compensates for the disadvantages in his two-handed backhand. "He plays with a total lack of inhibition, strictly on talent and inspiration," fellow professional Mark Cox has observed, "and it's enough."

Björn Borg was born on June 6, 1956, the only child of Rune and Margaretha Borg. He grew up in the Stockholm suburb of Södertälje, a manufacturing town known for producing auto parts as well as tennis and hockey stars. There his parents run a small grocery, an enterprise they had long dreamed about and were able to realize with capital given them by Björn from his tennis earnings. His father had previously been a clothing salesman. A competitive game spirit was early fostered in Björn Borg by his parents during family outings on an island near Södertälje, where they would tack a target to a tree and play darts with him. "I cried and cried when I lost," he has

recalled. "They would let me win then, and I would get confidence back."

His first tennis racquet was one his father brought home as a prize from a Ping Pong tournament, when Borg was nine. Borg immediately began practising with it, hitting the ball against the door of the family garage. Within a year he was playing at the Salk Tennis Club in Stockholm, charging around like a young bull and defeating youthful opponents despite badly timed serves and general awkwardness. Reluctant to leave the court, he was always pleading for someone to play or practise with him.

The tennis teacher Percy Rosburg, who remains Borg's mentor to this day, met Borg at the Salk Club, where Rosburg was scouting another player for the Swedish National Tennis Federation. "He was ten and he hit the forehand the same way as now," Rosburg has said. "All wrist, like a Ping Pong shot. I had to run well even then to get it back. He didn't know how to serve and he kept bothering with questions. But there was this looking in his eyes. He has always played 'working tennis,' too technical, not much style. The federation wanted to change the two hands. But he could put the ball where he wanted it—that was the point. Oh, how he hit so hard. And, boy, he fought like hell."

Borg was also good at hockey (the probable source of his two-handed backhand), but tennis prevailed. At fourteen, having already won all the scholastic and junior championships within his reach, he dropped out of the Blomback School in Södertälje to concentrate on the latter sport. He says he has no regrets about cutting his education short: "I hate school. I can never sit for hour listening to teacher talk. . . . I never go back as long as I live."

Within a year after leaving school Borg was the best junior player in the world, having capped the Berlin, Barcelona, and Milan junior crowns with the Wimbledon junior and the Orange Bowl (Miami Beach) title, tantamount to the junior world championship. At fifteen he made his debut in Davis Cup competition with the Swedish national team, winning both his singles matches against New Zealand in Baastad, Sweden. Lennart Bergelin, the leader of the Swedish Davis Cup team was—and still is, after Rosburg—the man most responsible for Borg's development. Bergelin, who insists that his players be aggressive, steel-willed, and gluttonous for daily practice, considered Borg an extraordinarily "lucky" find. He explained, "I recognized his mental toughness at an early age. This can never be given. He is a nice chap but so tough mentally."

Early in 1973 Borg made a strong contention for the French (senior) championship, beating Cliff Richey, Pierre Barthes, and Dick Stockton. Later in 1973 he made a bad showing in Rome and a good one at Wimbledon, where he felt his game improve by a quantum jump. "I played and won some long matches in front of big crowds," he explained later. "It was my confidence that grew first and that helped my strokes." Because of an Association of Tennis Professionals boycott, there was a dearth of male stars at Wimbledon that year, and Borg became an overnight idol. He would never again be able to walk onto a British court without hordes of youthful fans, especially girls, shrieking around him, pressing to touch him.

In the 1973 Swedish Open, Borg defeated Ilie Nastase and Jimmy Connors but lost to Tom Gorman in the final. In the semifinals of the Grand Prix he lost to Stan Smith. Early in 1974 Borg joined the "green group" on the thirteen-tournament World Championship Tennis circuit. Among the other twenty-seven top-class competitors in the group were Tony Roche, Vincenzo Franchitti, Rod Laver, Arthur Ashe, Jan Kodes, Roger Taylor, Mark Cox, and Roscoe Tanner. He began the WCT tour badly, losing to Roche in Philadelphia and Franchitti in Bologna, but in London he defeated Ashe, Tanner, and, in the finals, Cox. He made it to the finals in Barcelona, by defeating Laver, and in São Paulo, by beating Ashe. In the first round of the WCT championship tournament in Dallas in May 1974 Borg overwhelmed Ashe and Kodes but lost to Newcombe in the final. It was estimated that half of Sweden's 9,000,000 population remained up until five o'clock in the morning to hear the play-by-play broadcast of the title match on radio.

On June 3, 1974 Borg easily bested Ilie Nastase to take the Italian Open, 6-3, 6-4, 6-2, and thus became the youngest player ever to win a major international tournament. Two weeks later he won the French title—generally regarded as the world clay-court championship—by rallying against Manuel Orantes, 2-6, 6-7, 6-0, 6-1, 6-1. When he appeared at Wimbledon toward the end of June, the hysterical young fans spilled over the barriers onto the court in their effort to get close to him. Police had to strong-arm him through the shrieking crowd before and after matches, and he was restricted to the center court, the furthest away from the spectators. "This is a problem we have not had to deal with before," referee Mike Gibson explained. "It is not entirely fair to the other competitors, but public safety must come first." Egypt's Ismael el Shafei knocked him out of contention in the third round at Wimbledon, 6-2, 6-3, 6-1.

In Brookline, Massachusetts on August 26, 1974 Borg took the United States Professional Tennis Championship by trouncing Tom Okker of Holland in straight sets, 7-6, 6-1, 6-1. Five days later India's Vijay Amritraj ousted him from the United States Open at Forest Hills, 6-1, 7-6, 3-6, 1-6, 6-3. On October 13, 1974 Ilie Nastase, seeded number four, defeated Borg, seeded number two, in the finals of Melia International Open in Madrid, 6-4, 5-7, 6-2, 4-6, 6-4.

Borg plays hard, thrashing away for a win on every serve and every return. "It's very difficult to get on him because he keeps coming at you, putting on the pressure, and you can't get any rhythm," Mark Cox has said. "Of course, he still doesn't think; he is smacking, smacking the ball

BJÖRN BORG

always." In an article in Sports Illustrated (June 24, 1974), Curry Kirkpatrick wrote, "Borg administers his lethal topspin off the forehand from a western grip and attacks the ball with such ferocity on every stroke that he seems to be in imminent danger of breaking his wrist in half."

Rod Laver told Kirkpatrick, "He plays the big points, the big matches, super. But I think he has one weapon only—the forehand. When we create speed for him, he is murder. But I try to dink him around, pull him to the net, then mix garbage with passing shots." But most opponents, wary of Borg's forehand, overplay his backhand. Anticipating that, he is usually in position to respond murderously. "What makes Borg additionally difficult to contend with is his ability to disguise his stroke," Kirkpatrick observed. "Being double-handed from the left side is a natural decoy, and the western grip makes it hard for opponents to pick up the ball from the forehand side as well. Exceptional speed affords him time for concealment. Then the ball seems to zoom off the racket with, as Newcombe calls them, 'such different googly, dipping actions' that a man doesn't know whether to get in position for a return or call the bomb squad for help."

Judith Elian, tennis correspondent for L'Equipe in Paris, who has known Borg since the beginning of his career, has observed, "Björn, he has never been dummy. He has never been little boy." His parents, according to a friend of the family, "treat him both as old man and kid," and Borg himself tends to identify with the twenty-four and twenty-five-year-olds he associates with in the tennis world. In his press conferences and other activities that are, as he calls them, "part of the job," he acts with a businesslike maturity. As Kirkpatrick said in his article in Sports Illustrated, "Sometimes he appears so cold, wise, and frighteningly right that it is easy—no, inescapable—to forget his age."

When playing the circuit Borg always gets nine hours of sleep, practises at least two hours daily, and never goes to parties. Knowing that "plenty of promising tennis talent has fallen for the Dolce Vita," he never responds to the amorous invitations slipped or sent to him by his innumerable "groupies." He does wear the initials of Helen Anliot, a female Swedish tennis player his own age, on a chain around his neck, but he has no intention of getting married, at least for a few years.

Slim, blue-eyed, long-legged Björn Borg wears his golden locks long. He walks with a rocking motion that has been compared to the gait of Charlie Chaplin. The equanimity he displays on the court is carried over into private life, where he is said to approach everything with level-headedness and discretion. Those who have traveled the tennis circuit with him say that he never grumbles and never manifests melancholy or irritation.

Borg's tennis earnings are supplemented by a retainer he receives from Scandinavian Airlines for promotional work. In addition to the grocery store, he has bought his parents a summer home, and for himself, having recently obtained a driver's license, Björn Borg has bought a Mercedes-Benz. That purchase is untypical, for Borg tends to be very thrifty. His wardrobe, for example, is small and simple, consisting chiefly of jeans, warm-up jackets, loafers, and T-shirts (which he wears as long as three days consecutively). For recreation, he likes to read comic books—especially *Kalle Anka* (Donald Duck)—and listen to recordings by Shirley Bassey, Elvis Presley, the Beatles, and Cat Stevens.

References

Christian Sci Mon F p5 Jl 2 '74
London Observer p22 Je 23 '74 por
N Y Sunday News p143 S 1 '74 por
Parade p4 Ag 4 '74 por
Sports Illus 40:37+ My 20 '74; 40:70+ Je 24 '74 pors

BRANDO, MARLON

Apr. 3, 1924- Actor
Address: b. c/o United Artists Corp., 729 7th Ave., New York 10019

NOTE: This biography supersedes the article that appeared in *Current Biography* in 1952.

In 1947 Marlon Brando created the role of Stanley Kowalski in the original Broadway production of *A Streetcar Named Desire*, and his singular performance still reverberates in the memories of those who saw it. Dispensing with niceties of speech and gesture, Brando struck a new and disquieting note of reality. In 1950 his screen debut in *The Men* so emphatically demonstrated the cinematic value and commercial viability of his Stanislavski-inspired, Actors Studio-oriented "Method" that it spawned a multitude of mini-Brandos. The *International Encyclopedia of Film* credits him with having revolutionized the concept of acting in American films.

Brando has twice been named Best Actor of the Year by the Academy of Motion Picture Arts and Sciences: first, for his portrayal of the decent but slack-witted ex-boxer in *On the Waterfront* (1954) and, more recently, for his characterization of an elderly Mafia chieftain in *The Godfather* (1972). On March 27, 1973 he declined to accept his second Oscar, in protest against the movie industry's treatment of the American Indian. Many consider the finest work of his career to be the disillusioned hero of Bernardo Bertolucci's controversial *Last Tango in Paris* (1973).

Marlon Brando Jr. was born in Omaha, Nebraska on April 3, 1924, the third child and only son of Marlon and Dorothy (Pennebaker) Brando. His father was a manufacturer of chemical feeds and insecticides. His mother acted in a number of productions at the Omaha Community Playhouse and served on its board of directors.

In 1930 the Brandos moved to Illinois, living for a time in Evanston, but eventually settling down in the small town of Libertyville. At the local high school Brando preferred the athletic field to the classroom, and he became a rebellious disciplinary problem. His father shipped him off when he was fifteen to the Shattuck Military Academy in Faribault, Minnesota, but he was expelled a few weeks before the end of his senior year.

At home again, he thought of entering the Protestant ministry, until his parents talked him out of it. He tried to enlist in the Army but was judged physically unfit for service because of a trick knee. He took a job with a drain construction company, but quit after a month and a half. Assured of his father's financial support if he acquired some kind of professional training, Brando went to New York City, where his sister Frances was enrolled at the Art Students League and his sister Jocelyn was taking classes at the American Academy of Dramatic Art.

Perhaps influenced by his stagestruck mother and sisters, Brando entered the Dramatic Workshop of the New School for Social Research. Its director, Erwin Piscator, recognized Brando's talent at once, discerning beneath his callowness a virtually infallible "inner rhythm." *Bobino*, a Workshop production of Stanley Kauffmann's musical fantasy for children in which Brando played a small part, was transferred to the Adelphi Theatre during Easter week in 1944. It thus marked Brando's first appearance on a Broadway stage. He gained further experience that year as a member of the company that Piscator recruited to do summer stock under his direction at a theatre in Sayville, Long Island. Before the season ended, Brando was fired, but one day after his dismissal playwright-director John van Druten invited him to join the cast of the Broadway-bound production *I Remember Mama*, as the fifteen-year-old son, Nels.

A gently comic chronicle of Norwegian-American family life, *I Remember Mama* opened at the Music Box Theatre on October 19, 1944. During its long run Brando began to study acting with Stella Adler, who is generally conceded to have been a major influence on the development of his acting technique. Miss Adler recommended him to director Harold Clurman for the brief but demanding role of a wife-murderer in Maxwell Anderson's *Truckline Cafe,* but Clurman, doubting Brando's ability to execute such a startling transformation, was reluctant to entrust him with the part. With the aid of another Brando enthusiast, Elia Kazan, who was coproducing the play, Miss Adler finally persuaded Clurman to hire him. Apart from his performance, reviewers could find little to applaud in the blatant melodrama of *Truckline Cafe,* and the Broadway engagement lasted less than two weeks.

On April 3, 1946, just one month after the closing of *Truckline Cafe,* Brando took on the difficult role of the poet Marchbanks in a revival of George Bernard Shaw's *Candida* that starred Katharine Cornell. His notices were mixed. The following fall he appeared with Paul Muni in *A Flag Is Born.* Written by Ben Hecht and sponsored by the American League for a Free Palestine, it was more of a pageant than a play and was charitably reviewed for its good intentions rather than its merits. Early in 1947 Brando was signed by producer John C. Wilson to act opposite Tallulah Bankhead in an adaptation of Jean Cocteau's *The Eagle Has Two Heads,* but his "Method" and her "Grand Manner" failed to mesh and, during the tryout tour, he was replaced by the more malleable Helmut Dantine.

Soon Brando was himself a replacement, in the sense that he had not been producer Irene Selznick's primary choice for the male lead in *A Streetcar Named Desire.* She had sought John Garfield to play the part of Stanley Kowalski, and it was only after Garfield had turned it down that Brando became a serious contender for the role. Elia Kazan, who was slated to direct, favored using Brando and, once he had heard him read, so did Tennessee Williams.

In none of the many *Streetcar* revivals that have been staged since its Broadway opening on December 3, 1947 has any actor essaying the role of Kowalski managed to escape comparison with Brando's definitive performance. By slurring his words to suggest real speech, by exhibiting a physical grossness that was true to the character as well as subliminally significant, and by flaunting the sort of sexuality that had hitherto been implied rather than asserted, he defied a trio of stale stage conventions. His innovative approach led the way to greater freedom for actors in their interpretation of human behavior.

Hollywood wooed Brando with contract offers, but he turned a deaf ear to them all. In 1948 an interviewer, Lorenzo Semple Jr., elicited Brando's opinion of the dream factories: "They've never made an honest picture in their lives," he said, "and they probably never will." He did not change his mind until, having withdrawn from the cast of *Streetcar* in the middle of its second year on Broadway and gone to Paris for a vacation, he received a story outline that had been submitted

MARLON BRANDO

to him through his agent by independent movie producer Stanley Kramer.

The project that Kramer asked him to participate in was *The Men,* and its aim, to convey in semidocumentary fashion the plight of a returning soldier paralyzed from the waist down, appealed to Brando, who agreed to star in the proposed picture for a fee of $40,000. To achieve authenticity he lived for several weeks among the paraplegic patients at the Birmingham Veterans Hospital in Van Nuys, California, where large segments of *The Men* were subsequently shot, under the direction of Fred Zinnemann. When United Artists released *The Men* in the summer of 1950, it confused unsophisticated members of the moviegoing public, who assumed that Brando was an authentic casualty of World War II like Harold Russell, whom the makers of *The Best Years of Our Lives* had induced to play himself in that movie.

Many people thought that Brando's work in *The Men* deserved an Academy Award, and, when none materialized, they theorized that the Hollywood hierarchy had withheld the honor to chide him for his nonconformist behavior offscreen. Then, in 1951, Brando immortalized on film the riveting loutishness of his Stanley Kowalski, and his right to be an Oscar nominee for Best Actor could no longer be ignored. Yet he was a losing entrant in that year's Oscar sweepstakes while, ironically, Vivien Leigh, his costar in the film version of *Streetcar,* went on to win, as did Kim Hunter and Karl Malden, the principal supporting players, in their respective categories.

For his sensitive interpretation of the title role in Twentieth Century-Fox's *Viva Zapata!* (1952) and his incisive portrayal of Marc Antony in MGM's *Julius Caesar* (1953), Brando was twice again an unsuccessful nominee. Perhaps even more memorable was his performance as Johnny, the leather-jacketed leader of a gang of rampaging motorcyclists, in *The Wild One* (Columbia, 1953), which Molly Haskell, a film critic on the staff of the *Village Voice,* called "his most mythic performance" in her nine-part series on Brando that appeared in the *Village Voice* from June through September 1973.

With *On the Waterfront* (Columbia, 1954), Brando consolidated his position as the top screen actor of his time. About one now classic scene, in which he berated his brother for having robbed him of the chance to amount to something as a prizefighter, Pauline Kael wrote that Brando seemed to speak "for all our failed hopes." "It was," she concluded, "the great American lament." New York's movie critics voted *On the Waterfront* the best picture, and Brando the best actor of 1954, an opinion that was seconded by the judges of the Academy of Motion Picture Arts and Sciences.

Because of a contractual dispute with Twentieth Century-Fox, on whose production of *The Egyptian* he had walked out, Brando's only other 1954 vehicle represented an unhappy compromise. To avoid being the defendant in a $2,000,000 damage suit, he agreed to impersonate Napoleon Bonaparte in the studio's slick film version of the novel *Desiree*. In his own words, he "let the make-up play it." Jean Simmons, his leading lady in *Desiree,* also appeared as the object of his affections in 1955's *Guys and Dolls,* a disappointing transfer to the screen of Frank Loesser's Runyonesque stage musical.

Both of Brando's next films entailed journeys to the Far East for location shooting. In *Teahouse of the August Moon* (MGM, 1956), he was Sakini, the wily Okinawan; in *Sayonara* (Warner Brothers, 1957), he was a Southern-bred United States Air Force officer involved in an interracial love affair in Japan. In 1958 he gave further proof of his versatility with a telling portrait of Christian Diestl, the Nazi lieutenant who yearns for an end to the holocaust of World War II, in *The Young Lions* (Twentieth Century-Fox).

Brando revisited Tennessee Williams country in *The Fugitive Kind* (United Artists, 1960), an adaptation of the playwright's *Orpheus Descending,* which had flopped on Broadway three years before. It fared little better in its screen incarnation, despite the volcanic presence of Anna Magnani in a costarring role. Brando directed himself in Paramount's *One-Eyed Jacks* (1961), a technicolor western notable for its visual beauty and (within the motion picture industry) for the fact that in terms of time and money it had far exceeded its budget.

Blame for the prohibitive expense of *One-Eyed Jacks* was indisputably Brando's. Whether, as reported, he was also responsible for the troubles that plagued MGM's remake of *Mutiny on the Bounty,* sending production costs spiraling up to a record sum of $18,500,000, is still a subject of debate. Charles Lederer, who wrote the screenplay, has been quoted by John C. Waugh of the *Christian Science Monitor* (November 14, 1962) as saying that the press's "misinterpretation" of Brando's motives was "criminal," that any delays caused by him were in the interest of making "the best picture he could." In any event, the finished film was not a huge commercial success, and the critics were divided in their opinion of Brando's performance as Fletcher Christian.

After the furor over *Mutiny on the Bounty* subsided, Brando starred in *The Ugly American* (1963) at Universal, playing the United States ambassador to a Southeast-Asian country who unwittingly foments a revolution. *Bedtime Story* (1964), in which he tried his hand at farce, was a Universal release, too. While working on *Morituri,* a spy thriller, at Twentieth Century-Fox, Brando was asked by reporters to explain why an actor of his stature would busy himself with such a routine chore. He told them that an occasional "good-paying picture" had become an economic necessity for him. In 1965, when the film was released, it attested to his sincerity: fiscal considerations, not aesthetic ones, had obviously dictated his willingness to appear in it.

The Chase (Columbia, 1966), which *Life* magazine's Richard Schickel called "a disaster of awesome proportions" and *The Appaloosa* (Universal, 1966), a standard horse opera photographed with arty irrelevance, accelerated the downward trend of Brando's luck. When Charles Chaplin emerged from retirement to write and direct *A Countess from Hong Kong* (Universal, 1967), it was hoped that his comic touch would rub off on Brando and, perhaps, revitalize his career. Instead, Brando's characterization of a rich diplomat entangled in a shipboard romance with "stowaway" Sophia Loren was wan and wooden.

Increasingly, since his foppish Fletcher Christian in *Mutiny on the Bounty,* Brando's screen portrayals had polarized reviewers, especially after John Huston filmed Carson McCullers' *Reflections in a Golden Eye* (Warner Brothers-Seven Arts, 1967) with Brando as the latently homosexual Major Penderton. Richard L. Coe of the Washington *Post* (October 12, 1967) maintained that he was guilty of "lofty condescension" to the audience, and that his acting had degenerated into "sophomoric attitudinizing." On the other hand, Joseph Morgenstern contended in *Newsweek* (October 30, 1967) that Brando's depiction of the repressed officer was "brave and sometimes beautiful."

To accommodate his costar, Elizabeth Taylor, *Reflections in a Golden Eye* had been shot largely in Rome. Brando's next four movies were also European-based productions: *Candy* (Cinerama, 1968), which cast him as a Jewish-accented guru; *The Night of the Following Day* (Universal, 1969), a suspense melodrama marred by the directorial pretensions of Hubert Cornfield; *Burn!* (United Artists, 1970), a picture with a political "message" made by Gillo Pontecorvo; and *The Nightcomers* (Avco-Embassy, 1972), a presumptuous endeavor to explain the origins of the evil only hinted at by Henry James in *The Turn of the Screw.*

After that string of box-office failures, Paramount officials balked when director Francis Ford Coppola broached the possibility of giving Brando the title role in *The Godfather.* Not until after they had been shown a screen test videotaped in the actor's own home did the studio heads relent, and even then it was with reluctance that they gave in to Coppola's wishes. Their decision to gamble on Brando in the small but crucial role of Don Vito Corleone paid off handsomely. Since its release in March of 1972, *The Godfather* has amassed a worldwide gross of about $150,000,000, and may prove the most lucrative venture in cinematic history. It brought Brando his second Academy Award, which he delegated an aspiring actress named Sacheen Littlefeather to refuse on his behalf at the ceremony. Prevailed upon not to read Brando's five-page statement of his reasons for renouncing the Oscar, she said simply that he wanted to register his disapproval of the way Hollywood had, in its films, degraded the American Indian.

For the final attraction in their 1972 series of screenings at Lincoln Center, the organizers of the New York Film Festival chose Bernardo Bertolucci's *Last Tango in Paris*. Two weeks later, on October 28, 1972, the *New Yorker* published Pauline Kael's rapturous verdict: "This must be the most powerfully erotic movie ever made.... Bertolucci and Brando have altered the face of an art form." A legal technicality prevented United Artists from releasing the X-rated film here until the following February. Then, as Mrs. Kael had predicted, it drew its detractors, who professed to find such sexual explicitness disgusting. Although some of Miss Kael's colleagues challenged her judgment that *Last Tango in Paris* would rank as a milestone, they united in chorusing their praise of Brando. His portrayal of Paul, the middle-aged American expatriate trying to anaesthetize his despair over his wife's suicide by embarking on a frenzied but anonymous affair, was hailed as a triumph, and as positive proof that his comeback in *The Godfather* had not been a fluke. The ostensibly lean years that preceded it had been misread, for instead of auguring the abdication of a talent, they betokened its resilience; they were, in fact, signposts to its ultimate ascendance. Paul D. Zimmerman of *Newsweek* (March 13, 1972) exulted that "the king has returned to reclaim his throne."

Marlon Brando is a man of medium height with graying hair. His weight, which used to be notorious for its tendency to fluctuate widely, seems to have stabilized, and his former muscularity has been supplanted by a mature fullness of figure. He has always hated having to dress up, and T-shirts and blue jeans have been the staples of his wardrobe. The slightly crooked nose that imparts a Roman cast to his face is the product of a boxing accident he had while appearing in *A Streetcar Named Desire* on Broadway.

In October of 1957 Brando wed actress Anna Kashfi, and in 1959 they were divorced. Custody of their son Christian Devi has been a bone of bitter contention between the couple. Brando's second marriage, in 1960, to Mexican actress Movita Castenada was of shorter duration than his first, lasting barely one year. Since 1966 the actor has owned a private Polynesian atoll known as Tetiaroa. It is there, with Tarita, the native girl who played his lady love in *Mutiny on the Bounty*, and their son, Tehotu, and daughter, Cheyenne, that he spends most of his free time.

Besides espousing the cause of the oppressed American Indian, Brando has concerned himself with other social issues: marching with CORE pickets in Alabama; attending a Black Panther rally to decry the killing of Bobby Hutton; pledging a percentage of his income to the late Martin Luther King's Southern Christian Leadership Conference; demonstrating against capital punishment; and condemning the treatment of Jews in Soviet Russia.

References

Ladies Home J 90:76+ Ap '73 pors
Newsweek 81:54+ F 12 '73 pors
Time 101:51+ Ja 22 '73 pors
Carey, Gary. Brando (1973)
Fiore, Carlo. Bud: The Brando I Knew (1974)
Morella, Joe, and Epstein, Edward Z. Brando; The Unauthorized Biography (1973)
Offen, Ron. Brando (1973)
Thomas, Bob. Marlon; Portrait of the Rebel as an Artist (1974)

BRONFMAN, EDGAR M(ILES)

June 20, 1929- Corporation executive
Address: b. Distillers Corporation-Seagrams Ltd., 1430 Peel St., Montreal 110, Quebec, Canada; Joseph E. Seagram & Sons Inc., 375 Park Ave., New York 10022

After two decades in various executive positions with Distillers Corporation-Seagrams Ltd. and its chief United States subsidiary, Joseph E. Seagram & Sons, Edgar M. Bronfman took over as president, treasurer, and director of the parent firm on July 22, 1971 following the death of his father, the company's founder. Incorporated in Montreal, Canada in 1928, the firm rapidly grew during the Prohibition era in the United States, when Bronfman liquor found its way, via "Rum Row," to American customers. After Prohibition ended, in 1933, Seagrams grew at an even faster rate, and by the late 1940's the corporation was the number one distiller in the United States.

Sales declined during the 1950's but programs of expansion and development launched by Edgar Bronfman revitalized the firm's competitiveness in the American and international liquor markets. By the time he assumed full corporate power in the early 1970's, Seagrams owned thirty-nine distilleries and eighteen wineries throughout the world, was the largest importer of wines in the United States, and produced approximately 114 different brands of alcoholic beverages, including the American best-sellers Chivas Regal, Seagram's Seven Crown, and Seagram's V.O. Today the Bronfman family's wealth is estimated to be well over $400,000,000.

Edgar Miles Bronfman, who was born on June 20, 1929 in Montreal, Quebec, Canada, is the elder son of Samuel and Saidye (Rosner) Bronfman. He has two older sisters, Minda, the wife

EDGAR M. BRONFMAN

of French baron Alain de Gunzberg, and Phyllis, who is an architect. His brother Charles is also in the family firm. Bronfman's maternal grandfather and both grandparents on his father's side of the family were Jewish immigrants to Canada from Bessarabia. Yechiel Bronfman built up a profitable hotel business, eventually owning hostelries in both Eastern and Western Canada. Later his sons, Samuel and Allan Bronfman, established a successful mail-order liquor business, which they were forced to abandon when the Canadian Provincial governments took over the retail sale of liquor.

Unable to sell liquor, they decided to try their hands at producing it and in 1925 built their own distillery on the outskirts of Montreal, where the Bronfman children grew up in a suburban Victorian mansion. Protected and indulged, they were separated from the surrounding community by "faith and fortune," as Philip Siekman observed in *Fortune* magazine (December 1966). Siekman quoted Charles Bronfman remembering his brother Edgar in childhood as "always a sort of tougher guy" than he was, a boy who "would try to make the school bow to him." More often than not his defiance of authority brought him corporal punishment. After attending local schools he entered Trinity College School, a prep school in Port Hope, Ontario. In his spare time and during school vacations he earned his own pocket money, working as a golf caddy and department store employee, and when older, in two New York City investment firms, The Empire Trust Company and Carl M. Loeb, Rhoades & Company. Bronfman has explained his youthful industriousness as simply a matter of practicality: "If you went to father to ask for money, you had to explain why. If you earned it, you didn't have to explain."

After three years at Williams College in Massachusetts, Bronfman transferred to McGill University in Montreal, from which he graduated with a B.A. degree and honors in history in 1951. While working for his father in Montreal dur-

ing college vacations, he acquired a knowledge of the various aspects of the distilling business. Considering and rejecting careers as a Wall Street broker, a rabbi, and a lawyer, Bronfman opted to enter the family business. "Nobody ever told me I had to get in," Bronfman has recalled. "But a kid gets the feeling early that joining the business is his natural destiny. . . . I felt my father . . . expected more from me as the No. 1 son. At first, I resented . . . it. But when I was about twenty or twenty-one, I began to enjoy it."

For his part, Samuel Bronfman had made certain that if his sons were to take over the firm's leadership, they would do so alone and without the interference of relatives. Before acquiring Joseph E. Seagram & Sons in 1927, the elder Bronfman had seen the company flounder and decline under a management divided among too many heirs, and he was determined that a similar fate would not befall his own business. To that end, by buying out nephews and similar maneuvering, he assured the two Bronfman brothers of unhampered leadership of the Distillers Corporation. Dividing up their power, they decided in 1953 that Edgar would control the United States subsidiary, Joseph E. Seagram & Sons, while Charles would remain in Montreal to head the Canadian branch, the House of Seagram.

Edgar Bronfman was responsible for all Canadian plants from 1953 until 1955, when he left for New York City to become chairman of Seagram's administrative committee. Because of the young man's inexperience, the cautious elder Bronfman was at first reluctant to grant his son the presidency of Seagrams. It was not until 1957, when Bronfman implied that he might go elsewhere to work, that the father relented and permitted his son to take over as head of the American subsidiary, which today accounts for 86 percent of the parent corporation's sales. During Edgar Bronfman's first year as president of Joseph E. Seagram & Sons, the monumental new Seagram building on Manhattan's Park Avenue was completed by the noted architect Ludwig Mies van der Rohe, who had been hired on recommendation of Phyllis Bronfman.

Once in the presidency, Bronfman overhauled production and finance at the New York office, but he met with his father's objections when he attempted to revitalize the marketing of Seagram's brands. Finally, after five years of close supervision by Samuel Bronfman he was permitted to make more of the decisions himself. "I became president de jure in 1957," he has said, "and de facto in 1962." The first major change Bronfman initiated was the replacement of Calvert Reserve with the lighter-blended Calvert Extra. That fairly drastic measure was prompted by the changes in Americans' drinking habits during the 1950's. The emphasis at Seagrams had always been on blended whiskeys, but Americans were turning towards Scotch, bourbon, and the non-whiskeys—gin, vodka, rum, brandy, and wine.

In an attempt to recapture the company's once predominant role in the liquor market, Bronfman brought about an expansion of brands. He introduced bottled cocktails, Hawaiian, Puerto Rican, and Jamaican rums, four liqueurs, a gin, and a vodka; developed new Scotches such as 100 Pipers and Passport; lightened the Four Roses blend; and began importing wines and liqueurs. According to a reporter for *Time* (March 5, 1965), it was the "most ambitious marketing program ever undertaken by any distiller."

To modernize the management of the firm, Bronfman improved the methods of distribution, poured more money into advertising and sales promotion, and placed a greater emphasis on market research. Realizing that by the end of the decade the greatest potential for growth would be in the international market, he accelerated the expansion programs into Latin America and Europe. As a result of his efforts, by 1965 the firm was selling its products in 119 countries and was the first liquor company to exceed one billion dollars in annual sales.

Besides attending to his interests at Seagrams during the 1960's, Bronfman, in cooperation with his brother and sisters, increased the family wealth through investments made outside of the liquor industry. As his source of capital Bronfman utilized the four interlocking trust funds created by his father to perpetuate the family's control of the Distillers Corporation. The trusts, managed by the family-controlled Cemp Investments Ltd., were first used to invest in Canadian real estate, including the construction of shopping centers and office buildings. By 1966 Cemp owned twelve shopping centers, had made "semi-philanthropic" investments in a food store chain and some orange groves in Israel, and held stock in such firms as Allied Chemical, British-American Oil, and Bell Telephone Company of Canada. In the same year, reports indicated that as a result of wise investments, more than half of the family's wealth came from sources outside of the liquor industry. By 1969 the Bronfmans were the largest private landowners in Canada. Investments were also made in the brewing, packaging, and computer systems industries.

The marriages of Edgar Bronfman to Ann Loeb and of Minda Bronfman to Baron Alain de Gunzberg, a Parisian banker, eventually led to further business ventures. Loeb, Rhoades & Company aided the Bronfmans in their purchase of the Texas Pacific Coal and Oil Company Inc., while Cemp participated in such Loeb deals as the investments made in Curtis Publishing, Twentieth Century-Fox, and Pure Oil. Along with de Gunzberg, the Bronfmans bought into European real estate and insurance, purchased a fleet of butane and propane tankers, and invested in the Club Méditerranée chain of resorts. Most of the European ventures were carried out in partnership with de Gunzberg's distant relatives in the famous Rothschild family.

Edgar Bronfman's personal interest, however, was in expansion into the entertainment industry, which he considered "the best one to invest . . . money in over the next ten to fifteen years." After failing to gain control of Paramount Pic-

tures in 1965 because of the many competing investors, Bronfman turned his interests toward Metro-Goldwyn-Mayer Inc. With the Cemp purchase of 820,000 shares of MGM stock in 1967, the Bronfman family became the largest single stockholder. In 1968, after the acquisition of more stock, four of the eighteen seats on the board were controlled by the family; they were occupied by Edgar Bronfman, John J. Loeb Jr., and two Cemp officials.

Following MGM losses approximating $25,-000,000 in 1969 and failure of the chairman, Robert H. O'Brien, to expand the corporation according to Bronfman's wishes, Bronfman took over the chairmanship of MGM in May 1969. But the high hopes held by Bronfman for the future of the corporation under his control ended in August 1969, when Kirk Kerkorian, a Las Vegas hotel and casino owner, announced that he had obtained controlling interest with a purchase of 24 percent of MGM's common stock. At a meeting on October 21, 1969, Bronfman and Loeb resigned from their seats on the board of directors. "With the kind of money that he's putting up—$100,000,000—he can call the shots," Bronfman commented shortly afterwards. "Now, we'll be in there for the ride." According to a reporter for *Business Week* (November 11, 1969), it was the "first time in his well-capitalized career [that] he was outbid for something he really wanted."

Although disappointed with the outcome of his involvement in MGM, Bronfman retained a keen interest in the entertainment industry, and he had a great deal of success with a number of other investments made in the late 1960's and early 1970's. In 1966 he made a fairly large investment in *The Apple Tree*, a successful Broadway show produced by Stuart Ostrow. The following year he joined forces with Ostrow to form the Theater 28 Company for producing stage plays and films and investing in music publishing companies. Bronfman invested $250,000 in another of Ostrow's long-running Broadway productions, *1776*, which opened on March 16, 1969. In early 1970 Bronfman became the chairman of Sagittarius Productions, Inc., a firm that manages the Centaur Publishing and Bow Man Music corporations and produces stage shows and films.

After the death of Samuel Bronfman on July 10, 1971, the transition of corporate power he had planned many years before took place when Edgar Bronfman was elected president, treasurer, and director of Distillers Corporation-Seagrams Ltd. at a board meeting on July 22, 1971. His brother Charles stepped into the vice-presidency of the parent firm, and Jack Yogman succeeded Bronfman in the presidency of Joseph E. Seagram & Sons. In Edgar Bronfman's view, taking his father's place was an "awesome responsibility." "I was trying to explain [the business] to *my* son the other day," Bronfman remarked shortly after assuming his new corporate role. "I guess this is the final step of growing up."

Bronfman is a director of the Adela Investment Co., S.A.; the International Executive Service

Corporation; the Clevepak Corporation; the Metropolitan Applied Research Center, Inc.; and the Rheingold Corporation. He is a trustee of the Mount Sinai Hospital and School of Medicine, the Salk Institute for Biological Studies, the National Urban League, and the John F. Kennedy Center for the Performing Arts. He is a member of the Federation of Jewish Philanthropies and Delta Phi. Bronfman serves as president and trustee of the Samuel Bronfman Foundation.

Edgar M. Bronfman and Ann Loeb, who were married on January 10, 1953, have five children: Sam Jr., Edgar Jr., Matthew, Holly, and Adam. After their divorce in 1973, Bronfman married Lady Carolyn Townshend. The marriage ended in an annulment granted in New York State on November 21, 1974. Bronfman is of slender build and stands over six feet tall. Although he has been described as a "party loving" man, he is reputed to be as tough-minded, strong, and ambitious as his father was. He is a naturalized United States citizen. Bronfman, who has a liberal political outlook, was a major contributor to George S. McGovern's Presidential campaign in 1972. He enjoys hunting, especially on African safaris, and he has the heads of wildebeests, antelopes, and Cape buffaloes that he has killed mounted on a wall in his office. His favorite drink is Seagram's V.O. and soda.

References

Fortune 74:145+ N '66 pors; 74:176+ D '66 por
N Y Post p33 O 23 '71
Toronto Globe and Mail B p10 Jl 30 '71
Who's Who in Finance and Industry (1974-75)
Who's Who in America, 1972-73
Who's Who in Canada, 1970-72

BROOKS, MEL

1926 (?)- Comedy writer; performer; film director
Address: c/o Warner Brothers, Inc., 4000 Warner Blvd., Burbank, Calif. 91505

For twenty-five years, the humor of Mel Brooks—manic, outrageous, and steeped in its Borscht Circuit origins—has been a mainstay of American television. More recently, its lunacy has helped to revitalize film comedy. During the 1950's Brooks, a former musician and comic in the Catskills resorts near New York City, wrote for comedian Sid Caesar, whose *Your Show of Shows* and *Caesar's Hour* are remembered by nostalgia buffs as the high point of early live television. With Caesar's straight man, Carl Reiner, Brooks later recorded an antic series of records in which Brooks created the character of the 2,000-Year-Old Man, a crusty old Jew who has seen everything and been impressed by nothing.

After creating and collaborating on the writing of the long-running television spy spoof *Get Smart*, Brooks turned to films and won an Academy Award for his first effort, a cartoon short called *The Critic.*

Since 1968 he has written and directed three feature films: *The Producers,* a show business farce for which he won his second Academy Award; *The Twelve Chairs,* a comedy about greed in post-Revolutionary Russia; and *Blazing Saddles,* his satire of Hollywood westerns. Although his iconoclastic humor has offended some orthodox sensibilities, Brooks has become a hero to hip young audiences, for whom he and Woody Allen have become, in the words of Arthur Cooper of *Newsweek* (April 22, 1974), "the official satirists of a world that badly needs a hot needle in the posterior."

The grandson of a Russian Jewish immigrant, Mel Brooks was born Melvyn Kaminsky, in the then largely Jewish Williamsburg section of Brooklyn around 1926. His mother was Kitty Kaminsky, who raised Mel and his three older brothers alone after her husband died. "My father died when he was 34. I was 2½," Kaminsky told Joseph Gelmis of *Newsday* (January 21, 1971). "I think that, unconsciously, there's an outrage there. I may be angry at God, or at the world, for that. And I'm sure a lot of my comedy is based on anger and hostility. Growing up in Williamsburg, I learned to clothe it in comedy to spare myself problems—like a punch in the face."

"My mother had this exuberant joy of living, and she infected me with that," the comedian told Joanne Stang in an interview for the New York *Times* (January 30, 1966). "By the time my other brothers were old enough to work, she could stay at home and she was my company . . . she really was responsible for the growth of my imagination." His brothers went to work in factories in Brooklyn, and one of them became a chemist by going to night school. Acknowledging his role as the indulged baby of the family, he told Harry Stein, as quoted in *New Times* (February 22, 1971), "I was the baby in the family, so I just assumed I was adorable. Everybody threw me up in the air, punched my feet and told me I was terrific."

Although Kaminsky started his clowning early, it was years before he thought of becoming a comedian. After discarding his early ambition to be a pilot, he aspired to a career in science, like his brother, the chemist. That goal seemed unrealistic, however, because although he was an excellent science student, he got poor grades in mathematics. In the meantime, he had learned to play the drums, inspired by Buddy Rich, who lived in his neighborhood. Although he did not regard drumming as a "serious" career, Kaminsky was talented enough to earn money by playing after school and during the summers. After he graduated from high school, he attended Brooklyn College for a year, then joined the United States Army. Stationed first at Fort Sill, Oklahoma and later at Virginia Military Institute, he underwent training as a combat engineer. His job was to deactivate land mines before the infantry was sent into action, and the first battle in which he saw combat duty against the German forces was the Battle of the Bulge, in Belgium in December 1944.

After World War II, Mel Kaminsky returned to playing drums at nightclubs and at resorts in the Catskill Mountains, along the so-called Borscht Circuit. To avoid being confused with the famed trumpet player Max Kaminsky, he began calling himself Mel Brooks. He got his first chance to do comedy while playing for the band in a small Catskills hotel. The regular comic became sick and Brooks successfully stepped in for him. He later played in summer stock in Red Bank, New Jersey, and did some radio work as well as comedy engagements in the Catskills. During that period he was also employed as a social director at the big Catskills resort, Grossinger's. In 1949 Sid Caesar, who had become Brooks's friend while playing the saxophone in the Catskills, asked him to write material for an NBC television series called *Broadway Revue*. He responded with a series of comic sketches called "Nonentities in the News," which included the first of Caesar's performances as a daffy German professor. Brooks's salary at that time was $50 a week, which Caesar paid for out of his own pocket.

In 1950 Sid Caesar launched *Your Show of Shows* for NBC, which also featured Carl Reiner, Imogene Coca, and Howie Morris. Although Brooks was hired as one of the writers, he occasionally appeared on the program as a performer. He thrived in the frenetic atmosphere of the show's story conferences, which was described by Albert Goldman in *New York* magazine (April 22, 1968) in this way: "The years with Sid were an endless jam session. Every morning they would run from their analysts to . . . the City Center. They'd light their cigars, form a circle around Sid and watch him improvise like a one-man band until they were turned on. Then they'd jump up, start throwing lines, capping each other, doing business and screaming, until finally they fell down again, worn out with laughter. By the time they were through, Sid had the bit memorized and they would go on to the next *shtick*—six complete routines, a whole Broadway review every week." *Your Show of Shows* ran for four years and was succeeded in 1954 by *Caesar's Hour* (NBC), featuring the same format, essentially the same stable of writers, and the same cast of performers (except for Imogene Coca). Eventually the popularity of *Caesar's Hour* dwindled, and in 1957 it went off the air. The Caesar team tried once more with *Sid Caesar Invites You*, but the show left the ABC network after one season in 1958.

"For 18 months after the [Sid Caesar] show went off I'd wake up at 6:30 every morning and bang my head against the bathroom wall," Brooks told Richard K. Doan in an interview for the New York *Herald Tribune* magazine (December 12, 1965). For a time he occupied himself by writing for television specials, including shows for Andy Williams and Victor Borge. Then, in 1960, he made the first of his 2,000-Year-Old Man recordings with Carl Reiner, *2,000 Years with Carl Reiner and Mel Brooks*, on the Capitol label.

For years Reiner and Brooks had been convulsing friends with their ad lib interviews, with Reiner always playing straight man, as he did for

MEL BROOKS

Caesar on television, and with Brooks performing roles that ranged from Tibetan monk to Peruvian Indian to "astronaught." But the role that always got the most laughs was the centuries-old man with a Yiddish accent and a down-to-earth philosophy. This 2,000-Year-Old Man had been around at the dawn of mankind, and he had known most of the important personages of history since then. When asked if he had known Jesus Christ, for example, he replied, "Yes, thin, thin, nervous, wore sandals. Came into the store a lot. Never bought anything."

So successful was the first Reiner-Brooks recording that it was followed by two more (*2,000 and One Years* and *At the Cannes Film Festival*, both on Capitol), as well as by television appearances in which Brooks, looking no more than forty years old, would show up wearing a ridiculous black cape. By 1965 the series of recordings had sold over 2,000,000 copies. A lucrative spinoff of the 2,000-Year-Old Man for Brooks was a contract with Young & Rubicam advertising agency to play the 2,500-Year-Old Brewmaster for a series of Ballantine beer commercials that by 1965 were heard on more than 200 radio stations. "My tongue just threw a party for my mouth," the normally cranky old brewmaster would rhapsodize while tasting his sponsor's product.

Over the years Mel Brooks had worked on several Broadway shows. The first was the successful revue *New Faces of 1952*, for which he wrote a skit entitled "Of Fathers and Sons," which was a parody of *Death of a Salesman*. During his Sid Caesar years he collaborated on a short-lived musical called *Shinbone Alley* (1957), based on Don Marquis' stories of a cockroach and a cat, and in 1962 he coauthored the book for another musical comedy, *All American*. In Hollywood he created a trailer for the film *My Son, the Hero* (United Artists, 1963), and although the film was a flop, many people found the trailer funny. His first genuine film project was *The Critic* (1963), a cartoon short that he conceived, wrote, and narrated in the flat accents of a viewer of modern art who knows enough about the subject to know what is dirty. Brooks shared an Academy Award for the cartoon with Ernest Pintoff, who did the art work.

With Buck Henry, Brooks created *Get Smart*, which premièred on NBC-TV in the fall of 1965. A lampoon of James Bond spy thrillers, the show starred Don Adams as bumbling Agent 86, who ineptly subdued the villain while muttering things like, "If he could only turn his evil genius into— niceness." By October 1965 the show was number seven in the Nielsen ratings, and it ran until the spring of 1970. (During the last two seasons it was aired on CBS.) While the show was filmed, Brooks commuted from his home in New York to Hollywood, where he wrote some scripts and contributed ideas to others. The success of *Get Smart* reportedly led to his being offered his own TV series, but he declined because, as he explained to a *Newsweek* reporter (April 22, 1974), television "grinds you up, makes a sausage out of you every week."

In the early 1960's Brooks had thought of a song title called "Springtime for Hitler." Deciding to develop the idea, he wrote first a novel, then a play, and finally a film script. After persuading Sidney Glazier and Joseph E. Levine to back the film venture, Brooks directed his story, which was given the more circumspect title of *The Producers* (Embassy, 1968). The film is about Max Bialystock, a seedy, has-been Broadway producer (played by Zero Mostel), who raises money for plays by making amorous advances to little old ladies. With the reluctant assistance of a neurotic young tax accountant (Gene Wilder), Bialystock hits on the plan of choosing a sure-fire flop, raising much more money than is needed to produce it, and then pocketing the excess, since backers do not expect to make any profits on a play that closes after the first night. He decides on a musical comedy called "Springtime for Hitler" (subtitled "a gay romp with Adolf and Eva at Berchtesgaden"), chooses Broadway's worst director, a transvestite named Roger DeBris, and casts a spaced-out hippie called L.S.D. in the role of Hitler. The plot backfires, however, when the play becomes a camp hit, and Bialystock and the accountant end up in jail.

Although some critics complained that *The Producers* was vulgar and tasteless and that Brooks's direction was too frantic, the majority applauded its wild humor, and the film is now regarded by many as a classic of American film comedy. Made for under $1,000,000, the film had reportedly earned $5,000,000 by late 1970, and it is often revived in cities and college towns. For his debut feature film, Brooks won an Academy Award for the best original screenplay.

Brooks's second film, *The Twelve Chairs* (UMC Pictures, 1970), was adapted, by Brooks, from a satirical novel about post-Revolutionary Russia by Ilf and Petrov. Brooks had read the novel as a child and had always dreamed of making a movie out of it. Once again financed by Glazier, Brooks directed the film in Yugoslavia, on a relatively modest budget of $1,500,000. *The Twelve Chairs*, about three men who dash across Russia looking for a chair in which a fortune in jewels is hidden, received mixed reviews. Pauline Kael (*New Yorker*, November 7, 1970), for example, gave the film qualified approval, observing that the post-1917 Russian setting "gives Brooks an opportunity to show his nostalgic affection for the slapstick and mugging and innocent nuttiness of earlier periods . . . but, gifted as he is, he still doesn't go beyond gag comedy." Several reviewers, including Miss Kael, thought that the highlight of the film was Brooks's own bit performance as an ex-serf who still yearns for his former master's beatings.

Blazing Saddles (Warner Brothers) has, since its release early in 1974, shown promise of being Brooks's biggest box office success to date. A no-holds-barred travesty of westerns, *Blazing Saddles* is about a black sheriff (Cleavon Little) and his trusty sidekick the Waco Kid (Gene Wilder), who manage to save their town from the machinations of the villainous Governor, who is portrayed by Mel Brooks himself. (He also takes another small part as a Yiddish-speaking Indian chief.) The film was based on a novel by Andrew Bergman, and for the first time Brooks used collaborators, including Bergman and black comedian Richard Pryor, on the screenplay. A cornucopia of scatological humor, racial epithets, and four-letter words, the film outraged the sensibilities of many critics. But, as Peter Schjeldahl wrote in the New York *Times* (March 17, 1974), *Blazing Saddles* is a movie "that some people are bound to despise; it wouldn't be for real if some people didn't despise it. Brooks is America's current patron saint of 'going too far,' a manic yak-artist in the checkered tradition of burlesque, the Marx Brothers and Mad magazine. A show-biz primitive, he specializes in the humor of affront—affront to civilized sensibilities, good taste and common sense—and makes us believe that he would do absolutely anything for a laugh." Brooks's latest film project is "Young Doctor Frankenstein," a parody of 1930's horror movies that he wrote with Gene Wilder, who will star in the Twentieth Century-Fox release.

In 1972 Brooks directed and narrated a series of commercials for a soft-tipped pen called the Bic Banana. "If you write with a peach, you'll get a very wet letter," the comedian would warn in the commercials, which were put out by Wells, Rich, Greene advertising agency. "Let's face it, the only fruit you can write with is a banana. The Bic Banana," Brooks would conclude with a certain surreal logic. In 1973 Warner Brothers Records reissued Brooks and Reiner's three 2,000-Year-Old Man records along with a new disc entitled *2,000 and Thirteen*. One side of the new album consists of what Brooks calls the "Dead Sea Scrolls," tapes from impromptu sessions between the two comics at parties during the 1950's. The other side was recorded in Burbank in August 1973. A frequent guest on television talk shows, Brooks is an occasional panelist on the TV quiz show *The Hollywood Squares*.

"Mel is, quite simply, a study in nervous energy," observed Harry Stein in *New Times* (February 22, 1974). "He talks the way he moves, in short, sporadic bursts, and his Gatling gun mind frequently intrudes on his conversation in mid-sentence with a cogent—albeit tangential—thought." Short and stocky, Brooks has black hair, blue eyes, and what Jerry Talmer of the New York *Post* (January 16, 1971) called a "ferocious but somehow endearing Cro-Magnon grin." In August 1964 he married actress Anne Bancroft; they have one child, Maximilian, born in 1972. By a former marriage to Florence Baum, Brooks has three teen-age children, Stefanie, Nicky, and Edward. Brooks and Miss Bancroft own a brownstone on West 11th Street in Greenwich Village and a summer house on Fire Island. In recent years, however, they have spent much of their time in Hollywood.

References

Guardian p8 F 13 '71 por
N Y Times II p17 Ja 30 '66 por
New Times 2:55+ F 22 '74 pors
New York 1:3+ Ap 22 '68 pors
Biographical Encyclopaedia and Who's Who of the American Theatre (1966)
Who's Who in America, 1972-73

JOEL T. BROYHILL

BROYHILL, JOEL T(HOMAS)

Nov. 4, 1919- United States Representative from Virginia
Address: b. Room 2109, Rayburn House Office Bldg., Washington, D.C. 20515; h. 4845 Old Dominion Dr., Arlington, Va. 22207

Apparently unaffected by the shifting fortunes of his party at the national level until he lost at the polls on November 5, 1974, the conservative Republican Representative Joel T. Broyhill had consistently defeated all opposition in every election since he rode into office on the coattails of Dwight D. Eisenhower in 1952. Broyhill represents Virginia's Tenth Congressional District, which is just across the Potomac River from Washington, D.C. and has a population dominated by white employees of the federal government. With an outlook neither rural nor urban, but one reflecting the suburban character of his territory, he has set a style for a new type of Southern politician. More jobs in Washington for his constituents, better pay for government employees, more bridges across the Potomac for commuters, and federal aid to local schools are the issues that occupy a greater part of Broyhill's time than the larger national questions. Another Congressman, James T. Broyhill, Republican Representative from North Carolina, is the Virginian's third cousin.

The son of Marvin Talmadge and Nellie Magdalene (Brewer) Broyhill, Joel Thomas Broyhill was born on November 4, 1919 in Hopewell, Virginia. He attended public schools in Hopewell, Fork Union (Virginia) Military Academy, and George Washington University in Washington, D.C. During World War II he enlisted in the Army and attained the rank of captain, serving as company commander in the 106th Infantry Division. The Germans captured him during the Battle of the Bulge and held him in a prisoner of war camp for about six months, until he escaped and joined advancing American troops. By the time he was released from active duty on November 1, 1945, he had completed four years of military service. After the war he returned to Virginia and became a partner and general manager in his father's prosperous building and real estate firm, M. T. Broyhill & Sons, in northern Virginia.

Along with taking part in Arlington's business, community, and civic organizations, Broyhill entered local Republican politics. By 1952 he had gained enough prominence to run for the Tenth Congressional District seat, which he won by a slim margin of 322 votes over his Democratic opponent, Edmund D. Campbell. During his first term in office Broyhill set the pattern that he has followed for twenty-two years. That pattern includes fidelity to the Republican party line in regard to national and international issues, a vigorous role in legislating for larger salaries and more benefits for the government employees who make up a large part of his constituency, and a strong influence in the local government affairs of the District of Columbia, particularly on the question of "home rule." In addition, as a consistent anti-integrationist, Broyhill has opposed major civil rights legislation throughout his Congressional career.

During the Eisenhower administration Broyhill was one of the most faithful supporters of the President's programs in Congress. In the 1953-54 session, according to the Congressional Quarterly report, Broyhill voted 83 percent of the time in favor of Eisenhower's legislative programs. Pointing out, however, that he had a mind of his own, he once said, as quoted in the Washington *Post* (June 10, 1956), "Not more than 10 members of Congress have a better record of supporting the President than I. But my record isn't 100 percent and it's not going to be. I'm not a rubber stamp. There are a few things on which I disagree with him."

With the advent of the Democratic administration of President John F. Kennedy, Broyhill joined the "conservative coalition" in Congress, opposing Kennedy's New Frontier legislation, just as later he opposed President Lyndon B. Johnson's Great Society programs. The 1962 election campaign brought some sniping between Broyhill and the Kennedy camp. When his Democratic opponent, Augustus C. Johnson, was feted by White House Press Secretary Pierre Salinger, a resident of the Tenth District, Broyhill described Salinger as a "two-bit assistant" of the President, whom he termed a "Cape Cod carpetbagger." Kennedy quipped at a news conference in reference to Broyhill that he had never read so much about a Congressman "and seen less legislative results."

Representative Broyhill continued winning elections in the 1960's in spite of his antiadministration stand. Even in the 1964 election, which gave President Johnson two out of three votes in Virginia's Tenth District, Broyhill, who had campaigned for Barry M. Goldwater, achieved victory again. When the Republicans regained power with the election of Richard Nixon in 1968, Broyhill resumed a proadministration stance, voting approximately 70 percent of the time in support of Nixon's legislation. Broyhill's solid Republican position on national issues is apparently supported by his constituents. Since 1954 he has periodically polled the voters in his district to ascertain their feelings about local and national issues. By the mid-1960's he was sending out more than 100,000 IBM card questionnaires at a time.

Political commentators have suggested that Broyhill's victories at the polls are dependent on his role as ombudsman to his constituents in northern Virginia. During the 1950's he served on the House Post Office and Civil Service Committee, as well as the House District of Columbia Committee, which is concerned with the governing of Washington, D.C. Of twenty-four bills he introduced by 1962 that became law, none dealt with national legislation, while four were concerned with matters affecting federal employees and eight were concerned with the District of Columbia. Four consisted of legislation important to the area, and the rest were minor bills. Analyzing his appeal, Richard Corrigan wrote in the Washington *Post* (November 13, 1966), "The voters obviously believe Broyhill is always in there pitching on their behalf. The name Broyhill seems to convey the ideal of more federal benefits for them—personally or en masse—and less federal spending elsewhere." Broyhill claims that he has personally come to the aid of some 60,000 of his constituents during his years in the House of Representatives. Although opposed to government "handouts," he has backed federal spending in Impact Aid funds for schools in his district, as well as federal contributions to local park projects.

Broyhill's most widely publicized work has been his accomplishments on the House District Committee, where he was once ranking Republican member. He left the committee briefly when he attained a seat on the powerful House Ways and Means Committee in 1964. House tradition holds that a member of the Ways and Means Committee cannot serve on another committee, but Broyhill broke precedent by returning to the District Committee in 1965. As a member of the District Committee, he has influenced building programs in the city, prompted bridge and highway construction, and favored the development of mass transit.

Home rule for the District of Columbia has been an issue of particular concern to Broyhill since his first term in Congress. He supported proposals that would allow D.C. residents a voice in the election of the President and Vice-President, as well as voting or nonvoting representation in the House of Representatives. But although he conceded that D.C. residents should have a vote in national government, he consistently opposed any moves to give them a voice in their local government. At the time of his initial election to Congress, legislative powers for the District were centralized in the House and Senate District Committees, and a three-man commission appointed by the President administered the laws of the city. Broyhill fought bills that would revise the system by giving the city an elected mayor and council government.

"Every American has the right to vote, . . . [but] Washington is a federal city," Broyhill once said in explaining his attitude toward home rule. "The line where federal government ends and local government begins is difficult to draw." He reportedly believes that a local government run by D.C. residents would consider federal interests secondary. Arguing that Congress will never give up its Constitutionally guaranteed powers to rule the city, he opposes home rule bills that he predicts will only be defeated. In a talk before the Arlington Optimist Club in September 1960, he maintained that the District's large black population had caused "a great deal of resistance in Congress to home rule," but added, "This shouldn't be a reason for denying it."

Despite Broyhill's efforts to retain fully his committee's power to govern Washington, in 1967 reform of the city government brought about an attempt at a more efficient system with a Presidentially appointed mayor and an appointed city council. Broyhill opposed as "confused and inept" the government of the new mayor, Walter E. Washington, a black administrator, and urged Nixon to remove him from office. He continued to fight home rule proposals in Congress by proposing such alternatives as giving half the city of Washington back to Maryland and setting up a nine-man council to run the city, six members of which would be chosen by Congress.

Although Broyhill admits that his district in northern Virginia has proportionately fewer prosegregationists than other parts of the state, he early went on record against the principle of integration. In March 1956 he and one hundred other members of Congress from the South signed a declaration, the so-called "Southern manifesto," urging "all lawful means" to resist the Supreme Court decision on integration of schools. Explaining his position, he asserted, "I'm for segregation. I am in favor of giving every citizen equal opportunity and justice under the law. But I recognize that cannot be accomplished while men's minds and hearts won't accept it as a matter of custom." A gradual educational process could solve racial problems, but not a court order, Broyhill said. When asked how legal segregation might be achieved, he answered that although the Supreme Court's position made a solution "difficult," such means as aptitude tests, adjustment of school boundaries, and selection of courses could provide "a higher degree of segregation."

The civil rights programs of neither the Republican nor the Democratic parties have had the endorsement of Broyhill. He takes a strong-man stand against ghetto rioters, and a few days after the death of Dr. Martin Luther King Jr., in March 1968, he said, "If we are obliged to act in memory of Dr. King [by passing the 1968 civil rights bill], then I submit that the next time a policeman or a fireman, or an innocent citizen, is slain in a riot caused by agitators, this House is obligated to pass legislation, as another memorial to the dead, making it mandatory that all police, National Guardsmen and militiamen shoot to kill each and every looter or rioter henceforth." He added, however, that he proposed "nothing of the sort." Broyhill is an avowed admirer of the viewpoint of Alabama Governor George C. Wallace on law and order and has been outspoken in deploring the crime rate in Washington, D.C.

Representative Broyhill has, moreover, opposed antipoverty programs as a waste of money and an infringement by the federal government on the responsibilities of the states. "The Bible says 'For ye have the poor always with you,' and . . . I have a good deal more faith in the Bible than in some politicians' promises," Broyhill commented in 1964 in reference to the Economic Opportunities Act. During the Poor People's Campaign in 1968 he warned the marchers against violent demonstrations. On a TV discussion program he called for strong police action and suggested that a looter be made to understand that "when he is actually involved in some action that might result in the destruction of life or the loss of property, he might be taking a chance of losing his own life."

Campaigning in a generally low-key style, Broyhill runs on his record of action on bills directly affecting his constituents, such as federal employees, although he occasionally does become involved in crucial national issues. In 1968, for example, he accused President Johnson of "dilly-dallying" on the Vietnam war. During the 1970 election campaign when Edmund S. Muskie criticized Broyhill's stand on environmental problems, he took inspiration from then Vice-President Spiro T. Agnew and called Muskie, "the mournful mummer from Machiasport, this mucilaginous muckrake from Maine, this mousy meddler named Muskie, who carpetbags across the nation running for a radical-liberal Presidential nomination." In a speech at a Salvation Army banquet in November 1973, Broyhill said in regard to the Watergate scandal that if President Nixon failed to regain the confidence of the American people, resignation or impeachment would be necessary. Broyhill himself is known for scrupulously revealing his campaign contributions and expenditures.

The Virginia Congressman prides himself on his record of attendance in the House. "It is one of the most outstanding records in the country," he has claimed, adding that he works "an 18-to-20 hour day, day in, day out." Richard Corrigan commented in the Washington *Post* (November 13, 1966) on Broyhill's electoral appeal: "Going beyond the matter of Congressional favors, Broyhill represents his constituents in another way. He is, simply, one of them. He is a war hero turned postwar booster, a hell-of-a-fellow in a new green Caddy, a hard-driving salesman who sells himself, a middle-brow who is comfortable in his convictions and tells the voters what they want to hear but can wink in the middle of a platitude, too."

On May 17, 1942 Joel T. Broyhill married Jane Marshall Bragg, of Arlington, and they have three daughters, Nancy Pierce, Jane-Anne, and Jeanne Marie. His wife and children have long helped him in his campaigns, and at political rallies Mrs. Broyhill sometimes answers voters' questions about her husband's stand on campaign issues. "Joel and I made a good swap when we married," she told Sue Cronk of the Washington *Post* (October 21, 1962). "I became a Republican and he switched from the Baptist church to the Lutheran. I probably would have ended up a Republican anyhow. The [Democratic] party already was losing me as it became more liberal." Broyhill is a member of several veterans, fraternal, and professional organizations. He and his wife both play the electric organ. Among his other recreations are swimming and fishing, and he belongs to the Izaak Walton League.

References

Washington Post C p1+ O 26 '66; p13 Je 16 '67; B p1+ S 2 '68 por
Biographical Directory of the American Congress, 1917-1961 (1962)
Congressional Directory, 1973
Who's Who in America, 1972-73
Who's Who in American Politics, 1971-72

BYRNE, BRENDAN T(HOMAS)

Apr. 1, 1924- Governor of New Jersey
Address: b. State Capitol Bldg., Trenton, N.J. 08625; h. "Morven," The Governor's Mansion, Princeton, N.J. 08540

Despite the protestations of Nixon administration spokesmen that the Watergate scandals would fail to influence voters at the polls, many observ-

BRENDAN T. BYRNE

ers of the New Jersey gubernatorial election in 1973 considered the victory of Democrat Brendan T. Byrne over his Republican opponent on November 6 as proof that a backlash was inevitable. Byrne's avowed aim in seeking the Governor's office was to restore public confidence in government in a state plagued with political corruption of its own. As prosecutor and state Superior Court judge, he had gained a reputation for honesty that served him well in his bid for election as an anticorruption candidate. Although relatively unknown at the outset of his campaign because of his career as a rather obscure appointed official, his background eventually worked in his favor, since he appealed to voters who had grown cynical of politicians.

Brendan Thomas Byrne was born on April 1, 1924 into a family long active in local New Jersey politics. His father, who died in 1973 at the age of eighty-six, had been the public safety commissioner of the family's hometown, West Orange, New Jersey, and president of the Essex County tax board. After serving in the United States Air Force during World War II, Byrne attended Princeton University. After graduating in 1949, he went on to Harvard Law School, where he obtained his LL.B. degree in 1951.

Byrne began his own career in public service in 1955 as an assistant counsel to New Jersey's former Governor, Robert B. Meyner. The following year he was appointed Meyner's executive secretary, a post he held until 1959, when the Governor named him prosecutor of Essex County. While serving in that office he first came to public attention when he prosecuted dishonest construction contractors and the powerful underworld figure Anthony ("Tony Boy") Boiardo. Under Byrne's leadership, the prosecutor's office successfully dealt with scandals involving the Housing Authority and the Martland Medical Center in Newark. After serving nine years as prosecutor, he accepted the presidency of the New Jersey public utilities commission in 1968 and occupied that post until 1970, when Governor William T.

Cahill appointed him to a judgeship on the New Jersey Superior Court. One of his most important judicial decisions was the one that he handed down in 1971 declaring the state's seventy-eight-year-old law on capital punishment unconstitutional.

In early 1973 Byrne's career took a major turn when a number of influential Democrats suggested that he might be the right man to oppose the powerful Republican Governor Cahill in the November gubernatorial election. They hoped that a Byrne candidacy would appeal to all elements in the Democratic party, which was weakened by a split between reform-oriented veterans of the George S. McGovern campaign and the machine regulars. The party's prospects for winning the election were further dampened by the number of reputable Democrats who had already announced their candidacies, creating a situation that was certain to confuse and divide the Democratic voters.

Despite the support of Mrs. Helen Meyner, the wife of the former Governor, Mayor Francis Fitzpatrick of Bayonne, Joel Jacobson of the State United Autoworkers, and Archibald Alexander, the chairman of the state prison board of managers, Byrne hesitated before joining the primary race. Not only was he unsure that he would obtain the backing of the large county Democratic organizations but he was also waiting to see if indictments would be returned against members of Governor Cahill's administration who had been accused of corruption.

Byrne later described his predicament to Fred Ferretti of the New York *Times* (May 19, 1973): "I was happy on the bench, but they kept calling me. During the week of April 16 I made up my mind to make some determination because I found I was listening to the calls. I really didn't make up my mind until I went to Governor Cahill's office that morning." When Byrne met with the Governor on April 24, 1973, he presented Cahill with his resignation and, then, to the bewilderment of the Governor's aides, announced his candidacy in the Governor's outer office.

In his speech Byrne sounded what was to become the keynote of his campaign when he referred to the accusations of corruption made against some members of the Governor's administration and the investigations of the financing of Cahill's 1969 campaign and the possible misuse of state funds after that election. "An administration that must contend almost daily with corruption by its own," he said, "can have little time for anything else." With increasing numbers of Democrats declaring their support for Byrne after his announcement, he soon became a leading contender for his party's nomination. After pressure was brought to bear on other candidates to withdraw, only two remained in the primary race with Byrne: state senator Ralph DeRose and Morris County assemblywoman Ann Klein.

As his campaign activity gathered momentum, Byrne found that he had to discard some of his "judge's habits along with the robes." Accustomed to a judge's highly scheduled daily routine and explicit language, he had to adjust to rigorous campaigning and a manner of public speaking that required him to generalize. One observer of his campaign style noted that he exhibited a sense of humor despite the fact that he seemed to feel uncomfortable in the limelight. Although he was judged most effective when dealing with the corruption issue, Byrne expressed his hope that he would be elected not "as another Dick Tracy, but rather as another Woodrow Wilson." On June 5, 1973 both the Republican and Democratic parties held primary elections. Defeated largely because of the charges of corruption leveled against his administration, Governor Cahill lost his bid for the Republican nomination to Charles W. Sandman Jr., while Byrne won in the three-way Democratic race.

With the field narrowed down to two candidates, the election attracted the interest of political observers throughout the United States, who were curious to see if the outcome indicated voter retaliation toward the scandal-ridden Nixon administration. Both Republican John B. Connally, the former Treasury Secretary, and George Bush, the Republican party's national chairman, lent credence to the political importance of the race by expressing their opinion that the results would certainly be a sign of the electorate's sentiments about the national leadership. Not only the national scandals were of significance, however, since in New Jersey, between 1970 and 1973, seventy-eight public officials from both parties had been indicted by federal grand juries. With polls showing increasing voter apathy and suspicion of politicians, a low turnout was anticipated on election day.

Against that background of political corruption Brendan Byrne campaigned on the slogan that "one honest man can make a difference." His supporters widely publicized a Federal Bureau of Investigation tape recording of racketeers' conversations on which Byrne was described as "a man who couldn't be bought." To capitalize further on his image as a "clean" politician aloof from all the scandals, Byrne's career as an appointed official, not an elected one, was stressed.

Byrne promised to seek legislation providing for public financing of campaigns; to elicit financial statements periodically from members of his administration; to choose judges according to their ability and in a nonpolitical manner; and to strengthen the Attorney General's office in an attempt to combat corruption. In answer to criticisms by his opponent that he failed to take definite stands on such controversial issues as abortion, school busing, and the introduction of a state income tax, Byrne explained that he opposed giving facile answers to complex questions and that it would be an affront to the voters' intelligence to do so. Instead, he preferred to write position papers on complicated and emotionally charged issues. He, in turn, attacked Sandman for his conservative voting record in the state legislature and for appealing to voters' fears and prejudices.

To some Democratic and Republican leaders, Byrne seemed the most likely candidate to win,

especially since his opponent was considered a divisive force within his own party. Sandman's conservatism alienated many of his moderate and liberal colleagues, including the state's two most influential Republicans, United States Senator Clifford P. Case and Governor Cahill. On the other hand, Byrne succeeded in uniting his party by winning the support of labor and by appealing to the state's political moderates. On November 6, 1973 Byrne overwhelmingly defeated Sandman by 721,000 votes.

In what was described as the "biggest gubernatorial victory in the state's history" by a reporter for *Newsweek* (November 19, 1973), Byrne won by a margin of more than two to one, carrying some districts that had never before given their support to a Democrat and some areas where registered Republicans outnumbered Democrats by three to one. The Democrats took control of the state legislature, winning twenty-eight of the forty Senate seats, and sixty-six of the eighty Assembly seats. As had been predicted, there was a low voter turnout, with only 61 percent of the eligible voting, as compared with the usual figure of 70 percent.

Alluding to national scandals in a speech he gave after the election results were in, Byrne said, "Too many victories have been tarnished by the public stewardships that have followed them. My first obligation is to restore integrity in government." Some Republicans as well as Democrats viewed his victory as an indication of voter displeasure with the Nixon administration, with the head of the Republican county leaders organization calling it "a total rebellion and outrage on the part of the American people."

Even before his inauguration Byrne demonstrated his enthusiasm for his new role by vigorously taking part in the affairs of New Jersey and concerning himself with its problems. In late 1973 he discussed the mass transportation problems common to both New Jersey and the New York City metropolitan area in meetings with mayor-elect Abraham D. Beame of New York City and the Governor of New York, Nelson Rockefeller. He went on record as being opposed to a planned extension of the New Jersey Turnpike, citing environmental and energy-crisis concerns as the reason. Included in his announced plans were the simplification of voter registration procedures and the study of cable television development in New Jersey.

Byrne also planned to ask for a special session of the legislature for June 1974 to deal with the problem created by a State Supreme Court decision of 1973, later upheld by the United States Supreme Court, which ordered the state to find a new way to finance public education. Since the old system based the financing on 70 percent of local property taxes, many observers suspected that the only other way for the state to raise an equivalent sum of money was through the introduction of an income tax during the June session. Although an income tax bill was eventually introduced, it was defeated by the New Jersey Senate in August 1974.

Among Byrne's first official acts as Governor after his inauguration on January 15, 1974 was the launching of a mandatory gas rationing plan for New Jersey based on an even-odd day system and the introduction of the country's first auto emission testing program. He introduced bills in the legislature calling for the public financing of the 1977 gubernatorial campaign and for the creation of a department of public advocate, both of which were later voted on and passed. Byrne also promised to lend his support to a group of bills dealing with tenants' rights.

Although the budget that Byrne presented to the legislature on February 14, 1974 contained no new programs or taxes, he did suggest that there should be increased allocations to cities and schools. In choosing his cabinet members he by-passed the regular machine-backed interests to appoint some of his former campaign staff members and other close colleagues. After observing the new Governor in action for less than one month, John McLaughlin of the New York *Sunday News* (February 10, 1974) was moved to comment, "In short, he has shown every indication of being his own man."

Brendan T. Byrne now lives in "Morven," the Governor's mansion in Princeton, with his wife, the former Jean Featherly, whom he met in high school, and the couple's seven children. His son Brendan was elected "boy governor" of New Jersey in an American Legion program in 1971, prompting the older Byrne to comment during his campaign that he hoped to follow his son's lead. The other children in the family are named Susan, Nancy, Timothy, Mary Anne, Barbara, and William. Looking remarkably like Charlton Heston, Byrne is a tall and handsome man with "deep-set green eyes" and an average weight of about 170 pounds. He played tennis or squash as often as five times a week before his gubernatorial campaign and always enjoyed a game of basketball or football with his children. He neither smokes nor drinks. His religious affiliation is Roman Catholic. In May 1974 Rutgers University awarded him an honorary LL.D. degree.

Although often described by journalists as soft-spoken and "shy in public," Byrne is actually a self-assured man not particularly given to self-effacement. A colleague characterized him as a "cautious" person with "an infinite capacity for hard work, a deep sense of personal privacy, and a passion for intellectual growth." Once, when asked by a reporter why he wanted to be Governor, Byrne replied, "I have a real feeling that the Democratic party has a chance at leadership in the state, a chance to turn the state around. Maybe the people who said I can do it are right." When then asked if he thought he could do it, he responded, "Yeah, I think I can."

References

N Y Daily News p40 O 22 '73 por
N Y Times p1+ Ap 25 '73 por; p41 My 19 '73 por; p61 N 7 '73
Nat Observer p5 S 22 '73
Time 102:33+ N 19 '73 por

CAHN, SAMMY

June 18, 1913- Songwriter
Address: b. c/o Edward Traubner, 1800 Century Park East, Los Angeles, Calif. 90067

After nearly four decades as one of the most successful lyricists of popular songs, mainly for films and musicals, Sammy Cahn emerged as a Broadway star in his own right in 1974, with his revue *Words and Music,* a reminiscence of his life and work. In partnership with Saul Chaplin, Jule Styne, Jimmy Van Heusen, and other composers, Cahn has written hundreds of popular songs, some of which, such as the Oscar-winning "Three Coins in a Fountain" (1954), "All the Way" (1957), "High Hopes" (1959), and "Call Me Irresponsible" (1963), and the Emmy award winner "Love and Marriage" (1955), have become standards. For the Broadway stage he crafted the lyrics for the musical hits *High Button Shoes* (1947) and *Skyscraper* (1965).

A native New Yorker, Sammy Cahn was born Samuel Cohen, on June 18, 1913. (Early in his career he changed his surname to Kahn, because there was at the time a popular comedian named Sammy Cohen; later he became Sammy Cahn to distinguish him from the lyricist Gus Kahn.) His boyhood home, on Cannon Street, was in the "lowest part" of Manhattan's Lower East Side. Cahn was the second of the five children, and only son, of Abraham Cohen, who operated a tiny restaurant, and of Elka (Riss) Cohen. His parents were immigrants from Galicia. Over the years Sammy Cahn has maintained a close relationship with his sisters, Sadye, Pearl, Florence, and Evelyn. "My mother was the Jewish Lourdes," Cahn has recalled. "People always came to her with problems."

At his mother's urging Cahn became proficient at playing the violin. She was less successful, however, in her efforts to instill in him the ambition to become a doctor or lawyer. At Public School 147 and at the Seward Park High School—where he set something of a record for truancy—he failed to distinguish himself as a student, preferring to hang around poolrooms racking balls to earn pocket money for admission to the movies. At thirteen, on seeing his mother pay the musicians who played at his bar mitzvah, he suddenly realized that one could make a living playing music. The following year he played the violin at "borsht belt" resorts in the Catskills, and on his return to New York City he joined a small orchestra that played at weddings, bar mitzvahs, and other social functions.

After dropping out of school for good, Cahn worked as a violinist in Bowery burlesque houses, occasionally making up ribald parodies of songs to accompany the strip acts. Between musical engagements he worked as a porter, elevator operator, tinsmith, usher, and restaurant cashier. At sixteen, after hearing a young vaudevillian named Jackie Osterman sing a song of his own creation to an enthusiastic audience, Cahn wrote his first lyric, "Like Niagara Falls, I'm Falling for

You." Having learned to strum a few chords on the piano, he then wrote a series of songs, both words and music.

Because he felt more self-confident writing just lyrics, Cahn persuaded Saul Chaplin, the pianist in the orchestra in which he was then playing violin, to join him in a songwriting partnership. The first product of their collaboration, an arrangement by Chaplin of Cahn's song "Shake Your Head From Side to Side," was published but failed to net them any royalties. Under pressure from his parents to earn a living, Cahn then spent nearly three years "under refrigeration," working for the United Dressed Beef Company, while devoting his spare time to writing lyrics. Eventually, in the early 1930's, Cahn and Chaplin managed to make a modest living writing special material for singers, comedians, and vaudeville acts, and they rented space in a midtown office. Among their early customers were Bob Hope, Milton Berle, and Henny Youngman.

One day in 1935 Cahn met a boyhood friend, Lou Levy, who was performing a dance act with Jimmy Lunceford's orchestra at the Apollo Theatre in Harlem. On Levy's recommendation, Lunceford hired Cahn and Chaplin to provide him with special material, and they wrote "Rhythm Is Our Business," which was recorded by Lunceford on the Decca label and became an immediate hit. They followed it up with "Rhythm in My Nursery Rhymes" and "Posin'." Soon Cahn and Chaplin were much in demand. Glen Gray hired them to write "The Glen Gray Casa Loma Corporation" for his orchestra's opening at the Paramount Theatre, and Decca Records executive Jack Kapp engaged them to produce songs for Ella Fitzgerald, Andy Kirk, and other recording artists. It was their "Until the Real Thing Comes Along" that helped to place Andy Kirk's band in the limelight. For a revue at the Cotton Club in Harlem, Cahn and Chaplin wrote several songs, including "Shoe Shine Boy," performed by Louis Armstrong in the show's finale. It was a major hit in 1936, the year that Cahn and Chaplin were admitted to ASCAP.

Soon thereafter, the partners were placed under contract by the Warner Brothers Vitaphone Studios in Brooklyn, an organization that, according to Cahn, seemed to have the motto "We don't want it good—we want it by Thursday!" There they worked for about four years grinding out material for short films featuring such performers as Bob Hope, Betty Hutton, and Edgar Bergen. Their "Please be Kind" became the first song from a short subject to rise to the top of the Hit Parade. While working for Warner Vitaphone, Cahn attended a show at the Apollo Theatre, where he heard the song "Bei Mir Bist Du Schoen"—written for the Yiddish stage by Sholom Secunda and Jacob Jacobs. Encouraged by Lou Levy, Cahn wrote English lyrics to the Yiddish song, and Chaplin made a new arrangement of the tune. After the partners acquired the rights from the original publishers, the Cahn-Chaplin version of "Bei Mir Bist Du Schoen" was recorded for Decca by the Andrews Sisters, who were thus catapulted

SAMMY CAHN

to stardom. It became the top novelty song of 1938, earning some $3 million, and over 1,000,000 copies of the recording were sold. Subsequently, Cahn and Chaplin supplied the Andrews Sisters with another popular song adapted from the Yiddish—"Joseph, Joseph."

When the Vitaphone Studios in Brooklyn closed down about 1940, Cahn and Chaplin, still under contract to Warner Brothers, were sent to Hollywood. There they continued to draw their salaries for about two years but failed to receive any assignments. After their contract expired, they made the rounds of the studios. But apart from a story and accompanying score entitled "You'll Never Get Rich" that they sold to Republic Studios, they were unsuccessful, and eventually they decided to part company.

Meanwhile, shortly after Pearl Harbor, Cahn tried to enlist, but was turned down because of ulcers. Not long afterward he began his fruitful collaboration with composer Jule Styne. During their first meeting Styne played one of his own compositions, and Cahn remarked, "I've heard that song before!" When Styne expressed dismay at what he thought to be Cahn's implication that he had "borrowed" the tune, Cahn hastened to add that he was merely suggesting a song title. "I've Heard That Song Before" became the first of the many Cahn-Styne songs to reach the Hit Parade.

Frank Sinatra, whom Cahn had met early in his career through Tommy Dorsey, and with whom he established an enduring friendship, popularized a number of Cahn-Styne hits, including "I'll Walk Alone," which was nominated for an Academy Award after it was introduced by Dinah Shore in *Follow the Boys* (Universal, 1944); "I Fall in Love too Easily," nominated for an Oscar in 1945; "Saturday Night Is the Loneliest Night in the Week"; "As Long as There's Music"; "Come Out, Come Out"; "Five Minutes More"; and "The Things We Did Last Summer." At Sinatra's request Cahn and Styne were engaged to write the score for

MGM's gala musical *Anchors Aweigh* in 1945. The partners also wrote the songs for *Tonight and Every Night* (Columbia, 1945); the Danny Kaye vehicles *Wonder Man* (RKO, 1945) and *The Kid From Brooklyn* (RKO, 1946); and *The West Point Story* (Warner, 1950). Doris Day achieved motion picture stardom when she sang "It's Magic," another Oscar nominee by Cahn and Styne in *Romance on the High Seas* (Warner, 1948), and she also popularized their "It's a Great Feeling."

Other Cahn-Styne hits of the 1940's included "Let It Snow! Let It Snow! Let It Snow!" which became identified with Vaughn Monroe; "There Goes That Song Again," popularized by Kay Kyser's orchestra; "It's Been a Long, Long Time"; "Time After Time"; and "Victory Polka." As a writer for *Time* (August 30, 1948) observed, Cahn and Styne did for popular music what Rogers and Hammerstein did for the Broadway musical theatre.

Cahn and Styne first tried to write for the Broadway stage in 1944, when they supplied the songs for the musical *Glad to See You*. Although the show never reached Broadway, it afforded Cahn the opportunity to appear on stage as a replacement for the male lead during the show's Philadelphia run. The two songwriters were more successful when they produced the score for the musical hit *High Button Shoes*, which opened at Broadway's Century Theatre on October 9, 1947 and ran for 727 performances. Written by Stephen Longstreet, with choreography by Jerome Robbins, the musical featured Phil Silvers and Joey Faye and brought stardom to Nanette Fabray. It yielded several Cahn-Styne hits, including "Papa, Won't You Dance With Me?" and "I Still Get Jealous."

After *High Button Shoes*, Styne remained in New York while Cahn returned to California. For a time, Cahn collaborated with composer Nicholas Brodszky, and together they received Oscar nominations for the songs "Be My Love," introduced by Mario Lanza in *Toast of New Orleans* (MGM, 1950); "Wonder Why" (1951); "Because You're Mine" (1952); and "I'll Never Stop Loving You" (1955). They also collaborated on songs for *Serenade* (Warner, 1956), starring Mario Lanza, and for the MGM musical *Meet Me in Las Vegas* (1956). Cahn also worked with Sammy Fain on songs for Walt Disney's *Peter Pan* (RKO, 1953); with Arthur Schwartz on the Dean Martin-Jerry Lewis film *You're Never Too Young* (Paramount, 1955); with Sylvia Fine on the Danny Kaye comedy *The Court Jester* (Paramount, 1956); with Bronislau Kaper on *Forever Darling* (MGM, 1956); and with Vernon Duke on *April in Paris* (Warner, 1953). Other composers with whom he collaborated included Axel Stordahl, Paul Weston, and Gene de Paul. In 1953 Cahn tried his hand as a film producer, presenting *Three Sailors and a Girl* (Warner), which starred Jane Powell and Gordon MacRae.

Cahn and Styne were reunited professionally in 1954, when at Frank Sinatra's request they were commissioned by Twentieth Century-Fox to write the score for "Pink Tights," a Cinemascope musical planned for Sinatra and Marilyn Monroe. Although the score they created was in Cahn's view the best they had ever written, the production had to be shelved when Miss Monroe disassociated herself from it. Soon afterwards Cahn and Styne were asked by Twentieth Century-Fox producer Sol C. Siegel to write a title song for a romantic comedy, to be called *Three Coins in a Fountain*, that had just been filmed in Italy. Since the song was needed immediately, they had no opportunity to see the film and were given only a vague idea of the plot. Nevertheless they completed the music and lyrics within less than an hour. Made into a best-selling Capitol recording by Sinatra, who also sang it on the soundtrack of the film, "Three Coins in a Fountain" was named the best song of 1954 by the Academy of Motion Picture Arts and Sciences, earning Cahn his first Oscar award. Cahn also collaborated with Styne on the score of *The Seven Year Itch* (Twentieth Century-Fox, 1955), a comedy starring Marilyn Monroe.

In 1955 Cahn teamed up with composer Jimmy Van Heusen. For their first assignment they prepared special material for Bing Crosby's stage show at the Paramount. Then they wrote the title song for *The Tender Trap* (MGM, 1955), which was turned into a major hit by Sinatra and received an Oscar nomination. That same year, they wrote the songs for a musical version of *Our Town*, which was presented in September 1955 on *Producer's Showcase* over NBC-TV. One of its songs, "Love and Marriage," earned Cahn and Van Heusen a special Emmy award as well as a Christopher Award, and another, "The Impatient Years," also became a hit.

Their song "All the Way," written for *The Joker Is Wild* (Paramount, 1957), in which Sinatra portrayed the comic Joe E. Lewis, earned Cahn and Van Heusen an Oscar as well as a National Cash Box Award. "High Hopes," sung by Sinatra and Eddie Hodges in *A Hole in the Head* (United Artists, 1959), also netted them an Academy Award. A parody of that song by Cahn became John F. Kennedy's Presidential campaign song in 1960. The partners received another Oscar for "Call Me Irresponsible," originally written in 1955 for Fred Astaire and performed by Jackie Gleason in *Papa's Delicate Condition* (Paramount, 1963). Cahn and Van Heusen received Academy Award nominations for "To Love and Be Loved" from *Some Came Running* (MGM, 1959); "Second Time Around" from *High Time* (Twentieth Century-Fox 1960); "My Kind of Town" from *Robin and the Seven Hoods* (Warner, 1964); and the title songs from *A Pocketful of Miracles* (United Artists, 1961), *Where Love Has Gone* (Paramount, 1964), *Thoroughly Modern Millie* (Universal, 1967), and *Star* (Twentieth Century-Fox, 1968). Cahn wrote the lyrics for the theme song of *The Man With the Golden Arm* (United Artists, 1956), starring Sinatra. Four new songs by Cahn and Van Heusen were included in the film version of Cole Porter's *Anything Goes* (Paramount, 1956).

For television, Cahn and Van Heusen produced *The Frank Sinatra Show,* a series of four star-studded spectaculars, presented during the 1959-60 season. The first of them won a Sylvania Television Award as the outstanding variety program. In 1961 they wrote the title song for the CBS-TV series *Hazel,* with Shirley Booth, and in 1962 they wrote the song "Joey" for Joey Bishop's ABC-TV talk show. Their songs for Gene Kelly's television spectacular *Jack and the Beanstalk* written in late 1966, helped to win for that show an Emmy award as the best children's program.

Cahn and Van Heusen won critical acclaim for the songs they wrote for *Skyscraper,* a musical based on Elmer Rice's play *Dream Girl.* Starring Julie Harris, the show ran for 241 performances, beginning on November 13, 1965, at the Lunt-Fontanne Theatre, and it included several Cahn-Van Heusen hits, such as "Everybody Has a Right to Be Wrong." They also contributed the lyrics and music for *Walking Happy,* a British musical that opened at the Lunt-Fontanne in November 1966 and ran for 161 performances.

For Frank Sinatra, Cahn and Van Heusen wrote such hits as the title songs of the best-selling albums *Come Fly With Me* (1958); *Only the Lonely* (1958); *Come Dance With Me* (1959); *No One Cares* (1959); *Ring-a-Ding Ding* (1961); and *September of My Years* (1965). They also prepared songs and special material for theatre and nightclub acts for Nat King Cole, Sammy Davis Jr., and others.

By late 1969 Cahn had dissolved his partnership with Van Heusen. Once again he collaborated with Jule Styne, writing the lyrics to Styne's music for *Look to the Lilies.* Directed by Joshua Logan, the show opened at the Lunt-Fontanne Theatre on March 29, 1970 but closed after three weeks. More recently, Cahn collaborated with George Barrie on the score of the adult comedy *A Touch of Class* (1973). The song "All That Love Went to Waste" from that film brought Cahn his thirty-first Oscar nomination.

In 1972 Cahn gave a recital of his songs at the YM & YWHA on Manhattan's East 92d Street. Broadway producer Alexander H. Cohen, after hearing a tape recording of that performance, suggested that Cahn do a "one-man show" on Broadway. The result was *Words and Music,* coproduced by Cohen and Harvey Granat and directed by Jerry Adler, which opened at the Golden Theatre on April 16, 1974. Assisted by pianist Richard Leonard and singers Kelly Garrett, Shirley Lemmon, and Jon Peck, Cahn evoked rave reviews by informally presenting a nostalgic cross-section of his songs and punctuating his musical renditions with colorful anecdotes of his life and career. The performance brought Cahn the Outer Circle Critics Award for the best new talent on Broadway, as well as a Theatre World Award, and it qualified him for membership in Actors' Equity. In London, where it opened in September 1974 with the title *Sammy Cahn's Songbook,* the show was equally a hit.

Cahn emphasizes the art of "selling" a song. "I am the king of the demonstrators," he has said. "When we finish a song, my collaborator . . . and I get down to what we consider the most important work. We *learn* the song—'woodshedding' we call it—find the right tempo and phrasing, the right attitude. Then comes the moment of truth: the demonstration." Although he is one of the world's highest-paid songwriters —he has on occasion earned over $1,000 a word —he donates much work to charitable causes.

A recipient of Israel's Freedom Cup, Cahn holds many awards from humanitarian organizations, and he was cited by the armed forces for his work in behalf of the USO. Elected to the Songwriters Hall of Fame in 1972, he now serves as its president. At a party sponsored by his wife and by singer Paul Anka, honoring him on his sixtieth birthday, Cahn was presented with an honorary diploma from Seward Park High School. To accompany his stage show, Cahn compiled a songbook, *Words and Music* (1974). His autobiography, *I Should Care; The Sammy Cahn Story,* was published by Arbor House in 1974.

From his first marriage, on September 5, 1945, to Gloria Delson, a former Goldwyn girl, Sammy Cahn has a son, Steven, and a daughter, Laurie. The marriage ended in divorce in 1964 ("the day I won the Oscar for 'Call Me Irresponsible'," he has recalled). His second wife, the former Virginia Basile, known as Tita, whom he married on August 4, 1970, is a fashion consultant and former actress. They have a home on New York's East Side and another in Beverly Hills.

Described by Barbra Streisand as looking "like a Jewish dentist," by C. Robert Jennings in *Show* (July 1963) as having the appearance of "a chipmunk that has just poked its head blinkingly out of a dark nest," and by Max Wilk as "very much the elegant world traveler and bon vivant," Cahn stands at five feet eight inches and weighs 160 pounds. He has dark brown eyes, a fringe of graying dark hair, and a thin mustache. His singing voice was described by Tom Topor in the New York *Post* (April 27, 1974) as that of "a vain duck with a hangover." Although he had long been suffering from ulcers, he was cured of that condition by surgery in the early 1960's. According to Jimmy Van Heusen, Cahn "has such a brain for comedy, he can get in a room with professional gag-writers and just deal in punch lines." His favorite recreation, he has said, is "merely sitting and typing, either lyrics, or letters, or whatever." His interest in baseball is reflected in "The Dodgers' Song," which he wrote with Van Heusen.

References

> Sat Eve Post 232:26+ D 12 '59 pors
> Ewen, David. Great Men of American Popular Song (1972); New Complete Book of the American Musical Theatre (1970)
> Stambler, Irwin. Encyclopedia of Popular Music (1965)
> Who's Who in America, 1974-75
> Wilk, Max. They're Playing Our Song (1973)

CARL XVI GUSTAF, KING OF SWEDEN

Apr. 30, 1946-
Address: Royal Palace, Stockholm, Sweden

After years of well-rounded preparation for monarchical responsibility, Carl XVI Gustaf—who ascended the throne of Sweden on September 19, 1973, four days after the death of his grandfather, King Gustaf VI—is slated to be the first monarch in Swedish history with virtually no royal authority. A new Constitution, scheduled to become effective on January 1, 1975, establishes Sweden as a parliamentary democracy in which "all power emanates from the people" and divests the King of virtually all of his royal prerogatives. The question of whether monarchy in any form has any place in a modern welfare democracy like Sweden, has been the subject of much debate. The Social Democrats, Sweden's largest political party, had been committed to ending the monarchy for some time, but refrained from such action because of the popularity of the last two kings. Although Carl XVI Gustaf is popular in his own right, especially among the younger generation, some observers believe that his chances of remaining on the throne depend on his ability to cast off his playboy image and to cultivate the affection and esteem that his grandfather had acquired over the years.

Carl XVI Gustaf was born Carl Gustaf Folke Hubertus at the Haga Castle on April 30, 1946, the fifth and youngest child of Prince Gustaf Adolf and of the German-born Princess Sibylla, formerly the Princess of Saxe-Coburg-Gotha. He is the seventh sovereign of the French house of Bernadotte, which has ruled Sweden since 1818. In that year, after King Carl XIII of the old Swedish house of Vasa died without a direct heir, Jean-Baptiste Bernadotte, a marshal of Napoleon I, having been elected Prince Royal of Sweden eight years earlier, accepted the Swedish crown and became King Carl XIV.

At the time of Carl Gustaf's birth, his great-grandfather Gustaf V Adolf was King of Sweden. As an only son, in direct succession to the throne, Carl Gustaf was born heir apparent and was created Duke of Jämtland shortly after his birth. When on January 26, 1947 Prince Gustaf Adolf died in a plane crash, nine-month-old Carl Gustaf became second in line of succession to the Swedish monarchy. With the death of Gustaf V and the accession to the throne of Gustaf VI on October 29, 1950, Carl Gustaf at the age of four and a half years became Crown Prince, and his unmarried uncle, Prince Bertil, became second in the line of succession. Since the Swedish Constitution forbids the succession of women, Carl Gustaf's four older sisters, Princesses Margaretha, Birgitta, Désirée, and Christina, are ineligible to ascend the throne.

Prince Carl Gustaf was brought up by his mother, Princess Sibylla, who died in 1972, and by his grandfather, the late King. "My grandfather gave to us, his family, his deep human warmth, his friendship, and his concern," Carl

Gustaf has testified, as quoted in the London *Times* (September 20, 1973). "After the premature death of my father, Prince Gustaf Adolf, my grandfather became our central figure and the never failing mainstay of my family." His earliest education was undertaken at the royal court by a council of three specially appointed advisers. At two he was photographed returning a salute from his great-grandfather, King Gustaf V, while making his first official appearance at the Royal Calvary Club to receive an honorary membership.

When Carl Gustaf was old enough to begin school, the royal family decided that he should be educated like other upper-class Swedish children, and he was sent to a coeducational boarding school in Sigtuna, near Stockholm. Taking a liberal arts course, he studied there until he was twenty, growing up among ordinary young people as well as children of diplomats and the nobility. He soon demonstrated that, like his father, he preferred sports and outdoor life to scholarly pursuits. He became an excellent marksman and was chosen a member of the school's rifle team. According to one of his teachers, Carl Gustaf was especially fond of people and of nature and he liked to write essays about those subjects. His interest in archaeology, which he shared with his grandfather, led him to take part in the excavations of the 1,000-year-old ruins of Sweden's first capital at Sigtuna.

After graduating from the Sigtuna school in 1966, in the bottom half of his graduating class, Carl Gustaf spent two years in the different branches of the armed forces, a period he remembers as the most pleasurable of his life. His training included an around-the-world cruise aboard the minelayer *Älvsnabben* in 1966-67, several weeks with a coast artillery unit, and four months at the military cadet schools of the army and air force. In the fall of 1968 he received a commission as a navy officer. He also holds the rank of second lieutenant in the Royal Svea Lifeguards, the commando regiment of Jämtland, and the Swedish air force.

On completion of his military training, Carl Gustaf spent the academic year 1968-69 at the University of Uppsala, where he concentrated on history, sociology, political science, and economics and was active in the student union. During the summers of 1968, 1969, and 1970 he traveled to his ancestral France to study its culture and language. In 1969 Carl Gustaf embarked on a two-year study program of Sweden's social and governmental institutions. Designed to give him a practical knowledge of his country, the program began with study periods at government agencies, including the Stockholm county administration, the national labor market board, the national board of health and welfare, the national board of agriculture, and the national environment protection board. He acquainted himself with the work of the Swedish international development authority, at its Stockholm headquarters and at its centers in Tanzania, Kenya, and Ethiopia. In early 1970 Carl Gustaf visited major industrial companies, small industries in the provinces, and labor cooperatives. Later in the year he observed the work of the courts, the schools, and the police. At the 1970 World's Fair at Osaka, Japan he headed the Swedish delegation. That fall he spent a month at the United Nations in New York and several weeks at the Swedish Embassy in London and acquainted himself with the functioning of Swedish trade unions and employer organizations. He completed his formal training program with studies of the activities of the established Lutheran Church, the press, and the banking system.

On his twenty-fifth birthday Carl Gustaf was legally assured of succession to the throne and empowered to act as regent. At a news conference later that year, he expressed confidence that he could fulfill the role of King and credited his comprehensive training with giving him "the kind of background fit for a king in the world of today." Referring to the $30,000-a-year government stipend he received on his birthday, he quipped: "Quite a difference. When I was little, I only got thirty cents a week." In recognition of his new status, his grandfather asked him to take his place as regent during his trips abroad, to receive the credentials of foreign ambassadors, and to act as host at official luncheons. In December 1972, Carl Gustaf attracted international attention when he replaced the ailing King as host at the Nobel Prize ceremony. Further study since completing his formal training has broadened his understanding of his country. He has made frequent visits to the Cabinet ministries, the Royal Chancery, and the Riksdag (Parliament); attended a government course for diplomats; studied economics at Stockholm University; and received additional military training. Twice in 1972 he visited London, to observe the functioning of a private bank and of the Swedish Chamber of Commerce there. At the time of his grandfather's death, on September 15, 1973, Carl Gustaf was attending a command course at the Royal National Defense College.

On September 19, 1973 he was formally installed as King Carl XVI Gustaf, taking the oath of allegiance in a glittering ceremony at the Stockholm Palace. Dressed in an admiral's uniform, draped with two elaborate orders, the young King presented a "striking, dignified figure," according to news reports. From his solid silver throne, flanked by a squad of soldiers outfitted in eighteenth-century tricorns, he delivered a eulogy to his grandfather, whom he characterized as "a model king for a democratic society" and as an inspiration to him. He announced that his royal motto would be "for Sweden—moving with the times," reflecting "the significant new orientation of our society." After his installation, the King, his four sisters, and other members of the royal family were summoned to the palace balcony five times by people gathered in the courtyard chanting, "We want to see our King!"

Carl Gustaf—who at twenty-seven is the world's youngest reigning monarch—prefers the title "Swedish King" to the more formal title "King of Sweden, the Goths, and the Wends," by which his predecessors were known. "I want to be a

CARL XVI GUSTAF, KING OF SWEDEN

modern monarch," he has said, as quoted in the Vancouver (British Columbia) *Sun* (September 17, 1973). "I will try to understand the reactions of young people and to keep up with the rapid developments in Sweden and abroad." In practice, the King's traditional duties and prerogatives are becoming practically nonexistent. According to the English-language labor monthly *Sweden Now* (June 1971), while most Swedes continue to look with indulgence on their monarchy, "whose members open exhibits and races, and add a bit of color to the weekly magazines," the King is expected to "become primarily a public relations representative for his country." Under the new Constitution, effective in 1975, the King keeps the formal title of head of state but forfeits his traditional rights to act as supreme commander of the armed forces, to appoint a Premier in a Cabinet crisis, to preside at weekly Cabinet meetings, and to open the Riksdag—except at the request of its president. Another constitutional revision, yet to be approved, would divest the King of his role as head of the established Lutheran Church. His sole link with the nation's governing process under the new Constitution is a report on state affairs, to be submitted to him by the Premier three times a year.

Six feet one inch tall, with longish, wavy blond hair and blue eyes, Carl XVI Gustaf is "affable and easygoing." Considering himself an "ordinary guy," he prefers to be addressed simply as Carl Gustaf. He once said, "I would rather have chosen a career as an officer or a farmer if I had not been predestined to become King." According to a profile in the New York *Times* (September 17, 1973), he indulges in exercise to restrain a "tendency to portliness, caused by a liking for French and Italian food and the appropriate wines." Fond of the outdoors and of hunting and fishing, he likes to relax by driving a tractor or working in the stables of his private manor, Stenhammar, where he runs a large modern farm.

Once described in an Italian magazine as "Europe's leading Lothario," Carl Gustaf has often been seen dancing in chic night spots, and his love for attractive women, fast cars, and stylish clothes, especially colorful ties, is well known. Fond of revelry, he once arrived at a Swedish winter carnival disguised as Muhammad Ali's manager, in blackface, with baggy suit, dark glasses, and a large cigar. Officials of the royal court take pains to refute the King's image as a "swinger," and in fact, that image appears to be changing. According to the Vancouver *Sun* (September 17, 1973), "The playboy prince of a few years ago, who was fond of skiing, sailing, and whooping it up with pretty girls in Stockholm or Mediterranean discotheques, has developed into a more serious young man who knows what is required of him."

References

Keesing's Contemporary Archives p26,133 + 1973
N Y Times p8 S 17 '73; p7 S 20 '73
Washington Post A p24 S 20 '73 por

CASALS, ROSEMARY (kä-säls')

Sept. 16, 1948- Tennis player
Address: b. United States Lawn Tennis Association, 51 E. 42d St., New York 10017

Close behind Billie Jean King in money-making clout on the women's professional golf circuit is her friend Rosemary Casals, a fiery, plucky little player and one of the quickest on the courts. Among other titles, Miss Casals has won the United States indoor doubles, with Mrs. King in 1967, 1968, and 1971 and with Virginia Wade in 1972. Many Americans not ordinarily interested in tennis will remember her best perhaps for her acerbic commentary during the network televising of the celebrated "battle of the sexes" on September 20, 1973, when Billie Jean King trounced the hubris out of "macho" tennis hustler Bobby Riggs.

Rosemary Casals was born in San Francisco, California on September 16, 1948. In the paternal line of descent, which goes back to Barcelona, Spain by way of El Salvador, Central America, she is the grandniece of the late great cellist Pablo Casals—a relationship she can never be accused of exploiting. "I get wild when people keep bringing up Pablo . . . ," she told Hugh McIlvanney of the *Observer* (July 9, 1967). "I've never met the man. . . . When I'm asked about him I feel that he is taking part of my identity away. If people know me I want it to be because of what I've done."

Miss Casals grew up in a modest home at Grove and Buchanan streets in San Francisco, where her father, Manuel Casals y Bordas, an immigrant from San Salvador, ran a small stamp-machine business until his retirement. Once an excellent soccer player, he turned to tennis after suffering a serious injury on the playing field, and he introduced Rosemary—as well as her older sister, Victoria—to his new game. From the time he taught her the fundamentals, on a court near Golden Gate Park when she was eight and nine, he has been her chief mentor. "He knows me so well, and I think it's easier for him to tell instinctively when something is wrong with my game," she told Kim Chapin of *Sports Illustrated* (October 24, 1966). "I've heard of tennis parents who put too much pressure on their kids, but that's not the way it is with my father and me."

A bright student who liked to read, Miss Casals had high academic potential, but by the time she entered George Washington High School in San Francisco she had been winning junior tournaments for several years and was more interested in tennis than in school. "I made them [the teachers] understand that school was secondary and tennis was my life," she told Catherine Stott of the *Guardian* (May 7, 1971). "I never graduated out of any classes because I was never there; always off playing tennis." She pursued tennis on her own, rejecting membership on the high school tennis team as "a waste of time."

By the end of her fifteenth year Rosemary Casals, already possessing virtually every trophy available in California, was ready for national and international competition. In 1964 Billie Jean King asked her to be her doubles partner at Forest Hills, and Miss Casals gladly accepted. She dismisses any suggestion that there was ever anything Svengalian about her relationship with Mrs. King, as Hugh McIlvanney reported after interviewing her for the *Observer*. McIlvanney quoted her: "I knew I was capable of being a good effective partner for her. We've been close friends ever since, but when we get out on the court it's mainly just to discuss each other's mistakes or to talk about strategy. She doesn't coach me."

The United States Lawn Tennis Association ranked Miss Casals eleventh in 1965 and third in 1966, when she and Billie Jean King won the national hard-court and indoor doubles and reached the quarter-finals in the women's doubles at Wimbledon. Also in 1966, she had two victories over Mrs. King (who then shared first place among American women players with Nancy Richey) and wins over Kerry Melville and Maria Bueno (then the best woman player in the world).

At Forest Hills during the United States nationals in September 1966 Kim Chapin of *Sports Illustrated* (October 24, 1966) heard more than one spectator remark that Miss Casals had "a lot of courage." Chapin observed, "That is an accurate summation of her game. Her forehand is hit with tremendous overspin; and when she serves, it is sometimes hard to believe that Rosie is not a man. Her service is rarely tempered and is hit with all the twist and body gymnastics of a Tony Trabert. . . . The missing fraction is her backhand, which so far tends to be a defensive chop."

Chapin quoted Harry Hopman, the elder statesman of Australian tennis, regarding Miss Casals: "Lack of experience in choosing the right ball to bear down on makes her erratic, but her court sense is so strong and her balance so good that it won't be long before she is able to control her tendency to overhit. If I judge her temperament right she is going to have the confidence not only to attack courageously and go for the lines on her passing shots, but also to lob effectively in defense—and that is something the present top women players sadly lack." Hopman added: "Rosemary is the tomboy type and a little wayward, and I think this will help her game, although I must add she is sure to shock a few officials before she arrives at the top."

In February 1967 Miss Casals won the women's singles crown in the Wills Invitational tournament in Auckland, New Zealand by defeating Françoise Durr of France in straight sets. By the time she reached Wimbledon she was being called that tournament's most improved player. "I've played a lot more internationally," Miss Casals explained. "I've tightened up and don't play many careless points. And I've improved my concentration. I realized that most of my reason for losing was lack of concentration. You just can't allow your mind to drift away. You've got to control your mind as well as your play."

She lost to Britain's Ann Jones in the semifinals at Wimbledon that year but at Berlin in June she and Billie Jean King won the Federation Cup for the United States by their victories over, respectively, Virginia Wade and Mrs. Jones. In July Miss Casals beat Mrs. King in the semifinals of the national clay court matches in Milwaukee, and in November she prevailed over Mrs. Court in the quarter-finals of the Victoria championships in Melbourne. In the semi-finals of the United States championships she lost to Maria Bueno.

In February 1968 Billie Jean King and Rosemary Casals added the United States indoor crown to their United States grass-court and Wimbledon doubles titles, by defeating Mary Ann Eisel and Kathy Harter 6-2, 6-2 in Winchester, Massachusetts. Later in the same year Miss Casals again reached the semi-finals of the United States championships, and again she was beaten, by Nancy Richey.

On April 1, 1968 George MacCall, president of the National Tennis League, announced that Miss Casals and Mrs. King, along with Ann Jones and Françoise Durr, had signed professional contracts and would therefore join the pro tour. In her first open victory on the tour, Miss Casals upset Maria Bueno 6-4, 6-1 for the first prize of $1,500 in the Pacific Southwest tournament at Los Angeles on September 22, 1968.

In the final of the Tasmania open in Hobart, Australia on January 5, 1969 Kerry Melville defeated Rosemary Casals 6-3, 6-3. In the United States open at Forest Hills in September 1970 Miss Casals vanquished Virginia Wade in the semi-finals but lost the finals to Margaret Court 6-2, 2-6, 6-1. At that point her expected income for the year was about $25,000, sixth highest among women players. "For a woman," she commented, "that isn't bad." On September 7, 1970 she led a group of female players in issuing a threat to boycott future tournaments unless three demands were met: purses for women at least

ROSEMARY CASALS

a third as high as those for men; equal exposure in center-court matches; and better coverage in the news media. She explained that the *ad hoc* protest against sexist discrimination in tennis did not necessarily reflect blanket agreement with the women's liberation movement in general.

The protest was effective. With better spotlighting of their matches, women players began attracting larger crowds, and the prizes were boosted accordingly. In March 1971, when she was the second-leading money winner on the Virginia Slims tour, Rosemary Casals defeated Jane Bartkowicz in the quarter-final round of the $15,000 Virginia Slims invitational tournament. In 1972 she won a total of $70,000 in prize money, an amount second among women only to that garnered by Billie Jean King, $119,000. In third place was Kerry Melville, with $55,000.

The richest single prize in the history of women's sports was the $30,000 Miss Casals took in the 1973 Family Circle tournament, in which she defeated Nancy Gunter in the final match, 3-6, 6-1, 7-5. According to a report in the New York *Times* (May 6, 1973), "Miss Casals has had many brilliant moments in her international career . . . but never has she displayed such commitment to purpose and concentration as she did during this four-day tournament."

"Most of her career so far has been spent chasing the two top stars on the women's pro tour, Billie Jean King and Margaret Court," Phil Elderkin wrote in the *Christian Science Monitor* (August 27, 1973). "Their matches are always close, eye-compelling, and highly competitive. And right now, according to her rivals, Rosemary Casals is playing the best tennis of her career. . . . Miss Casals, who may have the fastest legs in women's tennis, says that any slow surface [clay or synthetic] is great for her game." He quoted her as saying, "I don't like hard surfaces where somebody hits the ball bangbang and it's all over. And I hate to play on grass. In fact, you have no control on grass." She has made great progress in overcoming what she has long regarded as her two main weaknesses: dwelling on her errors—she sometimes scolds herself audibly—and "tightening up" her forehand. Aside from her speed, her strongest points are generally recognized to be the variety of her volleys, her strength of service, and the arrow-like trajectory of her shots.

At five feet two and a half inches and 118 pounds, Miss Casals is, in the hyperbole of Phil Elderkin, "so small she could hide in a match box." In his *Christian Science Monitor* article Elderkin continued: "But there is power in her legs and a dash of Pancho Gonzales in her serve. And with an elastic head band holding her black hair, she looks as though she might have wandered off some cowboy and Indian movie set." In his article in the *Observer* Hugh McIlvanney described her face and manner: "Her features are not fine and the slightly projecting mouth makes her habitual expression an unsurly pout. When she speaks she frequently closes the lids over her dark eyes, breaks without warning into a shrugging smile. She is sharp and lively, and few are in a hurry to leave her company."

Rosie Casals, as she is known to her friends, lives in San Francisco, where she leads a single life. "I don't feel an urgency to get married, nor to get involved with anyone," she has said. "I'm happier doing what I'm doing and being my own boss." She has a reputation for brash, outspoken nonconformity. According to newspaper accounts, she keeps late hours; reads herself to sleep (Maugham and Metalious have been among the soporifics); has a big appetite ("tennis makes you hungry"); smokes an occasional cigar; and has been known to drink, among other exotic mixtures, gin and green chartreuse with a beer chaser. She plays the guitar "often," as she has said, "but not well."

References

Christian Sci Mon p13 Ag 27 '73 por
Guardian p11 My 7 '71 por
London Observer p16 Jl 9 '67 por
N Y Post p19 S 12 '70 por
Sports Ill 25:68+ O 24 '66 por
World Who's Who of Women (1973)

CHAPIN, SCHUYLER G(ARRISON) (chā'pən skī'lər)

Feb. 13, 1923- Opera manager
Address: b. Metropolitan Opera House, Lincoln Center, New York 10023; h. 901 Lexington Ave., New York 10021

With the sudden death of Goeran Gentele in the summer of 1972, Schuyler G. Chapin was unexpectedly thrust into the stagefront spotlight at New York's vast Metropolitan Opera as acting general manager for the 1972-73 season. Before the end of that season, Chapin had done so well that President George S. Moore and the board of directors of the Metropolitan Opera Association voted unanimously to strike "acting" from his title and confirm his appointment to the Met's tough but prestigious top post for a three-year term. It was a bittersweet achievement for Chapin, who had been brought to the Met the season before by his good friend Gentele. Ironically, Chapin had first dreamed of being manager of the Metropolitan Opera at the age of thirteen; his subsequent experience in the business end of the performing arts may now enable him to save the Met from its massive deficit and labor problems.

The oldest of three sons, Schuyler Garrison Chapin was born on February 13, 1923 to L. H. Paul Chapin, a lawyer turned investment counselor, and Leila (Burden) Chapin at Miss Lippincott's Hospital in New York City. His family, which dates back to the Nieuw Amsterdam origins of New York, numbers among its eminent ancestors Philip Schuyler, a Revolutionary War general. One of Chapin's aunts founded the multilingual international literary review *Botteghe Oscure* and another aunt, Katherine Garrison Chapin, became a respected poet. Raised by nurses and governesses in a townhouse on New York's fashionable upper East Side, the three Chapin boys seldom saw their socially prominent parents. "I didn't even know my parents," Schuyler Chapin told Stephen E. Rubin in an interview for a New York *Times Magazine* profile (September 23, 1973). "They used to come in and say good morning and good evening. We didn't meet very often." Although the family was not especially interested in music, Chapin recalled, as quoted in *Opera News* (September 1972), that "whenever *Manon* was broadcast . . . , the house was commanded into silence and my father would sit and listen, a box of Kleenex at the ready." Chapin's passionate interest in opera began in 1936 when, at the age of thirteen, he attended his first opera at the Metropolitan Opera House, escorting Mrs. August Belmont, a friend of his mother's and a celebrated Met patroness, to a performance of one of Wagner's operas.

Chapin spent much of his youth in Washington, D.C. visiting his aunt Katherine, who was married to Francis Biddle, Attorney General under President Franklin D. Roosevelt. When Chapin's father died in 1938, Biddle, an equitable disciplinarian, assumed responsibility for the boy's welfare. Chapin looks back fondly on the Biddles as surrogate parents who took him into their lives and encouraged him to follow his own interests. After studying at the Allen Stevenson School, a private school in Manhattan, Chapin attended Millbrook Prep School in Millbrook, New York, where by his own admission, he was "a rotten student," but had the good fortune to come in contact with Nathaniel Abbot, a Latin teacher whose informal music appreciation class was decisive in shaping the youngster's musical tastes and appetite. Chapin credits a recording of Paul Dukas' orchestral work, *The Sorcerer's Apprentice*, with convincing him that he should seriously study music.

In 1940 Chapin enrolled at the Longy School of Music in Cambridge, Massachusetts to study piano and composition with the famed Nadia Boulanger. Miss Boulanger, after examining several of Chapin's compositions, ended her student's dream of a creative career in music by telling him plainly, "My dear, you haven't any talent." However, she encouraged her disappointed pupil to investigate the other possibilities open to him in music, including a career as an impresario. Impatient to begin his career, Chapin left school before receiving a degree. After a brief sojourn at Harvard as a special unenrolled student, Chapin accepted a $15-a-week job as an NBC page in October 1941, aspiring to a position on the network's Artists Bureau. The federal government, however, ruling that networks could not be both buyers and sellers of talent forced the national broadcasting companies to close their artists' bureaus. Chapin remained with NBC as a page and as a newsroom assistant. During World War II he served as a newscaster for the Voice of America and for NBC, broadcasting in English to the Arab nations. A chance for more active service came in January of 1943 when Chapin joined the United States Army Air Force as an aviation cadet. Assigned to the China-Burma-India Theatre, he flew ninety-five round-trip missions over the Himalayas at the controls of a twin-engine C-47 ferrying troops and materiel, racking up some 2,000 flight hours. Chapin, who attained the rank of first lieutenant, was awarded the Air Medal for his wartime efforts.

Discharged from the Air Force in April 1946, Chapin returned to NBC, where he sold television time for several years before joining the staff of Jinx Falkenberg and Tex McCrary, the popular radio and television personalities. As the general manager of their daily TV and radio show, Chapin supervised a staff of twenty people. After two "difficult" years he got in touch with Arthur Judson of Columbia Artists Management, Inc., the world's largest booking and concert management agency, who promised the eager young war veteran a job if he first acquired some experience elsewhere. Following Judson's advice, Chapin, in collaboration with Skitch Henderson, organized a pop concert series at Carnegie Hall in the spring of 1953. The budding impresarios "lost [their] shirts," as Chapin has put it.

Returning to see Judson at CAMI, Schuyler Chapin was given a minor job in the publicity department. Later in 1953, he was named tour manager for Jascha Heifetz and, for the next few years, he accompanied the artist on his frequent cross-country road trips. Promoted to Midwest sales representative, Chapin handled concert bookings and personal appearances for CAMI clients in the "Kansas-Nebraska-Oklahoma circuit." Dispirited by long separations from his family, he decided to take several months' vacation and, with his wife and four young sons, moved to the isle of Eigg off the western coast of Scotland where the Chapins set up housekeeping in a seventeenth-century stone farmhouse belonging to

SCHUYLER G. CHAPIN

Lord Runciman, a cousin by marriage of Chapin's father. "We had no electricity and no icebox," Chapin recalled to an interviewer for the New Yorker (March 7, 1964). "It was a marvelous place—a great place for taking stock." A transatlantic telephone call from Goddard Lieberson, president of Columbia Records, interrupted Chapin's idyll. When Lieberson offered Chapin the codirectorship of Columbia's Masterworks division, Chapin readily accepted. Beginning work in October 1959, Chapin supervised the recordings of such composers, conductors and artists as Igor Stravinsky, Eugene Ormandy, George Szell, Isaac Stern, and Rudolf Serkin. Six months later, he became sole director of the Masterworks division, making it, in his words, "the best damn classical-music department in the world." In 1962 he was named vice-president of creative services at Columbia Records.

Gradually, Chapin began to feel trapped in the business end of the musical profession. When asked by William Schuman, then President of the Lincoln Center for the Performing Arts, to recommend a new program director, Chapin suggested himself, as Schuman had hoped he would. As vice-president of programming, a position he held from 1964 to 1969, Schuyler Chapin was responsible for all professional theatrical and musical activities at Lincoln Center. Among the highlights of his administration were the inauguration of the famous annual New York Film Festival, the National Student Film Festival, and the memorable 1967 and 1968 Lincoln Center Festivals that introduced the Rome Opera and the Hamburg State Opera to American audiences. Chapin tried to bring Gentele and his opera company to Lincoln Center for a brief season in 1969, but insufficient funds made that impossible. When financial difficulties forced a cutback in the Center's programming activities, Chapin accepted an offer from Leonard Bernstein to join Amberson Productions, his television and motion picture production company, as an executive producer. His activities for the Amberson group included coproducing Leonard Bernstein's *Mass*, which Mrs. Aristotle Onassis had commissioned for the opening of the John F. Kennedy Center for the Performing Arts in Washington, D.C. Chapin was awarded an Emmy for *Beethoven's Birthday*, a Bernstein television special filmed in Vienna to commemorate the composer's 200th anniversary.

It was during his tenure at Lincoln Center that Chapin first met Goeran Gentele, who was then heading the Stockholm Royal Opera Company. According to Fern Marja Eckman of the New York *Post* (August 12, 1972), Isaac Stern was responsible for bringing the two men together. The violinist reportedly suggested that Chapin contact Gentele in 1964 while the New Yorker was in Europe. The two impresarios immediately hit it off and their families became fast friends.

With the approaching retirement of the Metropolitan Opera Company's general manager, Sir Rudolf Bing (at a reported annual pension of $47,000) at the end of the 1971-72 concert season, the Met was in the market for a new man to fill the top post. Such prominent musical figures as Leonard Bernstein, Julius Rudel, Erich Leinsdorf and Peter Mennin were widely discussed as possible successors to Bing, but Schuyler Chapin vigorously promoted the candidacy of Goeran Gentele and, on December 9, 1970 Gentele was chosen to assume the post at the opening of the Metropolitan Opera's 1972-73 season.

After he was appointed to head the Met, Goeran Gentele asked Schuyler G. Chapin to join him in the difficult task of managing the gargantuan opera company, which has a payroll of some 1,000 full-time employees. Chapin, who was then in London for a Bernstein recording of the Verdi *Requiem* at St. Paul's Cathedral, resisted the temptation at first, but a letter from his wife Betty (who had never before intervened in Chapin's job decisions) urged him to reconsider. Finally, with Bernstein's blessing, he accepted the offer to become Gentele's right-hand man as assistant manager of the Metropolitan and his chief administrative aide.

During the 1971-72 Met season, the Swedish manager and his assistant Chapin were on the scene as observers only, but nonetheless managed to make many friends. One of their most important moves was to appoint Rafael Kubelik as the Met's first artistic director, and James Levine as principal conductor. The tragic death of Gentele on July 18, 1972 in an auto accident on the island of Sardinia, just eighteen days after taking over from Sir Rudolf Bing, led the Metropolitan Opera Association to name Schuyler G. Chapin as acting general manager with the mission of carrying out the original Gentele plans for the following season. One of Chapin's first decisions was to go ahead with the opening night performance of a striking new production of Bizet's *Carmen* that Gentele himself had intended to direct; Bodo Igesz was called upon to fill in as director. Another Chapin decision was to proceed with low-cost productions of old chamber operas or avant-garde works for small audiences that the

Swede had destined for the Forum or "Mini-Met," on the lines of Milan's Piccolo Scala. He also decided to carry out the "look-ins" that his friend Gentele had designed to show youngsters what goes into making an opera performance; Chapin's personal contribution was obtaining the services of Danny Kaye to act as master of ceremonies.

By the end of his improvised first season as interim replacement, it was clear that Schuyler Chapin had done better than anyone dared hope. Writing in *New York* magazine (April 23, 1973), critic Alan Rich undoubtedly spoke for his colleagues in noting that Chapin's season as acting manager had been "resoundingly successful" and expressed the conviction that it would be "cruel, wasteful and unrealistic to throw [Chapin's] position to the wolves at this juncture." The Opera Association apparently shared that conviction, because a month later it unanimously voted to give Chapin a three-year contract to carry on as full general manager of the Met, probably the most powerful job in music today.

In the opinion of most observers, Schuyler G. Chapin is a hard worker and a considerate, tactful listener who catches on quickly and holds firmly to his decisions once he has made up his mind, as more than one temperamental diva is said to have discovered. One of his avowed goals is to attract the world's most exciting talent to the Met, and he likewise plans to try new methods for covering the company's mounting deficit, probably his most pressing problem. One possible step might consist of cable television. The Met's staggering $7,700,000 deficit, brought down to $2,800,000 since last season, thanks to public and corporate contributions, forced Chapin to announce reluctantly towards the end of October 1973 that he was cancelling Gentele's Mini-Met project as a fund-saving gesture, although he regretted having to forego even temporarily what he considers an important artistic development. The Met's plans for free opera performances in New York parks in the summer of 1974, and for a new production of Mozart's *Don Giovanni* slated for the spring of 1974, also had to be cancelled in September of 1973. The current financial crisis, described as the Met's worst since 1932, seems to confirm Chapin's belief that the end of private philanthropy is probably in sight, and that federal funds will hereafter be needed to support such cultural institutions.

In his demanding new job as head of the Met's twelfth administration Chapin is aided by his wife, the former Elizabeth Steinway of the celebrated family of piano manufacturers, whom he married in 1947. As official Metropolitan Opera hostess, Betty Chapin, a former harpist, tries to be on hand in the general manager's box four or five nights a week to accompany the varied assortment of guests they make it their policy to invite. The Chapins' four college-age sons are Henry Burden, Theodore Steinway and Samuel Garrison (who are twins), and Miles Whitworth. The Chapin family, when at home, occupy a comfortable nine-room East Side co-op apartment in

Manhattan; they also maintain a rustic hideaway outside Plymouth near Cape Cod.

Schuyler G. Chapin credits three "terrible" years of analysis with having saved his life after he collapsed on the street one day in 1966 with severe bleeding ulcers. Six feet tall and weighing 176 pounds, blue-eyed and with a thick shock of brown hair, Chapin is an early riser who smokes eight or ten filter cigarettes a day but not until after lunch, and refrains from drinking until it is time for a couple of vodka martinis before dinner. He is a Democrat and a Unitarian, and is listed in the Social Register. Chapin is thought to earn between half and three-quarters of the $100,000 annual salary that was given Bing towards the end of his twenty-two-year reign. He is vice-president of the Bagby Music Lovers Foundation and a trustee of the Naumburg Foundation and the LeRoy Hospital. His clubs are the Century and the Coffee House. He holds the New York State Conspicuous Service Cross and a Christopher Award.

References

N Y Post II p13 Ag 12 '72 por
N Y Times p24 Jl 20 '72 por; p39 My 9 '73 por
N Y Times Mag p36+ S 23 '73 pors
New Yorker 40:40+ Mr 7 '64
Newsday II p3+ Ag 27 '72 pors
Opera News 37:13 S '72
Time 101:51+ Mr 5 '73 por
International Who's Who, 1973-74
Who's Who in the East, 1974-75

CHER

May 20, 1946- Singer; entertainer; actress
Address: b. c/o CBS Television Network, 51 W. 52d St., New York 10019

Until mid-1974 the most glamorous sex symbol on TV was Cher Bono, the lithe costar of CBS-TV's *The Sonny and Cher Comedy Hour*. Every Wednesday Cher dazzled television viewers with her decolletage, her comic vamp routines, the well-timed putdowns she directed to her husband and costar, Sonny, and her belting delivery of songs in a voice that according to one admiring critic sounds "like a cross between a mating call and a sonic boom."

Cher began her matrimonial and professional partnership with Sonny in 1964, while she was still a teen-ager. Within a year Sonny and Cher were the acknowledged sweethearts of the rock world, singing before ecstatic sold-out audiences and toting up a series of best-selling records. When, in the late 1960's, their youthful audience proved fickle, the couple proved their versatility by performing for more mature nightclub audiences. They also became the stars of their own TV show, which premièred during the summer of 1971 and was a staple of the CBS network until the middle of 1974. Once again a popular record-

CHER

ing star, Cher may be heard on albums both alone and with her husband. One of her best-selling discs was "Half-Breed," a song that alluded to her part American Indian ancestry. Sonny Bono filed court papers for a legal separation from Cher in February 1974. The couple's show business act ended shortly thereafter.

Besides being part Cherokee, Cher is of Armenian, Turkish, and French ancestry. She was born Cherilyn LaPiere in El Centro, California on May 20, 1946, the daughter of Georgia, a former fashion model, and Gilbert LaPiere, a bank manager. Her parents were divorced when she was young, and she grew up in Los Angeles with her mother and her sister, Georgeanne.

Determined to be an actress, Cher LaPiere dropped out of high school in her junior year and began studying drama with Jeff Corey. A year or so later she met a young songwriter and record producer, Salvatore "Sonny" Bono, on a double date, and the two became inseparable. Because her parents thought she was too young to marry, the couple eloped to Tijuana, Mexico, where they were wed on October 27, 1964.

"Cher seemed to be going in no direction at all," Sonny Bono recalled for James Bawden in an interview for the Toronto *Globe and Mail* (September 11, 1971). Impressed by her robust contralto, Sonny persuaded Cher to concentrate on singing instead of acting. The pair began singing backgrounds for recordings by famous soloists and graduated to small nightclubs. At first they called themselves Caesar and Cleo, but soon switched to their own long-time nicknames, Sonny and Cher.

Financed by a borrowed $168, Sonny and Cher recorded Sonny's song "Baby Don't Go," early in 1965. When it caught on in Los Angeles and Dallas, they quickly brought out a second cut, "Just You." Their next record, "I Got You, Babe," which was released in June 1965 and established them as recording stars, has sold more than 3,000,000 copies over the years. By the fall of 1965 Sonny and Cher had five records on the best-seller charts, an achievement that has only been rivaled by Elvis Presley. With their records on the best-seller charts, Sonny and Cher began drawing crowds at rock concerts and other appearances. Late in 1965 they were mobbed at the Los Angeles airport by 10,000 adoring young fans, and the following year they conducted a triumphant four-week European tour.

Sonny and Cher's success owed as much to their image as to their talent. They became the symbol of teen-age love and marriage (even though Sonny was twenty-nine when they married), and their young fans doted on their playful, affectionate way with each other, and their kooky, look-alike fashions. When Sonny's Beatle haircut and Cher's hip-hugging bell-bottoms got them kicked out of restaurants and hotels, such adult disapproval only enhanced their popularity with the young. Besides bell-bottom trousers, the couple favored brightly colored shirts, knitted tops, and fur vests. Most of their outfits were designed by Cher, who successfully marketed some of her designs for distribution in stores under her own label.

In 1967 the Bonos starred in *Good Times* (Columbia), which New York *Times* film critic Richard Shepard (August 3, 1967) called a "colorful, sprightly bit of good-humored silliness." Playing themselves in the film, the couple had the opportunity to clown, sing, and show off their wardrobes. It was, in short, an ideal vehicle for the dynamic duo, but it failed to score with the youth market. By mid-1967 young Americans had become infatuated with drugs and acid rock, and the innocent folk rock sound and wholesome image of the Bonos seemed bland to them. Sonny and Cher were not only outside the mainstream of the drug culture, but campaigned against drug use, even making an anti-marijuana film for the federal government that was distributed to high schools.

Attempting to woo back the young, the Bonos made *Chastity* (American International, 1969), an earnest nonmusical saga about an alienated young runaway (Cher) and her Search for Meaning in Life and a way out of her identity crisis. Critics panned the film, which was written and produced by Sonny, as superficial and banal, but some were impressed by Cher's performance. "Cher has a marvelous quality that often makes you forget the lines you are hearing. Her manner can be described as a combination of tough, disinterested, unhappy, self-critical, and deadpan, offset by sudden jaunty movements of her flexible body," wrote William Wolf of *Cue* (August 16, 1969).

The Bonos reportedly lost $500,000 when *Chastity* bombed at the box office. Realizing that their future as entertainers depended on their ability to recruit a new audience, the Bonos made the difficult decision to go into nightclubs. "It was Sonny's idea," Cher told a *Life* magazine reporter (March 17, 1972). "I've got to admit I fought him all the way." Abandoning their hippie garb, the couple dressed more conventionally for their nightclub appearances, and Cher began wearing the low-cut dresses for which she has become famous. Persevering through a series of one-night stands, the couple began to receive more prestigious bookings. In June of 1970 they made their debut in New York City at the Empire Room of the Waldorf-Astoria Hotel. Gradually the couple refined their comedy routine, which was based on Cher's deadpan delivery of putdowns of her husband. "At first Sonny didn't like it much," Cher told the *Life* reporter. "He'd say, 'Cher, you've got a smart mouth.' But it worked out."

By 1971 the Bonos were making guest appearances on TV shows, one of which they made as substitute hosts for *The Merv Griffin Show*. CBS programming director Fred Silverman so liked the way they handled that spot that he signed them for six one-hour shows in the summer of 1971. *The Sonny and Cher Comedy Hour* had its première on Sunday, August 1, 1971 at 8:30 P.M. Although the critical response was mixed, viewer reaction was unequivocal, and CBS scheduled the Bonos for its midseason lineup, beginning on Monday, December 27, 1971 at 10:00 P.M. Soon they were pulling in 40 percent of the audience in their Monday night time slot, or about 30,000,000 viewers. During the 1972-73 season *The Sonny and Cher Comedy Hour* was shown at 8:00 P.M. on Friday nights, and in the fall of 1973 it began its third year at 8:00 P.M. on Wednesdays.

Although Sonny and Cher conveyed the idea that they were hip young marrieds with their cool blend of love and sarcasm, their popularity proved that they bridged the generation gap, perhaps because the concept of their show—the man who plays fall guy to a mischievous woman or child—has long been a standby of mass entertainment. As Henry Ehrlich wrote in *Good Housekeeping* (May 1972), "The show sometimes echoes *Laugh-In*, but its real ancestors are George Burns and Gracie Allen, Edgar Bergen and Charlie McCarthy, Fred Allen and Portland Hoffa." For many TV critics, however, the chief attraction of the Sonny and Cher show was Cher's supercharged song delivery and her exotic beauty, which was enhanced by the $10,000 worth of clothes she wore for each show.

In recent years Cher has become a recording star in her own right, with hit songs like "Gypsies, Tramps and Thieves" and "Half Breed" to her credit. Her solo albums include *Cher's Golden Greats* (Liberty), *3614 Jackson Highway* (Atco), *This Is* (Sunset), *Cher* (Kapp), *Foxy Lady* (Kapp), *Superpak* (United Artists), *Superpak II* (United Artists), *Half Breed* (MCA), and *Bittersweet White Light* (MCA). Her recent albums with Sonny include *All I Ever Need Is You* (Kapp), *Live* (Kapp), which was recorded during one of their nightclub performances, and *The Two of Us* (Atco), which consists of old releases of their hit songs.

Like the silent film stars of the palmy days of the 1920's, Cher Bono and her husband lived in old-fashioned Hollywood splendor in a twenty-five-room mansion in the exclusive Bel Air section of Los Angeles. Their home abounded in antiques, servants (a housekeeper, cook, chauffeur, full-time secretary, and a bodyguard), and automobiles (three Mercedeses, a Ferrari, a Cadillac, and a jeep). The Bonos are the parents of a daughter, Chastity, born in 1969, who occasionally appeared in their nightclub act and on their television show.

With her willowy five feet seven and a half inches of height and her 110 pounds of weight, the black-haired, brown-eyed Cher has the ability to look elegant in almost anything. A lover of clothes, with an acute fashion sense, she has been voted one of America's ten best-dressed women and often adorns the glossy pages of *Vogue*. Besides amassing her large wardrobe, Cher enjoys collecting jewelry of all kinds, especially handmade American Indian pieces of turquoise and silver. In the future, Cher Bono hopes to pursue an acting career in films.

References

Good H 174:105+ My '72 pors
N Y Sunday News mag p6 My 21 '67 pors
N Y Times II p5 Jl 9 '67 por
Toronto Globe and Mail p23 S 11 '71 por
Who's Who in America, 1972-73
Who's Who of American Women, 1974-75

JAMES COCO

COCO, JAMES

Mar. 21, 1929- Actor
Address: b. c/o Agency for the Performing Arts, 120 W. 57th St., New York 10019

No fewer than twenty years of struggle brought James Coco the overnight stardom he had dreamed of while attending movies as a boy in the Bronx. Beginning his acting career as a teen-ager in the late 1940's, he performed in more than one hundred plays before his big break came in the 1968 Off-Broadway production *Next*. As the fat, nearly bald, forty-year-old Marion Cheever, mistakenly called for induction into the Army, he won not only glowing reviews, but also the lead in *Last of the Red Hot Lovers*. When the Neil Simon comedy opened in December 1969, Coco was proclaimed a Broadway star. Besieged with offers, he appeared on TV specials and talk shows and at the conclusion of his run in *Lovers* portrayed Sancho Panza in the film version of *Man of La Mancha*. During the fall of 1973 he starred in his own television series, the short-lived but critically admired *Calucci's Department*.

James Emil Coco, the son of Feliche and Ida (Detestes) Coco, was born in the Little Italy section of Manhattan on March 21, 1929. When he was still an infant, the family, including an older brother and sister, moved to the Pelham Bay section of the Bronx, where he lived until his late teens. Generously fed the customary pasta of an Italian-American family, he was an overweight child and, except for a period or two of careful dieting, always remained heavy. At about the age of eight he began to attend neighborhood movies regularly with his mother. Fasci-

nated by the film stars he saw, he dreamed of becoming an actor—an ambition that did not have the approval of his somewhat strict father, a shoemaker who made the boy, from the age of ten, work at shining shoes in the shoe shop. His mother died when he was thirteen years old. To absorb some of the glamour of the theatre, he spent his early teen years hanging around the stage doors of Manhattan theatres, seeking autographs from famous Hollywood entertainers making personal appearances.

As soon as he had graduated from Evander Childs High School, at the age of seventeen, Coco embarked on his career in the theatre as stage manager and actor for Clare Tree Major's Children's Theater. For the next three years he traveled about the country by truck, playing such parts as Old King Cole, Humpty Dumpty, and the Kublai Khan. After returning to New York he auditioned for Broadway and appeared with stock companies out of town. Often unemployed, he supported himself with a variety of jobs outside the theatre, such as short-order cook, hotel switchboard operator, messenger for a dental supply company, and a Santa Claus impersonator at Gimbel's. He lived at that time in several cheap rooming houses in Manhattan's West Fifties. Not until he reached his late twenties did he finally get a part in a Broadway show, the minor role of Tabu in *Hotel Paradiso*, a riotous bedroom farce that starred Bert Lahr and Angela Lansbury and opened at the Henry Miller Theatre on April 11, 1957 for a three-month run. Later that year he went on national tour in the Constance Bennett company of *Auntie Mame*, playing the roles of Dr. Waldo and Mr. Shurr for the 1957-58 road season.

Back in New York, Coco studied with Uta Hagen at the Berghof Studio, continued to seek work in the theatre, and won occasional small parts on television. He was signed for the revue *Darwin's Theories*, which proved an instant flop at the Madison Avenue Playhouse on October 18, 1960. Early the following year he played in the Denis Johnston drama *The Moon in the Yellow River*, which premièred at the East End Theatre on February 6, 1961. Although the play was not a popular hit, Coco's portrayal of Tausch, the intense Austrian engineer, earned him the Off-Broadway Obie award for that year. His name next appeared in the cast of two Broadway plays, John Patrick's comedy *Everyone Loves Opal*, presented on October 11, 1961, and Santha Rama Rau's dramatization of the E. M. Forster novel *A Passage to India*, presented on January 31, 1962. Fairly good notices failed to prolong the run of either production.

In the fall of 1962 Coco went back on the road to play Morestan in the national tour of *A Shot in the Dark* through the 1962-63 season. He also made his first movie, having been assigned a small role in the Joshua Logan production of Warner Brothers' *Ensign Pulver* (1963). Then, in November 1963, he opened as O'Casey in his third Broadway show, *Arturo Ui*, at the Lunt-Fontanne Theatre. Like his previous two Broadway efforts, it did not make the grade, closing within a week. Off-Broadway again, at the East End Theatre, beginning on February 24, 1964, he was among the principals in a pair of one-act plays, *The Sponge Room* and *Squat Betty*, which lasted for only forty-nine performances. During the following October at another Off-Broadway theatre, the Astor Place Playhouse, he acted in *5 A.M.—A World's Fair*, the first of two plays by Will Holt presented under the collective title *That 5 A.M. Jazz*. Again the show folded quickly.

Following the now familiar pattern of moving back and forth between Broadway and Off Broadway, Coco opened on March 25, 1965 in *Lovey*, a presentation of the Cherry Lane New Playwrights Series; on November 16, 1965 in *The Devils*, staged by the Greek director Michael Cacoyannis at the Broadway Theatre; on January 12, 1967 at the Helen Hayes Theatre in David Merrick's suspense melodrama *The Astrakhan Coat*; on October 2, 1967 at the Cherry Lane in Murray Schisgal's *The Basement* and *Fragments*, winning another Obie for his work in the latter comedy; and on March 4, 1968 at the Billy Rose Theatre in *Here's Where I Belong*, a musical version of John Steinbeck's *East of Eden*. The chief attention that Coco received in his role of the Oriental servant, Lee, in *Here's Where I Belong* came on opening night from Oriental members of Actors' Equity picketing outside the theatre in protest against his casting. Between engagements he played The Barber as a replacement in the long-running musical *Man of La Mancha* in 1966 at the ANTA Theatre in Washington Square.

By the late 1960's Coco had become used to appearing in plays whose rehearsal periods were often longer than their runs, and believed he would remain an often unemployed character actor for the rest of his career. Over the years he had made twenty-three television commercials, the most successful ones as Willie the Plumber for Drano, and with the fees from them earned a fairly decent living. Then, in the summer of 1968, he went to Stockbridge, Massachusetts to appear in the Berkshire Theatre Festival's presentation of the Elaine May play *A Matter of Position*. When the production scheduled to follow *Position* was suddenly canceled, Coco offered the script of *Next*, a play Terrence McNally had written for him. The producers accepted it and opened on schedule with Coco and Elaine Shore cast in the two-character comedy. Coco explained to Patricia Bosworth of the New York *Times* (January 4, 1970) how *Next* had come to be written: "We were sitting around the apartment one night and I think I'd just done another Drano commercial and I was feeling depressed and I said, 'Why doesn't anybody ever write a play for a fat character actor?' A few days later Terrence phoned me and said, 'I'm writing a play for you.' When I read 'Next' and read the part of Marion Cheever, that flabby, pathetic little assistant movie house manager who has to subject himself to a series of hilarious indignities at an Army induction center, I thought, 'My God, what a beautiful role!' At the time nobody wanted to produce it."

Elaine May was so impressed with the comic values in the McNally script that she persuaded the two actors to stay on when the season closed to work further on it with her, with the idea of presenting it Off Broadway. Guiding McNally in revising and reshaping the play, she insisted the humor be credible and cut many of the incidental jokes and sight gags.

On his return to New York, Coco began rehearsals for *Witness*, one of two McNally plays presented at the Gramercy Arts Theatre in November 1968. Although he scored personally with his portrayal of a talkative window washer, the double bill quickly closed. He then began preparing for *Next*, which was paired with an Elaine May play at the Greenwich Mews Theatre on February 10, 1969. *Adaptation-Next* was an immediate hit and for his creation of Marion Cheever, Coco received rave reviews. Clive Barnes commented in the New York *Times* (February 11, 1969), "This is gorgeous acting, rich, stylish, impeccable. Mr. Coco, with every gesture and inflection, brings an entire man to life."

Finding himself finally in a hit, Coco was inundated with offers, many of them from movie producers. While still in Stockbridge he had been filmed in the small role of the School Man in the X-rated screen version of John Barth's novel *End of the Road* (Allied Artists, 1970). Then, in two New York-based pictures, he portrayed Mr. Blatto in William Goodhart's film adaptation of his play *Generation* (Avco Embassy Films, 1969) and the usurious Uncle Harry in Elaine May's *A New Leaf* (Paramount, 1971), which was filmed on Long Island in the summer of 1969. Also during that summer Coco took a short leave from *Next* to go to Boston for location shooting of Otto Preminger's *Tell Me That You Love Me, Junie Moon* (Paramount, 1970), in which he played the fishmonger who befriends the hideously scarred title character. His later movie roles included the Grocer in *The Straw-*

berry Statement (MGM, 1970) and the more substantial part of the fat, blundering doctor in *Such Good Friends* (Paramount, 1971).

During the run of *Next,* Coco came to the attention of the playwright Neil Simon, who had recently completed the first act of his new play, *Last of the Red Hot Lovers.* When he saw Coco's performance, he knew he had the man to play the leading role of Barney Cashman, owner of a seafood restaurant who, in his late forties, decides to have an extramarital affair. Signing him for the part, Simon then wrote the rest of the play around Coco's comic talents.

At the end of about seven months Coco left the company of the New York production of *Next* to lead the cast of a roadshow presentation of the play in Los Angeles for six weeks, beginning in October 1963. He then returned for rehearsals of the Simon comedy, which had its première at the Eugene O'Neill Theatre on December 28, 1969. In the smash reviews of the play James Coco was hailed as a new Broadway star. The appraisal of his performance by Richard Watts Jr. in the New York *Post* (December 29, 1969) typified the notices: "Mr. Coco, who is constantly on stage, combines the humor and wistfulness of Barney Cashman in a really magnificent characterization."

Settled down for the eighteen-month run of his contract, Coco periodically visited the *Johnny Carson Show,* whose audience had met him on several earlier occasions. Both as guest and substitute host, he ran up a total of sixty appearances. He was also seen on the Mike Douglas, Dick Cavett, and David Frost talk shows and on an Alan King comedy special. After withdrawing from *Last of the Red Hot Lovers,* he suffered the disappointment of not being cast in the film version of the play, when the part of Barney Cashman went to Alan Arkin. As if in compensation, however, a short time later he was assigned the role of Sancho Panza in *Man of La Mancha,* an Arthur Hiller motion picture. In the fall of 1971 he went to Italy to make the film, in which he costarred with Sophia Loren and Peter O'Toole. When United Artists released *Man of La Mancha* in late 1972, critics differed over the merits of Coco's interpretation. Martin Knelman of the Toronto *Globe and Mail* (December 14, 1972) thought him "somewhat of an embarrassment as Sancho Panza doing a costume version of the buffoon he's been doing regularly." But one reviewer called him "deftly funny," and Joseph Gelmis, commenting in *Newsday* (December 12, 1972), found his contribution "the standout performance" of a "lackluster production." Gelmis went on to say, "Granted that Sancho is a potentially juicy role under any conditions, but Coco exploits it for what it's worth and gets the few laughs the film has."

During 1972 Coco kept busy on TV, filling engagements on *Marcus Welby, M.D.,* the *Flip Wilson Show,* and a Neil Simon special, *The Trouble With People.* On October 9, 1972 he appeared on the NET Public Television Special *VD Blues,* a playlet written by his friend Israel Horovitz, in which he had the part of Gonorrhea. Another friend, the actor Robert Drivas, portrayed Syphilis. Although written in a comic vein, the show had the serious purpose of providing information on venereal diseases. It made a strong impression on audiences and was repeated in 1973 and 1974.

Among the new shows on CBS-TV's fall schedule for 1973 was *Calucci's Department,* starring James Coco. Produced in New York by Ed Sullivan Productions, with scripts by Renée Taylor and Joseph Bologna, the comedy series premièred on September 14, 1973 to excellent critical reception. In their praise of the warmth and humanity of the show, reviewers singled out Coco for his performance as Joe Calucci, the supervisor of a state unemployment office, battling bureaucracy and trying to teach compassion for people to a disinterested staff. " 'Calucci's Dept.' is a rare species of American TV comedy," wrote the reviewer for *Variety* (September 18, 1973). ". . . There is an overcast of real satire and wit here, and the regular cast throughout is comedic rather than cute and/or slick plastic." Despite continued enthusiastic support from the press, the series fared badly in the Nielsen ratings, probably because of its time slot, which placed it opposite popular comedy series on the other networks. CBS therefore canceled the show at midseason, in December 1973.

In the spring of 1974 Coco was signed for the lead in a film titled "The Wild Party," to be produced jointly by Lansbury-Beruh and Merchant-Ivory Productions. He plays a character described as "Jolly Grimm—funny man of the films," a role based on Fatty Arbuckle, a fat comic star of Hollywood's silent era.

Brown-eyed, brown-haired James Coco is five feet ten inches tall and weighs 250 or more pounds. He likes to cook as well as eat, particularly Italian specialties. Although he described himself in *After Dark* (May 1973) as "a professional worrier," he insisted, "I never get tension headaches. If I'm sick, it's not psychosomatic. I'm in amazingly good shape for the shape I'm in." He enjoys being with people, going to parties, playing cards, especially poker, and collecting antiques and paintings. Still a film buff, he often goes to the movies and watches the old pictures on television. Coco has strong ties with his sister Lucy and spends much time at her Long Island home. Besides his bachelor apartment in Manhattan, he has a cottage in the lake region of Maine, where he goes for brief vacations.

References

After Dark 6:20+ My '73 pors
N Y Daily News p38 D 30 '69 por
N Y Post p17 D 16 '72 por
N Y Sunday News III p17+ Ag 26 '73 por
N Y Times II p1+ Ja 4 '70 por
Newsday A p36 S 9 '69 pors
Time 95:65 Ja 22 '70 por
Variety 257:65+ Ja 21 '70
Who's Who in the East, 1974-75
Who's Who in the Theatre (1972)

COGGAN, F(REDERICK) DONALD (cŏg'ən)

Oct. 9, 1909- Anglican prelate
Address: Bishopthorpe, York, England YO2
IQE

In May 1974 Dr. F. Donald Coggan, Archbishop
of York, was appointed to succeed the retiring Dr.
Arthur Michael Ramsey as Archbishop of Canterbury and Primate of All England. Dr. Coggan, an
able Biblical scholar and homilist, is the first Evangelical, or Low Church, Anglican in 126 years to
become spiritual leader of the Church of England,
with its 28,000,000 members, and of the Anglican
Communion, with its 45,000,000 members worldwide, including 3,500,000 Episcopalians in the
United States. Although conservative by Anglo-
Catholic, or High Church, standards, Coggan is
a noncontroversial churchman with a solid reputation as an administrator. His Evangelical antip-
athy toward permissiveness does not preclude
publicly expressed compassion for homosexuals,
receptivity to opening the priesthood to women,
and opposition to apartheid in South Africa. As
Archbishop of Canterbury he will, he says, address himself particularly to urban and Third
World problems. Dr. Coggan's enthronement as
Archbishop of Canterbury was scheduled for January 24, 1975.

Frederick Donald Coggan was born in London,
England on October 9, 1909 to Cornish Arthur
Coggan, a prosperous business executive, and
Fannie Sarah Coggan. With his sisters, Beatrice
and Norah, he grew up in London, where he
attended Merchant Taylor's School. "Even as a
boy at a good private school he was drawn to the
church," Joseph Collins wrote in a New York
Times (May 15, 1974) "Man in the News" profile
of Coggan, "and as an undergraduate at St. John's
College, Cambridge, he avoided the frivolous."

Coggan established a brilliant record in Oriental languages and theology at Cambridge, where
he received a B.A. degree in 1931 and an M.A.
in 1935. Before his ordination, to the diaconate
in 1934 and the priesthood in 1935, he was assistant lecturer in Semitic languages and literature
at the University of Manchester, from 1931 to
1934. For three years after his ordination he was
curate at the Church of St. Mary in Islington,
a working-class district in North London. According to James Collins in his New York *Times*
profile of Coggan, it was at St. Mary's, a center
of the Evangelical Movement, that he became "an
energetic evangelist."

From 1937 to 1944 Coggan was New Testa-
ment professor at Wycliffe College in Toronto,
Canada. His first book, *A People's Heritage*, was
published in Toronto in 1944 by the Supplies
Department of the Church of England in Canada.
The following year Canterbury Press in London
published *The Ministry of the Word*, in which
Coggan examined the New Testament concept of
preaching and its relevance for today. In 1950
Coggan's slim volume *The Glory of God: Four
Studies in a Ruling Biblical Concept* was issued
by the Church Missionary Society in London.

On his return to England Coggan became principal of the London College of Divinity, and he
remained in that post for twelve years, until his
consecration as Bishop of Bradford in 1956. During his tenure at Bradford he published *Stewards
of Grace* (Hodder & Stoughton, 1958), which
was concerned with preaching, and he became
chairman of the College of Preachers, founded
in 1960 to stimulate and help the clergy of the
Church of England in the ministry of preaching.

On the occasion of his nomination to the arch-
bishopric of York, in January 1961, Coggan told
the press that he believed an archbishop ought
to travel far afield in the cause of a union of the
churches. "I am prepared to do that," he said,
"and I would like to add that my relations in
Bradford with Nonconformists have been extremely happy." He also said, "Britain's youth will be
one of the main things I shall bear in mind when
I move to York. It is only natural, for they are
the people of tomorrow."

At his enthronement at York in September 1961
Coggan appealed to the Church of England to
reorder its priorities in the expenditure of money
and manpower. His chief point was that the work
of the missions abroad and the church at home
should be one. "The world is on our doorstep,
whether we like it or not," he said. "It is much
more important that the Christian task should be
got on with in Africa than that my church should
have a new organ." The following month he told
the York Convocation that the "church must give
a lead" on three fronts: prayer, support for the
United Nations, and "a sacrificial effort to improve
the conditions of the underprivileged."

Among the books Coggan published while at
York were a collection of his sermons, *Christian
Priorities* (Lutterworth Press, 1963; Harper &
Row, 1963), *The Prayers of the New Testament*
(Hodder & Stoughton, 1967), and *Word and
World* (Hodder & Stoughton, 1971). While help-
ing to coordinate the translation of *The New
English Bible* from the Greek and Hebrew he wrote
a short book about that project, *The English Bible*
(Longmans Green, 1963). A revised Psalter, pre-
pared by a seven-man committee headed by Cog-
gan, was presented at the Church of England's
Canterbury and York convocations in May 1963.

In one of his repeated deplorations of the
growth of pornography, which he considers pes-
tilential, Coggan observed, "The literacy rate
rises but the standard of books does not." In October 1964 he launched a "Feed the Minds of Millions" campaign, aimed at providing "wholesome
reading" for the new literate millions of Africa,
Asia, and South America. When the British Council of Churches issued its report on sex and morality in October 1966, Coggan condemned as a
"disservice to the personal and family life of the
nation" the failure of the document to condemn
premarital and extramarital sex.

At a Church Assembly debate on the place of
women in the ministry of the church in November 1962 Coggan expressed the hope that Canterbury would follow the example of the North

of England (the province of York) in allowing qualified women church workers to conduct church services, other than Holy Communion, and to speak at them. At the Lambeth Conference of 1968 he formally proposed that women be admitted to the priesthood.

In January 1970 Coggan took the unprecedented step of hiring an independent management consultant to streamline the organization and administration of the diocese of York. At Easter 1972, in a move toward church "renewal" of an ecumenical nature in the North of England, the Archbishop joined with the Roman Catholic Archbishop of Liverpool and the moderator of the Free Church Federal Council in issuing a letter entitled "Call to the North." In a follow-up letter at Easter 1973 the three prelates reported that the original letter was read in some 7,000 churches of the North of England and that since that time "some thousands of groups of Christians of all traditions have been meeting to pray and to learn the meaning of the Christian faith and its bearing on human needs." Fifty-two denominational leaders, including Salvation Army officers and Roman Catholic priests, began the practice of meeting regularly at York to discuss the best ways for spreading the Christian message.

Coggan's nomination to succeed Michael J. Ramsey as Archbishop of Canterbury, announced on May 14, 1974, took place in the traditional manner: Queen Elizabeth II made the nomination on the recommendation of the Prime Minister, Harold Wilson. Through his appointments secretary, the Prime Minister always consults church leaders before making an episcopal recommendation, but there is a growing movement in the Church of England for formal autonomy in that and other ecclesiastical matters, especially changes in the liturgy. Coggan goes along with those church leaders who want expanded power independent of the government, but he is against complete "disestablishment" because he believes that "a radical break would be taken as a sign of abandonment of the Christian faith on the part of the nation."

At the time of the announcement of Dr. Coggan's nomination to Canterbury, the Bishop of Southwark, Dr. Mervyn Stockwood, compared him to Pope John, "in that he is a devoted Christian and there is no telling where that will lead him." Writing in the London *Times*, Stockwood said: "Donald Coggan . . . is well aware of the problems that confront a generation that has been reared in a scientific era. . . . [He] is increasingly aware of the need for the church to concern itself with practical affairs." In an editorial in the *Church Times* Coggan was called a churchman of "true evangelistic zeal and fervor," and Baden Hickman in the *Guardian* described him as "a theologian with a tape recorder handy for prompt dictation and [with] a meticulousness equal to that of any managing director."

Coggan's sermons and other public statements are forthright and unadorned. He once told a congregation that included Princess Margaret that

F. DONALD COGGAN, ARCHBISHOP OF YORK

English churchgoers generally "pay lip service to Christian principles" but "few are convinced Christians." On the occasion of his nomination to the see of Canterbury he told the press that Britain had a "sick society" that would be healed "only when we start living by the rules again."

F. Donald Coggan and Jean Braithwaite Strain were married in 1935. They have two grown daughters, Ruth, a physician, and Ann, a teacher. The Archbishop has said that family life keeps him "from going crazy." When offered the Canterbury see he delayed replying for four days, explaining, "I want to say my prayers and I want to talk with my wife, who, after all, shares the work with me." His favorite recreation, outside of motoring and gardening, is listening to the women in his family play the piano. He is also fond of organ music and used to be an organist himself.

Dr. Coggan is a bespectacled man, five feet eleven and a half inches tall, with blue eyes, gray hair, and a slight stoop. Those close to him describe him as kindly and genial, with a relaxed and open manner and an air of informality. But, as James Collins observed in his New York *Times* profile, he does not engage easily in small talk. "He shines when giving expositions of the Bible and clarifying with a fine phrase some complex theological point," Collins wrote. "In debate in Convocation, the church's parliament, he is at his best, thinking acutely on his feet and speaking with force and precision."

Ever since becoming an archbishop Coggan has been a member of the Queen's Privy Council. He is pro-chancellor of Hull and York universities and a holder of ten honorary degrees. His club is the Athenaeum, London. The Reverend John Andrew, rector of St. Thomas Episcopal Church in New York City, described Dr. Coggan as a man with whom "average people. . . will be able to identify," explaining: "He speaks simply and directly to social issues. He is a plain man, almost New England plain. He lives in great simplicity. He's entirely unpretentious."

References

N Y Daily News p90 My 26 '74
N Y Times p14 My 15 '74
Time 103:88+ My 27 '74 por
Washington Post A p3 My 15 '74 por
Who's Who, 1973-74

COLEMAN, JOHN R(OYSTON)

June 24, 1921- Educator; economist
Address: b. Haverford College, Haverford,
Pa. 19041 h. 1 College Circle, Haverford, Pa.
19041

Although long respected and well known as an educator and labor economist, the president of Haverford College, John R. Coleman, remained obscure to most Americans until 1973, when his secret two-month adventure as a manual laborer was publicized by newspapers and magazines across the nation. The publication by J. B. Lippincott in 1974 of his witty and sensitive diary, entitled *Blue Collar Journal: A College President's Sabbatical*, brought further public attention to Coleman and to his creed that a student's education should consist of informal learning experiences outside the classroom as well as of academic studies. Before he accepted the presidency of Haverford College in 1967, Coleman had combined a career as an economic consultant in both the United States and India with his duties as a teacher of economics in a number of American colleges and universities.

The son of Richard Mowbray Coleman and Mary Irene (Lawson) Coleman, John Royston Coleman was born on June 24, 1921 in Copper Cliff, Ontario, Canada. He has a brother, Richard L. Coleman, and one sister, Mrs. Mary MacLeod. According to Coleman's own description of his ancestry, he is "descended from a United Empire loyalist family who left upper New York State for Canada in 1776." "[There is] a long line of proud, college-educated loyalists on my father's side [and] an equally long line of proud laborers on my mother's side," he has explained. Coleman's father, who grew up in a financially comfortable and conservative Church of England home in Toronto, moved to the isolated town of Copper Cliff early in his career to work as a metallurgical engineer in the town's smelter. His mother, the daughter of a laborer in the same smelter, was an intelligent woman whose formal education ended after high school. In his book, *Blue Collar Journal*, Coleman depicted his mother as a contented housewife who "never assumed that there was any positive connection among diplomas, intellect, and worth."

After studying at Sudbury High School for three years, Coleman entered the newly built high school in Copper Cliff in 1937, where he was active in dramatics and the student government. Despite his admitted lack of prowess in athletics, he played basketball, but, as he has explained, "only because without me there weren't enough

bodies to make up a full team." In 1939 Coleman was the valedictorian in his graduating class of only fifteen students.

Responding to his father's expectations and encouragement, Coleman then entered the University of Toronto. After a diligent freshman year, he began attending classes less frequently because of his newly discovered interests in the social aspects of college life: dramatics, debating, the student union, the dormitory council, and the glee club. During summer vacations he labored on a bull gang cleaning out sewers for the smelting firm in his hometown, and in the winters he held a part-time job as a porter. In *Blue Collar Journal*, Coleman explained his decision to major in political science and economics: "I toyed with the idea of studying more about the only subject outside of English that I had truly enjoyed at the University of Toronto, labor economics. The professor wasn't exciting and his materials weren't the best, but he reached me as no one else did and persuaded me that the ways by which people earn their living could be a lively subject to study."

After receiving his B.A. degree from the University of Toronto in 1943, Coleman entered the Royal Canadian Navy as an ordinary seaman. He graduated at the top of his class from an officers' training school in Halifax and then served on Atlantic escort duty aboard H.M.C.S. *Lanzon*. Following his discharge from military service in 1945 with the rank of lieutenant, he decided to study labor economics at the graduate school of the University of Chicago.

"Once I enrolled, I began for the first time to take academics seriously," Coleman remarked in his *Blue Collar Journal*. "I had flirted with intellectual ideas at a distance in Toronto; now I had to make up for lost time in a world where disciplined thought was the stock-in-trade. I was thrilled by the university, by ideas, themselves, [and] by my special field. . . . Soon there was no career I was considering except the academic one." He worked as a research associate at the university from 1947 until 1949, when he received his M.A. degree in economics and embarked on his college teaching career at the Massachusetts Institute of Technology.

During his first year at M.I.T., Coleman received his doctorate from the University of Chicago. His dissertation was called "Models of Labor-Management Relations: A Typology Based on Case Studies in the United States and Great Britain." After his appointment as an assistant professor, in 1951, he continued teaching at M.I.T. during the day, and at Tufts College and Brandeis University in the evenings, until 1955, when he accepted an associate professorship at Carnegie Institute of Technology (now Carnegie-Mellon University). Coleman served as assistant head of the Carnegie economics department from 1955 to 1960, as full professor and chairman of the department from 1960 to 1963, and as dean of the division of humanities and social sciences from 1963 to 1965. He wrote in *Blue Collar Journal*: "I still don't know any pleasure to match the one of seeing a student come alive with the thrill of a new thought. A good teacher is a bit of a ham. He is probably oversold on the importance and originality of his own thought, and he is sometimes pathetic in his search for immortality through his students. With it all, teaching affords him more chance to give of himself, both in his learning and in his loving, than just about any other field."

Besides engaging in teaching, Coleman found time during the 1950's and early 1960's for a variety of activities that enhanced his professional standing. His publications during that period include *Goals and Strategy in Collective Bargaining* (Harper, 1951), *Readings in Economics* (McGraw-Hill, 1952), *Labor Problems* (McGraw-Hill, 1953) and *Working Harmony in Eighteen Companies* (National Planning Association, 1955). He served as an arbitrator in labor-management disputes, as a lecturer and consultant on economic education for secondary schools and colleges, and as a consultant for major business firms in management and union development programs. From 1960 to 1961 he worked as a consultant in industrial relations research for the Ford Foundation in New Delhi, India. On two educational television series aired over CBS-TV in 1962 and 1963, Coleman was involved as an economics instructor. The first program, a five-part series entitled "Money Talks," was broadcast during the week of August 20, 1962. The second, part of an educational series called "College of the Air," was entitled "The American Economy" and was shown on CBS and educational stations from September 1962 until mid-1963.

Coleman's career took a major turn in 1965, when he accepted a position with the Ford Foundation in New York City to develop programs for increasing economic and social opportunities for minorities. He worked as the associate director of economic development and administration during his first year and, from 1966 to 1967, as program officer in charge of social development. While serving with the foundation, Coleman was approached by the board of managers of Haverford College, in Pennsylvania, in the fall of 1966 with an offer of the presidency. At first Coleman declined the position, believing that his work with the foundation was far too vital to abandon for a return to the ivory towers of academe.

The offer became more seductive during the winter of 1966, however, as Coleman began to worry that he might someday become as complacent and haughty as some of his colleagues, who behaved as if the foundation money they distributed were their own. When Haverford again made overtures to Coleman in March 1967, he accepted the presidency. To Coleman, as he explained in *Blue Collar Journal*, there was the "prospect of making a difference" in the college presidency: "A man accepts a presidency when he feels deep inside that he can do some part of the job better than anyone else can. Modesty requires, of course, that he say it was the urge to serve youth which called him to

JOHN R. COLEMAN

the post. More often it was a private conceit about his own worth that he heard."

Coleman became the ninth president of Haverford College, an undergraduate liberal arts school for men in Haverford, Pennsylvania. In his inauguration speech he expressed an opinion that later was to become one of his basic educational philosophies—that students should combine their formal studies with experiences outside the scholastic world. He has since suggested that college students might break their educational "locksteps" between their sophomore and junior years, or perhaps, by taking time off from formal studies before their freshman year, believing that students who take time off to travel or work are often more mature when they return and more aware of what they want from a college education. To Coleman, as he observed in *Blue Collar Journal*, the "case for a better mix between on-campus and off-campus lives for all of us isn't one that rests on pleas for getting in touch with reality. It is a case that springs instead from an awareness of how much isolation there is in *all* our lives. The numbers of people anywhere who have experiences that cross and recross lines of class, race, or job in anything but the most superficial way are small indeed."

After a year in the Haverford presidency, Coleman felt isolated and restive in a lifestyle that limited most of his personal contacts to members of the academic community. He continued to urge his students to vary their experiences and contacts with the nonacademic world, but his own desire to do so remained an unrealized dream for several years. In May 1970 he finally made up his mind to break his own lockstep.

Coleman had become distressed by an attack on student peace demonstrators by construction workers in the Wall Street area of New York City on May 8, 1970 and by the building trades council parade against the peace movement that was held shortly thereafter. It seemed to Coleman that the nation was being torn apart. He explained in *Blue Collar Journal:* "That was when my resolve to enter the blue-collar world once again, no matter how briefly or tentatively, changed from a vague thought to a firm commitment to myself. I didn't fancy myself a missionary, a healer, or even a teacher. I still don't. I didn't think I was going to put America together again. My motive was much more selfish than that. I felt compelled to try to learn some lessons forgotten or never understood about the world of work. Until I did that, I'd be less alive than I wanted to be in the rest of the 1970's."

While on sabbatical leave from his duties at Haverford during the spring semester of 1973, Coleman kept his promise to himself to return to manual labor. He worked, first, as a sewer laborer and ditch digger in Atlanta, Georgia for two weeks; then, as a sandwich and salad man in a Boston seafood restaurant for nearly a month; and finally as a garbage collector for nine days in a Maryland suburb of Washington, D.C. During that two month period the only contacts Coleman had with his own professional and personal life were the two meetings he attended as chairman of the board of directors of the Federal Reserve Bank of Philadelphia.

In his published diary Coleman summed up his reactions to his experiences as a manual laborer: "If I am clearing cobwebs and anxieties out of my mind through this work experience, it is not because I have come to live among simpler, happier, or even better folks. It is because I am not fully engaged here, and their work and a small glimpse of their lives let me see my own work and life in a new light. I'm learning more about what we have in common than about what drives us apart. The truth is that we are all somewhat mixed-up and some of us in both worlds are happy about even that fact." Most reviewers reacted sympathetically to Coleman's diary and were delighted by his perceptiveness.

In a 1974 report on the state of the college for *Horizons*, a magazine that Haverford publishes for its alumni, Coleman described some of the changes instituted under his administration: an increased number of psychological counsellors; the introduction of a career planning office; an enlarged student body; an increase in alumni gifts; and the greater cross registrations and dormitory exchanges made in cooperation with Bryn Mawr College. In addition to his administrative duties he has taught an economics course each semester at the college.

Coleman's publications include *The American Economy: A TV Study Guide* (McGraw-Hill, 1962), *The Changing American Economy* (Basic Books, 1967), *Comparative Economic Systems* (Holt, Rinehart and Winston, 1968), and articles for professional journals. He is a member of the Commission on the Study of Peace, the Industrial Relations Research Association, and the American Economic Association; a vice-chairman of the National Joint Council on Economic Education; and a trustee of the NAACP Special Development Fund, the Committee for Economic Development, and the AFL-CIO Labor Studies Center. Coleman is also on the board of directors

of the Council on Foundations. During the presidency of Lyndon Johnson, he served on two national task forces; one dealt with employment services and the other with measures to decrease urban unemployment. His honors include two LL.D. degrees, one from Beaver College in Glenside, Pennsylvania in 1963 and another from the University of Pennsylvania in 1968.

John Royston Coleman and Mary Norrington Irwin, who were married on October 1, 1943, have five children: John, Nancy, Patty, Paul, and Stephen. The couple was divorced in 1966. Coleman, who has graying brown hair, is six feet one inch tall and weighs 170 pounds. He became a naturalized United States citizen in 1954. For recreation, he cooks, jogs, listens to the music of Mahler, and reads his favorite authors, such as George Orwell, Elizabeth Bishop, and Robert Coles. He belongs to the Unitarian-Universalist church. Coleman, who considers himself an independent Democrat, led most of the students at Haverford College to Washington, D.C. in May 1970 to protest the American invasion of Cambodia. Following the advice of their father, four of Coleman's five children have broken the educational lockstep.

References

American Men and Women of Science 12th ed (1973)
Coleman, John R. Blue Collar Journal: A College President's Sabbatical (1974)
Who's Who in America, 1974-75
Who's Who in the East, 1974-75

COMFORT, ALEX(ANDER)

Feb. 10, 1920- Physician; scientist; author
Address: b. Center for the Study of Democratic Institutions, Box 4068 Santa Barbara, Calif. 93103

In an era of cramped specialization, the protean Dr. Alex Comfort has incontrovertibly achieved the Renaissance ideal of the well-rounded man. One of the world's leading authorities on the biology of the aging process, he is also an advocate of greater freedom in sexual behavior—a gospel he has preached in books ranging from the scholarly *Sexual Behavior in Society* (1950) to the best-selling *The Joy of Sex* (1972). Although a physician and surgeon, Comfort first won international recognition as a poet and playwright, and as a novelist with eighteen works of fiction to his credit, many of them vehicles for his lifelong anarchism. He has written critical essays, added lyrics to songs composed by Pete Seeger, lectured on radio and television, and organized political protest groups. In 1972, after two years as director of research in gerontology at University College, London, he joined the staff of the Center for the Study of Democratic Institutions in Santa Barbara, California.

The only son of Alexander Charles and Daisy Elizabeth (Fenner) Comfort, Alexander Comfort was born on February 10, 1920 in Palmers Green, a neighborhood in north London, England. An incorrigible child who ran away from a "crazy co-ed" school when he was seven years old, he was taught the basic elementary school subjects by his mother, a former schoolteacher. He then attended several grammar schools, among them the Highgate School in Middlesex. At the age of fourteen, he lost all but the index finger of his left hand in an accident.

Entering Trinity College, Cambridge, in 1938 as a Robert Styring Scholar, Comfort at first planned to study the classics but eventually switched to medicine. He won a First Class in the National Science Tripos, the final honors examinations, in 1940, and a Second Class in the pathology examination in 1941. After receiving a bachelor of medicine degree and a bachelor of surgery degree from Cambridge University in 1944, Comfort was licensed to practise by the Royal College of Physicians and accepted for membership in the Royal College of Surgeons. The following year, he obtained an M.A. degree from Cambridge and a Diploma in Child Health from London Hospital.

The World War II years were eventful for Comfort. Besides continuing his medical studies, he forged a promising literary career and began his lifelong political activism. A conscientious objector to military service, he was temporarily blacklisted from broadcasting because of his bitter attacks on Allied policies, especially the indiscriminate bombing of nonmilitary targets. His early plays, novels, and poems advocated a system of ethics based on individual freedom tempered by mutual human responsibility.

Comfort published his first book, *The Silver River: Being the Diary of a Schoolboy in the South Atlantic* (Chapman and Hall), in the late 1930's, when he was still an adolescent. Between 1941 and 1945—the most productive period in his literary career—he wrote three novels, two plays, and four books of poetry. Of the novels, *The Almond Tree: A Legend* (Chapman and Hall, 1942) best expresses that combination of "pessimism and idealism" crucial to his philosophy. In that novel, the grandchildren of an authoritarian patriarch rebel in a futile attempt to escape from his possessive dominance. The almond tree in the garden is the one constant in their rapidly changing world. *No Such Liberty* (Chapman and Hall, 1941) and *The Powerhouse* (Routledge, 1944), novels that one critic described as "anarcho-pacifist," were vehicles for Comfort's political and social beliefs.

The Powerhouse, like most of his novels, has a European setting, in this case a French industrial town during the 1930's. The main characters, an intellectual who becomes a soldier in the Resistance and a blue-collar worker, press their compatriots to follow a course of civil disobedience and noncooperation with the German occupation forces. As one character remarks, "The weak do a great deal—every woman who hides a deserter, every clerk who doesn't scrutinize a pass, every worker who bungles a fuse saves

DR. ALEX COMFORT

somebody's life for a while." When *The Powerhouse* was published in the United States by Viking Press in 1945, reviews were mixed. Although the majority of the critics disagreed with the author's controversial political thesis, several found the carefully detailed novel "deeply moving," "challenging," and "remarkably well written." Others objected to Comfort's "disjointed" and "erratic" style, and one disgruntled reviewer complained in the *New Yorker* (March 31, 1945): "At the end of 464 pages of this, you feel as if you had traveled from New York to San Francisco on a pogo stick."

Some of the same criticisms were leveled at *The Song of Lazarus* (Viking, 1945), a collection of contemplative poems about death that was widely reviewed in the United States. "His emotions, as well as his language, keep slipping into a haze," Louise Bogan observed in the *New Yorker* (November 3, 1945). "He can use ordinary language with good effect . . . but usually he is merely murmuring about eerie, obsessive pictures." On the other hand, Ruth Lechlitner praised him in the New York *Herald Tribune Weekly Book Review* (December 23, 1945) as "one of the most interesting writers of his generation."

Routledge published Comfort's book of verse, *The Signal to Engage*, in 1946, and a collection of stories, *Letters from an Outpost*, in 1947. Between 1947 and 1949 the appearance of four books of literary criticism and social history and of his fifth novel, *On This Side Nothing* (Viking, 1949), enhanced his international reputation as a writer of uncommon intelligence and sensitivity. Comfort's most recent belletristic works include the novel *A Giant's Strength* (Routledge, 1952) and two volumes of poetry, *And All But He Departed* (Routledge, 1951) and *Haste to the Wedding* (Eyre and Spottiswoode, 1962).

While serving as the resident medical officer at the Royal Waterloo Hospital for Children and Women, Comfort completed a textbook on physiology and biology, *First Year Physiological Technique* (Staples Press, 1948). In 1949 he received a Ph.D. degree in biochemistry for his doctoral dissertation on the pigmentation of mollusca. After several years as a lecturer in physiology at the London Hospital Medical College, he joined the zoology department of University College, London, as a Nuffield Research Fellow in gerontology in 1951. Twelve years later he was named director of University College's medical council research group on the biology of aging, a post he held until 1970. Although he specialized in gerontology, he continued to study a variety of subjects, ranging from human sexual behavior to the medical ethics of abortion and euthanasia.

In *The Anxiety Makers* (Nelson, 1967), the first volume of a proposed series with the working title "The Natural History of Society," Comfort argued that the medical profession was largely responsible for the "programmed" anxiety of modern man. Concerned about the apparent lack of responsibility among doctors, Comfort defined the complex role of the doctor in society, taking into consideration such controversial issues as the inequality of medical care available to the public and the prevailing fear of death. Originally presented as a lecture at the University of British Columbia in 1971, *What Is a Doctor?* was released as a long-playing recording by the Center for the Study of Democratic Institutions in 1972.

For more than twenty years, Comfort conducted experiments on the aging process of animals with short, easily studied life spans. In an article for *Scientific American* (August, 1961), he summarized many of the theories of gerontology that he and others had tested during the 1950's. In the University College laboratories, for example, guppies were used to test the theory that animals age because they cannot grow beyond a biologically predetermined fixed adult size. Comfort's experiments tended to disprove this hypothesis. Although guppies grow continuously and, theoretically, could grow indefinitely, the experimental fish died as they aged, having survival curves similar to those of small mammals. Guppies were also used to replicate earlier studies in which the life spans of rats were doubled by restricting caloric intake. Comfort found that young guppies on a restricted diet were significantly smaller than their normally fed siblings. When the experimental fish were switched to a normal diet, they rapidly attained full size and lived longer than the guppies that had been on an unrestricted diet from birth.

Commenting on the possibility of increasing the human life span in a 1971 UNESCO report on aging, Comfort predicted that within fifteen years American scientists, by using "selective starvation" and drugs to control cancer and heart disease, would be able to extend the average man's life. According to Comfort, the United States provides an ideal atmosphere for gerontological research because Americans consider old age to be "an intolerable state, which we are obliged to prevent if possible." On a lecture tour of the United States in 1972, he outlined the results of his research and explained some of the methods used to measure the human aging

process, such as skin elasticity, hearing, and mental ability. Although he rejected popular rejuvenation theories, he maintained that aging could be controlled and eventually retarded by "dietary tricks," such as the substitution of vegetable protein analogs for animal fats, and "maintenance chemicals."

Speaking in favor of a Congressional bill to establish a National Institute of Aging with the National Institutes of Health, Comfort urged the American public to support the legislation, which guarantees funds for biomedical, social, and behavioral research in gerontology—research once estimated to cost "the equivalent of one Saturn rocket or one big-dish antenna." President Nixon pocket vetoed the bill in 1972, but a similar bill was passed by Congress and sent to Nixon in May 1974.

Comfort has promoted an international approach to the problems of overpopulation and food shortages. At a scientific conference in San Juan, Puerto Rico in January 1973 he agreed with many of his colleagues that the attainment of zero population growth was necessary to insure an adequate food supply and enough living space for future generations. He set forth his theories in *Aging: The Biology of Senescence* (Holt, Rinehart, 1964), a revised and updated edition of a standard work on the aging process that was originally published in England in 1956, and in *The Process of Aging* (New American Library, 1964), a layman's introduction to gerontology. In *The Nature of Human Nature* (Harper, 1965) Comfort reviewed man's biological, cultural, and sociological development and discussed such problems peculiar to modern society as overpopulation, destruction of the environment, and the disintegration of traditional human relational patterns. Central to the book is Comfort's Freudian conviction that more and better sexuality will foster more affection and charity among human beings. Comfort further explored the ramifications of "better sexuality" in *The Joy of Sex: A Cordon Bleu Guide to Lovemaking* (Crown, 1972). Based on the work of an anonymous couple and edited by Comfort, *The Joy of Sex* is an informative and uninhibited sex manual. Its simple line illustrations won a design award from the American Institute of Graphic Arts.

A champion of a wider range of permissible sexual relationships, Comfort separates sex into parenthood, "relational" sex between two people emotionally involved with each other, and purely "recreational" sex. In an article for the *Center Report* (August, 1973) he argued that sexual "swinging" could benefit "bored" and "unrealized" individuals: "Unless the result disturbs children and leads to a backlash generation, the genuine insight present in 'swinging'. . . could expand into something far more like institutionalized socio-sexual openness." In his opinion, group sex will be accepted and widely practised in the future, although he acknowledges that group sex could "devalue relationships." A sequel to *The Joy of Sex*, titled *More Joy* (Crown, 1974), examines some of the psychological and sociological problems of a freewheeling sexual life-style, such as the role of marriage and the family and the effect of serial polygamy on children.

As a lifelong anarchist, Comfort has opposed both communism and social democracy through-out his career. A member of the Peace Pledge Union, the Author's World Peace Appeal, and Bertrand Russell's Committee of 100, he has taken part in "agitatorial activities" that promote socio-logical analyses of global tensions. During the 1940's and 1950's, he expounded his views as a lecturer at the Anarchist Summer School in London, as an occasional commentator for the British Broadcasting Corporation, and as a writer. He has published several political pamphlets, in-cluding *Peace and Disobedience*, and a long, dis-cursive essay, *Authority and Delinquency in the Modern State: A Criminological Approach to the Problem of Power* (Routledge, 1950). In 1962 he was arrested and jailed for helping to organize a massive "ban the bomb" demonstration in Lon-don's Trafalgar Square.

After twenty-nine years of marriage, Comfort divorced Ruth Muriel Harris in April 1973 to wed Jane Henderson, a sociologist at the London School of Economics and a longtime friend. He has one son, Nicholas Alfred Fenner, by his first wife. As of late 1973, the Comforts were planning to purchase a home in Santa Maria, California, near the Center for the Study of Democratic Institutions in Santa Barbara. Com-fort was appointed an associate of the center in 1969, when its director, Robert M. Hutchins, "refounded" the organization as an international community of scholars devoted to the solution of the fundamental problems of the contemporary world. Comfort's work has earned him several major awards, among them the Ciba Foundation Prize in 1958 and the Karger Memorial Founda-tion Prize in Gerontology in 1969.

References

Contemporary Authors vol 4 (1963)
International Who's Who, 1973-74
Twentieth Century Authors (1942; First Supplement, 1955)
Vinson, James, ed. Contemporary Novel-ists (1972)
Who's Who, 1973-74
Who's Who in America, 1972-73
Who's Who in the World, 1974-75

COOKE, (ALFRED) ALISTAIR

Nov. 20, 1908- Journalist; broadcaster
Address: b. c/o British Broadcasting Company, 630 5th Ave., New York 10020; h. 1150 5th Ave., New York 10028

NOTE: This biography supersedes the article that appeared in *Current Biography* in 1952.

Probably no one man has better served the cause of Anglo-American relations than the Brit-ish-born American journalist and radio and tele-

ALISTAIR COOKE

vision commentator Alistair Cooke, who has been interpreting the American experience to audi-ences on both sides of the Atlantic with urbanity, wit, and grace for thirty-six years. Until 1972 Cooke was correspondent for Britain's *Guardian*, and he continues to broadcast a weekly *Letter from America* on the BBC. In the United States, he hosted the prestigious *Omnibus* program on NBC-TV, for eight years beginning in 1952; nar-rated the BBC-produced, NBC-imported series *America: A Personal History of the United States*, which won four Emmy awards in 1972-73; and acts as master of ceremonies for National Edu-cational Television's *Masterpiece Theatre*, a pre-sentation of British television drama. His books include *Alistair Cooke's America*, a literary adap-tation of his 1972-73 television series. Published in 1973, the superbly illustrated volume was still on the best-seller list in April of 1974 and was ex-pected by its publisher, Alfred A. Knopf, to sell 500,000 copies or more.

The articulate, ultra-civilized Cooke, who has never lost his British accent, is known for his crisp style, warm, charming manner, and knack for giving a once-over-lightly treatment to com-plex subjects. "Alistair Cooke covers a story the way a short dress covers an attractive girl," Rob-ert G. Kaiser observed in the Washington *Post* (November 28, 1968), and Cooke himself has said (in explaining how he went about creating his *America* television series): "The whole busi-ness is selection. It's boiling down."

Alfred Alistair Cooke was born in Manchester, England on November 20, 1908 to Samuel and Mary Elizabeth (Byrne) Cooke. His Anglo-Irish father, a Wesleyan Methodist lay preacher, found-ed the Wood Street Mission in the slums of Man-chester. Terry Coleman, who interviewed Cooke for the *Guardian* and the *Guardian Weekly* (May 5, 1973) reports that in adolescence he "revolted against chapel and was allowed to stay at home and read the *Observer* and the *Sunday Times* instead of the Bible but not to play the piano, which was regarded as frivolous on Sundays."

Cooke was educated at Blackpool Grammar School in Manchester and Jesus College, Cambridge University, where he edited the campus literary journal the *Granta*. At that time primarily interested in theatre, he helped to found the Cambridge University Mummers in 1929, the year in which he won First Class honors in the English Tripos. He received his B.A. degree *summa cum laude* in 1930 and a diploma in education the following year. In November 1931 he began contributing theatrical reports and criticism to the American periodical *Theatre Arts Monthly*, which is now defunct. When he won a Commonwealth Fund fellowship to study theatre in the United States he was, in keeping with custom, received in audience by the late Duke of Windsor (then the Prince of Wales). The Duke was reported to have remarked, in observing the resemblance between Cooke and himself, "My God, my brother!"

On his Commonwealth Fund fellowship Cooke did research in drama at Yale University in 1932-33 and at Harvard University in 1933-34. During his first summer in the United States he traveled the length and breadth of the country. "That trip was an absolute eye-opener for me," he told George Michaelson when Michaelson was doing an article on him for the American Sunday supplement *Parade* (March 3, 1974). "Even then, even in the Depression, there was a tremendous energy and vitality to America. The landscape and the people were far more gripping and dramatic than anything I had ever seen. It truly changed me. You see, from then on my interest in the theater began to wane, and I began to take up what I felt was the real drama going on—namely, America itself."

During his second summer in the United States, Cooke worked in Hollywood with Charlie Chaplin, writing the script for a motion picture about Napoleon (to be played by Chaplin) that was never produced. He might have stayed in Hollywood had not the terms of his Commonwealth Fund fellowship required him to spend some years working professionally within the British Empire. When the British Broadcasting Company fired film critic Oliver Baldwin in 1934, Cooke applied for the vacated job and got it. In 1937 Jonathan Cape Ltd. published *Garbo and the Night Watchmen*, an anthology of British and American film criticism edited by Cooke, and three years later the Museum of Modern Art in New York City issued his critical biography *Douglas Fairbanks: The Making of a Screen Character*. While reviewing cinema on BBC radio he also served as London correspondent for the National Broadcasting Company.

After three years in London, Cooke returned to the United States to take up permanent residence there. He began commenting on American affairs for the BBC in 1938, and in the late 1930's and early 1940's he also wrote for the *Times* of London, the British Labour newspaper *Daily Herald*, and, occasionally, the *Fortnightly Review* and the *Spectator*. In the *Parade* interview he recalled that in his early years as a for-

eign correspondent there were few other British journalists covering America, which was then "only one of several powers in the world" and looked upon as "rather uncivilized and unexciting." His broadcasts and dispatches helped to change the latter European view.

In 1945 Cooke covered the charter conference of the United Nations for the *Guardian*—as well as the BBC—and three years later he became the chief American correspondent of that newspaper. His current weekly fifteen-minute chat for the BBC, *Letter from America*, was inaugurated in 1946. From the beginning he found the radio program a more satisfying vehicle than his *Guardian* column, as he explained to Alan Bunce of the *Christian Science Monitor* (April 26, 1973): "I've never liked the idea of 'doing a column'—you know, spinning it out three times a week. Then you just have to invent it. I've always liked a news peg. There's so much to go at in a weekly talk, you go all over the shop. Sometimes you go four weeks without politics."

In his *Christian Science Monitor* article Bunce wrote of *Letter from America:* "English friends tell me what a delight it is to hear his weekly BBC broadcast . . . , a healthy antidote to the windy summations of many commentators." Reviewing *One Man's America* (Knopf, 1952), the first collection of *Letter from America* talks, Gerald W. Johnson wrote in the New York *Herald Tribune* (April 20, 1952): "Any intelligent American will congratulate himself that we have an interpreter at once so genial and so well informed."

Among the events covered by Cooke for the *Guardian* in the late 1940's and early 1950's was that in which Richard M. Nixon, then a Communist-hunting member of the Un-American Activities Committee in the United States House of Representatives, gained prominence: the Alger Hiss affair. A State Department official accused of having passed department secrets to Communists in the 1930's, Hiss was investigated by Nixon and the committee beginning in 1948 and sentenced to prison for perjury by a federal court in 1950. Without departing from his base in the transcripts of the House hearings and the court trials, Cooke cut through the clutter of detail to retell the Hiss episode with his usual succinctness and clarity in *Generation on Trial: U.S.A. v. Alger Hiss* (Knopf, 1950). The book was widely praised for its combination of objectivity and liveliness. Richard Rovere ranked it as "one of the most vivid and literate descriptions of an American political event that has ever been written"; Merle Miller observed that Cooke had brought a mass of familiar facts "into magnificent focus"; and Perry Miller found the account to be, "on the level of pure narrative, more fascinating than any contemporary novel." Other reviewers described it as "fluent," "fresh," "compassionate," and as demonstrating "a keen sense of dramatic and legal values."

For his radio work Cooke won the Peabody Award for international reporting in 1952. According to Cooke, it was "pie, absolute jam reporting America" until the "McCarthy period," those years of anti-Communist hysteria in the 1950's instigated, or at least abetted, by the late Senator Joseph McCarthy's "witch-hunting." "That was," he told Alan Bunce in the *Christian Science Monitor* interview, "the worst time" for his BBC program's "acceptance . . . or what they now call credibility." Knopf published the slim volume *Christmas Eve,* comprising three seasonal stories broadcast by Cooke, in 1952, and the *Vintage Mencken,* an anthology, edited by Cooke, of the writings of the iconoclastic sage of Baltimore, in 1955.

The vast American television audience came to know Cooke through *Omnibus,* an hour-long highbrow magazine of the air that he hosted and narrated on Sundays from 1952 to 1961. That program, which offered viewers a smorgasbord of fare, from news documentaries to such literary essays as a tribute to Dylan Thomas, won Emmy after Emmy during its long run on the NBC network. In his dispatches and broadcasts to Britain in the 1960's, Cooke dismissed the conspiracy theories regarding the assassination of President John F. Kennedy; was sympathetic to President Lyndon B. Johnson (who, he believes, will be "rediscovered as a great President" despite the Vietnam war, "where all his worst qualities came out"); and described, among other experiences, what it was like to be a witness to the assassination of Senator Robert F. Kennedy, a mourner at the funeral of Martin Luther King, and an innocent target of police violence in the street rioting in Chicago during the 1968 National Democratic Convention. He once described the eight years that began in 1964 as "a bad time . . . the worst time I've known," adding the qualification: "A lot of the things that we deplore as being American are actually world problems. They happen a little sooner here, and they happen on a bigger scale."

Reviewing *Talk About America* (Knopf, 1968), Cooke's second collection of BBC chats, in the New York *Times Book Review* (December 8, 1968), Denis Brogan, himself no mean authority on American institutions, praised Cooke's "political penetration" and "flashes of wit, humanity, and wisdom." Brogan wrote: "The fact that he is of Irish origin perhaps accounts for the subtlety of the *doigté* with which he insinuates surprising or awkward truths into the British, even the English mind. There is no mere flood of information; there is no hectoring; there is no lecturing. . . . The American reader of this fascinating volume is eavesdropping on a highly skilled educational performer."

Cooke made the thirteen-installment television series *America* on location, traveling 100,000 miles to historical sites throughout the United States over a period of two years. No actors, no dramatizations were used. Everything depended on the scenery and the still shots of paintings and documents—brought alive by Cooke's commentary. The style was impressionistic, reflecting Cooke's interests and biases and capturing, as always, small but striking details. When the NBC tele-

vision network unveiled the series in the United States, Harry F. Waters of *Newsweek* (November 27, 1972) hailed Cooke for proving himself "equal to" the "formidable task" of compressing some 500 years of American history into 650 minutes of television time. "By text-book standards, *America* is hardly definitive history," Waters wrote. "But like the NBC's old *Omnibus* series, it is vintage Alistair Cooke—and that is more than enough. Avoiding stilted dramatizations, Cooke guides American viewers on an unabashedly subjective tour of their heritage, from an Indian graveyard to a Minuteman missile silo. . . . The show's liveliest moments come whenever Cooke pauses for some telling asides. 'Like the Vietcong,' he says of the Revolutionary Army, 'the Americans would not fight by the rules.' "

Waters ended by saying: "What charms in *America* is the presence of a sort of kindly stepfather, who is intensely interested in his adopted offspring but is not about to nag. The series is the first, and perhaps the finest, gift to the nation for its 200th birthday." In addition to the awards it received from the National Academy of Television Arts and Sciences, *America* won a Peabody Award and the British Society of Film and Television Arts' Richard Dimbleby Award. Reviewing *Alistair Cooke's America,* the book based on the television series, John Barkham wrote in the New York *Post* (November 6, 1973): "Cooke sees clearly the dangers inherent in the moral, social and racial crises now confronting this nation. . . . As its powers have grown, so have its problems. Cooke candidly considers these in a closing chapter which leaves the reader sobered rather than exhilarated."

In the *Parade* interview Cooke told George Michaelson that he thought the Nixon administration's Watergate scandal was "unique." "Even with Harding and Grant you never had the Presidency under such continuous fire as it is now. You never had such a wide range of charges hurled at the White House. No, this is something quite unprecedented in American history—something that has struck at the root of our system. . . . I think there is still a lot of idealism to be tapped here. . . . But that is the big question: In post-Watergate America, . . . will America's idealism prevail. . . ? I'm afraid that is something everyone is going to have to answer for himself."

Cooke and his present wife, the former Jane (White) Hawkes, were married on April 30, 1946. They have one child, a daughter, and Mrs. Cooke has two additional children by a previous marriage. Cooke himself was previously married to Ruth Emerson, from 1934 until that marriage—by which he has a son—ended in divorce. With his present wife he lives in Manhattan, where he records his weekly talk for the BBC. In preparing his scripts he writes and rewrites until the presentation is, as he has described it, "enormously tight." He told Alan Bunce of the *Christian Science Monitor*: "The easier it sounds . . . the harder it is to do."

Alistair Cooke is a tall, handsome, silver-haired man who speaks with a voice that is simultaneously cool and friendly and an accent that has been variously described as "NATO" and "Lancashire sprinkled with Manhattanisms." Endowed with a sense of humor, especially of irony, he punctuates his conversation with laughs, chuckles, and wry sallies. His favorite section of the United States is the West. As he told the interviewer for the *New Yorker*, he has "fallen out of love with New York." "I'm not sure the cities here aren't through. Human relations in them are impossible."

In 1973 Queen Elizabeth II named Cooke an honorary Knight Commander of the British Empire. (As an American citizen, since 1941, Cooke is not allowed to use "Sir" before his name.) The broadcaster and writer is a member of the National Press Club in Washington, D.C. and the Savile and Athenaeum clubs in London. His favorite recreations are listening to jazz and playing it on the piano, golf, going to movies, and reading. The walls of his study are lined with some 3,000 books, which he sifts through regularly, giving about 500 a year to the Merchant Marine. The majority of the books are in the fields of American geography and history and of political science, from, as Cooke says, "Plato to Tom Hayden." In response to the charge that he tends to see the lighter side of serious subjects in his journalism, he has said: "It is a crime . . . to take the crisis of the world so solemnly as to put off enjoying those things for which we were presumably designed in the first place."

References

Christian Sci Mon p11 Ap 26 '73 por
Guardian Weekly p18 My 5 '73 por
New Yorker 44:48+ O 28 '68
Parade p6+ Mr 3 '74 pors
Who's Who, 1973-74
Who's Who in America, 1972-73

COOPER, IRVING S(PENCER)

July 15, 1922- Neurosurgeon
Address: b. St. Barnabas Hospital of Chronic Diseases, 4422 3d Ave., Bronx, N.Y. 10457; h. 76 Mount Tom Rd., Pelham Manor, N.Y. 10803

Driven by his devotion to helping the presumably hopeless, Dr. Irving S. Cooper has developed more significant innovations in brain surgery than any other man alive. Early in the 1950's he developed the first brain operation to relieve the tremors and rigidity of Parkinson's disease without causing paralysis in the patient. In refining that treatment he became the first surgeon to use the technique of freezing or cryosurgery, and that technique has since become an important method of surgery in treating many of the body's ills. After relieving the symptoms of thousands of patients suffering from Parkinsonism, dystonia, and other crippling and disfiguring neurological disorders with brain cryosurgery, Dr. Cooper in

1972 began pioneering what will perhaps prove an even more important innovation, a brain stimulator or "pacemaker." By carrying electrical impulses to the brain, the pacemaker has proved able in many patients to relieve the convulsions of untreatable epilepsy, the spastic paralysis that often follows a stroke, or the spasticity of cerebral palsy. Furthermore, it is expected that the pacemaker will reveal new knowledge about how the human brain works. Since 1954 Cooper has been director of the department of neurosurgery at St. Barnabas Hospital for Chronic Diseases in the Bronx, New York.

Irving Spencer Cooper was born on July 15, 1922 in Atlantic City, New Jersey, the son of Louis and Eleanor Lillian (Cooper) Cooper. After high school, where he played football, Cooper entered George Washington University, in Washington, D.C. He completed his premedical studies in 1942 with a B.A. degree, and was granted his M.D. degree in 1945. After completing a one-year internship at the United States Naval Hospital in St. Albans, New York, Dr. Cooper studied at the University of Minnesota, where he held a fellowship from 1949 to 1951 and obtained an M.S. and a Ph.D. degree in 1951. Meanwhile, he completed his residency requirements at the Mayo Foundation, in Rochester, Minnesota, where he was a fellow from 1948 to 1951. From 1946 to 1948 Cooper served in the Medical Corps of the United States Naval Reserve, rising to the rank of lieutenant (j.g.).

In 1951 Dr. Cooper became an assistant professor of neurosurgery at the New York University postgraduate medical school. A year later, in October 1952, he accidentally discovered his first innovative treatment for Parkinson's disease, the progressively debilitating disease that cripples its victims with uncontrollable trembling and rigidity. He had set out to perform an established operation for the malady, in which a major motor pathway in the brain is cut, thereby replacing the victim's shaking palsy with partial paralysis. In the course of the surgery, however, Cooper accidentally cut open a tiny artery called the anterior choroidal artery, which leads to the globus pallidus and the thalamus, areas of the brain that control motor functions. To stop the bleeding he closed off the artery with silver clips and ended the operation without performing the planned surgery. When the patient came out of anesthesia, the tremor and rigidity of Parkinsonism had disappeared without any paralysis or other impairment to his motor functions.

After testing his new surgical procedure on baboons in the animal laboratory, Dr. Cooper repeated the surgery on fifty patients suffering from Parkinson's disease. At the same time he began looking for other ways to accomplish the same result, because the surgery was hard on the patient and risky. Since the choroidal artery nourishes slightly different portions of the brain in different people, the results of the operation were always unpredictable. By 1955 he had devised the startling new technique of chemopallidectomy and chemothamectomy (chemical removal of the globus pallidus or the thalamus). A tiny hole was drilled in the patient's skull, and minute amounts of pure alcohol were injected into the globus pallidus or the thalamus, deadening the brain cells that were triggering the symptoms of the disease. When the alcohol was applied to the right location, its effects could be seen immediately, and Cooper could therefore perform the procedure on his patients without having them lose consciousness. (The brain itself is insensitive to pain, so that only local anaesthetic was necessary.) In that way he could make sure that he had reached the right area by having the patient move the affected limb.

By the late 1950's Dr. Cooper had performed nearly a thousand chemopallidectomies or chemothalamectomies, and other doctors were performing similar operations in hospitals in the United States, Europe, and South America. Cooper had discovered that the surgical procedure could benefit not only victims of Parkinson's disease, which usually strikes adults, but those afflicted with a similar childhood disorder. Victims of dystonia are wracked with uncontrollable muscle contractions and spasms that leave their limbs contorted into grotesque shapes. Relatively safe, Cooper's operation had a 2 percent mortality rate, which is about the same as for gall bladder surgery. About three quarters of the patients operated on found substantial relief, with many returning to relatively normal lives. The operation came to national attention in 1959, when the *Life* photographer Margaret Bourke-White, a victim of Parkinson's disease, underwent surgery at the hands of Dr. Cooper. Afterward she vastly improved, was able to resume her work, and lived for twelve more years before her death from Parkinsonism in 1971. (Cooper could only treat the debilitating symptoms of the disease, not provide a cure, as he has pointed out.)

The scene of most of Dr. Cooper's innovative surgery was St. Barnabas Hospital, a small facility in the Bronx, where he became director of neurosurgery in 1954. He remained an assistant professor of neurosurgery at the N.Y.U. postgraduate medical school until 1957. For the next nine years he was director of neuromuscular diseases and professor of research surgery at the N.Y.U.— Bellevue Medical Center. Since 1966 he has been research professor of neuroanatomy at New York Medical College.

Despite his successes with injecting alcohol into the brains of his patients, Cooper kept experimenting with other methods, including injecting hot water or various drugs, or using electrical impulses or ultra high frequency sound waves. Then one day a Christmas present that he received set him thinking of a radically new method of treatment. The gift was a carbon dioxide winebottle opener, which lifts the cork by injecting it with CO_2 gas. What fascinated the surgeon was the fact that the gadget could cool a small area, since CO_2 is a coolant. He began developing an idea for an instrument that would consist of a hollow tube or cannula insulated like a thermos

DR. IRVING S. COOPER

bottle except at the tip. Chilled by liquid nitrogen, a more efficient coolant than CO_2, the tip of the probe could take the place of the surgeon's knife in disposing of diseased tissue. In 1961 such an instrument was built to Cooper's specifications by the head of the instrumentation laboratory of Columbia University. With it, the technique of cryosurgery was born.

With the cryoprobe, Dr. Cooper could perform thalamectomies more quickly, more simply, and with less risk to the patient. Once he has drilled a small hole in the patient's head, the surgeon positions the cannula, with the help of X-rays developed in ten seconds on Polaroid film, until the tip touches the correct location in the brain. At that point he sets the temperature at minus ten degrees Centigrade, cold enough to inhibit the function of the thalamus, but not cold enough to destroy cells. He then asks the patient to move the arm or leg that is being treated, while assistants test for side effects. If the indications are that he has not struck exactly the right spot, he merely lets the area warm up and moves his probe. When he has the tip positioned correctly, the doctor lowers the temperature to minus 70 degrees Centigrade and keeps it there for a few minutes to freeze the diseased cells solid.

After a year of performing cryothalectomies, Dr. Cooper reported to the American Medical Association in June 1962 that of the 150 operations he had performed, he had had no fatalities, two complications, and a spectacular success rate of 90 percent. By 1967 he had performed 3,800 such operations on patients crippled with Parkinson's disease or dystonia, and his success rate had not fallen. The mortality rate was only about 1 percent. Symptoms returned in about 11 percent of all cases, many of which were helped by follow-up freeze treatments.

After Dr. Cooper's success with cryothalectomy, other doctors began performing the operation in hospitals around the world. Surgeons also began adapting the technique of freezing to a wide range of surgical procedures, including removal of the pituitary gland, the prostate, tonsils, cataracts, tumors in the uterus, and certain skin cancers, correcting retinal detachment, and relieving the pain caused by large, incurable tumors.

In recent years a drug called L-dopa has become the standard treatment for Parkinson's disease, and Cooper operates only on those cases that have failed to respond to it. However, he still uses cryosurgery to treat dystonia, a variety of other involuntary movement disorders, and certain stroke victims. By 1972 he had developed a new surgical procedure to freeze the pulvinar, a section of the brain in the rear of the thalamus, in order to relieve the form of paralysis known as spastic hemiplegia, which afflicts many stroke victims and cerebral palsy sufferers. That paralysis cripples the limbs on one side of the patient's body. Dr. Cooper has also had some success with removing advanced brain tumors by freezing.

For some years research has shown that muscle spasticity could be moderated by stimulation of the cerebellum, a fist-sized section of the brain located at the base of the skull, which directs the body's coordination of movement. Reasoning that a mechanical stimulator could be planted surgically in a patient's brain to provide constant relief from spasticity, Dr. Cooper developed, with Roger Avery of the Avery Laboratories in Farmingdale, New York, an electrical "pacemaker" for the brain. It consists of two or four sets of tiny platinum electrodes embedded in Dacron-fiber mesh. During surgery a hole is made in the back of the skull and the electrodes are placed on the cerebellum. They are connected, by means of wires running under the skin, to two receivers implanted under the skin of the chest. An antenna is taped to the chest directly over the receivers, and the antenna is connected to a battery-powered transmitter that the patient can wear attached to his belt or in his breast pocket.

Late in 1972 Dr. Cooper implanted the first pacemaker in the brain of a young epileptic. When that operation turned out to be a success, the doctor continued to perform implant surgery, and by the end of 1973, he had given pacemakers to sixty-one patients with epilepsy, cerebral palsy, spasticity following strokes, dystonia, and other movement disorders. Of those, forty-two had experienced relief of symptoms. With Roger Avery and scientists from the Johns Hopkins University applied physics laboratory, he was reputedly working during 1974 on a more compact pacemaker system that would combine the exterior battery-pack and antenna and the internal receivers into one small power unit that would be implanted in the chest. It would be recharged with an external recharging unit that could work automatically while the patient sleeps at night.

From 1951 to 1966 Dr. Cooper served as associate attending neurosurgeon at the university hospital of New York University. Since 1951 he has been associate visiting neurosurgeon and consulting neurosurgeon of the institute of rehabilitation of Bellevue hospital and assistant attending neurosurgeon of the Hospital of Special Surgery and St. Joseph's Hospital. He has toured the world

four times to lecture on his work and was Eliza Savage visiting professor in Australia in 1962. He has published three books on his findings: *The Neurosurgical Alleviation of Parkinsonism* (C. C. Thomas, 1956), *Parkinsonism: Its Medical and Surgical Therapy* (C. C. Thomas, 1961), and *Involuntary Movement Disorders* (Hoeber, 1969).

Many honors have been conferred on Cooper, including the Lewis Harvey Taylor award of the American Therapeutic Society (1957); the St. Barnabas Hospital award (1959); the Modern Medicine award (1960); the alumni achievement award (1960) and the merit award (1967) of George Washington University; the humanitarian award of the National Cystic Fibrosis Foundation (1962); the merit award of the United Parkinson Foundation (1965), the gold medal of the Worshipful Societies of Apothecaries, London (1967); the Henderson Lecture award (1967); the bronze award of the American Congress of Rehabilitation Medicine (1967); and the Comenius University medal (1971). The American Medical Association has awarded him its Hektoen Bronze Medal (1957; 1958) and its certificate of merit (1961). Cooper is a member of the A.M.A., the Harvey Cushing Neurological Society, the Neurosurgical Society of America, and the American Academy of Neurology. He is governor of the Society of Cryobiology, president of the Society of Cryosurgery, and a fellow of the American College of Surgeons, the American Geriatric Society, the New York Academy of Medicine, and the New York Academy of Science. He has membership or honorary membership in professional societies in Scandinavia, Argentina, Egypt, Cuba, Spain, Portugal, and Czechoslovakia.

Despite the worldwide recognition that has been accorded to Dr. Cooper, he has had to weather a considerable amount of criticism during his pioneering career. Many of his surgical treatments have had to be tried for the first time on human beings, because no animal models exist for many of the diseases he treats, and his methods have been considered so radical that he has never been able to obtain government research grants. To help finance his work, he has put 20 percent of his income into his research. He has flatly refused to accommodate critics who say that he should conduct a controlled study in which some of his patients would receive dummy pacemakers. "That to me would be the most unethical of all," he told Jane E. Broday of the New York *Times* (September 22, 1973). "I'm treating desperate patients who have come to me for help, not an experiment."

Dr. Irving S. Cooper is a tall, energetic man with curly blond hair, blue eyes, and a muscular build. He plays a fast game of tennis and enjoys reading, the study of languages (he speaks six), and sampling vintage wines. By his first marriage, to Mary Dan Frost on December 15, 1944, he has three children, Daniel Alan, Douglas Paul, and Lisa Frost. Since January 31, 1970 he has been married to the former Sissel Holm. Cooper has toyed with the idea of quitting medicine to write and has published an autobiographical book,

The Victim is Always the Same (Harper, 1973), which recounts the moral and ethical self-questioning that he experienced before he first operated on a patient with dystonia, an eleven-year-old girl. The book received enthusiastic reviews. Calling it "a profoundly human book," Lord C. P. Snow wrote in the New York *Times Book Review* (August 12, 1973) that Cooper is "one of the most remarkable men alive. . . . He is regarded with intense respect, and something much warmer than that, by his English colleagues. They have told me that he attracts some envy, presumably because he appears to have all of the gifts that a man might conceivably wish for."

References

N Y Herald Tribune mag p20+ Ag 1 '65 por
N Y Times p1+ S 22 '73 pors
Sat R/World 1:66+ Ja 26 '74 por
American Men and Women of Science 12th ed (1971)
Who's Who in America, 1972-73

COPPOLA, FRANCIS FORD (cŏp'ə-lə)

Apr. 7, 1939- Motion picture director; screenwriter
Address: c/o Paramount Pictures Corp., 1 Gulf & Western Plaza, New York 10023

Foremost among the *wunderkinder* to achieve substantial recognition as a motion picture talent during the past decade is Francis Ford Coppola, the brilliant young director of *The Godfather*. One of a handful of directors with a graduate degree in film making, Coppola initially earned a modicum of success as a scriptwriter of "B" pictures for Seven Arts and as a directorial jack-of-all-trades for Roger Corman, the motion picture producer. Drawing on his wide-ranging experience, he wrote and directed his first major motion picture, *Dementia 13*, at the age of twenty-three. *The Godfather*, his fifth film, already occupies a secure niche in the history of motion pictures. Critically and popularly acclaimed, it earned three Academy Awards and was ranked as the screen's biggest box-office attraction as of early 1974.

The second of three children, Francis Ford Coppola was born in Detroit, Michigan on April 7, 1939. Shortly after his birth, his family moved to Queens, New York, where he grew up. His father, Carmine Coppola, of Neapolitan descent, was a concert flutist, composer, conductor, and occasional musical arranger for Radio City Music Hall, and his mother was a film actress. At an early age he developed a keen interest in the gadgetry and mechanics of film making. Using his family's 8-millimeter motion picture projector and a tape recorder, he created synchronized sound tracks for the Coppolas' home movies and edited segments from several films into "features" with such titles as "The Rich Millionaire" and "The Lost Wallet." Stricken by polio in the late

FRANCIS FORD COPPOLA

1940's and confined to bed for about a year, he began experimenting with puppets and puppet theatres. "The technical thing for gadgetry and the interest in plays and puppets and theatre and musical-comedy sort of came together in film, which was like a playground for all those things," he has explained.

An expert tuba player, Coppola attended the New York Military Academy at Cornwall-on-Hudson on a music scholarship, but he became piqued when his original book and lyrics for the class musical were considerably rewritten before presentation and he transferred to Great Neck (Long Island) High School for his senior year. After graduating in 1955, he enrolled at Hofstra University at Hempstead, Long Island to study theatre arts. In emulation of his cinematic idol, Sergei Eisenstein, the innovative Russian film director, he learned set design, lighting, script writing, and directing. Coppola was elected president of the Green Wig, the university's drama group, and the Kaleidoscopians, the musical comedy club, in the same semester, and brought about a merger of the two organizations into the Spectrum Players. Under his leadership the Spectrum Players presented a new production each week, many of them directed by students. Coppola wrote both the book and the lyrics for *A Delicate Touch*, an original musical comedy, and directed several musicals as well as a production of *A Streetcar Named Desire*. He founded the Cinema Workshop and contributed short stories to *The Word*, the campus literary magazine.

On taking his B.A. degree in theatre in 1959, Coppola entered the film school at the University of California at Los Angeles. Many of the graduate students were older than he and more pessimistic about the likelihood of succeeding in the Hollywood market place without compromising their integrity. Although he shared their mistrust of the established film industry, he was eager to work for a major motion picture producer. "I pattern my life on Hitler in this respect," Coppola explained, as quoted in *Newsweek* magazine (February 20, 1967). "He didn't just take over the country. He worked his way into the existing fabric first." Clarifying his admittedly "shocking" statement in an interview for WVHC-FM, Hofstra University's radio station, on April 8 and 15, 1968, he told reporter Richard Koszarski, "I was trying to say that as long as I believed in . . . film and film making it didn't matter that I became part of the Hindenburg government, because I was going to make it my own. The way to come to power is not always to merely challenge the Establishment, but first make a place in it and then challenge, and double-cross, the Establishment."

While at UCLA, Coppola accepted a position as an assistant to Roger Corman, the prolific producer of low-budget horror films. His first assignment was to write an English-language script that would transform a Russian science fiction adventure film into a standard monster movie. Retitled *Battle Beyond the Sun*, the film was released by American International in 1963. Impressed by his young assistant's tenacity and adaptability, Corman kept Coppola on as an all-purpose assistant to serve as dialogue director for *The Tower of London* (American International, 1962), sound man for *The Young Racers* (American International, 1963), and associate producer for *The Terror* (American International, 1964).

While on location in Ireland for *The Young Racers*, Coppola took advantage of his employer's passion for thrift and suggested that the camera crew shoot a second, less expensive feature. With Corman's enthusiastic approval, Coppola completed the script for *Dementia 13* (American International, 1962), a chilling tale of axe murders, in just three days. The film, his directorial debut, received generally favorable reviews. "It was the only film I've ever enjoyed working on," he told Stephen Farber in an interview for *Sight and Sound* (Autumn 1972).

On the strength of his having won the Samuel Goldwyn Award, the annual prize for the best screenplay submitted by a UCLA film school student, Seven Arts hired him to adapt Carson McCullers' novel *Reflections in a Golden Eye* for the screen. Pleased with his efforts, Seven Arts raised his salary and assigned him to a variety of script writing projects. During the next few years, Coppola wrote or collaborated on nearly a dozen films for Seven Arts, including *This Property is Condemned* (Paramount-Seven Arts, 1966), which was loosely based on Tennessee Williams' one-act play of the same title. While a "house writer" for Seven Arts, he contracted with Twentieth Century-Fox to write the script for *Patton*. His conception of the American general as "a man out of his time . . . a Don Quixote figure" won him the 1970 award for the best story and screenplay from the American Academy of Motion Picture Arts and Sciences, an honor he shared with his cowriter, Edmund Worth.

The original script for *Is Paris Burning?* (Paramount, 1967), written by Coppola and Gore Vidal,

was so drastically revised by a team of patriotic French writers that the American pair would have preferred to remain anonymous. To maintain his sanity during the tedious filming of *Is Paris Burning?* Coppola wrote a screenplay based on *You're a Big Boy Now*, a novel by David Benedictus. With the aid of Phil Feldman, a Seven Arts executive, he obtained the necessary financial backing. "The way we worked was the way I work now," he told Richard Koszarski. "I don't ask anybody if I can make a movie. I present them with the fact that I am going to make a movie, and if they're wise they'll get in on it." Having persuaded Geraldine Page, Julie Harris, and several other top professionals to tackle the bizarre character roles, Coppola entrusted the leads to Peter Kastner and Elizabeth Hartman, both relative newcomers. After three weeks of videotaped rehearsals, he began filming in June 1966 at such New York City landmarks as the Public Library, Times Square, and Central Park. Before the two-month shooting schedule had run its course, Seven Arts increased the budget from $250,000 to $1,000,000—an unprecedented vote of confidence in a fledgling director.

Exhibited in Los Angeles late in 1966 in order to be eligible for that year's Academy Awards competition, *You're a Big Boy Now* was released nationally in February 1967 to enthusiastic reviews. A film critic for *Newsweek* (February 20, 1967) raved: "Not since Welles was a boy wonder or Kubrick a kid has any young American made a film as original, spunky or just plain funny as this one." Howard Thompson, in his New York *Times* review of March 21, 1967, saluted the film as a "vibrantly visual comic strip" and compared Coppola's color camera to "a frenetic, kaleidoscopic blotter." Besides offering evidence that he was a director of uncommon promise, *You're a Big Boy Now* satisfied the graduate requirements of UCLA's film school and earned Coppola his Master of Arts degree.

Abandoning his resolve to avoid the lures of the major Hollywood studios, Coppola agreed to direct Warner Brothers' long-delayed film version of *Finian's Rainbow*. Scornful of the studio's intention to update the twenty-year-old musical comedy, he scrapped a "topical" adaptation in favor of faithful adherence to the original stage play. Working from his own screenplay, he treated the story, in his words, as "a fantasy without time or place." Some critics, however, objected to *Finian's Rainbow*'s anachronistic blend of social consciousness and whimsy. In *Newsweek* (October 21, 1968) Joseph Morgenstern commended Coppola's attempt "to lift the face of this period piece," but found the film "a shuffling relic [trying] valiantly to be modern."

Eager to return to independent film making, Coppola declined an offer to direct Warner Brothers' production of *Mame* and selected for his next project *The Rain People*, based on a short story he had written for a creative writing class in college. *The Rain People*, which was filmed entirely on location for Warner Brothers-Seven

Arts by a skeleton crew of technicians, starred Shirley Knight Hopkins as the well-educated, pregnant, and bored housewife who runs away from her conjugal responsibilities and drives aimlessly around the United States. Although the film received generally lukewarm reviews after its release in 1969, many film critics praised Coppola's technical expertise, citing its "gorgeous composition," "cinéma vérité realism," and "unusually sensitive sound effects." The film won an award at the San Sebastian (Spain) International Cinema Festival in 1970, and it remains Coppola's personal favorite.

Unhappy about the financial and supervisory "over control" of the major studios, in 1969 Coppola established and became the president of American Zoetrope, a production center for young independent film makers. Located in a San Francisco warehouse, American Zoetrope, named after a nineteenth-century optical toy, had facilities for editing, mixing, sound recording, and camera repair as well as a completely outfitted camera truck for location shooting. During its first year the company made more films than several Hollywood studios. Besides George Lucas' THX-1138, American Zoetrope produced a number of lesser-known films, such as Vesuvia, Naked Gypsies, and Have We Seen the Elephant?, and it made television features, educational films, and several documentaries for the Office of Economic Opportunity and the President's Committee for Voluntary Action. Although Coppola poured much of his time, energy, and money into the struggling enterprise, American Zoetrope foundered in the midst of a film industry recession and plunged him into debt.

To recoup his financial losses, Coppola signed with Paramount to direct the movie version of The Godfather, Mario Puzo's best-selling novel about the Mafiosi. Although top studio executives objected strenuously to Coppola's scenario for The Godfather, the young director was adamant in his insistence on making a "period" film on location rather than a typical backlot gangster melodrama. Demanding casting control, he was determined to cast Marlon Brando as Don Vito Corleone and Al Pacino as his son Michael. "I was getting 'fired' every other week," he recalled for Stephen Farber. "The things they were going to fire me over were . . . the very things that made the film different from any other film." Plagued by internal disputes over the film's cast, runaway budget, and script, which had been written by Coppola and Puzo, the project was further harassed by repeated confrontations with the Italian-American Civil Rights League. In return for its cooperation, the League exacted a pledge to delete all references to the Mafia and the Cosa Nostra. Coppola and producer Al Ruddy readily agreed. "It's not really about the Mafia," the director contended, as quoted in New York magazine (August 23, 1971). "It could just as well be about the Kennedys, or the Rothschilds, about a dynasty which demands personal allegiance to a family that transcends even one's obligation to one's country."

Filmed in what Coppola has described as a "forties" style, The Godfather was acclaimed by critics for its powerful visual images and its cool, detached direction. "In its blending of new depth with an old genre," wrote Jay Cocks in his Time review of April 13, 1972, "it becomes that rarity, a mass entertainment that is also great movie art." Since its opening on March 15, 1972, The Godfather has broken worldwide motion picture attendance records. During the first few months of its long run, the film grossed more than $1 million a day. At the forty-fifth annual awards presentation of the Academy of Motion Picture Arts and Sciences on March 27, 1973, The Godfather was honored with Oscars for the best picture, the best actor, and the best screenplay based on material from another medium. A sequel to the film, The Godfather, Part II, which began production under Coppola's direction in September 1973, is scheduled for release in December 1974.

In September 1972 Coppola and two other successful young directors, William Friedkin and Peter Bogdanovich, formed the Directors Company. The company, conceived by Coppola and Charles Bluhdorn, the chairman of Gulf & Western Industries, Paramount Pictures Corporation's parent company, is jointly owned by the three directors, who control 50 percent of the stock, and by Paramount. In return for the studio's guarantee of $31,500,000 to finance the company, each director agreed to make four films over a twelve-year period for Paramount release. The first major motion pictures produced by the firm were Bogdanovich's Paper Moon (1973) and Friedkin's The Bunker Hill Boys, not yet released. The Conversation, a psychological horror story about an American bugging expert that Coppola both wrote and directed, was released on April 7, 1974 in New York City. The film, which featured Gene Hackman in the leading role, was well received by most critics, who admired its manipulation of suspense and its technical ingenuity. On May 24, 1974 The Conversation received the Cannes Film Festival's highest award, the Golden Palm.

Continuing his interest in all forms of dramatic art, Coppola directed a 1972 revival of Noel Coward's Private Lives for the American Conservatory Theatre in San Francisco and staged the American première of The Visit of the Old Lady by Gottfried von Einem for the San Francisco Opera Company in October 1972. He also continued to work as a scriptwriter and completed the screenplay for Paramount's long awaited The Great Gatsby (1974). Despite a heavy schedule of personal commitments, he finds time to encourage young talent. He served, for example, as the executive producer for George Lucas' phenomenally successful American Graffiti (Universal, 1973).

Black-haired, bearded, bespectacled, and somewhat portly, Francis Ford Coppola has been described by one journalist as looking "more like an aging graduate student than a directorial hotshot." He and his wife, the former Eleanor Neil, a graphic artist he met in Ireland while shooting *Dementia 13*, live with their three children, Sophia, Gian-Carlo, and Roman, in a huge house overlooking San Francisco Bay. The thirty-room mansion includes a fully equipped studio, a projection room, and an "electric train room." In a recent interview, he confessed to Stephen Farber that he was "in a real state of transition," personally as well as professionally. "I was raised to be successful and rich. . . . I now am as successful as I ever want to be, and I'm pretty rich. . . . I do not really wear well being famous or successful. . . . I don't know the real answer, I just want honestly to follow my inclinations."

References

Films in Review 19:529+ N '68 pors
N Y Post p15 Apr 8 '72 por
New Times 2:55+ My 3 '74 pors
Newsday A p48 N 14 '68 por
Sight and Sound 41:217+ Autumn '72

Gelmis, Joseph. The Film Director as Superstar (1970)

CORTÁZAR, JULIO (kôr-tä′zär)

Aug. 26, 1914- Argentine novelist and short story writer
Address: 9, Place du General Beuret, Paris XV, France

An Argentine novelist who lives in France, Julio Cortázar is both one of the best—and one of the most unsettling and difficult—of the writers who have contributed to the present renaissance of Latin American literature. His literary career consists of three phases, each marked by his weird imagination, uncompromising intellectuality, and tireless experimentation. Cortázar first won a reputation with three books of short stories in the fantastic vein, much influenced by his compatriot and master, Jorge Luis Borges. Then followed three novels—*Los premios* (*The Winners*, 1960), *Rayuela* (*Hopscotch*, 1963), and *62: modelo para armar* (*62: A Model Kit*, 1968)—which are honeycombed with metaphysical and psychological preoccupations, and which move progressively further away from traditional approaches to form, plot, and character. The third phase was heralded by his fourth novel, *Libro de Manuel* (*Book of Manuel*, 1973), an overtly political book that is grounded on his fervent belief in humanistic socialism as the answer to Latin America's problems. Cortázar is perhaps best known internationally as the author of the short story "*Las babas del diablo*," which became the source of Michelangelo Antonioni's film *Blow-Up*. Pablo Neruda once said: "Anyone who doesn't read Cortázar is doomed. Not to read him is a grave invisible disease which in time can have terrible consequences. . . . I don't want those things to happen to me, and so I greedily devour all the fabrications, myths, contradictions, and mortal games of the great Julio Cortázar."

Julio Cortázar was born on August 26, 1914, in Brussels, Belgium, the son of Julio José and María Herminia (Descotte) Cortázar, two upper middle-class Argentines who were traveling in Europe at the time. Some sources say that his father was abroad as a member of the diplomatic corps. Rita Guibert, in her book *Seven Voices* (Knopf, 1973), quotes Cortázar as saying: "My birth was a product of tourism and diplomacy. . . . I happened to be born during the days when the Germans occupied Brussels at the beginning of the First World War. I was four years old by the time my family were able to return to Argentina; I spoke mostly French, which left me with a way of pronouncing 'r' that I could never get rid of." That early displacement partly accounts for Cortázar's cosmopolitanism, his living abroad, and the feeling of many of his deracinated characters that they have no home, no place where they belong.

On returning to Argentina, the Cortázars settled in the Buenos Aires suburb of Bánfield. Julio's father left home when the boy was still very young, and the family had little money. Nevertheless, Julio's mother made sacrifices to send him to the Teachers College of Buenos Aires, from which he graduated in 1936, qualified to teach literature. After another year of study at the University of Buenos Aires, Cortázar was offered a job teaching high school in a town in Buenos Aires province. He accepted because of his family's financial straits and spent the next seven years teaching in small provincial towns. In Luis Harss' book *Into the Mainstream* (Harper & Row, 1967), Cortázar says of that period: "I was always very ingrown. . . . I used to spend the day in my room in my hotel or boardinghouse, reading and studying. . . . It was useful in the sense that I consumed thousands of books. . . . It was dangerous in that it probably deprived me of a good share of vital experience."

Cortázar's intellectual development paralleled that of Jorge Luis Borges, the great Argentine poet and short story writer. Like Borges and many other Latin Americans, he looked to Europe for literary inspiration. An important milestone was his discovery of Cocteau's *Opium: Journal d'une Désintoxication*, which prompted his passionate interest in French literature. He told Harss that "My generation was considerably at fault in its youth in that it lived . . . with its back turned towards Argentina. We were great snobs. . . . We read very few Argentine writers and were almost exclusively interested in English and French literature, with a bit of Italian and American literature thrown in, and some German. . . ."

Although Cortázar had been writing since he was a child, it was not until he was almost thirty that he judged any of his efforts worthy of publication. His first book, a collection of sonnets composed under the spell of Stéphane Mallarmé, appeared in 1941, under a pseudonym; he prefers that it be forgotten. In 1944 he took a post at the University of Cuyo in Mendoza. There he became involved in a movement that unsuccessfully tried to block Juan Domingo Perón's drive to power. When Perón was elected President in 1946, Cortázar resigned because he knew he would be fired. Moving to Buenos Aires, he studied to become a translator, and followed that métier from 1946 to 1951.

Cortázar's second book, *Los reyes (The Kings)*, a series of dialogues in verse concerning the Minotaur myth, appeared in 1949. The book contains an interesting reinterpretation of the myth, in which Theseus is viewed as a crass hero, while the Minotaur is portrayed as the poet, locked in the labyrinth because of his unconventionality. Nevertheless, *Los reyes* attracted little or no attention in Buenos Aires, perhaps because of the hyper-intellectuality that characterizes Cortázar at his least inspired moments.

For some years Cortázar had been writing short stories, but they failed to measure up to his standards. It was not until 1951, when he was thirty-six years old, that his first book of any import was published. Although *Bestiario* (Bestiary) contained only eight short stories, it established Cortázar's literary personality. The stories belong to the literature of fantasy, and thus are in the tradition of Borges, the master of that genre, but Cortázar escapes the danger of being overwhelmed by Borges' influence. His tales are the product of a singular imagination, marked by his wit, by his shrewd observation of the Buenos Aires milieu and idiom, and by an uneasy sense of something lurking in the shadows. Ordinary situations skid into weird or crazy realms where the reader becomes unsure of his footing. The technical effects in *Bestiario* are already accomplished, testifying to Cortázar's long years of silent apprenticeship.

Bestiario appeared in the same month that Cortázar, depressed by the Perón regime, left Argentina for Europe. He took up residence in France, married Aurora Bernárdez in 1953, and continued to write. Eventually he found work as a freelance translator for UNESCO. *Bestiario* had attracted little attention outside literary circles in Argentina, and his second collection of stories, *Final del juego* (End of the Game), did not appear until 1956, when it was published in Mexico. Like the stories in *Bestiario*, those in *Final del juego* rely on expert technique to toy with bizarre ideas and effects. Often the stories are circular in structure, proposing fantastic juxtapositions of time, location, or dimension. In "Continuity of Parks," a man reading a novel becomes the murder victim of the novel's hero; in "Axolotl," a man becomes obsessed with a strange salamander in a Paris aquarium, and one day finds himself transformed into the salamander.

Cortázar's third collection of stories, *Las armas secretas* (The Secret Weapons, 1959), contained a novella titled "El perseguidor" (The Pursuer), which introduced a new tone into his work. The hero of the story is a jazz musician modeled on the great Charlie ("Bird") Parker, who, like Cortázar, is bedeviled by his metaphysical sense, most notably by an obsession with time. More than just a means of expression, his music is a

JULIO CORTÁZAR

tool in his search for his truest self. The novella marks Cortázar's first real exploration of the labyrinths of personality, in both a psychological and philosophical sense. "Fantasy for its own sake had stopped interesting me," he told Harss. "In 'El Perseguidor' I wanted to stop inventing and stand on my own ground, to look at myself a bit. And looking at myself meant looking at my neighbor, at man."

"El Perseguidor" made Cortázar famous in Argentina. A year later he published his first novel, which would eventually win him an international reputation. *Los premios* (translated as *The Winners* by Elaine Kerrigan, Pantheon, 1965), concerns a motley group of Argentines who are thrown together on a cruise that they have won in a lottery. Almost as soon as they board the ship, mysterious events take place. Since the whole stern is closed off, rumors begin to circulate about the terrible things going on there. Finally a group of passengers go below and try to reach the stern through the entrails of the ship. Because of the cross-section of Argentine types involved, the book has been interpreted as a satire or an allegory, but on a deeper level it constitutes yet another chapter in Cortázar's search for the essence of self, depicting how various human types look for what Cortázar calls the "way out"—out of their miseries and problems.

As with all of Cortázar's books, critical reaction to *Los premios* was mixed, although favorable enough to lead to translations into French and English. When *The Winners* appeared in the United States, William Goyen wrote in the New York *Times Book Review* (March 21, 1965): "This formidable novel should be welcomed here, for it introduces an outstanding writer of immense scope. . . . He creates a language and rhythm and sensuality as mysterious and terrible as Melville's but all in his own voice." Less impressed, Anthony West of the *New Yorker* (May 8, 1965) complained that the book was condescending, and other critics objected to metaphysical asides delivered by one of the characters.

Although written a decade earlier, Cortázar's *Historias de cronopios y de famas* (translated into English by Paul Blackburn as *Cronopios and Famas*, Pantheon, 1969) did not appear in Buenos Aires until 1962. In that collection of humorous short pieces Cortázar classifies three human types: *cronopios*, who are artistic, temperamental, impractical, and optimistic; *famas*, who are cautious and well-organized pessimists; and *esperanzas*, dull people who "never take the trouble." The book also contains sections on "The Instruction Manual," "Unusual Occupations," and "Unstable Stuff," all viewed from his unique perspective.

First published in 1963, the book that most critics call Cortázar's masterpiece is *Rayuela* (translated by Gregory Rabassa as *Hopscotch*, Pantheon 1966). Its hero, an Argentine named Oliveira, is a dedicated *cronopio*, perhaps the definitive incarnation of Cortázar's searcher. The story takes place in Paris and Buenos Aires, and follows Oliveira through various phases of seeking his "way out." As Harss describes him, Oliveira is "a triumphantly backboneless character" who makes "a concerted effort . . . to subvert rational barriers and collapse logical categories. . . . Oliveira lives in extremities, a ruinous shadow of himself, going from stranglehold to deadlock."

Enormously popular in Latin America, *Rayuela* was praised for its mad humor and bold experiments with form. It is, in reality, two books. One is to be read in the normal manner, following chapters one through fifty-six; the other is to be read by hopscotching between the first fifty-six chapters and 100 additional, "expendable" ones in an order prescribed by the author. What most impressed European and American critics was the intensity of Cortázar's investigation of life, language, and literature. As C. D. B. Bryan pointed out in the *New Republic* (April 23, 1966): "The book is hard going. Deliberately. It is a spiraling, convulsive, exploding universe of a novel. . . . And if it does not render every other novel written about a search for meaning obsolete, it certainly emphasizes their inadequacy." Other critics, however, while noting Cortázar's remarkable technical skills, felt that his experimentation was not wholly successful. In the *Saturday Review* (April 9, 1966), Emile Capouya remarked that "at first, from moment to moment, the reader has the conviction that he is in the hands of a master artist. It is only after some time that he finds the art to have been improvisation only."

Cortázar's next novel, *62: modelo para armar* (*62: A Model Kit*, Pantheon, 1972), is an outgrowth of a chapter in *Rayuela*, and stems from the author's fascination with the concept of "figures" or "structures." He has said: "I'm constantly sensing the possibility of certain links, of circuits that close around us, interconnecting us in a way that defies all rational explanation and has nothing to do with the ordinary human bonds that join people." *62: A Model Kit* is a complex novel about a group of people who form such a "figure," who are tied together like a constellation without being fully aware of it. As Cortázar

had predicted, the novel did not find many readers, although it was respectfully reviewed.

Throughout the 1960's Cortázar's thinking had been taking an increasingly political turn. That drift finally gave a radically new direction to his work, as witnessed by the novel *Libro de Manuel* (Book of Manuel), which was published in Buenos Aires early in 1973. The book is about a group of young exiles, mostly South American, living in Paris, who kidnap an important political figure in an effort to free some of their compatriots from jail. Those activists are contrasted with their vacillating friend, Andrés, an aesthete unable to decide whether or not he should commit himself to political action. In *Libro de Manuel*, Cortázar's experiments with language are muted, and his philosophical preoccupations, though still present, yield to political ones. The novel makes a plea for humanism in leftist politics: his young heroes are working for a revolution that salvages its sense of humor and its tolerance of differences. It is significant that Cortázar, while an outspoken admirer of Castro's Cuba, has been equally vocal in his opposition to the persecution of dissident Cuban intellectuals. Cortázar's fourth collection of short stories, *Todos los fuegos el fuego* (*All Fires the Fire*), was published by Pantheon in 1973, to a generally favorable critical reception. He has also published the whimsically titled miscellany *La Vuelta al día en 80 mundos* (Around the Day in 80 Worlds).

Julio Cortázar has an unusual appearance for a Latin American. Over six feet tall, and lean and gangly, he has a boyishly handsome face that makes him look much younger than he is. He is a reticent, sometimes withdrawn man who loves solitude and who maintains a certain formality with interviewers. Passionately fond of jazz, he plays the trumpet and maintains a huge record collection. Since the 1950's he and his wife, Aurora Bernárdez, who is a literary figure in her own right, and known for her translations of Sartre and Camus into Spanish, have divided their time between houses in Paris and the south of France. Cortázar has also travelled widely in South America and Europe, and has visited North Africa, India, Cuba and the United States. He finds exploring Paris a never-ending occupation. Cortázar's intellectuality is always tempered by his wit, but he is extremely serious about his quest for something new: "The question is: can one do something different, set out in another direction?" he told Luis Harss. "Beyond logic, beyond Kantian categories, beyond the whole apparatus of Western thought—for instance, looking at the world as if it weren't an expression of Euclidian geometry—is it possible to push across a new border, to take a leap into something more authentic? Of course I don't know. But I think it is."

References

Américas 15:39+ Mar '63 por
Guibert, Rita. Seven Voices (1973)
Harss, Luis and Dohmann, Barbara. Into the Mainstream (1967)

CRUMB, GEORGE (HENRY)

Oct. 24, 1929- Composer; educator
Address: b. Dept. of Music, University of Pennsylvania, Philadelphia, Pa. 19104; h. 240 Kirk Lane, Media, Pa. 19063

GEORGE CRUMB

Unwilling to settle for the superficial gimmickry that some of his colleagues consider an end in itself, the composer George Crumb has used his daring effects and haunting sonorities to establish a new communication with audiences and for his subtle meshing of old and new sounds has won the enthusiastic applause of his listeners and the admiration of critics. He is the recipient of a 1968 Pulitzer Prize, for *Echoes of Time and the River*, as well as the more significant musical grants and commissions. Because of his tendency to involve interpreters of his works in unorthodox, ritualistic action, he has been termed a "musical dramatist." He has also been called a "tone poet," Beethoven's phrase for himself. The critic Paul Hume of the Washington *Post* has described Crumb as a foremost composer of our time who expands his own horizon and that of the music-loving public with each new composition.

Among the diversified sources of Crumb's musical inspiration are the poetry of García Lorca, signs of the zodiac, and the "whale songs" investigated in recent years by marine biologists. The mixed media employed to perform his compositions include masks, colored lights, and vocal expressions and range from standard orchestral instruments, some of which are electronically expanded, and off-beat instruments such as the banjo, harmonica, and jew's harp, to Japanese Kabuki blocks, Tibetan prayer stones, a musical saw, and even a pail of water.

George Henry Crumb was born on October 24, 1929 to George Henry and Vivian (Reed) Crumb in Charleston, West Virginia, where he grew up and went to school. Both of his parents were musicians: his father played the clarinet, taught music, and directed a band until his death in 1950; his mother was a cellist. Another musical member of the family, his brother, William Reed Crumb, who now lives in Annandale, Virginia, played the flute. Teaching himself to play the piano by ear, from the age of nine or ten George Crumb composed Mozart-like pieces to be performed by his parents and brother, who in the Depression years could afford as entertainment only the music they created for themselves at home. At Charleston High School he belonged to the track team, but otherwise devoted himself almost entirely to music, reportedly to the extent of disconcerting his teacher by composing tunes in his English class.

In 1947, after finishing high school, Crumb enrolled in Mason College, a Charleston conservatory of music no longer in existence. He graduated with his B.Mus. degree in 1950, earned his M.Mus. degree at the University of Illinois in 1952, and enrolled at the University of Michigan to work for his doctorate. But before fulfilling requirements for his D.Mus. Arts degree, conferred in 1959, he

studied during the summer of 1955 at the Berkshire Music Center in Tanglewood, Massachusetts and then for a year, 1955-56, under a Fulbright fellowship at the Hochschule für Musik in Berlin. One of his teachers at the University of Michigan was Ross Lee Finney, with whom he studied composition. In the course of his lengthy formal musical training he also studied composition with Eugene Weigel and piano with Stanley Fletcher and Benning Dexter.

Although less derivative than much of his earlier work, Crumb's 1954 String Quartet, which he considers the first of his mature compositions, suggests "a lot of Hindemith, Bartók, and Berg," as he admitted in an interview with Donal Henahan for the New York *Times* (December 13, 1970). His next important work, Sonata for Solo Violoncello of 1955, was followed in 1959 by *Variazioni*, for large orchestra, which vaguely echoes Schönberg and Dallapiccola in its experiment with a twelve-tone theme. Crumb has never seriously used the twelve-tone technique of composition, but his work does show a certain receptivity to the influence of serialism on post-World War II music, as Henahan pointed out, "in a Weberian concern for economy, for delicate shades of dynamics (a Crumb score is always asking someone to play 'tenderly, hauntingly, as if from afar' or 'incredibly soft, almost inaudible'), and for sparse, wispy textures."

Variazioni had been written during an eventful year in which Crumb not only graduated from the University of Michigan, but also left his one year's teaching post as instructor of theory at Hollins College for an appointment as assistant professor of composition and piano at the University of Colorado, where he taught from 1959 to 1964. One of his fellow teachers at Colorado was the pianist David Burge, who urged him to compose music for the piano. After Crumb completed *Five Pieces for Piano* in 1962, Burge performed the work in an extensive concert tour and then recorded it for the Advance label.

Not a prolific composer, but steady and painstaking, Crumb produced *Night Music I* for soprano, keyboard, and percussion in 1963 and *Four Nocturnes: Night Music II* in 1964. His *Madrigals, Books I and II* for solo voice and instruments, written in 1965, was commissioned by the Koussevitzky Music Foundation. When *Madrigals, Book I* was performed at Lincoln Center's Philharmonic Hall in New York by the Festival Chamber Ensemble in July 1968, along with five other foundation-commissioned works, the New York *Times* critic Allen Hughes thought it one of the "furthest out in terms of sonorities" of the presentations of that avant-garde concert.

In the poetry of García Lorca, Crumb found a simple, melancholy imagery suitable to the somber mood of much of his own music. Crumb reads, but does not speak, Spanish. While attending the University of Michigan, he became aware of the beauty of Spanish in song when he heard Lorca's "Casida of the Boy Wounded by the Water" set to music by Edward Chudacoff, a fellow graduate student. Crumb himself eventually used that poem in one of his compositions. Both in his early *Madrigals* and in the work that followed, *Eleven Echoes of Autumn, 1965* (1966) for violin, alto flute, clarinet, and piano, Crumb included excerpts in Spanish from Lorca. The latter, which he wrote for the Aeolian Chamber Players, also introduced many technical directions—in bowing and plucking violin strings, for example, and speaking across the mouthpiece of a flute—to produce sounds that stir the imagination.

Another of Crumb's technically brilliant and inventive compositions, *Echoes of Time and the River* (1967), was commissioned by the University of Chicago and premièred by the Chicago Symphony Orchestra. The composer requires his musicians not only to whisper or shout out occasional phrases, but also sometimes to play their instruments in untraditional ways to achieve sounds suggestive of poetic ideas. At one point in the performance, for instance, the percussionist produces a "bent" pitch by beating a tremolo on a gong that he lowers and raises in and out of a bucket of water nine inches deep.

The enigmatic use of a fragment from Lorca, ". . .y los arcos rotos dónde sufre el tiempo" (and the broken arches where time suffers), in both *Eleven Echoes* and *Echoes of Time and the River* supplies one of several links between the two works. Besides alluding in its title to the Thomas Wolfe novel, the orchestral piece contains a reference to Crumb's home state of West Virginia in its inclusion of the Latin motto "Montani semper liberi" (Mountaineers always free). *Echoes of Times and the River* was awarded the 1968 Pulitzer Prize for the best work by a composer of established American residence. When it was presented at Tanglewood in August 1970 by the Berkshire Music Center's Festival of Contemporary Music, with Gunther Schuller conducting, the reviewer for the New York *Times* (August 18, 1970) declared *Echoes of Time and the River* to be "a four-movement masterpiece," adding that the incorporation of the ritualistic processions, omitted at the Chicago première, gave life to the work in its music-theatre form.

Songs, Drones and Refrains of Death, scored for baritone with guitar, piano, and double bass (all three instruments amplified) plus percussion for two players, is a García Lorca cycle on which George Crumb worked from 1962 to 1968. An intense treatment of death and violence, the piece features some elements common to most Crumb music: vocal impressions of chanting, whispering, and shouting together with colorful instrumental effects such as that produced by the percussionist's malleting on bass or guitar strings. The New York *Times* critic Allen Hughes called a late-April 1973 performance of the work at Carnegie Recital Hall another instance to rejoice in George Crumb's talent and admired the impact of the cycle as a whole despite some minor qualifications. A year later a new performance of the same work was given in the same hall by the Philadelphia Composers Forum, an ensemble in which Crumb has occasionally played and which is known for its special sensitivity in interpreting his music. "The piece sounds as evocative as ever," John Rockwell wrote in the New York *Times* (May 7, 1974), "even if the staid theatrics and academically proper approximations of Spanish passion are beginning to look a little silly."

Of the only eighteen compositions that Crumb in early 1974 said he was prepared to acknowledge, two were written in 1969: *Madrigals, Books III and IV* for soprano and instruments and *Night of the Four Moons* for alto and instruments. The latter reflects his ambiguous reaction to the Apollo 11 flight of 1969, when man first landed on the moon, although again he is indebted to Lorca for his text. Commenting on the 1974 Columbia recording of *Night of the Four Moons,* by the mezzo-soprano Jan DeGaetani with the Aeolian Chamber Players, Henahan pointed out in the New York *Times* (April 21, 1974), "Alongside his exotic sounds and his sometimes esoteric excursions into mysticism, Crumb almost always places startling ordinary material. In this he follows, no doubt consciously, the path of Mahler and Ives." Crumb sprinkles quotations from other musicians through his compositions, as Henahan further observed, and in *Night of the Four Moons* he refers directly to Mahler, marking the ending "Berceuse, in stilo Mahleriano." In several performances of his piece the composer himself has played the banjo.

In 1970 George Crumb completed *Black Angels (Thirteen Images from the Dark Land)* for electric, or amplified, string quartet, commissioned by the University of Michigan, and *Ancient Voices of Children* for soprano, boy soprano and seven instruments, including a musical saw. Described by one reviewer as "grim but poetic" when given its New York première at Lincoln Center in mid-November 1971 by the Bowling Green String Quartet, *Black Angels* is structured on a numerological formula revolving around seven and thirteen, with themes from the *Dies Irae* and Schubert's *Death and the Maiden.* Crumb directs the musicians to speak, count, or whisper in French, German, Russian, Japanese, and Swahili, besides whistling, shaking maracas while playing pizzicato with the same hand, or drawing their bows across twenty water-filled, tuned glasses in accompaniment to the "God-Music" produced by the electric cello. Such "oddities," as he called them, tempted Henahan to quip in his review for the New York *Times* (November 16, 1971) that "no tone is left unturned" in Crumb's search for the right sound. He also went on to note that *Black Angels* proved a "perilously but craftily poised piece," with "mysteriously poignant moments balancing the violence." Comparing a Composers Recordings, Inc., and a Vox recording of *Black Angels* in *High Fidelity* (November 1973), Robert P. Morgan remarked that it was "an extraordinary piece that holds up well under repeated hearings."

Quite often the title of a Crumb piece prepares the listener for its predominant sound. One such composition is *Ancient Voices of Children*, which was commissioned by the Elizabeth Sprague Coolidge Foundation for premièring at the Library of Congress' fourteenth Festival of Chamber Music at the end of October 1970. That work, counted by some critics among his masterpieces, marked a return to the poems of García Lorca for Crumb, who was rewarded by the deeply impressed, musically sophisticated audience in Washington with a standing, cheering ovation seldom witnessed at concerts of modern music. When performed at Hunter College in New York later that year, again with the singers of the Washington presentation, Jan DeGaetani and the boy soprano Michael Dash, the critic Harold C. Schonberg praised it in the New York *Times* (December 19, 1970) as a "brilliant, even slick piece of writing, completely eclectic yet with a great deal of personality." Schonberg also commented that Crumb—"hypnotized by pure, sheer, sensuous sound" and capable of some extraordinary acoustical achievements—went beyond sound for sound's sake by aiming for expressivity and often succeeding. Once more performed at the Library of Congress in late March 1972, *Ancient Voices* was enhanced by the simple choreography designed by Lynda Gudde for four dancers. On that occasion Paul Hume wrote in the Washington *Post* (March 27, 1972) of the "formidable strengths," "unchanging beauties," and "powerful evocations" of the score and of Crumb's "glorious array of instruments."

Other distinguished performances of *Ancient Voices of Children* include that of the New York Philharmonic, with Pierre Boulez conducting, at Philharmonic Hall in January 1973. According to the Canadian music critic John Kraglund of the Toronto *Globe and Mail* (April 1, 1974), *Ancient Voices* was probably the most moving work of a sold-out, all-Crumb concert presented by the Music Concerts series in Toronto in late March 1974. Kraglund acclaimed Crumb's music in general for being "consistently engrossing and frequently emotionally involving." Presented at the UNESCO International Roster of Composers in May 1971, *Ancient Voices* was judged the best of eighty-nine competing compositions. It also won the Koussevitzky International Recording Award for 1971.

Crumb's *Vox Balaenae,* or *Voice of the Whale,* for an electrified trio of piano, cello and flute, written for the New York Camerata in 1971, was suggested by the recordings of the sounds or "songs" of the humpback whale. It is intended to be performed in a hall completely dark except for the light concentrated on the players, who wear black masks to blot out the world of man. At its second New York performance in the spring of 1973, Henahan reported in the New York *Times* (April 7, 1973), the "endlessly inventive" work held the Lincoln Center audience at Alice Tully Hall fascinated "with its delicately amplified sounds and soundings." The reviewer concluded that *Vox Balaenae* was certainly one of the most successful examples of amplified music to date. Another dramatic Crumb composition employing similar theatrical devices is *Lux Aeterna.* Five musicians, including flutist and sitarist, wearing black masks and robes, are grouped within an area bathed in red light around a burning candle. The work, which is subtitled *For the Children of the Night,* was premièred at New York University in mid-April 1972 by the Philadelphia Composers Forum.

Unanimously favorable reviews greeted Crumb's 1972 composition, *Makrokosmos, Volume 1* (Twelve Fantasy Pieces after the Zodiac for Amplified Piano), at its première in Manhattan on November 5, 1973 by pianist David Burge, to whom the work is dedicated. *Makrokosmos,* which calls for plucking and strumming the piano strings, striking the hammers on metal, and other instrumental, as well as vocal, effects by the pianist, "strengthened the composer's reputation as one of the most imaginative and mesmerizing creators around," according to Raymond Ericson of the New York *Times* (November 7, 1973). Alan Rich wrote in *New York* magazine (November 26, 1973) that the piano piece as played by Burge proved "an exhilarating, dazzling, moving experience," refuting the contention that serious music no longer has anywhere to go. Rich, on the basis of *Makrokosmos* and other Crumb scores, unhesitatingly placed the author among today's major world composers.

Since 1965 Crumb has been teaching composition at the University of Pennsylvania, for the past four years as a full professor. He reportedly receives well over 1,000 commission offers a month, but accepts very few, preferring to take his time on one or two pieces a year. He composes in a den in the basement of his home in the Philadelphia suburb of Media, where he has collected a great variety of musical and other sound-producing instruments on which to experiment. Among the tributes to his music are honorary doctorates conferred on him by Morris Harvey College, in 1969, and Marshall College, in 1973. He belongs to the National Institute of Arts and Letters, and his Greek-letter societies are Pi Kappa Lamba and Phi Mu Alpha. He is a Democrat and a nominal Presbyterian.

In a harmony class in high school George Crumb met Elizabeth May Brown, whom he married about two years later, on May 21, 1949. They have three children, Elizabeth Ann, David Reed, and Peter Stanley. Mrs. Crumb is a piano teacher, but is said to find her husband's work too difficult for her to play. The brown-haired, brown-eyed composer is five feet eight inches tall and weighs 155 pounds. His recreation is reading books on astronomy, archaeology, and other nonmusical subjects. He has been described by press interviewers as quiet and self-effacing, and in his New York *Times* profile of Crumb, Henahan quoted his wife as saying, "George is one of those gentle people." During the 1960's he took part in the Composers and Musicians for Peace effort.

References

BMI p26 My '72 por
N Y Times II p15+ D 13 '70 por
Toronto Globe and Mail p15 Mr 29 '74 por
Wall St J p 1+ Ag 15 '74 por
Who's Who in America, 1974-75

DAVID, EDWARD E(MIL), JR.

Jan. 25, 1925- Corporation executive; scientist
Address: b. Gould, Inc., 8550 W. Bryn Mawr, Chicago, Ill. 60631

After occupying major research management positions for twenty years at Bell Telephone Laboratories, in 1970 Dr. Edward E. David Jr. was appointed science adviser to President Richard Nixon, a post that one Washington wit has said is like "being bartender to a teetotaler." The first science adviser to be recruited from the ranks of industry, David took on his responsibilities as director of the Office of Science and Technology and chairman of the President's Science Advisory Committee in September 1970, with a pledge to harness technology to the service of mankind. "Science and technology can do a great deal toward solving the problems of this country," he once remarked, as quoted in *Saturday Review of Science* (September 30, 1972). "I look on science and scientists as the antidote to politics. . . . In all these arguments about pollution, energy, drugs, product safety—some group has to stand up for reality. That's what science is all about."

During his twenty-eight months in office, David reorganized the federal government's vast scientific complex, initiated reciprocal research agreements with several countries, reestablished a technological partnership between government and private industry, increased the federal science budget, and applied esoteric research techniques to such mundane problems as food production, mass transit, and the conservation of natural resources. He resigned in January 1973, shortly before the Nixon administration overhauled the scientific advisory system and abolished his office, to accept an executive position with Gould, Inc., a Chicago-based manufacturer of electronic equipment, engine parts, and other products.

Edward Emil David Jr., the son of Edward Emil and Beatrice (Liebman) David, was born in Wilmington, North Carolina on January 25, 1925. He was raised in Atlanta, Georgia, where he attended the local schools. After receiving his B.S. degree in electrical engineering from the Georgia Institute of Technology in 1945, he enrolled at the Massachusetts Institute of Technology, where as a graduate student, he studied microwaves and noise theory and worked as an assistant in the university's electronics research laboratory. David earned his M.S. degree in 1947 and submitted his thesis, "Analysis of Beginning of Oscillation of a Magnetron," for an Sc.D. degree in 1950.

In 1950 David joined the technical staff of Bell Telephone Laboratories in Murray Hill, New Jersey. A specialist in underwater sound, he concentrated on the development of undersea warfare techniques and on communication acoustics. Working with Dr. Henry S. MacDonald and Dr. Max V. Matthews, two Bell colleagues, he connected a computer to a recording and playback apparatus to produce a prototype telephone answering device. The Bell management was so impressed by his technological expertise that it named him engineer in charge of acoustics research in 1956 and director of visual and acoustic research in 1958.

During the early 1960's, David conducted research in acoustical psychophysics and in the interpretation of neural information by the brain. In "The Reproduction of Sound," an article he contributed to the August 1961 issue of *Scientific American*, he discussed the relationship between electronic sound reproduction and aural reception: "In the design of systems to record and replay complex sounds, the acoustical engineer seeks not to re-create sounds exactly but to satisfy the peculiar requirements of the ear and brain." To improve the sound quality of live performances, he suggested that electroacoustic sound reinforcement equipment be included in the design and construction of auditoriums, theatres, and concert halls. In addition to conducting his theoretical research, David assisted in the development of practical sound reproduction devices, such as a low-cost artificial larynx for the correction of speech disorders following surgery.

In 1962 David turned his attention to computer technology and information sciences, investigating methods of man-machine communication. After his appointment as executive director of communications systems research in 1965, he supervised 200 scientists who were engaged in research in computer science, communications principles, and electronic systems, including aircraft anti-hijack devices. While an employee at Bell Labs, he was granted eight patents for the inventions stemming from his experiments in underwater sound, sound localization, and speech processing.

Throughout his corporate career, David maintained close contact with the academic world and regularly attended scientific symposiums. Spurred by the 1963 meeting of the National Science Foundation, which considered new approaches to the teaching of physics, he and Dr. John G.

Truxal, the academic vice-president of Brooklyn Polytechnic Institute, developed a new science course emphasizing the scientific principles behind technological advances. The course, which was officially known as the Engineering Concepts Curriculum Project, was specifically designed as an alternative to laboratory science courses for the "science-shy" college preparatory student.

To increase the technical literacy of high school students who do not intend to follow a career in science or engineering, the two scientists stressed the human factor rather than the scientific one and concentrated on socially relevant technological concepts. In an article for *Science* magazine (May 19, 1967), David and Truxal explained that their course "concerns the artifacts man has created to cope with nature and helps students understand the basic principles on which devices, systems, and processes depend." The course includes units on the construction and use of models, logic and digital computation, prediction based on scientific measurement, feedback systems, and field projects in which students apply technological concepts to actual community problems, such as traffic control, road flooding, and air and water pollution. The text for the course, which has been used by approximately 200 high schools, was published in 1968 by McGraw-Hill as *The Man Made World; A Course on Theories and Techniques That Contribute To Our Technological Civilization.*

At a news conference on August 19, 1970 President Richard Nixon announced that David had been chosen to succeed Dr. Lee A. DuBridge as director of the Office of Science and Technology and as science adviser to the President. The selection of David, the first industrial scientist to be named to the potentially influential administrative post, prompted speculation in some quarters that the choice may have been made because of Bell Telephone's high-level Washington connections rather than David's scientific standing. Many scientists, however, applauded David's nomination and expressed faith in his ability to serve as a link between the government and the scientific community. "I wouldn't take the job to downgrade science," the new science adviser told Daniel S. Greenberg in an interview for *Science* magazine (October 23, 1970). "I was satisfied after talking cold turkey that [the White House] agreed." Determined to maintain an independent course, he refused to act as "a lobbyist" for any one of his four divergent constituencies: scientists, President Nixon's staff, government research organizations, and the public.

Summarizing his plans during an interview for *Product Engineering* (October 26, 1970), David told reporter Will Lepkowski that he intended to "throw the spotlight" on significant scientific developments. He conceded that there were "tremendous things happening today," but not, he pointed out, in computer technology, solid-state physics, and biomedical research and development. After a round of meetings with former Presidential science advisers, he reorganized the federal science complex, drafted a program of

EDWARD E. DAVID JR.

"priorities" rather than "wish lists," and invited suggestions from industry and the general public as well as from academic institutions. Anxious to convert scientific knowledge into improved social conditions, he proposed applying research techniques to the improvement of mass transit, the construction of aesthetically pleasing low-cost housing units, the development of inexpensive pollution-free fuels, the biological control of insects, and the expansion of health care services.

At a press conference in the late autumn of 1970, Philip Handler, the president of the National Academy of Sciences, challenged David's program, charging that the Nixon administration failed to provide enough financial support for science and science education. In a rebuttal letter published in the New York *Times* on December 3, 1970, David pointed out that the administration's budget proposals showed an 8.7 percent increase in research and development funds for colleges and universities. "At a time when all funding is severely limited because of the strenuous effort to fight inflation," he concluded, "science has fared very well and in doing so is self-evidently among the high priorities of the administration."

Acting on David's advice, President Nixon allotted additional funds for academic research, increased the budget of the National Science Foundation, established 500 fellowships in government-owned laboratories for unemployed Ph.D.'s, and increased federal spending in environmental and medical research. At David's insistence, in March 1972 Nixon sent to Congress his first Presidential message on science and technology, in which he outlined a national program designed to insure American preeminence in technology and, at the same time, improve the quality of American life. Addressing a meeting of the Electronics Industries Association in Washington, D.C. in the spring of 1972, David commended Nixon's "pro-technology" program and its assumption "that quality and quantity can be reconciled and that economic growth *per se* is not inimical to better life, the natural surroundings, or the national environment." Among other things, the program authorized partial federal funding of hazardous projects, such as the fast-breeder nuclear reactor, immunity from antitrust suits for companies that pooled their talents to solve technical problems, and guaranteed loans for smaller companies willing to test experimental devices.

As the principal architect of Nixon's "clean energy" plan submitted to Congress on June 4, 1971, David was a resolute spokesman for federal and state legislative controls over public utilities. Speaking before the Edison Electric Institute on June 9, 1971, he exhorted the power companies to support governmental pilot programs for coal gasification, sulfur oxide control, and the perfecting of a fast-breeder reactor. "The ball is now in your court," he warned, "and the whole country is waiting to see how the electric power industry responds to the challenge." To conserve existing energy supplies, he recommended consumer restraint and increased industrial research.

A longtime advocate of international technological cooperation, David made several official visits to scientific facilities abroad. In July 1972, during a week-long visit to Poland, he signed a joint United States-Poland communiqué authorizing cooperation in such fields as medical science, agriculture, ecology, and urban planning. A similar agreement with the Soviet Union, a result of the Moscow summit conference in May 1972, sanctioned joint research in medicine, solar power, geothermal energy, crop genetics, and weather modification.

Despite his many accomplishments, David often clashed with President Nixon or with members of his staff over policy matters. In September 1971, for example, the President named William M. Magruder, the former director of the supersonic transport plane program, to head the New Technology Opportunities Program. Several Washington observers interpreted the Magruder appointment as a challenge to David's position. Although Nixon had authorized larger allocations for science in compliance with David's plans, much of the money had been impounded. Analyzing the situation for *Saturday Review of Science* (September 30, 1972), Daniel S. Greenberg commented: "The problem . . . is that Mr. David is politically chaste and Mr. Nixon is scientifically illiterate."

Contending that two years as the President's science adviser "was enough," on January 2, 1973 David resigned to return to private industry as an executive vice-president of Gould, Inc. Concurrently he is the president of Gould Laboratories, the corporation's research and development subsidiary. At Gould, David has established a technology transfer department, which he calls "the incubator," for developing and marketing new products. Among the new products being tested are auto emission control devices, transistorized zinc-air batteries, and lithium cells for electrically powered vehicles.

A slender and youthful man, Dr. Edward E. David Jr. stands five feet seven inches tall and has light brown hair and hazel eyes. To keep fit, he plays tennis, skis, and rides horseback. Every summer he spends several weeks camping in the West, where he selects rocks and mineral samples for his extensive rock and gem collection. For recreation, he enjoys photography and tinkering with his sports car. On December 23, 1950 he married Ann Hirshberg. They have a daughter, Nancy.

Dr. David was a professor of electrical engineering at Stevens Institute of Technology from 1967 to 1970 and served as a special academic consultant to Carnegie-Mellon University, Georgia Institute of Technology, the University of Rochester and Princeton University. He has also acted as a consultant to various federal and civilian agencies. A member of the National Academy of Sciences and the National Academy of Engineering, David headed the latter's committee on education and co-directed its Engineering Concepts Curriculum Program. In 1968 he helped to found the Summit (New Jersey) Speech School to assist deaf preschoolers. David often contributes to scientific and technical journals, and he is the joint author of *Man's World of Sound* (Doubleday, 1958) and *Waves and the Ear* (Doubleday, 1960) and coeditor of *Human Communication: A Unified View* (McGraw-Hill, 1972). In his writing David often argues in favor of the development of a symbiotic relationship between the humanities and the hard sciences. "What we're seeing in the attack on science and technology is a power struggle between the two cultures—the arts and sciences," he told a symposium conducted by *Forbes* magazine (November 15, 1971). "I'm unhappy to see this kind of warfare. Basically, society needs a mix of science, humanities and religion."

References

Chemical Week 112:40+ My 2 '73 por
N Y Times p1+ Ag 20 '70 por; p27 S 15 '70 por
Newsweek 76:63 Ag 31 '70 por
U S News 71:53+ O 18 '71 por
American Men and Women of Science 12th ed (1972)
Who's Who in America, 1972-73

DAVISON, FREDERIC E(LLIS)

Sept. 28, 1917-   United States Army officer
Address: b. Ft. McNair, Washington, D.C. 20315; h 4205 18th St., N.W., Washington, D.C. 20011

The ranking black general in the United States Army is Frederic E. Davison, commander of the Military District of Washington, D.C. Davison, whose combat command career goes back to World War II, was made a brigadier general in 1968, when he was serving in Vietnam, and a major general three years later. Only two Negroes in the history of the American armed forces attained silver star rank before him: Brigadier General Benjamin O. Davis Sr., an Army officer, no longer living, and the latter's son, Lieutenant General Benjamin O. Davis Jr., an Air Force officer, now retired. Today in the Army alone there are twelve blacks with silver star status, ten of them brigadier generals and two major generals.

Frederic Ellis Davison was born in Washington, D.C. on September 28, 1917 to Sue (Bright) Davison and the late Albert Charles Davison. His early education, like his life well into his career, was segregated. At all-black Dunbar High School in Washington he earned membership in the National Honor Society. After graduating from Dunbar, in 1934, he entered Howard University, then also all-Negro, where he starred in track and majored in zoology. He took his B.S. degree *cum laude* at Howard in 1938 and his M.S. degree there two years later.

Davison might have become a scientist or—if his wife had had her way—a physician, if the military had not obtruded. Having completed ROTC training, he was commissioned a lieutenant in the United States Army Reserve in 1939 and ordered to active duty in 1941, a few months before America entered World War II. During the war, in the rank of captain, he led the all-Negro B Company, 371st Infantry, 92nd Division, in fighting up from Sicily through Italy.

He has recalled that his men, resenting their segregated status, were an unruly group for whose conduct he was often called on the regimental commander's carpet. But in action, "considering their disadvantages," he was "sometimes just truly amazed that they did as well as they did." He told a reporter for *Ebony* (November 1968): "We didn't feel we were given the true opportunity to show our capabilities. On the other hand, we tried to prove that even under these handicaps the job could be done." His World War II decorations included the Distinguished Service Medal, the Legion of Merit, the Bronze Star, and the Army Commendation Medal.

After World War II, at his wife's urging, Davison enrolled in the College of Medicine at Howard University, but at the end of a year he dropped out to accept a commission in the regular Army. Between 1947, when he was training an ROTC unit at South Carolina Agricultural and Mechanical College, and the early 1950's, when he was a battalion operations officer in Germany, the United States Army gradually rid itself of segregation.

In 1954 Davison was groomed for higher rank at the Command and General Staff College, Fort Leavenworth, Kansas. In 1957, after a stint as a personnel management officer in Washington, he was advanced from the rank of major to lieutenant colonel, and then, in 1959, was sent to Korea as chief of GI personnel services with the Eighth Army. Back in the United States, he studied at the Army War College, in 1962-63, and received an M.A. degree in international affairs at George Washington University, in 1963. During the following two years he was in charge of manpower and reserve matters at the Pentagon. From 1965 to 1967 he commanded the Third Training Brigade at Fort Bliss, Texas.

MAJ. GEN. FREDERIC E. DAVISON

At his own request, Davison was sent to Vietnam in November 1967 as deputy commander of the 199th Light Infantry Brigade, which was deployed in the defense perimeter around Saigon. When the North Vietnamese and National Liberation Front demonstrated their military and popular power in the astounding Tet offensive of February 1968, the brigade's commander was absent. Davison led the defense of the United States base at Long Binh in such close rapport with the men under him that they continued to treat him as their *de facto* leader even after the *de jure* commander returned. In August 1968 Davison, then a full colonel, was made brigade commander, and the following month General Creighton W. Abrams, the United States commander in South Vietnam, pinned the silver stars of a brigadier general on his collar in a promotion ceremony at Binh Chanh.

After the ceremony Davison told an AP correspondent that he was disturbed by the breakdown in communication between "our generation and the young people" but had no sympathy for militant black power separatists. "In this brigade," he said, "I'm not going to put up with black power, or white power, or yellow power, or red power. . . . I envision one America, an integrated America."

The *Ebony* article that appeared two months after Davison's promotion to brigadier general stressed his regular trips into the field by helicopter for "eyeball-to-eyeball contact" with the men in his command. Davison was quoted: "It's in the field where you really learn what's going on. Reports filter up to you and of course they may or may not be messaged. Certainly they reflect much of the view of the commander. Unquestionably these reports are honest. The commanders are certainly men of integrity. However, if you want to get to the grass roots and know exactly what the problems and the attitudes of the men are, you've got to talk to them." On Sundays, the *Ebony* reporter noted, General Davison visited the hospitalized.

Among Davison's Vietnam decorations were the Gallantry Cross with Palm and the Distinguished Service Order First Class. In May 1969, after eighteen months in Vietnam, General Davison returned to the United States, and two months later he became the United States Army's inspector general in the Pentagon, a post he held for nearly one year. From September 1971 to May 1972 he was deputy chief of staff for United States Army personnel in Europe. Meanwhile, in April 1971, he had been elevated to the rank of major general.

While serving as commanding general of the 8th Infantry Division in Germany, from May 1972 to November 1973, Davison was asked by an AP correspondent how his soldiers reacted to being commanded by a black. "I'm sure that some blacks resent me," he replied. "I've been told that. Sure, I guess some blacks call me an Uncle Tom and I guess there are lots of whites that call me 'that damn nigger.' . . . But . . . they can call me anything they want under their breath as long as they are soldiers and do what is supposed to be done." As commanding general of the 8th Infantry he relieved three battalion commanders of their posts for failure to enforce new regulations calculated to foster racial tolerance. He also cracked down on the use of drugs ("the toughest thing we face"), ordered harsh punishment for drunken driving by GI's, and exhorted his officers to set good examples.

Davison returned to his native city to take command of the Military District of Washington on November 12, 1973. The military district has 3,600 troops, whose chief responsibilities are ceremonial functions, contingency plans for the security and rescue of the occupants of the Executive Mansion, aid to civil authorities in times of domestic disorder, and ground and air transportation support for the White House. Its units include the 3rd Infantry Regiment ("the Old Guard"), which provides troops for ceremonies at the White House and elsewhere; the United States Army Band; and the United States Army Herald Trumpets, who play key roles in Presidential funerals and other such rituals. Fort McNair, the headquarters of the district, houses the National War College, the Industrial College of the Armed Forces, and the Inter-American Defense College. The district also runs Fort Myer in Arlington, Virginia, Cameron Station in Alexandria, Virginia, and Davison Field at Fort Belvoir.

Frederic E. Davison and Jean Brown, a schoolteacher, were married on April 6, 1941. They have four daughters: Jean Marie, Andrea, Dayle Antoinette, and Carla Molis. Davison is a graying man of medium height, slender but husky. He has been described by interviewers as "articulate" and "sophisticated" and by his troops as "tough." Woody Dickerman of *Newsday* (June 2, 1969) wrote of him: "Davison has a reputation as a stern though not unreasonable disciplinarian, and he is a hot-tempered man with a salty vocabulary. Aides recall his 'chew-outs' with nervous awe. The belief in discipline and

respect for authority, his aides say, is one of the strongest features in Davison's solid character. As a result, he is deeply concerned by home-front disturbances, whether they are white student demonstrations or Negro riots." General Davison is a member of the Roman Catholic Church and the Kappa Alpha Psi fraternity. His recreations, when he has time for them, are photography and listening to music.

In addition to his other decorations, General Davison holds the Valorous Unit Award, the Meritorious Unit Award, the Combat Infantryman's Badge, the Vietnam Ranger Badge, the Distinguished Flying Cross, the Air Medal, the World War II Victory Medal, Army of Occupation Medal, and the National Defense Service Medal with Oak Leaf Cluster. Regarding the civil rights struggle, General Davison has said: "One thing that's essential for everyone to understand is that regardless of the approaches being taken by various Negro organizations, the basic urge is to be full participants in American life. The guy who's been . . . doing his full share—I believe very strongly that he has a right to full participation."

References

Ebony 24:128 N '68 pors
N Y Times p1+ S 16 '68 por
Newsday p4 Je 2 '69 por
Newsweek 72:35 S 30 '68 por
Toronto Globe and Mail p4 S 16 '68 por
Washington Post B p7 Jl 13 '68 por; B p1+
    N 13 '73 pors
Who's Who in America. 1972-73

DELORIA, VINE (VICTOR), JR.

Mar. 26, 1933- Writer; lawyer; social activist
Address: b. c/o Macmillan Co., 866 3rd Ave., New York 10022

"American society is unconsciously going Indian," Vine Deloria Jr., a Dakota Sioux who is the leading spokesman for native American nationalism, wrote in his *We Talk, You Listen* (1970). Deloria believes that the surge of interest in Indian culture among non-Indians in the United States springs from an instinct for survival and a sense that Indian tribalism, imbued as it is with community spirit and religious respect for the land, may provide the most viable model for a solution to the problems of individual alienation and destruction of the environment. Once a candidate for the Lutheran ministry, he now views Christianity, the theological handmaiden of the plundering invaders from Europe, as a failure, and sees "within the traditions, beliefs, and customs of the American Indian people . . . the guidelines for mankind's future," as he wrote in *God Is Red* (1973).

Deloria first came to public attention with his best-selling "new" Indian manifesto, *Custer Died for Your Sins* (1969), which is both a scathing indictment of white America's treatment of the

Indian up to now and a statement of what Indian activists want from the American government in the future: a "cultural leave-us-alone agreement" that would not involve the "termination" of federal economic services that is advocated by whites, some of them well-intentioned, who want to force Indians off the reservations and into the mythical "melting pot." A lawyer and head of the Institute for the Development of Indian Law, Deloria has provided students and activists with the legal and historical sourcebooks *Of Utmost Good Faith* (Straight Arrow, 1972) and *Behind the Trail of Broken Treaties* (Delacorte, 1974). As an editor of *Mademoiselle* (April 1971) has noted, in his popular writings Deloria "never uses rage to make his points, but rather an ironic intelligence that is all the more effective for its cool."

Vine Victor Deloria Jr. was born in the town of Martin on the Pine Ridge Reservation in South Dakota on March 26, 1933 to the Reverend Vine Deloria Sr. and Barbara (Eastburn) Deloria. His great-great-grandmother was the daughter of a Yankton chief who married a French fur trader named Des Lauriers early in the nineteenth century. The name was anglicized by Vine's grandfather, one of the first Indian converts to the Episcopal Church. Both the grandfather, Philip Deloria, and Vine's father became Episcopal priests and worked in the Indian mission field. Deloria has a sister, Barbara Deloria Sanchez, and a brother, Philip Samuel Deloria, now director of the American Indian Law Center at the University of New Mexico.

Deloria was educated in reservation schools, at the Kent School in Connecticut, and at Iowa State University, where he majored in general science and took his B.S. degree in 1958. His studies were interrupted from 1954 to 1956 by a tour of duty in the United States Marine Corps. Intending to enter the ministry, he earned a master's degree in theology at Augustana College, a Lutheran seminary in Rock Island, Illinois, in 1963 and then joined the staff of the church-founded United Scholarship Service in Denver, Colorado.

Deloria's assignment in the United Scholarship Service was the development of a prep school placement program for Indian students. In pursuing that task he tried to lay down high academic standards of qualification for scholarships. "It seemed to me that this was the only way for Indians to gain the white man's respect," he later explained. "I didn't think we should cry our way into schools; that kind of sympathy would destroy the students we were trying to help." But the financial backers of the scholarship program objected to what they considered his "elitist" approach, and Deloria left the United Scholarship Service, disgusted with the church's paternalism and dubious about its attitudes and objectives in general.

From 1964 to 1967 Deloria was executive director of the National Congress of American Indians, with offices in Washington, D.C. "I learned

VINE DELORIA JR.

more in my three years with the NCAI than I had in the previous thirty years of my life," he has recalled. "Every conceivable problem that could occur in an Indian society was suddenly thrust at me from 315 different tribal directions. I discovered that I was expected to solve these problems and I found that Indian people locally and on the national level were being played against each other by unscrupulous individuals with ego or income at stake. There were solutions, but few could be successfully put into effect or even tried because of those who worked night and day to destroy the unity we were seeking as a people."

As head of NCAI, Deloria dealt constantly with officials in the Interior Department's Bureau of Indian Affairs. The bureau was an easy target of criticism, because there was little evidence that it had done anything to improve the lives of Indians during a century and a half of administration. Indian unemployment was ten times the national average, family income averaged $1,500 a year, infant mortality was double the national rate, and life expectancy was a third less than that of whites. But Deloria, as concerned as he was, spent less time in belaboring such surface statistics than in advocating a radical reform: greater Indian autonomy in Indian affairs. "We want the right to plan and program for ourselves," he said. "We want the right to talk with people as equals. We want to be free to go to all the federal departments, including Agriculture, Labor and Commerce, for technical help with programs we can develop ourselves."

Deloria entered the University of Colorado School of Law in 1967 and took his J.D. degree three years later. His reason for studying law, as he expressed it at the time, was to help "smaller tribes and Indian communities to achieve a balanced program in which their rights are clearly outlined." He explained: "I have talked with enough leaders of small tribes to feel that they would respond with enthusiasm to anyone who could bring them the necessary technical skills to begin working out their problems."

Deloria's stated purpose in writing his first book was "to raise some issues for younger Indians which they have not been raising for themselves" and "to give some idea to white people of the unspoken but often felt antagonism . . . Indian people [have] toward them and the reasons for such antagonism." The topics he covered in *Custer Died for Your Sins* (Macmillan, 1969) included aboriginal rights (perhaps the major factor distinguishing Indians from other minorities); broken treaties ("Until America begins to build a moral record in her dealings with the Indian people she should not try to fool the rest of the world about her intentions on other continents"); the Indian wars; genocide; and neo-tribalism as an improvement over rugged individualism. "Indian tribes riding the crest of tribal and nationalistic waves will be able to accomplish a great many things previously thought impossible by Indian and non-Indian alike," he wrote. "There is every indication that as Indians articulate values they wish to transmit to the rest of society, they will be able to exert a definite influence on social developments."

The reviewer for *Newsweek* (October 13, 1969) said of Deloria's achievement in *Custer Died for Your Sins*: "With ironic, mordant wit . . . he resolutely destroys the stereotypes and myths that white society has built up about the Indian." In *Newsday* (September 17, 1969), Robert Mayer wrote, "Deloria lives with the knowledge that the white men who settled America systematically murdered his ancestors, burned their homes, stole their cattle, confiscated their land, and herded the survivors into rural slums called reservations. He is tired of the Indians' being polite about these indiscretions, and his book is a sharp indictment of American hypocrisy, Catholic missionaries, self-serving anthropologists, and the Bureau of Indian Affairs, all of which helped make Indians the true forgotten Americans."

In *We Talk, You Listen* (Macmillan, 1970), Deloria examined the deteriorating core of contemporary technological society and came to two conclusions: a return to tribal social organizations may be necessary if that society is to survive, and tribalization is in fact taking place in it among off-center groups, from Chicanos to hippies. Reviewing the book in the Washington *Post* (October 13, 1970), William Greider wrote, "His caustic wit, the hallmark of his best seller, *Custer Died for Your Sins*, surfaces only irregularly (as though the author feared his ideas would be taken less seriously if his perspective was too cynical). . . . His description of the environmental crisis . . . is so apocalyptic . . . it obscures his central point —that the land-based tribal groups of Indians were, by definition, required to live in harmony with the natural world, not to rape it."

In an interview with Peter Collier that appeared in *Mademoiselle* (April 1971), Deloria complained about "the anthropologists, missionaries, and other friends who've been swarming all over us and our reservations for generations and guiding our lives." Regarding "the policies and programs that are thrown at us by Congress" he said: "They're not made to help Indian people [but rather] to put certain white cultural characteristics into a process that is meant to *change* Indians. . . . Congress . . . should pass what you might call 'neutral legislation,' legislation aimed only at solving Indians' economic problems, not changing their lives. But always, things get twisted around so that the issue becomes how they can get us into the mainstream and make us as neurotic as middle-class whites."

Deloria's purpose in *God Is Red* (Grosset & Dunlap, 1973) was to contrast Indian tribal religions and their "centered" world view and "method of framing questions from a predominantly spatial conception of reality" on the one hand with, on the other, Christianity and its "linear," time-oriented point of view. "The contemporary Christian mythos has been developed over a period of two centuries in which the exploitation of human and natural resources has become increasingly sophisticated," he wrote. "With the singular concern for historical reality seen in its propensity to missionize, Christianity has avoided any rigorous consideration of ecological factors in favor of continuous efforts to realize the Kingdom of God on earth. As the twentieth century of Christian existence closes with social and political chaos . . . we can conclude that the effort to build the nations of Western civilization as prototypes of the Kingdom of God has been largely for naught." That has been especially true in the United States, he pointed out. "The deterioration of American community life . . . would seem to indicate that rootlessness has become the major feature of American existence." He quoted a statement Chief Luther Standing Bear made early in this century: "The white man does not understand America. . . . The roots of the tree of his life have not yet grasped the rock and soil. . . . But in the Indian the spirit of the land is still vested. . . . Men must be born and reborn to belong. Their bodies must be formed of the dust of their forefathers' bones."

Deloria asserted that "it is doubtful if American society can move very far or very significantly without a major revolution in theological concepts," and that non-Indian Americans generally sense this. "In seeking the religious reality behind the American Indian tribal existence, Americans are in fact attempting to come to grips with the land that produced the Indian tribal cultures and their vision of community. . . . American Indian tribal religions certainly appear to be more at home in the modern world than Christian ideas and Western man's traditional concepts." Deloria explained: "Christianity has traditionally appeared to place its major emphasis on creation as a specific event while the Indian tribal religions could be said to consider creation as an ecosystem present in a definable place. . . . In the Indian tribal religions man and the rest of creation are cooperative and respectful of the task set for them by the Great Spirit. In the Christian religion both are doomed from shortly after the creation event until the end of the world." Reviewing *God Is Red* in *Best Sellers* (November 15, 1973), Peter Mayer wrote, "Deloria could have made his point —that Indian religious practices are far more in accord with the necessities of contemporary life than are Christian—without dredging up the many failures of the sons of the Church upon the earth. . . . But read the book. I found it hard to put down."

Deloria has been a member of the Board of Inquiry on Hunger and Malnutrition in the United States and of the National Office for Rights of the Indigent, and he has served as a consultant to the Senate Select Committee on Aging. Through his Institute for the Development of Indian Law he has helped to obtain federal recognition for four tribes. Friendship Press published his new book *The Indian Affair* on November 15, 1974. He is working on a political history of the Sioux nation and a compilation of treaties and other agreements between Indian tribes and federal and state governments.

Vine Deloria Jr. and Barbara Jeanne Nystrom, a librarian, were married on June 14, 1958. With their three children, Philip, Daniel, and Jeanne Ann, they live in Golden, Colorado, where Deloria maintains his office. Deloria is six feet tall and weighs 225 pounds. His eyes and hair are brown. When Douglas N. Mount of *Publishers' Weekly* (December 1, 1969) met him he was "wearing spectacles, a white shirt and tie, a plain business suit, very long hair, and heavy, decorated western boots," and Robert Mayer in his *Newsday* article described him as "a round-faced gentleman with a wry sense of humor." Deloria is a member of the Authors Guild, P.E.N. International, the American Bar Association, Amnesty International, Associates for the Arts, and the American Judicature Society.

Deloria's favorite recreations are bowling and collecting coins and old books. In politics he used to be a liberal Democrat but lately he has been labeling himself a Republican. Deloria praised the Nixon administration's Indian policy, especially its return of 48,000 ancestral acres to the Taos Pueblo in New Mexico. "My white friends in New York and Washington really get worked up at me . . . ," he told Peter Collier in the *Mademoiselle* interview. "But I tell them . . . I've come to the point now where I'd vote for George Wallace if he had a good Indian program, one that would let us hold on to our land and help us survive as a culture." Whatever the political contingencies, he is optimistic. "Indians will survive," he has said, "because we are a people unified by our humanity, not a pressure group united for conquest."

References

Christian Sci Mon p15 F 26 '70 por
Mademoiselle p202+ Ap '71
Newsday B p3 S 17 '69 por
Gridley, Marian E. Contemporary American Indian Leaders (1972)
Who's Who in America, 1973-74

DENT, FREDERICK B(AILY)

Aug. 17, 1922- United States Secretary of Commerce
Address: b. United States Department of Commerce, 14th St., between Constitution Ave. and E St., NW., Washington, D.C. 20230

President Richard Milhous Nixon chose as his third Secretary of Commerce Frederick B. Dent, who was appointed in December 1973. He came to his post from the presidency of Mayfair Mills in Arcadia, South Carolina and the directorship of the American Textile Manufacturers Institute. Because of that background, some critics viewed his appointment as "a favor to both Strom Thurmond and the textile industry" (*Newsweek*, December 8, 1972) and as a Nixon administration move toward protectionist barriers in foreign trade. But Dent, whose executive efficiency was patent from the start, has proved himself to be a level-headed internationalist of sorts, a contributor to the thaw in trade between the United States on the one hand and the Soviet Union and the People's Republic of China on the other.

The Cabinet department that Dent heads is concerned with the economic life of the United States—the exchange of goods and services and the technology involved therein. In addition to its more obvious divisions, such as the Domestic and International Business Administration, the Department of Commerce includes the National Bureau of Standards, the Patent Office, and the Office of Telecommunications. It has 35,000 employees and an annual budget of $1 billion.

Frederick Baily Dent was born in Cape May, New Jersey on August 17, 1922 to Magruder and Edith (Baily) Dent. He received his preparatory education at St. Paul's, an elite Episcopalian school in Concord, New Hampshire, where John V. Lindsay, destined to become a Congressman and mayor of New York City, was a fellow member of the class of 1940. At St. Paul's, Dent was a chapel warden and a member of the student council, the Isthmian and Shattuck athletic clubs, the Glee Club, the Forestry Club, the Library Association, and the baseball and football teams. At Yale University he majored in government, played varsity football and hockey, was president of the Yale Key Club, and also belonged to the Torch Honor Society and Scroll and Key. After taking his B.A. degree, in 1943, Dent, a member of the United States Naval Reserve, saw World War II service in the Pacific, as an ensign and as a lieutenant (j.g.).

Dent's apprenticeship in his family's textile business began in 1946 with Joshua L. Baily & Co., Inc., a New York City textile sales firm founded by his maternal great-grandfather. The following year he began climbing the executive ladder at the family-owned Mayfair Mills in Arcadia, South Carolina. "I well recall that we were the first postwar Yankees in town," he once told an interviewer. "Another couple came and we were always invited out together so there'd be someone to talk to us."

FREDERICK B. DENT

In 1958 Dent became president of Mayfair
Mills. Under his presidency the company expanded from a one-mill industry to a four-plant,
159,000-spindle, 17,000-employee operation producing drip-dry synthetics and new-blend fabrics
in addition to traditional prints, broadcloths, and
sheets. On the personnel front, he set out, with
deliberate speed, to give fair employment opportunities to blacks. His clout as chairman of the
Spartanburg County Planning and Development
Commission played a significant role in the allocation of $600,000,000 in government funds for the
local textile industry.

As president of Mayfair Mills, Dent ranked relatively low in the American business hierarchy.
But by dint of personal effort he rose from directorship of the Carolina Textile Manufacturers Association to the same position with the American
Textile Manufacturers Institute in 1967, and he
won membership in the prestigious sixty-five-mem-
ber Business Council, the exclusive ruling circle
of titans of American industry.

In the late 1960's, as the hidden cost of the
Vietnam war finally boomeranged and the American economy began to reel, the textile industry
was numbered among the casualties. In behalf of
the industry, and with the backing of Senator
Strom Thurmond of North Carolina, Dent traveled
the world, making extended visits to those countries exporting cloth and clothing at prices with
which American companies could not compete.
In Japan, Korea, Taiwan, and Hong Kong he
helped work out agreements whereby manufacturers there would voluntarily limit their exports
to the United States.

While "protectionist" regarding textiles, oil,
steel, and sugar, the Nixon administration was
generally "free" in its international trade policy,
even when, in the early 1970's, the balance of
trade dipped unfavorably (more imports than exports). When the Burke-Hartke bill calling for
quotas on most imports was introduced in Congress in 1972, the then Secretary of Commerce
Peterson asserted that the proposal would be "a

national disaster for the United States and an international disaster for the world in which we live."

The appointment of Dent to Peterson's Commerce post in December 1972 was generally regarded as an about-face on the administration's
part, but in his confirmation hearings the new
Secretary made clear that he opposed across-the-
board compulsory quotas on foreign goods. He
attacked the key features of the Burke-Hartke bill,
saying he favored instead a trade bill providing
for an examination of each industry on an individual basis, with the government instituting
controls only where needed.

On April 19, 1973 President Nixon sent to Congress a request for authority to raise or lower
tariffs and to impose import taxes or quotas as
circumstances might dictate. Earlier, John M. Lee
had commented on Nixon's trade policy in the
New York *Times* (February 18, 1973): "The
President's true trade purpose seems ambiguous.
Free traders hope he is holding off protectionists
with devaluation and using devaluation to get a
liberal trade bill, albeit with standby protectionist features, through Congress. But protectionists
are also encouraged by his apparent readiness to
wield the big stick to get what he wants, namely
a trade improvement."

In an interview with Vernon Louviere of *Nation's Business* (September 1973), Dent said that
the purpose of Nixon's trade bill was to open up
all markets to freer trade while refusing open access to United States markets to those nations
that have thrown up barriers against American
goods. Unless Congress passed Nixon's trade bill
intact, he said, he saw little hope for generating
more foreign trade—the key, in his view, to solving the trade deficit ($6.3 billion as of 1972).
"If we are going to import goods and services
with the voracious appetite we have recently experienced, and add to this imports of petroleum
and other energy products, we are simply going
to have to make a greater national commitment
to export markets."

To expedite the outward flow of goods, Dent
reduced from 550 to seventy-three the number
of products that needed special government license to be exported. He also set up within his
department the Bureau of East-West Trade, a
service agency that informs American businessmen
of trade opportunities in Communist countries.
The East-West flow of goods, opened up in 1973,
will greatly improve America's international economic position, he believes, and he predicts that
China in particular will provide a vast new market for American goods in the future. Aided by
two devaluations of the dollar, the trade deficit
has apparently been turned back, at least temporarily. By the beginning of 1974 the United
States already had behind it several consecutive
months of export surplus.

Frederick Baily Dent and the former Mildred
Carrington Harrison were married on March 11,
1944. They have five children: Frederick, Mildred,
Pauline, Diana, and Magruder. Before going to
Washington, Dent was a director of the General
Electric Company, the South Carolina National

Bank, the Scott Paper Company, and the Mutual Life Insurance Company. Dent is six feet tall, weighs 195 pounds, and is youthful in appearance. Having lost one leg to cancer in the mid-1950's, he wears an artificial limb and walks with a slight limp. Despite that handicap, he remains a vigorous athlete, golfing in the 90's, bowling, swimming, and playing tennis. He also enjoys dancing, especially square dancing.

Those who know the Secretary report that he has an easy manner, a bright, open mind, a dislike of big government, and a "deep personal regard, almost love, for Mr. Nixon." One of his assistants at Mayfair Mills recalls what a stickler for detail he was there: "He not only worked at the machines. He got underneath the machines and counted teeth on the gears." A close associate says that Dent "takes pride in his flag, the American way of life and the free enterprise system."

References

Commerce Today p18 F 19 '73
N Y Sunday News p98 D 10 '72
N Y Times p69 D 7 '72 por
Nat Observer p7 D 16 '72

Who's Who in America, 1972-73

DE PAUW, GOMMAR A(LBERT) (de-pô')

Oct. 11, 1918- Roman Catholic priest
Address: Catholic Traditionalist Movement, Suite 303 East, Pan Am Bldg., 200 Park Ave., New York 10017; h. 210 Maple Ave., Westbury, N.Y. 11590

Spurred by his conviction that the liturgical reforms recently introduced into Roman Catholic worship are historically and theologically wrong, in 1964 Father Gommar De Pauw drew up a manifesto for the Catholic Traditionalist Movement. Since then the movement has become a rallying point for ultraconservatives who feel that English-language rites are destroying the Church they love. A decade later, Father De Pauw remains the visible head of what is probably the best-known American faction within the unauthorized and almost schismatic movement to retain the centuries-old celebration of the Mass and the Sacraments in Latin for those who prefer them that way. His Manhattan office and Long Island chapel have become the focal gathering places of his followers, who believe that the directives of Vatican Council II have been improperly applied.

With a holy wrath reminiscent of an Old Testament prophet, the otherwise affable Father De Pauw has unremittingly assailed what he contends is an unjustified and invalid abandonment of ancient Roman Catholic rites and doctrines. But although he has incurred the displeasure of virtually all of the hierarchy, so far no attempt has been made to excommunicate him or his followers.

Born to a family that has ties with America that date back as far as the early seventeenth cen-

REV. GOMMAR A. DE PAUW

tury, Gommar Albert De Pauw was born in Flanders, Belgium in the town of Stekene on October 11, 1918 to Desiré and Anna (Van Overloop) De Pauw. Anna De Pauw's parents had immigrated in 1911 to the United States, where they settled in Paterson, New Jersey. Desiré De Pauw was a cofounder of the Christian Labor Movement and the Roman Catholic school system in Belgium. The De Pauws, whose lineage stems from medieval Flemish crusaders, are descendants of New World pioneers who first arrived in America in 1627. One ancestor, Michael De Pauw, was the first white proprietor of Staten Island; another, Charles De Pauw, was aide-de-camp to the Marquis de Lafayette during the American Revolution. De Pauw University in Greencastle, Indiana is named after Washington Charles De Pauw, a Hoosier great grand-uncle of Father De Pauw, because his generous financial help saved the school, which was formerly called Indiana Asbury University. Gommar De Pauw's oldest sister, a missionary nun, served in the Congo for many years; his brother Adhemar is a Franciscan friar in New York. Other sisters and brothers are married and have children.

In 1936 Gommar De Pauw graduated *magna cum laude* in classics as the top student in his class from the College of St. Nicholas in East Flanders, in Belgium. He then entered the diocesan seminary in Ghent, Belgium for courses in theology and philosophy, but his studies were interrupted by the outbreak of World War II. For a while, in 1942, he taught algebra at the College of St. Nicholas, his alma mater, and then, although nominally a seminarian, served in Belgium, Holland, and France as a medical corpsman with the Ninth Belgian Infantry Regiment. Taken prisoner at the Battle of Dunkirk, he managed to escape from the prison camp where the Germans had interned him and made his way back to the seminary in Ghent. There he completed his theological studies and was ordained a priest later in the year 1942 by special dispensation from the Vatican.

During the liberation of northern Belgium and southern Holland, the newly ordained Father De Pauw accompanied the Belgian Underground Army and the First Free Polish Armored Division as an auxiliary chaplain and was decorated with the Medal of Honor of the Free Polish Forces. After engaging for three years in postgraduate studies at the University of Louvain in canon law, moral theology, and church history, along with some courses in archaeology and international law, he obtained the J.C.B. and J.C.L. degrees (Bachelor and Licentiate in canon law). De Pauw has said that the idealism of his father, the zeal of dedicated priests, and the example of Leo De Kesel, chaplain of a Catholic youth organization and later auxiliary bishop of Ghent, inspired him to join the priesthood. He still considers himself Bishop De Kesel's spiritual son.

From 1945 until 1949, when he joined his family in the United States, Father De Pauw served as a parish curate and Catholic social action chaplain in Ghent. For several years he worked in a New York City parish while undertaking advanced studies at the Catholic University of America. After submitting his doctoral thesis on "The Educational Rights of the Church," he obtained a doctorate in Canon Law from the Catholic University of America in 1953.

In 1952 Father De Pauw joined the faculty of Mount St. Mary's Seminary in Emmitsburg, Maryland as professor of theology and canon law, a post he held until 1965; concurrently he served for part of that period as dean of studies. In 1960 he served as substitute chaplain at the Army War College in Carlisle, Pennsylvania, in recognition of which the Second Army awarded him its certificate of achievement for his outstanding contribution to the religious welfare of military and civilian personnel.

During the momentous years of Vatican Council II (1962-65), the international conclave of bishops convoked in Rome by Pope John XXIII for reforming and updating the Roman Catholic Church, Father De Pauw served as a "personal expert" on theological matters. According to his 1967 pamphlet called The "Rebel" Priest, he was repeatedly consulted during the course of the Council deliberations by his former professor, the Belgian Bishop Charles J. Calewaert of Ghent. The latter officially presented and interpreted to the Council Fathers assembled in St. Peter's Basilica the 1962 Constitution on Liturgy that was to produce a major and far-reaching change in the ritual of the Roman Catholic Church. In The "Rebel" Priest Father De Pauw wrote: "In all honesty I can find little or no fault with this particular Council document."

What Father De Pauw did find fault with, however, was the interpretation and application of the Constitution on Liturgy of Vatican Council II. In his view, it gave rise to what he has called "a hootenanny liturgy" marked by the "chaotic conditions of a three-ring circus," and to the "regimented kindergarten antics" that, according to the advocates of greater participation by the

faithful and use of the vernacular, were necessary under the new norms of worship.

By late 1964 Father De Pauw was genuinely alarmed at what he viewed as the seeds of a new Reformation bent on the "Protestantization" of Roman Catholicism. On December 31 of that year he privately sent a communication to the Pope, all cardinals of the Vatican Curia, all members of the United States Roman Catholic hierarchy, and selected prelates around the world. Made public on March 15, 1965, that communication came to be known as the Catholic Traditionalist Manifesto, and it set forth a dozen major tenets that were to motivate all action by Father De Pauw's group over the following decade. At its core was the request that what was described as "the permissive nature" of the Constitution on Liturgy be safeguarded on the local level to avoid "any form of regimented compulsion" regarding innovations. (The Traditionalists maintain that the Constitution on Liturgy did not make innovations mandatory but permitted them as privileges.) The manifesto also requested that clergy and laymen be given the same freedom to promote and defend the use of traditional practices and languages as that accorded to the supporters of vernacularism.

Another key petition in the manifesto, based on articles 36 and 53 of the Constitution on Liturgy, was that the Latin Mass be allowed to co-exist with the new vernacular forms, so that priests and laity could choose between the new ritual or the traditional Mass in Latin on both Sundays and weekdays. The manifesto also petitioned for a renewal of such familiar Roman Catholic customs as devotion to the Virgin Mary, loyalty and obedience to the Pope, and the celibacy and traditional attire of priests and nuns.

After his first three years as a professor at Mount St. Mary's Seminary, during which time he often spent his weekends and vacations in parish work, Father De Pauw transferred his canonical jurisdiction from the Diocese of Ghent to the Archdiocese of Baltimore. The publication of his Catholic Traditionalist Manifesto in the spring of 1965 unleashed such a storm of controversy that Lawrence Cardinal Shehan, Archbishop of Baltimore and Father De Pauw's ecclesiastical superior, soon urged him to dissociate himself immediately and completely from the movement, on the ground that his activity in support of the manifesto was incompatible with his position as priest and seminary professor.

Obedient to the wishes of the Baltimore Archdiocese, on April 8, 1965 De Pauw announced that, although he felt Cardinal Shehan had made a mistake in ordering him to sever his activity in the group, he would hand over its leadership to laymen and accept Shehan's directive in what the Cardinal's office called "a spirit of loyalty to his lawful superiors." But he also declared he was going to appeal to Francis Cardinal Spellman of New York, whom he considered the senior United States prelate, to the Vatican's Holy Office, and to Pope Paul VI himself.

On July 26, 1965 Cardinal Shehan ordered De Pauw transferred from his seminary teaching post to Baltimore parish duty, to be effective the following September. Four days after he received the notification of his transfer, Father De Pauw was given permission to attend the concluding session of Vatican Council II as a private theologian and adviser to the Most Rev. Blaise Kurz, an exiled Franciscan bishop from China. While in Rome he took the opportunity to obtain a private audience with Pope Paul, and to plead his case with the conservative Alfredo Cardinal Ottaviani, who reportedly arranged to introduce him to the Bishop of nearby Tivoli and effect his transfer from Baltimore to that diocese. Lawrence Cardinal Shehan tentatively agreed to the move, but Bishop Luigi Faveri apparently signed the document accepting De Pauw into his Tivoli Diocese before Shehan actually sent his final, formal permission for reincardination, as the process of priestly jurisdictional transfer is known. Faveri thereby set off a series of confusing ecclesiastical misunderstandings.

Meanwhile, Father De Pauw had moved to Manhattan to set up headquarters for the Catholic Traditionalist Movement, Inc., which was incorporated under New York law. He insisted that he was now under the jurisdiction of Bishop Faveri of Tivoli, Italy, who, he said, had given him permission to return to the United States or any other country of his choice "to do research work." De Pauw has said that he was given tacit support and private encouragement by Cardinal Spellman in efforts to foster the preservation of the Latin Mass, a claim that has been denied by New York chancery office sources at St. Patrick's Cathedral. In the meantime, the Baltimore Archdiocese declared that it still had authority over Father De Pauw in view of the lack of any final letter of "perpetual and unconditional excardination" signed by Cardinal Shehan, as required in canon 112 of the Roman Catholic code of canon law.

On January 28, 1966 Cardinal Shehan forbade Father De Pauw from publicly functioning as a priest and he ordered him to report to Baltimore within twenty-four hours. Two weeks earlier, Bishop Faveri of Tivoli had reportedly changed his mind about accepting De Pauw nominally into his diocese if canonical formalities were incomplete, but De Pauw replied that he belonged to the Diocese of Tivoli and that he intended to continue celebrating daily Mass. He also indicated that he planned to ignore further directives and notes from the Diocese of Baltimore. Both Newsweek and the liberal Catholic weekly Commonweal suggested that there seemed to be little difference between Shehan's suspension of De Pauw and Los Angeles Cardinal McIntyre's silencing of liberal priests.

In the middle of January 1966 the Most Rev. Blaise Kurz, titular bishop of Terenuti and exiled prefect apostolic of Yungchow, China, who was then living on Staten Island, issued a statement in support of Father De Pauw, who had been his theology consultant at Vatican Council II. Bishop Kurz was the only prelate to offer De Pauw public backing, declaring him to be under his own "direct episcopal jurisdiction" as personal secretary while technically remaining a priest of the Diocese of Tivoli, directly subject to the Holy See. Later he said that he had directed Father De Pauw, as his secretary, not to report to Baltimore. Replying to continuing charges that the canonical transfer of Father De Pauw to Tivoli from the Baltimore Archdiocese had been properly and fully completed, Bishop Kurz issued a public declaration on May 22, 1966 repeating that there were in existence "documents of unquestionable canonical authenticity and validity" supporting the claim that De Pauw had been duly incardinated into the Italian diocese. He added that De Pauw was serving as personal secretary to Kurz and under his direct episcopal authority. On the same date, Bishop Kurz accepted the post of Bishop-Moderator of the Catholic Traditionalist Movement.

Despite that episcopal vote of confidence from Kurz, Father De Pauw soon discovered that the suspension decree of Cardinal Shehan carried far more weight in practice. In late February his attempts to celebrate a traditional Latin Mass in Detroit, Michigan and at the University of Notre Dame in Indiana proved fruitless. When his efforts to give an address on campus at the invitation of a Notre Dame student group were similarly thwarted, he was forced to give his talk at a South Bend hotel. Those repeated disappointments led Father De Pauw and his backers to buy a Westbury, Long Island church from a Ukranian Orthodox group for a reported sum of $34,000 in the summer of 1968 after failing in the previous year to obtain recognition from the Vatican as an authorized traditionalist Latin rite within the Church, similar to the various Oriental rites.

Renamed the Ave Maria Chapel, the church quickly became the spiritual haven for hundreds of nonconformists unhappy with the new English Mass and other innovations. When Charles Osgood interviewed Father De Pauw on a CBS television news program that was carried coast-to-coast on Easter Monday, April 3, 1972, the traditionalist priest explained that he feels his mission is that of a religious leader rather than that of a social leader. He therefore excludes politics 'either from the Left or the Right', from the movement, leaving such matters as social and civic needs to qualified laymen, and he lists himself as an independent in politics. In its February 4, 1974 issue Newsweek magazine reported that as many as 1,000 dissident Catholics flock to Father De Pauw's Ave Maria Chapel on Sunday to attend his Masses in Latin, which are carried on some seventeen radio stations each week. Of his personal celebration of the Mass each Sunday Father De Pauw has said, "I give the communions out myself. I don't have nuns, undertakers and flunkies giving out communion as other priests do."

Father Gommar A. De Pauw, who stands five feet ten inches tall and weighs about 200 pounds, has brown hair that is now intermixed with gray and green eyes that are usually framed by thick-rimmed glasses. He regrets that his frequent lecture tours around the United States leave him no time for vacations or for such recreations as the soccer, cycling, and mountain climbing he once enjoyed. Once a heavy smoker, he stopped indulging in cigarettes during World War II. He has contributed to such publications as the *Encyclopedic Dictionary of the Bible,* the *New Catholic Encyclopedia,* and *Homiletic and Pastoral Review,* has cut half a dozen recordings, and has appeared on such radio and television talk shows as the *Today Show* and the *Long John Nebel Show.* Since he believes that the faithful should be offered a choice between the new and the old liturgies, he maintains that he is essentially more liberal than "unliberal liberals."

References

> Life 60:74 Je 24 '66 por
> N Y Herald Tribune p14 F 6 '66 por
> N Y Times p17 Ap 3 '65 por; p1+ Je 6 '66 por
> Nat Observer p1+ My 10 '65 por
> Newsweek 67:76+ F 7 '66 por
> Who's Who in America, 1972-73
> Who's Who in the World, 1974-75

DEWHURST, COLLEEN

1926(?)- Actress
Address: h. South Salem, N.Y. 10590

An impressive string of *succès d'estime* that brought her one personal triumph after another preceded the first both critical and commercial Broadway hit of Colleen Dewhurst's twenty-seven years in the theatre, *A Moon for the Misbegotten,* which reached New York in late December 1973. The women of Eugene O'Neill's plays have long had a special appeal for Miss Dewhurst, who finds them magnificent in their strengths and weaknesses. She won an Obie award as Abbie Putnam in *Desire Under the Elms* about a decade before her portrayal of Josie Hogan in *A Moon for the Misbegotten* earned her a Tony award. Colleen Dewhurst is a thoroughly disciplined actress of sometimes electrifying stage presence whose subtle, multilateral characterizations have delighted not only theatre audiences, but also television viewers in dozens of first-rate performances on both educational and commercial channels.

Of Irish-Scotch-English ancestry, Colleen Dewhurst was born in Montreal, Canada in the mid-1920's. Her father was a professional Canadian hockey, baseball, and football player who raised her as an athlete and often took her to sports events with him. Her mother was a Christian Science practitioner. Before the divorce of her parents, when Colleen was in her early teens, the family traveled about a good deal, mainly in the United States. Over a period of some twenty years she attended fifteen schools. In several press interviews, she has recalled her childhood as a particularly happy period.

Colleen Dewhurst's first ambition was to be a flyer. Later, as a student at Downer College for Young Ladies, a Milwaukee finishing school, she decided to become a journalist. Then, when she acted in a skit she had written for the freshman class, she discovered that the stage was her true goal in life. In response to the dean's criticism of her lack of academic seriousness, she left college after about a year and went to Gary, Indiana, where she had a close friend, to work as a dentist's receptionist.

Acting remained Miss Dewhurst's aspiration. Moving eventually to New York City, she enrolled in the American Academy of Dramatic Arts, where one of her teachers was Joseph Anthony. She also later studied with Harold Clurman. To pay for her classes and to meet expenses while acquiring acting experience, she worked as a switchboard operator, an usher at Carnegie Hall, and an instructor at a reducing gymnasium. During the off-season of the New York stage she toured with summer stock companies. According to some accounts of her career, she made her debut in a stock company production of *Personal Appearance* in Gatlinburg, Tennessee. Most sources, however, regard her first professional performance to be the one she gave while a student at the American Academy, in the role of Julia Cavendish in *The Royal Family* on October 15, 1946 at New York's Carnegie Lyceum.

Slightly less than six years later Miss Dewhurst was seen for the first time on Broadway as one of the neighbors in a revival of O'Neill's *Desire Under the Elms,* staged by Clurman at the ANTA Playhouse in early 1952. Her New York engagements were then so few that she did not appear again on Broadway until January 1956, when she portrayed both a Turkish Concubine and a Virgin of Memphis in *Tamburlaine the Great* at the Winter Garden.

Insisting that her career has had no intentional grand design, Colleen Dewhurst has explained that she became an actress identified with classical roles simply because she accepted the parts that happened to be offered to her. Generally, her plays were those she "believed in." The producer probably most responsible for boosting her early fortunes in the theatre was Joseph Papp, founder and director of the New York Shakespeare Festival. In her first Papp production she played Tamora in *Titus Andronicus* at the East Side Amphitheatre in August 1956.

Then, after heading the cast as the title character in a revival of *Camille* at the off-Broadway Cherry Lane Theatre in September 1956, she returned to the Shakespeare Festival two months later to portray Kate in *The Taming of the Shrew,* a role that she once said provided her "first important chance." In Shakespearean tragedies presented by Papp she played Lady Macbeth in *Macbeth,* at the Belvedere Lake Theatre in Central Park in August 1957, and Cleopatra in two productions of *Antony and Cleopatra,* at the Heckscher Theatre in January 1959 and at the new, outdoor Delacorte Theatre on Belvedere Lake in June 1963. A taped performance of the latter was shown simultaneously over WCBS-TV on June 20. Again at the Delacorte in the summer of 1972, she made Gertrude of *Hamlet* a sympathetic and understandable woman in love.

Meanwhile, Miss Dewhurst had been steadily gaining recognition among New York theatregoers for performances in distinguished plays other than the Shakespeare Festival's. In late 1956 she had the lead in Jean Cocteau's *The Eagle Has Two Heads* at the Actors Playhouse. For her portrayal of the Queen in that revival, along with her performance in *The Taming of the Shrew*, she won her first Obie, the *Village Voice* off-Broadway award.

Maiden Voyage, in which Colleen Dewhurst appeared as Penelope, opened and closed in Philadelphia on its pre-Broadway tour in early 1957. In the fall of that year the Playwrights' Company production of Wycherley's seventeenth-century ribald classic *The Country Wife*, reached New York, at the Adelphi Theatre, after a successful run in Washington, D.C. For the Broadway presentation she switched from the role of Mrs. Dainty Fidget to Mrs. Squeamish.

London of a century later was the setting of Colleen Dewhurst's next play, a revival of Edwin Justus Mayer's sardonic tale of cynicism and corruption in Newgate Prison. The well-received *Children of Darkness*, directed by José Quintero and starring George C. Scott, opened at the Circle in the Square in late February 1958. Of her interpretation of Laetitia, the only woman in the cast, Walter Kerr wrote in the New York *Herald Tribune* (March 1, 1958), "One must stand in honest awe of Colleen Dewhurst's sultry-mouthed, stony-eyed trollop; as bad girls go, she is a beaut to be remembered." The role of Laetitia won her the *Theatre World* award.

"I'm the revival girl," Miss Dewhurst once quipped, as quoted by Sidney Fields in the New York *Mirror* (March 4, 1958). "And I always imagine the audience saying, 'Here she is again! Didn't we see her three weeks ago?' But my attitude is, 'I'll act every chance I get.'" Then, on February 16, 1960 at the 54th Street Theatre, she appeared in the first of several nonrevivals, the American première of Albert Camus' philosophical melodrama *Caligula*. As Caesonia, the mistress of the despotic Roman emperor, she played her first substantial Broadway role. It seemed, however, to Richard Watts Jr. of the New York *Post* (February 28, 1960) that "Colleen Dewhurst has a part that makes comparatively few demands on her remarkable talents as an actress."

Watts later wrote enthusiastically about the dramatic scope offered Miss Dewhurst as Mary Follet, a role she created in *All the Way Home*, Tad Mosel's sensitive and somber dramatization of James Agee's *A Death in the Family*. That play, which opened at the Belasco Theatre on November 30, 1960, overcame audience neglect to sus-

COLLEEN DEWHURST

tain a fairly long run only with the support of critics and others associated with show business. Arguing for its survival in a second favorable appraisal, on December 11, 1960, Watts called special attention to the acting of Miss Dewhurst as "one of the most beautiful performances of recent seasons" and to "the depth, simplicity, warmth and emotional range of her superb characterization of a young wife and mother who grows in stature and understanding through . . . tragic experience." Many professionals in the theatre agreed, including those who selected the actress for the 1961 Lola D'Annunzio Award and the Antoinette Perry (Tony) Award.

Some other prominent Broadway critics, such as Howard Taubman of the New York *Times,* thought that probably the chief dramatic merit of Alice Cannon's play about an Irish-American family in St. Louis in 1928, *Great Day in the Morning,* was the opportunity for acting it afforded its star, Colleen Dewhurst. After the première of the comedy at Henry Miller's Theatre on March 28, 1962, Taubman wrote, "As a marvelously big, slovenly, truculent and sentimental Phoebe [Flaherty], she is virtually a one-woman show."

Miss Dewhurst's director in *Great Day in the Morning,* Quintero, also staged an off-Broadway revival of *Desire Under the Elms* in which she portrayed Abbie Putnam, the young third wife of the tyrannical septuagenarian Ephraim Cabot, played by Scott. O'Neill's brooding tragedy of love and greed in a New England farm family of the mid-nineteenth century enjoyed a run of several months at Circle in the Square, beginning in January 1963. But Miss Dewhurst, whose Abbie won her a second Obie, left the cast before the play's closing to fulfill other commitments.

For several challenging roles in her repertoire Miss Dewhurst is indebted to another American playwright, Edward Albee. She created the strapping Miss Amelia Evans, in love with a dwarf, in Albee's stage adaptation of Carson McCullers' novella *The Ballad of the Sad Café,* which premièred at the Martin Beck Theatre on October 30, 1963. Despite several rave notices, including that of John Chapman of the New York *News* the play failed financially. During the summer of 1965 she toured in the role of Martha, the abrasive wife in Albee's *Who's Afraid of Virginia Woolf?*

Returning to Broadway, at the Broadhurst Theatre on October 31, 1967, in O'Neill's *More Stately Mansions,* Miss Dewhurst played the daughter of an Irish tavern keeper in nineteenth-century New England—Sara Melody, whose marriage became a contest with her mother-in-law. Even before its American première, in Los Angeles in September 1967, the play had been nationally publicized because it brought the reappearance on the United States stage of Ingrid Bergman after an absence of more than two decades. Although Miss Dewhurst was uniformly praised in New York reviews, a predominance of only mixed notices on the play itself contributed to shortening its New York run. Several critics objected to director Quintero's pared and edited adaptation of an unfinished drama that some O'Neill scholars say he had not wanted ever to be produced.

"I love the O'Neill women," Colleen Dewhurst asserted in a Rex Reed interview soon after the somewhat disappointing New York response to *More Stately Mansions.* "They move from the groin rather than the brain. To play O'Neill you have to be big. You can't sit around and play little moments of sadness or sweetness. You cannot phony up O'Neill"(*Conversations in the Raw,* 1969). She was soon to be rewarded for her faith in O'Neill, but meanwhile her career more or less continued to follow the pattern of enriching the New York stage with loudly applauded memorable performances in fugitive productions.

In September 1969, for example, Miss Dewhurst appeared in Kermit Bloomgarden's presentation of the South African playwright Athol Fugard's *Hello and Goodbye* at the Sheridan Square Playhouse. Her portrayal of the embittered prostitute Hester in that two-character play won her the 1969-70 Drama Desk Award. She starred in the title role of Bertolt Brecht's *The Good Woman of Setzuan,* which in November 1970 opened the sixth season of the Lincoln Center Repertory Theatre at the Vivian Beaumont Theatre. The following spring she was seen as the loving, gratifying mistress in Albee's drama of the ritual of dying, *All Over,* during its brief occupancy of the Martin Beck.

Then, giving what some critics consider the finest performance of her career, Colleen Dewhurst costarred with Jason Robards in a revival of O'Neill's *A Moon for the Misbegotten,* which began its long run at the Morosco Theatre on December 29, 1973. She seemed a natural for the role of Josie Hogan, a self-described "great cow" of a girl whose pretended promiscuity masks virginity and a need for love. "No woman has been big enough for the part before," T. E. Kalem wrote in *Time* (January 14, 1974), "not only

physically but in that generosity of heart, mind and spirit which Josie must convey."

In his review for the New York *Times* (December 31, 1973) Clive Barnes observed, "She spoke O'Neill as if it were being spoken for the first time." Miss Dewhurst's skill in achieving freshness and immediacy came in part from familiarity with the character of Josie over a long period. Quintero, who staged the current Broadway production, had first directed her in *A Moon for the Misbegotten* for a presentation during the summer of 1958 at the Festival of Two Worlds in Spoleto, Italy. In October 1965, again under Quintero's direction, she played Josie at the Studio Arena in Buffalo. For her most recent recreation of O'Neill's heroine she won her second Tony.

The professional integrity ascribed to Colleen Dewhurst because of her work in the Shakespeare Festival and meritorious off-Broadway plays has been made possible partly through her readiness to appear in comparatively well-paying TV shows. During the fall of 1959 she had major roles in WNTA-TV's *Medea* and *Burning Bright* and in WCBS-TV's *I, Don Quixote,* for which as Aldonza she won a Sylvania Award. In 1962 she was nominated for an Emmy for her performance in WNBC-TV's *Focus,* an adaptation of Arthur Miller's novel about anti-Semitism. Also notable among more than a score of television plays in which she acted were Sartre's *No Exit,* as the Lesbian, Inez, in 1961; Miller's *The Crucible* in 1967; *My Mother's House,* a play based on Colette's autobiography, in 1967; and *The Story of Jacob and Joseph* in 1974.

Colleen Dewhurst's roles in motion pictures, which she once referred to as "my famous cameos," include a violent lunatic in Fred Zinnemann's *The Nun's Story* (1959); the psychiatrist Dr. Vera Kropotkin in *A Fine Madness* (Warner Brothers, 1966); and the madam of a group of traveling prostitutes in *The Cowboys* (Warner Brothers, 1972), which starred John Wayne. In a later Wayne movie, *McQ* (Warner Brothers, 1974), she played Myra, a bar waitress. "Dewhurst is outstanding in her two scenes," a reviewer for *Variety* (January 23, 1974) commented. "She and Wayne play extremely well together in one of those magic pairings possible only on the screen."

While at the American Academy of Dramatic Arts, Colleen Dewhurst met James Vickery, a fellow student whom she married in 1947. The marriage ended some twelve years later, and in 1960 she married George C. Scott after a courtship that began with their working together in *Children of Darkness.* Before their first divorce, in 1965, she had two sons, Alexander and Campbell. She and Scott were remarried in July 1967 and divorced again on February 2, 1972. Miss Dewhurst's home is a 200-year-old farmhouse in northern Westchester County, New York, where she lives with her sons and several dogs, cats, and other pets.

Much admired for "honesty of performance," Colleen Dewhurst seems to detest what she would call "phoniness" not only on the stage, but also in her manner and appearance and relationships with others offstage. She is tall (five feet eight inches) and robust and has blue-green eyes, long dark hair, a generous smile, and a broad and well-formed face that even without makeup can carry changes of expression far out into the audience. In his review of *More Stately Mansions* in the New York *Times* (November 12, 1967) Walter Kerr described her voice as "husky, warm" and her laugh as "wolverine." One of her tributes, in which she takes a somewhat amused pride, is an honorary doctorate in fine arts conferred on her in 1972 by Lawrence University, which had merged with Downer College, her alma mater.

References

Christian Sci Mon p9 Je 5 '63 por
N Y Post p15 Jl 8 '72 por
N Y Sunday News III p1 D 24 '72 por
N Y Times II p1+ F 17 '74 por
Newsday LI p12+ Ap 28 '74 por
Theatre Arts 47:16+ Jl '63 por
Biographical Encyclopaedia & Who's Who of the American Theatre (1966)
Who's Who in the Theatre (1972)

FINLEY, CHARLES O(SCAR)

Feb. 22, 1918- Baseball team owner; insurance company executive
Address: b. Oakland Athletics, Oakland-Alameda County Coliseum, Oakland, Calif. 94621

The major-league owner mold has been broken with scandalous *éclat* by brash, impetuous Charles O. Finley, the autocrat of the American League's Oakland (California) Athletics and past master of the art of business ballyhoo. The flamboyant and controversial Finley, a self-made insurance millionaire, bought, in his words, "a little extra happiness" in the form of the Athletics (then located in Kansas City, Missouri) in 1960, and he proceeded to run the team first-hand, in breach of pro baseball etiquette. For years Finley was the pariah of the baseball Establishment, a parvenu disdained by other owners for his "bush-league" promotional stunts, from "Hot Pants Night" to greased-pig and cow-milking contests on the diamond. Eventually some of his innovations and suggestions—including night World Series games and colorfully garbed, hirsute line-ups—gained acceptance, and despite his tempestuous relationships with managers and players he built the hang-dog Athletics into world champions. When the A's won their second consecutive World Series, in 1973, Charlie O., as his men call him, upstaged the players with illegal antics and maneuvers, including use of the stadium lights to the Athletics' advantage, which drew penalties from the Commissioner of Baseball. His team went on the following year to win their third series in a row, defeating the Los Angels Dodgers in four games out of five. In addition to the A's, Finley owns teams in the National Hockey League and the American Basketball Association.

CHARLES O. FINLEY

The great-grandson of Irish Protestants from County Offaly, Charles Oscar Finley was born in Ensley, Alabama on February 22, 1918. His father is Oscar Finley, who worked in the steel mills of nearby Birmingham to supplement his meager farm income. Charles helped out on the family farm—mostly by feeding the hogs—and when his chores there were done he earned pocket money by selling newspapers, magazines, and rejected eggs (which he bought for five cents a dozen and sold for fifteen). During his boyhood he also formed a sand-lot baseball team and was batboy for the Birmingham Barons, a minor-league team.

In 1934 the Finleys moved to Gary, Indiana, where the father obtained a better steelworking job than the one he had in Birmingham. At Horace Mann High School in Gary, Finley was known to his male peers for his love of baseball, but one female classmate has recalled him differently: "Charley Finley was a strange boy. We looked on him as quite a dude because he wore a sport coat to school. I'd say the girls remember him more as a good dancer than as an athlete."

After graduating from high school, Finley worked in the Gary steel mills, studied salesmanship in a junior college, and organized the Gary Merchants, a Michigan-Indiana industrial league baseball team for which he played first base. In 1941 he married Shirley McCartney, his high-school girl friend. During World War II Finley worked in a defense plant in La Porte, Indiana, not too far from South Bend, where he settled with his young, growing family and bought the first 300 acres of the farm he still owns there.

While employed at the defense plant, Finley sold insurance at night. Working for the Travelers Insurance Company full-time after the war, he set a sales record but paid for the energy expended with his health. Stricken with pneumonic tuberculosis, he was confined to the James O. Parramore Hospital in Crown Point, Indiana from 1946 to 1948. During that time his wife supported the family by working as a proofreader for the Gary *Post-Tribune*.

His illness, he says, was the turning point in his life. Determined "not to die," he came through the initial crisis with a new philosophy of life, an indelible realization that "money is secondary" to health and happiness. And his convalescence gave him "a lot of time to just lie around and think" about an easier way to make more money. Pondering his own lack of health insurance, he extrapolated the plight of a professional man whose career would be ruined by protracted sickness or injury and came up with an insurance plan for physicians, a plan that would protect earning power at rates based on the statistical fact that doctors are better-than-average risks.

Although Finley's idea for providing the medical profession with group disability insurance was not new, it offered much more coverage than rival plans for a modest increase in premiums. Sold first through the Continental Casualty Company and then by Finley's own company, Charles O. Finley & Company of Chicago, it was bought by doctors all over the country. Within two years Finley had made his first million, and eventually his company's gross revenues surpassed $40,000,000 annually.

Finally having enough money to realize a lifelong dream, Finley in 1954 began shopping for that most jealously guarded and coveted commodity, a major league baseball franchise. For six years he made bid after unsuccessful bid, for the Athletics, the Detroit Tigers, the Chicago White Sox, and the American League expansion franchise in Los Angeles. "I never saw anybody who wanted to get into baseball so badly," one baseball executive has said. "He'd have bought anything. Why? I guess he wanted to wear a cap with a big-league team's name on it." In December 1960 Finley at long last acquired a 52 percent interest in the Kansas City Athletics for $1,975,000, and two months later he bought up the rest of the stock for another payment of the same magnitude. "I put every cent I could scrape up into this team," Finley said at the time. "It's more than a hobby for me. It's a total commitment."

"When I came into baseball in Kansas City . . . they told me I'd have to have this and I'd have to have that," Finley recalled in an interview with Wells Twombly for the New York *Times Magazine* (July 15, 1973). "I went out and hired Frank Lane, who was supposed to be the best manager available. I found out one thing about baseball people right away. They like to make the game sound so complex that nobody but them can run it. It doesn't take a genius to run a ball club. . . . I fired Lane and became my own general manager."

He also became his own manager. Traditionally, the general manager of a baseball club confines his activities to the front office, leaving day-to-day team operations and game strategy to the manager. Breaching that tradition, Finley, sitting in his private box surrounded by telephones, from the beginning acted as a commander-in-chief at games. Wells Twombly described the scene: "He listens to the radio broadcast and calls in orders.

He complains to the scoreboard. He phones the dugout with instructions. . . . The language that comes through the other receiver is acerbic, tough, profane, direct, suspicious." Not surprisingly, manager after manager either quit or was fired. The turnover was approximately a manager a year.

In last place when Finley bought them, the Athletics continued to flounder in the American League basement as long as they remained in Kansas City. Finley lost large sums on the team annually, and his relations with city fathers and citizens were less than ideal. He stepped on some important toes, such as those of the favorite local sportswriter (to whom he presented his first annual Poison Pen Award); the municipal council feuded with him over such matters as the terms of the Athletics' financial contract with the city; and residents did not always appreciate his promotional gimmicks, such as the fireworks that kept people living near the baseball stadium awake at night.

His other innovations included a mechanical rabbit in an Athletics uniform that popped up near home plate in Municipal Stadium with fresh baseballs when needed; a picnic area near left field; a flock of sheep, tended by a shepherd, to keep the grass cropped on an embankment behind right field; pink fluorescent lights to mark the foul lines; and Charlie O., the mule that is still the A's mascot. When he garbed the Athletics in their green and gold uniforms in 1963 baseball purists laughed or groaned, but colorful double-knit uniforms are now common in the major leagues. His suggestion that World Series games be played on weekends and at night for the benefit of fans who work in the daytime Monday through Friday, a suggestion ignored when Finley made it in 1964, was finally adopted eight years later.

After abortive attempts to move the Athletics to Dallas-Forth Worth, Texas and to Louisville, Kentucky, Finley succeeded in transplanting the team to Oakland, California in 1968. In Oakland the Athletics climbed from sixth place in American League standings to second place in the league's western division in 1969 and 1970, to first place in 1971, and to the world championship in 1972 and 1973.

In Dick Williams, who guided the Athletics to their World Series victories in 1972 and 1973, Finley thought he had finally found a manager with whom he could get along, or, as he put it, one who "could really make a difference in a ball club." But Williams' patience ran out during the 1973 series, against the New York Mets. In the second game of the series two errors by second baseman Mike Andrews contributed to the loss of the game to the Mets. After the game Andrews put himself on the inactive list by signing an injury report. According to newspaper accounts, the report was spurious and Andrews was forced into signing it by Finley, as a punishment for fielding inefficiency compounded by "arrogance."

"The seventieth World Series will be treasured in history as the occasion when Charles O. Finley got his comeuppance," Red Smith observed in the New York *Times* (October 19, 1973). "The egregious busher who owns the Oakland A's may be too insensitive to realize it yet, but when 54,817 baseball fans stood up to applaud Mike Andrews Wednesday night, they were also deriding the man who had tried to shove Andrews around."

Regarding Dick Williams, who had sent Andrews out for the ovation, Smith wrote: "Williams . . . has done Good Time Charlie's bidding for three years and managed to keep a civil tongue behind his mustache, but the Andrews caper was too much for his stomach." Moments after the series ended on October 21, Williams' resignation was announced. Finley seemed willing to let him go, until the New York Yankees attempted to hire Williams. At that point, on October 23, 1974, Finley told Yankee owner George Steinbrenner that he intended to hold Williams to his Oakland contract, and American League president Joe Cronin ruled in Finley's favor.

There have been several altercations between Finley and Baseball Commissioner Bowie Kuhn. Early in the 1972 season Kuhn angered the Oakland owner by interceding in a contract dispute with pitcher Vida Blue. Later in 1972 the commissioner fined Finley $2,500 for violating the major-league rule against the payment of bonuses or other incentives during a World Series. For his various indiscretions during the 1973 series, including the Mike Andrews affair, Finley was fined $7,000.

When he suffered a second heart attack, in 1973, Finley was advised by physicians to slow the pace of his activities. Accordingly, in January 1974, he announced that he was offering the Athletics for sale to "responsible parties" for $15,-000,000. "But if I don't sell the A's," he said, "I'll just continue to operate the club as before." He added that he was also open to bids for his National Hockey League team, the California Seals, and his American Basketball Association club, the Memphis Tams. Under Finley's absentee ownership, neither team has been prospering. Purchased in 1970, the Seals finished no higher than sixth in NHL standings during the following three years, and one former player has reported that "some of the things he [Finley] did or didn't do killed our spirit." The Tams, acquired in 1972, lost sixty out of eighty-four games and cost Finley $490,000 in 1972-73.

Before moving from Kansas City, Finley negotiated a contract with the Oakland municipal government under the terms of which the Athletics pay relatively low rent for the use of the Oakland-Alameda County Coliseum and share heftily in television, concession, and parking revenues. Since the move, the Athletics have netted between $600,000 and $1,300,000 a season. Finley budgets his money more carefully than his occasional big gifts to players would seem to indicate. "I can turn a profit because I don't have many unessential employees to pay big money to," he has pointed out. "I put my money into player development and don't worry about paying $20,000 to

a public-relations man who can't put any extra people in the seats anyway. . . . There's a feeling that every ex-player has to be put on the payroll as a $25,000-a-year scout. I don't see that I'm a charitable organization."

"He's the fairest man I've ever worked for in baseball," Oakland coach Vern Hoscheit has said of Finley, but contrary opinions are more prevalent. Oakland slugger Reggie Jackson has recalled: "I told Dave Duncan that Finley treated his black players like niggers. Dave told me not to worry or feel hurt. He said Charlie treats his white players like niggers too." Kansas City *Star* sports editor Joe McGuff has observed: "If you try to figure Finley out, you'll only succeed in confusing yourself. His capacity for turmoil is incredible. He thrives on it. He enjoys tough times so he can work his way out of them and give himself credit."

Charles O. and Shirley Finley have seven children: Sharon (Mrs. David Kesling), Charles Jr., Kathleen, Paul, Martin, Luke, and David. By buying up adjacent land over the years, Finley has increased the size of his cattle farm in La Porte, Indiana to 1,280 acres. His parents at last report were living nearby, on a farm he purchased for them. Because of the demands of his insurance business in Chicago and, above all, his baseball team in Oakland and on the road, Finley has never been able to spend as much time in La Porte as he would like to. "I'm really ashamed of the time I've put in on baseball to the neglect of my family," Murray Chass, writing in the New York *Times* (October 23, 1972), quoted him as saying. "My wife and kids have really sacrificed." According to a report in *Newsweek* (April 8, 1974), Mrs. Finley initiated divorce proceedings against her husband.

The Oakland owner is a cigar-chomping, beetle-browed six-footer with thinning white hair, a voice that has been described as a "walrus monotone," and a habit of shrugging his shoulders with what Wells Twombly in his New York *Times Magazine* article called "characteristic inscrutability." Finley told Twombly that, having only average intelligence, he has had to work "harder than anybody else" to achieve success: "I'm no brain. I take care of every detail because that's my formula for success." Phil Seghi, general manager of the Cleveland Indians, a former Finley employee, has testified: "Give Charles his due. He's a worker. He's a fanatic for details. People claim he's tough to work for. It's true, everything has to be checked with him. But he wants workers around him. He'll go until 4 A.M. and be up and going again at 8:30 A.M. If you work for him you can't worry about your own sleeping habits."

In Oakland, Finley lives in an apartment overlooking Lake Merritt. A good cook, he enjoys serving guests his favorite meal, calf's liver and bacon followed by T-bone steak. As chairman of the National Tuberculosis Association in 1961, the Oakland baseball magnate raised more money for the association than any previous chairman. In his New York *Times Magazine* article Wells Twombly wrote: "Never has there been anyone in baseball to match Charles O. Finley, who doesn't give a damn what anybody thinks. . . . He is capable of great generosity and great parsimony. . . . He is a man of long memory and short temper. He is at once earthy and capable of the grand gesture. He does not like to be corrected, defied, or challenged. He loves the game of baseball with an overriding passion and yet there is hardly anyone in it he hasn't offended."

References

N Y Times p44 O 23 '72 por
N Y Times Mag p12+ Jl 15 '73 pors
Nat Observer p7 Ja 13 '64 por
Parade p10+ Ja 28 '73 pors
Sat Eve Post 337:73+ Ap 4 '64 pors
Sports Illus 23:36+ Jl 19 '65 por

Who's Who in America, 1972-73

FONDA, HENRY

May 16, 1905- Actor
Address: b. c/o John Springer Associates, Inc., 1901 Avenue of the Stars, Los Angeles, Calif. 90067

NOTE: This biography supersedes the article that appeared in *Current Biography* in 1948.

If any actor can be said nearly to embody the ideal American, it is Henry Fonda, the veteran of some eighty motion pictures and of the theatre and television. During a career spanning nearly half a century, he has come to represent, in the words of director Joshua Logan, "a kind of synthesis of all the heroes of Mark Twain, Bret Harte, James Fenimore Cooper, Hawthorne, Poe, and Irving." Fonda's fame derives chiefly from his performances in such movie masterpieces of Americana as *Young Mr. Lincoln, The Grapes of Wrath, The Ox-Bow Incident,* and *My Darling Clementine.* On the Broadway stage he has scored a number of spectacular successes, including *Mister Roberts* and, more recently, the one-man show *Clarence Darrow.*

Henry Jaynes Fonda, the oldest of the three children, and only son, of William Brace and Herberta (Jaynes) Fonda, was born in Grand Island, Nebraska, on May 16, 1905. On his father's side, he is descended from a titled Italian who emigrated from Genoa to the Netherlands in about 1400, and whose descendants settled in the seventeenth century in upper New York State, where they established the town of Fonda. His maternal grandfather, Henry Jaynes, is said to have provided the inspiration for his artistic talents. Henry Fonda and his sisters, Harriet and Jayne, grew up in Omaha, where his father owned and operated a printing company.

At ten, while living in the Omaha suburb of Dundee, Fonda had his short story "The Mouse" published in the Dundee *News* as the winning entry in a contest. That sparked his ambition to be a writer and, after graduating

from Omaha Central High School in 1923, he enrolled as a journalism major at the University of Minnesota. To supplement a modest allowance from home, Fonda worked part-time as a "troubleshooter" for the Northwestern Bell Telephone Company and as director of sports at a Minneapolis settlement house. Eventually the routine of work and study proved too strenuous, and at the end of his sophomore year he left the university for good.

Although the idea of becoming an actor seemed out of keeping with his shy nature, Fonda was persuaded by Dorothy Brando, the mother of Marlon Brando and a friend of the family, to audition for the juvenile lead in Philip Barry's *You and I,* which opened in September 1925 at the Omaha Community Playhouse under the direction of Gregory Foley. After his successful stage debut, he remained with the Playhouse for three seasons, climaxed at mid-point by his performance in the title role of *Merton of the Movies.* Between theatrical assignments, Fonda tried unsuccessfully to obtain a newspaper job and worked intermittently as a window dresser, garage mechanic, iceman, and office boy.

Learning that the Lincoln impersonator George Billings was in need of new material, Fonda devised a dramatic sketch with a secondary part in it for himself. Billings bought the playlet and, with Fonda as his on-stage foil, used it during the summer of 1927 in a vaudeville tour of one-night stands. Returning to Omaha, Fonda accepted the salaried post of assistant director at the Community Playhouse and that season, besides designing sets, appeared vis-a-vis Dorothy Brando in Eugene O'Neill's *Beyond the Horizon.*

Equipped with savings of $100, Fonda came to New York City in June 1928. Discovering that all was somnolent on Broadway, he turned to summer stock. After a rebuff from the Provincetown Players, he obtained an unpaid job with the Cape Playhouse in Dennis, Massachusetts, as third assistant stage manager and also replaced one of the company's regular actors in a minor role in *The Barker.* Later that season Fonda joined the newly established University Players Guild in Falmouth, Massachusetts and was offered a part in *The Jest.* According to Joshua Logan, one of the founders of the group, Fonda's portrayal of a mature Italian nobleman was "disastrous," but later, cast in roles more appropriate to his age and background, he excelled. He appeared with the University Players at Falmouth for five summer seasons, from 1928 through 1932, and also during its winter 1931-32 season in Baltimore. From 1929 to 1931 Fonda was also associated with the National Junior Theatre in Washington, D.C., working occasionally as director and appearing in a number of roles, including that of the Cowardly Lion in *The Wizard of Oz.*

Meanwhile, after becoming a member of Actors Equity and contacting all the major New York booking agents, Fonda made his first Broadway appearance in November 1929, in a walk-on role in the Theatre Guild production of Romain

Rolland's *The Game of Love and Death.* In the
fall of 1932 he had a bit part in *I Loved You
Wednesday* at the Harris Theatre, and in the
spring of 1933 he understudied Fred Keating
and appeared in a small role in *Forsaking All
Others* at the Times Square Theatre. Fonda
finally broke out of the supernumerary mold when
he appeared in comedy skits with Imogene Coca
in the first of Leonard Sillman's *New Faces* re-
vues, which opened at the Fulton Theatre in
March 1934. His appearance in that revue brought
him to the attention of agent Leland Hayward,
who then became his personal representative.

While appearing in a stock production with
the Westchester Players in Mount Kisco, New
York in the summer of 1934, Fonda was summoned to Hollywood by Hayward for a meeting with movie producer Walter Wanger. Enamored of the theatre, Fonda had no desire
for a film career, and, thinking that he would
quash the incipient deal, asked for $1,000 a week.
To his astonishment, the demand did not faze
Wanger, and a contract calling for two pictures
a year was negotiated.

Once assured of a future in Hollywood, Fonda
returned to Mount Kisco. June Walker, who
saw him there in *The Swan,* chose him as her
costar in the Broadway production of *The Farmer
Takes a Wife.* But although Fonda, in his characterization of Dan Harrow, was praised by
critics, including Brooks Atkinson of the New
York *Times* (October 31, 1934), who cited his
"manly, modest performance in a style of captivating simplicity," the production ran only
thirteen weeks at the 46th Street Theatre. Fonda
made his motion picture debut with Janet Gaynor
in Twentieth Century-Fox's film version of *The
Farmer Takes a Wife* (1935). That year he also
appeared in that studio's *Way Down East* and in
the RKO-Radio musical *I Dream Too Much,*
with Lily Pons.

For Paramount, the home base of Walter
Wanger's production unit, Fonda appeared in
*The Trail of the Lonesome Pine, The Moon's Our
Home,* and *Spendthrift* in 1936. Of the pictures
he made in 1937, *You Only Live Once,* with
Sylvia Sidney, was by far the most memorable.
Directed by Fritz Lang and released by United
Artists, it recounted a tragic tale of persecution
and flight and, as one reviewer wrote, was "acted
with terrifying honesty." His other films of that
year were *Wings of the Morning* (Twentieth
Century-Fox) and the Warner Brothers releases
Slim and *That Certain Woman.*

Meanwhile, to keep his instincts as a stage
actor from atrophying, Fonda returned to Mount
Kisco in the summer of 1935 to appear in
The Virginian. In September 1937 he re-entered
the Broadway arena as star of the comedy *Blow
Ye Winds,* which despite his own commendatory
notices, closed after thirty-six performances at the
47th Street Theatre. Back in Hollywood, Fonda
made ten pictures in two years. They included,
in 1938, *Blockade* (United Artists), one of the
early anti-fascist films; *Jezebel* (Warner); *Mad
Miss Manton* (RKO); *Spawn of the North* (Para-

HENRY FONDA

mount); and *I Met My Love Again* (United
Artists). During 1939 he made *Let Us Live*
(Columbia), and won favorable notices for Twen-
tieth Century-Fox's *Young Mr. Lincoln* and *Drums
Along the Mohawk,* which marked the beginning
of his association with director John Ford. He
also appeared in supporting roles in that studio's
Jesse James and *The Story of Alexander Graham
Bell.*

Ford chose Fonda for the part of Tom Joad
in the screen version of John Steinbeck's epic
novel *The Grapes of Wrath,* but Darryl F. Zanuck,
chief of production at Twentieth Century-Fox,
maintained that such a plum should go to a
contract player. To obtain the role—which netted
him an Academy Award nomination as best actor
of 1940—Fonda was obliged to sign a seven-year
agreement with the studio. Reviewing the film
in his *Seventy Years of Cinema* (Barnes, 1969),
Peter Cowie wrote: "It is Fonda, with his cat-
like walk and his deep-etched gaze, who takes on
the features of an Everyman, suffering with grace
and every so often lashing out against exploitation."

Although Fonda was proud of *The Grapes of
Wrath,* he did not relish his long-term indenture
to Twentieth Century-Fox and the long series of
routine assignments that went with it. They included *Lillian Russell, Chad Hanna,* and *The
Return of Frank James* (1940); *Wild Geese Calling* (1941); *Rings on Her Fingers, The Magnificent Dope,* and *Tales of Manhattan* (1942); and
The Immortal Sergeant (1943). "On loan" to
Paramount, he played in Preston Sturges' farce
The Lady Eve, which one New York *Times* critic
named the best picture of 1941. In 1942 he appeared in *The Big Street* (RKO) and *The Male
Animal* (Warner) and served as the narrator
for two war documentaries.

Joining forces with director William A. Well-
man, Fonda obtained grudging permission from
Zanuck to film an adaptation of Walter van
Tilburg Clark's controversial novel *The Ox-Bow
Incident,* dealing with the lynching of three in-
nocent men. Although the film was not a box of-

fice success, critics hailed its release in 1943 as a landmark in movie history and termed Fonda's performance one of the highlights of his career.

In August 1942 Fonda enlisted as an apprentice seaman in the United States Navy. He saw active duty in the Pacific as a quartermaster, third class aboard the destroyer U.S.S. *Satterlee* and later served as an assistant operations and air combat intelligence officer under Admiral John Hoover, earning a Bronze Star and a Presidential citation. In October 1945 he was discharged as a lieutenant, senior grade.

Among the half dozen films that Fonda made right after the war, the three directed by John Ford stand out: *My Darling Clementine* (Twentieth Century-Fox, 1946) which afforded him the opportunity to play the legendary Western lawman Wyatt Earp; *The Fugitive* (RKO, 1947), an adaptation of Graham Greene's novel *The Power and the Glory;* and *Fort Apache* (RKO, 1948). Fonda's other films of that period include *Daisy Kenyon* (Twentieth Century-Fox, 1947), *The Long Night* (RKO, 1947), and *On Our Merry Way* (United Artists, 1948).

While visiting New York in 1947, Fonda listened to a reading of the *Mister Roberts* script, which Joshua Logan, in collaboration with Thomas Heggen, had fashioned from the latter's best-selling book, and expressed his desire to play the title role, unaware that the authors had him in mind for the part. When the elaborate Broadway production of *Mister Roberts* opened at the Alvin Theatre on February 18, 1948 it was given, according to *Life* (March 1, 1948), "the critical equivalent of a twenty-one-gun salute." The comedy-drama depicted life on a supply vessel plying the backwaters of the Pacific during World War II and described the plight of an idealistic young naval officer who, weary of the "regular run from Tedium to Apathy," keeps applying for a transfer to a combat area. Fonda's sensitive portrayal of the action-hungry lieutenant won him, among other distinctions, an Antoinette Perry award as best actor of the 1947-48 season. He remained with the show through October 1950, withdrawing only because of an operation on his knee. In January 1951 he took over the lead in the touring company. By his own reckoning, Fonda played Mister Roberts on stage 1,700 times and "never got tired of it."

As Charles Gray, the ambitious young bank executive of *Point of No Return,* Paul Osborn's dramatization of John P. Marquand's popular novel, Fonda won acclaim for what Wolcott Gibbs of the *New Yorker* (December 22, 1951) called a "singularly relaxed, touching, and humorous performance." After the play's 364-performance run, beginning December 13, 1951, at the Alvin Theatre, Fonda headed the cast on its national tour, from November 1952 to May 1953. His next Broadway appearance was in *The Caine Mutiny Court Martial,* Herman Wouk's expansion of the climactic scene from his Pulitzer Prize-winning novel, which toured extensively before arriving at the Plymouth Theatre under Charles Laughton's direction on January 20, 1954. As the naval defense lawyer Barney Greenwald, Fonda was, according to the consensus of the critics, superb.

Fonda relinquished his part in that production far in advance of its closing so that he would be free to act in the movie version of *Mister Roberts* (Warner, 1955). Although he clashed with director John Ford over how the material should be interpreted and had misgivings about the final product, most of the critics liked the film. John McCarten of the *New Yorker* (July 26, 1955), while echoing Fonda's complaint that the comedy had been "unconscionably broadened," nevertheless found the star's performance "consistently admirable throughout the picture."

Fonda played Pierre in King Vidor's visually stunning version of Tolstoy's *War and Peace* (Paramount, 1956) and starred in the Alfred Hitchcock thriller *The Wrong Man* (Warner, 1957) and the popular western *The Tin Star* (Paramount, 1957). He won acclaim for his performance as a persuasive juror in a murder case in *Twelve Angry Men* (United Artists, 1957), which he coproduced with writer Reginald Rose. But although the film won a Golden Bear award at the International Film Festival at Berlin in 1957, it was not a box office success in the United States.

Returning to Broadway in William Gibson's two-character comedy *Two for the Seesaw,* which opened at the Booth Theatre in January 1958, Fonda contributed a competent performance as Jerry Ryan, the newly divorced Nebraska lawyer. But, as several critics pointed out, the role was one-dimensional compared to that played by Anne Bancroft, of Gittel, the thirtyish waif from the Bronx. The year that he had to spend in the guise of a glorified "straight man" was, for him, a frustrating time. Meanwhile, he had completed *Stage Struck* (RKO, 1958), and for Twentieth Century-Fox appeared in the off-beat western *Warlock* (1959) and Nunnally Johnson's comedy *The Man Who Understood Women* (1959).

With Barbara Bel Geddes as his leading lady, Fonda opened at the Morosco Theatre on Broadway on December 3, 1959 in Robert Anderson's monochromatic *Silent Night, Lonely Night,* which closed after 124 performances. He then appeared as Parker Ballantine, a New York drama critic, in *Critic's Choice,* a featherweight comedy by Ira Levin that ran for 189 performances, beginning in December 1960, at the Ethel Barrymore Theatre. In addition to his stage work, he was seen during 1959-60 in *The Deputy,* a weekly half-hour western adventure series on NBC-TV. He also appeared in such specials as *The Good Years,* which was televised in January 1962 by CBS-TV.

During the filming of Otto Preminger's version of Allen Drury's best-selling novel *Advise and Consent* (Columbia, 1962), in which he played a Secretary of State, Robert Leffingwell, Fonda became captivated by the script of Garson Kanin's *Death of a Man,* about the last months in the life of the cancer-stricken novelist Charles Wertenbaker, and he persuaded Kanin to cast him in the lead. Retitled *A Gift of Time,* and co-starring Olivia de Havilland, the play opened at the Ethel Barrymore Theatre on February 22, 1962. But although the high quality of the performances received due recognition from reviewers, the grim theme caused audiences to stay away, and the production foundered after twelve weeks.

Fonda was cast as a President of the United States in the doomsday melodrama *Fail Safe* (Columbia, 1963) and as an American statesman in *The Best Man* (United Artists, 1964), an adaptation of Gore Vidal's play. He also appeared in *The Longest Day* (Twentieth Century-Fox, 1962); *How the West Was Won* (MGM, 1963); *Spencer's Mountain* (Warner, 1963); *Sex and the Single Girl* (Warner, 1964); *The Rounders* (MGM, 1964); *A Big Hand for the Little Lady* (Warner, 1966); *The Dirty Game* (American International, 1966); *In Harm's Way* (Paramount, 1965); and *The Battle of the Bulge* (Warner, 1966).

On Broadway, Fonda's genial performance as a Chicago advertising executive nervously awaiting the birth of his first grandchild in a Lower Manhattan loft was credited with turning the William Goodhart comedy *Generation* into a hit. Its tenure at the Morosco Theatre extended from October 1965 through June 1966. His next films included *Welcome to Hard Times* (MGM, 1967); *Stranger on the Run* (NBC-TV, 1967); the police drama *Madigan* (Universal, 1968); the domestic comedy *Yours, Mine, and Ours* (United Artists, 1968); the western *Firecreek* (Warner, 1968); and *The Boston Strangler* (Twentieth Century-Fox, 1968).

Fonda helped to organize the Plumstead Playhouse, a repertory theatre in Mineola, Long Island that included among its performers Robert Ryan, Estelle Parsons, and Anne Jackson. In its opening season, in the fall of 1968, Fonda starred as the Stage Manager in a two-week revival of Thornton Wilder's *Our Town* and then made a cameo appearance as the reporter McCue in *The Front Page.* When the Plumstead production of *Our Town* was resuscitated for a five-week stand at Broadway's ANTA Theatre in the fall of 1969, Fonda again headed the cast.

The series of relatively undistinguished films that followed included *Once Upon a Time in the West* (Paramount, 1969); *Too Late the Hero* (Cinerama, 1970); *There Was a Crooked Man* (Warner, 1970); and *The Cheyenne Social Club* (Warner, 1970). Admittedly motivated by monetary considerations, Fonda then accepted an assignment to play Chad Smith, a detective sergeant and devoted family man, in ABC-TV's prime-time half-hour series *The Smith Family,* first shown in January 1971. Later that year he went on a try-out tour of James Damico's unusual drama *The Trial of A. Lincoln,* and in November 1971 he directed a Los Angeles production of *The Caine Mutiny Court Martial.* In January 1972 Fonda played Joe in a Washington, D.C. revival of *The Time of Your Life.* His performance in *The Red Pony,* a two-hour program based on John Steinbeck's short novel, won him accolades when it was presented on NBC-TV's *Bell System Family Theatre* in

March 1973. Fonda's recent films include *Sometimes a Great Notion* (Universal, 1972), adapted from Ken Kesey's novel; *Ash Wednesday* (Paramount, 1973), in which he was cast as Elizabeth Taylor's philandering husband; and Sergio Leone's "spaghetti western" *My Name Is Nobody* (1974), a satiric comedy with thoughtful overtones about an aging gunfighter.

A padded midriff and a shock of false hair were the only aids to a physical resemblance that Fonda resorted to in David W. Rintels' one-man biographical drama *Clarence Darrow.* "Magical" was the word one New York critic used to describe the way the actor metamorphosed his own personality into that of the famous liberal lawyer. Theatregoers in the five cities where *Clarence Darrow* was tried out paid tribute to his tour de force with standing ovations, and New Yorkers did the same after the opening at the Helen Hayes Theatre on March 26, 1974. Fonda played to sold-out houses until, a few nights before the conclusion of the limited engagement, he collapsed in his dressing room. Following implantation of a pacemaker to forestall recurrence of a heart rhythm disorder, Fonda returned to the stage in mid-June, this time in Los Angeles. During its four-week California run, NBC-TV taped a ninety-minute adaptation of *Clarence Darrow,* which was aired as an IBM-sponsored special in September 1974.

Henry Fonda was first married to the late actress Margaret Sullivan on Christmas Day, 1931, while both were appearing with the University Players in Baltimore. Although the marriage lasted less than a year, they remained on friendly terms. His second marriage, to New York socialite Frances Seymour Brokaw on September 16, 1936, ended tragically with her suicide in April 1950. Fonda's third marriage, on December 27, 1950, to Susan Blanchard, the stepdaughter of Oscar Hammerstein 2d, ended in divorce in 1956, and his fourth, to Italian countess Afdera Franchetti on March 9, 1957, ended in the divorce court in 1962. Since December 3, 1965 Fonda has been married to Shirlee Adams, a former airline stewardess and model. They have a brownstone on Manhattan's fashionable East Side and a large house in the Los Angeles suburb of Bel Air.

Fonda is enormously proud of Jane and Peter, the children born of his second marriage. Jane Fonda (now Mrs. Tom Hayden) became the family's first Oscar winner in 1972 and is perhaps even better known for her antiwar activities and devotion to social causes. Peter Fonda has begun to make his mark in Hollywood, as an actor and director. The youngest daughter, Amy, had been adopted at birth by Fonda and his third wife.

Six feet one inch tall and still youthfully slim, Fonda has graying dark hair and blue eyes and appears, according to Leo Seligsohn of *Newsday* (March 17, 1974), "like a man who has learned to slow down the clock." Fonda enjoys painting, and his canvases have been described by Leslie Radditz of *TV Guide* (January 10, 1970) as "reminiscent of Andrew Wyeth." His other recreations include photography, sculpturing, making model airplanes, and growing organic vegetables.

References

Biographical Encyclopaedia & Who's Who
of the American Theatre (1966)
Ross, Lillian and Helen. The Player (1962)
Springer, John. The Fondas (1970)
Steen, Mike. Hollywood Speaks (1974)
Who's Who in America, 1974-75
Who's Who in the Theatre (1972)

FOREMAN, GEORGE

Jan. 10, 1949- Prizefighter
Address: h. Hayward, Calif. 94540

George Foreman, the 1968 Olympic heavyweight
gold medalist, turned pro in 1969 and became
world boxing champion by defeating Joe Frazier
four years later. Foreman successfully defended his title against Joe Roman in
September 1973 and against Ken Norton in
March 1974. But, in a surprising and exhausting
eight-round bout with Muhammad Ali in Zaire,
Africa on October 30, 1974, Foreman lost his
world heavyweight championship. Although a
four-to-one favorite to win, he succumbed to Ali's
left-right combination and was counted out by
the referee at the end of the eighth round.

George Foreman was born in Marshall, Texas
on January 10, 1949. With his older brother, three
older sisters, and two younger brothers, he grew
up in Houston, Texas, where the Foremans lived
on Lee and Montgomery streets in the Fifth Ward,
a black slum. He was "the only athlete in the
family," according to his mother, Nancy Ree Foreman. "Monkey we called him, still do. When he
was a baby he just wouldn't keep still, and he
was so quick and fast."

After the father, J. F. Foreman, a railroad construction worker, left the family, Mrs. Foreman
supported her brood by cooking in a cafeteria,
until she had a nervous breakdown, when George
was fourteen. Chronically truant from school,
Foreman roamed the streets, looking for fights
and trying to be "bad." As he has recalled, "I
drinked a lot, and hung around corners and I had
these ambitions to be a great thief . . . an all-
around hustler. But I was a complete failure . . .
just couldn't stand to take no one's money."

A positive factor in Foreman's early formation
was sports. Boxing, in which he was always interested, was confined to street fighting, but, bigger and stronger than his peers, he played tackle
on the E. O. Smith Junior High School football
team for a short time before he dropped out of
school, and he played basketball at Hestor House,
a ghetto youth settlement. The strongest of the
positive influences on him was his mother. "My
mom gave me spiritual help," Foreman told Tim
Tyler in an interview for *Sport* (July 1973). "We'd
sit in the kitchen and have long discussions about
what I was gonna to do in life. . . . My life just
fell apart when she was sick. . . . I always wanted
to impress her, to do something out of the ordinary for her to make her proud of me."

In a Houston poolroom one day in 1965 Foreman's attention was drawn to the television set by
a public-service message done by pro football
stars Johnny Unitas and Jim Brown in behalf of
the Job Corps, a Johnson Administration antipoverty program in which disadvantaged young
people were paid a small wage while learning
employable skills. He spent two years in the corps,
doing construction and forest-preservation work
at the Fort Vannoy Conservation Center in Grants
Pass, Oregon and taking a high school equivalency
diploma at Camp Parks, an industrial training center sponsored by Litton Industries in Pleasanton,
California. Out of his meager earnings he sent his
mother fifty dollars a month.

Foreman was constantly on the verge of dismissal from the Job Corps because of his two-
fisted pugnacity and egregious breaches of its
quasi-military regimen. His behavior improved
somewhat after he came under the tutelage of
Nick (Doc) Broadus, the boxing instructor at
Camp Parks, who taught him how to box and
imposed a training routine on him. The athletic
discipline so appealed to Foreman that he made
it a way of life. "I haven't really stopped training
since 1967," he said recently.

In his first official amateur bout, Foreman scored
a first-round knockout in the San Francisco Golden
Gloves on January 26, 1967. Subsequently he won
another tournament in Las Vegas and lost one in
the final round in Milwaukee. "I wasn't a bit happy
with his fightin'," his mother has said. "I thought
he was doin' it because he . . . still had a mean
streak in him. But he talked to me, told me he
loved the game . . . told me he could make a livin'
from boxing."

In May 1967 Foreman graduated from the Job
Corps and returned to Houston, where he could
find no jobs above the level of dishwasher or floor
sweeper. "We wrote to each other . . . ," Doc
Broadus has recalled. "I told myself, 'Doc, do
something. Do it quick. Give up on this boy and
he'll be in the penitentiary.'" Broadus arranged
for Foreman to work as a physical education instructor on the staff of Camp Parks, beginning in
October 1967, while pursuing his career in boxing.

By winning the National Amateur Athletic
Union boxing championship, Foreman qualified
for the United States Olympic team. At the Nineteenth Olympiad, in Mexico City, Mexico in October 1968, Foreman took the heavyweight gold
medal by defeating Ionas Cepulis of the Soviet
Union. After his victory he pulled a small American flag from the pocket of his robe and waved
it as he circled the ring—a gesture that contrasted
sharply with the clenched fists raised earlier in
the Olympiad by "black power" track medalists
Tommie Smith and John Carlos. In the United
States, Foreman was hailed by Governor Ronald
Reagan of California, among others, as "proof
that the American dream is just as real as it was
192 years ago." In some black quarters he was
called an "Uncle Tom."

In his professional debut, on June 23, 1969 in
Madison Square Garden, Foreman knocked out
Donald Waldheim in the second round. Over the

next twenty-nine months he defeated thirty-two opponents, but many observers of the heavyweight scene belittled his unbroken string of victories, on the ground that the men he faced, with the exception of George Chuvalo (August 1970), were relative unknowns, or, in any case, comparatively easy conquests. Murray Chass, for example, in reporting the Foreman-Luis Pires fight in the New York *Times* (October 30, 1971), noted that "the second-ranked heavyweight contender often missed with punches" and that the outcome "was more a case of Pires looking bad than of Foreman looking good."

Muhammed Ali was world heavyweight champion from 1964 to 1967. In the latter year Ali, a conscientious objector to military conscription, was stripped of his title by the World Boxing Association for violating the federal Selective Service Act. The W.B.A. conferred the title on Joe Frazier in 1970, but Ali fans refused to recognize Frazier's claim to the crown until he actually defeated Ali, by a decision, in 1971. When Frazier and Foreman met in the ring, in Jamaica, British West Indies on January 22, 1973, Foreman, the three-to-one underdog, knocked Frazier down six times. After the sixth knockdown, two minutes and thirty-five seconds into the second round, the referee stopped the fight and Foreman became the new heavyweight champion.

Immediately after winning the championship Foreman said: "Boxing's the only way I got to buy food for my family. I'll fight whoever the public says. The public makes these fights, same as they demanded I get a chance to fight for the title." But he defended his title only once in 1973, against Joe (King) Roman in Tokyo, Japan on September 1. On that occasion Roman was counted out in the first round, after three knockdowns, and his manager complained that Foreman had hit his man illegally on the head during the first knockdown. On March 8, 1974 Foreman flew to Caracas, Venezuela, where he defended his title for the second time, against Ken Norton on March 26. In the second round he sent Norton reeling to the ropes twice and then, with a barrage of heavy rights and lefts, knocked him to the floor. At the count of nine, two minutes into the second round, referee Jimmy Rondeau stopped the fight at the request of Norton's trainer, Bill Slayton. "I was going to stop it anyway," Rondeau later told reporters.

In the Norton bout Foreman was guaranteed $700,000 against 40 percent of all income. His trainer-manager, Dick Sadler, and his business manager, Leroy Jackson, scheduled Foreman's fights in foreign countries apparently to avoid liens on his earnings. Sadler explained to Bob Waters of *Newsday* (March 3, 1974) that he and Foreman made some bad financial choices early in the fighter's career, when they mortgaged future earnings to obtain needed cash. The most regretted of the commitments was alignment with a Philadelphia group called George Foreman Associates, which offered $250,000 in cash and another $250,-000 in installments in return for a long-term substantial slice of Foreman's income.

GEORGE FOREMAN

Going into the Norton fight, Foreman had an undefeated professional record of thirty-nine victories, thirty-six of them by knockouts. He himself had never been knocked down. In his first fight with Muhammad Ali, Norton had beaten the former champion, but followers of Ali still viewed a match with their hero as a *de rigueur* championship test for Foreman. In an Associated Press dispatch published as Foreman was leaving for Caracas, Will Grimsley contrasted him with Ali: "Foreman is as low-key as Muhammad is loud, militant, and arrogant. Friends say he is a genuine square, a man devoted to love, duty, religion, and apple pie. . . . He is almost too good to be true. . . . He doesn't make a noise. He is so naïve and gullible that he has got himself tied in knots with legal entanglements because of loyalty to friends."

George Foreman is six feet three and a half inches tall and weighs about 246 pounds. His strength is "awesome," according to Will Grimsley, who compares his arms to "wagon tongues" and his chest to "an oak." Foreman delivers his most devastating blows with his right hand. In his public appearances he usually wears a white shirt, dark tie, black suit, and polished black shoes. Bob Waters of *Newsday* (March 3, 1974) described him as he appeared at Valley Forge (Pennsylvania) Military Academy to accept his second Freedom Foundation award: "Foreman was dressed like a department store floorwalker. . . . His voice was solemn . . . deep . . . reassuring. . . . He stood quietly gazing ahead. Hewn from rock. That's the appearance. Actually, a lot of the rock that is Foreman is fragmented. He holds himself together the way a jigsaw puzzle remains in one piece."

Foreman and his wife, Adrienne Ray, were divorced early in 1974, after three years of marriage. Their daughter, Michi, is in the custody of the mother. Foreman is still very much attached to his mother, for whom he has bought a new brick home in Houston. His favorite recreations are riding motorcycles and raising dogs (Doberman pinschers, shepherds, and one English bulldog). His tastes and needs are simple, as he told Bob Walters: "I don't really need much. A nice four rooms, some land, comfort, friends. That's it. Friends is mostly it. Being good in the ring isn't everything. A man must be accepted by his fellowmen. He must be accepted as a man."

In politics Foreman is apparently nonpartisan. He "thought a lot" of President Lyndon B. Johnson and, regarding former President Richard M. Nixon, he told George Minort Jr. of the Washington *Post* (March 9, 1974): "I like Nixon. He is a sports fan and sports is a means of getting people together." In accepting his second Freedom Foundation award, he said: "When I hear someone kicking the American system, I tell them I can't take that kind of talk. God gave me the opportunity and gave me the physical strength to take advantage of my opportunity. I thank my country, my mother, and my manager Dick Sadler."

References

Ebony 28:35+ Apr '73 pors
N Y Daily News p83 Ja 24 '73 por
N Y Post p22 Ja 27 '73 por
N Y Times p1 Ja 23 '73 por
Sport 56:79+ Jl '73 por
White Plains Reporter Dispatch p24 Ja 31 '74 por
Who's Who in Boxing (1974)

FOWLER, WILLIAM A(LFRED)

Aug. 9, 1911- Physicist
Address: b. Kellogg Radiation Laboratory 106-38, California Institute of Technology, Pasadena, Calif. 91109; h. 1565 San Pasqual St., Pasadena, Calif. 91106

In modern science the discoveries made in one discipline are often essential to the progress of another. Thus it is that the empirical work in nuclear physics of William A. Fowler, Institute professor of the California Institute of Technology, has contributed not only to nuclear physics but to astronomy, astrophysics, cosmology, and geophysics. "It is probably fair to say," reads the citation with which Columbia University conferred its 1973 Vetlesen Prize on the physicist, "that almost all of our quantitative information about the basic nuclear processes that enter into stellar energy generation and element synthesis is due to Fowler or to work directly instigated by him." Because of Fowler, scientists now have a basic understanding of the way in which stars produce light and heat while synthesizing the chemical elements from light to heavy. They now know that the sun, the earth, and the other planets in our solar system are made up of chemical elements that were generated in stars long extinct and that our sun is embarked on a process of element synthesis that will eventually enrich celestial bodies as yet unborn.

The oldest child of John McLeod Fowler, an accountant, and Jennie Summers (Watson) Fowler, William Alfred Fowler was born on August 9, 1911 in Pittsburgh, Pennsylvania. His brother, Arthur Watson Fowler, who is two years his junior, is an engineer, and his sister, Nelda (Fowler) Wood, eight years his junior, is a housewife. When William Fowler was two years old his family moved to Lima, Ohio, a railroad town and locomotive manufacturing center. As a child, Fowler has recalled, he was fascinated with trains and everything mechanical, including toy electric trains, steam engines, and erector sets. At Lima Central High School, he played varsity football and baseball, was a member of the student council, and served as president of his senior class. After four years with the highest grade point average in his school, he graduated in 1929.

At Ohio State University, Fowler specialized in engineering physics, obtaining the highest grade point average that any student had ever achieved in his major. To help support himself during his college years he washed dishes and waited on tables for campus fraternities and sororities; during the summers he worked as a playground director in Lima. He was elected to membership in Tau Beta Pi, the honorary engineering society, of which he became president in his senior year, and he joined the social fraternity Tau Kappa Epsilon. After submitting an undergraduate thesis on low voltage electron beams, Fowler obtained the bachelor of engineering physics degree in 1933.

That same year Fowler started graduate work in physics at the California Institute of Technology, becoming a graduate research assistant to Charles C. Lauritsen, the head of Cal Tech's High Voltage and Kellogg Radiation laboratories. While a graduate student, Fowler assisted Lauritsen in experiments in which boron and other chemical elements of low atomic number were bombarded with protons or deuterons, the nuclei of the lightest element, hydrogen, to create radioactive substances. After completing his dissertation on "Radioactive Elements of Low Atomic Number," Fowler received his Ph.D. degree in physics *summa cum laude* in 1936.

After obtaining his doctorate, Fowler continued his studies under the guidance of Lauritsen, as a research fellow in nuclear physics. In 1939 he was appointed assistant professor of physics at Cal Tech and in 1942 he was promoted to the rank of associate professor. With the onset of World War II the study of nuclear physics came to a halt at Cal Tech, and its scientists were mobilized for defense projects. Late in 1940 Fowler joined Lauritsen in Washington to work on proximity fuses for bombs, shells, and ordnance rockets. A year later, Lauritsen was directed by the National Defense Research Committee to set up a rocket development project at Cal Tech as part of the NDRC's Armor and Ordnance Division, and Fowler was appointed assistant director of research of the project, which came to be known as Section L. Most of the section's work was done for the United States Navy, and later in the war Fowler and other Cal Tech scientists helped to build the Naval Ordnance Test Station at China Lake, California. While Cal Tech's rocket work was being turned over to the test station, Fowler served as acting director of research for the naval installation. In 1944 he visited the South Pacific Theatre as a technical observer. During the last two years of the war Fowler and the other Kellogg researchers became involved in producing components of the atomic bomb.

After the war, Fowler and other Kellogg scientists returned to their study of light element nuclear physics. As early as the 1920's some scientists had theorized that the sun's energy came from nuclear reactions in which hydrogen is converted into helium. In 1939 the physicist Hans A. Bethe had suggested in detail the series of reactions that took place, and during the late 1940's Lauritsen, Fowler, and others tested the validity of his theories, exploring other aspects of nuclear structure with the aid of Kellogg's electrostatic accelerators. By the early 1950's the process by which hydrogen "burns," thus producing helium, was fairly well understood, and Fowler and his coworkers turned their attention to the problem of how helium "burns." In 1953 the British cosmologist Fred Hoyle came to Cal Tech, bringing with him his idea that all the elements beyond helium are built in various kinds of stars, and experiments with helium seemed to bear out his theory. Throughout the rest of the decade Fowler, working at different times with Hoyle, the British physicists Geoffrey and Margaret Burbidge, and astronomer Jesse L. Greenstein, worked out the widely accepted theory for the way in which elements are built in the stars.

According to the theory advanced by Fowler, about 15 billion years ago the universe consisted of a huge fog of hydrogen, roughly spherical in shape and slowly rotating. (The simplest and most primordial of elements, hydrogen has been designated with the atomic number of one, which means that each atom consists, in simplified terms, of one positively charged proton for its nucleus, around which circles one negatively charged electron.) As time passed, parts of the hydrogen fog condensed to form stars, and under the force of gravity the stars continued to condense and contract, producing intense heat. When the interior of a star reached about 10,000,000 degrees absolute, the hydrogen ignited, or, in other words, its atoms became unstable, and the atoms came "unglued," with protons and electrons moving about at high velocities.

During ensuing, violent collisions, two protons would fuse to form the deuteron, the nucleus of the "heavy" form, or isotope, of hydrogen. The deuteron consists of one proton and one neutron. (Neutrons are neutrally charged particles that are capable of transformation into protons and electrons under certain conditions.) Then, two deuterons collide to form the light isotope of helium, with a nucleus of two protons and one neu-

WILLIAM A. FOWLER

tron. In a subsequent collision, two light helium nuclei fuse to form the nucleus of ordinary helium, the second element in the atomic table, with a mass of four units, consisting of two protons and two neutrons. (In that fusing the extra two protons are given off.) Thus, the new element, helium, has been formed. As in the hydrogen bomb, which is triggered by nuclear fission, the nuclear fusion of hydrogen into helium releases energy, which escapes from the star in the form of heat and light.

Stars that are burning hydrogen, like our sun, remain stable until the supply of fuel in the hot interior is exhausted. At that point many of them explode, spewing their hydrogen and helium into their galaxies to become part of stars that, like our sun, are formed later in history. Others, the so-called "red giants," continue the process of element building. As the nuclear hydrogen fire extinguishes, gravity once more takes over, and the helium core contracts until the temperature is reached at which helium ignites (about 100,000,000 degrees absolute). As the helium burns, three helium nuclei, each with a mass of four units, fuse into a nucleus of the element carbon, with a mass of twelve units. Heavier elements are similarly formed, from atoms of helium, until the star has a core of iron—the element of highest atomic number that can be formed by this process—and layers of intermediate elements out to carbon, helium, and hydrogen in cooler outer levels.

In some red giants the temperature continues to rise, and a new process begins. The heat breaks up many of the iron atoms into helium and neutrons, which have an affinity for iron. Slowly but inexorably, the remaining iron in the star absorbs neutrons, which transform into protons and produce the elements up to the heaviest stable elements in the universe, lead and bismuth. As this process continues, the star throws out its created elements into the galaxy, where they become part of other stars that are condensing.

Other red giants continue element building in a more spectacular fashion. After such a star has formed a core of iron, it collapses under the tremendous pressure of gravity on its center. In ten minutes the star may collapse into half its size. The result is a cataclysmic event that astronomers call a supernova explosion. The explosion releases a mass of electrons, which rapidly fuse with iron to synthesize a new range of elements beyond bismuth to uranium and even to the transuranic elements like californium. Such elements are unstable, however, and they disintegrate in a space of time ranging from a fraction of a second to millions of years.

During the early 1960's Fowler continued to elucidate details of the synthesis of elements by stars, but he also addressed much of his attention to other matters. For some years radio astronomers had been receiving strong radio waves from certain galaxies, and in 1963 Fowler and Hoyle put forward a theory that the waves were the aftermath of cataclysmic events near the center of galaxies. Since nuclear fusion, such as takes place in ordinary stars, could not account for the vast amount of energy represented by the radio waves, Fowler and Hoyle suggested that they could have been caused by gravitational collapse. A huge ball of gas in the nucleus of a galaxy begins to behave like a star, burning hydrogen to produce helium, and then heavier elements. Eventually, its huge mass exerts such a strong gravitational force that the ball scoops up all the material around it while contracting to a tiny fraction of its original size. Under the immense pressure the temperature rises above 1 billion degrees and the whole mass suddenly explodes in a kind of "super-supernova."

In an effort to locate "super stars" that might cause such explosions, radio astronomers scanned the skies and in late 1963 discovered an even greater mystery of the universe. They called the new objects quasistellar radio sources or quasars, because they bore some resemblance to stars, yet they appeared to be far larger and to emit more radio energy than any star. Later several quasars were located by optical astronomers, and it was discovered that the objects emanate more light and are probably farther away than any objects yet discovered in the universe. One of the quasars is believed to be as many as 10 billion light years distant from the earth. Fowler and Hoyle suggested that quasars represent explosions of massive bodies through gravitation, similar to the radio galaxies, but on a far grander scale. Later, in 1967, they put forward the idea that because of gravitational effects predicted by Einstein's theory of general relativity, the indications that quasars are so distant may be misleading. The objects may in fact be much nearer to the earth than formerly thought. In recent years Fowler has been occupied with further research on the general relativistic effects in quasars and in pulsars, which he and his colleagues now generally believe to be the remnants of supernova explosions.

Over the past decade Fowler has devoted much of his time to the study of neutrinos, those elusive subatomic particles that lack both mass and electrical charge. Released by nuclear fusion, neutrinos escape from the sun and other stars and hurtle into space. It has been estimated that every second, the earth and everything on it is flooded by hundreds of billions of neutrinos per square inch. Since the particles are unaffected by magnetism or nuclear interaction they usually pass right through bodies in a never-ending journey. Despite the difficulty in detecting neutrinos, Dr. Fowler and others have developed ways in which to study them that may eventually reveal new secrets about the sun and the universe.

Since 1946 Fowler has been a professor of physics at Cal Tech, and in 1970 he was appointed its first Institute professor of physics. At the University of Cambridge, England, he was a Fulbright lecturer and a Guggenheim fellow at the Cavendish Laboratory (1954-55), a Guggenheim fellow of St. John's College and the department of applied mathematics and theoretical physics (1961-62), and a visiting fellow of the Institute of Theoretical Astronomy (summers, 1967-71). To honor his sixtieth birthday, Cambridge University held a Fowler Symposium on massive objects in 1971. The American universities where he has held visiting lectureships include the University of Washington, where he was Walker-Ames professor in 1963, and the Massachusetts Institute of Technology (1966). During the Korean War (1951-52) Fowler served as the scientific director of Project Vista for the department of defense. For the government he served as a member of the National Science Board and the National Science Foundation (1968-72), as a committee member on the Atomic Energy Commission, ONR, and NASA, and he is currently a consultant to NASA.

Fowler was chairman of the joint discussion on nucleogenesis at the Tenth General Assembly of the International Astronomical Union in Moscow in 1958, and he has served as a delegate to international conferences on astronomy, nuclear physics, astrophysics, and cosmology. He is a fellow of the American Physical Society (of which he is vice-president elect in 1974), the American Academy of Arts and Sciences, and the Royal Astronomical Society and Benjamin Franklin fellow of the Royal Society of Arts. Fowler is a member of the National Academy of Sciences (of which he is a member of the Space Science Board), the International Astronomical Union, the American Association for the Advancement of Sciences, the American Astronomical Society, the American Association of University Professors (the Cal Tech chapter of which he presided over from 1963 to 1967), the British Association for the Advancement of Science, the Royal Society of Arts, and a corresponding member of the Société Royale des Sciences de Liège. He has written more than 180 articles in books and professional journals.

Besides the 1973 G. Unger Vetlesen Prize, Fowler's honors have included the Naval Ordnance Development award of the United States Navy (1945); the United States Medal for Merit (1948); the Ohio State University Lamme Medal (1952); the Liège Medal from the University of Liège (1955); the California Co-Scientist of the Year award (1958); the Barnard Medal for Meritorious Service to Science (1965) from Columbia University; the Apollo Achievement award of NASA (1969); and the Tom W. Bonner Prize of the American Physical Society (1970).

William A. Fowler, who is called Willy by his friends and associates, married Ardiane Foy Olmsted, a cashier at a stock and bond company, on August 24, 1940. They have two daughters, Mary Emily Fowler and Martha Summers Fowler. Fowler is five feet eleven inches tall, weighs 200 pounds, and has green eyes and gray hair. A model steam engine buff, he has been a member of the Los Angeles Live Steamers and the Cambridge and District Model Engineering Society. He also likes to relax by watching professional baseball, pro football, and college football games. Fowler is a Democrat. His clubs are the Athenaeum in Pasadena and the Cosmos in Washington.

References

Engineering and Physics p8+ Je '69 por
American Men and Women of Science 12th ed (1972)
International Who's Who, 1973-74
Who's Who in America, 1972-73
Who's Who in Government, 1972-73
Who's Who in the World, 1971-72

FRASER, LADY ANTONIA

Aug. 27, 1932- British writer
Address: b. c/o Alfred A. Knopf, 201 E. 50th St., New York 10022; h. 52 Campden Hill Sq., London W. 8, England; "Eilean Aigas," Beauly, Inverness-shire, Scotland

In making history as absorbing as fiction, Lady Antonia Fraser combines sound scholarship with an engaging style, and she has a special talent for fluid narrative that illuminates the relationships between characters and events. "Gripping" and "glittering" are among the tributes that critics paid to her biography *Mary Queen of Scots*, which appeared for several months on British and American best-seller lists after its publication in 1969. As if to prove that her success could not be attributed simply to the special bond she had long felt with the beautiful, romantic Catholic Queen of Scotland, four years later Lady Antonia produced a 774-page biography of a contrasting historical figure, the formidable Puritan leader, Oliver Cromwell. Lady Antonia is married to Hugh Fraser, a Conservative Member of Parliament and former Secretary of State for Air. Once an ornament of London society, she now prefers the roles of wife, mother of six, and writer.

Lady Antonia Fraser was born Antonia Pakenham in London, England on August 27, 1932, to

LADY ANTONIA FRASER

Francis Aungier and Elizabeth (Harman) Pakenham. The oldest child in a distinguished Socialist-Catholic family of eight children, she had three sisters, one of whom is no longer living, and four brothers. Their father, an Oxford historian, politician, and social reformer, served as a Labour member of the House of Commons before entering the House of Lords as Lord Pakenham. In the 1960's he succeeded to an earldom, becoming the seventh Earl of Longford. Besides holding high government positions, including that of Lord Privy Seal from 1966 to 1968, he wrote several scholarly books and is the author of a recent report on pornography in England.

The career of her mother, now the Countess of Longford, provided Lady Antonia, as she has acknowledged, with an "admirable example." Under the name of Elizabeth Longford she wrote, among other books, best-selling biographies of Queen Victoria and the Duke of Wellington. (An abridged version of her *Victoria, R.I.*, which had won the 1964 James Tait Black Memorial Prize for Biography, was published in the fall of 1973.) In an interview for the New York *Times* (November 5, 1966) Lady Antonia recalled an incident in her adolescence when she accompanied her Labourite mother on her campaign for Pakenham's former seat in the House of Commons. Replying to a woman in the audience who asked how a mother having to care for eight children could justify her political ambitions, the candidate said, "Stand up, Antonia. Does this look like a child who's neglected?" She lost the election, however.

In keeping with the family tradition of literary-political endeavor, Lady Antonia's oldest brother, Thomas Pakenham, has written *The Year of Liberty; The Story of the Great Irish Rebellion of 1798* (1969) and other books. Two of her sisters, Rachel and Judith, have also had books published. "It is partly due to an upbringing that provided constant intellectual stimulation," Lady Antonia once pointed out, as quoted in *Welcome Aboard,* a BOAC publication. "I can't remember a time when my mother wasn't researching and writing *something*. Our home was knee-deep in books and the discussion that revolved around them."

To her early acquired fondness for reading Lady Antonia owes what she has called "a passion for the subject of Mary Queen of Scots," which possessed her from childhood. When she was eight years old, growing up in Oxford and enrolled in the Dragon School there, she happened upon a biography of Queen Mary in the town library. Immediately fascinated, she read through the book several times and then began a prolonged search to find out everything she could about that heroic queen. At home, with a supporting cast of brothers and sisters, she played the role of Mary in acting out historic events like the execution scene. Later, as a student at St. Mary's Convent in Ascot, she was encouraged by one of the nuns in her explorations in historical writing. Then, following her mother, she attended Lady Margaret Hall, Oxford University, from which she obtained a degree in history in 1953.

After leaving the university Lady Antonia worked for about three years as an editor for George Weidenfeld of the London publishing firm of Weidenfeld & Nicolson. For publication by the Heirloom Library she also wrote two juvenile books based on English folklore and history, retellings of the Arthurian legends in *King Arthur and the Knights of the Round Table* (1954) and the Robin Hood adventures in *Robin Hood* (1955). When the books were reissued in 1970-71, by Sidgwick & Jackson in England and by Alfred A. Knopf in the United States, reviewers admired their clear, simplified delineation of character and vigorous action against a spare but colorful medieval backdrop.

On September 25, 1956 Antonia Pakenham married Hugh Charles Patrick Joseph Fraser, a well-to-do Scot and a Conservative Member of Parliament whose constituency is Stafford and Stone in England's Midlands. Subordinating her Socialist background to the Tory views of her husband, Lady Antonia Fraser occasionally joins him in election campaigns. She told Robert Ottaway, who wrote the article about her in *Welcome Aboard,* that she enjoyed being the wife of an MP. "It makes one see one's own happiness and comfort in perspective," Lady Antonia said. "Going down to a constituency and looking at something like a mental health institution stops you being complacent. It makes you think about other people's lives. And that is important."

During the decade following her marriage, however, Lady Antonia's life, as reported in the society columns, sparkled with glamour and frivolity. Her journey, partly by muleback, through Ethiopia, like everything else she did, was duly reported in the glossy magazines. She was prominently featured in the pages of the British *Vogue,* of which she became a contributing editor. A witty conversationalist, a trend setter for the Beautiful People, and a party-goer and party-thrower, she acquired celebrity as a brilliant host-ess—a reputation that she found difficult to shed when in later years she lacked time and inclination for entertaining on a lavish scale. "I had become," she once admitted, as quoted in *Life* (February 20, 1970), "a press creation—the result of a lot of friends who are journalists, a London telephone number, an obliging nature and too little sense that these things can eventually snowball."

As her family increased with the birth of a child about every second year, Lady Antonia's concerns necessarily shifted more and more to home life. She was immersed in her children's interests when she wrote for Putnam's Pleasures and Treasures series a book entitled *Dolls* (1963; published in England by Weidenfeld). The same preoccupation, together with a growing appetite for historical research, led to her writing *A History of Toys* (Weidenfeld; Delacorte, 1966). One of her incentives was her curiosity about a child's preference for certain toys over others, an attachment possibly to an old wooden spool rather than a toy of exquisite design. Aesthetic, sociological, and commercial implications, along with psychological, are among the factors she considers in her comprehensive and handsomely illustrated book. In his recommendation of *A History of Toys* the reviewer for *Library Journal* (November 15, 1966) noted that "the text continually and brilliantly links past and present, drawing on art, verse and memoirs to make a point."

Over the years Lady Antonia's affinity for Queen Mary of Scotland had not diminished. She had modeled her wedding dress, for instance, on one worn by Mary, sharing her strong feeling for white. From time to time she had considered writing an historical biography, but she remained undecided about its subject until in the mid-1960's Elizabeth Longford suggested that she herself might become the biographer of Mary. Thus threatened with being deprived of a subject that she wanted to claim as her own, Lady Antonia secured a contract from Weidenfeld & Nicolson, so that she would be held to her ambitious task, and launched an intensive search through the archives and libraries of England, Scotland, and France.

"I delved into as many published and unpublished sources as I could discover," Lady Antonia wrote in the author's note to her biography, "taking as my starting-point Mary's own letters and the calendars of state papers." For Mary's letters she could rely on her academic training in French, and for some documents she used her knowledge of Latin, but for many other sources she had to teach herself to read the sixteenth-century Scots language. The written Scots dialect would be understandable to an educated Englishman of the period, she explained in a footnote in her book, "although today of course the transcription of documents in this language presents considerable difficulties."

Lady Antonia's first objective was to discover the truth about Queen Mary, whose life and personality had become more and more encrusted with apocrypha over the centuries. Her second aim was to take into account for the first time in a biography of Mary the vast amount of research that during the past fifty years had thrown new light on the sixteenth century. Her perceptive, well-documented study of Mary Stuart, *Mary Queen of Scots* (Weidenfeld; Delacorte, 1969), became an international best seller. In England it won the 1969 James Tait Black Memorial Prize for Biography. Although her scholarship is irreproachable, the author is by no means detached. While writing about the execution of her courageous heroine, reportedly over a period of some thirty-six consecutive hours Lady Antonia alternated between typing and weeping.

One of the many enthusiastic reviewers of *Mary Queen of Scots*, Jean Stafford wrote in *Book World* (November 16, 1969), "[Lady Antonia] has done superbly by her queen. She brings to this immense biography a vivid sense of the mores of the sixteenth century, so lucid a manner of presenting history that she succeeds in almost completely clarifying the muddled maelstrom in which Europe and the British Isles were thrashing and trumpeting, and a narrative dexterity that makes her sad tale seem told for the first time." In the *Economist* (June 21, 1969), Antonia Fraser was saluted for doing much "to rehabilitate Mary both as a person and as a queen."

When Lady Antonia soon afterward turned to Oliver Cromwell, she effected a comparable rehabilitation. In her prefatory note to *Cromwell: The Lord Protector* (Knopf, 1973; published in England by Weidenfeld under the title of *Cromwell: Our Chief of Men*), she explained that her purpose was different from that of "the living giants of seventeenth-century research": "I have wished more simply to rescue the personality of Oliver Cromwell from the obscurity into which it seemed to me to have fallen. . . . In hopes of explaining to the general reader something of this remarkable man, I have set about my task—as one historian put it to me, half in jest—of 'humanizing' Oliver Cromwell."

Even more detailed than Lady Antonia's biography of Mary, *Cromwell* is the result of four years of conscientious research that included not only reading all available relevant contemporary documents and later published studies of the man and his times, but visiting the scenes described in the book, walking, for example, over all the important battlefields of Cromwell's campaigns. With a few exceptions, scholars and critics commended her balanced and rounded analysis of an exceedingly complex personality—"warts and all," as Cromwell would have insisted. "To some extent the book lacks historical background and depth," Paul Johnson commented in the *New Statesman* (June 8, 1973). "But as a portrait of a man it is a genuine work of art: complete, subtle, understanding and convincing."

King James I of England, whose reign spanned part of the period between his mother, Mary Queen of Scots, and Cromwell, is the subject of Lady Antonia's third historical biography, scheduled for publication in England in 1974 and in the United States in early 1975. When inter-

viewed for an article in *Newsday* (January 20, 1974) by Stephanie de Pue, Antonia Fraser disclosed that she planned a lengthy biography of King Charles II. She is also, reportedly, looking for a producer for a play that she has written called "The Heroines," which has an historical setting, but is not so much about history as about life and conflict and, more specifically, different forms of courage in women.

Lady Antonia Fraser is a member of the Arts Council of Great Britain and a judge of books for the Booker Prize. She is known in her own country not only for her writings, but also for her appearances on the lecture platform and on radio and television. When at work on a book, she follows a rather tight schedule, devoting the morning hours to writing because her children are then in school. In her interview with Stephanie de Pue she said that having to divide her time between her family and her career disposes of the problem of the writer's block: whenever she has a few moments to spare, she "flies to the typewriter and pounds away like a bat out of hell."

The oldest of Hugh and Antonia Fraser's six children, Rebecca, was named after Rebecca West and the title character of Daphne du Maurier's famous novel. When Rebecca Fraser was twelve or thirteen she made the highly praised line drawings and paintings that illustrate the reissued editions of her mother's books on King Arthur and Robin Hood. Hugh and Antonia Fraser's other children are Flora, Benjamin, Natasha, Damian, and Orlando.

Favored with exceptional beauty, Lady Antonia is tall (five feet eight inches) and slender (about 120 pounds), has blond hair and blue eyes, and wears her fashionable and expensive clothes to their best advantage. The Frasers have a Georgian house with a garden in Kensington, and when Lady Antonia is in London she enjoys the theatre, opera, ballet, and art exhibitions. At the family's house in Scotland, she likes to play tennis and, especially, to swim, all year round in a heated outdoor pool.

References

Christian Sci Mon p17 N 28 '73
Life 68:42+ F 20 '70 pors
N Y Post p47 O 24 '69 por
N Y Times p42 N 5 '66 por
Newsday Ideas p19 Ja 20 '74 por
Time 102:109+ N 5 '73 por
Washington Post K p1+ N 2 '69 por
International Who's Who, 1973-74
Who's Who, 1973-74
Who's Who of American Women, 1974-75

FRIEL, BRIAN

Jan. 5, 1929- Playwright
Address: Ardmore, Muff, Lifford, County Donegal, Ireland

An increasing number of drama critics are joining in the opinion that Brian Friel may well be

BRIAN FRIEL

the best Irish playwright since Sean O'Casey. Friel's most successful play is *Philadelphia, Here I Come!*, which ran on Broadway for nine months in 1966, but some critics consider *The Freedom of the City*, which flopped in New York early in 1974, to be his best. As in *The Freedom of the City*, Friel often vents the anger and frustration of the Ulster Catholic that he is, but he never loses his delicate touch, his compassion, or his sense of humor. His forte is comedy, sometimes bittersweet, sometimes broad, sometimes sardonic, but always thoughtful and lyrical. As one critic has pointed out, a notable quality in the typical Friel play is "the melody of the dialogue—sparkling but unaffected, akin to the cadences of his own lilting speech." Most of the Irish productions of Friel's work have been staged by Hilton Edwards. The text versions of the plays are published in England by Faber & Faber and in the United States by Farrar, Straus & Giroux. Short stories written by Friel before he turned to the theatre have been collected in two volumes published in London by Victor Gollancz and in New York by Doubleday.

Brian Friel was born in Omagh, County Tyrone in west central Northern Ireland on January 5, 1929 to Patrick Friel, a schoolteacher, now retired, and Chris Friel. The family moved to the city of Londonderry, commonly called Derry City, in County Londonderry when the father joined the faculty of Long Tower School there in 1939. After graduating from Long Tower School, Friel entered St. Patrick's College in Maynooth, County Kildare, Republic of Ireland, the principal Roman Catholic seminary in Ireland. He described his experience at Maynooth as "awful" in an interview with Peter Lennon of the *Guardian* (October 8, 1964): "It nearly drove me cracked. It is one thing I want to forget. I never talk about it—the priesthood. You know, the kind of Catholicism we have in this country, it's unique."

Abandoning his plans to enter the priesthood, Friel left St. Patrick's College with a B.A. degree in 1948. In 1949-50 he studied at St. Joseph's

Teacher Training College in Belfast, and during the following decade he taught with the Christian Brothers in various primary and intermediate schools in Derry. "Nearly as bad as Maynooth" was the way he summed up his years of teaching in the *Guardian* interview. "I was with them [the Christian Brothers] for ten years. Then I gave it up altogether."

While teaching, Friel began to write short stories based on his experiences as a member of the Catholic minority in the northwestern counties of Northern Ireland. Although humor abounds, the predominant mood of the stories is somber and thoughtful. Desmond Maxwell wrote of them in *Brian Friel* (1973): "Friel's settings are mostly rural and the people he writes about poor. . . . Although the characters are often hardy, spirited, and their presentation lighthearted, the tone of the stories seems to me predominantly elegiac: for loves, friendships, observances, past or fated to pass." The stories, many of which first appeared in the *New Yorker*, were collected in *The Saucer of Larks* (Gollancz, 1962) and *The Gold in the Sea* (Gollancz, 1966).

As Maxwell notes, Friel's first plays, written for the radio, recall his short stories "The Illusionists," "The Flower of Kiltymore," and "The Gold in the Sea," "whose characters are similarly engaged in their various degrees of compromise with disappointment and the hard life." Early in 1958 the Northern Ireland BBC presented Friel's *A Sort of Freedom*, about the owner of a trucking company who persuades an employee to resist unionization, to the employee's ruin. Later in the same year the same network broadcast *To This Hard House*, about a schoolmaster whose enrollment is lost to a more modern school in a nearby town where new industries have sprung up.

The first play that Friel wrote for the stage was *The Francophile*, later retitled *A Doubtful Paradise*, which was produced at the Group Theatre in Belfast in 1959. That work, about a Derry post office foreman with cultural pretensions, is viewed by the author as "a very bad play" about which he would "like to forget." He holds a similar opinion regarding the second stage play he wrote, *The Blind Mice*, in which an Irish priest is given a hero's welcome home after five years in a Chinese Communist prison. The focus in that play is on the varying reactions to the revelation that the priest obtained his release by signing a confession renouncing his faith.

The Blind Mice lay unproduced for several years, until 1963, when it was staged at the Eblana Theatre in Dublin. In the meantime *The Enemy Within*, which Friel considers "not good, but . . . there's nothing very wrong with it," was produced at the Abbey Theatre in Dublin. That play is an attempt to discover how St. Columba, by nature a belligerent, earthy person, acquired sanctity, which Friel defines as "tremendous integrity and the courage to back it up." *The Enemy Within* was more favorably received than Friel's earlier plays.

On an Arts Council grant, Friel spent six months in 1963 observing producer Tyrone Guthrie at work at the Tyrone Guthrie Theatre in Minneapolis, Minnesota. That experience made him realize, as he later recounted, that the plays he had written were "tedious, tendentious, and terribly boring." From Guthrie he learned that theatre is "an attempt to create something that will . . . transport a few fellow travelers on our strange, amusing, perilous journey," that the playwright's first function is "to entertain, to have audiences enjoy themselves, to move them emotionally, to make them laugh and cry and gasp and hold their breath and sit on the edge of their seats."

A surer mastery of the theatrical medium was evident in *Philadelphia, Here I Come!*, Friel's play about the social and spiritual forces that make it necessary for a young Irishman, Gareth O'Donnell, to emigrate. When it opened at the Gaiety Theatre during the Dublin Theatre Festival in 1964, Peter Lennon wrote in the *Guardian* (October 2, 1964): "Five minutes after the curtain went up . . . it was clear that here at last was an authentic voice, and whatever apprehension we may have had about Mr. Friel's ability to sustain the note so truly sounded or to build his material into a theatrical entity was quickly banished by the ease and accuracy with which he proceeded to deal with his theme." Although Friel has confessed that he wrote the play in anger, *Philadelphia, Here I Come!* came across as "subtle and gentle," as Lennon observed.

When *Philadelphia, Here I Come!* began its triumphal run on Broadway, John McCarten, writing in the *New Yorker* (February 26, 1966), described it as burning "at least part of the time with an almost gemlike flame" and praised Friel's "ability to draw three-dimensional characters with warmth, wit, and sympathy." Later, when the New York production went on tour, the reviewer for the Washington *Post* (November 30, 1966), wrote: "Apart from his glowing language, naturally lyrical but never cloying, Mr. Friel's happiest inspiration is his device for portraying his central character. . . . We are given both the 'public' Gareth O'Donnell and the 'private' Gar, the thoughts of the inner character while his outer form speaks platitudes or does not speak what is really on his mind." The *Post* critic noted that Friel, viewing his Ireland with "affectionate frustration," is irked by its sentimentality while himself succumbing to it.

In an article in *Acorn* (Spring 1965), published by McGee College in Derry, Friel discussed the social purpose of art, especially theatrical art. While his work may lead the audience to action, a social message should not be the direct concern of the playwright, he asserted. "If one is moved then one should react accordingly," he wrote. "This is the responsibility of the reader or an audience, but I don't think it's the writer's." Later, when the Catholic civil rights movement in Northern Ireland began to take on its current militancy, he said it was difficult for him to approach that political struggle as material for his art because he was "emotionally too much involved about it," and he expressed the hope that

no one would attempt a play on the subject "for another ten or fifteen years."

The Loves of Cass McGuire, about a septuagenarian Irish-American barmaid who returns to Ireland and an old-people's home, flopped on Broadway in 1966 but became a hit the following year at the Abbey Theatre in Dublin. Richard Watts of the New York *Post* (October 29, 1966) attributed the play's failure in New York to its "moments of rowdy comedy" and salty dialogue. Watts wrote: "I suspect they [audiences] were made uncomfortable because the author was trying something that didn't appear to stem naturally from his writing style." Walter Kerr of the New York *Times* (June 4, 1967) thought the problem was the diffuse dramatic structure of the play: "The work wasn't written to be assimilated as an orderly sequence of events. It was meant to come at us from all quarters, simultaneously, undifferentiated, like so many pieces of spliced tape run at once, a summoning back of lost sounds that had strayed to the stratosphere. . . . Achieving this is a long, patient process; time and tenderness are wanted." Friel himself said, regarding the "fatal mistake" of giving *The Loves of Cass McGuire* its first staging in New York: "The best theater was always done, in history, with a writer working with a director and a resident company. This is, of course, what you don't have on Broadway and indeed what you don't have in Ireland except in the Abbey Theatre."

Lovers, first produced at the Gate Theatre in Dublin in 1967, comprises two one-act plays: *Winners*, a bitter-sweet drama about two young lovers bantering happily on a hilltop, unaware that they are spending their last hours on earth; and *Losers*, a comedy about a middle-aged couple trying to court within hearing distance of a bedridden, neurotic mother. During the plays' successful run in New York City—first at Lincoln Center's Vivian Beaumont Theatre and later at the Music Box—beginning in July 1968, Jack Kroll of *Newsweek* (August 5, 1968) proclaimed Friel "a minor master of the old-fashioned play of sagacious, ironic, compassionate, lyric realism." Most critics preferred the second of the two plays, but Marilyn Stasio of *Cue* (November 30, 1968) thought that Friel there failed to structure "his insights into viable dramatic form."

In *Crystal and Fox* Friel tells the story of self-destructive Fox Melarkey, leader of a troupe of traveling Irish players, who hankers for the days when he was a single act, before he married Crystal. That play, which had its première at the Gaiety Theatre in Dublin in 1968, was given a disappointing production at the McAlpin Rooftop Theatre in New York in the spring of 1973. Marilyn Stasio of *Cue* (May 5, 1973) was not alone in complaining about *Crystal and Fox's* "sentimentality, melodramatic excesses, and predictable plotting," but she detected, underneath the flaws, "hints of his characteristic lyrical style."

In *The Mundy Scheme* Friel satirizes political venality by relating an Irish Prime Minister's plan to save the country from economic collapse by turning large areas of western Ireland into burial lots for foreigners. Rejected by the Abbey Theatre, *The Mundy Scheme* was given its première at the Olympia Theatre in Dublin early in 1969. The reviews were generally negative when Friel's attempt at gallows humor reached the Royale Theatre in New York in December of the same year. "While its most talented young playwright can write plays as sloppily conceived and constructed as this," Clive Barnes wrote in the New York *Times* (December 12, 1969), "Ireland's troubles will never quite be over." *The Gentle Island,* produced at the Olympia Theatre in Dublin in 1971 and at the Lyric Theatre in Belfast the following year, is yet to have a New York production.

Freedom of the City takes place in Londonderry in 1970. Its protagonists are three participants in a protest march who take refuge in the city's Guildhall when the march is gassed. As the harmless refugees amuse themselves by drinking the mayor's liquor and other such acts of mischief, the rumor spreads that the Guildhall is being held by a revolutionary squad of fifty or more. British soldiers attack in force and the three—two young men, one of whom is a model of propriety and the other a cynical tough, and a middle-aged mother of eleven—are killed. The play is based on an actual incident, in which British soldiers massacred marching nationalists in Londonderry, in 1970. Although obviously sympathetic to the nationalists, Friel in his play directs his anger not so much at the frightened troops as at the British military judges who attempted a cover-up in the inquiry into the slaughter of the three innocent persons.

First produced at the Abbey Theatre in 1973, *The Freedom of the City* arrived at the Alvin Theatre in New York City in February of the following year. The quick closing of the Broadway production was mourned by George Oppenheimer of *Newsday* as "a crying shame" and by Richard Watts of the New York *Post* as "a tragedy." In a March 2, 1974 postmortem review, Watts wrote: "He [Friel] has written a genuine masterpiece in *The Freedom of the City*, which was being beautifully acted on Broadway. We haven't, I firmly believe, had a play from Ireland to equal it in quality since O'Casey's most brilliant drama, *The Plough and the Stars*."

Brian Friel was described by Jerry Tallmer of the New York *Post* (September 20, 1968) as "black Irish, going gray, with a beak and faintly tufted cheeks that give him an eaglish-owlish look." Tallmer went on: "His heart is a bird of sweeter song, as everyone knows who has gone to a Brian Friel play." Alan Bunce of the *Christian Science Monitor* (November 27, 1968) observed that Friel's face "fairly twinkles with self-deprecating glee" but that "the seriousness of his statements belies the leprechaun smile." Peter Lennon in his *Guardian* article described the playwright as speaking with "that familiar northern drone."

With his wife, the former Anne Morrison, and four children, Paddy, Mary, Judy, and Sally, Friel lives in the village of Muff, County Donegal and spends his summers in a cottage near Kincasslagh on the West Donegal coast. Despite his religious rebelliousness and what some observers construe to be an anticlerical attitude, Friel remains a practising Roman Catholic. In politics he describes himself as "still a nationalist" but not the "violent nationalist" he used to be. "I am getting to an age when I don't have these things as strongly as I used to," he told Jerry Tallmer in the interview for the New York *Post*.

References

Christian Sci Mon p14 N 27 '68 pors
Guardian p9 O 8 '64 por
N Y Post p47 S 20 '68 por
Maxwell, D. E. S. Brian Friel (1973)

FRISCH, KARL VON (frish)

Nov. 20, 1886- Austrian zoologist
Address: h. Über der Klause 10, 8000 Munich 90, German Federal Republic

As he was beginning his eighty-eighth year, Karl von Frisch, the distinguished Austrian zoologist and authority on the social life of bees, was awarded the 1973 Nobel Prize for Physiology or Medicine. With that award, which von Frisch shared with two fellow students of animal behavior, Konrad Lorenz and Nikolaas Tinbergen, the Nobel Committee of the Karolinska Institute broke with tradition and, for the first time, recognized major contributions in the relatively new science of sociobiology.

Widely recognized for his research on the complicated communication system or "dance recruitment" of bees, Dr. von Frisch has concluded that such a "language" is genetically programmed rather than learned. In the course of his long career, he has investigated the hearing of fish, examined the nature of their skin pigment and color adaptation, and determined the chemical senses of insects. Commenting on the innovative research of von Frisch, Lorenz, and Tinbergen, Professor Lars Cronholm, a Karolinska psychiatrist and head of the committee's investigation of the three recipients' experiments, predicted that the ethological methods that the three scientists had developed for the study of animals "can shed light on how certain psychosocial situations can lead not only to abnormal behavior but also to serious physical disease, such as high blood pressure and heart attacks."

Karl von Frisch was born on November 20, 1886 in Vienna, Austria, the youngest of the four sons of Anton Ritter and Marie (Exner) von Frisch. His father, a surgeon and urologist, was head of surgery at the Vienna General Polyclinic. His parental grandfather, Anton von Frisch, had been a surgeon in the Austrian Imperial Army and his maternal grandfather, Franz Exner, was a professor of philosophy at the University of Prague. In his autobiography, *A Biologist Remembers* (Pergamon Press, 1967), Karl von Frisch pays tribute to the stimulating intellectual environment of his youth and credits his mother's family with encouraging his "leaning towards research and scholarship."

Like many of his contemporaries, von Frisch was fascinated by the technological advances of the industrial age, but animals were his primary interest. A naturally inquisitive, observant child, he collected specimens for a "little zoo" at his family's summer home in Brunnwinkl on Lake Wolfgang. His diary listed "nine different species of mammals, sixteen species of birds, twenty-six of cold-blooded terrestrial vertebrates, twenty-seven of fish, and forty-five species of nonvertebrates." He was especially fond of a bright green Brazilian parakeet named Tschoki, a pet for fifteen years. Von Frisch kept careful notes of his observations, submitting some to journals for amateur naturalists. One article, describing the sensitivity to light of sea anemones, was published in the *Blätter für Aquarien -und Terrarienkunde.* "There was nothing deliberate or intentional in this intensive occupation with animals," he has explained in his autobiography. "I simply enjoyed watching the manifestations of their biological functions and mental stirrings in all the variety related to the different stages of animal development."

After several years of private tutoring at home, von Frisch attended a convent school of the Piarist Fathers and the *Schottengymnasium,* a prestigious Benedictine secondary school in Vienna. Admittedly "never good" at school, he was particularly baffled by mathematics and languages and required special tutoring in Latin and Greek. In 1905 von Frisch enrolled at the medical school of the University of Vienna. An enthusiastic Darwinian who hoped for an appointment to a scientific expedition following his graduation, he had yielded to his father's request that he study medicine, a field that promised a more lucrative variety of career options. Von Frisch so excelled during the first two years of his medical training, which were devoted to the natural sciences, that he passed his first examinations with distinction in all six subject areas. Working under the direction of Sigmund Exner, the noted physiologist, von Frisch investigated the distribution of pigments in the compound eyes of butterflies, beetles, and shrimps, as a special project.

Becoming disenchanted with medicine, he transferred to the Zoological Institute in Munich, Germany, the internationally recognized center for experimental zoology, to study under Richard von Hertwig. On the frequent scientific excursions to the Dolomites conducted by von Hertwig's assistant, von Frisch was assigned to study the behavior of solitary bees—the beginning of an interest that became so absorbing that, as he confessed in *A Biologist Remembers,* "Many a day in later years a walk planned for a day ended after a few hundred yards in front of a bees' nest from which I could not tear myself away." Convinced

KARL VON FRISCH

that "a biologist who has not studied the fauna of the sea at first hand is only half trained . . . [because] the sea is the cradle of life," he studied marine biology at the Biological Institute for Marine Research in Trieste during his Easter vacation. He returned to Vienna to complete his thesis research on the color adaptation and light perception of minnows under the experimental biologist Hans Przibram. In 1910 he obtained his Ph. D. degree.

Having taken his degree, von Frisch returned to the Zoological Institute in Munich as a teaching and research assistant to von Hertwig in the fall of 1910. At the prompting of Dr. Carl von Hess, the director of the Munich Eye Clinic, he began investigating colorblindness in fish. His experiments, in which minnows were trained to respond to colored objects, disputed von Hess's contention that fish and all invertebrates were colorblind. To expand his doctoral study of the color adaptations of fish, he was especially interested in observing the brilliantly colored fish of southern ocean waters. Taking advantage of his two-month Easter vacations in 1911, 1912, and 1913, he conducted experiments at the well-equipped laboratories of the world-famous Stazione Zoologica in Naples. Von Frisch's intellectual power and experimental ingenuity matured under those ideal conditions. "I have always felt," he has said, "that scientific research thrives best in beautiful and harmonious surroundings." After submitting a paper entitled "Color Adaptation in Fishes," von Frisch was accepted as a *Privatdozent* at the University of Munich in March 1912.

Motivated by the widely accepted theory that flowers are brightly colored and scented to attract insects, von Frisch determined to prove that bees have a color sense. Using a sugar-water solution and differently colored squares of cardboard, he conducted a series of experiments that proved conclusively that bees could distinguish hues as well as shades of color. Bees trained to associate food with a particular color square would alight on that square even though the food had been removed and the colored squares had been shifted. At the annual meeting of the German Zoological Society at Freiburg in 1914, von Frisch demonstrated the results of his research with a showman's flair. His trained bees settled on the blue squares that advertised his soon-to-be-published paper describing his experiments.

In 1914 World War I broke out, putting an end to the free intellectual climate that had been enjoyed by Karl von Frisch and his colleagues. Retreating to Brunnwinkl, he continued his experiments for several months, although he was hindered by laboratories reduced to rubble, a bombed-out house, and an inflation-shattered income that forced him to sell a pair of second-hand shoes to buy food. Because of poor eyesight he was not conscripted into the army but served under the direction of his brother Otto, the physician who had become superintendent of a hospital in the Vienna suburb of Döbling. He soon learned to take X-ray photos, serve as operating theater anesthetist, and dress wounds. At his suggestion, a bacteriological laboratory was established to diagnose such contagious diseases as cholera, typhoid, and dysentery. By the war's end, von Frisch was in charge of a seventy-bed ward and performing certain surgical operations under strict medical supervision. In addition, he instructed nurses in bacteriology.

In January 1919 von Frisch returned to the University of Munich as an assistant professor in the Zoological Institute. There he divided his time between lectures on comparative physiology and research on the social organization of bees. Through a series of relatively simple experiments, he had recently proved that bees were able to recognize scents as well as colors. In one of several cardboard boxes, each provided with a hole as an entrance for the bees, von Frisch placed a dish of sugar-water and a fragrant flower. The bees invariably entered only that box. After removing the food, the experiment was repeated with the same results. In the course of his research he noticed that once the food dish was empty, the bees ignored it, but if a scout bee discovered another source of food, the entire swarm of bees congregated within a few minutes. "It was clear to me," he wrote in his autobiography, "that the bee community possessed an excellent intelligence service, but how it functioned I did not know. This gave me no rest." In the spring of 1919 he observed a lone scout bee which, after feeding, performed a "round dance" on the hive. The dance aroused the other bees, who immediately flew to the nectar source. That observation, which von Frisch has termed "the most far-reaching" of his life, led him to embark on three years of intensive research.

During those years of concentrated study, he held posts of increasing responsibility at the zoological institutes of the University of Rostock, from 1921 to 1923, and the University of Breslau before returning to Munich in 1925. At the annual meeting of the German Society for Natural Science and Medicine in September 1924, he issued a report based on his study of the "language"

of bees, including a film of the dancing bees—a form of audio-visual demonstration that was at the time a novelty in scientific presentations. His experiments indicated that foraging bees acquire a particular flower scent from the dancing bee and will use that odor as an indication of the location of the food source; that the vigor of the dance depends on the sweetness of the nectar source; and that the worker bees themselves apply a scent to odorless flowers to attract other bees. In 1927 he published *Aus dem Leben der Bienen* as the first part of a projected Science You Can Understand series. That slim volume, a straightforward, well-illustrated report of his research, described the bees' communal organization, complex communication system, and foraging methods. A revised edition, issued in English as *The Dancing Bees: An Account of the Life and Senses of the Honeybee,* was published by Harcourt, Brace & World in 1955.

Appointed director of the University of Munich's Zoological Institute in 1925, von Frisch continued his experiments in the communication system of bees and in the acoustical training of fish. (He successfully trained a catfish to obey his whistles.) Awarded a grant, von Frisch supervised the construction of a new zoological research building on the Munich campus. The building, designed to his specifications, included an aquarium, an insectarium, a tropical house, a "bees' house," ant colonies, culture rooms on all floors, and a lecture hall equipped with the latest in audio-visual teaching aids. His work, however, was closely monitored by the Hitler regime and, as he complained in his autobiography, he was often "denied the right of freely choosing [his] own staff. . . . Assistants . . . were chosen for political motives." From 1940 through 1942 he devoted most of his efforts to eradicating an unexplained epidemic that was decimating the European bee population. When Munich came under Allied bombing attack, von Frisch once again moved his equipment and experimental data to the relative safety of Brunnwinkl, where he continued his research. In 1946 he accepted the chair of zoology at the University of Graz. Despite a generous grant from the Rockefeller Foundation, the university's zoology department lacked adequate funds. Because "the essentials for research and teaching were there," von Frisch returned to the Zoological Institute in Munich in 1950, remaining there until his retirement in 1958.

Von Frisch has published full and fascinating accounts of the failures and successes, the false starts, and brilliant insights of his decades of study. In *The Dance Language and Orientation of Bees* (Harvard Univ. Press, 1967), he explains how successful foragers inform other bees in the hive where a food source is located, how the nature and vigor of "round" and "tail-wagging" dances on the honeycomb indicate the direction and distance of food from the hive, and how plentiful or sparse the food supply may be. Noting that each subspecies of bee performs a rhythmic dance that cannot be interpreted by other subspecies, von Frisch concluded that the dances are biologically inherited rather than learned. First published in 1950, his *Bees: Their Vision, Chemical Senses, and Language,* reprinted in a revised edition by the Cornell University Press in 1971, traces the history of his pioneering research in the visual and olfactory senses of honeybees and describes the experiments that eventually verified von Frisch's contention that bees navigate by the sun, following a precise internal clock. To prove von Frisch's theory that bees adhere to an innate time schedule, two of his colleagues, Max Renner and Werner Loher, transported 5,000 bees from Paris to New York City's American Museum of Natural History. While in New York, the bees continued to operate on Paris time. *Man and the Living World,* a 1936 ethological review of the life sciences written for the general reader, illustrates von Frisch's essentially behaviorist approach to the nature of life. Containing chapters on comparative anatomy and physiology, organisms and their environment, heredity, and the evolution of different species, the first American edition of that biological summary for laymen, published by Harcourt, Brace & World in 1963, was enthusiastically received by critics. In November 1974 Harcourt Brace Jovanovich published von Frisch's *Animal Architecture,* a book on which he collaborated with his son, Otto.

In recent years some skeptical zoologists have contended that von Frisch's experiments lacked adequate controls and that any one of a number of variables could affect the bees' foraging behavior and dances, but subsequent experiments, conducted under controlled conditions, have confirmed von Frisch's theories. By applying some of von Frisch's discoveries, beekeepers have directed bees to more abundant sources of honey, insured the pollination of seed crops, and attracted bees to their hives by means of painting them in bright colors.

While Karl von Frisch was teaching bacteriology to nurses during World War I, he met Margarethe Mohr, a nurse and artist who eventually illustrated the published compilation of his lectures. The couple was married on July 20, 1917. They have four children: Johanna (Mrs. Theo Schreiner), Maria, Helen (Mrs. E. Pflueger), and Otto, a zoologist. Although he has been officially retired for more than fifteen years, the bespectacled, white-haired zoologist continues to pursue his lifelong hobby of collecting insects.

Von Frisch is a member of the Academies of Science of Munich, Vienna, Göttingen, Washington, Uppsala, Boston, and Stockholm, and a foreign member of the Royal Society of London. He holds honorary degrees from half a dozen universities, including Graz and Harvard. In addition to the Nobel award he holds the Magellan Prize of the American Philosophical Society, and the Kalinga Prize for the popularization of science. Unperturbed by his failure to solve fully the mystery of the bees' inner clock, von Frisch has remarked philosophically, "Science advances but slowly, with halting steps. But does not therein lie her eternal fascination? And would we not soon tire of her if she were to reveal her ultimate truths too easily?"

References

N Y Times p42 O 12 '73 por
Science News p244 O 20 '73 por
Frisch, Karl von. A Biologist Remembers (1967)
International Who's Who, 1972-73
Who's Who in Germany, 1964
World Who's Who in Science (1968)

FUKUDA, TAKEO

Jan. 14, 1905- Former Minister of Finance of Japan
Address: 1-247 Nozawa-machi, Setagagya-ku, Tokyo, Japan

Because of an unforeseen combination of pressures from both home and abroad, quite suddenly in the early 1970's Japan's astonishing postwar economic boom began to lose its momentum. Recognizing the imminent peril to his country, Takeo Fukuda accepted the vital Cabinet post of Minister of Finance that was offered to him in November 1973 by his political foe, Premier Kakuei Tanaka. Although both are members of the dominant Liberal-Democratic party, the conservative Fukuda and the progressive Tanaka champion disparate political and economic views. Fukuda had served as Minister of Finance on two earlier occasions and had held the position of Minister of Foreign Affairs from July 1971 to July 1972. On July 16, 1974 Fukuda resigned his post as Finance Minister, citing as his reason dissatisfaction with the handling of his party's political affairs by Tanaka.

Takeo Fukuda was born on January 14, 1905 in Gumma Prefecture, northwest of Tokyo, the son of Zenji Fukuda, a wealthy farmer. His social position by birth ensured him a place later on in the elite power structure that still rules Japan, though less exclusively in recent years. His childhood home was on the slopes of Mount Haruna, and as a teen-ager he walked five miles every day to attend school in the city of Takasaki. Fukuda graduated from the high school in 1926. Then, following the tradition of his class, he enrolled in the select Tokyo Imperial University, where he studied law and earned his LL.B. degree in 1929.

Immediately after leaving the university, Fukuda won an appointment in the Ministry of Finance. During the next two decades in government service he gained a reputation as a brilliant and efficient, if somewhat cold, bureaucrat. He served outside Japan briefly in London and Paris during 1930 and in China during World War II, from 1941 to 1943, as financial adviser to the Japan-sponsored government of Wang Ching-wei. At the end of the war, in 1945, he was deputy vice-minister, a post that he exchanged the following year for director of the banking bureau.

TAKEO FUKUDA

By 1947 he had risen to the office of director of the budget.

As reported in the New York *Times* (September 9, 1971), Fukuda was among many officials implicated in the so-called Showa Denka affair, a scandal of the hectic, early postwar years. Indicted in 1950 on the charge of accepting bribes, he resigned from the Ministry of Finance. After a two-year court battle to establish his innocence, his efforts were rewarded with acquittal in 1952, but he did not receive final vindication until 1958.

Prolonged litigation to exonerate himself did not, however, hinder Fukuda's entrance into politics. In 1952 he ran successfully for his first four-year term in the House of Representatives, the lower chamber of Japan's national Diet. When, in 1955, the Democratic party merged with the Liberal party, he became a member of the resulting Liberal-Democratic party, the most powerful of the groups forming the Japanese multiparty political structure. Although its leadership is divided among several factions, the Liberal-Democratic party is well organized and financially strong, and in favoring free enterprise and co-operation with the United States, it has appealed to voters in both rural and industrial areas. Largely because of the remarkable postwar growth of the national economy, the party was able to maintain a majority in both houses of the legislature. In 1959 Fukuda served briefly as secretary-general of the Liberal-Democratic party, then under the presidency of Nobusuke Kishi.

By virtue of his position as head of the ruling party, Kishi was also Premier of Japan. He appointed Fukuda to his first Cabinet post in 1959, as Minister of Agriculture and Forestry. Seesawing between political and government offices, Fukuda became chairman of the policy research board of the Liberal-Democratic party in 1960, Minister of Finance in 1965, and secretary-general of his party in 1966. Eisaku Sato, who had been made Premier in 1964 and had chosen Fukuda for the Finance Ministry, reassigned him to the same post in 1968. He served there until July 1971, when Sato named him Minister of Foreign Affairs.

A strong supporter and close associate of Sato, whose anti-Communist, pro-American sympathies he fully shared, Fukuda came to be suggested as a possible "crown prince," among the front-runners for the Premiership. According to Elizabeth Pond in the *Christian Science Monitor* (December 2, 1971), he was "cut out of the same Tory mold" as past candidates for Japan's top political and governmental posts: "without charisma, skilled in backroom maneuvers, adept at filling the party coffers, clever and cool enough to face down the barrage of questions by the opposition in the Diet without ever divulging any policies." When Sato announced after his 1970 reelection that he would not run for office again, Fukuda appeared for a time to be distinctly favored among Liberal-Democratic members as his successor.

To most Japanese the prosperity that followed their postwar recovery seemed to have a limitless future. By the late 1960's, however, they were paying the cost of industrialization in terms of pollution and overcrowding in the cities. In international trade they had become a leading exporter of high-quality goods produced with relatively cheap labor, while keeping a closed-door policy toward imports. The United States was, and remains, Japan's prime market. In 1971, however, the United States made a series of moves that strained its relations with Japan and that were labeled in the Japanese press "the Nixon shocks."

The first shock came on July 15, when Nixon announced his plans to visit Peking. That decision clearly heralded a change in United States policy from a "two-nation" representation for China in the United Nations to the recognition of Communist China as the representative of all Chinese people. Some observers believed that the Japanese, who had backed the earlier American attitude toward Red China out of loyalty to an ally, actually welcomed, for the most part, an entrée into the Chinese market. The shock resulted from Nixon's failure to notify Japanese officials in advance, thereby causing loss of face to Japan in the international community. Foreign Minister Fukuda, who had supported an alliance with Taiwan, found himself in a particularly difficult position.

Another Nixon shock was felt in Japan on August 15, 1971 with the news that the United States would impose a 10 percent surtax in an effort to reduce imports, especially from Japan, into the American market. That change in economic policy was viewed as an attempt to bring about a revaluation of the yen, as well as other major world currencies. A further blow to the Japanese economy occurred soon afterward when, on October 15, Japan formally accepted the American demand for restrictions on its textile exports to the United States.

Meanwhile, during a period that has been described as an all-time low in Japanese-American relations, Fukuda led a seven-man delegation to the eighth annual Japanese-American Cabinet-level meeting in Washington, D.C. in September 1971. The Foreign Minister felt confident of his country's economic place in the world community and expected that Japan would be treated as an equal. Instead, according to an account in *Newsweek* (September 20, 1971), Fukuda and his team received a lecture from Secretary of State William P. Rogers, who chided them on the Japanese closed-door policy toward foreign imports, among other matters.

In a startling demonstration of independence Fukuda showed the strength that had carried him through decades of political maneuvering. "When his turn came to speak," as reported in *Newsweek*, "Fukuda gave as good as he got. He suggested that America's economic plight was due less to its trade imbalance with Japan than to the failure of its self-indulgent fiscal and monetary policies." On that occasion Japanese officials refused to agree to unilateral revaluation of the yen. They later accepted a new exchange of 308 yen, instead of 360, to the dollar, in keeping with a world currency realignment accord reached by ten industrial nations in December 1971. Fukuda called that revaluation "the greatest economic shock" to his country since it suffered defeat in World War II.

The financial and psychological embarrassments of the Nixon shocks coupled with urban problems at home eventually affected the self-assurance of the Japanese people. By 1972 they had become eager to find a scapegoat for their country's plunge from a prosperous nation boldly forging ahead at an accelerated rate to one thrown into unexpected losses of revenue. The public's confusion and loss of confidence in the government were reflected in the Diet, where the Japanese Socialist and Democratic Socialist parties saw an excellent chance to crumble Sato's power. Political opponents brought forth motions of no confidence against the Sato regime and finally forced the Premier to announce his retirement in June 1972, well before the expiration of his term of office, in October. Sato's loss of popularity inevitably reduced the stature of Fukuda within his party. On July 5, 1972 at a special caucus of Liberal-Democratic leaders, he lost to Kakuei Tanaka by a vote of 190 to 202 in a runoff election for party president, a post tantamount to Premiership. A few months after his defeat, in December 1972, Fukuda became director-general of the Administrative Management Agency.

Tanaka's election clearly indicated disenchantment with conservative government. Unlike Fukuda, the Premier was not a long-standing member of the party's inner circle, but a dynamic, flamboyant, self-made man with wealth gained through the construction business. While Fukuda is cautious and somewhat pessimistic, Tanaka is an optimist. Among one of his proposals to aid the Japanese economy was a plan for redistributing industry and population throughout Japan, thus "remodeling the Japanese archipelago." Opposing what he regarded as a grandiose scheme, Fukuda argued that it would only aggravate inflation.

Continued runaway inflation, together with the Arab oil boycott that stunned Japan in the fall of 1973, forced Tanaka to strengthen political support in attempting to deal effectively with a severe economic crisis. Upon the death in November 1973 of his Finance Minister, Kiichi Aichi, the Premier assigned Aichi's important post to Fukuda in a Cabinet reshuffle that signaled a decided shift in economic policy. Political observers considered the appointment a major political coup for Fukuda, who accepted the post with the understanding that he was to have a strong voice in economic planning. In a televised speech on November 23 the new Finance Minister said, "I have reaffirmed in my talk with the Premier that we forget the past and wrestle with the situation with a clean slate. . . . Various growth policies should be undertaken only after we have overcome inflation. In that sense, we cannot afford to have large expenditures for public works incorporated in the next fiscal year's budget."

By the spring of 1974 Fukuda was reported to believe that Japan's rampant inflation was coming under control, although labor strikes for higher wages threatened to reverse that trend. Richard Halloran of the New York *Times* (April 10, 1974) noted that even though the yen had been floating since February 1973, it had not recently dropped on the foreign exchange markets. "The fundamental reason that the yen has shown strength in recent weeks," Halloran wrote, "is that the Japanese economy is more sound and resilient than supposed when it was hit with the oil crisis last fall." Prospects moreover for an easing of the energy shortage had followed negotiations of Japanese-Arab agreements to exchange oil for technical assistance and other benefits.

About two years earlier Fukuda, then Foreign Minister, had explained the significance of Japan's economic well-being in its role in international affairs. Pointing out that the development of annihilating nuclear weapons makes a third world war unthinkable, he went on to say, as quoted in the New York *Times* (March 10, 1972), "Consequently economic strength becomes much more important than military strength. Instead [of making nuclear weapons], we wish to employ our economic strength to gain an increasing voice in the international community. The tradition once was that a nation uses its economic power to become a military power, but that is not the case with us today. I think this is unprecedented in history, at least in modern history."

Disturbed by the growing disunity within the Liberal-Democratic party, Fukuda resigned his Cabinet position on July 16, 1974. In a press conference following his resignation he called for the "reorganization and modernization" of his political party in order to prevent its collapse.

Takeo Fukuda is the recipient of the Grand Croix de l'Ordre de Léopold (Belgium), the Grand Cross First Class of the Order of Merit of the Federal Republic of Germany, the Grand Cross of the Order of St. Michael and St. George (England), and the Gran Cruz de la Orden de Isabel la Católica (Spain).

According to Japanese tradition, a politician generally receives visitors at his home in the morning before leaving for the office. His status is measured by the number of shoes left at the door. Early one morning when some twenty pairs of shoes were lined up, Fukuda quipped to a visiting newsman, "I keep an open-door policy." He is an intense, slender man with expressive hands and an affable, self-effacing air. Fukuda lives in the suburbs of Tokyo in a traditional Japanese-style house with his wife, Mie (Arai) Fukuda, whom he married on May 31, 1933. They have two daughters, Mrs. Kazuko Ochi and Reiko Fukuda, and three sons Yasuo Fukuda, Ikuo Yokote, and Tsuneo Fukuda. One of his recreations is the Japanese game go, played with black and white stones, or counters, on a board made up of 361 squares. In his *New Yorker* "Letter from Tokyo" (December 11, 1971), Joseph Kraft wrote that Fukuda "is known as the Eel, in tribute to his manipulative abilities."

References

Christian Sci Mon p19 D 2 '71 por; p16 N 28 '73 por
N Y Times p34 S 9 '71 por; p3 N 26 '73
International Who's Who, 1973-74
Who's Who in the World, 1971-72

GARFUNKEL, ART

Oct. 1942- Singer; actor; teacher
Address: b. c/o Columbia Records, 51 W. 52nd St., New York 10019

In all of his careers, as a singer, musical arranger, actor, and teacher, Art Garfunkel has enjoyed extraordinary success. Often hailed as "the voices of their generation," Simon and Garfunkel, the popular folk-rock singing duo, made the transition from the folk singing craze of the early 1960's to the post-Beatles rock explosion. The combination of Paul Simon's meditative, poetic lyrics and Art Garfunkel's clear, expressive tenor sold millions of records. Each of their seven albums earned a Gold Record and their last joint effort, *Bridge Over Troubled Water*, ranks as one of the best-selling LPs in the history of popular music. In addition to being a singer, Garfunkel is a talented motion picture actor who won critical acclaim for his performances in *Catch-22* and *Carnal Knowledge,* and a respected mathematical scholar. During a working vacation from his recording career in 1971, he taught mathematics at a private school in Connecticut.

Art Garfunkel was born in October 1942 in Forest Hills, New York, a middle-class residential area in the New York City borough of Queens. His father was in the garment packaging and container business. While a sixth-grade student at a local public school, he was cast in the role of the Cheshire Cat in the school graduation play, *Alice in Wonderland*. During rehearsals, he became acquainted with Paul Simon, a classmate who portrayed the White Rabbit. During back-stage breaks and walks home together, the two boys discovered that they shared an interest in sports and music. "Neither of us was a one-of-the-group type," Garfunkel recalled to Walter C. Meyer in an interview for the New York *Sunday News* (March 26, 1967). "I guess that's why, as outsiders, we were drawn together. Music was the big mutual interest."

Together Paul Simon and Art Garfunkel listened to the radio programs of such teenage idols as Alan Freed and Dick Clark, the popular disc jockeys of the day who featured rock 'n' roll music, played the recordings of Elvis Presley, Frankie Lymon and the Teenagers, and Bill Haley and the Comets, and attended rock concerts. The only member of his family to be musically inclined, Garfunkel sang in a high holiday choir at the local synagogue and even served as cantor at his own bar mitzvah. "I hated my bar mitzvah, though," Garfunkel told Josh Greenfield in an interview for a New York *Times Magazine* (October 13, 1968) profile. "I was acutely uncomfortable being the center of attention."

In the mid-1950's Paul Simon and Art Garfunkel started singing together as a team. Accompanied by Simon's acoustic guitar, they spent long hours rehearsing to blend and balance their voices, increase their small repertoire, and perfect their stage act. Encouraged by their success at school-sponsored activities and private parties, they cut a demonstration record at a Manhattan recording studio. A representative of Big Records, impressed by their first effort, signed them to a contract. Renamed Tom and Jerry, the duo recorded simple, adolescent rock 'n' roll tunes that Garfunkel later dismissed as "pretty crude stuff."

One of the singles, "Hey! Schoolgirl," released in 1957, rose to the number fifty-four position on *Billboard's* "Top 100" and sold 100,000 copies. They appeared on *American Bandstand*, Dick Clark's teen-oriented television show, and were booked for several rock 'n' roll tours, but none of their subsequent recordings was as successful as "Hey! Schoolgirl." When Big Records declared bankruptcy in the late 1950's, the musical career of Tom and Jerry ended. Partly because of their protracted close association as performers, the two boys' friendship had become somewhat strained. In a joint interview published in the May 1968 issue of *Seventeen* magazine, Simon explained the break to reporter Edwin Miller: "Take two teenagers who both sing and each one thinks he's the greatest; they become competitive and jealous, trying to show one's better than the other and you end up with trouble." Garfunkel, admittedly a "rebellious" youth, added, "[It was] nothing particular, just trying to assert my own identity, be a person."

After graduating from high school, Garfunkel enrolled at Columbia University as a liberal arts major. Two years later, inspired by *The Fountainhead,* Ayn Rand's popular novel about an individualistic architect, he transferred to the architecture department. Before completing his undergraduate education, he temporarily dropped out

of school to tour Europe on a motor scooter. He
also worked as a practical draftsman in New York
City, as a construction carpenter in San Francisco, and as a folk singer in the student union
at the University of California at Berkeley. He returned to Columbia and earned a B.A. degree in
art history in 1965, and an M.A. in mathematics
education in 1967. "I like an arena in which the
subject material is all settled . . . ," he told
Edwin Miller, "and math was the most closely
suited to my purposes." He is currently completing work toward a doctoral degree in mathematics.

While a student at Columbia, Garfunkel became reacquainted with Simon, and although
neither of them seriously considered a musical career, they began to sing again as a team. In the
interim, their musical preferences had shifted from
rock to folk. Garfunkel was especially influenced
by the Kingston Trio, the enormously popular
singing group often credited with ushering in
the folk revival in popular music. By singing at
impromptu "concerts" in Washington Square Park
and at folk cafes such as the Gaslight club and
Gerde's Folk City in Greenwich Village, the two
quietly gathered a small group of staunch supporters. In 1964 Simon showed some of his songs
to a producer for Columbia Records. At his suggestion, Simon and Garfunkel cut their first LP,
Wednesday Morning, 3 A.M. Released in October
1964, the folk-oriented record album made little
impression on the Beatle-crazed record-buying
public.

In the fall of 1965 a hard rock disc jockey in
Miami, Florida noticed that he was receiving an
inordinately large number of requests for "The
Sounds of Silence," one of the songs on the *Wednesday Morning, 3 A.M.* album. Encouraged by
that response, Columbia Records decided to release it as a single record. To attract a wider
audience, engineers electronically added a rhythmic, hypnotic rock accompaniment to the original acoustical guitar track. Hitting the charts on
November 20, 1965, "The Sounds of Silence" remained on the "Hot 100" for fourteen weeks.
It eventually reached the number one position and
sold more than 1,000,000 copies. A follow-up LP,
Sounds of Silence, which was released by Columbia Records in February 1966, earned the
singing duo a Gold Record for album sales and
"I Am a Rock," a cut from the album issued as
a single that spring, climbed to the number three
spot among best sellers.

Parsley, Sage, Rosemary and Thyme was the
source for four hit singles: "Homeward Bound,"
"The Dangling Conversation," "The 59th Street
Bridge Song (Feelin' Groovy)," and "Scarborough
Fair." Those songs, considered by pop music
critics to be among Simon's best compositions,
were arranged by Garfunkel. In a typical recording session, Garfunkel was ensconced in a glass
booth, listening intently to each successive vocal
and instrumental track, accepting one, suggesting
changes in another. Eddie Simon, Paul Simon's
younger brother, compared the singing team's
working relationship to that of a winning base-

ART GARFUNKEL

ball battery. "Paul works a record like a pitcher
who's working a batter," he told Josh Greenfield.
"And Artie's like the smart catcher who knows
just what to call for." In commenting on Garfunkel's arrangements for *Parsley* in a retrospective review for *The Rolling Stone* (August 3,
1972), Stephen Holden wrote: "Listening to *Parsley* today is almost as staggering an experience
as it was nearly six years ago. One glorious
melody follows another, each brilliantly arranged
and impeccably sung. . . . *Parsley* was a kaleido-
scope of moods and ideas communicated with
unprecedented tenderness and intimacy."

Captivated by the intense, personal lyrics and
melody of "The Sounds of Silence," Mike Nichols,
the motion picture director, commissioned Simon
and Garfunkel to compose and perform original
music for *The Graduate*, a phenomenally successful film about the coming-of-age of Benjamin
Braddock, an alienated young American. Both
the soundtrack album, which topped the charts
for six months, and the hit single "Mrs. Robinson," a tongue-in-cheek paean to Benjamin's older
mistress, earned Gold Records. At the Eleventh
Annual Awards of the National Academy of Recording Arts and Sciences in 1969, Simon and
Garfunkel were awarded Grammys for the Record
of the Year—"Mrs. Robinson"—and for the best
performance by a pop vocal group.

Their next two LPs were equally successful.
Bookends, their fifth album, replaced *The Graduate*
as the best-selling LP in the United States. Released early in 1970, *Bridge Over Troubled Water*
was acclaimed as a "model of consistency and
professionalism." In his review for *The Rolling
Stone*, Stephen Holden noted that the title cut,
sung by Garfunkel in his overriding tenor, was
"the ultimate Simon and Garfunkel hit. Though
[it] suffers from too much echo and syrupy
strings, it contains Garfunkel's finest inspirational
singing." Released as a single, "Bridge Over
Troubled Water" sold more than 1,000,000 copies
and appeared on *Billboard's* "Hot 100" for fourteen successive weeks. As of May 1973 the album

had sold more than 6,000,000 copies, reputedly making it, along with the soundtrack from *The Sound of Music* and Carole King's *Tapestry,* one of the top-selling pop LPs in history. For their efforts, they won six Grammy awards for 1970, including the coveted prizes for the best album, the best single record, and the best song of the year.

To manage their business affairs, Simon and Garfunkel hired an agent, Mort Lewis. An astute veteran of show business, Lewis turned down lucrative nightclub offers in favor of weekend concert performances, usually at colleges and universities. He restricted their television appearances to carefully selected, uninterrupted guest segments on the *Ed Sullivan Show,* the *Red Skelton Show, Hullabaloo,* and the *Kraft Music Hall,* and to such specials as the *Fred Astaire Show* and *Simon and Garfunkel,* an hour-long concert packaged and produced by the pair and broadcast by CBS-TV on November 30, 1969. By going along with Lewis' strategy, Simon and Garfunkel established themselves as polished concert artists, outdrawing such popular performers on the college circuit as the Smothers Brothers. In concerts at Carnegie Hall, Philharmonic Hall in Lincoln Center for the Performing Arts, and Forest Hills Stadium, they played to standing-room-only audiences. Their concert fee rose to 90 percent of the house gross, with two-thirds of the proceeds going to Simon, the song-writing half of the team, and the remaining third to Garfunkel.

Commenting on the extraordinary appeal of Simon and Garfunkel to young and old alike in a New York *Sunday News* (March 26, 1967) profile, Walter C. Meyer wrote: "They exhibit a smooth, hand-in-glove blend of singing and playing. Though the song may be gentle, angry, humorous, intense or hard-driving, their voices unite, separate, interweave and sing counter to each other with delicacy and ease. . . . It's a winning combination. . . ."

In an inspired bit of casting, Mike Nichols signed Garfunkel to play Captain Nately, the aristocratic bomber pilot, in his multimillion-dollar motion picture version of Joseph Heller's popular best seller, *Catch 22,* which went into production in Mexico in January 1969. "I like the idea of having another string to my bow," the singer-turned-actor told Edwin Miller. Major reviewers, such as Stanley Kauffmann, Judith Crist, and Vincent Canby, while disagreeing about the merits of the film, praised Garfunkel's acting debut. In her *New York* magazine (June 29, 1970) critique of the film, Miss Crist observed that "his major scene . . . , discussing national futures and survival with . . . a 107-year-old pimp, is one of the unforgettable moments of *Catch-22.*" Gary Arnold, writing in the Washington *Post* (June 25, 1970), added, "He embodies a kind of youthful sweetness and idealism that the material desperately needs in the face of so many manic and inhuman characters."

For his next film, *Carnal Knowledge,* Nichols capitalized on Garfunkel's ability to convey an appealing naïveté and cast the young actor as Sandy, the good-natured, innocent collegian who evolves into an arrogant, "superannuated swinger." The antithesis of his roommate Jonathan, a "macho" womanizer powerfully played by Jack Nicholson, Sandy eventually leaves a loveless marriage with his college sweetheart to embark on a series of empty affairs. In her lengthy review of the "grimly purposeful satire" for the *New Yorker* (July 3, 1971), Pauline Kael commended Garfunkel's "pleasantly non-actorish" portrayal of the college-aged Sandy but found his interpretation of the mature Sandy less satisfying. "He has no projection," she contended, and "becomes such a limp presence that you forget he's on the screen." Reviewing the film for *Newsweek* (July 5, 1971), Paul D. Zimmerman agreed with Miss Kael's analysis: "Garfunkel's idealist is suitably fuzzy and foggy-eyed—drifting from one perfect match to the next. But he is nearly blasted off the screen by Nicholson's power."

Divided by diverging careers and irreconcilable musical interests, Simon and Garfunkel formally dissolved their partnership in 1970 to go their separate ways. "There was an inevitability about the split-up, a sense of having done something and repeated it," Garfunkel remarked to Hubert Saal in an interview for *Newsweek* magazine (October 8, 1973). "In a marriage, changes can be made to coincide. In other relationships, changes go against the grain." In June 1972, in their only public performance as a team since their amicable separation, they sang at a McGovern-for-President rally at Madison Square Garden in New York City.

Garfunkel's first solo record album, which was released by Columbia Records in the fall of 1973, was well received by somewhat skeptical critics. Two weeks after it first appeared on *Billboard*'s chart of best-selling LPs, *Angel Clare,* a collection of tunes written by such top rock composers as Jimmy Webb, Van Morrison, and Randy Newman, was a solid hit. In her review for the New York *Times* (September 9, 1973), Loraine Alterman wrote: "Not only does Garfunkel emerge as the excellent singer we all knew him to be but he also reveals himself as a romantic not afraid to luxuriate in lush sounds." Although he has repeatedly referred to his acting career as "just a diversion," he took time off from his recording chores to appear in the March 1973 television production *Acts of Love,* in which he portrayed Marlo Thomas' unfaithful boyfriend.

A lean five feet ten inches tall, Art Garfunkel has pale blue eyes and curly blond hair that one interviewer compared to "a huge dandelion gone to seed." Shy and introspective, he avoids the public life of a rock star. At the height of his concert career he told Josh Greenfield, "I enjoy success. . . . And the recognition is fun, though it's just beginning to get more annoying than enjoyable. . . . When this whole bit no longer engages me creatively—or just isn't fun, I'll quit. Because I want to have a married life and a family life. . . . I want to make sure I have time for that." In October 1972 he married Linda Marie Grossman, an architect.

References

N Y Post II p17 My 26 '73
N Y Sunday News Mag p4 Mr 26 '67 por
N Y Times Mag p48+ O 13 '68 pors
Seventeen 27:140+ My 28 '68 pors

GENEEN, HAROLD S(YDNEY) (jǝ-nēn′)

Jan. 22, 1910- Business executive
Address: b. ITT Corp., 320 Park Ave., New
York 10022

HAROLD S. GENEEN

When Harold S. Geneen became chief executive
officer of International Telephone and Telegraph
in 1959, that corporation was a stagnating mono-
lith, with annual sales of $765,000,000, mostly
from communications businesses it held in loose
rein around the world. Under Geneen's aggressive, strong-willed management, ITT diversified,
acquiring scores of varied companies, from the
Sheraton hotel chain to the Hartford Fire-Insur-
ance Company, and grew into the biggest of the
multinational conglomerates, with annual revenues exceeding $8.5 billion. Despite its size and
power, ITT remained virtually anonymous. It was
either unknown to the average citizen or confused
with AT&T (the American Telephone and Telegraph Company), until its name emerged in Nixon
administration influence-peddling scandals overlapping the Watergate affair. As one stockholder has complained, the corporation's reputation is
now mired in "a morass of deals, plots, and intrigues," with a resultant drop in the price of its
stock. Profits, however, have not been affected.
According to a report in *Business Week* (November 3, 1973), "Only such an unexpected setback
as a massive penalty for the alleged acts being investigated will keep earnings—$483,000,000 last
year—from growing this year by close to the 11.3
percent they have averaged throughout Geneen's
tenure." The directors of ITT appointed Geneen
chairman of the company's executive committee
on August 29, 1974.

Harold Sydney Geneen was born in Bourne-
mouth, England on January 22, 1910 to Russian-
born S. Alexander Geneen, a concert manager, and
English-born Aïda DeCruciani (spelled Da Cru-
ciana in some sources). When he was one year
old he moved to the United States with his
parents, who later separated. Although he had a
close relationship with his mother until her recent death, he saw little of her in his growing
years, which he spent in boarding schools and
summer camps.

After graduating from Suffield (Connecticut)
Academy, at sixteen, Geneen studied accounting
evenings at New York University while working
as a page on the New York Stock Exchange. In
1934, armed with a B.S. degree, a nearly photographic memory, and an enthusiasm for and understanding of business rare in an accountant, he
joined the Manhattan accounting firm of Lybrand
and Ross Bros. & Montgomery. After eight years
at Lybrand, he worked as chief accountant at

the American Can Company (1942-46), as comptroller of the Bell and Howell Company (1946-
50), and as vice-president and comptroller of the
Jones and Laughlin Steel Corporation (1950-56).
As a comptroller he inspected ledgers like "a
bloodhound on the trail of a wasted dollar," as
one early colleague observed.

Eager for a position of real managing power,
Geneen left Jones and Laughlin in 1956 to accept
the executive vice-presidency of the then ailing
Raytheon Manufacturing Company, with headquarters in Waltham, Massachusetts. Mandated by
Raytheon's president, Charles Francis Adams, to
"make some money," he imposed strict cost controls, eked out more and more working capital,
and persuaded banks to open new lines of credit.
Losing no opportunity to pinch pennies, he insisted that Raytheon pay its bills within the time
limit for the standard discount while dunning its
own customers for debts outstanding.

At Raytheon, Geneen developed the basic system for which he became renowned in management circles. The company was divided into
twelve semiautonomous divisions, but the head
of each division was responsible, in detail, for all
aspects of operation and was under constant
scrutiny by top management. In an article he
wrote for the *Christian Science Monitor* (May 19,
1959) he described his management system, with
its emphasis on "comprehensive analysis covering
[each division's] policies and plans as to sales,
returns, and capital requirements for five years
ahead." Essential to it, he said, were "internal
controls, monthly management reviews, . . . constant pressures and samplings to measure progress."

Although he increased the company's earnings
fourfold, Geneen was never given absolute power
at Raytheon. He later explained his position there
as "driving at high speed when every so often,
without warning, somebody else would try to
put their hand on the wheel." In May 1959 he
abruptly resigned as executive vice-president of
Raytheon to accept the presidency of ITT.

The founder of ITT was Sosthenes Behn, a Danish Virgin Islander who accrued American citizenship when the United States bought the Danish Virgin Islands from Denmark in 1917. As Anthony Sampson recounted in his book *The Sovereign State of ITT* (1973), Behn established the corporation in 1920 for the immediate purpose of controlling several small Caribbean telephone companies he had acquired and with the long-range goal of building an international telephone network to rival and complement the American system. Sampson wrote: "Behn's grand design soon came up against the obstacles of nationalism and the insistence of governments on controlling their own communications; and in trying to hold his system together, Behn gradually wove a web of corruption and compromise which left his company with deep kinks in its character." Sampson examined meticulously the deals Behn made with the Nazis on the eve of World War II insuring that whoever emerged victorious from the war, ITT would be among the survivors.

Behn remained in control of ITT until 1956, the year before his death. A caretaker administration under Edmund H. Leavy filled the vacancy at the top until a subcommittee of directors, after combing the ranks of American management for three years, chose Harold Geneen to lead the corporation. When Geneen took it over, the cartel bequeathed by Behn, for all its international machinations, was in his view an anarchy, a loosely knit holding company operating far below its potential in net earnings ($29,000,000, or 3.8 percent of sales, in 1959). Whereas Behn had remained aristocratically aloof from the internal affairs of the member companies, Geneen made it known from the beginning that no nook or cranny of the corporation would escape his eye.

Implementing his dicta that "management must manage" and that he would tolerate "no surprises," Geneen abolished the traditional autonomy of ITT units and instituted the system of strict accountability that still prevails. The comptrollers of all subsidiaries report directly to the corporation's overall comptroller. All unit heads are required to draw up careful five-year plans, amendable annually, and to participate in marathon monthly meetings, held in New York and in Brussels, ITT's European headquarters. At those gatherings, presided over by Geneen, they present voluminous reports setting forth in detail accounts receivable, inventories, capital spending budgets, and analyses of administrative and marketing expenses. Each knows that any departure from strict fact or realistic prognostication will inexorably invoke the terrible wrath of Harold S. Geneen on some future judgment day. Geneen carries the monthly reports (those from Europe alone fill about thirty inch-thick books) as permanent luggage wherever he goes, reading and digesting them constantly.

In the 1960's, especially after Latin American governments began nationalizing telephone companies owned by ITT, Geneen made many new acquisitions, mostly in the United States, without regard to what they produced as long as they were likely to add to corporate earnings. In 1961 he bought up all remaining stock in American Cable and Radio (of which ITT was already the major shareholder), and subsequently he acquired, among other companies, the Gilfillan Corporation, a radar technology company; General Controls, a manufacturer of thermostatic equipment; Bell & Gosset, a pump manufacturer; the Aetna Finance Company (which merged into the Great International Life Insurance Company); Howard W. Sams & Company, the major stockholder in the Bobbs-Merrill publishing house; Levitt and Sons, builders of the "Levittown" housing developments; the Hamilton Management Company, a mutual fund firm; the Cannon Electric Company; and the Sheraton Corporation. An attempt to acquire the American Broadcasting Company was thwarted by the Department of Justice.

The juiciest plum plucked by Geneen, in 1970, was the Hartford Fire Insurance Company, a huge source of constant fresh cash. The United States Department of Justice filed an antitrust suit to divest ITT of the Hartford company, but in 1971 an out-of-court agreement was reached whereby ITT was permitted to keep the insurance company while divesting itself of several others, including Avis Rent-a-Car and the Canteen Corporation, a large but ailing automatic food vending company.

The scandals now clouding the public image of ITT began in February 1972, when syndicated newspaper columnist Jack Anderson published a memo written by Dita Beard, ITT's Washington lobbyist, connecting the Hartford "deal" with an ITT pledge of $400,000 for the 1972 Republican National Convention. Later there were strong allegations that President Nixon himself intervened to block the Justice Department's antitrust suit against ITT; that tax and securities-and-exchange laws were violated in the Hartford acquisition; and that ITT had offered the Central Intelligence Agency a substantial sum of money first to sabotage the election of President Salvador Allende of Chile (whose intention to nationalize ITT's Chilean Telephone Company was known) and then to undermine his regime by the creation of economic chaos in Chile.

Geneen has acknowledged the essential veracity of most of the anti-Allende allegation. (After Allende died in the Chilean military coup of September 1973, the company's Zurich office and one of its two Manhattan skyscrapers were bombed by unknown pro-Allende militants.) Their possible involvement in perjury in connection with the Hartford Fire Insurance Company affair contributed to the downfall of former Attorneys General Mitchell and Kleindienst, and the tax evasion and other charges against ITT have been the subject of investigation by many government agencies, including the Securities and Exchange Commission, the Internal Revenue Service, the special Watergate prosecutor, a federal grand jury, and Congressional committees. One of the subjects under investigation has been the alleged manipulation of stocks for ITT by Lazard Frères, the investment banking house.

One of the partners in Lazard Frères, Felix Rohatyn, is on the board of directors of ITT, which also includes John A. McCone, former head of the CIA, and Eugene Black, former head of the World Bank. Paul-Henri Spaak, former prime minister of Belgium, heads the corporation's Belgian subsidiary. In 1972 Geneen turned over the presidency of ITT to Francis J. Dunleavy without relinquishing his positions as chief executive officer and chairman of the board.

While no one faults the fabled efficiency of the unique accounting methods used in ITT, some experts in the field charge that those methods are calculated to magnify the corporation's growth rate. Whatever validity there is to that charge, there is no doubt that ITT is still thriving, growing at an annual rate of more than 10 percent and expecting sales of $10 billion in the current year and more than $20 billion by 1980. The recent scandals have shaken its stock price, however. In October 1973 the stock was selling for $38 a share, down 43 percent from its all-time high price of two years before.

ITT now manages approximately 250 companies in some sixty countries. They include the British insurance group Excess Holdings; the Continental Baking Company, makers of Wonder Bread; Groko, which wholesales and retails prepared food in European supermarkets; Standard Elektrik Lorenz of West Germany, mammoth manufacturer of a broad range of telecommunications and other electronic equipment; ITT Telecommunications; World Communications Inc; Bell Telephone Manufacturing Company; and the Pennsylvania Glass Sand Corporation.

Geneen's salary is just under $1,000,000, and he owns millions of dollars' worth of ITT stock. He has no taste for the usual trappings of wealth, preferring simple food (such as hamburgers) and modest surroundings, but in his position as chief executive of ITT he travels in high style—in a chauffeur-driven limousine or company airplane in the United States and a chartered Pan American jet (with an office especially for him) when flying abroad.

Harold S. Geneen is a short, balding man who looks, in the words of Anthony Sampson, "the complete accountant, bespectacled and trim." Possessing the energy and ambition of a man half his age, he does everything fast, from walking to thinking, and his speech is spirited, accompanied by the flailing of arms and jabbing of fingers. "When Geneen begins to argue or enthuse . . . ," Sampson wrote, "you can see that glint in his eye that has brought so many under his spell." Some former subordinates, not spellbound enough to keep pace with his relentless drive and dedication, have described him as a "flinty" despot who works with "ruthless efficiency," pays no attention to time, and expects the same from others. But one former associate testifies that he can be "surprisingly affable."

Geneen's first marriage ended in divorce in 1946. Three years later he married his present wife, the former June Elizabeth Hjelm, who was his secretary at Bell and Howell. He has no children by either marriage. In New York City Geneen lives in an apartment just across the street from his office. He also has homes in Key Biscayne, Florida, and Centerville, Massachusetts. His favorite recreation is fishing from his yacht, *Genie IV*, off Cape Cod or the coast of Florida, but the fishing expeditions are usually thinly veiled business meetings. Writing in the New York *Times* for August 6, 1973, Michael C. Jensen observed: "Mr. Geneen . . . , never an easily accessible man to outsiders, . . . has virtually isolated himself from the news media in recent months as the investigations of his company have intensified. Much in the manner of President Nixon, he has shunned all but the most superficial interviews. Insiders say, however, that he is deeply disturbed by the growing criticism of I.T.T., much of which he considers unfair."

References

Bsns W p60+ My 9 '70 por; p102+ Ag 11 '73 por; p43+ N 3 '73 por
Forbes 101:27+ My 1 '68 pors; 107:186+ My 15 '71 pors
Fortune 73:81+ Jl '66 por
N Y Times p43 My 21 '59 por
New York 6:33+ Ap 23 '73 por
Time 90:86+ S 8 '67 pors
Sampson, Anthony. The Sovereign State of ITT (1973)
Who's Who in America, 1972-73

GENET, JEAN (zhe-nā')

Dec. 19, 1910- French writer
Address: b. c/o Editions Gallimard, 5 Rue Sebastién Bottin, Paris 7e, France; c/o Rosica Colin, 4 Hereford Sq., London, England

Jean Malignon, the author of the *Dictionnaire des écrivains français* (1971), is hardly alone among French literary critics in ranking Jean Genet, that blasphemous and narcissistic genius, alongside Audiberti and Beckett as "without doubt the greatest dramatic poet of our literature in this second half of the twentieth century." Jean Cocteau, who discovered him and sponsored his first publications, dubbed Genet "the Black Prince of letters," and Jean-Paul Sartre canonized him as a criminal "martyr" in his massive study *Saint Genêt* (1952). Genet, who began writing while imprisoned for theft, male prostitution, and pimping, is *le grand fantaisiste* of inversion, constructing with his deviate imagination a demonic value system exactly counter to the "bourgeois" moral order against which he has steeled himself.

Out of Genet's private hell has come a wealth of confessional literature: the autoerotic poems and novels (including *Our Lady of the Flowers*) in which he glorifies criminal homosexuality, and such absurdist, revolutionary dramas as *The Maids*, *The Blacks*, and *The Screens*, in which he vilifies all that society holds sacred and exalts all that it considers sordid. Not surprisingly, Genet's reprobate works have been greeted with shock and con-

JEAN GENET

demnation by moralists of the establishment, although, ironically, Genet is himself a moralist in his intense preoccupation with the confrontation of good and evil. On the other hand, avant-garde critics and readers have rejoiced with him in his achievement of "salvation" through the beauty of the crafted word, in which he has created, *ex nihilo*, what has been described as "a grammar of reversal and negation." Genet is published in France by Gallimard, which periodically updates his *Oeuvres Complètes*, in England by Blond Ltd., and in the United States by Grove Press.

Jean Genet's surname derives from *genêt*—originally *genest*, and hence the circumflex—a wheat-like evergreen with a flower shaped like the butterfly, nature's most ostentatious symbol of metamorphosis. (It is interesting to note that the royal Plantagenet line got its name when, nine centuries ago, Geoffrey IV of Brittany, ruler of Anjou, conqueror of Normandy, and father of King Henry II of England, began wearing a sprig of *genêt* in his cap.) Jean Genet was born in a maternity hospital at 22 rue d'Assas in Paris, France on December 19, 1910. As he discovered twenty-one years later, when he had occasion to see his birth certificate, his mother was Gabrielle Genet. His father is unknown.

Genet lived in a state foundling home until the age of seven, when he was placed with peasant foster parents in the Morvan district of France's *Massif central*. There, as an altar boy, he impressed the local parish priest with his "religious nature." But his heart leaned to another altar, as he confessed in his autobiographical *récit Journal du voleur* (1949; *Thief's Journal*, 1965). "When I came across the *genêt* flowers in the heath—especially at sunset, when returning from the ruins of Tiffauges, where Gilles de Rais lived—I experienced a profound sympathy. . . . I am alone in the world, and I am not sure but that I may not be the king, perhaps the *fée* of those flowers. . . . They are my natural emblem, and through them I have roots in French earth nourished by the powdered bones of infants, of adolescents sodomized, massacred, burned by Gilles de Rais. Through that prickly plant of the Cévennes [mountains east of the *Massif central*] I embark on my criminal adventures. . . . It is to the tree-ferns and their swamps, to the algae that I wish to descend."

In his book *Saint Genêt: Comédien et Martyr (Saint Genet: Actor and Martyr)* Sartre—who by "actor" means inveterate trickster or role-player, a person who is radically, willfully dishonest, never showing his true face to society—relates Genet "to that family of people who are nowadays referred to by the barbaric name of *passéistes* [those who move through the present time "unalive," as aliens from the past]." According to Sartre, at some point early in puberty Genet underwent a horrible "metamorphosis," a "sacred drama" in which he, as "officiant," lost his innocence. "Genet lives and continues to relive this . . . fatal instant. . . . The argument of this liturgical drama is as follows: a child dies of shame; a hoodlum rises up in his place; the hoodlum will be haunted by the child. One would have to speak of resurrection, to evoke the old initiatory rites of shamanism and secret societies, were it not that Genet refuses categorically to be a man who has been resuscitated. There was death, that is all. . . . This original crisis appears to him as a metamorphosis. . . . He lives in terror lest the original crisis recur."

From the time his foster mother called him "you little thief" because he took some change from her purse, Genet deliberately and maliciously inverted his heart. "I answered 'yes' to every accusation made against me, no matter how unjust. 'Yes' from the bottom of my heart. . . . Yes, I *had* to become what they said I was. . . . I was coward, thief, traitor, queer: whatever they saw in me." Thus, Genet has explained, he "decisively repudiated a world that had repudiated" him.

"He seizes upon the curse which goes back to the depths of his past, of his mother's past . . . and he projects it before him," Sartre wrote. "It will be his future." During the score of years he spent in reformatories and prisons, Genet established, in Sartre's word's, "a black ethic, with precepts and rules, pitiless constraints, a Jansenism of Evil."

Like an outlaw priest saying underground Mass, the imprisoned Genet devoutly practised his secret rituals. In Fresnes Prison at the age of thirty-two he began to express his fantasies in the written word—chiefly to preserve them for his own future reference in ceremonial masturbation. Writing on the crude brown paper used in the prison's bag-making industry, he sumptuously transfigured his criminal homosexual underworld and its denizens, in a masterful, elevated style that seems to have sprung out of nowhere, given the paucity of his reading opportunities.

His first literary work was the solemn incantatory elegy "Le Condamné a mort" ("Under Sentence of Death"), dedicated to the memory of Maurice Pilorge, a young male prostitute executed in 1939 for murdering one of his clients. Written at Fresnes Prison in 1942, that poem was published along with "Un Chant d'amour" ("The Love Song"), on which Genet and friends later based a film (which was suppressed in France), and other poems under the title *Poèmes* by Éditions de l'Arbalète in 1948.

In his cell at Fresnes, Genet also wrote his first novel, *Notre Dame des Fleurs*, published in a limited edition by Éditions de l'Arbalète in 1943 and in a full, revised edition by Gallimard in 1951. The English translation by Bernard Frechtman (the major translator of Genet's work), *Our Lady of the Flowers*, first published by Éditions Paul Morihien in 1949, was later issued by Olympia Press, in 1957, and by Grove Press, in 1963.

In *La Folie en tête* (1970; *Mad in Pursuit*, 1971) the novelist and memoirist Violette Leduc reports the reaction of Paul Valéry when he first read the manuscript of *Notre Dame des Fleurs:* "Il faut brûler ça" ("that has to be burned"). In the novel a dying Parisian male prostitute named Divine looks back over the love affairs in his life, especially that with a "queenish" young hoodlum who is the title's namesake. Some critics complained about the book's loose episodic structure and shallowness of characterization—common criticisms of Genet's work—but others accepted that structure and characterization as expected features of masturbatory fiction and heaped praise on the novel. Susan Sontag asserted that "only a handful" of other twentieth-century writers, such as Proust and Kafka, have had "as important, as authoritative, as irrevocable a voice and style," and Alfred Chester went so far as to call it "the greatest novel . . . probably . . . produced during the past twenty years."

The prose-poem *Miracle de la Rose* (1951; *Miracle of the Rose*, 1965) was written in La Santé and Tourelle prisons in 1943. Keith Botsford in an article on Genet in the New York *Times Magazine* (February 27, 1972), called it "a celebration of love, death, and betrayal set in the penitentiary." Botsford went on: "It is Genet's most deliberately lyrical and literary novel, the rose of the title being at once the anus, love and death, a perversion of our normal ethic and esthetic of the true, good, and beautiful."

Obsessed with perverse ritual, Genet found his forum *par excellence* in theatre, the perfect sanctuary for the "Black Mass." His first play, *Haute surveillance (Deathwatch)*, which premièred in Paris in February 1949, is about sadism among three prisoners in a cell. Written later but staged earlier, by Louis Jouvet in 1947, was *Les Bonnes (The Maids)*, based on the story of the Papin sisters, who systematically mutilated-murdered their mistress. In the play two servants act out the roles of lady and attendant in a ritual of domination and humiliation that ends in ceremonial suicide. In New York *The Maids* ran Off Broadway for sixty-two performances in the 1963-64 season.

Death, a subtle theme running throughout the canon of Genet's work, became overt in *Pompes funèbres*, first published privately in 1947 and issued by Gallimard six years later. Grove Press published the translation, *Funeral Rites*, in 1969. The funeral is that of Jean Descarnin, a young lover of Genet's who was killed fighting with the Resistance in Occupied France. Genet's next novel, *Querelle de Brest* (1953; *Querelle of Brest*, 1967), has as its hero a sailor who sleeps with the ship's captain, commits a murder, and shifts the blame for the crime to a friend.

With his tenth conviction for theft, in 1948, Genet faced an automatic life sentence; but a petition signed by André Gide, Paul Claudel, Cocteau, Sartre, and other eminent writers won his pardon. Publication of *Journal du Voleur* in 1949 brought him to wide public attention, and he was already being lionized by the French café literati. Full financial reward came slower than fame, however, and Genet supported himself for several years by running a bookstall along the Seine. He supplied the stall by stealing books from bookstores, using a false-bottomed briefcase for the purpose. He considered himself, proudly, an "artist" at theft. The publication of Sartre's book on him (which he could not bring himself to read) in 1952 upset Genet. A superstitious man who felt that the book had entombed him, he suffered writer's block for a couple of years.

In his play *Le Balcon* (1956) Genet dramatized the idea that the ruling class is as corrupt as the criminal population that it punishes. The setting is a brothel in which the clients act out their sex and power fantasies in such roles as bishop and judge—while outside, in the streets, a revolution is taking place. In the United States *The Balcony* ran for 672 performances in 1960-61 and 1961-62, and the American film *The Balcony* (Continental, 1963) has become a counter-culture classic. In his introduction to his book *The Third Theatre* (1969), Robert Brustein observed that Genet's intention in *The Balcony* was to bring the audience into the production—into the brothel—and thus "annihilate" it (the audience): "*The Balcony* was based on his understanding that since revolution is dedicated to the destruction of artifice, its greatest enemy is play-acting."

Les Nègres, first performed at the Théâtre de Lutèce in October 1959, became another Off-Broadway hit as *The Blacks*, in 1961. Written for an all-Negro cast—some in whiteface—that "clown show" dramatizes fantasies of racial revenge (including a ritualized rape-murder of a white woman) but the audience eventually learns that the most important action is taking place offstage: the trial and execution of a black who has betrayed the cause of his people. "He loves French society as the Negroes love America, with a love that is full of hatred and, at the same time, desperate," Sartre wrote in *Saint Genêt*. "As for the social order which excludes him, he will do everything to perpetuate it. Its rigor must be perfect so that Genet can attain perfection in Evil."

His most sordid play, *Les Paravents* (*The Screens*), was inspired by sympathy for the underdogs in the Algerian war. It was published in 1960, but production difficulties delayed its staging until 1966, when Roger Blin directed it. Genet's correspondence with Blin about the production has been published under the title *Lettres à Roger Blin* (1966; *Letters to Roger Blin*, 1969).

The play—over five hours long and requiring a cast of more than forty—used colonialism in North Africa to epitomize the vilest aspects of human nature as affected by Western culture and to portray the absurdity of the Algerian war, a sensitive subject in France at the time. The stir—including police action—that it created was relished by Genet and apparently instigated his current interest in politics. The Brooklyn production, given by the Chelsea Theatre Company in 1973, was naturally less volatile.

In his New York *Times Magazine* article Keith Botsford observed: "The novels represent an inner Genet; the plays are Genet's fantasies acted out in public. . . . The plays show much greater inner development, as well as more consistent and forceful understanding of language and theme. . . . The growth of Genet's ability to externalize fantasy is paralleled by an even deeper understanding of theatre as ritual and ceremony, a place to act out extremes of emotion and ethical opposites. . . . In all three of these latter plays (*The Balcony, The Blacks,* and *The Screens*), all is illusion and defeat."

Genet visited the United States in 1968, to cover the Democratic National Convention in Chicago for *Esquire*, and again in 1970, when he lived for two months with members of the Black Panther party. During that time he formed a close friendship with Angela Davis, who acted as his interpreter. Later, when Miss Davis was imprisoned for her revolutionary activities, he mustered all the influence and money at his disposal to help her win her freedom. Genet wrote of the death of George Jackson: "It is rarer than ever to find a man in Europe who accepts his own death as the price to be paid for an idea he believes in. The blacks in America do so every day."

Jean Genet is, in the description of actress Madeleine Renaud, "a little round man" with a "funny high-pitched voice," an "extraordinary" theatrical ear, and a "sense of actors and what they could be made to do." Keith Botsford quoted her: "But love. How he needed love. . . . He talked about himself as though there were something inside him that made it impossible for him to be happy." Miss Renaud mentioned his abuse of sleeping pills, which nearly killed him on at least one occasion.

In manner Genet is quick, and he is alternately nonchalant and furtive. His head, almost completely bald to begin with, is clean-shaven. His living quarters, like his wardrobe, are simple to the point of asceticism, except when he indulges in luxury to please a lover. According to Keith Botsford, he often mothers the objects of his affection. (Genet has pointed out that the male role makes one vulnerable, whereas "the female will survive.")

All his belongings fit into a little suitcase, and he is indifferent to food and most other creature comforts (although he smokes). He often seems cold and aloof, but, a lover of word-play and argument, he can converse with gusto if he is accepted as the *maître* and as long as there is no small talk. Erratic, he can at times coolly be logical and at others given to tantrums. (In a fit of pique over a trifle during a carefully prepared dinner at Violette Leduc's, he pulled the tablecloth, sending the food and drink to the floor, before making his exit.)

Paradoxically, the rebellious author respects those in authority, especially the police, because he knows their power and because "they kill with their own hands, not at a distance or by proxy." But he continues to be dishonest toward the society that now accepts him, explaining, "Theft is individual action. I've gone in for more universal action with poetry. . . . Don't think it's made me any happier." He is reportedly writing a book with the working title "Toward Death."

References

N Y Times Mag p7+ F 27 '72 pors
Coe, Richard. The Vision of Jean Genet (1968)
Contemporary Authors vol 13-14 (1965)
Who's Who in France, 1971-72

GISCARD D'ESTAING, VALÉRY (zhē-skar' des-taɴ' va-lā-rē')

Feb. 2, 1926-   President of France
Address: Palais de l'Elysée, Paris 8ᵉ, France

NOTE: This biography supersedes the article that appeared in *Current Biography* in 1967.

The youngest head of state since Napoleon, Valéry Giscard d'Estaing was elected the third President of the Fifth French Republic in May 1974, succeeding Georges Pompidou. Often described as the "Gallic Kennedy," Giscard—as he is generally called—survived a bitter, hard-fought, personal campaign to defeat François Mitterrand, the leftist candidate, by only a narrow margin. A brilliant economist, the wealthy Giscard served in Gaullist Cabinets for more than a decade before his election to the presidency. As the Minister of Finance under Presidents de Gaulle and Pompidou, he was the principal architect of France's austerity program during the early 1960's and of her remarkable economic growth in the early 1970's. Since his election he has cautiously modified his conservative positions to support federally funded social welfare programs at home and a united economic community abroad.

The second of five children born to Edmond and May (Bardoux) Giscard d'Estaing, Valéry Giscard d'Estaing was born on February 2, 1926 in Koblenz, Germany, where his father, a prominent economist, was the financial director of the French High Commission in the Rhineland following World War I. Edmond Giscard, who owned land near the village of Estaing in Auvergne, officially added "d'Estaing" to the family name shortly before Valéry's birth. The aristocratic family has a tradition of government service. Giscard's maternal grandfather, Jacques Bardoux, and great-great-grandfather, Agenor

Bardoux, were politicians; his younger brother Olivier is an industrialist and a deputy in the National Assembly.

After graduating from the Lycée Janson-de-Sailly in Paris, Giscard enrolled at the prestigious École Polytechnique. In 1944 he interrupted his education to enlist in the French Army. Attached to a tank regiment, he served in North Africa and in Germany and won a Croix de Guerre. After the war he returned to the École Polytechnique to complete his degree. From 1949 to 1951 he attended the École Nationale d'Administration, a special school that provides training for the higher ranks of the civil service.

In 1952 Giscard began his civil service career as an assistant in the Ministry of Finance and Economic Affairs. Two years later he was made an inspector of finance in the ministry and played a major role in reorganizing the national economy. Impressed by Giscard's ability, Edgar Faure, then Minister of Finance and president of the Council of Ministers, appointed him assistant director of his staff. An active member of the conservative National Center of Independents and Peasants, Giscard was elected to the National Assembly from the district of Puy-de-Dôme, the seat once held by his grandfather, on January 2, 1956. He was reelected in 1958.

As a deputy, Giscard continued to attract notice because of his extraordinary intelligence and talent. After serving as a delegate to the United Nations General Assembly from 1956 through 1958, he was named Secretary of State for Finance in President Charles de Gaulle's first government of the Fifth Republic in January 1959. Among his responsibilities in that post were the formulation and implementation of the national budget. When Wilfrid Baumgartner, de Gaulle's second Minister of Finance, resigned on January 18, 1962, Giscard succeeded to the post.

In his first term as Minister of Finance, Giscard emphasized austerity. As Bernard Nossiter noted in an article for the Washington *Post* (January 10, 1966), he became "the very symbol of hard-nosed, old-fashioned economics." He chopped government spending, restricted credit, imposed tight controls on prices and wages, and increased taxes. Under Giscard, France achieved a balanced budget for the first time in thirty-six years.

Internationally, Giscard followed a course calculated to promote monetary cooperation between economically interdependent countries. He sought to limit American financial influence in Europe and to reduce the world's dependence on the dollar by restricting commercial investments in France and by repaying foreign debts. Although his rigorous economic program succeeded in lowering France's annual rate of inflation from 5 percent to 2.5 percent, it triggered a temporary economic recession. Faced with mounting opposition from business and labor, President de Gaulle and Premier Georges Pompidou dismissed Giscard in January 1966. "I was sacked like a servant," he remarked, as quoted in the London *Observer* (May 26, 1974).

VALÉRY GISCARD D'ESTAING

Relieved of his Cabinet-level responsibilities, Giscard concentrated on strengthening his own political party, the Républicains Indépendents, which was formed when a split developed between the pro- and anti-Gaullist factions of the National Center of Independents and Peasants in 1962. Under his leadership the essentially pro-Gaullist Independent Republicans gained an additional ten seats in the legislative elections on March 5, 1967, giving the party a total of forty-four seats in the National Assembly. Reelected to the Assembly from Puy-de-Dôme, Giscard adopted a more independent attitude. He roundly criticized de Gaulle's "strongman" regime for condemning Israel during the 1967 Arab-Israeli war, for its "free Quebec" policy, and for its determination to exclude Great Britain from the Common Market. Giscard opposed de Gaulle's call for proposed constitutional reforms to expand regional political authority and severely limit the powers of the Senate. Contending that de Gaulle's plan reduced the Senate to the status of an advisory council "without any practical effect," Giscard campaigned against the reforms.

When French voters rejected his proposals in a national referendum in April 1969, de Gaulle resigned, and in June, Giscard joined the new government of President Pompidou as Minister of Finance and Economic Affairs. Trying to stabilize the French economy, considerably weakened by student-worker disturbances in 1968, Giscard announced the devaluation of the franc by 11.1 percent. "Our monetary situation . . . exposed us to the threat of international speculation," he explained to the nation in an address broadcast on August 8, 1969. The devaluation was merely a "recognition of the franc's real value on the foreign currency market." That drastic and unexpected measure was followed by a five-week price freeze and by similar moves to curtail domestic spending and protect the devalued franc against inflationary pressures.

Reserves flowed back into the country, and in May 1970 Giscard announced substantial government gains in balancing trade, repaying short-term loans from foreign banks, and controlling inflation. During each of the next three years industrial production increased at an annual rate of about 6 percent—the fastest rate of economic growth in Western Europe. An optimistic Giscard predicted that continued economic expansion would give Frenchmen "the highest living standard in the world after the Americans" by 1980. His economic plan for 1974, outlined before the National Assembly on May 24, 1973, called for a 12 percent increase in industrial production, a 30 percent increase in the export of manufactured goods, and the creation of 400,000 new jobs.

To curb an inflationary spiral fed by the skyrocketing prices of Arab oil during the worldwide energy shortage in 1973, Giscard cut government spending, restricted credit, imposed a rent freeze, and placed a ceiling on corporate dividends. Concerned by the rate of wage increases, he asked management and labor to practise restraint in collective bargaining sessions. He announced several tax reform measures, such as a compulsory withholding tax, an increase in the capital gains tax, and higher taxes on upper-income families. Although Giscard was largely responsible for increased government allowances to families and to disabled and elderly persons, his critics argued that his economic policy ignored the problems of the poor. For example, in an article for the *Economist* (April 13, 1974), one foreign observer acknowledged the country's "remarkable economic growth," but criticized the economic system's "still more remarkable failure to distribute the fruits of growth equitably."

In addition to his domestic problems, Giscard was confronted with an unexpected international monetary crisis when President Richard M. Nixon suspended the convertibility of the American dollar to gold on August 15, 1971. As part of a currency realignment, he demanded the immediate devaluation of the dollar, and recommended a return to gold convertibility and fixed rates of exchange. In December 1971 the ten major industrial nations reached a compromise agreement to devalue the dollar, to appreciate other currencies, including the franc, and to permit fluctuating rates of exchange. The following September, at a joint meeting of the International Monetary Fund and the International Bank for Reconstruction and Development (World Bank), Giscard outlined a three-point French proposal for restoring financial order. The program included provisions for the adjustment of exchange rates, the convertibility of currencies, and the supply of new monetary reserves for the international system.

By January 1974, however, Giscard was convinced that an early reform of the international monetary system was impossible because of the oil crisis and the huge payments deficits in most countries. On January 19, 1974 he announced that the French government had decided to float the franc for six months to effect a *de facto* devaluation of 4 to 5 percent. He acknowledged that the surprise move, designed to reduce France's expected trade deficit for 1974, would cause "a temporary halt in the progress of the European economic and monetary union."

Following the death of President Pompidou on April 2, 1974, Giscard announced his candidacy for the presidency. Speaking from his home district in Auvergne on April 8, he pledged to champion "all those who reject bureaucratic society" and to make France "an equal partner of the biggest and smallest nations." His two main rivals for the office were Jacques Chaban-Delmas, the official Gaullist candidate, and François Mitterrand, a Socialist. Recognizing that voters were eager for substantial policy changes, Giscard promised "change without risk" and called for a "new majority" to replace Gaullism. His proposed domestic program, announced on April 19, emphasized social issues, such as guaranteed income for the aged, job security, equal rights for young people and women, the right to privacy, and income redistribution. In international affairs he favored closer cooperation among European nations, continued détente with the Communist bloc countries, and a cautious partnership with the United States. France must be "liberal in the modern sense of the term," he explained in an interview telecast by Europe One on May 13, 1974. He warned that without a union of European states, "by the end of the century none of our countries will be existing."

An admirer of Kennedy-style politicking, Giscard mounted an Americanized, image-oriented campaign. Youthful volunteers wearing T-shirts emblazoned with the slogan "Giscard à la barre!" ("Giscard at the helm!") canvassed neighborhoods to drum up support for their candidate; Giscard's attractive, energetic family staffed campaign headquarters and addressed political rallies; the candidate himself crisscrossed the country in a chartered jet and engaged in broadcast debates with his major opponents.

When no single candidate received a majority of the votes cast on May 5, 1974, a run-off election between the two top vote getters, Giscard and Mitterrand, was scheduled for May 19. Endorsed by the Gaullists as "the only defender of liberty," Giscard played on the voters' fears of Communism. Stumping the country, he charged that his opponent would "embark on collectivism." Mitterrand countered with his claim that Giscard was a tool of "these princes, these dukes, these millionaires [who] have not had a new idea in fifteen years." Eighty-seven percent of the electorate voted in the run-off, choosing Giscard by one of the narrowest margins in French political history. According to the official returns released by the Ministry of the Interior, Giscard polled 50.7 percent of the votes to Mitterrand's 49.3 percent.

In his election-night victory speech to the nation, given first in French, then repeated in English, Giscard commented on his victory. "One could have imagined a larger margin," he said, "but what counts in a presidential election is decision and responsibility. You have taken the decision. I will exercise the responsibility. . . .

You want changes—politically, economically and socially. You won't be disappointed."

After his inauguration in a brief ceremony on May 27, at which he wore a business suit instead of the morning coat hallowed by tradition, Giscard consolidated his base by appointing three trusted and experienced Independent Republican leaders and four nonpolitical technicians to key posts in his sixteen-member Cabinet. He appointed Françoise Giroud, editor of *L'Express*, as first Junior Minister of Feminine Affairs. As part of his program to make France "not only up-to-date, but ahead of its time," Giscard backed legislation to raise the minimum wage, to increase pensions and family welfare allowances, to reform the antiquated penal systems, to distribute free contraceptives such as *le pill* to any Frenchwoman who wanted them, married or not, and to "humanize" hospitals and homes for the aged.

Concerned by governmental infringements of constitutionally guaranteed freedoms, Giscard ended political wiretaps, ordered the destruction of existing dossiers, and recommended the establishment of an appeals system to handle citizens' complaints of violations of civil liberties. To stimulate competition and encourage quality programming, he endorsed the breakup of the state-owned radio and television system. He outlined a tough program to deal with France's galloping rate of inflation, the worst in the Common Market, with estimates ranging from 15 to 18 percent. Among his belt-tightening measures were an income tax surcharge, drastic cuts in government spending, a reduction in fuel consumption, and curtailed urban development.

Aware of the large opposition to his presidency, Giscard stressed the importance of the Gaullist-controlled National Assembly and promised to meet regularly with its members to explain and defend his policies. He supported the reform of campaign financing and the enfranchisement of eighteen-year-olds. "My idea is to have an exemplary political life, very democratic and very modern," he explained to George Taber in an interview for *Time* (June 3, 1974). In foreign affairs he seemed willing to cooperate with all friendly nations "to bring about a new international order." Within a few weeks of his inauguration Giscard negotiated trade pacts with Iran and the Soviet Union, signed several economic agreements with Great Britain, and discussed the revitalization of Europe with West German Chancellor Helmut Schmidt. A longtime advocate of mutual disarmament, he banned arms sales to those countries at odds with France's "liberal mission" and, succumbing to political and economic pressures, cancelled one of France's controversial atmospheric nuclear tests.

The quintessential patrician, Valéry Giscard d'Estaing is tall and slender and, despite his receding hairline, is youthful in appearance. A methodical and pragmatic man, he has been described by his colleagues as "cold" and "distant," and has been compared by one of his associates to a "calculating machine" because of his mental agility. For outdoor recreation Giscard enjoys hunting, skiing, and soccer; his domestic pleasures include playing the piano and the accordion. On December 23, 1952 he married the former Anne-Aymone Sauvage de Brantes, a descendant of the Schneider steel dynasty. They have two daughters, Valérie-Anne and Jacinte, and two sons, Henri and Louis Joachim. The Giscards, who do not plan to use the President's official country residences, maintain a house in Paris and two chateaux.

References

London Observer p2 My 26 '74 por
N Y Times p62 Ja 21 '72; p16 Ap 4 '74
Time 103:34 My 27 '74 por; 103:20+ Je 3 '74 pors
International Who's Who, 1973-74
Who's Who, 1973-74
Who's Who in France, 1973-74

GOTTLIEB, MELVIN B(URT)

May 25, 1917- Physicist
Address: b. Plasma Physics Laboratory, Forrestal Campus, Princeton University, P.O. Box 451, Princeton, N.J. 08540; h. 24 Lake Lane, Princeton, N.J. 08540

A distinguished, farsighted leader in one of the most challenging enterprises of contemporary science—the taming of the hydrogen bomb to meet the future demands for electric power in an economical and environmentally acceptable way—Dr. Melvin B. Gottlieb has been associated with important developments in high-temperature plasma technology since its infancy. As director of the Plasma Physics Laboratory at Princeton University, where he succeeded Lyman Spitzer Jr. on July 1, 1961, he has supervised the expenditure of millions of dollars in research. At one time regarded as a distant goal, atomic power plants generating 5,000,000 kilowatts of power, which exceeds the power generated by the Hoover Dam, may be a reality within this century. In Gottlieb's laboratories a complex of machines for accurately confining, controlling, and studying plasma has been built. Funded mainly by the United States Atomic Energy Commission, the work that Gottlieb directs is part of a concerted drive to bridge a stupendous technological gap between present-day fission and tomorrow's fusion reactors. "This is probably the greatest international effort of our time," Gottlieb said in an interview for *Intellectual Digest* (September 1972). "Almost every industrialized nation is working on it."

The son of Ezra Benjamin and Sara (Holtz) Gottlieb, Melvin Burt Gottlieb was born on May 25, 1917 in Chicago, Illinois. He attended the University of Chicago, where he majored in mathematics, was elected to Phi Beta Kappa and Sigma Xi, and took his B.S. degree in 1940. For two years after graduation he remained at the University of Chicago as an instructor in electronics. The Office of Scientific Research and Development, which was set up after the United

MELVIN B. GOTTLIEB

States entered World War II to provide research on scientific problems relating to the defense effort, assigned Gottlieb to the radio research laboratory at Harvard University. He carried out research on radar countermeasures as a staff member there from 1943 to 1946.

During the mid-1940's Gottlieb began to participate in James A. Van Allen's program on the study of cosmic ray particles, using balloons and captured German V-2 rockets that carried measuring instruments high into the atmosphere. In 1946-47 he led a University of Michigan team making observations on phenomena in the ionosphere. At the end of the war he had returned to the University of Chicago to teach the physical sciences. Then as a research assistant in physics there he continued his investigations in cosmic ray physics, concentrating on a study involving cosmic ray penetrating showers through cloud chambers. In 1950 he published findings that showed protons are primarily responsible for initiating penetrating showers and the ionizing particles initiate high-energy phenomena.

Awarded his doctorate from the University of Chicago in 1950, Gottlieb accepted an appointment as assistant professor on the faculty of Iowa State University, where along with teaching physics he made considerable progress on his research on high-energy particles in the upper atmosphere and space. In collaboration with Van Allen, who became head of the physics department at Iowa in 1951, he went on several expeditions under the auspices of the Office of Naval Research to study cosmic ray intensity near the north geomagnetic pole.

For their pioneering work on the measurements of the particles at the low-momentum end of heavy primary cosmic rays, Van Allen and Gottlieb used rocket-launched ion chambers. Geomagnetic theory had indicated a sharp drop in the intensity of heavy nuclei below a specific value of magnetic rigidity, a phenomenon that their measurements confirmed. Geiger-Muller counters were also used in another series of experi-

ments, for further measurements on the charged particles at high altitudes, with similar results. Later in the 1950's extensive measurements made possible with the launching of Pioneer rockets and the Explorer series of artificial satellites confirmed the decrease in the radiation intensity at extreme altitudes and showed it to be a part of what is now known as the Van Allen radiation belts.

Gottlieb's investigations so far, centered on the nuclear interactions of high energy particles at high altitudes, had been conducted largely in nature's laboratory. But in 1954 he became associated with the Plasma Physics Laboratory at Princeton, where he soon took over much of the responsibility for experimental physics as research associate on the then secret project Matterhorn, which aimed at developing the technology for nuclear fusion reaction. The study had its theoretical origins in the facts that vast amounts of energy are released, through conversion of matter into energy, when two deuterium (heavy hydrogen) atoms combine and that the supply of deuterium atoms in the oceans is so plentiful that it can provide energy for the earth for over a billion years.

In Gottlieb's opinion, continued growth in population and industrial production makes it impossible for environmentalists to reduce the world's demand for increased power. Since conventional sources of energy, such as gas and coal, will someday be depleted, he has argued, nations should make a greater effort to improve fission reactors, an immediately viable solution to the energy shortage, instead of deprecating that method of power generation because of pollution and radioactive waste. Although the operation of fusion power plants will also present problems of disposal of heat and radioactive products, Gottlieb has estimated that radioactive pollution will be a thousand times less than that now resulting from fission reactors.

The problem in harnessing energy from nuclear fusion lies in creating the conditions for the fusion reaction to take place and still be amenable to control. The positively charged atomic nuclei can overcome electric repulsion and achieve fusion only at temperatures of over 100,000,000 degrees, in the plasma state of matter. The plasma must have a particle density high enough so that the nuclei can get close enough and be sustained long enough for fusion actually to take place. More precisely, the multiplication product of the density and the containment time should exceed 10^{14} seconds per cubic centimeter, in order to achieve a net production of energy over and above the amount expanded in raising the thermal energy of the plasma to the required temperature and the amount lost through radiation from the plasma. The Princeton thermonuclear program has concentrated on the confinement of plasma in externally produced magnetic fields with thermal energy being supplied by induced electrical currents.

When Melvin Gottlieb arrived at Princeton, Lyman Spitzer's Stellarator model B-1 was in a stage of fairly early development. The magnetic field was produced by electric currents flowing in the 110 flat circular magnetic coils physically arranged in the shape of a twisted torus surrounding the discharge tube holding the plasma. The ensuing mechanical forces caused considerable packing and shifting of coils, destroying the accuracy of the magnetic field structure. Since the desired plasma energies and the confining fields could only be produced intermittently, the information relating to relationships between actual configurations of current-carrying condensers and the corresponding magnetic field was important. A redesign of pulse circuitry and the mechanical mounts supporting those coils led to a steady and reliable operation of the Stellarator at magnetic fields of increasingly greater strength.

One of the persistent problems impeding the growth of thermonuclear energy research has been inadequate financial support. The Plasma Physics Laboratory's annual electricity bill of $400,000 is only one indicator of its huge expenses. Melvin Gottlieb appeared before the Joint Congressional Atomic Energy Committee on February 10, 1958 to justify increased funding for the Model C Stellarator, then being built at Princeton, to enable its operation within a year rather than two as originally scheduled. In September of that year he attended the Atoms-for-Peace Conference at Geneva, Switzerland, where scientific exchanges led to worldwide declassification of thermonuclear research. The resulting extensive exchange of scientific information and collaboration on an international scale have partly offset the impediments due to insufficient funding.

Experience has shown that the fusion problem is tougher than initially anticipated. Gottlieb once described the undertaking as "probably the most difficult task that has ever been attempted, bar none." A major complication is the electroconducting behavior of the plasma. The fact that the electric currents flowing through the plasma also contribute to the magnetic field makes plasma temperature dependent on the shape of the magnetic field, or rather the geometry of the device itself. As Gottlieb explained to an interviewer for *Business Week* (September 12, 1970), the detection of cause-and-effect relationships, therefore, is almost impossible: "We cannot tell which results are due to the state of the soup, and which to the shape of the pot itself." The instability of the plasma has been the bane of scientists ever since they began fusion research. Even though nobody can predict which of the experimental techniques will be ultimately successful, impressive advances have been made since the 1950's in confining and stabilizing high temperature plasma. When the excellent results from the Russian tokamak device, a "magnetic bottle" to control fusion, were announced in 1969, scientists of other nations were skeptical of such significant steps forward until a British team spent six months checking them out.

In June 1972 Gottlieb announced that his laboratory had been authorized by the Atomic Energy Commission to build the PLT (Princeton Large Torus), a $13,000,000 fusion research device based on the Russian tokamak concept. At the end of that year results from experiments on a tokamak device in the Princeton laboratory called the Adiabatic Toroidal Compressor was also announced. A doughnut-shaped helium plasma was heated by electromagnetic induced currents and then a different set of magnets was used to produce yet another magnetic field that compressed the already confined plasma. That technique tripled the temperature of both deuterium ions and electrons. Scientists have projected that a plasma heated and compressed similarly in a device with larger physical dimensions could reach the ignition temperature of the fusion reaction. Recent developments in the field of superconducting alloys that are unaffected by strong magnetic fields are considered "very encouraging." The availability of magnets with resulting high efficiency may chop off a few years from the long wait for fusion power. In another successful experiment, announced in July 1973, using Princeton's Adiabatic Toroidal Compressor, the temperature of ions in a tokamak plasma was raised significantly by injection of energetic neutral atom beams.

Once the scientific feasibility of nuclear fusion as a source of power has been demonstrated, Gottlieb estimated in 1971, it will probably require at least fifteen years to work out and test engineering details. Even so, electric utilities have started chipping in cash contributions for development of fusion reaction. The Plasma Physics Laboratory, which has a staff of over 300 members, is one of four major laboratories where the Atomic Energy Commission's fusion research and development program is being carried out. The AEC, which has so far spent about $125,000,000 on the Princeton effort, also finances related work at the Los Alamos Scientific Laboratory in New Mexico, the Lawrence Livermore Laboratory in California, and the Oak Ridge National Laboratory in Tennessee, as well as several smaller laboratories.

Dr. Gottlieb has contributed articles on cosmic ray and plasma physics to scientific journals. Much of his work was not publicly known until after the declassification of fusion research in 1958. He is a member of the editorial boards of *Physics of Fluids* and *Nuclear Fusion*. As a fellow of the American Physical Society and a founder of its plasma physics division, he has presided over symposiums on the physics of hot compressed hydrogen and plasma physics. He is a member of the Atomic Energy Commission's standing committee on controlled thermonuclear reactions and also of the Air Force Office of Scientific Research's physical sciences evaluation group. The recipient of a NATO senior foreign fellowship in science, during 1971 he visited plasma physics research facilities in Italy, West Germany, and England. Some years earlier he had been one of the first Americans to visit Russia's Institute of Atomic Energy in Moscow.

The novelist Fletcher Knebel, who interviewed Melvin B. Gottlieb for *Intellectual Digest*, described him as "an informal type [who] prefers sweaters to jackets, wears his hair to the collar, dangles a pair of reading glasses by a neck cord and usually goes to work with a jackknife attached to his belt. ('I like to tinker.')." Knebel went on to say, "One has the impression of a man who enjoys life with a quiet self-confidence that needs no mask." He is six feet four inches tall, robust, and forthright in manner. His highly complicated and seemingly endless project has not shaken his enthusiasm or optimism. "My worst headache is fighting the government for more money," he said in answer to a question from Knebel. "... My big kick comes when a new favorable result comes in. That's a wonderful feeling. After that, I can take the headaches for weeks without complaint." Gottlieb and his wife, the former Golda Gehrman, who were married on June 26, 1948, have two daughters, Martha Ellen and Paula Gay. Interested in civic affairs, he once served as president of the Princeton Community Democratic Organization and as a director of the Council of Community Services in Princeton.

References

Bsns W p28+ S 12 '70 por
Intellectual Digest 3:6+ S '72 pors
American Men and Women of Science 12th ed (1972)
Who's Who in America, 1972-73
Who's Who in Atoms (1969)

GRANT, LEE

Oct. 31, 1929(?)- Actress
Address: b. 3000 W. Alameda Ave., Burbank, Calif. 91505

The American actress Lee Grant appeared to be well on her way to stardom in the early 1950's, when on the basis of the standards of "guilt by association" that prevailed during the McCarthy era she was suddenly placed on a blacklist of alleged subversives in the entertainment industry. Although she had been highly acclaimed for her performance in a supporting role in the Broadway production of Detective Story in 1949 and in its 1951 film version, she was forced to interrupt her promising career for some twelve years, during which she worked only intermittently on stage and in occasional independent film productions and noncommercial television. After her name was cleared in the mid-1960's, she began what amounted to a second career, giving distinguished performances in television's popular Peyton Place, in the Broadway hit The Prisoner of Second Avenue, and in a series of films, including The Landlord. Shaun Considine noted in After Dark (December 1969) that "on screen, Lee Grant has probably played more caustic swingers, shrieking shrews, and yenta-type broads than any other actress—with the possible exception of Shelley Winters," but that "off screen she's spirited, yet gentle; sophisticated, yet warm; and very, very much her own woman."

The daughter of A. W. ("Abe") and Witia (Haskell) Rosenthal, Lee Grant was born Lyova

Haskell Rosenthal in New York City, where she grew up at Riverside Drive and 148th Street. Her birthday is October 31; some sources indicate that the year of her birth was 1929; others suggest that she was born in 1928 or 1931. (The origin of her stage name is not quite clear, but she has insisted that it has nothing to do with Civil War generals.) Her father taught at the experimental Speyer School for boys and later became a realtor and deputy mayor of East Rockaway. Her mother, a model, actress, and teacher, who had come from Odessa, Russia as a young woman, encouraged her from her earliest childhood to pursue a career in the performing arts. Lee Grant made her stage debut as a child on January 20, 1933, when she appeared as the abducted princess, Hoo-Chee, in the Metropolitan Opera's production of Franco Leoni's L'Oracolo. By the time she was six, she was dancing with the Metropolitan Opera Ballet at $2 a performance, and when she was ten she was taking classes at the Art Students' League. She also attended the Juilliard School of Music for voice and violin training and went to the High School of Music and Art and George Washington High School, where she graduated before she was fifteen. Having obtained a scholarship to the Neighborhood Playhouse school of the theatre, she studied acting with Sanford Meisner for several terms. "I was overwhelmed by acting," Miss Grant told Tom Burke in an interview for the New York Times (July 5, 1970). "It was a religious experience to me."

Miss Grant made her professional stage debut as an adult at eighteen, when she toured in the national company of Oklahoma!, as understudy to Celeste Holm in the role of Ado Annie. In 1946 she appeared at the Camp Tamiment Summer Theatre in Pennsylvania and in 1947 she was seen at the Green Mansions Theatre in Warrensburg, New York in such plays as Liliom and This Property is Condemned. Her first stint on Broadway was at the Plymouth Theatre in the spring of 1948, when she succeeded Lois Hall in the role of Mildred in Allan Scott's Joy To The World. Later that year she appeared with Henry Fonda in a series of one-act plays at the American National Theatre and Academy. Impressed by her talent, playwright Sidney Kingsley asked her to read for the ingenue in his new play, Detective Story, but she was much more excited by a smaller part in the script, that of the neurotic young shoplifter, and persuaded Kingsley to let her play it. When Detective Story opened at the Hudson Theatre on March 23, 1949, she nearly stole the show from stars Ralph Bellamy and Meg Mundy, and critics called her the "find of the year."

Miss Grant left Detective Story to appear in February 1950 in the short-lived production of All You Need Is One Good Break, a new play by Arnold Manoff, whom she later married. After starring in the role of Raina Petkoff in a revival of Shaw's Arms and the Man, which had a limited engagement at the Hotel Edison's Arena Theatre beginning in October 1950, she went to

Hollywood to repeat her stage role in Paramount's film version of *Detective Story* (1951), starring Kirk Douglas. Her performance earned her the best actress award at the International Film Festival at Cannes, France, as well as nomination for an Oscar award of the Academy of Motion Picture Arts and Sciences in the best supporting actress category, in the spring of 1952. Meanwhile she had also appeared on Broadway in the Theatre Guild's production of John Patrick's *Lo and Behold*, which opened at the Booth Theatre on December 12, 1951. Although the play closed after thirty-eight performances, Miss Grant was singled out for critical praise. Commenting on her portrayal of Daisy Durdle, a "cheap and humorously garrulous housemaid," Brooks Atkinson of the New York *Times* observed that there was "nothing cheap in Miss Grant's discriminating acting."

Lee Grant's budding career as an actress was interrupted in 1952, when she became what television critic Bob Williams of the New York *Post* (April 13, 1971) called "one of the most innocent and tragic victims of the . . . political blacklist" inspired by the witch hunts of Senator Joseph R. McCarthy. Because her husband, playwright and novelist Arnold Manoff, was on the blacklist, and because she had spoken at the memorial service of a blacklisted actor, her name was also placed on the list of actors, writers, directors, and producers barred from working in films or television for alleged Communist connections. For the next dozen years she was restricted from both media, except for an occasional minor role.

During the long hiatus in her career, Miss Grant centered her attention on the role of homemaker for her husband and his three children by a former marriage. As she told Tom Burke in the New York *Times* interview: "Suddenly I had this whole lovely family to take care of. The blacklist freed me from thinking about what I should become or not become." When money was short, she acted on the stage, which was not affected by the blacklist. During summers she performed at the Mount Kisco (New York) Playhouse, as Sally Bowles in *I Am a Camera* in 1952, as Amy in *They Knew What They Wanted* in 1953, in the title role in *Gigi* in 1954, as Eliza in *Pygmalion* in 1956, and as Lizzie in *The Rainmaker* in 1957. On Broadway, Miss Grant appeared as Stella in Theodore Reeves' *Wedding Breakfast*, which began its 113-performance run on November 21, 1954, and as the widow Mrs. Rogers, in Arnold Schulman's *A Hole in the Head*, starring Paul Douglas, which opened on February 28, 1957 and ran for 156 performances.

In the fall of 1957 producer Fred Coe asked Miss Grant to read for the female lead in William Gibson's play, *Two for the Seesaw*. Although her New York City background made her eminently right for the role of the thirtyish Bohemian Gittel Mosca, she was not enthusiastic about the script and felt that a two-character play might not be successful. Deliberately, she read out of character and the role went instead to Anne Bancroft, who

LEE GRANT

opened in the play at the Booth Theater on January 17, 1958 to rave reviews. As Miss Grant told Robert Wahls of the New York *Sunday News* (July 12, 1959), "I was in shock for three days. It was a trauma. I'd turned down my biggest opportunity." She did, however, act as understudy to Miss Bancroft for a year and a half, and during the summer of 1958 she was her vacation replacement, but she turned down an offer to star in the play's London production because she did not want to be separated from her family. On June 29, 1959 she succeeded the departing Miss Bancroft in the role of Gittel in *Two for the Seesaw*, opposite Hal March, for the remainder of the play's run, which ended on October 31, 1959.

Miss Grant next appeared on Broadway in the role of Rose Collins in *The Captains and the Kings*, which closed after seven performances in January 1962. Later that year she toured in *The Tender Trap*, and in 1963 she played Ninotchka on a tour of the Cole Porter musical *Silk Stockings*. On November 14, 1963 she opened Off-Broadway at the One Sheridan Square theatre as Solange in *The Maids*, Jean Genet's early drama, and was garlanded by the critics, including Richard F. Shepard of the New York *Times*, who cited her "mastery of low-keyed, intense passion." In the summer of 1964 she was engaged by one of her favorite producers, Joseph Papp, to play the title role in Sophocles' *Electra* in his New York Shakespeare Festival production in Central Park. The following summer she appeared in Papp's Central Park production of *Love's Labour's Lost*.

Her motion picture career during her period of eclipse was relatively undistinguished. Cornel Wilde cast her in his independently produced *Storm Fear* (United Artists, 1956), which, she told Shaun Considine of *After Dark*, "had to be the worst movie ever made." In 1959 she appeared with Fredric March and Kim Novak in Columbia Pictures' *Middle of the Night*, and in 1963 she was seen as Carmen, the bookkeeper of the brothel that served as the setting of Jean Genet's drama *The Balcony*, in the film version produced independently by Ben Maddow in Hollywood. She also appeared in Maddow's *An Affair of the Skin* (Zenith International, 1963), and in the Allen Baron-Merrill Brody productions *Pie in the Sky* (1964) and *Terror in the City* (1966).

On television, Miss Grant gave a highly rated performance in the female lead, opposite Ben Gazzara, in *Mooney's Kid Don't Cry,* one of a trio of one-act plays by Tennessee Williams presented on NBC-TV's *Kraft Theatre* in April 1958. She also appeared on WNTA-TV's *Play of the Week* productions of *The World of Sholom Aleichem* in 1960 and *The House of Bernarda Alba* in 1961. In January 1964 she was seen on British television, as Lizzie, in a BBC production of Jean-Paul Sartre's *The Respectful Prostitute.* Apart from those productions, however, television provided scant outlet for her talents during the 1950's and early 1960's, other than occasional guest spots —on the detective series *Brenner* in 1959, on *The Defenders* and *The Nurses* in 1963, and on *East Side/West Side* in 1964.

For some time, Lee Grant had been attempting to clear her name, and she had become a leader in the movement to abolish the insidious blacklist altogether. Approached by members of a government committee who suggested that if she named her husband or others as Communists, she could be cleared, she steadfastly refused to do so. "I prepared a statement saying that I loved my husband, that our relationship was not a political one," she told Tom Burke in the New York *Times* interview. Finally, through the help of friends, she got her name removed from the blacklist and was able to begin a new career in films and on television.

In 1965 Miss Grant went to California to appear in the featured role of Stella Chernik in the prime time television soap opera *Peyton Place.* Her performance on the popular series won her the Emmy award of the Academy of Television Arts and Sciences as the best supporting actress of the 1965-66 season. She also resumed her motion picture career, appearing as a "swinger-for-hire" in the Norman Lear-Bud Yorkin comedy *Divorce American Style* (Columbia, 1967), as the widow of a murder victim in the detective drama *In the Heat of the Night* (United Artists, 1967), starring Rod Steiger and Sidney Poitier, and as Miriam Polar in the critically panned film version of Jacqueline Susann's best-selling novel *Valley of the Dolls* (Twentieth Century-Fox, 1967). For her next venture she went to Rome, where she spent four months on location for the filming of the comedy *Buona Sera, Mrs. Campbell* (United Artists, 1969), starring Gina Lollobrigida. As the tart-tongued but good-natured wife of war veteran Telly Savalas, Miss Grant received much praise from critics, and her comic exchanges with Savalas were among the highlights of the film. Back in California, she appeared with Ryan O'Neal and Leigh Taylor-Young in *The Big Bounce* (Warner, 1969), which evoked little enthusiasm.

Returning to her first love, the stage, Lee Grant opened in September 1968 at the Huntington Hartford Theater in Hollywood in Neil Simon's three-part comedy *Plaza Suite* with Dan Dailey. Capacity audiences caused the limited run to be extended for six months. While on stage at night, she spent her days on a movie set, playing the wife of an ill-fated astronaut in *Marooned* (Columbia, 1969), with Gregory Peck; and a lusty ranch widow in Joseph L. Mankiewicz's satirical western *There Was a Crooked Man* (Warner, 1970), with Kirk Douglas and Henry Fonda. Her performance in a *Judd for the Defense* episode entitled "The Gates of Cerberus," on ABC television in 1968, earned her an Emmy nomination.

In 1969 Lee Grant was approached by director Norman Jewison, who was then casting for his forthcoming film *The Landlord* and felt that she might be right for the role of Beau Bridges' mother, although he had some doubts as to whether she was old enough. Inspired by Vanessa Redgrave's recent performance in *Loves of Isadora,* Miss Grant worked hard at achieving the appearance, attitude, voice, and walk of an aging woman and persuaded Jewison to give her the role. When *The Landlord* (United Artists, 1970) opened, Miss Grant was acclaimed for her characterization of a WASP society matron exposed to a black ghetto environment and, in particular, for a memorable scene with Pearl Bailey. Gary Arnold of the Washington *Post* (July 5, 1970), referring to her "crazy balance between silliness and tough, hip self-awareness," called her the "comic sensation of the show." The performance brought her a second Oscar nomination in the best supporting actress category, in 1971. That year she was also twice nominated for Emmy awards, for her performances in two television films presented in 1970. Her next projects included the film version of *Plaza Suite* (Paramount, 1971), in which she was one of Walter Matthau's three costars; and *Portnoy's Complaint* (Warner, 1972), in which she gave a creditable portrayal of Sophie Portnoy, the caricatured Jewish mother, but which failed to match the success of Philip Roth's best-selling novel, on which it was based.

When *The Prisoner of Second Avenue,* Neil Simon's comedy about the trials of a middle-aged couple in the New York City high-rise jungle, opened at the Eugene O'Neill Theatre in New York on November 11, 1971 under the direction of Mike Nichols, Lee Grant received a generous share of the critical acclaim accorded to the production. In her role as the long-suffering wife of an unemployed former Madison Avenue executive, played by Peter Falk, Miss Grant was described as "tart, perky, and warmly sympathetic" by a critic for *Time* (November 22, 1971), and George Oppenheimer of *Newsday* (November 12, 1971) observed that she had "never been so appealing." She was among the nominees of the *Variety* poll of New York drama critics for a citation as best female performer of the 1971-72 Broadway season.

Returning to California in the summer of 1972, Miss Grant directed her energies to television and also pursued her goal to become a film director. With George Schlatter she codirected a television special, *The Shape of Things,* presented on

CBS on October 19, 1973. As a change of pace, she sang in a guest spot on the *Flip Wilson Show* shortly after her directing debut. She has also tried her hand as a theatrical director, staging a recent West Coast production of the play *The Adventures of Max and Jack* by Harvey Perr. Among her forthcoming films is *After a Long Time Lonely*, about two women engaged in a lesbian relationship, in which she costars with Tuesday Weld.

By her first husband, Arnold Manoff, whom she married in the early 1950's and who died in 1965, Lee Grant has a daughter, Dinah, born in 1958. Since 1967 she has been married to Joseph Feury, an independent film maker with whom she plans to collaborate professionally. Now an "ex-New Yorker," she lives with her husband and daughter on a hillside overlooking Zuma Beach, near Malibu, within comparatively easy commuting distance of the Hollywood television and film studios, as well as Actors Studio, of which she has been an active member since 1949. She enjoys painting, and her work has been exhibited in art galleries. During the 1972 Presidential campaign, she took part in benefits for Senator George S. McGovern's candidacy.

Delicate-featured and youthful-looking, with a full, distinctive mouth, auburn hair, and eyes that have been described as "blueish-brown," Lee Grant is slightly under five feet four inches tall, and weighs 119 pounds. Robert Wahls described her in the New York *Sunday News* (July 12, 1959) as an "early Luise Rainer . . . without Rainer's continental schmaltz." In his New York *Times* profile, Tom Burke observed that Miss Grant "smiles like a drowsy Cheshire cat, . . . sounding sometimes like an Americanized Greer Garson, other times like a softened Kay Medford, still other times like a funnier Phyllis Diller."

References

N Y Post p52 F 21 '70 por; p17 N 28 '70 por

N Y Sunday News III p1 N 18 '73 por

N Y Times II p9 Jl 5 '70 por; p1+ Ag 12 '73 por

Biographical Encyclopaedia & Who's Who of the American Theatre (1966)

International Motion Picture Almanac, 1973

Who's Who in America, 1972-73

GREENSPAN, ALAN

Mar. 6, 1926- Economist; United States government official

Address: b. Council of Economic Advisers, Executive Office of the President, Washington, D.C. 20506

Alan Greenspan, the chairman of the President's Council of Economic Advisers, is considered by many to be the high priest of the "old time religion," the traditional Republican economic policy of budget balancing and fiscal restraint. Before succeeding Herbert Stein as head of the three-

ALAN GREENSPAN

member council on September 1, 1974, Greenspan had for over fifteen years been president of the New York consulting firm of Townsend-Greenspan & Company, Inc. One of Richard Nixon's top advisers in the 1968 Presidential campaign, Greenspan filled several advisory posts during the Nixon administration and was nominated to his present position shortly before Nixon's resignation early in August 1974. His retention by President Gerald Ford was seen as evidence of the new chief executive's intention to pursue a conservative policy in the face of the nation's economic woes.

Classifying himself as neither a liberal Keynesian nor a conservative monetarist but as a "free enterpriser," Greenspan believes in as little government intervention as possible in the free market system. In common with such disparate economic theorists as Milton Friedman and John Kenneth Galbraith, he considers inflation to be the chief menace in the combination of skyrocketing prices and sluggish business activity that currently plagues the United States. Opposed to wage and price controls, the New York economist advocates continued tight credit, reduced government spending, and stringent budget cuts to solve inflation.

The only child of Herbert Greenspan, a broker, and Rose (Goldsmith) Greenspan, Alan Greenspan was born in New York City on March 6, 1926. His parents were later divorced. After graduating from George Washington High School (where he was two classes behind Henry Kissinger), Greenspan studied music at the Juilliard School and toured the country for a time playing clarinet in a dance band. (Another member of the band was Leonard Garment, who later went on to be one of Richard Nixon's law partners and a Presidential counsel.) After a year of one-night stands, Greenspan decided that he would rather go to college than be a musician. At New York University he majored in economics and received his B.S. degree *summa cum laude* in 1948. In 1950 N.Y.U. granted him the M.A. degree in economics, and that year he began doctoral studies at Columbia University under Arthur Burns, who is now the chairman of the Federal Reserve Board.

In 1948 Greenspan had also gone to work as an economist for the Conference Board, a non-profit research group largely supported by business. In that post he often advised businessmen, and in 1953 he left the Conference Board to form his own consulting firm with William Townsend, an investment counselor. Along the way, he dropped out of his doctoral program. "Study had become less and less interesting," he later recalled. Until 1958 Greenspan was vice-president of Townsend-Greenspan & Company, Inc. After Townsend's death in that year his junior partner became president and 99 percent owner of the firm. From 1953 to 1955 Greenspan was an instructor of economics at New York University.

Townsend-Greenspan began as a small operation employing six people, and its expansion has been carefully limited. "We have deliberately suppressed growth to maintain the quality of the operation," Greenspan explained to Lindley H. Clark of the *Wall Street Journal* (October 26, 1972). Unlike other consulting firms, Townsend-Greenspan has never aggressively sought new business. Yet its clients comprise about 100 major industrial and financial institutions, including most of the nation's top ten banks. The firm serves them with research, forecasts, and other economic consulting services. Townsend-Greenspan has its offices at 1 New York Plaza, a new building in lower Manhattan, and it employs a staff of twenty-five economists and other personnel.

"It is difficult, perhaps impossible to understand . . . [Greenspan] without understanding as well his twenty-year relationship with Ayn Rand and her philosophy of Objectivism," wrote Soma Golden in the New York *Times* (July 28, 1974). Greenspan met the controversial Russian-born philosopher and author of such best sellers as *The Fountainhead* and *Atlas Shrugged* in 1952. He has credited her with weaning him away from an early liberalism with her philosophy of Objectivism, which posits the morality and ultimate desirability of complete laissez-faire capitalism and what she calls "rational selfishness." "When I met Ayn Rand I was a free enterpriser in the Adam Smith sense—impressed with the theoretical structure and efficiency of markets," the economist told Soma Golden. "What she did—through long discussions and lot of arguments into the night—was to make me think why capitalism is not only efficient and practical but also moral."

As a friend and disciple of Miss Rand, Greenspan developed his profoundly conservative economic philosophy, which some observers have likened to a quasi-religious or mystical belief. According to Greenspan, the federal government has perpetrated a tangled web of mistaken policies, including commodity price supports, antitrust policy, consumer protection laws, welfare legislation, and even the progressive income tax. In a 1963 issue of *The Objectivist*—a periodical put out by Miss Rand's coterie, to which Greenspan contributed frequently during the 1960's—the economist wrote, "Capitalism is based on self-interest and self-esteem; it holds integrity and trustworthiness as cardinal virtues and makes them pay off in the market place. . . . It is this superlatively moral system that the welfare statists propose to improve upon by means of preventive law, snooping bureaucrats, and the chronic goad of fear." In a later issue (July 1966) he defined "the welfare state" as "nothing more than a mechanism by which governments confiscate the wealth of the productive members of a society."

Both Ayn Rand and Greenspan admit that the laissez-faire utopia of Objectivism, like other utopias, must be tempered by reality. Greenspan took his first plunge into practical politics in 1967, when Richard Nixon recruited the longtime Republican to be one of his top economic aides in the 1968 election race. During the campaign Greenspan held the title of director of domestic policy research for Nixon, and after the election he served as the President-elect's personal representative to the Bureau of the Budget during the period of transition between administrations and as chairman of the Task Force on Foreign Trade Policy. After Nixon took office in January 1969, however, Greenspan returned to his New York consulting firm, and, despite reportedly frequent importunings, refused to join the Nixon administration on a full-time basis. He did, however, serve as an informal adviser and accepted appointments to the Task Force on Economic Growth (1969), the Commission on an All-Volunteer Armed Force (1969-70), and the Commission on Financial Structure and Regulation (1970-71).

Because of his close ties to the Nixon administration, Greenspan became a frequently quoted forecaster of economic trends during the early 1970's. In September 1970, for example, the *Wall Street Journal* reported that in his latest newsletter to clients, Greenspan had contradicted the optimistic predictions of administration officials to forecast—correctly as it later became apparent—that sluggish economic growth would persist throughout the summer of 1971. On the other hand, at the same time he erroneously foresaw declines in defense expenditures with the winding down of the Vietnam war. "In the forecasting game," Soma Golden (New York *Times*, July 28, 1974) summed up, "Mr. Greenspan plays about par with the rest of the pros in his league."

Although he disagreed with some of Nixon's economic policies, most notably the program of economic controls that was instituted in August 1971, Greenspan campaigned for the President in 1972. In his many speeches and debates with Democratic economists, Greenspan accused George S. McGovern of fiscal irresponsibility in his advocacy of broad new social programs. After Nixon was reelected, Greenspan remained a frequent part-time adviser to the administration, serving as a consultant to the Council of Economic Advisers, the United States Treasury, and the Federal Reserve Board. He continued to resist joining the administration, however, and declined Nixon's offer early in 1974 of the chairmanship of the Council of Economic Advisers. The CEA's head since 1971, Herbert Stein, was scheduled to resign late that summer in order to begin teaching at the University of Virginia. Later that year, in July, Greenspan agreed to take the job, according to Hobart Rowen of the Washington *Post* (August 8, 1974), "after a desperate search by the administration failed to turn up an alternate candidate."

"I changed my mind," Greenspan told Soma Golden of the New York *Times* (July 24, 1974), "because some people in Washington destroyed my absolute conviction that I could do nothing to make things better." Before accepting the nomination, Greenspan reportedly was assured by the Watergate-besieged administration that it would pursue a stringent anti-inflation policy. Soon after President Nixon resigned in early August, his successor, Gerald Ford, announced his support of the Greenspan nomination, and the economist was confirmed easily by the Senate on August 21. He assumed his duties as chairman of the Council of Economic Advisers on September 1, 1974.

Greenspan became the first business economist —as distinguished from academic economist—to head the CEA since Leon H. Keyserling in the Truman administration. He is also only the second CEA chairman since the organization was established in 1946 not to have a Ph.D. degree. In accepting the $42,500-a-year position, the New York consultant is, by his own account, taking about a 90 percent income loss. While he is in Washington, his lucrative consulting firm is to be run by an executive committee of three women, M. Kathryn Eickhoff, Bess Kaplan, and Lucille Wu. (The three are longtime veterans in the firm, which began hiring women long before the Women's Liberation movement made it fashionable.) All of Greenspan's stock in the firm has been placed in a blind trust over which he has no control, and all profits made by the firm in his absence will be distributed to employees or charities.

Although some economists believe that the nation's stagnating economy is at least as much of a problem as its double digit inflation rate, Greenspan is confident that the economy will revive if the inflation rate is brought under control. To do that the government must cut spending, because deficit spending, in his view, is the primary cause of inflation. When the budget is in the red, the government must borrow, thereby competing with private business for money and driving up the money supply and interest rates. Although he acknowledges that the unemployment rate will rise for a time as the government pursues a stringent anti-inflationary policy, he questions the orthodox Keynesian view that decreased spending invariably leads to higher unemployment. He suggests that the opposite may be true. Ultimately, he believes, unemployment rates will fall if inflationary expectations are reduced and consumers feel confident enough to spend more. Greenspan is totally opposed to economic controls because they hold down business profits, thereby preventing new capital investment. He is skeptical of raising taxes to balance the budget, pointing out that in the past such tax hikes have usually spawned new spending programs. His economic prescription is an immediate cut in the 1975 budget and, in the longer run, a reexamination of such ever-expanding spending programs as Social Security and veterans' benefits.

Greenspan's CEA predecessor, Herbert Stein, had often been criticized for his overly optimistic assessments of the economy and his heated attacks on critics of administration economic policies. When Greenspan came to Washington, he pledged to "depoliticize" the council, explaining that he saw his role as a coordinator of economic research available to the President rather than as a public advocate of White House policy. Since taking office, the economic consultant has assumed a nonpartisan stance in his public statements, as well as a candor that observers have sometimes found disconcerting. For example, at one of the preliminary meetings that preceded President Ford's two-day summit conference on inflation on September 27 and 28, Greenspan drew catcalls and boos when he told angry representatives of the poor, the aged, and sick that "percentage-wise" Wall Street brokers had been most hurt by the nation's economic problems. Although most commentators had to agree that stockbrokers probably had lost more income proportionately than the poor, they almost unanimously felt that it had been tactless if not insensitive of Greenspan to make such a statement.

At the time that he accepted his appointment to the Council of Economic Advisers, Greenspan held directorships of General Cable Corporation, Sun Chemical Corporation, the Dreyfus Fund, and the Bowery Savings Bank, among other large enterprises. He has served as a member of *Time* magazine's board of economists, senior adviser to the Brookings Institution Panel on Economic Activity, past president (1970) and fellow of the National Association of Business Economists, director of the National Economists Club of Washington, D.C., and chairman of the Conference of Business Economists. In Washington he has been a member of the Secretary of Commerce's Economic Advisory Board (1971-72), the Security and Exchange Commission's Central Market System Committee (1972), and the GNP Review Committee of the Office of Management and Budget (1974). Over the years Greenspan has lectured widely on business and economic subjects and contributed to professional and business journals. He was one of the contributors to *Capitalism: The Unknown Ideal* (New American Library, 1966).

Brown-eyed and black-haired Alan Greenspan is six feet tall and weighs 180 pounds. He has been described as a candid, witty, articulate, and soft-spoken man with a mastery of business statistics. Although many liberal economists are put off by the strong ideological underpinnings of his theories, most are won over by his personal reasonableness. "Alan has never been one of those insufferable ideologues," one former Democratic official has said, "he's always willing to argue his points quietly and reasonably." Before taking up residence in Washington, Greenspan lived in a five-room apartment in the United Nations Plaza in midtown Manhattan. He usually arrived at his Wall Street office before eight in the morning and would often work a twelve-hour day. For relaxation the economist likes to play golf and listen to music, especially Mozart. Now a bachelor, Greenspan was married for about a year to the woman who introduced him to Ayn Rand. The marriage ended in divorce.

References

N Y Times p57+ Jl 24 '74 por; III pl+
    Jl 28 '74 por
Time 104:61 Ag 5 '74 por
American Men of Science 11th ed (1968)

GUINAN, MATTHEW

Oct. 14, 1910- Trade unionist
Address: b. Office of the President, Transport Workers Union, 1980 Broadway, New York 10023

When feisty, blustering Mike Quill, founder of the AFL-CIO's Transport Workers Union, died in 1966, he was succeeded in the TWU presidency by his long-time lieutenant, Matthew Guinan. A quiet but tough bargainer, Guinan dispelled any speculation about his strength when, during his first two years in office, he renegotiated all twenty-seven TWU contracts to union advantage, and in the years since then he has come away from the bargaining table with record pacts for his men. Particularly notable has been his success in dealing with the Metropolitan Transit Authority in New York City. In addition to the subway and bus workers of New York City, the 150,000-plus membership of the TWU includes mass transit workers in several other cities, and a variety of other transport personnel, from airline, railroad, and parking lot employees to taxi drivers in San Juan, Puerto Rico and workers at the government rocket installation in Jackass Flats, Nevada.

Matthew Guinan was born in County Offaly in Southern Ireland, or what is now the Irish Republic of Éire, on October 14, 1910, five years after Michael Joseph Quill's birth in County Kerry. The years when Guinan was growing up on a farm in Offaly were a time of turbulence in the Irish labor movement, which joined in the proud, bitter struggle for independence from Britain. Like many another Irish youth, he was inspired by the brave members of the fledgling Irish Transport and General Workers Union who risked their jobs in the Dublin tram strike of 1913 and their lives in the bloody insurrection of 1916 and 1919-21.

Leaving Ireland when he was eighteen, Guinan arrived in New York City in 1929, a few months before the great Depression struck and three years after the arrival of Mike Quill. In 1933 he became a trolley-car operator on the Kingsbridge (Bronx) line of the Third Avenue Railway, where he considered the pay, the hours (fifty-four a week), and the working conditions to be deplorable. After Mike Quill organized the Transport Workers Union, in 1934, Guinan, with some other workers, went to talk to Quill.

"Mike listened to us," Guinan recalled in an interview with Jack Mallon of the New York *Daily News* (December 27, 1967). "He didn't speak much, but when he did he knew where he was going. He instilled us with a lot of pride. We recruited the workers and when Mike felt we had enough strength we all put on our TWU button." When the Third Avenue Railway Corporation suspended Guinan and the other union organizers, the union struck. Eventually it prevailed, winning recognition from the Third Avenue Railway Corporation in 1937.

After six years as an unpaid union worker, in 1943 Guinan became a paid organizer. In 1948 he spearheaded the purge of Communists from the Transport Workers Union, and the following year he was elected president of Local 100, the largest unit within the TWU, with 35,000 members. The members included 8,000 drivers for private bus lines in New York City and its environs. For those drivers he won a five-day, forty-hour work week after a twenty-nine-day strike in 1953.

Meanwhile, in 1952, he was elected international executive vice-president of the Transport Workers Union, and in 1956 he became, in addition, secretary-treasurer of the TWU. In 1961 he quit the presidency of Local 100 to devote himself full-time to his positions with the TWU International, where he had become Quill's right-hand man. At Quill's insistence, the union's constitution was amended to insure Guinan the right of automatic succession. Four years later both Quill and Guinan were reelected to their positions at the top of the TWU International.

While Quill was playing a prominent role in union negotiations in New York City, Guinan traveled afield, to such places as Philadelphia, where he shut down the transit system to win union demands in 1963. In New York in January 1966 he was one of eight TWU leaders sentenced to jail along with Quill because the union defied a court order in calling a strike that paralyzed the city for twelve days.

Shortly after his release from jail, Quill died, on January 28, 1966, and Guinan took over the leadership of the Transport Workers Union. In the New York *Post* (January 30, 1966), Hope McLeod and Richard Montague commented: "Quill not only chose a successor in advance, but also moved to insure a smooth change of command. The new president of the Transport Workers . . . may have a bit of trouble forging some of the lower links in the union's large chain of command. But he faces no challenge for the presidency now and he has almost four years [before the 1969 union election] to consolidate his position. Great changes in personal style, both on the platform and at the bargaining table, are to be expected from Guinan. Quill was colorful, flamboyant, given to bombastic bellowing and conciliatory purrs by turns. Guinan is quiet, somewhat reserved. Quill was an artist with the fast quip. Guinan measures his words at length, tends to be terse. Quill basked in the spotlight. Guinan stood to one side and listened." Another observer, an expert closer to the union scene, said: "Matt's . . . been in the shadow. He undoubtedly will develop his own personality, give his own imprint to negotiations. The projection will be different."

And different it was. During Guinan's negotiating with the Metropolitan Transit Authority in New York City in December 1967, Transit Authority member John J. Gilhooley said: "Quill was like Rocky Graziano, who could knock you out with one punch, but Matt is like Jake LaMotta, who would doggedly and persistently just pound away at you and wear you down. . . . The bargaining this time is not being conducted in an atmosphere of a Roman circus." In the negotiations, Guinan won for the New York City transit workers a contract package valued at $70,000,000. It included a 5 percent wage hike immediately; an additional hike of 6 percent effective the following July; and pensions equal to half pay for workers with twenty years of service in the transit system.

In March 1969 striking ground service employees of American Airlines went back to work when Guinan won a pay increase of 25.5 percent for the key group of line mechanics, and the following month a strike at Pan American World Airways was averted when Pan Am agreed to a similar hike. In October 1969 the membership of the TWU voted to keep Guinan in the presidency. Two months later, when Guinan, like Quill before him, threatened a New York City transit strike, a writer for the New York *Times* (December 30, 1969) observed: "The words—'If we do not get a contract . . . not a bus or subway will roll in this city come 5 A.M., January 1'—were familiar, but to many who heard the president of the Transport Workers Union deliver the biennial threat they seemed out of character, and it was noted that his tones were far milder than his words."

The threatened strike was averted by a contract with the Metropolitan Transit Authority calling for an immediate wage increase of 8 percent, with an additional increase of 10 percent to follow on July 1, 1970. During the contract negotiations a writer for the New York *Times* (December 30, 1969) observed that as Guinan "wanders through the maze of rooms in the Americana Hotel where the present talks are being carried on he greets and is greeted by members of both negotiating teams with equal pleasantness."

Guinan negotiated a new two-year contract for New York City transit workers on March 31, 1974, seven hours before a strike deadline. The pact, covering 37,000 subway and bus workers, called for an immediate 6 percent wage increase; an additional increase of 3 percent on December 1; another increase of 5 percent in April 1975; and cost-of-living increases to be added to the wage base in July 1975 and January 1976. In 1973 and 1974 major negotiations were also underway with the Penn Central Railroad, American Airlines, and Pan American World Airways.

MATTHEW GUINAN

Matthew Guinan and Margaret Glynn were married in 1935. The Guinans, who still live in the Kingsbridge section of the Bronx, have three daughters, all of whom are Roman Catholic nuns: Mother Mary Eucharist of the Order of the Religious of Jesus, Sister Regina Matthew, a Dominican, and Sister Regina Margaret, also a Dominican. At the bargaining table he is, as those who have sat there with him have testified, a businesslike negotiator, straightforward in his demands, clever in his strategy, and determined in pursuing it. "He's a man of real integrity," labor mediator Theodore Kheel has said, "direct, and understanding of other viewpoints." He is especially strong in marshaling economic data to support his arguments.

Journalists have described Guinan as "short," "stocky," "granite-faced," and "ham-fisted." In both public and private life he is reputed to be even-tempered. In his speech there is only the slightest trace of an Irish brogue. His favorite recreations are fishing, golf, singing and listening to Irish songs, and watching news and documentaries on television. He is conservative in his tastes and his dress and usually serious in manner, but according to one associate he nonetheless has "a good sense of humor." The writer of his "Man in the News" profile in the New York *Times* (December 30, 1969) observed, "Understatement is the characteristic quality of his life. He is described, for instance, as being 'devout but not pious.' After leaving a bargaining session at the Americana on Sunday, he went to Mass and then quietly proceeded on to the union strike meeting." The same writer, observing that Guinan has not "lost touch with the rank and file," gave an example: "One associate recalls a taxi ride with Mr. Guinan during which the union leader chatted with the driver about his problems and his union needs."

References

N Y Daily News p60 D 27 '67 pors
N Y Times p31 D 30 '69 por
N Y World Journal Tribune p7 Ja 29 '66

HAMPSHIRE, SUSAN

May 12, 1941(?)- British actress
Address: b. c/o Michael Linnit, 179 New
Bond St., London W. 1, England

At first a priceless asset, the glow of innocence
that the British actress Susan Hampshire emanates
once threatened to become a professional liabil-
ity. Then, in the 1960's, her career took a gigantic
upward turn when instead of being cast as another of the giggling girls she had played in
dozens of films and also in some of her stage
productions, she was assigned the role of Fleur,
the not-so-innocent spoiled and spiteful darling
in BBC-TV's dramatization of John Galsworthy's
The Forsyte Saga. That role made her an international star. Although the television Saga has
been called a soap opera, it appealed to an audience interested in history and literature that followed Miss Hampshire's adroit portrayals in later
BBC series, her Becky Sharp in Vanity Fair and
Sarah Churchill in The First Churchills. For Fleur
and Sarah she won the American Emmy twice in
a row, in 1971 and 1972. London theatregoers
more recently saw Miss Hampshire as Nora in
A Doll's House, one of well over a hundred of
the parts she has performed on stage, screen, and
television.

Susan Hampshire was born in London, England on May 12 in the early 1940's, the youngest of four children of George Kenneth and Jane
Olive Hampshire. She has two sisters, Jane and
Ann, both of whom teach school, and a brother,
John, a restaurateur. Her father, a scientist, was
director of the Imperial Chemical Industry. Interviewers often describe Susan Hampshire as
"bright" and "brainy," but in childhood she was
considered slow and stupid because she suffered
from dyslexia, or word blindness, a congenital
brain condition that impairs ability to read. Although she had the advantage of attending London's Hampshire School, a private school founded
and directed by her mother, her education was
painful. "I remember standing up in class trying
to read Shakespeare," she has recalled, as quoted
in Time (June 22, 1970), "and I could hear all
the other children sniggering and laughing because I'd be literally making it up."

By the time the much-ridiculed child was nine
years old, she had made up her mind to win
respect someday by becoming a film star. At the
urging of her mother, who was probably aware
of the enormous handicap that dyslexia presents
to an actress, Susan Hampshire took ballet lessons for several years. But when she grew to a
height of five feet six inches, she thought she
would be too tall for a career in the dance and
with considerable relief returned to her ambitions
in acting. Her early training in ballet decidedly
influenced her technique as an actress, in her
tendency to approach each role from what she
has termed "the physical aspect," with concern
for the appearance and movements of the character. Dancing lessons also helped her to reach
the legitimate stage by way of musicals.

At about the age of sixteen Susan Hampshire
left school to join a small, obscure repertory company as assistant stage manager. She had learned
to read moderately well to herself and was able
to memorize parts. But first readings aloud remained so difficult a struggle for her that at auditions the interesting roles were assigned to other
performers. "As a result I often did mediocre
things with mediocre people," she told Catherine
Stott of the Guardian (November 1, 1972). She
made her stage debut at the Roof Top Theatre
in the seaside resort town of Bognor Regis in
April 1957 as Dora, the kitchen maid, in the
Emlyn Williams thriller Night Must Fall. A year
later she arrived in London's West End in the
small but attention-winning role of Cynthia in
the musical Expresso Bongo, which starred Paul
Scofield and enjoyed a fairly long run at the Sayville Theatre. In the less successful musical, Follow That Girl, staged at the Vaudeville Theatre
in March 1960, she portrayed the fluttery, beguiling heroine, Victoria.

From song and dance Miss Hampshire moved
on to the challenging roles of Elaine Musk, Miss
Kelly, Gertrude Gentle, and Charlotte Groves in
J. P. Donleavy's Fairy Tales of New York. She
shared the critical accolades for good performances given to all four members of the cast when
that comedy-drama in four acts, or four vignettes,
opened at the Pembroke theatre-in-the-round in
Croydon in December 1960. The following month
she played the same parts in a presentation at
the Comedy Theatre. Another Donleavy comedy-
drama, The Ginger Man, provided Miss Hampshire with her next stage role, Marion Danger-
field, the prim, middle-class, disappointing wife
of the title character, played by Nicol Williamson. Again she accompanied a Donleavy play in
a move from the suburbs to the West End, as the
production was transferred in November 1963
from the Ashcroft Theatre in Croydon to the
Royal Court Theatre.

In between her appearances in the two Donleavy black comedies Susan Hampshire had ventured to Hollywood, which she discovered, as
quoted in Time (June 22, 1970), to be "the land
of the Bottom Pinchers," of men who have "crocodile wives and ulcers and gold-and-diamond
rings," and long, entwining arms. Before leaving
the film capital in disgust, she portrayed a win-
some recluse of the forest whose amazing healing
powers lead children to believe that she is a witch.
As Lori MacGregor, she restores the health of
the title character, a cat, in The Three Lives of
Tomasina (1963), Walt Disney's adaptation of
a story by Paul Gallico.

Home again in England, Miss Hampshire
tended a flourishing career on the stage, screen,
and television, becoming so popular that during
1964-65 some thirty British magazines chose her
to adorn their covers. Her stage roles included
Miss Jones in Past Imperfect, which ran at the
St. Martin's Theatre from June 1964 into the next
year; Kate Hardcastle in a revival of She Stoops
to Conquer at the Ashcroft in Croydon in early
1966; and Helen Hayle in On Approval at the

Arnaud in Guildford the following summer. In a revival of Terence Rattigan's *The Sleeping Prince* at the St. Martin's in the spring of 1968, she played Mary, the character created by Vivien Leigh on the stage and by Marilyn Monroe in the film *The Prince and the Showgirl*. When Sir Noel Coward saw Susan Hampshire's interpretation, he reportedly said that she excelled her predecessors.

Meanwhile, moviegoers had the chance to enjoy Miss Hampshire's acting in a string of post-Hollywood films of varying merit, beginning with a British remake of the unnerving *Night Must Fall* (MGM, 1964). As the frightened Olivia, she was both understandably repelled and oddly fascinated by a hatchet murderer, played by Albert Finney. The comedy *Wonderful Life* (Warner-Pathé, 1964), which starred Cliff Richard, provided her first opportunity to do justice on the screen to her talents in singing and dancing. For her work in *Paris au Mois d'Août* (*Paris in the Month of August*, Films Sirius, 1965) Miss Hampshire, like the movie itself, received mixed notices. That French production, which had Pierre Granier-Deferre as director and Charles Aznavour as star, seemed coy and trite to several American reviewers. The British critic Harold Hobson, however, thought Susan Hampshire "altogether enchanting" as the vacationing English photographers' model who falls in love with a married Frenchman: "I have never seen happy English youth, with all that it can hide of sadness and disappointment, so beautifully or so touchingly presented as in Miss Hampshire's performance" (*Christian Science Monitor*, May 2, 1966).

The gifts that Hobson admired cannot be said to have found an adequate vehicle in Walt Disney's British-made adventure *The Fighting Prince of Donegal* (1966), in which Miss Hampshire, playing Kathleen MacSweeney, supplied the romantic interest. Her role, as a fake nun, was hardly more rewarding in *The Trygon Factor*, an involved Scotland Yard whodunit that was filmed in England in 1966 and released in the United States by Warner Brothers-Seven Arts in 1969. She joined an international cast for a featured but undistinguished part in *Those Daring Young Men in Their Jaunty Jalopies* (Paramount, 1969), about the racing-car Monte Carlo Rally of the 1920's.

Meanwhile, only too fully aware that many of her films were "pretty well junk," as she once described them in an interview, Susan Hampshire had taken advantage of the opportunity that BBC-TV afforded her in the middle and latter half of the 1960's to break away from a more or less one-dimensional debutante stereotype. Her experience on television had included performances in *The Improbable Mr. Clayville*, *The Lady Is a Liar*, *An Ideal Husband* and the title role in *Andromeda*. When offered the part of Fleur in BBC-TV's epic serialization of John Galsworthy's *The Forsyte Saga*, Miss Hampshire, though tempted, at first balked at the thought of spending nine months on a television role. But after reading some of the volumes of Galsworthy's novel and discovering that Fleur was supposed to be "the villainess of the piece," she changed her mind.

SUSAN HAMPSHIRE

"In films I've always played all those soppy, really boring girls who are very sweet and lovely and just say 'yes' and 'no' to the guy," she complained to James Day, president of National Educational Television, in a 1970 interview on TV in New York. "And all those girls are really there for is to fill in the gap, you know; they're not there for any real reason." The complexity of Fleur's personality therefore attracted her. She recognized that while Soames's daughter is self-centered, self-indulgent, rapacious, and often otherwise disagreeable, she is also intelligent and at times charming and lovable. Miss Hampshire's object was to show Fleur as "totally human."

Portraying a principal character in the last thirteen of the twenty-six installments of *The Forsyte Saga*, Susan Hampshire became widely known in hundreds of cities where the serial had been presented by 1970. In England the entire *Saga* was shown four times. "It's really incredible," the actress told Judy Klemesrud of the New York *Times* (March 30, 1970). "When the series was first shown in England, I'd walk out my front door and there would be people waiting, and they'd hug me and kiss me and say, 'Oh, you wicked girl, you wicked girl.'" In the United States the *Saga* no sooner ended its first run on NET-TV in the spring of 1970 than it immediately began a rerun. For her performance as Fleur, Miss Hampshire won an Emmy as the best actress in a dramatic series in 1970.

Then, as if to answer speculation about whether she could sustain the caliber of performance in her creation of Fleur, Susan Hampshire earned another Emmy the following year for her portrayal of Sarah Churchill in the BBC-TV Masterpiece Theatre series *The First Churchills*. In his review of the first segment, shown in the United States in early 1971, Alan Bunce of the *Christian Science Monitor* (January 11, 1971) praised the "wit and aplomb" of the performers: "Miss Hampshire's Sarah is comely and natural, lustrous even, . . . with a wry good sense that subtly foreshadows Sir Winston." The formidable challenges of characterization for Susan Hampshire were yet to come, as a redoubtable Sarah falls out of favor with an implacable Queen Anne in later episodes of that complicated historical drama set in the remote context of seventeenth-century England.

Although it did not arrive on the American home screen until 1972, Masterpiece Theatre's five-part serialization of *Vanity Fair*, made in England in 1967, falls chronologically in production between *The Forsyte Saga* and *The First Churchills*. The BBC lavished special care on its version of Thackeray's biting comedy of manners in Regency England, which was selected to be its first major venture into color television. Susan Hampshire as Becky Sharp portrayed a social climber who owes some of her traits more to her interpreter than her inventor. Several critics objected to a Becky Sharp who was both the novelist's unfaithful, predatory embodiment of evil and the actress' humanized, sympathetic victim of working-class deprivation. A critic for *Life*, however, approved: "I don't know how happy William Thackeray would have been with what Miss Hampshire did to his novel, but I was ecstatic."

Her television triumphs increased the demand among film makers for Susan Hampshire's presence, whether or not her talents could be fully employed. In Omnibus Productions' new film version of *David Copperfield* (Twentieth Century-Fox, 1970), notable for its distinguished cast of British stars, she played Agnes Wickfield, the girl who remains loyally devoted to the unhappily married David. Moving from Dickens' nineteenth-century London to twentieth-century Paris, Miss Hampshire next appeared in Christopher Miles's *Time for Loving* (1972), whose setting is Montmartre just before and during World War II. She then traveled to Kenya to portray the author and wildlife conservationist Joy Adamson in *Living Free* (Columbia, 1972), which tells the story of the cubs of Elsa the Lioness in a pallid and disappointing sequel to *Born Free*.

Having fulfilled a momentary desire to make "a nice family-type picture," Miss Hampshire went to Belgium to take on the three roles of Nancy, Alice, and Euryale in *Malpertius* (United Artists, 1972), a surrealistic psychological horror film. For her performance in that Société d'Expansion du Spectacle production, which was shown at the Cannes Film Festival, she was awarded the 1972 Prix de Cinéma Fantastique as best actress. The puzzling *Neither the Sand Nor the Sea* (Tigon, 1972), possibly of the same genre as *Malpertius*, starred Miss Hampshire as an older, discontented married woman in love with a moody young man who, after moving from the Channel Island of Jersey to Scotland, dies, or appears to die, but remains a lover. Derek Malcolm commented on the film in the *Guardian* (December 7, 1972), "It can't seem to make up its mind whether it is a naturalistic love story, fantasy romance or out-and-out horror fodder. . . . Still, Susan Hampshire does her considerable best."

During the month of November 1972 Miss Hampshire realized a long-held ambition of playing Nora in Ibsen's *A Doll's House*, when she performed in London before an audience that Harold Hobson of the London *Sunday Times* (November 19, 1972) described as "larger, more enthralled and excited" than he had ever seen at the Greenwich Theatre. Along with other London critics, Hobson commended Miss Hampshire's sensitive response to Ibsen's demand for a convincingly changing, maturing Nora to express the multiple values and themes of his drama.

On May 6, 1967 Susan Hampshire, who speaks French as well as she does English, married the French director Pierre Granier-Deferre, whom she had met at the time of the filming of *Paris au Mois d'Août*. Their son, Christopher Paris Granier-Deferre, born in August 1970, was only four months old when his mother took him along with her to the *Living Free* location in Africa. Miss Hampshire generally spends weekends with her husband in Paris and devotes most of the rest of her time to her career, living and working mainly in London. The couple have an apartment in Paris, a house and garden in London, and a house by the sea in Sandwich. Although Miss Hampshire is not domestically inclined, she enjoys cooking occasionally and collecting antiques for her English houses. Her other hobbies are gardening, music, collecting semiprecious stones, and the study of painting.

When Susan Hampshire visited New York in the spring of 1970 on the occasion of the rerunning of *The Forsythe Saga*, Eugenia Sheppard, fashion writer of the New York *Post* (April 10, 1970), observed that enthusiastic crowds welcomed her with "the fanfare the public used to give the old-time movie stars. . . . Not that she is heavy on glamor, mystery or any of the other old-time ingredients. There is no put-on or phony business about Susan Hampshire." She has brown eyes, reddish gold hair, and a well-proportioned 120-pound figure that enabled her to wear to their advantage the thirty, most of them glittering, costumes of Becky Sharp and even Fleur's dresses of the 1920's. Beautifully groomed in private life too, Miss Hampshire favors the Dior style, which she considers classical and practical.

In one of her interviews for an American newspaper Susan Hampshire said that temperamental behavior was repugnant to her. She seems to cherish her reputation for being professionally cheerful and cooperative. Along with her gaiety and at times dazzling frankness, she shows a serious-mindedness that startles some interviewers. Shortly before the death of Albert Schweitzer she went to Lambaréné to offer her help in his undertaking. Later she contributed financially toward the education of Biafran children, and she has a continuing interest in another educational project, to benefit dyslexic children, for whom she has been at work on an improved reading book.

References

Guardian p11 N 1 '72 por
Look 35:28+ F 23 '71 pors
N Y Times p50 Mr 30 '70 por
Time 95:53 Je 22 '70 por
Who's Who in the Theatre (1972)

HARDIN, GARRETT (JAMES)

Apr. 21, 1915- Ecologist; educator; author
Address: b. Department of Biological Sciences,
University of California, Santa Barbara, Calif.
93106; h. 399 Arboleda Rd., Santa Barbara,
Calif. 93110

GARRETT HARDIN

A persuasive voice for ecological sanity is Garrett Hardin, who in his lucid, penetrating, and often witty prose urges man to consider the complex problems that attend his populous inhabitation of the earth. Trained as a biologist, Hardin began writing about the moral and social implications of his science in the 1950's, and since that time he has ranged over a wide field including genetics, evolution, and the problems of pollution and population growth. A Malthusian who believes that human beings must curb their reproduction or face the ravages of starvation, disease, and social disorder, Hardin campaigned for the legalization of abortion during the 1960's and is now calling for widespread and effective birth control programs. His books include Nature and Man's Fate (1959), Exploring New Ethics for Survival (1972), and Stalking the Wild Taboo (1973), and he is the author of an influential essay on overpopulation entitled "The Tragedy of the Commons" (1968). At the University of California, Santa Barbara, where he has taught since 1946, he is professor of human ecology.

The younger son of Hugh and Agnes (Garrett) Hardin, Garrett James Hardin was born in Dallas, Texas on April 21, 1915. His brother John H. Hardin, five years his senior, is now a lawyer in Springfield, Illinois. Garrett's father was an office employee of the Illinois Central Railroad, a job that required him to move to a different city every few years. Hardin grew up in five cities in the Midwest, and he recently recalled that "as a result I grew up an unconscious and natural anthropologist in my own culture." The one fixed point in his childhood was his grandfather's 160-acre farm near Butler, Missouri, where he spent his summers. He has recalled the farm as a "lonely, but wonderful" place, where he worked hard and had time to read and think.

At the age of four, Garrett contracted polio, which left him with a weakened and shortened right leg. Because of that handicap he avoided sports, except swimming, in which he excelled. At Bowen High School in Chicago, he worked on the student newspaper, edited his class yearbook, and was active in dramatics. When he graduated from high school in 1932, he was awarded two scholarships, one to the University of Chicago and the other to a drama college. For a time he attended both schools, but then he abandoned drama to study science at the university. His decision was influenced by his realization that as an actor his physical handicap would restrict him to certain character roles. As a zoology undergraduate at Chicago, he was inspired by three of his teachers, the geologist J. Harlan Bretz, the ecologist W. C. Allee, and the philosopher Mortimer Adler.

After receiving his B.S. degree in 1936, Hardin did graduate work in biology at Stanford University and supported himself with a variety of fellowships and assistantships. He was a teaching assistant at Stanford in 1936-37 and from 1938 to 1942 and at Chicago City Junior College in 1938. He obtained his Ph.D. degree in 1941, after submitting a dissertation on microbial ecology entitled, "The ecology and physiology of Oikomonas termo, and the significance of Oikomonas in the nutrition of Paramecium multimicronucleatum."

In 1942 Hardin became a researcher for the Carnegie Institution of Washington at the division of plant biology on the Stanford campus, and for the next four years he did laboratory work on the culture of algae, the production of algal antibiotics, and the development of algae as a large-scale food source. He was appointed acting assistant professor of biology at Stanford University in 1945. Hardin withdrew from his research in 1946 because he had come to believe that the production of more food aggravates, rather than cures population problems.

That same year Hardin joined the faculty of the small liberal arts college that is now the University of California, Santa Barbara, as assistant professor of bacteriology. In 1950 he was promoted to associate professor of biology and in 1957 to professor. Since 1963 he has also been professor of human ecology there. For about his first fifteen years at Santa Barbara Hardin was mainly involved in updating the college biology curriculum. An important product of that activity was Biology: Its Human Implications (W. H. Freeman, 1949; expanded second edition, 1952), which became a widely used college textbook. During that period he pioneered a closed circuit television program in biology on the Santa Barbara campus, and he appeared in various teaching films, for which he wrote the scripts.

During the 1950's Hardin turned his attention increasingly toward genetics and evolution, and out of his reflections on those matters arose Nature and Man's Fate (Rinehart, 1959), which has been called one of the best general introductions to the problems of evolution ever written. In that book Hardin explains the history of evolutionary theory since Darwin and points out its provocative moral and social implications for man both now and in the future.

More and more interested in problems of population and preservation of the environment, around 1960 Hardin originated a course in "human ecology" to discuss those and related controversial subjects. One of the most explosive subjects he broached was abortion, and he began to urge its legalization in 1963. During the 1960's he lectured throughout the United States on the need to free women from "compulsory pregnancy," and his efforts undoubtedly contributed to the climate of opinion that resulted in the United States Supreme Court's historic January 1973 decision to legalize abortion on request.

Perhaps Hardin's best known work is his essay "The Tragedy of the Commons," which first appeared in the December 13, 1968 issue of *Science*. In it he makes a powerful argument for the concept that the human race must forfeit some of its freedoms in order to control population and pollution. Before man will do that, he contends, demographers must divest themselves of the belief, first popularized by the eighteenth century economist Adam Smith, that decisions individually reached will automatically tend to contribute to the social good. To refute that idea, Hardin draws on the work of a little-known nineteenth century mathematician who was able to show mathematically how a common pasture would eventually become overgrazed if each herdsman were allowed to decide the number of cattle he would graze there. The tendency would be for each herdsman to graze as many animals as he could because he would realize all the profits from the sale of each animal, while he would share with the other herdsmen the losses resulting from the overgrazing of the land.

"Such an arrangement may work reasonably satisfactorily for centuries because tribal wars, poaching, and disease keep the numbers of both man and beast well below the carrying capacity of the land," Hardin wrote. "Finally, however, comes the day of reckoning, that is, the day when the long-desired goal of social stability becomes a reality. At this point, the inherent logic of the commons remorselessly generates tragedy. . . . Each man is locked into a system that compels him to increase his herd without limit—in a world that is limited. Ruin is the destination toward which all men rush, each pursuing his own best interest in a society that believes in the freedom of the commons."

Hardin concludes that the commons can only be justifiable when population density is low. As human population has increased, he points out, the commons has had to be abandoned in one aspect after another. For some time the commons has been abandoned with respect to food gathering, with most farmland, pastures, and hunting and fishing areas restricted in use. More recently man has moved to abandon the commons as a place for waste disposal. Restrictions on the disposal of domestic sewage are nearly universal in the Western world, but we are still struggling to close the commons to the pollution caused by automobiles, factories, insecticides, fertilizers, and atomic energy installations. What we must now do, Hardin insists, is to recognize the necessity of abandoning the commons in breeding. "No technical solution can rescue us from the misery of overpopulation," he warns. "Freedom to breed will bring ruin to all." Nor will it help if we merely make appeals to the conscience, he argues, for those who are conscientious will only be outbred by the irresponsible. The only answer in Hardin's view is for humans to relinquish the freedom to breed through laws or other means of "mutual coercion mutually agreed upon."

Since its first publication, "The Tragedy of the Commons" has been reprinted in several journals and in more than thirty anthologies devoted to conservation, population, sociology, biology, political science, law, and economics. It has also been made into a Biological Sciences Curriculum Study film for instructional use. Enlarging on the ideas advanced in the essay, Hardin published *Exploring New Ethics for Survival: The Voyage of the Spaceship Beagle* (Viking, 1972), which consists of a straightforward discussion of environmental problems interspersed with four chapters of a science fiction parable about overpopulation. Hardin's thesis is that population control is inevitable, but it is up to us whether it will be achieved by humanly imposed birth control programs or by nature's more drastic methods. "In some respects, [this] is a disquieting work, masquerading under an innocuous title and written in witty, sensible prose," wrote Richard S. Lewis in *Science and Public Affairs* (November 1972). "Hardin isn't out to frighten anybody, but readers may find that their view of the future has been shaken. . . . The message of the book . . . is quite clear and credible. It is not likely to become dated by new facts and will not be easy for scoffers to deny." The book was nominated for a National Book Award in the field of science.

In his years of lecturing and writing, Hardin has come to believe that people resist certain ideas irrationally because those ideas are under a sort of taboo. He therefore sees himself as a stalker of taboos who through patience, cunning, and courage cautiously approaches the taboo and by exposing it to public thought and inquiry, strips it of its power. Around the concept of that "noble sport," he published *Stalking the Wild Taboo* (William Kaufmann, 1973), a collection of his previously published essays interlarded with commentary. The first section of the book includes some of the articles and lectures that Hardin created to break down the taboo against abortion; the second, called "Religion," consists of two essays satirizing the Roman Catholic Church for its failure to recognize the need for birth control. "Technology," the next section, takes on one of America's more recently created sacred cows, the space program, and the concluding section

"Competition," is an attempt to banish the taboo from the concept of competition, which Hardin sees as a basic human drive and a fundamental aspect of nature. "Unlike so many of his fellow scientists, he continues to prove in . . . [*Stalking the Wild Taboo*] that it's possible to write with engaging clarity, candor, perspective, and a refreshing absence of shrill zealotry masquerading as incontrovertible data, about the human implications of often complex and obscure scientific concepts," wrote Ralph Miller in *Equilibrium* (July 1973). "It's good to have a man who won't flinch from telling you the unpleasant truth but who also has a fine sense of how self-defeating it would be to ram it down your throat."

Garrett Hardin's other books include *Birth Control* (Pegasus, 1970), a review of birth control methods for the layman and a discussion of the moral and psychological issues connected with them; *Population, Evolution, and Birth Control* (Freeman, 1964; second edition, 1969), a series of essays, many by Hardin himself, which he edited; and *39 Steps to Biology* (Freeman, 1968) and *Science, Conflict and Society* (Freeman, 1969), two collections of reprints from *Scientific American,* which he edited and annotated. He is also a coauthor of *Fatty Acid Antibacterials* (Carnegie Institution of Washington, 1949) and *Laboratory Studies in Biology: Observations and Their Implications* (Freeman, 1955). Hardin has published some 130 essays and reviews in professional journals, magazines, and newspapers, many of which have been anthologized.

In 1952-53 Hardin was a Ford Fellow at the California Institute of Technology. He has been a visiting professor at the University of California, Los Angeles (1961), University of California, Berkeley (1964), and the University of Chicago (1970). Hardin often addresses professional societies devoted to psychiatry, semantics, fisheries, conservation, gerontology, education, and the computer sciences, and he has given the Nieuwland Lectures at the University of Notre Dame, the Remson Bird Lectures at Occidental College (1964), and the Messenger Lectures at Cornell University (1972). He was national visiting lecturer for Phi Beta Kappa in 1970-71 and Sigma Xi in 1972-73. When he was named Faculty Research Lecturer at the University of California, Santa Barbara in 1966, Hardin was cited for reinforcing "what he has called the 'humanistic' bearings of biology—the active, experimental understanding that one's choice of a subject matter, or a method of investigation, or indeed of a hypothesis is rarely without its moral implications, and that these implications need to be faced."

Since September 7, 1941 Garrett Hardin has been married to Jane Coe (Swanson) Hardin, who is active in community work for Planned Parenthood and the League of Women Voters. The Hardins have four children, Hyla, Peter, Sharon, and David. After visiting the ecologist in Santa Barbara, where he makes his home, Ralph Miller of *Equilibrium* wrote, "[Hardin] wears a string tie and a sports coat with a tiny gold pin in the lapel, a circle-and-arrow that looks like a Volvo ad but is really some sort of ecology symbol. If it were a Masonic pin instead, you'd take him immediately for a tourist from Kalamazoo." Hardin is five feet five inches tall, weighs 150 pounds, and has blue eyes and graying brown hair. In recent years he has been able to walk only with the aid of Canadian crutches. An amateur violinist, Hardin plays in the "Salsi Puedas" ("get out if you can") string quartet, with a fellow biologist and two philosophers. He also enjoys swimming and reading the novels of P. G. Wodehouse. Hardin is a Republican and a Unitarian. His memberships in professional societies include the American Association for the Advancement of Science, the American Academy of Arts and Sciences, the Ecology Society of America, the American Eugenics Society, the International Society of Genetic Semantics, Phi Beta Kappa, and Sigma Xi.

References

Equilibrium 3:30+ Jl '73 pors
American Men and Women of Science 12th ed (1972)
Hardin, Garrett. Stalking the Wild Taboo (1973)
World Who's Who in Science (1968)

HARKNESS, REBEKAH (WEST)

Apr. 17, 1915- Patron of dance; composer
Address: b. Harkness House for Ballet Arts, 4 E. 75th St., New York 10021

The role of patron of the arts, well-known in aristocratic Europe but rare in America, was adopted with flair and commitment in the early 1960's by Rebekah Harkness. While distinguishing herself as a composer of music, Mrs. Harkness has also directed her energy, her talents, and much of her fortune for the past fifteen years to the cause of dance. During that time her projects have grown more ambitious. When the Harkness Ballet was formed in 1964, she explained, "What I have in mind to do for the ballet will take not only a fortune but the almost total dedication of the rest of my life." Today she is the artistic director of a new forty-member Harkness Ballet, the creator of Harkness House—a ballet school and home for her company—and the owner of a 1,250-seat-theatre that opened in the spring of 1974 to present the Harkness Ballet and other dance companies to New York audiences.

Rebekah Semple West was born on April 17, 1915 in St. Louis, Missouri, the youngest of three children of Allen Tarwater and Rebekah (Semple) West. She has a brother, Allen West, and a sister, Mrs. Anne Whitemore. Their grandfather had founded the St. Louis Union Trust Company, of which their father, a stockbroker, was an official. After attending two private schools in St. Louis, the Rossman and the John Burroughs, Rebekah West was sent to a finishing school, the Fermata, in Aiken, South Carolina, which offered,

REBEKAH HARKNESS

she recalls, "a lot of fox hunting." She made her formal entrance into society in St. Louis and at the age of twenty went with her brother on a world cruise, a trip that confirmed her taste for travel and exotic places.

In adolescence Rebekah West had become fascinated with dance when she began taking ballet lessons as a means of losing weight. Her professional debut, in a St. Louis production of *Aïda*, however, brought objections from her father, who was offended by her scanty costume and put a stop to any consideration his daughter might give to a dancing career. Although she apparently felt, moreover, that she had begun training too late to develop into a first-rate dancer, she continued to love ballet and to take lessons. She also studied sculpting, which has remained a lifelong hobby. Her interest in the arts probably counterbalanced volunteer hospital work and similar community activities in which she was involved in St. Louis. In 1938 she married Dickson Pierce, an advertising man. "I had nothing *else* to do," she said of that marriage in an interview with Judy Michaelson for the New York *Post* (January 25, 1969).

After a divorce six years later and an interval of work in an advertising agency in Manhattan, Rebekah West on October 1, 1947 married William Hale Harkness, New York attorney and businessman. A philanthropist himself, he was a member of the Harkness family whose Standard Oil fortune has endowed many projects in medicine and education. When he died in the summer of 1954, Rebekah Harkness inherited his wealth and eventually the presidency of the charitable foundation named after him.

By that time Mrs. Harkness was gradually acquiring recognition as a composer. Beginning in about 1947 she had studied harmonic structure and composition, in Fontainebleau, France with Nadia Boulanger and in New York at the Dalcroze School and the Mannes College of Music. Her teacher at the latter school was Frederick Werle. She has written a hundred or more popular songs

and many orchestral compositions. A record album of her semiclassical pieces, *Music With a Heartbeat,* appeared in 1957. Much of her own music is inspired by her travels in Europe, Africa, and Asia—such as "Safari Suite," which premièred at Carnegie Hall in 1955, and "Il Palio," first performed in Washington, D.C. in 1957. Among her other compositions are "Mediterranean Moods" (1956), "Gift to the Magi" (1959), "Letters to Japan" (1960), and "Macumba" (1965). She has orchestrated Schumann's Six Etudes in the Form of a Canon, Schubert's Variations in B Flat, and Rachmaninoff's Cello Sonata, among other works.

The suggestion to write music for dance came from a friend, the Marquis de Cuevas, who commissioned a ballet score from Mrs. Harkness in 1957 for his Grand Ballet, to be performed the following year at the Brussels World's Fair. The success of the score, called "Voyage vers l'amour," which earned twelve curtain calls, may have encouraged her to begin in 1959 a foundation of her own, devoted to dance. One of the first projects of the new Rebekah Harkness Foundation revived Jerome Robbins' Ballets U.S.A. in 1961 and enabled the choreographer to create a new work for his company, tour Europe, and give a season in New York. Robbins' aim, to take American dance to the major cities and arts festivals of Europe, matched Mrs. Harkness' own interest in defining an American style of ballet and sharing it with audiences in other countries. In 1962 the foundation gave Pearl Primus backing for a four-month tour of west and central Africa, where Miss Primus put together performances using local dancers and musicians.

For Mrs. Harkness, to give to any project has always meant a close involvement with the work itself and the people concerned in it. She and her third husband, Dr. Benjamin Harrison Kean, whom she married in 1961, accompanied Miss Primus on part of the African tour. Later in the year Mrs. Harkness took an entire dance company under her wing when she created the first summer workshop at her Watch Hill, Rhode Island estate. The project encompassed twenty dancers from the Robert Joffrey Company (begun on a shoestring in 1952), along with several other ballet soloists, five or six choreographers, musicians, and designers, all of whom were to spend twelve weeks working together on possible new dances for the Joffrey repertory. Rarely had a dance company had enough time, amenities, collaborating artists, production money, and rehearsal wages for the dancers, to concentrate just on creating dances. "The step made by Mrs. Kean, no matter what the result . . . is to be cherished by the choreographers and cheered by the dance world itself," Walter Terry wrote in the New York *Herald Tribune* (May 13, 1962). During the session of that workshop Alvin Ailey choreographed *Feast of Ashes;* Brian Macdonald, *Time Out of Mind;* Gerald Arpino, *Sea Shadow;* and Joffrey himself, *Gamelan.*

During the next two years the Rebekah Harkness Foundation sponsored the Robert Joffrey Ballet, financing its tour of the Middle East, Europe, and Russia under the auspices of the United States State Department. At home the foundation helped several other projects aimed at increasing the dance public: several dance companies touring public schools, a winter season of modern dance at Hunter College, and a free, open-air summer dance festival as part of the New York Shakespeare Festival at Central Park's Delacorte Theater. The dance festival, which Mrs. Harkness began in 1962, continued annually until 1972, although she withdrew her support in 1969.

Rebekah Harkness may well have continued as a fairy godmother to the dance world in general if disagreements over artistic direction had not led to a break with Robert Joffrey, who charged that Mrs. Harkness had presented him with an ultimatum to change the name of the Joffrey Ballet to the Harkness Ballet. Deciding to consolidate her efforts in a new company, in April 1964 she announced the formation of the Harkness Ballet, endowed by both of her foundations with about $2,000,000. Fourteen of the twenty-six dancers in the new company were Joffrey dancers under contract to Mrs. Harkness, who denied that she had intended to "raid" Joffrey's company or take over his repertory. George Skibine left Europe, where he had been ballet master in opera companies, to become director of the new Harkness Ballet, which Mrs. Harkness wanted to be "an open forum" to many fine choreographers, dancers, and musicians. In residence with the company during the 1964 summer workshop at Watch Hill were Vera Volkova, Alexandra Danilova, Alvin Ailey, Brian Macdonald, Michael Smuin, Richard Wagner, Thomas Andrew, and Donald Saddler.

To give her dancers a working home in New York, in 1964 Rebekah Harkness bought the former Thomas J. Watson town house, which she named Harkness House for Ballet Arts. The transformation of the five-story, thirty-five-room mansion, built in 1896, was planned by Mrs. Harkness on the elegant scale of the European royal dance schools and was completed in November 1965. Resplendent with opulent details, the house has a wide marble staircase, an enormous crystal chandelier, ornately painted ceilings in the dance studios, French blue-silk window shades, and works of art on the subject of dance. It also provides a cafeteria and reading, listening, and massage rooms for the students. Mrs. Harkness explained to Jack Anderson of Dance Magazine (February 1966) that she wanted to impress potential ballet benefactors: "I hope the beauty of Harkness House will persuade some of these people that ballet need not be dingy and that by their patronage, they are contributing to the splendid and glamorous. I want to make sure ballet has status."

The Harkness emphasis on glamour also affected the new company's repertory. Some of its early ballets were "tastelessly overproduced, to the detriment not only of their visual attractiveness but also of their choreographic concepts," in the opinion of Marcia B. Siegel in Arts in Society

(Summer-Fall 1968). The critic Clive Barnes, although he complimented the company on its "smart professional look," thought that the attempted union of traditional and modern styles gave it the look of "going in two directions at once" (Dance Magazine, April 1965). After the company's first New York season in 1967, critics praised the soloists—Finis Jhung, Helgi Tomasson, Lone Isaksen, Brunilda Ruiz, Elisabeth Carroll, and Annette av Paul—and some of the dances—The Abyss, Monument for a Dead Boy, Zealous Variations, and Canto Indio. Douglas M. Davis of the National Observer (November 20, 1967) found that the principals "tower above their choreography, . . . which is bland and uninspired for the most part." Some critics protested that the repertory as a whole was overburdened with violent themes, and Doris Hering wrote in Dance Magazine (January 1968) that the dances "seemed to hark back to the anti-Victorian, neo-Freudian churnings of the thirties and early forties." Still, in spite of unresolved questions about the repertory, the public was aware of a major new ballet company that had emerged in the unheard-of period of two and a half years.

As the company grew, Mrs. Harkness' close involvement with artistic direction caused several shifts in its leadership. Brian Macdonald replaced the original director, Skibine, in 1965, and in 1968 Macdonald himself was replaced from the inside by the company soloist Lawrence Rhodes. A year later Rhodes, trying to dance major roles as well as direct the company, brought in Banjamin Harkarvy, a founder-director of the Netherlands Dance Theatre to codirect. The team of Harkarvy and Rhodes proved to be unusually effective—the dancers' morale and artistic standards improved and the repertory became more balanced when the addition of several Harkarvy ballets gave it the abstract and classical slant it had lacked. A New York season in the fall of 1969 was appreciatively and favorably received.

Mrs. Harkness has always wanted her company to be versatile. "We're a pioneering company. We try Adagio, jazz, Spanish, Hindu, modern, ethnic; we hope to find, eventually, a free American style," she once told Agnes Ash of Women's Wear Daily (March 30, 1969). But, it has been theorized, Rhodes' and Harkarvy's success with the company might have caused Mrs. Harkness to consider the "pioneering" expendable, because in March 1970 she called the company home from midpoint in a European tour, explaining that problems in the current economic conditions called for a reevaluation. Only sixteen of the thirty-one company dancers were offered new contracts, but almost all of the dancers chose to leave, once they understood that the company was being abruptly dissolved. No clear story of Mrs. Harkness' motives has ever been told in the press, and speculations on the subject have heightened the controversy attached to the Harkness name. The development of the Harkness Youth Dancers, first seen publicly in the 1968 summer dance festival at the Delacorte, may have influenced Mrs. Harkness' decision to abandon the company under Rhodes and Harkarvy. "I think I just may find myself with a second company," she said at the opening of the festival, as reported by Walter Terry in the *Saturday Review* (September 28, 1968). Through a merger of the two troupes, in May 1970 the Youth Dancers, trained almost exclusively at the Harkness School, became the nucleus of the new Harkness Ballet under the artistic direction of Rebekah Harkness, with Ben Stevenson as resident choreographer.

In addition to Harkness House, which continues as a school for groups of trainees, Mrs. Harkness owns a theatre that she bought in 1972, the former RKO Colonial movie theatre at Broadway and 62nd Street. Decorated with customary Harkness luxuriance, it boasts marble and crystal imported from Spain, wall coverings and velvet seats in a shade of blue borrowed from the Maryinsky Theatre in Leningrad, and a 3,500-square-foot stage. It is the first theatre in New York designed only for dance. The Harkness Ballet Foundation, Inc., which on January 1, 1974 became the new name of the former Rebekah Harkness Foundation, administers the theatre. The first dance company to perform in the theatre, on April 9, 1974, was the Harkness Ballet, now under the choreographer Vicente Nebrada, who has added several of his own works to the repertory.

Not only artistic director of the Harkness Ballet, Rebekah Harkness is also president of both her own and her former husband's foundations. She is proud of the grants to medicine made through the William Hale Harkness Foundation, such as those for the construction of the William Hale Harkness Medical Research Building at the New York Hospital, Dr. Irving S. Cooper's research on Parkinson's Disease, and the work of the New York University Medical Center's Institute of Rehabilitation Medicine. Mrs. Harkness serves on the board of directors of the Society to Beautify the Nation's Capitol, the President's Council on Youth Opportunities, and the John F. Kennedy Center for the Performing Arts in Washington, D.C. Her awards include New York City's Bronze Medal of Appreciation and its Handel Award, the Marquis de Cuevas Prize of the Université de la Dance in Paris, and the Shield award of the American Indian and Eskimo Cultural Foundation. In 1966 she was named an Officier Merité Culturel et Artistique, France.

Rebekah Harkness is the mother of three children—Allen Pierce and Mrs. Terry Pierce McBride, by her first marriage; and Edith Harkness, by her second marriage. She was divorced from Dr. Kean in 1965. Besides her homes in Manhattan and Watch Hill, she has residences in Sneden's Landing, New York; Gstaad, Switzerland; and Nassau, the Bahamas. She has little time or regard for jet-set events, and she customarily rises at 6 A.M. to work on composing. Six days a week she takes dancing lessons. For mental and physical well-being she practises yoga. She is a blond, slender, smartly dressed woman who stands five feet seven and a half inches tall. Reportedly somewhat shy, though on occasion redoubtable, Mrs. Harkness has appeared only two or three times on the stage, most recently, in the fall of 1973, as a flamenco dancer during a benefit program in New York. She sometimes writes scores for her choreographers' dances. "I am an artist," she once asserted, as quoted in the New York *Times* (April 18, 1964). "I see no reason why I shouldn't participate when and where I have the ability to contribute. The set-up is like a large family, and why should one member be forbidden to use the kitchen if he has an interesting new recipe to try out?"

References

Dance Mag 40:49+ F '66 por
N Y Herald Tribune mag p35 Ag 16 '64 por
N Y Post p25 Ja 25 '69 por
N Y Times p39 Ag 26 '66 por; p50 Jl 18 '71 por
Newsday A p3 Ag 29 '69 pors
Newsweek 70:100 N 13 '67 por
Chujoy, A., and Manchester, P.W., eds. Dance Encyclopedia (1967)
Who's Who of American Women, 1972-73

HAUGHTON, DANIEL J(EREMIAH)

Sept. 7, 1911- Corporation executive
Address: b. Lockheed Aircraft Corp., 2555 Hollywood Way, Burbank, Calif. 91503; h. 12956 Blairwood Dr., Studio City, Calif. 91604

An aerospace executive who, in his own words, "came up by hard work," Daniel J. Haughton, board chairman of Lockheed Aircraft Corporation since 1967, has won wide recognition in the business world for his effective handling of the crises that have beset the company in recent years. Totally dedicated to Lockheed, Haughton has taken risks by encouraging the development of new designs of commercial and military aircraft. Those risks have taken Lockheed to the brink of bankruptcy, but Haughton finds uncertainty a norm in the aerospace business. "We're in the business of taking risks—the business of developing new systems," he once said. "Engineering is not an exact science, and we have to invent as we go along."

Daniel Jeremiah Haughton, the son of Gayle Haughton Sr. and Mattie (Davis) Haughton, was born on September 7, 1911 near the town of Dora, in Walker County, Alabama, in the coal region northwest of Birmingham. His father was a farmer who also worked as a timekeeper at a coal mine and ran a country store. As a boy, Daniel Haughton helped on the family farm and in the store, did odd jobs at the coal mines, and sold newspapers. By his own admission, he further enhanced his financial status by lending money to friends at usurious rates, charging as much as 20 percent interest for a two-week loan.

Haughton did not enter school until he was eight, because, as he told Harold B. Meyers of *Fortune* (August 1, 1969), "I just plain wanted to stay on the farm and look after my calves and goats." He spent six years in grammar school and three years in high school and then studied accounting at the University of Alabama, working his way as a loader and dynamiter in the coal mines, and as a bus driver. He graduated with a B.S. degree in commerce and business administration in 1933 and then headed for the West Coast.

Although jobs were scarce during those Depression years, Haughton found work with the Dwight P. Robinson Construction Company at Trona, California, which employed him in 1933-34 as a timekeeper and distribution checker. After working in 1934-35 as timekeeper and payroll superviser with the American Potash and Chemical Corporation at Trona, Haughton spent a year in a supervisory training program as a member of the "flying squadron" production group with the Goodyear Tire and Rubber Company in Los Angeles. Having decided to enter the aircraft industry, he worked from 1936 to 1939 as a cost accountant with Consolidated Aircraft Corporation in San Diego.

Haughton began his long association with the Lockheed Aircraft Corporation in 1939, when he was hired at its Burbank, California headquarters as a systems analyst and coordinator, responsible for establishing procedures for accounting, industrial security, production controls, and manpower. At the time that Haughton joined Lockheed, the corporation was headed by board chairman Robert Gross who, with his brother Courtlandt Gross and a group of other investors, had bought Lockheed for $40,000 in 1932. Courtlandt Gross later recalled, as quoted in *Fortune* (August 1, 1969): "I first met Dan Haughton in 1939. . . . It was evident then that he had managerial and leadership qualities, loyalty, and very good judgment. . . . He proved himself a good soldier on every assignment. He was always willing to subordinate his own time and rest to the overall good of the company."

Moving up through the ranks at Lockheed at a time when the aircraft industry was experiencing its World War II boom, Haughton served from 1941 to 1943 as assistant to the vice-president of Vega Aircraft Corporation, a Lockheed subsidiary, with responsibility for planning, procurement, production, and deliveries. In 1943 he was works manager at Vega, with direct responsibility for production programs. As Lockheed's assistant general works manager from 1944 to 1946, Haughton assumed production responsibilities at the corporation's factories. He was assistant to the vice-president in charge of manufacturing from 1946 to 1949.

Haughton's talent for salesmanship was tested during his tenure, from 1949 to 1951, as president of two Lockheed subsidiaries—Airquipment Company and Aerol Company—that were later sold. Both companies had been losing money in 1949, but under Haughton's management they were soon financially solvent. In 1951 Haughton was named assistant general manager of Lockheed's Georgia Division in Marietta. He became general manager of the Marietta operation in January 1952 and was elected a Lockheed vice-president in May of that year.

DANIEL J. HAUGHTON

In 1956 Haughton moved back to Southern California to assume the post of executive vice-president, with authority over all of Lockheed's operating divisions and subsidiaries. He became a director of the company in 1958. When Robert Gross died in September 1961 and Courtlandt Gross became chairman of the board, Haughton succeeded the latter as president of Lockheed. On May 2, 1967, three months after Courtlandt Gross announced his coming retirement, Haughton replaced him as chairman of the board.

When Haughton became chairman, Lockheed was the third-largest aerospace firm in the United States, despite the fact that it had abandoned the commercial passenger plane market in 1962 to concentrate on military equipment. Its sales volume—$2.1 billion in 1966—was exceeded at the time only by those of Boeing and the McDonnell-Douglas Corporation. Lockheed not only produced missiles, including the Navy's Polaris and Poseidon, but space and electronic equipment. It was even involved in shipbuilding.

Haughton and his second-in-command, the company's president A. Carl Kotchian, took control of Lockheed with optimism and enthusiasm. Their announced goal of doubling sales in ten years was based on current defense contracts, which included orders for a super-transport plane, the C-5A, and a high-speed helicopter, the Cheyenne. In addition, in 1968 Lockheed embarked on a program to recapture some commercial airline business with the development of the L-1011, or Tri-Star, jet passenger plane. But Lockheed soon ran into serious difficulties.

Its troubles began with the Cheyenne rigid-rotor helicopter, which Lockheed had started to develop in 1957. In 1966 the Army, needing a helicopter to be used in close support of combat troops, signed a contract with Lockheed for the Cheyenne, then still in the experimental stage. The confidence of Lockheed officials in the design prompted them to accept a contract that limited the cost to the government to no more than 115 percent of the bid price. But unforeseen delays and problems in development drove costs up, so that Lockheed had to absorb over $54,-000,000 in excess costs. Despite delays, however, in 1968 the Army awarded Lockheed the contract for production of 375 Cheyenne planes. Then, early in 1969, the Army began to complain about the Cheyenne's performance, and in May of that year, Army officials suddenly announced the cancellation of the production contract. Facing a possible $68,000,000 loss, Lockheed officials went to court to contest the Army's action.

About that time, a controversy arose over the super-transport, the C-5A Galaxy. The largest plane in the world, the C-5A can carry virtually every type of equipment required by an army division, including tanks and helicopters. When Lockheed made its bid on the C-5A in 1965, the Pentagon predicted that the cost of its development and production would be $2.2 billion, but Lockheed submitted a low bid of $1.9 billion and won a contract for the production of 115 C-5A planes.

In the spring of 1969 both the Pentagon and Lockheed agreed that, mainly as a result of inflation, the cost of the 115 planes would be $3.2 billion, as compared with the 1965 bid of $1.9 billion. The Pentagon insisted that under those conditions Lockheed might lose as much as $285,000,000, but Haughton went before the Senate and House Armed Services committees to assert, on the basis of production-cost estimates and contract interpretations, that Lockheed's losses would amount to only $13,000,000. He expressed the hope that future sales of the C-5A as well as the production of a civilian version of the plane would enable the company to reap a "normal profit" from the overall program.

But although Lockheed, with a labor force of 97,000 and government contracts totaling $2.4 billion in 1969, had become the largest defense contractor in the United States, the company appeared to be moving rapidly toward bankruptcy. A financial report indicated that while in 1968 Lockheed had made a profit of $44,500,000, in the following year it suffered losses amounting to $36,200,000. In March 1970 Haughton sent a letter to the Defense Department, in which he contended that Lockheed had run out of operating capital and demanded that the Pentagon provide interim financing of up to $655,000,000 to enable the company to fulfill its contracts for four projects: the C-5A, the Cheyenne, rocket engines for the Air Force's short range attack missile (SRAM), and construction of destroyer escorts and amphibious floating docks for the Navy. The company's demands met with hostility in Congress, where an antiwar mood had given rise to opposition to increased military expenditures.

When, in December 1970, the Pentagon proposed a "contingency fund" for Lockheed, offering to absorb all but $200,000,000 of the large cost overrun on the C-5A, Haughton threatened to go to court rather than accept the fixed loss. But financial problems forced Haughton in February 1971 to concede to the Pentagon. "We continue to feel that if we had the resources to fund the program through a multi-year battle in the courts, we could obtain a favorable decision," he wrote to the Defense Department at the time. "We thus consider that the imposition of a $200,000,000 fixed loss isn't an equitable solution."

Those negotiations were barely settled when a problem arose concerning the L-1011, or TriStar jet. In March 1968 Haughton had announced orders, amounting to $2.16 billion, for 144 of the L-1011 jets, from Eastern Airlines, TransWorld Airlines, and the British-owned Air Holdings, Ltd. Lockheed engineers decided to use an improved jet engine, the RB-211 turbofan, for the plane, to be designed and produced by Rolls-Royce Ltd. of England. The British government backed the Rolls-Royce production with loans, while Lockheed borrowed $400,000,000 from American banks to finance the project. But in February 1971 Rolls-Royce spokesmen announced the impending bankruptcy of their company. In view of the huge amount already invested in the engines, the Rolls-Royce predicament constituted a severe setback for the L-1011 project.

After weeks of negotiations, during which Haughton shuttled back and forth between England, New York, and California, Rolls-Royce and the British government agreed to continue production of the engines at a higher price, provided that the American government would guarantee loans to Lockheed to save the company from possible bankruptcy. That offer took Haughton back to Congress, with a request for government guaranteed bank credit amounting to $250,000,000. Although President Nixon supported the Lockheed request, many Congressmen opposed government backing of defense contractors. Suggesting that the company's cost overruns on military projects raised "a presumption of mismanagement," California Senator Alan Cranston insisted that a guarantee be granted only if the entire Lockheed board of directors, including Haughton and Kotchian, resigned. Resorting to an aviation metaphor, Haughton offered to step down if that were needed to get the guarantee, but added that he did not want to resign "until we get out of this rough weather and into the blue again." The guarantee was narrowly approved by a 192 to 189 vote in the House on July 30, 1971 and by a vote of forty-nine to forty-eight in the Senate three days later.

With the help of additional loans from banks and other private sources, Lockheed continued to operate, but only on a low margin of profit. Sales of the L-1011 slumped as the boom in commercial air travel waned, partly as a result of the fuel crisis of 1973. To cash in on growing Soviet-United States trade, Haughton visited Moscow in early 1974, where he discussed possible sales of Tri-Star jets to the Soviet Union. Morale at Lockheed also improved when the company received an offer of a $160,000,000 loan from the government of Iran to resume production of the C-5A. The Iranians planned to buy six of those planes.

Lockheed's mounting economic woes, compounded by a staggering long-term debt—amounting to $850,000,000 as of May 1974—led Haughton to approach several firms, including General Dynamics and the Ford Motor Company, to discuss the possibility of a merger, but without success. Acting on the advice of the investment banking firm of Lazard Frères & Company, which had been engaged in late 1973 to aid Lockheed in strengthening its equity base, the Lockheed directors, on June 3, 1974, tentatively approved a far-reaching financial arrangement with Textron Incorporated, a conglomerate based in Providence, Rhode Island. Under the agreement (not a merger), Textron would acquire a 45 percent controlling interest in Lockheed by investing some $85,000,000 in Lockheed stock, and Textron chairman G. William Miller would become Lockheed's chairman and chief executive officer, while Haughton would assume the new post of vice-chairman. Tentatively scheduled to go into effect on November 30, 1974, and later extended until the end of December of that year, the plan hinged on Lockheed's ability to obtain forty-five additional firm orders for the L-1011 Tri-Star by that date.

Haughton is a director of the Southern California Edison Company, the United California Bank, and the Los Angeles World Affairs Council. Among other civic and philanthropic activities, he is director and board chairman of the National Multiple Sclerosis Society and a past director of the Atlanta and Los Angeles chapters of the American Red Cross. He has several honorary doctorates and organizational "man of the year" awards, including a 1973 citation as "employer of the year" from the National Industrial Recreation Association.

Daniel J. Haughton was married on September 28, 1935 to Martha Jean Oliver, who is a victim of multiple sclerosis. The Haughtons, who have no children, live in a two-story stucco house in Studio City, California. According to Harold B. Meyers, writing in *Fortune* (June 1971), Haughton is "a lean six-footer with a florid face, thinning hair, and a ready smile." An acquaintance, quoted in the same article, described Haughton's style as one of "red-dirt Southern courtliness." Haughton's stamina is legendary. He usually rises at 4 A.M., arrives at his Burbank office at 6 A.M., works steadily until 6 P.M., and gets along on four or five hours of sleep a day. Whenever he can take a few days off he and his wife visit their 425-acre farm near Marietta, Georgia, where they breed Black Angus cattle and fish in the farm's pond, which is stocked with bass and bream. The Haughtons belong to the United Methodist Church of Sherman Oaks, California.

References

Fortune 80:81 Ag 1 '69 por; 83:67+ Je '71 por
N Y Times p67 My 7 '71 por
Nat Observer p7 Ap 19 '65 por
International Who's Who, 1973-74
Who's Who in America, 1972-73
Who's Who in California (1968)
Who's Who in Finance and Industry, 1974-75

HAWKINS, ERICK

1917(?)- Dancer; choreographer
Address: c/o Erick Hawkins Dance Company, 104 5th Ave., New York 10003

One of the most original contributors to contemporary choreography is Erick Hawkins, whose serene, ritualistic dances transform body movement into a kind of Haiku poetry. Plotless, characterless, and devoid of emotion or tension, Hawkins' dances are metaphors that try to capture the essence of things in nature in much the same way that the sculptor Brancusi created his bronze columnar bird not to resemble a real bird but to embody the essence of flight. Hawkins' departure from the traditional, psychology-oriented school of modern dance, with its dramatic expressions of unresolved conflict, has left some critics baffled, exasperated, or merely bored, but he has long been a cult hero among those who appreciate his art.

Hawkins began his dance career in the 1930's as a member of George Balanchine's American Ballet Company, but gained his early reputation as Martha Graham's dance partner. After thirteen years with the Martha Graham Dance Company, in 1951 he started his own group, for which he dances and creates all the choreography. Particularly sensitive to the relationship of dance to music, Hawkins uses live music to accompany all of his pieces, much of it composed and performed by his inventive collaborator, Lucia Dlugoszewski. Among Hawkins' creations are *Early Floating*, *Geography of Noon*, *8 Clear Places*, *Lords of Persia*, *Naked Leopard*, *Black Lake*, and *Of Love*.

Erick Hawkins was born around 1917 in Trinidad, a small town in southeastern Colorado. He received his dance training at the School of American Ballet in New York City, where he studied under George Balanchine, and in 1935 he joined the American Ballet, for which Balanchine was the chief choreographer. When Ballet Caravan was formed by some members of the American Ballet in 1936 he began dancing with them, and in 1937 he left the American Ballet permanently for the newer company.

In 1938 Erick Hawkins appeared as a guest artist with the Martha Graham Dance Company, and the following year he left Ballet Caravan to join that illustrious modern dance group. Miss Graham's first and probably best-known male partner, Erick Hawkins created principal roles in such Graham masterpieces as *Appalachian Spring* and *Cave of the Heart*. While with her company he also began choreographing dances himself, including *John Brown* (1947), which he revived for his own company twenty years later, and *Stephen Acrobat* (1949).

By the early 1950's Hawkins had formulated a concept of dance technique alien to the percussiveness and tension that characterize Graham dance movement. After suffering an injury while dancing, he came to believe that ballet and modern dance technique force the body to move unnaturally, and he therefore evolved a vocabulary

ERICK HAWKINS

of "free-flow" dance movement that would avoid injury by allowing dancers to move in a natural, unforced manner. Based on a sound knowledge of anatomy, Hawkins' technique aimed at training dancers in "self-sensing," or becoming aware of how much effort they could expand on a movement before it became forced.

To start his own group with which he could develop his concept of "free-flow" dance, Hawkins left the Martha Graham Dance Company in 1951. Because he believed that dance should no more violate the spirit than it does the body, he shunned the expressions of angst and stress that had characterized traditional modern dance. Instead he began developing a mode of dance expression that would celebrate nature—the natural body and its metaphoric relationship to things in nature. Two of his early dances that reflect that concern are *Early Floating*, a study in liquescence that is still part of his repertoire, and *Here and Now With Watchers*, a seventy-minute *pas de deux* that explored different metaphors in each of its eight parts. The latter work remained in the Hawkins repertoire for several years, even though most critics found its lack of drama tedious. Allen Hughes (New York *Times*, July 16, 1962), for example, called it "one of the most trying theatrical experiences of our time."

In 1964 Hawkins gave his *Geography of Noon* its première at the annual Connecticut College dance festival in New London, Connecticut. For that piece Hawkins began with the idea of butterflies and went on to create an elegant ceremonial in which four dancers wove discreetly varied patterns around Lucia Dlugoszewski, who played gently percussive music on stage with her own specially invented boxes, rattles, and metal sheets. As Jack Anderson of *Dance Magazine* (December 1969) later wrote, "There are butterflies fluttering through *Geography of Noon*, but they are recognizable to lepidopterists of the imagination, rather than to researchers at the Natural History Museum." Most critics who sat through the dance in New London, however, agreed with

Walter Terry of the New York *Herald Tribune* (August 14, 1964), who complained that *Geography of Noon*, as well as Hawkins' other pieces, "are all too long and too much alike."

The following year Hawkins was commissioned by the Connecticut College dance festival to create a work, which he introduced there in August. Entitled *Lords of Persia*, it is loosely based on the game of polo. Characteristically, in Hawkins' treatment, polo is represented not as a competitive sport but as a stately ritual observance. Briefer, less abstract, and more structured than his previous pieces, *Lords of Persia* elicited a generally favorable response from critics.

By 1965 Hawkins and his dance group were making regular appearances in New York City. Among the pieces that they introduced to the demanding audiences in the world's dance capital over the next few years were *Naked Leopard*, a solo for Hawkins that he describes as "a celebration of animal innocence"; *Dazzle on a Knife's Edge; Cantilever;* and *Tightrope*, a representation of circus performing that showed the choreographer's idiosyncratic use of constant lateral exits and entrances to particular advantage.

After attending the première of *Tightrope* at the Brooklyn Academy of Music in November 1968, Anna Kisselgoff of the New York *Times* (November 15) more or less summed up the New York critical opinion of Hawkins when she wrote, "Although Mr. Hawkins has certainly one of the most interesting minds at work in dance, his very individual dance style requires an acquired taste." Despite his reputation as an avantgarde artist who was caviar to the general, on tour Hawkins enjoyed considerable success with less dance-sophisticated audiences around the country, especially with youthful college audiences. Each year he made nationwide tours, and in June 1967 *Dance Magazine* reported that his 1966-67 tour, during which the Hawkins company gave seventy performances in sixty United States and Canadian communities, was one of the most extensive North American tours in the history of modern dance.

When Hawkins presented eight performances to enthusiastic audiences at Riverside Church in October 1969, it appeared that he had at last begun to receive the kind of appreciation in New York City that he had come to expect elsewhere. Among the programs presented at the church was an unusual one in which his well-known *8 Clear Places* was performed twice, with an intermission between performances. A Haiku-like eight-part work for Hawkins and a female dancer, *8 Clear Places* was characterized by Jack Anderson of *Dance Magazine* (December 1969) "as sweetly ceremonious as an entertainment from some undiscovered and still uncorrupted Oriental land." On another evening Hawkins premièred *Black Lake*, a work which, like *8 Clear Places*, uses subtle movement and costuming to suggest various phenomena in nature.

At the ANTA Theatre in New York City in March 1971, Hawkins introduced *Of Love*, for which the artist Helen Frankenthaler had painted large hanging panels of yellow, green, and purple. The paintings formed a kind of bower for the virtually nude male and female dancers, who wore only G-strings. Nancy Goldner of the *Christian Science Monitor* (March 17, 1971), like many critics, found *Of Love* to be one of Hawkins' most successful creations. "Erick Hawkins' style is one of stillness punctuated by movement, and most of the movement is miniscule ripplings," Miss Goldner wrote. ". . . Hawkins, in fact, de-energizes dance, forcing one to study the body rather than regard the body as the given, the instrument that produces dynamic movement. . . . Hawkins' new *Of Love* . . . treats his implied eroticism in an explicit way, the body itself being the literal as well as the stylistic subject. Perhaps because of this joining of form and content, Hawkins' idiosyncracies seem crystalized and dramatic as never before. Minimal movement can mean lack of movement, but in *Of Love* it is a positive state."

When Hawkins and his troupe appeared at the ANTA Theatre in the fall of 1972, their performances attracted full houses who gave them standing ovations. During that engagement Hawkins introduced three new works, *Angels of the Inmost Heaven*, *Dawn Dazzled Door*, and *Classic Kite Tails*.

One of the most striking features of an Erick Hawkins dance concert is the music by Lucia Dlugoszewski, who has collaborated with the choreographer for over twenty years. Miss Dlugoszewski, who was recently nominated for a Pulitzer prize for her compositions, sets music to Hawkins' pieces after they are choreographed, inventively punctuating the stillness of his dances with her infinitely varied percussions. For many of his works she herself plays the piano or a variety of percussion instruments; for others she has composed chamber music. Occasionally Hawkins has turned to other sources for his music; *Naked Leopard* is set to a cello sonata by Zoltán Kodály, and *Classic Kite Tails* is accompanied by a David Diamond score.

Erick Hawkins, who used to be married to Martha Graham, has been called "one of dance's more charismatic figures," a tall, striking man with the look of a "fierce mystic." Clive Barnes (New York *Times*, November 16, 1968) has described his dancing as "febrile, athletic," and "explosive yet gentle." A student of anatomy, Zen Buddhism, and Oriental philosophy, Hawkins is an articulate spokesman for free-form dance. In 1971 he spent a month as a teacher-in-residence at the Wolf Trap-American University Academy for the Performing Arts in Washington, D.C. His own school of dance is located in New York City.

References

Dance Mag 46:24+ O '72 pors; 48:38+ N '74
N Y Times II p32 N 5 '72; II p16+ D 17 '72 por
Newsday A p4+ N 26 '73 pors
Chujoy, A., and Manchester, P. W., eds. Dance Encyclopedia (1967)
Who's Who in America, 1974-75

HAYS, WAYNE L(EVERE)

May 13, 1911- United States Representative from Ohio
Address: b. 2264 Rayburn Office Building, Washington, D.C. 20515; h. "Red Gate Farms," Belmont, Ohio 43718

A relatively conservative Democrat who has been a fixture on Capitol Hill for a quarter of a century, Congressman Wayne Hays of Ohio is the powerful and influential chairman of the House Administration Committee. First elected to Congress in 1948, the aggressive and articulate legislator came to national attention during the "Red scare" of the early 1950's, when, as a member of the notorious Reece Committee, he brilliantly defended a number of tax-exempt philanthropic organizations against spurious charges of Communist activities. Hays is a skilled practitioner of cloakroom politics, and, as Albert R. Hunt noted in the *Wall Street Journal* (July 24, 1972), "threats, bluster and intimidation are integral parts of his arsenal." In a recent interview he explained, "Up here, mealy-mouth nice guys finish last."

The son of Walter Lee and Bertha Mae (Taylor) Hays, Wayne Levere Hays was born in Bannock, Ohio on May 13, 1911. Although inactive in politics, his family had talked and voted Republican for several generations. The sole exception was his maternal grandfather, J. W. Taylor, a Confederate Army veteran who relished political arguments, in which he often played the role of devil's advocate. As a result, Hays grew up hearing both sides, and when he voted for the first time in 1932, he chose Franklin D. Roosevelt, the Democratic candidate, over President Herbert C. Hoover, the Republican incumbent. "Until then, I considered myself a Republican, I guess," he said to Tom Fitzsimmons in an interview for the *New Republic* (June 28, 1954). "Most of the boys around [the Ohio State University] campus did. But everyone was fed up with Hoover."

Hays graduated from Ohio State University in Columbus, Ohio in 1933 with a B.S. degree and then enrolled in the prelaw program at Duke University, in Durham, North Carolina. Two years later he left school to become a teacher of history and public speaking at the Flushing, Ohio high school. He was a popular and successful instructor, but he resigned when a member of the town's board of education criticized his unorthodox teaching methods, especially his alleged disregard for the accomplishments of the Republican party. Turning his attention to Flushing politics, Hays was promptly elected to the board of education and, in 1939, to the first of three consecutive two-year terms as mayor. In 1941 he was elected to the state senate, where he guided the passage of a tenure law to protect elementary and secondary school-teachers against summary dismissal. A member of the Officers' Reserve Corps of the United States Army since 1933, he volunteered for active duty two days after the surprise attack by the Japanese on Pearl Harbor in December 1941. After his honorable

WAYNE L. HAYS

discharge in August 1942 he resumed his duties as mayor of Flushing, Ohio in which post he served until 1945, when he left office to operate a large dairy farm.

In 1948, in his first bid for national elective office, Hays entered the race for the United States House of Representatives from the Eighteenth Congressional District, an agricultural and industrial area in southeastern Ohio near the West Virginia border. Since 1936 the district had sent a Democrat to Congress in a Presidential election year, and a Republican in an off-year. Pledging to give his constituents a voice in Washington, Hays garnered 54.1 percent of the votes cast and easily defeated his Republican opponent. Acutely aware that 1948 was a favorable year for Democrats, the young Congressman kept in close contact with his idiosyncratic constituents through a weekly newsletter and frequent weekend visits home. His painstaking political fence mending paid off in steadily increasing pluralities over the years. In the 1972 contest, for instance, he trounced his Republican challenger, Robert Stewart, a thirty-five-year-old dairy farmer, winning reelection to his thirteenth term by more than 74,000 votes. Hays was reelected to the House on November 5, 1974.

As a freshman legislator, Hays determinedly maintained a noncontroversial course, voting with the bipartisan majority on 92 percent of all roll call votes during his first term. Domestically he supported federally funded public housing, expanded health services to children in public schools, price supports for poultry and dairy products, and the repeal of the poll tax as a prerequisite to voting in national elections. A militant Cold Warrior, he favored increased military aid to the member nations of the North Atlantic Treaty Organization (NATO) and economic assistance to Korea. To halt Communist activity within the United States, he approved the Internal Security Act of 1950, which established the Subversive Activities Control Board and required members of Communist organiza-

tions to register with the Attorney General and proposed closing the mails to Communist literature. During the much publicized Whittaker Chambers-Alger Hiss Communist conspiracy trial in 1949, he publicly defended Federal Judge Samuel H. Kaufman's conduct of the trial and accused the House Un-American Activities Committee of using the case to make "unwarranted, vicious, partisan political accusations against the [Truman] Administration."

One of Congress' most outspoken opponents of political witch-hunting, Hays was named to a special House committee investigating the activities and expenditures of tax-exempt educational and philanthropic organizations in 1953. The committee's public hearings occasionally degenerated into bitter personal disputes between B. Carroll Reece, the five-member committee's Republican chairman, and Hays, the ranking Democrat. After listening to several hours of testimony based on the twenty-year-old published statements of some of the witnesses, he asked the committee members, "Is it not possible that some if not most of these alleged socialistic ideas of 1934 have been taken care of by the New Deal, whose programs were being denounced as being socialistic but still are supported avidly by Republicans?" Outraged by the tactics of Thomas M. McNiece, a staff researcher who quoted out-of-context statements as proof of a witness' Communist sympathies, Hays maneuvered the staffer into identifying as Communist propaganda the published remarks of two Popes. On one occasion the Ohioan stalked out of a meeting to protest the "loose" testimony and the "character assassination by inference" of the "Alice in Wonderland" investigation.

In September 1954 Hays demanded that the investigation be expanded to include a scrutiny of Facts Forum, the tax-exempt radio and television production company funded by H. L. Hunt, the Texas oil millionaire and staunch defender of Senator Joseph R. McCarthy. In his statement Hays charged that the programs produced by Facts Forum, such as Americans For Freedom and State of the Union, used "the technique of smear . . . by half-truths, distortions, generalizations, and exaggerations." A favorite ploy, he said, was "the deliberate and constant repetition of language discrediting liberals in general . . . and lumping them with Socialists, Communists, and totalitarians." When the hearings concluded, Hays and Congresswoman Gracie Pfost of Idaho submitted a minority report disputing the committee's contention that some foundations supported "subversion." In their 6,000-word dissent, the two Representatives deplored the majority report as the "crackpot view" of people with "fear sickness" and denounced the "barbaric" conduct of the inquiry as "an evil disregard of fundamental American guarantees."

Throughout his career Hays has been attentive to the needs of his constituents in the economically depressed Eighteenth Congressional District. He approved, for example, the Appalachian Regional Development Act of 1965 that provided federal monies for road construction, health care, vocational training, housing, and land reclamation. To protect the farmers' precarious livelihood, he backed flexible price supports and approved agricultural reform legislation; to guarantee an adequate income for coal miners, steelworkers, and other laborers, he supported minimum wage standards and right-to-work laws. He was equally responsive to urban problems and approved appropriations for public housing construction, slum clearance, and the "demonstration cities" program.

A longtime consumer advocate, Hays supported passage of the truth-in-lending bill and the creation of an independent Consumer Protection Agency. In addition, he approved rent supplements to low-income families, a basic, compulsory, tax-financed health program for the aged, increased aid to education, and open housing. Although he had voted for every major piece of civil rights legislation passed by Congress during the 1950's and 1960's, he opposed busing to achieve racial balance in the schools.

In foreign affairs, Hays preferred technical and economic aid to military aid, especially in underdeveloped nations where, in his words, "the guns will not maintain the regime in power." Specifically, he supported measures to eliminate military aid to certain Latin American countries and to Greece and to impose economic sanctions on Cuba. Although he once requested President Dwight D. Eisenhower to rescind trade agreements with Communist countries, in later years he recommended a relaxation of such restrictions. As a Vietnam War hawk, he regularly approved Pentagon requests for additional funds as well as the transfer of monies from other Department of Defense programs to the Southeast Asian war theatre. In a floor speech in October 1969 he rebuked a bipartisan group of seventeen Senators and forty-seven Representatives—"the self-appointed emissaries of Hanoi"—who sanctioned the nationwide Vietnam Moratorium. Although he vigorously defended President Nixon's Indochina policy and his conduct of the war, Hays opposed the administration's plan to assist financially in the reconstruction of North Vietnam. Such aid, the Congressman announced to the House, would be granted "over [his] dead body." Furthermore, he joined his colleagues to override Nixon's veto of the War Powers Bill, which restricted a President's war-making powers and guaranteed Congressional access to privileged information and decisions that could result in war.

For more than two decades Hays had resisted the Presidents' increasing reliance on "executive privilege." For example, during the confirmation hearings of Secretary of State Henry A. Kissinger in 1973, the legislator maintained that the issue was "whether the Congress has a right to know and whether the Congress has any power and whether the Congress is going to do what the American people want it to do, and that is to reassert its power and prerogatives that were granted to it by the Constitution."

In late 1973 Hays' voting record was rated at 48 percent by the liberal Americans for Democratic Action, while the conservative Americans for Constitutional Action measured it at 28 percent. The National Farmers Union and the AFL-CIO Committee on Political Education placed it at 100 percent.

Incensed by the slowly unraveling skein of Watergate-related scandals, Congressman Hays called for President Nixon's resignation in January 1974. (He had previously added an amendment barring aid to "indigent, abandoned Watergate defendants" to the bill creating an independent legal services corporation.) Like the majority of his colleagues, he recognized the need for campaign finance reform to prevent another Watergate. In the late 1960's and early 1970's he opposed several bills that strengthened the provisions of the 1925 Corrupt Practices Act. Among other things, he objected to a federal elections commission as an unwarranted extension of executive authority and to frequent campaign reporting requirements as "too cumbersome." He also disagreed with the proposed repeal of the equal time provision of the Communications Act of 1934. Explaining his position to the House on November 11, 1971, he said, "I do not . . . trust [the broadcasters] to be fair about how and to whom they give time and from whom they withhold it. I do not think there is a remote possibility that they would not be prejudiced and do exactly as they please."

In place of a tough Senate campaign reform plan, Hays offered a bill that provided public funding for Presidential campaigns with lower spending ceilings, that limited Congressional candidates to $60,000, and that relaxed the reporting requirements of the 1971 Federal Election Campaign Act. Some veteran Washington observers considered the relatively low limitation on campaign spending in Congressional elections a boon to incumbents. When Common Cause, the public interest lobby, charged that his "loophole-ridden" proposal was "a grossly inadequate response to the money-in-politics that have been the underpinning of the Watergate story," Hays replied, as quoted in the Washington *Post* (March 29, 1974), "Common Cause is just trying to raise an issue so it can bilk the suckers who subscribe to it for more funds."

As chairman of the House Administration Committee, Hays oversees such housekeeping functions as committee budgets, office expenses, stationery, and travel vouchers. In his official duties as head of the United States delegation to NATO and as chairman of the House Foreign Affairs Subcommittee on State Department Organization and Foreign Operations, he frequently travels abroad at government expense. On one of his trips to Paris for a NATO conference he was accompanied by Ernest Petinaud, the bilingual head waiter of the House of Representatives dining room, who, according to the Congressman, served as a "liaison man." Because of the public uproar, Hays later offered to pay Petinaud's expenses.

In a copyrighted article for the Knight Newspapers and for *Life* (June 6, 1966) magazine investigative reporters Don Oberdorfer and Walter Pincus charged three dozen Representatives, including Hays, with alleged expense account abuses. That same year the House passed a bill creating a bipartisan select committee on standards of conduct. Branding the measure "a self-immolation bill for the members of the House," Hays warned that frivolous accusations might be made for the sake of publicity. Eight years later he engineered the passage of a provision eliminating the requirement for public disclosure of foreign travel in the *Congressional Record*. "We decided we weren't going to spend eight or nine thousand dollars to let you guys do your stories on Congressional travel," he remarked to a group of Capitol Hill correspondents in May 1974.

Wayne L. Hays and the former Martha Judkins were married on June 3, 1937. They have one daughter, Martha Brigitte, a German orphan whom they adopted in 1955. The couple also cared for a young English girl during the early 1950's. Hays owns and operates Red Gate Farms in Belmont, Ohio, where he breeds Angus cattle and Tennessee walking horses. He was awarded honorary LL.D. degrees by Ohio University in 1966 and by the College of Steubenville (Ohio) in 1968, and received the Caritas medal in 1969.

References

Christian Sci Mon p10 Ja 24 '69
Newsday p35 N 12 '63 por
Who's Who in America, 1974-75
Who's Who in American Politics, 1973-74

HICKS, LOUISE DAY

Oct. 16, 1919(?)- City official; lawyer
Address: b. 11 Beacon St., Boston, Mass., 02108; h. 1780 Columbia Rd., South Boston, Mass. 02127

"No one in their right mind is against civil rights, against integration," Louise Day Hicks, a champion of the neighborhood school concept and one of the first Northern critics of busing to achieve racial balance, once insisted to Ira Mothner in an interview for *Look* magazine (February 22, 1966). "Only, let it come naturally. What will Negroes learn by sitting in class with white children?" Mrs. Hicks, who reached national prominence in the mid-1960's when the mass media covered her determined assault on the Supreme Court's school desegregation order, served three consecutive terms on Boston's School Committee and commanded substantial majorities in three elections. Described by one political observer as "the white hope of these panicky parents," she prevented until 1966 the implementation of massive cross-busing to alleviate *de facto* segregation. An indefatigable campaigner, she enlisted the support of the "little people" in ten political contests for five different offices in twelve years, including successful bids for the Boston City Council and the United States House of Representatives. As

the first woman to run for mayor in the city's history, she was twice defeated by Kevin H. White, her antithesis in politics.

One of several children of William J. and Anna (McCarron) Day, Anna Louise Day was born in the city of Boston, Massachusetts on October 16, 1919. (Some sources give 1923 as the year of her birth.) She was raised in a huge, three-story frame house in South Boston, at that time a tightly knit Irish Roman Catholic community, where she attended local parochial schools. After her mother's death, her father, who was a popular Democratic District Court judge, was especially attentive toward his only daughter, then fourteen years old. "He was the best friend I ever had," she told Jane Howard in an interview for a *Life* magazine profile (October 13, 1967). "He was such a good scout. I've yet to hear anyone say a word against him. As for me, he thought anything I said was the answer to the atomic bomb."

Following her graduation in 1938 from Wheelock College, a small teachers college in Boston that issued no degrees, Louise Day taught first grade in suburban Brookline, Massachusetts until her marriage to John Hicks, a design engineer, on October 12, 1942. She also clerked in her father's Boston law office. Several years later, Mrs. Hicks completed her education at Boston University, earning a B.S. degree in education in 1952 and a J.D. degree in 1955. Recalling her graduate training for Jane Howard, she said, "My best friends at law school were a Negro girl and a Jewish girl. One time the three of us said a novena together. They were both praying to find a husband and I was praying to pass the bar exam. All three of us got what we wanted." In partnership with her older brother John, she established Hicks and Day, a Boston law firm specializing in land and property transfers, and as a counsel to the Boston Juvenile Court, she also provided free legal advice to underprivileged youngsters.

Prompted by neighbors concerned about the quality of public education, Mrs. Hicks announced her candidacy for the five-member School Committee—the Boston equivalent of a municipal board of education—in the spring of 1961. Campaigning as a liberal, she promised to take "politics out of the School Committee." In his analysis of Mrs. Hicks's political career for the *Reporter* (October 19, 1967), Martin Noble summarized her first term on the School Committee as "noncontroversial." Mrs. Hicks charted her initial political course carefully and avoided a direct confrontation with the black community by asking Negro leaders for "advice and support" in developing "compensatory education" programs for black children. Her moderate and reasonable approach led civil rights leaders, as well as a number of local reform groups, to consider endorsing her for reelection. But on June 11, 1963, while chairing the first of several strained meetings, Mrs. Hicks clashed with representatives from the Boston chapter of the National Association for the Advancement of Colored People. Although she accepted some of the NAACP's complaints and recommendations, she squelched a discussion of *de facto* segregation in the Boston public school system and advised the black delegates to "kindly proceed to educational matters."

When blacks organized a one-day boycott of classrooms and held a peaceful demonstration outside the headquarters building of the School Committee to protest her rebuff, Mrs. Hicks reportedly remarked to an aide, "God forgive them, for they know not what they do." Her pledge to protect the "neighborhood school" clearly impressed the ethnically isolated communities in the city. Polling a phenomenal 74 percent of the votes cast, in November 1963 Mrs. Hicks was elected to a second term on the School Committee. In 1964 she tried to broaden her political base in an unsuccessful bid for the Democratic nomination for state treasurer.

Acting on a report issued by the state board of education, in 1965 the Massachusetts legislature passed a bill requiring local school districts to correct racial imbalance in the classroom or risk the loss of state aid. Mrs. Hicks, who was then chairman of the School Committee, denounced the report as the "pompous pronouncements of the uninformed" and vetoed a locally sponsored busing proposal. As a result, Boston's schools were deprived of an estimated $6,300,000 in aid. Arguing that "we can help the Negro child more by education than transportation," she formulated "Operation Counterpoint" as a viable alternative to busing. The program provided for field trips, books and other printed materials, audio-visual equipment, and learning resource centers. To correct the racial imbalance in two Boston schools immediately, the Committee reclassified Oriental pupils from "non-white" to "white."

With the full support of "Mothers for Neighborhood Schools," a politically active antibusing group she had helped to organize, in 1965 Mrs. Hicks campaigned for a third two-year term on the School Committee. In response to accusations of racism, she defended her position in an interview published in the Washington *Post* on October 31, 1965. "I know I've been called the Bull Conner of the North, a bigot, and anti-Negro," she told Jean M. White, the *Post's* correspondent. "But I haven't said 'no' to the Negroes. I have said 'no' to civil rights leaders using children as pawns in their national struggle. Civil rights infiltrators are not interested in good education for the children of Boston." Polling 64 percent of the vote in the November election, Mrs. Hicks easily defeated the five "anti-Hicks" candidates. Despite her opposition, the School Committee finally approved a modified busing plan in 1966.

Undeterred by the opposition of civil rights leaders, many civic groups, and the Boston mass media, Mrs. Hicks entered the mayoral contest on May 1, 1967. Employing the ambiguous campaign slogan "You Know Where I Stand," she skirted the inflammatory racial issue and contended that the central issue of the election was "the alienated voter." To reestablish the confidence of voters in their city government, she recom-

LOUISE DAY HICKS

mended additional federal aid, a nonresident head tax, the revitalization of ethnic neighborhoods, lower taxes, and a new athletic stadium. She reassured worried citizens after riots erupted in the Roxbury district of Boston by pledging to increase the salaries of law enforcement officers so that "no police officer . . . will be sacrificed on the altar of civil disobedience." Mrs. Hicks, who drew considerable political strength from blue-collar and middle-class white citizens, received slightly less than 30 percent of the total votes cast in the ten-candidate, nonpartisan preliminary election on September 26, 1967. Appalled by her success, the New York *Times* (September 27, 1967) editorialized: "Mrs. Hicks has no visible qualifications for this demanding post. . . . It would be a tragedy if Boston, with its unique place in the history of American liberty and equality, should elect a leader so lacking in an understanding of these fundamentals." The Washington *Post* (September 28, 1967) editorialized: "Her election would give Boston a bigot as its chief executive." Mrs. Hicks's opponent in the general election, Kevin H. White, the Massachusetts secretary of state was endorsed by the influential Boston *Globe,* by Senator Edward M. Kennedy, and by Republican Governor John A. Volpe. A civil rights liberal, White attacked Mrs. Hicks's platform of "Boston for Bostonians" and warned that her election could turn Boston into "an armed camp." On November 7, 1967 Mrs. Hicks lost to White by slightly more than 10,000 votes. She had failed to win the expected large majorities in her home district.

At a news conference on June 25, 1969 Mrs. Hicks announced her decision to run for the Boston City Council and told reporters that "the issues had not changed" since her mayoral campaign but "had grown more pressing." To attract a larger number of voters, she adopted a more moderate stance and deliberately avoided the controversial racial issue, emphasizing instead the problems of overcrowded schools, street crime, and a "soaring tax rate." In the September primary she led the eighteen-candidate field with nearly 47,000 votes. Since she was virtually assured of election, she made few public appearances and focused her efforts on those areas of the city most receptive to her point of view. Mrs. Hicks polled 28,000 votes more than her nearest rival in the November general election. While on the Boston City Council, she served as chairman of the committees on urban affairs, public service, and health and hospitals.

When John W. McCormack, the septuagenarian Speaker of the United States House of Representatives, stepped down in 1970, Louise Day Hicks decided to run for his vacant Ninth Congressional District seat. The best-known of a dozen candidates for the position, she campaigned on a law and order platform specially tailored to her urban constituents and won the official endorsement of the International Longshoremen's Association as "man enough for us." Although she publicly supported the invasion of Cambodia, she called for an "orderly withdrawal" from Vietnam, on the ground that the money wasted on military operations and on the space program could be better spent on the inner cities. On election day Mrs. Louise Day Hicks defeated her Republican opponent, former Congressman Lawrence Curtis, and Daniel Houton, a dovish Vietnam veteran who ran as an independent.

As a freshman legislator, Mrs. Hicks made no major speeches and took part in few floor debates, prompting considerable Capitol speculation that she was planning a second mayoral bid. "Some mornings, I wake up and I'm positive that I'm going to run for mayor again," she told Marjorie Hunter in an interview for the New York Times (May 16, 1971). "Then other times I'm not sure at all. If I could only take the Congress to Boston I'd be perfectly happy." Assigned to the House Education and Labor and Veterans Affairs committees, Mrs. Hicks approved legislation to provide standby wage-price controls, to expand the public service jobs program, to permit voluntary prayer in the public schools, and to postpone court-ordered busing. On other domestic issues, she opposed the appropriation of funds for the construction of the supersonic transport aircraft, the federal loan guarantee to Lockheed Aircraft Corporation, and the expenditure of federal monies to improve Washington, D.C.'s mass transit facilities. Although a former defender of American policy in Southeast Asia, she supported the Mansfield amendment to end United States military involvement in Indochina within six months of the bill's enactment.

One of five candidates for the post, Mrs. Hicks entered her name on the Boston mayoral ballot on June 14, 1971. In a public statement explaining her decision, Mrs. Hicks told Bostonians she could no longer "remain on the sidelines, safe in [her] Congressional seat and witness the destruction and demise of Boston." Noting that the Ninth Congressional District was one of several electoral districts to be reapportioned before the 1972 elections, some observers commented that her decision was based more on political expediency than on civic obligation. Mrs. Hicks conducted a low visibility campaign. Promising to appeal or amend the state's tough desegregation laws, she doggedly stumped the neighborhoods and visited supermarkets and subway stations, but shunned the mass rallies, fund-raising dinners, and broadcast interviews and debates favored by her chief opponent, incumbent Mayor White. "The technique has always been personal," one of Mrs. Hick's political advisers told Bill Kovach in an interview for the New York Times (October 24, 1971). "Run an advertising campaign to attack the opponent, but spend your time . . . at rallies stirring up your voters—but you can't do that when you're behind, you've got to bring out more voters." Mrs. Hicks carried only four of the city's twenty-two wards, lost to White by more than 40,000 votes, and became the underdog for the first time in her political career.

During the second session of the Ninety-second Congress, Mrs. Hicks continued to support legislation to guarantee quality education to all American children. Following extensive hearings conducted by the House Ways and Means Committee, she urged the passage of laws allowing tax credits to parents of nonpublic school children and permitting direct federal aid to needy students. To return a measure of self-government to local communities, she backed President Richard M. Nixon's revenue-sharing plan. All in all, Mrs. Hicks cast 59 percent of her votes in approval of legislative programs identified with President Nixon's administration.

Facing increased opposition from Republicans and liberals in the reapportioned Ninth Congressional District, Mrs. Hicks lost her House seat to John J. Moakley, an independent Democrat who polled 72,968 votes to her 67,143, in a three-way contest on November 7, 1972. Undaunted, Mrs. Hicks continued to press for reform of the Massachusetts desegregation plans. Observers have credited her with preventing violent antibusing demonstrations in Boston. Outpolling all other candidates, she was reelected to the Boston City Council on November 6, 1973.

Tall and large-boned, Louise Day Hicks has small, dark eyes and perfectly coiffed brown hair. Once described by a political reporter as looking "more like an enraged housewife than a politician," she ignores the fads of fashion, preferring royal blue or bright green suits worn with spotless white cotton gloves. Although her schedule allows her little time for recreation, she enjoys bowling, golf, and deep-sea fishing. A widow since 1968, Mrs. Hicks continues to live in her childhood home in South Boston, defiantly refusing to join the white middle-class flight to the suburbs. "Why, we all like to live with people of our own race, color, creed or place of origin," she once said. "Call it a neighborhood or call it a ghetto, you shouldn't be forced to move out of it." In 1964 Louise Day Hicks was given the local Woman of the Year award and in 1965 she was honored with Boston's Outstanding Citizen award.

References
  Life 63:89+ O 13 '67 pors
  Look 60:72+ F 22 '66 pors
  N Y Post p25 O 14 '67 por
  N Y Sunday News II p1G+ N 5 '67 pors
  N Y Times Mag p31+ N 5 '67 pors
  Newsweek 70:29+ N 6 '67 por
  Who's Who in America, 1972-73

STANLEY HILLER JR.

HILLER, STANLEY, JR.

Nov. 15, 1924-   Industrialist; inventor; entrepreneur
Address: b. Hiller Investment Co., 3000 Sand Hill Rd., Menlo Park, Calif. 94025; h. 150 Elena Ave., Atherton, Calif. 94025

The inventor-entrepreneur Stanley Hiller Jr. began manufacturing the world's first coaxial helicopter three decades ago, before he was twenty. In 1965, after Hiller Aircraft merged with Fairchild Industries Inc., Hiller left the helicopter business as a millionaire. In the following years he devoted himself to venture capitalism, journeying from his base in the Hiller Investment Company like a free-enterprise knight errant in search of mini-conglomerates in need of rescue. Since 1972 he has concentrated his time, energy, and money on the Reed Tool Company of Houston, Texas, a previously over-diversified enterprise that he has stripped down to its healthy, profitable core: the manufacture of metal and rock bits used in drilling for oil and gas. "Few investors have timed the energy crisis better than Hiller," a writer for Business Week (August 24, 1974) has observed. "Whether through foresight or sheer luck, Hiller could hardly have scheduled his entry into the oil equipment business any better." Hiller is also a partner in the Lathrop Company and a director of Bernicia Industries and the ELTRA Corporation.

Stanley Hiller Jr. was born into a wealthy family in San Francisco, California on November 15, 1924. His mother was Opal (Perkins) Hiller and his father was Stanley Hiller Sr., an owner of the Hillicone Shipping Company. Stanley Sr. was also a professional airplane pilot, an electrical engineer, a master mechanic, and, like his father before him, an inventor. He held forty patents, including one for a plane in which he taught his son to fly at a tender age. Stanley Jr.'s mother tried to interest him in music but the father won out by "throwing tools at him" (as the elder Hiller once explained to an interviewer) when most boys his age were still playing with blocks. Growing up in Berkeley, California, young Hiller spent most of his spare time tinkering with motors and engines and using them to power such homemade contraptions as a miniature backyard railroad, a motorized scooter, and model planes and racing cars.

At sixteen Hiller began mass-producing toy racers, and that enterprise, nourished by capital borrowed from his father, developed into Hiller

Industries, a war production company. At nineteen, after attending prep schools in Berkeley and in Milford, Connecticut and spending a few months at the University of California, he dropped out of school to devote himself full time to his company, which was producing aluminum castings for West Coast airplane manufacturers. Meanwhile he had begun developing the Hiller-copter, a helicopter whose two main rotors, moving in opposite directions, made unnecessary the conventional tail rotor. On August 31, 1944, the day before he was to report for military induction, he demonstrated a model of his revolutionary counter-roter flying machine for representatives of the Navy, the Army, and the National Advisory Committee for Aeronautics. On the basis of the demonstration he was deferred from the military draft at the request of the Navy so that he might continue to work on the Hiller-copter, which the Navy envisioned as a rescue and air-ambulance vehicle. Henry J. Kaiser bought the patent rights to the copter and hired Hiller to direct the helicopter division of Kaiser Cargoes Inc.

At the end of World War II Hiller left Kaiser to found his own company, United Helicopters Inc., later renamed the Hiller Aircraft Corporation, in Palo Alto, California. In the postwar years he concentrated on the development of an "air flivver," the Hiller Commuter, described as "a sort of coaxial flying goldfish bowl," which he hoped to sell to businessmen and suburbanites in quantity, and the "360," a light-weight conventional helicopter with a large single rotor blade and a stub rotor both revolving in the same direction. The 360, which could easily be maneuvered in any direction and was capable of darting into and out of corners quickly, was bought by some large farm owners, who used it for crop dusting, cattle surveillance, and other agricultural purposes, but the civilian market for the Commuter—and its ram-jet descendant, the Hiller Hornet—was disappointingly small. His company did not go into full production until the early 1950's, when he supplied millions of dollars' worth of helicopters to the armed forces for use in the Korean conflict.

In the mid-1950's Hiller Aircraft built for the Office of Naval Research the Flying Carpet, an experimental one-man disk without wings or visible helicopter blades. First publicly tested in April 1955, the flying metal "doughnut" was propelled by an interior ducted air fan. The pilot, standing inside a protective railing, steered the' craft by leaning in the desired direction. Among other prototype helicopters designed by Hiller for the government was a giant turbo-jet flying crane and the X-18, a tilt-wing transport capable of vertical takeoff.

In 1964 Hiller Aircraft merged with Fairchild Stratos, which was doing a $68,000,000-a-year business in the manufacture of space systems and electronic equipment. Hiller became an executive vice-president of Fairchild Stratos, in charge of the Hiller-Fairchild Corporation. In the industry-wide competition for a Pentagon contract to supply a light observation helicopter (LOH) for use in Vietnam, the field finally narrowed down to Hiller-Fairchild and Hughes Tool's Aircraft Division. Determined to get into the helicopter business by hook or by crook, Hughes, knowing it could raise the price later, underbid Hiller-Fairchild by nearly one-third, offering an LOH for the ridiculously unrealistic price of $19,860. It not only won the LOH contract but took away from Hiller-Fairchild its $5,500,000 Army contract for 215 primary helicopter trainers.

With all his military business taken away, Hiller quit his post at Hiller-Fairchild in disgust in 1965. After his departure, Hiller-Fairchild brought out a civilian version of his turbine-powered LOH. Eighty-two Hiller FH-1100's came off the assembly line before the end of 1966 and 144 were manufactured in 1967, and Hiller-Fairchild embarked on a $6,000,000-plus program to put a new twin-engine craft on the market before 1970.

In the meantime Hiller himself was turning his time, energy, and money to venture capitalism. In the late 1960's and early 1970's he poured capital into many new companies while looking for a major older enterprise in which to invest. "I was looking for a financially troubled company with lots of assets that I felt were not properly employed," he has recounted. "If you score there, the payoff will be big." After several frustrated attempts at corporate takeovers elsewhere, Hiller learned about G. W. Murphy Industries Inc., through contacts at the Bank of America, which had loaned George W. Murphy the money to buy the Reed Roller Bit Company. The Reed investment was sound, but otherwise Murphy over-diversified, acquiring more marginal operations—including hand tools, plastic artificial shrubs, and gears—than his company could profitably handle.

Murphy had put up his company stock as collateral on the loan from Bank of America, and when he was unable to meet the loan payments the bank forced him to sell. In partnership with a subsidiary of American Express and some rep-

resentatives of the firm of Blyth, Eastman & Dillon Union Securities, Hiller assumed the Murphy loan and bought Murphy's 42 percent interest in Murphy Industries in 1972. "Our philosophy is that we don't make a passive investment," he said at the time. "We are going to return Murphy to its basic field, where its knowledge and principal strengths are."

Hiller changed the name of Murphy Industries to the Reed Tool Company and set about concentrating the company on the manufacture of oil-drilling bits. He put in a seven-day week at Reed Tool in the beginning, before he hired Terrell L. Ruhlman, a petroleum equipment manufacturing veteran, as general manager. He added twenty people to the financial staff of the company, which had been limping along without a finance officer, a tax specialist, or even a legal counsel. To pay off insurance companies to which Murphy had gone heavily into debt, he used a combination of five-year bank financing and long-term loans from other insurance companies.

Within two years Hiller sold seven of the marginal businesses that had been putting the company in the red, and he introduced a new, improved line of rock bits while trimming away those items in the oil-tool line with the lowest margins and giving salesmen incentive rewards for selling high-margin products. "Before, they didn't even know what the high and low margin products were," he told an interviewer for *Business Week* (August 24, 1974). "They were just selling all the iron they could." He also introduced a three-year, $42,000,000 capital improvement program to double capacity and modernize facilities. As a result of his efforts—and a 30 percent rise in the total market for bits—the profits of the company increased 250 percent, to $2,500,000. Gross sales rose 20 percent, to $80,000,000.

The Bank of America asked Hiller in 1974 to take over another of its debtor companies, the Memorex Corporation, recording-tape manufacturers, but he turned down the offer and helped to recruit in his stead Robert C. Wilson, former president of Collins Radio, for the position of chief executive at Memorex. In declining the Memorex job, Hiller explained that Reed Tool was absorbing almost all of his attention and would continue to do so for the foreseeable future. "This is the best opportunity I've ever seen," he said, as quoted in the August 24, 1974 *Business Week* article.

Stanley Hiller Jr. and Carolyn Balsdon, who met as classmates at the University of California, were married on May 25, 1946. They have two children, Jeffrey and Stephen. Back in 1951 the United States Junior Chamber of Commerce named Hiller one of the top ten outstanding young Americans. His other honors include the Fawcett Award (1944); the Grand Trophy of the World Inventors Congress (1947); the Distinguished Service Award of the National Defense Transportation Society (1958); and an honorary fellowship in the American Helicopter Society. He is a member of the American Institute of Aeronautics and Astronautics, the American Society of

Pioneers, and the Phi Kappa Sigma fraternity. In the midst of the stepped-up tempo (which he describes in terms of "foot-pounds of energy") at the Reed Tool Company, Hiller retains his characteristic calm manner.

References

Bsns W p22 Jl 29 '72 por; p66+ Ag 24 '74 por
Sat Eve Post 224:25+ Je 28 '52 pors
Who's Who in America, 1974-75
Who's Who in Aviation (1955)

HOLLEY, EDWARD G(AILON)

Nov. 26, 1927- Librarian; educator; organization official
Address: b. 100 Manning Hall, University of North Carolina, Chapel Hill, N.C. 27514; h. 1508 Ephesus Church Rd., Chapel Hill, N.C. 27514

EDWARD G. HOLLEY

Before he joined the faculty of the University of North Carolina in 1972 as Dean of the School of Library Science, Edward G. Holley was director of libraries and professor at the University of Houston. There Philip G. Hoffman, the university president, described him as "a rare combination of scholar and administrator" with "a broad range of knowledge that cuts across many disciplines" and a "quiet and effective" method of working. In 1974-75 those attributes were expected to enhance his efficacy as president of the American Library Association, a nonprofit educational association of approximately 30,000 librarians, library trustees, and others committed to the advancement of library science and service. Founded in 1876, it is the oldest and largest national library association in the world.

Perhaps Holley's most significant contribution to scholarship so far is his book *Charles Evans, American Bibliographer,* which in 1964 won the Scarecrow Press Award of the American Library Association for its "outstanding contribution to library literature." It is the first comprehensive biography of the man to whom historians and other scholars will permanently be indebted for compiling *American Bibliography: A Chronological Dictionary of All Books, Pamphlets, and Periodical Publications Printed in the United States of America from the Genesis of Printing in 1639 down to and Including the Year 1820.*

Edward Gailon Holley, who prefers to be called Ed, was born in the farming community of Pulaski, Giles County, Tennessee on November 26, 1927 to Abe Brown Holley and Maxie Elizabeth (Bass) Holley. His father was, successively, a factory worker and milkman. He has two sisters, Mary Ellen (Mrs. Marion W. Jones), an elementary school teacher, and Elizabeth Ann, a federal government employee.

At Giles County High School Holley played in the band, belonged to the Beta Club, and co-edited the school yearbook. During his high school days he was strongly influenced by the principal,

R. B. Stone, and Stone's wife, who taught him Latin and English. After school he delivered newspapers and worked in a grocery store, and on Sunday afternoons he filled in for librarian Frances Hampton Moose, another important influence on him, at the local public library. At David Lipscomb College in Nashville, Tennessee, where he had a modest scholarship, Holley majored in English, minored in history and French, and worked on the college literary magazine. An assistant in the campus library, he was *de facto* librarian during his senior year, when there was no regular librarian.

Holley was persuaded by his college dean to change his vocational aspiration from that of high school English teaching to librarianship. Accordingly, after taking his B.A. degree *magna cum laude* at David Lipscomb College in 1949, Holley entered the George Peabody College for Teachers, also in Nashville. There he was elected to Kappa Delta Pi, the honorary education fraternity, and took his M.A. degree in library science and English in 1951.

From George Peabody College, Holley went to the University of Illinois in Champaign-Urbana, where he was a librarian in the photographic reproduction laboratory while beginning work on his doctorate. A member of the United States Naval Reserve, he was called to active duty in 1953 and spent two years as an intelligence officer in the Pentagon in Washington, D.C., and an additional year as an administrative and personnel officer aboard the USS *Botetourt.*

After his return to the University of Illinois, Holley was graduate assistant in the Graduate School of Library Science, in 1956-57, and librarian of the Education, Philosophy, and Psychology Library, for five years beginning in 1957. He received his Ph.D. in library science, with a minor in American History, in 1961. His doctoral dissertation on the pioneering American librarian and bibliographer Charles Evans (1850-1935) was suggested to him by his thesis advisor, Leslie W. Dunlap, and facilitated by Eliot H. Evans, the elder son of the bibliographer, who gave him access to Evans' papers. In his preface to *Charles Evans, American Bibliographer* (Univ. of Illinois Press, 1963), Holley explained the genesis of his interest in the man. "Five years ago," he wrote, "the name Charles Evans meant to me what it means to most people in the library profession—a name which conjured an image of twelve massive volumes, uniformly bound in rich crimson buckram, covering the first 160 years of printing in America. Beyond that not much was known about the man, his background, his method of work, or the real meaning of his efforts. When it was suggested that the library world needed a good biography of Charles Evans, I immediately became interested. . . . Despite an awareness of Evans' bibliographical work, the significance of his contributions to librarianship and bibliography are not well known. It is the purpose of this biography to remedy that deficiency."

When *Charles Evans, American Bibliographer* was published, David Kaser praised it in the *Mississippi Valley Historical Review* (March 1964) for being "full," "well-researched," and "competent." Jesse H. Shera, who long ago deplored the fact that one of the most neglected fields of American library history was that of biography, wrote in the *Library Journal* (December 1963) that Holley "has written a biography that will doubtless stand as the definitive treatment of Charles Evans' life."

Holley went to the University of Houston in Texas as director of libraries and assistant professor in 1962 and three years later was promoted to full professor. During his tenure in Houston a $3,300,000 annex added 126,000 feet to the original 93,000 feet of the M. D. Anderson Memorial Library, and a total of $3,589,015 was expended on books, periodicals, and binding. More than 300,000 volumes were added to the collections of the university libraries, making a total of 664,469, and the number of periodicals tripled. The number of microfilm reels reached 10,267, and the holdings in microcards, maps, and manuscripts came to comparable figures. Holley acquired a trove of Aldous Huxley papers and added the Pat H. Candler Collection of Texana and the Joseph W. Evans Memorial Bibliography Collection to the special collections.

While researching the life and work of Charles Evans, who was the first treasurer of the American Library Association, Holley had come across the charter scrapbook of the ALA, which contained the documents and letters of Melvil Dewey and the other founding fathers of the ALA relating to the association's creation. From those papers he compiled *Raking the Historic Coals; The ALA Scrapbook of 1876* (Beta Phi Mu Chapbook No. 8, 1967). With Donald D. Hendricks he wrote *Resources of Texas Libraries* (Field Services Division, Austin, Texas, 1968, which was also published as *CB Study Paper No. 8* by the Coordinating Board, Texas College and University System).

On a Council on Library Resources fellowship in the spring of 1971 Holley traveled throughout the United States, visiting publicly supported urban universities and such major private universities as Columbia, Chicago, and Southern California. He found that although "support for some of these institutions . . . was substantial during the decade [the 1960's], none of these increases really kept pace with the expansion of enrollments and new library programs, and most publicly supported urban universities have far too few staff . . . to do much more than operate as service-station libraries."

In his tour of urban university libraries Holley noted with some concern what seemed to be a decline in the spirit of service. As he told a group of librarians in Fayetteville, North Carolina the following year, he was "particularly depressed to see what has happened to library service in one major library system which has achieved all the goals dear to the heart [faculty status, optimum salary, and so forth]." He warned: "If we do not recapture our service ideal . . . the consequences will not only be more frustration and unhappiness for us as we pursue our legitimate personal goals, but there will also be decreasing public interest in and support of our libraries, which are rapidly becoming peripheral to the major concerns of most citizens."

While in Houston, Holley served as chairman of the United States Office of Education's Advisory Council on College Library Resources, from 1969 to 1971, as editor of the Association of College and Research Libraries' series *Publications in Librarianship*, from 1969 to 1972, and as president of the Texas Library Association, in 1971. At the TLA conference that was held in Corpus Christi on April 1, 1971 he quoted John Hersey's statement that two elements will be essential for higher education if it is to have a tolerable future: "an atmosphere of trust and decentralization of power." He applied the statement to the Texas Library Association, just as he would later call for federation, or decentralization of power, in the American Library Association.

Holley resigned his post at the University of Houston in December 1971 and assumed his present position at the University of North Carolina the following month. The School of Library Science that he heads at Chapel Hill has a faculty of fifteen, not counting guest lecturers, and an enrollment of approximately 150. It awarded ninety-eight master's degrees in 1972, and Holley and his colleagues at the school are currently planning the introduction of a doctoral program and the expansion of staff necessary for implementing such a program.

A member of the American Library Association since 1949, Holley was chairman of the ALA's publishing board at the time of his election to the top position in the association, in June 1973. Installation in the presidency takes place during the ALA's annual conference the year following election. The 1974 conference, the ninety-third such meeting of the association, was held at the Americana, New York Hilton, and other New York City hotels from July 7 to 13.

At the time of his nomination for the presidency of the ALA, Holley made the following "statement of professional concerns": "One of the fundamental issues of our time is how organizations can centralize some functions for efficiency and economy and decentralize other functions for service. . . . Almost certainly for ALA decentralization of power means a reorganization of the divisions to give them more control over their own programs, staffs, and budgets, while at the same time preserving for the national organization a few core functions such as federal legislative activities, intellectual freedom, and the welfare of librarians. Unless decentralization can be accomplished soon, ALA, which already faces fiscal disaster, may collapse of its own bureaucratic weight. The leadership of the presidency can best be exercised not in the day-to-day administrative details but by becoming the forceful advocate for a new structure, by encouraging the restoration of a sense of trust among librarians, and by becoming the tireless voice of libraries and librarians before those who do not see either as essential to our society."

As a representative of the American Library Association, Holley has appeared before United States Senate subcommittees to endorse a resolution calling for a White House conference on library and information services in the nation's bicentennial year, 1976, and to support extension of the federal subsidization of elementary and secondary school libraries, textbooks, and other instructional materials. Regarding the latter program he testified that he was "aware of the existense of school libraries in . . . communities [that] would never have been able to establish school libraries without federal assistance."

Holley's many contributions to professional journals include "Looking Forward to 1976," in *Southeastern Librarian* (Winter 1974), "Academic Library Finance in the Seventies: The Picture Blurs," in the *Texas Library Journal* (March 1974), "Federation: An Idea Whose Time Has Come," in the *Library Journal* (February 1, 1974), and "Who Runs Libraries? The Emergence of Library Governance in Higher Education," in the *Wilson Library Bulletin* (September 1973). In the last mentioned article he asserted that the best strategy for an academic librarian seeking a power base "is to ally himself with the faculty . . . the most powerful group on campus." He concluded: "In trying to sort out the various options, librarians must consider two fundamental questions: 1. How do they want to participate in library management? 2. Will staff participation benefit not only the staff but the library's clientele as well?"

Edward G. Holley and Robbie Lee Gault, a school teacher, were married on June 19, 1954. They have four children: Gailon Boyd, Edward Jens, Amy Lin, and Beth Alison. The Holleys are members of the Church of Christ. Mrs. Holley spends much of her time writing for religious publications and lecturing to religious groups, and Holley himself not only chairs the business meetings of the Church of Christ congregation in Chapel Hill but occasionally occupies the pulpit.

Holley is five feet seven inches tall and weighs 160 pounds. He has blue eyes and graying black hair. Tom Mulvany of the Houston *Chronicle* (February 25, 1968) described him as "a jolly extrovert with a contagious enthusiasm and a ready smile." Otherwise "very unathletic," as he has described himself, Holley enjoys swimming in the neighborhood pool with his family. The president of ALA is a member of the Democratic party, the library science honorary society Beta Phi Mu, the American Association of University Professors, the Southeastern Library Association, and the North Carolina Library Association, and he is a trustee of the Disciples of Christ Historical Society. In 1968 he retired from the United States Naval Reserve with the rank of lieutenant senior grade.

References

Houston Chronicle F 25 '68 por
Raleigh News and Observer Jl 7 '74
Biographical Directory of Librarians in the United States and Canada (1970)
Contemporary Authors, vols 7-8 (1964)
Who's Who in America, 1972-73

JACKSON, REGGIE

May 18, 1946- Baseball player
Address: b. Oakland Athletics, Oakland-Alameda County Coliseum, Oakland, Calif. 94621

In 1973, his sixth full season with the Oakland Athletics, Reggie Jackson was named the Most Valuable Player both in the American League and in the World Series, which Oakland won for the second consecutive time. The effervescent Jackson, who plays center field, is a fleet defensive man, with an extraordinary range and arm, but he is best known for his slugging at the plate, where he holds the "clean-up" position. His league-leading thirty-two home runs and 117 runs-batted-in in 1973 brought his major-league career totals in those departments to 189 and 536 respectively. An intelligent, articulate man with "class" and an intense player with a keen sense of team responsibility, Jackson is a natural leader during games, pep-talking his fellow players through crises, and off the field he acts as Oakland's player representative.

One of six children of mixed Afro-American and Spanish descent, Reginald Martinez Jackson was born in Wyncote, Pennsylvania on May 18, 1946 to Mr. and Mrs. Martinez Jackson. Early in Reggie's childhood his parents were divorced. Three of the children went with the mother to Baltimore and three, including Reggie, with the father to Cheltenham, Pennsylvania, near Philadelphia, where Martinez Jackson Sr. still runs a small tailoring and dry-cleaning business.

Encouraged by his father, who played semipro baseball, Jackson became an all-around athlete at Cheltenham High School. On the basketball court he was peerless; in track he ran the 100-yard dash in 9.7 seconds; on the football team he

REGGE JACKSON

was the star halfback; and in his senior year he pitched three no-hitters and batted .550 with the baseball team. From high school he went on an athletic scholarship to Arizona State University, in Tempe, where he was outstanding in both football and baseball. As a baseball player he hit a home run out of Phoenix Municipal Stadium, something no collegian had ever done before.

After his sophomore year at Arizona State, Jackson was lured into professional baseball by Charles O. Finley, the idiosyncratic owner of the Athletics, then located in Kansas City. "Mr. Finley opened with a bonus bid of $60,000, and when he got to $95,000 I signed," Jackson recalled in an interview with Bill Libby for *Sport* (September 1970). The New York Mets, having the first free agent draft selection in 1966, could have beaten Finley to Jackson's doorstep if they had wanted to. Instead, they chose Steve Chilcott, who never made it out of the Mets' farm system. "It is one of baseball's most whispered about stories," Maury Allen wrote in the New York *Post* (October 26, 1973). "The Mets didn't . . . [pass up] Jackson because they thought Chilcott was better. They picked Chilcott because they thought Jackson might be just too hot to handle."

With Lewiston, Oregon and Modesto, California in the Athletics' farm system in 1966, Jackson batted just under .300, and the following year he proved himself to be a power hitter with Birmingham, Alabama, where he led the Southern League in total bases, with 232. Called up to Kansas City toward the end of the 1967 season, Jackson moved with the Athletics to Oakland in 1968. In his first full season in the majors he hit twenty-nine homers and drove in seventy-four runs but otherwise performed inauspiciously, making eighteen errors and striking out 171 times, the second worst seasonal strikeout record in baseball history. The following year, 1969, he again led the American League in strike-outs, with 142, but that negative tally was overshadowed by his magnificent record of forty-seven home runs.

Ironically, his 1969 home-run pace contributed to a slump, after he reached his thirty-ninth homer. "I couldn't handle all that pressure," he told Glenn Dickey in an interview for an article in *Sport* (July 1973). "Everyday somebody was coming up to me and asking me if I could pass Ruth and Maris. It really got to me." Also demoralizing was his deteriorating relationship with his Mexican-American wife, Jenni (from whom he eventually separated). "Reggie looked like a superstar now," Glenn Dickey wrote, "and there were plenty of women eager to show their appreciation. Reggie didn't always resist the temptations."

The final seven of Jackson's 1969 homers were eked out over a period of two nervous months. Despite the deterioration of his performance in those months, he expected a healthy raise in pay. The post-season contract negotiations were acrimonious, with Jackson demanding $60,000 and Charles O. Finley insisting that $40,000 was the limit, considering the bonuses Jackson was getting. (The eventual settlement was $46,000 and $400 a month for the rent on Jackson's Oakland apartment.) As Harold Peterson observed in *Sports Illustrated* (June 8, 1970), "bitterness" clouded Jackson's "sunny, nice-guy nature." In 1970 his average dropped to .237 and his homers to twenty-three and when he struck out (135 times, again the highest in the league) he would often throw his bat in a fit of anger.

For therapy—in effect, if not intent—Jackson spent the winter of 1970-71 playing under veteran black player-manager Frank Robinson, an old idol of his, in Santurce, Puerto Rico. "He was trying to do too much," Robinson has recalled. "He'd get down on himself. . . . He had to be told he can't carry a whole club, that he can't expect to get a hit every time up." Jackson had been told that before, but coming from Robinson, the advice was more meaningful, and effective.

His morale restored, Jackson returned to Oakland a maturer person, "able to live with" himself, as he said, even if he "never hit another home run." In the 1971 All Star game he and Robinson paced the American League to its first victory over the National League in nine years. (Jackson hit a stupendous home run with a man on third to begin the scoring by the American League, which had been trailing 3-0.) In regular season play Jackson led the league in strikeouts (161) for the fourth consecutive time but his batting rose to .277 and his slugging was capped with thirty-two home runs. Oakland won the American League's western division title but in the pennant playoffs lost to the Baltimore Orioles of the eastern division. A disconsolate Jackson, who batted .333 in the championship series and hit two homers in the final game, sat in the dugout alone, his head in his hands, for ten minutes after the loss to the Orioles.

In 1972 Jackson batted .265 and belted out twenty-five homers. In the field he was tied for most double plays by an American League outfielder (five). His career totals at the end of the season were a batting average of .258, 128 doubles, twenty triples, 157 home runs, 419 runs batted in, and a fielding average of .965. In the post-season playoffs he stole home to score the decisive run in the final game against the Detroit Tigers. Emerging from the slide into home plate with a torn leg muscle (which still bothers him), he had to sit out the World Series, which the Athletics took from the Cincinnati Reds.

Jackson batted .293 and led the league in homers (thirty-two) and RBI's (117) in 1973, when the Athletics defeated the Baltimore Orioles in the playoffs and the New York Mets in the World Series. Just before the playoffs an anonymous letter arrived in the Oakland front office, with the warning that if Jackson played in the championship games he would never play again. Because of the death threat he was guarded by private and FBI agents throughout the playoffs and the World Series. In the series he batted .310 and drove in six runs, but fans of Oakland shortstop Bert Campaneris (who does not speak English well and does not have Jackson's presence) thought that Campy's contribution was more valuable. Some alleged that Jackson was chosen *Sport* magazine's Most Valuable Player in the series because it was known that he would be "bright, clever, and funny" in accepting the award (a new automobile, along with the citation). No such complaints were conspicuous when, in November 1973, the sportswriters of the United States unanimously voted Jackson the Most Valuable Player in the American League.

On the playing field Jackson is still aggressive, but he has learned to control his temper and to maintain his concentration, thanks to the tutoring of Frank Robinson "reinforced"—Jackson's word—by Dick Williams (manager of the Athletics through the 1973 season). Lefthanded at the plate as in the field, Jackson hits best against righthanded pitchers. He admits that his glaring weakness is indiscriminate swinging at pitches that are too high or low. "The pitchers learned how to pitch to me faster than I learned how to hit them," he told a reporter during the 1973 season. "I still need to learn the strike zone."

Mustachioed Reggie Jackson, six feet tall and weighing 200 pounds, is in better physical condition than any other member of the Athletics, with the possible exception of Vida Blue. "His strength is just unbelievable," former teammate Dave Duncan, still a close friend of his, has testified. His will is strong too, and it was only after long conflict that he accommodated himself to the autocracy of Charles O. Finley. "You have to play his game," he told Glenn Dickey of *Sport* with typical candor. "Life is too short and I've got too much going for me to let that SOB spoil it for me."

Dickey, who remembered Jackson the rookie as "fiery, emotional, and sometimes abrupt with newspapermen," found "the new Jackson" to be "affable" and "cooperative in the extreme" but, beneath "an unnatural calm" and "a surface confidence," still basically "insecure." In the past Jackson's insecurity often expressed itself in a strutting attitude that irritated some of his colleagues. At one point, for example, he was in the

habit of referring to himself as "Mr. B and B," meaning that he was the bread-and-butter member of the team.

Now divorced, Jackson lives alone, in Oakland during the baseball season and the rest of the year in the Phoenix suburb of Tempe, where he is a partner in a flourishing real estate business and a pillar of the community. At low points in his career he was tempted to go into business full time, but, as one sportswriter observed, the "ego" satisfaction he finds in baseball always prevailed. According to Jackson, his thirst for recognition, for feeling "needed," is an important factor in his determination to become "the A's first $100,-000 ballplayer." (In 1973 his salary was reported to be $75,000.) Despite his "thin-skinned" temperament, Jackson says that he is now "at peace" with himself. A friend in Tempe has characterized him as "a competent man who once had some problems."

References

Ebony 24:26 S '69 por; 24:92+ O '69 pors
N Y Post p87 O 26 '73 por
N Y Times p38 O 22 '73 pors
Sport 50:66+ S '70 por; 56:53+ Jl '73 pors
Sports Illus 32:56 Je 8 '70
Baseball Register, 1973
Who's Who in Baseball, 1973
Who's Who in Professional Baseball (1973)

JAMIESON, J(OHN) K(ENNETH)

Aug. 28, 1910- Corporation executive
Address: b. Exxon Corporation, 1251 Ave. of the Americas, New York 10020; h. 1310 E. Flagler Dr., Mamaroneck, N.Y. 10543

Described in the New York *Times Magazine* (April 21, 1974) as "the single most powerful man in the American oil industry," Canadian-born J. K. Jamieson rose through corporate ranks to become, in 1969, board chairman and chief executive officer of the Standard Oil Company of New Jersey, known since 1972 as the Exxon Corporation. As head of the world's largest oil company, with more than 150,000 employees and some 300 subsidiaries and affiliates in over 100 countries, Jamieson has been increasingly preoccupied with finding means of alleviating the current worldwide energy crisis. He has also been devoting much of his time to defending the oil industry against charges that it is responsible for the fuel shortage and accompanying high prices and to justifying Exxon's high profits, estimated at a record $2.44 billion in 1973.

John Kenneth Jamieson, whose family roots are in Nova Scotia, was born on August 28, 1910 in Medicine Hat, Alberta, Canada to John Locke Jamieson, a member of Canada's Northwest Mounted Police, and the former Kate Herron. He grew up in Medicine Hat, then a remote prairie outpost with a population of some 5,600. One of the boyhood memories that have re-

J. K. JAMIESON

mained with him is that of his shooting a bear
that was prowling near his family's home. Ken
Jamieson attended the University of Alberta at
Edmonton for two years and then entered the
Massachusetts Institute of Technology. At MIT
he studied civil engineering and business administration and belonged to Lambda Chi Alpha
fraternity. He earned a B.S. degree in 1931.

Unable to obtain an engineering job during
those early Depression years, Jamieson returned
to Alberta, where he found work straightening
rails for the Canadian Pacific. A six-foot snowfall
brought his second job, as a member of a road-
building gang in British Columbia, to an end.
"I thought that if I ever got an interesting, steady
job that someday might pay $10,000 a year, life
would be just fine," Jamieson recalled in an interview with William D. Smith in the New York
Times (April 26, 1970). "There weren't any good
steady jobs though. There weren't any jobs,
period."

In 1932 Jamieson's reply to a newspaper ad
launched his career in the oil business. Northwest
Stellarene Company of Alberta hired him as foreman of a construction gang at its Moose Jaw
(Saskatchewan) refinery. But when, after a year,
his employers told him that they would have to
reduce his pay because of the continuing Depression, he resigned, deciding to try his luck prospecting for gold along the Fraser River in British
Columbia's Cariboo Mountains. Four months later,
convinced that he would not strike it rich, he
asked Northwest Stellarene to rehire him and
accepted an even lower salary. After the firm
became part of the British American Oil Company
in 1934, Jamieson rose to the position of manager of the Moose Jaw refinery. During World
War II, he spent considerable time in Washington, D.C., handling liaison between the Canadian
controller's department and the United States government's Petroleum Administration for War.
After the war he went back to work at British
American and was promoted to manager of the
manufacturing department.

Although Jamieson was initially concerned
about the prospect of "just ending up in the back
room," in 1948 he joined Imperial Oil Ltd., the
70 percent owned Canadian subsidiary of the
Standard Oil Company of New Jersey. There he
worked as assistant to Michael Haider, whom he
later followed up the corporate ladder, and he
helped to revive the Canadian oil industry by
taking part in the development of a major oil
field at Leduc, Alberta. In 1949 Jamieson was
placed in charge of the engineering and development division of Imperial's Sarnia (Ontario) refinery. A year later he was promoted to assistant
general manager in the company's manufacturing
department. After spending the early months of
1951 "on loan" to the Canadian Government's
Department of Defense Production, helping to
set up that department's petroleum division, Jamieson returned to Imperial. He became a director
of the company in 1952 and was elected a vice-
president in 1953.

Jamieson changed his permanent residence from
Canada to the United States in 1959, when he
succeeded Michael Haider as president of the
International Petroleum Company, an affiliate of
the Standard Oil Company of New Jersey, based
in Coral Gables, Florida. As head of International, he dealt in particular with Latin American
affairs and traveled to Colombia, Ecuador, and
Venezuela, where the company has exploration,
production, refining, transportation, and marketing operations.

In 1961 Jamieson was named a vice-president,
director, and member of the executive committee
of the Humble Oil and Refining Company in
Houston, Texas, the principal affiliate of Standard
Oil of New Jersey, in control of all domestic operations. He became executive vice-president of
Humble Oil in January 1962 and president in
November 1963. Originally organized in 1917
by Texas and Oklahoma investors, Humble Oil
had a tradition of independence from the parent
company. Charged with the task of bringing it
more directly under the control of New Jersey
headquarters, Jamieson used considerable skill in
guiding the delicate negotiations that led to the
consolidation of five affiliates into one smoothly
operating division with assets totaling more than
$3 billion. At the same time, he reduced the
work force from 40,000 to 28,000. He also broadened the executive training program so that it
would produce men with a well-rounded knowledge of the oil industry rather than mere specialists.

Jamieson's success at Houston led to his promotion to executive vice-president of Standard Oil
of New Jersey in the fall of 1964. That same
year he became a naturalized citizen of the
United States. "It only made good sense," he told
an interviewer for Time (February 18, 1974),
"because when you're dealing with United
States government people you can't deal with
them adequately if you're a foreigner representing a United States company." Although he had
less seniority than eight other vice-presidents,

Jamieson was elected president of Standard Oil of New Jersey in February 1965, when Haider was designated chairman and chief executive officer. Addressing the eighty-fourth annual stockholders' meeting in Cleveland, Ohio in May 1966, Jamieson reported record first quarter earnings and predicted a bright economic future for the company, noting that continued economic growth in the United States, the European Common Market countries, Latin America, and Japan would lead to increasing demands for energy.

During Jamieson's presidency, Standard Oil of New Jersey carried on an extensive three-year, $700,000,000 crude oil exploration program, initiated in 1964 under former board chairman Monroe J. Rathbone to give the company more resources outside of the Arab-dominated Organization of Petroleum Exporting Countries (OPEC). The successful program, considered by Jamieson as one of the most important activities ever undertaken by Standard Oil of New Jersey, made it, according to *Forbes* (April 1, 1973), "far and away the most geographically and economically balanced company in the industry."

When Haider reached the mandatory retirement age of sixty-five in October 1969, J. K. Jamieson succeeded him as chairman and chief executive officer of Standard Oil of New Jersey. Milo Brisco, an executive vice-president who had worked with Jamieson at International Petroleum, stepped into the position of president. The appointments of Haider, Jamieson, and Brisco had marked a change in the company's custom of picking its top management from the Baton Rouge, Louisiana refinery complex. The three executives, each of whom had at one time served as president of International, were dubbed the "Coral Gables Mafia" by company associates.

While encouraging the company's expansion into such diverse areas as natural gas, fuel for nuclear plants, food and chemical production, and the hotel and restaurant business, Jamieson did not neglect its primary role as a producer of oil. The expropriation of properties of International Petroleum by the military government of Peru in 1968 and 1969, and the increasing demands by the governments of OPEC countries for greater taxes and royalties led to an accelerated search for domestic oil resources by Jersey Standard and other companies. In November 1969, Jamieson disclosed that an estimated 30 billion barrels of oil were located on Alaska's north slope in what was said to be the largest oil field in North America. The announcement coincided with the successful completion by the ice-breaking tanker S.S. *Manhattan* of a pioneering eighty-day, 10,000-mile voyage through the legendary Northwest Passage. Sponsored in part by Humble Oil at a cost of $40,000,000, the project was designed to provide information on the feasibility of shipping oil from Alaska's north slope to the East Coast of the United States and to Europe as a possible alternative to a projected transcontinental pipeline.

In May 1970 Jamieson announced a major reorganization of the top ranks of Jersey Standard's management, giving broader operational authority to individual department heads, with the aim of strengthening and modernizing the company's departments. During 1970 and 1971 Jersey Standard expended some $183,000,000 to combat environmental pollution. The company also stepped up its efforts to provide greater opportunities for training and employment to members of minority groups. In response to antiwar demonstrators who condemned Jersey Standard's role in the Indochina war at the May 1971 stockholders' meeting, Jamieson denied that his company had any relations with the South Vietnamese government but defended its role in supplying United States military forces in Southeast Asia.

At the stockholders' meeting of October 24, 1972—the first to be held at the company's new fifty-four story headquarters on Manhattan's Avenue of the Americas—Jamieson announced that by a vote of 97 percent of the shareholders the name of the Standard Oil Company of New Jersey was changed to Exxon Corporation. The name change, which became effective on November 1, 1972 was the latest of a sequence of events dating back to 1911, when John D. Rockefeller's Standard Oil Trust was dissolved. Over the years, the federal courts supported the complaints of several former Standard Oil group members against the use of the name Standard Oil and the Esso trademark. As a result, Jersey Standard was allowed to use the trademark in only eighteen states, a restriction that placed the company at a serious competitive disadvantage. The change of the company's name to Exxon—chosen from 10,000 computer-produced possibilities—was followed by a massive advertising campaign, featuring posters depicting the familiar Esso (now Exxon) tiger, and bearing the caption "We're changing our name, but not our stripes." On January 1, 1973 all company affiliates officially joined the parent corporation in using the Exxon name, and the Humble Oil and Refining Company became Exxon Company, U.S.A.

At a Tokyo meeting of businessmen in April 1973, Jamieson spoke out against reported proposals by the Nixon administration for the creation of a bargaining bloc of oil-consuming nations, which, he felt, might create an atmosphere of opposition between producers and consumers. "It could lead to a series of reprisals and counter-reprisals that would rule out the possibility of rational compromise in future negotiations," he asserted. Jamieson also took a dim view of proposed special preference agreements, contending that they might "inhibit the multilateral exchange of goods that has fostered economic growth in the past." In September 1973, Jamieson and other Exxon officials, foreseeing the impending Arab oil embargo, urged leaders of European Common Market countries to prepare an international allocation plan in the event the flow of oil to the West were cut off.

Testifying in January 1974 at hearings called by the Senate Permanent Investigations Subcommittee, Jamieson did not deny Senator Henry M.

Jackson's charge that Exxon had cut off supplies to United States military forces on orders of the Saudi Arabian government. He explained, however, that the company had no choice in the matter, and that the action taken was promptly reported to the Defense Department. A few days later, in keeping with "Operation Candor," launched by the oil industry to improve its public image, Jamieson called an unprecedented press conference, giving what John M. Lee of the New York *Times* (January 27, 1974) described as "a sincere presentation, the very model of corporate soundness and sobriety." He revealed that company earnings for the last quarter of 1973 had risen 59 percent over the corresponding period in 1972. He hastened to add that Exxon was not making "windfall profits" and attributed the increase in earnings to the devaluation of the dollar and the high volume of sales before the Arab embargo, among other factors. Asserting that the 1973 profits were needed to finance investments required to develop new oil resources, he announced that Exxon planned to spend $16 billion for capital expansion—including exploration, transportation facilities, and the development of new sources of energy—by 1978. He expressed concern about Congressional threats of legislation that would curb oil company profits by ending the favorable tax treatment that United States corporations enjoy in foreign countries.

According to Jamieson, the energy crisis was "real and serious" well before the 1973 Middle Eastern war and is likely to hover over us for the foreseeable future. He regards the Nixon administration's Project Independence, under which the American consumer would be freed from dependence on overseas energy supplies by 1980, as unrealistic, and he believes that as long as energy demands increase, Americans will become more and more dependent on Middle Eastern oil. The only remedy, in his view, is a sharp cutback on fuel consumption while alternative sources of energy are being developed.

The top management of Exxon has been compared to a loosely organized world government. While maintaining local autonomy, Jamieson has tightened his control of the corporation somewhat by giving the parent company a more active advisory role with subsidiaries and affiliates. Jamieson rarely makes a crucial decision without first consulting the nine-member management committee and the seventeen-member board of directors. His earnings at Exxon were reported to be about $600,000 for 1973. He emphasizes the international character of the corporation by giving non-American employees the opportunity to serve as his personal assistants and then sending the men home to executive jobs.

Jamieson is a director of the Chase Manhattan Bank, the Equitable Life Assurance Society of the United States, the International Nickel Company of Canada Ltd., and the American Petroleum Institute. He is a member of the Massachusetts Institute of Technology Corporation and the Council on Foreign Relations, and chairman of the Community Blood Council of Greater New York Inc. He serves on the executive committees of the United States Council of the International Chamber of Commerce, the Business Council, the National Petroleum Council, and the National Industrial Pollution Control Council.

J. K. Jamieson and his wife, the former Ethel May Burns, whom he married on December 23, 1937, have a son, John Burns, and a daughter, Anne Frances. A tough-minded, self-assured, and ruggedly handsome man, Ken Jamieson is six feet two inches tall, weighs 200 pounds, and has graying hair. He is an Episcopalian. His favorite recreations include golf, bicycling, quail hunting, salmon fishing, and working in the garden of his Mamaroneck, New York home. He travels extensively for Exxon and has a number of mementoes of meetings with statesmen, including a cigarette box given to him by the late President Sukarno of Indonesia. "The oil industry has done some bad in its day, but it has also done a lot of good," Jamieson told William D. Smith of the New York *Times* (April 2, 1970). "It serves a very real and valid function in the United States and the world that will not decrease in the years to come despite attacks that are often unreasoned and unjustified."

References

N Y Times III p3 Ap 26 '70 por
Time 103:24 F 18 '74 por
Wall St J p14 Ag 28 '69 por
Who's Who in America, 1972-73
Who's Who in Finance and Industry, 1974-75
Who's Who in the East, 1974-75

JAWORSKI, LEON

Sept. 19, 1905- Lawyer
Address: h. 3665 Ella Lee Lane, Houston, Texas 77027

On November 5, 1973, when Houston lawyer Leon Jaworski was sworn in as special Watergate prosecutor, he capped a long and distinguished career by taking on a historic task. In charge of investigating the Watergate scandal in all its labyrinthine ramifications—and thus of uncovering evidence that might bear on the possible impeachment of President Nixon—he knew that he would have to make ground-breaking legal decisions on extremely important and touchy issues and would be subjected to intense pressures and scrutiny from all sides. His predecessor, Archibald Cox, had been dismissed by Nixon when he refused to abandon the court battle for White House tape recordings and other evidence from the Oval Office that might indicate involvement in or knowledge of illegal campaign practices, influence peddling, bribery, perjury, political espionage and sabotage, or other betrayals of public trust. Confounding those who suspected that he might be "Nixon's man," Jaworski proved himself to be, as one of the thirty-eight lawyers on the special prosecution staff put it, "even tougher than Archie."

In April 1974 Jaworski obtained a subpoena for sixty-four White House tapes and related materials. Refusing to accept the assertion of the President's chief Watergate lawyer, James D. St. Clair, that transcripts made public by the White House contain "everything we know," he continued to press with vigor for the tapes themselves, which were needed for use in the trial of seven Watergate cover-up defendants, which began in September 1974. As of May 1974, the special prosecutor had eight appeals to handle, two corporations and sixteen individuals under indictment, twenty-three corporations and individuals whose cases had closed, and five individuals awaiting sentencing. Jaworski's involvement in the Watergate prosecutions ended when he resigned his post on October 25, 1974.

The third of four children of a Polish immigrant father and an Austrian immigrant mother, Leon Jaworski was born in Waco, Texas on September 19, 1905. His mother, Marie (Mira) Jaworski, died when he was five and his father, Joseph Jaworski, an Evangelical minister, remarried four years later. Jaworski's sister Mary, who married into Texas high society, knew Claudia Alta Taylor even before "Lady Bird" became Mrs. Lyndon Johnson. His brother Hannibal Joseph is a surgeon in Waco.

"We were as poor as church mice," Hannibal Joseph Jaworski told Mark Arnold of the *National Observer* (November 24, 1973). "Father would ride a buggy to various churches for five dollars a sermon, earning about twenty-five dollars a month. He was a very strict disciplinarian. To him the law was the law. He taught us to love our country and to respect the law." Eventually the Reverend Jaworski established his own congregation and the family financial situation improved.

Mature beyond his years, Leon Jaworski was an ambitious, diligent student, and as a member of the debating team at Waco High School he won statewide debating contests. After graduating from high school at fifteen, he went on scholarship to Baptist-owned Baylor University, where the president was a friend of his father's. To supplement his scholarship, he worked as a student assistant, correcting papers for seventeen cents an hour. In 1925 he received his LL.B. degree and became the youngest person ever admitted to the Texas bar. The following year he took an LL.M. degree at George Washington University.

In his first courtroom performance, Jaworski successfully defended a man charged with operating an illegal whiskey still in Moonshine Valley, near Waco. In another of his early cases he failed to win acquittal for a poor black accused of murdering a white couple. He joined the Houston firm of Fulbright, Crooker, Freeman & Bates as an associate in 1931 and became a partner three years later. During the 1930's he became increasingly well-known in the Texas legal fraternity as

LEON JAWORSKI

a deft courtroom strategist and tactician, capable of quickly digesting and masterfully using huge amounts of complex information.

During World War II Jaworski served as a colonel in the United States Army, and after the war he was chief of the war crimes trial section of the Judge Advocate General's Corps. He rejoined Fulbright, Crooker, Freeman, Bates & Jaworski in 1946 and became senior partner in the firm five years later. When Lyndon B. Johnson's narrow victory in the 1948 Texas Democratic Senatorial primary was contested, Jaworski helped Crooker and Abe Fortas win the electoral fraud suit brought against Johnson.

In the ensuing years Jaworski served terms as president of the Houston Bar Association, the Texas Bar Association, and the Texas Civil Judiciary Council. An independent Democrat, he broadened and tightened his relationships with Texas political and industrial leaders, and in the financial world he was by 1960 a director of the Bank of the Southwest and the Benjamin Franklin Savings and Loan Association. Later he joined the boards of directors of Anderson Clayton & Company, the Intercontinental National Bank, the Coastal States Gas Producing Company, and the Gulf Publishing Company. The last mentioned company published his account of his experiences as a Nazi war crimes prosecutor, *Fifteen Years After* (1961). The introduction to the book was written by Lyndon Johnson, then Vice-President of the United States. The previous year Jaworski had supervised the litigation that enabled Johnson to run simultaneously for the Vice-Presidency and the Senate.

Over the years, as Roy Reed pointed out in the New York *Times* (November 4, 1973), there was less and less doubt where Jaworski's interests lay, as his law firm represented "bankers and big business" and "his political loyalties . . . never strayed far from those of his clients." But by Texas standards Jaworski was progressive, at least in the area of race relations. His firm was the first in Houston to take on Jewish and black staff members, and from 1962 to 1965 he worked under Archibald Cox as special assistant to United States Attorney General Robert F. Kennedy in pressing contempt charges against Governor Ross R. Barnett of Mississippi for defying a federal court order desegregating the University of Mississippi. On the other hand, he represented the University of Texas in its effort to maintain segregated dormitories in 1963 and opposed the seating of poor people on the Houston antipoverty agency's board in 1965. He did, however, come out in favor of higher welfare expenditures.

With some exceptions—such as his opposition to electronic eavesdropping other than on grounds of national security—Jaworski's positions on national issues in the socially turbulent 1960's were generally hard-line "law and order" stands. He favored more power for law enforcement agencies, deplored Supreme Court decisions that he considered too permissive toward criminal suspects, opposed gun-control legislation that he viewed as too drastic, and called for strong action against student rioters and other disruptive protesters. Civil disobedience, he asserted on one occasion, should be limited to "one individual or a small group" testing the constitutionality of a law. "All other dissenters should abide by the law until it is declared unconstitutional."

As president of the American Bar Association, from July 1971 to July 1972, Jaworski stressed his concern over "errant lawyers" and "the vanishing respect for law . . . , a disquieting development spreading like a cancerous growth." His words, which seemed rather bland when he uttered them, have taken on new significance in the light of Watergate, the "cancer" of the Nixon administration, as John W. Dean, one of that administration's errant lawyers, now repentent, has described it.

The first major hint of the "cancer" at the top of the Executive branch became public in February 1972, nine months before the Presidential election of that year. That hint was a memorandum written by Dita Beard, the Washington lobbyist for the International Telephone and Telegraph Corporation. Published by Jack Anderson in his syndicated column, the memo suggested a connection between the out-of-court settlement of an antitrust suit that had been pending against ITT and ITT's contribution of $400,000 to the 1972 Republican Presidential campaign. (Later there were strong allegations that President Nixon himself had intervened to block the Justice Department's prosecution of ITT.) As soon as the memo was published, Miss Beard was declared "ill" and whisked to sequestration in a hospital.

Early in the Presidential campaign, the Committee to Reelect the President (CREEP) began wiretapping the offices of the Democratic National Committee at the Watergate Hotel in Washington, apparently as part of a strategy devised to insure President Nixon the weakest possible opponent in the November election. That fact came to light on June 17, 1972, when burglars paid with CREEP funds returned to the scene of their crime and were caught in the act of rifling files and installing additional electronic equipment. Publicly minimizing the break-in as a "third-rate caper" perpetrated by "overzealous" Nixonites acting on their own, Nixon administration officials all the way up to the highest levels of the White House allegedly scurried to suppress incriminating evidence.

Whatever cover-up there was must certainly have become stickier after October 1972, when evidence emerged suggesting that contributions made to the Nixon reelection campaign by dairy associations were actually political payoffs for an administration-approved rise in the price support for milk and that Watergate figures E. Howard Hunt and his wife Dorothy were the chairmen of the dummy committees set up to funnel the money. (Two months later Mrs. Hunt died in a jetliner crash with $100,000 in $100 bills in her possession.) But the lid remained on the scandal sufficiently to see Nixon through a landslide victory at the polls in November 1972.

Dauntless Washington *Post* investigative reporters Bob Woodward and Carl Bernstein would not let the issue drop, however, and Chief Judge John J. Sirica refused to be satisfied that the trial of the Watergate burglars had brought out "all the facts." Gradually it became clear that the Watergate "caper" was only the tip of what Woodward and Bernstein described as a vast administration "plot" in existence since 1969. The pattern of illegal and quasi-legal activities uncovered by Woodward, Bernstein, and others included use or attempted use of the Federal Bureau of Investigation, the Secret Service, the Central Intelligence Agency, and the Internal Revenue Service in political espionage and sabotage. Where "national security" could not be invoked, private squads were set up, such as the "vigilantes," who infiltrated "enemy" groups and the "plumbers," who burglarized the office of Dr. Daniel Ellsberg's psychiatrist. Much of the clandestine activity was allegedly financed with "laundered" campaign money, at least some of which had apparently been extorted from intimidated or favor-seeking businessmen and companies in violation of federal law.

Hoping to minimize the damage the Watergate scandal was inflicting on the image of their party, Republican leaders brought heavy pressure on Nixon to do some drastic housecleaning. Accordingly, on April 30, 1973, the President announced the resignations of his top White House aides and his Attorney General, Richard G. Kleindienst. The United States Senate agreed to confirm the appointment of Kleindienst's successor, Elliot L. Richardson, only after two demands were met: the naming of a special Watergate prosecutor and the word of Richardson that the prosecutor would have an absolutely free hand in probing the scandal and bringing all guilty parties to justice. Both demands were met, and Richardson was confirmed as Attorney General on May 23, 1973.

Two days after Richardson's confirmation, on May 25, 1973, Harvard Law School professor Archibald Cox was sworn in as special Watergate prosecutor. When the Ervin Committee hearings in the Senate uncovered the fact that Presidential conversations had been recorded, Cox obtained a subpoena for nine tapes relevant to Watergate. Refusing to comply with the command of the courts, Nixon on October 19, 1973 instead offered "summaries" of the tapes in question, to be verified by Senator John C. Stennis of Mississippi. When Cox rejected Nixon's "compromise" and insisted on pressing for the tapes through the courts, the notorious "Saturday night massacre" occurred, on October 20, 1973. On that occasion Attorney General Richardson and Deputy Attorney General William D. Ruckelshaus resigned rather than obey the President's order to fire Cox. The firing was then done by Acting Attorney General Robert H. Bork and the office of special prosecutor was abolished.

But public indignation over the "massacre" forced Nixon to revive the office of special prosecutor, to give assurances that the new prosecutor would not be dismissed without consultation with the leaders of both parties in the House and Senate, and to modify John's defiance of the courts in the matter of the tapes. After Jaworski took over as special prosecutor, the President surrendered seven of the nine tapes Cox had asked for. According to the White House, two others were "nonexistent" and the key section of a third tape had been erased "accidentally." Not content with that explanation or with the release of edited transcripts of White House conversations in the spring of 1974, Jaworski obtained a subpoena for sixty-four tapes. While trying to quash the subpoena, the White House resorted to various other maneuvers to evade full compliance with the law.

Jaworski's job basically was to collect evidence, present it to the Watergate grand juries, and direct the prosecution in any resulting trials. The two major Watergate cases were the cover-up case, in which Jaworski tried to prove that H. R. Haldeman, former White House chief of staff, and six other defendants conspired to obstruct justice, and the indictment of the "plumbers" for conspiracy. Under Jaworski, the special prosecutor's inquiry into illegal campaign donations broadened into an investigation of federal officials who may have done favors for major contributors. As Anthony Ripley wrote in the New York Times (May 1, 1974), "Few observers ever thought the job of Watergate special prosecutor would be quick and tidy. . . . Now, eleven months after the job was created . . . there seems no end in sight for the sprawling, shifting series of court actions and investigations."

Calling Jaworski "a pragmatic and informal man with a prosecutor's instinct for the kill," a writer for Time (March 11, 1974) said: "Quietly, efficiently, going his own way, Jaworski has turned out to be nobody's man but his own, determined that justice be done. . . . From the White House point of view, he is no improvement on Cox. He is often even more tenacious and less tolerant of anything that stands in his way." He was, however, as the Time writer took pains to point out, sensitive to the legal, political, and moral consequences of every decision he arrived at, and he was "scrupulously open-minded." Jaworski's resignation as special prosecutor became effective on October 25, 1974. According to Jaworski, most of his work as special prosecutor was complete at the time of his resignation.

Well-tailored Leon Jaworski is five feet eleven inches tall and speaks with a drawl. "The Colonel," as friends call him, is a hard worker who demands hard work from those under him. Linda Charlton of the New York Times (February 25, 1970) described him as "a benign, blue-eyed picture of a man content with himself." According to a report in Newsweek (March 11, 1974), "He is not universally admired in Houston —but to friends he's best known for warmth, unfailing courtesy, and an iron will. 'He's a real, soft-spoken, gentle, tough s.o.b.,' says one old friend."

Married in 1931 to the former Jeannette Adam, Jaworski has three children and five grandchildren. His home in Wimberly, Texas is a 400-acre ranch. In Washington he lives in a hotel. Before resigning from his law firm and severing his corporate connections he was earning $250,000 a year. As special prosecutor he makes $38,000. In 1961-62 Jaworski served as president of the American College of Trial Lawyers, and in 1965 he was appointed to the Permanent International Court of Arbitration in the Hague.

References

N Y Times p40 Jl 6 '71 por; p22 N 2 '73
Washington Post A p6 Ag 30 '64 por; A p1+ N 1 '73
Who's Who in America, 1972-73

JORDAN, BARBARA (CHARLINE)

Feb. 21, 1936- United States Representative from Texas; lawyer
Address: b. Room 1725, Longworth Office Building, Washington, D.C. 20515

When, in 1972, Barbara Jordan was elected to the House of Representatives by the voters of the Eighteenth Congressional District in Texas, she became the first black Congresswoman to come from the Deep South. Before that, Miss Jordan had been an articulate and assertive member of the Texas state senate since 1966. She first attracted national attention when President Lyndon B. Johnson, ignoring more prominent civil rights leaders, invited her to the White House for a private preview of his 1967 civil rights message. Impressed by her social reform legislation, Johnson praised the young lawmaker as "the epitome of the new politics" in the United States. "She proved that black is beautiful before we knew what it meant," the President continued, as quoted in The Ebony Success Library. "She is involved in a governmental system of all the people, all the races, all economic groups."

As a member of the House Judiciary Committee, Miss Jordan was one of thirty-eight Congress-

BARBARA JORDAN

men charged with the task of examining and evaluating the evidence bearing on the possible impeachment of President Richard M. Nixon. The freshman legislator, whom CBS News correspondent Bruce Morton once called "the best mind on the committee," subscribed to a broad definition of impeachable offenses that included "neglect of duty" and "subversion of the system of government."

Miss Jordan outlined her position on the January 22, 1974 edition of *Bill Moyers' Journal*, a public affairs program produced by the Educational Broadcasting Corporation. The task of the Judiciary Committee, in her opinion, was to determine whether or not probable cause existed to support articles of impeachment against the President. She viewed the Watergate affair as a "cleansing experience" for the political process. On November 5, 1974 Miss Jordan was reelected to the House for a second term.

Barbara Charline Jordan was born on February 21, 1936 in Houston, Texas, the youngest of the three daughters of Benjamin M. and Arlyne Jordan. Her two older sisters, Mrs. Bennie Creswell and Mrs. Rose Mary McGowan, teach music in Houston. Benjamin Jordan, a Baptist minister, supplemented his income by working as a warehouse clerk. "We were poor," Barbara Jordan told Molly Ivins in an interview for the Washington *Post* (October 22, 1972), "but so was everyone around us, so we did not notice it. We were never hungry and we always had a place to stay." She attended Houston public schools. Her father, a strict disciplinarian, reprimanded Barbara whenever she deviated from her straight "A" average, and she set equally high standards for herself. "I always wanted to be something unusual," she told Molly Ivins. "I never wanted to be run-of-the-mill. For a while I thought about becoming a pharmacist, but then I thought, whoever heard of an outstanding pharmacist?" After hearing an address by Edith Sampson, a black lawyer from Chicago, at the

Phyllis Wheatley High School "Career Day" assembly, Barbara Jordan decided to become a lawyer.

When Barbara Jordan graduated from Phyllis Wheatley High School in 1952, she was ranked in the top 5 percent of her class. She enrolled at Texas Southern University, an all-black college in Houston, where she majored in political science and history and ran unsuccessfully for president of the freshman class. A spellbinding orator, she led the debating team of Texas Southern to a series of championships. In 1956 she obtained her B.A. degree, *magna cum laude*. She earned an LL.B. degree at Boston University in 1959 and later that year was admitted to the bar in both Massachusetts and Texas.

Returning to Houston, Miss Jordan moved in with her parents and began to practise general civil law, with the dining room table as her desk. Three years later, she managed to scrape enough money together to open an office of her own. In addition to engaging in private practice, she worked as an administrative assistant to a county judge in Harris County, Texas. Convinced of the effectiveness of legitimate political change, she became active in the county's Democratic party organization. "All blacks are militants in their guts," she has explained, as quoted in *Time* (May 22, 1972), "but militancy is expressed in different ways." During the 1960 Presidential campaign, she directed Houston's first black "one person-per-block" precinct drive to drum up support for Democratic nominee John F. Kennedy and his running mate, Lyndon B. Johnson.

Barbara Jordan first ran for public office in 1962. In a losing bid for a seat in the Texas House of Representatives, she gathered a respectable 46,000 votes and, undaunted, ran for the same seat in 1964. "I figured anybody who could get 46,000 people to vote for them for any office should keep on trying," she explained to Louie Robinson in an interview for *Ebony* magazine (October 1972). Defeated for the second time, she turned her attention to the Texas senate and in 1966 defeated former state representative J. C. Whitfield, a white liberal, to become the first black woman elected to the state senate. "I didn't play up the fact of being a Negro or a woman," she has said of her first political victory. "It feels good to know that people recognize a qualified candidate when they see one." She ran unopposed in 1968 and was reelected to a four-year term.

So effective was Miss Jordan as a state legislator that she saw about half of the bills she submitted for consideration enacted into law. Among the legislation credited to her efforts were a law establishing the Texas Fair Employment Practices Commission, an improved workmen's compensation act, and the state's first minimum wage law designed specifically to include workers not covered by federal minimum wage standards —"the really poor people, laundry workers, domestics, [and] farm workers." Angered by the discriminatory hiring practices of the state, she forced the government to include antidiscrimination clauses in its business contracts. With her support and advice, the state created a special department of community affairs to deal with the problems of Texas' burgeoning urban areas. To insure the participation of minority groups in the electoral process, she prevented the passage of a restrictive voter registration act.

During her two terms in the state senate, Miss Jordan chaired several committees, including the Labor and Management Relations Committee, and her impressive record on that committee won her considerable political support from organized labor. Miss Jordan was named the outstanding freshman senator during her first year in office and was chosen senate president pro tempore in March 1972. On June 10, 1972, as the state's traditional "governor for a day," she became the first black chief executive in the country. Some political observers belittled her brief gubernatorial term as a "publicity stunt." Unperturbed, she told reporters at a news conference following the official swearing-in ceremony, "Someday, I may want to retain the governor's seat for a longer period of time."

In late 1971 Miss Jordan announced her candidacy for the Democratic nomination to the United States Congress from the newly drawn Eighteenth Congressional District, a populous and ethnically mixed section of Houston. Curtis Graves, a black man and her principal opponent in the hotly contested primary race, accused her of "Uncle Tom-ism" and of "selling out" to the state's political Establishment. Denouncing Miss Jordan as "the best black Congressman money can buy," state representative Graves contended that she had cooperated with other members of the predominantly white redistricting committee to create a Congressional district at the expense of a "safe" black state senate seat. Refusing to be drawn into a bitter personal battle, Miss Jordan concentrated on the issues and on her legislative record in the senate. "I can get things done," she told Thomas A. Johnson in an interview for the New York *Times* (September 26, 1971). "I've pushed a good deal of important legislation through the state senate. I'll run on my record."

With her astonishing 80 percent of the total votes cast in the May 1972 primary contest, Miss Jordan soundly defeated the three male contenders for the nomination. "If I got 80 percent of the votes, lots of white people voted for me," she said shortly after her victory, "and it was because they felt their interest would be included." In the national election on November 7, 1972 she trounced her Republican opponent, Paul M. Merritt, polling more than 85,000 votes for a plurality of 66,000 votes. By comparison, Senator George S. McGovern, the Democratic Presidential nominee, carried the heavily Democratic Eighteenth Congressional District by a plurality of 37,000 votes.

After taking office on January 3, 1973 Representative Jordan surprised some of her colleagues in the Congressional Black Caucus, who considered her an articulate spokesman for civil rights, by announcing that she intended to restrict her role to that of lawmaker. "We are legislators, and we ought to remember that this is our role," she explained to Jo Ann Levine. "I think blacks have begun to recognize that our future is in the political process. . . . It is not a very sexy way to proceed in civil rights, but it is now an accepted, legitimate way to achieve gains for black people." For example, following the constitutionally prescribed course, she joined forces with thirty-five like-minded Democrats, including all but one of the black Congressmen, and attempted to block the confirmation of Gerald R. Ford as Vice-President, charging he was weak on civil rights. Unlike many of her black colleagues, she questions the reliance on busing as the answer to the problem of racially segregated schools. Although she supports "the letter and the spirit" of the 1954 Supreme Court decision that held that segregated education was inherently unequal, she believes busing to achieve racial balance in the schools "should be resorted to only where the ends of equal educational opportunity, an education of quality, will result."

On the House floor, Barbara Jordan consistently backed legislation to raise the standard of living of impoverished Americans. She approved, for example, of the continuation of the programs of the Office of Economic Opportunity, the establishment of an independent public corporation to provide free legal services to the poor, and the creation of a powerful Consumer Protection Agency. Miss Jordan voted for an increase in the minimum wage and, with Representative Martha W. Griffiths of Michigan, sponsored a bill to extend Social Security coverage to American housewives. To ease the economic pressures of inflation, she recommended the continuation of the Nixon administration's wage and price controls program. An advocate of nationally coordinated, long-range planning to combat disease, she vigorously supported bills to create federally funded programs for the treatment and prevention of diabetes, cancer, and alcoholism. She also endorsed the creation of a National Institute on Aging and the expansion of a program to guarantee nutritionally balanced meals to elderly citizens.

In other domestic affairs, Miss Jordan backed increased federal aid to cities and recommended direct grants from the Law Enforcement Assistance Administration to metropolitan police departments and the subsidization of the operations of urban mass transit systems. She voted for increased aid to elementary and secondary schools, the continuation of the guaranteed student loan plan, and the extension of the national school lunch program. An environmentalist, she disapproved of the construction of the Alaska oil pipeline because of the potential ecological threat it posed to the Alaskan wilderness, and because of the fuel shortage in the winter of 1973, voted to suspend temporarily auto emission standards except in high pollution areas. Appalled by the huge profit margins reported by some of the major oil companies during the crisis, she approved a rollback on the price of domestic crude oil and called for a limitation on windfall profits.

An outspoken opponent of increasing military expenditures, Miss Jordan voted to reduce the number of United States troops stationed abroad, to impose a ceiling on military aid to South Vietnam, and to override President Nixon's veto of the War Powers Bill limiting Presidential war-making authority. To limit American military involvement in the continuing war in Southeast Asia, she approved of a bill forbidding the Department of Defense to divert money from other military programs to South Vietnam. One of a handful of Congressmen with a 100 percent voting record in the House, she voted with the majority of her party on 88 percent of the issues during her first year in office. The liberal Americans for Democratic Action rated her at 92 percent and the conservative Americans for Constitutional Action at 4 percent.

A handsome, large-boned, imposing woman, Barbara Jordan stands five feet eight inches tall. She never weighs herself. Because of her serious, no-nonsense approach to her profession, she has been described by one journalist as being "as cozy as a pile driver, though considerably more impressive." For recreation, she enjoys playing the guitar and reading. She is especially fond of political biographies, particularly those dealing with Presidents John F. Kennedy and Lyndon B. Johnson. Although she does not discount the possibility of marriage, she prefers to remain single, so that she can dedicate herself exclusively to her engrossing career. "Politics is . . . almost totally consuming," she told Louie Robinson. "A good marriage requires that one attend to it and not treat it as another hobby." In Houston she lives with her mother in a modest home painted a bright pink color.

Despite the added pressures of the impeachment hearings, Miss Jordan remains in close contact with her constituents. While Congress is in session, she returns to her district every other weekend to catch up on local affairs. A "progressive" liberal, she intends to concentrate on the "substantive" issues—"how a person eats and sleeps and lives." "My approach is to respect the humanity of everybody," she said in a recent interview. "Their position on anything is not relevant to the way I can relate to them as a human being. *That* we have in common."

References

> Christian Sci Mon p6 Mr 18 '74 pors
> Ebony 27:48+ O '72 pors
> Washington Post K p1+ O 22 '72 pors
> The Ebony Success Library vol II (1973)
> Who's Who in American Politics, 1973-74

KAEL, PAULINE (kāl)

June 19, 1919- Film critic
Address: c/o The New Yorker, 25 W. 43d St., New York 10036

Lively, witty, and irreverent, Pauline Kael has in the past twenty years established herself as the nation's preeminent exponent of that most twentieth-century of literary genres, motion picture criticism. One of the few of her profession who prefers the term "movie" to "film," she is as quick to ridicule a pretentious art film or a preachy "message" picture as she is to put down a crassly commercial Hollywood screen venture. Miss Kael began writing for film monthlies during the 1950's. After managing two art film houses in Berkeley, California and broadcasting for the Pacifica radio network, she came to national prominence when her first book of collected reviews, *I Lost It at the Movies,* became a best seller in 1965. Since then she has reviewed films for *McCall's,* the *New Republic,* and the *New Yorker.* She has published three more books of collected movie criticism, *Kiss Kiss Bang Bang* (1968), *Going Steady* (1970), and *Deeper Into Movies* (1973), and one long essay on film history, "Raising Kane," in the *Citizen Kane Book* (1971). All of her books have been published by Atlantic-Little Brown in hardcover and by Bantam in paperback.

Pauline Kael was born north of San Francisco in Petaluma, a city in Sonoma County, California on June 19, 1919, the fifth child of Isaac Paul and Judith (Friedman) Kael. She has two sisters —an English teacher and an educator—and two brothers. During the early years of her life she lived on a farm in Sonoma County run by her father, a Polish Jew whom she described in *I Lost It at the Movies* as "adulterous," "a Republican," "generous and kind," and "democratic in the western way that Easterners still don't understand." She later told Nora Ephron in a New York *Post* (May 11, 1966) interview that her father was an agnostic and a moviegoer.

When the Great Depression closed down the family farm, the Kaels moved to San Francisco. There, in 1936, Pauline Kael graduated from Girls High School. As a child she was an omnivorous reader and an avid moviegoer. Among her favorite films were those comedies of the late 1920's in which Bebe Daniels played a carefree, wisecracking flapper; *Million Dollar Legs,* with W. C. Fields; and the Marx Brothers' *Monkey Business* and *Duck Soup.*

Although Miss Kael majored in philosophy at the University of California at Berkeley, she read poetry and fiction extensively, and most of her friends were English majors. After her graduation in 1940, according to Nora Ephron, "there then followed what she lightly and vaguely refers to as a 'checkered story' of bohemian living, mostly in San Francisco, a little in New York, experimental film-making and unsuccessful playwriting."

Miss Kael published her first movie review in 1953 in the San Francisco little magazine *City Lights.* It was an appraisal of Charles Chaplin's bathetic *Limelight,* which she called "Slimelight." After that her work began to appear in *Sight and Sound, Partisan Review, Kulchur, Film Culture,* and *Moviegoer,* and she started writing regular short reviews for *Film Quarterly.* For several years she broadcast her film criticism without pay for the listener-supported Pacifica radio network. From 1955 until the early 1960's Miss Kael managed the Berkeley Cinema Guild Theatres, the first twin art film houses in the country. The theatres became renowned for her programming—she was among the first to revive W. C. Fields, Mae West, and musicals by Busby Berkeley—and for her one-paragraph program notes. During the 1950's Miss Kael contributed to several film anthologies, and by the 1960's she was a frequent lecturer on film at universities in San Francisco and Los Angeles.

"In ten years I made under $2,000 from film criticism," Miss Kael told a *Newsweek* reporter in 1966. To supplement her income during those lean years she worked as a seamstress, cook, and textbook ghostwriter, among other jobs. Her fortunes changed in 1965, however, when Atlantic Monthly-Little Brown published *I Lost It at the Movies*, a collection of her previously published or broadcast movie reviews and essays on film criticism.

Brash, witty, and acerbic, *I Lost It at the Movies* placed Miss Kael in the front echelon of American film critics. In the book she praised such vintage favorites of hers as *La Grande Illusion*, *Shoeshine*, and *Forbidden Games*, and a few recent pictures like *Hud* ("one of the few entertaining American movies released in 1963"). She attacked many of her fellow critics, derided the porcine materialism of American movie moguls, and ridiculed the overblown pretensions of such art films as *Last Year at Marienbad* ("the snow job in the ice palace"). Although some reviewers of the book professed to be scandalized by her feisty, nonacademic tone and her autobiographical comments, Richard Schickel expressed the opinion of many when he wrote in the New York *Times Book Review* (March 11, 1965): "Her collected essays confirm what those of us who have encountered them separately over the last few years . . . have suspected—that she is the sanest, saltiest, most resourceful and least attitudinizing movie critic currently in practice in the United States."

After the publication of *I Lost It at the Movies*, Pauline Kael no longer had any trouble earning her living as a movie critic. She moved to New York City and began free-lancing for such mass circulation magazines as *Life*, *Holiday*, and *Mademoiselle*. During the first half of 1966 she was the regular film reviewer for *McCall's*, but she was fired, reportedly for panning *The Sound of Music*, of which she wrote: "Wasn't there perhaps one little Von Trapp who didn't want to sing his head off, or who screamed that he wouldn't act out little glockenspiel routines for Papa's party guests, or who got nervous and threw up if he had to get out on a stage?" "I had realized that I would sock the ladies right between the ears," Miss Kael told a *Newsweek* reporter (May 30, 1966) after her dismissal, "but what the hell is the point of writing, if you're writing banality."

After a stint with the *New Republic* in 1967, Miss Kael began her association with the *New*

PAULINE KAEL

Yorker in January 1968. Each year she writes for the *New Yorker* during the fall and winter months, and the fiction and film writer Penelope Gilliatt, the author of *Sunday, Bloody Sunday*, takes over for the other six. In the spring of 1968 Miss Kael published her second book, *Kiss Kiss Bang Bang*, whose title, she explains, is taken from an Italian movie poster and is "perhaps the briefest statement imaginable of the basic appeal of movies." The book consists of a section of her movie reviews; essays on the frustrated greatness of Marlon Brando and Orson Welles; a withering appraisal of the career of Stanley Kramer; a long, angry piece, previously unpublished, on the making of *The Group*, which she considers a paradigm of what goes wrong in Hollywood movie making; and an alphabetical listing of pithy notes on 280 films.

In *Kiss Kiss Bang Bang* Miss Kael's fascination with the sociology of film began to be apparent. As she wrote in her review of *Morgan!*, "Conceivably it's part of the function of a movie critic to know and indicate the difference between a bad movie that doesn't matter because it's so much like other bad movies and a bad movie that matters . . . because it affects people strongly in new, different ways. And if it be said that this is sociology, not esthetics, the answer is that an esthetician who gave his time to criticism of current movies would have to be an awful fool. Movie criticism to be of any use whatever must go beyond formal analysis—which in movies is generally a disguised form of subjective reaction to meanings and implications, anyway." To some critics, like Joseph Morgenstern (*Newsweek*, May 20, 1968), Miss Kael's insistence on considering movies in the context of their audiences is both a strength and a weakness. "She has a way of mixing together the film, her attitudes toward it, the audience's attitude toward it and her attitudes toward the audience," the *Newsweek* writer pointed out. "I don't think *Blow-Up* and *La Guerre Est Finie* were intrinsically as pretentious as she found them, though the audience's solemnities were certainly a riot." Eliot Fremont-Smith of the New York *Times* (May 21, 1968), however, had only praise for her methods. "On individual movies . . . Miss Kael is the most quotable critic writing," he observed, "but what is important and bracing is that she relates movies to other experience, to ideas and attitudes, to ambition, books, money, other movies, to politics and the evolving culture, to moods of the audience, to our sense of ourselves—to what movies do to us, the acute and self-scrutinizing awareness of which is always at the core of her judgment."

By the time that *Going Steady* was published early in 1970, *I Lost It at the Movies* and *Kiss Kiss Bang Bang* had become the best-selling books in the history of movie criticism. In *Going Steady* Miss Kael presents, in chronological order, the movie reviews that she wrote for the *New Yorker* between January 1968 and March 1969. Allowed by *New Yorker* editor William Shawn to write whatever she wanted and at whatever length, Miss Kael revealed in *Going Steady* a more relaxed and more discursive writing style. Less concerned with attacking fellow critics, she more fully explored issues she had never had the space to discuss before. Although she conceded in her introduction that films in the late 1960's had boldly moved into new areas, thanks to gifted young directors, she had unqualified praise for only a relatively few movies, including Bergman's *Shame*, Carol Reed's *Oliver!*, Buñuel's *Simon of the Desert*, Bellocchio's *China Is Near*, and Godard's *Weekend* and *La Chinoise*.

In a chapter entitled "Trash, Art and the Movies," the only piece not previously published in the *New Yorker*, Miss Kael contends that the best thing about movies is that people enjoy them, and that they enjoy them because they lack the good intentions and moral uplift extolled by schoolteachers and other upholders of the "art" of establishment culture. "Movie art," she therefore insists, "is not the opposite of what we have always enjoyed in movies, it is not to be found in a return to that official high culture, it is what we have always found good in movies, only more so. It's the subversive gesture carried further, the moments of excitement sustained longer and extended into new meanings."

"Raising Kane" was first published in two installments in the *New Yorker* in February 1971. Later that year it came out as the introduction to an Atlantic-Little Brown and Bantam edition of the shooting script of *Citizen Kane*, the 1941 film classic that almost libelously portrayed the life of publisher William Randolph Hearst. Orson Welles, who starred in the film, directed it, and was listed as its coauthor with Herman J. Mankiewicz, has generally been accorded all the credit for what many *cinéastes* feel is the best movie ever made. But in "Raising Kane" Miss Kael makes a strong case for the thesis that Mankiewicz actually conceived the film and was responsible for most of the final script. As proof she points out, among other things, that Mankiewicz, unlike Welles, was an acquaintance of the

publisher and his mistress, Marion Davies, and apparently used that acquaintanceship to provide authentic details for the film. Furthermore, after the movie's release, Hearst vented his ire on Mankiewicz, not on Welles, and essentially ruined the scriptwriter's career.

"['Raising Kane'] is probably the best thing Kael has written, a mixture of journalism, biography, autobiography, gossip, and criticism, carried along by a style so exhilarating that one seems to be reading a new, loose kind of critical biography," J. A. Avant wrote in the *Library Journal* (August 1971). Some film critics, however, protested Miss Kael's dethronement of Welles, among them Andrew Sarris of the *Village Voice* and Peter Bogdanovich. The latter raised the standard for Welles in a long rebuttal published in *Esquire* (October 1972).

"This collection of my reviews from The *New Yorker* for September 1969 to March 1972," wrote Miss Kael in the introduction to her fifth book, *Deeper Into Movies* (1973), "is also a record of the interaction of movies and our national life during a frantic time when three decades seem to have been compressed into three years and I wrote happily—like a maniac—to keep up with what I thought was going on in movies—which is to say, in our national theatre." In her view, movies as pop culture—with the exception of an occasional brilliant throwback like *The Last Picture Show*—are dead, having been supplanted by television, and in its place a new, more artistic culture of movies is developing for a smaller, more hip film audience. That most of the results so far have been disappointing may be chalked up to the inevitable confusion and chaos that occur when new forms are explored. Despite the failures, she finds the present situation exciting and hopeful.

In the winter of 1972-73 Miss Kael caused a stir when she declared that Bernardo Bertolucci's *Last Tango in Paris* was the most important movie she had ever reviewed—a major "breakthrough" film comparable in its cultural impact to the 1913 première of Stravinsky's *Le Sacre du printemps*. Her fellow critics unanimously found the praise a bit excessive. Other films for which Miss Kael has campaigned include *M*A*S*H*, *McCabe and Mrs. Miller*, *The Garden of the Finzi Continis*, *Weekend*, and *Klute*.

Pauline Kael has lectured at colleges and universities across the United States and has served as a judge at film festivals. She currently fills many speaking engagements and is a frequent guest on television talk shows. Miss Kael is a member and past chairman (1970) of the National Society of Film Critics. She was the 1970 recipient of the George Polk Memorial award for criticism, and has been awarded several honorary degrees, including a doctor of laws from Georgetown University (1972) and a doctor of letters from Smith College (1973). In 1964 she studied in Europe on a Guggenheim fellowship.

Blue-eyed and brown-haired Pauline Kael is five feet tall and weighs 108 pounds. Interviewers have described her as a restless, mobile woman, a lively conversationalist with a salty vocabulary and "a nervous, almost wicked laugh." Married and divorced several times, Miss Kael now makes her home in a large sparsely furnished Central Park West apartment in Manhattan that she shares with her daughter, Gina James, who is a dancer, and her dogs. She maintains she can remember every film she has ever seen and never feels the need to see an old film again, except for pleasure. Her list of the greatest movies ever made includes D. W. Griffith's *Intolerance;* Buster Keaton's *Steamboat Bill Jr.;* Jean Renoir's *Rules of the Game, Day in the Country,* and *La Grande Illusion;* John Huston's *The Maltese Falcon,* and the Marx Brothers' *Duck Soup.* Perhaps Martin Knelman best summed up the appeal of Pauline Kael's writing when he wrote in the Toronto *Globe and Mail* (March 3, 1973), "It is Kael's special gift that she makes movies highly personal events, bringing all her experience to bear on them and channeling everything she knows into them, including a feeling for politics and literature and all the arts, high and low. . . . One has the sense that movies are for her, part of a very rich, very full life—and that's what makes her responses to them often far more interesting than the films themselves."

References

Book World p17 F 23 '69 por
N Y Post p47 My 11 '66 por
Pub W 199:31+ My 24 '71 por
Time 92:38+ Jl 12 '68 por
Kael, Pauline. I Lost It at the Movies (1965)
Who's Who in America, 1972-73
Who's Who of American Women, 1974-75

KELLEY, CLARENCE M(ARION)

Oct. 24, 1911- United States government official
Address: b. Office of the Director, Federal Bureau of Investigation, 9th St. and Pennsylvania Ave., N.W., Washington, D.C. 20535

To head the highly specialized far-flung operations of the Federal Bureau of Investigation, President Richard Nixon appointed Clarence M. Kelley, a "cop's cop," a dedicated professional who had spent twenty-one years in the FBI before becoming chief of police in Kansas City, Missouri, where he transformed a demoralized, scandal-ridden department into a model of efficiency. When Kelley took office on July 9, 1973, his honesty and competence were unquestioned, although charges of racism had threatened to mar his record. As the first permanent director of the FBI since the death of J. Edgar Hoover, Kelley, who received bipartisan support, has been attempting to modernize procedures and refurbish the bureau's reputation, a bit damaged in the Watergate affair. "I don't see any great difficulties," he told B. Drummond Ayres Jr. of the New

CLARENCE M. KELLEY

York *Times* (June 18, 1973). "The people of the United States kind of accept motherhood and the FBI." He has had to work, however, with a Congress determined to oversee the agency and increasingly concerned about civil liberties, including protection against police intrusion upon privacy.

Clarence Marion Kelley was born in Kansas City, Missouri on October 24, 1911 to Clarence Bond and Minnie (Brown) Kelley. He was an only child. His father, an electrical worker whose formal education had been interrupted in the primary grades, attended night school for seventeen years to earn a college degree. He became an engineer with the Kansas City Power & Light Company and provided a comfortable, middle-class home for his family. In his high school years as an outfielder for a crack amateur league, Clarence Kelley batted .300, but he gave up baseball because he struck out on curves. He graduated from Northeast High School in the upper third of his class, obtained the B.A. degree from the University of Kansas in 1936, and then studied at the University of Kansas City Law School (now part of the University of Missouri) for the LL.B. degree. At his graduation exercises in 1940 the Federal Bureau of Investigation agent in charge of the Kansas City office delivered the commencement address; a few months later, on October 7, 1940, Kelley himself joined the FBI.

While advancing steadily through the ranks, Kelley served in ten cities in all sections of the country, including Pittsburgh, Des Moines, Kansas City, Washington, Houston, Seattle, and San Francisco. His string of more or less routine assignments was broken by a stint at the FBI Academy at Quantico, Virginia and later by a World War II tour of Naval duty, from 1943 to 1946, in the South Pacific. "I am not cosmopolitan," he once told a Kansas City reporter, "but I have been around." For the most part, he handled criminal cases and administrative operations rather than security investigations. When he headed the Birmingham, Alabama office in the late 1950's, Kelley in accordance with FBI policy remained generally aloof from such local incidents in the integration crisis as Police Commissioner Eugene ("Bull") Connor's clash with black alleged bus boycotters. After a year as special agent in charge of the FBI office in Memphis, he retired from the agency, in 1961, to become chief of police in Kansas City, a $32,000-a-year position for which he was recommended by Attorney General Robert F. Kennedy, among other sponsors.

The former chief and four high-ranking officers of the Kansas City police department had recently been indicted for corruption. They were not convicted, but police morale sank and factions multiplied. Kelley found it necessary to fire some of the men and slowly rebuild the department around officers whom he could trust. His reputation for sternness toward certain kinds of wrongdoing was confirmed by his warning to a class of recruits in 1969, "I cannot abide a thief. I cannot abide a liar. These are the errors of the heart, which go to the center of a man's character." Except for a small burglary ring uncovered in 1963, the department remained free of scandal after the cleanup, its new image reflected in increased public confidence.

Like most police departments throughout the country, however, Kelley's force also remained racially lopsided. By 1968 Kansas City's population was over 20 percent black, but its police force was 95 percent white. Since salary was not competitive with that of private industry, most recruits were high school graduates, often from outlying rural areas. Kelley instituted a rudimentary human relations course in 1966, but, as William D. Tammeus reported in Newsday (June 18, 1973), "he discovered . . . that to be publicly sympathetic to black complaints of police prejudice meant that morale among his predominantly white officers would shrivel." The police were distrusted in the black community, while in Kansas City as a whole, racist attitudes hardened in reaction to the civil rights movement. It is unlikely that Kelley, the watchdog against crime and corruption, recognized the explosive nature of the situation.

On the day of the funeral of assassinated Dr. Martin Luther King Jr., April 9, 1968, a crowd composed mainly of schoolchildren marched first to the Kansas City Board of Education and then to City Hall to demand that schools be closed in honor of King. They were met by police in full riot gear and dispersed with tear gas and billy clubs. Two hours after the march had begun, Kelley requested National Guardsmen from the Governor. He adopted a hard-line policy in dealing with the ensuing riots, refused to join the mayor in apologizing for the use of tear gas at City Hall, and made television statements alleging provocation. Six unarmed black men were shot during the disorders; at least four, according to Christopher Bigsby in the Manchester Guardian (September 18, 1973), were "completely innocent of any wrongdoing." In retrospect, Kelley, claiming "minimal" errors, admitted that some officers might have acted unwisely, but he took no disciplinary action. "What elsewhere might have been described as a 'police riot' was seen here as firm law enforcement," Bigsby wrote.

With a majority of the taxpayers behind him and with enthusiastic support from his own men, Kelley began a series of innovations that made his department a national model. In 1968 he introduced around-the-clock helicopter patrols, the first in any major American city. During the same year a municipal bond issue funded the computerization of police records, an operation Kelley had advocated back in 1966. When the Safe Streets Act of 1968 made federal funds available, smaller towns in the area applied for money to hook into Kelley's system, the Automated Law Enforcement Response Team. ALERT, which eventually covered 10,000 square miles, enabled a patrolman to report a name or license number and receive information in ten to fifteen seconds. Stolen cars could thus be recovered more easily, fugitives captured, and persons with a history of assaulting policemen approached with the proper caution.

"At first, admittedly, we were pretty generous with the categories we included," Kelley told the Senate Judiciary Committee in 1973 when questioned about possible abuses arising from computerization. The names of "mentals," activists, and militants were fed into the computer along with the names of convicted criminals. But a visit from an Eastern civil rights group led to the elimination of many of those names, and strong pressure from the local American Civil Liberties Union and the threat of a lawsuit by the Italian American Unification Council forced the police to purge their files again. Discovering that an overzealous policeman had been asking university officials for the names of student demonstrators, Kelley put a stop to the practice. "I don't like that sort of thing," he asserted before the Senate committee. He also reprimanded officials of Lenaxa, Kansas for passing ALERT information about newcomers on to landlords and employers, apparently in an effort to preserve the suburban character of their town, but he allowed Lenaxa to retain its ALERT connection. At a 1970 police convention the computer demonstrated its ability to trace aliases and nicknames and identify parole violators. It also turned up entries like "molestation subject" and "known narcotics user."

To make the resources of the Kansas City police available to smaller towns in six adjoining counties, Kelley created the "metro squad," a sort of mini-FBI that could be called in for homicides and other major crimes. He also experimented with a more open administration—in some precincts, regular discussions between patrolmen and officers provided an alternative to the traditional quasi-military relationship. Police pay was raised and educational incentives were offered. Kelley credits modern equipment and the addition of some 400 men to the force for a remarkable 24 percent drop in the city's crime rate from 1969 to 1972. The actual number of crimes also declined from 1970 to 1972.

In the aftermath of the riots Kelley also tried to improve relations with the black community. Overreactive patrolmen were transferred from ghetto duty, and the chief himself set an example by keeping cool when addressed as "Pig." Twelve storefront community relations offices were opened; when all but one failed, Kelley installed a community worker in each precinct. Recruitment of blacks remained low, however, officials explaining that qualified blacks were hard to find—a situation that eventually led Kelley to assign ten Negro policemen to full-time recruitment duty. By 1973 there were nearly 100 blacks, including several officers, on the 1,300-man force. Several observers felt that the police chief had made a sincere effort, and police-community relations were further improved through compliance with federal programs.

In 1969 Kelley was called to testify before the Senate permanent investigatory subcommittee in connection with his having given 113 captured weapons to Major General Carl C. Turner, former provost marshal of the Army, who later sold them. Kelley explained that Turner had told him the guns were being collected for a military police museum. The Kansas City police chief came to wider attention in the summer of 1972 as chairman of the five-man security advisory board at both the Democratic and Republican national conventions in Miami Beach.

Following disclosure of his having destroyed documents pertaining to the Watergate affair, L. Patrick Gray 3d resigned as acting director of the Federal Bureau of Investigation in late April 1973, after almost a year in that post. William D. Ruckelshaus, administrator of the Environmental Protection Agency, was named caretaker head of the FBI, and twenty-seven candidates were surveyed for a permanent appointment. On June 7, 1973 President Richard Nixon designated Clarence M. Kelley, and on June 19 the Senate Judiciary Committee opened confirmation hearings on the nomination.

Although some political commentators had expected the committee to probe the issue of racism, the Senators were primarily concerned about establishing Kelley's freedom from the Watergate scandal and his willingness to cooperate with Congress. "I have never bowed to political pressure and I don't mean to start now," Kelley assured the committee. (In press interviews he has indicated he would resign if subjected to improper pressure.) He also informed the Senators that he would report to Congress regularly, work with a new Congressional committee overseeing the FBI, and possibly submit an itemized budget. "I subscribe very strongly to the notion that all government agencies must make a public accounting periodically," Kelley told Mark Arnold of the *National Observer* (November 24, 1973). "You can't get people's support unless they know what you're doing and how you're doing it."

With respect to the criminal history division of the National Crime Information Center (NCIC), a computer network by which the FBI exchanges information with state police, Kelley surprised the Senators by insisting that it would be extremely difficult to record all dispositions and remove the names of persons acquitted of crimes from the computer. Critics of NCIC believe that stringent regulation is needed to ensure the accuracy of data fed into the file and to prevent information from falling into the wrong hands, and one state, Massachusetts, has refused to join the system until the Justice Department establishes safeguards. Although not opposed to safeguards, Kelley feels that the danger to privacy is exaggerated and has pointed out that the computer is far more secure than the files in a typical police station.

On the whole, Kelley gave committee members the impression of living up to his billing as an honest and competent cop. His appointment, confirmed by the Senate 96-0 on June 27, was received with relief at the FBI. "Kelley's experienced in the business and that's good enough for me," one agent told Sanford J. Ungar of the Washington *Post* (October 24, 1973). After he was sworn in on July 9, Kelley appointed John Coleman, former head of a police training academy in Missouri, to draw up a management course for field agents emphasizing press relations, an area in which the new director intends to allow agents more leeway, and he asked William Reed, head of the Florida Law Enforcement Bureau, to review all operations, NCIC in particular. Kelley has suggested that in some respects the FBI may have fallen behind the times. "We must always remember," he said in a *U.S. News & World Report* interview (October 15, 1973), "that all this sophisticated new equipment is available to the criminal world."

Meanwhile, the Justice Department began to conduct its own review of the FBI, to determine, among other questions, whether the criminal investigatory branch of the bureau should be merged with other federal law enforcement agencies and a separate agency created to handle political and security matters. Pointing out certain drawbacks to that plan, Kelley argued that leads uncovered in criminal investigations can prove useful in security work. On the subject of tenure, the new director, who is nine years away from retirement, has suggested a fixed term covering more than two administrations, to reduce political influence.

Kelley has taken a cautious middle-of-the-road position on most issues. "I subscribe to the theory that society has to place some restrictions on the police," he said in a Kansas City interview. "After all, the police are constantly depriving people of their liberty. . . . But the pendulum can swing too far in the other direction." The exclusionary rule, barring evidence seized in an illegal search, strikes Kelley as unduly restrictive; however, he believes that court decisions strengthening the rights of the accused have raised the level of police work. "It used to be that most cases were brought to court as a result of a confession," he told Mark Arnold. "There was really very little investigation conducted. Now much more is required, and it should be." Kelley foresees an expansion of FBI activity against "white-collar crime," such as stock market frauds perpetrated by syndicate conmen. Another of his concerns is the spread of terrorism.

Clarence M. Kelley was described in the New York *Times* (June 8, 1973) as "a 6-foot, 200-pounder, with thick hands, bull neck, and slicked-back silver hair." He carries a .38-caliber revolver and is tough and decisive in action. His somewhat hawklike nose and square jaw earned him the nickname "Chief" in high school; now he is sometimes called "Dick Tracy" because of his delight in gadgetry. In conversation he is affable and low-keyed. He occasionally jokes with reporters, likes chili con carne, and sometimes wears blue shirts and flashy ties. Kelley and his wife, the former Ruby Dyeantha Pickett, whom he married on August 28, 1937, have two grown children, Kent Clarence and Mary Ruth (Mrs. Edward R. Dobbins Jr.). In Kansas City he served on the board of directors of the Boys' Club, the United Fund, and the Starlight Theatre Association. His Greek-letter societies are Phi Delta Phi and Sigma Nu. A deacon in the Christian Church, he also taught Sunday school for a time in his hometown.

References

Christian Sci Mon p8 Je 19 '73 por
Guardian p14 S 18 '73 por
N Y Times p32 Je 6 '73 por; p19 Je 8 '73 por
Nat Observer p12 N 24 '73 por
Newsday p45 Je 18 '73 por
Newsweek 82:21+ Jl 2 '73 por
Time 101:12+ Je 18 '73 por
Washington Post A p14 Je 9 '73 por;
    A p1 Je 17 '73 por; A p22 Ja 14 '74 por
Who's Who in America, 1972-73

KENYATTA, JOMO

Oct. 20, 1891(?)- President of the Republic of Kenya
Address: b. Office of the President, P.O. Box 30510, Nairobi, Kenya; h. Ichaweri, Gatundu, Kenya

NOTE: This biography supersedes the article that appeared in *Current Biography* in 1953.

Although he was once described by a British colonial governor as "a leader to darkness and death," Jomo Kenyatta, President of the Republic of Kenya, has become one of the world's most respected elder statesmen. Of humble tribal origin, Kenyatta is a veteran of a half century of struggles for the rights of his fellow Africans, and during the 1950's he was imprisoned by the British as the alleged leader of the Mau Mau terrorist organization. Since taking over the leadership of Kenya when it attained independence in 1963, he has guided it into a relative tranquility and economic well-being that contrasts sharply with the turbulence and poverty of many newly independent African nations.

Jomo Kenyatta, known in childhood as Kamau, is a member of the Kikuyu tribe which, comprising some 20 percent of Kenya's black population, is the largest, as well as the most progressive and industrious, of the country's tribes. The grandson of a medicine man, he was born at Ngenda in the heart of the Kikuyu country of what was then the British East Africa protectorate, to Muigai, a small farmer and herdsman, and his wife, Wambui. He had a younger brother, Kongo, and a half-brother, James Muigai, from his mother's marriage to his paternal uncle, Ngengi, following his father's death. Although Kenyatta is uncertain as to his age, some sources give his birthdate as October 20, 1891. Other accounts suggest that he may have been born in 1889, 1890, 1893, or 1897.

Like other Kikuyus, Kenyatta received his early education from his mother, who introduced him to tribal laws, customs, and folklore, and from his father, who taught him agriculture. Relatives remember him as being intelligent, ambitious, and something of a loner. While tending the family's flocks in the pasture lands surrounding his home community, Kenyatta was dismayed by the injustice of the colonial system. The most fertile lands in what became known as the White Highlands were appropriated by foreign settlers, while the natives could barely make a living on their own poor lands.

In November 1909 Kenyatta entered a mission school of the Church of Scotland at Thogoto, near Kikuyu, under the name Kamau wa Ngengi. There he not only studied academic subjects but was trained as a carpenter, earning his keep by performing mission chores. In keeping with tribal tradition, Kenyatta underwent circumcision rites in February 1913. When, in August 1914, he was baptized into Christianity at the mission, he took the name Johnstone Kamau. He then left to seek his fortune in Nairobi, where he worked as a courier with a sisal company. In 1917 he took refuge with the Masai tribe, to escape being forced into wartime service in the Carrier Corps, a contingent of young Africans who transported supplies overland for British military forces.

After the end of World War I he returned to Nairobi. It was about that time that he acquired the nickname "Kenyatta" from the beaded Masai belt (*kinyata*) that he wore, and he adopted the name as his own. (Some years later, during his stay in England, he decided to Africanize the name Johnstone and hit upon "Jomo," a Kikuyu word that has been translated as "burning spear" or as the act of "drawing a sword from a scabbard.") In 1919 Kenyatta acted as interpreter for a Kikuyu chief in a land dispute at the Nairobi Supreme Court. From 1922 until 1928, he worked for the Nairobi public works department as a stores clerk and water meter reader, a job that gave him some measure of financial security. Kenyatta entered politics in 1925 with the Kikuyu Central Association (KCA). In 1928 he accepted the full-time post of general secretary of the KCA and founded and edited its journal, *Muigwithania* (Conciliator), the first periodical in the Kikuyu language. In order not to jeopardize his position or that of the KCA, Kenyatta cautiously stressed the importance of self-advancement and tribal unity, while at the same time defending the British Empire.

In March 1929 Kenyatta went to London to present the KCA's objectives to the British Colonial Office. They included demands for recognition of the Kikuyu tribe's legal rights to lands it held before the arrival of foreign settlers; for government-financed educational facilities; and for native representation on the Kenya Legislative Council. Although he failed to gain an audience with the Colonial Secretary, he won at least one concession by persuading the authorities to permit the tribe to establish its own schools. In 1929 he visited Moscow, and in 1930 he attended the Communist-sponsored International Negro Workers' Congress in Hamburg, Germany.

After his return to Kenya in September 1930, Kenyatta promoted government schools for natives and clashed at times with church authorities. He returned to London in May 1931, where he renewed his government contacts, presented his tribe's demands to the Colonial Office, and testified before the Kenya Land Commission. To improve his English, he studied at Woodbrooke College, a Quaker institution in Birmingham, in 1931-32. During part of 1932 and 1933 he was in the Soviet Union, where he attended Moscow University and studied at a revolutionary institute. On his return to England he wrote militant articles for radical publications, demanding "complete self-rule" for Africa, and calling for "evacuation of the imperialist robber from the land." For a time he shared a flat with Paul Robeson, and in 1934 he appeared with the great actor and singer in the small role of an African chief in Alexander Korda's film version of Edgar Wallace's *Sanders of the River.*

Supported by a grant from the International African Institute and by income from his contributions to a textbook on the Kikuyu language, Kenyatta did postgraduate studies in anthropology under Bronislaw Malinowski at the London School of Economics and Political Science. One product of his anthropological studies was the book *Facing Mount Kenya; The Tribal Life of the Gikuyu* (Secker & Warburg, 1938). Acclaimed by Malinowski as "one of the first really competent and instructive contributions to African ethnography by a scholar of pure African parentage," it polemicized against colonialism and defended Kikuyu culture as superior to anything the Europeans could offer.

During World War II, Kenyatta worked as a farm laborer in Sussex and lectured on the Workers' Educational Association circuit. His writings during that period include *My People of Kikuyu and the Life of Chief Wangombe* (United Society for Christian Literature, 1942) and the pamphlet *Kenya: Land of Conflict* (International African Service Bureau, 1945). While his outlook was

JOMO KENYATTA

anti-Fascist, his continued attacks on British colonialism led some governmental authorities to consider him a security risk, but they found nothing damaging enough to warrant prosecution.

Kenyatta's involvement in Pan-Africanism dates to 1935 when, following the invasion of Ethiopia by Italian forces, he helped organize the International African Friends of Abyssinia and became its honorary secretary. Later he became active in the International African Service Bureau, organized in 1937. At the end of World War II he joined with Kwame Nkrumah, George Padmore, W.E.B. DuBois, and others in organizing the fifth Pan-African Congress, which assembled at Manchester in October 1945 with the theme "Africa for Africans."

Returning to Kenya in September 1946, Kenyatta became vice-principal of the Independent Teachers' College at Githunguri, a potential center of the independent schools movement. He became its principal the following May. In June 1947 he was elected president of the Kenya African Union (KAU), an intertribal political party founded in 1944. Determined to build KAU into an orderly and unified party, Kenyatta exhorted his people to hard work, integrity, and discipline while pressing demands for African voting rights, the elimination of race discrimination, and the return of foreign-held lands to their original owners. He met with resistance from British colonial authorities and white settlers, who feared his growing power and prestige. When in 1948 a terrorist organization, sworn to kill whites and their African supporters, emerged under the name "Mau Mau," the authorities tried to link the movement to KAU and to Kenyatta. He, in turn, tried to disassociate his party from it. "We do not know this thing Mau Mau," he declared in July 1952. "KAU is not a fighting union that uses fists and weapons."

On October 20, 1952, following a wave of Mau Mau terror, a state of emergency was declared and Kenyatta was arrested along with five associates and charged with masterminding the Mau Mau. The trial opened on November 24, 1952 at

Kapenguria, a small outpost near the Uganda border. Although much of the government's testimony rested on one key witness (who had allegedly been bribed and who refuted his own testimony some years later), Kenyatta was found guilty on April 3, 1953 of managing and being a member of the Mau Mau and sentenced to concurrent prison terms of seven and three years, to be followed by restriction to a remote area for an indefinite period. Protesting his innocence, Kenyatta told the court: "We have not received justice. None of us would condone the mutilation of human beings. We have families of our own." Confined to Lokitaung prison in Kenya's northern frontier district, Kenyatta suffered considerable hardship. On April 14, 1959 his term of imprisonment at Lokitaung ended, and he was sent ninety miles south to Lodwar, where he was permitted greater freedom.

Meanwhile, Kenya was making headway toward self-government. In May 1960 a new party, the Kenya African National Union (KANU), mostly comprising members of the Kikuyu and Luo tribes, was formed, and Kenyatta was elected its president in absentia. A few weeks later a second party, the Kenya African Democratic Union (KADU), composed of members of the smaller tribes, came into being. In the election of February 1961, KANU, campaigning with the slogan "Uhuru na Kenyatta" ("Freedom and Kenyatta"), emerged as the strongest party in the Kenya Legislative Council, but its members refused to form a government as long as Kenyatta remained in confinement. The colonial governor, Sir Patrick Renison, who had previously refused to release Kenyatta, now realized that his ultimate release was inevitable.

In April 1961 Kenyatta was taken from Lodwar to Maralal, some 180 miles from Nairobi, for the last stage of his confinement. Unconditionally released four months later, he made a triumphal return to his home territory. In October he assumed the presidency of KANU. A special by-election in January 1962, in which he was unopposed, enabled him to enter the Legislative Council as representative of the Fort Hall constituency. In the new coalition government, he assumed the post of Minister of State for Constitutional Affairs and Economic Planning in April of that year. On June 1, 1963 he became the first Prime Minister of self-governing Kenya, as well as Minister for Internal Security and Defense. The country officially attained independence under its new constitution on December 12, 1963, when the Duke of Edinburgh, representing the British Crown, turned over the instruments of sovereignty to Kenyatta. In compliance with Kenyatta's wishes, Kenya became a one-party state in November 1964, when the opposition KADU party underwent voluntary dissolution. On December 12, 1964 Kenya became a republic within the British Commonwealth, with Kenyatta as President.

Taking the Swahili logger's cry "Harambee!" —meaning "let's all pull together!"—as his watchword, Kenyatta has steered his people into what he calls "African Socialism," a nondogmatic philosophy stressing self-help, mutual assistance, and patient planning. While adhering to a policy of non-alignment in the cold war, he has resisted Communist efforts to gain a foothold in Kenya. In 1965 he directed the government's takeover of the Soviet-sponsored Lumumba Institute, and in 1967 he expelled mainland Chinese diplomats for allegedly trying to meddle in Kenya's internal affairs. Branding Communism "somebody else's nationalism," he has promised that Kenya "shall not exchange one master for a new master." By 1966 the Kenya government had established some 5,000 local self-help groups to build roads, schools, and hospitals, as well as a National Youth Service that provided work and education for unemployed young people.

In recent years Kenyatta has implemented a "good neighbor policy" by concluding treaties that ended disputes with neighboring Ethiopia and Somalia, and by acting as mediator in a longstanding conflict between Tanzania and Uganda. At the same time, he has firmly opposed white rule in South Africa, Rhodesia, and the Portuguese colonies. During 1973 his government played host to the annual conference of the World Bank and International Monetary Fund, and that same year the secretariat of the United Nations Environment Program opened offices in Nairobi. Kenyatta is a founder of the Organization of African Unity and of the East African Common Market.

Among Kenya's population of some 12,500,000, including 43,000 Europeans, 130,000 Asians, and about forty African tribes, Kenyatta has maintained a remarkable degree of harmony. Although he has embarked on a program of "Africanization" to bring native Kenyans into the economic mainstream, he has refrained from following Uganda's example of large-scale expropriation and expulsion of non-Africans. Aware of their importance to the economy, he has encouraged Europeans and Asians to remain, as long as they agree to identify with African aspirations. Kenyatta has kept some useful aspects of the British colonial structure, and he has retained Europeans in some key posts in the government and the civil service.

Despite Kenyatta's practice of carefully balancing his Cabinets and other representative bodies among the country's major tribes, the persistence of tribalism in the consciousness of many Kenyans has remained a major obstacle to national unity. It reached a harrowing climax in July 1969 with the assassination of Kenyatta's protégé and possible successor, Minister of Economic Planning and Development Tom Mboya. Kenyatta's effort to forge a "government of consensus" within a one-party system received a setback in April 1966, when his Vice-President, Oginga Odinga, once one of his most loyal supporters, resigned from KANU and formed a leftist opposition party, the Kenya People's Union (KPU). Since 1969, when KPU was dissolved and Odinga was placed under house arrest after outbreaks of violence that followed in the wake of the Mboya murder, Kenya has again been a de facto one-party state.

Kenyatta is an honorary fellow of the London School of Economics and a Knight of Grace in the Order of St. John of Jerusalem. He holds honorary LL.D. degrees from the University of East Africa and Manchester University. Some of his representative speeches are contained in *Harambee! The Prime Minister of Kenya's Speeches 1963-64* (Oxford Univ. Press, 1964), and *Suffering Without Bitterness* (Nairobi, 1968). He continues to consider himself a Christian. In December 1973 Kenyatta was honored at a three-day gala celebration marking "Ten Great Years" of progress since Kenya's attainment of independence.

Jomo Kenyatta is affectionately called "Mzee" ("grand old man") by his people. From his first marriage, to Grace Wahu, on November 28, 1922, he has a son, Peter Mugai, and a daughter, Margaret Wambui, his closest confidante, who was elected mayor of Nairobi in 1970. On May 11, 1942 Kenyatta married Edna Grace Clarke, a British schoolteacher and governess, who has remained in England. He has a son, Peter Magana, from that marriage. His third wife, Grace, a daughter of the late Kikuyu senior chief Koinange, bore him a daughter, Jane Wambui, and died giving birth to a second child. In the early 1950's Kenyatta married Ngina, the daughter of Kikuyu chief Muhoho, known popularly as "Mama Ngina." They have two sons, Uhuru and Muhoho, and a daughter, Nyokabi.

The President lives with his wife on his estate at Ichaweri, in the Gatundu district, not far from his birthplace. He often rises at dawn to work on his farm, and he commutes daily to Nairobi, some thirty miles away. A broad-shouldered, muscular man of average height, with a graying beard, penetrating dark eyes, a resonant voice, and remarkable energy and vitality, Kenyatta seems equally at home in Savile Row suits, open-necked shirts, or tribal robes. The former British High Commissioner in Kenya, Malcolm MacDonald, once described Kenyatta as "a very great man and a very good man," with a "terrific sense of humor" and "a sense of destiny but also a sense of humility."

References

Cox, Richard. Kenyatta's Country (1966)
Howarth, Anthony. Kenyatta: A Photographic Biography (1967)
Kenworthy, Leonard and Ferrari, Erma. Leaders of New Nations (1968)
Murray-Brown, Jeremy. Kenyatta (1973)
Segal, Ronald. Political Africa (1961)

KING, CAROLE

Feb. 9, 1941- Singer; songwriter
Address: b. c/o Ode Records, 1416 N. La Brea Ave., Los Angeles, Calif. 90028

In the brutally competitive world of pop music, Carole King's successful transition from songwriter to singer-composer constitutes one of the music industry's happier survival stories. Author of

CAROLE KING

"golden shlock-rock" hits for more than a decade, the gifted Miss King is considered by many pop music critics to be the queen of her specialty, which she has identified as "soft rock," a jazz-based acoustic sound emphasizing lyrics rather than heavy beat. One of her albums, *Tapestry*, has compiled an enviable sales record of more than ten million copies. *Tapestry*, her second solo LP, won for Miss King one of her four Grammy awards for 1971.

Carole King was born in Brooklyn, New York on February 9, 1941 to middle-class parents. Her father, an insurance salesman, was formerly a fireman; her mother was a public school teacher. After graduating from Madison High School in Brooklyn, Carole enrolled at Queens College, where her classmates included Neil Diamond and Paul Simon. She dropped out of college after her freshman year to marry Gerry Goffin, a laboratory assistant and aspiring chemist who shared her interest in popular music.

Introduced to pop music publisher Don Kirschner by Miss King's childhood friend Neil Sedaka, the newlyweds signed contracts with Aldon Music, a small music publishing firm owned by Kirschner and Al Nevins, for a salary variously reported to be from fifty to several hundred dollars a week. Kirschner, who eventually launched "bubble gum" music and fabricated such pop groups as the Monkees and the Archies, employed a group of apprentice rock 'n' roll songwriters, among them Sedaka, Barry Mann, Cynthia Weil, and Howard Greenfield. Cramped into a "musical chicken coop" in the Brill Building on Broadway, each songwriting hopeful churned out one tune after another. "We each had a little cubby hole with just enough room for a piano, a bench and maybe a chair for the lyricist—if you were lucky," Miss King recalled to Grace Lichtenstein in one of her rare interviews, which was published in the New York *Times* on November 29, 1970. "You'd sit there and write and you could hear someone in the next cubby hole composing some song exactly like yours. The pressure . . .

was really terrific because Donny would play one songwriter against another."

Such constraints were not particularly conducive to inventiveness and the songs, according to Miss King, were written "interchangeably." Concentrating on "uptown R & B," a money-making musical style that tried to capture the frustrated, plaintive lament of Harlem adolescents, the songwriting team of Goffin and King produced its first hit in 1960. Hitting the charts on November 27, 1960, the Shirelles' version of "Will You Love Me Tomorrow?" remained on the *Billboard* "Hot 100" for nineteen weeks, reaching the number one position during the week of January 30, 1961. In the next few years Goffin and King wrote a number of hits including "Take Good Care of My Baby," a 1961 number one disc for Bobby Vee; "Go Away, Little Girl," Steve Lawrence's 1962 chart-topper; "Up On the Roof," a best-selling single for the Drifters in 1962; "The Loco-motion," the 1962 number one hit recorded by the Goffins' maid, who billed herself as Little Eva; and "He's a Rebel," a 1962 Crystals' hit that followed "The Loco-motion" to the top of the charts.

In the early 1960's the standard approach to rock 'n' roll songwriting and promotion was to write a song, cut a demonstration record, and distribute it to pop singers on the prowl for new material. "I saved all my Carole King demos," singer Don Everly admitted, as quoted in the Washington *Post* of May 24, 1973. "They always sounded better to me than the final versions of the songs." One demo—"It Might As Well Rain Until September"—was released as a single on Kirschner's Dimension label in 1962. On the best-selling record charts for nine weeks, the single, which was Carole King's first release as a performer, climbed to the twenty-second position on *Billboard*'s "Hot 100" chart. In Great Britain it reached the number one spot.

The tidal wave of British hard rock groups during the mid-1960's brought about a minor revolution in music publishing. Because many of the new groups preferred to write their own material, some songwriters saw in that new trend the end of their separate usefulness. After several lean years, Goffin and King managed to score a big hit in the soul field with "A Natural Woman," recorded by Aretha Franklin, and they also hit the jackpot with "Hi-De-Ho," a 1970 release by Blood, Sweat and Tears. In 1968 Gerry and Carole Goffin dissolved both their songwriting partnership and their marriage. In explaining her decision in an interview for *BMI; The Many Worlds of Music* (Summer 1971), Miss King told Arnold Shaw, "It's very hard to maintain a marriage writing together."

Moving to the West Coast with her two daughters, Carole King determined to find "a new identity." In 1969 she joined The City, a Los Angeles-based musical group, singing and playing piano for an album called *Now That Everything's Been Said*. The album of Goffin and King songs produced by pop entrepreneur Lou Adler was not commercially successful, but it gave Carole King the self-confidence to perform as a solo vocalist. Before summoning the courage to strike out on her own, Miss King performed publicly with James Taylor, the pop singer and songwriter.

Her first solo recording effort for Adler's Ode label was *Writer: Carole King*. It featured Goffin and King's hit song "Up on the Roof," which spoke of the escape from the world's problems to be found at the top of the stairs. Released in 1970, the album made it clear that Carole King had struck out on her own. Unlike many current popular songs, Miss King's lyrics ignored the drug-induced fantasies favored by some rock stars and made only slight references to political issues of the day, addressing themselves instead to questions of love, friendship, and lost youth. "Without howling sexuality or exotic mysticism, Carole King reached a pinnacle in rock," James Lichtenberg wrote in *Cue* magazine (November 13, 1971). "The openness of her straightforward, human intensity as a performer plus her songwriting talent are what put her in the vanguard of this new movement. Whether you are a young woman working as a secretary . . . or Carl Wilson of the Beach Boys . . . , Carole King talks to you."

Tapestry, Carole King's second solo album, took the pop music industry by surprise. Released in 1971, its unprecedented sales were estimated to have surpassed 10,000,000 copies by May 1973. In analyzing Carol King's music for *Newsday* (November 5, 1972), Robert Christgau praised her "honesty and innovation." Taking inventory of its contents, he reported that although *Tapestry* contained the obligatory "chin-up song ('Beautiful') . . . , pastoral-escape song ('Way Over Yonder') and . . . inane life-is-cosmic song ('Tapestry') . . . , it also evoked the joys of physical (not necessarily sexual) love and the pain of the geographical separation that is the curse of romance in our mobile paradise." He went on to say that "it contained a true and sentimental standard about friendship and a true and ironic standard about breaking up. . . . But most of all, it established Carole King's individuality as a woman."

When the members of the National Academy of Recording Arts and Sciences assembled in New York City on March 14, 1972 to announce their Grammy awards for the outstanding discs of the previous season, they voted Carole King's *Tapestry* the best album of the year. Miss King also earned Grammy awards for the best song of 1971 ("You've Got a Friend"), for the best record ("It's Too Late"), and for the best female vocal performance in the pop field ("Tapestry"). Her friend and sometime artistic partner James Taylor won the best male vocal award in the pop field with his version of the King song "You've Got a Friend." Noting that it was "Carole King's year," pop music commentator Robert Christgau, in his *Newsday* review (March 17, 1972) of the Grammy award presentations, expressed the opinion that "only a sorehead could gainsay these choices."

When *Music,* Carole King's third LP for the Ode label, was released in the winter of 1971, it received only mixed reviews. In his New York *Times* pop music column (January 2, 1972), Don Heckman conceded that "there was no way" Miss King could surpass the "mind-boggling success" of *Tapestry,* but that, nevertheless, *Music* was a "fine collection of tunes" that indicated "the King wizardry with phrases." Late in 1972, when Ode Records released *Rhymes & Reasons,* Heckman posed the inevitable rhetorical question of whether the talented Miss King could continue to meet the competitive standards set by her previous hits, especially since she and her lyricist, Toni Stern, were "not yet able to match the almost symbiotic musical interaction" that made her professional relationship with Gerry Goffin so memorable. Nevertheless finding the album indispensable, Heckman explained that "her total musical conception is what makes everything work: hard piano rhythms, chugging percussion and a roving, contrapuntal bass all combine to provide a pulsating, endlessly moving vehicle for her gospel-blues-tinged vocals. Style is inseparable from, but never a substitute for, substance."

Fantasy, Carole King's first attempt at a "concept album," was released by Ode Records in mid-1973. Explaining that "in fantasy I can be black or white, a woman or man," Miss King sings about racial and sexual inequality, the dangers of drug addiction, and the need for human understanding. Commenting on the album for the *National Observer* (September 1, 1973), Daniel Henninger wrote that although the music was "funky" and "catchy," the lyrics were "downers" and "exceedingly bittersweet, not my favorite flavor." In her New York *Times* review (July 15, 1973), Loraine Alterman selected "You Light Up My Life," a joyful, romantic love song, and "Corazón," a "rhythmically compelling" Spanish song, for special praise. But, taken as a whole, she considered *Fantasy* to be musically "monotonous," with a "slow to middling" tempo and "rather bland string arrangements, and uninspired horn parts that added up to a total effect of smooth, rock-flavored Broadway orchestration with a bow to rock."

An admitted victim of stage fright, Miss King rarely performs in public. "I'm really kind of . . . reticent about singing," she confessed to Grace Lichtenstein. "As a writer, it's very safe and womblike, because somebody else gets the credit or the blame. . . . I worry that I'm going to forget the words!" In December 1970 James Taylor introduced Carole King to his audience at Toronto's Massey Hall. Accompanying herself at the piano, she sang ten songs. In so doing, she entranced Toronto *Globe and Mail* critic Jack Batten, who in his "Pop Scene" column (December 12, 1970), described her sound as "genuinely ferocious" and compared her vocal interpretations to those of "Barbra Streisand without the wretched excess." Although he acknowledged that Miss King was "a most effective interpreter of her own work," John S. Wilson, in his New York *Times* review (June 20, 1971) of her two standing-room only Carnegie Hall concerts, remarked that the "steady unvarying consistency of her songwriting manner, her singing manner and her piano-playing manner became a bit too much of what might otherwise be a good thing."

In May 1973 some 8,500 Washington, D.C. fans braved a steady downpour with undampened spirits to attend Carole King's open-air recital at the Merriweather Post Pavilion, and several days later, defying overcast skies and wet ground, a crowd estimated at 65,000 to 70,000 persons thronged to her free concert in Central Park. Making her only local appearance in two years, Miss King gave the Central Park concert out of gratitude and affection for New York City. "New York has given me such an awful lot—stimulus, ideas, feelings to write," she told friends. "The concert is just a small way of giving something back to it." With James Taylor, Barbra Streisand, and Quincy Jones, Miss King took part in April 1972 in a fund-raising concert organized by actor Warren Beatty that raised about $300,000 for the Presidential campaign of Senator George S. McGovern.

Carole King and her second husband, Charles Larkey, a former bass player for The City, live in the Laurel Canyon district of greater Los Angeles with their infant daughter Molly, and Miss King's two daughters, Louise and Sherry, from her previous marriage. In addition to the California home, she has a farm near New Canaan, Connecticut. Carole King's special brand of beauty, noted by several critics, has been attributed to her "open, pleasant, honest, warm" face. According to Robert Christgau, Miss King "is the greatest thing to happen to the Jewish nose since Barbra Streisand." Her long, thick dark hair, once a virtual trademark, was cropped and curly when she appeared in New York City in May 1973. Like several of her songwriting contemporaries, among them Carly Simon and Joni Mitchell, she prefers jeans and sweaters to designer fashions. A contented homebody, she drives her children to and from school in her battered white Volkswagen and enjoys preparing meals for her family, especially Japanese-style raw fish. She often plies the studio technicians at her recording sessions with her home-baked cookies. For relaxation, Miss King practises yoga and stitches samplers. Jealous of her privacy, she seldom grants interviews. "The main reason I got into performing and recording on my own was to expose my songs to the public in the fastest way," she told Arnold Shaw some years ago. "I don't consider myself a singer. . . . I don't want to be a star with a capital S."

References

BMI p20 Summer '71 por
Life 72:R My 19 '72 por
N Y Post p22 Je 21 '71
N Y Times II p31 N 29 '70 por; II p21 Jl 15 '73 por
Newsday II p17 N 5 '72 por
Washington Post C p1 My 24 '73
Who's Who in America, 1974-75

KNUDSEN, SEMON E(MIL) (nūd′sən)

Oct. 2, 1912- Corporation executive; industrialist
Address: b. c/o White Motor Corporation, 100 Erieview Plaza, Cleveland, Ohio 44114

When Semon E. ("Bunkie") Knudsen took over in May 1971 as chairman and chief executive of the White Motor Corporation, to embark on the miracle of nursing that moribund firm back to health, he carried with him unimpeachable credentials, based on personal achievement as well as family background. The son of the late William S. ("Big Bill") Knudsen, who had been president of General Motors Corporation from 1937 to 1940 and was director of United States industrial production during World War II, he followed in his father's footsteps into GM corporate ranks, serving with distinction as head of the Pontiac and Chevrolet divisions and as a GM executive vice-president. For nineteen months, in 1968-69, Knudsen was president of the Ford Motor Company before being forced out in a power struggle among its top executives. During his first two and a half years at White, Knudsen totally reorganized the corporation and turned its deficits into profits. Professor Eugene E. Jennings of Michigan State University, who has followed Knudsen's career closely, has observed, as quoted in the *Wall Street Journal* (April 5, 1973): "The White Motors of the world, the companies that are truly sick, are the situations in which the manager's managers—I call them heroes—are made."

Semon Emil Knudsen was born in Buffalo, New York on October 2, 1912, the oldest of the four children, and the only son, of Danish-born William S. Knudsen and of Clara Elizabeth (Euler) Knudsen, a native of Buffalo. In 1913 his father, then an employee of the Ford Motor Company, brought the family to Dearborn, Michigan, where Semon and his sisters, Elna, Clara, and Martha, spent their early childhood. It was his father who gave him the nickname "Bunkie"—army slang for "bunkmate" or "close companion"—that has remained with him through the years. When Knudsen was fourteen, his father, who in the meantime had become vice-president in charge of the Chevrolet division at General Motors, gave him a new Chevrolet car, unassembled, and told him that it was his if he could put together the 1,000 or more parts unaided. Knudsen accomplished the task within two months.

After attending Dartmouth College in 1931-32, Knudsen studied engineering at the Massachusetts Institute of Technology, from which he graduated in 1936. Turning down a job offer from General Motors, he went to work in a Detroit machine shop, and later, to obtain experience in mass production, took a job in a roller bearing plant that turned out 100,000 units a day. He joined the manufacturing staff of the Pontiac division of General Motors in January 1939 and worked successively as chief inspector of its defense plant, superintendent of the car assembly

plant, and assistant general master mechanic. In 1949 he became director of the process development section at GM's central office. He moved to Indianapolis in 1953 as assistant manufacturing manager of aircraft engine operations at GM's Allison division and became manufacturing manager there the following year. In March 1955 he was named general manager of GM's Detroit Diesel engine division.

Appointed in July 1956 as general manager of the Pontiac division, and elected a GM vice-president, Knudsen took immediate steps to streamline Pontiac's management committee and to revitalize its dealerships and national sales organization. Although the Pontiac had long had a reputation for solid engineering, it conveyed something of an "old maid image" that Knudsen was determined to change to popularize the car among younger buyers. He ordered drastic changes in the style of the 1957 model, including the removal of Pontiac's traditional chrome streaks and Indian-head hood ornament. He entered Pontiac cars in racing competition, and he personally test-drove selected models. Among his innovations were a 225-horsepower economy engine for the 1959 model; the compact Tempest, a leader in the small-car field since its introduction in 1960; and the Grand Prix, a sedan with a sports car look. During his first three years as general manager, Knudsen moved Pontiac from sixth place in sales among American auto makers to third place, where it has remained.

In November 1961 Knudsen was appointed to succeed Edward N. Cole as general manager of the Chevrolet motor division, which, as the nation's top auto producer, accounted for nearly 60 percent of GM car sales. Under his management, Chevrolet established three successive industry sales records and delivered more than 9,000,000 Chevrolet cars and trucks, becoming the first auto maker to surpass the 2,000,000-mark in car sales for a single year. Knudsen maintained close contact with Chevrolet dealers from coast to coast and took a personal interest in styling and engineering developments, with emphasis on appeal to women and youth. Among the models he introduced was the popular Chevelle, modeled on the Pontiac Grand Prix.

In June 1965 Knudsen was elected to the GM board of directors and named a group vice-president, in charge of Canadian and overseas operations. The following February he was elected an executive vice-president and given additional responsibility for the Dayton, household appliance, and engine divisions. When the GM management was reorganized in November 1967, Knudsen—who was then considered the fourth-ranking executive at GM and, with 42,507 shares, was one of its largest stockholders—hoped to succeed James M. Roche as corporation president, but lost out, reportedly by a small margin of the directors' votes, to Edward N. Cole. Knudsen continued to serve as executive vice-president, with responsibility for all GM international operations, as well as all domestic non-automotive and defense divisions, until January 31, 1968, when he resigned from his $482,000-a-year GM post for "personal reasons." As he noted at a press conference, the recent changes in management at GM had convinced him that "the corporation had decided on its organization for a minimum of the next four years," and therefore he was ready for "another assignment."

On February 6, 1968 Henry Ford 2d, the chairman and chief executive officer of the Ford Motor Company, announced that Knudsen had been named to succeed Arjay Miller as company president. Knudsen's move from GM to Ford was said to be the most significant shift in the executive ranks of the automobile industry since his father had left Ford in 1921 to become head of GM's Chevrolet division. Determined to increase his company's share in the medium-priced car field, then dominated by GM's Pontiac, Oldsmobile, and Buick, Henry Ford 2d had reportedly been seeking a manufacturing specialist like Knudsen to replace the financial expert, Miller, who was given the newly created post of company vice-chairman. To compensate Knudsen for the more than $1,000,000 in accrued bonus awards that he forfeited when he left GM, Ford gave him a stock bonus valued at about $750,000 and a guaranteed annual base salary of at least $200,000 for a five-year period.

As president of Ford, Knudsen—who was also named a director of the company and a member of its executive committee—was in direct charge of North American automotive operations, overseas automotive and tractor operations, and the Philco-Ford Corporation, as well as the central staffs for manufacturing, personnel and organization, scientific research, engineering, product planning and design, labor relations, marketing, and purchasing. In April 1968 he was elected a director of the subsidiary Ford Motor Company of Canada. According to a report in the New York *Times* (July 12, 1968), Knudsen took charge of the Ford Motor Company with "a speed and determination that . . . impressed Ford insiders." Shortly after taking office he introduced two new safety features to be included in 1969 Ford cars: an anti-skid braking system and an electrically heated rear window. Although during the last quarter of 1968 Ford sales still comprised only 26.5 percent of the car market in the United States, as compared to GM's 53.3 percent for the same period, Ford outstripped Chevrolet in the production of trucks that year for the first time since 1935. The 2,313,208 cars sold by Ford during 1968 represented a 26 percent increase over the preceding year.

On September 2, 1969, amid growing rumors of discord among Ford's top executives, Knudsen was suddenly dismissed by Henry Ford 2d, who gave no explanation for the action, other than that "sometimes these things don't work out." The dismissal was made official by a unanimous vote of the board of directors nine days later. "I want to make clear that today's decision, in my opinion, is unwarranted in view of the accomplishments the company has made during my brief tenure," Knudsen said at the time. "Further,

SEMON E. KNUDSEN

it is completely inconsistent with what Mr. Ford said to me at the time I was offered the presidency." He relinquished the post only after being assured in writing that the remainder of his five-year contract would be honored. Knudsen's dismissal was said to have resulted from his tendency to "move too fast" and too far; his difficulty as an outsider, coming from GM, in gaining acceptance from the "insiders" at Ford; and the strong competition he faced within the company, notably from the young and ambitious executive vice-president Lee A. Iacocca.

In February 1970—after reportedly turning down an offer of the presidency of General Dynamics Corporation—Knudsen founded Rectrans, Inc., a company for the manufacture and marketing of a new style of luxury motor homes, and he became its chairman and chief executive and the owner of some 60 percent of its stock. Convinced that motor homes were "in tune with what the young people today want" and also appealed to older, retired people, he bought an old mobile home factory at Brighton, Michigan and recruited a young and competent staff from Ford and General Motors. But it looked as if Rectrans might not be successful because of the stiff competition that it faced in its field. Therefore when the White Motor Corporation—a major manufacturer of on-highway and off-highway trucks, farm machinery, construction and industrial equipment, and recreational vehicles—offered Knudsen the post of chairman and chief executive, to be effective on May 1, 1971, he accepted. As part of the arrangement, the White Motor Corporation bought Rectrans, which became part of its recreational products group, for 400,000 shares of its common stock. Relinquishing his Ford contract when he joined White, Knudsen was given an annual salary of $200,000 plus another $100,000 a year for the ten-year period beyond 1975.

The White Motor Corporation was beset by serious problems, but for Knudsen it presented the sort of challenge he liked. The firm had been losing some $30,000,000 annually, overseas operations were in a chaotic state, morale at its Cleveland headquarters was at its lowest ebb, and some of the company's dealers were saddled with four-year-old tractors. There was virtually no centralized control, and public relations, financial management, engineering, manufacturing staff operations, labor relations, and personnel records were practically nonexistent. Three attempts at mergers, aimed at bringing the corporation out of its financial straits, had been turned back by the Justice Department.

As a first step in transforming the White Motor Company into a going concern, Knudsen arranged for bank credits amounting to $290,000,000 "to keep the company afloat." To replenish its decimated executive corps he raided the Detroit automobile companies and other major firms. He undertook a thoroughgoing centralization, reorganizing the farm equipment division from top to bottom and bringing together all tractor operations in a single plant in Iowa. After selling the only marginally profitable Diamond Reo truck line he consolidated the company's remaining four lines under a single marketing group and advertised them as the "Big Four." He poured substantial sums of money into such neglected areas as product development and engineering, instituted vitally needed control systems for inventory and other crucial areas, and replaced antiquated plants with new ones.

Knudsen established personal rapport with regional dealers of White's products, many of whom had become discouraged by the decline in the company's fortunes, and restored their confidence with pep talks. At White's home office he stressed efficiency and brevity. "If you had something you would normally explain in fifteen minutes, you learned damned fast that you'd better be prepared to explain it in three minutes," one employee of the company observed, as quoted in the *Wall Street Journal* (April 5, 1973). "Knudsen was intensely interested, but not for long."

After two years with White Motor, Knudsen continued to be faced with problems involving certain unprofitable enterprises. These included an idle tractor and truck engine plant in Canton, Ohio, that Knudsen had been trying to sell; the debt-ridden Italian subsidiary Arbos S.p.A. of Milan, a manufacturer of harvest combines; and Knudsen's own creation, Rectrans, which was struggling to overcome competition. To those who advised him to eliminate all operations not making a profit, Knudsen said, as quoted in *Forbes* (November 15, 1972): "You know, I could have come into White, really chopped everything out of it, and showed a tremendous improvement in a year's time. But then it would have fallen to pieces. I didn't come here for a one-year job."

On the whole, Knudsen's tenure at White Motor has been remarkably successful. From the time he joined the company until late 1972 White's stock rose from $22 to $71. During the first half of 1973 sales reached a record $582,-000,000, an increase of 25 percent over the corresponding period in 1972, and earnings for the same period rose by 113 percent to $8,000,000.

Figures released in the summer of 1973 indicated that within a year truck sales had risen 29 percent, North American farm equipment sales had increased by 33 percent, and European farm equipment sales had doubled.

In addition to fulfilling his role as chairman and chief executive, Knudsen succeeded Henry J. Nave as president of the White Motor Corporation in January 1972. His business associations also include membership on the boards of directors of United Air Lines, Cowles Communications Inc., the Michigan National Bank, and the First National Bank of Palm Beach, Florida. He is a director of the National Multiple Sclerosis Society and of the Greater Cleveland Growth Association; a trustee of the Oakland University Foundation of Rochester, Michigan and of the Cleveland Clinic Foundation; and a member of the Massachusetts Institute of Technology Corporation and of the national board of Boys Clubs of America. Knudsen is treasurer of the Motor Vehicle Manufacturers Association and a member of the Society of Automotive Engineers, the American Ordnance Association, the American Society of Tool Engineers, and Delta Upsilon fraternity.

Semon E. "Bunkie" Knudsen and his wife, the former Florence Anne McConnell, whom he married on June 16, 1938, have a son, Peter, three daughters, Judy (Mrs. Howard Christie), Lisa (Mrs. Henry Howard Flint 2d), and Kristina (Mrs. S. A. Gregg), and several grandchildren. A broad-shouldered man with a mane of graying hair, who is given to wearing ankle boots and aviator glasses, Knudsen does not quite conform to the Fabian Bachrach image of the typical corporation executive. As a hobby he owns a racing car that finished in twenty-sixth place at the Indianapolis 500 in 1973. Deceptively soft-spoken and nondynamic in outward appearance, Knudsen has a reputation as a "no-nonsense executive" noted for his singlemindedness, determination, and organizational skill. His personal fortune has been estimated at well over $30,000,000.

References

N Y Post p39 F 8 '68 por
N Y Times p60 F 7 '68 por
Wall St J p1+ Ap 5 '73
Who's Who in America, 1972-73
Who's Who in Finance and Industry (1972-73)

KOHOUTEK, LUBOŠ (loo'bosh kä-hō'tek)

1935(?)- Czech astronomer
Address: b. Hamburger Sternwarte, 205 Hamburg-Bergedorf 80, West Germany

The unwitting discoverer of a comet variously described as "the celestial extravaganza of the century" or "the Edsel of the firmament," Luboš Kohoutek, a Czech astronomer and lecturer at the Hamburg University Observatory, is among the top astronomical observers in the world. A specialist in galactic astronomy, he earned an international reputation for his detailed analyses of the physical characteristics of planetary nebulae and investigations of interplanetary matter. His fortuitous discovery of an unusually large comet in March 1973, nine months before its optimum viewing period, offered an uncommon opportunity for a well-coordinated, worldwide observation and research program. Monitored by ground observatories, unmanned satellites, balloons, rockets, high-flying aircraft, and a manned orbiting space laboratory, Comet Kohoutek became the most studied comet in history.

Luboš Kohoutek was born in northern Moravia, a province in central Czechoslovakia, in 1935. Interested in astronomy from childhood, he was especially fascinated by the minor bodies of the solar system and spent many nights on meteor- and comet-watching expeditions in the Sudeten and Carpathian mountains. That early interest in astronomy determined the course of his education. After studying for several years in Brno, the Moravian capital, he enrolled at Charles University in Prague, where he majored in physics, mathematics, and astronomy.

After his graduation in 1958, Kohoutek accepted a research position at the Astronomical Institute of the Czechoslovak Academy of Sciences. Under the guidance of Professor Luboš Perek, the director of the Institute and a specialist in stellar studies, Kohoutek concentrated on planetary nebulae—the small, dense, generally ring-shaped clouds of gases that slowly expand outward from a hot central star. For the next several years he investigated the particular physical characteristics of planetary nebulae and speculated on their possible origin. Among his published studies on planetary nebulae are "A New Distance Scale and the Optical Thickness of Planetary Nebulae," "Some Physical Characteristics of Very Young Planetary Nebulae and of Their Nuclei," and *Catalogue of Galactic Planetary Nebulae*, written in collaboration with Dr. Perek and published in Prague by Academia in 1967. He also wrote a number of articles for the Czechoslovak Academy of Sciences *Bulletin of the Institute of Astronomy*, of which he was associate editor. Named to the Institute's Stellar Department in 1965, he was awarded several research grants to Hamburg Observatory. He was in Hamburg when the Soviet invasion of Czechoslovakia took place in 1968, and, deciding to remain, he accepted a position as an assistant professor at the University of Hamburg.

In 1969 Kohoutek discovered his first comet, while photographing the stars. It was officially designated "1969b" by the International Astronomical Union, the "b" indicating that the comet was the second to be charted in 1969. (In addition to the formal nomenclature, it is customary to name comets after their discoverers.) "It was very faint, without interest to the public," Kohoutek recalled to Victor K. McElheny in an interview with the New York *Times* (December 9,

LUBOŠ KOHOUTEK

1973). "It was normal. Most comets are faint." Two years later he became much interested in an article appearing in a circular published by the International Astronomical Union. Written by Dr. Brian G. Marsden, the head of the Central Bureau for Astronomical Telegrams at the Smithsonian Astrophysical Observatory, it included calculations for the possible position of fragments of Biela's comet, a lost periodic comet that split in two in 1846. Using a Schmidt-type telescope, he located some fifty asteroids orbiting the sun between Mars and Jupiter. Although the planetoids could have been cometary fragments, their origin was not immediately evident.

Continuing his study of the asteroids, Kohoutek plotted their returning orbital course and trained the Hamburg Observatory's thirty-one-inch telescope upon the night sky. He found eight of the asteroids, although he had hoped to spot at least fifteen, and, on February 28, 1973, his second comet: "1973e." Several weeks later, while scrutinizing a series of photographic plates exposed on March 7, he discerned a moving object in the constellation Hydra. After consulting sky atlases to see if the object had been charted previously, he examined other plates and found a "prediscovery" image of the object on a plate taken January 28, 1973. On March 23 he notified Dr. Brian Marsden that he had found an unusually large comet more than 400,000,000 miles from the sun, well beyond the orbit of Mars. Marsden confirmed the comet's position and asked Harvard College Observatory to make an independent verification of the comet's existence. It was then assigned the official name "1973f."

Because the comet was visible at such a great distance from earth a full nine months before its perihelion, both scientists and laymen predicted a dazzling celestial display, with most agreeing that Comet Kohoutek would be larger and brighter than Halley's Comet. Dr. Elizabeth Roemer, an astronomer at the University of Arizona, estimated that the comet's nucleus, or solid, tightly-compacted core, measured approximately twenty-five miles in diameter, more than twice the size of the nuclei of past comets. Their early calculations of the comet's sun-grazing elliptical orbit, which would bring it within 13,000,000 miles of the sun at perihelion, led other astronomers to expect a spectacular 100,000,000-mile tail and a magnitude as bright as -5 to -10. (The sun measures -26.84 on the scale.) Only one in twenty comets sweeps around the sun at such close range. "Although several new comets are found each year, it's only when they come close to the sun that they become spectacular," Kohoutek explained.

With an unprecedented nine months for preparations, astrophysicists, astronomers, National Aeronautics and Space Administration project engineers, and other scientists cooperated on an observation and study program. NASA's "Operation Kohoutek," under the direction of Stephen P. Maran, an astronomer formerly at Kitt Peak National Observatory, included plans for an airborne infrared observatory and special assignments for two orbiting satellites designed to monitor solar and astronomical phenomena and for the Mariner Venus/Mercury probe. The previously scheduled third Skylab orbital mission was altered to permit study of the comet without atmospheric interference. Equipped with an impressive array of specially designed telescopes, an ultraviolet camera, and a white-light coronagraph to block out the blinding effects of the sun, the three Skylab astronauts planned additional spacewalks to observe the comet.

Complementing NASA's extensive preparations, ground observation stations aimed their radio and optical telescopes at Comet Kohoutek. The New Mexico Institute of Mining and Technology, for example, hurriedly completed construction of its new cometary observatory with its sixteen-inch reflecting telescope to photograph the comet through different filters and a special device to study comet tails. By comparing the photographs taken by the observatories, Skylab, and the Mariner 10 spacecraft, scientists hoped to obtain their first three-dimensional view of a comet. Other scientists planned to study the comet in visible, ultraviolet, and infrared light; to observe the third magnitude star Scorpius through the comet's coma, the nebulous light that surrounds its nucleus; to bounce radio pulses off the nucleus; and to examine the effect of solar activity on the comet's density and structure.

Because many astronomers believe comets to be the most primitive members of the solar system, cometary study may offer important clues to the origin and development of the solar system. That theory, proposed by Jan Henrik Oort, the former director of the University of Leiden Observatory in the Netherlands, holds that comets are composed of the gases and space dust that condensed billions of years ago to form the sun and the planets. The remaining primordial matter, known as "Oort's cloud," encircles the solar system beyond Pluto's orbit and includes an estimated 200,000,000 comets. Some astronomers maintain that those comets are formed when bits

of matter drift together and, in the absolute zero temperature of deep space, coalesce into a glacial nucleus, or "dirty snowball," of frozen water vapor, methane, ammonia, dust particles, and perhaps some hydrocarbons.

Like many of his colleagues, Dr. Kohoutek supports the "dirty snowball" theory developed by Dr. Fred L. Whipple in 1950. According to that theory, solar heat vaporizes the frozen gases as the comet swings around the sun and the dust particles expand to form the comet's head and tail. Other scientists accept British astronomer Raymond A. Lyttleton's "gravel bank" hypothesis that a comet's nucleus consists of dust particles and bits of space debris with little or no ice. On the basis of his early observations, Dr. Kohoutek expected his especially dusty comet to form an extensive luminous tail and provide conclusive evidence to support one of the two theories.

The Czech astronomer, who had seen his comet only in telescopic photographs, made his first visit to the United States early in December 1973 to join the "Hunt-the-Comet" cruise, a three-day excursion aboard the *Queen Elizabeth II* that was sponsored by the Earth Society. Before boarding the ship on December 9, he told reporters at an impromptu news conference that Comet Kohoutek was "nothing extraordinary—just a comet." All that ballyhoo, he made clear, was largely unwarranted. In addition to the planned observation of the comet itself, the shipboard program included displays of cometary structure and behavior, a series of lectures by noted astronomers, and an address by Dr. Kohoutek. Although he acknowledged that "this comet [was] something special" to him personally because it had "changed" him, he told his rapt audience that a comet was "something normal" to astronomers. "Perhaps as many as fifty comets have been discovered in the last ten years," he explained. "But there's something disturbing in a comet to ordinary people. Perhaps that is because a comet appears suddenly as something wild and extraordinary in the sky. It is not usual to see the sky in motion."

Following the cruise, Kohoutek returned to Hamburg briefly before visiting American astronomers and space researchers in Washington, D.C., Cambridge, Massachusetts, Houston, Texas, and Tucson, Arizona. At a joint news conference, held in conjunction with NASA administrator Stephen P. Maran on December 27, 1973, he offered several explanations for Comet Kohoutek's less than "spectacular" appearance as it rounded the sun. First, although the comet had formed a long "plasma tail" of ionized molecules that register on telescopic photographs, the dust tail, normally visible to the naked eye, was shorter than expected. Secondly, the comet appeared low in the sky, close to the horizon. Finally, "light pollution" from metropolitan areas interfered with unaided observation. "I'm really sorry people overestimated this thing," he said, as quoted in *U.S. News & World Report* (December 31, 1973). "I hope it will not be a big disappointment and

I hope people will understand that it's difficult to make exact forecasts of such things." In January 1974 Kohoutek, who had providentially booked telescope time at the European Southern Observatory atop Cerro La Silla in northern Chile to study planetary nebulae, examined the comet at its viewing peak.

Although Comet Kohoutek was hardly the "comet of the century" from the viewpoint of the public, it was, in the opinion of one astronomer, "the most [scientifically] important comet that we've had since Halley's." Two Canadian researchers, Nobel laureate Gerhard Herzberg and Hin Lew of the National Research Council of Canada, detected electrically charged water molecules around the comet's head, lending support to the "dirty snowball" theory of cometary composition. Other scientists found traces of the solar wind in the plasma tail and monitored radio noise emitted by the comet. The Skylab astronauts photographed an "anti-tail," composed of larger particles than those found in the dust tail, which stretched out before the comet for 2,000,000 miles.

Some astronomers computed Comet Kohoutek's nucleus to be approximately four miles in diameter, much smaller than was originally predicted, and the coma to be 7,000 miles in diameter. The dust tail measured some 20,000,000 miles in length. Corrected orbital calculations confirmed previous speculation that the comet had originated in the outer fringes of the solar system and was making its first passage around the sun. The presence of methyl cyanide and hydrogen cyanide in the coma provided additional evidence of an extraplanetary origin. In a speech before the American Astronomical Society on April 5, 1974 Dr. Fred Whipple hailed that discovery as "the most significant finding of all the observations made of Kohoutek." The existence of the two chemical compounds, he explained, "definitely increases the suspicion that comets were formed . . . out at about twenty trillion miles or halfway to the nearest star."

A rather shy, retiring man, Luboš Kohoutek jealously and successfully guards his privacy. Inundated with telephone calls, letters, and requests for interviews after his discovery of Comet Kohoutek, he once complained to newsmen, "I have no free time . . . , no time for my family . . . [and] no time to do my work." He has been married twice. By the first marriage, which ended in divorce, he has a daughter, Ivana. He and his second wife, Christine, have two small daughters, Eva and Martina. According to Kohoutek, when Eva was two she could read a sky photograph well enough to distinguish a star from a comet.

References

Christian Sci Mon pF10 F 19 '74
N Y Post p20 F 11 '74
N Y Times p36 D 12 '73; p61 Ja 7 '74 por
Nat Observer p1+ D 22 '73 por
Newsday p7 D 10 '73 por
Time 102:88+ D 17 '73 por

KOLLEK, TEDDY

May 27, 1911- Mayor of Jerusalem
Address: b. Municipality of Jerusalem, 22 Jaffa Road, Jerusalem, Israel; h. 6 Rashba Street, Jerusalem, Israel

More than most cities, Jerusalem, the capital of Israel, is a tinderbox. Its eastern sector, inhabited largely by Arabs, was annexed by Israel in 1967, after having been part of Jordan for nearly twenty years. Because the city is sacred to three world religions, it is constantly in the international eye. Fortunately for Jerusalem, it has been governed since 1965 by Teddy Kollek, a man with great love for the city and with a grand vision of its future. Earlier in his serried career he had been an undercover agent, an arms smuggler, an Israeli minister to the United States, and a ranking official in Premier David Ben-Gurion's government. His greatest dream, he says, is to make Jerusalem a major international cultural center and the new home of the United Nations.

Theodore Kollek was born on May 27, 1911, in Vienna, Austria, the son of Alfred and Margaret (Fleischer) Kollek. He has a younger brother, Paul, now a businessman in Israel. Alfred Kollek, a director of the Vienna branch of the Rothschild Bank, was an ardent supporter of Zionism, and from an early age, Teddy Kollek shared his father's enthusiasm. As a boy he joined the Zionist-oriented youth group T'khelet-Lavan (meaning "Blue-White," the Jewish national colors), which emphasized colonization in Palestine. Kollek remained active in T'khelet-Lavan after completing his secondary-school education. He also took part in the activities of He-Halutz, an international organization, based in Palestine, that trained Jewish youth for pioneering and self-defense. During the years from 1931 to 1934, which witnessed a great upsurge in anti-Semitism, he was an instructor at Jewish youth convocations sponsored by He-Halutz in Austria, Germany, Czechoslovakia, and England. On one occasion, while on a Sunday excursion in the countryside outside Vienna, he and some companions were beaten up by an anti-Semitic gang.

The Kollek family—sailing on the Italian steamer *Jerusalem*—emigrated to Palestine in 1934 and settled in the port city of Haifa. During the next few years, while continuing to work for He-Halutz, Teddy Kollek also served for a time as a *mukhtar,* or village headman, with the British administration that then governed Palestine under a League of Nations mandate. In July 1937, as one of a small band of young people from Germany, Austria, Czechoslovakia, and the Baltic countries, Kollek helped to found the kibbutz of Ein Gev on the eastern side of the Sea of Galilee. Because the Arab revolt of 1936-39 was then at its height, Ein Gev was established with a stockade-and-tower defense system, and its young inhabitants, isolated from their compatriots on the opposite shore, had to fight off frequent Arab attacks. As his first job on the kibbutz, Kollek filled bags with sand and trans-

TEDDY KOLLEK

ported them by boat to construction sites at Tiberias, on the western side of the sea.

Although retaining his membership in the kibbutz—which he did not relinquish until 1950—Kollek was released from his duties at Ein Gev in 1938 in order to be able to work full time for He-Halutz. During the next two years he went on educational missions to Zionist youth groups on the European continent and in England. While in Vienna, he came into contact with Adolf Eichmann, then the head of the Gestapo unit that controlled Jewish emigration from Austria. Kollek persuaded Eichmann to authorize the release of 3,000 Jewish youngsters from concentration camps for resettlement in England as farm laborers. Recalling his encounter with Eichmann, Kollek told J. Robert Moskin of Look (October 1, 1968): "He was very civilized, very businesslike. . . . I had no idea he would be the murderer of six million Jews and I would see him years later in a glass box in Israel."

In 1940, while stranded in England for nearly a year as a result of wartime conditions, Kollek met David Ben-Gurion, who headed the Jewish Agency, the governing body of the Jewish community of Palestine. Under Ben-Gurion's tutelage, Kollek became an agent of the Jewish Agency's political department. From about 1942 on his duties involved the Jewish underground in German-occupied Central and Eastern Europe. In 1943 he opened a Jewish Agency office in Istanbul, and from that base he established communication links with Jewish resistance groups and escape organizations. He also worked for the United States Office of Strategic Services and for the British military intelligence, in England, Egypt, Turkey, and elsewhere.

In 1946 Kollek took part in the massive operation that brought scores of thousands of Jewish refugees from Europe to Palestine, circumventing immigration restrictions imposed by the British authorities. Meanwhile, it became apparent that the United Nations decision to partition Palestine, and the impending withdrawal of British troops,

would be followed by an Arab-Jewish war. In anticipation of that conflict, Haganah, the military force of the Palestinian Jews, sent a clandestine weapons-buying mission to the United States. In 1947 Kollek was appointed its head—or, as he preferred to term himself, its "traffic cop." As detailed by Leonard Slater in his book The Pledge (Simon & Schuster, 1970), Kollek, from headquarters in a hotel on New York City's East 60th Street, directed the secret and often illegal operations of a small but far-ranging band of agents. They were often aided by American Zionists and by non-Jewish sympathizers—among them anti-British Irish longshoremen on the New York docks. Kollek and his operatives smuggled out of the country a store of surplus war supplies that ran the gamut from canteens and helmets to dismantled aircraft and small naval vessels.

On completion of that mission in mid-1948, Kollek returned to Ein Gev. He left the kibbutz again in 1949 to take charge of the United States desk at the Israeli Foreign Ministry in Jerusalem. In 1950 Kollek—who speaks English fluently and is strongly pro-American in his outlook—became Israel's minister plenipotentiary to the United States. While in Washington he negotiated for American technical and financial aid to Israel and organized the first Israel Bond drive. In 1952 David Ben-Gurion, who was now Israel's Premier, recalled Kollek to Jerusalem from the United States mission, and appointed him director general of the Premier's office.

In that key administrative post Kollek became known as an unorthodox and somewhat bohemian doer and fixer who bypassed official bureaucracies and concentrated on practical solutions rather than ideological considerations. As Yoel Marcus wrote in Israel Magazine (September 1971), "Ben-Gurion believed in him blindly and always backed him. The words 'Ask Teddy' were frequently on his lips. He loved Teddy as a son and treated him as such."

Refusing, however, to take advantage of his close relationship with the Premier, Kollek avoided political entanglements and concentrated on matters that did not involve patronage. In addition to organizing Ben-Gurion's trips abroad and other activities, Kollek headed the Department for Applied Civilian Scientific Research, the Bureau of Statistics, and the Government Press and Information Office. He was also in charge of water desalinization projects and of Israel's aid program for developing countries in Africa and Asia. It was largely as a result of Kollek's efforts that Ben-Gurion, who had long opposed television on cultural grounds, was finally persuaded to permit its introduction into Israel.

Kollek was the first ranking Israeli official to grasp the potential importance of tourism as a means of earning foreign currency, and to further that end he founded the Government Tourist Office in 1952. He became the first chairman of its successor agency, the Government Tourist Corporation, in 1956, and by the time he left that office in 1965, Israel's income from tourism averaged about $150,000,000 a year.

When Ben-Gurion retired in June 1963, his successor, Levi Eshkol, asked Kollek to stay on as director general of the Premier's office. Before long, however, Ben-Gurion had become an outspoken critic of the new Premier. In turn, Eshkol developed an intense distrust of Ben-Gurion's associates, and in that abrasive atmosphere Kollek decided, in 1964, to tender his resignation. Leaving the government service, Kollek devoted a major part of his effort to a longtime pet project, the creation of a national museum. Since the early 1950's he had been engaged in fundraising and other activities for the development of such an institution. Now, as board chairman of the Israel Museum, he assumed full administrative responsibility for the project. The $3,000,-000 museum, situated in the Judaean hills overlooking Jerusalem, opened on May 11, 1965.

Meanwhile, Ben-Gurion had decided to stage a comeback in the general election of 1965. Since his old party, Mapai, was solidly under Eshkol's control, he founded a new political group, R'shimat Po'ale Yisrael, or Rafi, that did not differ greatly from Mapai in ideology and program. Kollek was asked by spokesmen for Ben-Gurion to become the Rafi candidate for mayor of Jerusalem, but he at first refused, protesting that he was a nonpolitical public servant, and that, in any case, it would be impossible for him to win. Ben-Gurion's emissaries persisted, however. In addition, Kollek was barraged with spontaneous appeals from Jerusalemites who were fed up with their city's stagnation. Finally tossing his hat into the ring, Kollek rang doorbells and shook hands with constituents in a nonpartisan "good government" campaign, in which he played down his connection with Rafi and focused on his hope of "restoring Jerusalem to its ancient glory."

In the multiparty proportional-representation election of November 2, 1965 the national hopes of Ben-Gurion and Rafi were dashed, but Kollek garnered 20.4 percent of the votes cast, as compared with 23.4 percent won by the incumbent mayor, Mordecai Ish-Shalom, who was Eshkol's choice. Although Kollek's share of the vote fell short of a plurality, his ability, as the candidate of a newly founded minority party, to obtain nearly as many votes as the incumbent was seen by political analysts as a spectacular achievement. After the election Kollek succeeded in organizing a coalition of four parties—Rafi, the right-wing Gahal, the National Religious party, and the ultra-Orthodox Agudath Israel—that controlled fourteen of the twenty-one seats on the municipal council, and on November 12, 1965 the council designated him mayor of Jerusalem.

Although Kollek's demand for legislation permitting direct election of mayors went unheeded, he agreed to be a candidate again in the general election of October 28, 1969, running on the Mapai-Mapam alignment ticket of Golda Meir, who had become Premier after Eshkol's death earlier in the year. Meanwhile, Jerusalem had become reunited following Israel's victory in the Six-Day War of June 1967, and Kollek openly campaigned among the Arabs of the Old City, most of whom were experiencing universal suffrage for the first time. Although his opponents conducted a vigorous campaign charging that he had gone too far in conciliating the Arabs, Kollek, with about 45 percent of the popular vote and a majority of the municipal council members on his side, was reelected mayor of Jerusalem.

Terence Prittie, in his book *Israel: Miracle in the Desert* (Praeger 1968), called Kollek one of Ben-Gurion's "Three Musketeers"—along with Moshe Dayan and Shimon Peres. A social democrat in the Mapai tradition, Kollek is perhaps the best vote-getter and the most popular public figure on the present-day Israeli scene. Yet he does not consider himself a politician, and he takes little interest in party business and factional alignments, striving to conduct himself in the best spirit of nonpartisanship and service. As Yoel Marcus explained in *Israel Magazine* (September 1971), "Teddy injected a new spirit into the municipality. He raised productivity and the tempo of work among his staff by introducing a system of financial and moral incentives and by acting forcefully with those employees whose work was unsatisfactory."

But combating the civil-service mentality and providing adequate municipal services are only part of the challenge of governing Jerusalem. The city's 291,700 people include such diverse elements as the anti-Zionist, ultra-Orthodox Jews of the Mea Shearim district, and the 75,000 Arabs—many of them of dubious loyalty—who suddenly found themselves under Israeli jurisdiction as a result of the administrative reunification of 1967. Moreover, reunification gave the Jerusalem city administration the added responsibility for care of the ancient walled city, which encompasses historical sites and holy places sacred to Christians, Moslems, and Jews.

The fact that Jerusalem is sacred to hundreds of millions throughout the world poses problems for the city's development. For example, a projected high-rise building that might not harmonize with the Old City's historic vistas would attract international criticism. Working diligently to attract business and industry to the city, Kollek has tried to accommodate growth while preserving the treasures of antiquity. To that end, in 1969 he invited to the city foreign dignitaries in the fields of art and architecture, including Lewis Mumford, Buckminster Fuller, and Sir Nikolaus Pevsner, who have from time to time proffered advice and assistance in drafting Jerusalem's master plan. Kollek has on occasion scrapped projects, such as a proposed multilane expressway, of which the advisors disapproved. Aware that the Jerusalem Arabs are not under Israeli jurisdiction by choice, Kollek understands their concern for maintaining their own way of life. He has repeatedly asserted that a kind of biculturalism, like that of Montreal, Canada, is his goal for the city. Through his even-handed and sympathetic approach, Kollek has, by and large, kept the peace in Jerusalem, winning some measure of trust and cooperation from its Arabs.

Teddy Kollek was married in May 1937 to Tamar Anna Schwartz, a rabbi's daughter from Vienna. They have a son, Amos, and a daughter Osnat. Amos Kollek is the author of *Don't Ask Me if I Love* (Evans, 1971), an English-language novel about the generation gap in Israel. Blue-eyed and sandy-haired, Teddy Kollek is of medium height and portly build, and he favors khaki shirts with rolled-up sleeves as his daily attire. Noted for his warm personal manner, his informality, and his infectious broad grin, Kollek is an outgoing, amiable man who reportedly has occasional critics but no enemies. According to Yoel Marcus, he has so many friends that he "never buys his own cigars."

Despite his schedule as mayor, which keeps him occupied as much as eighteen hours a day, Kollek is available at all times for calls and visits from ordinary citizens. By avocation he is a student of archaeology and history, and for more than forty years his hobby has been collecting old maps and books dealing with Jerusalem. In collaboration with Moshe (or Maurice) Pearlman, Teddy Kollek has written two books: *Jerusalem; A History of Forty Centuries* (Random House, 1969) and *Pilgrims to the Holy Land; The Story of Pilgrimage Through the Ages* (Harper, 1969).

References

Look 32:6+ O '68 pors
N Y Post p35 Ja 12 '67 por
N Y Times p44 My 2 '65 por
Encyclopedia of Zionism and Israel (1971)
International Who's Who, 1973-74
Who's Who in Israel, 1972
Who's Who in World Jewry (1972)

KOSINSKI, JERZY (NIKODEM) (ye'zhi)

June 14, 1933- Writer
Address: c/o S.F. Inc., 60 W. 57th St., New York 10019

Twentieth-century evil is cataloged with a hawk-like eye and a conjurer's hand in the novels of Jerzy Kosinski, whom one critic has gone so far as to call "our Dante." Like Joseph Conrad before him, the Polish-born Kosinski writes only in his foster tongue, English, which he learned in adulthood. He broke into print in 1960, just three years after he arrived in the United States, and catapulted to fame in 1965 with his bizarre, best-selling *The Painted Bird*, a mythic rendering of a nightmarish childhood spent adrift in Nazi-occupied Eastern Europe. In the National Book Award-winning *Steps* (1968), he evokes in loosely connected tales of abomination and perversity the cruel mutual manipulation for which human beings are preconditioned by their culture, both in the totalitarian East and the "free" West. The inevitable control of mass behavior in a television-oriented society is the target of his satire in the fable *Being There* (1971), and his fourth novel, *The Devil Tree* (1973), is an exposure of success, American style.

The materials with which Kosinski depicts the living hell in which individual human freedom is either usurped or surrendered to images and illusions are often violence, sex, and corruption. But even at his most grim he writes with a lucidity and control that allows him to intimate the possibility of the antithesis: goodness. The canon of his work thus far offers a vision of life which, however harrowing, affirms the possibility of choice—for the nonconformist determined to exercise it—in an increasingly programmed world. Although a moralist, Kosinski never preaches, but insinuates his ideas through irony, paradox, and a deceptively simple style. Whether discrediting the image-making of Washington politicos or the youth cultists of Woodstock, he reminds his readers that he is no partisan missionary: "I speak for no one but myself."

An only child, Jerzy Nikodem Kosinski was born in Lodz in central Poland on June 14, 1933. His ancestry was Jewish, according to Rita Delfiner of the New York *Post* (July 20, 1971), who quoted him: "I was never at home in my native country, therefore I was never at home in my native tongue." Kosinski's mother, Elzbieta (Liniecka) Kosinski, was a pianist of professional calibre who never performed in public. His father, Mieczyslaw Kosinski, was a felt manufacturer and philologist who fled Russia during the Bolshevik Revolution.

When World War II broke out the Kosinskis sent their son eastward into the countryside for refuge. Thus Jerzy Kosinski escaped the direct brunt of Nazi brutality, but not the ramifications of the Nazi spirit among the terrified and superstitious peasantry. Separated from the person into whose care he had been entrusted, the protagonist of *The Painted Bird* wandered from village to village throughout the war. Marked as a victim (if not a Jew, then a Gypsy with the "evil eye") because of his swarthy visage and "magnetic" hair, he was persecuted by fairer-skinned, lighter-haired rural folk and experienced so traumatic a series of physical and spiritual horrors that he was struck dumb for five years. While denying that *The Painted Bird* is autobiographical, Kosinski has admitted that "every incident is true."

Reunited with his parents after the war, Kosinski quickly caught up with his schooling. While working as a ski instructor and photographer in the early 1950's, he studied at the University of Lodz, where he took M.A. degrees in history and political science in 1953 and 1955, respectively. Both of Kosinski's dissertations dealt with nineteenth-century Russia, and he continued his pursuit of that subject under the auspices of the Polish Academy of Sciences, Lomonosov University in the U.S.S.R., and the Soviet Academy of Sciences. During his stay in the Soviet Union he and his father would converse long-distance on the telephone in Latin to confound eavesdropping censors.

By temperament Kosinski has always been a "painted bird," in the sense of being a nonconformist. Bridling under Communist pressures toward conformity, he took advantage of the relative permissiveness of the Khrushchev regime to obtain a passport on the fraudulent ground that he had been offered a grant to study in the United States. He did in fact obtain a grant, from the Ford Foundation, but only after his arrival in America. Between December 1957, when he docked in New York, and July 1958, when his grant to work for a doctorate in political sociology at Columbia University took effect, he worked at odd jobs, including those of parking lot attendant, cab driver, and ship scraper.

Kosinski taught himself English by memorizing words from a Russian-English dictionary, listening to the radio, going to the same movies repeatedly, comparing good English translations word for word with their Russian and Polish originals, and memorizing poems by Shakespeare, Poe, and others. "It is easier to memorize poems than individual words," he observed in an interview with Dick Schaap for *Book Week* (November 14, 1965). "The rhythm makes it easier." Also, until his death in 1962, his father twice weekly sent him Polish and Russian interlinear translations of such works as the speeches of Franklin Delano Roosevelt and the plays of George Bernard Shaw with detailed grammatical explanations.

Recalling his early efforts at writing in English, Kosinski told Dick Schaap: "I was acquiring a new tradition. I could never write fiction, for instance, in Polish or Russian because I was suppressed by the linguistic tradition, suppressed by the grammar. And English is so much a richer language." In another interview, with Martha McGregor of the New York *Post* (October 24, 1965), he revealed that he often resorted to the zero on the telephone for help in grammar and syntax: "Late at night you have no one to ask. I would dial the telephone operator. . . . I got incredible advice. I did it hundreds of times—I still do it." He was never too proud to show the imperfect preliminary drafts (as many as fifteen) of his manuscripts to friends for revision.

His first two books were works of nonfiction published under the pseudonym Joseph Novak, in which he analyzed the mechanisms of Soviet collective society and gave a profile of the Russian mind through conversations he had had with a representative cross section of citizens in the Soviet Union. Critics described *The Future Is Ours, Comrade* (Doubleday, 1960) as "readable," and "grimly fascinating." Emanuel Litvinoff wrote of it in the *Guardian* (October 21, 1960): "The book is something of a revelation. It will fit scarcely anybody's preconceptions. . . . This is the Russian people . . . talking with passion, vigor, intelligence, and disconcerting candor." Regarding *No Third Path* (Doubleday, 1962), a reviewer for the *Christian Science Monitor* (April 13, 1962) wrote: "The story Mr. Novak tells is deeply disturbing. It suggests that the leaders have succeeded to a higher degree than would have been believed possible in replacing individual reflection by conditioned reflexes."

Kosinski's achievement in *The Painted Bird* (Houghton Mifflin, 1965) was, in his words, to use

JERZY KOSINSKI

"the stones" of his childhood "to build a new wall," to take "the literal and turn it into something symbolic." In *Notes of the Author* (Scientia-Factum, 1965) he described *The Painted Bird* as "not an examination or a revisitation of childhood" but rather a "vision," a "search for something lost" that "can only be conducted in metaphor, through which the unconscious most easily manifests itself." He added: "Just as the setting is metaphorical, so do the characters become archetypes."

Critics, like readers in general, found *The Painted Bird* "staggering" and "haunting," and they were virtually unanimous in their praise of Kosinski's success in translating brute emotion into language so exquisite and controlled that beauty and terror are perfectly poised. Arthur Miller was prompted to write to Kosinski: "The surrealistic quality . . . is a blow on the mind. . . . You have made the normality of it all [the Nazi experience] apparent."

The Painted Bird was published in most of the major countries of the world but not in Poland, where those who read it in other languages generally took offense despite Kosinski's presentation of the peasantry in the book as a generalized paradigm of all humanity. "The cruelty and primitiveness of the peasants . . . ," the author pointed out, "is extremely defensive, elemental, sanctioned by traditions, by faith and superstition, by centuries of poverty, exploitation, disease." Of all the characters, he observed, only the child hero "hates consciously . . . thirsts to hate others for all that happened to him in this world." In France, *The Painted Bird* was awarded the Prix du Meilleur Livre Étranger.

In *Book World* (November 3, 1968) Alice Glaser quoted Kosinski as saying that *The Painted Bird* was "a very mild book" as compared, say, to the horrors retailed in the *National Enquirer*. On the other hand, he admitted that his second novel, *Steps* (Random House, 1968), was "cruel." *Steps*, written in a spare style with macabre wit, consists of twenty-four incidents interspersed with fragments of conversation between the narrator-protagonist and a woman before and after the sex act. Kosinski has described the central male character as a person "always in step with the culture, unable to walk any other staircase," and he has explained that the intentionally loose structure was designed to be filled in with the reader's "own formulated experiences."

The reviewer for *Time* (October 18, 1968) wrote: "The narrator of *Steps* reveals a condition of obsession that is all the more horrifying because of its controlled willfulness and absence of passion and spontaneity. . . . Comic relief is overwhelmed by the savage purity of Kosinski's vision—that of a man stripped of all humane conventions and in complete control of his impulses and appetites." The *Time* critic summed up the novel as "a rather abstract expression of a pathological state of mind."

One of the central themes of *Steps* was Kosinski's concept, taken from Sartre, that "hell is the inability to escape from others who prove and prove again to you that you are as they see you." That theme was dealt with more gently in the author's *Being There* (Harcourt Brace Jovanovich, 1971), a fable about a retarded but handsome gardener of uncertain origin named Chance whose only contact with the reality outside his garden is a television set. When he is thrown out into the world, his narrow range of talk about gardening is misconstrued as deep worldly wisdom expressed with artful obliqueness in pregnant metaphors. Telegenic to boot, he becomes a national celebrity, consulted by financial and political leaders.

"Written in deliberately stale, totally imageless language," it [*Being There*] is a fable for the television generation . . . ," Henry Allen observed in the Washington *Post* (August 30, 1971). "His [Chance's] identity shifts with the channels. . . . Because he tries to be only what people want him to be, to tell them what they want to know . . . he becomes an adviser to the President. . . . Politicians realize the nation is full of Chances, their ability to create reality for themselves destroyed by television. . . . It's a book that is pure intellectual technique, a critic's delight."

Allen, who interviewed Kosinski, quoted him: "The cycle is historically completed. The world of *The Painted Bird* began because of some Chances who came across well enough on the screen of the twentieth century: non-persons, nobodies like Hitler and Mussolini." In other interviews Kosinski expressed his convictions that television, unlike the cinema ("when you went to the movies you were not going to see reality") blurs the distinction between the real and the unreal ("the war in Vietnam is a half-hour program"), and that a generation reared before this "patient babysitter" is unprepared to bear up in difficult real-life confrontations. Of young people today he has said: "They are the most idealistic and the purest generation I have ever encountered. . . . However, . . . television castrated them as individuals, instilling the belief that you can't

accomplish something by yourself, that you can't confront the system, not only collectively but also individually."

The need for self-definition, a theme integral to all of Kosinski's works, figures prominently in *The Devil Tree* (Harcourt Brace Jovanovich, 1973), the title of which alludes to the African myth about the "cursed" baobob tree, which grows upside down, with its branches in the earth and its roots reaching absurdly skyward. The bedeviled hero of the novel is the young heir to an American industrial fortune who tries everything, from the kinky to the criminal, that money can buy, and finds that it is never enough. As his quest for self grows more frenzied and joyless, he is entrapped by the roots of his own heritage, the illusions of power fostered by money. Eventually he realizes that his freedom exists only in the eyes of his beholders: in Kosinski's terms, the ultimate hell.

Several reviewers of *The Devil Tree* remarked on Kosinski's ability to dramatize his ideas through episodes that amount to a steady accretion of horror and to create blank spaces in which apocalyptic meaning may magically manifest itself to the adept reader. In *Newsday* (February 7, 1973) Hal Burton wrote: "The book may seem unsatisfying because it is so episodic. Yet that may be, precisely, its virtue. Kosinski has an eye like a laser beam; he cuts through the pretensions to the heart of what makes America tick; and, as you might expect, that heart is rotting away within the national body."

Kosinski has published articles in the *American Scholar*, the *Boston Review of the Arts*, and *Exile*. Selections from his most famous novel are read by Kosinski on the recording *The Painted Bird*, released by CMS Records in 1967. The novelist was a fellow of the Center for Advanced Studies at Wesleyan University in 1968 and he taught English prose at Princeton University in 1969-70. From 1970 to 1973 he was a professor of English prose and criticism at Yale. In the legend of Kosinski the first day of his seminar on "Death and the American Imagination" at Yale stands out. No more than twenty students were expected —or wanted—but 2,000 showed up. Kosinski whittled the crowd down to twelve by explaining, in the course of his introductory lecture, that the seminar would confront the experience of death as directly as possible, through visits to hospitals, morgues, and mortuaries. "Regrettably," he solemnly added, "in order for the experience to be complete, it will be necessary for one member of the seminar to die." There was a mad, mass rush for the exits.

Regarding the subject of death he has said: "You don't die in the United States. You underachieve. . . . Dying is merely a stage of being alive, slightly below the top." Kosinski believes that a person cannot live fully until he has faced and accepted his own mortality. His own many brushes with death included the occasion in 1969 when he was delayed by airline baggage problems in New York just long enough to miss being at the Tate-Polanski home in Los Angeles the night of the tragic party there.

Kosinski was for several years married to Mary Hayward Weir, the widow of an American steel magnate. She died in 1968. His constant companion since then has been the Baroness Katharine von Fraunhofer. The fastidious author, as meticulous in his life as in his craft, lives in a leanly appointed apartment on Manhattan's Upper East Side, where he likes to "hide." He spends much of his time in the summer at the beach. Besides swimming, his recreations include skiing and photography (his second craft). In the arts he particularly likes Bosch, Auden, Beethoven, Pushkin, Faulkner, and Kuprin, and Socrates is his greatest historical hero.

Jerzy Kosinski is five feet eleven inches tall and weighs about 132 pounds (eating is the least of his interests). He has thin lips, an aquiline nose, a hurried but graceful manner, an intense disposition, and a quick, sardonic sense of humor. He speaks slowly, with a slight accent, in English. In addition to the latter language and Polish and Russian he speaks French and reads Italian, Spanish, Ukrainian, and Esperanto. He had a Guggenheim fellowship in creative writing in 1967 and received the National Institute of Arts and Letters Award for Literature in 1970. He is currently president of the American Center of P.E.N.

A pessimist about the course of civilization generally ("one disaster created to solve another"), he takes an especially bleak view of the immediate future: "This century, I am convinced, will totally and totalitarianly get rid of the liberal mind, the Renaissance man. This is the first time there is a perfect match between crude political ideas and the complex technology that makes those ideas acceptable." His motto is a phrase from Descartes, *Larvatus prodeo*: "I go forth disguised."

References

Guardian p10 Je 25 '73 por
N Y Times Bk R p8 O 3 '65
Newsday A p4+ Jl 1 '71
Sat R 54:16+ Ap 17 '71
Washington Post B p12 My 24 '71; B p1+ Ag 30 '71 pors
Contemporary Authors vols 17-18 (1967)
Who's Who in America, 1972-73

KRASNER, LEE

Oct. 27, 1908- Painter
Address: b. c/o Marlborough Gallery, 40 W. 57th St., New York 10019; h. The Springs, East Hampton, N.Y. 11937

Along with Jackson Pollock, Willem de Kooning, Arshile Gorky, and similar experimental artists, Lee Krasner belongs among the first-generation action painters. They founded abstract expressionism, which expanded the definition of what a painting is and became the dominant movement in American art after World War II. Because of

LEE KRASNER

a combination of circumstances—including the expense to her career of her role as the wife and later the widow of Pollock, abstract expressionism's towering genius—Lee Krasner's place in contemporary painting has only recently been acknowledged. After abstract expressionism had fallen out of fashion, her work helped to restore the vitality of that idiom, while proving its own aesthetic merit, through a retrospective in Great Britain in 1965-66, appreciative articles in influential art magazines, and a prestigious exhibition in 1973-74 at the Whitney Museum in New York. Her multivalent paintings are perhaps primarily both pensive and energetic celebrations in color of movements and moods in nature—the rhythm of the sea, the process of growth.

Lee Krasner was born Lenore Krassner on October 27, 1908 in Brooklyn, New York, where her parents, Joseph and Anna (Weiss) Krassner, Jewish emigrants from Odessa, Russia, owned a small fish and vegetable store. She was the next to the last of their seven children, six daughters and one son, and the first child born to them in the United States. In childhood Lee Krasner was exposed to much discipline at home but to little culture. She can recall only a few Caruso records that her brother Irving occasionally brought in and a large picture of Queen Isabella of Spain that hung on the wall. She did, however, read fairy tales and Russian classics. Independent-minded from an early age, she rebelled at P.S. 72 in Brooklyn against singing Christmas carols because they celebrated beliefs she did not share.

Deciding at the age of thirteen to become an artist, Lee Krasner transferred from Girls High School in Brooklyn to Washington Irving High School in Manhattan, which permitted girls to specialize in art. Although she was academically less successful in art than in other subjects, she enrolled in 1926 in the Women's Art School of Cooper Union, where the curriculum was rigorously classical. One of her teachers, Victor Perard, was impressed enough by her drawings from life to use some of them for his textbook of drawing. While still at Cooper Union she attended classes in 1928 at the Art Students League, studying life drawing with George Bridgman.

From 1929 to 1932 Miss Krasner studied at the National Academy of Design, where her teachers included Sidney Dickenson and Leon Kroll. To advance from antique to life classes at the academy she had to submit an oil painting to a jury. A 1930 self-portrait with trees in the background, which she painted outdoors, earned her only a promotion on probation, but her picture holds interesting promises fulfilled in her later work. With several other students from the academy she went to the Museum of Modern Art to see an exhibition of contemporary French painting. "I flipped my lid," she has related, as quoted in *Newsday* (November 12, 1973). "When we came back to the academy . . . , we staged a revolution. We pulled the model stand away from the wall to the center of the room to free it from the eternal red and green background, and irritated the teachers."

To help meet expenses as an art student, Miss Krasner waited on tables in Greenwich Village restaurants. During 1933, while considering the possibility of becoming an art teacher, she took courses at City College of New York. She was employed for a few months early the following year as an artist on the Public Works of Art Project, the first of the Depression-spawned New Deal art programs. From mid-1935 to 1943 she worked intermittently for the federal Works Projects Administration. As assistant to the muralist Max Spivak in the project's mural division, she was associated with Harold Rosenberg, who became a prominent art critic.

Many WPA artists were regionalists or social realists or leftists reflecting their political tenets in their style. Discussing her alienation from a group whose work she considered banal and provincial, she commented in an interview with Bruce Glaser for *Arts Magazine* (April 1967), "Painting is not to be confused with illustration." In the development of her own style, she was profoundly affected by Matisse, Picasso, Mondrian, and other European painters. Her preferences, especially for Matisse, were reinforced by her study from 1937 to 1940 with Hans Hofmann, who, on his way to abstract expressionism, synthesized cubist structure with the exuberant colors of the French moderns.

In June 1940 Lee Krasner exhibited her paintings for the first time with the avant-garde American Abstract Artists in its fourth annual show in New York. At the invitation of the painter John Graham she took part in January 1942 in an exhibition of American and French paintings organized by him at the McMillan Gallery. Among the French painters represented were Picasso, Matisse, and Bonnard. Some of the Americans participating were WPA painters, such as Willem de Kooning and Jackson Pollock. Miss Krasner, as she later realized, had met Pollock a few years earlier, in 1936, at a party given by the Artists Union, an organization set up to protect the rights of WPA

artists. She had apparently been unimpressed, however, by the meeting and knew nothing about his work until just before the 1942 show when she went eagerly to his studio to satisfy her curiosity about the type of pictures that would be shown with hers. "I was totally bowled over by what I saw," she told John Gruen (*Close-Up*, 1967). "One work—the painting he later titled 'Magic Mirror'—just about stunned me. We talked about this painting and the others. . . . We met again, and a courting period began."

Lee Krasner and Jackson Pollock were married on October 25, 1945 and the following month left the city for The Springs, a community in East Hampton, Long Island, where they settled in an old $5,000 farmhouse. Largely because of Pollock's severe drinking problem, which he was able to control with only sporadic success, the marriage was a difficult one, but it lasted until his death in an automobile accident in August 1956. During those eleven years they had much enthusiasm and respect for each other's painting. They customarily visited one another's studio by invitation. Lee Krasner worked in an upstairs room of the farmhouse and Pollock used a barn near the house as his studio. According to Lee Krasner, there was no rivalry between them. One of the ways in which Pollock encouraged his wife was to help arrange for her first solo show, held at the Betty Parsons Gallery in New York in the fall of 1951.

For Lee Krasner, the marriage meant the eclipse of her career by Pollock's. Both painters, however, made important contributions to the New York School of abstract expressionism. After she had absorbed or discarded various elements of surrealism and cubism and other outside influences, Miss Krasner went through a period of intense introspection and stylistic groping from which she emerged in 1946 with the first of her series of Little Image paintings. From that year through 1949 she produced thirty-five or more small, exquisite canvases pulsating with an assortment of tiny, crowded images.

Many of the Little Image paintings are untitled; among those to which Lee Krasner gave titles are *Noon* (1947), *Shell Flower* (1947), *White Squares* (1948), *Continuum* (1949), and *Night Light* (1949). Although the paintings fall into three general groups, they all share certain characteristics, including, as Cindy Nemser described them in *Artforum* (December 1973), "an unceasing flow of movement sustained by a non-hierarchical organization of line, shape, and color." She went on to point out, "All these works manifest an intensely personal, highly distinctive kind of handwriting, 'a calligraphy of the soul.'"

While working on the Little Image paintings in East Hampton, in 1946-47 Miss Krasner used broken glass, tessarae, coins, and other flat objects to make for her new home a mosaic tabletop that was related in motif to her current paintings. Besides several other small mosaics, she designed two mosaic glass murals, one of which is eighty-six feet long, for the Uris Building in Manhattan. Completed in 1959, the mosaics were constructed from collages designed in collaboration with Ronald Stein, her nephew.

After her 1951 show Lee Krasner cut up some of the paintings exhibited at the Parsons gallery to work on a new series of pictures, this time of collage-paintings made in part from fragments of canvas and paper. *Black and White* (1953), *Forest No. 1* (1954), *Bald Eagle* (1955), and *Porcelain* (1955) belong to that series. Some of the collages were shown at a solo exhibition at Eleanor Ward's Stable Gallery in the fall of 1955.

At her next one-man exhibition, in March 1958 in New York at the Martha Jackson Gallery, Lee Krasner showed seventeen canvases that she had painted during the year and a half since the death of Pollock. Larger on the average than the collages, just as the collages had for the most part exceeded the Little Image pictures in size, the new paintings also followed a tendency toward freer, more aggressive gesture in sweeping forms and whirling shapes, an opening out of images. To Emily Genauer, then of the New York *Herald Tribune* (March 2, 1958), the principal mood of the series was "evolution, that of masses burgeoning with growth, within the canvas." Miss Genauer saw in the painter's light but virile color a "concern with the feeling of flowers as much as with the spirit of fish-laden streams, and the transmutation of the seasons." The critic for *Time* (March 17, 1958), however, remarked on "somber blacks and greys on white, shades of fuchsia and ochre in thinly applied paint," and suggested that the abstract designs "mostly seem to express death-haunted themes." One of them, entitled *Birth*, struck "a lonely note of hope."

The question of Pollock's influence on Lee Krasner's painting recurs persistently in critical discussions of her work. While maintaining that she preserved her own artistic independence and identity, she has acknowledged his influence—an influence, she has pointed out, that she would have felt even if she had not been married to him, since he changed the whole art world. Marcia Tucker, who wrote the introduction to the catalogue of Miss Krasner's Whitney show, has argued that Pollock's influence became more pronounced after his death and that a stylistic relationship is apparent in the umber and off-white canvases of 1959 and the early 1960's.

Of the large, sweeping, almost violent canvases like *The Gate* (1959-60), *The Eye Is the First Circle* (1960), and *Night Birds* (1962), Miss Tucker wrote, "The oppositions in these works—light and dark, opacity and translucence, detail and immensity—are visual metaphors for natural events, as well as formal elements that focus attention on the reality of the canvas as an event in itself." The very characteristics that suggest Pollock, however, prevail in her work in almost all periods. As Cindy Nemser observed, the Little Image paintings contained "all the stylistic and subjective themes" that appear in her later work: "the wild, rhythmic patterns, the mysterious hieroglyphic traces, the organic references to natural phenomena." In a recent article in *Art in America*

(November-December 1973) Bryan Robertson regarded Lee Krasner's search for images expressing her preoccupation with nature as an "initial premise" of her work.

In her more recent paintings Lee Krasner's individuality seems to have asserted itself through increased lyricism in line and color. *Kufic* (1965), for example, has a Klee-like delicacy. Reaffirmation of early affinities, especially with Matisse, is evident in *Pollination* (1968), *Palingenesis* (1971), *Mysteries* (1972), and *Peacock* (1973). However, as Hilton Kramer wrote of her pictures in the New York *Times* (November 22, 1973), "There is no suggestion of anything secondhand or merely appropriated." Much of the imagery and symbolism in her work, moreover, is probably personal rather than formal, perhaps derived from her early reading of fairy tales or related to the analysis she underwent during her marriage.

A major retrospective exhibition of Lee Krasner's paintings, drawings, and collages at the Whitechapel Gallery in London in 1965 went far toward redressing the neglect that her work had long suffered. The show was well received in the press and was later circulated by the Arts Council of Great Britain to museums in York, Nottingham, Manchester, and other cities. Since then she has had solo shows in Tuscaloosa (Alabama), Detroit, and San Francisco, and her several shows of recent paintings and gouaches at the Marlborough (formerly Marlborough-Gerson) Gallery in New York have been both critically and commercially successful. One of the many group shows in which she has been represented was the "Twenty-one Over Sixty" exhibition at Guild Hall in East Hampton in the summer of 1973, a show that she herself suggested. The Whitney Museum of American Art in New York accorded her probably the most important acknowledgement she has so far received when, from November 13, 1973 to January 6, 1974, it showed a group of eighteen of her large-scale works of the period from 1953 to 1973.

On several occasions in her direct and outspoken manner Lee Krasner has attributed her failure to win earlier recognition to controversies and resentments surrounding the obligations she assumed as an "art widow." After Pollock's death she was faced with pressing and complex problems regarding the exhibition and sale of his pictures. "I had to make decisions, and I stepped on a lot of toes," she explained in an interview for *Newsday* (November 12, 1973). ". . . So there were a lot of vendettas against Mrs. Pollock, the widow, that had to be paid back to Lee Krasner, the artist." Although she reasons that the market rose with demand, she has been credited with almost singlehandedly bringing on inflated prices for works by modern American artists because of the control she exercised over the selling of Pollock's paintings.

Lee Krasner divides her time between the East Hampton farmhouse and a large East Side Manhattan apartment, which is decorated with Victorian furniture. She has studios at both homes and paints constantly. Gardening, tending house plants, and cooking are her hobbies. A woman of medium height, she stands at about five feet five inches tall; she has graying-brown hair that is styled by the hairdresser Kenneth. Vivien Raynor described her in the New York *Times Magazine* (April 2, 1967), "She has a long nose and a very full, wide mouth; the eyes—seen when she briefly removes her dark glasses—are pale blue-gray. She both speaks and listens in a deliberate way."

Aware that she has shared the fate of other artists whom the art world is slow to honor because of their sex, Lee Krasner joined the picket line at the Museum of Modern Art in 1972 in protest against the museum's reluctance to show the work of women artists. She is a supporter of the Women's Lib movement, and her own marriage was one in which husband and wife split up the housework. The art critic Barbara Rose, who interviewed her for an article in *Vogue* (June 1972) wrote admiringly of Lee Krasner's courage in pioneering her particular life-style: "As her paintings are visionary statements providing mysterious insights into the inner life of an artist, so, too, is Lee Krasner a visionary and a revolutionary personality as a woman."

References

Art in Am 61:83+ N-D '73 por
Art N 67:43+ Mr '68 por
Artforum 12:61+ D '73
Arts Mag 41:36+ Ap '67 por
N Y Post p41 D 6 '73 por
N Y Times p50 N 22 '73
N Y Times Mag p50+ Ap 2 '67
Time 102:76 N 19 '73 por
Vogue 159:118+ Je '72 por

Gruen, John. Close-up (1967)
Who's Who in American Art, 1973
Who's Who of American Women, 1972-73

KRISHNAMURTI, JIDDU (krish'nə-mo͞or'tē ji' do͞o)

May 22, 1895- Religious philosopher
Address: c/o Krishnamurti Foundation, Box 216, Ojai, Calif. 93023

India-born Jiddu Krishnamurti, who has described himself as "sort of a philosopher," was in his youth lionized by the Theosophical Society as, literally, a new Messiah. Without breaking friendly relations with Theosophy, Krishnamurti in 1929 abdicated his Buddha-like position and embarked on a mission to set human beings "absolutely, unconditionally free" from all conditioning, including that imposed by organized religion and dependence upon spiritual leaders. In the forty-five years since then he has traveled the world, speaking, and leading Socratic-type dialogues and discussions, talk sessions that have invariably found their way into print, under such titles as *Think on These Things* (1964), *The Urgency of Change* (1971), and *You Are the World* (1972).

"Krishnamurti's lectures, like his books, are all variations on his central theme: the current world crisis is psychological—the basic problem is how to achieve the 'right relationship between human beings,'" a reporter for *Time* once wrote. "The ultimate answer," says Krishnamurti, "is to see things as they really are, unclouded by the deceptions of self-concern. To accomplish this one must be 'empty' of all preconceptions and all teachers." Put most simply and broadly, what Krishnamurti seems to be saying is that the universal is to be found within the individual self only by direct experience, and outside helps are in reality only crutches at best and cages at worst.

Jiddu is Krishnamurti's family name, but the order of the names is reversed in keeping with the custom in South India, his birthplace. Also in keeping with custom, as a male eighth child in a Brahmin family he was called Krishnamurti in honor of the Hindu divinity Shri Krishna. Krishnamurti was born in Madanapalle, a small town near Madras, on May 22, 1895. After his mother died, in 1905, his father, Narayaniah, a civil servant of meager means, moved with his children to Madras.

An ardent Theosophist as well as a devout Brahmin, Jiddu Narayaniah became a part-time staff worker in the Madras office of the Theosophical Society. The term theosophy comes from two Greek words meaning "divine wisdom." Generically, in its widest sense, it is a religious philosophy that may be traced back at least as far as the sixth century B.C. In that sense the term would apply to the thought of Pythagoras, the Cabalists, Emanuel Swedenborg, and other mystical philosophers stressing the essentially spiritual nature of the universe and the human capacity for preternatural, intuitive perception of supersensible reality. The German mystic Jakob Boehme (1575-1624) is generally regarded as the father of modern theosophy.

The contemporary formal syncretistic system known as Theosophy (with a capital T) began when Madame Helena Petrovna Blavatsky and others brought together the strands of various occult movements, including Spiritualism, prevailing in the late nineteenth century into the Theosophical Society, which was founded in New York on November 17, 1875. Later Madame Blavatsky went to India, where she imbibed the Hindu concepts of the transmigration of souls and the universal, eternal principle underlying all things. The chief contribution of Hindu philosophy to Theosophy was the idea that there are seven levels in life, from the grossly physical to the completely developed, perfect, universal self. The soul must pass through seven existences, accruing occult knowledge (in the soul itself, not the mind) as it transmigrates. According to Theosophical teaching, this spiritual evolution can be accelerated by the study of religious literature giving enlightenment concerning the laws of the universe, and the esoteric teachings of the mahatmas are especially helpful in the development of the latent inner senses that are capable of responding to invisible reality.

Before her death in 1891 Madame Blavatsky prophesied that humanity was on the verge of a new age, a development of the evolutionary spiral in which a new "root race" would be led to truth by an avatar of the Lord Maitreya, the "World Teacher." In Hindu mythology Maitreya is the messianic Buddha, the divine spirit who periodically—every two thousand years or so—takes human form. Two of Madame Blavatsky's successors in the leadership of the Theosophical Society, Mrs. Annie Besant (1847-1933) and Charles Webster Leadbeater (1847-1934), became convinced that Krishnamurti was the chosen vehicle for the next appearance of the World Teacher. The cult of the new Messiah was fostered by the World Order of the Star in the East, founded by Mrs. Besant on December 28, 1911, with Krishnamurti at its head. "From that time on," as James Webb notes in *The Occult Underground*, a book scheduled for publication by the Library Press in LaSalle, Illinois before the end of 1974, "Krishnamurti was brought up 'at the feet of the Master'—to borrow the title of the book which was passed off as written by him." Originally published by the Theosophical Publishing House in Madras, India without date, *At the Feet of the Master* was later issued by the Rajput Press in Chicago, in 1911. The book, which carried the pseudonym "Alcyone," contained the foreword: "The teachings . . . were given him by his master . . . and were written down by him from memory."

After his adoption by Mrs. Besant, Krishnamurti was sent to study in England, where Lady Emily Lutyens, wife of the architect Sir Edwin Landseer Lutyens and the granddaughter of the English novelist and playwright Bulwer-Lytton, became his devoted "foster mother." Lady Lutyens and her daughter, Mary (Mrs. Anthony Sewell), have recalled their experiences with Theosophy and especially with Krishnamurti in, respectively, *Candles in the Sun* (Lippincott, 1957) and *To Be Young; Some Chapters of Autobiography* (Hart-Davis, 1959).

Mary Luytens recounted how the Lord Maitreya allegedly took possession of the body of Krishnamurti, on December 28, 1925: "He [Krishnamurti] had been saying, 'He comes to lead us. He comes only to those who have understood, who have suffered, who are unhappy, who are enlightened. He comes only to those who want, who desire, who long.' And then the voice changed and rang out, 'And I come for those who I come to reform, not to tear down. I come not to destroy, but to build.' "

However, Krishnamurti refused to remain in the role that the members of the World Order of the Star in the East expected him to play. In 1929 he dissolved the order and repudiated the very concept of seeking salvation by adherence to a cult leader. "Truth is a pathless land," he explained to his shocked followers. "You cannot approach it by any religion, any sect. You must look within yourselves for the incorruptibility of the self. . . . I desire those who seek to understand me to be free, not to follow me, not to make out of me a cage. . . . Rather they should be free from all fear, from the fear of religion, from the

JIDDU KRISHNAMURTI

fear of salvation, from the fear of spirituality, from the fear of love, from the fear of death, from the fear of life itself. For eighteen years you have . . . looked for someone who would . . . transform your whole life. . . . You are accustomed to being told how far you have advanced, what your spiritual status is. How childish. Who but yourself can tell you whether you are beautiful or ugly within? You are all depending for your spirituality on someone else."

A newspaper reporter, marveling at Krishnamurti's audacity and courage in dissolving his large, flourishing organization, asked him, "What will you do afterwards? How will you live? You will have no following. People will no longer listen to you." Krishnamurti's response was: "If there are only five people who will listen, who have their faces turned towards eternity, it will be sufficient. Of what use is it to have thousands who do not understand, who are fully embalmed in prejudice, who do not want the new, but would rather translate the new to suit their own sterile, stagnant selves?"

Early in his career Krishnamurti occasionally wrote verse, such as that contained in the collection *The Song of Life* (Liveright, 1931). But most of his books were then, as they are now, transcripts of his talks and dialogues. *The Kingdom of Happiness* (Boni & Liveright, 1927), for example, consisted of talks given by him in Ommen, Holland. "Authentic reports" of talks given by Krishnamurti at his headquarters in Ojai, California were regularly published by the Star Publishing Trust in Hollywood during the 1930's and 1940's. Later Krishnamurti Writings Inc. issued similar verbatim reports of his talks in Ojai, Benares, London, and elsewhere.

Aldous Huxley, who compared listening to Krishnamurti to hearing "a discourse by the Buddha," wrote the foreword to the sage's *The First and Last Freedom* (Harper, 1954). Of that book the critic for the London *Times Literary Supplement* (March 14, 1954) wrote: "Doubtless to the dualist who regards conflict, actual or dialectic, as an unchangeable condition of human life and truth, Krishnamurti's teaching will seem to offer a delusive short-cut to a vaguely beatific freedom. But there is nothing vague about it. It is precise and penetrating."

Commentaries on Living, edited from the notebooks of Krishnamurti by D. Rajagopal, were issued in three volumes by Krishnamurti Writings Inc., in 1956, 1958, and 1960. Like some of his other books, those were later published in Quest Book editions by the Theosophical Publishing House in Wheaton, Illinois. Anne Morrow Lindbergh once said, regarding the *Commentaries*: "The sheer simplicity is breathtaking. The reader is given, in one paragraph, often in one sentence, enough to keep him exploring, questioning, thinking for days."

In his autobiographical *The Quiet Mind* (Harper & Row, 1971), John E. Coleman recounts how he met Krishnamurti in the early 1960's by serendipity, during an airplane flight from Benares to New Delhi. "Had I known at that moment what I was to learn later about Krishnamurti," Coleman wrote, "I might have been awed with the significance of the occasion. . . . I ventured to ask him what was the meaning of his name. . . . He told me, with no trace of self-consciousness, [it] meant 'in the likeness of God.' " When Coleman asked if it was correct to assume that he was, therefore, a religious man, Krishnamurti answered: "I believe all philosophies and all religions are wrong. The spoken or written word is not the truth. Truth can only be experienced directly, the moment it happens. Any thought or intellectual projection of the truth is a step away from the truth, sir. . . . No organization, however old or however recent, can lead man to truth. It is a hindrance. . . . It blocks a man from sincere study. The truth comes from within, by seeing for yourself."

Coleman countered, "If you described a book or a motor car or the plane we are traveling in I would understand." To that Krishnamurti answered: "That is the purpose of the intellect, sir —to communicate. Mechanical or materialistic things can be understood but . . . what God is . . . what reality is . . . what love is . . . this you must understand by direct experience, without interpretation and without intellectualisation. The thought and the word are not the thing but a distortion of the reality."

In *Life Ahead* (Harper & Row, 1963) Krishnamurti addressed himself particularly to young people, in discussing the essentials of right education. In his introduction to that book he wrote: "There is a revolution which is entirely different [from economic and social revolutions] . . . which *must* take place if we are to emerge from the endless series of anxieties, conflicts, and frustrations in which we are caught. This revolution has to begin, not with theory and ideation . . . but with a radical transformation in the mind itself. . . . At present we are tinkering with results, with symptoms. . . . We are not . . . uprooting the old ways of thought, freeing the mind from traditions and habits. . . . Learning in the true sense of the word is possible only in that state of attention in which

there is no outer or inner compulsion. . . . A generation educated in this manner will be free of aquisitiveness and fear, the psychological inheritance of their parents and of the society in which they are born; and because they are so educated, they will not depend on the inheritance of property . . . [which] destroys real independence and limits intelligence; for it breeds a false sense of security. . . . It is only when the mind understands [both] the superficial and the hidden that it can go beyond its own limitations and discover that bliss which is not of time."

In 1969 the Krishnamurti Foundation of America was established in Ojai, California, where Krishnamurti usually lives when he is not traveling. The British Krishnamurti Foundation is located in Beckenham, Kent, England, and the Krishnamurti Foundation of India runs the Rishi Valley School in the Chittoor District of Andhra Pradesh, India. Krishnamurti talks and leads discussions on a more or less regular basis at Ojai, Beckenham, and the Rishi Valley School. Among the other stops on his routine itinerary are Carnegie Hall and Town Hall in New York City. *Time* (June 7, 1971) reported: "Once the darling of the solid and middle-aged, he has now been adopted by the young. At four packed lectures in New York City's Town Hall recently there was only a handful of the aged faithful in the college-age audiences."

Discussions and dialogues led by Krishnamurti in the summer of 1970 were published under the title *The Impossible Question* (Harper & Row, 1973). In his recapitulation Krishnamurti said: "If any person seriously concerned with and actively involved in social change . . . is not aware of his own conditioning, then this conditioning makes for fragmentation in action; and therefore there will be more conflict, more misery, more confusion. . . . Fragmentations divide. . . . Attention is a state of mind in which all energy is highly concentrated; and in that attention there is no observer, . . . no center as the 'me' who is aware. . . . The 'me' is the monkey who is incessantly active . . . with its problems, with its anxieties, fears and so on. This restless thought—the monkey—is always seeking security, because it is afraid to be uncertain in its activity, in its thoughts, in its relationships. It wants everything mechanical. . . . The mind that is seeking security cannot be stable in the sense of being mobile, swift, and yet immensely immovable."

Talks and discussions given and led by Krishnamurti in Santa Monica, San Diego, London, Brockwood Park (Hampshire, England), and Rome on the subject of the "appalling brutalities" in the society we have built were reported in *Beyond Violence* (Harper & Row, 1973), in which he suggests that the urgent need for a change in human values can come about through the growth of a religious mind, "extraordinarily silent, but highly awake in that silence." *The Awakening of Intelligence* (Harper & Row, 1973) consists of transcripts of talks, conversations, dialogues, and discussions that took place in New York City, Madras, Saanen (Switzerland), and Brockwood

Park. Intelligence and its relation to thought was central in those sessions. At one point Krishnamurti, who distinguishes the temporal, measurable mechanism of thought from the transcendent potential of intelligence, said, "Intelligence comes into being when the brain discovers its fallibility." At another, he stated, regarding the transcendent, "If you cannot find it, you will always be cruel, you will always be in conflict."

He was at his most eloquent in *The Awakening of Intelligence* when talking about death and love, time and eternity: "How does one find out about this strange thing [death] that we all have to meet one day or another. . . ? To die to your pleasure, to your attachment, your dependence, to end it without rationalizing, without trying to find ways and means of avoiding it . . . to put an end to that which has continuity; to put an end to your ambition, because that is what is going to happen when you die, isn't it. . . ? When you actually die, you have to end so many things without any argument. You can't say to death, 'Let me finish my job, . . . my book . . . —you have no time. So can you find out how to live a life now, today, in which there is always an ending to everything you began. Not in your office, of course, but inwardly to end all the knowledge you have gathered . . . your experiences, your memories, your hurts, . . . comparing yourself always with somebody else. To end all that every day, so that the next day your mind is fresh and young. Such a mind cannot be hurt, and that is innocence . . . that is eternity . . . that is the quality of the mind that has come upon this timeless state, because it has known what it means to die every day to everything it has collected during the day. . . . In that there is love. Love is something totally new every day. But pleasure is not, pleasure has continuity. Love is always new and therefore it is its own eternity."

George Bernard Shaw once described Krishnamurti as the most beautiful person he had ever seen. The writer of the *Time* article described him as "ascetically slim, darkly handsome," and John E. Coleman gave this description of him: "He was a striking figure . . . tall, with a full head of graying hair. . . . He spoke quickly and directly in an impeccable Oxford accent." When Coleman noted that Krishnamurti was carrying no luggage, the Indian sage responded, "I am only going as far as New Delhi. I have no need of possessions and carry none. I have no money with me either. I never handle it." Coleman asked, "What will you do without money or clothes in Delhi? What will you do for food and accommodation?" Krishnamurti answered: "I shall be among friends. . . . As a matter of fact, I have no permanent home or possessions. I spend my life traveling from place to place and my friends everywhere look after my needs." Krishnamurti is a lifelong vegetarian, teetotaler, nonsmoker, and practitioner of yoga. He dresses and acts in accordance with the style of the country he is in. As the *Time* writer observed, "In the United States he lectures while seated in a chair, impeccably dressed in Western-style clothes. In India

he may wear the traditional white robe and sit cross-legged in a yoga position to speak, but he refuses to pose that way for Western photographers."

References

Time 97:63 Je 7 '71 por
Besant, Annie. How a World Teacher Comes (1926)
Coleman, John E. The Quiet Mind (1971)
Lutyens, Lady Emily. Candles in the Sun (1957)
Lutyens, Mary. To Be Young (1959)
Menen, Aubrey. The Mystics (1974)
Webb, James. The Occult Underground (1974)
Who's Who in America, 1972-73

KRISTOFFERSON, KRIS

June 22, 1936- Singer; songwriter; actor
Address: c/o Columbia Records, 51 W. 52d St., New York 10019

The songs of Kris Kristofferson, who has been called the Johnny Cash of the counter culture, are "country" in their strength and simplicity and urban in their wit, sophistication, and poetry. That apparently paradoxical combination has made him one of the most popular artists in the Nashville country music industry. Kristofferson broke into the music world as a protégé of Cash, after an erratic career as a Rhodes scholar, rock 'n' roll singer, Army helicopter pilot, and day laborer. Since 1969 his ballads have been recorded by Johnny Cash, Roger Miller, Janis Joplin, and scores of other performers, and he himself has achieved star status by singing them in nightclubs, at concerts, and on records. An actor as well as a singer, Kristofferson has had roles in *Cisco Pike*, *Pat Garrett and Billy the Kid*, *Blume in Love*, and *Bring Me the Head of Alfredo Garcia*.

The son of an Air Force officer stationed in Brownsville, Texas, Kris Kristofferson was born in that Gulf city on June 22, 1936. He grew up in Brownsville and in San Mateo, California. Kristofferson's father retired from the Air Force as a major general and then worked for some years in Saudi Arabia as air operations manager for Aramco Oil. He died in 1971, and his widow lives in California. Kristofferson has a sister who is married to an Army officer and a brother who is a Navy jet pilot.

"In school I was always a straight arrow," Kristofferson told Sally Quinn in an interview for *Newsday* (September 11, 1971). "They even called me 'straight' in college." After an unperturbed adolescence as a model student and altar boy, he attended Pomona College in California, where he was a football star, Golden Gloves boxer, sports reporter for the campus newspaper, member of the honor society, and the top-rated ROTC cadet. In college he started a novel and won four prizes in the *Atlantic Monthly's* national collegiate short-story contest. Encouraged by one of his pro-

KRIS KRISTOFFERSON

fessors, he tried out for a Rhodes scholarship, won it, and after graduation went to Oxford University to study English literature. In England, Kristofferson started another novel and began writing songs, inspired by Hank Williams, who had long been his musical idol. Songwriting led to performing, and a London promoter launched him into a short-lived rock 'n' roll career under the name Kris Carson. "I did a TV show that was really awful, man," the singer recalled to Craig McGregor of the New York *Times* (July 26, 1970). "I got so embarrassed about the whole durn thing I said to myself, 'I'll never get into the music business'." During his brief career as Kris Carson, Kristofferson was publicized in *Time* magazine as a rising young pop-singing idol who had written two unfinished novels. The report prompted a couple of publishers to ask to see his manuscripts, but the novels were summarily turned down. Crushed by the rejections, Kristofferson left Oxford and within two months had married his childhood sweetheart and joined the United States Army.

In the Army, Kris Kristofferson went through jump school, Ranger school, and flight school. He was then assigned to Germany as a helicopter pilot. After his first two-year hitch was ended, he signed up for three more years in order to bring his wife overseas at government expense. "I dug flying, but I hated the Army," Kristofferson told Paul Hemphill of the New York *Times Magazine* (December 6, 1970). During his years overseas he drank heavily and cracked up two cars and four motorcycles. Eventually he resumed songwriting and began traveling with a musical group that played at clubs for enlisted men and noncommissioned officers.

Although Kristofferson volunteered for Vietnam duty in 1965, he was assigned instead to teach English literature at the United States Military Academy at West Point. On his way to West Point he stopped in Nashville, Tennessee to show some of his songs to an Army buddy's relative who was a music publisher there. His two-day visit stretched to two weeks, after which he went to the Pentagon and managed to obtain a discharge from the Army. He recalls that his family and friends thought he was crazy, but he nevertheless moved to Nashville at the age of twenty-nine to carve out a new career for himself as a songwriter. He quickly sold one song, "Vietnam Blues," but further success was slow in coming. Not wanting to take a full-time job that would interfere with his writing, Kristofferson worked part time as a ditch digger, a bartender, and a janitor. After two separations, his wife, then pregnant with their second child, left him and moved to California. His parents in effect disowned him, and they ordered him never to visit any of their relatives because they considered him an embarrassment. After his son was born with a defective esophagus, Kristofferson found a job for two weeks each month near New Orleans flying helicopters on oil rigs, so that he could pay for the hospital bills and support his children. He held that job for two years, until April 1970.

During that period of loneliness and struggle, Kristofferson wrote many of the songs for which he was later to become famous, including "For the Good Times," about the painful but inevitable breakup of a marriage, and "Sunday Mornin' Comin' Down," which captures the essence of urban loneliness with the refrain. "On the Sunday mornin' sidewalks,/ wishin' Lord that I was stoned;/ 'cause there's somethin' in a Sunday,/ makes a body feel alone./ And there's nothin' short of dyin'/ Half as lonesome as the sound/ On the sleepin' city sidewalks/ Sunday mornin' comin' down." He received a great deal of encouragement from Johnny Cash, who started singing his songs and introducing him around after meeting him at Columbia Recording Studios, where Kristofferson worked for a time as a janitor. His fortunes really began to change in mid-1969, when Roger Miller recorded his song "Me and Bobby McGee" and made it into a country hit. A bouncy tune about two young hitchhikers with the striking refrain "Freedom's just another word for nothin' left to lose," "Me and Bobby McGee" later became a national hit when sung by Janis Joplin. By 1972 the song had been recorded by over fifty artists.

To promote his songs, Kristofferson began singing them himself, and in the summer of 1969 Johnny Cash got him an engagement at the Newport, Rhode Island, Folk Festival. By 1970 he was appearing on Cash's television show and had formed his own band. Kristofferson made his nightclub debut in June 1970 at the Troubadour Club in Los Angeles, where he stole the show from the headliner Linda Ronstadt, and two months later he made his New York bow at the Bitter End. That year he also cut his first album, *Kristofferson*, for the Monument label, which sold a respectable 60,000 copies in its first months on the market. In between his club and college concert dates, Kristofferson cut three songs for the soundtrack of the Dennis Hopper film, *The Last Movie* (Universal, 1971). He wrote about a dozen songs for the Hopper movie and sang several of them on screen, including "The Pilgrim: Chapter

33," which for many of Kristofferson's fans contains the quintessential statement of his years of searching: "Once he had a future/full of money, love and dreams,/ Which he spent like they was/ goin' out of style;/ And he keeps on a-changin'/ for the better or the worse,/ And searching for a shrine/ he never found;/Never knowing if believing/ is a blessing or a curse,/ Or if the going up/ is worth the coming down." For the soundtrack of *Fat City* (Columbia, 1972) Kristofferson recorded his "Help Me Make It Through the Night."

In 1971 Kristofferson continued to fulfill almost nightly engagements across the United States and Canada, and the following year he toured Great Britain. A casual, poised performer, he was described by Jack Batten of the Toronto *Globe and Mail* (November 29, 1971) as "a dark, rangy, good-looking man who projects a terrifically attractive aura." Although Kristofferson has self-deprecatingly described his husky baritone as sounding like "a goddamned frog," he uses its limited range effectively to put across his highly autobiographical songs. Essentially a storyteller, he becomes for his audiences a romantic road-weary troubadour relating what he has been through.

Although most critics dismissed the film as just another youth-and-drugs movie, Kristofferson received generally favorable reviews for his acting debut in *Cisco Pike* (Columbia, 1972). Martin Knelman of the Toronto *Globe and Mail* (January 31, 1972) found his screen personality "too limp to carry a feature movie," but many other reviewers were impressed with Kristofferson's relaxed, sardonic portrayal of Cisco, a has-been rock singer who turns to dope dealing to make a living. The singer-composer fared less well in *Pat Garrett and Billy the Kid* (MGM, 1973), a disappointing Sam Peckinpah Western in which Kristofferson created a Billy the Kid who, according to Vincent Canby (New York *Times*, June 3, 1973), looked more "like a fellow who's fond of drinking double-thick malteds and reading good books" than a hunted desperado. Canby had only praise, however, for Kristofferson's portrayal of an unemployed musician in the offbeat comedy *Blume in Love* (Warner Brothers, 1973), which he called "most relaxed and debonair." Sam Peckinpah's perverse and quirky *Bring Me the Head of Alfredo Garcia* (United Artists, 1974) afforded him little opportunity to exhibit his talents in the minor role of Paco, a motorcyclist and rapist. He was killed off after appearing in only one episode.

Kristofferson is considered the foremost singer and songwriter of what has been called "progressive Nashville." Although most of the songs retain the uncomplicated melodies and simple, emotional themes of love and heartbreak that characterize country music, he has added a liberal measure of wit, sophistication, and poetry, as well as a blunt, earthy sensuality. He has also introduced an anti-establishment note to country music by satirizing straight society in such songs as "The Law Is for the Protection of the People" and "Blame It on the Stones."

The music industry has bestowed many awards on Kristofferson, including the Country Music Association's 1970 song of the year award for "Sunday Mornin' Comin' Down," the 1971 songwriter of the year award by the Nashville Songwriter's Association, BMI's Robert J. Burton award for the most performed country song of 1972 ("Help Me Make It Through the Night"), and two 1972 Grammy best song nominations for "Help Me Make It Through the Night" and "Me and Bobby McGee." BMI also honored Kristofferson in 1974, when it named his "From the Bottle to the Bottom," as performed by him and his present wife, Rita Coolidge, the winning entry in its "Best Country Vocal Performance by a Duo or Group."

By the middle of 1971 Kristofferson had published some 130 songs. His songwriting slackened off during the first couple of years that he was performing; since that time he has adjusted his schedule to allow time for composing. His recently recorded hit songs, mostly of his own composition, include "Just the Other Side of Nowhere," "Give It Time to be Tender," "Help Me," and "Why Me?" Among his record albums on the Monument label are *The Silver Tongued Devil and I*, *Border Lord*, and *Jesus Was a Capricorn*. Although all of his albums have enjoyed brisk sales, many music critics still regard his first one, *Kristofferson*, as his best. It has been rereleased by Monument under the title *Me and Bobby McGee*. Kristofferson's latest album is *Big Sur Festival* on the Columbia label.

Since 1972 Kristofferson has often been joined in his concerts by the blues rock singer Rita Coolidge, whom he married on August 19, 1973 in a Baptist ceremony performed by her father in Malibu, California. The couple have recorded several singles together and the album *Full Moon* (A&M), on which they sing country, folk, and pop numbers. By his previous marriage, Kristofferson has a daughter, Tracy, and a son, Kris. After interviewing the singer-songwriter, Sally Quinn (*Newsday*, September 11, 1971) described him as "a series of contradictions. He's totally open and completely inaccessible. He's shy and gregarious, honest and devious, rude and polite, smart and dumb." Five feet eleven inches tall, Kristofferson has deep-set blue eyes and, according to Miss Quinn, "sensuous lips, white teeth, a gravelly, sexy whisky voice, [and] a disarming grin." He chain-smokes Bull Durham cigarettes. Until his alliance with Miss Coolidge, at least, Kristofferson had a reputation as a hard-drinking, hard-loving man who exerted an irresistible attraction on women, an image emphasized in his songs. That image might be changing, however; some of his more recent music, according to a *Saturday Review* (February 3, 1973) record critic, contradicts "Kristofferson's established *macho* image" by being "uncharacteristically tentative and gentle." But Kristofferson might still prefer to be described by the self-portrait he paints in "The Pilgrim: Chapter 33": "He's a poet, he's a picker/ he's a prophet, he's a pusher/ He's a pilgrim and a preacher/ and a problem when he's stoned/ He's a walking contradiction/ partly truth and partly fiction/ Taking every wrong direction/ on his lonely way back home."

References

BMI p10 O '70 por; p23 Jl '72 pors
N Y Times II p8 Jl 26 '70 por
N Y Times Mag p54+ D 6 '70 pors
Newsday W p13+ S 11 '71 por
Shestack, Melvin. The Country Music En-
cyclopedia (1974)

KRISTOL, IRVING (WILLIAM)

Jan. 22, 1920- Editor; author; educator
Address: b. Public Interest, 10 E. 53d St., New
York 10022

As coeditor of the quarterly journal the *Public
Interest*, which he helped to found in 1965,
Irving Kristol is a leading spokesman for a small
but articulate group of scholars seeking to provide an antidote to the alienated intellectuals
whom they regard as a major factor in the ero-
sion of traditional American values. Described
by Joseph Epstein in *Dissent* as "perhaps the
quintessential new Conservative," Kristol ranks
among those academicians whose counsel was welcomed in the White House under the first Nixon
administration. A product of New York's liberal
intellectual establishment, Kristol has served as
editor of *Commentary, Encounter,* and the *Reporter* magazines and as executive vice-president
of Basic Books, Inc. Since 1969 he has occupied
the chair of Henry R. Luce Professor of Urban
Values at New York University. As a possible
remedy for the "crisis in values" that in his view
largely resulted from the too rapid changes in
American life in the 1960's, Kristol has suggested
in his book *On the Democratic Ideal in America*
(1972) a "combination of the reforming spirit
with the conservative ideal."

The son of Jewish immigrants from Europe,
Irving William Kristol was born in New York
City on January 22, 1920 to Joseph Kristol, a
men's clothing subcontractor, and Bessie (Mail-
man) Kristol. He has a sister, Mrs. Lillian O'Sullivan. Kristol grew up in Brooklyn, where he
graduated from Boys' High School in 1936, and attended the City College of New York as a history
major. Described as "a kind of Jewish, proletarian
Harvard," tuition-free CCNY was a fountainhead
of intellectual activity during the Depression years,
and a number of its alumni became leading
scholars of the "Eastern establishment." Among
Kristol's classmates at City College were the sociologists Daniel Bell, Seymour M. Lipset, and
Nathan Glazer, and the literary critic Irving Howe.

Although Kristol had not been profoundly influenced by political ideas during his adolescence,
he was swept up by the political debates that
were raging at CCNY during the 1930's. Casting
his lot with the anti-Communist left, he became
a member of the Young People's Socialist League.
In the general philosophical sense, Kristol later
cited the literary critic Lionel Trilling and the
political philosopher Leo Strauss as the thinkers
who had the strongest influence on his ideas.

In 1940 Kristol graduated *cum laude* with a
B.A. degree from CCNY, where he had become
a member of Phi Beta Kappa, and he then went
to work as a machinist's apprentice at the Brooklyn Navy Yard. He entered the United States
Army in 1944 and saw combat in France and
Germany with the 12th Armored Division. After
his discharge with the rank of staff sergeant in
1946, he went to England with his wife, the
former Gertrude Himmelfarb, who had won a
scholarship to Cambridge University. While in
England, Kristol completed work on a novel, but
he became dissatisfied with it and burned the
manuscript. At that time he also began to write
for *Commentary*, a monthly journal of opinion
sponsored by the American Jewish Committee.

On his return to New York in 1947, Kristol
was engaged as managing editor of *Commentary*
by its founder and then editor in chief, Elliot
Cohen, who gave the magazine a marked anti-
Communist orientation during the McCarthy era.
Kristol remained with *Commentary* until 1952,
when he went to London to collaborate with the
British poet Stephen Spender in founding the
British-American intellectual magazine *Encounter*.
Coedited by Spender and Kristol from 1953 to
1958, the monthly was considered one of the
most prestigious publications of its kind. Some
years later, *Encounter* became a subject of controversy as a result of reports that the United
States Central Intelligence Agency had given financial support to the magazine through the vehicle of the Paris-based Congress for Cultural
Freedom, which had financed its first issue in
1953 with a $30,000 grant and continued to sup-
ply it with funds until 1964. Confirmation of the
reports by Thomas W. Braden, a former CIA
official, in a *Saturday Evening Post* article in May
1967, led to Spender's resignation as contributing
editor. When asked whether he had known about
the CIA funds, Kristol replied that he had investigated such rumors while he was coeditor
but had been assured by his backers that the
rumors were false. "As for myself," he said, as
quoted in the New York *Times* (May 8, 1967),
"I have never been, am not, and have no intention of becoming a CIA agent."

After leaving *Encounter* in late 1958, Kristol
returned to New York to become editor of the
liberal, anti-Communist fortnightly the *Reporter*,
succeeding the magazine's founder and publisher, Max Ascoli, who became its editor in chief.
"The appointment," Ascoli said at the time, "is
intended to ease my burden and to strengthen
the editorial staff, so that the *Reporter* may continue to broaden its political and cultural coverage." In 1960 Kristol left the *Reporter* to join
Basic Books, Inc., a small but prestigious publishing firm, as its executive vice-president and
senior editor for the social sciences. He continued
to serve Basic Books on a part-time basis as a
consulting editor after his appointment, in 1969,
as Henry R. Luce Professor of Urban Values in
the faculty of arts and science at New York
University.

In 1965 Kristol and Daniel Bell, who had remained in close contact since their student days at CCNY, founded and became the unsalaried coeditors of the *Public Interest,* a scholarly journal dealing with domestic affairs. Published quarterly in New York City under the sponsorship of various individuals and foundations, the magazine increased the number of its subscribers from 5,000 in 1965 to some 11,000 in 1973. Its title refers to a statement by Walter Lippmann, defining the public interest as "what men would choose if they saw clearly, thought rationally, acted disinterestedly and benevolently." In their introductory article in the magazine's first issue, published in October 1965, the editors indicated that it was designed as a counterweight to those members of the literary intellectual establishment whose ideological rigidities prompt them to "insistently propose prefabricated interpretations of existing social realities . . . that bitterly resist all sensible revision."

The *Public Interest* addressed itself to what Kristol called "a new class, a policy-making intellectual class," consisting of government administrators concerned with such topics as housing, urban development, poverty, automation, and scientific progress, as well as sociologists, political scientists, and others seriously interested in public affairs. Its aim was to present precise information based on statistical studies, and to formulate non-ideological analyses of current issues, with an emphasis on seeking viable solutions to pressing social problems. Although the *Public Interest* has been described as representing the "new conservatism," it has presented a variety of viewpoints. During the 1972 Presidential election campaign, for example, the magazine featured conflicting articles by its co-editors, with Bell backing the candidacy of George McGovern and Kristol supporting Richard Nixon. Its contributors over the years have included such noted scholars as Jacques Barzun, Daniel P. Moynihan, Leo Rosten, James Q. Wilson, and Robert L. Heilbroner, among others. In June 1973 Daniel Bell stepped down as coeditor of the *Public Interest* because of other commitments and was succeeded by Nathan Glazer.

While working as a research associate with the Russell Sage Foundation in 1968-69, Kristol wrote a series of articles on such topics as urbanization, education, utopianism, and the role of the historian that were brought together in the book *On the Democratic Idea in America* (Harper & Row, 1972). Its basic theme is what Kristol saw as a breakdown of American democratic ideals, exacerbated by the "utopian" liberalism of the 1960's and the emergence of the New Left. "I regard the exaggerated hopes we attach to politics as the curse of our age, just as I regard moderation as one of our vanishing virtues," he wrote in the preface. While recognizing the need for reforms in American political, economic, and educational institutions, Kristol believes that such reforms should be carried out "by moderate men using moderate means," that they should "wed

IRVING KRISTOL

themselves to the national tradition and become part of the accepted way of life," and that they should make "the bonds of the community stronger rather than weaker."

Predictably, critical comment on the book—which became recommended reading for President Nixon's staff—was divided along ideological lines. Writing in the *Wall Street Journal* (May 3, 1972), Robert L. Bartley called *On the Democratic Idea in America* "a brilliant and incisive commentary on our times" presenting "an exceptionally strong and valuable outlook, . . . sensitive to both detail and the broad sweep, [and] relevant both to important political battlegrounds and to the diffuse hunger of our times," and suggesting "the immense difficulty of reform by rational prescription." On the other hand, Yosal Rogat commented in the *New York Review of Books* (September 21, 1972): "The book is littered with . . . assertions, some outright falsehoods, some misleading, some cleverly tendentious, some quite possibly accurate, but all without supporting authority."

With Stephen Spender and Melvin J. Lasky, Kristol edited *Encounters* (Basic Books, 1963), an anthology of writings from *Encounter* magazine over a ten-year period. He collaborated with Daniel Bell in editing *Confrontation; The Student Rebellion and the Universities* (Basic Books, 1969), a collection of articles on the student unrest in the 1960's. Typical of the divergent viewpoints with which the book was evaluated were P. G. Altbach's comment in *Christian Century* (July 2, 1969), calling it "a balanced analysis of student activism . . . by well-known academics who place great emphasis on the university as an important and positive institution in American life"; and criticism of the book by Paul Osterman in *Commonweal* (September 26, 1969) for its "sustained attack on student activists," its espousal of the viewpoint of the "academic elite," and its defense of the status quo in higher education. Kristol and Bell were also coeditors of *Capitalism Today* (Basic Books, 1971), a reprint in book form of the special issue of the *Public Interest* that appeared in the fall of 1970.

Kristol has contributed a number of articles to symposiums, including one entitled "Machiavelli and Political Science" in *Essays on Personal Knowledge* (Routledge, 1962), and another, "The Negro and the City," in *A Nation of Cities; Essays on America's Urban Problems* (Rand McNally, 1968). He is the author of the essay "Equality" in the *International Encyclopedia of the Social Sciences*. Over the years he has published more than fifty articles in the New York *Times Magazine, Harper's, Atlantic Monthly, Fortune, Commentary, Foreign Affairs, Yale Review, New York Review of Books, Partisan Review, Horizon,* and other publications. He is a member of the board of contributors of the *Wall Street Journal.*

From 1962 to 1966 Kristol was cultural correspondent in New York for the London *Observer,* and in 1964 he was a Regents' Lecturer at the University of California at Riverside. During 1967 he served as chairman of a Ford Foundation delegation of American intellectuals visiting West Germany and as a member of the RAND Corporation Study Group on Urban Problems. In 1968 he was a member of the Vice-President's Task Force on Income Maintenance and cochairman, with Daniel P. Moynihan, of the Conference on the Future of New York City, sponsored by National Affairs, Inc., the Ford Foundation, and the Carnegie Foundation. Although he voted for Hubert H. Humphrey in 1968, after Nixon's election Kristol served, in 1968-69, on the President-Elect's Task Force on Voluntary Urban Action. Appointed in December 1972 to the board of directors of the Corporation for Public Broadcasting, Kristol hoped to counteract the influence of young activists involved in public television who, in his view, "sincerely believe that they have the right—the responsibility, even—to use taxpayers' funds to excoriate the taxpayers' way of life."

Despite his disillusionment with the domestic reform programs of the Kennedy and Johnson administrations, which he felt were put into effect too quickly and were alien to the country's traditions, Kristol has remained a registered Democrat. He credits the Nixon administration with having stabilized the country, although he admits that its effectiveness was weakened by the Watergate affair. Among his chief targets on the domestic scene are the utopian philosophies, anti-American attitudes, and hostility to the business establishment prevailing among intellectuals. Kristol believes that the proliferation of pornography is debasing America and should be subjected to "liberal censorship;" that much of the press is incompetent to report on the complexities of modern life; that public broadcasting has been dominated to too great a degree by the "counterculture," and that the "mindless" expansion of higher education in the 1960's contributed considerably to the alienation and disorientation of youth. He has also criticized the modern corporation as looking "more and more like a dinosaur on its lumbering way to extinction," and he believes that if capitalism is to be saved, corporations should undergo extensive reform and improve their public image.

Kristol admits to an occasional nostalgia for the cold war and the "relatively forthright way it posed unambiguous moral issues." He believes that the United States should accept its role as an "imperial power," and in the early 1960's he argued in favor of American intervention against Fidel Castro's Cuba. Kristol defended United States military intervention in Indochina, arguing that the "domino theory" was valid and that the Soviet Union and China were responsible for the hostilities there. With regard to the fate of Israel, Kristol wrote in the *Wall Street Journal* (October 18, 1973): "I am not an Orthodox Jew, and only a barely observant one. I am not a Zionist and I did not find my two visits to Israel to be particularly exhilarating. . . . Still, I care desperately . . . because I sense, deep down, that what happens to Israel will be decisive for Jewish history." Convinced that the Arab countries "will not in the foreseeable future accept the existence of a non-Arab nation in 'their' Middle East," Kristol believes that Israel, in order to survive, "must be to a considerable degree a garrison state."

In 1972 Kristol was elected a fellow of the American Academy of Arts and Sciences; appointed to the National Council on the Humanities; and awarded an honorary LL.D. degree by Franklin and Marshall College in Pennsylvania. In February 1973 he was asked by the President to assemble a group of scholars for a White House session dealing with current social policy. Kristol is a member of the American Political Science Association, the American Sociological Association, the Council on Foreign Relations, and the Century Club.

Irving Kristol and Gertrude Himmelfarb were married on January 18, 1942. Mrs. Kristol, who uses her maiden name professionally, is a professor of history at the City University of New York and has written several important books on the intellectual history of the nineteenth century. The Kristols live in New York City with their two children, William and Elizabeth. A deceptively mild-mannered man of slight build, Kristol is five feet six inches tall, weighs 160 pounds, and has graying brown hair and blue eyes. His favorite recreation is watching sporting events on television.

References

Forbes 113:74+ My 15 '74 por
Los Angeles Times II p7 Ja 11 '73
N Y Herald Tribune Mag p7+ O 24 '65 por
N Y Times p41 Je 3 '73
Nat Observer p1+ D 30 '72 por
Wall St J p20 My 3 '72
Washington Post A p2 Ap 15 '73 por
Contemporary Authors vols 25-28 (1971)

KUHLMAN, KATHRYN

1910(?)- Faith healer; Protestant minister
Address: Kathryn Kuhlman Foundation, Carlton House Hotel, Pittsburgh, Pa. 15230

The most celebrated Christian charismatic leader in America today is Kathryn Kuhlman, at whose "miracle services" thousands claim to have been spontaneously cured of illness or physical handicaps. Since discovering her healing powers, in 1946, Miss Kuhlman has reached millions through her preaching, her books, and her radio and TV programs. Personally she is a member of the American Baptist Convention, but her services are interdenominational. Her preaching is Pentecostal, with the emphasis on the power of the Holy Spirit. "I have nothing to do with these miracles," she insists. "I have nothing but the power of the Holy Spirit."

Kathryn Kuhlman, who reportedly does not discuss her age, was born around 1910 in Concordia, Missouri. Her father, Joe Kuhlman, whom she revered, was for many years the mayor of Concordia. A nominal Baptist, he seems to have despised the clergy, for Miss Kuhlman recalls that he would cross the street to avoid speaking to a minister. Her mother, whose maiden name was Emma Walkenhorst, belonged to the Methodist Church.

When Miss Kuhlman was about thirteen she underwent an intense religious experience. Feeling "a definite call to the ministry," she dropped out of high school at the end of her sophomore year and began preaching when she was sixteen. "Had I chosen a profession," she wrote in her first book, *I Believe in Miracles* (Prentice-Hall, 1962), "in all probability my choice would have been either medicine or law. But I had no choice: I was called of God to preach the Gospel."

After studying the Bible informally for two years, Miss Kuhlman was ordained a minister by the Evangelical Church Alliance. Regarding her lack of formal theological schooling and other negative aspects of her background, she once told an audience: "Without the Holy Spirit, I haven't a crutch, I haven't anything to lean on. I don't have a thing. . . . You see, if I had been born with talent, I might have been able to lean on that. Had I had education, I might have used that as a crutch. But I don't have a thing."

Miss Kuhlman began itinerant preaching in Idaho and for almost twenty years worked among poor farming congregations throughout the Midwest. From the beginning her sermons focused on Christian faith, which she has defined as "that quality or power by which the things desired become the things possessed." In *I Believe in Miracles* she wrote, "You cannot have faith without results any more than you can have motion without movement. . . . Although we trust in the Lord, it is *faith* which has action and power."

During her early preaching years Miss Kuhlman attended traditional divine healing services and found them deplorable. "I knew why the evangelist asked people to fill out those cards to get into the healing line," she has said. "It was

KATHRYN KUHLMAN

to get a mailing list, that's all. I used to sit there and watch this kind of thing and I wasn't satisfied it was real." After visiting one such service and seeing the despairing faces of those who were told they had not been healed because their faith was deficient, she went home and cried all night. However, she continued to believe that miracles and healing through faith could occur.

In 1946, while minister of a congregation in Franklin, Pennsylvania, Miss Kuhlman underwent a second profound religious experience, which she has described only to the extent of calling it her "baptism of the Holy Spirit." It inspired her to begin preaching regularly about the Holy Spirit, and during one of her Pentecostal sermons a woman in the congregation was cured of a tumor. Miss Kuhlman learned about the cure only afterward, when the woman reported it to her. After that initial spontaneous cure, others in her congregation experienced healings, and Miss Kuhlman started preaching about God's power to cure.

In 1947 she moved to Pittsburgh, which has remained her home base ever since. As her fame spread, the sick and the crippled came from far and wide to Pittsburgh for her miracle services, which were held in local churches or auditoriums. For many years Miss Kuhlman refused to travel, because she felt that the saving of souls through divine healing could best be accomplished "by staying in one place," where she would be in a position "to follow through" and "insist that those who claim healings procure medical verification." During the 1960's, however, she began to carry her ministry to other parts of the country, and by 1970 she was drawing large crowds in major cities on the East and West coasts.

When Kathryn Kuhlman comes to a city, crowds wait for hours to be admitted to the hall where she is to appear, for fear of being turned away. Some people are in wheelchairs, some on crutches, some even on stretchers. The miracle service begins with music. Miss Kuhlman appears on stage, a tall, slim figure usually dressed in a simple white chiffon dress with large sleeves. For a while she may chat and joke with her audience in a folksy, friendly manner, then move on to an impassioned talk on the Holy Spirit. James Morris in his book *The Preachers* described one of her services in this way: "While she spoke she constantly moved about the platform. Her sermon seemed to be built around an emotional tribute to the Holy Spirit. The full sleeves and the long, dazzling white dress billowed and wafted as she glided and turned. At first her voice seemed halting and slow, then more vibrant and mellow. Suddenly it was mixed with throaty sobs, and she was almost crying. Her audience was carried along on the tide of emotion, and many dabbed at their eyes, and more than a few wept openly and unashamedly."

After she has preached for an hour or more, the "miracles" begin. In place of the healing lines of other preachers, Miss Kuhlman has a system of diagnosing disease by supernatural means. She announces the cures as she becomes aware of them happening, identifies those cured, and points out their locations in the auditorium. The healed persons surge into the aisles and are guided onstage by ushers. There the evangelist congratulates them and puts her hands on their heads. Almost invariably each person collapses under her touch into the arms of waiting ushers. Although this phenomenon, known as "falling under the power of the Spirit," is for some observers the most extraordinary aspect of the Kuhlman service, others consider it similar in nature to the highly emotional responses of most Pentecostal services.

Unlike other Pentecostal faith healers, she apparently has seen miracles worked on nonbelievers as well as the faithful. Atheists, agnostics, and curiosity seekers have regularly claimed to have been cured at her services. Miss Kuhlman has no explanation for such occurrences. She wrote in the Afterword of *God Can Do It Again* (Prentice-Hall, 1969), a book in which she brought together the first-person stories of numerous persons who were healed or who witnessed healing: "When I was twenty years of age, I could have given you all the answers. My theology was straight and I was sure that if you followed certain rules, worked hard enough, obeyed all the commandments, and had yourself in a certain spiritual state, God would heal you. . . . Lo and behold, my theology came tumbling down and was crushed into a thousand pieces when one day a man who had just entered the auditorium during a miracle service stood silently against the back wall, and after not more than five minutes walked boldly to the stage and freely admitted, "My ear has just opened and I do not believe!" . . . . He never recanted. . . . He had not been to church for more than twenty-five years and had put himself in the category of an atheist. It is possible for me to relate many cases where people have been healed who were amazed, who freely admitted that they did not expect to be healed. . . . Until we have a way of defining it, all that I can tell you is that these are mercy healings."

Miss Kuhlman refuses ever to predict or guarantee a healing. "I can't," she has said. "That's the

sovereign act of God." When she is preaching she sometimes has physicians on the stage with her to verify the cures. However, a reporter for *Time* magazine (September 14, 1970) has reported that her staff spends little time medically documenting healings, except in the most dramatic cases. It has been pointed out that at least some people who claim to have been cured at Kuhlman services were suffering from self-diagnosed maladies, and many do not bother to verify their cures with doctors. Although skeptics dismiss the healings as purely psychosomatic, some objective reporters come away believing the miraculous has occurred.

In *Kathryn Kuhlman: The Woman Who Believes in Miracles* (1970), Allen Spraggett attempts to explain the cures in terms of parapsychology. Spraggett, a psychic researcher and former religion editor with the Toronto *Evening Star*, is skeptical of the healing powers of such legendary faith healers as Oral Roberts and the Rev. A. A. Allen, but he calls Miss Kuhlman "the greatest faith healer since Biblical times" and "one of the most extraordinary Christian mystics and clairvoyants of our time." Convinced that miracles do occur at her meetings, Spraggett defines them as "supernormal" rather than supernatural occurrences. He maintains that when the Holy Spirit "comes upon" her, she is experiencing "an altered state of consciousness" that psychics refer to as an "out-of-the-body" experience. He also suggests that her Holy Ghost power is a "field phenomenon" similar to an electric or magnetic field.

Although Spraggett maintains that Kathryn Kuhlman possesses special qualities that make her a healer, the charismatic leader insists that she is only an intermediary for God's power and has nothing to do with the healings. "There never was a more ordinary woman than the one standing before you," she told her audience in a familiar Kuhlman refrain at one meeting. "I have nothing, nothing to do with these healings. I have only yielded my life to Him. Do not try to reach out and touch Kathryn Kuhlman. Reach up and touch Him."

Miss Kuhlman is president of the Kathryn Kuhlman Foundation, a religious, nonprofit, charitable organization with headquarters in Carlton House Hotel in Pittsburgh. In fiscal 1972 the foundation reportedly grossed nearly $2,000,000, most of which came from donations collected during miracle services. As of 1970 Miss Kuhlman herself drew a straight annual salary of $25,000. Most of the rest of the foundation's gross income, after operating expenses, goes to a variety of charities, including foreign missionary churches of various denominations; drug rehabilitation; the education of blind children; a college scholarship and loan fund; the foundation's twenty-two mission projects around the world; and grocery commissaries for the needy.

In Pittsburgh the Kathryn Kuhlman Foundation has a radio studio where the faith healer broadcasts her daily half-hour programs, which reach most of the United States on tape over sixty stations. Her weekly television broadcasts go out over sixty-five stations. Miss Kuhlman's first book, *I Believe in Miracles,* sold millions of copies, going through many printings in hardcover and paperback editions, and her second book, *God Can Do It Again,* was also a best seller. In 1973 she published a third book, *Captain Le Vrier Believes in Miracles* (Dimension), about a Houston, Texas police captain cured of terminal cancer. The faith healer has also made a popular record entitled *I Believe in Miracles.* Her most recent book, *Nothing Is Impossible with God,* was published in 1974. Miss Kuhlman holds an honorary Doctor of Humane Letters degree from Oral Roberts University in Tulsa, Oklahoma.

The possessor of a compelling stage presence that fairly crackles with spiritual electricity, Kathryn Kuhlman is a slender woman with auburn hair. Described by one reporter as "joyfully middle-class," she enjoys expensive clothes and believes that preachers need not be ashamed of living comfortably. Yet, according to James Morris, she admits to living a lonely life when she is not conducting her services. Aware of the prejudice against women preachers among many of her conservative, middle-class followers, Miss Kuhlman is at pains to minimize her position. "I never think of myself as a woman preacher . . . ," she has said. "I am a woman . . . and I try to keep my place as a woman. . . . I never try to usurp the place of authority of a man—never! That's the reason I have no church. I leave that to the men."

References

Time 96:62+ S 14 '70 por
Kuhlman, Kathryn. I Believe in Miracles (1962)
Morris, James. The Preachers (1973)
Spraggett, Allen. Kathryn Kuhlman: The Woman Who Believes in Miracles (1970)

LEAR, NORMAN (MILTON)

July 27, 1922- Television producer
Address: b. Tandem Productions, Inc., Century City, 1901 Ave. of the Stars, Los Angeles, Calif. 90067

"I don't want to deal with TV's old drivel about the wife burning the roast just before the boss comes home to dinner," television producer Norman Lear once said in an interview. "I want to entertain, but I gravitate to subjects that matter and people worth caring about." Challenging the entrenched myth that the average television viewer has the mental capacity of a twelve-year-old, Lear introduced controversial adult themes, strong language, and true-to-life characters in his precedent-shattering series *All in the Family.* Unparalleled audience response reinforced Lear's opinion and, by the end of its first season, *All in the Family* was the most popular comedy series ever presented on television. Lear's succeeding shows,

NORMAN LEAR

Sanford and Son and *Maude,* ranked respectively, second and fifth in the Nielsen ratings shortly after their debuts in January and September 1972.

Norman Milton Lear, the son of Herman and Jeanette Lear, was born on July 27, 1922 in New Haven, Connecticut. His father, a second-generation Russian Jew, was an ineffectual salesman of everything from vacuum cleaners to garages. Though likeable, Herman Lear was an intolerant man who asserted his position as head of the household by ordering his wife to "stifle herself" and by belittling his son as "the laziest white kid I ever saw," expressions later favored by Archie Bunker. After graduating from Weaver High School in Hartford, Connecticut in 1940, Lear attended Emerson College in Boston for one year before enlisting in the United States Army Air Force in 1942. A technical sergeant in the Fifteenth Air Force stationed near Foggia, Italy, he flew fifty-seven missions as a radioman. Although Lear never returned to college, Emerson awarded him an honorary Ph.D. in the late 1960's.

Influenced by his financially successful uncle, a theatrical press agent, Lear accepted a position with the New York publicity firm of George and Dorothy Ross in 1946. Laid off one year later, he founded his own company to produce novelty ashtrays. When that venture failed, he moved to Los Angeles, where he worked as a door-to-door furniture salesman and as a sidewalk photographer specializing in baby pictures. To earn extra money, Lear and his friend Ed Simmons began writing comedy skits. Their modest success inspired Lear, the bolder of the two men, to offer material to Danny Thomas, the popular nightclub and theatre entertainer. He contacted Thomas' agent and, pretending to be a New York *Times* reporter, obtained the comedian's private telephone number. Impressed by the ruse, Thomas read the team's comedy sketch, liked it, and, according to Lear, bought it for "five bills." When Thomas used the routine at a benefit performance in Hollywood, David Susskind, then a New York agent, immediately signed the promising writing team of Lear and Simmons to *The Ford Star Review*, a regular television series. Lear was soon earning an annual salary of $100,000. In the next few years, he was, successively, a writer for the *Colgate Comedy Hour,* starring Dean Martin and Jerry Lewis, cowriter of the *Martha Raye Show,* and writer-director of the *George Gobel Show.*

While working on the *Colgate* show, Lear became friends with the show's associate director, Bud Yorkin, and in 1959 the two men formed Tandem Productions, Inc., of which Lear serves as the vice-president. "We [called] ourselves Tandem," Lear has often explained, "because we think of ourselves as two guys on a bicycle, going uphill." Deliberately designed to permit each partner to pursue his own interests, Tandem is a loosely structured organization. As an independent production company, Tandem produced motion pictures as well as packaged television specials showcasing such stars as Fred Astaire, Jack Benny, Danny Kaye, Carol Channing, Don Rickles, Andy Williams, and Henry Fonda. Tandem's first film *Come Blow Your Horn* (Paramount, 1963), starring Frank Sinatra, was a box-office smash. Adapted by Lear from a Neil Simon play and directed by Yorkin, the film was denounced by critics as "tiring," "garish" and "lushly overproduced." *Never Too Late* (Warner Brothers, 1965), another Broadway hit transferred to the screen by Lear as producer and Yorkin as director, fared slightly better with the critics. Although some objected to the plot's "questionable joke" of a late-life pregnancy, the majority praised the faithful interpretation of the Sumner Arthur Long play and the exacting performances of Paul Ford and Maureen O'Sullivan. Lear's original screenplay for *Divorce, American Style* (Columbia, 1967) earned him an Academy Award nomination. Produced and directed by Yorkin, the film, starring comedian Dick Van Dyke and Debbie Reynolds, had a moderate box-office success.

Striking out on his own, Lear wrote a script in collaboration with Arnold Schulman and Sidney Michaels about an innocent Amish girl who joins Minsky's Burlesque and inadvertently invents the striptease. Produced by Lear and directed by William Friedkin, *The Night They Raided Minsky's* (United Artists, 1968) accurately evoked the sleaziness of a New York burlesque house of the 1920's. A reviewer for *Time* magazine praised the "engaging blend of mockery and melancholy" in this "surprisingly successful musical." A stage version, with additional music and lyrics by Henry Mancini, has been scheduled for an opening on Broadway in the fall of 1974. Lear made his debut as a director with *Cold Turkey* (United Artists, 1971), a film he also scripted and produced. In *Cold Turkey*, the citizens of an Iowa farming community accept the challenge of a tobacco tycoon and collectively kick the cigarette habit to win a $25,000,000 prize. In his review for the Washington *Post* (March 9, 1971), Gary Arnold dismissed the "shallow, self-deluding sort of comedy" as "an honest-to-goodness turkey." Although acknowledging the film's "decent, comic idea," Paul D. Zim-

merman, in his *Newsweek* review of April 19, 1971, criticized Lear for "trying to harness a sweeping satire of American society to his small vehicle. . . ."

Because profits in the declining movie industry were relatively low, Tandem's business manager advised the partners to concentrate on the more profitable television market. Struck by an item in *Variety* describing the popular BBC-TV series, *Till Death Do Us Part*, a broad, satirical comedy of working-class mores, Lear obtained the American rights to the series. As he read about Alf Garnett, the bigoted central character of the British program who constantly bickered with his liberal son-in-law, Lear immediately remembered his father and their squabbles over political and social issues. "My father and I fought all those battles," he told Martin Kasindorf in an interview for a New York *Times Magazine* article (June 24, 1973). "I thought: 'My God, if I could only get this kind of thing on American television.'"

Adapting *Till Death Do Us Part* for American audiences, Lear and Yorkin wrote a pilot script centering around the conflicts between blue-collar bigot Archie Bunker and his liberal "Polack" son-in-law Mike Stivic. Under the title "Those Were The Days," he presented the series idea to ABC programming executives, who enthusiastically agreed to finance a pilot film. An astute casting director, Lear hired Carroll O'Connor and Jean Stapleton for the leading roles. Although ABC officials agreed that the two pilot films were hilarious, the network's top executives came to the decision that the program's language and frankness were too shocking to the sensibilities of American viewers and canceled the project.

Intent on changing CBS's program roster, too long dominated by corn-fed rural situation comedies, network president Robert D. Wood encouraged Lear to revive "Those Were the Days," which, he felt, would attract a young urban audience. Wood approved a third pilot, retitled *All in the Family,* starring O'Connor and Miss Stapleton in their original roles with Sally Struthers as the daughter, Gloria, and Rob Reiner as her husband. Despite Wood's unqualified support, William Tankersley, the director of CBS's department of program practices, balked at the "vulgarity" and "irreverence" of the script. Although Lear agreed to a few minor script changes, he adamantly refused to accede to Tankersley's demands to tone down the initial episode. "I felt we had to get the network wet completely," Lear told Arnold Hano in an interview for the New York *Times Magazine* (March 12, 1972). "I wanted the audience to hear all of Archie's epithets. . . ."

Slotted into the CBS prime time schedule, *All in the Family* had its première at 9:30 P.M. on Tuesday, January 12, 1971 with a voice-over disclaimer describing the program as "a humorous spotlight on our frailties, prejudices, and concerns." Expecting angry calls from irate viewers protesting the show's content and Archie's candid remarks about race, color, nationality and the church, CBS hired dozens of extra telephone operators. Of the comparatively few calls, most favored the program. Opening to mixed reviews, *Family* was not an instant hit. "This show proves that bigotry can be as boring and predictable as the upthink fluff of *The Brady Bunch*," Richard Burgheim gibed in his *Time* (February 1, 1971) review of the series. On the other hand, in the *National Observer* (March 15, 1971), Clifford A. Ridley called the show "at least the brightest new thing on commercial TV since the early *Laugh-In*." Favorable viewer reaction and increasing critical support boosted *Family* near the top of the Nielsen ratings. By the time the show went into re-runs in May, it had become the nation's most popular program and had won three Emmy awards, including one for the best comedy series. Shifted to the lucrative 8:00 P.M. slot on Saturday night at the beginning of the 1971-72 season, *All in the Family* averaged fifty to sixty million viewers weekly, an audience it continued to hold into its third full season. Under the overall supervision of producer-director John Rich, the show earned six Emmys for its 1971-72 run and two for the 1972-73 television year.

The spectacular success of *All In The Family* immediately spawned imitations, with the Tandem team providing the most successful spinoffs. Purchasing the adaptation rights to another BBC-TV series, *Steptoe and Son*, based on the lives of a crotchety Cockney junkman and his layabout son, producers Lear and Yorkin, working with writer Aaron Ruben, created *Sanford and Son*. In Americanizing the series, Lear solved initial problems in the pilot film by changing the show to an ethnic comedy with black performers. Redd Foxx, an experienced comedian, led the cast as the engaging fraud, Fred Sanford, when the program, an NBC-TV midseason entry, made its debut on Friday, January 14, 1972.

While Bud Yorkin handled the executive production chores for *Sanford and Son*, Lear continued to experiment with *All in the Family*, broaching more controversial topics such as impotence, menopause, Jewish defense organizations, and breast cancer, and introducing new characters. One of the characters, Edith's liberal-minded cousin Maude Findlay, originally a one-shot guest appearance created for Beatrice Arthur, so delighted the viewers that Lear developed *Maude*, a separate series that premièred on Tuesday, September 12, 1972. As tolerant as Archie Bunker was prejudiced, Maude presented the other side of the coin, showing in her outspoken manner that liberalism can be as ludicrous as bigotry.

Despite its resounding successes, Tandem's shows, particularly *All in the Family*, had their detractors, who felt that serious social comment and comedy were strange bedfellows. In her open letter to the New York *Times*, published September 12, 1971, Laura Z. Hobson, the author of *Gentleman's Agreement*, the controversial 1947 best-selling novel about anti-Semitism, protested the presentation of a "lovable bigot." Dr. Eugene Kusielewicz, the director of a Polish-American cultural and historical society, disapproved of the term "dumb Polack"; the late Whitney Young Jr., executive director of the National Urban League, called the show a "new low in taste"; and Dr. Benjamin R. Epstein, national director of the Anti-Defamation League of the B'nai B'rith, objected to racial slurs directed against Jews in a comedy that made prejudice "tolerable." Countering those arguments, Lear contended that *All in the Family* merely reflects the bigotry that exists in all people. Explaining his position in an interview for *New York* magazine (May 21, 1973), Lear told James Brady, "We don't ... try to sensationalize and create controversy on the show, but we reflect what people are thinking. ... Television comedy used to act as if there was no black and white hatred in the country, no drug problem, no friction. That was taking . . . a negative position. I'm a positive sort of fellow and I like to tackle those things." Lear does admit however, that for dramatic purposes, Archie is deliberately "a little larger than life."

Maude, too, has its adversaries. "Maude's Dilemma," a two-part episode in which the pregnant forty-seven-year-old Maude decides to have an abortion, was opposed by anti-abortion groups who picketed CBS network headquarters in New York City and pressured affiliates to cancel re-runs of the controversial segments. In spite of a loss of advertising revenues and forty affiliate cancellations, CBS refused to back down and reran the episodes, winning praise from Lear. "Because CBS stood up, others eventually will," Lear remarked, as quoted in the Toronto *Globe and Mail* (September 21, 1973). "And because when they stood up no wind blew them down, they will stand up again and again."

The "creative end" of Tandem Productions, Lear is a compulsive sixteen-hours-a-day worker. At CBS Television City in Hollywood, he oversees rehearsals of his shows, particularly *Maude*, making frequent script revisions. Between performances of his programs, he meets with cast and crew to discuss additional script changes. Taking the best scenes from the two live performances, Lear supervises the editing of the final videotape for telecast several weeks later. Searching for fresh approaches to contemporary social issues, he is constantly inventing plot lines for new Tandem series. *Good Times*, a comedy series about a black ghetto family starring Esther Rolle, who played the maid Florida on the *Maude* series, began as a CBS midseason replacement in January 1974. Lear's plans include a weekly dramatic series, an afternoon "soap-opera-comedy," a drama anthology, and the television production of his screenplay based on the life of John Henry Faulk, an author and radio commentator who was blacklisted during the McCarthy era.

Of slight build and medium height, Norman Lear is a dapper man with blue eyes and an oversized, drooping white mustache. Quiet and gentle-mannered, he has the air of melancholy that often hangs like a pall over comedy writers. Lear, who has spent four years in psychoanalysis, often presents young writers with gift certificates for initial professional counseling sessions. He married Frances Loeb, a former buyer for Lord and Taylor, in 1956. The Lears live in a ten-room colonial-style house in Brentwood, California. The couple has two teenaged daughters, Kate and Maggie, and Lear also has one married daughter, Ellen, by his first wife. For recreation, Lear visits New York City, where, in one week, he takes in as many as fifteen stage productions to scout promising actors. As president of the Southern California affiliate of the American Civil Liberties Union Foundation, he regularly writes letters to government officials and others in influential positions. His files contain a voluminous correspondence with the officials of four Presidential administrations.

On May 10, 1973 Lear was named 1972's Broadcaster of the Year by the Independent Radio and Television Society. In his acceptance speech, Lear told the audience of broadcasting and advertising executives that the shift from inane, inoffensive situation comedies to "social opinion in a situation-comedy format" was inevitable. "The so-called adult themes that television is currently dealing in are themes for which the American people have always been ready. We in television simply weren't trusting the people . . . to accept or reject as they saw fit. . . . We, especially in the media, must start to trust the American people more. And to do that, we must begin to trust ourselves."

References

> Broadcasting 41:51 Jl 3 '72 por
> N Y Post p31 F 19 '72 por
> N Y Times Mag p31+ Mr 12 '72 por;
>   p13+ Je 24 '73 por
> Newsweek 78:52+ N 29 '71 por
> Time 100:48+ S 25 '72 pors
> Toronto Globe and Mail p15 S 21 '73

LE CARRÉ, JOHN (le kə-rā')

Oct. 19, 1931- British novelist
Address: c/o Black, Geoghegan and Till, Kingsbourne House, 229/231 High Holborn, London MC1V 7DA, England

In the early 1960's, when Ian Fleming's "imperialist thug" James Bond was still murdering and wenching his way onto the best-seller lists, John le Carré quietly introduced a new image of the British secret agent. Le Carré's spies are tired, lonely, decent men, more likely to be cuckolds than seducers, more interested in literature than baccarat, and justifiably uncertain whether the humane values they defend are more deeply threatened by enemy agents or their own employers. A large sector of the reading public evidently shared his belief that the sun had set on the empire of the glamorous superspy, and welcomed the compassionate subtlety of his characterization, the verisimilitude of his seedy espionage establishments, and the brilliance of his plot-

ting. His third book, *The Spy Who Came in From the Cold* (1963), was one of the most successful British novels published since World War II. By 1974 its worldwide sales were said to be approaching 20,000,000 copies.

Le Carré's next two books, *The Looking-Glass War* (1965) and *A Small Town in Germany* (1968), were also best sellers, but *The Naïve and Sentimental Lover* (1971), the author's first attempt at a "straight" novel, fared less well, and was harshly treated by most critics. *Tinker, Tailor, Soldier, Spy* followed in 1974 and seemed to many reviewers an even better book than *The Spy Who Came in From the Cold*. Le Carré has received the Somerset Maugham Award (1964), the British Crime Novel of the Year Award (1963), and the Edgar Allan Poe award of the Mystery Writers of America, Inc. (1965).

John le Carré is the pseudonym of David John Moore Cornwell. He was born on October 19, 1931 in Poole, Dorset, the son of Ronald Thomas Archibald Cornwell and the former Olive Glassy. His grandfather had been a builder and lay preacher who became mayor of Poole; his father was a wealthy businessman of sporting tastes, who owned racehorses and once sought election to Parliament as a Liberal. Le Carré was educated at St. Andrew's Preparatory School, Pangbourne, in Berkshire, at Sherborne School in Dorset, and elsewhere. In a BBC television interview published in the *Listener* (September 5, 1974), he says that he had "no consistent family life" as a child. "We lived an itinerant life . . . and I went from school to school and developed a very wary eye for each new place that I was attached to." He sees in these experiences the beginnings of that half-admiring, half-horrified fascination with English social institutions that is so important a factor in his books.

A lonely boy, with a great fondness for animals, le Carré wrote his first story at preparatory school—a sad tale about a heroic old racehorse flogged to victory by an unscrupulous jockey. His headmaster thought the story trash, but when considered with hindsight it sounds remarkably like an apprentice version of le Carré stories in which heroic old spies are driven blinkered by their unscrupulous masters into dubious battle. At Sherborne, le Carré has said, his efforts to write were "largely discouraged," although in 1948 he won the school's prize for English verse. He was not happy there and one day simply walked out, never to go back. There followed a year (1948-1949) in Switzerland, where he had relatives, studying French and German at Berne University and learning to ski. Then came his national service, which took him to Vienna with the Army Intelligence Corps—useful training for a future writer of spy stories.

Resuming his education, le Carré read modern languages at Lincoln College, Oxford University. He was married in 1954 to Alison Ann Veronica Sharp, and left the university to teach for a year at a preparatory school, Millfield Junior School in Glastonbury, Somerset. He then returned to Oxford, graduating with a first-class honors degree in 1956. The same year he went as a tutor in French and German to Eton College, the most famous of English public schools, which has for centuries educated and molded the sons of Britain's richest and most powerful families. "In some ways," le Carré said in his BBC interview, "those who knock the upper classes have no idea how awful they are. Eton, at its worst, is unbelievably frightful. It is intolerant, chauvinistic, bigoted, ignorant. At its best, it is enlightened, adaptable, fluent and curiously democratic." In any case, le Carré did not feel that he was intended for a lifetime of teaching, and in 1958 he left Eton, tried without success to make a career as a painter and illustrator, and then for some two years drifted from job to job.

By that time le Carré, an ardent student of Britain's remarkable social institutions, had been able to examine at first hand a generous selection —his own preparatory and public schools, the army, Oxford, and Eton. He added another specimen to his collection in 1960, when he answered an advertisement for late entrants into Her Majesty's Foreign Service. It was then, while commuting by train from Great Missenden in Buckinghamshire to the Foreign Office in London, that he wrote his first book, *Call for the Dead,* published in England by Gollancz (1961) and in the United States by Walker (1962) as written by "John le Carré." Taken from a London shopfront he had once passed on a bus, the pseudonym was used simply because it was not considered proper for Foreign Service officials to publish books under their own names.

Call for the Dead introduced George Smiley of the British secret service, an agent who might have been conceived as the deliberate antithesis of Ian Fleming's James Bond (but was not, according to le Carré, who says merely that the material available to him was "entirely different from the material available to Fleming"). Smiley is plump, bespectacled, middle-aged, and diffident—intellectually and morally attractive, but physically not at all so. He is repeatedly cuckolded by his aristocratic wife, and increasingly disgusted with his profession. Smiley reaches a personal and professional crisis with the apparent suicide of a Foreign Office clerk to whom he has just given security clearance, and the book is an absorbing account of his attempts to resolve his emotional and career problems. *Time's* reviewer was impressed by the novel's atmosphere of "grubby realism and moral squalor, the frazzled, fatigued sensitivity of decent men obliged to betray or kill others no worse than themselves." It was filmed in 1967 under Sidney Lumet's direction as *The Deadly Affair,* with James Mason, Simone Signoret, Harriet Andersson, and Maximilian Schell in the cast.

From 1960 to 1963 le Carré served as second secretary in Great Britain's embassy in Bonn, where he wrote his second book, *A Murder of Quality* (Gollancz, 1962; Walker, 1963). Smiley reappears, conducting a private investigation into the death of a schoolmaster's wife at a great English public school. Anthony Boucher in the New

JOHN LE CARRÉ

York *Times Book Review* (September 8, 1963) called it "a model of the whodunit-of-locale, in which all actions and motivations are conditioned by the setting. . . . Puzzling and well-plotted, it is also an admirably written study in levels of snobbery and cruelty, rich in subtle explorations of character." Indeed a reviewer in the *Times Literary Supplement* (August 31, 1963) thought that, as a murder mystery, the book suffered from an excessive attention to characterization.

Le Carré himself is not much interested in literary classifications of that kind. He acknowledged in his BBC interview that there are thrillers in which "the plot is imposed upon the characters," but he himself favors "the other kind of book where you take one character, you take another character and you put them into collision, and the collision arrives because they have different appetites, and you begin to get the essence of drama. The cat sat on the mat is not a story; the cat sat on the dog's mat is the beginning of an exciting story, and out of the collision, perhaps, there comes a sense of retribution. Now you may call that God, or you may call it the presence of fatalistic forces in society, or you may call it man's inhumanity to man."

That last phenomenon predominates in the book that made le Carré famous, *The Spy Who Came in From the Cold* (Gollancz; Coward-McCann, 1963). Written like its predecessor while le Carré was commuting to work in Bonn, it again features George Smiley, but this time in only a minor role. It tells the story of a fifty-year-old British spy, Alec Leamas, who has been too long in the field. Recalled from Germany after the death at the Berlin Wall of his last East German contact, he is stale, tired, and bitter. All the same, Leamas allows himself to be talked into accepting one last assignment—a pretended defection in which he is cynically deceived by his masters, and spiritually destroyed.

The novel was universally admired for the bleak precision of its prose and the authenticity of its settings and characterization. It addresses itself with a new directness and urgency to the moral problems implicit in the author's first book, raising large questions about espionage, patriotism, and more generally about ends and means; it asks, le Carré says, "How long we can defend ourselves . . . by methods of this kind, and still remain the kind of society that is worth defending?" Widely translated, it became one of the great international best sellers of the 1960's and was successfully filmed, with Richard Burton in the starring role. According to Anthony Boucher in the New York *Times Book Review* (January 12, 1964), *The Spy Who Came In From the Cold* established its author "beside Ambler and Greene in the small rank of writers who can create a novel of significance, while losing none of the excitement of the tale of sheer adventure." It seemed to Graham Greene himself "the best spy story I have ever read."

In 1963 le Carré had left Bonn and gone to Hamburg as consul. The following year, thanks to the success of *The Spy Who Came In From the Cold,* he was able to resign from the Foreign Service and devote himself full-time to writing. He and his family lived abroad for a year, on the island of Crete and then in Vienna, while he wrote *The Looking-Glass War* (Heinemann; Coward-McCann, 1965). That novel is about an obsolescent British espionage establishment and its pathetic attempt to regain its wartime glory with a single coup. Smiley is on hand to pick up the pieces, after the attempt ends in a disaster that to the reader is never for a moment in doubt. *The Looking-Glass War* illustrates even more clearly than *The Spy* le Carré's preoccupation with the way in which the institutions man creates for his own purposes may take on a monstrously antisocial life of their own. It had a mixed reception: a reviewer in the *Times Literary Supplement* (June 24, 1965), for example, found it confused and imprecise, and thought that "the spy thriller in this case just does not seem the right vehicle for [le Carré]," but D. B. Hughes in *Book Week* (August 8, 1965) called it "a superb spy story, unflawed."

During his years at Bonn, le Carré had been one of those responsible for reporting on movements in Germany's internal politics. Out of that experience he wrote *A Small Town in Germany* (Heinemann; Coward-McCann, 1968), in which a British agent named Alan Turner, a working-class avenging angel, arrives at the Bonn embassy to investigate the disappearance of an employee who has apparently absconded with important secret papers. The book was praised both for its evocation of Bonn during the cold war and for what it implies about the British social system, which can produce an elite as able, charming, but ultimately sterile as the diplomats Turner is obliged to deal with. Some reviewers, however, found the plot less compelling than in earlier le Carré books, and Malcolm Muggeridge went so far as to call it "remarkably silly."

More than one critic had speculated that le Carré was growing restive with "the conventions of the thriller genre," and he dispensed with them altogether in *The Naïve and Sentimental Lover* (Hodder & Stoughton; Knopf, 1971). The title derives from Schiller, who said that a poet either *is* nature, and naïve, or *seeks* nature, and is sentimental. The sentimental lover is Aldo Cassidy, a dull businessman with a duller wife, who meets and is swept up in the violent wake of a naïve lover, the wild and protean artist Shamus. Aldo, inevitably, "doth the wingèd life destroy." The book had its defenders, but they were few; most reviewers agreed with the critic in the *Times Literary Supplement* (September 24, 1971) who called it "an unhappy venture in the metaphysics of love" and a "disastrous failure."

In Le Carré's own view, *The Naïve and Sentimental Lover* was less of a departure than its critics thought, since it dealt like its predecessors with a man imprisoned by the institutions he has created—in this case his business and his marriage —and describes his attempt to escape into a more natural way of living. Its reception made him angry, he says, but failed to deject him. He returned to the thriller genre with immense success in *Tinker, Tailor, Soldier, Spy* (Hodder & Stoughton; Knopf, 1974), suggested by the case of the double agent Kim Philby. The chief of British Intelligence is dying, and it suddenly becomes clear that one of the men in the line of succession is a traitor. George Smiley is brought out of an enforced retirement to find out which one.

Tinker, Tailor, Soldier, Spy seemed to most reviewers the best of le Carré's books since *The Spy Who Came in From the Cold*—if not simply the best. Richard Locke, writing in the New York *Times Book Review* (June 30, 1974), called it "a full recovery, which in many ways consolidates le Carré's career." Locke goes on: "Le Carré has learned a lot since he first created Smiley; he now can handle complementary heroes and intertwining plots. . . . In yet a further reclamation of old territory, le Carré also sets the subplot at a public school, which is much more vividly portrayed than that in his second novel. His characterization too has become richer: we meet Cabinet ministers, Whitehall officials, aides, journalists, old office hands; and there is an extremely dextrous off-stage portrait of Smiley's faithless wife. Le Carré has never presented so much detail about the intelligence Establishment, and he moves easily from past to present, from adventure to research to induction, and keeps one guessing right to the end which of the five top men is the double agent."

Le Carré has also published two short stories and a play, *Dare I Weep, Dare I Mourn*, which was produced by ABC Television's Stage 66. The author attributes his exact and elegant style to his training as a civil servant—"certainly the most rigid, the most astringent training" he ever had. He is said to have "a remarkably accurate ear" for dialogue and a sharp eye for visual detail, but maintains that he has "absolutely no geographical sense." Perhaps partly for that reason he makes a practice of photographing the places that feature in his books, especially the buildings around Cambridge Circus in London, where he has located his fictive secret service headquarters. "The face of London changes so quickly," he says. "I want to use all these buildings for future books . . . so I've frozen them and put them in the bank."

John Le Carré is a tall, brown-haired, personable man, and an articulate speaker, accomplished raconteur, and mimic. He has three sons—Simon, Stephen, and Timothy—by his first marriage, which ended in divorce in 1971, and one son, Nicholas, by his 1972 marriage to Jane Eustace. He and his family live in seclusion on a cliff-top near Lands End in Cornwall. Living in England means that the greater part of le Carré's very large income goes to the tax authorities, but England is the source of his material and of his values and he is not inclined to seek a tax haven. "Wouldn't it be the most asinine thing in the world if success *limited* your freedom?," he asked in his BBC interview. Le Carré said in that same interview that he knew, when he had finished writing *The Spy Who Came in From the Cold*, that he "had the makings of some sort of literary or artistic strength." "What makes me go on . . . writing," le Carré added, "is the hope that one day I'll do something I'm really proud of."

References

Life 56:39+ F 28 64 pors
Listener 92:306+ S 5 '74 por
N Y Times Mag p55 S 8 '74 pors
Contemporary Authors 5-8 1st revision, 1969
International Who's Who, 1973-74
Vinson, J. (ed.) Contemporary Novelists, 1972
Who's Who, 1974-75
Who's Who in America, 1972-1973
Writers Directory, 1974-1976

LEE, SHERMAN E(MERY)

Apr. 19, 1918- Museum director
Address: b. The Cleveland Museum of Art, 11150 East Blvd. at University Circle, Cleveland, Ohio 44106; h. 2536 Norfolk Rd., Cleveland, Ohio 44106

"An art museum, when you look closely at it, is a subversive institution," Sherman E. Lee, the director of the Cleveland Museum of Art, once observed. According to Lee, a habitué of art galleries must eventually become "dissatisfied with the world . . . outside." During his more than three decades of experience as a museum administrator, Lee has supervised the growth of the Oriental art collections of the Detroit Institute of Art, the Seattle Art Museum, and the Cleveland Museum of Art. Since coming to the Cleveland Museum of Art in 1952, he has added major works from many periods and styles to that museum's superlative permanent collection. Often described as the "intellectual aristocrat of American museum directors," Lee condemns the fund-

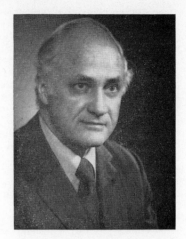

SHERMAN E. LEE

raising galas, crowd-pleasing purchases, and trendy exhibitions favored by some administrators. "Our museum has never been show business nor a therapy," he told David L. Shirey in an interview for *Newsweek* magazine (September 12, 1966). "It is quality and quality alone."

The son of Emery H. I. and Adelia (Baker) Lee, Sherman Emery Lee was born on April 19, 1918 in Seattle, Washington. He attended American University in Washington, D.C., where he obtained a B.A. degree in 1938 and an M.A. degree in 1939. He then enrolled in the doctoral program of Western Reserve University (now Case Western Reserve University) in Cleveland, Ohio, specializing in Far Eastern art, and received his Ph.D. from that institution in 1941.

Later that same year, Lee was appointed curator of Far Eastern art at the Detroit Institute of Art, a post he held until 1946. In 1944 he enlisted for a two-year tour of duty in the United States Naval Reserve, and when World War II ended, he elected to remain in Japan as an advisor on art collections. As the officer in charge of the Arts and Monuments Division, he was attached to General Douglas MacArthur's headquarters in Tokyo from 1946 to 1948. After his return to the United States in 1948, he joined the staff of the Seattle Art Museum, where he served as assistant director and, later, as associate director. At the same time, he lectured in art history at the University of Washington. In 1952 he resigned both positions to become the curator of Oriental art at the Cleveland Museum of Art, a privately endowed museum that first opened its doors to the public on June 16, 1916.

Compared to such venerable institutions as the Metropolitan Museum of Art in New York City and the Museum of Fine Arts in Boston, the Cleveland Museum of Art was not an especially distinguished repository for Oriental art until Dr. Lee's appointment. Under his aggressive but discriminating acquisitions program, the Cleveland staff assembled a large, well-balanced collection of Far Eastern, Indian, and Southeast Asian art that one awe-stricken critic has described as "staggering." The impressive array includes airy landscape scrolls and glazed ceramics dating from the Sung Dynasty, Shang and Chou bronzes, magnificent Cham and Khmer sculpture, Japanese folding screens, and a unique seventeenth-century Mughal manuscript. Commenting on the museum's fiftieth anniversary for *Art in America* (May/June 1966), Joseph Alsop described the collection as "an intoxication of the eye and spirit," and added, "One comes away reeling from the experience." Dr. Lee modestly attributes his astonishing success to an active postwar market in Near Eastern and Far Eastern art objects, to the astronomical price increases and tight market for European art, and to the increased interest in Oriental art in the United States.

While advancing through the ranks of the museum's hierarchy—he was appointed assistant director in 1956, associate director in 1957, and director in 1958—Lee redefined his ambitious acquisitions program to benefit all the departments of the Cleveland Museum of Art. "While there is planning—the strengthening of strengths, the solid replacement of voids, the insistence on high quality and excellent condition—there must also be improvisation . . . ," he explained in an article in the Cleveland Museum of Art *Bulletin* (September 1966). "Like a military campaigner, one begins with strategy, continues with tactics, and ends with responses to local situations. The day is long past when one could determine to have, for example, a really fine collection of Italian High Renaissance painting or Medieval sculpture. But easy despair finds solace in the still continuing, if irregular, appearance of riches on the art markets of the world."

Part of Lee's strategy in the 1960's was to strengthen and expand the museum's small collection of Spanish paintings. To that end, he purchased two superb examples of Spanish art from different periods, Francisco de Goya's *Portrait of the Infante Don Luis de Borbón* and Jusepe de Ribera's *The Death of Adonis,* and, in a brilliant coup, one of the few available full-length paintings by Diego Rodríguez de Silva y Velázquez. When Velázquez's *Portrait of the Jester Calabazas* came up for auction in London in 1965, Lee rushed to Europe to bid on the painting. After consulting with the curator of the Museo del Prado in Madrid and examining x-ray photographs of the painting, he bought the portrait for $518,613.75—considerably less than he was prepared to pay. The painting, restored to its original brilliance by Lee's talented associate, William Suhr, perfectly complemented the museum's growing collection. "It was also a very beautiful picture, which was the fundamental thing," Lee told Robert Ostermann in an interview for the *National Observer* (December 27, 1965).

In his continuing role as curator of Oriental art, Lee added a number of important pieces to the museum's Far Eastern art collection: a pair of six-fold, ink-on-paper screens painted by the sixteenth-century Japanese artist Sesson; a bronze group of Shiva and his consort Parvati; a thirty-inch, wooden figure of a grimacing warrior and its companion piece, a graceful *Amida,* both representative of Japan's Kamakura Period; and a Yüan Dynasty celadon plate with an oxblood dragon design, one of three in existence.

Because he has occasionally been criticized for allegedly neglecting Occidental art in favor of Oriental art, Lee defended his record in the March 1973 issue of the museum's *Bulletin.* From 1958 to 1972, 71.25 percent of the acquisitions budget went toward the purchase of Western art, 16.25 percent for Oriental art, and 12.5 percent for Ancient, African, South Pacific, and Pre-Columbian art. His purchases include Rembrandt van Rijn's *An Old Man Praying,* Antonio Pollaiuolo's *Battle of Naked Men,* an almost intact royal portrait of the pharaoh Amenemhet III carved in black Aswan granite, and a five-by-seven inch, fifteenth-century panel of St. John the Baptist attributed to the Master of Flémalle, which Lee has described as "one of the great coups of acquisition in our century." Nevertheless, he concedes that it is becoming increasingly difficult to assemble a balanced collection due to the "inflationary nature" of the market and the "gradual depletion" of works of art.

Sherman E. Lee sees the functions of a museum as "preservation, exhibition, research, and education." Commenting on the problem of preserving fragile, time-worn art objects for a *Christian Science Monitor* (June 5, 1970) profile, he told interviewer Christopher Andrews: "All works of art are by their very nature condemned to death. . . . But if we expose these works . . . send them on trips . . . [or] bus them out to regional or neighborhood museums, we are . . . hastening that dying. . . . I insist that it is easier to move people than it is to move pictures. . . . People travel thousands of miles to see a football game and I think we have every right to expect that they should do the same thing to see great works of art. This is not because of an elitist or snobbish point of view; I think it really simply is a matter of common sense."

To attract visitors to the museum, Lee recommends free admission and frequent special exhibitions. The Cleveland Museum of Art mounts a major new show every two months as well as the annual "Year in Review" exhibition of all art objects acquired by the museum during that particular year. Among the museum's recent exhibits were "Color and Field," a survey of contemporary painting; "Caravaggio and His Followers," an examination of the influence of Michelangelo Amerighi da Caravaggio on baroque art; "Chinese Art Under the Mongols"; and the superb "Golden Anniversary Acquisitions," a display of more than 200 pieces which, in Dr. Lee's words, celebrated "the *raison d'être* of an art museum: the collection, preservation and display of important, rare, and beautiful works of art."

Unlike several of his counterparts at other major metropolitan museums, Lee steadfastly refuses to transform the Cleveland Museum of Art into an instrument of "social action." For instance, he vetoed the proposed construction of several neighborhood storefront "mini-museums" and opposed a special showing of art by black artists. "I think it's condescending," he explained to Grace Glueck in an interview for *Art in America* (May 1971). "How would it fit in with other exhibitions in terms of quality?" On the other hand, the Cleveland Museum maintains a number of educational branches to encourage museum attendance and featured a traveling exhibition of works by Henry Tanner, the noted Negro impressionist painter. "There are various ways of education," he told students at ceremonies marking the fiftieth anniversary of the Dayton (Ohio) Art Institute, "and appropriate times for its application—in the museum, before and/or after contemplation." Under Lee's guidance, the educational staff of the museum, which includes more than fifty full- and part-time instructors, teaches painting, drawing, puppetry, art history, and art appreciation; conducts film, music, and dance workshops; and sponsors special summer programs for ghetto youngsters. Most of the classes are held in a recently completed, $10,000,000 wing. Designed by Marcel Breuer, the wing includes classrooms, lecture and recital halls, an audio-visual center, a library, and the Gartner Auditorium as well as additional galleries.

To appreciate and understand a work of art, Lee suggests that the viewer adopt what one admiring critic has called a "bifocal approach." In his introduction to the second edition of his *Chinese Landscape Painting* (The Cleveland Museum of Art, 1962), Lee acknowledges that it is impossible for a contemporary museum visitor to know precisely what a painting, a porcelain bowl, or a piece of sculpture meant to those for whom it was created, "but we can discipline ourselves to understand something of that country's approach to her own painting. . . . We can try to see what it was; we see what it is. Both visions are valid." Originally published in 1954, *Chinese Landscape Painting* was the first of nearly a dozen books that Lee has written on Asian art. Covering more than 1,000 years and scores of artists, the book was enthusiastically received by laymen as well as by scholars.

History of Far Eastern Art (Harry N. Abrams, Inc., 1964), the first major English-language survey of Oriental painting, sculpture, architecture and ceramics, is perhaps Lee's most well-known and widely read book. In a lengthy review for *Art in America* (July 1964), Francine du Plessix praised Lee's "well-balanced and beautifully organized" work: "He is least at home in India, a comfortable traveler in China. But when he gets to Japan his prose and his ideas become elevated by the power of love; his history comes alive with richness of background and heightened perceptiveness." Most recently, Lee wrote *The Colors of Ink* (The Asia Society, 1974), the descriptive catalog of a special exhibition of classical Chinese paintings on silk and paper at the Asia House gallery in New York City. He contributes to a number of art magazines and scholarly journals, such as *The Burlington Magazine*, the *Journal of*

Aesthetics and Art Criticism, Art Quarterly, and *Ars Orientalis.*

Long interested in establishing an international communications network among the world's museum directors, Lee, as president of the Association of Art Museum Directors, arranged a curator exchange program for museums in the United States, Europe, and Asia. In November 1973 he headed an American delegation of twelve specialists in Oriental art during a month's visit to the People's Republic of China. In addition to discharging his duties as director of the Cleveland Museum of Art, he has been a professor of art at Case Western Reserve University since 1962 and has lectured at many colleges, art schools, museums, and galleries. He is the vice-chairman of the National Council for the Humanities, a member of the American Association of Museums, the American Academy of Arts and Sciences, the American Oriental Society, and the College Art Association. Lee is the recipient of the Swedish Order of the North Star and is a Chevalier of the Legion of Honor.

Sherman Emery Lee and the former Ruth A. Ward were married on September 3, 1938 and have four children: Katharine, Margaret, Elizabeth, and Thomas. An urbane, handsome, grayhaired man, Lee epitomizes the popular image of the art collector and connoisseur. "Not a few of the errors of connoisseurship in the past have resulted from the passion for big names," he wrote by way of advice, in *The Burlington Magazine* (May 1972). "The illustration of the history of art with originals is an expensive and often foolish industry. The Chê school of Ming painting is well represented in Japan and the United States because the owners of these works were convinced they were acquiring masterpieces by . . . Southern Sung masters." He has often cautioned would-be collectors to ignore an art object's monetary value and concentrate on its aesthetic appeal. "If you keep looking at it and it still gives you a bang, that's a good sign."

References

Christian Sci Mon p8 Je 5 '70 por
Newsweek 68:96+ S 12 '66 por
Who's Who in America, 1972-73
Who's Who in American Art, 1973

LINK, EDWIN (ALBERT)

July 26, 1904- Oceanologist; inventor; industrialist
Address: h. 10 Avon Rd., Binghamton, N.Y. 13905

The human race's occupation and exploitation of the ocean floor has been brought a giant step closer by the tireless efforts of Edwin Link, inventor of aquanautic devices, from improved diving equipment and versatile submarine vehicles to underwater housing. Before turning to oceanography and oceanology—the term now increasingly used for marine engineering—Link was a pioneer-

EDWIN LINK

ing creator of simulator pilot trainers, blind-flying instruments, and other avionic devices. He is the founder of the Link divisions of the General Precision Equipment Corporation and Ocean Systems Inc.

"If man could work freely on the world's continental shelves, an area the size of Africa would be added to his world . . . ," Link has pointed out. "Riches await us under the sea . . . and we can harvest them. If three-quarters of our planet awaits us, the great age of discovery did not end with Columbus, Magellan, or Cook. It may well lie in the future." One of Link's colleagues has observed, "We're like Lewis and Clark crossing the Rockies. We don't know what all is down there on the ocean floor, but we're making it possible to live and work there."

Edwin Albert Link was born in Huntington, Indiana on July 26, 1904 to Edwin A. and Katherine (Martin) Link. He grew up in Binghamton, New York, where he attended public schools and the Lindsley Institute. While working at the organ and piano factory his father ran in Binghamton, he pursued flying as a hobby and eventually earned a commercial pilot's license, in 1927.

Learning to fly even the simple planes of the 1920's required hours in the air, at a minimum cost of $25 an hour. In 1929, with his brother George, Link built a cockpit-like contraption, with a simulated instrument panel and control stick, and offered training at bargain rates. He manufactured additional simulators for sale, but there were few customers until 1934, when the United States Army Air Corps was, without notice, given the task of transporting air mail. The corps's pilots, taught to watch the ground while flying, found it difficult to cope with the rigors of sustained flight in inclement weather, and many lost their lives in crack-ups. To give its men a good, safe grounding in instrument flying, the corps began using Link trainers.

From then on, Link's enterprise expanded rapidly. In 1935 he founded Link Aviation Inc., with headquarters in Binghamton, and he was president of that company for eighteen years.

During those years, Link simulators enabled more than two million military and commercial pilots to get the feel of flying while still on the ground. The AN-T-18 Basic Instrument Trainer, popularly known as the Blue Box, was standard in the training procedure for American and Allied pilots during World War II. In the postwar years, as planes became more sophisticated, so did Link Aviation's research and development. Later Link expanded beyond avionics to meet such needs as transpolar navigation and missile-firing controls, which were eventually applied to space shots.

In 1954 Link Aviation Inc., became a subsidiary of the General Precision Equipment Company, a conglomerate involved in the manufacture of missile parts and industrial control devices, among many other items. Link became president of General Precision in 1958, when the company's sales were near the $200,000,000 mark, and he remained in that position for approximately a year.

In June 1958, shortly after assuming the presidency of General Precision, Link announced that the company had developed HIDAN (High Density Air Navigation), a system of air traffic control entirely independent of fallible ground signals. In a statement to the press he explained that the new system was designed, in conjunction with flight plans, to lessen the likelihood of aircraft collisions. "Airplanes have no quick and simple way of determining accurately by their own instruments the angle of drift caused by the wind or their true ground speed, and hence have no constant check on their exact positions," he said. "They have to rely on periodic positions from ground-based equipment. But at the speeds of modern flying, aircraft cannot continue long to depend principally on ground-controlled navigation. There is too much room for error and too little time for computation and correction." The HIDAN instrument, a two-cubic-foot black box, would automatically calculate any divergence of the aircraft from its planned position and enable the pilot to correct the dangerous situation.

Three months later, in September 1958, Link and his associates installed in the United Air Lines flight school in Denver, Colorado a $1,000,000 trainer simulating the interior of a Douglas DC-8 jet airliner cockpit. Other major airlines soon bought the jet trainer, which enabled them to school their pilots for $36 per hour on the ground as opposed to $1,000 an hour in the air. As the United States space program progressed, Link and General Precision directed their attention to the development of astronautic as well as avionic devices.

But Link was really more interested in hydro-space than outer space. For many years skindiving had been a hobby of his, and during the 1950's that hobby took a practical turn. In April 1955 he and his wife, also a diver, found in the coral reef in Cape Haitien Bay, Haiti an anchor believed to be from Columbus' flagship, the *Santa Maria*. Four years later, in August 1959, off Mexico's Yucatan Peninsula, Link recovered relics from the ruins of one of the treasure ships of Spanish conquistador Hernando Cortez.

One of the earliest salvage ships owned by Link was the *Monadnock*, which he rented out to the William J. Cari American Salvage Company. Later he codeveloped a bullet-shaped underwater scooter, designed to tow a diver along behind it. The first vessel built from keel up specifically for underwater archaeology was the *Sea Diver*, designed by Link and built in 1959. That 164-ton, ninety-one-foot motor cruiser was used by Link in exploring the sunken Biblical harbor city of Caesarea, off the coast of Israel, in May 1960. That exploration yielded ancient jewelry, pottery, and mosaic tiles, among other precious items.

With two of his long-time associates, Gunne Lowkrantz and Karl A. Kail, Link invented the "Shark," a mobile, unmanned television apparatus patented in December 1960. So named because of its appearance, the Shark was designed to probe the sea bottom and send pictures up to the mother ship via cable. Link used it extensively in undersea archaeological research along the Florida coast in the early 1960's.

Link's archaeological work eventually led him to an area of interest of much more significance for man's future, the occupation of the continental shelves, the submerged land masses that slope out from the world's continents. As population, food, and energy problems have become more pressing, the untapped potential of these offshore plateaus, comprising more than 10,000,000 square miles, has become more obvious. Petroleum and mineral deposits, known and unknown, might be exploited, aquaculture, or undersea agriculture, might be widely practised, and fish might be herded like cattle—if men could travel to the ocean depths more easily and live and work there for prolonged periods.

To facilitate deep-sea exploration and exploitation, Link designed underwater breathing devices to combat the "bends" and other dangerous somatic side-effects, a heated diving suit, and an aluminum diving chamber that also serves as a decompressor, among other inventions. But something more was needed, as he explained to a reporter on one occasion: "What I am seeking is a practical way of staying at great depths long enough to do something useful. . . . By putting up portable, inflated living quarters on the ocean floor and using diving chambers as 'elevators' to take men down and bring them up . . . we could maintain underwater forces on the continental shelf long enough to do a job. If they could stay down for days or weeks, there would be only one time-consuming decompression period when they come up."

By the summer of 1963 Link's SPID (Submersible, Portable, Inflatable Dwelling) was ready for testing. A sturdy, metal-weighted balloon with a rubber sleeve underneath for entrance and exit, it was, when inflated, nine feet long and six feet high. With two bunks, a hot plate, and other conveniences, it could serve as a home base for undersea workers, a living compartment where they might sleep, eat, and relax. It was air-conditioned, so that the occupants would have

to don face masks only when leaving for their outside work. SPID was first tested on the bottom of the Potomac River in Washington, D.C. in August 1963, when Link himself entered the dwelling, took off his diving mask, and spent half an hour inside. A year later Jon Lindbergh and Robert Stenuit spent ninety-four hours in SPID 430 feet underwater off the Bahamas.

The first major United States company solely dedicated to the development of mineral and petroleum resources on the continental shelf was Ocean Systems Inc., formed by Link, the General Precision Equipment Corporation (from which he had already retired as an executive officer), and the Union Carbide Corporation in 1965. For Ocean Systems, Link designed *Deep Diver*, a little submarine, a sort of undersea Jeep, which may be parked on the ocean bottom at any time and place the occupants wish to disembark for exploration or work. The versatile sub, first tested off Grand Bahama Island early in 1967, can operate at a maximum depth of 1,250 feet and be used in connection with an underwater dwelling and workshop. Its potential uses include repair and splicing of transoceanic cables and offshore oil prospecting and drilling.

Link has pointed out that by extending his technology from a depth of 400 feet to levels of 5,000 feet beneath the sea, man would have access to another 10 percent of the earth's surface, an area roughly equivalent to the surface of the moon. In the late 1960's descents to 1,000 feet were being simulated in Ocean System's high pressure tanks at Tonawanda, New York. At the same time Link was developing a "rotorless helicopter" able to "fly" four occupants down to a maximum depth of 1,500 feet. That odd-looking vehicle, called *Sea Link*, began operating as an oceanographic research vessel for the Smithsonian Institution in 1971. Two years later, in June 1973, it was on a routine mission off of Key West, Florida when tragedy struck. Scouting around a sunken Navy destroyer, the *Fred T. Berry*, it became entangled in the old ship's debris and cables. When it was finally extricated, after thirty-one hours, two of the four crew members were dead of CO_2 poisoning. They were Al Stover and Link's son, Edwin Clayton.

Edwin Link is a big man with a tanned face, a balding head, a quiet, self-effacing manner, and, as one reporter noted, nerves of "steel." In semiretirement, he remains a director of and consultant to the Link division of General Precision Equipment Corporation, with offices in Binghamton. He is a trustee of the Woods Hole Oceanographic Institution, a director of the Binghamton First-City National Bank, and an adviser to various governmental and private agencies concerned with oceanography and oceanology. His honors include the Exceptional Service Award of the United States Air Force and the Brewer Trophy. He is a member of several professional organizations and of the Binghamton, University, and New York Yacht clubs. With Philip Van Horn Weems, Link wrote *Simplified Celestial Navigation* (Weems System, 1940).

The multimillionaire oceanologist and his wife, the former Marion Clayton, were married on June 6, 1931. They have one surviving son, William Martin. When their other son died aboard *Sea Link*, the Links were heartbroken, but brave. "We're not going to stop," Edwin Link declared at that time. "This shows the magnitude of the problem and the challenge." Marion Link said: "We are going to learn as much from this as we can—and then just go forward."

References

Newsweek 82:44+ Jl 2 '73 por
This Week p7 F 13 '66 por
Time 72:80+ S 22 '58 por
Washington Post B p1+ Ag 20 '63 por
Link, Marion C. Windows in the Sea (1973)
Who's Who in America, 1972-73

LOEB, WILLIAM

Dec. 26, 1905- Newspaper publisher
Address: b. 35 Amherst St., Manchester, N.H. 03105; h. 1750 Skyline Blvd., Reno, Nev. 89502; Prides Crossing, Mass. 01965

The Manchester *Union Leader* (circulation 64,000), the dominant newspaper in New Hampshire, becomes a national force once every four years, when candidates for the United States Presidential nomination go to the Granite State for the first of their primary-election battles. Outspoken William Loeb, the publisher and chief editorialist of the *Union Leader* since 1946, is a crusty but idealistic conservative of the old-fashioned school who backs only those candidates who share his view that the United States government should carry a big stick abroad and a small one at home. For example, he supported the candidacies of Barry Goldwater and Richard Nixon (until Nixon's rapprochement with China and the Soviet Union). Among Democrats he has generally been able to find his ilk only in such long shots as Sam Yorty, whom he persuaded to run in 1972.

While some outsiders may consider Loeb harmlessly quixotic, people within the state are well aware of his wide influence, and he is generally acknowledged to be the man most responsible for Senator Edmund Muskie's failure to gain the Democratic Presidential nomination in 1972. Locally, Loeb's editorial energy is directed chiefly against taxation, governmental skulduggery, and political cant. The controversial publisher owns several other New England newspapers, but he concentrates his attention on the *Union Leader*. The other papers are virtually autonomous, running his hard-hitting front-page editorial columns only on special occasions.

William Loeb 3d has described himself as both a "nineteenth century liberal" and a "Teddy Roosevelt conservative." When he was born in Washington, D.C. on December 26, 1905, his father, William Loeb Jr., was the private secretary and trusted confidant of President Theodore

Roosevelt. Mr. and Mrs. Roosevelt were the godparents at his christening, and the hero of San Juan Hill not only exerted a close, constant influence on him throughout his formative years but remains his exemplar to this day.

Loeb's mother was Katharine W. (Dorr) Loeb. An only child, Loeb grew up in Washington and on his parent's estate in Oyster Bay, Long Island, near the Sagamore Hill residence to which Roosevelt retired. After leaving the White House, Loeb's father headed the New York Customs House and later became president of the Yukon Gold Company.

Loeb was educated at the Hotchkiss School and at Williams College, where he was an honor student in philosophy. At Williams he resigned from a social fraternity in protest against its refusal to admit a Jewish applicant, and he again created a stir when he invited William F. Green, the president of the American Federation of Labor, then considered a "radical" organization, to address a student group.

Loeb's journalistic career began while he was still in college. Besides editing the campus newspaper, he worked part time as a reporter for papers in Springfield, Massachusetts and as a stringer for the New York *World*. But he was unsure of his vocation until, after taking his B.A. degree at Williams, in 1927, he had put in two years of study at the Harvard University School of Law. He began full-time journalistic work as a reporter with the Hearst National News Service. During the 1930's he held a number of reporting jobs and, in between them, was employed in sales and public relations.

Even as a cub reporter Loeb displayed the fervent, single-minded idealism that is a distinguishing feature of his personality. Assigned to cover a round-table discussion on the question of independence for India, he was outraged to see that the chairman of the meeting was a leading British colonialist. Abandoning his newsman's objectivity, he began vociferously to take part in the discussion, and his rash intrusion might have cost him his job if an older colleague had not restrained him.

When Japan invaded China in 1937, Loeb joined an organization advocating a boycott of Japanese goods. The group, it turned out, was Marxist. Embarrassed and angry at being duped by a "Communist front," he from that time on used his "special knowledge" of the Communist party to fight the "Communist conspiracy." Discussing the time he "infiltrated the Communist party" in an interview with Bill Kovach for the New York *Times Magazine* (December 12, 1971), he said: "I guess seen from the viewpoint of that age I was an idealist, but seen from the viewpoint of today, I'm called reactionary. I just haven't changed much from those days."

In 1941, in fulfillment of a long-standing ambition, Loeb, with the financial assistance of his mother, bought the small St. Albans (Vermont) *Daily Messenger,* and the following year he acquired the Burlington (Massachusetts) *Daily News.* He bought into the Manchester *Union*

Leader in 1946 and gained complete control of the paper two years later. In 1948 he also acquired what is now the Sunday edition of the *Union Leader*, the New Hampshire *Sunday News*.

In his article in the New York *Times Magazine* Bill Kovach described Manchester at the time of Loeb's arrival as "a defeated town," explaining: "The [textile] mills had dwindled. . . . Left behind were row after row of company houses attesting to a culture of paternalism among the predominantly French-Canadian mill workers. They had been conditioned by work and the Catholic religion to look to a higher authority for leadership. Loeb quickly turned the paper into an aggressive watchdog, exposing waste in government, conflicts of interest, and rigged bidding. Investigative reporters—well-paid and devoted to the publisher—dug out stories to embarrass political enemies."

Loeb founded the Haverhill (Massachusetts) *Journal* in 1957, when the city's only other paper, the *Gazette*, was gravely weakened by protracted labor difficulties. A bitter war between the two competing papers ensued, and in 1958 the *Gazette* was purchased by a group of anti-Loeb New England publishers who had borne a grudge against him ever since the Boston newspaper strike of 1957, during which he increased the pressrun of the *Union Leader* in order to supply the news-hungry big city. Loeb was eventually sued for violation of the antitrust laws because of his effort to entice Haverhill merchants, through cash rewards, into signing exclusive long-term advertising contracts with the *Journal*. He was fined approximately $3,000,000, an amount which he managed to raise only through a loan from the pension fund of the Teamsters' Union. According to many observers, that loan, which is still not fully repaid, is the explanation for Loeb's staunch backing of former Teamster president James R. Hoffa during his long court duel with Robert F. Kennedy and his subsequent successful effort to gain a parole.

In the early 1950's Loeb's favorite candidate for the Republican Presidential nomination was Robert Taft (he never forgave Dwight Eisenhower for displacing Taft) and he expressed admiration for Senator Joseph McCarthy. In 1964 he supported Barry Goldwater while dismissing Nelson Rockefeller as a "wife swapper." Four years later he hurled the epithet "skunk's skunk's skunk" at Eugene J. McCarthy, and his harsh words over the years about the Kennedys finally brought a rejoinder from Robert F. Kennedy: "If there's anyone more reckless with the truth, I don't know him."

When Loeb headed the Coordinating Committee for Fundamental Human Freedoms, a lobby against the 1963 Civil Rights Act, an inter-religious group headed by Father Philip Kenney took out ads in the *Union Leader* to charge that Loeb's policies "undercut the social gospel of the church" and fostered "an atmosphere of hatred, bigotry, and racism." Throughout the remainder of the 1960's Loeb retaliated by attacking the "pulpit politics" of Father Kenney and other priests and

WILLIAM LOEB

ministers like him. In 1971 Loeb's editorials against socially and politically militant clergy reached such intensity that the Roman Catholic Bishop of Manchester, who had tried to remain aloof from the struggle, was forced to speak out in defense of his priests and the social mission of the church. (The Bishop's action was a rare act for a man in the public eye in New Hampshire, where Loeb had been generally considered sacrosanct.)

Senator Muskie, the front-running Democratic candidate for the Presidency in 1972, was thrown out of the race primarily on the basis of two items in the *Union Leader*. One was a letter appearing in the *Union Leader* on February 24, 1972, eleven days before the primary. Datelined Deerfield Beach, Florida, the letter was signed by one "Paul Morrison," who has never been located. In the letter "Morrison" suggested that Muskie in an offhand campaign remark in Florida had mocked "Canucks," and he, "Morrison," not being from New England, wondered what he meant. Since 60 percent of the voters in Manchester are of French-Canadian descent, and the Manchester vote swings the state, the alleged insult was devastating to Muskie's chances, which were diminished further by a front-page editorial, some of it in capital letters, calling attention to the letter. Investigative reporters for the Washington *Post* later reported that the letter had been fabricated by White House aide Ken Clawson. According to James M. Perry in *Us and Them: How the Press Covered the 1972 Election* (1973), Clawson had been in personal contact with B. J. McQuaid, editor in chief of Loeb's paper.

The destruction of Muskie's candidacy was clinched on the following day by a guest editorial (actually a reprint of a breezy society column item from *Women's Wear Daily* via *Newsweek*). In it Mrs. Muskie was quoted as saying to reporters and aides such things as, "Let's tell dirty jokes" and "I can't mix booze and wine." On Saturday, February 26, Muskie, standing in the Manchester snow, branded the "Morrison" letter "a lie" and then, as he defended his wife ("a good woman . . .") he broke repeatedly into sobs and tears. Recovering, he said of Loeb: "This man doesn't walk. He crawls. . . . It's an insult to the people of New Hampshire that you have to pick up this rotten newspaper every morning."

In his irascible editorials he demonstrates his showmanship and iconoclasm in a style that is unadorned and aggressive. He pulls no punches, especially in the front-page editorials, which are often printed in three colors, with an idiosyncratic variety of typefaces and formats. Among other quirks, Loeb persists in spelling the word "Negro" with a lower-case "n" and he occasionally publishes lists of registered voters who fail to turn out for elections. His political views are intense and unequivocal and his hatreds well-delineated, but he keeps his paper's letters section open to expressions of other opinions. It is generally estimated that the *Union Leader* prints more letters-to-the-editor than any other paper in the country.

As an employer, Loeb is innovative and fair-minded, admired by those who work for him. He was one of the first newspaper publishers in the United States to introduce profit sharing. Fifty percent of the paper's profits go to the employees, and half of Loeb's 50 percent is contributed to the pension fund. The terms of Loeb's will provide that the paper's staff will inherit the *Union Leader* after he and his wife die.

In state politics Loeb's backing of conservative candidates in his own image has had such a divisive influence on the Democratic party that the electoral spoils usually fall to a coalition of upstate Republicans and maverick Democrats. But he has a major influence on issues. "The result," one leading Democrat was quoted as saying by Kovach in his *Times Magazine* article, "is that a campaign on the state level never revolves around services, but always around taxes." New Hampshire is the only state in the Union without a sales or income tax.

The late syndicated columnist George Sokolsky once observed that Loeb "will take on any fight for human liberty if it is not a phony." A true believer in absolute verities, he sees himself as a sort of last-bastion defender of the traditional American way of life. More complicated than his opponents tend to acknowledge, he is at once a vigilant anti-Communist who sees Red encroachments everywhere and a staunch supporter of the labor movement. While condemning such far-right organizations as the John Birch Society—whose head, Robert Welch, he once described as a "bloody nut"—he once worked unsuccessfully to establish a new conservative political party. A writer for *Newsweek* (February 28, 1972) described him as opposed to "almost the entire political spectrum to the left of Louis XIV." Loeb has said that he deliberately aims at the extreme, the controversial, and the shocking in his editorials in order to "stir the pot" of thinking and discussion about issues and personalities. "We believe that the electorate has the right to see every political candidate at his worst as well as at his cellophane-wrapped, pre-packaged best," he once asserted.

Loeb is a trustee of the Lahey Clinic Fund and a director of the National Rifle Association of America and of the American China Policy Association. He served as president of the latter group from 1941 to 1943. A former secretary of the American Foundation for Tropical Medicine (1940-44) and chairman of the Council of Profit-Sharing Industries (1949-52), he has also served as national chairman of the Coordinating Committee for Fundamental American Freedoms. On May 10, 1972 at its annual awards banquet, the National Economic Council honored him as an outstanding American conservative.

William Loeb has been married three times and divorced twice. By his second wife, Eleanor McAlister, he has one daughter, Penelope. He has two other daughters, Elizabeth and Edith, by his present wife, the former Nackey Scripps, a painter, sculptress, and horsewoman and a granddaughter and heir of Edward Wyllis Scripps, the founder of the Scripps-Howard newspaper syndicate. Before his present marriage, Loeb was jailed briefly in connection with an alienation-of-affection suit brought against him by the current Mrs. Loeb's first husband, New York businessman George Gallowhur.

Standing about five feet nine inches tall and weighing a solid 160 pounds, Loeb is brown eyed and bald, and he has thick, prominent eyebrows. Some see in him a resemblance to Little Orphan Annie's Daddy Warbucks. Although his editorials are noted for their blunt and fiery invective, all who have met him agree that Loeb is a soft-spoken, gentle, sincere, and personally charming man in private.

Loeb and his wife maintain two homes: their legal residence, a ranch near Reno, Nevada, and their New England dwelling, a 30-room neo-Tudor mansion on a 100-acre estate in Prides Crossing, Massachusetts. The latter is well protected by an elaborate arsenal of security devices, and both Loeb and Mrs. Loeb usually carry firearms on their persons. Loeb's favorite recreations, in which he is usually joined by his wife, are skiing, horseback riding, tennis, trap shooting, goose shooting, and salmon fishing. He is a member of Zeta Psi, the Seawanhaka Corinthian Yacht Club in Oyster Bay, the Harvard Club of Boston, and the Prospectors' Club in Reno. Raised in the Episcopal Church, he became a Baptist in 1952 because he was attracted to the Baptist Church's fundamentalism. In some quarters Loeb has been mistaken for a Jew because of his name and his support of Israel, which he considers, "like the United States, a bulwark against the heathen, non-Christian world."

References

N Y Times p14 F 21 '72 por
N Y Times Mag p14+ D 12 '71 por
Newsweek 79:51+ F 28 '72 por
Time 99:38 Ja 31 '72 por
Wall St J p1+ O 30 '68 por
Washington Post A p1+ S 7 '70 por; A p1+ Mr 1 '72
Who's Who in America, 1973-74

LON NOL

Nov. 13, 1913- Khmer Head of State
Address: b. Office of the President, Phnom
Penh, Khmer Republic

In his forty years of government service, Lon Nol,
the first President of the Khmer Republic that
superseded the 1,100-year-old Kingdom of Cambodia on October 9, 1970, has held an assortment
of judicial, military, and administrative posts.
President Lon, a six-star general, served as Prince
Norodom Sihanouk's Premier and Defense Minister before conspiring with other disaffected anti-
Communist officials to oust the neutralist prince
in March 1970. Since the coup, Lon's government
has watched helplessly while the steadily increasing strength of the Khmer Rouge—the blanket
term covering several opposition groups, including indigenous Communists, Sihanouk loyalists,
Hanoi-trained Cambodians, and freebooters—
eroded Phnom Penh's sphere of influence. As of
mid-1973, the insurgents controlled more than 75
percent of the land and nearly half the civilian
population. Inflation, governmental corruption, administrative disorganization, military incompe-
tence, and the devastating effects of years of B-52
bombing strikes have compounded President
Lon's difficulties. Although the eccentric, deeply
religious general initially enjoyed some measure
of public acceptance, his apparent inability to
deal with Cambodia's pressing economic problems
and repeated enemy assaults on the capital has
prompted criticism that democratic government
under Lon Nol is merely "Sihanoukism without
Sihanouk."

Of Khmer and Chinese ancestry, Lon Nol, one
of several children, was born in the southern
province of Preyveng, near the Vietnamese border, on November 13, 1913. His grandfather had
been the provincial governor of Preyveng; his
father, Lon Hin, was a minor government official in the provincial capital. After attending elementary school in Phnom Penh, Lon Nol enrolled
at the Lycée Chasseloup-Laubat in Saigon, an
upper-class secondary school also attended by
Prince Norodom Sihanouk and other members of
Cambodia's royal family and by Sisowath Sirik
Matak, who was to become one of Lon's most
trusted advisers. A devotee of French colonial
culture, Lon Nol, in his six years at the Saigon
school, refrained from taking part in the frequent
anti-French demonstrations. Although his classmates remember him as an earnest, diligent, and
religious student, he also enjoyed sports, especially boxing and soccer.

On graduating from the *lycée* in 1934, Lon Nol
entered the civil service, accepting a post as a
magistrate at Siem Reap, a town near the temple
ruins of Angkor Wat. Transferring to the administrative service in 1937, Lon rose quickly through
the ranks to the governorships of Kratie and Battambang provinces, where he gained recognition
as a pacification expert. He was appointed head
of administrative services for the state in 1949

LON NOL

and, two years later, chief of the national police
force. Commissioned as a lieutenant colonel in
1952, Lon, who led his infantry battalion in several successful campaigns against Vietminh guerrillas, joined the first class of the Khmer Royal
Military Academy in 1954. The general secretary
of the Renewal party, Lon supported Prince
Sihanouk, who had renounced his throne in favor
of a more participatory role in Cambodian government, in the 1955 legislative elections. Sihanouk rewarded Lon's support with a succession
of military and cabinet posts, among them army
chief of staff, commander-in-chief of the Khmer
Royal Armed Forces, Deputy Premier, and Minister of National Defense in each of Sihanouk's
many cabinets from 1955 to 1966.

Elected Premier in 1966, Lon originated a far-
reaching program of direct assistance to the Cambodian peasant farmers. To publicize his unprecedented program, he labored in the rice paddies, always making sure that he was accompanied by
members of the press corps. When disputes over
land ownership erupted in the agricultural province
of Battambang, Sihanouk, acting through Premier
Lon, ordered a crackdown on the rebellious farmers
and on the leftist members of parliament who encouraged their revolt. When the rebellion had been
quelled, Sihanouk forced Lon's resignation, in an
attempt to pacify his political critics. Returning to
the government as Defense Minister several
months later, Lon cautiously followed Sihanouk's
nonpartisan position. In August 1968 he guided
newsmen to Ratanakiri province in northeastern
Cambodia to disprove American allegations that
North Vietnamese troops were transporting maté-
riel from Laos to South Vietnam through the
sparsely populated, jungle-infested area. A few
months later, he submitted a detailed report of
widespread Communist activities in that sector.

When deteriorating economic conditions, the
result of North Vietnamese encroachments originally sanctioned by Sihanouk, forced the prince
to form a new government, he chose Lon Nol to
succeed the retiring Premier, Penn Nouth. Before

accepting the position, Lon demanded substantial administrative powers, including the authority to select his own ministers. Sihanouk's ready acquiescence to Lon's conditions was interpreted by some observers as a successful bloodless coup.

Taking office on August 12, 1969, Lon announced immediate measures to denationalize certain sectors of the economy, such as the chemical and petroleum industries; to facilitate private investment; to encourage the establishment of foreign bank branches; to ease trade restrictions; and to coin new money to discourage the Viet Cong from using counterfeit *riels* to purchase supplies. Working with his Minister of the Interior, Sisowath Sirik Matak, Lon drafted new laws to funnel taxes directly into the treasury rather than into the office of the chief of state. Also he closed the state-owned gambling casino, which earned enormous sums of money for corrupt high government officials, including members of Sihanouk's family.

While Sihanouk was abroad on one of his periodic "cures," General Lon met with the governors of Cambodia's nineteen provinces, many of whom openly objected to the prince's tolerance of North Vietnamese and Viet Cong troops on Cambodian soil, and encouraged "spontaneous" anti-Vietnamese demonstrations to force the Hanoi government to restrict Communist activity within Cambodia. According to Laura Summers, writing in *Current History* (December 1972), that well-orchestrated "propaganda campaign [was designed] to aggravate racial tensions between Khmers and Vietnamese for the dual objectives of mobilizing support for the coup and soliciting military aid from the United States."

The campaign had its desired effect. Cambodian dissidents burned the North Vietnamese and National Liberation Front Embassies and much of the Vietnamese quarter in Phnom Penh and engaged in similar activity in the border provinces. In a retaliatory attack by the Vietnamese, Lon's younger brother Lon Nil, a provincial police commissioner, was killed and—according to some reports—cannibalized. Lon demanded the immediate withdrawal of all Vietnamese troops from Cambodian territory. Charging that Sihanouk's appeasement of Hanoi had resulted in a political and economic crisis, the National Assembly, on March 18, 1970, unanimously declared "no confidence" in the Sihanouk government and voted "full power" to Premier Lon Nol.

In an interview with newsmen on March 23, General Lon justified the "constitutional" overthrow of Sihanouk with the contention that the former ruler had a "tendency not to respect" Cambodia's neutrality and territorial sovereignty. Indicating his determination to maintain a position of "active neutrality," Lon appealed to Great Britain and the Soviet Union, cochairmen of the Geneva Convention, to enforce the 1954 accords that guaranteed Cambodian neutrality, invited assistance from the International Control Commission, which Sihanouk suspended in 1969, and asked that the Communists demonstrate a willingness to negotiate. To strengthen his position,

Lon initiated a media campaign to discredit the Sihanouk regime, intimidated or jailed pro-Sihanouk citizens, prescribed curfews, mobilized army reservists and veterans, and met with leaders of all political persuasions to outline his programs and enlist their support. Surprised by the swift coup, many diplomatic observers regarded the ouster as evidence of a strong anti-Communist, pro-Western sentiment in Cambodia. Veteran war correspondent Robert Shaplen, in his "Letter From Indo-China" in the *New Yorker* (May 9, 1970), interpreted the coup as "an unexpected psychological boost" for the Communists—"similar to the one they received from the Tet offensive, and at far less physical cost."

In a series of carefully worded public announcements, the Lon Nol government, asserting its "neutrality," vigorously protested the increased bombing and shelling of Cambodian border areas by United States and South Vietnamese troops. Believing that properly equipped Cambodians, eager to defend their homeland from its ancient enemy, could repel the insurgents, Lon initially refused offers of direct military assistance other than the donation of weapons by "friendly countries." When Communist forces moved to within artillery range of Phnom Penh in April, Lon amended his statement and welcomed "all unconditional foreign aid from all sources." Specifically, he appealed to President Richard M. Nixon, requesting arms, ammunition, and several detachments of the ruthless American-trained and-equipped Cambodian mercenaries who fought with United States Special Forces units in South Vietnam. Having been uninformed of the impending allied invasion of Cambodia in May 1970, General Lon termed the operation a "violation" of Cambodian territorial integrity and suggested that the United States was behaving "a little like the Vietcong." He later conceded that the invasion had been a "positive" response to his personal appeal for assistance and that its immediate effect had been "favorable."

Faced with the task of leading Sihanouk's army of 35,000 lackadaisical soldiers, who were more accustomed to performing as extras in one of the Prince's cinematic extravaganzas than to defending a strategic military position, Premier Lon played upon Khmer racial and religious pride and quickly recruited 150,000 men to defend Buddhism against the "atheist Vietnamese Communist aggressors." To indoctrinate his young recruits, he prepared a military manual of Buddhist aphorisms. Calling upon his experience as a provincial governor, he organized "community development" or pacification programs to discourage enemy recruitment. He optimistically devised a long-range military strategy to defend "the essential Cambodia"—Phnom Penh, the seaports, and vital transport routes—regain territory lost to the insurgents, and expel the Communists.

Hauled to the front in civilian buses and commandeered soft-drink trucks, the ill-equipped, inexperienced government soldiers were no match for the battle-toughened Communist guerrillas. In a December 1971 operation known as Tchenla II, government troops who were attempting to advance into enemy-occupied areas of northeastern Cambodia were defeated by the Khmer Rouge. Many government soldiers, refusing to fight other Khmers, fled to Phnom Penh; others defected. In Laura Summers' view, "Tchenla II marked the turning point in the Cambodian war because it was a political as well as a military defeat for Lon Nol; it signalled the beginning of widespread public recognition of civil war." In spite of increasing evidence to the contrary, Lon had steadfastly insisted that the Communist rebels were North Vietnamese or Viet Cong and that no Cambodians were involved in the "Communist plot" to overthrow the Phnom Penh government.

Severely criticized by opposition leaders and, increasingly, by disgruntled Cambodian citizens for neglecting domestic economic policy and ignoring the corruption and favoritism practised by his ministers, Premier Lon resigned on April 20, 1971, citing poor health. Although he had suffered a debilitating stroke two months earlier, Indochina watchers speculated that he had tendered a tactical resignation to effect a reshuffling in his cabinet. While Lon's right-hand man, Sirik Matak, wielded active executive power, Lon remained the titular head of the Cambodian government.

Taking advantage of the confusion and dissension in the government as Sirik Matak and Lon Non, the premier's vain and devious younger brother, vied for power, the Khmer Rouge made extraordinary gains in the provinces and eventually controlled more than 80 percent of Cambodia. Furious, Lon Nol declared a state of emergency. In an October 20, 1971 broadcast announcing rule by "ordinance," he said that the Khmer Republic could no longer afford to "vainly play the game of democracy and freedom. . . ." Although he insisted he had not established a military dictatorship, he tightened press controls, curtailed civil rights, strengthened the military, and stripped the National Assembly of its powers.

A few months later, Lon nullified the nearly completed democratic constitution of the new republic by substituting his own proposal for a presidential form of government with a bicameral legislature. Seeking a popular mandate, he called for a presidential election, in which he headed the Social Republican ticket. After an openly fraudulent election, Lon garnered 55 percent of the votes cast, handily defeating his rival, In Tam, a former president of the National Assembly. (Some foreign observers maintain that Lon's correct vote count was closer to 35 or 40 percent and that In Tam may have been the victor.) By taking advantage of an attempted assassination and a bombing raid on the presidential palace in March 1973, Lon further consolidated his absolute power.

Sustained by American military aid, which in early 1973 amounted to $5,000,000 a week, President Lon Nol agreed to a reorganization of government suggested by General Alexander M. Haig Jr., a special envoy from President Nixon. To facilitate truce talks with the Khmer Rouge and to broaden Lon's legitimate power base, the United States recommended the inclusion of opposition leaders in the administration. The new four-man ruling council, which took office on April 24, 1973, consisted of Lon Nol, who retained the title of President, Sirik Matak, In Tam, and Cheng Heng—all veterans of the 1970 coup. After American bombing raids ended on August 15, 1973, the new government scored a series of impressive and unexpected military victories. Despite a second attempt on his life, President Lon launched an extensive public relations campaign to restore confidence in his regime, which was faced with yet another reorganization following the resignation of In Tam on December 12, 1973.

Described by a popular Cambodian magazine as "a block . . . , a rock, massive [and] weighty," Lon Nol is a heavyset man with a broad, round face and graying dark hair. He is tall by Cambodian standards. According to Robert Shaplen, like most Cambodians, Lon "wears an almost constant smile—likely to be a defense mechanism, especially in the presence of Westerners." He walks haltingly, aided by a cane and a steel brace, because of the lingering effects of the stroke that partially paralyzed his left side in February 1971. The President also suffers from diabetes and hypertension. Out of consideration for his childless wife, Lon ignored the Cambodian custom permitting a man of his age and rank to take a concubine as a "minor wife." His four illegitimate children, now teenagers, live with his half-brother, a UNESCO official in Paris. A widower since 1969, Lon lives in a spacious but simply furnished suburban villa where he often houses as many as fifty relatives as well as a number of itinerant Buddhist monks.

To the annoyance of his ministers, Lon prefers to work at home. An inveterate early riser, he usually meditates for about an hour before taking his morning coffee at 6:00 A.M., a daily ritual that often includes a discussion of current events with Lon Non. The President shuns newspapers, radio, television, and telephones, and does not receive a regular news briefing. He prefers to depend on his astrologers. Superstition is deeply ingrained in Khmer culture, but even by Cambodian standards Lon Nol outstrips his subjects. Commenting on Lon's reliance on astrology in a New York *Times Magazine* article (April 24, 1973), Mark Gayn wrote: "He believes deeply in demons and spirits, including the wild crocodile which . . . will some day appear before the palace to herald the arrival of the millenium." Nevertheless, when some soothsayers predicted his fall from power, Lon promptly jailed them.

Although the introverted President dislikes public appearances, he has recently increased the frequency of his press conferences. Chain-smoking English cigarettes, he responds to screened questions, in fluent French, occasionally illustrating his remarks with an appropriate quotation from one of several leather-bound journals in which he records his thoughts. Excerpts from the journals have been published in Cambodia under the title *The New Khmer Way*.

References

N Y Times p16 Mr 19 '70 por
N Y Times Mag p28+ D 13 '70 pors;
  p27+ Je 27 '71; p13+ Ap 24 '73 por
Time 95:22+ Mr 30 '70 por
U S News & World Report 68:28+ Ap
  13 '70 por

Caldwell, Malcolm and Lek Tan. Cam-
  bodia in the Southeast Asian War (1973)
International Who's Who, 1973-74
Kirk, Donald. The Wider War (1971)

LOOS, ANITA

Apr. 26, 1893- Writer
Address: h. 171 W. 57th St., New York 10019

The overshadowing work in the abundant output
of Anita Loos is her witty minor classic of the
1920's, the novel *Gentlemen Prefer Blondes,* which
became a favorite also of audiences as a play, a
musical comedy, and a motion picture. The title
of Miss Loos's satire has been enshrined in the
Oxford Dictionary of Quotations, while its heroine, Lorelei Lee, the prototype of the not-too-
bright blonde, has enriched twentieth-century
Americana with such pithy observations as, "Kiss-
ing your hand can make a girl feel very good,
but a diamond bracelet lasts forever."

Besides other novels in the vein of *Gentlemen
Prefer Blondes,* Anita Loos has written countless
scenarios and many plays, some of them in collaboration with her late husband, John Emerson.
One of her plays, *Happy Birthday* (1946), she
wrote expressly for Helen Hayes, her coauthor of
a later memoir and guide book of New York City.
Throughout her enterprising career Miss Loos has
attracted wide attention not only as a writer of
sparkling and critical perception but as a personality, a consummate flapper of the Roaring Twenties and a devotee of haute couture. At a time
when all women had long hair, she gave herslf
the wind-blown bob that was soon copied by her
whole generation; and long before it became
fashionable for women to have a career, she herself preferred hard work to a life of leisure.

Anita Loos was born on April 26, 1893 in
Sissons (now Mount Shasta), California to Richard Beers and Minnie Ellen (Smith) Loos. Her
older brother, Clifford, became a physician; her
younger sister, Gladys, died in childhood. A native
of Ohio, R. Beers Loos had moved at the age
of fifteen to California, where he became founder,
editor, and proprietor of the weekly Sissons
Mascot. When papers all over the West began
quoting his articles, he felt ready for the challenges of a big city and moved with his family to
San Francisco. Although Anita Loos was then
only four years old, she can recall her relief at
escaping from a dull, admiring child who had
been following her about in Sissons. Throughout
her life she has abhorred boredom.

Combining his interest in journalism with his
enthusiasm for the stage, her father acquired a
San Francisco paper that he called the *Dramatic
Review.* He helped to launch his daughter's career
as a child actress by having her cast in *May
Blossom,* a play coauthored and directed by David
Belasco. Anita Loos also appeared in *Quo Vadis?,*
the American première of *A Doll's House,* and
other San Francisco productions. Eventually her
acting became the family's chief source of income,
since her scamp of a father neglected his paper
for theatrical ventures, parties, and the pursuit of
attractive women, as she related in her autobiography, *A Girl Like I* (Viking, 1966). One of
the highlights of her early years was the beginning of her interest in clothes, which dates
from the time she discovered Kate Greenaway's
illustrated children's books and persuaded her
mother, whom she once described as an "earth-
bound angel," to make her children's clothes in
the Greenaway style. That same year, at the age
of eight, she also broke into print, when a four-
line verse she had written was published in a
children's magazine as the winning entry of an
advertising contest for a floor polish.

From San Francisco, which Miss Loos regards
as her spiritual home, the family moved to Los
Angeles, where her father had found a job as
manager of the Cineograph theatre. Along with
offering an exciting new form of entertainment,
one-reel moving pictures, the Cineograph regularly presented comedy sketches like *Box and
Cox* in which Anita Loos and other resident
actors performed. A good student as well as a
full-time actress, she also contributed articles periodically to the *Morning Telegraph,* a New York
daily that she read for news of the theatre. She
had begun to write for the paper at the age of
thirteen when she won a prize for submitting the
best humorous anecdote about life in New York,
a city she had never seen.

In early 1906 the family moved to San Diego,
where R. Beers Loos helped to form a stock company for which he was producer and his daughter,
a featured player. She had reached her full height
of four feet eleven inches—small enough to play
the title role in *Little Lord Fauntleroy,* but credible, with high heels and piled-up hair, as the
villainess in *East Lynne.* In *The Prince Chap,*
opposite the unknown, young Harold Lloyd, she
portrayed a girl of eight, twelve, and eighteen
in successive scenes. Between the acts the stock
company management entertained audiences by
showing short movies, which Anita Loos watched
from backstage. When she realized that those
films must have been based on written outlines
of plot, she began writing scenarios and mailing
them to the Biograph Company. *The New York
Hat* (1912), her first filmed scenario, which had
D. W. Griffith as its director and Mary Pickford
and Lionel Barrymore as its costars, may still be
seen in film courses and film festivals at museums.

By 1915 the Biograph Company had bought
over a hundred of Anita Loos's scenarios, a few
of them serious scripts, but mainly comedies with
titles like *Saved by the Soup* and *A Hicksville
Epicure.* "Miss Loos's little stories prick the pulse
of the times," Gary Carey wrote in *Film Com-*

ment (Winter, 1970-71). "Those of her early films available for viewing show a keen eye for all contemporary pretensions, foibles and fads." When she joined the staff of a film studio as a writer on a regular salary, her scenarios were used by Mae Marsh, Lillian and Dorothy Gish, and Norma and Constance Talmadge, all of whom were her friends. Another friend, Constance Collier, starred with Sir Herbert Beerbohm-Tree in Miss Loos's adaptation of *Macbeth* (1916).

After moving from Biograph to Mutual studio and then to Triangle studio, Miss Loos began collaborating with the director John Emerson, who used her scripts to help compensate for the limitations of Douglas Fairbanks' acting ability. In *His Picture in the Papers* (1916), Emerson translated the wit of her script into screened subtitles, making that film the first to use subtitles for conveying more than basic information. The innovation brought stardom to Fairbanks and earned the comment from one New York critic that with the satiric *His Picture in the Papers* the movies had outgrown their infancy. Converted to subtitles by the success of the film, Griffith asked Miss Loos to help supply subtitles for his monumental *Intolerance* (1916). Soon she was writing subtitles not only for all the pictures that starred Fairbanks, but for every film made at the studio.

In 1919, about three years after the beginning of their collaboration, Miss Loos and Emerson were married. It was Anita Loos's second marriage. Her first, to Frank Pallma Jr., in June 1915, had been annulled after one day. With Emerson she moved to New York, where they produced their own films, partly in association with Joseph M. Schenck, who asked them to help boost the career of his sister-in-law, Constance Talmadge. Among the many movies of that actress based on Loos-Emerson scripts were *A Virtuous Vamp* (1919), *The Perfect Woman* (1920), *Dangerous Business* (1921), *Polly of the Follies* (1922), and *Learning to Love* (1925). The couple also collaborated on books about the motion picture industry, *Breaking Into the Movies* (1919) and *How to Write Photoplays* (1921)—a subject that Miss Loos, as author of more than 200 scripts, was singularly well equipped to handle. Besides her screenplays, she wrote two plays produced on Broadway, *The Whole Town's Talking* (1923) and *The Fall of Eve* (1925).

A devoted reader of the magazine *Smart Set*, Anita Loos had long admired its editor, H. L. Mencken, and its drama critic, George Jean Nathan, both of whom became her friends when she moved to New York. As she related in her autobiography, on the occasion of sharing a transcontinental train ride with Nathan's dim-witted, blond girl friend, to whom Mencken and Emerson had been absurdly attentive, Miss Loos began pondering the question of why she had been neglected for a young woman no prettier than she and far less intelligent. She concluded that men have a special affinity for fair hair. Piqued, especially at Mencken, she decided to expose and attack such folly with her customary weapon—the

ANITA LOOS

pen. By the end of the trip she had mapped out several hilarious chapters about a mindless, seemingly innocent gold digger from Little Rock, Arkansas named Lorelei Lee.

Lorelei's diary, *Gentlemen Prefer Blondes*, which first appeared in installments in *Harper's Bazaar* in 1925, was published the following year in book form by Boni & Liveright. It has since delighted millions of readers in more than sixty editions and in translations in thirteen languages. According to Miss Loos's own report, George Santayana once smilingly called it "the best philosophical work by an American." To Mencken the distinction of *Gentlemen Prefer Blondes* was that for the first time an American writer had made fun of sex. "Like most of Miss Loos' work," Carey observed in *Film Comment*, "the novel is haphazardly constructed and cast with caricature more than with character. But it captures a time. . . . Most of all, it is blessed with that crystal clear and balanced logic that characterizes the best comic writing."

By making Miss Loos internationally famous, *Gentlemen Prefer Blondes* served as an entrée to world celebrities ranging from H. G. Wells to Mussolini. Her stage adaptation of the story of Lorelei's progress had its première in New York at the Times Square Theatre in September 1926. On tour it was at one time played by four road companies. Together with Joseph Fields, Miss Loos wrote the book for the musical version of *Gentlemen Prefer Blondes*, which opened at the Ziegfeld Theatre on December 8, 1949 and ran for almost two years on Broadway with Carol Channing as the blonde, a role played on the screen in 1953 by Marilyn Monroe. Miss Loos's *But Gentlemen Marry Brunettes* (Boni & Liveright, 1928), though another best seller, never achieved the immense popularity of its predecessor.

At the height of her career Anita Loos retired in order to travel and have fun. "The biggest mistake I ever made," she told a reporter in 1960, ". . . I became sick and bored with life." Her health and happiness were restored by the stock market crash of 1929, which forced her to return to work, writing sound film scripts for MGM in Hollywood. Her script for *Red-Headed Woman* (1932) speeded recognition of Jean Harlow as a comedy star. In her own opinion, her screenplay for *San Francisco* (1936) is among her finest achievements, and some critics consider her movie version of *The Women* (1939) superior to Claire Boothe Luce's original satire.

Before turning her full attention to MGM scenarios, Anita Loos had joined Emerson in writing and directing *The Social Register*, a light, satirical comedy presented in New York at the Fulton Theatre in the fall of 1931. She abandoned Hollywood for Broadway in the mid-1940's, resuming work for the stage with *Happy Birthday*, which she wrote especially for Helen Hayes, who welcomed a change in characterization from eminent personages like Queen Victoria. Miss Loos's Saroyanesque comedy about a staid librarian who sheds her inhibitions in a Newark bar premièred at the Broadhurst Theatre on October 31, 1946 and ran for 564 performances.

Much of Anita Loos's later writing for the stage consists of adaptations from French literature. The comedy *Gigi*, her dramatization of Colette's witty classic about the rearing of a *grande cocotte*, was handsomely produced by Gilbert Miller at Broadway's Fulton Theatre, where on November 24, 1951 it began a 219-performance run. Critics and audiences were less receptive to Miss Loos's *Chéri*, an adaptation of two of Colette's other novels, which was performed during seven weeks in the fall of 1959 at the Morosco Theatre in New York.

Miss Loos also wrote the book for the musical version of two French plays. *The Amazing Adèle*, based on the play by Pierre Barrillet and Jean-Pierre Gredy, tried out in Philadelphia and Boston in the 1955-56 season, but did not reach New York. *Gogo Loves You*, derived from the 1918 comedy of manners *L'École des cocottes*, ran briefly at the Off-Broadway Theatre de Lys in October 1964. A comedy-drama about Anne of Cleves, *The King's Mare*, which Miss Loos adapted from a play by the French dramatist Jean Canolle, opened in London in the mid-1960's. Its farcical episodes seemed to some reviewers well suited to the talents of its stars—Glynis Johns as Anne and Keith Michell as Henry VIII.

Returning, meanwhile, to the idiom that had made her famous, Anita Loos lampooned the old-time Hollywood she had known so well in two hilarious novels that employed some of the techniques, such as satiric naïveté, of *Gentlemen Prefer Blondes*. Effie Huntriss, the bird-brained heroine of *A Mouse is Born* (Doubleday, 1951), gives a misspelled account of her movie career that becomes, as a reviewer for the New York *Times* (May 6, 1951) put it, "a sly and acid picture of the lunacies of those who puff and plot in the vicinity of Hollywood and Vine." Another amusing Loos novel, *No Mother to Guide Her* (McGraw, 1961), is a shortened, revised, and retitled version of *The Better Things of Life*, which was serialized in *Cosmopolitan* magazine in 1930. Edmund Wilson once called it "the novel about

Hollywood with most teeth in it." Although Miss Loos pokes unsparing fun at the extravagances of filmland in its heyday, she seemed to some reviewers to be too involved emotionally with the Hollywood scene to carry off satire effectively. A critic for the London *Times Literary Supplement* (October 27, 1961) thought that "her battle cries turn into nostalgic lullabies of affection."

New York has always been Miss Loos's preference over Hollywood as a place to live and work. *Twice Over Lightly: New York Then and Now* (Harcourt, 1972), which she wrote jointly with Helen Hayes, is a document to her enduring fondness for the city. The two friends explored well-known places like the United Nations, the Brooklyn Botanical Gardens, and the Bronx Zoo; introduced readers to out-of-the-way shops and restaurants; and made the most of privileged adventures seldom experienced by New York visitors or residents, such as taking a ride on a garbage scow and examining the storage rooms of the Museum of Modern Art. Miss Loos's most recent publication is the second volume of her autobiography, *Kiss Hollywood Good-By* (Viking, 1974). Except for disclosures about her marriage to Emerson, the book is not so much an account of her own life as a collection of highly readable anecdotes about Irving Thalberg, Clark Gable, Jean Harlow, Garbo, and other greats of the brassy Hollywood of the 1930's and 1940's.

Anita Loos has been a widow since 1956. Her home for the past twenty years has been an apartment opposite Carnegie Hall in the heart of Manhattan. Confessing that royalties from *Gentlemen Prefer Blondes* have filtered steadily over the years into the dress salons of Mainbocher and Balenciaga, she continues to regard clothes as "works of art." She welcomed the return in fashion of raised hemlines, which she believes take ten years off one's age. Short dresses, moreover, are becoming to her slight, ninety-four-pound figure. She has large brown eyes and brown hair still worn in a fringe of bangs. "I can't wait to get to my desk each morning," she recently told Israel Shenker of the New York *Times* (April 26, 1973). She customarily rises at four in the morning and writes until ten and then devotes the rest of the day to the pleasures of reading and conversation and to the diversions of the city.

References

Film Comment p51+ Winter '70-'71
N Y Post p29 D 30 '71 por; p2 S 19 '73 por
N Y Times p14 S 17 '66 por; p45 Ap 26 '73
Newsday A p40 Jl 11 '69 por
Toronto Globe and Mail p25 Ap 4 '72 por
Biographical Encyclopaedia & Who's Who of the American Theatre (1966)
Contemporary Authors vols 21-22 (1969)
Twentieth Century Authors (1942; First Supplement, 1955)
Who's Who in America, 1972-73
Who's Who in the Theatre (1972)

LOUD, PAT(RICIA RUSSELL)

1926- Television personality; author
Address: c/o Coward, McCann & Geoghegan,
Inc., 200 Madison Ave., New York 10016

Among the major "pseudoevents" (as Daniel
Boorstin would say) of 1973 one must certainly
rank the disintegration of the William C. Loud
family of Santa Barbara, California as viewed by
the national PBS television audience. For seven
months in 1971 the daily life of Bill and Pat Loud
and their five teen-age children was captured on
film by a Public Broadcasting System crew led
by producer Craig Gilbert. The 1973 twelve-epi-
sode documentary made from the 1971 footage
fascinated the public and caused many social
scientists to observe that the Loud family's crisis
represented the collapse of the nuclear family in
America. Perhaps the most compelling figure in
An American Family was Mrs. Loud, who after
twenty years as a housewife and mother found
her children growing up and her marriage falling
apart. Now divorced, Pat Loud lives in New York
City. She is the author of a candid autobiography,
Pat Loud: A Woman's Story (Coward, McCann &
Geoghegan, 1974), written with Nora Johnson.

Of Scotch-Irish origin, Patricia Russell was born
in Eugene, Oregon in 1926. Her father, a civil
engineer who had worked on the Panama Canal,
was at the time of her birth engaged in planning
a railroad connecting Oregon with points in northern California. Patricia was the Russells' third
child. Their first daughter had died in infancy;
their son Tom, now an engineer, was born in
1924. Pat and Tom were brought up in the
father's Roman Catholic faith rather than the
mother's Episcopalianism. Pat Loud has described
her childhood home as an "old-fashioned Victorian household" in which her father was "a
little Caesar."

When Patricia was three years old her family
moved to Brazil, where her father had a job
building a railroad through the Amazon jungle.
For two years the children and their mother
divided their time between Rio de Janeiro and
the jungle at Baixo Guandu. When a revolution
called a halt to the building job, the Russells left
for New York City, where they lived in the New
Yorker Hotel. Six months later they drove across
the country, back to Eugene. When Pat's father
took a job in Salem, Oregon, in 1936, the family
moved there. In Salem, Pat was sent to a Catholic
girls school, Sacred Heart Academy. During World
War II the Russells lived in Seattle while Mr.
Russell designed and constructed war installations
in Alaska and the Aleutians. In Seattle, Pat completed high school at Holy Name Academy.

As a growing girl, Pat Loud was, in her words,
"shy, tongue-tied, and a loner." Awkward with
boys, she had few dates. Having been taught by
her mother that marriage was woman's highest
vocation, she had little ambition for a career, but
her parents had decided that she and her brother
were to go to Stanford University. As she wrote

PAT LOUD

in *Pat Loud: A Woman's Story,* "College for wom-
en was a refinement whose main purpose was to
better prepare you for your ultimate destiny . . .
to make you a more desirable product." At Stanford her social life scarcely improved, since she
entered in 1944, when most of the men were
away at war. After toying with the idea of becoming an archeologist, Pat eventually majored
in history, because it was the subject in which
she had the most credits. During the summer of
her sophomore year, in 1946, she returned to
Eugene, where her parents had settled at the
end of the war. There she began her first real
romance, with Bill Loud, who was six years her
senior and the older brother of her brother's best
friend.

After attending college and serving in the military during the war, Loud had settled down in
Eugene to run the logging supply company he
had inherited from his father. Pat and Bill dated
steadily through her last two years of college. In
her book Mrs. Loud wrote that after she obtained
her B.A. degree, in 1948, Bill was anxious to
get married, but she hesitated, torn between a
desire to make her mark in the world and a
desperate need to cling to her parents. She went
to San Francisco to look, unsuccessfully, for a
job, and then lived at home with her family
in Eugene. Early in 1950 she visited her brother,
who was married and living in Syracuse, New
York. While she was in Syracuse, Bill Loud tele-
phoned her from Acapulco, Mexico and asked
her to join him there. "It was like Daddy calling
from Rio," she recalled in her book. "I could no
more have said no than I could have resisted a
tidal wave."

Bill and Pat Loud were married in Acapulco
on March 1, 1950. After a brief honeymoon, they
returned to Eugene. In her autobiography Pat
recalled that she was afraid to tell her parents
about their elopement and therefore insisted that
they return to their respective homes and keep
the marriage a secret. They continued to live
apart for months, even after Pat became pregnant,

until Bill was called back to active duty for the Korean war and transferred to San Diego. At that point she broke the news and moved in with Bill in La Jolla.

In June 1951 Pat Loud gave birth to their first child, Lance. Shortly afterward, Bill was shipped overseas, and Pat and the baby returned to Eugene, where they lived until Bill returned eight months later. After a few more months in Southern California, the Louds moved back to Eugene, living briefly with her parents and then in their own home. Bill resumed control over his father's business, the Coast Cable Company, which required him to spend much of his time traveling. Meanwhile, the family continued to grow: Kevin was born in January 1953, Grant in May 1954, and Delilah in October 1955.

"What essentially was going on with me all the time was kids," Pat Loud wrote of this period. "Life was diapers and little jars of pureed apricots and bottles and playpens and rectal thermometers, and all those small dirty faces and all those questions." A new factor intruded upon her consciousness when, in 1957, she discovered a love letter from another woman in her husband's wallet. In her book she tells how she packed up her four children—she was then pregnant with the fifth, Michele—and left Bill. But within a few hours she returned home and allowed herself to be mollified by her husband's alibi for the letter.

In 1962 the Louds moved to Santa Barbara, a small, affluent city located on a beautiful and perenially temperate strip of California's coast just north of Los Angeles' suburban sprawl. By that time William Loud had established American Western Foundries, which supplies parts for heavy-duty strip-mining equipment, and it kept him traveling throughout the Western states. After a year and a half in a rented house, the Louds moved into their own home, the large, comfortable ranch style house at 35 Wooddale Lane in which they were later to be televised.

In Santa Barbara Pat Loud continued to find clues to her husband's marital infidelities—lipstick smudges on his handkerchiefs, unexplained plane tickets, a brochure from a Las Vegas hotel—but she refused to let herself realize what was going on. Finally, in 1966, a set of her husband's cuff links, engraved "To Bill, Eternally Yours, Kitty," became the last straw. She managed to have an extra set of keys to her husband's office made, and while he was off on a business trip she went through his files. "It was all there," she wrote in *Pat Loud*, "as though it had been waiting for me for years—credit card slips telling of restaurants I'd never been to and hotels I'd never stayed at, plane tickets to places I'd never seen, even pictures of Bill and his girls as they grinned and screwed their way around the countryside."

When Bill Loud returned from his business trip, his wife has recalled, she confronted him with the evidence and the two ended up exchanging blows. After her discovery she suffered from severe depression, briefly consulted a psychiatrist,

and at her husband's urging took a turn at picking up businessmen at local bars. At least twice she went to a lawyer and began divorce proceedings. In an apparent last-ditch effort to save the marriage, the Louds, with all their children and Pat's widowed mother, went on a vacation to Europe in December 1970. When they returned, Pat and Bill went off by themselves to Hawaii. By the time that they were back in Santa Barbara, in February 1971, Pat was making plans for a trial separation. Into that atmosphere of tension and discord in May 1971 stepped Craig Gilbert, asking the Loud family to be the subjects of a one-hour TV program on "an attractive, articulate California family." The segment on them would be part of a series, he explained, on five families across the country. Before choosing the Louds, Gilbert had interviewed and rejected fifty other California candidates.

Despite their marital problems, the Louds agreed to let Gilbert and his television crew into their house. "Bill, of course, was dying to do it. What could be more perfect? This would be the height of his self-expression," Pat has said. "I dragged my feet a bit at first. . . . It might be too real. Bill, the phallic wonder, and Pat, the washed-up harridan. But, behold, there were other images that might eradicate that one. Pat, dedicated mother of five. . . . Pat, the gourmet among her copper pots. . . . Pat, the decorator in her lovely ranch house." She also admitted that she was attracted to the idea because she believed that Bill's women would see the show and be jealous.

Gilbert and his crew began filming in May 1971. According to the Louds, Gilbert told them after the filming was completed for the one-hour special that it had gone so well that he wanted to extend it to five hours, then a few more hours, until they finally consented to be the subject of an unprecedented twelve-hour documentary. The film crew remained with the Louds for seven months, leaving just after New Year's Day 1972. In the meantime Pat had begun divorce proceedings, in September 1971.

Ultimately, Craig Gilbert accumulated some 300 hours of film on the Louds, which was edited to twelve hours by the producer and eight editors. The whole project cost $1,200,000, put up by the Public Broadcasting System and the Ford Foundation. The Louds were paid nothing. Although the family members had veto power over scenes in which they were involved, they rarely exercised it, and the final version of the film was approved by Mrs. Loud.

The edited version of *An American Family* seemed mostly to be about Pat Loud, as wife and mother. The series pivoted around Pat and Bill's divorce, opening the first episode with a scene showing Pat alone on New Year's Eve, watching her children and their friends having a party in the garage. In subsequent episodes the viewer was shown the Loud family as it was before the separation: bluff, hearty Bill coming home from business trips to make small talk with Pat and the children, and Pat, caught up in the flow of life at the family's home, a large rambling house with a swimming pool and an endless swirl of children, dogs, cats, horses, cars, and rock music. The disintegration of the Louds' marriage is emphasized with the inclusion of scenes that show them quarreling bitterly at a local restaurant, Pat confiding to her brother and sister-in-law about Bill's infidelities, and, finally, Pat asking Bill to move out of the house. In counterpoint to the drama of Pat and Bill's marital troubles, the series dwells on the life of the oldest son, Lance, who is shown leading a precarious existence in New York City and Paris, spending his time with flamboyantly dressed homosexuals and asking for money from home.

During the year between the time the TV cameras left the Louds and the première of the series on educational television, the family lived in anonymity, Bill in a bachelor apartment in Santa Barbara and Pat with the children in the family house. Through a friend of Lance's, Pat Loud got a job in Santa Barbara in the spring of 1972 on the staff of the Forum of Contemporary History, which publishes a newsletter for which well-known people write, often on controversial subjects. In the autumn the Louds' divorce became final.

An American Family premièred on the Public Broadcasting System on Thursday evening, January 11, 1973. It became an immediate sensation, drawing a weekly audience estimated at 11,000,000. Sociologists, psychologists, novelists, and magazine columnists joined the TV critics in analyzing the family and what its members' lives said about family life in America. While some pundits were relatively sympathetic to the Louds, others deplored what they saw as the family's empty, materialistic lifestyle and the inability of the members to communicate with one another. For many critics, the Louds dramatically symbolized the decline of the nuclear family. Other authorities, however, argued over whether the Loud family was truly representative of American families. Rutgers University sociologist Irving Louis Horowitz, for example, felt that the family was exhibitionistic and atypical because it allowed itself to be filmed for TV. M.I.T. psychotherapist Dr. Thomas Cottle on the other hand contended that the Louds had only done what many others would have done in their place: they had fallen victim to the "compulsion of this culture—the compulsion to confess." Reviewers were also divided on the validity of Gilbert's *cinéma vérité* technique. "You cannot put human beings in an aquarium and expect them to act 'normally,'" objected Shana Alexander of *Newsweek* (January 22, 1973). But as formidable an authority as Margaret Mead called the television series "the most important event in human thought since the invention of the novel."

Caught up by the media once the TV series was launched and driven at least partly by a need to justify themselves against the attacks that had been made on them, the Loud family submitted to numerous interviews on TV and for newspapers and magazines. They were seen on the Mike Douglas, Dick Cavett, Jack Parr, Dinah Shore, and Phil Donahue shows as well as on the cover of *Newsweek* magazine.

In the fall of 1973 Pat Loud quit her job with the Forum of Contemporary History, where she had been promoted to associate editor, and moved to New York. Her husband remains in Santa Barbara, where he is trying to rebuild his business, which, as millions of viewers saw on TV, has been in grave financial difficulty for the past few years. Loud reportedly paid his former wife $1,300 a month in alimony and child support. In June 1974 she became New York sales manager of the American Essence, a firm that promotes Anne Klein and Rudi Gernreich perfumes.

Pat Loud: A Woman's Story received mixed reviews. Some critics dismissed it as a tasteless attempt by the author to cash in on her notoriety, but others found it an honest and moving statement of an individual's struggle for selfhood. "Despite its self-serving intent," wrote Nancy Mayer of *New Times* (April 5, 1974), "Pat Loud's story of stunted growth is an effective brief for the urgent feminist cry that women should take themselves and their lives seriously from an early age. Or be in for a brutal awakening much later." Mrs. Loud has also written articles for magazines, including *Viva* and the *Family Weekly*.

In New York City, Pat Loud lives in a one-bedroom, sublet apartment on East 79th Street with her younger daughter, Michele, who is a high school student. Much of the time she has shared her small home with other members of her brood, including Delilah, who works for a cosmetics firm; Lance, who has at various times expressed the ambition to become an actor, writer, or rock star; and Grant, who wants to be a rock musician. The next-to-eldest son, Kevin, lives in Santa Barbara, where he attends Santa Barbara City College and plays bass with a rock band. Frank about her financial difficulties, Pat Loud admits that she wrote her book largely to make money.

A tall, slim, handsome woman, with black hair and dark eyes, Pat Loud was described by Dr. Theodore I. Rubin of the *Ladies' Home Journal* (July 1973) as "direct, open [and] natural." She smokes Virginia Slims cigarettes and enjoys drinking Scotch and soda. She has not been a practising Catholic since her college years, and in politics she classifies herself as a liberal. Asked by Jerry Tallmer of the New York *Post* (March 16, 1974) if she would do the TV series again, she replied, "I guess if I'd known what would happen the day Craig Gilbert opened that door, I would have screamed and run up into the hills. But not knowing what would happen, I guess I'm stuck with it."

References

Ladies Home J XC:44+ Jl '73 por
Newsday p12+ Mr 24 '74
Newsweek 83:58 Mr 11 '74 por
Loud, Pat. Pat Loud: A Woman's Story (1974)

McCALL, TOM (LAWSON)

Mar. 22, 1913- Governor of Oregon
Address: b. Office of the Governor, State Capitol Bldg., Salem, Ore. 97310; h. 796 Winter St. N.E., Salem, Ore. 97301

A moderate Republican who firmly believes that issues are more important than party labels, Governor Tom McCall of Oregon is considered one of the most forward-looking and innovative public officials in the United States. Previously McCall was a newspaper, radio, and television journalist, and in that capacity he championed programs for the betterment of his state, particularly in the area of environmental control. As chief executive since 1967, he has been able to effect programs that significantly enhance Oregon's progressive reputation, which paradoxically overlays the tendency of Oregonians toward an ingrained conservatism. The pioneering measures he adopted to cope with his state's fuel shortage in 1973, several months before the energy crisis became recognized nationwide, have since served as models for programs in other states. Because of his reputation for far-sightedness and resourcefulness and his independence of the scandal-ridden Nixon establishment, McCall has been mentioned as a possible Presidential candidate for 1976.

Thomas Lawson McCall was born to Henry and Dorothy (Lawson) McCall on March 22, 1913 in the mansion of the Lawson family's thousand-acre estate in Egypt, Massachusetts, on the Bay State's fashionable South Shore, which was also the birthplace of his two sisters and two brothers. His grandfathers were, on the maternal side, Thomas W. Lawson, copper magnate and author of a history of the Republican party, and, paternally, Samuel W. McCall, Governor of Massachusetts, Congressman, and owner of the Boston *Advertiser*.

Tom McCall grew up on the family ranch near Prineville, Oregon. At the University of Oregon, where he was a member of Phi Delta Theta and Alpha Delta Sigma, he received a B.A. degree in journalism in 1936. The following year he went to work as an unsalaried public relations man for the Latah County Wildlife Association, a job in keeping with his deep interest in conservation of the natural environment. Later he became a founding partner of the public relations firm Goodrich, McCall & Snyder.

In 1944 and 1945 McCall was a Navy war correspondent in the Pacific. After his discharge from the Navy, in 1946, he became involved in journalism and politics in Portland, Oregon. As a journalist, he wrote a newspaper column and was a political news analyst for radio station KGW and television station KGW-TV. As administrative assistant to Governor Douglas McKay, from 1949 to 1952, he acted as executive secretary of committees on legislative agenda concerned with welfare, public employees' retirement, Indian affairs, sex offenses, and legislative procedures. In 1954 he made his first bid for elective office, entering the Congressional race in Oregon's Third District.

After defeating incumbent Representative Homer D. Angell in the Republican primary he lost to the Democratic candidate, Mrs. Edith S. Green, by some 6,000 votes in the November election. In 1960 McCall was a member of the governor's Blue Ribbon Committee on Government Reorganization.

While working at KGW-TV McCall produced *Pollution in Paradise,* a television documentary about the despoiling of the three-hundred-mile Willamette River that won him an award from Sigma Delta Chi, the fraternity of professional journalists, in 1962. In November 1964 he was elected to a two-year term as secretary of state, Oregon's second most important office. In addition, he became a member of the State Board of Control and the State Land Board. As a full-time public servant, he relinquished the name he had been using as a journalist, Lawson McCall, and became known as Tom McCall.

As early as June 1965 McCall was rumored to be a likely candidate to replace lame-duck Governor Mark Hatfield, and in the May 1966 primary he won the Republican nomination. On November 9, 1966, after a campaign fought largely on the issue of environmental pollution, McCall defeated the Democratic candidate, state treasurer Robert W. Straub, by a vote of 377,346 to 305,008. He took office as governor in January 1967, succeeding Hatfield, who had been elected to the United States Senate.

Already well-known to Oregonians because of his television appearances, the new governor soon brought their attention to his aggressive and far-reaching plans for the preservation and improvement of Oregon's natural, as well as human, resources. Appointing himself interim chairman of the State Sanitary Authority, he went into action to clean up the Willamette River, which had been almost totally polluted by sewage and industrial wastes. In May 1967, after preliminary hearings, he established standards of water quality for every river in the state and issued an enforcement plan for every city and industry on those waterways. By 1969 the salmon population of the Willamette, which had been nearing extinction, was flourishing, and soon the entire length of the river was clean enough for swimming, boating, and fishing. McCall also devoted much effort to expanding and improving the state's educational facilities on all levels. Rejecting a sales tax or increased property taxes, he proposed an adjustment in income tax rates as a means of financing his educational program.

In keeping with his campaign promise to make his a "citizens' administration," McCall conducted open house in his office for a half hour every day, and in the first four months of his governorship 17,000 Oregonians took advantage of the opportunity to discuss problems with him. In addition, he reported to the people in monthly television broadcasts and weekly radio talks. In preparation for the 1968 Presidential election and the important Oregon primary that preceded it, McCall tried to rally his fellow Republican governors to act "in concert toward selection of the

Republican who has the best chance of victory." Although he strongly favored a "balanced" ticket of Nelson A. Rockefeller and Ronald Reagan, he finally went along with the choice of Richard Nixon and Spiro Agnew at the Republican National Convention.

In December 1969 Governor McCall spearheaded a protest by residents of northwestern states against United States Army plans to ship 13,000 tons of lethal nerve gas from Okinawa to an ordnance depot in Oregon, and the shipment was cancelled. When, in the late summer of 1970, an antiwar group announced plans to stage massive demonstrations in Portland, to coincide with an American Legion convention there, McCall probably averted a violent confrontation between Legionnaires and youthful protesters by inviting the latter to a state-sponsored Woodstock-style rock festival at a state park some thirty-five miles from the city.

Again stressing environmental protection as one of the strong points of his platform, McCall won reelection as governor with 56 percent of the vote on November 5, 1970, defeating Democrat Robert Straub for the second time. By July 1971 he had maneuvered more than 100 environmental protection bills through the legislature. On October 1, 1972, Oregon became the first state to outlaw pull-tab cans and nonreturnable bottles, the cause of much roadside litter. Other bills that he originated or pushed prevent developers from building on Oregon's 359-mile Pacific Ocean coastline (and thus robbing the public of its beaches) and call for the allocation of 1 percent of all state highway funds for bicycle lanes and footpaths.

In keeping with his concern for preserving Oregon's natural resources, McCall has not been eager to welcome new industries, and he insists that those that do come into the state must have clean, nonpolluting plants. He takes a dim view of any great influx of new residents, and although tourism is a major industry of the Beaver State, he prefers to have visitors come in limited numbers so that its scenic beauty is not despoiled. Nevertheless, Oregon has a greater influx of new residents than the neighboring states of Washington and California, and tourism is constantly increasing.

In 1971 McCall created the Office of Energy Research and Planning to study possible solutions to power shortages that might arise in Oregon, which is heavily dependent on the great dams of the Columbia River for hydroelectric power. In the spring of 1973 a crisis arose when lack of snow and an unusually light rainfall brought reservoirs to their lowest level in nineteen years. After declaring a statewide emergency, on August 21, 1973, McCall instructed state employees to economize in the use of lights, heat, air-conditioning, and hot water in state buildings. Through such measures, a 30 percent drop in power consumption was attained within a month. He then ordered a ban on outdoor commercial lighting and a 50 percent cutback in highway lighting, lowered the state speed limit from seventy to fifty-five miles

TOM MCCALL

an hour, and enlisted public cooperation in the conservation of heating fuel and gasoline. On January 14, 1974, Oregon became the first state to adopt a program of voluntary gasoline rationing according to which cars with odd and even number plates were eligible for gas on alternate days. The "Oregon Plan" was soon adopted in other parts of the country.

In the New Yorker (February 25, 1974), E. J. Kahn Jr. noted that Oregonians "have laws so progressive that, by comparison, many other states look doddering," and he attributed much of the progress to McCall's policies. "Oregon is far ahead of the Supreme Court on abortions," Kahn observed. "Contraceptives can be sold from vending machines. . . . The Oregon legislature . . . has even discussed passing a bill legalizing some form of euthanasia." In an effort to reform the political process, McCall has encouraged adoption of a bill to limit the amounts candidates for public office can spend on their campaigns and another "specifying that all gatherings of state officials at which a decision could theoretically be arrived at . . . must be open to the press." His promotion of a methadone program for Oregon's drug addicts was in part personally motivated, since his youngest son, a former heroin addict, was helped by methadone. Although McCall is not in favor of legalizing marijuana, he signed a bill, effective July 23, 1973, that made the possession of less than an ounce of the weed a mere violation rather than a criminal offense, so that young people found guilty of using it would not be saddled with a lifelong criminal record.

Because of his outspokenness, McCall has on occasion been in trouble with the G.O.P. establishment. At the 1971 Republican governors' conference he clashed with then Vice-President Spiro Agnew over party strategy and was quoted as calling Agnew's address to the conference an "ignorant, rotten little speech." With reference to the Watergate scandals, McCall said in November 1973: "We're not going to be housemen for the White House and try to whitewash one of the sorriest pages in American political history." He called on President Nixon "to become more credible, more human." A few months later he asserted, as quoted by Russell Sackett in *Newsday* (February 4, 1974): "The President is *destroying* the power of the presidency. Why is he doing this to himself and the nation? To me, this is the most mystifying tragedy of public life since the assassination of Lincoln." When asked whether Nixon should resign, he said, "Well, I think [in his place] I'd say that I don't want to be where I'm not wanted."

In 1972 and 1974 McCall considered running for the United States Senate but on both occasions he decided instead to complete his term as governor. He reportedly intended to enter the 1972 race in opposition to the strong stand against the Vietnam war taken by incumbent Senator Mark Hatfield. According to Robert Shepard, writing in the Bergen (New Jersey) *Record* (March 7, 1974), "To the despair of Republicans, McCall has little regard for party labels. While considering the Senate races, McCall thought about switching to the Democratic party or running as an independent. His appointments have also cut across party lines, and some of his key staff members are Democrats."

As a lame duck governor, serving the last year of his second term, McCall is faced with several alternatives when his term expires in January 1975. He has considered teaching journalism or political science at Oregon State University or entering foundation work. Having undergone surgery for cancer of the prostate in the summer of 1973, he was reluctant to make any definite decisions until he received word from his doctors as to the success of his operation. On March 5, 1974 they gave him positive report, giving rise to speculation that he might be a candidate for the Presidency in 1976, possibly as head of a "third force," or as a Democrat. About his national ambitions, McCall has said, as quoted in the *New Yorker*: "America is beginning to open up. We've got an inherently good system. We've just got to get the right people to make it work. If I had to run for President to sell the Oregon message—to encourage more innovative and daring actions, that is—I would do it. But that will depend on a lot of things, and in any event the message is more important than the messenger."

Governor Tom McCall and his wife, the former Audrey Owen, whom he married on May 20, 1939, have two sons, Thomas Lawson and Samuel Walker 3d. The tallest among the governors of the fifty states, McCall stands at six feet five inches and weighs 217 pounds. His manner is open and candid and he speaks in a distinctive voice which, according to *Newsday* correspondent Russell Sackett "has been described as Ivy League barnyard." His accent is the upper-class Bostonian of his forebears, flavored by the ranch-hand talk of back-country eastern Oregon, where he was raised. He is an Episcopalian. His favorite recreational activities are golf, hunting, and fishing.

McCall is on the board of overseers of Lewis and Clark College in Portland. He has been a member or officer of many committees as well as civic, philanthropic, and professional organizations. His honors include the 1959 Golden Beaver Award of the Izaak Walton League, the 1964 Brotherhood Award of the Oregon Regional Conference of Christians and Jews, and the 1971 American Scenic and Historic Preservation Society Award. The Freedoms Foundation has conferred a special award on him for his weekly radio progress report to the people, and in 1965 he was awarded an honorary LL.D. degree by Linfield College in McMinnville, Oregon.

References

N Y Times p14 Jl 13 '71 por
New Yorker 50:88+ F 25 '74
Newsweek 83:49+ Ja 7 '74 por
International Who's Who, 1973-74
Who's Who in America, 1972-73

MAHARAJ JI, GURU (ma-ha-ra"ji' go͞o ro͞o)

Dec. 10, 1957- Indian spiritual leader
Address: b. Divine Light Mission, 411 16th St., Denver, Colo. 80202; P.O. Box 6495 Denver, Colo. 80206

The late psychic Edgar Cayce once prophesied that in 1969 a child born in the foothills of the Himalayas would come forth to lead the world. Devotees, or premies (from *prem*, the Hindu word for love), of Guru Maharaj Ji believe that their teen-aged "Perfect Master" is that child, the *Satguru*, or Messiah, of our time. Among the more prominent of Maharaj Ji's Western converts is Rennie Davis, the former antiwar militant, who regards him as "Lord of the Universe, the power of creation itself." (The plump young Guru himself claims only to be a "messenger.") Davis has said, "The Perfect Master is on the planet and we are standing on the edge of the greatest change in the history of the world." That change is in the direction of international peace and love, the aim of the Maharaj Ji's Divine Light Mission, which claims to have approximately seven million members around the world. The members are those who have received "the Knowledge" through a laying-on-of-hands technique taught to them in a secret rite by the Guru or one of his numerous mahatmas. That technique, according to those who use it, opens the "third eye" and enables one to "bliss out"—"to see the Divine Light, taste the Divine Nectar, and feel the Divine Vibration." The founding ashram of the Divine Light Mission is at Prem Nagar, India, and other headquarters are in Denver, Colorado and London, England. The mission is supported by members (many of whom turn over all their worldly goods to it) and by thrift shops and various other Divine Light business enterprises.

As telescoped conversationally by American premies, Guru Maharaj Ji's name is pronounced "Goom Rodgie." The Guru's full name, with title, is Pratap Singh Rawat-Balyogeshwar, Satguru Shri Maharaj Ji. According to the records of the United States Immigration and Naturalization

Service, he was born Prem Pal Singh Rawat in Hardwar, India on December 10, 1957. His widowed mother is Shri Mata Ji, known to the premies as "Holy Mother." The other members of the "Holy Family" are Guru Maharaj Ji's three older brothers, Bal Bhagwan Ji, Bhol Ji, and Raja Ji. Bal Bhagwan Ji, the eldest, has been described by close observers as the Mission's "mastermind." Bhole Ji is leader of the Blue Aquarius spiritual rock band, which plays at many of the Divine Light Mission festivals.

Like some of the other "holy men" who have come to the United States from India in recent years, Guru Maharaj Ji is regarded with skepticism in some quarters. For example, Agehananda Bharati, chairman of the Department of Anthropology at Syracuse University, sees him as a self-deceived fraud, "a typical phoney" who "believes in what he does." But he is no "ripoff," according to Khalid Shah, a correspondent for the *Illustrated Weekly of India*: "In India there is a guru on every corner, and every guru has a guru; the competition is very fierce. But I do not think Guru Maharaj Ji came here for the money. He is a member of the highest of the high Brahmin caste. His family is quite wealthy."

The father of the family was Param Sant Satgurudev Shri Hans Ji Maharaj, the anointed protégé of Perfect Master Shri Sarapanand Ji and the Perfect Master of his time. Shri Hans Ji Maharaj was a controversial figure among Brahmins, because he challenged the caste system by preaching to the lowest and poorest group in Indian society, the untouchables. He built up a large following, becoming recognized by thousands of Indian devotees as Satguru, the one living Perfect Master who reveals the ancient Knowledge of the inner self.

Shri Hans Ji Maharaj founded the Divine Light Mission in 1960. At the Prem Nagar ashram in June of the following year he gave a satsang in which he spoke of birth and reincarnation and differentiated between "rational" human life and all other forms on this planet, in which "instincts alone are working to guide actions." He said, "Non-human births are bestowed to suffer the fruits of actions—good or bad—performed with egoism and ignorance of true self during human life. . . . But human birth itself is not obtained because of the merit of previous actions. It is due only to the extreme grace of the Almighty. . . . When, through the grace of God, the soul obtains human life, a divine opportunity is opened to it to pierce the veil of delusion . . . and to realize . . . its true self, which is *satchitananda*: its existence, its life-force, and its bliss. . . . However . . . he who can bestow God-vision instantaneously within oneself is the Satguru of the time and no one else. In reality, he is God incarnate."

Before his death in 1966 Shri Hans Ji Maharaj gave his *pranams* (prostrations) to his youngest son, thus singling him out as the new Perfect Master. (Family members and others who knew Guru Maharaj Ji from birth testify that he exhibited spiritual precocity from the time he

GURU MAHARAJ JI

was a toddler.) "I didn't want to be Satguru," Maharaj Ji has said. "I didn't understand why it is me. I would have been satisfied to be the humblest servant of the Satguru." He has related what happened when his father died: "I went home [from St. Joseph's Academy in Dehra Dun] and everyone was weeping. I was just sitting there not weeping and something began to happen to me. I began to feel that I am not this body. . . . And this voice came to me saying, 'You are he, you are the one to continue.'" At the funeral the voice came again: "This is the last I will tell you. You are he. You must take this knowledge to the world." According to the Guru, "the satsang just came" and he found himself telling the mourners: "Dear children of God, why are you weeping? . . . The Perfect Master never dies. Maharaj Ji is here, amongst you now." His mother, his brothers, and all the mahatmas present immediately prostrated themselves before him and kissed his "lotus feet."

In 1969 the first Western premies arrived at the Divine Light ashram at Prem Nagar, on the banks of the Ganges, and in October of that year the first of Maharaj Ji's mahatmas, Guru Charnanand, was sent westward, to London, where he supervised the establishment of a Divine Light ashram. Among those who took knowledge from Mahatma Guru Charnanand at that time was Charles Cameron, a graduate in theology from Oxford University.

Cameron edited *Who Is Guru Maharaj Ji?* (Bantam, 1973), and in one of his own contributions to that book he told the story of his initiation: "This is the tale of a magical thing, of a goodness which came to pass. I received a gift from my Guru Maharaj Ji. By the laying on of hands, his disciple, Mahatma Guru Charnanand showed me the clear light of self inside me, a pure and living light, calm by nature, unselfish, loving, radiant, wise. . . . Guru Maharaj Ji, like all these saints [Jesus Christ, Mohammed, Krishna, Buddha] before him, graces his disciple with . . . a seed of light. But as those who read the *Gospels* know, if the field where the seed is planted is dry, the hopes of the seed are slight. . . . And I had a most dry and calculating heart. . . . So I set out for India . . . [where Maharaj Ji] opened my heart. . . . I have had no problems since that day, about my heart. It is a fine story, particularly when one remembers that Guru Maharaj Ji has already given the gift of illumination, which the Lord Buddha gave, to five million people, though he is no more than fifteen years old."

In November 1970 Guru Maharaj Ji, having quit school at the end of the ninth grade, inaugurated his international mission by riding through Delhi in a golden chariot with a retinue of camels, elephants, and devotees. The triumphal parade ended at India Gate in New Delhi, where a crowd estimated at a million and a half people assembled to pay homage to the Perfect Master. In addressing the crowd, Guru Maharaj Ji exploded what he called his "peace bomb" with the statement, "I declare that I will establish peace in this world."

Maharaj Ji made his first international tour in 1971, visiting Great Britain, Canada, and the United States. In preparation for his visit to Los Angeles his disciples there, who numbered seven at the time, distributed a flyer inviting "all brothers of love to come to welcome Guru Maharaj Ji" as he comes "in the clouds with great power and glory" in a "silver steed" that "will drift down at 4 P.M. at Los Angeles International Airport, TWA Flight 761." The flyer concluded: "The thirteen-year-old saint has come to this earth only to awaken mankind and usher in the age of spiritual revolution." Approximately 200 people (some of whom became converts) gathered at the airport as the disciples greeted their Lord, shouting "Bolie Shri Satgurudev Maharaj ki jai!" (Sing the praises of the Lord True-Revealer of Light, inexpressibly all-powerful majesty), pranaming, and strewing blossoms in his path.

Within a year Guru Maharaj Ji's following had grown so enormously that after his 1972 tour eleven jumbo jets were required to carry a small fraction of the Western devotees back to India with him to celebrate the annual three-day festival in honor of his late father. A hostile Indian religious group asked the government to arrest Guru Maharaj Ji at the airport in New Delhi and force him to submit to a medical examination to determine his true age, which, the group asserted, was twenty-two. The request was denied, but an embarrassing incident occurred nonetheless: customs officials found $80,000 in jewels, watches, and money in the briefcase of Joan Apter, who was then serving as the Guru's secretary. Spokesmen for the Guru explained that the money was to pay the expenses of Western devotees during their stay in India and that the watches and jewelry were gifts for the Guru's mother, brothers, and mahatmas. Smuggling charges were never filed, but the Indian government was at last report still looking into the Guru's taxes.

At the end of 1972 and the beginning of 1973 Guru Maharaj Ji established the Divine United Organization, or DUO, for the purpose, in his words, of remolding "this world as a humanistic society where people base their lives upon service rather than selfishness." In his DUO Proclamation he said: "The people who have experienced the Knowledge of Shri Sant Ji Maharaj . . . are compelled to reach out to the rest of struggling humanity to spread the solution to strife and suffering by a commitment to work in all fields of endeavor."

During an appearance by Guru Maharaj Ji in Detroit, Michigan on August 7, 1973 Pat Haley, an underground newspaper reporter, threw a shaving-cream pie in the Guru Maharaj Ji's face. Unruffled, the Guru gave his attacker his forgiveness blessing, but his followers were not so merciful. A week later Haley was visited by two devotees of the Guru and beaten almost to death, suffering a fractured skull. "They acted out of pure devotion," Dr. John Horton, a physician-devotee explained. "It was a crime of passion."

In November 1973 the annual three-day celebration in honor of Guru Maharaj Ji's father was made the occasion for "Millenium '73," a super spectacle held in the Astrodome in Houston, Texas and coordinated by Rennie Davis. The "cosmic" purpose of the spectacle was implicit in its name, an allusion to the thousand years of peace prophesied in the twentieth chapter of Revelation, the last book of the New Testament. It was promoted accordingly. Ballyhooed as "the most holy and significant event in human history" and staged at considerable expense (at least $400,000, not counting the $75,000 rental for the stadium and the cost of chartering thirty-three jet airliners to fly premies in from all over the world), it was expected to attract overflow crowds to the 44,500-seat stadium, but less than 20,000 people showed up. The disappointing attendance did not seem to disconcert Guru Maharaj Ji, who reigned serenely over the event from a flame-shaped throne atop a thirty-five-foot stage, enjoying the electronic fireworks, and the music of the Blue Aquarius band and giving satsang. Typical of the parables he uses in giving satsang is the comparison of the Knowledge to the taste of an orange, which cannot be known second-hand but must be experienced directly. In Houston, as he has on many occasions elsewhere, he advised his audience: "Try it. You'll like it."

At a press conference given during Millenium '73 a reporter asked Guru Maharaj Ji about his much publicized (and much criticized) Rolls Royce. "If you're going to feed a child this morning he's going to be hungry again this afternoon . . . ," he replied. "All a Rolls-Royce is, a piece of tin. If I gave poor people my Rolls-Royce they would need more tomorrow and I don't have any more Rolls-Royce to give them." When another reporter asked, "Are you the son of God?" he replied, "Everyone is the son of God. None of you ain't the uncle or aunt of God," and later in the news conference he said, "I am a humble servant of God." "Then why do your devotees say you're God?" he was asked. "Why don't you ask them?" the Guru shot back.

In the December 13, 1973 issue of the *New York Review of Books* Francine du Plessix Gray described a satsang given in New York City by one of the Guru Maharaj Ji's mahatmas: "His teaching is not vastly different from that of the Vedantists. . . . The rational everyday mind is the obstacle, the great demon that stands in the way of Understanding; suffering is created by the duality which that mind posits; Enlightenment is the resolution of that duality and the merging into the One Consciousness. The mahatma's principal departure from rigorous Vedanta doctrine is that Maharaj Ji does not want his devotees to leave the world. Quite the contrary, we must keep our jobs and enjoy our meals. . . . The new Divine Knowledge of Maharaj Ji will give us increased concentration and will make us *better* businessmen, musicians, writers. We can have our cake and eat it too."

The reaction to Guru Maharaj Ji by religious and spiritual leaders and scholars outside his own movement varies widely. Voga Dhyan Ahuja, author of numerous books on Asian culture and religion, sees him as "an enlightened soul . . . out to share his enlightenment," and the Rev. Daniel Berrigan S.J., noting that "many of our young people are without direction or hope, and our own churches are able to offer very little, being themselves complicit in many of our social crimes," has called the Guru's coming westward "a great blessing." But Swami Prabhupada, spiritual master of the International Society for Krishna Consciousness, has told his followers that Maharaj Ji is to be denounced for falsely claiming to be God; Swami Gitananda, president of the Worldwide Yoga Congress, has called him an "idiot" while conceding that he is apparently successful in "turning on thousands of young people," who might otherwise be on drugs, to "genuine spiritual experiences"; and the Rev. Robert Montgomery, a Protestant clergyman who engaged in public debate with representatives of Maharaji Ji in Houston during "Millennium 73," believes Maharaj Ji is "controlled by a demon." The Rev. Montgomery sees the Guru as "a peculiarly dangerous minion" of Satan, "helping to create" a robotized world in which "all the little white rats will do what they are told." The wittiest rejection of Guru Maharaj Ji came from the lips of political renegade Abbie Hoffman: "If the Guru Maharaj Ji is God, he is the God America deserves."

According to its own estimate, the Divine Light Mission has approximately 60,000 members in the United States, but that figure, along with its international membership claim, is based on the gross number of people who have taken Knowledge and not the net number who have remained faithful. Premies are encouraged to become renunciates (celibates as well as vegetarians, teetotalers, and abstainers from cigarettes and drugs), but there are ashrams for married devotees who do not wish to renounce sex. They are also encouraged to turn over their fortunes and incomes to the Mission. Complete devotees are provided with all necessities of life but receive no salary, unless they bring in one from a job outside the ashram. There are approximately fifty ashrams in the United States, in addition to the stores and other enterprises run by the Mission.

The headquarters of the Divine Light Mission is a plush seven-story office building in Denver, Colorado. From that base an unpaid staff, using computers, Telex machines, and other electronic equipment, coordinates the activities of all American ashrams and Divine Light commercial and professional enterprises. The latter include Divine Sales Thrift Shops; Shri Hans Engineering and Divine Electronics, wholesalers; Shri Hans Aviation, the Divine Light Mission's own little airline; Divine Travel Services and Divine Travel International, which arrange the transportation of devotees to and from Divine Light events; Shri Hans Publications, which issues the weekly newspaper *Divine Times* and the monthly glossy magazine *And It Is Divine*; the Cleanliness Is Next to Godliness handyman service; a vegetarian restaurant in New York City; Shri Hans Productions, which makes documentary films, records, and other educational and media items; and Shri Hans Humanitarian Services, which operates a medical clinic in New York City and a school for children in Denver and plans to open drug clinics and health centers. Eventually the Divine Light Mission hopes to realize the building of the Divine City, a Millenium abode for the elect that is, according to the plans premie-architect Larry Bernstein is working on, to be suspended between the cliffs of a great canyon.

In September 1974 Guru Maharaji Ji's business manager, Michael Clegg, and eight of his associates were indicted in New York for conspiracy, fraud, and sale of unregistered stock in the Pioneer Development Company of Reno, Nevada, described as a "shell" company in the indictment. The Guru was not named in the indictment, and a United States attorney made clear that he was not viewed as a participant in any of the alleged criminal acts. In Denver, state and city sales tax agents have been investigating the legality of some of the tax-exempt purchases made by the Guru and his followers. But it is unlikely that the tax-exempt status of the Divine Light Mission can be successfully challenged, so wrapped is it in constitutional protections. Tax experts cite a March 1, 1974 ruling in which a federal judge in California declared, "Neither this court nor any branch of this government will consider the merits or fallacies of any religion."

Guru Maharaj Ji and Marolyn Lois Johnson, a young woman who worked as a United Airlines stewardess before becoming private secretary to the Guru, were married in Denver on May 20, 1974. The site of the wedding was the $80,-000 home that the Divine Light Mission maintains for Maharaj Ji on Dahlia Street in the Colorado capital. The DLM also provides him with expensive residences in London, Los Angeles, Old Westbury (New York), and several Indian cities. In addition to his automobiles (a Rolls-Royce in Los Angeles and Mercedes-Benzes in Denver and New York), the Maharaj Ji has received, among other gifts from his followers, two Cessna airplanes (which he can pilot), a cabin cruiser, a motorcycle, and gold digital watches.

The chunky young Guru, always majestically imperturbable of mien, has a mobile face, capable of changing in an instant from a warm, childish grin to an inscrutable, aloof expression. He wears his neatly trimmed and styled black hair slicked back, and lately he has begun to grow a wispy mustache. His dress varies from occasion to occasion, but white satin robes or Nehru-style suits and patent leather boots are staples in his wardrobe. His English is full of current slang terms such as "dig it" and "far out." Despite an intestinal ulcer, he is usually jolly and has a lively sense of humor. Among his favorite *lilas* (divine pranks) is squirting people with a water pistol. He tops off his vegetarian meals with huge portions of ice cream, and he likes to watch "Little Rascals" comedies and horror movies on television. An aficionado of "Batman" comic books, he sometimes uses them in his parables. In a satsang in New York in 1973, for example, he explained the reluctance of many people to accept his message in terms of someone who has been looking all over New York City for Batman comics to no avail. If, after having given up, such a person were approached by a boy saying "Hey, you want Batman comic?" the reaction would probably be, according to Maharaj Ji, "What? Come on, don't make a fool of me. You don't have Batman comic. I search everywhere and there is none."

References

Denver Post mag p10+ Ap 21 '74 por
N Y Post p39 Je 18 '74 por
Nat Observer p 1+ N 3 '73 por
New Times 1:47+ D 28 '73 pors
Newsweek 82:157+ N 19 '73
Sat R World 1:18+ F 9 '74 por
Time 100:52 N 27 '72 por

Cameron, Charles. Who Is Guru Maharaj Ji? (1973)

MASSON, ANDRÉ (AIMÉ RENÉ) (mä″sôn′)

Jan. 4, 1896- French artist
Address: h. 26 rue de Sévigné, Paris 4ᵉ, France

Like Heraclitus, whose portrait he once painted, the philosophic French artist André Masson searches for unity in antithesis and diversity. His work is both a clash and resolution, sometimes, of conflict between the rational and spontaneous, the scientific and the metaphysical, between aesthetic loyalties, and between pure form and literary content. Heraclitean also in his elemental view of the cosmos and in his preoccupation with change and event, Masson has been credited by his compatriot Jean-Paul Sartre with "retracing a whole mythology of metamorphoses: [transforming] the domain of the mineral, the domain of the vegetable, and the domain of the animal into the domain of the human." Although he is considered to fall short in influence and achievement of Pablo Picasso and Joan Miró, two of his fellow pioneers of surrealism, he is a painter and graphic artist of important stylistic innovation, whose gestural, automatic thrust of bold, free forms into space forged a link between the School of Paris and the New York School of abstract expressionists.

André Aimé René Masson was born near Paris, at Balagny-sur-Thérain in the Oise department of France, on January 4, 1896 to Aimé and Marthe (Bénard) Masson. Unlike Miró, with whom he otherwise shares quite a number of significant characteristics, he seems to have derived little or no inspiration for his work from memories of childhood. But by adolescence he had become absorbed in the beauty, wildness, and drama of nature—a fascination that made itself felt throughout the many stages of his development as a painter.

The devotion to books that accounts for the abundance of philosophic and literary themes in Masson's oeuvre also thrived in his adolescence. At sixteen his hero was Nietzsche. Other writers who then or later influenced the direction of his thinking, in addition to Heraclitus, included the Marquis de Sade, Rimbaud, Lautréamont, and Kafka. Beginning his formal artistic training early, he attended the École des Beaux-Arts in Brussels before he enrolled, in 1912, in the École des Beaux-Arts in Paris to study fresco painting under Paul-Albert Baudouin. Among the painters whom he admired as a student were Poussin, Delacroix, Uccello, El Greco, and Piranesi.

When World War I broke out, Masson returned to France from a prolonged visit in Switzerland to join his country's armed forces in the romantic hope of experiencing the "Wagnerian aspects of battle." In a front-line assault early in the war he was so severely wounded that he believed himself dead. Despite prolonged medical treatment in several hospitals and confinement in a psychiatric institution, he remained deeply scarred, physically and mentally. Nightmares have plagued André Masson throughout his life.

His traumatic experience of war also left Masson engrossed in the theme of mortality, as persistent in his work as his convictions that brutality and sadism are integral components of human nature and that man's reason inevitably surrenders to irrationality. The war also confirmed his penchant for rebellion, leading him to an anarchistic rejection of philosophical and political systems and even of allegiance to any fixed school of art.

During the postwar years of recuperation Masson tried his hand at various skills, such as acting in motion pictures and making ceramics. In 1919 he spent some time at Céret in the Pyrenees, studying with the sculptor Manolo. By the time he returned to Paris in 1922, he was concentrating on painting. His early pictures, such as the somewhat Derain-like landscape *Trees* (1923) and tranquil still lifes, seem to seek through their order and subdued color to overcome the artist's inner chaos. They may be said to provide a calm against which Masson could balance a gradually emerging turbulence, setting a pattern of counterpose that the art critic Otto Hahn regarded in *Masson* (1965) as the artist's method of finding, establishing, rejecting.

Eagerly experimental along with many other artists in the Parisian aesthetic hotbed of the early 1920's, Masson veered toward the erratic mode of Dadaism before succumbing to a brief but clearly recognizable attraction to cubism in *The Card Players* (1923), *The Sleeper* (1924), and *Glass and Architecture* (1924). His cubist-derived style, suggestive especially of Juan Gris, continued in movement and feeling to be peculiarly his own. "Influences are the nourishment of artists," Masson once remarked, as quoted in *Newsweek* (November 15, 1965). "The lion eats the sheep but remains a lion."

In his association with surrealism, similarly, Masson retained his individuality, considering hmself a sympathizer with surrealism rather than a faithful follower of the tenets of *Manifeste de Surréalisme*, published by André Breton in 1924. Drawn, however, to the "psychic automatism" of surrealism, for some years Masson belonged to the inner circle of the movement. He had exhibited his pictures for the first time in February 1924 at the Galerie Simon in Paris and two years later joined Braque and Gris in an exhibition at the Galerie Jeanne Bucher in Paris. Between those two shows he took part in the first group exhibition of surrealist artists, at the Galerie Pierre in Paris in 1925, when his work was presented along with that of Picasso, Miró, Max Ernst, Paul Klee, and others of the first generation of surrealists.

Some of the paintings of Masson's early surrealist period, such as *Wreath* (1925), retain the organized structure and pictorial discipline of cubism. The many pictures, however, that he contributed to the review *La Révolution Surréaliste* during the 1920's show his command of automatic drawing, his exploitation of what Gertrude Stein called "the wandering line." In his study of Masson, Hahn pointed out that the artist's "inner rhythm" asserts itself in his automatic drawings, which Hahn described as "delirious germinations complicated to the point of becoming nothing more than labyrinthine tangles of vegetable, organic, or mental circuits."

Linear errantry lent spontaneity also to Masson's sand paintings, such as *Death's Head* (1927). On a canvas laid on the floor, he automatically drew lines in glue to hold sand sprinkled on them. In the quick execution of his work and in the exertion of his whole body in the process of painting, he anticipated the manner of the American action painters of post-World War II. Also significant for his relationship to the gestural artists of the New York School was his conception of "space as a totality without center," to use Hahn's phrase.

Blending a rapidly moving, convoluted line with a content of violent action, Masson depicted scenes of combat between animals, like *Battle of Fishes* (1928), of creatures devouring each

ANDRÉ MASSON

other, and, in his Massacre series (1932-33), of men and women in frenzied conflict. The eroticism implied and symbolized in many of the pictures became explicit in his Lovers series (1930) and such paintings as *Bacchanalia* (1934). A recurrent subject of Masson during the 1930's was the myth of the Minotaur, which combined his favorite themes of eroticism, mortality, and metamorphosis. The many pictures in which he explored the myth in different media include the drawing *The Lily and the Minotaur* (1932), the etching *Minotaur* (1933) of his Sacrifices series, the oil painting *Labyrinth* (1938), the oil and sand canvas *Story of Theseus* (1939), and the oil and tempera *Pasiphaë* (1943). Strife and suffering in Masson's art are sometimes relieved by visual wit, but more significantly, as H. H. Arnason explained in *History of Modern Art* (1968), by "a passionate hope, through painting, to be able to find and express the mysterious unity of the universe hinted at in primitive myths and religions."

From 1934 to 1936 Masson lived in Spain, first in Andalusia and then at Tossa de Mar in Catalonia. There, besides continuing to track the Minotaur, he painted insect forms, as in his lively and delicately colored *Summer Frolic* (1934), a Bullfight series, and Spanish landscapes. At the outbreak of the Spanish Civil War he returned to France, where he expressed his disgust with oppression in *Not Enough Earth* (1937) and *Dream of a Future Desert* (1938), among other drawings. Having been alienated from the surrealists since 1933, he became reconciled with Breton in the late 1930's, when during a second surrealist period he reexamined and summarized his earlier styles and themes, sometimes compressing into a single picture the forms and ideas he had developed previously in several pictures. He worked, characteristically, in series: the Metamorphoses, the Anthropomorphic Furniture, and the Mythology of Nature. One canvas of the period that illustrates his surrealist celebration of the fantastic, the grotesque, and the hallucinational is *House of Birds* (1939).

After the Nazi invasion of France during World War II, Masson found refuge in the United States, following stopovers in Martinique and the Antilles. Living in or near New York City from 1941 to 1945, he became fascinated, he has said, by "American energy" and painted what he felt to be the power and climate of the country. American Indian myths inspired such pictures as *The Grain of Millet* (1942) and *The Maize Myth* (1942). The vigor of his brushwork and intensity of emotion in, for example, *There Is No Finished World* (1942) and *Contemplation of the Abyss* (1943) and the sand-canvas technique of his *Cat and Fish* (1942) may very well have impressed Jackson Pollock and other young pioneers of abstract expressionism. They had an opportunity to see his work during the war years in exhibitions at the Baltimore Museum of Art and at the Paul Rosenberg and Buchholz Gallery in New York City.

Almost as soon as the war ended, Masson went home to France, in November 1945. In one creative outburst during a period of tension and restlessness in 1947 he produced in a single day twenty-two drawings on the theme of desire. Dividing his residence between Paris and Aix-en-Provence, in the south of France he resumed his study of nature and embarked on new experiments. In his oil painting *Pomegranate Branch* (1952), as L. M. Saphire observed in his notes for the catalogue of Masson's 1972 exhibition in New York, he "technically takes the Impressionist colors and applies them automatically in a virtuoso performance, merging Impressionist perception of light with surrealist dynamism."

In another postwar unfolding of his art Masson developed his gift for automatic writing into a mastery of calligraphic forms, as in the paintings *Abyss* (1955), *Constellation of the Lovers* (1958), and *Aquatic Migrations* (1959); in the etching *Chinese Actors* (1957); and in the ink drawing *The Life of a Flower* (1959). During the 1960's, while following his usual practice of retracing and extending earlier techniques and ideas, he painted many pictures in what had become the idiom of the abstract expressionists, leading some critics to suggest that he was copying the very artists to whom he had pointed the way.

Almost all of the major themes of Masson's paintings are paralleled in books of which he is both author and illustrator, among them *Mythology of Nature, Mythology of Being* (1936), *Anatomy of My Universe* (1943), and *Nocturnal Notebook* (1944). In the twelve lithographs on the beast in the human being that make up his *Bestiary* (1945), he expressed his pessimistic view of man as a fighter of world wars. Masson is also the illustrator of books, mainly erotic, by other writers, including the Marquis de Sade, Louis Aragon, Georges Batille, and André Malraux. It was to illustrate the poetry of Georges Limbour that Masson taught himself etching in the mid-1920's. His prints number well over 800.

Throughout much of his long career Masson also demonstrated a devotion to the performing arts in his designs, for instance, for the scenery of performances of Massine's ballet *Les Présages* (1933) and Cherubini's opera *Medea* (1940) and for several theatrical productions directed by Jean-Louis Barrault, including Cervantes' *Numances* (1937), *Hamlet* (1946), and Alban Berg's opera *Wozzeck* (1963). Commissioned by André Malraux, then the French Minister of Culture, to paint a new ceiling for l'Odéon Théâtre de France in Paris, Masson designed a 180-square-yard brightly colored circular panel crowded with symbols of tragedy and comedy, including depictions of Agamemnon, Lysistrata, and Falstaff. Of the ceiling, which was completed in 1965, he said, as reported in *Newsweek* (November 15, 1965), "It is the synthesis of all my various periods." The *Newsweek* writer also noted Jean-Louis Barrault's reaction to the ceiling upon first seeing it: "At last we have a sun over our heads."

Masson's work has been widely exhibited in Europe and the United States. His first retrospective in his own country was held at the Museum of Modern Art in Paris in March 1965. He later had retrospective shows in Lyons and Marseille. In 1973 the Blue Moon Gallery and the Lerner-Heller Gallery jointly organized in New York City an exhibition of fifty-two of Masson's paintings and drawings along with a selection of graphics. Emily Genauer, art critic of *Newsday* (November 9, 1973), found it "an arresting and absorbing retrospective," but Hilton Kramer complained in the New York *Times* (November 18, 1973) that the show lacked comprehensiveness, so that while Masson is "a figure of great interest," Americans still know his work "only in fragments." Masson's awards include the Grand Prix national des Arts (1954) and a São Paulo Biennale prize for theatrical design (1963). He is an Officer of the Legion of Merit and a Commander of Arts and Letters. Since 1962 he has been a member of the purchasing commission of the museums of France.

On December 28, 1934 André Masson married Rose Makles. By that marriage he is the father of Diego and Luis. He has another child, Gladys, by an earlier marriage. Almost a decade ago he was described in *Newsweek* (November 15, 1965) as a "white-haired, gentle old lion," still in pursuit of his "tranquility." His hobby is collecting Greek and Hindu sculpture and *objets exotiques*.

References

Arts 48:72+ N '73
Le Monde p7 Jl 15-21 '71
N Y Times II p21 D 3 '72; II p25 N 18 '73
New Yorker 37:87+ F 25 '61
Newsday p11 N 9 '73
Newsweek 66:106 N 15 '65 por
Arnason, H. H. History of Modern Art (1968)
Encyclopedia of World Art vol 13 (1967)
Hahn, Otto. Masson (1965)
International Who's Who, 1973-74
Praeger Encyclopedia of Art vol 4 (1971)
Who's Who in France, 1971-72

MAUCH, GENE (WILLIAM) (mok)

Nov. 18, 1925- Baseball manager
Address: b. Montreal Expos, P.O. Box 500,
Station R, Montreal, Quebec H2S 3G7, Canada

Tough, determined Gene Mauch, manager of the
Montreal Expos in the Eastern Division of the
National League, is regarded by many veteran
baseball observers as the best major league mentor to have come along in many a year, and the
number of manager-of-the-year awards Mauch
has collected confirm that assessment. Mauch began his professional career as a fringe infielder
who was constantly shuttled from team to team,
league to league, and majors to minors. During
seventeen years as a player he saw action in only
304 games with six major league teams. A steady
clinch hitter but no slugger, he came away from
737 times at bat with 176 hits, thirty-seven of
them for extra bases, and an average of .239. As
manager over the past fifteen years (nine in Philadelphia and six in Montreal), he has guided his
teams to a win-loss record of 992-1,142. "Gene
Mauch has the most fertile, inventive mind of any
manager in the game today," John Robertson
noted in an article on Mauch in *Maclean's* (June
1974). "He will resort to any tactic to beat you."

Gene William Mauch was born on November
18, 1925 in Salina, Kansas, where his father ran
a chain of bakeries and Gene himself early exhibited athletic prowess. Mauch has called his
father "the greatest man" he ever knew: "There
wasn't nothing he couldn't do. Nothing! The Depression ruined his business so he said, 'If I'm
going to work like a dog to make a living here,
I might as well go to California where Gene can
concentrate on being an athlete all year round.'
Now I never had great natural ability, but I was
a good all-round athlete. I was best at ball and
I was a red-ass, a helluva lot like Tom Foli [the
Expos' shortstop] . . . always agitating."

The Mauchs settled in Los Angeles, where
Gene was a star high school infielder. In 1943, at
the end of his junior year, Mauch dropped out of
school to join the Brooklyn Dodgers' organization.
The Dodgers assigned him to Durham, North
Carolina in the Piedmont League, where he batted
.322 and fielded .893 in the shortstop position.
He finished the 1943 season with Montreal, then
in the International League, where his averages
were .169 and .865. With Montreal he played
second base as well as shortstop.

In 1944 Mauch was called up to Brooklyn, and
in five games of National League play that year
he had averages of .133 and 1.000. During the
rest of the season he played fourteen games with
Montreal, batting .283 and tallying .889 at shortstop. For two years beginning in May 1944 he
was in military service. After his discharge he
went back into the Dodgers farm system, where
he batted .248 and fielded .918 with St. Paul.

On May 3, 1947 Mauch was traded to the Pittsburgh Pirates, also in the National League, and
playing with Pittsburgh in the 1947 season he
tallied .300 at the plate and .927 at shortstop. He

GENE MAUCH

finished the season with Pittsburgh's Indianapolis
club, where he played second base and had averages of .300 and .967. On December 7, 1947
Pittsburgh traded him back to Brooklyn, and early
in the 1948 season the Dodgers in turn sold him
to the National League's Chicago Cubs. In sixty-
five games of National League play in 1948 he
hit .199 and fielded .942.

The Cubs traded Mauch to the Boston Braves
in December 1949. In two seasons with Boston
he batted .231 and .100 and fielded .960 and .970.
In the midst of the 1951 season the Braves sent
him to Milwaukee, where his averages were .303
and .959 in thirty-seven games. "He wasn't fast,
he didn't have a great arm, he didn't have a lot
of power," Milwaukee manager Bobby Bragan
later observed. "But he got the most out of what
he had."

The New York Yankees of the American League
drafted Mauch following the 1951 season and
sold him via waivers to the St. Louis Cardinals
of the National League before the opening of the
1952 season. After his seventh game with St.
Louis, the Cardinals returned him to Milwaukee,
in the Boston Braves' organization. His 1952 averages were .000 and .500 in St. Louis and .324 and
.975 in Milwaukee.

The Braves transferred Mauch to Atlanta, where
he batted .268 and fielded .961 in 111 games as
second baseman in 1953. More important, he had
his first shot at managing in that season. John
Quinn, who was then general manager of the
Braves, recommended Mauch when the managing
opportunity presented itself. "Since that time,"
Quinn said seven years later, "I observed that he
had the qualities I like to see in a manager—
enthusiasm, knowledge of baseball, ambition,
alertness, and the ability to handle players."
Under Mauch, Atlanta won eighty-four games and
lost seventy, finishing third in the Southern
Association.

The Braves' organization released Mauch to
Los Angeles, in the Chicago Cubs' farm system,
in September 1953. During three seasons with

Los Angeles he played second and third base, batting .287, .296, and .348 and fielding .975, .978, and .969. Near the end of the 1956 season he was released to the Boston Red Sox, in the American League. Playing seven games with Boston in 1956, he had averages of .320 and .935. The following year he played sixty-five games with the Red Sox, batting .270 and fielding .962.

During his years as a player Mauch made good use of the frequent periods he spent on the bench. "Mauch would sit beside managers and study their tactics and, by his own testimony, say to them, 'Why in hell did you do that?'" Myron Cope observed in the *Saturday Evening Post* (August 1-8, 1964). "So far as is known, no manager resented him. 'I imagine I had as many friends in baseball as anybody,' insists Mauch, while admitting that his scrappy playing style led to many appointments with opposing players under the grandstands."

In 1958 Mauch went to Minneapolis in the American Association as player-manager. As manager, he guided the Minneapolis Millers to eighty-two wins and seventy-one losses in 1958 and ninety-five wins and sixty-seven losses in 1959, when the Millers won the Junior World Series championship. As infielder in 1958, Mauch played in sixty-five games, batting .243 and fielding .938. In 1959 he pinch-hit in eight games for an average of .500.

Meanwhile general manager John Quinn had moved from Boston to the National League's Philadelphia Phillies, and when Philadelphia field manager Eddie Sawyer quit, the day after the 1960 season opened, Quinn immediately brought in Mauch to replace Sawyer. Mauch's first two years as manager of the Phillies were inauspicious, with the team tallying 58-94 and 47-107 and finishing in last place both years. In 1962 Philadelphia moved up a notch, to seventh place, on the basis of a decent 81-80 record, and the following year, when it won sixty-seven games and lost seventy-five, it moved up to fourth place. In 1962 Mauch was named National League Manager of the Year in the annual poll of Associated Press sports writers.

Mauch's best year as manager in Philadelphia was 1964, when the Phillies almost won the National League pennant. Ahead six and a half games with two weeks to go in the season, they lost ten games in a row and finished in a tie for second place. Many observers blamed the end-of-season slump on a change in Mauch's usually audacious style. During most of the season he had juggled his lineup in the most untraditional ways, and he had used four-man rotation on the mound. But when the race for the pennant neared its end he became cautious and finished the season with just two pitchers, Jim Bunning and Chris Short, who were worked to the point of exhaustion. Despite the disappointing ending, Mauch was for the second time named National League Manager of the Year in the AP poll.

Philadelphia finished sixth in the National League with a record of 85-76 in 1965; fourth with 87-75 in 1966, and fifth with 82-80 in 1967,

when Mauch won the manager-of-the-year honors in both the Associated Press and United Press polls. Meanwhile, friction had developed between Mauch and the Phillies' star slugger, Richie Allen, chiefly because Mauch objected to Allen's off-the-field behavior. Siding with Allen, Philadelphia owner Bob Carpenter dismissed Mauch and replaced him with Bob Skinner on June 16, 1968, when the Phillies' record stood at 28-27.

Four days after Carpenter fired Mauch, Ed Rumill reminisced in the *Christian Science Monitor* (June 19, 1968): "Only the Phillies' clubhouse custodian and his aide would beat Mauch to the park and often they had to hustle to do it. . . . The sort of dedicated baseball man who started thinking about the chores of the day the instant he awoke in the morning, . . . Mauch demanded . . . 100 percent in effort from every player. . . . If you didn't hustle for Mauch, he let you know about it. But more than one player has told me that the dapper little Californian always did it in an adult manner, away from the eyes and ears of the others in the clubhouse. If the news got out, it came from the player. Mauch's impatience was generally with himself—his criticism with his own mistakes."

The Montreal Expos came into existence as a major league team when, following the 1968 season, the National League expanded from ten teams to twelve and split into two divisions. On September 5, 1968 Mauch was offered the job of building the new franchise from the ground up, and it took him only twenty seconds to decide to accept. His fledgling team finished sixth in the National League East with a record of 52-110 in 1969 and in the same place with 73-89 the following year. In 1971 it moved up to fifth place with 71-90, and in 1972 it again finished fifth, with 70-86.

Mauch was named *Sporting News* Major League Manager of the Year and Associated Press National League Manager of the Year in 1973, when he guided the Expos to seventy-nine wins and eighty-three losses and fourth place in the National League East. In 1974 the Montreal team again won seventy-nine games, as against eighty-two losses, and again finished fourth. On October 16, 1974 Mauch signed a new two-year contract with the Expos. On that occasion he told reporters, "This begins phase two of our program here. The first six years with the Expos was the reclamation phase as we worked with expansion players, etc. Now we are into the development stage where we have a surplus of youngsters to work with." Jim Fanning, the Montreal general manager, commented, "Actually, when we played ourselves out of the National League East race last August, it gave us a chance to play our farm kids, and they won eighteen of twenty-two games."

Gene Mauch, who was described by John Robertson in his *Maclean's* article as having a "rock-hard frame" and "ramrod carriage," is five feet ten inches tall and weighs 173 pounds. To keep in shape he does fifty pushups every morning before breakfast, and his favorite recreation, aside from vacationing with his wife,

Nina Lee, is golf. Mauch is an intense man, "a gritty, gutsy little thinker," as Jack Olsen described him a decade ago in *Sports Illustrated* (August 10, 1964). A sharp, rasping voice and a talent for invective contribute to the impression of a tough exterior, but deep beneath the surface he is, according to those who know him well, a soft-hearted "father" to his men.

An old-fashioned disciplinarian, Mauch imposes strict rules on the Montreal players. He will not allow them, for example, to follow the current hirsuite trend in baseball and grow long hair or mustaches. In the *Maclean's* article John Robertson explained why the players accept the restrictions without grumbling: "Because they know that just about every one of them came here with some real or imagined flaw which caused them to be set adrift by other organizations. And he instilled in them an unwavering belief that not only can they play in the National League, they can win in the National League."

References

Christian Sci Mon p4 Ap 22 '60 por
Maclean's 87:40+ Je '74 pors
N Y Daily News p101 O 17 '74 por
Baseball Register, 1975
Who's Who in Professional Baseball (1973)

MESKILL, THOMAS J.

Jan. 30, 1928- Governor of Connecticut
Address: State Capitol Bldg., Hartford, Conn. 06115

The first Republican Governor of Connecticut in sixteen years, Thomas J. Meskill was elected on November 4, 1970 after campaigning on a pledge to establish sound fiscal policies for his financially troubled state. During his first year in office, he was faced with a huge deficit of $260,000,000, but by August 1973, he was able to report a budget surplus of approximately $65,000,000, the highest in Connecticut history. His success, however, was clouded by two years of intense and bitter disputes with his embattled Democratic opposition in the state assembly. Citing personal reasons, Meskill announced on March 11, 1974 that he would not run for reelection in the following November. That election was won by Democrat Ella T. Grasso on November 5, 1974. A lawyer, Meskill had been a corporation counsel, mayor, and Congressman before his election as Governor of Connecticut.

The son of Thomas J. and Laura (Warren) Meskill, Thomas J. Meskill was born on January 30, 1928 in the small industrial city of New Britain, Connecticut, near Hartford. His father, a purchasing agent for the Stanley Works, was active in politics as a state central committeeman and chairman of the Republican town committee of New Britain. Sister Laura Marie, the governor's older sister, is a Roman Catholic nun. After attending local schools and the St. Thomas Seminary in Bloomfield, Connecticut, Meskill entered New Britain High School, from which he graduated with honors in 1946. He obtained his B.S. degree in 1950 from Trinity College in Hartford, Connecticut.

THOMAS J. MESKILL

In September 1950, just after the outbreak of the Korean War, Meskill enlisted in the United States Air Force. A graduate of the officers' candidate school in December 1951, he served in Alaska until 1953. After his discharge with the rank of first lieutenant he returned to his home state to attend the University of Connecticut Law School, where he edited the law review in his senior year. He received his LL.B. degree in 1956, and after some postgraduate study at the New York University School of Law, settled in New Britain, where he became a partner in the law firm of Meskill, Dorsey, Sledzik, & Walsh.

In 1960 Meskill made his first bid for public office, when he ran as the Republican candidate for mayor of New Britain, a city in which Democratic voters outnumber Republicans two to one. After losing the election, he bided his time by serving as assistant corporation counsel of New Britain from 1960 until 1962. Successful in his second attempt, he won the mayoralty election in April 1962 and served as mayor of his hometown for two years.

Having failed to hold on to his mayoral post after the April 1964 election, Meskill decided to challenge the incumbent Democratic Representative Bernard F. Grabowski for the newly formed Sixth Congressional District seat in the United States House of Representatives. Encompassing almost a quarter of Connecticut, the district consists of a number of industrial towns scattered throughout a predominantly rural area in the northwestern corner of the state. Throughout the campaign, Meskill bore down heavily on his effectiveness as mayor of New Britain, especially on his ability to obtain federal aid for his constituents. His opponent, however, making an issue of the Presidential tickets headed by Republican Barry M. Goldwater and Democrat Lyndon B. Johnson, associated himself with Johnson and implied that a vote for Meskill was a vote for Goldwater. Receiving 41.3 percent of the vote to his opponent's 58.7 percent, Meskill was defeated in November 1964 by over 34,000 votes.

While waiting for another opportunity, Meskill served as corporation counsel of New Britain from 1965 to 1966. He then once again campaigned for the seat in the Sixth Congressional District and this time beat his former rival by the slim margin of 2,000 votes in November 1966. According to a *Congressional Quarterly* election profile, Meskill's victory was, to some degree, the result of a splitting of Democratic votes by peace candidate Stephen Minot and increasing voter dissatisfaction with inflation and expansion in federal spending. It was no accident that Meskill was endorsed during his campaign by the Ripon Society, the Republicans for Progress, and the conservative Americans for Constitutional Action.

During his first session in the House, Meskill was assigned to the Judiciary Committee. The major bills that he supported during his first term in office dealt with the increasing of funds for the war in Vietnam; the cutting back of allocations for model cities projects; a civil rights open housing measure; an omnibus crime bill with provisions for wiretapping and gun controls; and a Labor and Health, Education, and Welfare appropriations bill that included a provision for withholding funds from Southern districts that violated busing and school closing laws. Key issues that Meskill opposed during 1967 and 1968 included a measure providing for additional rent supplements to the poor; a bill to cut antipoverty funds; and a 10 percent income tax surcharge.

Defeating his Democratic challenger, Robert M. Sharaf, by an overwhelming 50,000 votes, Meskill was reelected to a second term in the House in November 1968. Because he felt somewhat insecure as a public speaker, he relied heavily during his campaign on personal contact with the electorate at such places as factories and shopping centers. In debates with Sharaf he said that there could be no end to the United States's bombing in Vietnam so long as the lives of American troops were in danger and that the Viet Cong had to end their fighting before they could be included in peace negotiations. As for domestic civil disorders and street violence, he conceded that the best deterrent was social justice, while insisting that, to a certain extent, Communist agitation was responsible for the unrest. It was reported in the New York *Times* (October 17, 1968) that Meskill was delighted to see Nixon faring so well in the national polls.

Continuing on the Judiciary committee in his second term, Meskill was concurrently appointed to the Post Office and Civil Service committee. During 1969-70 he supported bills dealing with tax and Selective Service reform, including the introduction of the lottery; coal mine safety; President Nixon's family assistance plan; and the right of eighteen-year-olds to vote. He voted against Labor, HEW, and foreign aid allocations. According to James Quinn in the *New Republic*

(May 29, 1971), "Meskill, during two terms in Congress, had chalked up the most conservative voting record of any Connecticut congressman in decades." He fairly consistently supported the conservative coalition in the House, attaining scores of 72, 57, and 76 percent for the years 1967 to 1969, respectively. In 1968 he received a rating of 71 percent from the Americans for Constitutional Action.

Raising the sights of his ambitions, on February 23, 1970 Meskill announced his candidacy for governor of Connecticut. Although well-known and well-liked in his own district, he remained an unknown quantity to the rest of the voters until he campaigned in the first statewide primary race in Connecticut's history, which he won on August 12, 1970. During his primary campaign he berated the Democrats for mismanagement of the state's finances, which, he contended, was the reason for a deficit of over $200,000,000. He called for the use of wiretaps as a deterrent to crime, and for measures to fight pollution and drug abuse, the latter being the voters' major concern, according to the results of a statewide poll sponsored by Republicans.

Elected on November 4, 1970, Meskill became the first Republican governor of Connecticut since 1954, when Democrat Abraham A. Ribicoff defeated the incumbent governor, John Davis Lodge. Aided in his victory by divisiveness within the Democratic party organization, Meskill received 582,160 votes to Emilio Q. Daddario's 500,561. In his January 6, 1971 inaugural speech before the General Assembly, Meskill pictured Connecticut as a state "wallowing in debt" and stressed that austere administrative and legislative measures would be required to restore financial solvency. As an example of his intentions, Meskill's first official action as governor was to issue a directive ordering a ban on state hiring and purchasing of equipment.

By the time the Governor presented his $1.5 billion budget proposal to a joint session of the legislature on February 16, 1971, the state's deficit had soared to $230,000,000. Faced with ever increasing operating costs and determined to avoid similar deficits, by 1971 most state governments had resorted to the introduction of an income tax to balance their budgets. There were still six states, however, including Connecticut, without such a plan. Rhode Island and Pennsylvania finally introduced state income taxes in February and March of 1971, respectively. Despite calls from fiscal experts, including the members of a special revenue task force, and from certain civic groups for the adoption of a similar financing system in Connecticut, Meskill chose, instead, to ask for an increase in the sales tax, from 5 percent to 7; a rise in taxes on such items as cigarettes and liquor; no increase in educational allocations; and a 60 percent cut in the state's antipoverty programs.

Anticipating the inevitable objections to his speech, Meskill told hecklers in the legislature, "I fully expect the people of Connecticut to be very unhappy with this proposal." Nevertheless, the Governor, who partly based his opinions on polls taken by both political parties, was certain that the citizens of Connecticut would be even more dissatisfied with facing a year-end, accumulated payment of taxes than with the defrayal of the less visible and more widely dispersed sales tax. With the Connecticut unemployment figure standing at 7.2 percent in January, as compared with a 5.8 percent level for the rest of the nation, Meskill believed that the state needed to provide encouragement for industrial development, not a hindrance such as the income tax.

Disgruntled Democratic leaders immediately voiced their disapproval of the call for an increase in the sales tax, contending that Connecticut's workers and their families, one half of whom earned annual salaries of less than $10,000, would be the hardest hit by the regressive tax. Some observers felt, as reported in the New York Times (February 17, 1971), that the Governor's motive for presenting the unpalatable proposals was his desire to force the legislature to initiate income tax legislation, and, therefore, to shoulder the blame at election time. But despite the barrage of criticism directed at the Governor for his program, a study done for the Hartford Times, and reported in March 1971, showed most voters supporting Meskill's plan in the ratio of five to four.

Failing in three attempts to pass their own proposals in June 1971, the Assembly leaders finally reached a compromise with the Governor on June 28, 1971. When the plan was presented to the General Assembly on July 1, it met with unbridled hostility from the legislators, who anathematized it as a "hodgepodge" of "horrendous" and "rotten" taxes. The rank and file members then passed their own legislation, which included an income tax. The bill became law without the Governor's signature.

After a period of intense public opposition, manifested in demonstrations, petitions, and unfavorable newspaper editorials, the General Assembly was recalled into session on August 5 to consider an abrogation of the income tax legislation, and on August 23 the Governor signed a repeal. As it finally stood, the $1.07 billion budget was accompanied by a 6.5 percent sales tax, the highest in the country, and by Meskill's warning of a probable increase in the tax in 1972. Sensitive to widespread criticism of their lack of leadership during the bitter tax struggle of 1971, both the Governor and the legislators avoided a repetition of the previous year's financial haggling and on April 15, 1972 passed a 7 percent sales tax and a bond issue to repay the deficit in ten years. Since it was an election year, the legislators discreetly avoided any mention of an income tax in their 1972 planning.

Conflict between Meskill and the Democratic majority erupted once again in late 1972 over subsidies for Connecticut's financially troubled bus transportation system. While the Democrats pressed for direct state subsidization of the bus companies, the Governor supported a plan for providing only partial subsidies to those towns that organized their own transit districts. In the meantime, the bus companies, whose workers were striking for higher wages, shut down services to sixty-four towns between October 1972 and March 1973. The situation remained unresolved until the Governor relented and agreed to pay the entire deficit incurred by the new transit authorities for two years.

Despite two years of disagreement between Meskill and the Democrats, during which time he wielded his veto power 229 times, some fruitful legislation was passed by the Connecticut lawmakers. It included a no-fault auto insurance plan; the legalization of pari-mutuel and off-track betting; the creation of a state lottery; the establishment of a Department of Environmental Protection; and last, but not least, the selection of a state song, "The Hills of My Connecticut."

With the election of a Republican-controlled legislature for 1973, greater cooperation between Meskill and the lawmakers brought about a reduction in the sales tax from 7 to 6.5 percent; the establishment of the Connecticut Product Development Corporation to finance the transformation of technological innovations into marketable products; and the creation of Connecticut Nutmeg Securities, Inc., the first state-owned brokerage firm to gain a seat on a stock exchange for the purpose of managing the investment of pension and retirement funds. Having achieved his campaign promise to bring financial stability to Connecticut, the Governor announced a budget surplus of approximately $65,000,000 for the fiscal year 1972-73. Since he succeeded in 1973 in reducing allocations for welfare, transportation, higher education, and mental health he looked forward to even greater savings in 1974. As quoted by the New York Times (February 7, 1973), Meskill said, "We have come a long and sometimes bumpy way to reach this promising crossroads."

Thomas J. Meskill is married to the former Mary T. Grady. The couple has five children: Maureen, John, Peter, Eileen, and Thomas. Five feet five inches tall, Meskill has dark hair and what has been described as a "choirboy face." Nicknamed "Tough Tommy" by admirers and critics alike, he is reportedly a "bold, forceful, and aggressive governor" who possesses a "quick wit." According to Lawrence Fellows of the New York Times (December 3, 1972), Meskill "smiles easily, in spite of his reputation for toughness. When he speaks, he goes straight to the point, with an economy of movement and talk. . . . He is quick to make decisions." Although he has been criticized by some colleagues for a propensity to overcentralization of power, one Connecticut Republican summed up a fairly widely held opinion when he said that because of Meskill "the party's probably more united now than in 35 years."

The Governor of Connecticut is a member of the American, Connecticut, and Florida bar associations. He has served on the Cost of Living Council's committee on local and state government cooperation and as a member of Connecticut's constitutional convention, which met in Hartford in 1965. He is the chairman of the New England Governors' Conference.

References

N Y Times p29 S 19 '64; p40 S 17 '68; p1, 23 Ag 13 '70; p36 Ag 30 '71
Wall St J p38 My 3 '73
Congressional Directory (1970)
Who's Who in America, 1972-73
Who's Who in American Politics, 1971-72

MESSIAEN, OLIVIER (EUGÈNE PROSPER CHARLES) (me-syän')

Dec. 10, 1908- French composer; organist; educator
Address: 230 rue Marcadet, Paris 18°, France

Few composers have drawn upon such a complex array of source materials as Olivier Messiaen, whose musical vocabulary has been enriched by birdsong, oriental and South American rhythms, monastic plainsong, and Greek and Hindu modes. The foremost composer alive in France today, Messiaen has cultivated every musical form except opera, and he has also won acclaim as an organist and pianist. His pupils constitute a veritable Who's Who of contemporary composers, including such names as Pierre Boulez, Karlheinz Stockhausen, Luigi Nono, and Yannis Xenakis. Nevertheless his considerable influence has not molded his disciples into any homogeneous school or movement; each has developed an idiom different from that of the others and from that of Messiaen himself. That which irradiates and inspires Messiaen's music is his unwavering, mystical Roman Catholic faith.

Olivier Eugène Prosper Charles Messiaen was born in Avignon, France on December 10, 1908 to Pierre and Cécile (Sauvage) Messiaen, near the Dauphiné mountains where Hector Berlioz was born. Pierre Messiaen, of Flemish descent, was a scholar and teacher of English literature whose translation of Hamlet into French is still in use; Madame Messiaen was a noted poet who celebrated the birth of her son Olivier in verse with a poem called "L'Âme en bourgeon" (The Budding Soul).

The boy began to compose at seven years of age; taught himself to play the piano at eight; pored over the scores of Don Giovanni, Die Walküre, and Pelléas et Mélisande at ten; and entered the Paris Conservatory in 1919 at eleven, after studying music in Grenoble and Nantes, where he had spent his childhood. Messiaen remained for a decade at the Conservatory and won first prizes in harmony, piano accompaniment, fugue, organ, music history, improvisation, and percussion. One of Messiaen's teachers of composition at the Conservatory, Paul Dukas, interested him in the songs of birds, whom Dukas considered masters of music. Among his other teachers were Marcel Dupré for organ, Jean and Noël Gallon, and Maurice Emmanuel. He graduated in 1930.

Olivier Messiaen was only twenty-three when he was appointed organist at the Church of the Trinité, a few blocks behind the Opéra on the Right Bank in Paris. It is for that Trinité instrument that Messiaen has written his many compositions for organ, on which he himself plays so superbly. The organist-composer has remained faithful to his church post for over forty years, playing at Sunday services whenever he is in Paris.

About the time that he was appointed organist at la Trinité, Messiaen began delving into medieval and exotic music, including Greek and Hindu modes and the rhythms of China, Japan, Peru, Bolivia, and Bali. Meanwhile, the study of birdsong that would eventually dominate Messiaen's life and take him all over the world had begun in earnest.

In the early 1930's Messiaen produced such orchestral works as the devoutly religious Les Offrandes Oubliées (Forgotten Offerings), a symphonic poem for voice with chamber instruments, that was written in 1931 and performed by Serge Koussevitzky with the Boston Symphony before World War II. It was Forgotten Offerings that first brought Messiaen to the attention of the music world as a major talent. In 1935 another orchestral compositon of his entitled L'Ascension appeared, consisting of four symphonic meditations. Still other early works were Le Mort du nombre, for soprano, tenor, violin, and piano (1930), Thème et variations (1932), and Fantaisie (1933).

With fellow composers André Jolivet, Daniel Lesur, and Yves Baudrier, Messiaen formed a movement in 1936 known as "La Jeune France" for mutual support of their music and propaganda purposes. That same year Messiaen published nine meditations for organ called La Nativité du Seigneur (The Nativity of Our Lord) and a work for organ entitled Le banquet céleste, and first began teaching composition at the Schola Cantorum and the École Normale de Musique. During that period immediately preceding World War II, Messiaen composed a vocal work called Poèmes pour Mi ("Mi" was Messiaen's nickname for his first wife, the composer Claire Delbos, who died in 1959) and a song cycle for solo soprano and orchestra, Action de Graces, featuring a text by the composer, that had its première in Paris on June 4, 1937.

Messiaen's composing and teaching were interrupted by the outbreak of World War II in 1939, when he joined the French Army. Captured by the Germans, he spent two years in the Stalag VIII-A prison camp in Görlitz, Lower Silesia, where his perpetual undernourishment gave him "colored dreams" full of "halos and strange swirls of color." While interned, he managed to continue writing, and in 1940 he composed a chamber work that has remained one of his best-known pieces, Quatuor pour la Fin du Temps (Quartet for the End of Time) for violin, cello, clarinet and piano. It was given its first performance on January 15, 1941 in the Nazi prison camp with Messiaen at the piano and thousands of rapt prisoners in the audience. When it was presented in New York early in 1946 as part of a program of new French music, Virgil Thomson noted in his New York *Herald Tribune* review (January 31, 1946) that the work as a whole, was marked by harmonic and rhythmic originality. He found it weak melodically and lacking in shape, a charge often leveled against Messiaen's compositions, along with accusations of pomposity, bombast, and banality. According to Thomson, Messiaen is probably unequaled among living composers as a harmonic colorist.

Released from Görlitz in 1942, Messiaen resumed his interrupted career as composer and teacher. That year he became professor of harmony at the Paris Conservatory, and five years later he was appointed professor of analysis, aesthetics, and rhythm as well. Typical of the new sounds he was working with in that period and of his marked affinity for timbre was his *Trois Petites Liturgies de la Présence Divine* (Three Short Liturgies of the Divine Presence), published in 1944 and given its première in Paris on April 21, 1945, which is scored for soprano choir, piano, celesta, vibraphone, maracas, Chinese cymbals, gongs, Ondes Martenot (electronic music), and strings. The composer won the 1967 Koussevitzky International Recording Award for that work, which was recorded and released in France by Erato.

Despite the German occupation of Paris, Messiaen's harmony class at the Conservatory remained an enclave of progressive experimentation, indulging in free composition and the analysis of such contemporary composers as Alban Berg and Béla Bartók, who were officially forbidden by the Nazis. In the years just after the War, his classes were sought out by young European composers who were to form the élite of the postwar musical generation, the "new" Messiaen avant-garde in contrast to the "old" avant-garde of Igor Stravinsky. Messiaen has said that he adores teaching and will be unhappy the day he is forced to retire. Among his pupils were Karlheinz Stockhausen, Pierre Boulez, Luigi Nono, Yannis Xenakis, Marius Constant, Jean Barraqué, Gilbert Amy, and other young progressives. Despite his powerful influence, no "Messiaen school" of composition has come into being. Even when critics try to trace his musical lineage back to the nineteenth-century romantics through Franck and Massenet by way of Debussy, they recognize that Messiaen is an original with a style all his own that he has not forced upon his students. "Imitation of Messiaen's musical style would be difficult if not impossible," New York *Times* critic Allen Hughes has remarked, "even if he wanted his students to follow his example. But nothing could be farther from his wishes."

The result of one of the 1945 Koussevitzky Music Foundation commissions for symphonic works, the *Turangalila-Symphonie*, written between 1946 and 1948, is one of Messiaen's most celebrated compositions. He has described the ten-movement work, which lasts nearly an hour and a half, as "a hymn to joy, time, movement, rhythm, life and death," adding that it is also a

OLIVIER MESSIAEN

song of love based on the Tristan and Isolde love-potion symbol. The work was introduced by Leonard Bernstein on December 2, 1949 with the Boston Symphony and later with the New York Philharmonic. With rhythm as its basic element, *Turangalila* is composed in what Messiaen calls "a very special rhythmic language" and uses several new rhythmic principles.

Turangalila marks a watershed in Messiaen's career. It was followed by a period of creative exhaustion, described by the composer as a time when "all seemed lost, when the way is no longer clear, when one has nothing more to say," that lasted until the mid-1950's. Then Messiaen's intellectual bent became evident in his experiments in serialism and in his attempts to develop rhythm as an organizational principle. What kept him from following those experiments to their logical conclusion were his concern with birdsong, his Catholic mysticism, and his original temperament that fortified his refusal to fit into set "modern" patterns.

Another of Messiaen's commitments is his color fixation, which has led him to propose such audio-visual scoring directions as "play red," for instance. When added to his programmatic concert notes, the color fixation obliges the listener to adopt a frame of mind that submerges him in the Messiaen mood of such compositions as *Couleurs de la Cité Céleste*. To appreciate Messiaen's music, the listener must read all the program notes he has written about it, since the impact the works make upon the audience derives to a large extent from the composer's poetic commentary.

His obsession with color also invades the seven-part *Chronochromie*, his most monumental work based on birdsong, since the title itself might be translated from the Greek as "The Color of Time." Premièred under Hans Rosbaud at the Donaueschingen Festival on October 16, 1960, *Chronochromie* incorporates birdsongs and the sound of waterfalls into a work that leaves some listeners lost in a maze of eighteen-part polyphony. Other major compositions by Messiaen that introduce birdsong are *Couleurs de la Cité* and *Et Exspecto Resurrectionem Mortuorum,* the work honoring the dead of both World Wars that was first performed before Charles de Gaulle at a 1964 state ceremony in Chartres Cathedral.

Since first coming to the United States as a guest teacher at the Berkshire Music Center in 1949, Messiaen has visited and performed in that country several times. In November of 1970 he and Yvonne Loriod, the virtuoso pianist who is his second wife, were featured in a performance of his two-piano work *Visions de l'Amen* in the Lisner Piano Series in Washington, D.C. In the spring of 1972 they returned to the United States for the world première at Washington's Immaculate Conception Shrine of his first major organ work in two decades, entitled *Meditations on the Mystery of the Holy Trinity* and for the first American performance of his *Transfiguration of Our Saviour Jesus Christ* by Antal Dorati and the National Symphony at the John F. Kennedy Arts Center and at Carnegie Hall. Based on Gospel and Old Testament sources and Thomistic thought, the latter work enlarges the orchestra beyond anything Messiaen had done before. Although it may prove inaccessible to newcomers to Messiaen's music, Pierre Boulez views *The Transfiguration* as his former teacher's greatest work to date.

Always an articulate exponent of his theories, Messiaen has explained his *oeuvre* in a book entitled *Technique de mon langage musical* (Paris: Alphonse Leduc, 1944), which appeared in English translation as *The Technique of My Musical Language* (Chicago, 1957). The two-volume work acknowledged the factors that have exercised the strongest influence on his compositions, singling out the modal scales of Gregorian chant, Eastern elements such as Hindu rhythmic thought, and, above all, Nature with its bird songs, which he considers a composer's supreme resource. The book provides the key to Messiaen's compositional method, containing his theories on rhythm, modes, harmony, and structural problems. Other pedagogical works by the composer include "Traité de rythme" (begun in 1948) and "Mode de valeurs et d'intensité," both of which form part of *Quatre études de rythme,* published in 1949-50. In them Messiaean propounds, in opposition to Schönberg, a theory of rhythmic modes that not only applies to orthodox compositions, but also serves as a guide to electronic music.

On July 7, 1961 Messiaen married Yvonne Loriod, who was one of his first postwar pupils at the Paris Conservatory. She has performed his works in public hundreds of times since then. By his first marriage, to Claire Delbos, who died in 1959, Messiaen has one son, Pascal. The Messiaens live in Paris when not on concert tours, and they always try to spend the summer months in their chalet in the Alps. A commander of the Legion of Honor, grand officer of the National Order of Merit, and a commander of Arts and Letters of France, Messiaen is a member of the academies of Bavaria, Berlin, and Rome, and of the National Academy of Arts and Letters, in New York. He once inventoried the major influences on his career: "My mother, the poet Cécile Sauvage; my wife, the composer Claire Delbos; Shakespeare; Claudel; Reverdy and Éluard; Ernest Hello and Dom Columba Marmion (dare I speak of the Holy Scriptures, which contain the only Truth?); birds; Russian music; the great *Pelléas et Mélisande;* plainsong; Hindu rhythms; the mountains of Dauphiné; and, finally, that which pertains to stained glass windows and rainbows." Messiaen remains a musician of stained glass windows, having declared as his credo: "I want to write music that is an act of faith, a music that is about everything without ceasing to be about God."

References

N Y Times II p17 D 3 '67 por; II p34 Je 22 '69 por; II p24 Je 20 '71 por
Newsweek 76:138+ N 23 '70 por
Time 89:73 Ap 14 '67 por
Washington Post F p6 N 8 '70; K p1 Mr 26 '72 por

Ewen, David. Composers Since 1900 (1969)
Grove's Dictionary of Music and Musicians (1955)
International Who's Who, 1969-70
Rostand, Claude. Olivier Messiaen (1958)
Who's Who in the World, 1972-73

MILLER, ARNOLD (RAY)

Apr. 25, 1923- Labor union official
Address: b. United Mine Workers of America, 900 15th St., N.W., Washington, D.C. 20006; h. Ohley, W. Va. 25147

The first American labor union chief executive to come to office from the rank and file after defeating an incumbent, Arnold Miller began a five-year term as the twelfth president of the 205,000-member unaffiliated United Mine Workers of America on December 22, 1972. In the court-ordered union election earlier that month, Miller led an unlikely coalition of disgruntled miners and young activists to victory over W. A. ("Tony") Boyle in a grassroots rebellion against corrupt leadership, achieving what James A. Wechsler of the New York *Post* (December 22, 1972) called "the biggest upset in United States labor history." Under Miller, who is committed to union democracy, the U.M.W.A. has taken on a new militancy, and it struck the nation's coal mines for safer working conditions, wage increases, and other benefits on November 11, 1974 when its contract with the Bituminous Coal Operators Association expired. The strike, which lasted over three weeks, caused real concern, because the current international energy crisis made the country dependent on coal for much of its fuel.

The son and grandson of miners, Arnold Ray Miller was born on April 25, 1923 in Leewood, Kanawha County, in the heart of the bituminous coal region of West Virginia, to George Matt and Lulu (Hoy) Miller. Fond of the outdoors, Miller had an early ambition to study forestry, but economic considerations forced him to end his formal education at sixteen. After attending Leewood public schools to the ninth grade, he entered the Cabin Creek mines in 1939 and went to work with his grandfather handloading coal for wages of 77 cents a ton.

In 1942 Miller volunteered for the United States Army and was assigned to the infantry. Severely wounded on the left side of his head by machine-gun fire during the Normandy invasion, he spent two years in military hospitals and underwent about twenty operations. After his discharge in 1946, he planned to open a small auto repair shop but "just wasn't up to getting through the course," as he told Wesley Pruden Jr., of the *National Observer* (December 2, 1972). In 1948 he returned to the Cabin Creek mines, where he worked mainly as an electrician-repairman until August 1970, when he was forced to retire because of work-related arthritis and pneumoconiosis, or black lung disease.

During his years in the mines, Miller served as a member of mine and safety committees and as president of U.M.W.A. Local 2903 in Eskdale, West Virginia. Once he ran unsuccessfully as a candidate for the House of Delegates—the lower house of the West Virginia state legislature. In 1968, after his condition was diagnosed as black lung disease, Miller tried unsuccessfully to obtain help from U.M.W.A. headquarters in his effort to gain recognition of black lung as a compensable ailment under the state workmen's compensation law. Disillusioned when he found that union officials had no interest in campaigning for legislation to aid black lung victims, he became one of the founding members of the grassroots Black Lung Association (BLA). In February 1969 he played a leading role in organizing the BLA's statewide three-week strike and led a massive march of miners on the state capitol in Charleston. U.M.W.A. officials condemned the BLA members for "dual unionism" and telegraphed legislators to ignore the strikers' demands. "They were not just not with us, they were against us," Miller told Mary McGrory of the New York *Post* (December 18, 1972). Nevertheless, after intensive lobbying by miners, the legislators passed the first black lung compensation bill.

Miller has presented testimony before House and Senate committees in the hearings on the 1969 Coal Mine Health and Safety Act, which established standards for the regulation of dust in the mines and provided federal aid for black lung victims. In 1970 he became president of the BLA. By 1972, when he returned to Washington to argue with some success for amendments to the 1969 act that would provide additional benefits for black lung sufferers, the BLA had, in addition to its West Virginia constituents, gained members in Pennsylvania, Ohio, and Virginia. In connection with his activities for the BLA, Miller worked closely with Designs for Rural Action, an agency of the Office of Economic Opportunity. As that agency's vice-presi-

ARNOLD MILLER

dent for special projects from 1970 to 1972, he became acquainted with a number of young activists, lawyers, and fund raisers sympathetic to the miners' cause.

The success of the BLA underscored the widening rift between rank-and-file miners and the union leadership. Once the "shock troops of American labor," the U.M.W.A. declined in membership from about 600,000 in 1943 to 205,000 in 1973, as coal gave way to oil, while new machinery and strip mining eliminated many pick-and-shovel jobs. In 1950, U.M.W.A. president John L. Lewis accepted mechanization—and widespread unemployment in the coalfields—in exchange for a wage hike and a royalty on each ton of coal mined under union contract. The royalties, which went into the U.M.W.A. Welfare and Retirement Fund, in time made the union rich and disinclined to allow rank-and-file demands to interrupt production.

For miners on the job, Lewis and his successor, A. W. ("Tony") Boyle, obtained substantial wages, thus assuring their loyalty, but their contracts included no sick pay, no cost of living escalator, and no supplemental unemployment benefits. Boyle, who succeeded Lewis as president in 1963, appointed the district "representatives" and ruled by fiat and by strong-arm tactics. Unlike Lewis, he rarely visited the coalfields and seemed to demonstrate little economic insight. Mismanagement reached its apogee in the 1960's when large sums belonging to the Welfare and Retirement Fund were placed into checking accounts in the U.M.W.A.-controlled National Bank of Washington, rather than into interest-bearing savings accounts. From 1969 on, the fund showed a steadily growing deficit.

Joseph ("Jock") Yablonsky, a member of the national executive board of the U.M.W.A., became the spokesman for rank-and-file insurgents when he began to challenge Boyle for the presidency in May 1969, and Arnold Miller was one of his early supporters. After Boyle was reelected with 63 percent of the vote in the U.M.W.A. election of December 9, 1969, Yablonsky asked the United States Department of Labor to investigate some 100 separate claims of election fraud, but the department refused to impound the ballots. Nevertheless, Yablonsky vowed to continue the fight. A few days after the election Miller, who had served as his campaign coordinator for District 17 in central West Virginia, offered to provide him with a bodyguard of four retirees, but Yablonsky turned down the offer. On January 5, 1970 Yablonsky, his wife, and their daughter, were found shot to death in their beds at their home in Clarksville, Pennsylvania.

The Yablonsky murders brought the federal government into the affairs of the U.M.W.A. A three-year investigation led to the indictment of a number of high-ranking union officials. (In late 1973 Boyle himself, then already under sentence for making illegal political contributions, was indicted in connection with the case.) More immediately, the murders outraged the mining community and gave a new impetus to the reform movement. Assembling in a Roman Catholic church in Washington, Pennsylvania after the Yablonsky funeral, supporters of the late insurgent leader formed the nucleus of a new organization, which was formally established in April 1970, as Miners for Democracy (MFD). With the assistance of attorney Joseph L. Rauh Jr. and of Yablonsky's two sons, who are both lawyers, MFD took the battle into the courts.

In the months that followed, MFD attorneys obtained court orders establishing the right of miners to freely elect their local union officials; blocked Boyle's efforts to intimidate MFD members or to expel them from the U.M.W.A.; and won a suit against trustees of the pension fund, charging them with mismanagement and fraud. As a result of MFD's efforts, Boyle was convicted on charges of having illegally contributed nearly $50,000 of U.M.W.A. funds to 1968 political campaigns; in June 1972 he was sentenced to five years in prison and fined $130,000. Meanwhile, MFD in cooperation with the Labor Department succeeded in May 1972 in having Boyle's 1969 victory declared void. On June 16, 1972 Judge William B. Bryant of the United States District Court in Washington, D.C., invoking the Landrum-Griffin Act, ordered a new U.M.W.A. election, to be closely supervised by the Labor Department. Elaborate procedures were drawn up to insure the secrecy and integrity of the ballot and to prevent the resources of the union from being diverted to the campaign.

In May 1972 450 delegates of the MFD convened in Wheeling, West Virginia and selected Miller as their candidate over Michael Trbovich, who had been Yablonsky's campaign manager. Trbovich and Harry Patrick, were chosen for vice-president and secretary-treasurer. The campaign was extraordinarily bitter. Stigmatizing Miller and his running mates as the "three stooges" from "the Moscow fire department," Boyle asserted that the insurgents were seriously weakening the union and warned the 85,000 U.M.W.A. retirees that their pensions were in jeopardy in the event of an MFD victory. The

leaders of many large unions on the national scene tacitly supported Boyle, and some charged MFD with "union busting." According to Wechsler, AFL-CIO president George Meany, while remaining officially neutral, seemed to have viewed the insurgent movement in the U.M.W.A. with "quiet hostility . . . from its inception."

As Laurence Leamer observed in the New York Times Magazine (November 26, 1972), the MFD ran "a hybrid campaign, in part modern, media-conscious, in part miner-to-miner bathhouse electioneering." Miller and his running mates visited hundreds of the bleak changing rooms where miners prepare for the pits, and they ventured into pro-Boyle areas that Yablonsky had avoided. They called attention to corruption in the national office; they stressed the need for more adequate mine safety measures, greater union democratization, and increased benefits; and they promised to raise the monthly retirement pensions for miners from $150 to $200. They also dropped broad hints about the possible involvement of Boyle in the Yablonsky killings. Miller promised that, if elected, he would cut his own salary and those of other union officials and that he would move union headquarters from the nation's capital into the coalfields. "If I fell dead on this spot," Miller said during the campaign, "I'd figure that I'd done something these last four years. I realize, we all realize, that the only hope is for the miners . . . to clean up the union themselves." His identification with the rank and file seemed to have cost him some votes, since many miners doubted whether a man from the pits, like themselves, could negotiate successfully with the companies. On the other hand, the prison term facing Boyle seemed to work in Miller's favor. As one miner told a reporter for Life (December 8, 1972), "I don't want a man running my union from behind bars."

In the elections, held from December 1 to December 8, 1972 under the supervision of some 1,000 federal agents, Miller won by an unexpectedly large margin, receiving 70,373 votes to Boyle's 56,334. Sworn in on December 22, after certification by a federal court, Miller told some 200 cheering supporters at U.M.W.A. headquarters in Washington, D.C.: "The era of one-man rule in this union is over." One of his first acts as president was to cut his own salary from $50,000 to $35,000 a year. Staff salaries were also reduced and, in a symbolic gesture, Harry Patrick auctioned off the union's three Cadillac limousines. In restructuring the administrative machinery, the reformers took steps to give the rank and file a larger voice in union affairs. The district officers appointed by Boyle to the executive board were sent home to stand for election, and the results gave MFD a majority. The biweekly U.M.W.A. Journal was transformed overnight by the new administration from a vehicle of pro-Boyle propaganda into an objective labor newspaper reflecting various viewpoints.

At the U.M.W.A.'s forty-sixth constitutional convention, held in Pittsburgh in December 1973, four-fifths of the union's largely obsolete constitution was rewritten. Although Miller, who encouraged the widest possible debate at the convention, continued to encounter considerable opposition to his policies, he emerged from it stronger than before. He has tried to forge unity among disparate groups of miners traditionally kept isolated from one another by the union: the deep pit miners of the bituminous fields in northern and southern Appalachia; the anthracite miners of eastern Pennsylvania; and the strip miners of the Midwest and West. The Western regions have become a prime area of expansion for the coal industry, because the low sulfur level of the coal found there makes it easier for the mine operators to conform with federal clean air standards than the high-sulfur coal of Appalachia. Thus far the U.M.W.A. has made relatively little headway in unionizing Western mines.

Convinced that large companies can afford to pay some of the human and environmental costs of mining, Miller opposes any relaxation of air standards and is personally against strip mining, although he has indicated that he might support compromise legislation allowing strip mines where the land can be restored. On the issue of mine safety, Miller is unlikely to compromise. Flying to Itmann, West Virginia on December 27, 1972, after an explosion had killed five miners there, he cut short apologies by the Consolidation Coal Company president with the words, "I am sick of these disasters. . . . There's just too much plain ordinary irresponsibility here."

Miller has threatened to shut down unsafe mines and has allocated $1,500,000 and forty-two staff members to the safety division at U.M.W.A. headquarters, formerly a one-man office. In August 1974, he called a five-day industry-wide walkout as a memorial to miners killed or injured on the job. The stoppage reduced the nation's stockpiles of coal and enhanced the U.M.W.A.'s bargaining power, as did its victory in the thirteen-month strike against the Duke Power Company's Brookside mine in Harlan County, Kentucky, which ended in August 1974.

In bargaining for a new contract to succeed the one that expired on November 12, 1974, Miller presented Walter Wallace, president of the Bituminous Coal Operators Association, with a list of forty major demands, calling for a company-financed safety program, higher wages and pensions, a cost-of-living escalator, sick leave, and a substantial increase in royalties, then 80 cents a ton. Miller was convinced that the industry could well afford the increase in wages, since there had been a rise of as much as 800 percent in the profits of some companies. Before the strike began on November 11, 1974, Miller was confident of his bargaining powers. "I can negotiate a contract better than Boyle," he said, as quoted by Laurence Leamer. "I've been in the mines." The signing of a contract on December 5, 1974 ended the strike after twenty-four days.

Arnold Miller lives in West Virginia in a five-room frame house near Cabin Creek with his wife, the former Virginia Ruth Brown, whom he married on November 26, 1948. They have two grown children, Larry Allen and Vicki Lynn. According to Leamer, Miller has "thick, silvery hair, pinkish skin, and strong Anglo-Saxon features." The left side of his head bears the scars of his wartime injuries, and black lung has given him the look of a man ten years older. Reserved and somewhat shy with the press, Miller is courteous in demeanour but has, according to associates, a stubborn and independent mind. Using plain, occasionally pungent, language and speaking in a soft mountain drawl, Miller enjoys a great deal of rapport with working miners. He served on the board of directors of the Appalachian Research and Development Fund from 1970 to 1972, and he is a trustee of the U.M.W.A. Welfare and Retirement Fund. A liberal Democrat, he supported Senator George S. McGovern in the 1972 Presidential campaign.

References

Atlan 233:10+ Mr '74
Bsns W p44+ Ag 31 '74 por
N Y Post p33 D 28 '72 por
N Y Times Mag p40+ N 26 '72 pors
Washington Monthly p7+ Je '74 por
Finley, Joseph E. Corrupt Kingdom (1973)

MILLER, JASON

1939(?)- Playwright; actor
Address: b. c/o Public Theater, 425 Lafayette St., New York 10003

Jason Miller, author of *That Championship Season*, the triple prize-winning tragicomedy and successful Broadway show, has been acclaimed by critics as a master of stage dialogue and straight narrative who offers new hope for traditional, "well-made" drama. Playwright Miller's sensitivity to the dynamics of speech and character is no accident, for he is also an accomplished actor, with a repertory ranging from Shakespeare and O'Neill on stage to the title role of *The Exorcist* in cinema. As a playwright he had one previous three-act credit, *Nobody Hears a Broken Drum*, produced Off Broadway in 1970.

After suffering through a long period of experimentation in the theatre, critics and audiences alike have welcomed the work of Jason Miller as a refreshing return to the tradition of Ibsen-like realism. New York *Post* reviewer Jerry Tallmer has observed, "Perhaps, indeed some people maintain, not since *Death of a Salesman*, by another Miller, has a playwright of this order come along." In his syndicated column of May 9, 1972 Sidney Fields echoed the consensus of the critical fraternity when he ascribed to Miller "a searing and sardonic but understanding perception of human folly."

An only child, Jason Miller was born John Miller in Long Island City, New York about thirty-four years ago. (According to differing sources, the year of his birth was either 1939 or 1940.) Miller's parents are John Miller, an electrician, now retired, and Mary Miller, a teach-

JASON MILLER

er of brain-damaged children, now semiretired. His ancestry is Irish Catholic, with some admixture of German. "I had an Irish grandmother of eighty-five . . . ," he told Glenn Loney in an interview for *After Dark* (January 1973). "She had a faith that was enormous but not didactic." In another interview, with Jerry Tallmer of the New York *Post* (September 23, 1972), he said: "My first play was about the Irish miners of Pennsylvania, the Molly Maguires. My grandfather and my uncles on my mother's side were all miners. On my father's side? Sea people, from New England, Providence."

During Jason's infancy the Millers moved to Scranton, in Pennsylvania's Lackawanna Valley, where the maternal relatives had already settled. "I was in Scranton until I was twenty-one, twenty-two," Jason Miller recounted to Jerry Tallmer, "but I left there . . . periodically and went to Rhode Island and Block Island, went to the ocean a lot." He remembers the Scranton in which he grew up as a "poverty area," where the "main thing" was "survival"—but still, "it wasn't the potato famine."

Miller, who believes that "all good theatre has something religious about it," acknowledges that his "whole frame of reference, even toward the theatre, was built on being an altar boy and on the ritual and on Midnight Mass." At St. Patrick's High School (run by the Sisters of the Immaculate Heart of Mary) in Scranton he was an excellent football, basketball, and baseball player but an incipient delinquent—until he came under the influence of Sister Celine, who taught public speaking and coached the debating team. Trained and encouraged by her, he became an elocution contest champion, and from elocution he went on to acting. In his first stage appearance he played the Queen's private secretary in a high school production of *Victoria Regina*, when he was a senior at St. Patrick's.

His entrée to the University of Scranton, a Jesuit institution, was an athletic scholarship, but soon after his matriculation he dropped sports to concentrate on acting and writing for the theatre. His first experiment in playwriting, a one-act play about a prizefighter, *The Winner,* took first prize in the Jesuit Eastern Play Contest. After his graduation from the University of Scranton, in 1961, he studied drama for two years at the Catholic University of America in Washington, D.C.

In 1963 Miller married a fellow acting student at Catholic University, Linda Gleason, a daughter of the television comedian Jackie Gleason. Before their first child arrived, Jason and Linda toured high school assemblies in and around the Washington area performing a one-hour program of Shakespearean selections called *Shakespeare on Love.* After a couple of years they moved to New York, where they settled in Queens. In the beginning the only acting assignments Miller could find in New York were occasional bits in television commercials and soap operas and insignificant roles Off and Off Off Broadway. In between he worked as a messenger, truck loader and driver, waiter, and welfare investigator. His first substantial work as a professional actor was done in sojourns outside New York, at, for example, the Champlain Shakespeare Festival in Burlington, Vermont, the Cincinnati Shakespeare Festival, the Baltimore Center Stage, and the Hartke Theatre at Catholic University. On his return from the resident regional companies he would either scout around for an odd job or collect unemployment insurance.

Miller's first involvement with Joseph Papp, founder and producer of the New York Shakespeare Festival, was as an actor in *Subject to Fits.* Papp's company, which stages its Shakespearean productions in Central Park in the summer months, during the rest of the year presents the works of other playwrights at its Public Theatre, housed in the former Astor Library Building in lower Manhattan. *Subject to Fits,* a mad, fanciful "response" to Dostoevski's *The Idiot* by Robert Montgomery (not to be confused with the veteran actor of the same name), opened at the Public Theatre on February 14, 1971 with Miller in the role of Rogozhin. Under the direction of A. J. Antoon, an ex-Jesuit fresh out of Yale Drama School, the play had a successful run, and even the minority of critics who did not appreciate its audacity acknowledged that the acting, including Miller's, was "admirable." Miller remained in the cast until April 20, 1971, when he was replaced by Walter McGinn.

In his spare time, including that spent riding the subway between Manhattan and his home in Queens, Miller was writing plays. His short play *Lou Gehrig Did Not Die of Cancer* was one of the Equity Theatre's "informal" presentations at Lincoln Center early in March 1970, and several other one-act plays by Miller were produced Off Off Broadway by the Triangle Theatre. His full-length *Nobody Hears a Broken Drum* had a brief run at the Triangle before opening Off Broadway at the Fortune Theatre on March 19, 1970.

Nobody Hears a Broken Drum is Miller's panoramic account of the rebellion of oppressed immigrant Irish miners in the anthracite region of southern Pennsylvania in 1862. In Miller's version of the historic event, the hero is Jamie O'Hanlin, a fiery leader with the soul of a Celtic poet. Critics generally judged the work to be intrinsically interesting, if lacking sharp dramatic focus, but they found the Fortune Theatre production of it tedious and "passionless," and it closed after five performances. "This is one to wring your hands over," Marilyn Stasio wrote in *Cue* (March 28, 1970), "because it is at its core a good play, but one strangled by its flaws. . . . Jason Miller shows an exceptional gift for tough yet lyrical language." A disappointed Miller himself said, "Maybe someday I'll get it done properly."

Miller wrote most of *That Championship Season* while appearing as one of the poker players in a production of *The Odd Couple* at the Windmill Dinner Theatre in Fort Worth, Texas in 1970. For his setting he chose a "jock" reunion in a small Pennsylvania coal town that begins with hollow bonhomie and turns into a *Walpurgisnacht* of the soul. Twenty years after winning a state high school basketball championship, four members of the team gather to honor the coach who taught them how to win, and in the course of the gathering it becomes painfully clear to all five men that the values by which they have been living have been perverted and are as false as their basketball triumph (which, it turns out, was achieved by foul play). The play was written on several levels, or about several themes, as Miller has pointed out. On one occasion he said, "I am writing in *Championship* about men going into their middle age with a sense of terror and defeat." On other occasions he said that the play was "about Middle America" on the surface and more subtly about religion, "about the fall from grace."

When the engagement in Fort Worth was completed, the members of *The Odd Couple* cast drove to the airport in Dallas with some of their belongings, including the manuscript of *That Championship Season*, tied to the top of the car. En route, the manuscript blew off, forming what Miller later described as "a beautiful cloud of what seemed like yellow sunflowers floating over a field." In an interview for the *New Yorker* (May 20, 1972) he recalled, "We stopped the car and went into that lovely field and recaptured each and every one of the hundred and fifty-three pages. It was like picking strange flowers, blowing in the wind. I couldn't believe my luck, and I still can't."

Broadway producers were not taken with the play: it did not "read well," and its all-male cast and small-town locale seemed like box office poison. After two years of negotiating with directors who wanted to turn *That Championship Season* into a star vehicle, Miller jumped at the chance offered by director A. J. Antoon to audition the work for Joseph Papp. In a run-through with professional actors, the script came to life. Papp agreed to do the show, after Miller had cut some of the Broadway padding away from his original version, and sent the cast on a visit to Scranton to soak up atmosphere.

With a cast of excellent, team-working ensemble actors, *That Championship Season* opened to rave reviews at the Public Theatre in May 1972 and moved to the Booth Theatre on Broadway four months later. It won the New York Drama Critics Circle and Tony awards and evoked such praise as that heaped on it by Charles Michener of *Newsweek* (September 25, 1972), who called it "a major work of American theatrical realism with the best kind of popular appeal and a virtuoso job of writing for actors." Secondary productions were mounted in San Francisco, London, Oslo, Tel Aviv, and elsewhere. On May 7, 1973 Miller was awarded the Pulitzer Prize for *That Championship Season*.

Some critics saw in Miller's play an exposé of American public morality, but Miller himself in discussing the work is inclined to emphasize its ritualistic aspects and the plight of its five characters. "They're unable to make that rite of passage from youth to middle age," he explained to Allan Wallach of *Newsday* (July 3, 1972). "They're unable to do it; they're too terrified. . . . These are three-act people; these are people who have curtain lines to their lives."

For $112.50 a week, Miller understudied two of the characters in the Off-Broadway production of *That Championship Season*, but, with success assured he returned to writing, adapting the script of the play for a movie to be filmed by Playboy Productions and working with Papp and Antoon on a musical version of Studs Terkel's *Hard Times: An Oral History of the Depression*. As an actor, he played Father Damian Karras, the priest who battles the demons who possess a young girl in *The Exorcist*, the movie version of William Peter Blatty's novel, filmed by Warner Brothers in 1973. Intrigued by the questions raised in the story regarding the nature of evil, Miller worked his way into the part by reading the works of Teilhard de Chardin, the late Jesuit mystic, and saying Mass with a priest at Georgetown University. "The camera loves Jason's face," William Friedkin, director of *The Exorcist*, has observed. "He is potentially one of the most exciting film actors in America." Miller has been signed to star in a second film, "Nickel Ride," in which his role is a professional crook.

Jason and Linda Miller were separated in late 1973. They have three children, Jennifer, Jason, and Jordan. Physically, Miller is short (five feet seven inches), lean and wiry, with black hair and small, sharp features. Emotionally, he has been described as "intense" and "vulnerable." His voice is husky and his manner, like his wit, is quick.

Religiously, Miller classifies himself as "a vacationing Catholic." He told Charles Michener of *Newsweek*, "I'm beyond the institutional aspects of religion, but there's still an immense depth and mystery about it that appeals to me." In the *New Yorker* interview he said: "Funny thing. Until I finished the first draft of *That Championship Season* and read it over, I hadn't realized that all my characters are Catholics. . . . I know for myself that an Irish Catholic is a complex human being. I believe in God but the institutions of churches give me trouble. I certainly don't like the English Mass. The old ritual was better." In his *After Dark* article Glenn Loney quoted Miller on the subject of spiritual evil: "I'd say there are *forces* in this world which create people like Manson and Hitler. . . . We are in the middle of a plague right now. A deadly plague."

References

After Dark 5:49+ Ja '73 pors
N Y Daily News p46 My 9 '72 por
N Y Post p15 S 23 '72 por
N Y Sunday News II p3 My 14 '72 por
N Y Times II p1+ Mr 21 '72 por
New Yorker 48:32+ My 20 '72
Newsday 80:124 S 25 '72 por
White Plains Reporter Dispatch p20 Mr 27 '73 por

MILLER, JOHNNY

Apr. 29, 1947- Golfer
Address: b. c/o Uni-Managers International, Suite 1800, 10880 Wilshire Blvd., Los Angeles, Calif. 90024

In the not too distant future Johnny Miller's star is likely to outshine those of Lee Trevino and Jack Nicklaus in the firmament of professional golf. Twenty-seven-year-old Miller, who joined the pro tour full time in 1970, leaped to prominence a year later by finishing in a tie for second place in the Masters tournament. Last year he took both the World Cup and the United States Open, and in the first five months of the 1974 pro tour he won five tournaments, collecting almost $193,000, more than twice the amount garnered by the closest contender. Notwithstanding his success, he still ranks himself fifth best golfer in the world. In late 1974 Miller received the Professional Golf Association's player of the year award.

The son of Larry and Ida Miller, Johnny Miller was born into a devout Mormon household in San Francisco, California on April 29, 1947. With his older brother, Ronald—who died by accidental drowning at sixteen—and two sisters, he grew up in the Bay Area, where his father works as a cable traffic supervisor for the Radio Corporation of America. According to Louis Sabin in *Parade* (June 2, 1974), he credits his father with giving him a healthy attitude toward life in general and golf in particular. Sabin quoted him: "My dad is a good amateur golfer, and he started me in the sport when I was five. But, like other kids, I wanted to play a lot of sports. My father was smart to let me. He encouraged me to have fun, never pushed me, and that kept sports on the level of enjoyment rather than a job."

Starting out, Miller strengthened his swing by driving balls into a canvas bag set up by his father in the basement of the family home. At seven he began practising at the San Francisco Golf Club under the tutelage of the club's pro,

John Geertsen a Mormon friend of his father's. Later he played at Harding Park, where he paid his way around the course by winning nickel, dime, and quarter bets. As a teenager he had free access to the elite Olympic Country Club, through the good graces of the father of a friend, Leo Gregoire.

Without exerting undue pressure, his father taught him the necessity of positive thinking. "You must never learn to think the negative," he would tell him. "You can become a professional, but if you want to become a champion, you are going to have to do more." When Johnny was a five-feet-two-inch, 110-pound fourteen-year-old his father initiated a physical training regimen for him that included weight lifting and squeezing a rubber ball to strengthen his thin wrists. Two years later, as a sturdy six-footer, Miller won the 1964 United States Golf Association Junior Championship.

In 1966, while attending Brigham Young University in Provo, Utah on a golf scholarship, Miller entered the United States Open as an amateur alternate. He also signed as a caddie, in case he failed to qualify. As it turned out, he not only qualified but finished the tournament in a tie for eighth place, with a score of 270, three strokes ahead of the next closest amateur.

His success in the Open, coupled with a National Collegiate Athletic Association ruling that he was ineligible to compete on the collegiate level in his senior year, convinced Miller to leave Brigham Young University in 1968. ("A college degree is not going to help you sink those two-footers," he once said.) On winning the 1968 California Amateur Open he decided to turn professional, and after undergoing training at the Professional Golf Association school, he joined the pro tour, in 1970.

During his first year on the tour Miller was helped immeasurably by old pro Billy Casper, also a member of the Mormon Church, who taught him the importance of a proper mental approach to the game. Miller did not win any PGA tournaments until the following year, when he took the $20,000 Southern Open. But it was his dramatic attempt to capture the 1971 Masters tournament that propelled the Californian into national prominence. Entering the fourth and final round at Augusta, Georgia, Miller trailed Charles Coody and Jack Nicklaus by four strokes. He proceeded to erase that lead by completing the front nine in thirty-three shots, and he birdied the eleventh, twelfth, and fourteenth holes to vault himself to a two-stroke lead.

At that point Miller began to think he had the tournament won. "Up till then," he later recounted, "I had pretended it was just a practice round, but I began to think about what I'd say when they put the green jacket [symbol of the Masters champion] on me and how my dad would feel. It brought tears to my eyes." His concentration destroyed, he bogied the sixteenth and eighteenth holes and finished tied for second place with Nicklaus as Coody took the champion's jacket.

Rumors began to spread that Miller "choked" in pressure situations, that he tended to become nervous when championships were on the line. But he himself, although unhappy with his performance in the Masters, never questioned his ability to play his game under pressure, and his overall 1971 record vindicated his self-confidence. He shot par or better on the final day in 85 percent of the tournaments he finished, and his total earnings in tournament play were $91,081.

Constantly working to improve his game, Miller became a keen observer of his opponents' strengths and weaknesses. Quitting his incessant experimentation with new and different clubs, he settled on the old set that he has used ever since. It consists of 1947 Armour irons and an original Bullseye putter, considered a relic. Although his only victory on the 1972 tour was in the Heritage Open Classic, he had enough close finishes to earn $99,348.

A book by Bobby Locke, an ex-British Open titleholder from South Africa, helped convince Miller that everything on a golf course must be done as little by chance and as much by calculation as possible. He developed the habit of jotting notes—yardage calculations, reminders to keep his head down, and so forth—on the backs of old envelopes, so that it became a familiar sight to see Miller studying his notes during tourney play. Later, Bill Lyon observed in the Philadelphia Inquirer (June 7, 1974), "A lot of tour regulars will tell you that Johnny Miller is a thinking golfer, one of the new breed who has brought computer strategy to the land of double knits and 5-woods."

Shooting what many experts considered the greatest round of golf ever played, Miller scored a record-breaking 63 in the final round to win the 1973 U.S. Open. On the tough 6,921-yard Oakmont Country Club course, the twenty-six-year-old pro birdied nine of the first fifteen holes, winding up with a 31 on the back nine and a one-stroke victory over John Schlee. He had started the final round trailing twelve players, including six former Open champions. Looking back on his victory, he has said, "I think that I'll never equal that round. It set up my life."

Proving his Open win was no fluke, Miller finished a strong second in the British Open, and then, in late November, he teamed with Jack Nicklaus to win the prestigious World Cup for the United States. In the latter international event, held in Marbella, Spain, Miller led all scorers with a 11 under par 277 and established a course record of 65 in the second round. The victory brought his 1973 total earnings to $127,833.

In January 1974 Miller won three consecutive events: he opened the 1974 PGA tour with an easy four-stroke win in the Bing Crosby National Pro-Am, which was cut short by bad weather; birdied the final two holes to edge Lanny Wadkins in the Phoenix Open; and won the $30,000 Dean Martin Tucson Open by three strokes.

Because of a nagging cold, Miller took a three-week rest in March 1974. As usual, he spent the

JOHNNY MILLER

three weeks relaxing with his family, fishing, driving his sports car, and generally enjoying himself. After rejoining the tour he captured the Sea Pine Heritage Classic and the Tournament of Champions. Observing that Miller had not touched a golf club during his three-week rest, a reporter for the New York Times (March 24, 1974) wrote, "Johnny Miller . . . is an embarrassment to other golf pros because he performs so well without practice. . . . He is as sharp as he was when he took time off to cope with his allergies. . . . He practises only rarely, except for some limbering-up before the start of a round. . . . He says practice must have a purpose, a target, like correcting the flaw that was causing him to hit iron shots to the right."

By the end of April 1974 Miller had won $192,877. Jack Ludwig commented in Maclean's (July 1974): "Not even in Jack Nicklaus' two best years . . . did he have anything like Johnny Miller's $193,000 after only four months. And yet, to Nicklaus, Johnny Miller doesn't quite rate. Miller lacks the high seriousness Nicklaus associates with golf as a calling." Ludwig quoted Miller as saying that his aim in playing was to "score good" and Nicklaus as saying that his was to "win more major championships than anyone else." The Times reporter went on: "What made Nicklaus, Palmer, and Player unique, according to Nicklaus, was that they all 'felt a responsibility to win big golf tournaments, especially the major events.' . . . Miller's attitude is anything but Nicklaus-Olympian. 'Heck,' he says, 'I know I'm not in the class of a Nicklaus or Trevino. I've a long way to go and a lot to learn.'"

"The whole thing to me is tempo, alignment, and address position," Miller once explained about his game. "My swing hasn't changed in years except for tiny little things. . . . Most guys who practise too much fiddle with their swings on the practice tee and then screw up. All the practice is doing is confusing their muscle memory. They hit 300 balls and can't understand why they can't hit them right. . . . The reason is that they're tired, their reflexes are slow, their legs are dead, they're not taking time with the shots."

Johnny and Linda Miller, who met when both were students at Brigham Young University, were married in the autumn of 1969. As of June 1974 they had two children, a son, John Jr., and a daughter, Kelly, and they were expecting a third. The Millers live in Napa, California. A close family man, Miller takes his family on tour with him when possible. The recreations he enjoys in addition to sports-car driving and fishing include hiking, tennis, and duck hunting. In keeping with the proscriptions of his Mormon faith, the six-foot-two, 170-pound golfer neither drinks nor smokes, and he contributes 10 percent of his net income to the church. That income is swelled by exhibition fees ($10,000 a day) and remuneration for television and other media endorsements of MacGregor sporting goods, Sears clothes, and other products. His business affairs are handled by Uni-Managers International.

A Ford advertising executive explained on one occasion why his automobile company hired Miller to do commercials for its Thunderbird car: "We want an image young people can identify with. Miller fits that image. He's the college guy; young, virile, has a freshness about him, socially mature and well-spoken." Miller himself has said: "In my life, there are three things. First my family. Then my church. And, finally, there is golf. If I ever have to give up one of them, it'll be the golf." His honors include the 1973 Hickok Professional Athlete of the Year Award.

References

Parade p12 Je 2 '74 por
Sport 57:24+ Je '74 pors
Sports Illus 40:40 Je 10 '74 por
Time 102:60+ Jl 2 '73 por

MILLER, NEAL E(LGAR)

Aug. 3, 1909- Experimental psychologist
Address: b. Rockefeller University, 1230 York Ave., New York, 10021; h. 500 E. 77th St., New York, 10021

"Pure empiricism is a delusion," Dr. Neal E. Miller, the eminent behaviorist and experimental psychologist once commented. "Gathering all the facts with no bias from theory is utterly impossible." For more than forty years, Dr. Miller has worked to discredit the scientifically indefensible but generally accepted theory that the autonomic nervous system which regulates involuntary bodily functions such as heart rate and blood pressure was inferior to the voluntarily controlled central nervous system. His research, conducted at Yale University and, since 1966, at Rockefeller University, indicated that laboratory animals and humans can learn to regulate certain autonomic functions through a system of electronically ad-

ministered rewards and punishments. "We no longer view the brain as merely an enormously complicated telephone switchboard which is passive unless excited from without," the scientist reported in 1961. "The brain is an active organ which exerts considerable control over its own sensory input."

In a series of well-designed and carefully monitored experiments, Miller and his research associates at the Rockefeller Laboratory of Physiological Psychology proved that hypertensives could lower their blood pressures and that heart patients could slow and regularize their heart rates. Commonly known as biofeedback, this technique of behavior modification was enthusiastically received by the American public. Amateur experimenters purchased biofeedback devices manufactured for popular consumption, such as an apparatus for measuring "alpha wave" brain patterns. At the annual meeting of the Society for Psychophysiological Research in Boston in September 1972, Miller joined with some 650 colleagues to issue a resolution advising the public that "most of the research in the area of biofeedback [was] still in an experimental stage. . . . The therapeutic or psychological benefits of biofeedback training have not been established with any degree of scientific certainty." In recent experiments with rats, Miller was unable to replicate his earlier findings.

Neal Elgar Miller, the son of Irving E. and Lily R. (Fuenfstueck) Miller was born in Milwaukee, Wisconsin on August 3, 1909. He grew up in Bellingham, Washington, where his father, an educational psychologist trained by pragmatist John Dewey, was on the faculty of Western Washington State College. After receiving his B.S. degree in psychology from the University of Washington, in 1931, Miller studied at Stanford University under Dr. Lewis M. Terman, author of the Stanford-Binet I.Q. test, and at Yale University under Clark L. Hull, a leading behaviorist. He was granted an M.S. degree by Stanford in 1932 and a Ph.D. degree by Yale in 1935.

Intrigued by the possible relationship between the behavioristic "stimulus-response" theory of learning and psychoanalysis, Miller went to Vienna, Austria in 1936 on a grant from the Social Science Research Council. "The way you studied psychoanalysis in those days was to be analyzed yourself," he explained to Gerald Jonas in an interview for a *New Yorker* (August 19 and 26, 1972) profile, "preferably by someone at the Vienna Psychoanalytic Institute, or, even better, by Freud himself." Unable to pay Dr. Freud's fees, Miller submitted to eight months of psychoanalysis, which he later described as a useful "learning experience," under Dr. Heinz Hartmann, a student of Freud's. "If I had known then how many people would ask me what Freud was like, I'd have requested at least one hour's worth just to talk to him," he told Jonas. "But twenty dollars seemed like too much money at the time."

In the autumn of 1936 he returned to Yale, where he joined the faculty of the Institute of

Human Relations as an instructor and research associate in psychology. In collaboration with John Dollard, a Yale sociologist who specialized in the clinical applications and social manifestations of learning theory, he identified and traced the operation of "the higher mental processes" in the resolution of emotional problems. In *Frustration and Aggression* (Yale University Press, 1939), *Social Learning and Imitation* (Yale University Press, 1941), and *Personality and Psychotherapy: An Analysis in Terms of Learning, Thinking and Culture* (McGraw, 1950), the two scientists, as they explained in the third book, combined "the three great traditions" of psychoanalysis, experimental psychology, and sociology "to aid in the creation of a psychological base for a general science of human behavior."

Working from expanded "operational" definitions of "stimulus" and "response," they contended that a neurotic symptom is a "learned" instrumental response to a stress or conflict situation. By changing the label normally attached to that situation, they argued, it was possible to modify or alter an individual's emotional reaction. For example, a person suffering from anxiety may exhibit sudden fits of crying, outbursts of anger, or periods of depression. If the emotional response reduces the anxiety, the behavior is automatically reinforced. To correct the behavior, the psychotherapist, in effect, severs the "bad" stimulus-response association and substitutes a "better" response to the anxiety-producing stimulus. "It is desirable that the patient have some skill at the deliberate solution of emotional problems which we call self-study," Miller and Dollard wrote in *Personality and Psychotherapy*. "In the ordinary case, the skill is a by-product of the original therapeutic training."

In the early years of World War II, Miller and Dollard investigated a particular kind of emotional behavior: fear in battle. For their sample, they selected at random 300 veterans of the Abraham Lincoln Brigade, a group of American volunteers who fought with the Spanish Republican Army. Eighty-five percent of the men interviewed freely admitted that they were occasionally "scared stiff" during enemy attacks. Describing their fears to the researchers, the subjects identified a pounding heart, muscular tenseness, dryness of the mouth and throat, and physical trembling as the most common symptoms. Nearly all the men, however, had ignored their fears to become efficient combat soldiers. Miller and Dollard concluded that such fear was normal and had no effect on subsequent behavior. Noting that 94 percent of those questioned admitted that they fought better after observing a comrade's calm behavior, they emphasized the importance of a group discussion of fear and its symptoms before beginning a combat action. The study, *Fear in Battle*, was published by Yale University Press in 1943. Dr. Miller, a major in the United States Air Corps, continued his behavioral studies as the officer in charge of research for the Psychological Research Unit in Nashville, Tennessee from 1942 to 1944 and as the director of the

NEAL E. MILLER

psychological research project at Randolph Field, Texas from 1944 to 1946.

After the war, Miller returned to Yale as an associate professor. In 1950 he was appointed professor of psychology, and in 1952 he was named James Rowland Angell professor of psychology. He remained at Yale until 1966, when he joined the behavioral sciences faculty at Rockefeller University. While at Yale, Dr. Miller continued to conduct experimental research into emotional behavior. To pinpoint cerebral nerve centers, he inserted tiny electrical probes into the hypothalamic region of the brains of rats and cats. (The hypothalamus controls and regulates temperature and other involuntary bodily functions.) With this technique, he located the exact centers of pain, pleasure, hunger, and fear which lie within a few hundredths of an inch of each other. When he sent a small amount of electrical current into the probe imbedded in the "fear" center, the experimental animal showed signs of fear. By moving the probe to other centers, he produced corresponding responses of hunger, pleasure, and pain. By electrically punishing and rewarding the rats, Miller taught them to negotiate mazes and turn wheels.

In other experiments, he combined behaviorism and physiology to examine motivation and reward. For instance, he found that the hunger drive of a ravenous rat could be significantly reduced by injecting food directly into the animal's stomach. Using such an injection as a reward, he trained rats to select repeatedly the arm of the T-maze in which the food or sugar solution was injected. Although it produced the same amount of distension, the inflation of a balloon inside the rat's stomach served as a punishment, causing the rat to avoid the other side of the maze. In Miller's view, these experiments provided substantial proof that the motivating tendencies, such as hunger, thirst, and sex, are complex reactions governed by the nerve centers in the brain rather than simple, instinctual drives.

Discussing his research results at a five-day meeting of the American Association for the

Advancement of Science in December 1956, Miller asserted that his goal was "to find drugs that will accentuate the positive, rewarding functions and minimize the negative, punishing and fear functions." Such drugs could be used in the treatment of "mental diseases in which patients seem to have been overwhelmed by anxiety or lost hope of reward." He suggested, for example, that chlorpromazine, a tranquilizer he had used in several experiments, might aid patients "who have far too strong a striving for unrealistic or tabooed rewarding goals." For his work, the Association awarded Dr. Miller the Newcomb-Cleveland Prize. He shared the award with Dr. James Olds, a research psychologist at the University of California at Los Angeles.

In a radical departure from the classical conditioning techniques practiced by the Russian physiologist Ivan Pavlov, Dr. Miller began experimenting with operant conditioning. Without using any natural stimulus, such as rattling the feeding dish, he observed a dog. When the animal began to salivate spontaneously, he immediately rewarded it with a drink of water. Miller's dogs eventually learned to salivate whenever they wanted water. This was the first time that any animal had been known to control an "autonomic" or involuntary bodily response. Before Miller's groundbreaking experiments, most scientists thought that the only responses subject to control were those mediated by the cerebrospinal nervous system, but as the new concept gained acceptance in the scientific community, more and more psychologists agreed with Miller that visceral learning might hold the key to curing psychosomatic illnesses such as ulcers, irregular heartbeat, asthma, epileptic seizures, and hypertension.

At the annual meeting of the American Psychological Association in September 1961, Miller outlined the research that had correctly identified the weight-regulating mechanism located in a primitive area of a rat's brain. The experimenters discovered that a cerebral injection of adrenalin caused hungry rats to eat; a similar injection of a cholinergic substance provoked satiated rats to drink. Acknowledging that "it is very difficult to get people who eat little to eat more and people who eat too much to eat less," Miller suggested that it might be possible to control malnutrition and obesity through the intake of drugs which affect the weight-regulating center of the brain. Two years later, at a symposium on psychophysiology sponsored by the International Congress of Psychology, Miller maintained that it would be feasible and prudent to "reset man's food thermostat" to correspond with more nutritious food and more leisure time.

After several years of intensive research at Rockefeller University's Laboratory of Physiological Psychology, which he had founded in 1966, Miller and a colleague, Dr. Leo V. DiCara, were convinced that operant conditioning was a valuable tool in the correction of maladaptive human behavior. "We have developed a technique for using learning to modify glandular and visceral responses," Miller wrote in an article for *Science* magazine (January 31, 1969). "The success of this technique suggests that it should be able to produce therapeutic changes. If the patient who is highly motivated to get rid of a symptom (the bad habit) understands that a signal, such as a tone, indicates a change in the therapeutic direction, that tone should serve as a powerful reward. . . . As patients find that they can secure some control of the symptom, their motivation can be strengthened."

Miller and DiCara had established that rats and other experimental animals could be trained to increase or decrease their heart rates, regulate blood pressure, and control kidney functions and intestinal contractions in response to a tone signal. To convince skeptics that the visceral responses were not mediated by the cerebrospinal nervous system, Miller paralyzed the laboratory rats with curare, the poisonous plant extract that acts as a muscle relaxant. Using the direct electrical stimulation of the pleasure center in the brain as a reward, he trained the rats to regulate their heart rates. After ninety minutes of training, the rats learned to raise or lower their heart rates by as much as 20 percent. Subsequent tests confirmed that the animals remembered their training.

Assuming that "men are at least as smart as rats in this respect," Dr. Miller began applying his operant conditioning techniques to the modification of human behavior in 1969. In a cooperative project with the Cornell University Medical College, he taught patients with chronic tachychardia to slow their heart rates to a more normal level. Each patient was monitored electronically. Whenever his heart rate fell below a certain level, his behavior was rewarded and reinforced by an electronic tone. A similar series of tests at Rockefeller University proved that both healthy and hypertensive individuals could be trained to raise or lower their diastolic pressure.

Confirming Miller's results, a team of researchers at Harvard Medical School found that young men could be easily trained to raise or lower their blood pressures when the correct response was immediately rewarded by a five-second look at a photograph of a *Playboy* magazine "playmate." Buoyed by his considerable success, Miller suggested that doctors use operant conditioning methods to teach ulcer patients to regulate their gastric secretions and to train migraine headache victims to control their blood vessels. Nonetheless, Miller warned against "overoptimistic publicity" about the therapeutic possibilities of biofeedback training. "It leads to impossible hopes that will produce inevitable disillusionment," he explained in an interview for *Newsday* (November 24, 1972).

Miller insists that the brain, which he once described as "the greatest miracle in the universe," is the key to the universality of human behavior. As chairman of President John F. Kennedy's eight-man Science Advisory Committee, he exhorted the government to sponsor additional research into human behavior and urged the inclusion of behavioral science courses in high schools and colleges. A report issued by the committee in April 1961 recommended that governmental agencies utilize the existing studies on human communication, culture, and personality development; that the National Academy of Science broaden its scope to include research in behavioral sciences; and that the appropriate scientific and social organizations apply behavioral techniques to the study of public issues, such as the problems of the aged, the effect of increased leisure time on the middle class, occupational aspirations, and mental illness.

A dedicated teacher for more than forty years, Miller seldom practises the precepts of learning theory in the classroom. Teaching is "halfway between the realm of art and the realm of science," he told Gerald Jonas. "You can try to sharpen the problems for your students and help them avoid blind alleys, but essentially you have to give them practice in learning things on their own. . . . I regularly expect my students to know more than I do about at least one field. And I expect them to be able to put this knowledge to work in the laboratory."

Neal E. Miller and his wife, the former Marion E. Edwards, were married on June 30, 1948. They have two children, York and Sara. In addition to their Manhattan apartment near the campus of Rockefeller University, the Millers maintain a weekend retreat in Guilford, Connecticut and a summer home on a lake in Maine. For relaxation, Dr. Miller enjoys fishing and gardening. He tends exotic blossoming plants in his city apartment and raises tomatoes (because "they're so easy") and an especially sweet variety of corn in the country.

References

New Yorker 48:34+ Ag 19 '72; 48:30+
    Ag 26 '72
Science News 97:274 Mr 14 '70 por
American Men and Women of Science 12th
    (1972)
McGraw-Hill Modern Men of Science
    (1966)
Who's Who in America, 1972-73

MITFORD, JESSICA (LUCY)

Sept. 11, 1917- Writer
Address: h. 6411 Regent St., Oakland, Calif.
94618

An aptitude for polemics and a mastery of the techniques of investigation and exposure, enhanced by a grace of style, a moral zeal, and a lacerating wit, have made the British-born writer Jessica Mitford a remarkably effective practitioner of the old American way of muckraking. She has said in press interviews that she does not think of herself as a crusader or reformer or even a rebel, but as Lena Jeger pointed out in the *Guardian* (June 13, 1964), "Her life has been a protest—a protest against her own privileged, arid, aristocratic background; against snobbery and political selfishness

JESSICA MITFORD

and reactionary regimes wherever they existed." Whether scrutinizing the funeral industry, as in *The American Way of Death* (1963), or the penal system, as in *Kind and Usual Punishment* (1973), or the workings of the conspiracy laws or the practices of a mail-order writing school, Miss Mitford displays an uncanny gift for ferreting out fraud.

The daughter of a peer, Jessica Lucy Mitford was born at Batsford Mansion, Gloucestershire, England on September 11, 1917 to Lord Redesdale (David Mitford) and Lady Redesdale (the former Sydney Bowles). Her father had become the second baron of Redesdale only shortly before her birth, when his older brother died in World War I. Decca, as her friends call her, was next to the youngest girl of the seven children in an extraordinary family whose eccentricities have been recorded in *The Pursuit of Love* (1946), a novel of an older daughter, Nancy Mitford, a celebrated writer of fiction and biography, and in *Daughters and Rebels* (Houghton Mifflin, 1960), the autobiography of Jessica Mitford, which was published in England by Gollancz under the title of *Hons and Rebels*.

Growing up together at Swinbrook in the Cotswold country along with Nancy and Jessica were a brother, Thomas, and four sisters. Pamela, the oldest, longed to be a horse; Deborah, the youngest, became the Duchess of Devonshire. Two of the sisters turned to Fascism: Unity went to Germany as a disciple of Hitler; Diana married the British Fascist leader Sir Oswald Mosley. While their brother attended Eton, the Mitford girls acquired only a meager education at home. Tutored by her mother, however, by the age of six Jessica was expected to stand and read aloud faultlessly editorials from the London *Times*.

"I was an unhappy child," Miss Mitford said in an interview for the New York *Post* (November 10, 1963), recalling the restrictions of her upperclass rearing. The tone of her spirited autobiography is often sardonic. As a teenager when she shared a sitting room with her swastika-loving sister, Unity, she used her diamond ring to carve small hammers and sickles in the window panes on her side of the room. At nineteen she ran away from home with her second cousin, Esmond Romilly, a nephew of Winston Churchill and a Communist sympathizer, to aid the Loyalist cause in the Spanish Civil War.

A British destroyer was dispatched to retrieve the runaway pair, but that proved no more effectual than family efforts to separate them. They were married in 1937. Jessica Romilly quit work as a market researcher at the London office of J. Walter Thompson advertising agency in 1939 and moved to the United States with her husband in a bohemian lifestyle venture of traveling around the country and trying to make ends meet through jobs that required little training. In 1939-40 she was employed as a bartender at the Roma Restaurant in Miami, Florida and in 1940-41, as a salesgirl in Weinberger's Dress Shop in Washington, D.C.

Daughters and Rebels ends with the departure of Romilly for Canada to resume his fight against Fascism by joining the Royal Canadian Air Force. He was killed in action in World War II in November 1941. Remaining in Washington, Jessica Mitford worked from 1941 to 1943 in the Office of Price Administration, first as a typist and later as an investigator. Among her fellow employees in that wartime agency was the Brooklyn lawyer Robert E. Treuhaft, whom she married on June 21, 1943. The following year she became a naturalized United States citizen.

Fairly soon after their marriage the Treuhafts moved to California and settled in a racially integrated section of Oakland. In his law practice Treuhaft became involved in civil rights causes and labor relations in the San Francisco-Oakland area. During the late 1940's and early 1950's Jessica Mitford served as executive secretary in Oakland of the Civil Rights Congress. She was instrumental in bringing about in 1948-49 the first state legislative investigation into charges of police brutality.

Miss Mitford did not begin to write until she was about thirty-eight years old. Her first book, *Lifeitselfmanship*, was privately published in 1956. Through her autobiography, however, which was widely and warmly reviewed in 1960, she had come to the attention of many American readers well before the appearance of her best-selling *The American Way of Death* (Simon & Schuster, 1963). Her inquiry into the high cost of burial began with the concern of her husband that often much of the modest inheritance of his clients disappeared into the coffers of morticians. He therefore organized a funeral society in a cooperative community effort to reduce the cost and simplify the style of burial or cremation.

In funeral trade publications and in the opposition of undertakers to her husband's project, Jessica Mitford encountered an abundance of what she would call "bosh." Her indignant determination to write a book about unscrupulous funeral practices thrived on the response she received from her article "St. Peter, Don't You Call Me," which appeared in the California periodical *Frontier*, and

from her debate on a local TV show with representatives of the mortuary industry. The description in the *Guardian* (June 13, 1964) of her article as "a revelation of racket and rubbish" applies also to *The American Way of Death*, which assails the ornateness and commercialism of funerals in the United States. "She has documented her book with facts," Harold H. Brayman wrote in the *National Observer* (September 16, 1963), "and treats a dismal subject tastefully—yet often with hilarity, though she's never too flippant. Largely she lets the funeral industry insert its own satiric rapier, with unfunereal quotes from morticians and the funeral industry's 11 trade publications." Other reviewers compared her indictment to Evelyn Waugh's caustic novel about a deluxe Hollywood mortuary establishment, *The Loved One* (1948).

As expected, Miss Mitford's searching examination of America's rites of death aroused the anger of the nation's funeral directors. Also outraged, presumably by a chapter in the book on the Forest Lawn cemetery in Los Angeles, California, Representative James B. Utt denounced her in a statement in the *Congressional Record* as "pro-Communist, anti-American" and an enemy of Christianity. Others who attacked her personally recalled that the House Un-American Activities Committee had once criticized her for her association with the left-wing Civil Rights Congress. But aware of public support and gratitude for the author's stand in the funeral controversy, CBS presented in October 1963 a special documentary inspired by her book. Miss Mitford appeared on that and other TV shows, as well as many radio programs on the abuses of the American undertaking industry.

Timeliness of subject may have accounted considerably for the success of *The American Way of Death*. Since it involved the burning question of United States participation in the Vietnam war, Miss Mitford's next book held a similarly topical appeal, while commenting on ethical issues of continuing concern. In *The Trial of Dr. Spock; William Sloane Coffin, Jr., Michael Ferber, Mitchell Goodman, and Marcus Raskin* (Knopf, 1969) she gave a firsthand, factual, though openly partisan, account of the 1968 trial of the so-called "Boston Five" on charges of "conspiracy to aid, abet and counsel violations of the Selective Service Law." Although they were all engaged individually in antiwar activities, the five men scarcely knew one another. Besides covering day-to-day events in the courtroom of eighty-five-year-old Judge Francis Ford in Boston, Miss Mitford interviewed scores of persons connected with the trial.

In keeping with her longstanding interest in civil rights, Miss Mitford focused her attention on the prosecution of the accused on conspiracy charges. She showed in her book that the conspiracy laws endanger personal liberty by denying defendants certain procedural safeguards and privileges available in usual criminal cases. After the trial, in which four of the five were found guilty, she interviewed several jurors, one of whom explained that they had voted "guilty as charged by the judge." The August 1969 issue of the

Atlantic Monthly, carrying an excerpt from Miss Mitford's forthcoming book, was running on the press when a federal appellate court reversed the conspiracy conviction on the ground that the judge had improperly instructed the jury—a decision in accordance with one of Miss Mitford's arguments in The Trial of Dr. Spock.

"I've always gotten into these subjects by chance," Jessica Mitford told Jean M. White in an interview for the Washington Post (September 12, 1973)."I did that article of the Famous Writers School because my husband had a client, a 73-year-old widow, who was enrolled in the school." Her amusing and devastating article, "Let Us Now Appraise Famous Writers," first appeared in the July 1970 issue of the Atlantic and was excerpted in the Washington Post and the Des Moines Register. Charging the well-known mail-order school of Westport, Connecticut with deceptive practices, she attacked misleading advertising and high-pressure sales methods that enticed the elderly, the gullible, and the not-too-bright—along with qualified students—into signing contracts for expensive correspondence courses that would supposedly prepare them for a career in creative writing.

Among Miss Mitford's targets was the Guiding Faculty of the Famous Writers School, fifteen eminent and respected men and women, such as Bennett Cerf and Faith Baldwin, whose misrepresentation, she alleged, took the form in part of giving the impression that they were personally involved in judging aptitude tests and evaluating manuscripts. She recommended in her article that aspiring writers enroll in far less costly state university correspondence courses, which she regarded as superior to the Famous Writers offerings. Much to her delight the Famous Writers School later went bankrupt.

What Miss Mitford has called her "three-year odyssey of American prisons" began in early 1970 with her acceptance of a proposal by the American Civil Liberties Union that she write an article on prisoners' rights for publication as part of that organization's fiftieth anniversary program. Her research became a great deal more extensive than she had expected. As she corresponded with prisoners, interviewed lawyers and correctional officers, explored the published studies of criminologists and penologists, attended professional conventions, visited penitentiaries across the country, and spent a night in a women's detention center, her project grew into the 340-page, ironically titled Kind and Usual Punishment; The Prison Business (Knopf, 1973).

Like many other investigators of the American penal system, Jessica Mitford found that prisons, though now called "correctional facilities," are more likely to corrupt and brutalize than to correct and rehabilitate, and that inmates are subjected to much the same racial and class prejudices they had encountered in society at large. She went ahead to provide well-documented pioneering analyses of prison finances and crime statistics. In her grim study of what happens to men and women behind bars, she denounced the horrifying and dehumanizing use of experimental chemical, surgical, and psychiatric techniques as "behavorial modifiers," in Clockwork Orange fashion, and the practice of pharmaceutical firms of leasing prisoners for developing and testing drugs. She also argued persuasively against the sentencing of prisoners to indeterminate terms and other reforms of some well-intentioned liberal penologists, and against the parole system itself.

"The Mitford book, in sum, is a wonderfully readable, tough-minded, and in parts memorable account of the prison system today. No one volume better reports the scholarly literature or more compellingly describes the sordid state of incarceration," David J. Rothman asserted in the New York Times Book Review (September 9, 1973). Several reviewers of Kind and Usual Punishment criticized Miss Mitford for failing to detail concrete solutions to problems that she discussed. In interviews after its publication she replied that she had indicated that total abolition of prisons would be unrealistic without a reorganization of society, preferably through socialism—a subject beyond the scope of her book. She said that she had hoped, however, to stir public interest in changing the present penal system through her proposal of such reforms as the establishment of prisoners' unions.

In 1973 San Jose State College in California appointed Jessica Mitford to a distinguished visiting professorship in sociology and assigned her to teach a lecture class titled "The American Way" and to conduct a seminar on techniques of muckraking. At the beginning of the term, in October, she disclosed in a press conference that she had signed "under duress" a state-required oath of allegiance that she considered "obnoxious, silly and demeaning." When she later refused to be fingerprinted, college officials threatened to lock her out of her classroom. "I'm going to come and teach every day as long as my contract goes on," she promised, as quoted in the New York Times (October 12, 1973). "I shall fight this in the courts." Jessica Mitford's name was among those that had appeared on a list drawn up in 1970 by the House Internal Security Committee (formerly the House Un-American Activities Committee) of sixty-five persons with ties to "radical" organizations who had spoken on American college campuses.

By her first marriage Jessica Mitford has a daughter, Constancia Romilly, and by her second marriage she has a son, Benjamin Truehaft. A residence of more than thirty years in the United States has scarcely affected the British characteristics of her speech, including her slang preferences, although her sister Nancy, the inventor of the U and non-U designation for British speech, was once reported to have thought her accent shocking. She is a tall woman whose style of dress is subdued but chic. In contrast to her "formidable" books, Peter Gardner, who interviewed her for Publishers' Weekly (October 1, 1973), found that she "gives an initial impression of gentle amiability." He went on to say, "But her eyes, which are of striking shape and an almost alarming blue, begin to hint of steely qualities within—along with a mordant and highly developed sense of humor."

References

Christian Sci Mon p10 S 21 '73 por
Guardian p6 Je 13 '64 por
Guardian W p18 O 13 '73
N Y Post mag p2 N 10 '63 por; p51 S 30 '69 por
Newsday p56 O 30 '63 por
Pub W 204:32+ O 1 '73 por
Time 96:52 Jl 20 '70 por
Washington Post C p1+ S 12 '73 pors
Contemporary Authors vol 2 (1963)
Who's Who of American Women, 1973-74

MORRIS, DESMOND (JOHN)

Jan. 24, 1928-   British ethologist; author
Address: b. Dept. of Zoology, Oxford University, Oxford, England; h. 78 Banbury Rd., Oxford, England; Villa Apap Bologna, Attard, Malta

"Something of a Renaissance man, combining wit with learning and artistic sensibility with scientific research" is Anthony Storr's categorization of the peripatetic Oxford zoologist Desmond Morris, who has described himself as "a rare and vanishing species of twentieth century man, an anti-specialist." Morris is best known as a leader in the popularization of the relatively new science of comparative ethology, the study of human behavior through its animal roots. A former curator of mammals at the London Zoo and producer and host of popular animal programs on British television, Morris has since the late 1960's been concentrating on research and the writing of books concerned, in his words, with "making people think about what kind of animal they are and what sort of problems that animal's got himself into." The most successful of his audacious pop ethological works was the controversial international best seller *The Naked Ape* (1967), and *The Human Zoo* (1969) ran a close second in sales. On the side, Morris is an artist whose paintings are invariably typified by undefinable biomorphic forms set in Daliesque landscapes.

The son of Harry Howe Morris, a professional writer of fiction, and Dorothy Marjorie Fuller (Hunt) Morris, Desmond John Morris was born in Purton, Wiltshire, England on January 24, 1928, and he was raised in Swindon, also in Wiltshire. "I was born in . . . West Country, very beautiful, with some marvelous prehistoric monuments; Stonehenge is there and other prehistoric remains," he told Helen Dudar of the New York *Post* (February 3, 1968). "So you see, right from an early age I started asking about early man and what he was about. I was also surrounded by art as a child and later I took up painting seriously."

Growing up in the Wiltshire countryside, Morris became fascinated by the local flora and, above all, fauna. From a self-made canoe he observed the wildlife in and around the lake in what is now Queen's Park in Swindon. He collected a menagerie of crows, jackdaws, newts, lizards, tortoises, fish, rabbits, guinea pigs, toads, cats, dogs, and foxes, and he became a supplier of small animals to the Kidlington Zoo. At Dauntsey's School in Wiltshire he edited a natural history magazine. After discovering among the family heirlooms a microscope and set of slides that had belonged to his great-grandfather, he became interested in drawing and painting the shapes of microorganisms.

During his two years (1946-48) of service as a British Army conscript, Morris lectured in fine arts at an army college. For several years after his demobilization it was, as he has said, "touch-and-go" whether he would pursue a career in art or in science. As an artist, he had his first one-man exhibition in 1950, at the London Gallery. But on the scholastic level he had already opted for science, because, as he has explained, "the art schools were so bad" at that time. As an undergraduate at Birmingham University he was persuaded by one of his professors, Peter Medawar, to devote himself to zoology, and he took a first-class B.S. degree in that subject in 1951.

Besides Medawar, two other pioneer ethologists had strong influences on Morris: Konrad Lorenz, generally regarded as the founding father of the new science of animal-human behavior, and Nikolaas Tinbergen. From Birmingham, Morris went to Oxford University to study under Tinbergen, and he took his D.Phil. degree at Oxford in 1954. For his doctoral thesis he studied the courtship rituals and other sexual behavior of the small Northern Hemisphere fish the ten-spined stickleback, and his dissertation became his first published work, *The Reproductive Behavior of the Ten-Spined Stickleback* (E. J. Brill, 1958). Among his original discoveries was the finding that sticklebacks display homosexual behavior under certain conditions. While working for his doctorate at Oxford, Morris wrote and directed a surrealist film, *Time Flower*, featuring his wife, Ramona, stumbling across terrain on the North Downs, which was pocked with rabbit holes.

Following two years of postdoctoral research in bird behavior under Professor Tinbergen at Oxford, Morris became the founding host of *Zoo Time*, a popular Granada Television production aired over the ITV network. The favorite guest on the show in its original three-year run was Congo, a chimpanzee from the London Zoo. When abstract paintings by Congo and two other apes were exhibited at the Institute of Contemporary Arts in London in 1957, Julian Huxley observed in a dispatch to the New York *Times* (October 6, 1957): "The results show conclusively that chimpanzees do have artistic potentialities. . . . One of the great mysteries of human evolution is the sudden outburst of art of a very high quality in the Upper Paleolithic period. This becomes more comprehensible if our ape-like ancestors had these primitive esthetic potentialities, to which was later added man's unique capacity for symbol-making."

Years later Morris himself agreed with an interviewer's conclusion that the "ape art" suggested that "abstraction is in some way infantile." He explained: "The very young child is preoccupied with purely esthetic considerations. By the time a child is twelve or thirteen he is able to record outside events, and eventually the burden of recording becomes very heavy and the esthetic factors are weakened. . . . Painting is now going back to the infantile condition—and I want to make it quite clear that this is not a criticism. . . . The art of the twentieth century has thrown off these chains of recording information."

Morris wrote *The Story of Congo* (Batsford, 1958) for children, and he related the picture-making behavior of the great apes to human art in his adult book *The Biology of Art* (Knopf, 1962). Commenting on the latter in the New York *Post* (September 2, 1962), Irving Sandler wrote: "Morris has established . . . that the painting activity of apes is for its own sake; they do not require rewards for picture-making. If bribed, Morris writes, apes can become corrupt. One [ape] quickly learned to associate drawing with getting a reward, 'but as soon as this condition had been established the animal took less and less interest in the lines it was drawing.'"

As moderator of *Zoo Time*, from 1956 to 1959, and as an occasional host on Granada and BBC animal programs in the years following, Morris presented a total of some 500 television programs. From 1959 to 1967 Desmond Morris was curator of mammals at the London Zoo, or the Zoological Society of London, as it is more properly called. His experiences as curator confirmed many of the Freudian hypotheses about the influence of the early environment on infants, whether animal or human. For example, no matter what precautionary steps were taken, the keepers were unable to prevent one of the zoo's coyotes from constantly clawing itself, inflicting deep wounds. The self-destructive tendency does not occur simply as a result of confinement, however. Morris has observed that it is usually present in animals who have suffered untimely removal from the natal environment. With animals as with humans, such removal is traumatic if it occurs in the period between the time the infant becomes consciously attached to a parent or parents and the point when it is mature enough to cope with separation.

Morris made many innovations to liven up zoo life for the animals, such as slot machines for monkeys to operate and baskets of fish traveling along a water-side rail for seals to chase, and foliage and other such environmental items congenial to each species. "If zoos are to survive the twentieth century," he later said, "they must reform. . . . Animal enclosures must be as different from one another as the animals they contain. They must be as complex as possible. This is not simply a question of physical space; it is a matter of psychological space. . . . Zoos have a choice. They can change drastically and flourish. . . . Or they can continue along as the scruffy little animal slums they all too often are, and find themselves outlawed and condemned."

While at the zoo Morris wrote the juvenile books *Apes and Monkeys* (Bodley Head, 1964; McGraw-Hill, 1965), *The Big Cats* (McGraw-Hill, 1965),

DESMOND MORRIS

and *Zoo Time* (Hart-Davis, 1966) and the adult books *Introducing Curious Creatures* (Spring Books, 1961) and *The Mammals* (Harper, 1965). With his wife he wrote *Men and Snakes* (McGraw-Hill, 1965), *Men and Apes* (McGraw-Hill, 1966), and *Men and Pandas* (Hutchinson, 1966; McGraw-Hill, 1967). With Caroline Jarvis he edited the *International Zoo Yearbook* volumes for 1959-60, 1960-61, and 1961-62, published by the Zoological Society of London, and by himself he edited *Primate Ethology* (Aldine, 1967).

During a winter he spent in Moscow trying unsuccessfully to mate the London Zoo's giant panda Chi-Chi with the Moscow Zoo's An-An, Morris' health broke down. Curtailing his activities as zoo curator, he found himself with a surplus of leisure time, during which he turned to a project that had been gestating in his mind for years: a book calculated to stun readers into "examining a thesis that we are still subject to the basic laws of animal behavior and must recognize this in order to survive." He had never seriously considered putting it down on paper because, as he once explained, he "was frightened of what people would say, how they would react to this cold, very objective treatment of themselves." Encouraged by an editor at Jonathan Cape, he put aside his fear and set to work. In keeping with his routine, he holed himself up until he finished a first draft, and the final draft was completed within three months.

The Naked Ape: A Zoologist's Study of the Human Animal was published in England by Jonathan Cape in 1967 and in the United States by McGraw-Hill the following year. His opening paragraphs set the tone of the book: "There are 193 living species of monkeys and apes. One hundred and ninety-two of them are covered with hair. The exception is a naked ape self-named Homo sapiens. . . . He is proud that he has the largest brain of all the primates but attempts to conceal the fact that he also has the largest penis. . . . It is high time we examined his basic behavior."

There was hardly any area of civilized social ritual or mores that Morris did not ingeniously trace back to our animal or cave-man ancestors.

Small talk such as that engaged in at cocktail parties he interpreted as a sort of mutual grooming, similar to the friendly gestures of monkeys in picking fleas and dead skin off each other. Marriage he saw as an outgrowth of the "pair bonding" that hunting apes learned to practise as a means of keeping peace among themselves. Our obsession with deodorizing ourselves, he asserted, comes not so much from fear of "offending" as from fear of arousing strangers sexually and thus threatening our pair bonds. One of his more far-out speculations was that human female breasts have evolved into their present globular shape because after human beings emerged from the "all-fours" stage a frontal device resembling the buttocks was needed for sexual signaling. Fighting between groups and nations he traced to an instinct for domination, not destruction—to the territorial imperative that developed with the family and tribal units and their needs for fixed abodes. But global conflict, exacerbated by technology, he warned, is now threatening the very survival of our species. "The only sound biological solution to the dilemma," he concluded, "is massive de-population or a rapid spread of the species to other planets."

The reviewer for Newsweek (January 22, 1968) wrote of The Naked Ape: "Jumping right into the behavioral battle between social scientists—who believe that man is largely a product of his culture —and those who contend that behavior is genetically determined, Morris sides with the latter and argues that the patterns of behavior laid down in our early days as hunting apes still shine through all our affairs. It is, he claims, 'the biological nature of the beast that has molded the social structure of civilization rather than the other way around.'" The reviewer for Time (January 26, 1968) found the book "a little dramatic perhaps" but enhanced by "wit and graceful, untechnical prose." While William French, writing in the Toronto Globe and Mail (February 5, 1968), described Morris as using a "lecture" technique in The Naked Ape, others called his style entertaining," "stimulating," and "racy." Some critics admired his bold, imaginative explanations of civilized behavior and others were angered by his "flights of speculation." Among the most negative of the reactions was that of Robert Claiborne, who in his book God or Beast (1974) accused Morris of being "pseudoscientific" and "obnoxiously ethnocentric if not racist" and lumped him with other "pop evolutionists" under the label "Schlock Sociology."

Briefly, in 1967-68, Morris was director of the Institute of Contemporary Arts in London. In 1968 he retreated to Malta to write The Human Zoo (Cape, 1969; McGraw-Hill, 1969), in which he argued that the modern city is not, as the usual metaphor would have it, a jungle, but rather a zoo. In the jungle, he explained, the normal animal behaves in a free, healthy manner. In captivity it tends to become neurotic, and urban humanity is a tribal primate captive in a complex world where, like a caged animal, he tends to engage in meaningless pastimes and twisted forms of sexual and other behavior and to invent unnatural means of controlling the flow of stimuli. Like the animal in the zoo, when there is not enough input of stimulation from outside, humans tend to create unnecessary problems to solve or to magnify normal stimuli. When there are too many stimuli, they tend to turn off their receiving apparatus. Morris' mentor, Nikolaas Tinbergen, in reviewing The Human Zoo for the London Observer (September 28, 1969), wrote: "The specialist who grumbles because he disagrees with interpretations, generalizations, or oversimplifications is not quite fair; what Morris is trying to do is to shock people into an awareness of our ignorance of ourselves. In this he certainly succeeds, and I find it an important social service; it is a step in the important social process of cutting ourselves down to size."

In 1969-70 Morris was at Oxford doing research with Tinbergen into the ways in which the central nervous system organizes specific behavior patterns. From Oxford he returned to his villa on the island of Malta to write a book on the problems of basic human communication. "This is obviously going to be the central area where we're going to make or break ourselves as a species," he said at the time. Intimate Behavior, published in England by Cape in 1971 and in the United States by Random House in 1972, received mixed reviews. Among those who liked it was Anatole Broyard of the New York Times (March 3, 1972), who called Morris "a positive genius at interpreting our much abused body-language." Another was Alex Comfort, who in a review for Book World (February 27, 1972), observed that "it not only inculcates the cross-biologic viewpoint but deals with a number of our hangups in relation to the expression of our emotions, of which we are becoming increasingly aware."

Among those with negative reactions to Intimate Behavior were Arthur Koestler and Mordecai Richler. In the London Observer (October 10, 1971) Koestler wrote: "After a number of highly enjoyable books on snakes, pandas, and apes—including the naked one—Dr. Morris this time has indulged in filling a rag-bag with miscellaneous bits of information which add little to our knowledge of human nature but make it appear in a crude and grotesquely distorted form." Writing in the New York Times Book Review (March 5, 1972), Richler assessed Intimate Behavior as "on balance, a pseudo-book."

Papers by Desmond Morris published in such journals as Behaviour, New Scientist, and Zoo Life were collected in Patterns of Reproductive Behavior (Cape, 1970; McGraw-Hill, 1971). Forms "biological in concept but not representing a specific animal" is the way Morris describes the "creatures" in his paintings, which he continues to turn out, mostly for his personal satisfaction. "My biological knowledge—what I see under a microscope—gives me an understanding about spines and lobes and antennae. I let them evolve as though they were obeying some evolutionary role of which I'm not consciously aware. If one of the creatures or beings is identifiable as an existing kind of plant [or organism] then I have failed. They must all be invented."

Desmond Morris and Ramona Joy Baulch met at Oxford University, where she was majoring in history, and they were married in 1952. In addition to the books on which she has collaborated with her husband, Mrs. Morris has written many television scripts. With their son, Jason, the Morrises live alternately in Oxford and Attard, Malta, in what have been described as "luxurious" homes. Morris' study in the Oxford house contains a painting by Miró (one of his youthful artistic inspirations) and primitive art objects alongside paintings by chimpanzees, and there is a pet deer and an aviary in the back garden. Regarding the villa in Malta, Morris told Helen Dudar in the New York Post interview: "I've bought myself a piece of territory. I wanted the right kind of atmosphere where I could write. The snag is that the only property I could find that had the right kind of atmosphere happens to be a twenty-seven-room house with a fifteen-foot wall around an orange grove."

Morris is six feet tall and has brown hair and brown eyes. Helen Dudar found him to be "friendly, charming, and clever" and "running to chub below the shoulders and to bald above the ears." In her New York Post profile on him she wrote: "Cast in the modern TV mold, his conversation is instructive and his instruction is conversational." Other interviewers have described him as a "conservative" dresser, a "private" person, and a "rampageous, spontaneous man with bursting gestures and a wicked laugh." Morris himself admits to being "neurotically" productive. Reared in the Church of England, he now has no religious affiliation. Despite his peripateticism, his positions as a fellow of the Zoological Society of London and a research fellow at Wolfson College, Oxford University, remain constant. His favorite activity, outside of zoology, ethology, and painting, is archeology.

"I am a very typical member of my species," Morris has said. "I regard myself as very lucky to belong to it. It is not true that I want to reduce us to the level of animals. I am not one of those people who think animals are nicer than human beings." Among his favorite human beings are such youthful, rebellious talents as John Lennon and Dennis Hopper, both of whom he knows personally, and he regards counter-culture young people in general as society's best hope for saving the world. "Politicians . . . are without exception older men who do not seem to have woken up to the fact that they have to start looking at the people they control with a more biological eye." When, in 1968, the publishers of the Chicago Tribune and the Washington Post went to considerable trouble and expense to delete the word "penis" from a review of Naked Ape in the syndicated literary supplement Book World (the Tribune recalled the whole press run and removed the review entirely), Morris commented, as he was quoted in Newsweek (February 6, 1968), "Newspapers commonly use the word gun. They don't mind printing a word describing something that shoots death, but if it shoots life, they won't have it."

References

Arts R 18:570+ D 24 '66 por
Isis p18+ Mr 9 '70 pors
N Y Post p26 F 3 '68 por
New Yorker 33:32+ S 28 '57 por
Contemporary Authors vols 45-48 (1974)
Who's Who, 1974-1975

MURAYAMA, MAKIO

Aug. 10, 1912- Biochemist
Address: b. National Institutes of Health, Building 6, Room 143, Bethesda, Md. 20014; h. 5010 Benton Ave., Bethesda, Md. 20014

Since 1971 the federal government has poured millions of dollars into a war against sickle cell anemia, an incurable genetic blood disorder that afflicts blacks almost exclusively. In the United States about one in 400 blacks falls victim to the disease, and about another 10 percent of the black population carries the trait for it. Sickle cell anemia gets its name from the way in which the normally spherical red cells of the blood become weakened and distorted in shape. A genetic mutation that first occurred millions of years ago, blood sickling survived as a genetic trait among the tribes of equatorial Africa because it provided immunity to malaria, which at one time threatened to extinguish the human race. The toll exacted for that genetic immunity proved to be high, however. Although those who only carried the trait lived normal lives, those afflicted with the disease suffered the constant debilitating symptoms of anemia as well as periodic crises of excruciating pain. According to some figures, sickle cell anemia in the United States today kills at least half of its victims before the age of twenty, and only a few live beyond forty years.

Much of the basic research that has provided the springboard for current and future study on sickle cell anemia has been conducted by Makio Murayama, a Japanese-American biochemist at the National Institutes of Health in Bethesda, Maryland. Murayama first observed the devastating effects of sickle cell anemia on black children when he was working at a Detroit hospital during World War II. After studying blood sickling under Linus Pauling at the California Institute of Technology and at the Cavendish Laboratory in Cambridge, England, Murayama in 1958 joined the National Institutes of Health, where he was for many years the only scientist working fulltime on sickle cell research. Murayama's elucidation of the basic molecular process that takes place in sickling provided the theoretical basis for a chemical therapy, first announced in 1970, that holds promise of controlling the ravages of the disease.

Makio Murayama was born on August 10, 1912 in San Francisco, California, to Hakuyo and Namiye (Miyasaka) Murayama. His father, who died when Makio was four years old, was a philologist, and his mother was a midwife. Murayama has one brother, Yukio Murayama, director of

DR. MAKIO MURAYAMA

education of a pharmaceutical firm in Tokyo, and four sisters: Masuko (Murayama) Kishi, who lives in San Francisco; Fumiko, who is married to Dr. Charles Pentler of Cupertino, California; Dr. Ettsuko Murayama, a physician in San Francisco; and Motoko, who is married to Yutaka Nakazawa of San Francisco. His elder brother, Tamotsu Murayama, who was managing editor of the *Japan Times*, an English language daily newspaper, is no longer living.

Shortly after his father's death, Makio was sent to Japan to live with a great-aunt. He remained there for ten years, until he was fourteen, when he announced that he was "going home." Back in San Francisco, he attended Lowell High School. A lonely boy with a Japanese accent, he spent most of his spare time reading, playing with his microscope, and learning how to take pictures through it. "My first photography was photomicrography," the scientist told Victor Cohn for the Washington *Post Potomac* magazine (September 24, 1972). "I put an old, beat-up camera without a lens behind my microscope and took pictures of flies that I caught in my room and dismembered. That's how I gravitated toward science."

While in high school Murayama was president of the Mendeleev chemistry club, and he was employed as an assistant medical photographer at the San Francisco County Hospital, where he took all photomicrographs. After he graduated in 1933, he attended the University of California at Berkeley, where he majored in biochemistry and minored in bacteriology. Murayama worked his way through college by scrubbing hotel bathrooms or cleaning up at night, since they were the only jobs he could get. Sometimes he stayed out of the university for a while to work on a truck farm. At Berkeley, Murayama sang with the University of California Glee Club as a baritone. He obtained the B.A. degree in 1938.

Murayama went on to graduate work at Berkeley, majoring in biochemistry. He minored in nuclear physics, which he studied under Ernest

O. Lawrence and J. Robert Oppenheimer at Berkeley's Radiation Laboratory. He also worked as an assistant at the laboratory. Murayama's main interest in nuclear physics was not the atom's nucleus, but rather the radioactive elements that Lawrence's newly developed cyclotron could create and that could possibly be useful in tracing body processes. But with war looming on the horizon, most research effort was going into fission, and as a Japanese, it became clear to Murayama that he would not advance in nuclear research. He was awarded the M.A. degree in biochemistry and nuclear physics in 1940. Besides working in the Radiation Laboratory, between 1939 and 1942 he was employed as a research assistant in the university's biochemistry department and in Dr. Herbert M. Evans' Institute of Biology in Berkeley.

Shortly after Japan declared war on the United States on December 7, 1941, Murayama's family, along with other West Coast persons of Japanese extraction, were shipped to an internment camp in Idaho. Makio was not sent to the camp, but was ordered to report to the Manhattan Project in Chicago as a physicist. When he arrived at the top-secret atom bomb project, however, officials saw that he was Japanese and he was turned away. He finally succeeded in finding a job as a chemist in Detroit at the Children's Hospital of Michigan. Murayama has recalled that during the war he was often followed by an FBI agent, whom he came to recognize. "I told him, 'What a waste of the taxpayer's money,'" the biochemist recalled to Victor Cohn.

In January 1943 Murayama began working for Dr. James L. Wilson, director of the Children's Hospital in Detroit, as a research biochemist in pediatrics. Although he did most of his work there in the laboratory, he was also exposed to the clinical side of medicine, since he accompanied Dr. Wilson on his daily rounds and attended clinical pathological conferences. It was at Children's Hospital that Murayama first encountered sickle cell anemia. "Once you heard their raspy cry, you would know the next time—there was a kid in a sickle cell crisis," he told Victor Cohn. Asked by doctors if he could give them any help on the strange malady, Murayama searched the medical literature, but could find little information on it. About all that was known about sickle cell anemia at that time was that it is a disorder of the red blood cells, which causes them to become fragile and sickle-shaped. Because the sickled cells die off at a faster rate than normal cells—much faster than they can be replaced by the bone marrow—the disease victim suffers from persistent anemia. It was also observed through microscopic analysis that the sickled cells seem to stick to each other and to form clumps that become blocked in the small veins and capillaries. When the sickling is accelerated, that tendency becomes more pronounced and the victim's blood can no longer supply sufficient oxygen to the bones, tissues, and vital organs. When that happens, the patient is said to be in sickle cell crisis.

When Dr. James L. Wilson moved to Bellevue Hospital in New York City in July 1943, Murayama accompanied him, becoming director of the hospital's pediatric laboratory. He remained in New York until 1945, when Wilson became chairman of the department of pediatrics at the University of Michigan. Following his mentor, Murayama went to work for the University of Michigan in April 1945. During the period that Murayama was employed by Dr. Wilson he did much of his work on the blood analysis of babies, studying especially the acid-base balance and water-electrolyte equilibrium of premature and full-term infants. At that time large amounts of blood were needed to obtain chemical analyses, and Murayama became one of the early researchers to recognize the need for microchemical methods of analysis. While at the University of Michigan he developed several such methods. He also developed a therapy with sodium bicarbonate for infants in acidosis that is still used by some pediatricians.

While working for the University of Michigan, Murayama began studying toward his doctorate in microbiology. In 1948 and again in 1949 he was given National Institutes of Health predoctoral fellowships that allowed him to work full time on his doctorate. He received his Ph.D. degree in 1953, after submitting a dissertation on immunochemistry entitled, "A study of the adenosinetriphosphatase activity of leucocyte nuclei-free homogenate of the guinea pig and the rat; mechanism of host resistance against infections."

In 1950 Murayama had gone to work at Harper's Hospital in Detroit as research biochemist and supervisor of the clinical laboratory. After completing work on his Ph.D. degree in 1953, he applied for postgraduate study at the California Institute of Technology, in Pasadena, and was accepted for two years of study, beginning in July 1954, under Dr. Linus Pauling, who was at that time the foremost authority on blood cell sickling. In 1949 Pauling had shown that normal and sickle hemoglobin are different, thus proving that the disease occurs because of a malfunction in the hemoglobin, the red, oxygen-carrying protein constituent of red blood cells. At Caltech, Murayama studied immunochemistry and protein chemistry, especially the chemistry of normal and sickle hemoglobin. As a research associate in biochemistry at the Graduate School of Medicine of the University of Pennsylvania, he continued his study of hemoglobin from 1956 to 1958. In January 1958 he was hired by the National Institutes of Health in Bethesda, Maryland as a biochemist, and during the first eight months of his tenure continued his study of sickle hemoglobin as a special research fellow of the National Cancer Institute at the Cavendish Laboratory of Cambridge University. There he worked with Dr. Max F. Perutz and Dr. Vernon M. Ingram, helping to lay the groundwork that allowed Ingram a few years later to pinpoint the abnormality in the hemoglobin that causes sickling: the presence of the amino acid valine instead of glutamic acid in a mere two of the hemoglobin molecule's 574 links.

When Murayama returned to the National Institutes of Health from England in August 1958, he became the only scientist in that huge research facility to concentrate on the study of sickle hemoglobin. To facilitate his research, he began building in his home, in the evening and on weekends, a three-foot-high model of a hemoglobin molecule that represents an actual molecule magnified 127,000,000 times. Using the limited information that was available on the structure of hemoglobin, it took him six years to build it out of bits of plastic, aluminum, and steel, joined together by 70,000 tiny set screws, each representing an atom. When Murayama had finished, he understood the specific molecular mechanism for sickling, and he elucidated it in a paper that was published in *Science* in 1966. The valine units in neighboring hemoglobin molecules of the sickle cell protrude and hook onto each other like locks and keys, he explained. When the millions of hemoglobin molecules in a red cell begin to link up in that way, they form a kind of filament that pushes the normally spherical cell into a brittle, sickled shape. Furthermore, he showed that valine linkage is the same kind of chemical interchange, known as polymerization, that builds modern plastics and synthetics. He also proposed that the sickle-molecules join by the same "hydrophobic" bonding that holds oil drops together.

At the National Institutes of Health Murayama had always worked alone, with at most only one technician helping him. A lone scientist, without large amounts of money and a large staff behind him, Murayama attracted little attention with his landmark 1966 paper, especially since sickle cell anemia was then a neglected disease. One scientist who did pay attention to him, however, was Dr. Robert Nalbandian, a Michigan pathologist and hematologist. On the basis of Murayama's molecular description of sickling, Nalbandian drew up a list of properties that the ideal therapeutic substance should have. He found that he had described urea, which, besides being the main ingredient of urine, has many chemical and medical uses. After testing the urea treatment on a limited number of patients in 1969, Dr. Nalbandian held a press conference in 1970 to announce his success with the treatment in aborting the pain of sickle cell crises. His announcement was met with scepticism by most scientists, who pointed out that he had not run properly controlled tests. The scientific world was also shocked because Nalbandian had gone to the public instead of publishing his results in a scientific journal in the established fashion. Nevertheless, despite his unorthodox methods, Nalbandian's urea treatment has attracted the attention of many scientists, and most observers agree that the publicity he brought to sickle cell anemia brought that long-forgotten disease to public attention. The federal government is now spending about $540,000 to test urea and other chemical treatments, and in 1971 the United States Congress allocated $10,000,000 to fight sickle cell disease.

Murayama stoutly defends the research of Dr. Nalbandian and is confident that his urea treatment will prove effective in alleviating and preventing blood sickling. But his own research has shifted to another trail in solving the mysteries of sickle cell anemia. Since about 1968 he has been trying to track down a "sickle cell co-factor" that he believes must be present if cells are to sickle. He has succeeded in removing the mysterious substance from red cells by dialysis (a kind of filtering), but he has not been able to isolate and identify it. Ironically, Murayama continues to work alone at the National Institutes of Health and has been allotted none of the new money that has been poured into sickle cell research. Part of the reason is that the National Institutes of Health's National Heart and Lung Institute has been appointed to allocate the funds, and Murayama works in the National Institute of Arthritis and Metabolic Diseases. "I don't believe I have any apparent enemies," the frustrated scientist told Victor Cohn of the Washington *Post Potomac*. "I guess I'm just not a good politician. As far as NIH is concerned, I don't exist. Of course," he added, "if I were a politician, I wouldn't ask the right [scientific] questions to solve the problems." Because of his inability to gain increased support from NIH, he is now engaged in trying to raise funds privately to expand his research.

For his research in sickle cell disease, Murayama has received the 1969 Association for Sickle Cell Anemia award in research, the Martin Luther King Jr. medical achievement award of 1972, and the Japanese American Citizens League national recognition award of 1972. Murayama has served as adviser on oral urea therapy to the ministry of health in Ghana, West Africa. With Dr. Nalbandian, he is the author of *Sickle Cell Hemoglobin: Molecule to Man* (Little, Brown, 1973), and he has written about forty articles on sickle cell and other aspects of his research for professional journals. Murayama is a member of the American Chemical Society, the American Society for Biological Chemists, the American Association for the Advancement of Science, the New York Academy of Science, Sigma Xi, and the Association of Clinical Scientists. He is an honorary member of the West African Society of Pharmacology and a fellow of the American Institute of Chemists, Inc.

A small, slim man, Makio Murayama is five feet five inches tall, weighs 135 pounds, and has brown eyes and nearly white hair. Since December 16, 1972 he has been married to Diane Louise Diehl Robertson, a science illustrator. They have one child by her previous marriage, Bruce, and two by his, Gibbs Soga and Alice Myra. Murayama's previous wife was Sonoko Soga, whom he married on October 10, 1945. She died of cancer in August 1972. Murayama is a member of the Republican party and the Methodist church. In his spare time he enjoys photography, singing, and raising tropical fish. Although some of his colleagues have called him a loner who likes to work alone, he told *Current Biography* in a recently submitted questionnaire, "I am not a loner and I do not enjoy being alone. I have been forced to work alone due to lack of support by the National Institutes of Health."

References

Detroit Sunday News mag p16 Ap 15 '73 por
Life 64:51+ Je 2 '68 por
Washington (D.C.) Post mag p14 S 24 '72 por
American Men and Women of Science 12th ed (1972)
Who's Who in Government, 1972-73

NASTASE, ILIE (nä-stä'sē il'ē)

July 19, 1946- Romanian tennis player
Address: c/o U.S. Lawn Tennis Association, 51 E. 42nd St., New York 10017

The *enfant terrible* of today's tennis is Ilie Nastase, a Romanian whose off-court charm and on-court antics have made him the most colorful and controversial player on the international professional tennis circuit. He is also one of the best. In 1973 he was the most successful player in World Championship Tennis, winning $228,750 and the Martini & Rossi Player of the Year award. On the negative side in that same year the fines levied against him for misconduct on the court reached a record total of $10,000. Nastase is the first player from an "Iron Curtain" country to win the United States Open (in 1972), and with Ion Tiriac he has brought Romania into serious Davis Cup contention for the first time. "Nasty," as he is often called, has expressed the intention to join the Sets, the New York franchise in the new World Team Tennis organization, but he must first receive the approval of various tennis associations to which he already belongs, including the national association in his homeland.

Ilie Nastase was born on July 19, 1946 in Bucharest, Romania, into the family of a bank teller. His mother observed that on the day of his birth the sky was not blue, but yellow, which she interpreted as an ill omen, a sign that he would not easily achieve success. "I was always rather nasty," Nastase told Curry Kirkpatrick of *Sports Illustrated* (October 16, 1972) in his clear but fractured English. "I willing to be friends with devil just to cross the bridge [to success]."

In the interview with Kirkpatrick, Nastase recalled his childhood: "I was thin and raggedy, nobody bother with me much, a restless soul. I had chest like chicken and legs like matchsticks in the cartoons." With his three older sisters and his older brother, Costel (also a good tennis player), Nastase grew up in a home that adjoined the grounds of the Progresul Sports Club in Bucharest. Although he preferred soccer, he began playing tennis with his brother at the club when he was eight years old. "I hate to play," he told Kirkpatrick, "but I want him have to work hard. I made him play heart out to beat me. An uncle kept me at game by giving me candy and jelly beans to stay on court hitting balls."

Coached by Constantin Chivaru, Nastase won the Romanian national boys title in 1959, and seven years later he defeated Marty Riessen in Cairo and Jan Kodes in Paris. As a Davis Cup team, Nastase and his friend and mentor, veteran Ion Tiriac, in 1969 defeated Egypt, Israel, Spain, the Soviet Union, and India before losing to the United States in the final round. It was during Nastase's 1969 Davis Cup zone match against Mark Cox of Britain that the world first became aware of his unusual court manners. After a close call went against him, Nastase stomped all over the court, finally kicking a chair, and he played the rest of the match in a cold rage that so unnerved Cox that he dropped the final, decisive set. Nastase has not worried about his court demeanor since. "It's not good to hold anger in," he has explained. "It is bad for your insides."

In 1970 Nastase won the Italian championship by defeating Kodes of Czechoslovakia in four sets, and he took the United States indoor title by defeating Cliff Richey in five. In the spring and summer of the following year he amassed a string of victories in Omaha, Hampton, Nice, Monte Carlo, and Istanbul, as well as the Swedish Open, and he was runner-up in Madrid, Brussels, and the French Open. Again teamed with Tiriac in Davis Cup competition, he went unbeaten in twelve matches only to lose to Smith of the United States in the final round at Charlotte, North Carolina, three sets to love. When Romania lost the challenge to the United States, three matches to two, other Romanian players tended to blame, not Tiriac, but Nastase, because he allegedly had been neglecting practice out of preoccupation with his social life. Nastase's total earnings in 1971 were $114,000.

Because Nastase grew up on clay courts, he spent many years becoming accustomed to playing on grass, which is faster. "I was waiting for the ball too much on fast surfaces," he told Nick Seitz of the *Christian Science Monitor* (October 12, 1972). "You must go to the ball." In 1972 he suddenly gained confidence on the grass court, and that self-assurance was reflected in his performances at Wimbledon, where he almost beat Stan Smith in the final, and at Forest Hills, where he won the United States Open (and $25,000) by defeating Arthur Ashe. The crowd at Forest Hills booed Nastase several times, when he complained about line decisions and ridiculed linesmen. But there were also some catcalls for Ashe, who broke the code of the formal handshake. "This is a great player," Ashe said later. "When he tightens up his court manners, he will be even better."

In a dispatch from Forest Hills to the *Guardian* (September 12, 1972), David Gray wrote: "The Rumanian's behavior—his delaying tactics, his habit of falling over on every possible occasion, his continual arguments—certainly added to the pressures of the afternoon for Ashe. . . .'Nastephobia' is one of the current preoccupations of both the World Championship Tennis professionals and the United States Davis Cup team." As the 1972 Davis Cup finals turned out, however,

ILIE NASTASE

the United States team won, defeating Nastase and Tiriac on their home ground, at the Progresul Sports Club in Bucharest.

After several early line calls went against him in the United States National Indoor Open championships, in February 1973, Nastase deliberately hit balls at linesmen or into the net and failed to run after shots. He was eliminated from the tournament and later fined $1,000 by the United States Lawn Tennis Association. The latter organization also fined him $4,500, or half of his first-prize money, for his behavior in the finals of the Western championship in Cincinnati in August 1973, when he shouted obscenities at the tournament referee and slammed tennis balls into the crowd and at a linesman. And the Association of Tennis Professionals fined him $5,000 for playing at Wimbledon after a majority of the ATP membership had voted to boycott the tournament to protest the disciplining of Yugoslavia's Nikki Pilic. But there was little doubt about Nastase's mastery of the courts, as David Gray of the *Guardian* (December 15, 1973) observed: "Who is the best player in the world. . . ? Ilie Nastase proved his supremacy by winning the Commercial Union Masters title for the third year in succession with a victory, 6-3, 7-5, 4-6, 6-3, over Tom Okker. Some skeptics and statisticians may still dispute this. Stan Smith and John Newcombe have their supporters, but for your correspondent, Nastase's overwhelming victory in the Grand Prix, added to his success in the Master's round-robin event in which the eight leading players on the circuit competed for a first prize of fifteen thousand dollars, settled the issue."

In January 1974 an injury forced Nastase to withdraw from the United States Professional Indoor championship. After recuperation, he won the Xerox Tennis Classic, in March, and the Rothman's British title, in May. He was beaten by Björn Borg in the finals of the Italian Open, on June 3, by Harold Solomon in the quarter-finals of the French Open, on June 13, and by Dick Stockton in the preliminaries at Wimbledon, on July 2.

In August 1974, when he was only two games from victory in the $100,000 United States clay court championships at Indianapolis, Nastase was defaulted—in effect, expelled—for stalling and foul language. Commenting on the incident in the New York *Times* (August 20, 1974), Neil Amdur wrote: "Nastase's familiar response [to admonishment] has been a schoolboy shrug and an innocent smile. . . . Deep inside, however, Nastase knew that he could punch the winning volley in any rally with tournament promoters, who needed his handsome face, world ranking, and exciting game to fill empty seats. And what volunteer umpire or referee would have the guts to call Nastase's bluff and default him. . . ?" The umpire who did have the guts to default Nastase in Indianapolis was seventy-four-year-old Bill Macassin, who explained, "He called me an s.o.b. as loud as could be over the whole court. I couldn't take that."

Nastase was seeded seventh in the United States Open championships scheduled to take place in Forest Hills beginning on August 28, 1974. In his preview of the Open in *New York* magazine (August 26, 1974), Hamilton Richardson wrote under the subtitle "Who's Who at Forest Hills": "Ilie Nastase, probably the fastest human being ever to play tennis, stands several feet behind the base line to return serve. He is so quick that a wide serve (i.e., a serve to the sideline), which is beyond the reach of most players, is a cinch for him."

Ilie Nastase is six feet tall, weighs 175 pounds, and has long dark hair and thick eyebrows. He and Dominique (Niki) Grazia, a former Belgian fashion model, were married—twice, in a civil ceremony and again in a religious one—in December 1972. The couple live in the luxurious lake district of Floreasca, on the outskirts of Bucharest. Mrs. Nastase says that people misinterpret her husband's actions. "Ilie—he is not bad," she told a writer for the Associated Press in May 1974. "He just enjoys life. He is like a little boy. He has fun. He is mischievous. But he is no ogre."

On another occasion Mrs. Nastase said: "I worry sometimes because I know crowds don't understand my husband. Otherwise they would never boo or whistle at him. They think he is mad at them when he throws a racket or gets upset with calls. But he is really only mad at himself. All the time he likes to win. It means so much to him." Nastase himself told a writer for *Sports Illustrated* (October 16, 1972): "Sometimes I feel like tap-dancing, screeching, unscrewing light bulbs, pulling curtains, combing hair, doing kneebends, handstands and turning somersaults out there. I have no patience. I want the contest to be one yard from the net, to not have the time to pass the racket from one side to the other, to play until my opponent and I fall down with exhaustion, to beat him and then embrace."

Friends of Nastase say that behind many of his antics is an impish sense of humor, and that he can be very witty in conversation. Clark Graebner, who has almost come to blows with him on the court, has said of Nastase: "You have to give him credit. He can drive you nuts at times with all that nonsense of his. But he's got all the ability a man needs to be supreme in this sport. He's quick-footed. His reflexes are fantastic. He's got that lightning top-spin forehand. His backhand is beautiful. . . . He acts nutty on the court and you get the urge to kill him. I still call him the gypsy because he has so much dash. But he's worth the price of admission."

References

Christian Sci Mon B p5 D 17 '73 por
N Y Times p34 F 6 '74 por; p29 Ag 20 '74 por
N Y Times Mag p42+ O 22 '72 pors
Sports Illus 37:36+ S 18 '72 por; 37: 112+ O 16 '72 pors

NICHOLSON, JACK

Apr. 22, 1937- Actor; film maker
Address: c/o Sandy Bresler & Associates, Suite 206, 360 N. Bedford Dr., Beverly Hills, Calif. 90210

Jack Nicholson, long recognized by underground film makers as one of their own and as a revolutionary within the commercial film system, finally came to wide public attention when he stole the show from stars Peter Fonda and Dennis Hopper in *Easy Rider* (1969). He went on to star in *Five Easy Pieces* (1971), *The King of Marvin Gardens* (1972), *The Last Detail* (1973), and *Chinatown* (1974). Nicholson, who began his Hollywood career in lowly B-movie roles in the late 1950's, now chooses his parts carefully. While most of the roles he plays are those of outsiders, the characters are never similar. As Derek Malcolm pointed out in the *Guardian* (May 27, 1974), "He is lucky in that he is one of the few major screen actors around who, like Olivier, can change his physical identity from part to part." In addition to acting, he has produced, directed, and written for films.

Jack Nicholson was born in Neptune, New Jersey on April 22, 1937 to John Nicholson, a sign painter of Irish descent, and Ethel May Nicholson. After separating from her husband, during Jack's infancy, Mrs. Nicholson opened a beauty parlor in her home to support her son and two daughters. As a student Nicholson was bright but, as he has put it, "always a deportment problem." He told an interviewer for *Newsweek* (December 7, 1970): "I remember in fourth grade I got sent to the corner next to the blackboard . . . and I powdered my face with chalk dust and made myself into a clown. And that's the way I was all through high school, the class clown, performing on and off the stage." In another interview, with a reporter for *Time* (November 30, 1970), he explained his motivation for acting in high school plays: "I got sort of talked into it by a teacher. And all the chicks that I liked were doing plays."

"His smile was terrific," George Anderson, one of Nicholson's high school friends, has recalled. "He made plenty of friends who spanned several classes. Jack wasn't one of the heroes, but he made them his friends." After graduating from high school, Nicholson considered going to the University of Delaware, and he scored high on his college entrance exams. But, as he has said, he "hated school," and decided to do some drifting before committing himself to college. While visiting his older sister, June, a showgirl, in Los Angeles in 1957 he took a job as an office boy in the animated cartoon department at MGM, where producer Joe Pasternak "discovered" him. With Pasternak's encouragement, he joined the young resident troupe at the Players Ring Theatre in Los Angeles and studied under Jeff Corey. Regarding Corey, Nicholson has said: "Everything he teaches is from the basic root of improvisation. . . . Jeff's interested in character action, not in plot. He wants to know if you can feel and react as an actor, but he's into structure."

Roger Corman directed Nicholson in his screen debut, as the gunman in the movie *Cry-Baby Killer* (Allied Artists, 1958), in which, as the critic for *Variety* (June 18, 1958) observed, he was "handicapped by having a character of only one dimension to portray." Corman also directed *Studs Lonigan* (United Artists, 1960), based on the James T. Farrell trilogy, in which Nicholson had a supporting role. His score of other movie credits in the late 1950's and early 1960's were roles, often insignificant, in what Rex Reed has characterized as "low-budget go-out-and-grab-a-movie B flicks . . . beach blanket bikini flicks . . . horror flicks . . . the kind of trash only a mother or a *Cahier* critic could sit through and love." Nicholson himself told a reporter recently, "The people who never saw my [early] movies are better off in life than I am, man, but, like all actors, I needed the work. I did all those horror flicks [including *The Raven*, released by American International in 1963] because they were the only jobs I could get." As Jay Cocks noted in a *Time* (August 12, 1974) cover story on Nicholson, "The only real satisfaction Nicholson was to get from any of these films, besides a salary, was the chance to insert a little underhanded humor." Between films, Nicholson appeared in such television series as *Divorce Court*.

Two American International off-beat westerns made by Nicholson won several awards at European film festivals in 1966 and went on to attract a cult following in France, but both remain virtually unknown in the United States. One is *The Shooting*, which Charles Eastman wrote, and the other is *Ride the Whirlwind*, which Nicholson himself wrote. Nicholson, who coproduced and starred in both, has described the first as "a McLuhan mystery" and the second as "an existential western."

In *Hell's Angels on Wheels* (U.S. Films, 1967) Nicholson played the poetic leader of a raucous motorcycle gang. While generally condemning the film as an exercise in violence, critics tended to praise "the rather dazed performances" of the

JACK NICHOLSON

principals for rendering the picture "curiously convincing," as Howard Thompson put it in the New York *Times* (July 27, 1967). In the Toronto *Globe and Mail* (May 30, 1967) Joan Fox wrote: "[Adam] Roarke and Nicholson . . . both radiate intelligence . . . and strength of will that make them seem to be what they are. Nicholson is particularly good."

In 1968 Columbia Pictures released *Head,* a psychedelic musical fantasy co-scripted and co-produced by Nicholson and starring the rock group the Monkees, a film that Rex Reed has called "way-out, wonderful, and badly underrated." Meanwhile Nicholson met Peter Fonda and Dennis Hopper, when he wrote the screenplay for *The Trip* (American International, 1967), a film about a director of television commercials who experiments with LSD. Fonda and Hopper headed the cast of *The Trip,* which was produced by Roger Corman.

When Fonda (as producer) and Hopper (as director) gave themselves the starring roles of two gentle motorcycling hippies in *Easy Rider* (Columbia, 1969), they took on Nicholson in a supporting role. The part was that of George Hanson, a genteel but boozy and disillusioned ("this used to be a hell of good country; I don't know what happened") Southern lawyer who switches from whiskey to marijuana and "drops out," joining Captain America (Fonda) and Billy (Hopper) in a cross-country odyssey that ends in violent death at the hands of "freak"-hating back-country bigots. In that minor role Nicholson walked away with the movie. Even those who hated *Easy Rider,* such as Louise Sweeney of the *Christian Science Monitor* (September 29, 1969) found him "worth watching," and both the New York Film Critics and the National Society of Film Critics bestowed on him their awards for best supporting actor of the year.

Impressed with Nicholson's performance as a San Francisco hippie in *Psych-Out* (American International, 1968), Vincente Minnelli cast him in a similar role, as one of Barbra Streisand's suitors in the film version of the musical *On a Clear Day*

You Can See Forever (Paramount, 1970). In the latter movie Nicholson had one song to sing, and that was cut. "What is left," Rex Reed commented in *Holiday* (July-August 1970), "wastes him so criminally that he should have stayed in bed."

Bob Rafelson, whom Nicholson met when Rafelson was directing *Head*, directed him in *Five Easy Pieces* (Columbia, 1970), in which Nicholson plays a character specifically created for him by Rafelson and writer Adrien Joyce: Bobby Dupea, a maverick pianist who abandons a prospective concert career to become an oil rigger. Richard Roud of the *Guardian* (November 3, 1970) called *Five Easy Pieces* "probably . . . the best American film of the year," and Richard Schickel, writing in *Life* (September 18, 1970), asserted that Nicholson, on the basis of his "consummate" performance, "must now be regarded as one of the few truly gifted actors we have."

Nicholson's first directorial effort was the controversially honest *Drive, He Said* (Columbia, 1971), which he adapted for the screen in collaboration with Jeremy Larner, author of the novel of the same name. That film, starring William Tepper, Karen Black, and Michael Margotta, depicts the emotional and spiritual disintegration of two Midwestern college roommates, a basketball star who is sleeping with a professor's wife, with the professor's compliant knowledge, and a campus revolutionary who avoids the draft by following a no-sleep program into schizophrenia. The near-violent jeering and cheering of the movie at the 1971 Cannes Film Festival, especially in reaction to its deliberately unglamorous sex scenes, presaged its later commercial failure. "I thought I was Stravinsky for a moment," Nicholson said recently. "I had a major riot. But it hurt the picture. It was a disaster, this movie. I knew it was going to set me back."

Ingrained, pervasive male chauvinism was the theme of *Carnal Knowledge* (Avco Embassy, 1971), written by satirist Jules Feiffer and directed by former comedian Mike Nichols. In that film, according to William Wolf in *Cue* (July 3, 1971), "Jack Nicholson is more brilliant than he's ever been as the empty bastard of a guy who can be potent only with the ego-building, undemanding, totally sexual plaything." While critically acclaimed, *Carnal Knowledge* faced problems with local censors until the United States Supreme Court ruled it not obscene, in June 1974.

Out of loyalty to his director friend Bob Rafelson, Nicholson accepted the title role in *The King of Marvin Gardens* (Columbia, 1972), that of an introverted, stone-faced, self-deceptive radio monologist. While registering high with Nicholson cultists, the Kafkaesque film went over the heads of people generally and was a commercial and critical flop. Not so *The Last Detail* (Acrobat-Columbia, 1974), a heart-warming movie in which Nicholson portrays Billy "Bad-ass" Buddusky, a tough, veteran Navy shore patrolman with a soft heart. Assigned to escort a seventeen-year-old sailor from the Navy base in Norfolk, Virginia to the Navy prison in Portsmouth, New Hampshire, where the young swabby is to serve an obviously

unjust eight-year sentence, he does his ineffectual best to introduce the young sailor to the fun of life (via beer and brothels) before his loss of freedom. "Here at last the actor's almost throwaway style is tightly disciplined to his role," Betty Lee wrote in the Toronto *Globe and Mail* (February 23, 1974), echoing a wide critical sentiment. "Instead of slouching through the picture, he confidently struts away with it. And this is tough to do. The *Last Detail* is a thoughtfully crafted film, studded with glowing performances. . . . In the end, though, it is Jack Nicholson who holds the whole enterprise together. Cocky, belligerent, as sure of himself as Cagney at his Irish worst, Bad-ass Buddusky is still a fascinating picture of a man questioning himself and his reason for being alive. Nicholson's brilliant reading of the Buddusky character makes the answer apparent. No man is an island." Like his performances in *Easy Rider* and *Five Easy Pieces*, his portrayal of Buddusky brought him an Academy Award nomination.

In Roman Polanski's *Chinatown* (Paramount, 1974), Nicholson plays an updated version of the Hollywood private detective of thirty or forty years ago. As J. J. Gittes he is hired by Evelyn Mulwray (Faye Dunaway) to solve a marital case which gets more complicated the deeper he probes into it, like a Chinese box puzzle. "Jack Nicholson is one of the few actors in America today who can play a Bogart role and get away with it . . . ," Joseph Gelmis wrote in *Newsday* (June 21, 1974). "*Chinatown* is the movie's code word for the state of mind in which, as Nicholson tells Faye Dunaway, 'You can't always tell what's going on.' The mystery is that the world, our lives, the pieces of our realities, don't make any sense, don't add up."

In his *Time* magazine cover story Jay Cocks wrote of the real life Nicholson: "All the double-edged kidding and up-front aggressiveness stand in some contrast to the cool, measured, and often affectless character Nicholson has played so well on the screen. He looks, when he is not trying, like an all-night coach passenger who is just beginning to realize he has slept through his stop. But his features have great plasticity. His friend Candice Bergen speaks of his 'cobra eyes.' His energy level can vary with the most careful calibration."

Jack Nicholson is short and slim, with thinning hair. He has been described as a "laconic" man with "reckless charm" who is "very wry and funny but very cynical." Although he has a reputation for "turning on," and he can depend on his charm and intuition to see him through many difficult situations in life and on the screen, he is, as Jay Cocks noted in his *Time* cover story, "usually a careful and thorough craftsman." Cocks wrote: "Nicholson's patience and zeal are exceptional. When he works over a script, not only are key phrases underlined and notes made, but almost every word is assigned a number, which signifies beats and pauses." For five years, from 1961 to 1966, Nicholson was married to actress Sandra Knight, by whom he has a daughter,

Jennifer. At last report he was, as he would put it, "seeing" Anjelica Huston, daughter of John Huston.

References

After Dark 11:38+ O '69 pors
Guardian p6 My 27 '74 por
N Y Sunday News II p7 F 10 '74 por
N Y Times II p11 F 10 '74
Time 104:44+ Ag 12 '74 pors
Toronto Globe and Mail p26 Je 19 '71 por;
    p29 N 11 '72 por

O'NEILL, THOMAS P(HILIP), JR.

Dec. 9, 1912- United States Representative from Massachusetts
Address: b. Rayburn House Office Building, Washington, D.C., 20515; h. 2601 Woodley Place, Cambridge, Mass. 02138

THOMAS P. O'NEILL JR.

The Majority Leader of the House of Representatives, veteran Congressman Thomas P. O'Neill Jr. has compiled an enviable record of almost forty years in both state and federal government without encountering a significant political defeat. First elected to Congress from Massachusetts' Eleventh Congressional District, O'Neill has been regularly returned to Congress with such astonishing vote totals that the Republican party has not fielded a candidate against him since 1966. A shrewd and aggressive legislative manipulator, he once described politics as "the art of effective compromise." O'Neill prefers to work behind the scenes—in committees, conferences, and Congressional cloakrooms—rather than on the House floor, settling differences by arranging mutual concessions. "I have an ability to read the sense of the House," he has said. "I've never had a problem that I could not put the thing together." O'Neill was reelected to the House on November 5, 1974.

As head of the Democratic faction in the House, O'Neill was responsible for the equity of possible impeachment proceedings against Republican President Richard M. Nixon. Although he was appalled by the Watergate break-in and cover-up and fraudulent campaign tactics, O'Neill warned his colleagues in the House to "preserve a cool impartiality." With the help of House Speaker Carl Albert, he squelched a "premature" impeachment resolution submitted by Representative John Moss in the spring of 1973. During the House Judiciary Committee's deliberations, O'Neill urged Congressmen and their legislative and judicial staffs to refrain from partisan politics. The Majority Leader, who called publicly for the President's resignation, was convinced that Nixon would "step aside for the good of the country" before impeachment proceedings could be begun.

Thomas Philip ("Tip") O'Neill Jr., the son of Thomas Philip and Rose Ann (Tolan) O'Neill, was born on December 9, 1912 in Cambridge, Massachusetts. The senior O'Neill, the son of an immigrant bricklayer from County Cork, Ireland, directed the city's 1,700-man water department. A hardworking recruit of the local Democratic party, he was elected to the city council in 1900 and served for six years. O'Neill got his nickname from James Edward O'Neill, a player for the St. Louis Browns baseball club who was famous for hitting foul tips. At St. John's Parochial School in North Cambridge he was only an average student. Despite his unimpressive athletic skills, he was invariably chosen as captain of his school teams. Introduced to Boston's rough-and-tumble politicking at an early age, O'Neill gained first-hand, door-to-door campaign experience when, as a teen-ager, he solicited support for Democratic candidate Al Smith in his unsuccessful bid for the Presidency in 1928.

After graduating from the local parochial secondary school, O'Neill enrolled at Boston College. To pay for his education, he drove a truck and played poker. During his senior year, he announced his candidacy for a seat on the Cambridge city council, but in the excitement of his first campaign he neglected to make a direct personal appeal to the voters. O'Neill lost to his opponent by 150 votes, suffering his only political defeat to date. After taking his degree from Boston College in 1936, he took a job with a local insurance company.

Later that year, O'Neill was elected to the Massachusetts state legislature. Because of the Depression, many of his constituents were out of work, and he arranged for the hiring of several hundred local citizens for emergency snow removal and road maintenance. In 1946 and 1947 he studied educational problems at the local level as a member of the Cambridge School Committee, and he has remained an advocate of quality education for all students. In recognition of his ten years' experience in state government, O'Neill was elected minority leader in 1947. One year later, when the Democrats regained control of the legislature for the first time in 100 years, he became the youngest majority leader in the history of the state. Taking full advantage of his powerful position, he pushed a wide-ranging program of social legislation, popularly known as the "Little New Deal," through the State House. To "keep a fella from taking a walk" during a crucial vote, he occasionally locked the doors to the legislative chambers.

When Congressman John F. Kennedy launched his senatorial campaign in 1952, O'Neill decided to run for Kennedy's seat in the House of Representatives. Since he enjoyed strong support from the heavily Democratic Irish and Italian working-class wards of the Eleventh Congressional District, O'Neill was virtually assured of victory. As the protégé of fellow Bostonian John W. McCormack, who was then the House Democratic Whip, he was quickly introduced to the members of the Congressional power structure and invited to House Speaker Sam Rayburn's informal, after-hours "board of education" meetings, an unusual privilege for a freshman legislator. In Rayburn's office, O'Neill discussed upcoming bills and planned party strategy with fellow Democrats Lyndon Baines Johnson and Carl Albert, and, as a regular at late-night Congressional poker games, he played cards with a number of government leaders of both parties, including Vice-President Richard M. Nixon. During O'Neill's second term in the House, McCormack wangled him a position on the Rules Committee, which regulates the flow of legislation to the floor of the House and which was often deadlocked in the mid-1950's because of a split between liberals and conservatives. O'Neill, who managed to steer his bills around the legislative logjam, later approved a measure that enlarged the Rules Committee from twelve to fifteen members, thus providing the Democrats with a majority.

Throughout his Congressional career, O'Neill has carefully cultivated his constituency. On frequent weekend visits to his district, now reapportioned into the Eighth Congressional District, he takes a Saturday "ethnic walk" through his neighborhood to trade with local shopkeepers, question the shoppers, and lend a sympathetic ear to the voters' complaints. Mindful of his constituents' interests, O'Neill has consistently opposed legislation that he feels may be detrimental to their welfare. To maintain Boston's importance as a seaport and international trading center, he voted against the construction of the St. Lawrence Seaway and, in a clash with President Lyndon B. Johnson, stubbornly supported the continuation of the Boston Navy Yard. At a more grass-roots level, O'Neill arranged temporary employment in Boston's post offices for several thousand students during the Christmas mail rush.

On the House floor, Congressman O'Neill has generally voted with the Democratic liberals. He has, in the past, approved an omnibus housing redevelopment bill; legislation to improve and expand metropolitan mass transit facilities; the Economic Opportunity Act, which funded a variety of anti-poverty programs; and the Civil Rights Acts of 1956, 1957, and 1964. To insure adequate health care, he supported Medicare, recommended the construction of federally funded health care

centers, and submitted a bill that eliminated economic need as an eligibility requirement for vocational rehabilitation. Although he regularly voted for aid to education, O'Neill, in conjunction with a likeminded member of the Rules Committee, New York Representative James J. Delaney, threatened to delay indefinitely the Kennedy administration's massive school aid bill unless a companion bill authorizing federal aid to private and parochial schools was also cleared for floor debate. More recently, he approved strict gun control legislation, busing to achieve racial balance in the schools, and the creation of a strong Consumer Protection Agency within the federal government. An environmentalist, he supported air and water pollution control bills and opposed the expenditure of additional federal monies for the construction of a prototype supersonic transport plane.

Although he originally backed President Johnson's military policy in Southeast Asia, O'Neill yielded to a request from his children and re-examined his position on the war. Ultimately convinced that the Vietnam war was not an "invasion" but a "civil war," O'Neill openly broke with the President and denounced American involvement in Indochina. His student constituents immediately applauded his decision to back Senator Eugene McCarthy, the antiwar candidate in the Democratic Presidential race in 1968, but, as he explained to Myra MacPherson in an interview published in the New York *Post* on January 6, 1973, his strength came from the workingmen. "I had to sell them," he continued. "I had a helluva time."

In March 1971 O'Neill cosponsored a bill setting a date for total American withdrawal from Southeast Asia contingent upon the release of American prisoners of war. Despite lingering doubts of the bill's effectiveness, he supported a measure to cut off funds for the continuation of the air war after August 15, 1973. "There's enough money in the pipeline to keep this war going a lot longer than I want to see it last," he remarked, as quoted in the New York *Times* (January 20, 1973). In November 1973 he voted to override President Nixon's veto of the War Powers Bill effectively limiting executive warmaking powers. Speaking in behalf of the bill, O'Neill told his colleagues: "If the President can deal with the Arabs, and if he can deal with the Israelis, and if he can deal with the Soviets, then he ought to be able and willing to deal with the United States Congress. That is all we ask of him."

In his zeal for legislative reform, Congressman O'Neill offered bills to abolish the teller vote, to publicize votes taken in committee, and to limit each Representative to one subcommittee chairmanship. Furthermore, he favored a ban on floor recitations from the *Congressional Record*—the House equivalent of the Senate filibuster. In recent months, O'Neill has repeatedly urged Congress to recover its constitutionally guaranteed rights, particularly in budgetary matters. "The pivotal issue," he maintained during a floor debate on extending the federal debt ceiling, "is whether Congress is voluntarily going to abdicate its Constitutional responsibility in controlling the purse strings or . . . take a firm stand in retaining its rightful . . . review of federal government spending."

In 1971 Hale Boggs, the newly elected House Majority Leader, tapped O'Neill as his Whip. One month after Boggs disappeared in a flight over Alaska, O'Neill announced his candidacy for the leadership post. At a news conference on November 13, 1972 he acknowledged that he had "substantially over" the 123 required votes as well as "commitments from all sections of the country and all factions of the party." Florida Representative Sam M. Gibbons, his only rival, quickly withdrew from the contest. Since his unanimous election, O'Neill has generally encouraged revision of the traditional seniority system but has steadfastly opposed the imposition of an age limit on committee chairmen and the direct election of party whips, a move he supported in 1970. In February 1973 the House Democratic leadership, under O'Neill and Speaker Albert, formed a twenty-three-member steering committee to formulate policy, plan strategy, and revitalize the Democratic party. "The O'Neill move represents an historic shift in the balance of power," David Cohen, the legislative representative of Common Cause, an effective citizens' lobby, told Myra MacPherson. "Not only do the old guard like him but he has the support of the younger, change-oriented liberals. He's a House man, but he's made the bridge more than any other."

Described by one political journalist as a "great, shaggy bear of a man," Thomas P. O'Neill Jr. stands six feet two inches tall and weighs around 260 pounds. He has thick white hair and blue eyes. To control his fluctuating weight (he estimates that he has lost "a thousand pounds" over the years), he attends meetings of a local Weight Watchers group and keeps his refrigerator well-stocked with Fresca. The gregarious O'Neill throws an annual St. Patrick's Day party on Capitol Hill, complete with green beer and rollicking Irish music. For recreation he enjoys poker and golf. "Tip" O'Neill and his wife, the former Mildred Anne Miller, were married on June 17, 1941. They have five children: Rosemary, Thomas Philip 3d, who was recently elected to the Massachusetts state legislature, Susan, Christopher, and Michael. The O'Neills live in a 100-year-old frame house in a blue-collar neighborhood in Cambridge. They also have a summer home on Cape Cod. In Washington, D.C. O'Neill shares a three-room apartment with Massachusetts Representative Edward Boland, his Congressional roommate for more than twenty years.

References

N Y Post p28 Ja 1 '73 por
N Y Times p21 Ja 20 '73
Newsweek 81:15+ Ja 15 '73 por
Time 103:14+ F 4 '74 pors
Congressional Directory, 1973
Who's Who in America, 1972-73

PACINO, AL(FRED) (pə-chē′nō)

Apr. 25, 1940- Actor
Address: b. c/o Martin Bregman, Inc., 641 Lexington Ave., New York 10022

Al Pacino typifies the breed of actor who has risen to prominence at least partly as a result of the discovery by movie producers that today's audiences prefer reality to escapist fantasy. Pacino won laurels as a stage actor in the late 1960's, but his forceful and magnetic performances did not win him the status of superstar until he began playing true-to-life screen roles in the 1970's. He earned an Oscar nomination in the supporting actor category for his portrayal of a Mafia kingpin's heir in *The Godfather* (1972) and in the best actor category for his interpretation of the title role in *Serpico*, the story of an actual New York policeman who refused to be corrupted. *Godfather II*, a Paramount production directed by Francis Ford Coppola and starring Pacino, was scheduled for release in December 1974.

Of Sicilian ancestry, Alfred Pacino was born in New York City on April 25, 1940, the only child of Salvatore and Rose Pacino. His parents were divorced when he was two years old. Mrs. Pacino and her young son lived in a furnished room in East Harlem before moving to her parents' apartment in a poor neighborhood not far from the Bronx zoo. "My mother and grandmother never let me out of the house until I was seven," he recalled to Kathleen Carroll in an interview for the New York *Sunday News* (July 24, 1971). "I guess it was because I was very sensitive and they were afraid of what might happen to me." At night, he frequently accompanied his mother to the local movie house. Forbidden to venture outside during the day, Pacino, lonely and bored, staged one-man shows for his grandmother, describing in detail the film that he had seen the night before and acting out all the parts. His repertoire included impersonations of Al Jolson, James Cagney, and other movie greats.

At school Pacino used his flair for extemporaneous acting to fabricate a colorful past for himself. "I'd tell the kids stories, that I was from Texas, that I had ten dogs," he told Chris Chase in an interview for a New York *Times* (May 7, 1972) profile. "I used to say to them, 'I'll see you later. I gotta go to work now.' I was ten! I'd ride off on my red scooter, hide behind a billboard, read a book." The energy and imagination that went into his tall tales became a great asset when he began appearing in school plays. Impressed by his enthusiasm and his aptitude for dramatics, elementary school teachers who despaired of Pacino academically advised him to apply for admission to the High School of Performing Arts in Manhattan. He did so, successfully, but at the age of seventeen, when he was failing every subject but English, he dropped out.

For several years Pacino drifted from job to job, working successively as a mail delivery boy in the editorial offices of *Commentary* magazine, as a messenger, as a movie theatre usher, and as

AL PACINO

a building superintendent. The dream of becoming a professional actor remained uppermost in his mind, but it was not until he came under the influence of Charlie Laughton, a coach at the Herbert Berghof Studio, that he began to work seriously toward its materialization. After serving his apprenticeship as an actor, director, and comedy writer in such noncommercial, avant-garde Off-Off-Broadway theatres as Elaine Stewart's Cafe La Mama and Julian Beck and Judith Malina's Living Theatre, he was accepted for training at the Actors Studio in 1966. In December of that year, he appeared with James Earl Jones in a New Theatre Workshop production of John Wolfson's *The Peace Creeps*, and in the fall of 1967 he signed with the Charles Playhouse in Boston, where he performed in Jean-Claude van Itallie's *America Hurrah* and Clifford Odets' *Awake and Sing*. Returning to New York, he re-created Off Broadway the character of Murph in *The Indian Wants the Bronx*, a role he had played when the one-act drama by Israel Horovitz premièred in 1966 at the Eugene O'Neill Memorial Theater in Waterford, Connecticut.

Staged by James Hammerstein as the second and more substantial half of a double bill, *The Indian Wants the Bronx*, a one-act play in which two young hoodlums terrorize an aged Indian man, opened at the Astor Place Theater on January 17, 1968. Preceding it on the program was another play by Horovitz, *It's Called the Sugar Plum*. The critic for *Variety* (January 24, 1968) dismissed the latter as "an implausible, thin black comedy," but praised its companion piece as "a study of urban savagery" that was both "convincing and frightening" and lauded Pacino for his "particularly effective . . . use of an uncommonly naturalistic, unstagey style." *The Indian Wants the Bronx* enjoyed a run of 204 performances in New York City and was a featured attraction at the 1968 Spoleto (Italy) Festival. For his chilling performance as a brutal hood Pacino was awarded an Obie as the best actor in an Off-Broadway production in 1967-68.

A slightly heftier Pacino made his Broadway debut in February 1969. At the behest of director Michael A. Schultz, the actor had gained twenty-five pounds for the role of Bickham, the psychotic junkie in *Does a Tiger Wear a Necktie?*, Don Petersen's play about daily life inside a drug rehabilitation center. Although the play, which opened to lukewarm reviews on February 25, 1969, closed after thirty-nine performances, Pacino's interpretation of the sadistic, suicidal addict was acclaimed by critics as "one of the most brilliant performances of the season," as "magnificent," "sensationally menacing," and as "spectacularly good." In *Newsweek* (March 10, 1969) Jack Kroll qualified his praise: "Pacino . . . has the choreography of a hood (with a poetic soul) down pat—the ceaseless soft treadmill stance, sniffing nose and blinking eyes, the fingers that constantly scrabble at the air as if scratching the invisible monkey on his back. . . . Pacino's performance is indeed 'brilliant,' but there is also . . . a touch of the perfect academic demonstration. It misses the instant, total existential wallop of the early Brando and [James] Dean." Pacino was voted an Antoinette Perry (Tony) Award by his colleagues as the best dramatic actor in a supporting role and was named the "most promising new Broadway actor" in a *Variety* poll of metropolitan drama critics.

On November 3, 1969 *The Local Stigmatic*, a playlet by British dramatist Heathcote Williams, opened at the Actors Playhouse in New York City, along with seven one-act plays by Harold Pinter. In the Williams piece Pacino played a role very similar to the one he had in *The Indian Wants the Bronx*, a bully who, along with a partner, gets his kicks by inflicting violence on inoffensive strangers. Several critics mentioned the resemblance to the Horovitz play and chided Pacino for the essential sameness of his characterization. For instance, John Simon, *New York* magazine's acerbic drama reviewer, remarked in his November 17, 1969 analysis of the play, "If Pacino is an actor, not merely a highly efficient robot programmed for psychosis, evidence is urgently required."

When *The Local Stigmatic* and its companion pieces closed after only eight performances, Pacino anxious to broaden his scope, signed on with the Repertory Theater of Lincoln Center. He was immediately cast as Kilroy, the ubiquitous American hero with the symbolically oversized heart, in a revival of Tennessee Williams' *Camino Real*. Richard Watts Jr., writing in the New York *Post* (January 9, 1970), felt that Pacino's "touching portrayal" attested to his versatility. Jack Kroll disagreed, contending that the actor deserved "to be read the riot act." In his *Newsweek* (January 19, 1970) review Kroll conceded that Pacino was "a brilliant technician," but argued that "he simply cannot play every role as the same . . . sentence-chopping street urchin that has won him plaudits umpteen times in a row." In March 1970, Pacino got a respite from acting when the resident company of Boston's Charles

Playhouse hired him to direct its production of *Rats*, a short play by Israel Horovitz.

In his film debut, in *Me, Natalie* (National General, 1969), a commercially unsuccessful motion picture starring Patty Duke, he once again played a junkie. Two years later he starred in *The Panic in Needle Park* (Twentieth Century-Fox, 1971), a brutally realistic study of a drug-addicted couple during a temporary heroin shortage in New York City. As Bruce Cook noted in the *National Observer* (July 26, 1971), it was "almost physically painful to watch." The movie owed a large measure of its authenticity to the painstaking, on-location research of Pacino and his costar, Kitty Winn. Before shooting began, the pair talked to addicts and ex-addicts, attended methadone treatment sessions, and frequented the hangouts of drug pushers. "Cops began to think we were addicts and addicts began to think we were cops," Pacino recalled to Leo Seligsohn in an interview for the Washington *Post* (July 16, 1971). "I was afraid people might recognize me and say, 'Hey, look what happened to Pacino. He went all the way.'" Critics gave the film mixed reviews but were unanimous in their praise of Pacino's "marvelously alive," "remarkable," and "exceptionally successful" performance.

After viewing a twelve-minute segment of *The Panic in Needle Park*, Paramount Pictures executives agreed to consider Pacino for the role of Michael Corleone in the movie version of *The Godfather*. Previously they had been looking for a "name" star of the magnitude of Warren Beatty or Jack Nicholson. After submitting to two additional screen tests, Pacino was chosen, and in order to appear in *The Godfather* he bought his way out of a previous commitment to MGM's Mafia spoof, *The Gang That Couldn't Shoot Straight*. Although director Francis Ford Coppola shot the film out of sequence, Pacino conceived his *Godfather* role as a "slow, subtle transition." Michael, the college-educated, decorated war hero son of Don Corleone, was " a private person," he explained to Chris Chase. "He was the youngest, so he really had to observe, to look, and he was prepared when he finally took over because he'd learned a lot of things just by observing."

By virtue of its record-breaking grosses, *The Godfather* (Paramount, 1972) wrote a new chapter in movie box-office history; it also elicited preponderantly glowing notices for everyone connected with it, including Pacino. In the *New Yorker* (March 18, 1972), Pauline Kael marveled at the ingenuity with which he accomplished his character's metamorphosis "from a small, fresh-faced, darkly handsome college boy into an underworld lord." Pacino, she continued, "has an unusual gift for conveying the divided spirit of a man whose calculations often go against his inclinations." Commenting on his "unforgettably fine performance" in the Toronto *Globe and Mail* (March 18, 1972), Martin Knelman noted that the young actor "quietly takes over the movie until he towers over everyone except [Marlon] Brando." His perceptive portrayal earned him the best actor award from the National Society of Film Critics in addition to the nomination from the Academy of Motion Picture Arts and Sciences.

Eager to face a live audience again, Pacino readily accepted when David Wheeler's highly regarded Theater Company of Boston invited him to essay the title role in David Rabe's antiwar play *The Basic Training of Pavlo Hummel*. "Pacino's great," Chris Chase reported, adding that the world of difference between the ruthless Michael Corleone and the bumbling Pavlo Hummel had been "bridged by a virtuoso." The following year, he fulfilled a long-held ambition when he starred in a Theater Company production of *Richard III*. His interpretation of the Shakespearian villain was based upon the "profound insight" that Richard was "primarily an actor himself," according to Melvin Maddocks in *Time* magazine (February 26, 1973). "This Richard may be a monster," Maddocks declared, "yet how heroic and finally touching a monster Pacino makes him."

Scarecrow (Warner, 1973), Pacino's first post-*Godfather* film, represented a reunion with Jerry Schatzberg, his director in *The Panic in Needle Park*. His touching and, at times, amusing portrait of a shy, hapless drifter incongruously named Lion again testified to his versatility. His acting, and that of Gene Hackman, helped to alleviate the mawkishness of Garry Michael White's script, which the majority of critics faulted for containing too many echoes of *Midnight Cowboy*. In May 1973, when the jury at the Cannes Film Festival announced that *Scarecrow*, the official United States entry in the competition, would share the grand prize with Britain's *The Hireling*, it emphasized that the decisive factor had been the outstanding performances by the stars of the two motion pictures.

That he was a "star" in the full sense of that term, capable of carrying a picture on the strength of his personality and skill, Pacino proved beyond any shadow of a doubt in *Serpico* (Paramount, 1973). That true story of a scrupulously honest New York City cop whose untiring efforts to expose corruption within the Police Department culminated in the public Knapp Commission hearings in 1971 was, as one admiring critic noted, "a galvanizing and disquieting film." Because Pacino was onscreen for nearly all of the film's 130 minutes running time, the critical and commercial triumphs that *Serpico* scored were unquestionably his. Commending Pacino's "blockbuster performance" in *Cue* (December 10, 1973), William Wolf remarked, "There is electricity in virtually everything Pacino does, from the smallest gesture to the big emotional moments. . . . [It is] tour de force acting."

A compact, muscular man, Al Pacino stands five feet seven inches tall and has black hair and deep-set, dark eyes. Some reviewers have seen in Pacino a resemblance to Dustin Hoffman. To keep physically fit, he follows a self-imposed regimen of exercise at a YMCA gymnasium in New York City. For relaxation, he enjoys listening to rock 'n' roll and classical music. Until recently, Pacino, a bachelor, shared a Manhattan apartment with Jill Clayburgh, an actress. He accepts stardom and the adulation of thousands of fans as "another part" of his job. "With this bloody life, you can't think of success because that's not where the focus should be," he told Leo Seligsohn. "There are no rewards except in what you're doing —unless you consider money a reward, and I don't."

References

N Y Post p13 Jl 24 '71 por; II p15 Ja 5 '74
N Y Sunday News Mag p4+ Je 4 '72 pors
N Y Times II p1+ Mr 9 '69 por
Time 99:70+ Ap 3 '72 pors
Washington Post A p3+ Jl 16 '71 pors

PANOV, VALERY (SHULMAN)

Mar. 12, 1939 (?)- Israeli ballet dancer
Address: c/o Bat-Dor Ballet Company, Tel Aviv, Israel

The stubborn, twenty-seven-month refusal of the Kremlin to allow Valery Panov, a Jew and the leading male dancer of Leningrad's Kirov Ballet, to emigrate to Israel once again called attention to the high cost of dissent in the Soviet Union. Panov, considered by New York Times dance critic Clive Barnes to be perhaps the greatest dancer in the world, performed with the Kirov for nine years, but after a series of ideological disputes with Communist party cultural watchdogs, who objected to his unconventional choreography, he opted for the cultural freedom of the West. After Panov and his wife applied in April 1972 for exit visas, they became the targets of continuous government harassment and terror, as well as the subjects of mounting Western sympathy and outraged protest. In June 1974 the Soviet authorities capitulated. Greeted by a crowd of 100 cheering admirers at the Tel Aviv airport, Panov said, "I feel I have come home. My achievements will be Israel's. Israel will be our home, but art is for the world."

Of Jewish heritage, Valery Panov was born Valery Shulman on March 12, 1939 in Vilnius, or Vilno, the capital of Lithuania. (Some sources give his birthdate as 1938.) He has at least one brother, who still lives there. He began studying ballet when he was six and became a professional dancer at fifteen. In 1958 he joined the Maly Opera Theatre of Leningrad, then under the direction of Galina Isayeva, one of the Soviet Union's leading dancers. The company, which was formed in 1918, was known for its experimental ballets and for its lovingly reconstructed revivals of such classics as Petrouchka and Swan Lake. Five years later, the young dancer changed his name to Valery Panov and transferred to the Kirov Ballet, one of the leading ballet companies of Europe. "I couldn't join the Kirov Ballet until I called myself Panov," he explained to Herbert Gold in an interview for the New Republic (August 24, 1974). "I managed to change my passport from Jew to Russian. Many dancers are Jewish, but they don't admit it. Even ballet is ruled by politics here, though it seems far from ideology."

Studying under Alexander Pushkin, the celebrated ballet master who also instructed such premiers danseurs as Rudolf Nureyev and Mikhail Baryshnikov, Panov quickly achieved the coveted status of the principal dramatic dancer in the company. Among the major roles in his huge repertoire were Count Albrecht in Giselle, the Bluebird in The Sleeping Beauty, the leading role in The Creation of the World, and the title roles in Petrouchka, his favorite ballet, and in Hamlet, an imaginative new ballet choreographed by Konstantin Sergeyev. Despite his position as the Kirov's leading male soloist, Panov was regularly denied an assignment to the touring company. His one trip abroad was around 1960 when he appeared as a guest artist with the Kirov at Madison Square Garden in New York City. After only one performance, Panov was summoned home by a telegram alleging grave illness in his family. On his return he discovered that the telegram had been a hoax. Although Soviet authorities never issued an official explanation for their policy, Panov did not accompany the Kirov Ballet on its subsequent tours of Europe, Canada, and the United States. Foreign observers speculated that the decision was prompted by fear that Panov would defect to the West, since the Kirov had already produced such celebrated expatriates as Anna Pavlova, Vaslav Nijinsky, and George Balanchine. (Rudolf Nureyev, Natalia Makarova, and Mikhail Baryshnikov have defected since 1960.)

During Leningrad's "White Nights Festival" marking the 155th anniversary of the birth of Marius Petipa (1819-1910), the dancer and choreographer of the Russian Imperial Ballet who has been called the "father of the classic ballet," Panov danced the role of Basil in Petipa's Don Quixote. Commenting on his "fantastic" performance for the New York Times (July 1, 1968), Clive Barnes observed: "He is one of the few great male dancers of the world. His wit and humor in this were matched only by the elegance of his partnering and the flamboyant virtuosity of his perfect dancing." As a choreographer, Panov combined the traditional techniques of classical ballet with the abstract movements of modern dance to create startlingly different works. His unorthodox approach to the dance, especially his choreography for Alexander Pushkin's Queen of Spades and other Russian classics, outraged Communist party cultural arbiters who constantly demanded production changes for ideological reasons. His Pugachev was never staged, for instance, because several Kirov officials objected to a scene depicting the independent spirit of the peasants. Despite repeated threats, Panov steadfastly refused to adapt the scene. "I grew very tired of lies," he explained to Herbert Gold. "Individuality is not required, not allowed. I even had political trouble over choreography— political trouble."

Planning to immigrate to Israel, in the spring of 1972 Panov applied for exit visas for himself and for his non-Jewish wife, Galina Ragozina Panov. At a public hearing in the Kirov Theatre on April 29, 1972 his colleagues accused him of "crime and treachery," "betrayal of the creative arts," and "treason at the temple of . . . love, purity, and friendship." Because of his "amoral behavior and treason," he was summarily discharged from the Kirov Ballet. His wife, a Kirov soloist, was demoted to the *corps de ballet*, dropped from the roster for a forthcoming tour abroad, and—according to Panov's letter to United States Senator Henry M. Jackson, published in the New York *Times* on February 7, 1974— "advised to find another husband."

Following his dismissal from the Kirov Ballet, Panov encountered the first direct governmental opposition to his emigration from the Soviet Union when the visa department repeatedly ignored his petitions. The applications were finally accepted on the eve of President Richard M. Nixon's visit to the Soviet Union in late May 1972 but were returned immediately after his departure. Constantly hounded by the police, Panov was finally arrested for "hooliganism," beaten, and imprisoned for ten days in a cell with amputees and cripples. His mail deliveries were stopped, his telephone service was discontinued, and his Western friends were questioned about his activities. Blacklisted by the major dance companies, Valery Panov persistently and unsuccessfully searched for work as a dancer, teacher, or choreographer; Galina Panov, after several months of intimidation, resigned from the Kirov to protest her husband's treatment and, like him, was branded a traitor. The couple's financial situation became so desperate that they were forced to sell some of their possessions. When authorities disregarded their appeal for practice space, they converted their tiny ten-by-sixteen-foot Leningrad apartment into a primitive studio too small for all but the simplest exercises. On the grounds that Galina Panov's mother, Larisa Ragozina, refused to consent to her daughter's emigration, a requirement of Russian law, the government denied their applications for exit permits. "I have a little more strength left to fight," Panov told Anthony Lewis in a rare interview for the New York *Times* (April 9, 1973). "Then . . . I must get out or my life is over; there is no more me."

Panov's plight did not go unnoticed in the West. Clive Barnes, the influential dance critic for the New York *Times*, took up Panov's cause in April 1972. In an article published in the April 23, 1972 issue of the *Times*, he praised the Russian dancer as a "brilliant demi-caractère dancer and an extraordinarily subtle actor" with "few if any equals in the world." "It has always seemed strange that a dancer of such distinction has never been allowed to take part in the Kirov Ballet tours," Barnes wrote. "I have every reason to believe that had he had the opportunity to dance abroad in the way of his colleagues he would not have taken the grave step of trying to leave the country permanently. . . . It is to be

VALERY PANOV

hoped that the Soviet authorities will accede to his wish to leave for Israel and will cease penalizing him for a situation that has never been of his making."

The Ad Hoc Committee for Valery and Galina Panov, largely composed of concerned performers, critics, and balletomanes, mounted a massive media campaign to drum up public support for the Soviet artists, and Panov, who had been relatively unknown in the West, became an international celebrity. In June 1972 the Committee sent to the Soviet government the first of several petitions supporting the Panovs' request; in April 1973 United States Senator Henry Jackson wrote to Soviet Communist Party Chief Leonid I. Brezhnev in Panov's behalf; and in November 1973, when Panov began a hunger strike, an Anglo-American group that included Joanne Woodward, Barbra Streisand, Beverly Sills, and Clive Barnes, urged Secretary of State Henry A. Kissinger to intercede. Outside the Russian embassy in London demonstrators vowed to maintain their vigil as long as Panov continued his hunger strike. On the advice of his doctor, Panov ended the strike after three weeks. He had lost twenty-six pounds and had reached the point where he was suffering from hallucinations.

Faced with mounting Western outrage, the Russian authorities approved Panov's visa application in December 1973. Because of her mother's alleged objection to her emigration, Galina Panov's petition was denied. The situation was further complicated by Mrs. Panov's pregnancy. "I cannot leave her. Least of all now," Panov remarked in a statement to the press. In desperation Galina Panov appealed to Soviet Premier Aleksei N. Kosygin for permission to leave the country with her husband. "I am over eighteen and my marriage has been duly registered," she wrote in a letter to the Soviet leader, as quoted in the Washington *Post* (January 19, 1974). "The Soviet law on the family and marriage stipulates that my allegiance is to my husband. My desire to preserve my family is legal while the attempt to separate me from my husband by force is a gross and arbitrary act that tramples on the law."

Concluding that "the personal freedom of Mr. and Mrs. Valery Panov is essential to the successful appearances of the Kirov Ballet in this country," officials of New York's City Center threatened to cancel the company's scheduled appearances at Lincoln Center in July 1974. The entire Kirov tour was eventually cancelled by Columbia Artists Management, Inc., (CAMI), the theatrical agency in charge of arrangements for the American tour. Although CAMI insisted that the twelve-week tour had been dropped because of the energy crisis, Samuel Niefeld, a spokesman for the organization, admitted that "the Panov situation" figured in the decision. "We made it clear to the Russian authorities that feelings about the Panovs were running high in this country," Niefeld explained to David A. Andelman in an interview for the New York Times (January 16, 1974).

The Bolshoi's projected Western tour was also drastically curtailed ostensibly because of "transportation difficulties." In London, British Equity, the powerful theatrical union, threatened to block all Soviet cultural exchanges with Great Britain until the Panovs were freed. The Russian government responded by declaring the couple "parasites," often a first step toward imprisonment in a labor camp. At a meeting with Western journalists in Moscow in February 1974, Panov revealed that his wife had been permanently barred from leaving the Soviet Union and that he risked the revocation of his exit visa and government imposition of other "administrative measures" unless he agreed to emigrate without her.

In the West, despite Secretary Brezhnev's pledge to release the Panovs, the protest continued unabated. In New York City, some 400 people attended a "birthday party" for Valery Panov on the occasion of his thirty-fifth birthday. Speaking to the crowd assembled outside the Plaza Hotel, Clive Barnes denounced the Soviet government's "inhuman" treatment of Panov: "This very great man has not been able to practice his craft. He is constricted in a small two-room apartment. . . . It is like putting a man in a cage in a zoo." In London, British supporters presented to the Soviet Embassy poems, cables and a petition demanding the Panovs' release and pressured the Prospect Theatre Company into cancelling its forthcoming visit to Russia. The New York Times (March 18, 1974) editorialized: "During the long period in which the Panovs have struggled with the obdurate Soviet bureaucracy, they have . . . been deprived even of proper space to practice, a deprivation that is a living death for dancers. . . . No gesture would do more to promote genuine goodwill than for Moscow to cease its spiteful crime against marriage and art and permit the Panovs to dance again."

In early June 1974, while the Panovs were in Vilnius visiting Valery's brother, Soviet authorities suddenly announced that the couple's exit permits were waiting for them at the Leningrad visa office. Despite widespread media speculation that the Russians had capitulated in order to insure a "most favored nation" trading status with the United States and to safeguard the Bolshoi Ballet's imminent European tour, Soviet sources maintained that the decision was prompted by Larisa Ragozina's consent to her daughter's emigration. "For two years I have been at war with this system, banging my head against the wall," an incredulous Panov told Hedrick Smith in an interview for the New York Times (June 14, 1974). "And suddenly this tremendous change. It was too much for me. . . . I did not believe we were going until we got the exit visas." The Soviet officials simplified the usually complex clearance procedures and on June 14, 1974 the Panovs flew to Tel Aviv by way of Vienna with nineteen other Soviet Jews immigrating to Israel. The joy of their departure was marred when Galina Panov suffered a miscarriage several days before leaving the U.S.S.R.

Small, slender, and well-proportioned, Valery Panov has been described by Anthony Lewis as a "man modest in size but projecting tremendous physical power and beauty." Although clean-shaven in many of his photographs, at the time of his release Panov sported a fringe of light-colored beard. Anxious to get back into shape after two years of inactivity, he and his wife began taking daily ballet classes shortly after their arrival in Israel. They performed together for the first time outside of the Soviet Union on November 10, 1974 in the Mann Auditorium in Tel Aviv. Panov is interested in establishing a state-sponsored classic ballet school and company.

By his own admission, Panov is "not religious." "We are both atheists," he revealed in an interview for NBC News broadcast on June 25, 1974. "But we love this country and one of the reasons of our love toward Israel is because the people here love God so beautifully and purely." Valery and Galina Panov have become Israeli citizens and have taken an apartment in suburban Tel Aviv. A guest of Israel's famed Bat-Dor Dance Company during 1974, Panov received several tempting offers from American and European companies, including the San Francisco Ballet and the Stuttgart Ballet. "Galina and myself . . . want to dance all over the world. I want to choreograph, but also to dance," he explained, as quoted in the New York Times (August 6, 1974). "We have been imprisoned. Now we must fly."

References

Carousel 46:54+ N '72 pors
Christian Sci Mon pF12 F 15 '74 por
Guardian Weekly p9 Je 15 '74
N Y Post p35 Ja 18 '74 por; p26 F 13 '74
N Y Times II p8 Ap 23 '72; p24 Ja 16
    '74 por; p2 Je 14 '74 por
Newsweek 84:43 Jl 1 '74 por

PARK, MERLE

Oct. 8, 1937- British ballerina
Address: b. Royal Opera House, Covent Garden,
London W.C. 2, England

A member of the Royal Ballet since 1954 and one
of its principal dancers since 1962, Merle Park
originally made her mark as a brilliant soubrette,
but has gone on to become one of the world's
leading classical ballerinas. In her twenty years
with the British company, she has gradually accepted all of the great classical roles—Juliet, Giselle,
Princess Aurora, and Odette-Odile—as well as a
number of leading roles in such shorter contemporary ballets as *Jazz Calendar*, *Symphonic Variations*, *Les Rendezvous*, and *A Birthday Offering*.
A brilliant technician with an innate sense of timing, Miss Park has been compared to such superb
ballerinas as Galina Ulanova, Alicia Markova, Alicia
Alonso, and Dame Margot Fonteyn. Recognizing
her uncommon talent as a dramatic actress, one
reviewer has called her "a Julie Harris on points."

Merle Park was born on October 8, 1937 in
Salisbury, Rhodesia, the youngest of the three
daughters of Peter Joseph Park and Florence
(Winson) Park, who had emigrated from South
Africa. On the advice of their family physician,
the Parks sent their daughter, a frail child, to a
local dancing school where she studied acrobatics,
mime, and folk and tap dancing. "I loved them
all except tap," Miss Park recalled in an interview
with Linda Christmas for the *Guardian* (January
19, 1973). "I was always the one on the end who
went wrong." Encouraged by her father, a railroad
"engine driver" with an insatiable appetite for
classical music, she also took piano lessons and
eventually earned a music scholarship.

When Miss Park entered her teens, her ballet
instructor at the Betty Lamb School in Salisbury
suggested that her gifted pupil go to Capetown
or London for further study. "She told me I moved
my arms and legs together," Miss Park recalled in
an interview with Daniel Webster for a Philadelphia *Inquirer* (June 1, 1969) profile, to explain
why the teacher had first singled her out. Impressed
by the disciplined technique exhibited by a friend
who had trained in London, Merle Park enrolled
at the Elmhurst Ballet School near London in
1951. "I was terribly happy at the school," she
told Linda Christmas. "We had fried bread with
practically every meal and at last I started to put
on weight."

Three years later, in the spring of 1954, Miss
Park auditioned for the Royal Ballet School and
was accepted. In August 1954 she officially joined
the corps de ballet of the Royal Ballet (then known
as the Sadler's Wells Ballet) and made her professional debut as a mouse in the train of the evil
fairy Carabosse in Tchaikovsky's *The Sleeping
Beauty*. Her first appearances as a soloist came a
few months later, when she brilliantly substituted
for the ailing Rowena Jackson in *Variations on a
Theme of Purcell* and danced the role of the milk-
maid, a "planned" solo, in *Façade*, to music of
Sir William Walton.

MERLE PARK

In 1959, a year after being promoted to the
status of soloist, Miss Park achieved her first
notable success when she danced Swanilda in
Délibes' *Coppélia*. Some critics praised the young
dancer as the best Swanilda in their experience.
Two years later she became the first dancer after
Nadia Nerina to dance the role of Lise in Sir
Frederick Ashton's *La Fille Mal Gardée*. Since
both those roles are essentially comic, they eminently suited Miss Park's image as an engaging
soubrette. When she first performed *La Fille Mal
Gardée* at a matinee performance at the old Metropolitan Opera House in New York City in September 1960, she was partnered by Donald Mac-
leary, the company's youngest *premier danseur*.
Writing in the New York *Times* (September 26,
1960), John Martin called the pair "charming and
capable" and "personally winning." Walter Terry,
who reviewed the performance for the New York
Herald Tribune (September 26, 1960), singled out
Miss Park for special praise: "[Her] Lise is pretty,
vivacious and appropriately mischievous. . . . She
is a secure dancer with certain aplomb for turns
and balances, a clear action line, and feet which,
in fast movements, sparkle as brightly as do her
eyes."

Over the next several years Miss Park developed
a variegated repertory as a principal dancer. Her
assignments included the waltz in *Les Sylphides*,
the Neopolitan dance in *Swan Lake*, the roles of
Blue Bird and Fairy in *The Sleeping Beauty*, Fire
in *The Prince of the Pagodas*, and the demanding
role of Princess Aurora in *The Sleeping Beauty*.
During the Royal Ballet's tour of the United States
and Canada in 1963, she appeared regularly as
Princess Aurora. Writing in the New York *Herald*

Tribune (May 20, 1963), Lillian Moore found the perennial soubrette more than equal to the challenges of the classical role. "She carried off the bravura sections with warmth and grace as well as assurance," Miss Moore reported, "yet was equally successful in suggesting the remote, elusive quality so important in the Vision scene." The critic was especially enchanted by the dancer's "lovely *ballon*" and by her "natural, unforced charm."

Miss Park's growing technical and dramatic mastery became even more apparent when she danced the role of Juliet in Prokofiev's *Romeo and Juliet* at the Metropolitan Opera House in April 1965. As choreographed by Kenneth MacMillan as his first full-length evening ballet, *Romeo and Juliet* demands of its performers sensitive acting as well as virtuoso dancing. Critics noted a "fluid, lyrical quality" in her dancing and applauded her performance as "consistent and commendable." In his New York *Herald Tribune* (April 24, 1965) review, Walter Terry suggested that Merle Park's acute sense of timing helped make her interpretation of Juliet a success. "She gave the accent to pacing," Terry wrote. "Moving with the swiftness of mercury, she literally sped from one tempestuous episode to another as if she were showing us how much of life, with its discoveries, ecstasies, and tragedies, had to be crammed into a pitifully short span of time." Miss Park explained her affinity with the role to Hubert Saal in an interview for *Newsweek* (May 6, 1968): "I feel for that music. And that's all that matters. The music goes with that lady."

Because she is "good in allegro," Antony Tudor selected Miss Park for the female lead in *Shadowplay*, his first work designed specifically for the Royal Ballet since 1939. That imaginative ballet, inspired by Rudyard Kipling's *Jungle Book* and choreographed to music by Charles Koechlin, received accolades in both London and New York. As the Queen of the Celestials, who was borne aloft in a series of difficult lifts, Miss Park was "as breathtaking as a full moon on a dark night," according to one bewitched reviewer. *Shadowplay* was featured during the Royal Ballet's visit to New York City, when in addition to her principal part in that ballet, Miss Park danced the roles of Titania in *The Dream*, the one-act ballet that Sir Frederick Ashton choreographed to Mendelssohn's music; Juliet in *Romeo and Juliet*; Lise in *La Fille Mal Gardée*; and the title role in *Giselle*. Writing in the New York *Times* (May 15, 1967), Clive Barnes extolled her perceptive dramatic interpretation of Giselle, particularly in the "touchingly realistic" mad scene, as well as her "rapturous musicality." "Miss Park's Giselle is the kind of Giselle one dreams of," he concluded. "One looked at it, and wondered how it was that a young dancer could still extract something fresh and newly meaningful out of a ballet 126 years old. And that . . . is the measure of Miss Park."

Further proof of Merle Park's international status was the announcement by the management of the Royal Ballet in August 1967 that Rudolf Nureyev would be her partner in *Romeo and Juliet* during the company's autumn season. (Dame Margot Fonteyn, Nureyev's regular partner, was scheduled to appear as a guest artist with another company.) The Nureyev-Park partnership, although not as constant or well-known as that of Rudolf Nureyev and Margot Fonteyn or that of Antoinette Sibley and Anthony Dowell, continues to be important for both dancers.

In 1968 Nureyev created a new version of Tchaikovsky's *The Nutcracker* and selected Miss Park to dance the expanded role of the child Clara. To rejuvenate the perdurable but slightly tired ballet, the traditional Christmas showpiece for many of the world's major dance companies, Nureyev combined the roles of Clara and the Sugar Plum Fairy and those of Herr Drosselmeyer and the prince. With Nureyev as her partner, Miss Park danced (to quote Clive Barnes) "with the delicacy of lace and the sparkle of diamonds." Working with the Russian-trained Nureyev has enriched her technique. "A lot of what I've learned," she told Hubert Saal, "Rudolph taught me." But the partnership has not been without its tensions. For instance, during a performance of *The Nutcracker*, the temperamental Nureyev, annoyed by the conductor's tempos, stalked off the stage, leaving his disconcerted partner to finish the *pas de deux* alone. She continued to dance, and an apologetic Nureyev eventually returned to complete the duet.

As Miss Park's technical mastery became more and more evident, some critics complained that her dancing was impaired by a marmoreal kind of perfection. Winthrop Sargeant, for example, in the *New Yorker* (May 3, 1969), described her performance in *La Bayadère* as "wonderfully efficient . . . but quite cold." Others, however, have repeatedly praised her "formidable musicality" as the unique element in her performances. Commenting on her Princess Aurora in a May 1972 production of *The Sleeping Beauty*, Clive Barnes observed in the New York *Times* (May 13, 1972): "She phrases dances with a kind of careless precision that is beguiling to watch." Anna Kisselgoff of the New York *Times* (May 1, 1972) commended Miss Park's "convincingly Shakespearian" Juliet and "her extraordinary ability to act through movement rather than just the face."

Merle Park's career has been unusual in the way that it has evolved through many different kinds of roles. Unlike many ballerinas, she has been somewhat reluctant to add new roles, particularly classical ones, to her repertory. "I've never wanted to dance any of the big roles," she told Linda Christmas. "I'm much happier with a short solo. I'd rather do Bluebird than Beauty . . . flash on, do my stuff and off again. . . . I prefer to do a little and do it well. *Symphonic Variations* is my ideal role. Fifteen minutes and it's all over, but it says what it has to say in that time." In 1972 she added Sir Frederick Ashton's *Walk to the Paradise Garden*, a love duet fashioned especially for her and David Wall, to Frederick Delius' music, and in 1973 she finally accepted the principal role in Stravinsky's *Firebird* and Odette-Odile in *Swan Lake*.

The dual role of Odette-Odile, which one critic has called a "final, comprehensive exam" for a leading ballerina, requires the dancer to portray two women of opposite temperaments—a gentle, ethereal Odette and a brilliant, seductive Odile—and yet suggest that they are somehow similar. According to critics, Miss Park more than fulfilled the expectations of balletomanes who waited so long for her debut in that role, which took place on February 10, 1973 in London. In his review for the *Guardian* (February 12, 1973), James Kennedy noted that the key to the contrast between Odette and Odile, "seldom so effectively achieved, was her exceptionally variable technique; and the common denominators were her Fonteyn-like timing, or musicality, and a long-limbed liquefaction of movements which is not quite like any other dancer's." Teamed with Rudolf Nureyev as Siegfried, she danced the role for the second time at Covent Garden on August 1, 1973, prompting Clive Barnes to call her "a marvelous Odette-Odile," with a characterization "intuitively balanced between those sacred and profane sides of womanhood that continually confuse man."

Although the tiny and small-boned Merle Park stands only five feet two inches tall and weighs about 102 pounds, her long legs and arms lend her the illusion of height and the "gift of elegance." She has long, dark auburn hair and large, expressive blue-green eyes. In 1965 she married James Monahan, a dance critic who writes under the name of James Kennedy. They were divorced in 1969, two years after the birth of their son, Antony Joseph Henry James. The following year Miss Park married Sidney Bloch, a businessman and solicitor. They live in a house in London that commands a view of the Thames. To escape temporarily from her usual routine of classes, rehearsals, and performances six days a week, eleven months a year, Miss Park travels with her husband and plays with her young son. She intends to teach young dancers when she is no longer able to perform professionally. "I never wanted to be a so-called ballerina," she said in a recent interview. "I have been called unambitious, but I do have an ambition to do what I do well."

References

Dance Mag 48:43+ My '74
Guardian p11 Ja 19 '73 pors
N Y Daily News p19 My 9 '74 por

Chujoy, Anatole, and Manchester, P.W., eds. Dance Encyclopedia (1967)
Kerensky, Oleg, Ballet Today (1970)
Who's Who in the World, 1972-73

PAZ, OCTAVIO (päs)

Mar. 31, 1914- Mexican writer
Address: b. Harvard University, Boylston Hall, Room 401, Cambridge, Mass. 02138

Like Pablo Neruda of Chile and Miguel Angel Asturias of Guatemala, the Mexican writer and thinker Octavio Paz belongs to a distinctively

OCTAVIO PAZ

Latin American breed of literary titans—cosmopolitan, wide-ranging men who have profoundly influenced the politics of their native countries and have channeled their cultures into the mainstream of world literature. Paz is a poet, essayist, diplomat, critic, professor, translator, polemicist, and founder of literary journals. A tireless traveler both through continents and through the landscapes of the mind, he has preoccupations that range from surrealism and socialism to archaeology and Oriental philosophy. Among his best-known works are *El laberinto de la soledad (The Labyrinth of Solitude)*, a searching essay on the Mexican character, and the long and sensuous, yet metaphysical poems *Piedra de sol (Sun Stone)* and *Blanco*. One of his countrymen and colleagues, the novelist Carlos Fuentes, has called Paz the "greatest living Mexican writer, great renovator of the Spanish language, great universal poet and essayist."

Octavio Paz was born in Mexico City on March 31, 1914 into what he has somewhat inaccurately described as "a typical Mexican family." His mother's parents had emigrated from Andalusia in Spain; his father's ancestors were Mexicans from the state of Jalisco through whose veins flowed a considerable amount of Indian blood. The paternal grandfather, whom Octavio much admired, was a writer, journalist, and political activist, who espoused the cause of the peasantry. It was in his huge private library that the boy Octavio did his first extensive reading. The father, a lawyer, took part in agrarian reform, embraced with fervor the Mexican Revolution of 1910, and represented Emiliano Zapata in the United States. Because the Paz family was financially ruined during the upheavals of the civil war, Octavio spent his boyhood in Mixcoac, a suburb of Mexico City, in a large house that was, as he told Rita Guibert in an interview for her book *Seven Voices* (1973), "crumbling to bits" gradually. "As rooms collapsed," he recalled, "we moved the furniture into others." He lived for a time in a large room with only part of a wall.

While attending a French school run by the Marist fathers Paz abandoned Roman Catholicism, mainly out of boredom, and became an atheist. He obtained his higher education at the National University of Mexico, without taking a degree. In the early 1930's his first work appeared in two avant-garde literary journals, *Barrandal,* which he himself founded at seventeen, and *Cuadernos del Valle de Mexico.* At that time young Latin American writers were coming under the influence of José Ortega y Gasset, who was trying to jolt Spanish letters out of its contemporary backwardness. The resulting discovery of modern European literature, and especially of such French writers as Saint-John Perse and André Breton, was an epiphany for Paz and for others of his generation.

In 1933, at the age of nineteen, Paz published his first book of poetry, *Luna silvestre* (Forest Moon). Four years later he made the first of many trips to Europe, when he attended a congress of antifascist writers in Spain. After the congress Paz remained in Spain for a year, and he took up the Republican cause in the civil war. "Spain," he told Rita Guibert, "taught me the meaning of the word 'fraternity.'" His Spanish experiences went into another book, *Bajo tu clara sombra y otros poemas de España* (Beneath Your Clear Shade and Other Spanish Poems), published in Valencia in 1937. That year also brought the appearance of *Raiz del hombre* (Root of Man). Those two books led him to be viewed as one of the most gifted among the younger writers of his generation.

On his way back to Mexico in 1938, Paz stopped off in Paris, where through Alejo Carpentier and Robert Desnos he made his first contact with the surrealists, whose work and philosophy have been an enduring influence on him. Although his Spanish experiences during the civil war had fortified his revolutionary zeal, he had come to distrust revolutionary theories, and he thus found himself more and more drawn to the political attitudes of the surrealists. "Surrealism was not merely an aesthetic, poetic, and philosophical doctrine," he told Rita Guibert. "It was a vital attitude. A negation of the contemporary world and at the same time an attempt to substitute other values for those of democratic bourgeois society: eroticism, poetry, imagination, liberty, spiritual adventure, vision. . . . Well, the poetry I have written seems to me to form part of this current, or is trying to form part of it."

Paz then embarked on what he looks back upon as the years of his "most intense political activity." In 1938 and 1939 many Spanish Republican intellectuals took refuge in Mexico, and Paz worked with them in literary and political endeavors. He joined the editorial board of *El Popular,* a newspaper published by a union of Mexican workers, for which he wrote a daily column on international affairs. In 1938 he helped to found *Taller,* an important literary magazine. Although Paz had close ties to the Communists at that time, like many leftists, he was disillusioned by the German-Soviet pact. His disenchantment

led him to leave *El Popular,* break with the Communists, and virtually retire from political activity. In 1943 he collaborated in the founding of another avant-garde journal, *El hijo pródigo* (The Prodigal Son). In 1941 his book of poems *Entre la piedra y la flor* (Between Stone and Flower) appeared, and in 1942 he collected much of his previous work, along with new poems, in *A la orilla del mundo* (On the Banks of the World).

With the help of a Guggenheim Fellowship, in 1944 Paz visited the United States for the first time. "My stay in the United States was a great experience," he told Rita Guibert, "no less decisive than that in Spain. On one hand there was the amazing and terrible reality of North American civilization; on the other, my reading and discovery of a number of poets: Eliot, Pound, William Carlos Williams, Wallace Stevens, Cummings." But Octavio Paz's American sojourn was marred by financial worries, especially during the several otherwise exhilarating months that he spent in San Francisco. In 1945 he found himself so poverty-stricken in New York City that when two friends offered him a chance to join the Mexican diplomatic service, he gratefully accepted. Posted to Paris as secretary to the Mexican embassy, he met Sartre, Camus, Bréton, and other literary figures in the French capital, and during the next sixteen years he served in diplomatic posts in France, Switzerland, the United States, and Japan. The fact that he achieved no particular distinction as a diplomat and advanced only slowly through the ranks did not trouble him, since his career gave him the opportunity to write and to work in relative anonymity.

The first book that Paz wrote after entering the diplomatic service was one that some critics consider his masterpiece, *El laberinto de la soledad (The Labyrinth of Solitude),* a key document in Mexico's midcentury search for definition and identity. An investigation of the Mexican national character, Paz's long essay appeared in 1950 and touched off a whole movement of native writers interested in "Mexicanism." When it was published by Grove Press in a translation by Lysander Kemp in 1962, it was equally acclaimed in the United States. More than a decade later, Irving Howe wrote of *The Labyrinth of Solitude* in the New York *Times Book Review* (March 25, 1973): "This book roams through the phases of Mexican past and present seeking to define the outrages, violation and defeats that have left the Mexican personality fixed into a social mask of passive hauteur. . . . At once brilliant and sad, *The Labyrinth of Solitude* constitutes an elegy for a people martyred, perhaps destroyed by history. It is a central text of our time."

When, in 1951 and 1952, Paz visited India and Japan for the first time, he was introduced firsthand to Oriental architecture, painting, poetry, and religious and philosophical classics. He returned to Mexico in 1953 for six years of frenetic literary activity. *Aguila o sol?* (*Eagle or Sun?*), a collection of visionary prose poems about Mexican perspectives on history that has been translated into English by Eliot Weinberger, appeared in

1951, and was followed by *Semillas para un himno* (Seeds for a Psalm), another collection of poems, in 1954. In the next three years were published *El arco y la lira* (The Bow and the Lyre, 1956), a collection of essays on the nature and structure of poetry; *Las peras del olmo* (Pears of the Elm, 1957), a book of literary criticism; *Piedra de sol* (Sun Stone, 1957), his long poem to the planet Venus, which exists in at least four English versions; and two more collections of his poetry, *La estación violenta* (The Violent Season, 1958) and *Salamandra* (Salamander, 1962).

By the time that Paz reached his middle period, the contours of his poetry had clearly emerged. He is, first of all, a supremely *Mexican* poet, immersed in his country's history, geography, climate, and mythology, as evidenced by *Piedra de sol*, probably his best-known poem, which is saturated with Náhuatl mythology and symbolism. But above all he is a universal poet with breadth of interest, erudition, and intellectual curiosity, as interested in other Western philosophies, notably that of the existentialist Martin Heidegger, as he is in that of surrealism. Equally influenced by Oriental thought and poetry, he published his first poems in *haiku* form in 1955. In his search for reconciliation and synthesis, Paz combines the lyrical with the intellectual, fusing idea with exuberance. Rich with imagery drawn from nature and wide-foraging in its themes, his poetry can be explosively baroque or serenely simple. As such critics as Guillermo Sucre have pointed out, Paz took the two major trends of Mexican poetry of his day—the meditative, probing, metaphysical, and death-obsessed poetry on the one hand, and the sensuous, radiant, and impressionistic poetry on the other—merged them, and finally transcended them.

It was around 1962, the year in which Octavio Paz was appointed Mexico's ambassador to India, that he began to win the international recognition that he deserved. In the late 1950's translations of his work began to appear in France; the year 1962 brought the publication in English of *El laberinto de la soledad;* and in 1963 Paz was awarded the Grand Prix International de Poésie. When, in the latter year, his *Selected Poems* appeared in an English translation by Muriel Rukeyser (Indiana Univ. Press), Dudley Fitts praised Paz in the New York *Times Book Review* (January 26, 1964) for "a tenderness and a fierceness completely controlled; a mimetic flexibility of diction and intonation that is admirable in its rightness; a spiritual *élan* that is unembarrassed by elevation and indifferent to humiliation; and music, always the music of the running line. . . ."

Paz held his ambassadorial post to India until October 1968, when he resigned in protest against the brutal repression and massacre of student rebels at the National University of Mexico. The years in India were crucial, not only for his intellectual development but for his personal life, for in 1964 he married the young, vivacious, and attractive Marie-José Tramini, a Frenchwoman whom

he met there. "After being born," Paz has said, "that's the most important thing that has happened to me." Paz was not so much interested in Indian religion as he was in Indian traditional thought, particularly Buddhism, and as time went by the number of Oriental allusions in his work markedly increased. Paz told Rita Guibert that India taught his wife and himself such lessons as friendship, "a feeling of brotherhood for plants and animals," and the recognition that "we are all part of the same unity." "Above all," he said, "we learned to be silent."

That silence permeates *Ladera este* (Eastern Slope), a collection containing poems that Paz wrote between 1962 and 1968, the time span of his ambassadorship to India. He considers *Ladera este* to be his best book. The French critic Alain Bosquet observed in the weekly English airmail edition of *Le Monde* (February 3, 1971): "This is Paz's contemplative period. The contact with India must have fascinated him; but beyond mere fascination, what we find in these poems is the need to penetrate to the very essence of things and feelings. The poems are condensed, reduced to the essential as though a certain verbal economy gave words an entirely new dignity."

Since resigning his ambassadorship to India in 1968, Paz has lived in England, France, the United States, and Mexico. In recent years he has resorted increasingly to experimental and avant-garde modes for his poetry. He had his long and difficult poem *Blanco* (1967) printed on a folding scroll, thus making possible a number of alternative readings. In *Topoemas* (1968), a book of concrete poems, the arrangement of words and letters on the page is as important as the words themselves. That same year appeared the equally arbitrary *Discos Visuales* (Visual Disks). "They were a little gimmick of mine," Paz explained to Rita Guibert. "The object consists of two superimposed cardboard disks; as the upper disk is rotated, the 'windows' in it reveal the text of a short poem written on the lower disk. My purpose was twofold: firstly, to give the text mobility by means of visual rhythm; secondly, to ensure slower reading." *Renga* (1971) is a collaborative poem written by Paz and three other poets in Spanish, French, English, and Italian.

Since 1970 the number of translations of Paz's work into English has markedly increased. Collections of his poetry have included *Eagle or Sun?* (October House, 1970); *Configurations* (New Directions, 1971); and *Early Poems, 1935-1955* (Indiana Univ. Press, 1973), with translations by Muriel Rukeyser and other poets. Several books of essays ranging over a wide spectrum of topics have also appeared, including *The Other Mexico; Critique of the Pyramid* (Grove Press, 1972), a brief exploration of some of the motives behind his giving up of his ambassadorship; *Conjunctions and Disjunctions* (Viking, 1973); and *Alternating Current* (Viking, 1973), a collection of essays that he wrote between 1958 and 1964. In 1971-72 Paz had the honor of being appointed Charles Eliot Norton Professor of Poetry at Harvard University, where he lectured on "Modern Poetry: A Tradition Against Itself." The lectures were later published in *Children of the Mire: Modern Poetry from Romanticism to the Avant Garde* (Viking, 1974). Paz has also taught classes at the University of Texas and at Cambridge University in England, where he was Simón Bolívar Professor of Latin American Studies and Fellow of Churchill College in 1970-71. He is currently a visiting professor of comparative literature at Harvard University. Paz is an honorary member of the American Academy of Arts and Letters. Recently Paz has edited another Mexican journal, *Plural,* which, he says, "is fighting from a political and literary point of view for diversity in critical, political, literary, and intellectual spheres."

With his square, dark-skinned face, black hair, and slightly flattened nose, Octavio Paz bears some resemblance to the ancient Mexican Indians who generated the myths that so fascinate him. Writing by hand and avoiding the typewriter, he tries to work and to read a little each day, although his timetable is admittedly irregular. He tries to read poetry, which remains his first love, every day, along with the dictionary, which he has called "his adviser, his elder brother" and a source of "magic" and "surprises." Conversation and reading books on archaeology, travel, history, and philosophy are his favorite diversions. Writing, he confessed to Rita Guibert, is the thing he likes least, although it has sometimes brought him great happiness. In closing her interview with Paz in Cambridge, England, Miss Guibert asked the poet, "What are your plans for the future?" "To abolish it," he replied.

References

Guibert, Rita. Seven Voices (1972)
International Who's Who, 1973-74
Ivask, Ivar, ed. The Perpetual Present; Poetry and Prose of Octavio Paz (1973)
Who's Who in America, 1972-73
Who's Who in the World, 1972-73

PEALE, NORMAN VINCENT

May 31, 1898- Clergyman; author
Address: b. Marble Collegiate Church, 1 W. 29th St., New York 10001; h. 1030 Fifth Ave., New York 10028; Quaker Hill, Pawling, New York 12564

NOTE: This biography supersedes the article that appeared in *Current Biography* in 1946.

Perhaps the most influential Protestant clergyman in the United States, the Reverend Norman Vincent Peale has comforted a vast audience of angst-ridden Americans with his upbeat message of self-help through prayer and positive thinking. His famous *The Power of Positive Thinking,* first published in 1952, just before the dawn of the Eisenhower era, is one of the best-selling works in American publishing history. He has written several other best sellers, conducted a newspaper column, edited the inspirational monthly magazine *Guideposts,* broadcast his message over radio and television, and lectured tirelessly.

One of the first clergymen to understand the relationship between religion and psychiatry, Peale began doing pastoral counseling with a psychiatrist during the 1930's. Out of that grew the American Foundation of Religion and Psychiatry, now one of the largest psychiatric outpatient clinics in New York City. At times a controversial figure, Peale has been criticized by intellectuals for oversimplifying religion and for reducing the complexities of theology to pabulum for a midcult audience. To Peale "Christianity is a practical, usable way of life—a clearly defined system of workable formulas and techniques drawn from the Bible." A minister of the Reformed Church in America, he has been pastor of Fifth Avenue's Marble Collegiate Church in New York City since 1932.

The first son of the Reverend Charles Clifford and Anna (DeLaney) Peale, Norman Vincent Peale was born on May 31, 1898 in the rural Ohio town of Bowersville, where his father, a former physician, was then the Methodist pastor. Peale has two brothers, Robert Clifford, a physician, and Leonard, a clergyman. Glenn D. Kittler, writing in *Coronet* (September 1964), described Peale's father as "a quiet, reflective, literate man" and his mother, who was of Irish descent, as "a gregarious, decisive, persuasive woman who kept urging her sons to go out and get involved with life."

Since Methodist circuit ministers were rotated frequently, Peale spent his childhood in several Ohio communities, including Highland, Cincinnati, Greenville, and Bellefontaine. Because preachers' salaries were low, Norman delivered papers, worked in a grocery store, and sold pots and pans from door to door. At Bellefontaine High School he overcame his initial shyness to become a star debater. After he graduated from high school in 1916, he attended Ohio Wesleyan University in Delaware, Ohio. At college he majored in liberal arts, became president of his fraternity, Phi Gamma Delta, served in the students' army training corps until the end of World War I, and was associate editor of the campus newspaper, the *Transcript.* Peale obtained his B.A. degree from Ohio Wesleyan in 1920.

During college Peale was torn between the ministry and a career in journalism and, eventually, politics. He decided on journalism and, after graduation, took a job with the *Morning Republican* in Findlay, Ohio, where his parents had moved while he was in college. After a few months as a cub reporter with the Findlay *Republican,* Peale took a job with the Detroit *Journal,* which is now defunct. Within a year he was disenchanted with the newspaper world and decided to enter the ministry.

Peale began studying at Boston University in the fall of 1921 and was ordained into the Methodist Episcopal Church the following year. Shortly after his ordination he took up the duties of his calling in Berkeley, a small mill town in Rhode Island. Meanwhile he continued his theological studies at Boston University, and in 1924 he received the bachelor of sacred theology and master of arts in social ethics degrees. That year he was appointed minister of a small struggling congregation with forty members in Brooklyn, New York. During his three-year pastorate funds were raised to build a new church, the Kings Highway Methodist Church, which was completed in 1925, and membership in the congregation rose to 900.

In 1927 Peale was called to the University Methodist Church in Syracuse, New York which, although well established, had been poorly attended until Peale began to deliver his dynamic sermons there. After spending five years in upstate New York, Peale accepted an invitation to become pastor of Marble Collegiate Church in, New York City. In order to accept the call, he had to change his denominational affiliation to the Reformed Church in America, popularly called the Dutch Reformed Church. Located in what is now the heart of Manhattan, Marble Collegiate had been founded in 1628 by the Dutch settlers of Nieuw Amsterdam and is said to be the oldest continuous Protestant pastorate in the United States. When Norman Vicent Peale took over its pulpit, the membership of the venerable old church had shrunk to 500, and on the day that he preached his first sermon, only 200 persons attended. As the years passed, however, Peale's fame and his down-to-earth sermons drew overflow crowds to the church, which now has about 4,000 members. Since the 1950's Peale has been able to preach to about 4,000 people each Sunday morning by means of closed-circuit television set up in two rooms of an adjoining building.

Recognizing that he was unequipped to handle the complex psychological problems of the New York parishioners who came to him for guidance, Peale enlisted the aid of a psychiatrist, Dr. Smiley Blanton. At first the two men worked together, but as the caseload increased more staff was added. Their religio-psychiatric clinic, as it was then called, operated out of the basement of Marble Collegiate. In 1951 the clinic was organized into the nonprofit American Foundation of Religion and Psychiatry. Today the interfaith, interracial organization has its headquarters in an office building next door to Marble Collegiate but is no longer affiliated with it. Its large staff of ministers, priests, rabbis, psychiatrists, psychologists, and social workers treat some 600 patients a week, in addition to which there is a training program for pastoral counselors. Dr. Peale remains president of the foundation, which has counseling branches in Harlem, Chicago, and Green Bay, Wisconsin.

Propelled by what he has called "this obsession of mine to reach as many people as I could with the message of Jesus Christ," Peale became one of the country's first religious leaders to recognize the power of the mass media. While still in Syracuse, he had begun lecturing widely and for a time he had a radio show called The Angelus Hour. In 1935 he began a weekly radio program

REV. NORMAN VINCENT PEALE

on NBC called The Art of Living, which was sponsored by the National Council of Churches. By the mid-1950's Peale's radio talks were heard over 125 NBC affiliates and he had an estimated radio audience of 5,000,000. After World War II he began to distribute a weekly four-page leaflet called Guideposts, a kind of spiritual newsletter for businessmen, with unpretentious religious testimonials from clergymen and businessmen. By the 1950's Guideposts had grown to a monthly magazine studded with first-hand accounts from movie stars and other celebrities. It now has approximately 2,000,000 subscribers. Peale, who contributes one article each month, continues to be the editor; his wife, Ruth, has been coeditor since 1957.

In 1937 Peale published his first book, The Art of Living (Abingdon), a volume of short essays on such topics as "How to Live in a Time Like This," "How to Banish Worry," and "Meet Yourself." An appreciative reviewer for the Springfield Republican (June 21, 1937) wrote: "The style and terminology of these essays are such as everyday folks understand, and the subjects interest them." The same common touch was evident in You Can Win (Abingdon, 1939), a collection of essays pointing the way to achieving true success in living by cultivating a personal relationship with God. With Dr. Smiley Blanton, Peale wrote Faith Is the Answer (Abingdon, 1940), which reviewed some of the cases they had successfully treated with their combination of religious and psychiatric therapy. Peale's fourth book, A Guide to Confident Living (Prentice-Hall, 1948), was his first best seller. In A Guide to Confident Living, which went through twenty-five printings in four years, Peale set out to summarize what he had learned during his years of counseling about the interrelationship of fear, worry, guilt, tension, and ill health and the therapeutic effects of applied religion. The Art of Real Happiness (Prentice-Hall, 1950, which used case histories from the Marble Collegiate Church clinic, represented another collaboration with Dr. Blanton.

Peale's experience with psychiatric counseling had convinced him that the key to happiness is the cultivation of a positive attitude, for, as the Bible says, "As a man thinketh, so is he." Using that central idea, he wrote *The Power of Positive Thinking* (Prentice-Hall, 1952), containing chapters with such titles as "I Don't Believe in Defeat," "How to Get People to Like You," and "Expect the Best and Get It." The book received generally friendly reviews, although some critics found its formulas simplistic and its theology shaky. Within a few weeks it appeared on the New York *Times* best-seller list, where it zoomed to the top and stayed for three years, breaking the previous all-time record set by Lloyd Douglas' Biblical novel, *The Robe*, Over the years the book has continued to sell briskly, and its sales have now reached over 3,000,000 copies. The third best-selling inspirational book of all time, ranking behind only the Bible and Charles M. Sheldon's 1897 novel, *In His Steps, The Power of Positive Thinking* has been translated into thirty-three languages. In 1953 Peale recorded excerpts from the phenomenally successful book for RCA Victor, and in 1954 Prentice-Hall published a special abridged version called *The Power of Positive Thinking for Young People.*

In the wake of the success of *The Power of Positive Thinking* came a host of commitments that made Dr. Norman Vincent Peale one of the most sought after clergymen in the United States. From 1952 to 1968 he and his wife appeared on a nationally televised advice program called *What's Your Trouble?* Shortly after the publication of *The Power of Positive Thinking* Peale began to write his newspaper column, "Confident Living," which at the apex of its popularity, appeared in more than 200 newspapers, under the aegis of the Hall Syndicate. When, in 1954, Peale began to conduct a biweekly question-and-answer page for *Look,* the magazine was overwhelmed by an avalanche of reader response that was unprecedented in magazine publishing. In addition to his other commitments, he found time to contribute one article a year to *Reader's Digest* and occasional articles to other magazines.

With fame came criticism as well as praise. Reinhold Niebuhr and other Protestant religious leaders attacked Peale's message as moral pragmatism that watered down traditional doctrines of Protestantism and stressed the materialistic rewards of religion. Others criticized Peale because he seemed to be counseling people to accommodate to existing social conditions rather than urging social reform.

Peale's political views also evoked controversy. A Republican stalwart, he had opposed President Franklin D. Roosevelt and his New Deal during the 1930's, and he served for a time as acting chairman of the Committee for Constitutional Government, an influential and ultra-conservative anti-New Deal lobby. In 1948 he supported first General Douglas MacArthur and then Thomas E. Dewey in the Presidential race, and in 1952 and 1956 he urged the nation to vote Republican. In 1960 he provoked a storm of controversy when he acted as spokesman for a group of 150 Protestant clergymen who questioned whether John F. Kennedy should be elected President because his Roman Catholicism might subject him to pressures from the Vatican. He warned an audience at New York's Mayflower Hotel that "faced with the election of a Catholic, our culture is at stake." But Peale soon withdrew his support from the National Conference of Citizens for Religious Freedom and was warmly commended by Cardinal Cushing of Boston for his action.

A close friend of Richard Nixon since the early 1950's, Peale officiated at the wedding, at Marble Collegiate, of Julie Nixon to David Eisenhower on December 22, 1968. In 1969 Nixon sent Peale to Vietnam as a special envoy, and during the Nixon administration the clergyman often conducted religious services at the White House. Peale has declined to comment on the moral implications of the Watergate scandals, but in an interview with James Conaway of *New York* (May 20, 1974) he defended his continued White House visits by pointing out that "Christ didn't shy away from people in trouble."

Since the publication of *The Power of Positive Thinking*, Peale has written over a dozen books, many of them best sellers. His self-help books include *Inspiring Messages for Daily Living* (Prentice-Hall, 1955), *Stay Alive All Your Life* (Prentice-Hall, 1957), *The Amazing Results of Positive Thinking* (Prentice-Hall, 1959), *The Tough-Minded Optimist* (Prentice-Hall, 1961), *Sin, Sex and Self-Control* (Doubleday, 1965), *The Healing of Sorrow* (Doubleday, 1966), *Enthusiasm Makes the Difference* (Prentice-Hall, 1967), and *You Can If You Think You Can* (Prentice-Hall, 1974). He has written several books about the life of Christ, including *The Coming of the King* (Prentice-Hall, 1956) and *He Was a Child* (Prentice-Hall, 1957), which were written for children and *Jesus of Nazareth* (Prentice-Hall, 1966), which was first published as a pull-out feature in *Look* magazine. Peale is also the author of *Adventures in the Holy Land* (Prentice-Hall, 1963) and *Bible Stories* (Watts, 1973), a retelling of Old and New Testament incidents in modern English. He edited *Sermon on the Mount* with wood engravings by John de Pol for World in 1955 and has edited several volumes of religious testimonials culled from the pages of *Guideposts* magazine. He is also the editor of *Norman Vincent Peale's Treasury of Courage and Confidence* (Doubleday, 1970), an anthology of stories, poems, and quotations to inspire confidence and suggest solutions to common problems.

Another thriving Peale enterprise, the Foundation for Christian Living, had its genesis during World War II, when Ruth Peale organized a committee of volunteers to fill mail requests for her husband's sermons. Then Sermon Publications was organized to handle that activity, and in 1945 the Foundation for Christian Living was established, with Mrs. Peale as president, editor-in-chief, and general secretary. The organization moved its headquarters into a new building in Pawling, New York in 1953 and prospered so quickly that the building had to be enlarged three years later. By the 1960's the Foundation for Christian Living had about ninety employees on its staff and a mailing list of some 300,000 names at its disposal. The foundation continues, on a voluntary contribution basis, to mail out copies of Peale's sermons and inspirational booklets, and it also sells recordings of the standing-room-only sermons he has delivered at Marble Collegiate.

Peale served as a member of the mid-century White House conference on children and youth and the President's commission for the observance of the twenty-fifth anniversary of the U.N. He has been president of the National Temperance Association, the Reformed Church in America (1969-70), and the Protestant Council of New York (1965-69). Peale's awards include several honorary degrees, Freedom Foundation awards (1952-55), the Horatio Alger award (1952), National Salvation Army awards (1956-57), the International Human Relations award of the Dale Carnegie Club International (1958), and the clergyman of the year award of the Religious Foundation of America (1964). In 1941 he served as a technical adviser for the Warner Brothers film *One Foot in Heaven*, about the life of a minister, and in 1963 his own life became the subject of United Artists' *One Man's Way*, which was based on Arthur Gordon's book, *Minister to Millions*, and starred Don Murray. After seeing *One Man's Way*, Peale reportedly said: "The story is accurate in general, although they've put a little icing on the cake."

Norman Vincent Peale and Loretta Ruth Stafford were married on June 20, 1930. Mrs. Peale was named churchwoman of the year in 1969 by the Religious Heritage of America. The Peales have three children; Margaret Ann (Mrs. Paul F. Everett), the wife of a Presbyterian minister; John Stafford, an ordained minister who teaches philosophy at Stratford College, a liberal arts college for women in Danville, Virginia; and Elizabeth Ruth (Mrs. John M. Allen), whose husband is a senior editor at *Reader's Digest*. They have eight grandchildren.

The Peales divide their time between a twelve-room cooperative apartment on Fifth Avenue, which is provided by Marble Collegiate Church, and their sixteen-room home in Pawling, New York. Built in 1830 on land that covers 225 acres, the Pawling residence is equipped with a sauna and indoor swimming pool and is furnished with Norwegian antiques. There Peale and his wife have over the years entertained such neighbors as Thomas E. Dewey and Lowell Thomas at non-alcoholic get-togethers where grape juice is served. Fond of travel, the Peales often vacation in Switzerland, where they enjoy mountain climbing. Dr. Peale has commented that "there's nothing quite so peaceful as going to sleep to the mellifluous sound of mountain cowbells."

Gray-haired and portly, the five-foot-nine inch Peale displays a vigor that belies his seventy-six years. He still keeps up a busy schedule that includes writing, conducting weekly services at Marble Collegiate, and making lecture appear-ances. In the opinion of *Wall Street Journal* reporter Stephen Grover (May 7, 1969), public speaking continues to be Peale's most effective form of communication. "Peering over his glasses at his audience, the . . . minister sometimes has the look of a benign owl," Grover wrote. "Mr. Peale knows how to use his voice, raising it (but rarely to a shout), cutting it to a whisper, laughing one moment and exuding sincerity the next. He can be cornier than Ed Sullivan . . . and he can be completely square." In recent years he has conducted a daily five-minute radio show, and his taped sermons were, as of 1972, broadcast over 200 radio and television stations. Peale is a Rotarian and a Mason and his clubs are the Metropolitan and Union League.

References

Coronet 2:78 S '64
N Y Daily News p44 O 2 '72 por
Newsweek 42:43 D 28 '53 por
Gordon, Arthur. Norman Vincent Peale: Minister to Millions (1958)
Westphal, Clarence. Norman Vincent Peale: Christian Crusader (1964)
Who's Who in America, 1974-75

PERÓN (SOSA), JUAN (DOMINGO)

Oct. 8, 1895- President of Argentina
Address: Quinta Presidencial, Olivos, Provincia de Buenos Aires, Argentina

BULLETIN: Juan Perón died on July 1, 1974.
Obituary: N Y Times p1+ Jl 2 '74

NOTE: This biography supersedes the article that appeared in *Current Biography* in 1944.

In one of the most remarkable political comebacks in modern history, Argentine strongman Juan Perón returned from exile in 1973 and, after a landslide election victory, reassumed the Presidency of the country from which he had been ousted nearly eighteen years earlier. During his previous tenure as President, from 1946 to 1955, Perón exercised virtually dictatorial powers, relying on demagoguery and repression as well as social reform to maintain his enormous hold over Argentina's working masses. During the years he spent in exile, *peronismo* remained a dominant political force in Argentina. Perón exemplifies the Latin American tradition of *caudillos*—strong, semi-dictatorial populists whose power rests more on their captivating personalities than on any clear-cut political philosophy or party.

Juan Domingo Perón Sosa was born on October 8, 1895 in Lobos, a small country town in Buenos Aires province, to Mario Tomás Perón, who was of Italian ancestry, and Juana Sosa de Perón, whose background was Spanish Creole. Accounts differ as to whether his father was a well-to-do landowner or a small farmer. According to Arthur P. Whitaker in *Argentina* (Prentice-

JUAN PERÓN

Hall, 1964), "both sides of the family were middle class and neither was a newcomer to Argentina. . . . Perón's paternal grandfather had been a successful physician. . . . Whether from bad luck or bad management, however, Juan's father met with no success in a migratory life that took him from the banks of the Plata to sheep-raising Patagonia and back again to . . . the province of Buenos Aires. Young Juan thus grew up in an atmosphere of insecurity on the fringe of the rural middle class, sharing the resentment against the established order that runs through the pseudo-gaucho poem *Martin Fierro* . . . which he later . . . cited time and again in his public addresses."

Perón attended the Colegio Internacional de Olivos and the Colegio Internacional Politécnica. At fifteen he entered the Colegio Militar de la Nación, Argentina's military academy, from which he graduated with a commission as a sublieutenant of the infantry in 1913. In 1924 he graduated from the Sargento Cabral officers' school with the rank of captain, and from 1926 to 1930 he was a staff officer with the operations division while taking advanced training at the Escuela Superior de Guerra. In 1930 he played a minor role in the coup that toppled the democratically elected President Hipólito Irigoyen. From 1930 to 1936 Perón was a professor of military history at the Escuela Superior de Guerra, serving concurrently as private secretary to the Minister of War and as aide-de-camp to senior officers. During that period he wrote several books on military history and strategy.

Perón was sent to Chile in 1936 as military attaché in the Argentine Embassy in Santiago, but he was, according to some accounts, expelled from that country in 1938 for espionage. From 1939 to 1941 he headed a special military mission that visited European countries and spent some time in Italy, where he studied the tactics of mountain and ski warfare and became a fervent admirer of Mussolini and Hitler.

Returning from Europe in 1941, Perón, now a colonel, was placed in charge of training ski troops as commandant of a mountain detachment in Mendoza. Soon thereafter, he joined a cabal of right-wing officers known as Grupo de Oficiales Unidos (GOU), who sympathized with the fascist powers and hoped that Argentina would become predominant in Latin America. Perón's rapid rise to power began in June 1943, when he played a key role in the coup that deposed President Ramón Castillo. In the next government, headed by General Pedro Pablo Ramírez, he became undersecretary of war and chief of staff of the first army division. More important, however, was his appointment as director of the moribund National Department of Labor which he transformed into the powerful Secretariat of Welfare and Labor.

Aware that Argentina was changing from an agricultural to an industrial society and that the new working classes represented an untapped political force, Perón used his position as head of the labor secretariat to win a large and devoted following among the workers, whom he affectionately called *descamisados*, or "shirtless ones." He enacted measures bringing them such benefits as wage increases, bonuses, social security, and low-cost housing and established control over the labor unions, which he forged into powerful organizations loyal to him. As his power base grew, so did his political influence. By February 1944 he was sufficiently in control to force the resignation of Ramírez and the installation of General Edelmiro Farrell.

While Farrell was President, Perón, as Secretary of Labor and Welfare, Minister of War, and Vice-President, held the real power. But as he steered Argentina toward a corporate state, both domestic and foreign opposition grew. The Allied powers were dismayed by Argentina's pro-Axis stand and by Perón's anti-American statements. His rivals in the military resented his growing popularity, and Argentina's industrial and commercial interests assailed Perón's "social agitation."

The power struggle climaxed in October 1945, when generals opposed to Perón forced his resignation and jailed him. At that moment, Perón's strategy of courting labor produced its most dramatic result. Hearing of his imprisonment, hundreds of thousands of workers—Perón's loyal *descamisados*—staged a peaceful invasion of Buenos Aires. Frightened by the show of force, the generals released Perón. Not long after that, he married the young actress María Eva Duarte—popularly known as "Evita"—who had helped to rally the workers to his defense, and who soon shared his popularity.

In February 1946 Perón was formally elected to succeed Farrell as President, defeating his liberal opponent, José P. Tamborino, representing the Democratic Union, by a vote of 1,474,000 to 1,207,000. In the beginning, Perón—who had assumed the rank of brigadier general in 1946—was fairly successful. Argentina's coffers were filled with currency earned by exporting foodstuffs during World War II. Workers were given important benefits, such as the forty-hour week, paid vacations, and retirement pensions. Banks, railroads, and basic utilities were nationalized, and tens of thousands of public works projects were constructed. Through her government-financed Eva Perón Foundation, which had exclusive control of all charitable activities, Evita channeled some $10,000,000 a year into social benefits. An unprecedented number of small consumer industries were established to promote economic self-sufficiency. Women won the right to vote. The balance of political power in Argentina shifted, with the workers becoming an important force for the first time. Perón called his movement and his amorphous philosophy "*justicialismo,*" which he defined as a "middle way" between capitalism and Communism. To ensure his continued control, in 1949 Perón persuaded his rubber-stamp Congress to rewrite the Constitution to permit presidents to succeed themselves. In the national elections of November 1951 he was handily reelected to the Presidency by a two-to-one margin.

But the first years of the Perón regime sowed the seeds of the chaos that followed. The outpouring of government spending led to inflation. Corruption flourished, the treasury was depleted, and nationalized industries stagnated. Invoking national security, Perón stepped up his dictatorial repressions, establishing control over the judiciary, imposing censorship on the press, jailing dissenters, and smothering opposition in the trade unions, the political parties, and the universities.

As Juan and Eva Perón consolidated their hold on Argentina's masses, schoolchildren were taught to venerate them as if they were saints: the countryside bristled with statues of the Peróns, and public squares and railroad stations bore their names. The Peróns did little to discourage such iconographic adulation. Evita said of her husband: "He is God for us; . . . we cannot conceive of heaven without Perón. He is our sun, our air, our water, our life." As the passionate defender of women and of the poor, Eva Perón was—and still is—revered as a saint by Peronists, and after she died of cancer in 1952 the regime seemed to lose considerable direction and force.

Although during his second term Perón belatedly tried to save the economy by introducing anti-inflationary austerity measures and encouraging greater agricultural production, by 1955 opposition to his regime had crystallized. Large segments of the population, including the powerful land-owning class, the liberal political parties, the students, and much of the military, were aligned against him. By such actions as ending religious instruction in schools and legalizing divorce, Perón alienated the Roman Catholic Church, and his excommunication in June 1955 heralded his downfall. Finally, on September 16, 1955 a military revolt erupted. Three days later he resigned the Presidency and fled the country on a Paraguayan gunboat.

For the next five years Perón lived successively in Paraguay, Nicaragua, Panama, Venezuela, and the Dominican Republic before settling in Madrid in 1960. In Argentina the military did its best to obliterate his influence. The Peronist party was outlawed, many of its leaders were jailed, and statues of Perón were toppled. Meanwhile, Perón kept in touch with his supporters in Argentina from his luxurious villa in Madrid and continued to enjoy the loyalty of a large segment of the population. About the succession of civilian and military regimes that governed Argentina in the late 1950's and the 1960's, Perón has remarked: "It was not that we were so good, but those who followed us were so bad that they made us seem better than we were."

In 1966 General Juan Carlos Onganía wrested power from a struggling civilian president and embarked on yet another attempt to bring about order and progress by means of a harsh dictatorship. He cracked down on the Peronists and other dissenters, but his main achievement was to drive the opposition underground. Onganía was ousted in 1970 and replaced by General Roberto Lévingston; he, in turn, yielded a year later to General Alejandro Lanusse, who had once been imprisoned by Perón. Convinced that the only solution for Argentina lay in a return to civilian government with the full participation of the Peronists, Lanusse began long-distance negotiations with Perón, who still held sway over the single most potent political faction in Argentina. Lanusse, who hoped to gain Perón's endorsement of the elections, while finding a way to keep the Peronists from gaining control, agreed to remove the obstacles that had prevented his return to Argentina and vacated a long-standing charge of treason against him. In January 1972 Perón's Justicialist party was officially recognized as a legal political party.

Perón's long-trumpeted return to Argentina, on November 17, 1972, proved an anticlimax. He met with leaders of political factions and organized a coalition, the Frente Justicialista de Liberación, or Frejuli, around his Justicialist party, but he did not try to return to power or to overcome the residency requirement that the Lanusse government had imposed to prevent him from becoming a candidate in the coming presidential election. On December 14, 1972, four weeks after his arrival, Perón left Argentina. Two days later he sent a message to the Frejuli party congress, designating as his choice for presidential candidate Héctor Cámpora, a colorless figure whose only claim to distinction was his total loyalty to Perón.

In a relatively dull campaign, centering on the Frejuli slogan "Cámpora in government, Perón in power," Cámpora presented the Peronists as the only effective alternative to the military government. Juan Perón directed the presidential campaign from Spain, issuing statements calculated to irritate the military and to forge unity among the various segments of the motley Peronist movement, which had expanded to include most students and much of the middle class. Peronism now encompassed groups ranging from the extreme left to the far right, and many moderates viewed Perón as the only man capable of bringing unity and peace to Argentina.

In the elections on March 11, 1973 Cámpora received a plurality of 49.6 percent of the vote in a field of nine candidates. Inaugurated on May 25, Cámpora fulfilled Peronist promises, including the establishment of diplomatic relations with Cuba and the release of political prisoners. But Cámpora seemed impotent to cope with the country's economic woes or with the incendiary violence of urban guerrillas of the Trotskyist People's Revolutionary Movement that had spread into the ranks of the Peronist movement itself. Young leftwing Peronists hoped for a rapid socialist revolution, which conservative labor leaders and businessmen wanted to avoid. Violent confrontations multiplied, the worst erupting on June 20, when Perón made his second return to Argentina. More than a million people gathered to greet him but gunfire broke out between rival factions, leaving many dead. Shocked by the incident, Perón retired from public view for more than three weeks.

Cámpora suddenly announced his resignation on July 13, 1973, clearing the way for Perón himself to run for the presidency. In a nationwide television address that same day, Perón declared: "If God gives me health . . . , I will spend the last effort of my life to complete the mission that could be entrusted to me. . . . For me this is a tremendous sacrifice . . . because the years have not passed in vain." As his vice-presidential running mate, Perón chose his present wife, Isabel, whom he had tried to groom in the image of Evita. On September 23 Perón was elected President, winning 62 percent of the vote in a four-way race, in which his nearest rival, Ricardo Balbin of the Radical party received 24.5 percent. In a simple inauguration ceremony, on October 12, 1973 Perón took over the Presidency from Raúl Lastiri, who had acted as interim President since Cámpora's resignation.

The most serious problem facing Perón has been the continuing political violence. Within the three weeks following his election, four Peronist union leaders were assassinated, including José Rucci, the head of the powerful General Confederation of Labor. A wave of kidnappings of foreign businessmen culminated in the gunning down, in November, of an executive of the Ford Motor Company. Perón's attempts to purge the leftist elements in his movement not only failed to mitigate the violence but disenchanted many of his youthful followers, who felt that he had abandoned his revolutionary goals.

Nevertheless, many observers agree that Perón took power at a fairly auspicious time. By mid-1973 Argentine exports were on the upswing, and inflation had begun to decline. The powerful anti-Perón military had been eclipsed, during Cámpora's term. Determined to make Argentina more independent, both economically and politically, Perón plans to end what he sees as American domination by relying more on Europe for financial and technical aid, and he visualizes Argentina as a leader of non-aligned nations. In December 1973 Perón announced a far-reaching three-year economic program aimed at nearly doubling the economic growth rate and "recovering economic independence by demolishing foreign financial, technological, and commercial control" over the Argentine economy.

Juan Perón was first married in 1925 to Aurelia Tizón, who died of cancer in 1938. His third wife, the former María Isabel Martínez, has failed to rival the popularity of Evita. A former cabaret dancer, thirty-five years his junior, "Isabelita" met Perón during his exile in Panama, and they were married in Madrid in 1961. Perón stands slightly over six feet tall, weighs about 200 pounds, and has black hair that he touches up with dye. The power and charm that marked his rise to prominence have remained with him. Although in poor health, he is, according to the New York *Times* (July 14, 1973) "still a commanding figure of a man. His smile is still dazzling. His physique is that of a retired athlete. . . . He looks the part of a leader.'"

References

Ferns, H. S. Argentina (1969)
Luna, Felix. De Perón a Lanusse (1973)
Scobie, James R. Argentina (1971)
Whitaker, Arthur P. Argentina (1964)

PINOCHET UGARTE, AUGUSTO (pē-nō-chet')

Nov. 25, 1915- Chilean chief of state; army commander
Address: b. Santiago, Chile; h. Laura Neves 128, Las Condes, Santiago, Chile

On September 11, 1973 General Augusto Pinochet Ugarte, commander in chief of the Chilean army, led a four-man military junta in a bloody coup that resulted in the death of Marxist President Salvador Allende, ending his experimental attempt to lead Chile down "the democratic road to socialism." A career army officer, Pinochet—who assumed full power as chief of state in June 1974—has emerged as a strict authoritarian, determined to rid the country of all vestiges of Marxism. Although Chile's military government, during its first year in power, made some headway toward ending the political strife and economic chaos that had bedeviled the country during the Allende government, the atmosphere remains shrouded in repression and austerity. Under Pinochet, Chileans have little hope that they will return to their traditional democratic constitutionalism in the foreseeable future.

Augusto Pinochet Ugarte, whose ancestors came from Brittany, was born on November 25, 1915 in Valparaiso, Chile, the son of Augusto and Avelina Pinochet. Like most members of Chile's officer corps, he comes from the upper middle class. Educated in local schools, he entered the Escuela Militar, Chile's military academy, in Santiago, at eighteen and graduated with the rank of *alférez*, or second lieutenant, in the infantry in 1936. According to one authoritative source, he also spent two years at the University of Chile in Santiago, studying law and the social sciences.

Early in his military career, Pinochet served as an instructor at the Escuela Militar. In 1942 he attained the rank of *teniente,* or first lieutenant, and in 1946 he advanced to captain. The following year he was assigned to the garrison in Iquique in the desolate north of Chile. He returned to Santiago in 1949 to attend the Academia de Guerra, or War College, and completed his course of study there in 1952. Promoted to major in 1953, he was then assigned to the Rancagua regiment in Arica. In 1954 he joined the staff of the Academia de Guerra as a professor, teaching geography and artillery courses, and the next year he served as adjutant at the undersecretariat of war. During 1956 Pinochet spent some time in Washington, D.C. as a military attaché to the Chilean Embassy and also served in Quito, Ecuador as a member of his country's military mission. In 1961 he was appointed commander of the Seventh Infantry ("Esmerelda") Regiment in Antofagasta. He returned to the Academia de Guerra in 1964 as assistant director and professor of geopolitics and military geography. Fellow officers who knew him during the 1950's or 1960's remember him as a relatively colorless, conservative officer who, in keeping with the tradition of the Chilean military, remained aloof from politics. According to the New York *Times* (September 15, 1973), they also respected him as "intelligent, ambitious, and professionally competent."

Under the reformist government of Christian Democratic President Eduardo Frei Montalva, who took office in 1964, Pinochet continued to scale the military ladder. He was promoted to colonel in 1966 and became a brigadier general in 1968, the year he was appointed interim commander in chief of the First Army Division at Iquique. In 1965, 1968, and 1972 Pinochet visited the schools of the United States Southern Command in the Panama Canal Zone—where, among other subjects, counter-insurgency tactics are taught. During 1968 he also made an official tour of the United States.

By 1970 Frei's reforms had raised expectations and sharpened political consciousness, but had failed to satisfy most Chileans. In the Presidential elections in September of that year, the Christian Democrats and the rightist National party lost to the Popular Unity movement, a five-party leftist coalition. Its candidate, Dr. Salvador Allende Gossens, a Socialist, who proclaimed his intention to bring socialism to Chile, won a narrow plurality, with 36.3 percent of the vote, and became the hemisphere's first freely elected Marxist President. He was inaugurated on November 4, 1970.

Within a year after Allende's election, the Chilean government had nationalized most mining operations—including the mammoth American-owned copper mines that provided the country with most of its foreign exchange—as well as many other industries, banks, and large farms. In many cases, farms and factories were taken over by workers or peasants. Whether as a result of government blunders or the implacable opposition of the anti-Allende interests and the United States, inflation skyrocketed, industrial and agricultural production dropped, and critical food shortages developed.

AUGUSTO PINOCHET UGARTE

During the Allende years Pinochet served in various key army command posts in the Santiago area, including that of commanding general of the Santiago army garrison. It was in the latter post that he first won public attention. When rioting between pro- and anti-Allende groups in December 1971 caused the President to declare a state of emergency in the capital, Pinochet instituted a curfew, ordered over 100 arrests, and announced: "I hope the army will not have to come out, because if it does, it will be to kill." A few days later he temporarily closed the right-wing paper *Tribuna* for "insulting the military." He insisted at the time that "coups do not occur in Chile."

By mid-1972 Chile's economic and political situation was desperate. A middle-class strike in October and November, begun by truck drivers and ultimately embracing nearly the entire professional and mercantile sectors, almost sparked a civil war. To resolve the crisis, Allende brought several military men into his Cabinet in November, including General Carlos Prats Gonzalez, who became Minister of the Interior. Pinochet temporarily replaced Prats as commander in chief of the army. The move polarized the Chilean military into pro- and anti-Allende factions, ending its long-standing policy of noninvolvement in politics.

Opposition leaders hoped to win the two-thirds parliamentary majority that would enable them to impeach Allende, but in the March 1973 congressional elections Popular Unity received 43.4 percent of the vote. That result reinforced the widely held view that only a coup could remove Allende from the scene. In late June part of the military, sponsored by extreme right-wing forces, attempted an anti-Allende revolt. It was, however, suppressed by troops loyal to the government.

In July 1973 the truckers capped a series of debilitating work stoppages by resuming their strike and effectively throttling commerce. On August 9, in a last-ditch effort to placate the opposition, Allende again brought military men into the government and named Prats Defense Minister. But anti-Allende factions in the military forced Prats to resign his command and his

Cabinet post two weeks later. Pinochet, who had been serving as chief of staff, or second in command, of the army since 1972, was appointed commander in chief by Allende on August 24, 1973. Prats had reportedly assured Allende that he could depend on Pinochet, and although in the days preceding the coup some of the President's supporters tried to warn him that the general stood with the opposition, they apparently failed to convince him.

The stage was thus set for the military coup which, as Pinochet later revealed, had been in preparation since mid-1972. "I don't think even my wife knew of the planned coup," he later told reporters. On September 5 Pinochet held secret talks with the other members of the junta—air force chief General Gustavo Leigh, Admiral José Toribio Merino of the navy, and national police chief General Cesar Mendoza. Four days later the commanders made the irrevocable decision to overthrow Allende.

Even by Latin American standards, the coup was an extremely violent one. It began in the early morning hours of September 11, 1973, when navy units seized the port of Valparaiso. At La Moneda, the Presidential palace in Santiago, Pinochet gave Allende the ultimatum to surrender or face attack. After Allende refused, the palace was bombed, strafed, and shelled by tanks. In the afternoon infantrymen entered La Moneda and found Allende dead. According to the junta, the President committed suicide to avoid surrender. Others, including Allende's widow, have claimed that he was killed by the military insurgents.

To their own surprise, the military were in control of Chile by the end of the day, although bitter resistance by Allende supporters continued for some time. A twenty-four hour curfew was imposed, and soldiers warned that violators would be shot on sight. On September 13 General Pinochet was named president of the junta, an office that was to rotate among its four members, according to the original plan. He swore in a fifteen-man Cabinet that included ten military men.

One of the junta's first acts was to break off relations with Cuba, and to announce that some 14,000 leftist exiles in Chile would be tried or expelled from the country. In the days that followed, Allende supporters were rounded up and jailed or executed. A new constitution, giving a major role to the military, was promulgated by decree. The junta suspended civil rights, imposed heavy censorship, purged the universities, outlawed the Marxist political parties, placed all other parties in "indefinite recess," and abolished the country's largest labor confederation. Xenophobia was encouraged by the junta, and rightists blamed "foreign subversives" and Jews for Chile's plight.

Claiming to have found evidence of an Allende-supported "Plan Zeta" to assassinate military commanders and opposition leaders, members of the junta asserted that their takeover had been intended "to restore institutional normality" in Chile and to "stop a disastrous dictatorship from installing itself." Lashing out at "mentally deranged" Chileans who continued to resist the new govern-

ment, Pinochet declared, a few days after the coup: "I am not a murderer, but if people insist on fighting, we will act as we do in time of war." He described his government as "a junta of old generals without ambitions" and "men without a future who can bring a future," and he pledged that "democratic normality" would eventually return to the country.

Pinochet has emphatically denied that the United States had intervened to bring the junta to power, declaring that "the armed forces. . . . of Chile, with a pure tradition of respect for legitimate authority, will never accept foreign intrusion." (It was later revealed that, in addition to imposing economic sanctions, such as an "invisible blockade" that virtually isolated Chile's socialist government from the world money market, the United States government had authorized its Central Intelligence Agency to spend millions of dollars to "destabilize" the Allende regime.) On September 24, 1973 the United States granted full recognition to the Chilean junta.

In the months that followed, the junta moved to desocialize the economy and restore the "free market." Although some legally expropriated businesses remained under government control and parts of Allende's land reform program were continued, some 300 companies, including forty that had been under American ownership were returned to their former owners. Compensation was promised to United States companies for the copper mines that had been expropriated by the Allende government. Prices were allowed to rise to their natural levels while wages were held down, a move that eased shortages but placed a severe burden on the working class. Foreign investments were encouraged by the junta, and credit from abroad was again made available to Chile.

Whatever stability had been achieved by the junta during its early months in power was obtained at an enormous human cost. Estimates of the number of persons who died in the coup and its aftermath range from several hundred to as many as 20,000. Roman Catholic sources placed the number of political prisoners that were still being held by the junta at the end of 1973 at 10,000. According to various respected sources, including Amnesty International, the International Commission of Jurists, and the human rights commission of the Organization of American States, the torture of leftist prisoners was widespread, although Pinochet reportedly repudiated its use.

At first most members of Chile's powerful middle class backed the junta. But as it became clear that long-term repression was in store, and that the generals envisioned a corporate, technocratic, apolitical state resembling those in Spain or Brazil, opposition surfaced. In February 1974 the Christian Democratic leaders criticized the junta for "deeds that amount to a denial of justice and a grave violation of human rights." As reported by the New York Times (April 25, 1974) the Roman Catholic bishops of Chile accused the junta of "the use of torture, arbitrary and lengthy detentions, of causing large scale unemployment, of making job dismissals for political reasons, and of establishing an economic policy that . . . shifted the burden to the poor."

The first major shakeup in Chile's military government came on June 26, 1974, when Pinochet assumed sole power as "supreme chief of the nation," while the other junta members were relegated to subordinate roles as "a sort of legislative body." Explaining the move, a government spokesman said: "History has shown that collective leaderships simply do not work. We need one-man rule." The editors of the the New York *Times,* who had observed earlier that Pinochet seemed to favor a Gaullist type of government, rather than more extreme forms of authoritarianism, greeted the change in the Chilean government with guarded optimism in their editorial of June 27, 1974. They noted that Pinochet, alone among the junta leaders, had promised to preserve gains made by workers under Allende, that he showed some sensitivity to world opinion, and that he had established a dialogue with church leaders.

Addressing a crowd of several thousand Chileans in Santiago on September 11, 1974, the first anniversary of the coup, Pinochet offered to free most political prisoners, provided they agreed to leave the country, and challenged Cuba and the Soviet Union to free an equal number of prisoners. To alleviate the burdens of the working class, he promised that wages would be adjusted quarterly to increased living costs. He asserted that continued police surveillance of farms, factories, and schools was necessary "to provide tranquillity to the citizenry." Ruling out any early return to democratic government, Pinochet declared: "The recess for political parties must continue for several more years and can only be responsibly lifted when a new generation of Chileans, with healthy civic and patriotic habits, can take over the leadership in public life."

General Augusto Pinochet Ugarte and his wife, the former Lucia Hiriart (or Hieriarte) Rodriguez, who is of French Basque ancestry, have two sons and three daughters. The general, who speaks some French and English, is about six feet tall and of husky build, with graying hair, a military stiffness in his bearing, and a thin mustache. Although toughness, discipline, and energy are the qualities most often attributed to him, he is also said to have a sense of humor. His vehement anti-Communism has not prevented him from expressing admiration for the work of the late Pablo Neruda, Chile's Nobel Prize-winning Marxist poet. A member of the geographical society of Chile, Pinochet is the author of several books, including a standard text on the geography of Chile, a study of Latin American geopolitics, and a history of the War of the Pacific of 1879. His decorations include Colombia's Order of Merit and Chile's Star of Military Merit. He is a practising Roman Catholic.

References

N Y Times p13 S 15 '73 por
Time 102:38 S 24 '73 por
Diccionario biográfico de Chile, 1968-70

POMEROY, WARDELL B(AXTER)

Dec. 6, 1913- Psychotherapist; research psychologist
Address: 215 E. 68th St., New York 10021

A pioneer in the emancipation of Americans from the strictures of Victorian sexual attitudes, Dr. Wardell B. Pomeroy was a close associate of the late Dr. Alfred C. Kinsey during the 1940's and 1950's. With Kinsey he took thousands of sex histories from Americans in all walks of life, and he was a coauthor of the landmark studies *Sexual Behavior of the Human Male* (1948) and *Sexual Behavior of the Human Female* (1953), which became famous worldwide as the Kinsey Reports. After Kinsey's death in 1956, Pomeroy remained at Indiana University's Institute for Sex Research, familiarly known as the Kinsey Institute, as director of field research until 1963. Since that time he has practiced psychotherapy and marriage counseling in New York City. Pomeroy has written several books on sex education for children and their parents, and he is the author of *Dr. Kinsey and the Institute for Sex Research* (1972), an intimate account of Kinsey and his work.

Wardell Baxter Pomeroy was born in Kalamazoo, Michigan on December 6, 1913 to Percy Wardell Pomeroy, a patent attorney, and Mary Adelia (Baxter) Pomeroy. He has one sister, Vivian Ryan, who now resides in Tampa, Florida. Pomeroy grew up in South Bend, Indiana, where he attended South Bend Central High School, was active in sports, and worked at the local YMCA. After graduating in 1931 he attended Indiana University in Bloomington, where he met Dr. C. M. Louttit, a clinical psychologist who persuaded him to study psychology. Pomeroy obtained his B.A. degree in 1935. While pursuing his graduate studies in clinical psychology at Indiana University, Pomeroy worked in 1938-39 as a Department of Welfare clinical psychologist at the Mental Hygiene Clinic in South Bend. In 1940-41 he was a clinical psychologist at the Indiana Reformatory in Pendleton, where he gathered material for his master's thesis, entitled "Personality Factors in Mentally Superior Felons." He was awarded the M.A. degree in 1941. That same year he returned to South Bend and began working full time in the personnel department of the United States Rubber Company. In the evenings he moonlighted at the Mental Hygiene Clinic as a psychologist. While he was working in South Bend, Pomeroy became acquainted with Dr. Alfred C. Kinsey, an Indiana University biology professor who had begun teaching a course in sex and marriage in 1937. Appalled by the lack of scientific knowledge that was then available on sex, Kinsey decided in the late 1930's to launch the sex survey that was to make him world famous.

During his years as a student at Indiana University, Pomeroy had encountered Kinsey casually from time to time, but the two men had no meaningful contact until 1941, when Kinsey delivered

WARDELL B. POMEROY

a lecture on sex and prisons to an organization of social workers at South Bend. Impressed with Kinsey's knowledge of his subject, Pomeroy spoke to him after the speech and was persuaded to give him his sex history. In his book *Dr. Kinsey and the Institute for Sex Research* Pomeroy recalled: "I found myself telling him things I had never dreamed of telling anyone else. Occasionally, as he deftly and persistently questioned me, I hesitated a moment, but then I said to myself, 'Of course. I must.' When we were finished, Kinsey told me he was impressed by my attitudes about sex. I appeared to be relaxed, he said, and without fear or unwarranted modesty."

Pomeroy remained in contact with Kinsey, who eventually offered him a job as an interviewer. To meet Kinsey's exacting criteria, a prospective interviewer had to be happily married but free to travel extensively; he was required to hold a doctorate in a science related to the subject matter under study, and at the same time to have the ability to communicate with all classes of people; and he had to be American-born and brought up according to American mores but open-minded about sex. Pomeroy did not strictly meet the second requirement, and therefore, at Kinsey's insistence he embarked on a program of advanced graduate work. Although he did not complete his doctoral program until 1954, when he was awarded a Ph.D. degree in psychology at Columbia University after submitting a dissertation entitled "Sex Before and After Psychosurgery," he was hired as a full-time staff member of Kinsey's study group in early 1943.

Along with researchers Paul H. Gebhard and Clyde E. Martin, Pomeroy became a senior member of the Kinsey team, which was formally incorporated as the Institute for Sex Research in April 1947. "Looking back, I think I was more intense temperamentally and more extroverted than the others," Pomeroy wrote in *Dr. Kinsey and the Institute for Sex Research.* "I was less scholarly than Paul, and less esthetic than Clyde, but more interested in human contacts and inter-

reactions than either." Officially, Pomeroy's title was that of research associate, but he has recalled that actually the coworkers were like a family, with Kinsey as the father figure. "We were working for a genius who maddened us, delighted us, drove us to the point of exhaustion, but most of all inspired us to share something of his total dedication," he wrote. During his years with Kinsey, Pomeroy shared with him responsibility for the bulk of the interviewing. Of the 18,000 in-depth interviews that were ultimately recorded, they each did about 8,000, with the remaining 2,000 divided up among other interviewers. Concurrently with his work for Kinsey, Pomeroy also taught for a time at Indiana University.

The effectiveness of the interviewer in obtaining a subject's sex history was central to the success of Kinsey's research. From a relatively short series of questions that he began asking college students during the late 1930's, Kinsey evolved a systematic coverage of from 350 to 521 items, with even more questions added if the subject warranted it. The typical interview lasted from one-and-a-half to two hours. To put the subject at ease, the interviewer would at the outset show how all names of interviewees and answers to questions were recorded in a code that prevented unauthorized persons from reading them. The early questions in the interview covered such non-threatening subjects as the patient's age, birthplace, and education. Then the interviewer would go on to questions about the subject's marriage, early sex education, age at puberty, and age at first orgasm. Only after those areas were completed would the interviewer proceed to such subjects as nocturnal sex dreams, masturbation, heterosexual petting and intercourse, homosexual experiences, and contact with animals.

The sex researchers devised a number of ways to assure the accuracy of their histories. One method was the cross check. For example, before an interviewee was asked any direct questions about homosexuality, he would be required to answer a dozen inquiries that would provide a tip-off to such proclivities to anyone who was psychologically trained. Furthermore, the interviewers phrased their questions in such a way that it was assumed that everyone could have had every type of experience. They encouraged an atmosphere of honesty with their subjects by looking them straight in the eye, asking their questions without apology, and avoiding euphemisms.

Kinsey's *Sexual Behavior in the Human Male,* coauthored by Pomeroy and Clyde E. Martin and published by W. B. Saunders in 1948, was based on the histories of 5,300 white males. (Kinsey had excluded nonwhites because he was not sure of the typicality of his nonwhite subjects.) The book created a sensation with its unprecedentedly frank and complete treatment of sexual behavior. Although written in a serious, scientific manner and aimed at professionals rather than the general public, it became a best seller. It was generally well received by the scientific and professional community, but some experts argued that Kinsey's sample was not representative enough. A number of critics of the book faulted it on nonscientific grounds, claiming that Kinsey ignored the phenomenon of "love," that he saw human beings as animals, and that he was contributing to the breakdown of morality by reporting the nonconformist sexual behavior of certain portions of the population.

Nevertheless, Kinsey's name became a byword in American homes, and anticipation mounted for the publication of his next report, *Sexual Behavior of the Human Female* (Saunders 1953). Written by Kinsey, Pomeroy, Martin, and Paul H. Gebhard, it was based on the histories of 5,940 white American women. Like the book on the male, Kinsey's best-selling report on the American female received generally favorable comments from experts, but it was condemned even more vehemently by church groups and others who claimed to uphold the public morality. The virulence of the attacks on the study could be attributed to its shattering of the Victorian myth of female chastity. For example, Kinsey found that two-thirds of the women interviewed reported that they had experienced orgasm in some manner before marriage.

In the years since the Kinsey Reports first appeared, scientists have continued to argue over the Indiana biologist's methodology. Many social scientists, for example, now believe that empirical studies like Kinsey's are outmoded. Argument also continues over the reliability of his statistics, although most experts agree that whatever the shortcomings of his data, it remains the best sampling ever taken of human sexual behavior. Few scientists, however, debate the validity of Kinsey's major findings. As Dr. Pomeroy wrote in *Dr. Kinsey and the Institute for Sex Research*, "In retrospect, the controversy over the two Kinsey Reports seems slightly incredible. Harmful to youth? The present generation would consider their conclusions old-fashioned in the climate of freedom which now prevails. Shocking to the general public? How unmoved would a much larger part of that public be today, when nudity, four-letter words, explicit sexual situations and utterly frank discussion of sex are the characteristic of every medium of communication except newspapers and television. Debatable in its conclusions? They are nearly all accepted as a matter of course now, and Masters and Johnson have gone on to break new grounds of controversy and knowledge."

Despite history's vindication of Kinsey's work, the forces of reaction seemed to prevail at the time the reports came out. After the publication of *Sexual Behavior in the Human Female*, puritanical groups began putting pressure on Congress, and early in 1954 Republican Representative B. Carroll Reece of Tennessee formed a House Committee to Investigate Tax-Exempt Foundations. His specific target was the Rockefeller Foundation, the Kinsey Institute's chief backer. Ultimately Reece's investigations were denounced by a majority of the members of his own committee, but in the meantime the Rockefeller Foundation's new president, Dean Rusk, capitulated to the pressure and withdrew the foundation's support for research from the Kinsey Institute.

After the Rockefeller Foundation withdrew its support, in 1954, Kinsey was forced to continue his studies with sharply curtailed funding, relying mainly on book royalties and grants from Indiana University. Exhausted by overwork and financial worries, he died of a heart attack on August 25, 1956, at the age of sixty-two. Kinsey had intended to obtain 100,000 sexual histories; at the time of his death the institute had about 17,500. He left behind plans for nine more studies, including revised and racially more balanced versions of the studies on male and female sexual behavior. Other projects that Kinsey had planned concerned such topics as sex offenders and the law, development of sexual attitudes in children, sexual factors in marital adjustment, institutional sexual adjustments, the heterosexual-homosexual balance, sexual arousal and orgasm, sex education, the erotic element in art, and prostitutes viewed as persons.

After Kinsey's death, the Institute for Sex Research was reorganized, with Paul H. Gebhard as executive director and Pomeroy as director of field research. In 1957 it received a substantial grant from the National Institute for Mental Health, which has continued to support it. During the 1960's the Institute for Sex Research grew by leaps and bounds, and by 1971 it had published at least eight books and over fifty articles and book chapters. In collaboration with Gebhard and others, Pomeroy prepared the statistical studies *Pregnancy, Birth and Abortion* (Harper & Row, 1958) and *Sex Offenders; An Analysis of Types* (Harper & Row, 1965) for the institute.

Meanwhile, in the early 1960's, Pomeroy had become frustrated with the direction the institute was taking in its research techniques. In particular, he was dismayed by the departure from Kinsey's concept of the interview as the prime factor in research and the tendency to place the main emphasis on the analysis of data. A small evening practice that Pomeroy had built up in Indiana convinced him that he would find it more rewarding to be a consulting psychotherapist and marriage counselor than to continue in research. Consequently, in November 1963 he left the institute and moved to New York City. Within eight months he had established a full practice, counseling about thirty couples or individual patients a week. With the help of the professional writer John Tebbel, Pomeroy has written several books, including two informational volumes for teenagers and their parents, *Boys and Sex* (Delacorte, 1968) and *Girls and Sex* (Delacorte, 1970). In the *Saturday Review* (July 1968) J. H. Plumb called the former volume "a remarkable book, clear, sane and realistic about those ineradicable habits of male life that our immediate ancestors viewed with such stern disapproval."

Of Pomeroy's book *Dr. Kinsey and the Institute for Sex Research* (Harper & Row, 1972), P. A. Robinson wrote in the *Atlantic Monthly* (May 1972): "Although an official biography, and a sympathetic one at that, this is also an admirably candid book. No attempt has been made to disguise Kinsey's failings. Pomeroy characterizes him as warm, persuasive, enthusiastic, yet at the same time driven, authoritarian, and totally intolerant of criticism. Above all he emerges as a man of great passion." Pomeroy's most recent book is *Your Child and Sex* (Delacorte, 1974).

Dr. Pomeroy is on the faculty of the American Institute of Psychotherapy and Psychoanalysis and on the staff of Lenox Hill Hospital. He serves as associate attending psychologist of the Payne Whitney Psychiatric Clinic of New York Hospital-Cornell Medical Center. Active in all major professional societies dealing with sex education and marriage counseling, he is a fellow and past president of the American Association of Marriage and Family Counselors and of the Society for the Scientific Study of Sex, and he serves as president of the Sex Information and Education Council of the United States. He is a fellow of the American Psychological Association. Because of his concern about the increasing incidence of unqualified sex therapists practising in the field, he is on the board of directors of the Eastern Academy of Sex Therapists, which is taking steps to remedy that situation. Pomeroy has received the distinguished service award of the Massachusetts chapter of the American Association of Marriage and Family Counselors, the Educational Foundation for Human Sexuality award, and the Society for the Scientific Study of Sex annual award for outstanding contributions to the study of sex. He is a diplomate of the American Board of Examiners in Professional Psychology, a certified psychologist of the State of New York, and a licensed marriage counselor of the State of New Jersey.

Dr. Wardell B. Pomeroy conducts his practice in the study of his East Side Manhattan apartment, which he shares with his wife, the former Martha Catherine Sindlinger, a social worker who is now director of teacher placement of the Teachers College of Columbia University. The Pomeroys were married on September 4, 1937 and have three children, David Wardell, John Eric, and Mary Lynne, and six grandchildren. Pomeroy was married to Frances Wilson Hopkins, his high school sweetheart, from 1931 until her death in 1935. Barbara Yuncker of the New York *Post* (March 30, 1972) described Pomeroy as "a calm, handsome, silver-haired, pipe-smoking, friendly man." He is five feet nine and a half inches tall, weighs 180 pounds, and has gray eyes. His favorite recreations include billiards, correspondence chess, weekly poker sessions, going to the theatre, and vacationing in the Caribbean. He enjoys reading *Playboy*, news magazines, biographies, and professional journals in his field. Pomeroy is an independent in politics and has no church affiliation.

References

N Y Post p39 Mr 30 '72 por
Pomeroy, Wardell B. Dr. Kinsey and the Institute for Sex Research (1972)
Who's Who in America, 1972-73

PORTER, WILLIAM J(AMES)

Sept. 1, 1914- United States Ambassador to Canada
Address: b. Department of State, 2201 C St., N.W., Washington, D.C. 20520

For over thirty-five years William J. Porter, who was named United States Ambassador to Canada in January 1974, has represented his government under a succession of six Presidents in countries where and when world-shaping events were often taking place and crucial steps were being decided upon in the development of American foreign policy. A career diplomat fluent in Arabic, he became a top specialist in Middle East and North African affairs and was serving as Ambassador to Algeria in the mid-1960's when he was somewhat abruptly selected to assume a central role in the United States involvement in Vietnam. First he directed the "pacification" program in South Vietnam and later confronted Communist delegates as chief United States negotiator at the Paris peace talks. Then, as Under Secretary for Political Affairs, he held the third highest position at the Department of State in Washington for about a year before President Richard Nixon chose him for the Ottawa assignment.

A native of England, William James Porter was born on September 1, 1914 in Staleybridge, Cheshire. He is the only child of William and Sarah (Day) Porter, who had him baptized in the Catholic Church of St. Peter's in Staleybridge shortly after his birth. His father, an officer in the Royal Navy, was killed early in World War I. When the boy was two years old, his widowed mother took him to the United States to live with relatives. He attended St. Vincent's Elementary School in Fall River, Massachusetts and later, from 1927 to 1930, Durfee High School, also in Fall River. After graduating, he entered Boston College, where he studied for two years, but meanwhile, in 1931, he enrolled at Thibodeau College of Business Administration in Fall River in a secretarial course that he completed in 1933.

During the Depression years of 1933 to 1936 Porter sold men's clothing in a fashionable haberdashery in Fall River. One of his customers was John F. Montgomery, then the United States Minister to Hungary. After several conversations with the young salesman, who was interested in the Foreign Service and wanted to travel, Montgomery engaged him as his private secretary at the United States Legation in Budapest. Porter, who had become a naturalized United States citizen in March 1936, went to Hungary in the private employ of Montgomery rather than on the government payroll. But the post proved a stepping stone toward his goal, for in 1937 he obtained a Department of State appointment.

With his assignment in July 1937 as a clerk in the American diplomatic mission in Baghdad, Iraq, Porter began to acquire an expertise in Middle East affairs during the turbulent era of political intrigue and espionage just preceding and throughout World War II. In 1941 he was transferred from Baghdad to Beirut, Lebanon, again in the position of clerk, and in 1943 was sent to Damascus, Syria, where he had greater responsibilities, including political reporting and administrative and consular duties. Briefly in 1946 he filled the post of acting Palestine desk officer at the Department of State in Washington. Returning to the Middle East later in that year, he became political officer at the consulate in Jerusalem. He served there during the period of preparation for the partition of Palestine and the build-up of tensions that led to the Israeli-Arab armed conflict after the proclamation of the independent state of Israel in May 1948.

In early 1947, during his tour of duty in Jerusalem, Porter was promoted to Foreign Service officer class five. From that grade he advanced steadily in the Foreign Service over the years, receiving his next promotion in April 1949. He was at that time stationed in Nicosia, Cyprus as principal officer, a post to which he had been transferred in February 1948. Recalled to Washington in the fall of 1950, Porter was next assigned to the State Department's division of international broadcasting and spent several months of the following year in New York as political adviser to the chief of the Voice of America. In November 1951 he began another stint at the department in Washington, this time as officer in charge of Greek affairs.

On his next assignment in the field, Porter went in November 1953 to Rabat, French Morocco, where he became consul general about a year later. When Morocco gained its independence from France in 1956, the United States consulate general in Rabat was elevated to the status of an embassy and Porter was named its counselor and chargé d'affaires. With the appointment of Cavendish W. Cannon as the first American Ambassador to Morocco later that year, Porter took the post of deputy chief of mission. His first important task in Morocco after its liberation from French rule was to help renegotiate with the government the status of United States air bases that had been established in Morocco by agreement with the French in 1950, bases in which the United States had invested $410,000,000. Attesting to his success is the presence in Morocco today of important American communications facilities and other installations.

From 1957 to 1960 Porter directed the office of North African affairs at the department in Washington. Then for eighteen months during 1960 and 1961 he engaged in full-time study of the Arabic language at the Foreign Service Institute, also in Washington. Posted to Algiers in June 1961 he headed the United States mission

WILLIAM J. PORTER

there as principal officer with the personal rank of minister. Once again he had the opportunity to witness the birth of a new North African nation when, in July 1962, the French government proclaimed Algeria an independent state.

Soon afterward, President John F. Kennedy named Porter the United States's first Ambassador to Algeria. The head of the government with which Porter had to deal was the revolutionary hero Ahmed Ben Bella, whose bitter memories of United States-made artillery, trucks, and aircraft used against his Arab nationalist guerrillas by the French army in the war for independence gave his regime a decidedly anti-American tilt. With his fluency in both Arabic and French and his persistent persuasiveness, Porter protected and advanced his country's interests by encouraging among Algerian leaders a policy of nonalignment in regard to the Cold War and directing their attention to Algeria's need for economic aid from the West.

Porter's long involvement in Middle East and North African affairs ended, at least temporarily, in 1965, when instead of assuming the newly assigned post of Ambassador to Saudi Arabia, he became Deputy Ambassador to South Vietnam, reportedly at the request of Ambassador Henry Cabot Lodge. An embassy's second in command is normally called the deputy chief of mission. The unusual post of Deputy United States Ambassador to South Vietnam was created to provide an experienced diplomat to assist Ambassador Maxwell D. Taylor, a retired Army general (whose deputy was U. Alexis Johnson), and later Ambassador Lodge, regarded by official Washington as a specialist more in politics than in diplomacy. The job of the deputy ambassador also was to assure continuity of direction on many occasions when the ambassador was called back to Washington for consultations.

While retaining the title of deputy ambassador, in February 1966, a few months after his arrival in Saigon, Porter was relieved of the routine duties of his office. At that time he was instructed "to take full charge" of the nonmilitary aspects of the United States effort in the Vietnam war, the so-called "pacification" program. The program was designed to win the loyalty of the people of South Vietnam to the government in Saigon by raising their standard of living. Workers in health, education, and agriculture, together with community organizers, were to be trained and installed throughout the country. Before Porter's appointment as chief, pacification efforts were conducted by several different United States agencies—such as the Agency for International Development (AID), the United States Information Agency (USIA), and the Central Intelligence Agency (CIA)—with considerable overlap and duplication of function. Porter's task was to coordinate the efforts of the American agencies while maintaining close association with key South Vietnamese officials in the pacification undertaking.

The columnists Rowland Evans and Robert Novak, writing in the Washington *Post* (June 22, 1966), credited reports from Porter with reinforcing President Lyndon B. Johnson's conviction that a non-Communist Vietnam was obtainable. Ambassador Porter drew on his observations of the genuine nationalism of the uprisings, or insurgencies, in Morocco and Algeria, where rebels had maintained tight discipline and broad control over the population. By contrast, the Viet Cong appeared to Porter to be a false front lacking popular support. Thus, he pointed out, Americans could wander unharmed through South Vietnamese cities, unlike Frenchmen in Algeria during the civil war there. Porter's reports were said to buttress President Johnson's conviction that his government was on the right course and to help pave the way for the escalation of the bombing of North Vietnam.

After Porter had directed the pacification program for eighteen months, the entire operation was transferred from the control of the United States Embassy to that of the Military Assistance Command, Vietnam, General William C. Westmoreland, Commander. Porter, who had opposed earlier attempts to have pacification put under the authority of the military, was reassigned as United States Ambassador to South Korea in May 1967. Summoned from Seoul to Washington, Ambassador Porter was called upon in September 1970 to explain to a subcommittee of the Senate Foreign Relations Committee why the United States had kept secret the amount of more than one billion dollars it had paid during the preceding five years to South Korea to dispatch 50,000 of its troops to fight in South Vietnam. He also had to handle the delicate negotiations attendant upon the withdrawal in 1971 from South Korea of 20,000 American soldiers out of a force of some 60,000.

Apparently impressed by Porter's dexterous and realistic approach in negotiation, President Richard Nixon chose him in the summer of 1971 to replace the ailing veteran Ambassador David K. E. Bruce as chief United States delegate at the peace talks in Paris. The talks were begun in May 1968 by United States and North Vietnam negotiators in an effort to bring about a settlement of the Vietnam war. At the beginning of the following year representatives of the South Vietnamese government and National Liberation Front were admitted to the conference table. Porter, who attended his first Paris session on September 9, 1971, soon introduced a dynamic quality in United States tactics, particularly in counteracting what he considered to be Communist attempts to use the talks as a propaganda forum.

"Porter has a well-deserved reputation as an earthy and adroit negotiator," wrote a *Time* reporter (January 17, 1972), who also reported that the delegate had "totally changed the once patient and restrained U.S. style in Paris—not by negotiating but simply by talking tough." On some occasions he unnerved representatives of the other side by adopting their own ploy of postponing meetings and by replacing gentility with lectures challenging, for instance, Viet Cong claims of popular strength. His role as chief negotiator was to complement the efforts of Henry A. Kissinger, then Presidential adviser on national security affairs, in hammering out the technical details necessary to implement the broad agreements eventually reached between Kissinger and the North Vietnamese negotiator Le Duc Tho. Porter's bold offensive has been credited in part with bringing about the break in the deadlocked negotiations that led to withdrawal of United States troops, return of prisoners of war, and an agreed-upon, if not fully realized, cease-fire.

As part of an intensive overhaul of the Department of State undertaken by President Nixon shortly before beginning his second term in office, William J. Porter was named to succeed U. Alexis Johnson in January 1973 as Under Secretary for Political Affairs. In what is considered the "number three job" in the department he continued to play an influential role in further developments in United States policy toward Indochina. His responsibilities included the overseeing of United States political relations with more than 150 nations and international organizations and presiding over a Foreign Service Officer Corps of approximately 3,000 officers during a period of considerable restructuring and streamlining. His skill as a negotiator was again tested in discussions beginning in the fall of 1973 with Icelandic officials calling for a revision of the 1951 pact permitting United States forces to use the Keflavik air base on behalf of the North Atlantic Treaty Organization.

Certain aspects of United States relations with another Western ally, Canada, also came within Under Secretary Porter's sphere of responsibility. In early January 1974 he was named Ambassador to Canada to replace Adolph W. Schmidt, an appointment that reflected what he called the "deep interest in Canadian-American affairs" of President Nixon and Secretary of State Kissinger.

While in the Middle East during World War II, William J. Porter met Eleanore Henry, of Philadelphia, an Army nurse serving in Cairo. They were married on October 30, 1944 and have a son, William Jr., and a daughter, Eleanor. The Ambassador has been described in the press as a gracious man, but shrewd, tough-talking, and deceptively mild-looking. In recognition of his accomplishments Porter was presented with the Distinguished Honor Award of the Department of State in 1966, the President's Award for Distinguished Federal Service in 1967, and the Vietnam Service Medal in 1968.

References

N Y Times p6 My 17 '67 por; p2 N 12 '71 por
Time 98:20+ Ag 9 '71 por; 99:26+ Ja 17 '72 por
Toronto Globe and Mail p1+ Ja 9 '74 por
Department of State Biographic Register, 1973
International Who's Who, 1973-74
Who's Who in America, 1972-73

JANE POWELL

POWELL, JANE

Apr. 1, 1929- Actress; singer
Address: h. 1364 Stradella Rd., Bel Air, Calif. 90024

When the curtain rose in Broadway's Minskoff Theatre on February 7, 1974, it signaled the triumphal return to public acclaim, after a fairly long absence, of an actress and singer who had once been a popular Hollywood star. That evening Jane Powell took over the title role in a hit revival of the 1919 musical *Irene* from Debbie Reynolds, an old friend and former feature player in Miss Powell's film musicals of the early 1950's. Stereotyped for a decade as the wholesome girl-next-door in a string of frothy MGM comedies, she had nevertheless made a happy transition to adult stardom in the Hollywood movie classic *Seven Brides for Seven Brothers* (1954). During some thirty-five years in show business she worked in radio, films, television, summer stock, nightclubs, and recording studios, but for her Broadway debut she had to await the re-creation of *Irene*.

The daughter of a baby-food salesman, Jane Powell was born Suzanne Burce on April 1, 1929, in Portland, Oregon where her parents, Paul and Eileen Burce, lived in a modest three-room apartment. "We didn't come from the ghetto," Miss Powell recalled to Jan Hodenfield in an interview for the New York *Post* (February 16, 1974), "but we didn't come from a rich family by any means." To help make ends meet, her father also worked as manager of the building in which they lived.

At the age of seven Suzanne began singing on a local children's radio program. Impressed by the quality of her voice even at such a young age, neighbors urged the Burces to enroll her in singing classes. However, it was not until she was eleven that she began to receive professional instruction. Her exceptional singing talents prompted her teacher to introduce her to the manager of radio station KOIN in Portland. Suzanne was soon given her own program and within a year was heard on two local radio shows, singing songs and advertising a jewelry shop. About that time, as Oregon's Victory Girl, she supported the United States war effort by appearing at patriotic rallies and extolling in song the virtues of owning war bonds.

Her career might have stopped there, had it not been for a three-week holiday trip to Southern California with her parents. Two days after arriving in Los Angeles the Burces took their daughter to *Stars Over Hollywood*, a broadcast talent show, and the following week Suzanne made an appearance as one of the program's six contestants. The tiny soprano with a two-and-a-half-octave voice easily won the competition when she sang an aria from *Carmen* that brought the studio audience to its feet applauding and calling for more.

Metro-Goldwyn-Mayer talent scouts were so surprised by the appreciative audience response that they invited Suzanne to the studio for an audition. Shortly afterward she accepted a long-term contract from MGM, a contract unusual at that time because the studio offered it without having her first take a screen test. Although her parents had promised that she could give up acting after a year or two if she wanted, Hollywood quickly became her way of life.

While MGM was looking for an appropriate film in which to launch its new find, Suzanne was loaned to other studios so that she could gain practical, on-the-set experience. In her first film, *Song of the Open Road* (United Artists, 1944), she played a character named Jane Powell, a child star who runs away from home and fortune to live with a band of tomato pickers. The name has been hers ever since. As Jane Powell she led the cast of the musical *Delightfully Dangerous* (United Artists, 1945), in which she seemed to a reviewer for the New York *Times* (June 9, 1945) "a shimmering vision of youth in bloom, . . . sweet and charming—not the least bit cloying."

In 1946 Miss Powell appeared in her first MGM feature, *Holiday in Mexico,* a typical light-hearted Hollywood tale of romantic misadventure south of the border, produced by Joseph Pasternak and also starring Walter Pidgeon, Ilona Massey, and José Iturbi. Another teen-ager in the movie, Roddy McDowall, presented Jane with a photograph inscribed "To My First Screen Flame." Most memorable of Miss Powell's scenes in the film was the "Ave Maria" number, a lavish production described by one critic as "a Eucharistic Congress staged by Billy Rose." Nevertheless, her own notices were favorable enough to result in an upward renegotiation of her contract. On October 26, 1946 the New York *Times* reported that the new MGM agreement guaranteed $750 weekly for a three-year period, with lucrative bonuses and options.

Despite a star's salary and fame, Jane Powell's early days in Hollywood were not completely a dream come true. The MGM school, although filled with famous pupils such as Elizabeth Taylor and Margaret O'Brien, seemed to lack the hometown charm of Grant High School in Portland. According to an article in *Life* magazine (September 9, 1946), when asked about the celebrities of the movie capital's fabled social scene, the seventeen-year-old starlet wistfully commented, "I'm too young for the old ones, and too old for the young ones."

Following *Holiday in Mexico* came another Pasternak opus, *Three Daring Daughters* (1948), a film designed as both a showpiece for Miss Powell and a vehicle for the return to the screen of Jeannette MacDonald after a six-year absence. It was rather mercilessly panned by most critics, with Bosley Crowther of the New York *Times* (February 13, 1948) calling it "silly and schematically disgusting, not to mention downright embarrassing in some of the stickier scenes." However, Miss Powell emerged critically unscathed; her performance as Jeannette MacDonald's eldest daughter even won from Crowther the compliment "attractive and melodious."

The schoolgirl mold imposed on Miss Powell became one that she filled more than adequately in a spate of popular MGM productions during the late 1940's and early 1950's. As the bouncing stowaway daughter of a cruise ship's captain in *Luxury Liner* (1948) she delighted Eileen Creelman of the New York *Sun* (September 10, 1948): "Miss Powell is as expert a comedienne as a soprano." *A Date with Judy* (1948) offered similar routine, innocuous charm, as did *Nancy Goes to Rio* (1950), another Pasternak musical. Next came *Two Weeks with Love* (1950), featuring a newcomer named Debbie Reynolds, who more than two decades later would help Jane Powell reestablish herself as a musical star.

In a remarkable change of type, Miss Powell then costarred with Fred Astaire in *Royal Wedding* (1951). The two played a brother-and-sister dance team that travels to England on the eve of a royal nuptial ceremony. There they mix song and dance with romance as the sister falls in love with an English lord, and the brother with an English chorus girl. In view of the fact that Astaire was one of the screen's most sophisticated entertainers and his leading lady, though twenty-two years old, was playing the first adult role of her career, it would not have been surprising if her performance in *Royal Wedding* had been overshadowed by his seasoned stylishness. Miss Powell, however, handled the role of Ellen Bowen with considerable aplomb. The complementary talents of Miss Powell and Astaire were seen best in a lively song-and-dance duet to a tune reputed to have the longest title of any ever heard in a film musical—"How Could You Believe Me When I Said I Loved You When You Know I've Been a Liar All My Life?"

Under normal circumstances, MGM officials would probably never have considered casting Jane Powell in a role as mature as that of Ellen Bowen. But when both June Allyson and Judy Garland became unavailable, she was called to fill the vacant spot. The maturity of *Royal Wedding* proved not only new-found, but short-lived. Jane Powell returned to the ranks of love-struck bobby-soxers almost immediately. In *Rich, Young and Pretty* (1951), according to a New York *Times* review (July 26, 1951), she was "fetching and cheerful as the Texas miss who is ready to break out into song over Paris and l'amour." She continued in similar roles through *Small Town Girl* (1953) and *Three Sailors and a Girl* (1953) before arriving at another important milestone in her career—*Seven Brides for Seven Brothers.*

When *Seven Brides for Seven Brothers* opened at Radio City Music Hall in late July 1954, it garnered virtually unanimous critical acclaim. Loosely based on Stephen Vincent Benét's folk story "The Sobbin' Women," which was itself inspired by Plutarch's tale "Rape of the Sabine Women," the film combined Gene de Paul and Johnny Mercer's music with Michael Kidd's brilliantly imaginative choreography. Today it is considered by many to be one of the best movie musicals ever produced. Jane Powell played the educated bride of an oafish frontiersman, portrayed by Howard Keel.

A pleasant satire on Southern California health cults, *Athena* (1954) gave Miss Powell the opportunity once again to demonstrate her vocal gifts by singing "Chacun le Sait," a coloratura aria from *La Fille du Régiment.* Another musical of transparent plot and characterization, *Hit the Deck,* a 1955 release, placed her at the head of a cast that included Vic Damone, Debbie Reynolds, Ann Miller, and scores of juvenile singers and dancers as well as many older players on the Metro-Goldwyn-Mayer lot.

Despite her string of commercial successes at MGM, Jane Powell was growing increasingly eager to play more adult parts, roles denied her by the studio head, Louis B. Mayer, who insisted that she play teen-agers long after she had married and become a mother. Faced with the unfulfilling prospect of remaining locked into ingenue portrayals for an indeterminable time at MGM, she made the difficult decision to split from the company after eleven years under contract and try for an independent career. "They kept me the girl next door and nobody thought of me as anything else," she recalled in an interview years later with Rex Reed (New York *Sunday News*, February 10, 1974); ". . . I got frustrated and . . . finally left by mutual agreement. I can't even remember what my last film was at MGM. All of my life seems to have happened to somebody else. I just wish I could have been around to enjoy it. None of it sunk in."

Shortly after her break with Mayer, Jane Powell sang at a Hollywood Bowl concert before a sell-out audience of 20,000. Her first appearance before a live crowd seemed to be the harbinger of a new career as a recording and nightclub star. Once out from under the wing of MGM, however, Miss Powell found it impossible to maintain a star standing. There were a few more films, all of them "terrible," according to Rex Reed. "A silly, crawling little bore" is the way one reviewer described *The Girl Most Likely* (RKO, 1958). That appraisal is fairly typical of the critical response to her last films, which included *Female Animal* (Universal-International, 1958) and *Enchanted Island* (Warner Brothers, 1958). Before long, casting directors just stopped calling. "I didn't quit movies," she laughingly told Rex Reed; "they quit me."

For a few years Miss Powell primarily played supper clubs in New York and Las Vegas. In the spring of 1958 she had a warmly received engagement at the Persian Room of New York's Plaza Hotel, earning rave descriptions of herself as "a lark on the wing" and "scrumptious." During that year she performed as one of five rotating stars on the television suspense series *Goodyear-Alcoa Theatre*. On April 26, 1959 in a CBS-AV adaptation of the movie *Meet Me in St. Louis* she played the role made famous years before by Judy Garland.

Meet Me in St. Louis brought excellent notices for Miss Powell, but did little to better her professional lot. Her television performances remained limited to occasional specials such as *Give My Regards to Broadway* (December 6, 1959) and *Hooray for Love* (October 2, 1960). In the summer of 1963, however, Jane Powell proved that her name still had substantial drawing power, when, starring in *The Unsinkable Molly Brown* at Melodyland Theatre in Anaheim, California, she was credited with establishing the highest gross in summer stock theatre to that date. During a two-week run a total of $177,805 in box-office receipts was recorded. Encouraged by the success of that engagement, she and the producer James Fitzgerald prepared a revue called *Just Twenty—Plus Me*, which they hoped to take to Broadway following out-of-town tryouts. After a tour through Texas, the show's scheduled one-night, pre-Broadway presentation at Carnegie Hall in February 1964 was cancelled because of "technical problems," and the anticipated Broadway opening never occurred.

During much of the next decade, though not retiring from show business, Jane Powell customarily worked for only about sixteen weeks a year. But she retained all her professional discipline and polish, and when Debbie Reynolds relinquished the title role in *Irene* in early 1974, Miss Powell readily replaced her, even without the help of the show's director, Gower Champion, who was occupied elsewhere. As the plucky Irish-American piano tuner whose perseverance helps her to win her dream man, she not only achieved suitable freshness and vivaciousness, but also brought to the character a special softness and grace of her own. "She clearly has a gift for humor," Richard Watts wrote in the New York *Post* (February 8, 1974). ". . . She makes the girl from Ninth Avenue both believable and appealing, and she can play an emotional scene convincingly. Indeed, you might think the part had been created for her." Of the nostalgic musical *Irene*, which some dismissed as sentimental and stilted, the star herself said, "If it helps people laugh and relax, that's good." Miss Powell's contract called for her to appear in *Irene* through September 1, 1974, when Miss Reynolds returned for a final week on Broadway before taking the show on tour.

Jane Powell's first marriage, in 1949, to the professional ice skater and insurance broker Geary Steffen Jr., ended in divorce in 1953. She and the stockbroker Patrick Nerney were married in 1954 and were divorced in 1963. On June 27, 1965, in Sydney, Australia, where she was performing, she married James Fitzgerald, the Hollywood public relations man who had produced her revue *Just Twenty—Plus Me*. She has three children—Geary and Suzanne by her marriage to Steffen and Lindsey by her marriage to Nerney. Suzanne raises horses on her own ranch, and Lindsey, the younger daughter, hopes to become an actress.

Several recent interviewers have commented on Miss Powell's youthful appearance. Rex Reed, for example, remarked that she was "still as fresh as a peach blossom" and looked as "young and vibrant" as she had in the MGM musicals. Also as petite as ever, she is five feet one inch tall, weighs ninety pounds, and wears a size three. She has blond hair and blue eyes. "I do take care of myself," she said in the Reed interview. "Vitamins, exercise, no booze or cigarettes. . . . I live a healthy life." Boating is one of her recreations, but most of her hobbies are domestic, such as baking and embroidery.

References

Life 21:91 S 9 '46 por
N Y Daily News p44 Jl 9 '74 pors
N Y Post p19 F 16 '74 pors
N Y Sunday News III p5 F 10 '74 por; mag p33 Mr 3 '74 por
Variety 274:49 F 20 '74
Shipman, David. The Great Movie Stars (1972)
Who's Who in America, 1974-75

POWERS, BERTRAM A(NTHONY)

1922(?)- Union official
Address: b. New York Typographical Union
No. 6, 817 Broadway, New York 10003

As president of Local 6 of the International Typographical Union (ITU) since 1961, Bertram A. Powers is one of the most controversial figures in New York's beleaguered newspaper industry, a man whom many hold responsible for the demise of four major dailies in the past decade. A militant union leader who venerates the memory of John L. Lewis, he is a hard bargainer who distrusts bosses and relies on "muscle" as labor's chief weapon. Heading Local 6 in a period of crisis, Powers faced a seemingly insoluble problem: New York City's remaining newspapers claimed that without automated typesetting equipment, they could not survive; with it, his men's jobs would be eliminated. After protracted negotiations the apparent deadlock was broken by a new contract that was drawn up by Powers and the newspapers' managements at the end of May 1974.

A fourth-generation Irish-American (with one German grandparent), Bertram Anthony Powers was born in 1922 in Cambridge, Massachusetts. He has one brother and four sisters. During the Depression, Powers' father, who had been a civil servant with the U.S. Customs & Immigration Service, was thrown out of his job. For some time thereafter, according to a *Time* reporter (March 1, 1963), the Powers family lived on "relief money, dried fruit, [and] surplus food stamps ... using the public library for entertainment." During those grim years, in 1933, when Powers was about eleven, his mother died. The elder Powers worked for the WPA for a while, but he eventually found a civil-service job in Maine, leaving his children in the care of their maternal grandparents, a Cambridge policeman and his wife.

After attending a Roman Catholic parochial elementary school in Cambridge, Powers went on to high school, but he dropped out after two years to join the CCC (Civilian Conservation Corps). Although that marked the end of his formal education, he has always been an avid reader, and, as he once remarked to Stanley W. Penn of the *Wall Street Journal* (February 15, 1963), "[my] college was the composing room." With several hundred other city youngsters, Powers spent the year of 1939 at a CCC camp in the Maine woods, clearing the forest and climbing trees to destroy gypsy moth larvae. Three years earlier, however, Powers had sustained severe hip and leg fractures when hit by a truck, and when a previously unnoticed nerve injury was now discovered, he was hospitalized for six months and underwent two operations. He still walks with a noticeable limp and suffers considerable pain, especially when sitting.

That injury, as Geoffrey T. Hellman has pointed out in a profile of Powers in the *New Yorker* (March 7, 1970), determined Powers' lifework. On his discharge from the hospital in 1939,

he was sent by the Massachusetts Division of Vocational Rehabilitation to Fitchburg State Teachers College. There he learned printing and worked as a linotype operator on the school's newspaper for a weekly salary of $12, of which $9 went for room and board. Powers stayed at Fitchburg for a year to learn his new trade and then became an apprentice printer in Boston, where he earned $16 a week on his first job.

Innately restless and eager to improve his earning power by acquiring diversified experience, Powers soon became something of an itinerant. He held many jobs, all for relatively short periods —including a stint on the Boston *Globe*—and worked in many different places, including Bridgeport, Chicago, Detroit, and New Haven. While in New Haven, where he worked for the *Courier* and other firms, he finally amassed the requisite total of six years of composing-room experience, thus completing his apprenticeship and receiving his printer's card. He also became eligible for membership in the ITU, which he immediately joined.

In 1946 Powers moved to New York City, where he worked for a time as a typesetter for the newspaper *PM* and subsequently for the New York *Star*. He lost his job in 1949 when the latter paper folded, and in 1951 he took a job, at $110.58 a week plus a $15 efficiency premium (which he always received), for the Sorg Printing Company on South Street, a commercial outfit specializing in financial work.

When Powers settled in New York City in 1946 he had joined ITU's Local 6, an 11,000-member organization (divided into two branches, Book & Job and Newspaper) that encompasses all printers in New York City and in nearby Westchester and Rockland counties. Ninety percent of its membership works in Manhattan. Known popularly as "Big Six," the local was founded in 1850 by Horace Greeley as the New-York Printers' Union. Antedating both the New York *Times* and the ITU, it is the national union's largest and most powerful local.

Interested in union politics as early as 1943, Powers quickly threw himself into the affairs of Big Six by affiliating himself with the Progressives, one of the two parties (the other being the conservative Independents) operating in the local's democratic internal political system. In 1947, in his first bid for office, he ran for a seat on the local's eleven-member executive committee and was defeated, but in 1948 he won a seat as an alternate delegate. In 1949 he was elected a regular member of the committee, becoming its chairman in 1951. Elected a vice-president of the local in 1953, he left his job with Sorg to take on that full-time paid post, which entailed responsibility for enforcing contracts and settling disputes in all shops of the Book & Job branch. He also became one of the six trustees (three from the union and three from management) of the local's pension and welfare fund. Powers has remained a full-time paid official of the local ever since, achieving a longevity record unequaled in the history of the ITU.

During the next six years Powers assiduously consolidated his reputation with the membership of Big Six, despite the fact that the local's incumbent president, Francis G. Barrett, kept him in a relatively subordinate role. He particularly identified himself with an issue that had long been a bone of contention with many members: the fact that wage settlements in the Newspaper branch were tied to settlements previously worked out by the owners of the papers and the Newspaper Guild (representing writers, editors, and clerical workers), which, by a chronological accident, had a contract expiration date preceding that of the ITU and the other "mechanical" unions. Since the Guild, like many white-collar unions, was not especially aggressive or demanding, ITU settlements had not been very lucrative or satisfying.

When Barrett stepped down in 1961, Powers decided to run for the presidency. In the election of May 1961 he defeated his opponent by the impressive margin of 5,045 to 3,493, becoming the local's fiftieth president. In 1970 the post paid $502.55 a week plus a small amount for expenses, which Powers conscientiously itemizes for his members in the local's *Monthly Bulletin,* of which he is the editor. His popularity with the local's members increased considerably after the 1962-63 strike, and he was re-elected by ever greater margins in every subsequent election. Powers is currently serving his sixth term, which began in June 1973, after an election in which he defeated his opponent, Nicholas Vagenas, by a vote of 5,997 to 1,809.

The first real test of Powers' mettle came at the end of 1962, when Big Six's contract expired, bringing about a struggle between the local and the New York Publishers' Association, the trade body that represents the city's big dailies. Money, of course, was a key issue, especially since the rank and file members of the Newspaper branch were demanding wages and benefits as good as those customarily won by members of the consistently better-paid Book & Job branch, which includes workers on weekly newspapers. That the problem was much more complicated, however, was pointed out by Gay Talese in his history of the New York *Times, The Kingdom and the Power* (World 1966), when he wrote: "The publishers were beset by the rising costs of newspaper production, by the higher wage demands of workers and the intrusion of television for the advertising dollar, and they scrambled and experimented to keep pace with economic trends and a changing society, often taking wrong turns and going astray. The workers feared the new automatic machinery that the publishers saw as tools of survival; despite the vague promises and euphemisms of the new technologists, the workers knew that automation would ultimately destroy their craft and their security, and so they drove harder bargains. . . ."

Both labor and management reached an impasse in the dispute. When preliminary discussions, more or less as expected, failed to lead to a settlement, Powers, in Local 6's first such action

BERTRAM A. POWERS

since 1883, took his men out on December 8, 1962, striking the New York *Times,* the *Daily News,* the *Journal-American,* and the *World-Telegram and Sun.* Those papers were supported by the *Post,* the *Herald Tribune,* the *Mirror,* the Long Island *Star-Journal,* and the Long Island *Press,* all of which voluntarily shut down. Big Six, in turn, was soon joined by the New York Mailers Union No. 6 (an ITU affiliate), the New York Stereotypers Union No. 1, and the Photo-Engravers Union, while ten other newspaper craft unions, honoring the picket lines, refused to go to work even though they were not formally on strike.

Thus began the longest and most destructive newspaper strike in American history. Before it ended, 114 days later, on March 31, 1963, Powers had been condemned for his intransigence by President John F. Kennedy and by other national leaders. New York retail businesses suffered irremediable losses because of their inability to advertise during the crucial Christmas season, Broadway shows shut down prematurely because of their inability to get reviewed, and the struck and shutdown newspapers lost an estimated $108 million in advertising and circulation revenue. Driven to the brink of desperation, the New York *Post* bolted the Publishers Association to make its own settlement with the union. The 19,074 employees of New York City's daily newspapers, both strikers and nonstrikers, lost some $50,400,-000 in wages and benefits.

The disastrous dispute ended when both sides, somewhat reluctantly, accepted a settlement hammered out by New York's Mayor Robert F. Wagner. It included a wage-and-benefit package worth $12.63 a week, as compared to the union's initial demand for $38.62 and the publishers' offer of $9.20, and the establishment of a common expiration date for all newspaper-union contracts, which would strengthen the workers in future negotiations. Perhaps most important was Big Six's agreement to the limited use of automatic equipment, including Teletypesetter tape, a computerized means of setting type without human typesetters. Although restricted to the preparation of AP and UPI stock-market tables, the innovation was portentous in its implications for the future.

Wagner's settlement may have ended the strike, but it left in its wake many unsolved problems. The printers were still not especially well paid, the newspapers were besieged by more financial problems than ever, and automation still represented a major threat. In the sequel, with new union contracts being negotiated every two years, there ensued a grim saga of labor-management relations that left the key problem of automation agonizingly unsolved. It also left New York City with only three daily English-language newspapers. Crippled by the protracted strike, the tabloid *Mirror* folded in 1963, the *Herald Tribune* and the *Journal-American* suspended operations to 1966, and, after a lengthy Newspaper Guild strike, the ill-fated merger paper, the *World Journal Tribune*, gave up the ghost in May 1967. Writing in *Saturday Review* (July 11, 1970), the labor expert A. H. Raskin deplored the situation as "a labor-management jungle that has provided an eight-year demonstration of how to commit suicide via the bargaining table."

The issues haggled over and the positions advanced by both sides have remained so constant since 1963 that a writer for *Newsweek* (June 8, 1970), in summarizing contract negotiations in the spring of 1970, commented that "many New Yorkers were touched by a sense of *déja vu*." Similarly, the *Wall Street Journal* (February 9, 1973) headlined its account of the beginning of the most recent series of discussions with the words, "Once Again Automation Is the Issue." There were, however, some differences. In 1973 the publishers found themselves in even more dire straits than previously, for their advertising income had been dwindling, while they suffered tremendous circulation losses to aggressive new suburban papers in the New York metropolitan area, especially to Long Island's fast-growing *Newsday*. Meanwhile Powers had come to realize that automation, in one form or another, would have to be accepted as the wave of the future. Recognizing as early as the mid-1960's that the union's interests depended on the well-being of the city's three remaining dailies, he had for practical purposes given up the strike as a weapon. He had, in fact, formalized that in the 1971 contract, depending instead on slowdowns and other job actions.

Big Six's current contract expired on March 30, 1973, without Powers and the publishers arriving at a settlement, even though bargaining had begun several weeks earlier. The local's members remained on the job without a new contract and talks continued, but to no avail. During that round, Arthur O. Sulzberger, the publisher of the *Times*, revealed himself to be adamant on the introduction of IBM selector keyboards and other automatic equipment in the composing room. The *Times* obtained delivery of some new machinery and reportedly began secretly to train nonprinter strikebreakers to operate the devices. In retalia-

tion, Big Six began engaging in slowdowns. The most commonly used tactic, already familiar from the 1960's, was the holding of chapel meetings during working hours. (In the printing industry the term *chapel* designates an association of workers in a particular shop or plant).

Claiming to have suffered tremendous financial losses as a result of those tactics, the *Times* on September 14, 1973 secured a court order enjoining the union from engaging in stoppages and slowdowns. Powers, in turn, appealed to John J. Pilch, the president of the ITU, to release Local 6 from the contract provision forbidding strikes. He also continued the chapel meetings, and in consequence, on October 16, he and several other Big Six officials were found guilty of contempt and fined $250 each. The court warned that Big Six would be assessed to pay for any further damages suffered by the *Times*, but Powers called on Pilch to take over the negotiations and renewed his appeal to the international union for freedom to strike.

After months of continued haggling, including a nineteen-day work stoppage by printers at the *Daily News*, the managements of the *Times* and the *News* reached an agreement with the union on a new contract at the end of May 1974. It included provisions allowing for the introduction of new automated equipment and guarantees of lifetime job security for the printers. Union members ratified the contract on July 28, 1974.

Standing six feet two inches tall and weighing 175 pounds, "Bert" Powers, who is blue-eyed and white-haired, walks with a pronounced limp and speaks with a New England accent. Soft-voiced, articulate, and elegantly groomed, he was described by Geoffrey Hellman, in the *New Yorker* profile as having "an intense, penetrating, watchful look; a severe, guarded, defensive air that sometimes relaxes into a kind of tentative affability, punctuated by a fleeting smile; a controlled ruthlessness . . . an aversion to small talk . . . [and] a Celtic wit." According to a *Newsweek* reporter (January 7, 1963), he exudes "the self-conscious confidence of a self-made, self-educated man." Because of his hip injury, Powers often works standing up at an extra-high teakwood desk that was a gift from labor mediator Theodore Kheel. He enjoys surf-casting, walking on the beach, and cooking seafood. His personality and style were perhaps best summed up by labor journalist A. H. Raskin of the New York *Times*, who once described him as "honest, clean, democratic—and impossible."

Powers lives with his wife, Patricia (whom he met and married while working in New Haven in the early 1940's), in a house in Massapequa, Long Island. They have four children: Kevin (a high school history teacher), Patricia, Brian, and Moya. Mrs. Powers, a dark-haired woman who was born in Ireland, teaches senior English at Massapequa High School. An alumna of Hofstra College, she holds M.A. and Ph.D. degrees in English from New York University. Powers has been a director of the Urban Coalition and chairman of the publishing industry's Research and

Development Fund, a joint labor-management group. In 1967 he received the annual Labor Award of the Westchester County Central Labor Body of the AFL-CIO.

References

Newsweek 61:54 Ja 7 '63 por
New Yorker 46:43+ Mr 7 '70 por
Time 81:13+ Mr 1 '63 pors
Wall St J F 15 '63

PRITCHETT, V(ICTOR) S(AWDON)

Dec. 16, 1900- British author
Address: h. 12 Regent's Park Terrace, London N.W. 1, England

V. S. PRITCHETT

Cultivated taste, wry wit, balanced sensibility, and quiet authority are qualities that distinguish the prose of wise old V. S. Pritchett, the British critic, short-story writer, and novelist. Septuagenarian Pritchett's works of fiction are carefully crafted combinations of a dark pessimism and a comic irony that is usually subtle but sometimes, as in the novel *Mr. Beluncle* (1951), explodes into farce. With his finely tuned ear for dialogue, his sharp eye for significant details in behavior and body language, and his talent for narrative, Pritchett is an uncanny alchemist of fictional personality, adept at evoking the extraordinariness of unique characters in the most ordinary situations. His vision and deftness are especially manifest in his short stories, which rank among the best in the English language.

The perceptive eye of the painter *manqué* is also evident in Pritchett's nonfiction works based on his travels, the best of which is *The Spanish Temper* (1954), perhaps the most perspicacious such assessment ever offered by a non-Spaniard. As a writer of "familiar" literary essays in the intuitive tradition of Charles Lamb and William Hazlitt, he is widely considered to be the preeminent critic of fiction writing in English today, with a range and depth comparable to that of the late Edmund Wilson. Pritchett is a director of the *New Statesman* and a contributor to such American publications as the New York *Times Book Review*, the *New Yorker*, and the *New York Review of Books*.

"Autobiography at its most luminous and illuminating" is Jean Stafford's description of the memoirs—*A Cab at the Door* and *Midnight Oil*—in which Victor Sawdon Pritchett has with delicate candor recounted his life back to its lower-middle-class Edwardian beginning. Pritchett was born on December 16, 1900 in Ipswich, Suffolk, England to Walter Sawdon Pritchett, a Yorkshireman, and Beatrice (Martin) Pritchett, a Cockney. In *A Cab at the Door* (Chatto and Windus, 1968; Random House, 1968) he describes his father as a "cock-sparrow . . . , dressy and expansive with optimism, walking in and out of jobs with the bumptiousness of a god" and his mother as a "sulky, moody" woman, "either laughing or in tears," made "more and more a worn-out nervous wreck" by quarrels with her Micawber-like husband. The typical condition of the family was, he says, "hysteria."

Pritchett traces his "love of change, journeys, and new places" to the chaos and nomadism of his early life. With his two younger brothers and younger sister, he was raised mostly in London, but the children never knew when they were going to be bundled into a hansom and whisked away from his father's creditors. "I did not know that almost every time we moved house Father had lost his job or was swinging dangerously between an old disaster and a new enterprise." Very often the family would split up, with Pritchett usually going to Yorkshire to live with his paternal grandfather, a Congregationalist minister, or his great-uncle, an atheist.

While working as a commercial traveler the father was absent from the family for as long as a year at a time, but his influence on Pritchett prevailed over that of grandfather and great-uncle, at least in the matter of religion. Through adolescence and into early manhood—when he became disillusioned—Pritchett was by choice a Christian Scientist, like his father. (The father's adventures and misadventures in religion and business were the basis for the core of Pritchett's diffuse, Dickensian comic novel *Mr. Beluncle*—Chatto and Windus, 1951; Harcourt, 1951—which, Pritchett confesses, is about his "obsessive subject.") Ultimately it was the paganism of his mother (nominally an Anglican) that he would embrace. He was also influenced by his mother's "laughing eyes" and her penchant for tall stories. "My mother's laughter is what remains with me," he has said. "Everything turned into a tale in her talk."

The frequent changes of residence played havoc with Pritchett's education, until his father finally settled into a permanent, fairly lucrative position as managing director of an art needlework company and the family took up residence in Dulwich, on the outskirts of London. Even thereafter, as a student at the Rosendale Road School and Alleyn's Grammar School, both in London,

Pritchett had an unimpressive academic record, but a progressive teacher, a Mr. Bartlett, inspired in him a love of literature and writing. "I had previously been drawn to painting," he relates in his autobiography, "and now in poems and stories I saw pictures growing out of print."

On his own in his early teens Pritchett read through every volume of a series on the home bookshelf called the *International Library of Famous Literature,* where he first encountered Charles Dickens, one of his early idols, and Thomas Hardy, through whom he discovered "a lasting taste for the wry and ironical." In *A Cab at the Door* he recalls: "These volumes converted me to prose. I had never really enjoyed poetry, for it was concerned with inner experience and I was very much an extrovert and I fancy I have remained so; the moodiness and melancholy which fell on me in Dulwich and have been with me ever since must have come from the disappointments of an active and romantic nature; the forms of Protestantism among which I was brought up taught one to think of life rigidly in terms of right and wrong, and that is not likely to fertilize the sensibilities or the poetic imagination. . . . But in prose I found the common experience and the solid worlds where judgments could be made and in which one could firmly tread."

Later, while still a student, Pritchett read through the complete works of Shakespeare, loaned him by a fellow student, and when he could cadge the money from his mother he would buy a book by Marie Corelli, John Ruskin, or H. G. Wells, or another of his favorites. His first short stories, written in his early teens, were, as he has described them, "pure Corelli." The very first, written at the beginning of World War I, was based on a London air raid he had just experienced.

Discovering that he had a talent for foreign languages—it was only when he learned French and German that he began to understand grammar, he has pointed out—Pritchett contemplated becoming a schoolteacher. But, fearing that his son's literary aspirations would lead him to starvation "in a garret," Walter Sawdon Pritchett, on the advice of Grandfather Pritchett, took him out of school just before his sixteenth birthday and arranged for him to enter the leather trade.

For four years Pritchett worked as a clerk in the warehouse of one of the leading leather factories in the Bermondsey district of London. The trade, and especially the craft of tanning itself, fascinated him, but eventually he saw his job as a trap keeping him from further intellectual and literary growth. At the age of twenty he liberated himself by setting off for Paris.

By 1920, when Pritchett arrived in Paris, that city had become the home of a generation of brilliant British and American expatriate writers. Unaware that he was living in the midst of a literary revolution, he usually wandered about alone, enjoying the city, occasionally working as a salesman, and feverishly trying to read all the French and English literature he had missed. He sold sketches of his impressions of Paris and the French countryside to two British weeklies and to the *Christian Science Monitor,* but his freelance income barely kept him from starvation. In 1922 he applied for full-time work with the *Monitor* and was taken on as a correspondent. After a year in Ireland reporting on the civil war then raging there, he was sent successively to Spain, North Africa, North America, and then Ireland again. Because he "despised news and was confused by opinion," the quality of his articles deteriorated and the *Monitor* fired him, in 1927.

Back in London, Pritchett worked part time as librarian at the exclusive Bath Club while occasionally publishing short stories, book reviews, and sketches. All the while he was purifying his style, rewriting and polishing obsessively. Searching for a way both to live and to maintain his integrity as a writer, he hit on the idea of an original travel book, "the short, compact subject made personal." With this in mind, he took a ship to Portugal and thence walked across Spain, through an area that was relatively unknown, except for its poverty. He described the trip in his first published book, *Marching Spain* (Benn, 1928). The attention drawn to him by that book led to contracts for a novel and a volume of short stories.

The novel, *Clare Drummer* (Benn, 1929), an admittedly "nervous" and "uneven" attempt to translate his "private Irish experience" into fiction, was panned by critics and sold under one thousand copies. The short-story collection, *The Spanish Virgin* (Benn, 1930), had a much better critical reception and sold 3,000 copies. Both books have been out of print for more than four decades.

His second novel, *Shirley Sanz* (Gollancz, 1932), published in the United States under the title *Elopement into Exile* (Little, Brown, 1932), was a romance about an English girl who elopes to Spain with an Anglo-Spaniard. Pritchett's growing maturity, especially in the handling of characters, was evident in the difference between that novel and his third, *Nothing Like Leather* (Chatto and Windus, 1935; Macmillan, 1935), the story, set in drab industrial England, of a businessman who suffers a drastic change of fortune. A reviewer for the *Spectator* (January 18, 1935) considered *Nothing Like Leather* to be "one of the few really memorable creations in modern fiction."

Pritchett has described his first three novels as "machines for conveying my characters into a trap." In the second volume of his autobiography, *Midnight Oil* (Chatto, 1972; Random House, 1972), he relates the weaknesses and excesses of those novels to the crisis he was then going through in his personal life, a sustained trauma exacerbated by the deterioration of his first marriage (to an Irish journalist): "There is a theory among psychologists . . . that an eldest child . . . [may] become . . . adventurous and self-sufficient—but, untrained by conflict, breaks in a crisis, disperses himself and goes to pieces. I have certainly had to deal with that. . . . I ran into one nervous illness after another. . . . My habits of work cannot have been helpful. I rewrote and rewrote all day and half the night.... What . . . eventually cured me was success in love, and in my work."

In 1936 Pritchett was divorced from his first wife and married to his present wife, the former Dorothy Rudge Roberts. Personally more fulfilled, he was better able to achieve his intentions in fiction, to use the idiosyncracies of characters' language and behavior to expose the illusions by which they live or "protect their dignity." In 1937 Chatto and Windus published his novel *Dead Man Leading*, about a young man searching for his father, lost in a South American jungle. Over the next few years he wrote some of his best short stories, including "The Saint," "The Fly in the Ointment," and "Sense of Honour."

During World War II Pritchett wrote radio plays, did documentary reporting, and began writing book reviews for the *New Statesman*. He served as the literary editor of that publication for two years beginning in 1954, and he has been one of its directors ever since. For many years he wrote the column "Books in General" for the *New Statesman*, and most of the critical essays collected in *In My Good Books* (Chatto, 1942), *The Living Novel* (Chatto, 1946; Reynal, 1947), and *Books in General* (Chatto, 1953; Harcourt, 1953) were from that publication. A reviewer for the London *Times Literary Supplement* (February 27, 1953) wrote of the "insight and sympathy" exhibited in *Books in General*: "Such talents as these not uncommonly incline thoughtful men to melancholy. In Mr. Pritchett, however, they are held in balance by the free play of a natural gaiety that is perhaps an even rarer gift. He is the least Olympian, the most approachable of critics."

After thirty years of living in Spain on and off, mastering its language thoroughly, steeping himself in its literature, and traveling the whole country by foot and public conveyance, Pritchett wrote *The Spanish Temper* (Knopf, 1954), in which he brought a fresh insight into the Spanish character and compressed a remarkable analysis of the whole range of Spanish life and culture into some 60,000 words. Literary critics generally credited him with dispelling false romantic notions about Spain, and Honor Tracy wrote in the *New Statesman* (May 1, 1954): "Few people love Spain more than Mr. Pritchett does, or understand it better; and no English author, unless it is Mr. Gerald Brenan, writes of the country with such perception." Pritchett's lucid impressions and insights about other locales were presented in *London Perceived* (Chatto, 1962; Harcourt, 1962); *Foreign Faces* (Chatto, 1964), published in the United States under the title *The Offensive Traveler* (Knopf, 1964); *New York Proclaimed* (Chatto, 1965); and *Dublin; A Portrait* (Bodley Head, 1967).

Twenty-five of the best short stories written by Pritchett up to 1956—mostly gray-toned tragicomedies about lower-middle-class people in tearooms, pubs, offices, and the like—were brought together in that year by Chatto and Windus in the volume *Collected Stories*, which reviewers hailed for its "rich" and "many-faceted" portraiture. A critic for the *New Republic* (August 20, 1956) noted that Pritchett, seeing absurdity in human nature even at its grimmest, encourages us to "take our sadness pleasurably." Later stories were collected in *When My Girl Comes Home* (Chatto, 1961; Knopf, 1961); *The Key to My Heart* (Chatto, 1963; Random House, 1964), which was actually a trilogy; and *Blind Love* (Chatto, 1969; Random House, 1970). Reviewing *Blind Love* in the January 25, 1970 issue of the New York *Times*, Wilfrid Sheed wrote of Pritchett: "He has to get everything just right—dialogue, motive, the actuality of things." In 1974 Random House published a collection of his short stories entitled *The Camberwell Beauty and Other Stories*.

In the *Penguin Companion to English Literature* (1971), edited by David Daiches, Charles Osborne reviewed Pritchett's stories in general: "Pritchett's eye is for the bizarre incident, but his ear is for the natural rhythms of dialogue and narrative. The juxtaposition gives his stories a creative tension and individuality. . . . To the imaginative eye and the realistic ear Pritchett adds the mind of a poet.... He reveals..., at his best, the universal in the particular." Pritchett's longer fiction reviews were collected in *The Working Novelist* (Chatto, 1965). Regarding his literary criticism, Charles Osborne wrote: "His knowledge is extensive, his taste unfailing, and his essays always manage to convey the texture and flavor of the work under discussion." For Pritchett fiction and criticism are both a "kind of exploration" of character, situation, and theme, and in his literary commentaries he uses his "personal insights" and "experience of literature" rather than critical doctrines, which he thinks often miss the "real impulse in creative writing." Given the modern addiction to critical theory, his intuitive approach strikes some pedants as anachronistic and lacking rigor, but as Karl Miller in the *New York Review of Books* (July 20, 1972) noted, his precision is that of the imaginative writer to whom "surfaces and surmises are not only admissible and delightful . . . they are part of the truth." Pritchett has an almost unparalleled grasp of the unique features of writers as diverse as Charles Dickens, Samuel Beckett, and Saul Bellow.

Pritchett has lectured extensively in Britain and the United States. His Clark Lecture at Trinity College, Cambridge University in 1969 was published within the same year by Random House under the title *George Meredith and English Comedy*. Regarding his biography *Balzac* (Knopf, 1973), Martha Duffy wrote in *Time* (October 22, 1972): "Pritchett's knowledge of Balzac's body of writing is so well assimilated that he can call on it at will. There are no noisome transitions between 'life' and 'work.' "

V. S. Pritchett and his wife live in London. They have two children. An interviewer for the New York *Times Book Review* (April 25, 1954) found Pritchett to be "composed primarily of smile, pipe, wispy hair, and glasses" and to have "the laugh of a man who will seek out a good joke." Karl Miller, who met him a few years ago, described him in his *New York Review of Books* article as "good-natured" and "mischievous."

In an interview with Elie Abel on the NBC television network in 1965 Pritchett said that he has always tried to stay out of literary cliques partly because he "can't understand what they're talking about" and partly because he "cannot bear" the "jealousies," the "intrigues," and the "little wars." "There's only one war," he said. "That's you." In religion, Pritchett classifies himself as a "pagan" who is unable "to regard the doctrine of original sin as anything more than an intellectual convenience." He has written: "If I do think of a possible God, some image of the Berg [a mount near one of his boyhood homes in Yorkshire] comes at once to my mind now, or of certain stones in the ravine. To such things the heathen in his wisdom always bowed."

References

N Y Herald Tribune Bk R p2 Ap 25 '54 por
N Y Review of Books 12:17+ F 13 '69 por; 19:12+ Jl 20 '72 por
N Y Times Bk R p16 Ap 25 '54 por
Pritchett, V. S. A Cab at the Door (1968); Midnight Oil (1972)

RABIN, YITZHAK (rä-bēn yits'häk)

Mar. 1, 1922- Premier of Israel
Address: b. Office of the Premier, Jerusalem, Israel

The inauguration of Yitzhak Rabin in June 1974 as Israel's fifth and youngest Premier marked a shift in the top leadership of the Jewish state from the generation of pioneer settlers of European birth to the native-born Israelis, or sabras. Rabin succeeded Golda Meir, who resigned in the wake of criticism of the government's handling of the October 1973 war. A career military man, he fought with distinction in Israel's War of Independence, and as chief of staff of the Israel Defense Forces he engineered Israel's lightning victory in the six-day war of June 1967. From 1968 to 1973 Rabin was Israel's Ambassador to the United States, and in 1974 he served briefly as Minister of Labor in Mrs. Meir's last Cabinet. Committed, like his predecessors, to the establishment of recognized and defensible boundaries for Israel within the context of a general Middle Eastern peace settlement, Rabin is expected to take a more flexible and pragmatic approach to the pursuit of those goals than earlier Israeli political leaders.

Yitzhak Rabin was born in Jerusalem on March 1, 1922, shortly before the British mandate in Palestine went into effect. His father, Nehemia Rabin, a native of Russia, lived in the United States for fifteen years before coming to Palestine during World War I to fight in the British-sponsored Jewish Legion against Turkish rule. His mother, Rosa (Cohen) Rabin, also born in Russia, was a Zionist pioneer, a leader in the labor movement, and a member of the high command of Haganah, the Jewish underground army. Rabin, who received his early schooling in Tel Aviv and on a kibbutz, originally intended to become a pioneer farmer. In 1936 he entered the Kadoorie Agricultural School in Kfar Tabor, where he excelled as a soccer player and graduated in 1940 with honors. But World War II forced him to cancel plans to study irrigation engineering at the University of California in Berkeley, where he had applied for a scholarship. In 1941 he joined the Palmach, the highly trained commando force of Haganah.

Although Jews chafed under Great Britain's White Paper of 1939, which severely restricted immigration to Palestine at the time of their greatest peril in Europe, Haganah cooperated with the Allies against the Axis powers in the Middle East, and its troops were trained by the British in sabotage and other partisan activity. Rabin took part in Palmach operations against the Vichy French in Syria and Lebanon in 1941. On one occasion he led a scouting unit ten miles behind enemy lines in Lebanon to head off retreating Axis forces. By 1944 he was a deputy battalion commander in the Palmach.

Even before the end of World War II, however, the wartime alliance between the British and Haganah broke down, as Palestinian Jews resisted the continuing British blockade against efforts of Jewish survivors from Europe to enter Palestine. Moving underground with the Palmach in 1945, Rabin led a raid on Athlit, a British detention camp south of Haifa, to liberate some 200 illegal immigrants held in custody there. (A fictionalized version of that episode appears in the novel *Exodus* by Leon Uris, who is said to have used Rabin as a prototype for the character Ari Ben-Canaan.) Placed on the "most wanted" list by British authorities, Rabin was arrested in 1946 after dynamiting a police post and spent six months in a prison camp.

By the time of his release in early 1947, the debate over Palestine's future had entered a new phase. Weary of their mandate, the British referred the entire Palestine question to the United Nations, which in August 1947 approved partition of the Holy Land into Arab and Jewish sectors. At the end of 1947 Rabin was appointed deputy to Yigal Allon, the commander of the Palmach. Meanwhile, hostilities between Jews and Arabs intensified, culminating in the Israeli War of Independence on May 15, 1948, one day after the British mandate ended and Israel became a sovereign nation.

As commander of the Palmach Har-El Brigade, Rabin played a crucial role in the defense of Jerusalem. Although the desperate effort to retain the walled Old City for Israel failed, Rabin kept open the supply route between Jerusalem and the coastal plain. During the second phase of the war, in late 1948, Rabin, now a colonel, was second in command at the Southern Command Headquarters. He fought in the Negev and the Red Sea port of Eilat, pursuing Egyptian forces into the Sinai Desert until intervening U.N. troops forced him to retreat. At the Israeli-Arab armistice negotiations, held at Rhodes early in 1949, Rabin represented the Israel Defense Forces in meetings with Egyptian representatives.

After the 1949 armistice, Rabin, having decided on an army career, served successively as commander of an armored brigade in the Negev and acting commander of the southern front in 1949-50, and as chief of the tactical operations department at the general headquarters of the Israel Defense Forces from 1950 to 1952. In 1953 he went to England to complete a year's course of study at the British Staff College at Camberley. Promoted in 1954 to the rank of *aluf*, or brigadier general, Rabin served until 1956 as head of the training branch of the Israel Defense Forces. From 1956 to 1959 he was commanding officer of the northern front, and in 1959-60 he headed the manpower branch. As deputy chief of staff and chief of the general staff branch from late 1960 to late 1963, Rabin accompanied the chief of staff on tours of military installations in several countries, including the United States. In January 1964 he succeeded General Zvi Tsur as chief of staff of the Israel Defense Forces and was promoted to the rank of *rav aluf*, or major general.

Although Rabin's term as chief of staff should have ended when he reached the age of forty-five, the usual retirement age for Israeli generals, he served beyond that date at the request of Premier Levi Eshkol, who was impressed by the skill with which he handled the uneasy border situation that periodically erupted into land and air battles between Israel and its neighbors. Determined to use "all weapons without any reservations in defense against attacks," Rabin used retaliatory air raids in November 1964 to protect Israeli settlements in North Galilee from Syrian attack and to prevent Syria from sabotaging Israel's water system through diversion of the Jordan headwaters. He deviated from traditional patterns of border reprisal by using planes to blast artillery emplacements on the far slopes of hills that Israeli guns could not reach and allowing Israeli aircraft to pursue Syrian planes to Damascus. In 1966, after hostile Arab forces infiltrated into Israel from Jordan, Rabin initiated the first daylight reprisal in the history of Arab-Israeli border warfare.

At the same time, Rabin was responsible for formulating long-range defense policies and strategies, taking into consideration Israel's material resources, population, and strategic location. In an interview with Drew Pearson (New York *Post,* January 7, 1966) he cited as Israel's main problems its extreme vulnerability to air attack, and its small population and modest budget that limited its permanent standing army to 50,000. Israel thus had to depend on constant alertness, a highly trained reserve, and an adequate supply of armaments to offset the heavily equipped Arab forces.

YITZHAK RABIN

Those factors substantially determined Israeli strategy in the six-day war that erupted on June 6, 1967. Although Defense Minister Moshe Dayan has been widely regarded as the hero of that war, it was Rabin who was to a major extent responsible for planning the steps leading to Israel's sweeping victory: the swift mobilization of reserves to an army of 300,000; the sudden circular sweep of Israeli planes over the Mediterranean to evade Egyptian radar, and the virtual destruction of Arab air forces; the carefully laid groundwar tactics enabling Israeli troops to thrust into the Sinai peninsula and the Gaza Strip, into Sharm el Sheik, into the Old City of Jerusalem, into Jordanian territory on the west bank of the Jordan, and into the Golan Heights of Syria. The success of the strategy was apparent by the third day of the war, as Rabin proudly announced: "All this has been done by the Israel Defense Forces alone, with what we have, without anything or anybody else."

Although Rabin had not had any previous formal experience as a diplomat, his role in the six-day war gave him the prestige he needed for the crucial post of Ambassador to the United States, with responsibility for cementing Israeli-American friendship and ensuring the continued flow of vitally needed armaments to Israel. After retiring as chief of staff as of January 1968 Rabin was appointed to succeed Avraham Harman in the ambassadorial post, and on March 5, 1968 he presented his credentials in Washington, D.C.

As the chief interpreter of Israel's policies to the United States, Rabin was charged with the task of gaining support for Israel's basic demands, rejecting any settlement imposed from the outside while calling for political recognition by the Arab nations as a precondition of withdrawal from captured territory, for defensible frontiers, and for sufficient armaments to meet all defense needs. To win American popular recognition for his country's views, Rabin toured the United States extensively, averaging some twelve lecture meetings a week. In contrast to the elaborate parties staged by the Arab embassies, he hosted small dinner meetings at his residence, to which he invited key government officials and members of Congress.

Rabin criticized a peace initiative advanced by Secretary of State William P. Rogers in late 1969 for requiring Israel to make too many concessions and undermining Israeli policy in the Middle East. On the other hand, he endorsed U.N. efforts to arrange Arab-Israeli peace talks and expressed Israel's willingness to withdraw from occupied territory as part of an overall peace settlement, thus drawing fire from Israeli "hawks" who felt that he was "too soft." He was also criticized at home for his tendency to bypass Foreign Minister Abba Eban and report directly to Golda Meir, who succeeded Eshkol as Premier in March 1969. He established good working relationships with United States officials, notably with Henry A. Kissinger and with Assistant Secretary of State Joseph J. Sisco. Although he experienced some delays in obtaining delivery of American Phantom jets and other military equipment, he was largely successful in negotiating with Pentagon officials for his country's military needs.

In June 1972 Rabin provoked considerable controversy when in an interview broadcast in Israel he made comments that were interpreted as supporting President Nixon for reelection. The interview spurred speculation and protest among Democratic Jews and supporters of Israel; a demand by the editors of the Jerusalem *Post* that he be recalled; and a statement by Mrs. Meir that it was Israel's policy never to interfere in another country's domestic policies. Rabin explained that his statement was one of appreciation, not endorsement, adding that no American President had ever made as strong a commitment to Israel's survival as Nixon had done.

In March 1973 Rabin, who for some time had harbored an ambition to enter national politics, returned to Israel. Making his first bid for election to the Knesset (Parliament), with the hope of obtaining a key post in Premier Meir's Cabinet, Rabin campaigned throughout the country, cultivating Israel's dominant Labor party, the Mapai, at the grass roots level. When, on October 6, 1973 Syria and Egypt launched surprise attacks against Israel, Rabin visited the battle fronts and armed forces headquarters without assuming any command role. He thus bore no responsibility for the conduct of the seventeen-day Yom Kippur war, in which Israel scored some gains but suffered heavy casualties. In November, Rabin took charge of a national campaign to raise a voluntary war loan to ease the burden that the war had placed on the national treasury.

During the weeks preceding the national elections of December 31, 1973, Rabin campaigned in the shadow of the older Labor party leaders, refraining from joining in the widespread criticism of Mrs. Meir and Defense Minister Dayan, whom many Israelis held responsible for the country's lack of preparedness in the October war. The elections, in which Rabin won a seat in the 120-member Knesset, marked a setback for

Premier Meir's Labor Alignment, which saw its parliamentary plurality reduced from fifty-six to fifty-one seats, while the right-wing Likud opposition bloc increased its strength. In his maiden speech in the Knesset, in January 1974, Rabin presented a relatively "dovish" viewpoint, indicating that under a peace agreement with the Arab states Israel should eventually withdraw from most of the occupied territories. Although Rabin had originally been slated to succeed Moshe Dayan as Defense Minister in Mrs. Meir's new Cabinet, which was sworn in on March 10, 1974, he was given instead the post of Minister of Labor after Dayan, in view of continued tension on the Syrian front, withdrew his earlier offer to resign.

Continued public criticism and party factionalism prompted Mrs. Meir on April 10, 1974 to make the "irrevocable" decision to resign the Premiership, bringing down her month-old government, which remained in control on a caretaker basis until the formation of a new government. On April 22, 1974 the Labor party's 614-member central committee chose Rabin as Premier-designate by a vote of 298 against 254 cast for Information Minister Shimon Peres. The open election of Rabin by the central committee marked a democratization in the process of choosing candidates for Premier, who had previously been selected secretly by a small group of party leaders and then brought to the committee for approval. The allegation by one of Rabin's former associates, that he had suffered a "breakdown" shortly before the 1967 war and was therefore unfit to be Premier, was brushed aside by the committee after Rabin explained that the breakdown was physical —caused by nicotine poisoning, resulting from excessive smoking—rather than emotional.

On the following day, Israeli President Ephraim Katzir officially charged Rabin with the task of forming a viable coalition government within a three-week period, effective April 27, 1974—to be extended for an additional three weeks if necessary. If he failed to do so, then new national elections would be required. After weeks of painstaking negotiations, Rabin announced on May 28 the formation of a three-party coalition that gave the government a bare majority of one in the Knesset. Rabin's Cabinet excluded the conservative National Religious party, which had been part of Mrs. Meir's government, and it included two small progressive factions—the Independent Liberals and the "dovish" Civil Rights party, headed by Mrs. Shulamit Aloni. Conspicuous by their absence from the nineteen-member Cabinet were Moshe Dayan, whose post as Defense Minister was taken over by Shimon Peres; Abba Eban, succeeded as Foreign Minister by Yigal Allon, who also became Deputy Premier; and Finance Minister Pinhas Sapir, one of the Labor party's elder statesmen, who went into retirement. To remain in power, the government now depended for the first time on the votes of the five Communists and three Arab party members in the Knesset.

After the new coalition government was approved by the Knesset on June 3, 1974—by a vote of sixty-one to fifty-one, with five abstentions—Rabin called on Israelis to shake off the despondency that had enshrouded them since the October war and indicated that his policies were essentially those of the Meir government. Although he pledged himself to negotiate with the Arab countries, beginning with Egypt, he ruled out talks with Palestinian guerrilla groups and asserted that Israel would not return to pre-1967 borders, "even within the context of a peace treaty." Although in the weeks before his inauguration Israel had concluded military disengagement agreements with Egypt and Syria owing largely to the efforts of Henry Kissinger, the country continued to be plagued by Palestinian terrorist acts, for which Rabin ordered swift retaliation. On the domestic scene, Rabin has devoted his efforts to maintaining enough military strength and coping with serious economic problems, including a housing shortage and an inflation rate of some 35 percent a year.

Yitzhak Rabin was married on August 23, 1948 to German-born Leah Schlossberg, a former teacher whom he met in the Palmach during World War II. They have a daughter, Dalia, the wife of an army officer, and a son, Yuval, who is in the army. Rabin is a short, sandy-haired, blue-eyed, youthful-looking man of military bearing. He does not indulge in alcoholic beverages and has little patience with small talk. Described as self-effacing, taciturn, and withdrawn, he is also said to manifest a volatile temper as well as a wry sense of humor on occasion. According to columnist Joseph Alsop (Washington *Post*, April 9, 1973), "Rabin is not merely a brave man, a good companion and a good friend. He also has one of the most far-thinking yet down-to-earth strategic minds." His favorite recreation is making home movies. Now a member of the army reserves, Rabin was promoted to lieutenant general in July 1968. He holds honorary doctorates from the Hebrew University in Jerusalem and from several American colleges and universities.

References

N Y Post p39 Ap 18 '68 por; p22 Je 22 '74 por
N Y Times p16 Je 8 '67 por; p10 Ap 23 '74
Newsweek 96:28+ D 28 '70 por; 83:40 My 6 '74 por
Who's Who in America, 1972-73
Who's Who in Israel, 1973-74
Who's Who in World Jewry, 1972

REARDON, JOHN

Apr. 8, 1930- Opera singer
Address: b. c/o Metropolitan Opera Company, Lincoln Center Plaza, New York 10023; h. 155 W. 68th St., New York 10023

"Opera is a bastard art," John Reardon once wrote in an article for *Music Journal*. "It is probably the most artificial dramatic form. You can't fool an audience into 'believing' what's happening on the stage, even with the world's greatest

JOHN REARDON

singers, if the acting is bad." One of the most versatile singer-actors on the American lyrical stage, Reardon has achieved star status as a leading baritone with the Metropolitan Opera, capping a multifaceted career that has included Broadway musicals, operettas, summer stock, concerts, recitals, and appearances on television as well as grand opera. He recently became the artistic director of the Wolf Trap Company at Wolf Trap Farm Park for the Performing Arts.

Reardon's operatic repertory includes more than one hundred roles, nearly one-third of them in contemporary operas. As a principal with the New York City Opera, he created more roles than any other singer of his generation. "I'd go out of my mind if I sang nothing but *Tosca* and *Traviata*," he has declared. "I'd much rather be the first Grandier in *The Devils of Loudun* than the 600,000th Marcello in *La Bohème*." Several roles, such as the husband in Douglas Moore's *Carrie Nation*, Belaev in Lee Hoiby's *Natalia Petrovna*, and Orin in Martin David Levy's *Mourning Becomes Electra*, have been created especially for him. New operas are "no harder than Mozart," he argues. "The trick is to sing them like Mozart."

The son of John Joseph Reardon, an insurance agent and factory worker, and Thelma Claire (Fulton) Reardon, a professional singer, John Robert Reardon was born into an uncommonly musical family on April 8, 1930 in New York City. His maternal grandfather conducted the town band in Waterbury, Connecticut, and the family also included two sopranos, two instrumentalists, and a concert pianist. Encouraged by his talented relatives, Reardon quickly learned to play the piano and to sing snatches of grand opera in his "boy coloratura." After spending his childhood in the Northeast, he moved with his family to Lake Worth, Florida, where he attended Lake Worth High School.

On his graduation from high school in 1948, Reardon enrolled at Rollins College, a small liberal arts institution in Winter Park, Florida. Despite his training in piano and voice, he intended to become a banker and registered for a full program of business courses. Three days later he switched to the music curriculum. "The all-pervading influence of all that music in the family was just too much," he told *Current Biography* in a recently submitted questionnaire. Although he continued to study piano and composition, he eventually concentrated on voice under the tutelage of Ross Rosazza. He sang with the college's Chapel Choir and the Bach Festival Choir and was a soloist at the Winter Park Congregational Church. Since receiving his bachelor's degree in music in 1952, he has taken additional course work at the Mannes College of Music in New York City and at the Aspen (Colorado) Institute and has studied privately with Martial Singher, the renowned French baritone, and with Margaret Harshaw, a former soprano with the Metropolitan Opera.

In the early 1950's Reardon began his professional career at the Paper Mill Playhouse in Millburn, New Jersey as a member of the chorus in *Die Fledermaus*. As he gained more stage experience, he was assigned small roles in such dissimilar productions as *Carmen* and *Blossom Time*. After a successful audition for the New York City Opera, he made his debut with the company as Falke in *Die Fledermaus* in 1954. "I was a 'comprimario,'" he recalled to Meryle Secrest in an interview for a Washington *Post* (March 27, 1966) profile. "That means you only get to play the bit parts. But I didn't know what the word meant, so it didn't insult me." He quickly graduated to more substantial parts, such as Count Almaviva in *The Marriage of Figaro* and Olivier in *Capriccio*, and in 1956 sang the four baritone roles in Rolf Liebermann's new opera, *School For Wives*.

Throughout the 1950's Reardon pursued two distinct careers, singing with the New York City Opera during its regular winter season and with straw-hat musical stock companies during the summer. In 1959 he was Edvard Grieg in the Jones Beach (Long Island) Marine Theatre's production of the *Song of Norway*. On the Broadway stage he appeared in *New Faces of 1956*, Leonard Sillman's musical revue showcasing young talent, and in *Do Re Mi*, a musical comedy by Jule Styne, Betty Comden, and Adolph Green, as John Henry Wheeler, the debonair young business rival of Hubert Cram, the fast-talking music promoter.

As his Broadway successes continued, Reardon found it increasingly difficult to readjust to the more demanding operatic roles. Finally forced to choose between opera and musical comedy, he chose opera. "After each musical closed, it would take me the better part of a year to get swinging in opera again," he explained to James Clois in an interview for *Music & Artists* (February-March, 1968). "Opera managers were looking on me as a Broadway singer and . . . Broadway considered me somewhat as a square opera singer. I had to pick one or the other." Nevertheless, Reardon regards his theatrical experience as an invaluable training for opera. "Any company wants singers who know what they are doing and can produce more than a pear-shaped tone," he continued. "What is more boring than a fat singer standing perfectly still making singing noises that could just as easily be heard on your phonograph?"

Reardon relied on his musical comedy experience to vitalize his operatic roles. In the spring of 1963, for example, he appeared as the Count in Emmerich Kálmán's *Countess Maritza*, an operetta only infrequently performed in the United States. Widely praised for its "versatile" cast of "singing actors," the American Opera Society's production charmed the critics. Ronald Eyer, who noted in his New York *Herald Tribune* (April 2, 1963) review that music lovers "could use more of this old-fashioned yeast to leaven our musical fare," was surprised by Reardon's accomplished performance. "He not only sang his *csárdás*, he also danced it," Eyer wrote. Similarly impressed by Reardon's hilarious portrayal of the irate husband in Gian-Carlo Menotti's *Amelia Goes to the Ball*, which was presented by the New York City Opera in May 1963, Paul Henry Lang observed in the New York *Herald Tribune* (May 6, 1963) that Reardon's "very funny" performance put "real life on the stage." The singer also sang major roles in the New York City Opera's production of *Capriccio*, *Die Fledermaus*, and *The Merry Widow*, and was one of the three soloists in *Carmina Burana*. On October 8, 1964 he created the role of Belaev in the world première of *Natalia Petrovna*, Lee Hoiby's two-act opera based on Ivan Turgenev's *A Month in the Country*. The opera received generally lukewarm reviews, but Alan Rich, writing in the New York *Herald Tribune* (October 9, 1964), maintained that the "delicious" characterizations by Reardon—"as believable a Belaev as the libretto allowed"—and others atoned for the "blandness" of the "badly out of focus" opera.

His dramatic insight was even more evident when Reardon assumed the role of Scarpia, for which he claims "a particular affinity," in the (Washington, D.C.) Opera Society's production of *Tosca* in February 1964. One critic suggested that Reardon's overpowering portrait of the corrupt police chief was justification for changing the name of the Puccini warhorse from *Tosca* to "Scarpia." Appraising the singer's "truly memorable Scarpia" for the *Christian Science Monitor* (March 10, 1966), Richard D. Fletcher noted: "He . . . built a terrifying dramatic image, effectively served by fine and disciplined singing. . . . Subtle insinuations in the text were clearly delineated. Few other baritones successfully negotiate such dissimilar roles as Pelléas and Scarpia," he continued. "Reardon has done both, superlatively, on this same stage."

Reardon's New York City recital debut at Town Hall on April 28, 1964 was not particularly well received by the music critics. Although they admired his operatic skill, several reviewers considered his approach too dramatic for the art song. For example, John Gruen, writing in the New York *Herald Tribune* (April 29, 1964), contended that the "personable and charming" baritone was "hopelessly out of his depth" in the "highly specialized world of the art song." The very qualities that endeared Reardon to the opera-going public—a powerful, resonant voice, perfect diction, perceptive dramatic phrasing—proved a handicap at recitals. "I've discovered American critics don't like any emoting with their recitals—at least, not from Americans," he admitted to Meryle Secrest.

Cast as Mandryka in Richard Strauss's *Arabella*, John Reardon made his first appearance with the Metropolitan Opera during the 1965-66 season at the old, pre-Lincoln Center opera house on Broadway. In his New York *Times* (October 15, 1965) review, Howard Klein singled out Reardon's performance as the brightest spot in the production, applauding his "smooth and velvety" voice for being exceptionally strong in the high registers, and blurring only slightly in the middle and lower registers, and citing his keen rhythmic sense and almost perfect timing. Klein added that his intuitive matching of "graceful or angry movement to word ignited his scenes."

Among his other major roles in his first season with the Metropolitan Opera were Count Tomsky in Tchaikovsky's *The Queen of Spades,* Count Almaviva in *The Marriage of Figaro,* and Orin in *Mourning Becomes Electra.* More recently he has appeared as Escamillo in *Carmen,* Sharpless in *Madame Butterfly,* Mercutio in *Romeo and Juliet,* Taddeo in *L'Italiana in Algeri,* and Sergeant Belcore in *L'Elisir d'Amore,* one of his favorite roles.

In March 1966 Reardon returned to the New York City Opera to sing the title role in the American première of Gottfried von Einem's *Danton's Death.* "It is an exciting challenge to create a new role and to surmount the vocal problems posed," he explained to John Kraglund in an interview for the Toronto *Globe and Mail* (March 19, 1966). As presented in an English translation, the unfamiliar work was denounced in the press as "an artistic failure" and "a pretty bad opera," but Reardon earned praise for his sensitive portrayal of the doomed French revolutionary leader. In his New York *Herald Tribune* (March 10, 1966) review, Alan Rich hailed the "masterly creation" as "probably the best thing the young baritone has yet accomplished." Later in the year he participated in the company's Mozart festival at the Lincoln Center for the Performing Arts, singing Count Almaviva in *The Marriage of Figaro* and Papageno in *The Magic Flute.*

When the New York City Opera presented Lee Hoiby's *Summer and Smoke* in 1972, Reardon recreated the role of Dr. John Buchanan Jr., which he had originated in the world première of the opera in St. Paul, Minnesota in 1971. Hoiby adapted the opera from the Tennessee Williams play with the baritone in mind as the brilliant, self-indulgent young doctor. Commissioned by the St. Paul Opera, *Summer and Smoke* opened on June 19, 1971 to laudatory reviews. In his Washington *Post* (June 21, 1971) assessment of the first performance, Paul Hume commented: "Reardon is utterly magnificent, acting and singing with a mixture of cynicism and honest sweetness that makes his work one of the outstanding portraits on any stage today. His singing is at its finest," he added, "with every word clear, and every phrase filled with meaning."

In addition to his appearances with the major New York opera companies, Reardon has performed as a guest artist with companies in Philadelphia, Dallas, Seattle, Cincinnati, and Boston. Since the mid-1960's he has appeared regularly with the Santa Fe Opera, a young company with a deserved reputation for presenting adventurous works. In 1965 he sang the role of Kovaliov in the American première of Dmitri Shostakovich's satiric opera, *The Nose;* in 1967 he sang the taxing title role in Paul Hindemith's *Cardillac;* in 1968 he created the role of Pentheus in Hans Werner Henze's *The Bassarids,* a modern treatment of Euripides' *Bacchae;* and in 1969 he took on the assignment of the comical Dr. Stone in Gian-Carlo Menotti's fantasy, *Help, Help the Globolinks!* as well as the demanding characterization of Urbain Grandier, the worldly priest, in the first American performance of Krzysztof Penderecki's *The Devils of Loudun.* Equally at home in light opera, Reardon contributed his verve and polish as Count Danilo to the Canadian Opera Company's production of Franz Lehár's *The Merry Widow* at the O'Keefe Centre in Toronto in 1973.

Reardon has appeared as a soloist with leading American orchestras and as a concert artist in Benjamin Britten's *War Requiem,* Rachmaninoff's *The Bells,* Haydn's *Creation* and *The Seasons,* the oratorios of Bach and Handel, and songs by such composers as Mozart, Debussy, and Richard Strauss. Reviewing a performance of *The Seasons* by the Cleveland Orchestra and Chorus at Carnegie Hall on February 8, 1966, Harold C. Schonberg found that Reardon "held his own" despite the fact that the part ran "rather low for him." Moved by the singer's interpretation of the dramatic baritone passages in the *War Requiem* at a special Kennedy Center performance dedicated to the memory of the Israeli athletes slain during the 1972 Olympic Games in Munich, Germany, one critic marveled at Reardon's use of "immense power and sleepful quiet to range from bitter anger to utter acceptance."

Since the summer of 1973 Reardon has been the artistic director of the Wolf Trap Company at Wolf Trap Farm Park for the Performing Arts at Vienna, Virginia, a suburb of Washington, D.C. The first national park for the arts in the United States, Wolf Trap Farm Park provides valuable stage experience to gifted newcomers under the guidance of seasoned performers. In 1972 Reardon directed the Wolf Trap Opera Workshop. His previous teaching experience includes a season as the director of apprentices for the Santa Fe Opera and one and one-half years as a voice teacher at the Philadelphia Music Academy.

Recently Reardon concluded that only massive governmental support, including public funding, could save the performing arts from financial disaster. "The burden is simply becoming too great for the private sector to shoulder forever," he told *Current Biography.* "We will just have to take the chance that government will try to control the artistic content and guard against it." Despite his pessimistic forecast, he has refused to join his expatriate colleagues who have forged brilliant careers by singing with major European companies. "I frankly don't think singing is worth giving up the country you love," he explained to James Clois in an interview for *Music & Artists* (February-March 1968.) "If it came to a choice between selling neckties in the United States and singing full time in Europe, I think neckties would win."

A strikingly handsome man who has been described as looking like "a cross between Lawrence Tibbett and Errol Flynn," John Reardon has light brown hair and blue eyes. He stands slightly over six feet one and maintains his weight at a trim 180 pounds by swimming regularly. His hobbies include meteorology and horticulture. A bachelor, he lives on Manhattan's Upper West Side, within easy walking distance of Lincoln Center. His church affiliation is Christian Science.

References

Hi-Fi 23:MA-6+ Mr '73 pors
N Y Times II p15+ Mr 12 '72
Opera News 36:30 Ap 1 '72 por
Time 94:60+ Ag 22 '69 por
Who's Who in America, 1974-75

RIGG, DIANA

July 20, 1938- British actress
Address: c/o John Redway and Associates Ltd., 5-11 Mortimer St., W1N 7RH, London, England

Diana Rigg, who was once described by Laurence Olivier as "a brilliantly skilled and delicious actress," ranges in her accomplishments from Shakespeare and Molière to modern drama and television situation comedy. The British actress first gained recognition as a member of the Royal Shakespeare Company during the early 1960's and then gained worldwide fame as a sexy undercover agent in the internationally popular British TV spy-adventure series, *The Avengers*. After co-starring in the London and New York productions of the modern historical drama, *Abelard and Heloise*, Miss Rigg in 1972 joined the National Theatre of Britain, for which she created coruscating portrayals of Lady Macbeth, Célimène in *The Misanthrope*, and a neurotic pop singer in Tom Stoppard's *Jumpers*. In 1974 she was playing Eliza Doolittle to Alec McCowen's Professor Higgins in John Dexter's triumphant West End revival of Shaw's *Pygmalion*, the success of which more than made up for the failure of her short-lived American TV situation comedy series called *Diana*.

The only daughter of Louis and Beryl (Helliwell) Rigg, Diana Rigg was born on July 20, 1938 in Doncaster, an industrial city in Yorkshire, England. She has a younger brother, Hugh. When Diana was two months old, her family moved to Jodhpur, in northwest India, where her father, a civil engineer, became manager of the state railroad. She lived there until the age of eight,

when she was sent home to England to go to boarding school. The first school she attended was the Great Missenden School in Great Missenden, Buckinghamshire. Three years later Diana was transferred to Fulneck Girl's School in Pudsey, in the West Riding of Yorkshire, near Leeds, which she has grimly recalled as "very rigid, very strict, very cruel." "I was quite unhappy [there]," she told Arnold Hano of *TV Guide* (October 6, 1973). ". . . Classes were incredibly boring. I took to dreaming. They took to punishing me. I was always working off punishments for not doing what I was supposed to do."

The Fulneck School was hardly an unmitigated disaster for Miss Rigg, however, for it was there that she met Mrs. Sylvia Greenwood, a sympathetic teacher who introduced her to poetry, elocution, and the stage. Encouraged in her acting aspirations by Mrs. Greenwood, Diana Rigg performed in school plays, including *A Midsummer Night's Dream* in which she played Titania. Her theatrical ambitions were also fortified by her grandfather, with whom she stayed during school vacations. He would encourage her to recite poetry, and she came to love T. S. Eliot, Shakespeare, and the English lyric poets.

At seventeen Miss Rigg graduated from Fulneck and became engaged. Against the wishes of her parents (who had by that time returned to England and settled in Leeds), she had successfully auditioned for the Royal Academy of Dramatic Art instead of applying to enter a university. When her father informed her that she had to choose between school and getting married, she chose the former, thereby, as she told Catherine Stott of the *Guardian* (January 14, 1972), unintentionally giving her "a guiltless approach to relationships outside marriage."

For two years Miss Rigg studied at the Royal Academy of Dramatic Art and learned about life through what she has called "divers lovers." "[The Academy] was too rarefied," she told a *Time* reporter (December 18, 1972). "It had nothing to do with real life. As a matter of fact, I very nearly got thrown out of R.A.D.A. because I was having a dose of real life on the outside." With the Royal Academy of Dramatic Art she made her professional debut in the summer of 1957 at the York Festival playing Natella Abashwili in *The Caucasian Chalk Circle*. Over the next two years she appeared in repertory with the York and Chesterfield repertory companies, and she was an assistant stage manager with the Chesterfield company for a few months in 1958. To supplement her meager acting income, she worked as a waitress in a Greek sailors' bar and as a fashion model.

In 1959 Miss Rigg was accepted by the Royal Shakespeare Company in Stratford-on-Avon as an understudy. During that season she had walk-ons in several plays and appeared for six performances as Diana in *All's Well That Ends Well*. The following year she was signed to a five-year contract. In addition to walk-ons, during the 1960 Stratford season Miss Rigg got to play Andromache in *Troilus and Cressida*. Public recognition began to be accorded her during the Royal Shakespeare's

1961 season at its new London home, the Aldwych Theatre, where her first assignment was as second Ondine and Violanta in *Ondine*. On two days notice she subsequently took over the role of Phillipe Trincant in John Whiting's *The Devils*. Phillipe was followed by the roles of Gwendolen in Jean Anouilh's *Becket* and Bianca in *The Taming of the Shrew*. At the end of the season the London critics for *Plays and Players* named Miss Rigg one of the promising newcomers of the 1960-61 season.

After performing as Madame de Touruel in *The Art of Seduction*, based on *Les Liaisons Dangereuses*, at the Aldwych, Miss Rigg returned to Stratford, where her initial assignment was the role of Helena in Peter Hall's acclaimed production of *A Midsummer Night's Dream*. Her performance prompted a *Plays and Players* critic to write, "Diana Rigg's drooping, swooping Helena has the most outrageously comic invention and she makes the most of it." Helena was followed by Bianca in *The Taming of the Shrew*, Lady Macduff in *Macbeth*, Adriana in Clifford Williams' production of *The Comedy of Errors*, and Cordelia in Peter Brook's *King Lear*. Her performance as Adriana won her a citation by the London Critics Circle as one of the season's best actresses in a dramatic play.

In December 1962 Diana Rigg was back at the Aldwych, appearing as Cordelia and Adriana. After a stint there early in 1963 as Nurse Monika Stettler in *The Physicists*, she went on the road with the Royal Shakespeare Company, appearing in Paris as Cordelia and touring Northern England and Scotland as Helena. During the winter of 1963-64 she appeared at Stratford and at the Aldwych repeating her roles in *The Comedy of Errors*, *A Midsummer Night's Dream*, and *King Lear*. Sponsored by the British Council, the Royal Shakespeare Company set out in the spring of 1964 to tour Russia, Eastern Europe, and the United States with *The Comedy of Errors* and *King Lear*. In the United States the company appeared in Washington, D.C., Boston, Philadelphia, and New York City. After her appearance as Adriana at the New York State Theatre in Lincoln Center, New York, Richard Watts of the New York *Post* (May 21, 1964) wrote, "The beautiful Diana Rigg . . . reveals an enchanting gift of comedy in her spirited and attractive portrayal of a sorely puzzled wife." The critics were even more taken with her Cordelia, citing the monumental strength and independence that she brought to the role. "Cordelia was skillfully portrayed by Diana Rigg," wrote the critic for the New York *Journal-American* (May 9, 1964), "not as a fragile beauty whose pristine innocence prevents her from expressing her devotion. She is rather a chip off the old block—prideful and independent."

Declining to sign a second five-year contract with the Royal Shakespeare Company, Miss Rigg left it in 1964 and, late in the year, was hired as Emma Peel, the seductive spy in the British television series *The Avengers*. It was her first encounter with commercial television, since her previous performances on the home screen had

DIANA RIGG

been in the Royal Shakespeare production of *The Comedy of Errors* (January 1964), and in Donald Churchill's *The Hothouse* (December 1964), and Thomas Middleton's *Women Beware Women* (January 1965).

A tongue-in-cheek espionage-adventure series about a pair of free-lance undercover agents, *The Avengers* had been ranked in the top six of Britain's television programs since 1961. As Mrs. Peel, the "internationally educated daughter of a wealthy shipowner and youthful widow of a famous test pilot," Diana Rigg karate-chopped her way through adventures in which she and her suave partner John Steed (played by Patrick Macnee) solved diabolical murders and rescued kidnapped scientists. The relationship between Steed and Emma Peel was subtly erotic; the show's kinky touches were more obvious. Often clad in way-out leather outfits, Mrs. Peel was sometimes threatened by the sadistic advances of villains wielding whips and other instruments of torture, but she always managed to get the upper hand.

Miss Rigg made her British television debut as Emma Peel in September 1965, and shortly later the American rights to the series were sold to ABC-TV. When the show premièred in the United States in March 1966, Stanley Price of the New York *Times* (March 13, 1966) wrote that Miss Rigg "added an extra touch of wryness and humor to the old formula." As in Great Britain, both *The Avengers* and Diana Rigg were a critical and popular success in the United States, with the actress being nominated for Emmy awards as best actress in a dramatic series in 1967 and 1968. Emma Peel fan clubs were formed, and eventually Diana Rigg became known worldwide, when the show was televised in many countries.

While filming *The Avengers* Miss Rigg appeared in 1966 with the Royal Shakespeare Company—of which she had been made an associate artist—as Viola in *Twelfth Night*. The following year, after making fifty-two segments, she left *The Avengers*. Her next assignment was with the Royal Shakespeare in Peter Hall's televised version of *A Midsummer Night's Dream,* which was aired in the United States on CBS-TV in March 1969.

Miss Rigg made her film debut in *The Assassination Bureau* (Paramount, 1969), a comedy-adventure based on Jack London's unfinished novel of the same name. As a female journalist in the male world of Edwardian England, Diana Rigg prompted Vincent Canby of the New York *Times* (March 30, 1969) to observe, "In a role that is much too small for her and in a movie that has been made more often than necessary, she is still fine, pure, and very funny." Her next film assignment was as the international playgirl who marries James Bond and gets murdered in *On Her Majesty's Secret Service* (United Artists, 1969), a routine addition to the James Bond series. With an all-star British-American cast including Charlton Heston, Sir John Gielgud, and Jason Robards Jr., Diana Rigg appeared in *Julius Caesar* (American International, 1970), a disappointing treatment of Shakespeare's tragedy that was deservedly flayed by the critics. She managed to survive the film unscathed, however, in the small role of Portia, and Howard Thompson of the New York *Times* (February 4, 1971) said she was "excellent in her quicksilver precision and feeling." In January 1970 she costarred with Robert Culp in *Married Alive,* a television comedy that was aired in Great Britain on London Weekend Television and in the United States on NBC.

Returning to the stage, Miss Rigg costarred with Keith Michell in *Abelard and Heloise,* Ronald Millar's play about the tragic love of the twelfth-century schoolman and cleric and his brilliant seventeen-year-old student. After touring the provinces the play opened in the West End in May 1970, where it became one of the hits of the London season. For her interpretation of Heloise, Miss Rigg was named by the London Critics' Circle as one of the year's best actresses.

Michell and Miss Rigg left the London cast of the play late in 1970 to bring it to the United States, where, after a short run in Los Angeles, it opened on Broadway on March 10, 1971. Diana Rigg's performance captivated most of the critics, including Clive Barnes, who wrote in the New York *Times* (March 11, 1971), "Miss Rigg ... was I thought, perfect, as sensuous as a cat, with hidden fires beneath the surface, and a radiant beauty far more beguiling than that of many more obviously pretty women." She was nominated for a Tony award as best actress in a dramatic play. *Abelard and Heloise* gained a certain amount of notoriety because of a three-minute nude love scene between Michell and Miss Rigg, which made them the first major actors to appear in the nude on the London and Broadway stages. Although the London press raised a furor about it before the play opened, both British and American critics agreed that the scene was not only tasteful but important to the development of the play.

After completing her New York engagement in *Abelard and Heloise,* Diana Rigg appeared with George C. Scott in *The Hospital* (United Artists, 1971). To prepare for her part as an American nurse, the actress worked with tape recorders and voice coaches and she was rewarded for her efforts with a Golden Globe nomination as best supporting actress. "[Script-writer Paddy] Chayefsky has been responsible for some lovely lines in his life," wrote Vincent Canby in the New York *Times* (December 15, 1971) after viewing the film, "but nothing quite equal to the monologue by which this marvelous actress seduces her costar by word and well exposed leg."

In January 1972 Diana Rigg joined the National Theatre of England, and the following month she appeared at the Old Vic in the National Theatre production of Tom Stoppard's absurdist farce, *Jumpers,* which became one of the hits of that London season. For her performance as a prematurely retired West End musical comedy star married to an aging moral philosopher, Miss Rigg received such critical appreciations as that of Harold Hobson of the London *Sunday Times* (February 5, 1972), who wrote, "And if the radiant splendor of her appearance is not enough, Miss Rigg is witty and poised and returns Mr. Stoppard's intellectual service from the racket of a champion."

In November 1972 Miss Rigg returned to Shakespeare with a delineation of Lady Macbeth at the Old Vic that the *Variety* correspondent (November 29, 1972) said "reaffirms her classical training and creates an eloquent and persuasive characterization; one of authority and discipline." Her Lady Macbeth was named one of the outstanding performances of the London season by *Best Plays of 1972-73.* In John Dexter's modern-dress production of Molière's *The Misanthrope,* Miss Rigg early in 1973 added another jewel to her National Theatre repertoire with the role of Célimène. Robert Brustein (London *Observer,* March 4, 1973) noted that she had made of the usually giddy coquette the most complicated character in the play, thus confirming "her growing authority as an actress." For her portrayal of Célimène Miss Rigg was named one of the best actresses of 1973 by the London critics for *Plays and Players.*

To the chagrin of many Diana Rigg enthusiasts —one of whom said that it was like a *cordon bleu* chef cooking a McDonald's hamburger—the British actress starred in a stale NBC-TV situation comedy called *Diana* that premièred in September 1973 and was dropped in the middle of the season. Although critics panned the show, which they felt was a tired imitation of *The Mary Tyler Moore Show,* they had only praise for Miss Rigg, who played a divorced British dress designer newly settled in New York.

In May 1974 Diana Rigg opened in the West End in a revival of George Bernard Shaw's comedy *Pygmalion,* the first one allowed since 1956, when the success of the musical version, *My Fair Lady,* crowded it off the boards. Her Eliza Doolittle was hailed by Robert Cushman of the London *Observer* (May 19, 1974) as "a rare comic creation, compact of dignity, fire, and mischief." Before returning to the National Theatre in 1975 to play the title role in a new production of *Phèdre*, Miss Rigg is scheduled to recreate her Célimène at the Kennedy Center in Washington, D.C. Her most recent film is *Theatre of Blood* (United Artists, 1973), a black comedy in which she plays the devoted daughter of a British actor (Vincent Price), who sets out to kill off the members of the London Critics' Circle after they fail to give him the best actor award. All the murders are taken from the plays of Shakespeare.

Diana Rigg, who has been called "the thinking man's sex symbol," is five feet eight and a half inches tall, weighs about 121 pounds, and has brown eyes and auburn hair. Fiercely independent and blunt in her opinions, she has said that she identifies with the new woman evolving in our society but is not especially in sympathy with the women's liberation movement. "I don't think women's lib would exist if women had financial freedom. If every woman had financial freedom she'd have herself sorted out in no time," the actress told Andrew Smith of *Harper's Bazaar* (January 1974).

Long outspoken in her opposition to marriage, Miss Rigg lived for eight years, until the fall of 1972, with the British writer and director Philip Saville. She succumbed to matrimony, however, on July 6, 1973, after a stormy five-month romance with Menaham Gueffen, an Israeli painter. Eleven months later she and Gueffen agreed to a "trial separation." In London Miss Riggs lives in her house in Barnes; when on vacation she often goes to an old farmhouse that she owns on the Spanish Balearic island of Ibiza. Easily bored, she loves her many-faceted career and enjoys traveling and learning about new things. Her pastimes include reading, writing, cooking, and growing herbs. She dislikes exercise. Although she has expressed a desire to have children, she believes that "the timing has to be right."

References

Guardian p11 Ja 14 '72 por
Time 100:62 D 18 '72 pors
TV Guide 21:30+ O 6 '73 por
Who's Who, 1973-74
Who's Who in the Theatre, 1972

ROBBE-GRILLET, ALAIN (rob grē-ā')

Aug. 18, 1922- French novelist; film maker *Address*: b. Éditions de Minuit, 7 rue Bernard-Palissy, Paris 6°, France; h. 18 boulevard Maillot, 92 Neuilly-sur-Seine, France

The foremost practitioner and theoretician of the *nouveau roman* or so-called "anti-novel" is Alain Robbe-Grillet, whose novels, short stories, essays, and film scenarios comprise one of the most daring and experimental *oeuvres* in contemporary French literature. According to Robbe-Grillet, the anthropocentric attempts of traditional novelists to impose meaning on the world are naïve and irrelevant, because "the world is neither insignificant nor absurd. It simply *is*." Instead of relying

ALAIN ROBBE-GRILLET

on metaphor, the "new" novelist describes the world as meticulously and dispassionately as possible. He rejects linear plots, rounded characters, and psychological depth in order to record reality in the same fragmented way that the mind perceives, remembers, imagines, and dreams.

Robbe-Grillet published his first novel, *Les Gommes*, in 1953, and since then has published five more, including *Dans le labyrinthe*, *La Maison de rendez-vous*, and *Projet pour une révolution à New York*. All of them are characterized by a cool, detached tone at variance with the dark and turbulent side of human nature that they explore—a world of murder, jealousy, and sado-erotic obsessions. To the general public Robbe-Grillet is perhaps best known as the author of the screenplay for the celebrated—and controversial—film, *L'Année dernière à Marienbad (Last Year at Marienbad)*, which won the grand prize at the 1961 Venice Film Festival. An innovative, highly stylized love story, the film featured many of the techniques of Robbe-Grillet's novels, including circular structure, nonlinear chronology, and the unexplained juxtaposition of reality, memory, and imaginings. Since *Marienbad* Robbe-Grillet has written and directed four films. In France his works have been published by Les Éditions de Minuit; in the United States his publisher is Grove Press. Most of his output has been translated into English by Richard Howard.

Alain Robbe-Grillet was born on August 18, 1922 in Brest, Finistère to Gaston and Yvonne (Canu) Robbe-Grillet, who had moved there from the Jura, near Switzerland. As a child, Robbe-Grillet was fascinated with the lichens and rock plants of the Breton seacoast, and, after his early education at the Lycée Buffon in Paris, the Lycée de Brest, and the Lycée St. Louis in Paris, he decided to take up agronomy, like his father and sister before him. His chief American exegete, Bruce Morrissette, in *Alain Robbe-Grillet* (1965), however, speculates that the author's interest in flora and fauna bore results not in his scientific career "but rather in the habits of observation of microstructures and their scientifically phrased descriptions which lie, at least partly, at the source of his so-called objectal prose vocabulary of surface geometries."

During World War II Robbe-Grillet was deported to Germany to work in a German tank factory in Nuremberg. There he met Claude Ollier, who was later to become one of the French writers of the "new novel." After the war he obtained his diploma from the French National Institute of Agronomy and went to work in Paris for the National Institute of Statistics. While working as a statistician he published his first known work, a survey of French cattle. After three years at the institute, in 1948, he became restless and took an undemanding job at a small laboratory run by his sister. While working there Robbe-Grillet wrote his first novel, "Un Régicide," which has never been published. In need of money, in 1949 he took a job with the Institute of Colonial Fruits and Crops, studying the diseases of bananas and other tropical fruits in Morocco, French Guinea, Martinique, and Guadeloupe. In 1951, while working as the overseer of a banana plantation in Martinique, Robbe-Grillet fell ill with a tropical disease, and during his hospitalization he made the decision to abandon agronomy for a writing career.

Returning to Paris, Robbe-Grillet began to write, and in 1953 his novel Les Gommes (The Erasers, 1964) was published by Jérôme Linden's Les Éditions de Minuit. Not long after that, Linden hired Robbe-Grillet as his literary director, a position he holds at the present time. Over the years the Paris publishing house has published the works of the authors who have come to be associated with the avant-garde in general, and the nouveau roman in particular, including Samuel Beckett, Nathalie Sarraute, Claude Simon, Marguerite Duras, Michel Butor, and Claude Ollier.

Although Les Gommes received scant attention from the public and the popular press on its publication, it received some favorable reviews in literary magazines and was awarded a literary prize in 1954. A kind of ironic detective story, Les Gommes is about a special agent named Wallas who attempts to investigate the murder of Dupont, a recluse. Unknown to the detective, Dupont has only been wounded and is in hiding. Exactly twenty-four hours after the murder has been bungled, Wallas returns to the scene of the crime and kills Dupont, mistaking him for his murderer and thus making the imaginary killing a reality. Since there are hints in the text that Dupont may be Wallas' father, the novel has been read as a sardonic retelling of the Oedipus myth.

If in The Erasers Robbe-Grillet betrays an uncharacteristic interest in plot, the novel nonetheless displays many of the hallmarks of his later works, including a concern with the discrepancy between objective and subjective reality, circular structure, nonlinear chronology, repetitions, "false" scenes, disturbing quasi-symbolic objects (like the gum erasers that Wallas seeks in vain throughout the novel), and a labyrinthine setting. How-

ever, the characteristic of the book that intrigued many critics was its elaborate, compulsively precise descriptions of objects, such as the well-known passage in which Robbe-Grillet describes a wedge of tomato served in an automat: "A quarter section of tomato quite perfect and without defect, sliced by machine from an absolutely symmetrical fruit. The peripheral flesh, compact and homogeneous, of a fine chemical redness, is uniformly thick between a band of shiny skin and the semicircular area where the seeds are arranged, yellow, of uniform caliber, held in place by a thin layer of greenish jelly lying alongside the swelling at the heart. The latter, of a dilute and slightly granular pink, begins, near the lower hollow, in a network of white veins, one of which stretches out towards the seeds, in a somewhat uncertain manner. At the top, a scarcely visible accident has occurred: a corner of the skin, detached from the flesh over the space of one or two millimeters, sticks up imperceptibly." Such obsessive attention to the surface appearance of things led Roland Barthes and other critics to praise Robbe-Grillet as a *chosiste*, or one who insists on the non-referential, antimetaphysical reality of things divorced from human reference.

Robbe-Grillet's second book, Le Voyeur (1955; The Voyeur, 1958), is a strange, elliptical narrative viewed through the eyes of Mathias, an itinerant watch salesman who is peddling his wares on a small island. His increasingly hallucinatory perceptions reveal that he has apparently tortured and murdered a young girl on the island, but, even though the details of his movements are obsessively told and retold, the actual crime is never clearly described. The Voyeur won the prestigious Prix des Critiques and launched the author's reputation as a major literary figure in France.

Like Le Voyeur, La Jalousie (1957; Jealousy, 1959) is written in the third person, but its scenes take place in the tortured mind of a banana planter who imagines—whether correctly or incorrectly the reader never learns—that his wife is unfaithful. The husband rehearses over and over in his mind several incidents in which his wife and her putative lover interact. In one such incident the man kills a small centipede, which in the husband's mind gradually grows into a beast of gigantic proportions. Despite the emotion-charged potential of the narrative, it is presented, like Robbe-Grillet's other novels, in an objective, factual tone that forces the reader to bring his own imagination and feeling to the story.

In Dans le labyrinthe (1959; In the Labyrinth, 1960) Robbe-Grillet makes the novelist's creative process itself the central theme. The narrator, a nameless figure shut up in a room containing, among other things, a box wrapped in brown paper, creates a story about a soldier from a vanquished army who must deliver the box to someone in a city about to be occupied by the enemy. At one point the narrator intrudes himself into the story as a doctor, and by the end the soldier is dead and the narrator is again alone in the room with the box. *Dans le labyrinthe* quickly became the most popular of Robbe-Grillet's novels, selling 15,000 copies in its first year. Despite the author's warning that the book is only "a fiction" with "no allegorical meaning," some critics extolled it as an allegorical tale.

It was in order to prevent such misunderstandings and to explain his works to the reading public, Robbe-Grillet has said, that he began writing essays on what soon came to be known as the "new novel." His success in that venture is open to question, but there is no doubt that his periodic manifestos on literature served to publicize his works and those of the other authors associated with the *nouveau roman*. His first essay was published in the *Nouvelle Revue Française* in 1956 and in English in the *Evergreen Review* the following year. In 1963 his essays were collected in *Pour un nouveau roman* (*For a New Novel*, 1966).

In his essays Robbe-Grillet announces a new literature that disencumbers itself of the humanist burden of the traditional novel, a literature that rejects the "continuous fringe of culture" superimposed on objects to give them a less alien aspect. With the new freedom of observation thus achieved, readers will be able to see that the world "is neither significant nor absurd. It *is*, quite simply." In language he urges the abolition of anthropomorphic metaphors like "majestic" mountain, "pitiless" sun, or "huddled" village in favor of "the visual or descriptive adjective, the word that contents itself with measuring, limiting, defining." With the rejection of anthropomorphism comes the rejection of characters as the central aspect of the novel. Likewise the centrality of the plot is gone, its "innocent" naturalism replaced by an art that deliberately asserts its invention and artifice.

Robbe-Grillet's ideas found application not only in literature. The meticulously descriptive, quasi-photographic nature of his narrations had always seemed to have borrowed much from cinematic techniques, and it was perhaps inevitable that the author would eventually turn to motion pictures. Early in 1970 Robbe-Grillet and the French film director Alain Resnais agreed to collaborate on a film of a new type that would abandon linear plot and traditional flashback techniques for a work that juxtaposes past and present, memories, false imaginings, and reality without explanation or transition. Set in a labyrinthine baroque castle converted into a resort hotel, *L'Année dernière à Marienbad* is a story of persuasion. A handsome stranger at the hotel gradually convinces a beautiful young woman that she has had an affair with him "last year at Marienbad," that she made him promise he would wait a year for her, and that she must now break off with her companion (who may be her husband) and keep her promise. Photographed in black and white with a camera that moves slowly over the details of the hotel and its formal gardens, the film is narrated by the stranger, whose narration is sparse, repetitious, and incantatory. The acting, often outwardly emotionless, is highly stylized and even operatic in mode.

At the 1961 Venice Film Festival *L'Année dernière à Marienbad* captured the Golden Lion, and when it was released commercially in France it was lauded by many critics as the most important and original film in decades. Breaking art film records in France, the cool romanticism of *Last Year at Marienbad* captured the imagination of filmgoers who speculated endlessly—despite the author's protests that the question was irrelevant—over whether or not the woman and the stranger had actually met "last year." In the United States *Last Year at Marienbad* (Astor, 1962) was accorded a similarly enthusiastic reception, although some critics found it maddeningly obscure and pretentious.

In the decade after the release of *Marienbad*, Robbe-Grillet wrote and directed four films which, if they did not achieve the success of his first cinematic venture, nonetheless earned a measure of critical acclaim. The highest praised was *L'Immortelle* (1963), an eternal triangle story set in Turkey, which won the Prix Louis Delluc. After viewing Robbe-Grillet's next film, *Trans-Europ-Express* (1967) at the 1967 London Film Festival, Harold Hobson of the *Christian Science Monitor* (December 8, 1967) called it "an ingenious variation on the theme of reality, and philosophically absorbing." In the film Robbe-Grillet plays the part of a film director who creates a lurid story about a young man who is a passenger on the same train he is riding. In *L'Homme qui ment* (1968) Robbe-Grillet presents the story of a man who creates his own character, past, and emotions. Robbe-Grillet's latest film, *L'Eden et après* (1970) was dismissed by Jean De Baroncelli of *Le Monde* (June 3, 1970) as "simply an elegant pastiche that is spiced with a dash of surrealism and the sort of eroticism found in certain strip cartoons."

The novel *La Maison de rendez-vous* (1965; *La Maison de Rendez-Vous*, 1966) is a playful, erotic fabrication set in the Hong Kong of Westerners' fantasy, a place of political intrigue, white slavery, and unspeakable depravities. It mainly concerns the activities at the Blue Villa, an elegant brothel that stages exquisitely perverse spectacles featuring snarling black dogs and acquiescent servant girls. In his earlier novels Robbe-Grillet recounted several different versions of each incident; in this novel characters assume a variety of identities as well. Reality becomes irrelevant as the book shifts kaleidoscopically from one invention to another. Many critics enjoyed *La Maison*, agreeing with Eliot Fremont-Smith (New York *Times*, November 23, 1966), who called it "a funny book, a provocation, a do-it-yourself mystery or fairy tale."

Like the Hong Kong of *La Maison de Rendez-Vous*, the New York of *Projet pour une révolution à New York* (1970; *Project for a Revolution in New York*, 1972) is an imaginary city, a city of fear and violent crime reported by the mass media. The book is peopled by a shifting cast of characters who belong to a subversive underground organization that tortures young women and plans acts of murder, rape, and arson. The obsession with sado-eroticism, usually present in Robbe-

Grillet's works but especially prominent here, offended some critics, but others, like John Sturrock (London *Observer*, January 28, 1973) admired *Project for a Revolution in New York*: "As an allegory of the birth (or still-birth) of a fiction, [it] is an impossibly clever book and has got to be read with only half the mind on what is occurring on the page while the other half works out the reasons why it is occurring. The challenge is to reconstruct the novelist's own logic of events."

Robbe-Grillet's short stories, which explore many of the themes developed in his novels, are collected in *Instantanés* (1962; translated as *Snapshots* by Bruce Morrissette, 1968). For the photographer David Hamilton, Robbe-Grillet has written verses for two volumes of photographs of young women, *Rêves de jeunes filles* (Montel, 1971; *Dreams of a Young Girl*, Morrow, 1971) and *Les Demoiselles d'Hamilton* (Laffont, 1972).

Although to his detractors Robbe-Grillet remains a frivolous "anti-novelist," he has for almost two decades been a prominent figure in French letters, frequently appearing on television or at cultural institutes to talk about his literary theories. In 1965 he made a lecture tour of the United States and in 1972 he taught for a semester at New York University. As of 1970 Robbe-Grillet's works had been translated into twenty-three languages, and his French publishers had sold some 430,000 copies of his books. His works are generously represented in anthologies of twentieth-century literature, and he has been the subject of lengthy critical studies in France, the United States, and Great Britain.

Alain Robbe-Grillet is of medium height with a solid, athletic build. He has thick, curly black hair, a bushy mustache, and humorous brown eyes. Interviewers have described him as charming, warm, and unpretentious, although at least one of his interpreters, John Sturrock (*The French New Novel*, 1969) has warned that "he is not especially reliable as an interviewee, since his answers are sometimes too irreverently oblique not to mislead." Robbe-Grillet has classified himself as "anti-religious" and politically "rather on the Left." He considers his principal literary influences to have been James Joyce, William Faulkner, Franz Kafka, and Lewis Carroll, and his favorite contemporary author is Vladimir Nabokov. Robbe-Grillet has been married since October 23, 1957 to the former Catherine Rstakian, whom he met in Turkey.

References

Guardian p5 Ap 29 '67 por
Contemporary Authors vols 9-12 1st rev. (1974)
Encyclopedia of World Literature in the Twentieth Century vol 3 (1971)
Grigson, Geoffrey, ed. Concise Encyclopedia of Modern World Literature (1971)
International Who's Who, 1973-74
Morrissette, Bruce. Alain Robbe-Grillet (1965)
Who's Who in France, 1971-72

ROSEN, SAMUEL

1897- Ear specialist
Address: b. 101 E. 73d St., New York 10021; h. Orchard Hill Rd., Katonah, N.Y. 10536

Simple, unexpected happenings sometimes precipitate great discoveries, as the New York ear surgeon Dr. Samuel Rosen proved in 1952, when in performing a routine diagnostic procedure he stumbled upon a technique that would restore hearing to many sufferers of ostosclerosis. About one half of all conductive deafness is caused by ostosclerosis, a condition in which the bony wall lividing the middle and inner ear thickens. He discovered that by freeing the stapes, the third of the bones in the middle ear, allowing it to vibrate and thus function naturally, he could alleviate deafness. The operation that Rosen developed is exceedingly delicate because the stapes is the smallest bone in the body. Through his own work and those of the surgeons around the world to whom he has taught stapes surgery, Rosen is directly or indirectly responsible for improving the hearing of about a million persons. Besides revolutionizing ear surgery, he has pioneered in research on noise pollution and the connection between hearing and nutrition and cardiovascular disease.

The fourth of five children in a poor Jewish family, Samuel Rosen was born to George and Ella Rosen in 1897 in Syracuse, New York and was reared in that city's ghetto. His father, a peddler of crockery who had little aptitude for his trade, at times earned barely enough to feed his children. By the age of eight Samuel Rosen had decided to become a doctor so that he could try to find a cure for asthma, from which his mother suffered severely. In his teens, however, he was diverted from his ambition in medicine by his admiration for a kindly lawyer who helped him collect from a dishonest grocer the wages of $15 that he had earned as a delivery boy.

With the financial help of his brothers and sisters, Rosen enrolled in Syracuse University, a prelaw student and, as he has called himself, "a thoroughgoing court buff." About a third of the way through his training in law, he realized that what he actually wanted after all was to be a doctor. As soon as he transferred to Syracuse Medical School, he knew with certainty that he was temperamentally suited to a career in medicine rather than law. After obtaining his M.D. degree in 1921, he began a two-year internship at Mt. Sinai Hospital in New York City. "As my internship progressed, I found myself on the ear, nose, and throat service for several months," he wrote in *The Autobiography of Dr. Samuel Rosen* (Knopf, 1973). "Almost at once I knew I had finally found my place in medicine. The surgery in this specialty was especially satisfying to me, because it required a meticulousness and a precision that surgery in roomier parts of the human anatomy did not demand."

Specializing in otology, Rosen also completed his residency training at Mt. Sinai, under the guidance of Dr. Isadore Friesner, chief of the hospital's ear, nose, and throat service. He then accepted an appointment as attending surgeon on that service, and in association with Friesner he launched a private practice through which he soon became recognized as a highly skilled surgeon. When he began his practice a primary function of ear surgery was to stop the spread of infection by removal of the mastoid. With the development of antibiotics in the early 1940's, mastoidectomy became obsolete and otologists rechanneled their talents into relieving disorders of the middle ear. The accepted operation for ostosclerosis at that point was fenestration nov-ovalis, developed by Julius Lempert. The three middle-ear bones receive sound vibrations from the ear drum, magnifying and transmitting them to the inner ear. Ostosclerosis prevents the ossicles from working correctly so that sound does not reach the auditory nerve. By creating a window in the horizontal canal, fenestration provided an alternative route through which sound reached the inner ear. The long, difficult operation required a two-to-three-week convalescence. One of its possible side effects was severe vertigo because surgery carried the risk of tampering with the organ of equilibrium. Even when successful, fenestration could not fully restore hearing. The operation sometimes proved useless because midway through the procedure the stapes was found to be mobile, instead of being fixed by the thickening of the ostosclerotic bone.

To establish, therefore, that the stapes was rigid before subjecting the patient to the fenestration operation, Dr. Rosen decided to make a simple surgical diagnostic test. One morning in 1952 while he was performing his preliminary examination, his probing freed the fixed stapes. The patient immediately declared he could hear normally. Rosen was astute enough to grasp the significance of what had happened, although many of his colleagues later said that they themselves probably would have ignored the events of that April morning, considering them a freak exception.

Convinced that mobilization of the stapes had restored the middle ear to its natural functioning, Rosen prepared to duplicate his success by first experimenting and practising on cadavers so that he could familiarize himself with the variations in human anatomy and test the strength of the stapes. He also designed a new set of surgical instruments, a modification of a dentist's tools. After several months of intensive work to refine his technique, Rosen performed his operation on selected patients to whom he carefully explained the experimental procedure. With his precisely tuned sense of touch he was often able to free the stapes by pushing on it gently and rhythmically. Sometimes he was required to pry it loose. (He and others eventually developed techniques for handling problems involving stapes found to be permanently fixed.) A disinterested audiologist tested the patients before and after the operation to validate Rosen's work and generally recorded

DR. SAMUEL ROSEN

improved hearing and in some instances 100 percent recovery of hearing. Patients were normally discharged from the hospital the day following the operation.

Once Rosen could prove that he had made an important discovery, he tried to communicate his knowledge to his colleagues at Mt. Sinai. For months they ignored what he had to say and refused to observe his operation. Their skeptical reaction to demonstrable facts was difficult for Rosen to understand, but he proposed three reasons for their attitude in his autobiography—money, politics, and racism. His procedure, first of all, greatly lessened the importance of the fenestration operation that ear surgeons were accustomed to perform, a technique requiring years to master and earning high fees.

Because of his liberal political stand, such as in his support of Franklin D. Roosevelt, Dr. Rosen had, moreover, incurred among his conservative colleagues a cloud of suspicion that he felt had cost him an appointment some years earlier as successor to Friesner in the position of head of the ear, nose, and throat service. A close friend of Henry A. Wallace, he backed Wallace's Presidential candidacy on the Progressive party ticket in 1948. Furthermore, in 1949 Rosen agreed to allow the Civil Rights Congress to hold a rally at his summer place in Katonah, New York to protest right-wing disruption of a concert sponsored by the Congress to raise funds for the defense of American Communists. Although not a Communist himself, he strongly believes in the right of freedom of expression. By alienating many of his patients and colleagues, Rosen's liberal commitments threatened to destroy his practice and perhaps accounted in part for the early disappointing reception given his discovery in some medical circles. One other explanation for opposition occurred to him, as he wrote in his autobiography: "I am a Jew, and ours is a racist country, sad to say. Medicine is tainted with this disease just as are the other professions." Evidence of prejudice could not be ignored.

When he was able to claim good results of at least a year's duration from his operation, Dr. Rosen put his discovery on record by making a preliminary report at a meeting of a section of the Medical Society of the State of New York. It was not until 1955 that he was invited to present a paper on stapes mobilization before the American Laryngological, Rhinological and Otological Society, an occasion that enabled him to spread knowledge of the results of his work throughout the profession. By that time he had won considerable acceptance for his technique abroad, beginning in 1953 when he demonstrated stapes mobilization surgery in London. Since then he has taught ear surgery in at least forty countries throughout the world, including both Israel and Egypt. He travels at his own expense, accepts no fee for operations outside New York, and supplies his own set of instruments, which he then gives to the hospital with the condition that instrument makers be permitted to study their special design for manufacturing purposes.

Over the years in travel undertaken mainly for teaching, Rosen also learned much through research. Concerned about the deterioration of hearing in the form of nerve deafness, which seems an inevitable part of the aging process, he began to investigate the assumption that such degeneration is universal. One of his most widely publicized studies centered on the extraordinarily acute hearing of a tribe of Mabaans, who live in a remote part of the Sudan. The background noise of their society, in a Stone Age culture, measured one-tenth the sound made by an electric refrigerator. Mabaans were found to have better hearing in their fifties than Americans in their twenties and to lose their ability to hear high frequencies only very slowly as they aged. Besides measuring hearing acuity, Rosen's team of researchers made physical and psychological examinations. With their quiet, stress-free environment and a diet low in saturated fats, the Mabaans showed a remarkable absence of heart trouble, hypertension, duodenal ulcer, and other common ailments of Western man.

Other studies of Rosen document a relation between cardiovascular disease and hearing loss. The ear is the one sense organ not directly supplied by the blood vessels. Since the supply of vital nutrients is indirect, anything retarding the blood supply is most critical to the inner ear. The hardening of capillaries causes a drop in high-frequency hearing that seems to be the first indication of circulatory problems. Rosen took part in an experiment in two mental hospitals in Finland. For five years patients in Kellokoski Hospital ate the common Finnish diet high in animal fats, while those in Nikkila Hospital received food high in polyunsaturated fats. In the second group cholesterol levels declined, as did deaths due to heart attacks. Hearing also improved. Then the diets in both hospitals were reversed and patients in Kelloloski Hospital led in improved cholesterol levels and related conditions. At the same time hearing improved in Kelloloski while it worsened in Nikkila.

Quiet is an essential for good health, according to Rosen, who has studied the harmful effects of noise to which the body responds involuntarily. Even if an individual feels he has adjusted to the din of urban life, his nervous system never will. As quoted in *Life* (May 15, 1970), Rosen described the intensity with which the body reacts each time to a sudden noise: "The heart beats rapidly, the blood vessels constrict, the pupils dilate, and the stomach, esophagus and intestines are seized by spasms." He has warned against the dangers of rock music, which he classifies with jets, subways, and sirens as injurious to man's hearing, and in an attempt to publicize the deleterious effects of noise pollution, a likely contributor to heart disease, he has criticized existing laws and standards as inadequate.

Among the thousands of people throughout the world to whom Dr. Rosen restored hearing was Ratan K. Nehru, the cousin of the late Prime Minister of India, Jawaharlal Nehru. Since his patient happened to be the Indian Ambassador to the government of mainland China, the doctor's reputation penetrated the bamboo curtain. In 1965 the government of China invited him for a visit, but when the United States State Department publicized the invitation for propaganda purposes, the Chinese canceled the trip. Rosen, however, remained eager to see for himself what he has called China's "bold new social experiment," and in 1971 as a guest of the Chinese Medical Association he became one of four American doctors to enter China.

During his visit in 1971 and on a later visit Dr. Rosen obtained training in a complex process developed by the Chinese to treat nerve deafness by acupuncture. He then organized in New York a program of acupuncture therapy and testing involving 110 deaf children. The study, the first of its kind in the Western world, parallels a similar experiment in Peking, in the first collaborative medical research project ever undertaken between Americans and Communist Chinese. Rosen believes that Americans have much to learn from the Chinese in addition to medical knowledge. "The Chinese move quietly. There is a kind of basic tranquility to the pace of life," he asserted in his autobiography. ". . . There is something about both the Mabaans and the Chinese that makes them seem beautiful, natural people, in close harmony with nature."

Dr. Rosen's present title is Emeritus Clinical Professor of Otolaryngology at Mt. Sinai School of Medicine. The tributes paid him in recognition of his contributions to ear surgery include the American Medical Association's Gold Medal for original work in medicine (1956), the first Pietro Caliceti Award of the University of Bologna (1957), and the first Dr. S. G. Joshi Medal, presented by the Indian Association of Otolaryngologists (1959).

Despite the fact that New York is one of the noisiest cities in the world, Dr. Samuel Rosen continues to live and practise there. His wife, the former Helen van Dernoot, whom he married on November 26, 1928, works with him on research and accompanies him on his travels, assisting as his technician when he operates. They have two children, John F. Rosen, a pediatrician, and Judith (Rosen) Ruben, a teacher. Rosen is a sports fan and occasionally plays tennis and baseball at his Katonah home. According to his own description, he is "only 5 feet 7½ inches tall and not exactly slender." When Rita Delfiner interviewed him for the New York *Post* (June 4, 1973), he was wearing a blue blazer and his favorite bright red tie. She was attracted to his "jovial-wise-cherubic expression and an open manner that invites questions." Throughout his humanitarian career Dr. Rosen's extraordinary professional skill has been complemented by immense goodwill, compassion, and humor.

References

Life 68:R My 15 '70 pors
N Y Herald Tribune mag p8+ O 25 '64 por
N Y Post p29 Je 4 '73 por
N Y Times p73 O 27 '63; p9 S 15 '71; p20 O 31 '71

WILLIAM B. SAXBE

SAXBE, WILLIAM B(ART)

June 24, 1916- Attorney General of the United States
Address: b. Department of Justice, Constitution Ave. and 10th St. N.W., Washington, D.C. 20530

William B. Saxbe, the Attorney General *du jour* —to borrow a phrase from veteran Washington journalist Victor S. Navasky—was a disillusioned "law and order" Republican in the Senate when the "Saturday night massacre" occurred, on October 20, 1973. On that occasion Elliot Richardson, President Nixon's third Attorney General, resigned and Richardson's deputy, William D. Ruckelshaus, was discharged, when in turn they refused to obey the President's order to fire special Watergate prosecutor Archibald Cox. While Robert H. Bork filled in as Acting Attorney General, the White House sought to fill the Justice Department vacancy permanently with a person who was not only not "out to get Nixon" but also obviously not "soft" on him either, because it wished to avoid a prolonged and politically damaging confirmation battle in the Senate. It found such a man in Saxbe, a GOP maverick who tried to support the administration where he could despite his judgment that the Nixon regime was "one of the most inept" in our history.

Saxbe accepted the Cabinet appointment with alacrity because he was planning to retire from elective office anyway and because he is genuinely interested in the pursuit of justice. (Before his election to the Senate, in 1968, he was Attorney General of Ohio.) When he took charge of the Justice Department in January 1974 he did so with an expressed determination to restore the department's shattered morale and raise its credibility. Paradoxically, one of his chief means to

the latter end, an open, "fresh air" policy with the press, has boomeranged. Joining in the public outrage evoked by some of his blunt offhand remarks, an editorialist for the Washington *Post* (April 21, 1974) compared Saxbe unfavorably to Martha Mitchell: "Outburst for outburst and indiscretion for indiscretion, he makes her look like Calvin Coolidge."

Of English descent, William Bart Saxbe was born on June 24, 1916 in Mechanicsburg, Ohio, the town where his great-grandfather settled in 1825. His parents were Bart Rockwell Saxbe and Faye Henry (Carey) Saxbe. Some have suggested that his political independence comes from the maternal side of his family, on which Patrick Henry was an ancestor. But in tracing the genesis of his straightforward "country" style it is not necessary to look further than the Midwest farming community where he grew up and where his father was a cattle buyer.

Saxbe attended Mechanicsburg High School, where he played football, and Ohio State University, from which he graduated with a B.A. degree in political science in 1940. A member of the Ohio National Guard, he served for five years stateside in the Army Air Forces during World War II. Called up again during the Korean conflict, he was discharged in the rank of colonel after serving two additional years of duty within the United States. Before beginning the study of law, Saxbe thought seriously about becoming an Episcopal minister.

While studying law at Ohio State University, Saxbe was elected to the Ohio House of Representatives, where he spent four terms. In his third term (1951-52) he was majority leader and in his fourth (1953-54), speaker. In 1954, six years after receiving his law degree, he became a partner in the Columbus, Ohio law firm of Saxbe, Boyd & Prine. After three years in the private sector, practising law and raising cattle on his farm in Mechanicsburg, he ran for state Attorney General. He was elected to four terms in that office, for a total of eight years (1957-58 and 1963-68). At the polls he had the support of organized labor because, unlike Ohio Republicans generally, he had from the beginning opposed "right-to-work" legislation.

As Attorney General of Ohio, Saxbe was, in the words of an associate, "a tough, capable crime fighter." He favored capital punishment as a deterrent and stiff prison sentences for gun-related crimes, but, unlike some other hard-liners on crime, he backed such decisions of the Warren Court as that affirming the right of a defendant to counsel. He explained his stand as "conservative on money and crime" and "liberal on the rights of people." He opposed, as he still does, gun-control legislation, which he considers "an idealistic dream." Regarding his eight years as state Attorney General, Saxbe once said it was "one job" he "really liked." He explained: "It is a challenge, a challenge that I really like. It is a personnel job. It is a management job. It requires an understanding of lawyers, and I have probably hired a thousand lawyers in my days as Attorney General."

In 1968 Saxbe became the Republican candidate for United States Senator from Ohio, running against liberal Democrat John J. Gilligan, a former literature professor. Gilligan's campaign centered on the issue of the Vietnam war, while Saxbe campaigned on the law and order issue and called for a return to business-minded leadership that would give private enterprise a greater role in the solution of national problems. Making quiet but effective use of television and personal appearances, Saxbe's campaign was successful. In the closely fought election he defeated Gilligan by 116,476 votes.

Those who had expected Saxbe to follow a rigidly conservative line when he reached Washington in 1969 were surprised to find him taking unexpectedly liberal positions, such as his stand against the Pentagon's deployment of anti-ballistic missiles. Expressing his fear that the nation was becoming "militaristic" and a "national security state," he wrote in a law review article: "We are on the brink of a new round in the arms race, more costly and more dangerous than any which preceded it. To maintain our current foreign policy is a ticket on the Titanic." His independent stand prompted his erstwhile opponent, John J. Gilligan to comment, "If I had known he was going to be like this, I would have voted for him myself."

As a Senator, Saxbe supported the Supreme Court nominations of G. Harrold Carswell and William Rehnquist and opposed that of Clement Haynesworth. He was against the extension of the 10 percent tax surcharge sought by the administration; against a cutoff of funds for the Vietnam war; and for the controversial "no knock" search warrant clause in the 1970 crime control bill. John S. Lang of the New York *Post* (April 27, 1974) observed that "during his four years in the Senate his voting record appeared to have moved gradually to the right on most major issues." As evidence, Lang cited Saxbe's rating with the liberal Americans for Democratic Action, which dropped from 61 percent in 1969 to 15 percent in 1972, and his rating with the conservative Americans for Constitutional Action, which rose over the same period from 27 to 58 percent.

Early in his term in the Senate, Saxbe told reporters how appalled he was to find so many politicians in Washington, including those in the White House, out of touch with the electorate. "I think there is a real urgency and I've communicated my feelings to the President and everyone else who would listen...," he said. "I get terribly discouraged sometimes." After two years he admitted he was bored and disenchanted with the Senate and would probably not seek reelection. "The first six months I kept wondering how I got there," he said. "After that I started wondering how all of them did."

He was especially critical of the slow pace of the legislative process: "The future of the country lies with Congress—and in many ways it could do a better job. . . . [But] if they can take action by doing nothing, they will." With Senator Alan Cranston of California, Saxbe looked for ways to speed bills through Congress and to end the use of the filibuster as a weapon for stalling legislation. He and Cranston devised what is called the "two-track" system, a procedure for sidetracking legislation that threatens to become stalled in argument while allowing less controversial bills to pass through the legislative process quickly.

Reflecting Saxbe's disenchantment with the Senate was his decision to junket at every opportunity, to Japan, Thailand, India, Africa, Israel, and most of the countries of Europe, including the Soviet Union. "I've taken every free trip I could," he admitted. "I like to travel." One result of his traveling was a plea in the Senate on May 10, 1971, for aid to East Bengal and a cutoff of aid to Pakistan. He believes his action on that issue was one of his greatest achievements in the Senate.

Saxbe's maverick stance became increasingly obvious when, in 1971, he referred to Presidential aides H. R. Haldeman and John Ehrlichman as "a couple of Nazis." "I caught hell out in Ohio for that remark," he has recalled. "But I noticed that after the Watergate story broke a year or so later, people didn't criticize me any more." When President Nixon resumed the bombing of North Vietnam in December 1972, Saxbe's comment was widely reported in the press: "I have followed President Nixon through all his convulsions and specious arguments, but he appears to have lost his senses on this." In September 1973 Saxbe announced that he did not intend to seek reelection. When explaining why, he once again attacked the Administration: "Nixon had a chance to put businessmen back in the saddle and make the free-enterprise system respected again. He blew it. From now on, this town will be full of social planners like Walter Mondale [Democratic Senator from Minnesota]."

Scarcely a month after Saxbe made that statement, Nixon offered him the job of Attorney General and Saxbe accepted it. He delayed assuming office at the Justice Department until after the turn of the year in order to have enough time served in the Senate to qualify for a government pension. On January 4, 1974, the day he was sworn in, Saxbe found inspiration in the Bible's Book of Micah ("What doth the Lord require of thee but to do justice and love mercy and walk humbly with thy God?"). At his request, Senator Harold Hughes of Iowa, who is retiring from the Senate to go into religious work, prayed for the success of Saxbe's administration of the Department of Justice.

Saxbe was at first skeptical about President Nixon's innocence in the Watergate scandal, saying at one point, "It sounds like the fellow who played the piano in a brothel for twenty years, and insisted that he didn't know what was going on upstairs." But after a two-hour talk with the President before he accepted the nomination for Attorney General he appeared more willing to accept Nixon's version of the affair. "All I had was a general man-to-man confrontation; he says, 'I am telling the truth. I'll cooperate on any investigation.' I say, 'That's good enough for me.'" Saxbe promised the Senate that he would not interfere on Nixon's behalf with the impeachment process unless the House was proceeding on "obviously political grounds" and not on "criminal charges." The attorney general also excused himself from any Justice Department decisions regarding the 1970 shootings by Ohio National Guardsmen and the deaths of four students at Kent State University, because he is a retired member of the 107th Cavalry, the division involved in the shootings.

Among Saxbe's first actions as Attorney General was a push for legislation to limit access to criminal records of arrested and convicted persons and to investigatory files on individuals. In keeping with his reputation for accessibility and candor with the press, Saxbe instituted a regular, informal weekly coffee-and-doughnuts news conference at the Department of Justice. Among the explosive *faux pas* he let slip in those sessions were a premature derogation of Patty Hearst as a "common criminal" and a statement that "the Jewish intellectual" of the 1950's tended to be "enamored" of the Communist party. On April 24, 1974, in the wake of the uproars caused by his explosive statements, Saxbe suspended his weekly meetings with journalists, explaining through a spokesman that he was considering a less frequent, more formal press forum.

William B. Saxbe is a tobacco-chewing, earthy type who loves skeet shooting, quail hunting, fishing, golf, and gun collecting. He drives a red Cadillac convertible. Saxbe and the former Ardath Louise (Dolly) Kleinhans, who were married in 1940, have three children and three grandchildren. Primitive-style paintings by Mrs. Saxbe adorn her husband's office as well as the apartment the couple rents in Washington, which is also filled with Oriental art. In addition to their 238-acre cattle ranch in Mechanicsburg, with a bass-stocked lake, they own a cabin at a ski resort near Bellefontaine, Ohio and a vacation home in Costa Rica.

Representative Charles A. Vanik, Democrat of Ohio, has said of the Attorney General: "Saxbe's highly respected by Democrats of the state. We don't see eye to eye economically or philosophically, but we do know Bill to be forthright, open, and frank as a Senator and in his present role." In his article on Saxbe in the New York *Post,* John S. Lang wrote: "For all that his speech is sprinkled with epithets, Saxbe is a religious man." Lang quoted Saxbe: "Private life would be much easier . . . but if you have any flair for it at all I think you have the responsibility to try to serve." Elsewhere the Attorney General has been quoted as saying, "I feel very strongly that the Justice Department is the very heart and soul of our country, because government without law is tyranny, and I would like to re-establish a real sound belief in our system of justice and in our country."

References

N Y Post p22 Ap 27 '74 por
N Y Sunday News p54 My 5 '74 por
N Y Times p18 N 21 '73 por
N Y Times Mag p18+ My 5 '74 por
Newsweek 83:35+ Ap 20 '74 por
International Who's Who, 1973-74
Who's Who in America, 1972-73

SCHMIDT, HELMUT (HEINRICH WALDEMAR)

Dec. 23, 1918- Chancellor of the Federal Republic of Germany
Address: b. Bundeskanzleramt, Palais Schaumburg, Bonn, Federal Republic of Germany; h. Neubergerweg 80, 2 Hamburg 62, Federal Republic of Germany

On May 16, 1974 Helmut Schmidt became the fifth Chancellor of the Federal Republic of Germany, following the dramatic resignation of his predecessor, Willy Brandt, in the wake of a top-level spy scandal. Although Brandt's broad, statesmanlike vision helped to bring about détente between East and West in the late 1960's and early 1970's, it is Schmidt's tough-minded pragmatism—which he put into practice as Defense Minister in Brandt's first Cabinet and as Finance Minister since 1972—that seems best suited to the resolution of the immediate day-to-day problems of Germany and Western Europe. "No government can work miracles, but it must do everything in its power to achieve what is possible," Schmidt declared in his first policy speech as Chancellor. "In this respect we are making a new approach in that we are concentrating our energies on what *is* essential today."

Helmut Heinrich Waldemar Schmidt is a native of Barmbek, a tough working-class district of the traditionally Social Democratic city of Hamburg. He was born on December 23, 1918 to Gustav Schmidt, a secondary-school teacher, and Ludovica (Koch) Schmidt. His boyhood ambition

HELMUT SCHMIDT

was to become an architect. Although Barmbek was largely dominated by Communist dockworkers during the early years of the Weimar Republic, Schmidt's upbringing was anti-Communist. After Hitler came to power in 1933, Schmidt joined the Hitler Youth, eventually becoming a group leader in its maritime division. On the other hand, Nazi influences on him were minimal at the progressive Lichtwark-Schule in his native city, where he received his secondary education.

After a stint with the Reichsarbeitsdienst, the national labor service, Schmidt was drafted into the Wehrmacht in 1937. During World War II he served on both the Russian and Western fronts. As a member of the anti-aircraft artillery he became a battery commander with the rank of Oberleutnant (first lieutenant) and was decorated with the Iron Cross. During the Battle of the Bulge, in the final stages of the war, he was taken prisoner by the British. In the prisoner of war camp Schmidt was converted to the Social Democratic cause by his fellow captives.

Returning to his war-ravaged native city in 1945, Schmidt enrolled in the University of Hamburg, where he studied political science and economics while his wife worked as a schoolteacher and dressmaker to make ends meet. Among his professors at the university was Karl Schiller, who later became West Germany's first Social Democratic Minister of Finance. In 1946 Schmidt joined the Social Democratic party, and in the following year he became the first national chairman of the Socialist Student League, then a moderate organization that bore little resemblance to the revolutionary group it became in the 1960's. In 1949, after completing a thesis comparing German and Japanese currency reforms after World War II, he obtained his diploma in political economy from the university.

In 1948, while still a student, Schmidt joined the Social Democratic municipal government of Hamburg on Schiller's recommendation, becoming an adviser in its division of economic affairs

and commerce. By 1949 he was head of the division, where he acquired a reputation as an authority on municipal transportation problems. In the national elections of 1953 Schmidt was elected to the federal Bundestag in Bonn, where his audacity and gift of gab soon earned him the nickname "Schmidt-Schnauze" ("Schmidt the Lip").

Within Social Democratic ranks, Schmidt became known as something of a maverick of the right. In 1957, when most Social Democrats still opposed German rearmament, he supported it, and he became one of the first Bundestag deputies to accept a reserve commission in the Federal Republic's newly organized Bundeswehr. In 1959 he stormed out of a student congress meeting in Berlin in protest against a resolution calling on the Bonn government to consider interim confederation with Communist East Germany. On the other hand, when in 1960 the West German government considered acquiring military facilities in Spain for the Bundeswehr, Schmidt joined with other Social Democrats in protest, declaring that he had "about the same degree of sympathy" for Spanish chief of state Francisco Franco as he had for East German Communist leader Walter Ulbricht.

In 1961 Schmidt, who did not relish the prospect of being perennially in the opposition, decided to forego his candidacy for reelection to the Bundestag. Returning to Hamburg, he entered the state government as Senator (the equivalent of Minister) of the Interior. In that role he attained national prominence in February 1962 when, following a disastrous North Sea flood that took some 300 lives, he singlehandedly took control of rescue and salvage operations, relegating Hamburg's mayor and other officials to the sidelines.

Following his reelection to the Bundestag, Schmidt returned to Bonn in 1965. As the party's expert on defense matters, he criticized the defense establishment under Christian Democratic Chancellor Ludwig Erhard and Defense Minister Kai-Uwe von Hassel, and what he saw as the demoralization of the armed forces. Modifying his earlier anti-Communism, Schmidt proposed, after visiting the Soviet Union and Eastern Europe in the summer of 1966, that the Federal Republic abandon the Hallstein Doctrine, which had prevented it from recognizing governments that had established formal ties with Communist East Germany, and he called for diplomatic relations with Romania and Czechoslovakia. In early 1967 he outlined a "step by step" process to normalize relations between East and West Germany. His views accorded with the Ostpolitik of Willy Brandt, who had become Vice-Chancellor and Foreign Minister in a "grand coalition" government of Christian Democrats and Social Democrats under Chancellor Kurt Kiesinger in December 1966.

Elected in March 1967 to succeed the late Fritz Erler as floor leader of the Social Democratic parliamentary group, Schmidt consolidated his reputation as one of the Bundestag's most skilled and incisive speakers, especially on defense and foreign policy. Called by some observers the "John F. Kennedy of Germany," Schmidt was regarded as a potential candidate for the Chancellorship. He became second in command to party chairman Willy Brandt in March 1968, when the Nurnberg Social Democratic congress elected him vice-chairman.

The national elections of September 1969 placed the Social Democrats in the catbird seat for the first time, enabling them to form a coalition government with the small, old-line liberal Free Democratic party. In the new Cabinet, headed by Chancellor Willy Brandt, Schmidt agreed to head the Defense Ministry, a thankless job, but one for which he was eminently qualified.

On October 22, 1969 Schmidt was sworn into office, along with the other Cabinet members. His mission as Defense Minister, as he saw it, was to effect a reconciliation between the armed forces and the traditionally antimilitarist Social Democratic party, and to revitalize West Germany's moribund defense establishment. He modernized its arsenal of weapons, rejuvenated its antiquated officer corps, and improved military morale by making his Bundeswehr more democratic, improving barracks conditions, and allowing recruits greater freedom, including the privilege to sport long hair and beards. As a step toward making the Bundeswehr an all-professional force, he planned to establish armed forces universities.

In discussions with American officials in Washington, D.C., Schmidt stressed the importance of a continued United States military presence in Europe. He accepted Brandt's Ostpolitik of détente with the Communist bloc, but he considered the continued strength of the North Atlantic Treaty Organization of equal importance. "The balance between the two military pact systems in Europe . . . has been the vital condition for the preservation of peace . . . during the past twenty years," he asserted in a speech at Georgetown University in Washington in February 1971. "And I do not have the slightest doubt that it needs to remain that way."

On July 7, 1972, shortly after Karl Schiller resigned from his dual post as Minister of Economics and Finance in protest against a Cabinet decision to impose foreign-exchange controls, Chancellor Brandt appointed Schmidt as his temporary successor. Brandt indicated that the functions of Economics and Finance Minister, united into a single "super-ministry" under Schiller in May 1971, would again be separated following national elections later in the year, with Schmidt retaining one of the two portfolios.

As Economics and Finance Minister during the last half of 1972, Schmidt concentrated on combating inflation, West Germany's most urgent economic problem. An advocate, like Schiller, of a free-market economy, he favored tight-money policies rather than price and wage controls, thereby drawing criticism from some of the left-wing elements of the party. During the campaign that preceded the November 1972 elections, he defended the Brandt government's record on in-flation against attacks by the Christian Democratic opposition, thereby helping the Social Democratic-Free Democratic coalition to return to power with increased strength. In Brandt's new Cabinet, sworn in on December 15, 1972, Schmidt retained the portfolio of Finance, and he reorganized the Finance Ministry into a smoothly functioning machine.

To cope with the international monetary crisis of early 1973, partly brought on by what Schmidt termed the "worldwide frailty" of the United States dollar, six of the nine member countries of the European Economic Community, including West Germany, agreed in March to link their currencies in a common float against the dollar. The move was seen as a step toward the ultimate establishment of a Western European economic and currency union, long advocated by Schmidt as essential for the prevention of future crises. Also Schmidt announced a 3 percent upward valuation of the mark, aimed at curbing an anticipated inflationary boom. An additional 5.5 percent increase in the value of the mark, intended to safeguard European monetary unity and "restore calm to the currency markets," was announced by Schmidt in June.

In May 1973 Schmidt announced a stringent anti-inflation program, including an 11 percent tax on new investments and imported capital goods, a 10 percent tax surcharge on high personal and business incomes, and major reductions in public expenditures. In his budget message to the Bundestag in September, Schmidt revealed that the rate of inflation had dropped to 6.4 percent after having increased to nearly 8 percent in mid-1973, but he asserted that despite "indications of a price slow-down and a cooling-off of the economic climate" the anti-inflation measures would remain in effect for the time being.

During the height of the energy crisis, brought on by the embargo on crude oil shipments by Arab nations to the West in late 1973, Schmidt took the initiative in lining up all the Common Market nations except France solidly behind the United States for a united front to deal with the oil-producing countries of the Middle East. He emerged with heightened prestige from the thirteen-nation conference on the energy crisis held in February 1974 in Washington, D.C., where he joined with United States spokesmen in demanding a cutback in Middle Eastern oil prices and rebuking the French government for its independent dealings with the Arabs. In March 1974 Schmidt concluded a $2.28 billion agreement with United States officials in Washington for West German payments to cover the cost of the continued stationing of American troops in the Federal Republic.

By the early spring of 1974 the Brandt government seemed to be suffering from a malaise. The Social Democrats lost in one local election after another, and public opinion polls indicated that the party now had the support of no more than 30 percent of the population. The press abounded with rumors of Brandt's impending resignation. Schmidt, who according to a profile in

Newsweek (May 20, 1974) had been waging "a shrewd behind-the-scenes campaign to displace Brandt," became increasingly critical of some of the Chancellor's policies. In February, for example, he publicly described a 12.5 percent pay increase that Brandt had awarded, against his advice, to 3,500,000 striking public service and utility workers, as "a financial and economic calamity." Despite the opposition of the militantly leftist Young Socialists (Jusos), who made up about 25 percent of the party's ranks, Schmidt was now rated in opinion polls as the most popular Social Democrat in the Brandt government.

What occasioned Willy Brandt's resignation from the Chancellorship on May 6, 1974 was the discovery, a few days earlier, that Gunter Guillaume, a top member of his staff, was an East German Communist spy. Taking full responsibility for negligence in the affair, Brandt handed over the reins of government to Vice-Chancellor Walter Scheel, who became interim Chancellor of a caretaker government on May 7. On the same date the Social Democratic party, with the assent of the Free Democrats, nominated Schmidt to the Chancellorship. Brandt continued, however, to serve as party chairman, with Schmidt remaining as vice-chairman.

On May 16, 1974, after negotiations between the Social Democrats and Free Democrats, Schmidt was elected the fifth Chancellor of the Federal Republic of Germany by a Bundestag vote of 267 to 255. Sworn into office on the same day, Schmidt declared that he would carry on the foreign policy begun by Brandt, but that for the time being he would "concentrate more strongly on domestic political problems, in the broadest sense." In his Cabinet of eleven Social Democrats and four Free Democrats, Schmidt retained most of Brandt's appointees. The most significant change was the appointment of former Minister of the Interior Hans-Dieter Genscher, a Free Democrat, as Vice-Chancellor and Foreign Minister, replacing Scheel, who had been elected to succeed Gustav Heinemann as President of the Federal Republic.

In his policy speech to the Bundestag on May 17, Schmidt stressed the goal of "political unification of Europe in partnership with the United States" but warned Common Market partners that they must make "resolute efforts" to help themselves. With reference to the recent spy scandal, he asserted that political radicals had no place in public service. His domestic policies, he said, would be marked by austerity in public spending "to ward off all excessive demands," and he would seek to guarantee continued full employment and to safeguard West Germany's position as the country with the lowest rate of inflation and the largest volume of trade in Western Europe.

About two weeks after taking office, Chancellor Schmidt visited Paris to meet with newly elected French President Váléry Giscard d'Estaing, an old friend. The Schmidt government survived its first vote test on June 9, 1974, when in a state election in Lower Saxony the Social Democratic-Free Democratic coalition managed to retain control of the legislature by a narrow margin. It was also during his early weeks in office that a treaty, described by Schmidt as "the final stone" in the structure of Brandt's Eastern policy, was approved by the Bundestag. The treaty provided for the normalization of relations between West Germany and Czechoslovakia and nullification of the infamous Munich pact of 1938.

Schmidt has written two important books on Western defense strategy: *Verteidigung oder Vergeltung; Ein deutscher Beitrag zum strategischen Problem der NATO* (1961), translated as *Defense or Retaliation; A German View* (Praeger, 1962); and *Strategie des Gleichgewichts; Deutsche Friedenspolitik und die Weltmächte* (1969), translated as *The Balance of Power; Germany's Peace Policy and the Superpowers* (Kimber, 1971). His other writings include *Beiträge* (1967), a collection of his essays, lectures, and addresses. He has contributed to European and American periodicals, including *Foreign Affairs*. In 1972 he received the United States Medal for Distinguished Service. Newberry College in South Carolina conferred an honorary LL.D. degree on him in 1973.

Helmut Schmidt was married in 1942 to Hannelore Glaser (nicknamed Loki), whom he met at the Lichtwark school. They have a daughter, Susanne. A handsome, strong-featured man, Schmidt has thick, graying hair that he keeps neatly parted. Standing at five feet six inches, he wears thick-soled shoes in order to appear taller, and he watches his diet because of a tendency to overweight. He has been suffering from a chronic thyroid condition that caused him to be hospitalized several times during 1972 and 1973. A former chainsmoker of cigarettes, he now usually smokes a pipe.

A pragmatist who has little patience with philosophizing, Schmidt is noted for his efficiency and organizing ability, and for his boundless energy that often keeps him working eighteen hours a day. Although he has been described as arrogant, with a roughhouse style, an occasionally volatile temper, and a lack of warmth and compassion, he is also known for his sense of humor, his informality, and his knack for teamwork. When his busy schedule permits, he enjoys reading, painting, playing chess with his wife, listening to baroque organ and harpsichord music (he occasionally plays the organ himself), and sailing on the lake near his weekend home in Schleswig-Holstein that he built with the help of a local carpenter. He is a member of the synod of the Evangelical church of Hamburg.

References

London Observer p15 My 19 '74 por
N Y Times p16 My 8 '74; p3 My 17 '74 por
Newsweek 84:53 O 21 '74 por
Time 103:39+ My 20 '74 por; 104:55+ O 2 '74 por
Wirtschaftswoche p18+ My 17 '74 pors
International Who's Who, 1973-74
Wer ist Wer? (1973)
Who's Who in Germany (1964)

SCHMITT, HARRISON H(AGAN)

July 3, 1935- Geologist; astronaut
Address: b. Manned Spacecraft Center, National Aeronautics and Space Administration, Houston, Tex. 77058

Dr. Harrison H. "Jack" Schmitt, the only geologist among the scientist-astronauts in the United States space program, became the first scientist and the first civilian to walk on the surface of the moon in December 1972, during the Apollo 17 mission—the final moon probe under the Apollo program of the National Aeronautics and Space Administration (NASA). He entered the scientist-astronaut program in 1965 and was selected for the Apollo mission in 1971, after scientists persuaded NASA officials of the benefits that could be derived from sending a professional geologist to the moon. Although Schmitt has jokingly compared his lunar experience to that of "a kid playing in a sandbox," his explorations during his three days on the moon have yielded some of the most significant data of the entire Apollo project in the quest for an understanding of the moon's nature and evolution.

Harrison Hagan Schmitt was born on July 3, 1935 in Santa Rita, New Mexico, to Harrison A. Schmitt, a mining geologist, and Ethel (Hagan) Schmitt. As a boy he acquired the nickname "Jack" to distinguish him from his father. Growing up in Silver City, New Mexico, Jack Schmitt spent many hours working on the family farm, performing such tasks as mending fences and repairing the barn. He also visited mining camps and Indian reservations, searched for rocks in the surrounding desert areas, and went on geological field trips with his father, who was credited with discovering some of the major copper deposits in the Southwest. As long as he could remember, he had the ambition to become a geologist.

After completing high school, Schmitt attended the California Institute of Technology, where he studied with Professor Ian Campbell and other noted geologists and obtained his B.S. degree in 1957. As a Fulbright fellow in Norway during 1957-58, he studied at the University of Oslo and worked with the Norwegian Geological Survey. Schmitt continued his graduate studies under a Kennecott Fellowship in geology in 1958-59, a Harvard Fellowship in 1959-60, a Harvard Traveling Fellowship in 1960, a Parker Traveling Fellowship in 1961-62, and a National Science Foundation fellowship with the department of geological sciences of Harvard University in 1963-64. While he was a graduate student, he also worked for the United States Geological Survey in New Mexico and Montana. He obtained his Ph.D. degree in geology from Harvard in 1964.

In 1964-65, Schmitt worked with the astrogeological branch of the United States Geological Survey in Flagstaff, Arizona as project chief for photographic and telescopic mapping of the moon and planets. In that post he was responsible for

HARRISON H. SCHMITT

assembling photographs taken by unmanned Ranger spacecraft into detailed lunar maps for use by future moon explorers. He also took part in developing techniques and equipment for use during the early moon landings, and he instructed astronauts on geological field trips. During the course of his work with the Geological Survey, he "caught the space bug." When NASA began recruiting scientist-astronauts (candidates for the space program with specialized scientific training, as distinguished from jet pilots), Schmitt was one of the first to apply. On June 26, 1965 NASA officials announced the selection of six civilian scientists from among 1,500 applicants as trainees for the scientist-astronaut program.

Schmitt, the only geologist among them, was accepted after NASA physicians determined that a troublesome intestinal problem would not prevent him from meeting the space program's rigorous physical demands. As part of the three-year astronaut training program at the Manned Spacecraft Center near Houston, Schmitt completed a fifty-five-week flight training course. He also received advanced instruction in astronomy, physics, and geology, as well as training in spacecraft mechanics. When he completed flight training in 1966, he ranked second in his class of fifty at the Air Force flight school, and he was considered the best pilot among the scientist-astronauts, who numbered fifteen.

After completing the astronaut training program, Schmitt was assigned to train the Apollo 11 and 12 crews on the geological aspects of their missions. He guided them on field trips to such locations as Iceland and Hawaii, where he taught them how to recognize and select geologically important rocks. He also worked with NASA scientists in developing scoops, shovels, and other equipment to be used on the moon expeditions. At the same time he was required to maintain and improve his flying skills through continuous jet piloting, and by the time of his selection for the Apollo mission in 1971 he had logged 1,300 hours of flying time.

In an unofficial report in August 1969, a NASA spokesman indicated that Schmitt was the only one of the scientist-astronauts with enough flying ability to be considered for a moon landing. In December of that year, Schmitt became the first scientist to train actively for a lunar landing after being named backup lunar module pilot for the Apollo 15 mission. The move was, in part at least, a response to complaints by lunar scientists that NASA was sacrificing the opportunity of deriving maximum benefit from the $24 billion Apollo program by delaying the assignment of a scientist-astronaut to a lunar flight. NASA officials explained the delay by saying that the lunar landing was still a very hazardous undertaking and that the assignment of highly trained professional test pilots to Apollo crew positions took priority over the appointment of scientists until enough experience could be obtained.

In September 1970, NASA officials reluctantly decided, because of budget limitations, to end the Apollo program with the Apollo 17 mission, canceling the two final Apollo flights originally planned. Under the normal procedure for spacecraft mission assignments, the backup crew on one mission became the primary crew three flights later. Accordingly, Schmitt, having served as backup lunar module pilot for the Apollo 15 mission, completed on August 7, 1971, would have been scheduled to go to the moon with Apollo 18. But since that flight had been canceled, it appeared that neither he nor any other scientist-astronaut would be sent to the moon on an Apollo mission. (Most of the other scientists in the moon program had by that time been assigned to the Skylab space station project, which was scheduled to succeed Apollo.)

Contrary to expectations, however, NASA officials announced on August 13, 1971 that Schmitt was assigned to the Apollo 17 flight, replacing Air Force Colonel Joseph H. Engle, a former X-15 pilot. The assignment was seen as a victory for the space agency's scientific community, whose members had long been urging NASA to send Schmitt to the moon, contending that a trained geologist was more capable of making meaningful on-the-spot observations and judgments than a pilot-astronaut. Another factor that influenced the space agency in assigning Schmitt to Apollo 17 was his performance on the Apollo 15 backup crew. One unidentified NASA source, quoted in the Washington Post (August 8, 1971), indicated that Apollo 15 commander David Scott "set a furious pace during training, and Jack Schmitt stayed right with it all the way."

Defending his selection over that of Engle at a press conference on August 19, 1971, Schmitt declared his readiness to "compete with anybody" in flying a spacecraft. He emphasized that as a "professional observer," he could greatly add to the knowledge of the moon, the history of the sun, and the very early history of the earth. In preparing for Apollo 17, Schmitt worked diligently to make his participation a success. "He's spent more time with flight controllers and such than any astronaut that I know of," Apollo 17 flight

director Gerald D. Griffin told an interviewer for the New York Times (December 8, 1972). At a lunar science briefing at the Washington, D.C. headquarters of NASA on October 27, 1972, Schmitt predicted that Apollo 17 would bring back some of the oldest, as well as some of the youngest lunar rocks ever encountered by man, and that if his prediction proved to be correct, scientists would be able to expand their knowledge of the moon's evolution considerably.

On December 7, 1972, at 12:33 A.M. (Eastern Standard Time), the Apollo 17 spacecraft was launched from Cape Kennedy, Florida on its twelve-and-one-half-day lunar mission. In addition to Schmitt, it carried Navy Captain Eugene A. Cernan, who was in command of the spacecraft, and Navy Commander Ronald E. Evans, the command module pilot. Although Schmitt's official mission assignment was that of lunar module pilot, his actual duties on the flight consisted of monitoring backup systems and reading out data during the descent to the moon for Cernan, who piloted the lunar module.

Apollo 17 entered lunar orbit on December 10, 1972. The following day, Schmitt and Cernan, after donning their space suits, entered the lunar module Challenger and separated it from the command and service module America, which continued to orbit the moon with Evans at the controls. Challenger landed in the Taurus-Littrow valley, a region on the southeastern edge of the moon's Sea of Serenity, that was chosen in order to enable the astronauts to explore both highlands and lowlands. Apollo 17 was the longest space flight in history, both in distance (1,486,000 miles) and time (301 hours and fifty-two minutes, of which 147 hours and forty-eight minutes were spent in moon orbit). Cernan and Schmitt, who were the eleventh and twelfth man, respectively, to walk on the moon, also established records for the longest time on the lunar surface (seventy-four hours and fifty minutes, of which they spent twenty-two hours and five minutes outside of the space capsule). During their three days on the moon's surface, they spent from seven to eight hours a day in extra-vehicular activity (EVA) and collected 249 pounds of rocks and soil for scientific analysis.

On the first day, Cernan and Schmitt assembled their electrically operated lunar rover vehicle. It was equipped with a television camera, controlled by mission control in Houston, through which the spacemen's activities were monitored and pictures were sent back to earth for the benefit of television viewers. The astronauts set up a variety of scientific equipment for the collection of data on such phenomena as gravity waves, moonquakes, changes in the moon's shape, traces of lunar gas, the speed and mass of micrometeorites striking the moon, and radiation from lunar soil at various depths. Before embarking on their second excursion, they ingeniously repaired a fender on the rover vehicle that had been accidentally damaged, by taping several traverse maps together and clamping them to the rest of the fender.

During the second day's activities, Schmitt gave a detailed description, for the benefit of his fellow geologists, of the South Massif, a steep-walled mountain about four miles from the landing site that was believed to contain some of the oldest rocks ever viewed by man. Later, while exploring the rim of a deep crater called "Shorty," Schmitt made a startling discovery—a layer of soil that, in contrast to the surrounding gray material, was bright red to orange in color. According to Patrick Young of the *National Observer* (December 23, 1972), Schmitt's unexpected shout—"There is orange soil!"—caused "bedlam . . . in the science-support room at mission control. . . . Schmitt's description gave scientists reason to believe that . . . the first extinct volcano [had been] found on the moon. . . . One [scientist] grabbed a lunar traverse map of the area, and everyone in the room signed it as a memento of a historic event."

Whereas earlier samples had failed to turn up any evidence of water on the moon, the orange soil, which was believed to contain iron oxide, seemed to indicate the presence of water at some stage of the moon's development. Further exploration of the site suggested to Schmitt the presence of a fumarole—a vent in the moon's crust, through which volcanic gases and water vapor once escaped from the moon's interior. Schmitt's speculations, if proved correct, would establish that the moon had a complex volcanic history that extended over 3 billion years, refuting the widely held belief that it had always been geologically dead. The discovery of the orange soil, believed to be the most important single find of the six moon explorations, seemed to vindicate the scientists who had urged NASA to send a geologist on the final Apollo mission. "Schmitt's personal observations as a geologist and scientist were far superior to anything we have known in past moon landings," NASA geologist Farouk El-Baz said as the three astronauts completed their Apollo 17 mission. "Today I feel proud to be a geologist like Jack Schmitt" (Washington *Post*, December 15, 1972).

After a final day of moon exploration and gathering of geological samples, Schmitt and Cernan left the surface of the moon on December 14, and docked their lunar module with the command and service module piloted by Evans. The astronauts ended their Apollo 17 mission at 2:24 P.M. on December 19 with a perfect splashdown in the South Pacific, about 1.7 miles from their target point. Medical tests indicated that none of the three men suffered ill effects from their lunar mission.

In the months that followed the conclusion of Apollo 17, Schmitt spent much of his time in public relations and lecture tours for NASA and in the fall of 1973 he visited Norway to attend a scientific conference. He also worked extensively with other scientists in analyzing the more than 900 pounds of geological samples recovered from the moon during the six Apollo missions. In 1973 he had to revise his earlier theory that volcanoes had been active on the moon as recent-

ly as 10,000,000 years ago, when scientists at the State University of New York at Stony Brook determined that the orange soil sample he had brought back from the moon was as much as 3.71 billion years old. Dr. Noel Hinners, the chief scientist at NASA headquarters, has indicated that the wealth of information derived from the Apollo project should keep scientists occupied for at least a decade.

Dr. Harrison H. Schmitt is the only bachelor in the astronaut program. He lives a quiet life in an apartment complex near the Manned Spacecraft Center and drives to work in an old Volkswagen. He has been known to work more than sixteen hours a day, six days a week, and he allows himself little time for social life, except for an occasional date. Dark-haired and handsome, Jack Schmitt is five feet nine inches tall and weighs 165 pounds. He is an expert skier and an accomplished chef, especially with Mexican dishes, and he keeps in good physical condition by running and weightlifting.

References

N Y Times p30 D 8 '72
Time 100:35+ D 11 '72 por
Washington Post A p14 D 7 '72 por
International Who's Who, 1973-74
Who's Who in the South and Southwest, 1973-74

SCOTT, SHEILA

Apr. 27, 1927- British aviator
Address: h. 593 Park West, London W2 2RB, England

The British aviator Sheila Scott, who has broken over a hundred world flying records and won more than fifty racing trophies, learned to fly in 1959, while she was pursuing an acting career. Six years later she made the longest consecutive solo flight in history by flying 31,000 miles around the world. Since then, she has twice flown solo around the world and in 1971 made the first solo light aircraft flight over the North Pole.

A popular lecturer, television personality, and journalist, Miss Scott has written two autobiographical books, *I Must Fly* and *Barefoot in the Sky* (called *On Top of the World* in England). In his foreword to *Barefoot in the Sky* the British astronaut Dr. Philip K. Chapman, who worked with her on the Polar flight, wrote that Sheila Scott "belongs in the company of Lindbergh and Earhart and Saint-Exupéry. . . . She is a truly remarkable woman, an inspiration to all who know her. Her contributions to aviation and to the preservation of the individual human spirit of exploration and adventure are almost unparalleled in our time."

Sheila Christine Scott was born on April 27, 1927 in the city of Worcester in the English midlands, the only child of Harold R. and Edith (Kenward) Hopkins. When she was very young her mother deserted the family for another man.

SHEILA SCOTT

After the divorce of her parents she was raised in Worcester by her indulgent paternal grandparents until, when she was about eleven, she rejoined her father, who had remarried. She has described her stepmother as a generous and loving woman but a stern disciplinarian.

As a child, Sheila Scott was shy but adventurous. Her father used to dare her to ride fairground roller coasters or to dive from the highest board at the swimming pool. On her sixth birthday, she was taken for an unforgettable joyride in a canvas-covered biplane. By that time she was boarding at the Alice Ottley School, a private school for girls in Worcester, where she excelled at games, gymnastics, dancing, and drama, and loved biology, reading, and music, but could make nothing of mathematics. Her boredom and her rebelliousness brought her into conflict with the school authorities. Towards the end of her school career she was almost expelled, but was allowed to stay on to pass the school-leaving examinations she needed to fulfill her first ambition, which was to become a voluntary aid detachment nurse.

In 1944, after some basic training, she was posted as a trainee nurse to the Haslar Naval Hospital, serving the British naval base at Portsmouth. At that late stage in World War II, life held its horrors for a young nurse as the warships that put into Portsmouth unloaded their wounded. She sought distraction from the tragedies of the wards by dating young midshipmen on shore leave. "This had its effect," she wrote in *Barefoot in the Sky*, "and for many years I was to live for the moment, sampling everything for myself, never looking back or truly far ahead."

That feckless life continued after the war in London, where Miss Scott began a new career as an actress, when the film producer Sir Alexander Korda, father of one of her friends, employed her as a stand-in to Deborah Kerr during the making of a film at Denham film studios, near London. Miss Scott holds a low opinion of her abilities as an actress, but she secured small parts in films and in television, and worked in repertory theatres at

Aldershot, Watford, and Windsor. She eked out her tiny income by modeling. In 1945, while still in her teens, she married Rupert Leaman Bellamy.

The marriage ended in divorce in 1950. After it, Miss Scott went on acting and modeling, and also tried her hand at writing and clothes design. She traveled a great deal in Europe, skiing and bobsleighing in winter and summering in the South of France. Deeply insecure, she nevertheless sensed a pattern of coincidences in her own life that hinted at the existence of some universal order, and led her to study philosophy and some of the Oriental religions.

One day in 1959 she and some friends were "sleeping off a late party pretending to watch television" when, prompted by a magazine article she had just read, and mainly for effect, she announced that she was going to learn to fly. Spurred on by her friends' disbelief and teasing she began to take lessons, first at Elstree airport near London, then at Thruxton, in Hampshire, where she could stay overnight each weekend. By the time she had earned her private pilot's license, the following year, she had caught the "flying fever."

Wanting a commercial license that would enable her to fly larger aircraft and to carry fare-paying passengers, she bought on the installment plan an old Royal Air Force biplane, had it painted blue with silver wings and decorated with white upholstery, and gradually equipped it with navigation lights, brakes, and a radio. She christened it "Myth." Finding that Myth was an exceptionally fast example of its type, she fitted it for air racing. To her astonishment, she won the first races she entered, carrying off the 1960 De Havilland Trophy. Throughout that summer she entered every race and rally she could find, all over Europe, and by the end of 1960 had accumulated about three hundred flying hours—more than enough to start training for a commercial license. She passed the written and flying examinations, but a specialist ruled that she was too nearsighted for commercial flying. Miss Scott began a campaign to persuade the authorities that she should be reexamined, and meanwhile she solaced herself with the news that the British Women Pilots' Association had awarded her their Jean Lennox Bird Trophy for her achievements in races and rallies during 1960.

Miss Scott still held her private pilot's license, and during 1961 demonstrated Cessna aircraft in British and European races and rallies. As a reward she was sent to the United States to attend the Cessna Aircraft Sales Week and the annual convention of the Aircraft Owners' and Pilots' Association. American doctors pronounced her sight imperfect but adequate, and she remained in the United States long enough to secure a commercial license as a ferry pilot. On later visits she qualified herself to fly all kinds of aircraft, from helicopters to seaplanes. In the end she was given another eye test and was granted her British commercial license.

By that time, however, Miss Scott had become more interested in competitive flying. She sold

Myth and in 1964, in a rented single-engined Piper Comanche 400, went after fifteen European light aircraft records that had not been attempted for several years. Within thirty-six hours she broke them all and set her sights on a more formidable record—that established in 1964 by the American Jerrie Mock, the first woman to fly solo around the world.

The route Miss Scott chose was much longer than her predecessor's—a total of almost 32,000 miles. Many months of planning and fund raising followed the decision, until on May 18, 1966 she took off from London Airport in Myth Too, her almost untried Piper Comanche 260. From the very beginning there were such troubles as radio failure, bureaucratic obstructionism, partial or total failure of navigational aids and other electrical equipment, but Sheila Scott went on, often through appalling weather, sustained by the encouragement of air traffic controllers and fellow flyers, and by the morale-building crowds that met her at every airport. As her plane's problems were gradually solved, she herself neared collapse from lack of sleep, fever, and dysentery. But on June 20 she flew into London Airport, having completed the longest consecutive solo flight in history—over 31,000 miles in approximately one hundred and eighty-nine flying hours, at an average ground speed of one hundred and sixty-six miles per hour. She was the first British pilot, man or woman, to fly solo around the world.

For her feat Miss Scott received the most valued of her awards, the American Harmon Trophy as the year's outstanding aviatrix, as well as the Silver Award of Merit of the Guild of Air Pilots and Air Navigators—never before given to a woman—the Royal Aero Club's Silver Medal, and the Italian Isabella D'Este award. She was honored at banquets by aviation and sporting societies, and at lunch by the Queen. Sheila Scott wanted to return to flying, but the flight had cost her £31,000, and to keep up with her payments on the plane and other bills she had to devote all her time to giving lectures, writing articles, making personal appearances, and doing anything else that she and her growing secretarial staff could think of to raise funds.

Help came when she met Ken Wood, the food-mixer manufacturer, who sponsored her record-breaking flight from London to Cape Town in South Africa in July 1967. A string of similar achievements followed: the Cape to London record in July and August 1967; the North Atlantic east to west direct crossing record in October 1967; and the South Atlantic west to east record in November 1967. In May 1969 she broke her own North Atlantic records during the *Daily Mail's* Transatlantic Air Race, and on the way home took seven more records between New York and Copenhagen. She set further world records in October 1969: London to Kenya and South Africa, South Africa to London.

The worst ordeal of her career came in December 1969, when she was one of the three solo flyers who took part in the England to Australia Air Race. Because much money had been gambled on the race and because she received celebrity treatment from the organizers, she encountered hostility from some of her competitors. She has reason to suspect that her plane was sabotaged, and that unpleasant and unfounded rumors were spread about her throughout the race.

At one point, flying in thick cloud between Singapore and Darwin, Australia, she found that not only her autopilot but both radios were out of action, and that she was cut off from communication with the outside world. She had at that time been flying for nearly three days with only about two hours' rest. She emerged from cloud over the sea, and for some hours flew below the low-lying mist, which pinned her almost to the surface of the waves. Her fuel was running low and death seemed close when a gleam of light attracted her attention and she came down through lifting cloud onto the military airstrip at Makassar, in the Celebes. That was the worst in the long series of physical and emotional tribulations that dogged her throughout the race, and that she believes she could not have survived without some sort of guidance from superior forces. In spite of everything she reached Adelaide, Australia, a few hours before the deadline for completion of that section of the race, in the last part of which she carried off the $5,000 Ford Woman's Prize. Afterwards she went on to complete her second solo flight around the world.

The most remarkable of Sheila Scott's achievements followed in 1971, when she made the first solo light aircraft flight, equator to equator, over the North Pole, using a twin-engined Piper Aztec, Mythre. Her flight was monitored, with the help of the satellite Nimbus, by the United States National Aeronautics and Space Administration, which studied Miss Scott's physical and mental responses to the immense strains of the flight, and also measured air pollution along her route.

The flight placed her in acute financial difficulties. Although she received invaluable help from N.A.S.A., the Royal Air Force, equipment manufacturers, and many other individuals and organizations, she was forced to raise a large personal loan to finance the attempt. Just before it began, her London apartment was robbed and she lost all her trophies and valuables, including the video tape camera with which she had hoped to make a profitable film record of the flight. Although she never recovered financially from then on, she has no regrets.

After the Polar flight, Sheila Scott made a third round-the-world flight, breaking the Australia to England record on the way. It was her hundredth world class record. Apart from the awards already mentioned, Miss Scott received the Brabazon of Tara Award in 1965, 1967, and 1968 for outstanding achievement by a woman pilot, the Amelia Earhart Medal in New York in 1966, and the Sir Alan Cobham Achievement Award in 1965 and 1966. In 1968 she was named an Officer of the Order of the British Empire. She received the Royal Aero Club's coveted Britannia Trophy in 1968 and its Gold Medal in 1972. Miss Scott has also won over fifty racing trophies.

Sheila Scott was cofounder and first governor of the British Section of Ninety-Nines, Inc., the International Association of Licensed Women Pilots. She was the first British member of the "Whirly Girls," the association of the first hundred women helicopter pilots in the world, and the first British civilian woman to break the sound barrier. She was also one of the founders of the British Balloon and Airships Club. Miss Scott is among many other affiliations, a Fellow of the Royal Geographical Society, a council member of the Geoffrey de Havilland Flying Foundation, and a member of the Appeals Committee of the Institute of Sports Medicine.

I Must Fly (Hodder & Stoughton, 1968), which told the story of Miss Scott's life up to 1968, was largely superseded by her next book, *On Top of the World,* which was published by Hodder & Stoughton in England in 1973 and appeared in the United States the following year as *Barefoot in the Sky* (Macmillan). It covered virtually the same ground as *I Must Fly,* but brought Miss Scott's career up to date. A reviewer in the London *Sunday Mirror* found that it revealed "a courageous, sensitive—and truly feminine—spirit."

Sheila Scott's recreations include sailing, motor rallies, music, reading, "and being a beachcomber." She finds time for a number of civic and philanthropic activities, including work with the Girls' Venture Corps. She has no formal political affiliation, but says she believes "in world friendship and ecology regardless of nationality, religious belief or political creed," hastening to add that she is "a moderate rather than a nut in these fields!"

Interviewing Sheila Scott for the *Guardian* (April 25, 1969), Catherine Stott described her as "blonde and willowy" and observed that "she appears too tense, too fragile to be a sportswoman of any kind, smoking nervously and incessantly, speaking in a hushed and breathless voice, dressing with a model's elegance and care." She tries to look "like a woman," even when she climbs exhausted from a plane.

"Flying has been nearly as exciting as a love affair," Miss Scott says, "but far less dangerous." She has contemplated remarriage, but lives alone because her way of life would not be easy to share. She would have liked children but gives her affection instead to her plane; like Lindbergh, she speaks of herself and it as "we." When Catherine Stott asked her what she gained from flying that justified such enormous sacrifices Miss Scott replied: "It is not easy to explain. Physically you are alone in the air but that knowledge disappears and you feel in the presence of something, someone greater than yourself—is it God?—I don't know. It is as though there is some outside energy. Doctors have likened it to 'taking a trip,' this experience of heightened perception, this crystal clarity of mind. There is discomfort, even pain, and then suddenly something snaps inside you and there is peace . . . there is calm. And perhaps it *is* like taking drugs, because you cannot have it once without wanting to recapture it again and again."

References

Guardian p11 Ap 25 '69 por
London Observer p33 O 22 '67 por
Washington Post p3 My 25 '72 por
Who's Who, 1974-1975
World Who's Who of Women, 1973

SCULL, ROBERT C.

1917- Business executive; art collector
Address: b. Scull's Angels, 37-11 126th St., Corona, New York, 11368; h. 1010 Fifth Ave., New York 10028

Capitalizing on his uncanny ability to anticipate artistic trends, Robert C. Scull, a New York City taxi tycoon, has assembled one of the finest private collections of contemporary American painting and sculpture in the United States. Scull has been hailed as "the pop of Pop art," the "Medici of the Minimals," and as the "patron angel of modern art" by his admirers, but he has also occasionally been denounced by outraged art critics for contributing to the runaway prices of art speculation. On three occasions, sales of Scull-owned abstract expressionist and Pop art have set the price standard for contemporary American art. His disposal of fifty pieces at a highly publicized Sotheby Parke-Bernet auction on October 18, 1973, which brought a staggering total of more than $2,200,000, broke eighteen major auction records. In amassing their collection, which also includes more than forty small Italian Renaissance bronzes, Scull and his wife Ethel have themselves become, in a sense, creations of Pop art. They have been painted by Alfred Leslie and Robert Rauschenberg, silk-screened by Andy Warhol, and molded in plaster by George Segal. "They learned . . . how to turn themselves into objects through packaging . . . , media exposure, and sheer, unadulterated *chutzpa*," wrote Barbara Rose in "Profit Without Honor," a mordant commentary on Scull's promotional genius that appeared in *New York* magazine (November 5, 1973).

The son of Russian immigrants, Robert C. Scull was born on the Lower East Side of Manhattan in New York City in 1917. The family name, originally Sokolnikoff, was shortened to Scull by entry authorities when Scull's father Mayo, a twenty-four-year-old Jewish tailor from southern Russia, arrived on Ellis Island. At his wife's insistence, Mayo Scull, who worked as a tailor and designer at Bergdorf-Goodman, one of the city's most fashionable clothing stores, moved his family from the Lower East Side to the "better neighborhood" of the Upper West Side. Robert Scull attended DeWitt Clinton High School, a special public school for brighter students, until the economic realities of the Depression forced him to drop out. To supplement the family income, Scull refurbished and resold furniture, lamps, and store signs, manufactured homemade soap, and hustled pool. "The whole time was terrible for my father," Scull remembered in an interview with Tom Wolfe for a New York *World Journal Tribune* (October 23, 1966) profile. "My father liked art . . . and history and everything, and he only worked for a living. . . . Every job that sounded great would fall through. He was always involved with finding a job or keeping one. But we lived a pleasant life."

Concentrating on business courses, Scull attended a number of high schools and trade schools at night and, after nine years, graduated from Roosevelt High School. "I always dreamed of going to college," Scull told Wolfe, "some college like the one Alice Faye and Jack Oakie were at in the movies, with the campus and the columns and hamburger joints and everybody . . . wearing sweaters with big letters on them. . . . All I remember about school was the subways, no campus, no nothing." Spurred by a friend's efforts at self-improvement, Scull read literary classics and began writing plays, which he has described as being "all about hemophiliacs, and guys who kill themselves in the last act because they're twenty-six and life's all over for them." His paternal grandfather encouraged his interest in the arts and introduced him to the city's museums and to the opera.

Those museum visits with his grandfather kindled his latent passion for art. He purchased reproductions of paintings by Francisco de Zurbarán and Pablo Picasso to decorate the family flat and enrolled at art schools, such as the Art Students League, the Pratt Institute, and the Textile High School, which offered free night classes. During the day, Scull sold shoes, repaired gas stoves, and modeled men's clothing and uniforms for Peter Wild, an illustrator for mail-order catalogs. In exchange for his modeling services, Wild taught Scull to draw.

After several years of sporadic employment as a free-lance illustrator, Scull joined with Jacques Martial, a business associate, in founding Martial & Scull, a design office. At first the company specialized in fashion illustrations for New York department stores, principally Saks Fifth Avenue. Emulating Raymond Loewy, a successful industrial designer, the partners expanded their operations to design radios, automobile ornaments, plastic appliances, Estabrook pens, and Telechrome clocks. Despite a determined effort to adjust to the changed technological needs of World War II by designing such secret weapons as trick depth charges, the firm of Martial & Scull folded in the early 1940's.

In the autumn of 1943 Scull met Ethel Redner, a student at the Parsons School of Design. They married in January 1944 and moved into an efficiency flat with a Murphy bed close to the Museum of Modern Art in Manhattan. To augment their cramped quarters, further cluttered by Scull's photographic equipment and by his wife's easel and painting supplies, the couple began using the museum's restaurant and outside sculpture garden as an annex to their tiny *pied à terre* for entertaining guests, a rather daring parlay of the Sculls' $12 annual museum membership. Increasingly sensitive to the works on display

ROBERT C. SCULL

play at the museum, he compiled a shadow collection of the pictures he wished were his, meticulously recording the artists and titles on a scrap of shirt cardboard he carried in his wallet.

When Ben Redner, Ethel Scull's father, retired in the late 1940's, he transferred his profitable taxi business to the husbands of his three daughters. In 1948, after entering into a brief partnership with one of his brothers-in-law, Scull decided to use his share of the cabs as the nucleus of an independent company. Convinced that postwar prosperity would increase taxi patronage, Scull borrowed heavily at a time when banks were lending liberally to buy four more vehicles, using his first eight cabs as collateral. With the fleet of twelve as security, he bought an additional eight taxis. Within a few years he managed to pyramid his original eight cabs into the Super Operating Corporation, a fleet of 130 taxicabs operated by 400 drivers.

By 1966 the value of a New York City taxi medallion, or operating license, which had been free when Scull began acquiring taxis, had skyrocketed to $22,500, making Scull's fleet worth nearly $3,000,000. To project a high-class image of his company, now known as Scull's Angels and identified by the emblem of a pink Cupid, Scull recently hired Amy Vanderbilt, the etiquette expert, to teach courtesy and gracious manners to his drivers. In addition to his taxi company, Scull acquired several apartment houses, garages, warehouses, and factories in the Bronx, purchased an interest in several Broadway plays, and bought stock in Electronovision, an innovative film production company that has produced such motion pictures as *Hamlet* (1964), starring Richard Burton, and *Harlow* (1965), starring Carol Lynley.

In the mid-1950's Scull purchased his first painting—an oil that he had mistakenly attributed to Maurice Utrillo—for $245 at a New York City auction. Although the painting was not an Utrillo, Scull later sold it at the same auction gallery for a $45 profit. Enjoying his growing reputation among his neighbors as an important collector of postimpressionist art, Scull decided to begin collecting in earnest. At first, he concentrated on abstract expressionist artists, such as Willem de Kooning, Barnett Newman, Franz Kline, Mark Rothko, and other lesser-known American artists. By 1965 he had acquired more than thirty abstract expressionist paintings, many of which were stored in a warehouse.

Introduced to Pop art by Richard Bellamy, an enterprising patron of the popular arts whom he met at the opening of a junk sculpture exhibition in 1961, Scull became one of the first serious collectors of the Pop creations of James Rosenquist, Larry Poons, Mark di Suvero, John Chamberlain, and Robert Morris. His fascination with the ingenuity of those early Pop artists led Scull to agree to finance Bellamy's Green Gallery, a Manhattan showroom devoted to exhibitions of Pop art. Scull's patronage of the Green Gallery during its five years of existence confirmed his position as a major power in the New York art world, and before its demise, he drew a total of seventy-two works, including paintings, drawings, and pieces of sculpture, from the Green's collections. Among his more important acquisitions from that period Scull numbered Jasper Johns's *Painted Bronze*, a pair of cast-bronze replicas of Ballantine ale cans with painted labels, Andy Warhol's *Flowers*, and Rosenquist's *F-111*, an eighty-six-foot-long multicolor montage superimposed on a painting of a United States bomber.

Committed to obtaining funds to encourage the development of unknown artists, in the autumn of 1965 Scull auctioned off at the Parke-Bernet galleries a dozen of his best abstract expressionist paintings, among them four de Koonings and three Franz Klines. The proceeds from the sale, which amounted to $165,000, were assigned to a recently created family foundation for aiding deserving young artists. With the foundation's funds, Scull not only commissioned works from such struggling artists as Walter De Maria, a sculptor, and Michael Heizer, a conceptual artist, but also furnished art materials and supplies, purchased food and clothing, paid rents, and awarded regular living allowances. "What I really needed was to be *used*. Like the guy who sponsored Giotto's frescoes—used in the best possible way," he explained to Jane Kramer in an interview for a *New Yorker* (November 26, 1966) profile. "My artists use me, and I've learned how to support them and not get anything in return but that great feeling of being involved." A second Parke-Bernet auction five years later, in November 1970, brought Scull $197,500 for works by Ray Lichtenstein, Claes Oldenburg, Kline, and Rosenquist. Because he considered the respective bids of $85,000 and $105,000 as insufficient, he decided to "buy in" paintings by Rothko and Johns. At both auctions the low initial purchase prices meant that sale proceeds were nearly all profit.

Interesting as those sales were, they pale by comparison with the widely publicized and highly profitable auction of fifty works from the Scull collection at Sotheby Parke-Bernet on October 18, 1973. The unprecedented gavel total of $2,242,900 shattered auction records for contemporary American art in several categories. Jasper Johns's large canvas *Double White Map*, purchased by Ben Heller for $240,000, set a new record for Pop art, for a work by a living American artist, and for any twentieth century American work of art. His *Painted Bronze* went to a German dealer for $90,000. Scull reportedly paid $10,200 for the painting and $960 for the sculpture. Another painting by Johns, the often photographed *Target*, which cost $5,000 in 1961, was sold for $125,000 to a European collector. Scull selected the art objects to be sold, which involved about one-fifth of his collection, as if he were assembling an exhibition of contemporary art. "I'm selling them because they're completely useless in a warehouse and should be out doing their thing with everyone and everybody in every place," he remarked before the auction, as quoted in the *Christian Science Monitor* (October 20, 1973). "It's terrible to take six years out of the life of a painting which should be operating with people who love it and care about it and want to write about it."

The high prices paid for works that originally cost Scull comparatively little prompted art critic Barbara Rose to complain that the sale, which she labeled a "circus" replete with "gross avidity and naked cupidity," was a perfect illustration of the current crass relationship between art and society in America. At a news conference following the auction, Robert Rauschenberg, an artist whose paintings were sold at record prices, charged Scull with "infidelity" and accused Sotheby Parke-Bernet of encouraging the "profiteering of dealers and collectors." While agreeing that artists should receive "some benefits" from such sales, Scull disagreed with the 15 percent royalty proposed by some disgruntled artists, suggesting instead "a reasonable percentage—like 1 percent." Countering Rauschenberg's argument, Scull insisted that his early faith in and patronage of previously unknown artists increased their fame and boosted their profits. "People say I buy art for an investment, to get prestige," Scull told Arthur Cooper in an interview for *Newsweek* magazine (October 29, 1973). "They accuse me of being a social climber, of using art. You know, it's all true. You bet I'm a social climber—and I'd rather use art to climb than anything else!"

A tall, bulky man with graying black hair and a "black and white tweed-mix beard," Robert Scull presents a distinguished, well-groomed appearance, with his custom-made suits and designer accessories. To remain in vigorous health, he refrains from smoking and substitutes No-Cal cola for alcoholic beverages. For recreation, Scull enjoys reading and listening to music, and his extensive record collection includes over 300 recordings of works by Mozart, his favorite composer. Scull and his wife, affectionately nicknamed "Spike," have three sons, Laurence, Stephen, and Jonathan. The Scull family divides its time between a large, art-filled apartment on Fifth Avenue in Manhattan and a glass-walled villa on one and one-half carefully landscaped acres in East Hampton, Long Island. Built around a court-yard, the villa acts as a perfect foil for Scull's important outdoor sculpture by Mark di Suvero, Robert Morris, Alex Liberman, and other con-temporary American artists.

Although Scull has occasionally refused to lend works of art to certain museums because of "deep philosophical objections" to their policies, he has donated paintings to the Whitney Museum of American Art, the Museum of Modern Art, and the Solomon R. Guggenheim Museum, and loaned some 140 paintings, sculptures, and drawings to museums and art galleries in various nations. More interested in discovering new artists than in accumulating a collection of recognized master-pieces, Scull recently defined his desire to be-come directly involved in the creation of art. "I buy art because that way I become a part of the artist's life," he told Arthur Cooper. "A seg-ment of his life is bound up with mine. I find that very romantic. . . . Artists are the most heroic people in the world—next to cabdrivers."

References

Art N p78+ D '73
Christian Sci Mon p14 O 20 '73
N Y World Journal Tribune p16+ O 23 '66 pors; p21+ O 30 '66 pors
New Yorker 42:64+ N 26 '66 por
Newsweek 82:64+ O 29 '73 por

SEAGREN, BOB

Oct. 17, 1946- Pole vaulter
Address: c/o Sports Illustrated, Time-Life Bldg., Rockefeller Center, New York 10020

A leading attraction on the new professional track and field circuit is Bob Seagren, a charter mem-ber of the International Track Association, organ-ized in 1973. Before turning pro, Seagren, a grad-uate of the University of Southern California, vaulted to record heights both indoors and out and won two Olympic medals, a gold medal at Mexico City in 1968 and a silver one at Munich in 1972. On the pro circuit he has been vaulting against Dennis Phillips, Mike Wedman, and Greg Smith, among others. Seagren still holds the world outdoor pole vault record, with eighteen feet five and three-quarter inches.

Robert Lloyd Seagren was born on October 17, 1946. According to *Who's Who in Track and Field*, his birthplace was Fullerton, California. Other sources say he was born in Pomona, California. Seagren's father, Arthur Seagren Sr., the manager of a Pepsi-Cola plant, wanted him to become a baseball player, but, like his older brother, Arthur Jr., Bob Seagren preferred pole vaulting. "I guess I was about eleven when I started," he recalled in an interview for the New York *Times* (June 24, 1966). "The man in the [local] rug store let us take whatever bamboo poles we wanted. We used to ride the poles from a garage roof to the roof of a shed. We

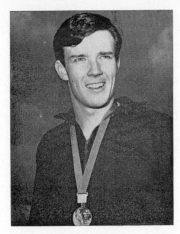

BOB SEAGREN

built our own set of uprights and vaulted over a homemade crosspiece."

"The strangest vaulting area, perhaps, was in a bomb shelter . . . ," Seagren continued. "A man built a bomb shelter and piled earth on the roof. He planted flowers there and watered them with sprinklers. One day he forgot to turn off the sprinklers and the extra weight caved in the roof . . . , so he abandoned it and piled lawn clippings, weeds, and stuff like that inside the crumpled walls. My brother and I used to vault over the wall and land on all the soft debris."

The first measured height Seagren cleared was six feet one inch, when he was twelve. By the time he was a tenth-grader he could do ten feet, and in April 1965 he cleared sixteen feet for the first time. At the 1965 Amateur Athletic Union championships in San Diego he met John Pennel, the first vaulter to clear seventeen feet, doing it outdoors. The two became close friends.

An indifferent scholar, Seagren would probably never have gone to college if he was not wanted on the track team. Because his high school grades were low, officials at the University of Southern California advised him to get some credits in junior college first. Accordingly, he studied at Mt. San Antonio Junior College and Glendale Junior College, both in California, before enter-ing the university in the fall of 1966. In Glendale he shared an apartment with Pennel, and to-gether the two would attend meets, study the competition, and watch films of themselves and other pole vaulters in action.

In March 1966 Seagren became the first vaulter to clear seventeen feet indoors, at a meet in Albu-querque, New Mexico. Two weeks later he vaulted seventeen feet three-quarters of an inch at the Knights of Columbus indoor meet in Cleveland. On May 15, 1966 Bob Seagren set a new world's record for outdoor competition, vaulting seventeen feet five and one-half inches at the West Coast Relays in Fresno, California. Pennel later re-claimed that record, vaulting seventeen feet six and one-quarter inches, but Seagren added to his indoor mark, leaping seventeen feet three inches, again at the Knights of Columbus meet in Cleveland.

In June 1966 at Sacramento, California Seagren eclipsed Pennel's outdoor record with a vault of seventeen feet seven inches. Two weeks later at the AAU championships in Bakersfield, California Seagren's mark was broken by Paul Wilson, who leaped seventeen feet seven and three-quarter inches. "It was the damndest thing you ever saw," said one witness to the record event. "It was about 11:45, maybe nearer midnight. When Wilson beat the record, there was Seagren, seemingly as ecstatic as the guy who'd just beaten him, jumping around and patting Wilson on the back. Pole vaulters are strange people."

In an article in *Sports Illustrated* for February 20, 1967 John Underwood described the then twenty-year-old pole vaulter thus: "Seagren . . . is . . . a handsome dog with a made-in-Los Angeles personality and a little boy smile that knocks girls out. He is obviously no intellectual, because he thinks we ought to be in Vietnam and ought not to take seriously those 'nuts' at Berkeley." Underwood noted that, like most pole vaulters, Seagren was "daring." He recounted how Seagren used to ride his motorbike "at breakneck speeds around the hills below Mt. Baldy" and how he had often climbed the mountain and crawled through the narrow underground passages of Cucamonga Canyon, "daring them to swallow him up."

As for pole vaulting, Underwood observed that Seagren was his own severest critic: "By his own appraisal, Seagren often 'slops up into the air' and then tries to muscle through to make up for his loss of form. . . . Seagren complains that he does not have the coordinated hand action of Hansen or Pennell, that he frequently pushes off with one hand instead of two and other times he just looks plain tired going over the bar. But these are things only he might see in himself, and the point is he *does* get over the bar, somehow, and usually at that moment when all would be lost if he did not."

In 1968 Seagren placed first in seven of his first nine indoor meets and in one of them, the Millrose Games at Madison Square Garden in New York, he raised his indoor record to seventeen feet four and one-quarter inches. Writing of the latter performance, Stan Isaacs of *Newsday* (January 26, 1968), noted: "And he enjoyed himself while doing it, strutted on that runway like a peacock. Every motion seemed studied and mannered as he walked up and down the runway. He gripped and regripped his pole; he stretched his legs and his arms; he breathed deeply and remained motionless in a last brief communion with himself and his sport of adventure. This was a good time for him. The crowd was almost on top of him, studying him, and he knew it. 'I like the indoors. I like having the crowd so close to me. It inspires you more, I think.'"

Seagren qualified for the American Olympic team with a record leap of seventeen feet nine inches at the Olympic trials in September 1968.

The following month at the Olympics in Mexico City he won the gold medal in the pole vault, and he did it on a typical bit of Seagren gambling. He elected to pass his turns until the bar reached seventeen feet six and three-quarter inches, partly to avoid adding misses to his record but mostly in hope of "psyching" the other competitors. He made that height but so did four others, including Pennel. Then the bar was raised to seventeen feet eight and one-half inches. Seagren missed on his first attempt but made it on his second. So did Claus Schiprowski of West Germany and Wolfgang Nordwig of East Germany. But when all three failed to negotiate seventeen feet ten and one-half inches Seagren was declared the winner of the event by virtue of fewer misses.

The thumbnail biography of Seagren in the *Trojan Track and Field* booklet published by the Athletic News Department of the University of Southern California in 1969 hailed him as "the greatest pole vaulter in history" and noted that he also did a considerable amount of running during the track season. Doubling as an intermediate hurdler on the track team, he clocked 53.4 seconds in his first-ever attempt in that difficult race.

In Albuquerque in January 1969 Seagren once again set a new indoor record, this time soaring to seventeen feet five and three-quarter inches. Later in the same year he added a quarter inch to that mark but lost his outdoor record to Pennel, who jumped seventeen feet ten and one-quarter inches. Plagued by illness and injuries, Seagren slumped badly in 1970 and 1971. Regaining his form, he vaulted eighteen feet four and one-quarter inches in a meet at El Paso, Texas in May 1972, tying the record set by Sweden's Kjell Isaksson. On July 2, 1972 he reclaimed the world's outdoor record when, competing in the Olympic trials at Eugene, Oregon, he cleared eighteen feet five and three-quarter inches.

Seagren was outspokenly bitter when the International Amateur Athletic Federation informed him that the Dura-Fibre carbon pole he was using would be banned at the Olympics in Munich in the summer of 1972 on the ground that it was not generally available through normal supply channels worldwide. "The pole that I used was one and a half ounces less in weight and 25/1,000 of an inch smaller in diameter than the one I used before," he told Leonard Shapiro of the Washington *Post* (August 19, 1972). "If that makes that much difference . . . well, I just don't believe it does. I can vault just as high with the older pole as with the new. It's not a physical handicap, it's a psychological handicap. A pole is like a golf club. You get used to the feel of it. . . . Now I've got to get used to a new one." At the Olympics he finished second to East Germany's Nordwig.

The first professional competition in which Seagren participated was a decathlon of superstars (Joe Frazier, Jean-Claude Killy, Johnny Bench, and seven others of like calibre from various sports) held in Rotonda, Florida in March 1973. Each athlete could compete in any seven of ten scheduled events, except his specialty. By winning four events—weightlifting, baseball hitting, half-mile running, and bike racing—Seagren had the highest total of points and won $39,700. The newly organized International Track Association opened its first regular schedule in Los Angeles later in the same month.

Bob Seagren and actress Kam Nelson were married on January 22, 1970 in Trinity Lutheran Church in Pomona. They live in a five-bedroom house in Westwood, California which Seagren hopes "to fill . . . up pretty soon—with children." The pole vaulter is five feet eleven inches tall and weighs 175 pounds. Aspiring to become a motion-picture actor, he would like, he says, "to develop eventually along the lines of a Steve McQueen or a Robert Redford—playing physical roles and doing my own stunts." But he has no intention of retiring from pole vaulting soon. "I love competition," he told one reporter, "and I'm sure I could go on for six or eight more years."

References

Christian Sci Mon p12 Ag 31 '72 por
Newsday A p28 Ja 26 '68
Sports Illus 26:22+ F 20 '67 por
Who's Who in Track and Field (1973)

SELDEN, DAVID (SEELEY)

June 5, 1914- Former labor union official; teacher
Address: b. American Federation of Teachers, 1012 14th St., NW, Washington, D.C. 20005; h. 7102 Rebecca Dr., Alexandria, Va., 22307

"I want to be thought of primarily as a social reformer," David Selden, the former president of the American Federation of Teachers (AFT) once remarked. "I want to be considered a creative person who leads the way for the country's teachers to become more dignified professionals, to make an impact on American education far more significant than they ever have in the past." For more than thirty years, Selden was a leading figure in the teachers' union movement at the local, state, and national levels. An experienced teacher as well as a skilled union organizer, he was aware of the mounting educational, social, economic, and legal problems of the teacher in contemporary American society. Although he believed in public control of the educational system, he was convinced that only a strong, militant union can insure the continued freedom of the schools from strict control by the government or by special interest groups. Selden, who was running for his fourth consecutive two-year term as president of the AFT's 400,000 members, was defeated by Albert Shanker, the powerful president of the United Federation of Teachers (UFT), the New York City local affiliate of the AFT, on August 21, 1974.

DAVID SELDEN

David Seeley Selden, one of five sons born to Arthur Willis Selden, a school principal, and Florence (Seeley) Selden, a teacher, was born in Grand Haven, Michigan on June 5, 1914. He was raised in Pontiac, Michigan, where he attended local public schools. In 1932 he enrolled at Michigan State Normal College (now Eastern Michigan University) to prepare for a career in teaching. The following year, he married the former Isobel Igel and temporarily dropped out of school. To support himself and his wife he worked at odd jobs in restaurants and factories and played in a dance band. He returned to college in 1934 and, with majors in history and political science, earned a B.A. degree in 1936. Several years later, he obtained an M.A. degree in government from Wayne State University.

Upon taking his undergraduate degree, Selden accepted a position as a social science teacher in a Dearborn, Michigan high school. Influenced by the political writings of George Bernard Shaw and H. G. Wells and by his admiration of militant unionist Walter Reuther, he joined the American Federation of Teachers in 1940. "When I joined the federation, there were only seven members," he recalled in an interview with Robert J. Braun for Braun's book *Teachers and Power* (1972). "By the time I left, we had 400 and had voted the local NEA affiliate out of existence." His success as a union organizer at the local level increased his frustration with his career as the "paternalistic" teacher of several dozen teenagers, the children of black migrants and East European immigrants. "I couldn't stand being father to all those kids," he remarked years later, as quoted in *Teachers and Power*. "I couldn't stand their dependence on me."

After three years on a destroyer as a lieutenant (j.g.) in the United States Navy, Selden moved to Jacksonville, Florida, where he sold and repaired x-ray equipment. In his spare time, he formulated a plan for an experimental college patterned after Antioch College in Yellow Springs, Ohio. In his plan, jobs would be filled from a student-run "labor bank" and credit would be given for "working" hours rather than "study" hours.

Selden taught briefly at public schools in Oak Hill, Florida and in Peekskill, New York, but he was anxious to return to the stimulating challenge of union recruitment. When William Green, the president of the American Federation of Labor, offered him a position as union organizer and national field representative for the AFT, he accepted without hesitation. From 1949 to 1953 he crisscrossed the eastern half of the United States, drumming up support for union affiliation. Despite the fact that he personally organized and chartered scores of union locals, he was disgusted by the AFT's catch-as-catch-can recruitment methods. To increase union membership and improve communication among the locals, he proposed the creation of area councils, financed by a ten cents-a-month dues increase, to handle the immediate organizational and financial problems of the fledgling locals. The proposal was vetoed by John Ecklund, the AFT president.

In 1953 the guild executive board named David Selden special representative and director of organization of the Teachers Guild, the New York City affiliate of the AFT. The Guild, with some 1,500 members, was the largest of the eighty-odd white-collar groups that represented New York City's teachers. With the substantial financial backing of the AFL-CIO's industrial union department, Selden made dozens of personal appearances, printed and distributed reams of promotional literature, and hired highly skilled assistants, among them, Albert Shanker. "The idea was for us to keep moving, to keep acting as if we were the power," he explained to Braun. He believed this would attract people in other organizations. The strategy worked, and in March 1960 prounion members of the High School Teachers Association, another powerful metropolitan local, merged with the Teachers Guild to form the United Federation of Teachers.

Intent on securing collective bargaining rights, the UFT repeatedly used strike threats and short-term walkouts to force the recalcitrant school board to accept the union as the legal representative of its members in contract negotiations. On November 7, 1960 5,000 teacher-members of the UFT staged a one-day walkout. Further strike action was halted when school board officials agreed to collective bargaining. By a three to one margin, the teachers voted in favor of a bargaining election and chose the UFT as their delegated representative, making it the first major urban teachers' union to win the right to collective bargaining.

When UFT president Charles Cogen was elected to the presidency of the national AFT in 1964, he made Selden his special assistant. Considered by many observers to be the *éminence grise* of Cogen's administration, Selden quietly and skillfully constructed a personal political base within the union leadership. Acting as Cogen's "spokesman," he represented the union at public meetings and in labor caucuses, issued joint directives with the president, and wrote dozens of policy-making articles and speeches, some of which advised members to find "a man like Walter Reuther" to lead the union. Selden devised the so-called "Co-organizational Plan" to decentralize effectively the AFT's operations by creating statewide organizations to assist the locals with collective bargaining, strike preparation, and contract negotiations and to raise money for organizing.

In August 1968 Selden, running on a radical platform that favored the use of strikes to win increased federal aid to schools and recommended an immediate merger with the one million-member National Education Association (NEA), defeated Mrs. Zeline Richards and Edward C. Bolstad to become the new president of the AFT. His two opponents, both of whom disapproved of the proposed merger with the NEA, polled 1,089 votes to his 1,321 votes. Calling his victory "an overwhelming endorsement for teacher unity," the newly elected president announced that he would fight for "a single militant teachers' organization." In a public statement issued after the election, he spoke again in favor of a merger with the NEA. He acknowledged the "fear on the part of black teachers that they will be swallowed up in [the] huge organization" but maintained that these fears could "be overcome through discussion within the union." As proof that the smaller AFT would not be engulfed, he cited the AFT's victories in bargaining elections in New York City, Detroit, Chicago, and Philadelphia.

Shortly after assuming office, Selden suggested that union members consider a nationwide strike as a means of increasing teachers' power. In October 1968 he proposed a national conference of teachers and interested citizens to discuss the problems of and formulate guidelines for school decentralization. "You can't have instant decentralization," he told reporters at a news conference in Washington, D.C. "It is something that has to be very carefully constructed. . . . We don't have a single benefit to be gained but we have a lot to lose." Along with job security and academic freedom, the "lot to lose" included the "dignity a teacher has on the job because he knows he can't be intimidated," he said. Unlike the NEA, the AFT backed a federally funded evaluation of schools to establish national standards of education. "Public officials [tend] to conceal the things that make our school systems less effective than they should be," Selden noted in a news release. "The National Assessment [project] will tend to reveal these deficiencies and to generate more support for reform. . . . We think a child in Alabama . . . should have, as a minimum, the same educational standards as the child in Massachusetts."

In his speech opening the AFT's annual convention in New Orleans in August 1969, President Selden argued that "no teacher anywhere in the nation [should] be forced to teach more than twenty children at one time or more than twenty classroom periods a week." This "twenty-twenty standard," he continued, should be the union's "top negotiating priority." Among the other changes he recommended were radical variations in class size, experimental modular programs, the establishment of day care centers for teachers' children, the direct involvement of teachers in curriculum development, and the diversion of a small percentage of each school system's operating budget to educational research. Later that year, he exhorted local union members to make the four-day week and the twenty-twenty plan high-priority demands in their upcoming contract talks.

On February 2, 1970 Newark, New Jersey teachers, ignoring a court injunction, struck for higher wages, increased job security, seniority rights, and the revision of the school system's promotion procedures. Selden joined the picket line on February 18 "to protest this antique law that treats teachers as if they were working for the King of England in the sixteenth century." He was immediately arrested, charged with contempt, and jailed for sixty days. He refused bail and his right to an appeal. Dissident union officials accused Selden of using the Newark strike and his well-publicized jail sentence to improve his image and increase his vote-getting potential before the biennial election in August 1970. At the bitterly divisive convention, Selden defeated Ken Miesen, an AFT national representative and one of the union's top strike strategists, by 105 votes. To insure unity within the organization, he purged the executive staff of his political opponents and sought AFL-CIO support for the Newark teachers' clemency campaign. In a powerful address to the AFL-CIO convention in November 1971, he demanded the immediate passage of public employee laws to guarantee basic civil rights: "What is involved . . . is the right to work under conditions which are satisfactory to you. When you do not have that right, you are under a system of forced labor, and forced labor is slavery. . . . The injunction rule that applies to teachers and other public employees is governmental repression." He went on to say, "If the opposite of humanity is brutality, then the courts of New Jersey are guilty of brutality."

In September 1972 Selden was elected to a third two-year term as president. He handily defeated challenger Ken Miesen by a two to one margin while his Progressive Caucus slate won all twenty vice-presidential spots. The victorious Progressive Caucus platform called for "growth, militancy, and unity," and recommended, among other things, union staff reorganization, affiliation with AFL-CIO groups at the local level, and the hiring of additional teachers' aides and paraprofessionals. Despite the outspoken opposition of Catherine Barrett, the president of NEA, Selden continued to push hard for a merger with the larger organization. "There'll be a wedding, whether it's shotgun or not," he told Elliot Carlson in an interview for the Wall Street Journal (May 22, 1972).

Fearing a takeover by Albert Shanker, who had recently been appointed representative to the AFL-CIO executive board, Selden moved to discredit his former protégé as a power-hungry "Meaney-organization man." (According to a New York Times report published August 25, 1973, the AFT's executive board had decided to name Shanker to the post because Selden was "unacceptable to the AFL-CIO brass.") Following several months of charges, countercharges, and backstage maneuvering, the union's executive council, at a meeting convened at Shanker's insistance, voted sixteen to three to request Selden's resignation. Selden refused. To combat Shanker's "highly centralized, bureaucratic, machine-type organization," he founded "Teachers' Cause" to lobby for the election of liberals to high AFT offices. After he published his reasons for refusing to accede to the executive council's demand for his resignation in the January 1974 issue of the American Teacher, the council, in his words, "clapped its censorship on the paper in the same way that military governments do after they take over." One month later, the merger talks between the AFT and the NEA, so carefully cultivated by Selden, collapsed. The major stumbling blocks were the AFT's insistence on AFL-CIO affiliation and the NEA's demand for a quota system to insure adequate representation of minority group members on the governing boards.

Under Selden's presidency, the American Federation of Teachers, traditionally a politically active union, took strong stands on such controversial issues as civil rights, busing to achieve racial balance in the schools, and increased federal aid to education. Selden was especially critical of President Richard M. Nixon's educational programs and urged union members to support the candidacy of Senator George S. McGovern in the 1972 Presidential campaign. In an article entitled "The Logic and Reality of Political Power," published in the American Teacher (November 1973), he reminded his readers that they had "only two alternatives—(1) put up, or (2) shut up" and that "working with other liberal forces in America" they could "elect a veto-proof Congress . . . and vote real federal aid for education."

A tanned, vigorous man, David Selden stands five feet ten and one-half inches tall and weighs 180 pounds. He has blue eyes, graying red hair, which he wears modishly long "to keep up with the times," and, as of early 1974, a bushy moustache. Although his busy travel schedule leaves him little time for recreation, he enjoys sailing and playing the banjo and guitar. Long a socialist at heart, he formally joined the Socialist Party in 1969, but he still regularly votes the Democratic ticket.

Selden's marriage to Isobel Igel Selden terminated in divorce in 1945. He divorced his second wife, the former Dolores Velez, in 1955 after ten years of marriage. In 1956 he and Bernice Shirley Cohen, a social worker, were married. They have one son, John Arthur. Selden also has two daughters, Ann Christine and Denise Dolores.

A member of several liberal organizations, including Americans for Democratic Action, he was twice elected president of the Council of AFL-CIO Unions for Scientific, Professional, and Cultural Employees. Selden also serves on the United States Advisory Committee on Intergovernmental Relations, the American Trade Union Council for Histadrut, the National Trade Union Council for Human Rights, and in the Industrial Union Department of the AFL-CIO. He has contributed articles to a number of popular magazines and professional journals, including the Saturday Review, Phi Delta Kappan, the Forensic Quarterly, and the Teachers College Record, and is currently completing two books, one on the history of teacher professionalism and one on sailing.

References

St. Louis Post-Dispatch p3+ Mr 4 '73 pors
Braun, Robert. Teachers and Power (1972)

SERT, JOSÉ LUIS

July 1, 1902- Architect; urban planner
Address: b. 44 Brattle St., Cambridge, Mass. 02138; h. 64 Francis Ave., Cambridge, Mass. 02115

So influential and far-reaching is the work of José Luis Sert that the social awareness and concepts of artistic collaboration that he brought to the practice of architecture have become almost commonplace. His early development coincided with the dawning of a new era in art and architecture, a time of revolutionary ferment that called upon the architect to use building techniques and designs and urban planning to help solve the problems of dehumanizing industrialization. Sert has been instrumental in moving architecture away from isolated attention to single buildings and toward the shaping of entire cities, and in a step further he has treated college campuses and even museums, such as the one he designed for the Fondation Maeght in France, as microcities.

For the whitewashed walls and rough concrete of his buildings, their patios and courtyards, sculpted "parasols," splashes of bright color, and textures of tile, Sert is indebted to his Spanish background, upon which he has drawn repeatedly in resourceful application to sites as remote as Chimbote in Peru, Baghdad in Iraq, and Cambridge in Massachusetts. From 1953 to 1969 he was professor of architecture and dean of the Graduate School of Design at Harvard University. He still has an architectural office in Cambridge.

José Luis Sert was born on July 1, 1902 in Barcelona, Spain to Francisco and Genara (López) Sert. A devotion to art seems to have been part of his Catalan heritage. One member of his family was a patron of the architect Antoní Gaudí, and his uncle was the painter José Maria Sert, best known in the United States for his murals at the entrance of the RCA building at Rockefeller Center in New York City. José Luis Sert himself began his career as a painter, expressing an inclination that may account in some measure for his abiding appreciation of the relationship between architecture and the visual arts, painting and sculpture.

As a student from 1921 to 1928 at Escuela Superior de Arquitectura in Barcelona, Sert became occupied with social as well as aesthetic concerns. He joined a student protest movement against the beaux-arts training, which ignored housing and community architectural needs arising from problems of post-World War I industrialization. On a trip to Paris in 1926 he had the opportunity to read the early books of the Swiss architect Le Corbusier, who was then living in France. Excited by the daring ideas in *Vers une architecture (Toward a New Architecture)* and *Urbanisme,* Sert took the books back with him to Barcelona, where they incited him and his fellow students at the academy in a cooperative effort toward the development of a contemporary architecture. One result of their work was the exhibition in 1929 at the Dalmau Galleries in Barcelona of plans for a resort community on the Costa Brava, a project that demonstrated Sert's interest in both urban design and the integration of the visual arts and architecture.

At the invitation of Sert and his fellow students Le Corbusier visited Barcelona in 1927 to lecture on his theories on the building of "the city of tomorrow." A year or two later, having completed his study at the academy and obtained his M.Arch. degree, Sert went to Paris, where he became part of an international group of experimental architects gathered at Le Corbusier's atelier on rue de Sèvres. Under the direction of Le Corbusier and his cousin, Pierre Jeanneret, he worked there on the second set of plans for a League of Nations building. Frequenting the Café de Flore in the evening, he discussed the new aesthetic order with artists who were to be his lifelong friends: Fernand Léger, Alexander Calder, and his Catalan compatriots Joan Miró and Pablo Picasso.

Meanwhile, in 1929 Sert opened his own architectural office in Barcelona and helped to organize a group of local architects that soon became affiliated with the International Congresses for Modern Architecture (CIAM). It was in 1929, moreover, that he attended a meeting of CIAM for the first time, at its second congress, in Frankfurt, Germany, where Walter Gropius and Alvar Aalto were also present. Stimulated by the lively exchange of ideas with his colleagues, Sert contributed prominently to the dissemination of the avant-garde principles of that far-flung organization, of which he served as president from 1947 to its last congress in 1956.

Sert's Barcelona group was a part of an association of Spanish architects that, like the CIAM, insisted on the importance of the role of the architect in city planning and renewal. A statement of principles quoted by Knud Bastlund in *José Luis Sert* (1967) included the objective: "To bring architecture to its natural expression related to actual technical, social and economic conditions from which it is now divorced, is the basis of the program that . . . the group proposes to carry out, coordinating our efforts and encouraging teamwork." On April 14, 1931, the day of the proclamation of the Spanish Republic, the Barcelona group moved into its first meeting hall. From the beginning, its fortunes were tied to the young, ill-fated government, which embarked on a public works program for the whole country. On one of its major projects, the redevelopment of Barcelona, Sert worked first in collaboration with Le Corbusier and Jeanneret in Paris in 1932 to diagram a master plan and then, from 1933 to 1935, with the local Catalan group to make studies and designs for rezoning, eradication of slums, and other specific goals. In a related project he prepared a study in 1934 for the construction of a proposed leisure city near Barcelona.

By 1937, when Sert designed the Spanish Pavilion for the Paris Exposition, his country had become embroiled in civil war. Constructed of prefabricated materials over a painted steel frame, his building, with its movable partitions, served as an effective showcase for stage performances, photographs, sculptures, and paintings that in many instances revealed to the outside world the current struggle of the Spanish people. Picasso's *Guernica* mural and Miró's *Catalan Peasant in the Revolt*, for example, were among the paintings for which Sert provided a setting. Sert's work and similar experimental efforts had come to an end at the outbreak of the civil war in June 1936, just after the completion of Casa Bloc, a Barcelona residential development of 200 dwellings and social service facilities. With the collapse of the Republican government in 1939, he moved to the United States.

"Sert is one of the strongest proponents of the Mediterranean mentality in contemporary architecture," S. Giedion wrote in his introduction to Bastlund's study. The influence of his Mediterranean origins became evident soon after he left Spain in the wide-ranging work in urban planning for South American cities that he undertook as a partner of Town Planning Associates, a firm that he helped establish in New York City in the early 1940's. In collaboration with Paul Lester Wiener and Paul Schulz he designed a series of pilot plans and master plans in Central and South America to bring about "a closer relationship between buildings and people."

Town Planning Associates enlisted the services of a New York engineering firm in its projects as well as the advice of local architects and engineers. Sert and his colleagues surveyed the entire region before any planning began and took great care to avoid destroying natural features of sites by poor development, as had happened repeatedly in some South American projects. Mountain streams, for instance, were integrated into towns as landscaped relief. Parkways became the organizing spines of city sectors. Pedestrians enjoyed private paths that concluded as quiet cul-de-sacs. Decentralized city sections were provided

JOSÉ LUIS SERT

with churches, shopping facilities, libraries, theatres, and playgrounds.

Among the first clients of Town Planning Associates was the Brazilian government, which commissioned studies for a new town of some 25,000 inhabitants, Cidade dos Motores (City of Motors), to be built on a clearing in the jungle about twenty-five miles from Rio de Janeiro. Plans for the town, which was to be constructed over a period of ten years, provided for two factories, modern farms, recreation areas, and residences. As reported in the *Christian Science Monitor* (November 23, 1946), "Its designers say it will be the first complete city in the world planned in accordance with modern scientific, sociological and industrial principles."

In another project, for the city of Chimbote on a desert coastline of Peru, Sert's firm employed a scheme of groupings of patio houses in varying scales from the small family dwelling to the civic center. The Chimbote plans, prepared in 1948, have since been applied repeatedly in developing African and Asian countries. The patio style of building around an open court is an integral part of Sert's Mediterranean manner. He was not the only modern architect to favor that style, but he was a prime mover in readapting it for contemporary needs.

Other new communities that Town Planning Associates blueprinted included two towns in the Orinoco Valley of Venezuela commissioned by United States Steel. Sert also took part in designing master plans for the Colombian cities of Cali, Medellín, and Tumaco and, in consultation with Le Corbusier from about 1949 to 1953, helped to develop a master plan for Bogotá. Engaged as a consultant to the National Planning Office of the Cuban government in 1955, Sert worked on a redevelopment plan for Havana that was to serve as a model for other cities of that country. Also in 1955 he was commissioned by the United States State Department to design the buildings for the American Embassy in Baghdad, Iraq.

Although Sert's academic experience had been limited to a year, in 1944-45, as professor of city planning at Yale University, he was chosen in 1953 to succeed Joseph Hudnut as professor of architecture and dean of the faculty of the Graduate School of Design at Harvard University. By the appointment of Harvard's President Nathan M. Pusey, in 1957 he also became consultant on technical problems in the university's long-range planning. He opened his own office in Cambridge in 1955, but continued his practice in New York until 1958, when the partnership of Town Planning Associates ended. Soon afterward he joined in forming the partnership of Sert, Jackson, Gourley & Zalewski, which in 1963 became Sert, Jackson & Associates in Cambridge. He had also served as chairman of the Cambridge Planning Board.

With his Harvard Graduate Center in 1949 Walter Gropius had begun a change at the university away from the Georgian country house style for student dormitories toward open planning. Following Gropius' lead, Sert succeeded in his Peabody Terrace for Married Students, completed in 1964, to integrate a complex of 500 apartments into the organism of the city. In Peabody Terrace, which received an honor award from the American Institute of Architects, he also agreeably solved one of the most perplexing problems of modern architecture: how to combine low buildings with high-rise buildings without resorting to difficult banks of stairs and uneconomical elevators. Sert linked buildings by bridges and made twenty-two story towers into stacks of neighborly walk-ups serviced by elevators at every third floor.

Also for Harvard, Sert helped to design the Holyoke Center, the Center for the Study of World Religions, and the library addition of the Fogg Art Museum. One of several other important buildings of Sert in Cambridge is his own house, built in 1958 on property leased from Harvard. "Maximum seclusion in minimum space," is the succinct description given of his home in Look (June 9, 1959). Adapting to a colder climate the patio style that he had used earlier to satisfy the simple living needs of Peruvian natives, Sert demonstrated to space-conscious urbanites a modest home looking inward to enable a family to live in a high-density area and still enjoy privacy and trees. Attractive fences pushed out to the property line formed double patios at either end. The living-dining room, kitchen, and bedroom wings were built around a third patio. The house contained picture windows facing completely private sculpture gardens and a Constantino Nivola mural on the back fence.

While using his architectural skill to enhance life in New England, Sert resumed designing buildings for a Mediterranean setting, including a studio for Miró in Palma de Mallorca, a house for Georges Braque in Saint-Paul-de-Vence in France, and a vacation house for himself in Ibiza, Spain. When the Flemish-French art dealer Aimé Maeght saw Miró's studio, he engaged the architect to design a museum for the Fondation Maeght

on a pine-covered hilltop at Saint-Paul-de-Vence. Sert's fusion of traditional and modern architectural elements tends to subdue architecture itself in fulfillment of the purpose of framing the works of Kandinsky, Bonnard, and other painters. The gardens and courtyards, as well as the natural landscape, were treated as part of the whole museum, for displaying the sculptures of Miró and Giacometti and the mosaics of Braque and Chagall. The museum opened in 1964.

Sert left his positions at Harvard in 1969, and the following year he lectured at the University of Virginia as the Thomas Jefferson Memorial Foundation Professor of Architecture. In addition to writing articles for professional publications, he is the author of Can Our Cities Survive? (Harvard Univ. Press, 1942); the coeditor, with Jacqueline Tyrwhitt, of The Shape of Our Cities (Cambridge, 1957); and the coauthor, with James Johnson Sweeney, of Antoni Gaudí (Praeger, 1960). He is a fellow of the American Institute of Architects; a member of the American Academy of Arts and Sciences, the American Institute of Planners, and the National Institute of Arts and Letters; and an honorary member of the Royal Institute of British Architects, the Sociedad Colombiana de Arquitectos, and the Peruvian Institute of Urbanism. He has been awarded the Gold Medal of the Architectural League and several honorary doctorates.

The Mediterranean outlook of José Luis Sert has been much sustained through the Catalan atmosphere preserved around him by his wife, the former Ramona Longás, whom he married on October 2, 1938. They have one daughter, Maria. Sert became a naturalized United States citizen in 1951. As his well-known ability to work harmoniously with sometimes temperamental artists and craftsmen would indicate, he is a tactful, affable man, unassuming in manner as well as appearance. Highly articulate about his work and never dogmatic, he has approved of the steel and glass skyscraper even though he is noted for reviving textured walls to relieve the monotonous uniformity and avoid the staring flatness of the glass tower. "We need now the variety of other materials and forms, other roof lines," Sert has said, "something to compare with the sculptural qualities of the vaults and domes of earlier days."

References

Washington Post G p7 Ag 9 '64; C p2 S 24 24 '67 por

Bastlund, Knud. José Luis Sert (1967)
Who's Who in America, 1972-73

SHULA, DON

Jan. 4, 1930- Professional football coach
Address: b. 16400 N.W. 32d Ave., Opa-Locka, Fla. 33054; h. 16220 W. Prestwick Place, Miami Lakes, Fla. 33014

Professional football's most dominant figure since the late Vince Lombardi, Don Shula, the six-time winner of the Coach of the Year award, is the only coach in National Football League history to win one hundred games in his first decade of coaching. He is also the only coach to lose two Super Bowls, having lost to the New York Jets, 21-7, while guiding the Baltimore Colts, and to the Dallas Cowboys, 24-3, as coach of the Miami Dolphins. In Super Bowls VII and VIII, however, Shula's Dolphins rebounded to become the first team to win back-to-back NFL championships since Lombardi's legendary Green Bay Packers. Shula "turned the Dolphins inside out," John Underwood wrote in *Sports Illustrated* (September 17, 1973), transforming the Miami club "from downstairs maid to belle of the ball in three dizzy years."

A shrewd, tough, demanding coach, Shula has occasionally been criticized by sports writers for his "parade ground manner" and brusque, businesslike approach to the game. "I can't see myself leading Larry Csonka in singing 'Hail to the Dolphins,'" Shula said at a news conference on January 10, 1973, shortly before the Dolphins' second Super Bowl appearance. "I don't go in for that 'Fight Team, Fight' stuff." Csonka, one of Miami's three star running backs, refers to Shula as "an ass-busting coach" in his *Always on the Run* (Random, 1973), written with teammate Jim Kiick. "If you win, it makes for an easier life," Csonka has said, "because if you lose, Shula goes crazy."

Donald Francis Shula, the third of six children of Dan and Mary (Miller) Shula, was born on January 4, 1930, in Grand River, Ohio. (Süle, the original surname, was Americanized to Shula.) His father, a Hungarian immigrant, worked as a nurseryman until the birth of triplets doubled his family, forcing him to take a more lucrative job with a Lake Erie fishery. An energetic, athletic youngster, Shula began organizing football games while he was a student at St. Mary's elementary school. "I spent all my spare time in the playground," he remembered in his autobiography *The Winning Edge* (Dutton, 1973). "I didn't have any ambitions other than to play ball.... The playground meant action and competition. Anything that interfered with sports upset me." Even as a small boy he hated to lose. "When he was eight years old, he would play cards with his grandmother," Mary Shula recalled to Michael Katz in an interview for the New York *Times* (January 15, 1973). "If he lost he would tear up the cards and run and hide under the porch."

At Harvey High School in Painesville, Ohio, Shula earned letters in football, baseball, basketball, and track. Despite the disapproval of his parents, who feared he would be injured, Shula played first-string on the varsity football squad. Named to the all-league high school team, he earned a partial scholarship to John Carroll University, a Jesuit college in Cleveland, where he majored in sociology. The Carroll coaching staff, impressed by Shula's performance as a freshman, awarded him a full scholarship and a starting position on the varsity team in 1948. Alternately

DON SHULA

playing defensive and offensive halfback, Shula quickly established a reputation as an intelligent, aggressive player. Because of injuries, he was benched during his junior year, but returned to the lineup in 1950. To make up for the lost season, Shula sparked the feckless John Carroll Blue Streaks to a respectable 8-2 season. As an offensive back, he gained 872 yards rushing, averaging 5.8 yards per carry, and caught twelve passes for an additional 208 yards. The highlight of his college career came in an end-of-season game with the powerful Syracuse University Orangemen. In that heavily scouted game, Shula rushed for 125 yards, leading his team to a 21-6 victory. He graduated from college in 1951 with a B.S. degree and received an M.A. in physical education from Western Reserve University in 1953.

A ninth-round college draft choice of the Cleveland Browns, Don Shula reported to the Browns' training camp in the summer of 1951. Under Blanton Collier, the defensive backfield coach, twenty-one-year-old Shula survived the cut to become the only rookie on the veteran Cleveland team. Shula began his first professional season as a reserve defensive back on the taxi squad. As a substitute for the injured Tommy James, he intercepted six passes in nine games. One spectacular interception, which led to a ninety-six-yard touchdown run, was called back for a roughing-the-passer infraction.

After two seasons with the Browns, Shula was traded to the Baltimore Colts in a multiplayer deal. In addition to filling his starting assignment as the right cornerback, Shula assisted defensive coach Ross Murphy in planning defensive maneuvers. When former Cleveland line coach Weeb Ewbank joined the Colts as head coach in 1954, he asked Shula to call defensive signals on the field. To bolster the slowly improving Colts, Ewbank recruited younger talent and, just before the beginning of the 1957 season released Shula. The Washington Redskins organization picked him up in time to join the team for the second game of the season. Disappointed by his performance as a player, he retired at the end of the season and returned to Painesville to look for a coaching job. "I guess I always wanted to be a coach," he told a reporter for the Associated Press. "I set my sights on coaching while in high school. I have never wavered."

On the recommendation of Frank Lauterberger, an ex-coach for the Baltimore Colts, Shula was offered a position as an assistant coach at the University of Virginia. Tough scholastic standards that kept some potential players off the squad, a series of injuries, and an apathetic student body combined to hamper the Virginia team so that it finished the season with only one victory. Disgusted, he accepted a job as an assistant under Blanton Collier, head coach at the University of Kentucky. After one year at Kentucky, Shula received coaching offers from the Chicago Cardinals and the Detroit Lions. In 1960 he joined the Lions as a defensive backfield coach. Three years later, in January 1963, he succeeded Weeb Ewbank as head coach of the Baltimore Colts.

In seven seasons with the Colts, Shula compiled a 71-23-4 record for a remarkable .755 percentage. During his tenure with the Baltimore club, he emphasized the importance of the special teams. He publicly praised his kicking unit and required Johnny Unitas, Bill Pellington, Raymond Berry, Gino Marchetti and other established Colt stars to attend screenings of game films and tactical meetings with the special squads. Working with poised professionals such as Unitas, Shula developed a patient, confident coaching strategy: "I . . . learned not to make mistakes, but to wait for the other team to, then to capitalize on their uneasiness and lack of poise to put the points on the scoreboard."

Despite his success, Shula was in danger of being tagged with the reputation that his teams were incapable of winning championship games. In 1964, for example, the Colts clinched the Western Division title by winning ten of their first eleven games, twice defeating the favored Green Bay Packers and the defending champion Chicago Bears, but they were beaten, 27-0, by the Cleveland Browns in the NFL championship game. In 1967 the Colts won eleven and tied two of their first thirteen games, but lost to the Los Angeles Rams, 34-10, in the final game of the season, which decided the Western Division title. Shula's most distressing setback, however, occurred in the January 1969 Super Bowl. The Colts had compiled a 13-1 record during regular season play and were considered to be one of the best teams in the history of professional football. Although Baltimore was rated a 17-point favorite, the Colts lost, 16-7, to the New York Jets, making Don Shula the first NFL coach to lose the Super Bowl to an AFL team.

Because of the Colts' mediocre 8-5-1 record for the 1969 season, Shula readily accepted when Joe Robbie, owner of the floundering Miami Dolphins, offered him a long-term, $70,000-a-year coaching contract, plus an option to purchase part of the Miami franchise. At a press conference announcing his decision, Shula told newsmen, "I'm no miracle worker. I don't have a magic formula that I'm going to give to the world as soon as I can write a book. I'm not a person with a great deal of finesse. I'm about as subtle as a punch in the mouth. I'm just a guy who rolls up his sleeves and goes to work."

Shula's first task was to assemble a coaching staff familiar with his system of "winning football." He hired defensive coaches Bill Arnsparger, Tom Keane, and Mike Scarry and offensive experts Howard Schnellenberger, Carl Taseff, and Monte Clark. To learn as much as possible about his players, Shula scrutinized films of the Dolphins' games and administered psychological tests to each player, measuring drive, motivation, and determination. Recognizing the weaknesses of the offensive line and the defensive secondary, he shuffled the lineup, recruited rookies, negotiated for experienced pros, such as Marv Fleming, a tight end, and Garo Yepremian, a field goal specialist, and joined BLESTO VIII, a professional scouting organization.

When a players' strike delayed the opening of the Dolphins' training camp, Shula ordered four daily practice sessions to assemble his offense and defense for the team's first exhibition game of the 1970 season. The young team of eager but inexperienced players, responding to Shula's tough regimen of daily workouts, field practice, and classroom instruction, won four straight exhibition games, including one against the Baltimore Colts. The Dolphins, whose four-year record was 15-39-2, had never before won more than two games in a row. The Miami offense, sparked by running backs Csonka and Kiick, went from last to first in total yards rushing as the Dolphins won ten of their fourteen regular season games, qualifying for the playoffs for the first time in their five-year history. The Dolphins lost to the Oakland Raiders in the first round of championship play.

The following year Shula led his team to the American Football Conference title, defeating the Kansas City Chiefs, 27-24, in a sudden-death, double-overtime playoff game and shutting out the Colts, 21-0, in the championship contest. In regular season play the Dolphins ran up a phenomenal 2,429 yards to top the NFL in yards rushing; Csonka led the league with an average of 5.4 yards per carry; Paul Warfield, whom Shula had obtained from the Browns in exchange for a first-round draft choice, caught eleven touchdown passes and averaged twenty-three yards per catch; Yepremian, with twenty-eight field goals, was the NFL scoring leader with 117 points; and quarterback Bob Griese was voted the outstanding player in the AFC. Despite their incredible performance in conference play, the Dolphins were trounced by the seasoned Dallas Cowboys, 24-3, in their first Super Bowl appearance, in January 1972. "It was actually the worst performance of our club in the two years we had been together," Shula wrote in his autobiography. "They tore us apart defensively and completely controlled our offense. . . . There wasn't any way I could console myself. . . . Only a victory could soothe the pain."

Thanks to Shula's aggressive "no-name" defense, which allowed a mere twelve points per game, and the blistering running attacks of Csonka and Mercury Morris, both of whom gained more than 1,000 yards rushing, a fired-up Dolphin squad ran up sixteen straight victories in 1972. The most one-sided Dolphin victory—a 52-0 romp over the hapless New England Patriots—marked coach Shula's one hundredth career victory. "I'd like to do something no one's done," Shula told the press at an impromptu celebration, "but only if it leads to something meaningful, like the Super Bowl." Under the guidance of veteran quarterback Earl Morrall, secured to act as a back-up to Griese, the Dolphins came from behind and, playing ball-control football, defeated the Pittsburgh Steelers 21-17. Against the Washington Redskins in Super Bowl VII, the Dolphins, two-point underdogs, contained quarterback Billy Kilmer and held the powerful Redskins' offensive backfield to forty-nine yards rushing in the first half. Led by Bob Griese, who connected on eight of his eleven pass attempts, the Dolphins confused the Washington defensive secondary by mixing play-action passes with ground-gaining runs on first-down plays. Miami racked up 184 yards on the ground —112 contributed by Larry Csonka—and sixty-nine in the air to defeat the Redskins, 14-7. Washington's only score came on an interception of a pass from place kicker Yepremian, who had been unnerved by a blocked field goal attempt. "The Super Bowl game meant a lot to me, personally," Shula has said, as quoted in the Washington *Post* (March 25, 1973). "My guys had to win it or I'd be known as the only coach ever to lose three Super Bowl games."

Shula began his fourth season with the Dolphins by beating the College All-Stars, 14-3, in a nationally televised game to continue the Miami winning streak. The string was snapped at nineteen games—one game short of the professional football record—by the Oakland Raiders, who had shrewdly adopted the Dolphins' game plan of a zone defense, three fast running backs, and a variation of Shula's patented "53 Defense." The Dolphins won all but one of their remaining games, earning their third trip to the Super Bowl in three years. Playing near-perfect football, Miami rolled up twenty-six first downs to humiliate the Minnesota Vikings, 24-7. The Dolphins, according to William N. Wallace's account of the game for the New York *Times* (January 14, 1974), "made no mistakes—no lost fumbles, no intercepted passes, and only one penalty for a loss of four unimportant yards."

Don Shula and his wife, the former Dorothy Alice Bartish, were married on July 19, 1958. The couple and their five children—David Donald, Donna Dorothy, Sharon Lee, Anne Marie, and Michael John—live in a sprawling, six-bedroom ranch house in Miami Lakes, Florida. Shula, who stands five feet eleven and one-half inches tall and weighs 215 pounds, has a ruggedly hand-some face with deep-set blue eyes and a prominent chin. To keep fit, he works out daily with his team, bikes with his children, and plays golf on weekends. He only occasionally indulges in the luxury of a Scotch and water and a good cigar. A devout Catholic, Shula regularly attends 7 A.M. Mass, "I enjoy going to Mass, thinking about Christ, giving thanks," he explained to John Underwood. "I consider it part of my day." During football season his entire life-style is geared to the sport. He arises early and is often in his office by 7:30 A.M., beginning a twelve- or fifteen-hour day. Although Shula has often insisted he does not "pattern [his] style after anybody," he admitted in an interview with William Gildea for a Washington *Post* profile (January 14, 1973): "Paul Brown was the greatest influence on me, especially in the teaching aspect of coaching. In football, it's not what you know but what your ballplayers know that counts."

References

Christian Sci Mon p11 Ja 22 '73 por
N Y Times V p3 Ja 14 '73 por; p37 Ja 15 '73
Sports Illus 33:16+ S 7 '70 pors
Time 100:91+ D 11 '72 por
Washington Post E p5 Ja 14 '73
Shula, Don. The Winning Edge (1973)
Who's Who in America, 1972-73

SIMON, WILLIAM E(DWARD)

Nov. 27, 1927-   United States government official
Address: Department of the Treasury, 15th St. and Pennsylvania Ave., Washington, D.C. 20220

In response to the fuel shortage, President Richard Nixon in June 1973 set up the Federal Energy Office. Since its first director, John A. Love, spent most of his time waiting to consult with the Watergate-distracted President about procedure, the F.E.O. remained ineffectual for six months until William E. Simon succeeded Love as director in December 1973. The self-confident Simon immediately took the initiative and built the F.E.O. into a full-fledged super-agency with a staff of 1,000 in Washington and another 500 in branches throughout the United States.

A former Wall Street bond trader, Simon has been in Washington since December 1972, when he became deputy Secretary of the Treasury, a post that he maintained concurrently with that of energy czar. Although he established a mandatory fuel allocation program and a contingency plan for gasoline rationing, his policy at F.E.O. was basically free-market, aimed at handling the energy crisis as much as possible by voluntary co-operation. Simon's influence in the Nixon administration grew with his appointments as Secretary of the Treasury on April 17, 1974 and chairman of Nixon's Energy Policy Council in June 1974. When

WILLIAM E. SIMON

Congress passed the administration's Emergency Energy Act, the F.E.O. became the Cabinet-level Federal Energy Administration in July 1974, with John C. Sawhill as administrator. In September 1974 Simon became President Ford's leading economic spokesman when he was named chairman of the Economic Policy Board.

The son of an insurance broker and the grandson of a French-immigrant textile-dyeing manufacturer, William Edward Simon was born in Paterson, New Jersey on November 27, 1927. His mother died when he was eight. With his brother and two sisters, he grew up in Spring Lake, on the Jersey shore. As a secondary school student, at Blair Academy and Newark Academy, Simon, was, according to one of his classmates, an excellent swimmer and a popular person generally but "nothing special" scholastically. In 1946 he graduated from Newark Academy and joined the United States Army. While serving in Japan he swam with the Army team in the Pacific Olympics. Discharged in 1948, he entered Lafayette College in Easton, Pennsylvania as a pre-law student specializing in economics. His academic performance was only average because, according to Steve Lawrence of the New York Post (January 12, 1974), he "apparently liked partying and sports a bit more than studying."

In 1952 Simon graduated from Lafayette and, having abandoned his plans to go on to law school, ventured into Wall Street, where he managed trade in municipal bonds for the Union Securities Company (until 1957), Weeden and Company (as a vice-president, through 1963) and Salomon Brothers (beginning in January 1964). After nine months he became a Salomon partner, in charge of federal bonds and securities.

Simon's arrival at Salomon Brothers marked the beginning of a period of spectacular growth for the company. According to John Allan of the New York Times (December 17, 1972), Simon was "a major force in directing the firm's expansion." By the late 1960's he was recognized throughout the financial world as one of the most brilliant bond experts. In 1969 he was elected the first president of the newly formed Association of Primary Dealers in United States government securities, and in October of the following year he was named to Salomon Brothers' seven-man management committee. His annual earnings for 1971 and 1972 are estimated to have been between $2 million and $3 million.

Simon's Wall Street reputation for quick, shrewd decision making and astute administrative ability did not escape the notice of George P. Shultz, Secretary of the Treasury in the Nixon administration. When Shultz asked him to come to Washington, Simon accepted with alacrity, and President Nixon nominated him to succeed Charles Walker as Shultz's deputy on December 6, 1972. The nomination was confirmed by the Senate three weeks later.

While managing the day-to-day operations of the Department of the Treasury for Shultz, Simon also chaired the administration's Interagency Oil Policy Committee. In the course of his consultations with people in the oil industry and the sixty or so government agencies concerned in one way or another with that industry, he gained an intimate knowledge of the energy problem. Americans, who comprise only one-sixth of the world's population, were consuming about one-third of the world's fuel in the 1960's, and, goaded by the siren ads of the fuel, utility, appliance, and auto companies, the rate of consumption was ever upward.

In 1970, according to some industry experts, available oil production in the United States reached its limit while demand continued to climb. From that time on a fuel crisis was inevitable. The "crunch"—as the industry likes to call it—came three years later, when the Arab countries stopped exporting oil to nations sympathetic to Israel.

At the request of President Nixon, John Love resigned the governorship of Colorado to take direction of the newly created Federal Energy Office in July 1973. Faced with the impossible task of coordinating the energy policy of some sixty government agencies in the face of a major national crisis with only a skeleton staff, Love sought consultation with President Nixon, to no avail. He did manage to see the President on at least a couple of occasions, but those meetings achieved very little. Aside from White House preoccupation with the Watergate matter, the crux of Love's failure to get Nixon's ear was, in the view of many journalists, not his lack of decisiveness but his divergence from White House policy. Whereas the Nixon administration opposed a system of gasoline rationing, Love was saying publicly that he considered such rationing a necessity.

Five months after Love's arrival in the nation's capital, he and the administration parted company. On December 4, 1973 the White House announced that Love would be succeeded by Simon. Asked by a reporter why he agreed to take on such a "thankless" job, Simon replied: "I suppose there are people who might call this a no-win situation. But that never bothers me. I would say what we have here is an infinitely soluble problem. And I enjoy getting things done." At a press conference following the announcement of his appointment, Simon said: "We have become a nation of great energy wastrels. We have been accustomed to an overabundance of cheap energy. That day is over. This country now faces the choice between comfort and convenience, or jobs."

With the specter of mass unemployment in mind, Simon made clear in the first presentation of his allocation program, on December 12, 1973, that industry would get the fuel it needed to maintain production. The next priority included home heating. Accordingly, Simon ordered gasoline refineries to cut their production by 5 percent, for the purpose of diverting that percentage of petroleum from driver use to factory and home consumption.

Before he assumed the post, Simon described his new job as "undoable." It was no surprise that the longer he occupied it the less he pleased all parties. The Gulf Oil Corporation took its fight against his mandatory allocation program to court. (The oil companies did, however, appreciate his efforts to obtain for them higher tax-credit incentives for exploring new resources.) The Pentagon balked when he tried to convert 1,500,000 barrels of military jet fuel to civilian use. (It gave up only half the amount.) And some Congressmen, needing a scapegoat to placate irate motorists lined up at gas stations back home, began to train their sights on him.

His most serious infighting was with the administration. When, in mid-February 1974, Roy Ash, Nixon's Director of the Budget, publicly described the energy crisis as short-term, Simon, in a fury, announced on television that Ash ought to "keep his cotton-pickin' hands off energy policy." Later in the same month, when the Shah of Iran said in a television interview that the United States was importing as much oil as before the oil boycott, Simon called the statement "irresponsible and reckless." The White House, which had a much needed friend in the Shah, was embarrassed. Also in February 1974, when Simon pushed his authority to the limit in order to supply twenty-six states with gasoline, John Schaefer, a White House loyalist, resigned as the F.E.O.'s chief of allocations.

Nobel Prize-winning economist Wassily Leontief blamed the energy crisis on oil industry mismanagement, and Ralph Nader went so far as to charge that there was no crisis at all. Simon had difficulty in getting the industry to provide him with full statistics on production, imports, and inventory, and in stopping hoarding of gasoline by trucking companies, but those problems were as nothing compared to his hardest task: to persuade the American public that the crisis was real and not a device by which the oil industry, abetted by a federal administration anxious to draw attention away from the scandal of Watergate, was raising the price of its product exorbitantly.

Driving to work in his Belair, William Simon arrives at his office before eight each morning. His whirlwind workday lasts an average of thirteen hours and his workweek includes Saturday and sometimes even Sunday. He pushes his staff as hard as he does himself, insisting, for example, that the briefings prepared for him when he goes to Capitol Hill be meticulous and exhaustive. Senators and Representatives appreciate his accessibility, openness, and responsiveness, as do journalists. He always returns the calls of reporters, and he holds candid press conferences. The fourth estate takes mischievous delight in beginning its reports on him with an allusion to the old children's game: "Simon says. . . ."

In his youth Simon was obese, until he lost more than forty pounds in a self-administered crash exercise program. He now keeps his weight at approximately 165, a lean tally for a man almost six feet tall. Colleagues and underlings report that he has a terrible temper but also a ready laugh. The ambience of his office is at once informal and orderly, reflecting the personality of the man. He is a good organizer partly because he tends to see everything, according to one associate, in "black and white" categories. Others have described him as a "bright," "honest," "action-oriented" person with a "take-charge" manner. He has little time these days for his favorite recreations: swimming, at which he is excellent, and golf and tennis, at which he is fair to middling.

William E. and Carol (Girard) Simon were married in 1951. With four of their seven children, they live in a large house on seven acres in McLean, Virginia. Their permanent home is a sixty-four-acre estate in northern New Jersey. Simon, whose net worth has been estimated at $3,000,000, put his investments in a blind trust when he became deputy Secretary of the Treasury.

References

N Y Post p22 Ja 12 '74 por
N Y Times III p5 D 17 '72 por; p35 D 5 '73 por
Time 103:25 Ja 21 '74 por
Washington Post G p1+ Ja 13 '74 pors

SIRICA, JOHN J(OSEPH) (sə-rik′ə)

Mar. 19, 1904- Federal judge
Address: b. United States District Court for the District of Columbia, United States Court House, Washington, D.C. 20001; h. 5069 Overlook Rd., N.W., Washington, D.C. 20016

The year 1973 is likely to be remembered as the one in which the sordid Watergate affair began to unfold. The developing series of events thrust a tremendous burden of responsibility on the shoulders of Federal Judge John J. Sirica, who presided at the key Watergate trial of 1973. Sirica met the challenge directly. As reported in *Time* magazine (January 7, 1974), by "stubbornly and doggedly pursuing the truth . . . regardless of its political im-

JOHN J. SIRICA

plications, [he] forced Watergate into the light of investigative day, . . . insisting that not all the panoply of the presidency entitled Nixon to withhold material evidence." In the course of his juristic career, which began in Washington in the mid-1920's, Sirica was a prosecutor, a defense lawyer, and a counsel to a Congressional investigation committee before being appointed to the United States District Court for the District of Columbia by President Dwight D. Eisenhower in 1957.

John Joseph Sirica was born on March 19, 1904 in Waterbury, Connecticut, the son of Fred Ferdinand Sirica, who immigrated to the United States in 1887 from his native village of San Valentino near Naples in Italy, and of Rose (Zinno) Sirica, who was born in New Haven. He has one brother, Andrew. Fred Sirica, who suffered constantly from a hacking tubercular cough until his death in 1940, was a barber by trade. At various times he also ran a restaurant, a grocery, and other small businesses, but each of his ventures failed, and in most instances he was cheated by unscrupulous partners. As a result, John Sirica's childhood was a difficult fight against persistent poverty, and even as a boy he helped support the family by greasing cars, waiting table, and selling newspapers.

Because the Siricas wandered from city to city in search of employment and business opportunities, John Sirica's early years were spent in Jacksonville, Dayton, New Orleans, and Richmond, where he attended the local public schools. The family settled in Washington, D.C. around 1918, and in that city Sirica completed his secondary education at the Columbia Preparatory School. Then, at the age of seventeen he entered the George Washington University Law School. Never having attended college, however, he found the work over his head and dropped out after a month. For a time he sold newspapers again while learning boxing at the YMCA and considered becoming an auto mechanic. When, however, his family returned to its itinerant existence, his resolve to study law grew stronger. He had also long been impressed by Fred Sirica's words, "I don't care what you do, John, but be somebody," as well as by a paternal threat to break his arm if he ever took up barbering.

Determined to succeed in his second attempt, Sirica enrolled in the law school at Georgetown University. To support himself he worked as a boxing coach for the Knights of Columbus and fought in occasional three-round stag matches. After receiving his LL.B. degree in 1926 he joined his family in Miami, where he became the sparring partner of the department store heir Bernard F. Gimbel and of the former welterweight champion Jack Britton. He also boxed in local smoker matches.

At the urging, however, of Rose Sirica, who thought her son was wasting his education, he soon gave up boxing. Later in 1926 he returned to Washington, secured admission to the District of Columbia bar, and set up a private law practice. At the outset he spent most of his time defending indigent clients without fee to get experience. Many of his frequent off-hours were passed as a courtroom spectator watching skilled lawyers in action. Eventually he met and came under the influence of William E. Leahy, one of the foremost trial lawyers of the period, whom he first saw when Leahy was defending Secretary of the Interior Albert Fall on the charge of having accepted a $100,000 bribe in connection with the Teapot Dome scandals.

On August 1, 1930, during the Hoover administration, Sirica was appointed an assistant United States attorney for the District of Columbia. In that role, according to Time (January 7, 1974), "he developed a reputation as a fair but somewhat excitable courtroom lawyer. Aroused by the tactics of opposing counsel in one trial, Sirica impulsively shouted: 'It ain't fair; it ain't fair!' "

Sirica resigned his post on January 15, 1934, during the Roosevelt administration when a Democrat was appointed United States attorney. With a partner, he resumed his private practice, which for a while depended mainly on cases given him by friends. Among his friends was the boxer Jack Dempsey, whom he met while serving as attorney to a local fight promoter. His unique personal style, however, soon began to capture public attention. On August 8, 1934, for instance, during a trial Sirica accused the arresting police sergeant of having framed his client on a vice charge, as John S. Lang related in the New York Post (April 7, 1973). Furious, the burly cop leaped up and attacked the smaller Sirica, who ducked and then slugged his assailant, leaving the courtroom spectators agog and the policeman with a puffy eye.

In one of his first important cases, in 1940 Sirica defended the head of a Missouri public-utility firm who was accused of perjury in connection with the investigation of a political slush fund. As Walter Winchell's attorney, he defended the noted columnist when the publisher Eleanor ("Sissie") Patterson sued him for $200,000 on a charge of libel. Through his shrewd tactics in the latter case he persuaded the plaintiff to withdraw the suit.

While building up a flourishing law practice, Sirica became active in politics as a Republican. During five Presidential campaigns, beginning in 1936, as well as in other elections, he acted as a kind of party emissary and spokesman to Italian-American organizations throughout the country. In 1938-39, moreover, he served as state chairman of the District of Columbia Junior Bar Conference of the American Bar Association. Turned down because of a minor physical defect when he applied to the Navy for an officer's commission in World War II, Sirica devoted much of his time during the conflict to accompanying Jack Dempsey on nationwide bond-selling tours.

The choice of Democratic Representatives, in 1944 Sirica was appointed general counsel to a House Select Committee investigating charges that the Federal Communications Commission had been misusing its power to license broadcasters. He angrily resigned on November 28, 1944, when it became apparent that the committee's Democratic majority intended to cover up evidence that high-ranking officials in the Roosevelt administration were involved in an effort to revoke the license of radio station WMCA in New York. In his final statement he asserted, "I don't want it on my conscience that anyone can say John Sirica . . . is a party to a whitewash." He returned to private practice, and when, in 1952, Senator Joseph R. McCarthy, a good friend, invited him to become majority counsel to his Government Operations Committee, Sirica declined. "Divine providence guided me away from that one," he once said, as Mary McGrory quoted him in her syndicated column of September 1, 1972.

Meanwhile, in 1949, Sirica had become chief trial lawyer for the prestigious Washington law firm of Hogan & Hartson. He remained with the firm until President Eisenhower appointed him in 1957 to the United States District Court for the District of Columbia. As a judge in one of the busiest district courts in the nation, Sirica tried a wide range of cases, many of which were highly complicated and controversial. In 1959, for instance, he ruled that the Army had the right to give an undesirable discharge to a reservist based on his conduct after leaving active service. In 1957 he presided over the contempt-of-Congress trial of the teamsters' union vice-president, Frank W. Brewster, and in 1966, over the trial on the same charge of the Ku Klux Klan wizard, Robert M. Shelton. In 1972 he tried the gruesome Ammidown murder case, in which a suburban husband was charged with hiring an assassin to rape and murder his wife. Perhaps the most complex case to come before Sirica during that period was a ten-month-long, $90,000,000 antitrust action brought against twenty-three railroads by a Kansas City trucking firm in 1960.

His decade and a half on the district court bench earned Sirica a reputation among Washington lawyers as a tough, hardworking, forthright man of impeccable integrity, although it was generally conceded that he was not a profound legal scholar. Because of his firm law-and-order stance and his tendency to give the longest sentences allowable under the law, he acquired the nickname of "Maximum John." Sirica's command of legal niceties and technicalities was sometimes questioned, however, and it is commonly said that he was the most frequently reversed judge in the District of Columbia. His award of $225,000 in the trucking firm antitrust action, for instance, was ultimately invalidated by the Supreme Court on the grounds that some of the evidence presented at the trial was inadmissible.

In an article for the New York *Times Magazine* (November 2, 1973) Howard Muson wrote, "Sirica's errors seem to run the gamut of all possible procedural pitfalls of the complex modern trial." Sirica's own record for all civil and criminal matters tried from 1957 to 1967 indicated he was affirmed seventy-seven times and reversed only thirty-five times. Muson concluded, "No complete figures are available, and even if they were, they wouldn't be a fair appraisal of a judge's competence because, for one thing, there might be philosophic differences between him and the appeals court, and, for another, the judge who always plays it safe with his eye on the appeals court may be shirking his duty to adapt the law to changing circumstances in the front lines of the trial court."

By virtue of seniority John Sirica became chief judge of the United States District Court on April 2, 1971. The duties of his new office were mainly administrative. He heard few cases and began to look forward to his impending retirement or semiretirement, which was to have taken place on his seventieth birthday. His plans soon changed, however, with the onrush of startling public events. In June 1972, during the election campaign in which President Richard Nixon won his second term in office, seven undercover Republican operatives were arrested while in the process of bugging the headquarters of the Democratic National Committee in Washington's Watergate building complex. As the investigation of the incident proceeded, a growing body of evidence suggested that many close associates of President Nixon were involved in a wide range of improprieties and illegal activities, and allegations began to be made that the President himself was personally involved and directly responsible.

John Sirica was quick to grasp the full dimensions of the developing Watergate scandal. When the case of the original seven Watergate defendants came before his court in January 1973, he did not assign it to any of the fifteen judges under his supervision, but decided to try it himself. According to *Time* (January 7, 1974), he took that action "partly because he felt that if he as a Republican judge handled the matter, and did so fairly and aggressively, no charges could be leveled that partisanship had entered the judicial process." Impatient at times with the ineffectiveness of the prosecutor, Sirica himself intervened to question the defendants more closely. When James McCord, an electronics specialist accused in the Watergate wiretapping, decided to take the fateful step of breaking an apparent conspiracy of silence and implicating higher-ups in the government, it was to Judge Sirica that he made his first disclosures.

The Watergate trial, like the televised Watergate investigation by Sam Ervin's Select Senate Committee, attracted nationwide attention, and John Sirica soon became perhaps the best-known and most admired judge in the country. He won particular acclaim for his courageous and thoroughly researched ruling, fraught with awesome constitutional implications and subsequently upheld by the United States Court of Appeals, that the concept of executive privilege did not absolve a President of the obligation to hand over tape recordings and other evidence in response to a subpoena.

Sirica's handling of the trial did not escape criticism, however. Some observers, including both civil libertarians and political conservatives, felt he had been guilty of prejudicial acts against the defendants and their attorneys and of many technical violations of proper courtroom procedure. Joseph L. Rauh Jr., former national chairman of the Americans for Democratic Action, commented, "It seems ironic that those most opposed to Mr. Nixon's lifetime espousal of ends-justifying-means should now make a hero of a judge who practiced this formula to the detriment of a fair trial for the Watergate Seven." On the other side of the political spectrum, William F. Buckley Jr., who quoted Rauh's censure in his column of November 23, 1973, charged Sirica with "singular cruelty" and "slovenly work," and reproved him for harsh sentences: "One wonders why Judge Sirica doesn't just keep a big noose in his courtroom, saving himself, and the Court of Appeals, no end of time."

Those extreme views were the exceptions, however, for to most Americans, whether liberal, conservative, or middle-of-the-road, Sirica was a hero —"a man for this season," in the words of the columnist Mary McGrory. Letters of praise poured into his office from lawyers, judges, and ordinary citizens throughout the United States. Even President Nixon, the target of his subpoena and, in the eyes of many, the person who was really on trial in his courtroom, publicly acknowledged Sirica's courage and honesty. The consensus was well expressed in the Christian Science Monitor (August 27, 1973): "He is nonpartisan in the administration of justice in the best tradition of the bench." Sirica was still chief judge of the district court when, on March 1, 1974, a Watergate grand jury handed up an indictment on conspiracy and other charges of former officials of President Nixon's administration, including former White House chief of staff H. R. Haldeman and former Presidential assistant John D. Erlichman. Later as senior judge of the court, after his seventieth birthday, Sirica tried the case, beginning on October 1, 1974.

John J. Sirica is a member of the American Bar Association and the Phi Alpha Delta law fraternity and an honorary member of the District of Columbia Bar Association, the National Lawyers Club, and the Lido Civic Club. In addition to carrying out his judicial duties, he lectures as an adjunct professor of law at the Georgetown University Law Center. For his pursuit of justice in the Watergate case he was chosen the 1973 Man of the Year by *Time* magazine and given the Award of Merit of the American Judges Association.

With Jack Dempsey as best man, Sirica, after a long period of bachelorhood, was married on February 26, 1952 to Lucille M. Camalier, the daughter of one of the proprietors of the chic Washington leather-goods firm of Camalier & Buckley. Since their marriage the Siricas have lived in a comfortable buff-brick Cape Cod house in Washington's exclusive Spring Valley residential district. They also have a beach cottage in Delaware. Their children are John J. Sirica Jr., a student at Duke University Law School; Patricia Ann; and Eileen Marie. The family pet is a poodle named Cocoa.

Of trim build and erect bearing, Judge Sirica stands five feet eight inches tall and weighs about 160 pounds. He has wavy black hair and thick eyebrows. "The pupils of his brown eyes are ringed in black," Mary McGrory wrote, "adding to the sternness of his air." A lifelong devotee of sports and athletics, he walks several miles a day and occasionally plays golf at the Congressional Country Club. He is an avid reader of newspapers and magazines, works of history and biography, and books by and about trial lawyers. He also enjoys organizational banquets and dinners. A Roman Catholic, he attends Mass regularly. His friends speak of him as a humble man with the intense love for America often characteristic of children of immigrants.

References

N Y Post p22 Ap 7 '73 por
N Y Times p12 Mr 24 '73; p18 Ja 16 '73 por
N Y Times Mag p34+ N 4 '73 pors
Time 102:8+ Ag 13 '73 pors; 103:12+ Ja 7 '74 pors
Washington Post D p1+ S 9 '73 por
Martindale-Hubbell Law Directory, 1973
Who's Who in America, 1972-73

SMITH, CHESTERFIELD H(ARVEY)

July 28, 1917- Lawyer
Address: b. Holland & Knight, 92 Lake Wire Dr., Lakeland, Fla. 33802; 245 S. Central Ave., Bartow, Fla. 33830 h. 1710 Mariposa St., Bartow, Fla. 33830

Chesterfield H. Smith, the president of the American Bar Association from August 1973 to August 1974, guided that influential organization through one of the most turbulent years in its ninety-six-year history. Aggressive and outspoken, he received more publicity than any other ABA president for his candid comments on politics, the Watergate scandals, controversial social and moral issues, and the legal profession.

Before accepting the presidency of the ABA, Smith served on the boards of several state and national bar associations and acted as president of the Florida Bar. From 1965 to 1967 he chaired a special commission to rewrite Florida's state constitution. More recently he has served on the board of trustees of the Citizens Conference on State Legislatures and as chairman of Governor Reubin Askew's Citizens for Judicial Reform. Succeeded as ABA president by James Fellers, Smith returned to practice in a large law firm in Florida. Law, he believes, is "the major bulwark between man and his government."

Chesterfield Harvey Smith, the son of Cook Hall Smith, a public school superintendent, and Grace (Gilbert) Smith, was born on July 28, 1917 in Arcadia, Florida. He took six years to complete his undergraduate education at the University of Florida, interrupting it with periods of work as a collection agent for a finance company and as a candy salesman. After serving as a major in the United States Army during World War II, he enrolled at the University of Florida College of Law. He earned his J.D. degree, *cum laude*, in 1948.

Admitted to the Florida bar in 1948, Smith began his career as an associate with Treadwell & Treadwell, a law firm in Arcadia. Two years later he joined Holland, Bevis & McRae, now Holland & Knight, in Bartow, Florida, and in 1952 he was named an executive partner in the firm. Holland & Knight, one of the largest law firms in the state, maintains offices in Bartow, Lakeland, Tampa, and Tallahassee. From his Lakeland office Smith represented some of Florida's biggest industries, including citrus growers and manufacturers of phosphate fertilizers. A persuasive lobbyist for the phosphate industry, he prevented the levy of a special "phosphate tax" for several years. By the early 1970's his lucrative practice brought him $100,000 annually, and in addition to his legal career he served on the boards of directors of the Exchange Bancorp, Ben Hill Griffin, Inc., DECOA, Inc., Mineco, Inc., and the Citrus and Chemical Bank of Bartow.

Smith has been a leading figure in state and national professional bar activities for many years. He was named vice-president of the Twelfth Judicial Circuit Bar Association in 1949 and president of the Tenth Judicial Circuit Bar Association in 1958. Later he was a member of the Board of Governors of the Florida Bar from 1958 to 1963 and served as its president in 1964 and 1965. As president, he helped draft uniform rules of procedure for Florida's courts. He also headed the Florida Bar Center Committee's fund-raising campaign to establish a permanent legal center in Tallahassee. From 1968 to 1971 Smith was Florida's representative to the ABA's House of Delegates and in 1969 and 1970 he was a member of the national organization's Board of Governors.

CHESTERFIELD H. SMITH

After being appointed chairman of the Florida Constitution Revision Commission by Governor Hayden Burns in 1965, Smith devoted more than half his time over a two-year period to rewriting the eighty-year-old state constitution. Although he expected opposition from hard-line political traditionalists, Smith was convinced that the constitution, which had been amended nearly 150 times, was "inconsistent," "ungrammatical," "increasingly inadequate," and "replete with . . . contradictions and obsolete provisions." As an example, he cited the stipulation providing for the election of United States senators by the state legislature. (Since 1913 United States senators have been elected by popular vote, according to the Seventeenth Amendment to the United States Constitution.)

Among the changes suggested by Smith were a bicameral legislature because "legislation should be slow for public education" and a strengthened, two-term chief executive. Smith contended that because the governor was limited to one term by the existing constitution, he was a "lame duck" before he had mastered the political know-how of his office. He also favored increased local autonomy. "Right now our executive branch is a seven-headed monster which directs the whole state," he explained in an interview for *Florida Magazine* (August 6, 1967), the Sunday supplement to the Orlando *Sentinel*. "Local government should be so flexible that the people, by their votes, should have any form of government they want." In a speech before the Florida State Legislature on August 8, 1967 Smith presented the Revision Commission's draft of a new state constitution and urged the legislators to make "proper provision . . . for further changes when conditions make changes desired." The most important thing, he continued, "is to give to the people forevermore the power to amend and revise their constitution in the future without the interference of the legislature, and without the interference or the veto of the chief executive." After the legislature approved a new constitution, Smith stumped the state to drum up popular support for its ratification. Floridians overwhelmingly approved the document in 1968.

At the ABA's mid-year meeting in New Orleans in February 1972 the 307-member House of Delegates, the association's policy-making body, selected Smith as president-elect nominee. In August 1972 at the annual convention he was officially named president-elect. Smith immediately made a favorable impression on the press corps covering the meeting when, in a news conference following his election, he candidly confessed that "there's not too many who can afford me." When asked to outline his position on the potentially explosive issue of busing to achieve racial balance in the public schools, he replied that busing was a "necessary evil" in certain areas of the country. "We may have to put up with it to rectify the sins of my ancestors and others' ancestors," he added. "I hate it . . . but I don't know any better way." He said he would like to see a black judge appointed to the federal bench in the South if the man was "qualified" for the position. "I would not want a black appointed just because he's black," he explained. To revive the ABA, he suggested "broadening the base" to include women, blacks, and members of minority groups and increasing the number of minority representatives on the governing boards "when they demonstrate the capacity for leadership."

At the ABA's annual convention in Washington, D.C. in the summer of 1973 Smith responded to consumer advocate Ralph Nader's charge that the organization was a "trade association" and a "bastion of economic and corporate power" controlled largely by a handful of wealthy and influential corporate attorneys." "We played the game or we wouldn't be here," he conceded to a group of reporters at a breakfast meeting on August 6, 1973. He acknowledged that there was "a fringe" of incompetent lawyers, but dismissed Nader's assertion that the ABA was essentially closed to "reformist" attorneys. "The only way to obtain change is to work within the existing structure," he responded. "I have tried hard to name chairmen from all sections of the country representing all parts of the legal profession. We don't have enough women, blacks, or chicanos, but we're trying."

After serving a one-year term as president-elect, Smith succeeded Robert W. Meserve as president of the ABA on August 9, 1973. One of his first actions on taking office was designed to limit the power of entrenched establishment attorneys. In an unprecedented move he ruled that no member could serve on the same committee for more than six years or act as its chairman for more than three years and that no person could sit on more than one committee. To "regain public acceptance," he suggested that federal law enforcement agencies, tainted by the Watergate scandals, be "depoliticized." An advocate of Chief Justice Warren E. Burger's recommendation that a new national court of appeals be created to lighten the Supreme Court's workload, he also agreed with Burger's harsh criticism of the quality of service provided by many trial lawyers and suggested periodic retesting to weed out incompetent attorneys. Furthermore, he endorsed the concept of prepaid legal service plans similar to medical insurance programs. At his insistence, the House of Delegates publicly deplored minimum mandatory criminal sentences for drug-related crimes, approved ending the popular election of judges, and proposed limiting the powers of appointment of state governors. As one solution to crowded court calendars, Smith suggested that small injury suits, such as auto negligence cases, be submitted to a voluntary community arbitration service.

Testifying before a Senate Judiciary Committee subcommittee investigating the adequacy of legal services in the United States, Smith denied subcommittee chairman John V. Tunney's allegation that the ABA catered to the special interests of wealthy clients. "I represent some of the biggest cruds in Florida, but I don't carry their viewpoints past the time that I go off the payroll," he said. Although he continued to dispute the notion that lawyers are the "handmaidens of the rich," Smith, in an interview for *Intellectual Digest* (March 1974), admitted to correspondent Jack Star that many of his colleagues "sell their services to whoever can pay for them—and the rich can pay for them, not the poor." Nonetheless he maintained that the situation had improved markedly in recent years because of such developments as the class action suit. To publicize the need for more comprehensive legal services, he asked R. Sargent Shriver to develop a wide-ranging public relations program. The program included a documentary promoting local legal clinics staffed by "paralegals."

Unlike many of his predecessors, Smith welcomed the opportunity to speak out on controversial issues. For example, he confidently predicted that "more than several" of the lawyers involved in the Watergate scandals would be disbarred. "No other matter is of more importance to the organized bar than that of insuring to our client public that only lawyers worthy of trust are allowed in the practice," he said, as quoted in the *Wall Street Journal* (August 15, 1973). In a public statement following Nixon's dismissal of Watergate special prosecutor Archibald Cox, Smith deplored the President's action as an attempt to "abort the established processes of justice" and urged Congress and the courts to take "appropriate action . . . to repel" his "defiant flouting of law and courts." Later, he testified before Congress in favor of a court-appointed, independent Watergate special prosecutor. Despite criticism from some members of the ABA, particularly John Leroy Jeffers, the president of the Texas Bar Association, and a vote of censure by the Louisiana Bar Association, the ABA's Board of Governors endorsed Smith's statement as well as his subsequent testimony before Congress.

Two months later, in an opinion piece published in *Newsday* (December 3, 1973), Smith contended that it was "in the national interest that the President be now given his day in a lawfully constituted tribunal absolutely independent of him to make a determination of whether or not he has violated the public trust." Arguing that a forced resignation of the President could be construed as "nothing more than a political assassination," he called on Congress to begin an impeachment investigation. After the release of the official Presidential tapes transcripts on April 29, 1974, he exhorted the House Judiciary Committee "to press for full compliance with its subpoena" requesting that Nixon turn over the actual tapes to the Committee as the "best evidence" available. Shocked by the President's apparent disregard for the "rule of law," Smith announced on June 14, 1974 that he no longer opposed resignation as a viable alternative to a prolonged, potentially divisive impeachment trial. Because he considered impeachment to be "primarily political in nature," Smith reiterated that he was speaking as a private citizen and not as a representative of the ABA.

Taking a defiantly nonpartisan approach to Watergate, Smith questioned the ethics of Judge John J. Sirica's use of the criminal sentencing process in order to further criminal investigation. He also argued that prosecutors should not grant limited immunity to suspected conspirators in order to solicit "questionable testimony." Although he vigorously defended a free press, he denounced grand jury and prosecutorial news leaks that interfered with the "civil rights of those under criminal investigation." In Smith's opinion, the Constitutional issues, including executive privilege, that President Nixon raised in his defense were properly rooted in American Constitutional history. At a meeting of lawyers in Atlanta on December 3, 1973, however, he called on the President to release all relevant materials "even if it had to damage our national security." "It's almost as important for justice to appear to be done as for justice to be done," he said. By April 1974 the ABA had prepared a list of 115 lawyers involved in Watergate to be considered for possible disciplinary action. That same month Smith told reporters that Nixon himself might be subject to professional sanctions for allegedly offering the directorship of the FBI to Federal Judge William Matthew Byrne while he was presiding over the Daniel Ellsberg trial.

After Nixon resigned from the Presidency on August 9, 1974, Smith cautioned against criminal prosecution. "We do not have time for vengeance," he said, as quoted in the *Christian Science Monitor* (August 20, 1974). At a news conference on August 12 he announced his opposition to the ABA's taking a position on immunity for the former President and other defendants, although he personally disapproved of granting immunity. Three days later the ABA, at Smith's insistence, unanimously approved a resolution calling for the impartial application of laws to all potential defendants "without fear or favor arising from the position of status."

Chesterfield H. Smith, a husky, white-haired man, has the affable manner of a seasoned political campaigner. He once described himself as an "overachiever" and as the one-time "loudest crapshooter" in Florida. For recreation he plays golf and goes hunting. He and his wife, the former Vivian Parker, were married on January 29, 1944. They have two children, Rhoda (Mrs. David B. Kibler, IV) and Chesterfield, Jr. For many years the Smiths have lived in Bartow, Florida, a small town not far from Lakeland, where Smith maintains his law office. Officially he is a Democrat, but he votes independently and supported Nixon for the Presidency in 1968 and 1972. He belongs to a number of professional organizations, such as the American Law Institute and the American Bar Foundation. Smith received the University of Florida's Significant Alumni Award in 1966 and has honorary degrees from the University of Florida and several other universities. In 1969 he was named the first "Distinguished Floridian of the Year" by the state Chamber of Commerce for his work as chairman of the state's constitutional revision.

References

Florida Law J 5:253 My '64 por
Newsweek 83:105 Ap 15 '74 por
Time 103:84 F 18 '74 por
Who's Who in America, 1974-75

SMITH, WILLIAM JAY

Apr. 22, 1918- Author; university professor
Address: b. Hollins College, Roanoke, Va. 24020; h. Upper Bryant Rd., West Cummington, Mass. 01265

When the National Institute of Arts and Letters conferred on William Jay Smith the Russell Loines Award for poetry in 1972, it paid tribute to his versatility as a man of letters, citing his translations from several languages, his writings for children, and his lyric poems "in which dark states of mind are made palpable." Smith, who is also a literary critic and a teacher of literature and creative writing, currently holds a professorship in English at Hollins College. In further verifying the values of literature he has conducted writers' conferences, served as consultant on poetry to the Library of Congress, and lectured in many parts of the United States and abroad. Some of his widely anthologized lyrical poems, published in five volumes, are contemplative expressions of the tragic in human experience, but he has a special aptitude for light verse inspired by the humor he finds characteristic of Americans. With a few hints of the macabre, his poems for children are whimsical, frolicsome adventures in imagination.

Although, like Conrad Aiken, he is sometimes identified as a New England rather than a Southern poet, William Jay Smith was born in Winnfield, Louisiana on April 22, 1918, the older of two sons of Jay and Georgia Ella (Campster) Smith. His native town counted among its founders the family of his grandfather, William Allen Smith, a soldier in the Confederate Army and Winnfield's postmaster. Earlier, in the eighteenth

WILLIAM JAY SMITH

century, the Smith family had left Ireland to help settle the Carolinas. From his mother's forebears, cattlemen of Oklahoma and Arkansas, William Jay Smith can claim a one-sixteenth blood relationship with the Cherokee Indians.

Part of Smith's early life was spent in Louisiana, where his family and the family of Huey P. Long were neighbors, and part in Missouri. A professional soldier and a clarinetist in the United States Army band, his father was stationed at the Jefferson Barracks near St. Louis. Even as a young boy—sensitive, imaginative, and perceptive—Smith wrote poetry. In his lecture "The Making of Poems" he recalled his childhood exploration of the woods along the banks of the Mississippi River in Missouri and his response to their terror and beauty, the experience of poetry itself, which he tried to express years later in a poem that he wrote in college called "Quail in Autumn."

Educated in St. Louis until his twenty-third year, Smith attended the Blow School from 1924 to 1931, Cleveland High School from 1931 to 1935, and then Washington University, which awarded him the B.A. degree in 1939 and the M.A. degree in 1941. His major subject at the university was French, a study that he later pursued at the Institut de Touraine, Université de Poitiers. During World War II he served to the rank of lieutenant in the United States Naval Reserve in both the Atlantic and Pacific theatres of operation. His knowledge of French won him commendation from the French Admiralty for his two-year performance as liaison officer aboard the French sloop La Grandière.

For about a year after the war, in 1946-47, Smith taught French and English at Columbia University, where he also enrolled in graduate courses in English and comparative literature. Then, in 1947-48, as a Rhodes Scholar he undertook further work in English literature at Oxford University. He spent the following two years in Italy, at the University of Florence, studying Italian literature and language.

Meanwhile, Smith's literary reputation had begun to catch up with his development as a poet. He moved to Pownal, Vermont in the early 1950's and spent the greater part of the decade there concentrating on writing. His first poem to be published nationally had appeared in Versecraft when he was fourteen. A few years later the College Society of America chose a poem that he had contributed to College Verse as the best lyric by an undergraduate. His first published collection, Poems (Banyan, 1947), consisting of twenty-one lyrics strikingly diverse in mood and style, won tribute from Dudley Fitts in the Saturday Review of Literature (February 21, 1948): "This beautifully made little book is an engaging and sometimes impressive contribution to contemporary poetry."

Celebration at Dark, Smith's second collection of poems, appeared in England under the Hamish Hamilton imprint shortly before Farrar, Straus published it in the United States in late 1950. It was admired by British and American writers alike, including Stephen Spender, Sir Kenneth Clark, and Eudora Welty. The American poet Richard Eberhart commented on the author in the New York Times Book Review (January 7, 1951). "He is in some ways a poet like a painter, sensuously conscious of colors, of words as plastic tones and of music in words as color. Above all, of the demand for controlled form, a blending of images and sounds and sights and imaginings in harmony."

Another American poet, Louise Bogan, who had been less than enthusiastic about some of Smith's poems in his first collection, endorsed his Poems, 1947-1957 (Little, 1957) in the New Yorker (March 29, 1958): "Mr. Smith's serious poems are filled with fresh observation and direct emotion. His light verse—'epigrams, satires, and nonsense'—sparkles and flies free, often straight to the center of a chosen target." Both Smith's third collection of poetry and his fourth, The Tin Can and Other Poems (Delacorte, 1966), were among the final contenders for the National Book Award. Allen Tate welcomed the publication of the latter book as "a literary event of the first importance."

In several of the poems of The Tin Can Smith used a long, unrhymed line of open cadence, having found, as he once explained, that the material he has dealt with in recent years "seems to lend itself to this form, which is often close to, but always different from, prose." The poet John Malcolm Brinnin singled out Smith's title poem, "The Tin Can," for special comment, describing it as "a Laocoon-like involvement in the toils of creative anxiety [and] a rage for freedom and identity. . . . A poem about itself, it begins with delicately quiet annotations, muted feelings, builds in a controlled extravagance of whirlings and whorlings and agonized self-recognitions, and arrives at a kind of epiphany. Wholly convincing, without a false syllable in its hundreds of lines, it is a recreation of experience that seems to make its statement not by calculations but by its processes."

From his four volumes of poetry Smith chose what he considered his best lyrics for inclusion, along with four additional poems, in his *New & Selected Poems* (Delacorte, 1971). The question of whether the cream of thirty years of work places him among the major poets or the more distinguished minor poets of contemporary American literature was variously answered by reviewers and may be left to time to decide. Less disputable is the integrity of his development independently of any school of poetry, or his achievement in terms of the aesthetic values of Smith himself, who does not hold that self-expression is the be-all and end-all of poetry. "I believe that poetry should communicate: it is, by its very nature, complex, but its complexity should not prevent its making an immediate impact on the reader," he has asserted, as quoted in *Contemporary Poets of the English Language* (1970). "Great poetry must have resonance: it must resound with the mystery of the human psyche, and possess always its own distinct, identifiable, and haunting music."

Smith's verbal agility and deft handling of a great variety of verse forms also characterize his poetry for children, which has, as he insists it should, the technical validity of poems for adults. He began writing for children in the early 1950's when his older son, David, was four years old. His first children's poem was inspired by the little boy's repeated, rhythmic recitation to himself of a sentence about Jack-in-the-Box. Later, by closely observing his son, he was able to recapture many of his own reactions and attitudes as a child so that he could communicate directly and vividly to children in his poetry.

By 1973 Smith's first collection of children's poems, *Laughing Time* (Little, 1955), had reached its twelfth printing and had become regarded as a classic by some historians of children's literature. Among his later collections of sprightly, well-executed poems of the same genre, principally nonsense verse, are *Boy Blue's Book of Beasts* (Little, 1957); *Puptents and Pebbles; A Nonsense A.B.C.* (Little, 1959); *Typewriter Town* (Dutton, 1960); *Ho For a Hat!* (Little, 1963); and *Mr. Smith and Other Nonsense* (Delacorte, 1967). His *The Pirate Book* (Delacorte, 1972) is freely adapted from the Swedish of Lennart Hellsing. Smith has read poems from some of his books for children in several recordings. Tapes from two of them, issued by the Library of Congress, were used in a television program *Mr. Smith and Other Nonsense*, first heard in Washington, D.C. on WETA-TV on Christmas Day 1969. That reading won the 1970 National Education Television award in the category of children's programs. The most highly regarded of Smith's anthologies for young people is *The Golden Journey* (Reilly & Lee, 1965), compiled with Louise Bogan.

Some of Smith's collections of poetry for adults had included his translations of the work of other authors, such as five poems by the Russian Andrei Voznesensky that appeared in *The Tin Can*. He has also read his translations of Voznesensky's poems in recordings. As a translator Smith is particularly well known for his *Selected Writings of Jules Laforgue* (Grove, 1956). Also from the French he translated *Valéry Larbaud; Poems of a Multimillionaire* (Bonacio & Saul, 1955), and from the Italian he translated Romualdo Romano's novel *Sirocco* (Farrar, 1951). Two books that he compiled and edited, *Poems from France* (Crowell, 1967) and *Poems from Italy* (Crowell, 1972), contain poems in the original language along with translations by American and English writers.

A selection of some of the best of the book reviews and literary essays that Smith had contributed to American and British periodicals since 1954 was published in *The Streaks of the Tulip; Selected Criticism* (Delacorte, 1972). It included a discussion of children's literature; his 1969 Library of Congress lecture, "The Making of Poems"; an essay on Robert Herrick, whose poetry he had edited for a volume published by Dell in 1962; and critical pieces on Marianne Moore, Louis MacNiece, Louise Bogan, Evelyn Waugh, Kavafy, and others. Smith's earlier book of literary criticism, *The Spectra Hoax* (Wesleyan Univ. Press, 1961), is particularly reflective of his interest in the craft of poetry and its practice in twentieth century literature as well as in the nature of criticism itself. Smith examined several literary hoaxes, principally the "experimental" poems published in 1916 under the title of "Spectra" to spoof the current craze over free verse.

Teaching, though intermittent, has been an important aspect of Smith's career. From 1959 to 1967 as poet in residence and lecturer in English at Williams College, he was in charge of the creative writing program and also taught courses in American and English literature. To somewhat similar responsibilities he added courses in children's literature and European literature as a member of the faculty of Hollins College, where he was writer in residence in 1965-66 and is at present professor of English. During the early months of 1973 he was also visiting professor of writing and acting chairman of the writing division of the School of the Arts of Columbia University.

On leave from Williams College, Smith spent the year 1964-65 in Washington, D.C. as writer in residence at Arena Stage, under a Ford Foundation grant. His play, *The Straw Market*, a comedy for which he also composed music, was given a public reading by the actors at Arena Stage in 1965, was performed at Hollins in 1966, and was read again at the YM & YWHA poetry center in New York in 1969. Smith also spent some years in Washington on leave from Hollins at the Library of Congress, to which he was appointed consultant in poetry in 1968 and reappointed in 1969. An international poetry festival that he, as consultant, took the lead in organizing was attended by poets from eight European and Asian countries and their translators. The festival's panel discussion on the subject of translation was published by the Library of Congress. Smith served also, from 1970 to 1973 as honorary consultant in American letters at the Library of Congress, a post to which he was nominated for a second term in 1973.

Under the American Specialists Program of the Department of State, Smith spent six weeks in 1969 traveling and lecturing in the Far East and more than two months in 1970 on a similar mission in the Soviet Union and several Eastern European and Mediterranean countries. During a visit to Budapest in the fall of 1971 as a guest of the Hungarian P.E.N. Club, he translated the poems of some of Hungary's prominent writers into English. A selection of his own poetry was translated into Hungarian by Szabalcs Várady.

The more recent of Smith's honors include the 1970 Henry Bellamann Major Award "for creative achievement in poetry," a grant from the National Endowment for the Arts in 1972, and a D.Litt. degree from New England College in 1973. He is a member of the Academy of American Poets and the Cosmos Club. While living in Pownal, he was elected on the Democratic ticket to serve in the Vermont House of Representatives for the two-year term from 1960 to 1962.

William Jay Smith married Barbara Howes on October 1, 1947, and by that marriage he is the father of two sons, David Emerson Smith and Gregory Jay Smith. He and his first wife were divorced in June 1964. On September 3, 1966 he married Sonja Haussmann, of Paris, a fashion and publishing consultant. Nearly six feet tall, Smith weighs about 200 pounds; he has brown eyes and graying brown hair. He was described in the Washington *Post* (December 8, 1967) as "suave, witty, and a blunt talker." His friend and fellow poet Allen Tate once placed him among "the least eccentric men in the world." Swimming is his favorite sport, and readers of his poem "Morels" know another of his outdoor recreations, what he calls "collecting mushrooms."

References

N Y Times p24 D 9 '67 por
Washington Post A p3 O 28 '64 por; B p3 D 9 '67 por
Washington Post Potomac p22+ Mr 9 '69
Contemporary Authors 1st rev vols 5-8 (1969)
Contemporary Poets of the English Language (1970)
Something About the Author vol 2 (1971)
Untermeyer, Louis. 50 Modern American and British Poets, 1920-1970 (1973)
Who's Who in America, 1972-73

SOLANDT, OMOND M(cKILLOP)

Sept. 2, 1909-   Canadian scientist; business executive
Address: b. Mitchell, Plummer & Co. Ltd., 18 King St. East, Toronto 210, Ontario, Canada; h. "The Wolfe Den," R.R. #1, Bolton, Ontario, Canada

The goal of medical research that Omond M. Solandt set for himself in preparing for his life-work expanded with his experience in public service into a broad interest in scientific research, development, and application, particularly in government and industry. Dr. Solandt is highly respected as the founder and first chairman of Canada's Defence Research Board and first chairman of the Science Council of Canada. In his executive positions in industry, such as vice-president for research and development of de Havilland Aircraft of Canada from 1963 to 1966, as well as administrative posts in government and also in education, as chancellor of the University of Toronto from 1965 to 1971, he has had an invigorating impact on the intellectual and economic life of his country.

Omond McKillop Solandt was born in Winnipeg, Manitoba on September 2, 1909, the younger of two sons of the Reverend Dr. Donald McKillop Solandt, a minister in the United Church of Canada, and Edith (Young) Solandt. His brother, Dr. Donald Young Solandt, became a professor of physiology at the University of Toronto. Like his brother, Omond Solandt attended Central Technical School and Jarvis Collegiate Institute, both in Toronto, and then the University of Toronto. He also followed his brother in academic preferences and extracurricular pursuits, such as photography. One of his few interests that he did not acquire from his brother was football, which he played in both secondary school and college.

The study of medicine consumed most of Solandt's time at the University of Toronto, where he was editor of the student medical journal. After taking his B.A. degree in biological and medical sciences in 1931, he engaged in graduate research under the supervision of Dr. Charles H. Best, of the department of physiology, who steered him toward a career in medical research. In 1933 he was awarded his M.A. degree in physiology and in 1936, his M.D. degree and the Gold Medal in Medicine.

With the intention of eventually concentrating on clinical cardiology as a medical researcher, Solandt began working in 1936 on a second M.A. degree, in pathology, studying under Dr. Allan Drury at Cambridge University, where he had a scholarship. At the end of his first year he left Cambridge to begin a rotating internship between Toronto General Hospital and London Hospital in England. In early 1939, on completion of his internship at London Hospital, he passed the M.R.C.P. (Member, Royal College of Physicians) examination. He then returned to Cambridge, which granted him his M.A. degree in pathology that same year and appointed him to a teaching position.

When World War II broke out in September 1939, Solandt tried to enter the Canadian Army while he was still in England. Before he could do so, he was offered a position, which he accepted, as director of the southwest London blood supply depot at Sutton, Surrey. Heading that unit, which was part of Britain's Medical Research Council, he had the responsibility until January 1941 for supplying blood transfusion equipment and advice and help on transfusion and treatment of shock to hospitals in southwest London, Surrey, and Sussex. He was next posted to the Armoured Fighting Vehicle School at Lulworth, England to establish what became the Medical Research Council's physiological laboratory. His study here of the physiological problems of tank crewmen and his research on tank design led to his assignment in 1942 to the Army Operational Research Group (AORG) as head of the tank section. The following year he was promoted to deputy superintendent of AORG and in 1944, to superintendent. While in the office of deputy superintendent he was commissioned a lieutenant colonel in the Canadian Army, which advanced him in rank to colonel before discharging him from service after the war, in 1946.

Meanwhile, obviously impressed with his work, the British Army had appointed Solandt in the summer of 1945 to the post of scientific adviser to Lord Louis Mountbatten in the Southeast Asia Command. He was on leave awaiting embarkation when the war ended. On assignment from the War Office he became, instead, in September of that year, a member of the British team that joined the United States Strategic Bombing Survey to evaluate atomic bomb damage in Japan.

On Solandt's return home and release from military duty, the Canadian government lost no time in enlisting his expertise as a scientist and administrator. In 1946 he accepted the challenging position of director general of defense research, with the mission of setting up a government agency in Ottawa to be responsible for the coordination of all research and development of Canada's three armed services—the army, navy, and air force. The following year he organized the Defence Research Board, of which he was appointed chairman, a post that carried with it membership on the Chiefs of Staff Committee. Considered a fourth service in the country's defense establishment, the Defence Research Board provided a link between technological activities of the armed forces and the civilian scientific community. During Solandt's tenure as chairman, from 1947 to 1956, the staff of the organization grew to about 3,000.

Dr. Solandt's career branched off again in a new, though not divergent, direction in 1956. At that time, having become assistant vice-president for research and development of the Canadian National Railways, he turned his attention from problems of defense to those of industry. A year later he was made vice-president for research and development of the government-owned transcontinental railroad. In that job he proved himself a strong advocate of an integrated system of rails and highways in which trains would haul freight over long distances and trucks would convey it from rail depots to the final destination. Because of his responsibilities in development and research, Solandt was intensely concerned with the problem of Canada's shortage of scientists and technicians, which by the mid-1950's seemed to some observers to be approaching a national emergency. At a conference of leaders in indus-

DR. OMOND M. SOLANDT

try and education, held in September 1956, he pointed out that Canada had been able to meet a part of its need for highly skilled personnel only by importations from Great Britain and other countries, and he urged that Canada prepare itself to train more of its own scientists and engineers.

An issue of grave international concern in which Solandt continued to be involved was the nuclear bomb. In October 1952, when Great Britain exploded its first atomic bomb in the Monte Bello Islands, off the northwest coast of Australia, he had served as an adviser to William George Penney of the British Ministry of Supply, the agency responsible for all atomic development in Britain. Taking time from his work at the Canadian National Railways, Solandt represented Canada at the East-West atomic test ban talks held in Geneva beginning on July 1, 1958. At the invitation of the United States, which insisted upon a balance of power, Canada became one of four Western countries sending experts to meet with scientists of the Soviet bloc for technical discussions on policing suspension of tests of nuclear weapons. As reported by Clark Davey of the Toronto Globe and Mail (June 21, 1958), Prime Minister John G. Diefenbaker "surprised and pleased the Commons" with his announcement that Solandt would take part in the negotiations. The leader of the opposition Liberal party, Lester Pearson, welcomed news of the appointment, asserting that no Canadian had better qualifications than Solandt.

In 1963, exchanging his role in government service for a similar one in private industry, Solandt left the Canadian National Railways to become vice-president for research and development and a director of de Havilland Aircraft of Canada and Hawker Siddeley Canada Ltd. Just as he had once argued the importance of Canadian universities' supplying engineers and scientists for defense and industry, he tried to encourage business organizations to appoint more scientists to executive positions and he maintained that the development of more research facilities in Canada would curtail the departure of researchers to the United States.

Receptive, as usual, to further opportunities for public service, in 1966 Dr. Solandt gave up his full-time positions in the aircraft industry for the chairmanship of the Science Council of Canada. The purpose of that newly formed organization, which in 1969 became a Crown Corporation, was to advise the government on scientific and technological matters, assessing requirements, available means, and potentialities. Shortly after the council's inaugural meeting in mid-1966, Solandt explained its objectives, as quoted in the Toronto *Globe and Mail* (July 13, 1966), "Basically, the science council will try to ensure that all that is known in science is brought to bear on the solution of Canada's economic and social problems." Efforts regarding the standard of living, pollution, and transportation were among those to which scientific knowledge would be applied.

The difficult and often frustrating task of trying to have the resources and views of the scientific community reflected in government policy occupied Solandt as chairman of the Science Council until 1972. At the same time he carried out the duties of chancellor of the University of Toronto for two three-year terms, beginning in 1965, and of vice-chairman of the board of the Electric Reduction Company of Canada Ltd. from 1966 to 1970. The diversity of his activities eventually led to his coming "under fire," to use the term of David Spurgeon, who reported in the Toronto *Globe and Mail* (February 5, 1970) on a Science Council press conference in December 1969 in which Solandt commented on a proposed banning of detergents containing phosphates to reduce water pollution. He called attention to his affiliation with the Electric Reduction Company, which was Canada's only manufacturer of sodium tripolyphosphate; argued that he was "at least well-informed," if "probably biased"; and maintained, "The people who say ban phosphates are grossly oversimplifying the problem." In thus opening the door to charges of conflict of interest in the highly controversial subject of water pollution, Spurgeon suggested, Solandt possibly raised a question regarding public confidence in his future statements as Science Council chairman.

By no means indifferent to threats of pollution and other environmental disturbances, Solandt had issued a warning in an address before the Canadian Council of Resources Ministers in Montreal in 1966: "The introduction of DDT has provided a recent and striking demonstration of the problems that arise when man intervenes in a complex ecological system." Environmental problems, moreover, figure prominently in Solandt's 1970 annual report of the Science Council, which recommended that the Canadian government establish an Environmental Council and a Department of Renewal Resources for the benefit of both the natural and urban environments.

Solandt's affiliation with industry also seemed to some students to compromise his position as chancellor of the University of Toronto. He laughed at the stereotype of himself as the big businessman, and while defending the university's deepening involvement with industry, he acknowledged a risk in that policy. During an interview reported in the Toronto *Globe and Mail* (December 16, 1968) he said, "One of the major problems of the university is to keep closely enough in touch with the society of which it is a part to be influential, yet not so closely identified with society that it cannot be objective and give leadership." Because of his past association with defense research some students called him a militarist. As if in answer to that charge he proposed that Canada consider transforming its armed forces into a worldwide public works corps to help underdeveloped countries by building roads, bridges, and power plants. Besides promoting peace by tending to reduce resentment of the have-not nations toward the affluent, the plan would probably boost the Canadian economy by increasing the sale of civilian goods to the underdeveloped countries.

In January 1971 Solandt joined Mitchell, Plummer & Company Ltd. as a director and consultant on capital placements in high technology industry. Since 1971 he has also been public governor of the Toronto Stock Exchange. His other business interests have included a directorship in the Huyck Corporation of Stamford, Connecticut and a trusteeship in the Mitre Corporation of Boston. He has served as president of the Canadian Operational Research Society, vice-president of the American Management association, and director of Expo '67.

At least a dozen colleges and universities have conferred honorary doctorates on Solandt. His other awards include the Order of the British Empire, the United States Medal of Freedom with Bronze Palm, the Civic Award of Merit of Toronto, and the Gold Medal of the Professional Institute of Public Service of Canada. He was appointed a Companion of the Order of Canada in 1970. He is a fellow of the Royal Society of Canada and of the Royal College of Physicians in London, England. His clubs are the York in Toronto, the Rideau in Ottawa, and the Athenaeum in London, England. He belongs to the United Church of Canada.

Dr. Omond M. Solandt married Elizabeth McPhedran on January 25, 1941. They had two daughters, Sigrid and Katharine, and a son, Andrew. Solandt's first wife died in 1971, and on February 1, 1972 he married Vaire Pringle, the daughter of Sir Gerald Woollaston, who as Garter Principal King at Arms was the head of the Royal College of Heralds in London. Mrs. Solandt is a professional dog breeder. A vigorous outdoorsman of sturdy build, he stands five feet ten and a half inches tall and weighs 190 pounds. He has brown eyes and graying dark hair. Over the years, beginning in 1952, he and a small group of other hardy adventurers have retraced by canoe the old fur-trade routes throughout western and northern Canada. He also enjoys skiing. His favorite indoor recreation is woodworking.

References

Chemistry and Industry 33:1113+ Ag 16
 '69 por
Toronto Globe and Mail p3 Ap 28 '65 por
American Men and Women of Science
 12th ed (1972)
Canadian Who's Who, 1970-72
International Who's Who, 1973-74
Who's Who in America, 1974-75
Who's Who in the East, 1974-75

WOLE SOYINKA

SOYINKA, WOLE (shô-yin′kə wô′lə)

July 13, 1934- Nigerian writer; teacher
Address: b. Dept. of English, University of
Ife, Nigeria; c/o Third Press, Joseph Okpaku
Publishing Co., 444 Central Park West, New
York 10025

The Nigeria that Wole Soyinka has been credited with introducing to the world, especially to readers of English, is potentially perhaps the most prosperous of the new African nations, but it is also a country of vast cultural upheaval. Soyinka's recurrent theme, therefore, is the ordeal of Africans beset by the contradictory demands of traditional practices and progressive ideals, the ancient and the modern. Among the targets of the satiric social criticism in his plays and novels is native self-deception about the past. But with his thorough understanding of the complexities of primitive cultures, he still rejoices in folk wisdom and humor, old mythology and ritual, the natural imagery and rhythm of an agrarian land. Since the Nigerian civil war of the late 1960's, when he was imprisoned for two years for political reasons, much of Soyinka's writing has concerned that bloody conflict and its tragic aftermath.

Africa's foremost black playwright was born Akinwande Oluwole Soyinka on July 13, 1934 near Abeokuta, western Nigeria, the son of Ayo and Eniola Soyinka. He has a younger brother, Kayode Soyinka, a dancer and actor who has also written plays. The father was a school inspector in the countryside of the Yoruba tribe, and Wole was educated in local schools until the age of eighteen, when he was admitted to the University College of Ibadan, about forty-five miles from home. During his two years as a student there his early poems were published in the Nigerian magazine *Black Orpheus*.

A scholarship enabled Soyinka to go to England in 1954 to attend the University of Leeds, where he studied world literature written in English. In 1957 he graduated with honors and in the summer of that year became a play reader at London's Royal Court Theatre. His study of the theatre in England and of American and European playwrights enormously influenced his own stagecraft. Years later, however, he told Brian Lapping of the *Guardian* (September 13, 1965) that Synge's *The Playboy of the Western World* was the only European play whose content really excited him. "And this, Soyinka agrees, may have

been because Synge sympathetically mocks Ireland as Soyinka does Nigeria," Lapping explained. Another affinity that has been suggested is that the first, native language of both Synge and Soyinka profoundly affected their writing in English. In the course of his eighteen-month association with the Royal Court Theatre at least two of Soyinka's plays were produced in London, *The Invention*, a one-act play set in South Africa, and *The Swamp Dwellers*.

After he returned home in 1959, Soyinka duplicated the "minor sensation" he had created in London with the production in Ibadan of *The Swamp Dwellers* and *The Lion and the Jewel*. A tragedy in verse, *The Swamp Dwellers* concerns the self-sacrifice of an unhappy son who returns from Lagos to his family in a swamp community oppressed by superstition. The jewel in the comedy *The Lion and the Jewel* is a village belle who prefers a wily old tribal chief to a progressive, partly Westernized schoolteacher. Another comedy written in the late 1950's, the satirical farce *The Trials of Brother Jero*, has as its title character a roguish charlatan, a false prophet—one of the more familiar figures in Soyinka's work. In his early plays, as well as his later, Soyinka interprets the clash between the old and the new in rapidly changing Nigeria, appraises African and Western values, and tends to act as a mediator in the conflict.

As a Rockefeller research fellow in drama at the University of Ibadan in 1960-61, Soyinka concentrated on a study of the folk drama of his country. His familiarity with the traditions and customs of its various cultures, which he acquired by traveling throughout Nigeria, greatly enriched his writing. In his plays he mingled staging techniques of the European theatre with the dance, mime, drums, and masks of native ritual. Indebtedness to his Nigerian heritage is particularly evident in *A Dance of the Forest*, which depicts a tribal religious ceremony in which spirits of ancestors are summoned in a vain effort to distort history and glorify the past.

Commissioned for the Nigerian independence celebrations of October 1960, *A Dance of the Forests* had its première in Lagos as the first important production of the 1960 Masks, an amateur company that Soyinka had just organized in Lagos. In 1961 he helped to found the Mbari Writers and Artists Club in Ibadan. That group of Nigerian intellectuals—writers, teachers, and civil servants—encouraged creative work in literature and the arts and shared with the 1960 Masks the goal of generating a modern Nigerian theatre with plays written in English but rooted in African folklore, festivals, and religious concepts. Protesting a facile, complacent idealization of the past in African literature, Soyinka attacked the concept of Négritude at a writers' conference in Uganda in 1962: "I don't think a tiger has to go around proclaiming his tigritude."

Besides producing his own plays and those of other African playwrights, Soyinka occasionally performed as an actor. He was also employed for a time as a teacher, having joined the faculty of the Ibadan branch of the University of Ife in 1962 as a lecturer in English. He resigned for political reasons in 1963 and spent the next two years mostly writing and producing plays, some of them as artistic director of the Orisun Repertory, a professional theatre company that he established in 1964. One of his plays premièred about that time, *The Strong Breed,* is a religious tragedy in verse that again explores the pull of opposing forces in a culture in transition. His Western-educated hero rejects the sacramental scapegoat role inherited from his father, but through altruism loses his life as a victim of a primitive purification ritual in a village away from home.

The characters of Soyinka's dramatic satire *The Road*—truck drivers and others who earn their living on treacherous African highways—make sacrifices of another kind to a demanding god that was once the god of iron. Soyinka's own fear of death by automobile accident on Nigeria's roads is reflected in that play, which he himself directed in London in 1965, when it was presented at the Commonwealth Arts Festival. Also in 1965 the London firm of André Deutsch published his first novel, *The Interpreters,* a complex, narratively skillful study of the dilemma of a group of young intellectuals in Lagos caught between African tradition and increasing modernization. Political corruption is one of the concerns of the novel, as it is of a play that Soyinka wrote about the same time, *Kongi's Harvest,* a satirical portrait of a dictator of a newly independent African state. Staged by the playwright, it was performed by the Orisun troupe in 1965 and at the Festival of Negro Arts in Dakar in 1966.

Meanwhile, in the unrest preceding the outbreak of civil war in Nigeria, Soyinka was becoming more deeply involved in politics not only as a writer, but also as a man. In the fall of 1965, soon after he had taken up an appointment as senior lecturer in English at the University of Lagos, he was arrested and tried for theft in connection with a disputed election. The charges brought against him were that he had confiscated from an Ibadan radio station the tapes of a victory statement by a regional leader and had substituted tapes claiming that the election was fraudulent. His eventual acquittal was attributed in part to an appeal signed by such distinguished writers as Lillian Hellman, Alfred Kazin, Robert Lowell, Norman Podhoretz, William Styron, and Lionel Trilling.

As Soyinka's literary reputation flourished in England and Nigeria, interest in his plays mounted in the United States. When the Oxford University Press collected his early published plays in *Five Plays* (1964), the drama critic Howard Taubman paid tribute to Soyinka in the New York *Times* (April 18, 1965). In the summer of 1967 Soyinka and the American actor-playwright Ossie Davis met in New York to plan the filming of *Kongi's Harvest,* a project completed in 1972. During Soyinka's visit the first professional productions in the United States of *The Trials of Brother Jero* and *The Strong Breed* were scheduled for the fall of 1967 and *Kongi's Harvest* was slated for a New York première by the Negro Ensemble Theatre in 1968. While he was planning those productions, Soyinka received word of imminent civil war in Nigeria and returned home immediately. He was arrested by government officials on August 17, 1967, imprisoned in Lagos without charge or trial, and a short time later removed to the harsh Kaduna prison in northern Nigeria, where he spent most of two years in solitary confinement.

Sifting through government allegations in which he purportedly confessed to various acts of subversion and spying, reporters of the Western press were able to establish certain facts. On August 4, 1967 Soyinka had published an article in Ibadan's *Daily Sketch* in which he deplored the divisive struggle in his country between forces of the federal government and secessionist Biafra: "There will be no victory for anyone in the present conflict, only a repetition of human material wastage and a superficial control that must one day blow up in our faces and blow the country to pieces." On August 6 he attempted to persuade Biafran leader Odumegwu Ojukwu to consider a cease-fire and a negotiated settlement. In a letter smuggled out of prison Soyinka denied that he had confessed to any crimes and that he had visited Biafra for any reason other than to try for an accord between Ojukwu and Nigeria's leader, Major General Yakubu Gowon.

News of Soyinka's imprisonment triggered strong remonstration in various liberal and literary circles in England, the United States, and other countries. Critical reception of his plays at the Greenwich Mews Theatre in New York in the fall of 1967 widened interest in his plight. Reviewing *The Trials of Brother Jero* and *The Strong Breed* in the New York *Post* (December 2, 1967), Richard Watts praised Soyinka as "the dramatist who has already done more than anyone else on the entire continent [of Africa] to demonstrate the richness and promise of the emerging culture of black Africa, and is surely the most effective propagandist for the potentialities of its spirit." The publication of *Idanre and Other Poems* (Methuen, 1967; Hill and Wang, 1968), which extended his theme of tradition versus industrialization into poetry and also paid tribute to the thousands of Ibos massacred in Biafra by his own tribesmen, further impressed Soyinka's name on British and Americans who had been made aware of the Biafran disaster.

Soyinka was set free in October 1969. His suffering in prison had not persuaded him to remain silent on political issues, as he demonstrated immediately in a press conference by twisting the wording of the national rallying cry from "To keep Nigeria one is a task that must be done" to "To keep Nigeria one justice must be done." Shortly after his release he returned to the University of Ibadan as head of the school of drama, a position to which he had been appointed before his arrest.

The following summer Soyinka visited the United States with a troupe of Nigerian actors, some of them his drama students, to present his play *Madmen and Specialists* at the Eugene O'Neill Memorial Theatre Center in Waterford, Connecticut. Soyinka described the theme of his somewhat difficult allegorical tragedy as "the betrayal of vocation for the attraction of power in one form or another." Although written in jail on assorted scraps of paper, the play does not deal with his prison experiences, but is rather an indictment of tyranny and corruption in postwar Nigeria, despite the fact that Soyinka has said that it is set "nowhere in particular."

The fragmented record of his arrest and imprisonment, *The Man Died: Prison Notes* (Collings, 1972; Harper, 1973), readily accounts for the bitterness of his outlook. He also wrote about his loneliness, rage, and despair in solitary confinement in A *Shuttle in the Crypt* (Collings, Hill and Wang, 1972), a collection of poems composed in prison. One of his poems, "Live Burial," had been smuggled out of prison and published by the *New Statesman* in May 1969. The opening lines refer to the size of his cell: "Sixteen paces / By twenty-three. They hold / Siege against humanity / And truth, / Employing time to drill through to his sanity."

In other work completed since leaving prison Soyinka has also shown exceptional versatility: *Jero's Metamorphosis*, a sequel to his comedy *The Trials of Brother Jero*; an adaptation of Euripides' *The Bacchae*, produced by the British National Theatre in London in 1973; *Season of Anomy* (Collings, 1973; Third Press, 1974), a novel about the struggle to preserve the best of the old ways of life amid oppressive forces threatening the freedom of a new African nation. He also edited *Poems of Black Africa* (Secker and Warburg, 1973). Disagreement meanwhile with the administration's policies had led to his resignation in 1972 from the University of Ibadan, leaving him free to accept a fellowship at Churchill

College, Cambridge University, and an appointment as research professor in drama at the University of Ife.

Appraising Soyinka's work in *African Authors* (1973), Donald E. Herdeck wrote, "Soyinka, possibly more than any other of the new African writers, seeks to break down his experiences into shards and then to reassemble them into new wholes neither African nor European, but universal." Joseph Bruchac pointed out in *Contemporary Dramatists* (1973), however, that Soyinka's plays "exist on so many levels at the same time that there is great richness—and the very real possibility that while a play of Soyinka's may mean one thing for everyone in the audience it may also mean something else in addition to those who are African or at least familiar with the subtleties of Yoruba culture and belief which he handles so masterfully." Among Soyinka's many international literary prizes are an award from *Encounter* magazine for *A Dance of the Forests* (1960), the 1966 African Arts Festival award for *The Road*, the £1,000 *New Statesman* literary prize for *The Interpreters* (1968), and the Jock Campbell-*New Statesman* Literary Award (1969). An honorary D.Litt. degree from the University of Leeds was conferred on him in 1973.

In 1963 Wole Soyinka married a fellow teacher, Laide Idowu. She is his second wife and the mother of their three daughters. He has a son from an earlier marriage, to an English girl, which took place when he was a student at the University of Leeds. Soyinka's bearing is said to be "princely," a description at variance with his lifestyle and his assertion that if writing were not compulsive for him he would turn out only a few well-polished poems a year and devote himself to farming on a small scale and searching for pieces of old African sculpture. He has said that his religion is man's freedom, but he has taken Ogun, the ancient creative god of metals and metal work, as his patron saint.

References

Guardian p7 S 13 '65 por; p8 N 27 '72 por
N Y Times p19 O 9 '69
N Y Times Bk R p6 D 24 '72 por
Contemporary Authors vols 15-16 (1966)
Dathorne, O. R. The Black Mind (1974)
Herdeck, Donald E. African Authors (1973)
International Who's Who, 1973-74
Vinson, James, ed. Contemporary Dramatists (1973)
Who's Who in the World, 1971-72

SPÍNOLA, ANTÓNIO (SEBASTIÃO RIBEIRO) DE (spē'nō-lä)

Apr. 11, 1910- Former provisional President of Portugal; army officer
Address: Lisbon, Portugal

When, on April 25, 1974, General António de Spínola assumed power in Portugal, that coup

ANTÓNIO DE SPÍNOLA

d'état differed from the usual military takeover. It not only toppled a long-established right-wing dictatorship but seemed to herald a return to democracy. The interim government of which Spínola became provisional President on May 15, 1974, succeeded the government of President Américo Thomaz (or Tomás) and Premier Marcello Caetano, the heirs of Antonio de Oliveira Salazar who had ruled the country for thirty-six years. A career army officer, Spínola became a national hero during his service in Portugal's African overseas territories, and his book outlining proposals for a peaceful solution to the country's debilitating colonial wars earned him great popularity. Although Spínola seemed an unlikely candidate to lead a liberal coup, many observers believed that only a man with his conservative and patriotic record could command allegiance from the ruling class and the military while coping with Portugal's problems and restoring representative government to its 9,800,000 people. But after only five months in power, Spínola resigned the Presidency on September 30, 1974, thereby leaving control of the government in the hands of the nation's leftist forces. In a farewell address to the nation he expressed his concern with the unstable political situation in Portugal and warned of the possible development of "new forms of slavery."

A member of a well-to-do aristocratic family, António Sebastião Ribeiro de Spínola was born in Estremoz, in southern Portugal, on April 11, 1910, the year the last Portuguese king, Manuel II, was overthrown and a republic established. When Spínola was sixteen, the republic was ended by a military coup that set the stage for Salazar's rise to power in 1932. Under Salazar's dictatorial regime Spínola's father served the government as inspector general of finance, and he was one of Salazar's top economic advisers.

After attending the Colegio Militar, a military preparatory school, António de Spínola entered the Escola Militar, Portugal's national military academy, in 1930. He graduated in November

1933 with the rank of *alferes,* or second lieutenant, in the cavalry. In December 1937 he was promoted to lieutenant. During the Spanish Civil War, Spínola commanded a detachment of Portuguese volunteers fighting on the side of Francisco Franco's Falangist forces. Later he was sent by the Portuguese high command to Nazi Germany for training with the Wehrmacht. Although Portugal remained neutral in World War II, Spínola was an observer with German troops on the Russian front, where he witnessed the siege of Leningrad. In March 1944 he was promoted to captain, and the following year he was assigned to the Azores.

For the next fifteen years Spínola gradually rose in the army hierarchy, occupying a succession of staff positions. He attained the rank of major in December 1955. When in 1961 African guerrillas in Angola began a war for independence that soon spread to Portugal's two other African overseas territories, Mozambique and Portuguese Guinea, Spínola, who had become a lieutenant colonel in January of that year, volunteered for service in Angola. There, as commander of a cavalry battalion, he acquired a reputation as a courageous officer who often led his men into battle. He won a number of decorations, and in December 1963 he was promoted to colonel. After his return to Portugal in February 1964, Spínola was appointed second in command of the National Republican Guard, a paramilitary police force. In December 1966 he attained the rank of brigadier general.

As the wars in Africa continued, Spínola was named in May 1968 to succeed General Arnaldo Schultz as commander in chief of military forces in Portuguese Guinea and later also became provincial governor. In July 1969 he was elevated to the full rank of general. Concerning his five-year tenure in Guinea, a correspondent for *Time* (May 6, 1974) remarked that "Spínola created a MacArthur-like aura around himself.... Unlike [Douglas] MacArthur, however, he believed in cultivating the enlisted man, and he would pop from his helicopter in hazardous spots to see personally how the fighting was going." Although a disciplinarian, Spínola was popular among his troops, who appreciated his fairness and his concern for their well-being.

Realizing that the Portuguese army could not win a strictly military victory, Spínola instituted a policy of "total war" in Guinea, combining military action and socio-economic measures. Soldiers built roads, schools, and hospitals. Native "people's congresses" were established to give Africans a measure of self-rule. Spínola also organized a native fighting force loyal to Portugal, and by 1973 about half of the army in Guinea was native African.

Those efforts failed, however, to placate the guerrillas, who continued their struggle for independence and at one time claimed to control as much as three-fourths of the territory of Guinea. Raiding from bases in neighboring countries and supplied with modern weapons by Communist nations, the African party for the Independence of Guinea and the Cape Verde Islands (PAIGC) showed no signs of weakening, even after its leader, Amilcar Cabral, was assassinated in early 1973. Meanwhile, some 27,000 demoralized Portuguese troops were tied down in Guinea. In Spínola's view, the rebels' territorial claims were inflated, but he reportedly negotiated in secret with PAIGC leaders, and his outlook on the protracted colonial struggle seems to have changed as he witnessed his own lack of progress. In September 1973, shortly after Spínola's departure from Africa, the PAIGC proclaimed the independent Republic of Guinea-Bissau, which was soon recognized by most Communist nations and by a number of African and Arab states.

Now a national hero and enormously popular with the armed forces, Spínola returned to Portugal in the summer of 1973. He was awarded the country's highest military decoration, thus becoming the only living grand officer of the Order of the Tower and Sword with Palm. In December 1973 he was named deputy chairman of the joint chiefs of staff of the armed forces, a post created for him. But his disillusionment with the struggles in Africa increased as he observed conditions at home. After almost half a century of dictatorship, Portugal remained the poorest and most backward country in Western Europe. Because of the African wars, many essentials had been ignored at home, with 40 percent of the national budget going down the military drain. Hundreds of thousands of Portuguese had left home to work in the more prosperous countries of Europe, and many young men had fled the country to avoid military conscription.

Spínola's views coincided with those of the younger army officers, who were discontented with army pay, the promotion system, and repeated tours of duty in Africa. In the October 1973 election campaign, opposition candidates, forbidden to criticize the government's African policy, called for a boycott of the election, and as a result the official government party won all seats in the National Assembly. Meanwhile, dissatisfaction continued to spread in the armed forces.

That dissatisfaction found a catalyst in Spínola's book *Portugal e o Futuro* (Portugal and the Future), published in February 1974. Permission for its publication had come from Spínola's immediate superior, armed forces chief of staff General Francisco da Costa Gomes, and from Premier Caetano, who apparently did not anticipate its bombshell effect. Painting a bleak picture of the country's plight and calling for an end to the stalemated African wars, the book expressed the feelings of many Portuguese, who had never seen such sentiments in print before. Within a month 100,000 copies were sold, an unprecedented number for Portugal.

In his book Spínola pointed out that "trying to win a subversive war by military means is to accept defeat in advance, unless one possesses un-

limited capacity to prolong the war indefinitely." Instead of calling for outright independence for the African territories he proposed a referendum to establish a federation in which the former colonies would have virtually equal status with Portugal. His arguments were not radical, but coming as they did from a respected soldier, they caused a sensation. Spokesmen for the wealthy classes and right-wing military men and government officials demanded that Spínola be punished. Premier Caetano, who had mildly liberal leanings, resisted their demands for a time, but on March 13, 1974 he gave in to pressure to dismiss Spínola and Costa Gomes. That move further incensed the junior officers who shared Spínola's views.

On March 16 some 200 soldiers loyal to Spínola staged an abortive military coup. The government then began a purge of liberal officers and rounded up leftist civilians but was hesitant to move against Spínola. According to *Time* (April 1, 1974), "President Thomaz and Portugal's rightist ultras are faced with a highly uncomfortable dilemma. The general's arrest or exile would surely shatter already shaky morale, if it did not lead to open revolt by the military. On the other hand, Spínola at liberty represents a viable symbol of an alternative to the moribund colonial policies of the regime."

The government's hesitation proved its undoing. In the early hours of April 25, 1974, in classic coup d'état style, armored units seized key points in Lisbon. Most government troops soon defected to the rebels, and there was little fighting. Caetano, who had taken refuge in the barracks of the National Republican Guard, demanded to see Spínola, who replied: "I am not the leader of this movement. I did not act against the Government. If it has the good sense to find a solution, I think I will be doing a good service by speaking to the rebels."

Known by the code name "Operation Oscar," the coup was in fact not the work of Spínola, although it apparently had his tacit approval. It had reportedly been secretly planned for some seven months by the twelve-member coordinating committee of a group of several hundred aggrieved junior officers, mainly captains and majors, that became known as the Armed Forces Movement. The rebels gave Spínola a mandate to negotiate for them, and Caetano agreed to hand over power to him, "so that the government would not fall in the streets." On April 26 Spínola emerged as head of a seven-man "Junta of National Salvation" elected by the armed forces coordinating committee.

Spínola's early actions and declarations brought about sweeping changes. Press censorship was abolished. Freedom of speech and assembly was restored. Political parties other than the official party of the old dictatorship were declared legal. An interim government of soldiers and civilians was to arrange free elections for a constituent national assembly within a year. Political prisoners were released, and military deserters and draft evaders were given amnesty. Caetano, Thomaz, and other deposed leaders were exiled to the island of Madeira and were later permitted to leave for Brazil. Socialist leader Mario Soares and Communist party chief Alvaro Cunhal were allowed to return to Portugal after years in exile and were warmly received by Spínola.

The Portuguese responded with several days of joyful celebration. The "flower revolution," as the upheaval was popularly known, was symbolized by pretty girls decorating soldiers' rifles with red carnations. Exercising liberties that they had almost forgotten during half a century of repression, citizens talked politics, staged demonstrations, painted leftist slogans on monuments, and bought up uncensored newspapers as fast as they appeared. They wrecked offices of right-wing publications and helped to hunt down members of the General Directory of Security, the hated secret police of the late dictatorship. Spínola and his fellow officers were hailed by the crowds. The celebrations peaked on May Day—newly established as a national holiday—with enormous marches and gatherings.

On May 15, 1974 a left-leaning interim government was established, with Spínola as provisional President and Costa Gomes as armed forces chief of staff. A fourteen-member Cabinet, headed by Adelino da Palma Carlos, a moderately liberal law professor, included three Socialists, two Communists, and only one military officer. Soares became Foreign Minister and Cunhal was named Minister Without Portfolio in the new government. In his inaugural speech, Spínola promised that after elections for a constituent assembly in the spring of 1975, he would leave politics.

Meanwhile, the initial euphoria of the revolution began to fade as Portugal's problems became increasingly serious. Although the Moscow-oriented Communist party, emerging as Portugal's best organized political force, took a relatively moderate position, extremist splinter groups, described variously as Maoist, Trotskyist, or anarchist, menaced the country's precarious stability. At the same time labor unrest threatened to cripple large segments of the economy. On barnstorming tours throughout the country, in May and June, Spínola appealed to the Portuguese for moderation and warned them against playing into the hands of "reactionaries and counter-revolutionaries."

With regard to the African question, Spínola continued to call for a referendum to approve the federation of states he had proposed in his book. But leading spokesmen for the Africans rejected the referendum idea, and the Portuguese government itself was split, with many civilians and junior officers on the left favoring immediate independence for the territories. On the other hand, some political observers saw the possibility of a counter-coup by white settlers in the African territories, supported by the white supremacist governments of Rhodesia and South Africa. In mid-May Soares began negotiations with rebel spokesmen in Africa.

In negotiating with Communist countries and independent African states for the establishment of diplomatic relations, the Portuguese government met with success, but official spokesmen for neighboring Spain expressed apprehension over the Portuguese revolution and its possible effect on their own country. Spínola won praise from President Richard Nixon, who visited Portugal in June, and he assured Nixon of Portugal's continued support of the North Atlantic Treaty Organization.

Amid continued unrest, the Portuguese government in June imposed new controls over radio, television, and the press and instituted censorship regulations against "ideological aggression" and the publication of "false news." At Spínola's insistence, in July the government decreed an elaborate social and economic program, combining incentives to business and foreign investors with such social reforms as construction of low-cost housing, along with limitations on the right to strike and measures to combat Portugal's mounting rate of inflation.

Portugal's civilian Cabinet collapsed on July 9, 1974, when Premier Palma Carlos resigned, along with several of his ministers, contending that the predominantly military twenty-one member Council of State—the country's interim constitutional body—did not grant him enough authority to cope with crises. Nine days later, Spínola swore in a new Cabinet, headed by Colonel Vasco dos Santos Gonçalves and including six other military men. Although the new Cabinet had about the same ideological composition as the preceding one, it was believed to be "tougher and more decisive" than its predecessor. Its appointment was considered a setback for Spínola, whose own choice for Premier had been passed over by the Council of State. Unhappy with the political instability in his country, Spínola resigned on September 30, 1974. The immediate assumption of the Presidency by General Francisco da Costa Gomes was expected to meet rather violent reaction from the conservatives.

General António de Spínola, who is married and a devoted family man, resembles the type of character played by Erich von Stroheim in films of the 1930's—a craggyfaced, ramrod-stiff Prussian officer. A profile in *Time* (May 6, 1974) refers to "his bushy eyebrows, the flashing monocle in his right eye—an adornment he picked up in Berlin—the gloves, and the riding crop." A teetotaler and nonsmoker, Spínola is decidedly conservative in his habits. He is a member of an elite group of equestrians and has won a number of trophies in national and international riding competitions on his horse, Achilles. Spínola has often been compared to Charles de Gaulle.

References

London Observer p13 Ap 28 '74 por
N Y Times p12 Ap 26 '74 por
Newsweek 83:32+ My 6 '74 pors
Toronto Globe and Mail p7 Mr 13 '74
Washington Post A p28 Ap 26 '74 por

STEINFELD, JESSE L(EONARD)

Jan. 6, 1927- Physician; cancer specialist; former public health official
Address: c/o Department of Oncology, Mayo Clinic, Rochester, Minn. 55901

As Surgeon General of the United States Public Health Service during the first Nixon administration, Dr. Jesse L. Steinfeld vigorously pursued the government's campaign to dissuade Americans from smoking and presented the first government report linking violence on television to aggressive behavior in children. A cancer specialist, Dr. Steinfeld taught at the University of Southern California from 1959 to 1968 and served on National Cancer Institute committees before becoming associate program director of the National Cancer Institute in 1968. In 1969 he became deputy assistant secretary of health and scientific affairs of the Department of Health, Education and Welfare, and later that year he succeeded Dr. William H. Stewart as Surgeon General. Since leaving government service early in 1973, Dr. Steinfeld has directed tumor research at the Mayo Clinic in Rochester, Minnesota.

Jesse Leonard Steinfeld was born in West Aliquippa, Pennsylvania on January 6, 1927. He received a B.S. degree from the University of Pittsburgh in 1945 and his M.D. degree four years later from Western Reserve University. Dr. Steinfeld joined the United States Public Health Service as a commissioned officer in 1951 and remained on active status until 1958. At the same time he was an instructor of medicine at the University of California at Berkeley (1952-54), a fellow of the Atomic Energy Commission (1952-53), and an instructor at George Washington University (1954-58).

After serving as assistant director of the blood hospital at the City of Hope Medical Center in Duarte, California in 1958-59, Dr. Steinfeld joined the staff of the University of Southern California Medical School as an assistant professor in 1959. He was promoted to associate professor in 1963 and to professor in 1967. During his affiliation with the University of Southern California, Dr. Steinfeld was chairman of the interdepartmental cancer research committee (1960-68), chairman of the radioisotope committee (1960-66), and cancer coordinator (1966-68).

In 1968 Dr. Steinfeld became associate program director of the National Cancer Institute and the following year he was appointed deputy to Department of Health, Education and Welfare assistant secretary of health and scientific affairs Dr. Roger O. Egeberg. As deputy assistant secretary, Dr. Steinfeld was, according to a Washington *Post* reporter (November 14, 1969), "the nation's No. 2 health official." He was chiefly responsible for the 1969 ban on cyclamates, which had been found to cause bladder cancer in rats.

On November 1969 Dr. Steinfeld was nominated by President Richard Milhous Nixon to be Surgeon General of the United States Public Health Service. The office had been vacant since

DR. JESSE L. STEINFELD

that summer, when Dr. William H. Stewart had resigned, and there had been some debate within the Department of Health, Education, and Welfare as to whether the post would be filled. Nominally the head of the Commissioned Corps of the Public Health Service, the Surgeon Generalship had once been a powerful position, but its importance had dwindled during the Johnson and Nixon administrations because of their lack of interest in the Commissioned Corps. When Dr. Steinfeld was named to the post, however, the White House indicated that the job's responsibilities would be increased. In order to become Surgeon General, Steinfeld was recalled from reserve status in the Public Health Service Commissioned Corps and sworn in as an active officer with a rank equivalent to brigadier general. While Surgeon General he retained his post as deputy assistant secretary in Health, Education, and Welfare.

In December 1969 Dr. Steinfeld was confirmed as Surgeon General. Besides heading the Commissioned Corps, the Surgeon General is responsible for a wide range of governmental health programs handled within the Public Health Service, whose divisions include the Food and Drug Administration and the National Institutes of Health. The Surgeon General reports to the HEW assistant secretary for health and scientific affairs.

After cancer had been discovered in rats that had been fed cyclamate, Dr. Steinfeld appointed a committee of eight scientists recruited from the National Institutes of Health and from the American academic community to prepare a report on cancer prevention. Submitted in April 1970, the report flatly rejected the concept of "toxicologically insignificant" levels of carcinogens in foods, a concept that had served as a guideline for the Food and Drug Administration. Instead, it maintained that it is "impossible to establish any absolutely safe levels of exposure to a carcinogen for man." As a "first screening of the environment" the report recommended that up to 20,000 substances should be tested at an estimated cost of $1 billion. Although the report was not publicized and was disputed within government health agencies, it was credited, at least in part, by Dr. Steinfeld with increasing the budget for testing chemical carcinogens from $11,000,000 in fiscal 1971 to $19,000,000 in fiscal 1972.

As Surgeon General, Steinfeld proved to be an implacable foe of the American tobacco industry. In a speech before the National Interagency Council on Smoking and Health in January 1971 he called for a major campaign to alert women to the dangers of cigarette smoking. The physician, himself a nonsmoker, cited figures showing that the number of women and girls smoking was increasing, while their male counterparts were dropping the habit. That trend was especially dangerous, he warned, because of increasing evidence that smoking can cause fetal damage in pregnant women.

In his annual Surgeon General's reports to Congress on smoking and health, Dr. Steinfeld enumerated the mounting evidence of the ills caused by smoking. In 1971 he cited studies showing that the nicotine in cigarettes increases the work of the heart and its need for oxygen, thus heightening the risk of heart attack. In 1972 his report emphasized for the first time the dangers to smokers and nonsmokers alike of carbon monoxide, which is a component of all tobacco smoke. He cited studies showing that the carbon monoxide levels in poorly ventilated smoke-filled rooms sometimes exceed the maximum air pollution limits permitted in several states and cities. Such exposure to carbon monoxide is particularly dangerous to people suffering from heart or lung ailments.

Dr. Steinfeld urged that smoking be banned in restaurants, theatres, airplanes, buses, and trains. He also recommended that the tobacco industry develop cigarettes with lower nicotine, tar, and carbon monoxide levels. Other measures to deal with the tobacco problem that Steinfeld proposed include graduated federal taxes based on the tar and nicotine content, a ban on all cigarette advertising, and an end to federal subsidies to tobacco farmers.

One of the biggest controversies that Dr. Steinfeld was involved in during his term as Surgeon General involved the government's stand on phosphate detergents. During the 1960's there was growing concern among ecologists about the damage done to waterways by excessive phosphorus, which leads to eutrophication or the premature aging of waters. Since the phosphates in detergents are one of the principal sources of phosphorus pollution, environmentalists urged that they be banned. In response the Nixon administration early in 1970 called upon the major detergent companies to replace phosphates with a little-tested chemical called NTA (nitrilotriacetic acid). Steinfeld shocked both environmentalists and the detergent industry in December 1970 when he announced that NTA had been implicated in tests as a cause of birth defects in rats. Pending further tests he urged the detergent companies to suspend the use of NTA. Over the next few months subsequent studies implicated NTA as a possible carcinogen. In the face of the cancer threat, Dr. Steinfeld and the heads of the En-

vironmental Protection Agency, the Council on Environmental Quality, and the Food and Drug Administration held a joint press conference on September 15, 1971 at which they announced that NTA should not be used until adequate data proved whether or not it was harmful.

The Surgeon General maintained that since most phosphate substitutes other than NTA were so caustic that they could cause injuries, people should return to using phosphates until a safe replacement was discovered. His remarks were widely criticized since they constituted a complete turnabout in governmental policy, but he remained steadfast. In an article written for the *Reader's Digest* (November 1973) after he left government service, Dr. Steinfeld called the phosphate detergent flap "a classic case of environmental extremism and governmental ineptitude." To avoid such mistakes in the future, he wrote, "the public and the government must realize that the simple, hasty, politically expedient solution to a complex, scientific, regulatory issue may create more problems than it solves."

In January 1972 Dr. Steinfeld became embroiled in another controversy when he released the Surgeon General's Scientific Advisory Committee on Television and Social Behavior report on the effects of television violence on children. Commissioned in 1969, the report analyzed forty-three studies conducted at a cost of $1,000,000. The Surgeon General's advisory committee consisted of twelve scientists, five of whom were either television network officials or social scientists with close ties to the TV industry.

In a nineteen-page summary of the report, the advisory committee wrote that "violence in television programming does not have an adverse effect on the majority of the nation's youth but may influence small groups of youngsters predisposed by many factors to aggressive behavior." After the summary was released, the report was denounced by critics as "a political whitewash." Furthermore, many of the forty social scientists who had worked on the studies on which the report was based protested that the committee had slanted their findings to play down the harmful effects of TV violence that they had documented. The critics' case was further strengthened by the revelation that Steinfeld's predecessor had allowed the major networks to blackball seven nominees to the advisory committee, because they were believed to be too critical of television.

While acknowledging the criticism of the way in which the advisory committee was chosen, Dr. Steinfeld contended that the report was not a whitewash. However, he conceded to Elizabeth Peer of *Newsweek* (March 6, 1972), "If I had written this report alone, I would have written it somewhat more strongly." At Senate communications subcommittee hearings in March, the Surgeon General declared, "It is clear to me that the causal relationship between televised violence and antisocial behavior by children is sufficient to warrant appropriate and immediate remedial action." On his recommendation a television violence rating system will eventually be established to advise viewers of the degree of violence in dramatic programs.

After President Nixon was reelected for a second term in 1972, he did not reappoint Dr. Steinfeld as Surgeon General. The physician had given up his post as deputy assistant secretary of HEW in 1972, and he left the Surgeon General's office early in 1973. He is now director of the department of oncology at the Mayo Clinic in Rochester, Minnesota.

In an interview with Richard D. Lyons of the New York *Times* (September 10, 1973), Dr. Steinfeld charged that the Nixon administration failed to implement medical programs needed by the United States and that federal health affairs were in "a kind of chaos." In a press conference that same month he announced that he was joining the Committee for National Health Insurance, which is backing the national health insurance program proposed by Senator Edward M. Kennedy and other liberal Democrats. The Nixon administration was backing a rival proposal.

Dr. Steinfeld's research specialties have been oncology (the scientific study of tumors), the chemical treatment of cancer, and hematology (the scientific study of the blood). For the National Cancer Institute he has served as a clinical investigator (1954-58), member of the Krebiozen review committee (since 1963), member of the clinical studies panel (1964-66), consultant (since 1966), member of the chemotherapy advisory committee (1967), and member of the cancer special progress advisory committee (1967). He has been a consultant to the Veterans Administration Hospital in Long Beach, California since 1959; the City of Hope Medical Center since 1960; and Kern County General Hospital in Bakersfield, California since 1964. Since 1961 Steinfeld has been a member of the California State Cancer Advisory Council.

According to Richard D. Lyons of the New York *Times*, Dr. Jesse L. Steinfeld's "outspoken remarks and feisty character had not endeared him to the Administration during his tenure." The former Surgeon General has been married since 1953, and he has three children. Steinfeld is a member of the Surgical Society of Nuclear Medicine, the American Association of Cancer Research, and the American Medical Association. He is a fellow of the American College of Physicians; the American Federation of Clinical Research; the American Society of Hematology; the New York Academy of Sciences; and the International Society of Hematology. In 1971 he served as president of the American Society of Clinical Oncology and in 1972 he was president-elect of the Association of Military Surgeons of the United States. Steinfeld was awarded an honorary LL.D. degree by Gannon College (Erie, Pennsylvania) in 1972.

References

N Y Times p1 S 10 '73 por
Washington Post A p6 N 14 '69

American Men and Women of Science 12th ed (1973)

STEVENSON, ADLAI E(WING) 3D

Oct. 10, 1930-   United States Senator from Illinois
Address: b. Room 456, Old Senate Office Building, Washington, D.C. 20510; h. 1519 N. Dearborn St., Chicago, Illinois 60610

Adlai E. Stevenson 3d, who was elected to the United States Senate by a landslide vote in the November 3, 1970 by-election, has always considered politics to be the "art of the possible." A practical and strong-minded maverick, Stevenson bucked the awesome power of the Illinois Democratic party machine to win the party's nomination to the Senate seat formerly held by Everett M. Dirksen, the venerable Senate Republican Majority Leader. Coming up through the ranks of state politics as a state representative and as state treasurer, Stevenson was an unofficial spokesman for reform within the Democratic party. While a member of the Illinois House of Representatives he sponsored legislation to eliminate conflicts of interest, reform the electoral process, and control campaign financing. To involve citizens in grass-root politics, he recruited young talent for the state treasurer's office and used state monies to support community projects. "We need to restore the confidence of everyone . . . in our capacity for self-government," he explained to Godfrey Sperling Jr. in an interview for the *Christian Science Monitor* (May 11, 1970). "People are losing their faith in our public institutions and in our public men." Stevenson was reelected to the United States Senate on November 5, 1974.

Adlai Ewing Stevenson 3d was born on October 10, 1930 in Chicago, Illinois, the oldest of the three sons of Adlai Ewing and Ellen (Borden) Stevenson. The Stevenson family had been involved in state and national politics for three generations. Young Adlai's great-grandfather, Adlai E. Stevenson, was the twenty-third Vice-President of the United States during President Grover Cleveland's second term; Lewis Green Stevenson, his grandfather, served for a time as Illinois' Secretary of State; his father, one of the better-known Democratic politicians of the twentieth century, was the governor of Illinois from 1948 to 1952, the Democratic Presidential candidate in 1952 and 1956, and the United States Permanent Representative to the United Nations from 1961 until his death in 1965. Determined to create an intellectually stimulating environment for their children, his parents conversed only in French at the dinner table and, after dinner, read aloud from literary classics. Not particularly inclined to scholarly pursuits, Stevenson preferred solitary fishing expeditions on the family farm in Libertyville, Illinois.

Because of the frequent moves that accompanied his father's burgeoning political career, Stevenson was educated at several schools in the United States and in Great Britain, including Harrow. In 1948 he graduated from Milton Academy in Milton, Massachusetts, and after several hectic

ADLAI E. STEVENSON 3D

months of campaigning on behalf of his father's successful gubernatorial bid in 1948, he enrolled at Harvard University. He obtained his B.A. degree in government in 1952 and then enlisted in the United States Marine Corps Reserve. Commissioned a second lieutenant and assigned to duty as a tank battalion platoon commander, he served in Japan and Korea from July 1953 to July 1954. The poverty he saw in the latter country deeply impressed him, and he remembers dogs coming into his camp area to keep from being eaten by the Koreans. Stevenson enrolled at Harvard Law School after his discharge in 1954, and he obtained his LL.B. degree in 1957.

Admitted to the Illinois bar in 1957, Stevenson worked in Springfield, the state capital, for several months as a law clerk to an Illinois Supreme Court justice. He then joined Mayer, Friedlich, Spiess, Tierney, Brown & Platt, a prestigious corporate law firm in Chicago. Stevenson, who was made a partner in 1966, remained with the firm until 1967. While practising law, he was active in a number of political and civic organizations, including the Chicago Crime Commission and the Governor's Committee for Distinguished Foreign Guests, and earned a reputation as a hard-working public servant.

When the Republicans and the Democrats failed to agree on a compromise reapportionment scheme for the Illinois House of Representatives in 1964, Democratic slate makers asked Stevenson to run for one of the 118 seats in an at-large election. In that unusual situation, both parties nominated "blue ribbon" candidates with well-established names or proved political records. Stevenson was an obvious selection. "I never had a choice," he explained to Myra MacPherson in an interview for the Washington *Post* (November 24, 1970). "It was ordained at birth that I would go into a life of public service. The question was never 'whether'—it was always 'when' and 'how.'" To save time and money in the statewide campaign, the frugal Stevenson joined forces with a dozen likeminded liberal Democrats to plan a

cooperative strategy. Under that plan each candidate representing the entire "Adlai strategy group" concentrated on a particular issue or canvased a specific district. Emphasizing the need for election reform, tax revision, civil rights legislation, and improved law enforcement, the Stevenson team led the field of 236 candidates in the November elections. Stevenson polled a phenomenal 2,147,-978 votes, more than any other candidate.

In his one term in the state house, Stevenson sponsored or cosponsored eighty-four bills, including a tough law to control lobbying and conflicts of interest in the legislative and executive branches. His support of a graduated state income tax, open housing, credit reform, and other liberal legislation was enthusiastically approved by the Independent Voters of Illinois, who named him "best legislator" in the House. Recognizing his vote-getting potential, the Democratic State Central Committee selected Stevenson as the party's candidate for the office of state treasurer, with the endorsement of the powerful Cook County machine headed by Mayor Richard J. Daley. Thanks to his indefatigable campaigning he survived a Republican landslide to become the only Democrat elected to a state office in 1966.

Stevenson transformed the routine administrative post into a force for change. To eliminate patronage and favoritism, he trimmed the size of his administrative staff by one-third and opened the account ledgers to public scrutiny. Withdrawing state funds from low-interest banks and from banks that practised racial or religious discrimination, he devised a complex computerized system to search out the most promising investments. To broaden the economic base of the inner cities, he funneled state monies to black-owned banks to finance small businesses, middle-income housing, and community development projects. His astute fiscal management of idle tax monies earned the state of Illinois an additional $7,000,000 in revenues in one year.

Although he was regarded by many political observers as the logical Democratic candidate to oppose incumbent Republican Senator Everett M. Dirksen in the 1968 elections, Stevenson offended party regulars by refusing to endorse President Lyndon B. Johnson's military policies in Southeast Asia. The Democratic slate makers retaliated by approving the senatorial candidacy of state attorney general William G. Clark. After the violence at the 1968 Democratic National Convention in Chicago, where he was a convention delegate and vice-president of United Democrats for Humphrey, Stevenson issued a 2,500-word white paper calling for "reform" and "change" within the party. In that newsletter, released September 17, 1968, Stevenson deplored the "feudal structure" of the Illinois Democratic machine, which employed "storm troopers in blue" to stifle dissent and rewarded "homage with favors and jobs." As a member of Senator George S. McGovern's party reform commission, Stevenson pressed for greater representation of minority groups. "If we don't give blacks, women, and others more voice," he warned, as quoted in the Washington *Post*

(April 6, 1969), "then August and Chicago will be just a prelude."

When Senator Dirksen died in September 1969, leaving a vacancy to be filled by a special election in 1970, Stevenson mobilized a number of well-organized Citizens for Stevenson committees, signaling to party leaders that he had both the manpower and the political efficiency to mount an effective primary campaign. To avoid a split in the party, Mayor Daley reluctantly endorsed Stevenson's candidacy.

Stevenson's opponent was Ralph T. Smith, a Republican who had been appointed by Governor Richard Ogilvie to fill Dirksen's seat until the by-election. Trying his best to portray Stevenson as being soft on crime, campus unrest, and violence, Smith conducted a virulently emotional and media-oriented campaign. Party leaders, including President Richard M. Nixon and Vice-President Spiro T. Agnew, stumped the state for the Republican candidate and appeared at $250-a-plate Smith dinners. But Stevenson maintained a low media profile, preferring to take his campaign directly to the people at dozens of 99 cents-a-plate dinners throughout the state. "People are tired of noisy politicians, the Agnew approach," he explained to James R. Dickenson in an interview for a *National Observer* (September 21, 1970) analysis of the Illinois race. Concentrating on substantive issues, Stevenson called for an immediate end to the Vietnam war, fiscal restraint to slow spiraling inflation, and a reordering of national priorities to divert funds from "unnecessary weapons systems" to public housing, education, mass transit, crime control, health care, and environmental protection. With the support of independent as well as Democratic voters, Stevenson polled 2,065,054 votes to Smith's 1,519,718 for a plurality of 57.4 percent.

Taking office on November 17, 1970, Stevenson eagerly cast his first vote in favor of overriding President Nixon's veto of a bill limiting the amount of money a political candidate could spend to purchase television time. He subsequently introduced legislation to control televised "spot" political advertisements and approved public financing of campaigns. Stevenson, who was assigned to the Banking, Housing and Urban Affairs Committee, voted for federal funding of public works projects, for the continuation of the Office of Economic Opportunity, and for the creation of a National Legal Services Corporation to furnish legal counsel to the poor. On other domestic issues, he has favored strict gun control legislation; the establishment of a Consumer Protection Agency; the diversion of federal monies from the Highway Trust Fund to mass transit; an increase in personal income tax exemptions; and federal supervision of welfare programs. He opposed revenue-sharing on the grounds that it invited the misuse of public funds by corrupt government officials. Since he has often called for a halt to the stockpiling of "arsenals of ugly and unusable instruments of human destruction," it is not surprising that he opposed additional appropriations for the Safeguard antiballistic missile

system, the Trident nuclear submarine, and multiple warhead intercontinental ballistic missiles. To minimize the possibility of nuclear war, Stevenson cosponsored a bipartisan amendment requesting President Nixon to achieve mutual troop reductions with NATO and Warsaw Pact forces in Central Europe. Outraged by the administration's "corruption" and "concealment" during the investigations of the Watergate break-in and related incidents, Stevenson urged complete independence for the special prosecutor to "give the President a last chance to keep his promise to uphold the Constitution."

A longtime opponent of the war in Indochina, Stevenson condemned continued American military and economic support of the dictatorial regime of South Vietnamese President Nguyen Van Thieu. After visiting Southeast Asia in 1971, he proposed an unsuccessful amendment to establish a ten-member on-site commission to insure impartiality in the 1971 Vietnamese elections. On the Senate floor he repeatedly cast his vote in favor of an end to United States involvement in Indochina, approving the Mansfield, Cooper-Church, Brooke, and Eagleton amendments. In November 1973 Stevenson joined his colleagues to override President Nixon's veto of a bill limiting executive war-making powers. "The only thing we can do for these people now is to get out," Stevenson argued, as quoted in Mary McGrory's syndicated column of September 3, 1971. "We keep giving them helicopters and military supplies. What they need is leadership, and they can only get that if we leave them alone."

Stevenson is an equally vocal critic of the Nixon administration's "impulsive, convulsive economic policy," and he chaired a series of traveling hearings on the impact of the fuel shortage for the Senate Commerce Committee's consumer subcommittee. After listening to testimony in Chicago, Illinois on May 29, 1973, he announced to the press that he had "evidence that major oil companies [were] using the fuel shortage they helped to create to drive out their competition." Because they anticipated the oil shortage, Stevenson and Senator Edward M. Kennedy urged Nixon to suspend temporarily the oil import quotas in January 1973, along with nineteen other Senators. To stop the soaring prices of gasoline and heating oil, Stevenson suggested placing a ceiling on the cost of oil and petroleum products to consumers and on oil industry profits during the energy crisis, recommended mandatory fuel rationing, and approved the construction of the Alaska oil pipeline. As an alternative to an administration-backed bill for the deregulation of natural gas prices, Stevenson submitted a compromise plan to end regulation for all but the largest companies and to extend coverage to intrastate sales.

Adlai Ewing Stevenson 3d strongly resembles his father, who years ago affectionately nicknamed him "Bear." Although the Senator is taller and slimmer, he has the same deeply set eyes, the distinctive sharp-nosed profile, and the "Stevenson balding dome." Like his father, he wears large horn-rimmed spectacles for close work. More reserved and introspective than his father, Stevenson lacks his eloquence. He dislikes public speaking, campaigning, and the ceremonial aspects of politics. In his interview with Myra MacPherson he explained that he tries to strike a balance between politics, which is admittedly the "consuming interest" of his life, and "the things that are really important: catching your breath, maintaining equilibrium, communing with yourself." For recreation, he enjoys a fast game of tennis, hunting, and fishing. The Senator and his wife, the former Nancy Lewis Anderson, were married on June 25, 1955. They have four children: Adlai Ewing 4th, Lucy, Katherine, and Warwick. Besides their Washington, D.C. residence, the Stevenson homes include a brick Victorian townhouse on Chicago's Near North Side and a farm of several hundred acres near Galena, Illinois.

In December 1973 Adlai Stevenson was unanimously slated for reelection by the Illinois Democratic Party. After seven leading Republicans, including former United States Attorney General Elliott L. Richardson, declined the nomination to challenge the incumbent Stevenson in the 1974 Senate contest, the Illinois Republican Party drafted George M. Burditt, a former member of the General Assembly, who was virtually unknown in the state. In a public statement following his endorsement, Stevenson promised to conduct a "positive" campaign rather than to "belabor [the] sorry record" of the Nixon administration. Stevenson described his political convictions to Nobuo Abiko in an interview for the *Christian Science Monitor* (January 8, 1965): "I suppose I'm . . . a liberal Democrat. . . . I think basically that government shouldn't be called upon to do anything that individuals can do for themselves. But as the world grows . . . more complex . . . , I think government can and must be an active force for good in society. . . . I want desperately to be of public service." He concluded, "I've been thinking of running for one thing or another all my life."

References

N Y Post p39 Je 12 '64
N Y Times Mag p28+ F 22 '70 pors
Washington Post B1+ N 24 '70 pors
Americana Annual, 1971
Congressional Directory, 1973
Douth, George. Leaders in Profile (1972)
Who's Who in America, 1972-73

STEWART, THOMAS (JAMES)

Aug. 29, 1928- Opera Singer
Address: b. Metropolitan Opera Company, Lincoln Center for the Performing Arts, Lincoln Center Plaza, New York 10023; h. Placido Via Remorino, Locarno, Minusio, Switzerland

Thomas Stewart of New York's Metropolitan Opera is widely regarded as the world's leading *Heldenbariton* (heroic baritone). A vocal actor with a formidable stage presence and a rich, round bass-baritone voice, Stewart is an American who achieved status as a *Kammersänger* only by going to Europe, where he performed with the Berlin Städtische Oper and other companies from 1958 until he joined the Met, in 1966. Although his forte is the Wagnerian villain, Stewart is a flexible singer, equally at home in Puccini's Scarpia, the four villains in *Les Contes d'Hoffmann*, and such Verdi roles as Amonasro in *Aïda*, Rodrigo in *Don Carlo*, and Renato in *Un Ballo in Maschera*. Audiences attending the concerts given jointly by Stewart and his wife, the soprano Evelyn Lear, can attest to his versatility.

Thomas James Stewart was born in the town of San Saba, Texas on August 29, 1928 to Gladys (Reavis) Stewart and Thomas Stewart, a Texas state highway engineer. His childhood was a "terrible struggle," he recalled in an interview with John Gruen of the New York *Times* (February 20, 1972). "We were very poor and . . . I was an unattractive child—fat, and full of complexes. I had no girl friends. I was not witty or funny. I was shy." When he was ten he began to sing because, he told Gruen, it "made people notice" him and gave him "an identity."

Stewart's first voice teacher was a high school physics instructor who also conducted an a cappella choir. His Baptist mother wanted him to become what she called an "evangelistic soloist," but that did not appeal to him. He did, however, do some "Billy Graham gospel kinds of things" in California after his family moved there, as he told Robert Jacobson in an interview for *After Dark* (April 1974). "I was pretty cramped by the church bit, a rebellious youth chafing under the restrictions. I had heard concerts."

Gradually Stewart became more interested in music for its own sake, but he was also interested in electrical engineering and chose that as his major when he entered Baylor University, in Waco, Texas. His studies at Baylor were interrupted by a three-year enlistment in the United States Air Force, where he worked as a statistician on an IBM prototype computer project at Randolph Field in San Antonio, Texas. After his discharge from the Air Force, in 1949, he worked as a civilian in the Randolph Field research lab for a short time and then returned to Baylor, where he switched his major to music.

After taking his B.A. in music at Baylor, in 1953, Stewart studied under Mack Harrell and Frederick Cohen at the Juilliard School of Music Opera Workshop in New York City. Among his fellow students in the workshop was Evelyn (Kwartin) Lear, daughter of singer Nina Kwartin, granddaughter of cantor Zavel Kwartin, and cousin of Paul Kwartin, who conducts the "Wings of Song" program of Jewish liturgical music on radio Station WQXR in New York City. The name Lear is retained from her first marriage.

Miss Lear and Thomas Stewart were married on January 8, 1955. For two years they scrounged minor jobs together in musical comedy choruses, summer stock, radio, and television, and on his own Thomas Stewart won a radio talent contest and performed with Mae West's troupe at the

Latin Quarter, in New York City. Out of desperation he learned to play the guitar with a view to becoming a singing cowboy, but he abandoned that detour in his career when he flunked an audition for Arthur Godfrey's *Talent Scouts* television show (because he sounded "too professional.")

With the help of Frederick Cohen, the Stewarts obtained Fulbright grants to study at the prestigious Hochschule für Musik in Berlin, Germany in 1957. While studying at the Hochschule, Stewart successfully auditioned for Berlin's Deutsche Oper. (Some sources suggest that it was rather Berlin's Städtische Oper to which Stewart first belonged.) "I was a bass, but they needed a baritone, so that's what they got," he told an interviewer for the *New Yorker*'s "Talk of the Town" column (January 22, 1972). Miss Lear joined the Berlin opera company a year after her husband. As she has recalled, they worked tirelessly, "night and day," to be ready to move into major roles whenever the opportunities arose. Soon Stewart's repertoire included Don Giovanni, Iago, Golaud, the Flying Dutchman, and Dr. Falke. "His German is often easier to understand than that of the German singers," one of the company's officials told an Associated Press correspondent in 1960. "Stewart has a definite gift for languages." During his early years in Berlin, Stewart suffered a vocal crisis, which he surmounted by singing nothing but exercises for several months.

The first of Stewart's annual performances in major roles at the Wagner Festival in Bayreuth, Germany was in 1960, when he filled in for the ailing George London as Amfortas in a production of *Parsifal*. As his reputation grew in the early 1960's his international tours took in such distinguished houses as Covent Garden in London, the Vienna State Opera, and the Teatro Colón in Buenos Aires. In a brief visit to his homeland in 1963 Stewart sang with the San Francisco Opera Company in the role of Prince Yeletsky in Tchaikovsky's *Queen of Spades*. Reviewing the production for the New York *Times* (October 29, 1963), Harold C. Schonberg called Stewart "a clear-voiced baritone, a fine figure of a man, and an admirable artist."

When Stewart made his debut at the Metropolitan Opera on March 9, 1966 as Ford in Verdi's *Falstaff*, his "finesse, style, and vocal prowess" were such that the reviewer for the next morning's New York *Times* "found it hard to believe that he had not been a part of the [Franco] Zeffirelli production before or that he had never set foot on the Met's great stage to orchestral accompaniment." When he performed in *Tannhäuser* at the Met later in the same month Eric Salzman of the New York *Herald Tribune* (March 21, 1966) described him as "a consummate artist . . . able to make something strong and moving out of even such a stick as Wolfram."

In the recording of the complete *Der Ring der Nibelungen* directed by Herbert von Karajan and released in separate albums by Deutsche Grammophon Gesellschaft in the late 1960's and early

THOMAS STEWART

1970's, Stewart sang Wotan. "There are times when he threatens to break under the strain," Herbert Glass wrote in the *American Record Guide* (May 1967), "but in the end one feels that he has transcended the difficulties admirably, and what emerges is a powerful, tragic figure."

In the autumn of 1971 Stewart and his wife sang the leads in a San Francisco Opera production of *Eugene Onegin*, and at the Metropolitan Opera during the 1971-72 season they performed together (for the first time there) as the Count and Cherubino in *Le Nozze di Figaro*. Among Stewart's other roles in the same Met season were Golaud in a new production of *Pelléas et Mélisande* and Jochanaan in *Salome*. "The baritone brings to the role of Mélisande's jealous, murderous husband [Golaud] the sort of strength and virility that gives a new-found focus and dimension to this most incantatory of operas," John Gruen observed in his New York *Times* article. "Indeed, Stewart's tall, imposing presence, the warmth and richness of his voice, and his dramatic believability create a sense of tension not usually encountered in productions of this work."

Reviewing the *Salome* production in the New York *Times* of March 8, 1972, Harold C. Schonberg reported: "The evening's complete fusion of singing and acting came with the Jochanaan of Mr. Stewart. This was handsomely delivered, with a dignity and naturalness that are the mark of a fine singing actor. He did not have to indulge in any exaggerated movements; everything about his conception conveyed the burning fanaticism of the Prophet. And his singing was resonant, secure, and intense."

After attending Stewart's solo recital debut in a program of German lieder at Alice Tully Hall of Lincoln Center, Harriett Johnson observed in the New York *Post* (February 21, 1972): "There is no doubt, judging by this recital, that Stewart is a natural villain—on-stage, we hope—with a wicked sense of humor, all of which adds dimension to his personality." In January 1972 Thomas Stewart and Evelyn Lear gave a much acclaimed joint recital at Hunter College, and in March

1973 the two performed together as Dido and Aeneas in Purcell's opera, inaugurating the experimental "Mini-Met" at Lincoln Center. The following winter the couple toured the United States with a concert of songs by Purcell, Wolf, Ives, and Brahms. After their initial concert, in Lincoln Center's Philharmonic Hall, Speight Jenkins commented in the New York *Post* (December 3, 1973): "Mr. Stewart sang with an abundance of lyric beauty and a warm, rich tone. The flexibility of his voice is amazing." Among Stewart's roles at the Metropolitan in the season of 1973-74 was that of Gunther in the new production of *Götterdämmerung*, which he sang, according to Harold C. Schonberg of the New York *Times* (March 10, 1974), "with more freedom than he recently has." The characterization, Schonberg wrote, "was thought all the way through."

The neatly bearded, blue-eyed, burly Stewart is as imposing in person as he is on stage, according to John Gruen, who visited the Stewarts in their West Side New York apartment, near Lincoln Center. "He presents the image of a benevolent though somewhat forbidding schoolmaster," Gruen observed in his New York *Times* article on the couple. "Actually, Stewart is an outgoing, friendly, and articulate Texan who nevertheless reveals a certain reserve and shyness." At Miss Lear's urging, Stewart showed Gruen his "devil's look," fixing the *Times* writer with the piercing glower he has perfected for his Machiavellian roles. "It is a startling transformation," Gruen reported.

In marrying Evelyn Lear, Thomas Stewart became father to Jan and Boni, her son and daughter by her previous marriage. In addition to their New York City apartment, the Stewarts have a two-story home in the Italian section of Switzerland. According to Miss Lear, they lead "a very quiet life," the social part of which is limited chiefly to playing golf and having a few friends to buffet dinner. (Both enjoy cooking.) "We make it a point of being together as much as possible," she told John Gruen. "The fact is we need each other emotionally and we enjoy each other. I think Tom would agree with me that we're really happiest when we're together."

Stewart's approach to operatic roles is more cerebral than his wife's. "I sometimes question whether I get as much sensual pleasure out of music-making as Evy does," the baritone told John Gruen. "Frankly, I doubt it. With me it's more a matter of pride. I really do take pride in what I do and how I do it." Miss Lear agreed: "He constructs within his mind how a role should be sung. He'll go to the libretto first and he'll read it over and over again. I go directly to the music. I'm an instinctive singer." But Stewart is hardly emotionless in his performances. "I've experienced lots of emotions on the stage for the first time in my life—and it can really shake you up. I feel that's how it should be because then the emotion is so much fresher, so much more alive," he has said. "I have had more experiences on the stage than in my private life."

References

N Y Herald Tribune mag p40 Mr 20 '66 por
N Y Post p33 F 10 '73 por
N Y Times II p13+ F 20 '72 por
Who's Who in America, 1973-74

STOPPARD, TOM

July 3, 1937- British playwright; author
Address: h. "Fernleigh," Wood Lane, Iver Heath, Buckinghamshire, England

"I write fiction because it's a way of making statements I can disown, and I write plays because dialogue is the most respectable way of contradicting myself," the British playwright Tom Stoppard once said in a television interview, revealing his commitment to the exposition of enigma and paradox. Since achieving his initial triumph at the age of thirty with his award-winning play *Rosencrantz and Guildenstern are Dead*, Stoppard has remained one of the most successful young British dramatists, and has won the favor of playgoers on both sides of the Atlantic. *The Real Inspector Hound* and *Jumpers*, his most recent productions to be seen in the United States, won considerable praise from the critics for their intricately designed plots and literate dialogue. Stoppard is the author of several dozen plays for radio and television and one novel, *Lord Malquist and Mr. Moon*.

Tom Stoppard was born Thomas Straussler in Zlin, Czechoslovakia on July 3, 1937, the second son of Dr. Eugene and Martha Straussler. Dr. Straussler was a company doctor for the Bata shoe manufacturing company. In 1939 he and his family were transferred to a factory in Singapore, thereby escaping the Nazi invasion of Czechoslovakia. When the Japanese invaded Singapore in 1942, Mrs. Straussler and her two sons were evacuated to India by the retreating British; Dr. Straussler remained behind and was killed. In 1946 Mrs. Straussler married Kenneth Stoppard, an officer with the British Army stationed in India, and Tom and his brother assumed that surname.

For a time the Stoppards remained in India, where Tom attended an American-run boarding school. The family eventually settled in Bristol, England. Tom Stoppard completed his formal education at the Dolphin School, a prep school in Nottinghamshire, and at a public school in Pocklington, Yorkshire. "[My] Czecho-Chinese-American accent made me a subject of interest," he remarked to an interviewer for a *Newsweek* magazine (August 7, 1967) profile. "It also gave me a certain cachet."

At the age of seventeen Stoppard began his writing career as a reporter for the *Western Daily Press* in Bristol, a job he held from 1954 to 1958. At that time his professional goals were exclusively journalistic. "My ambition then was to be lying on the floor of an African airport while machine gun bullets zoomed over my typewriter," he recalled, as quoted in the London *Observer* (April 9, 1967). Bored with his career as a general news reporter assigned to cover "flower shows and funerals," he joined the staff of the Bristol *Evening World* as a feature writer and drama critic in 1958. For two years he reviewed the dramatic productions of the flourishing Bristol theatres before turning to free-lance writing. In 1962 he was briefly associated with *Scene*, a satirical magazine conceived by Peter Cook.

His first play, *A Walk on the Water*, which he wrote in 1960, was produced on British television in November 1963. A domestic drama about the family of an unsuccessful inventor, the play received little notice at the time. It was revived as a stage play in Hamburg, Germany in 1964 and in London in 1968. *A Walk on the Water* was followed by a number of radio plays, including *The Dissolution of Dominic Boot* (1964), *M is for Moon Among Other Things* (1964), *If You're Glad I'll be Frank* (1965), and *Albert's Bridge* (1967) and several teleplays, among them *A Separate Peace* (1966), *Teeth* (1967), *Another Moon Called Earth* (1967) and *Neutral Ground* (1968). In addition to the plays he wrote during that early, prolific period, Stoppard wrote a number of short stories, often inspired by his favorite short story writers, Damon Runyon, Ernest Hemingway, and Nathanael West. Some of his short stories were published in *Introduction 2; Stories By New Writers* (Faber & Faber, 1964). Stoppard won the John Whiting Award from the Arts Council of Great Britain in 1967.

In 1964 Stoppard went to Berlin on a Ford Foundation grant. For five months he lived and worked with a group of twenty other writers who had received similar grants. During his stay in Berlin he wrote a one-act verse burlesque entitled *Rosencrantz and Guildenstern*, which bore little resemblance to Stoppard's later hit, *Rosencrantz and Guildenstern are Dead*. In an interview with Dan Sullivan for a New York *Times* (August 29, 1967) profile, Stoppard admitted that initially he saw the situation of Rosencrantz and Guildenstern in terms of a farce. "Then," he went on to explain, "something alerted me to the serious reverberations of the characters. Rosencrantz and Guildenstern, the most expendable people of all time. Their very facelessness makes them dramatic; the fact that they die without ever really understanding why they lived makes them somehow cosmic."

In Shakespeare's *Hamlet*, Rosencrantz and Guildenstern are the pawns of King Claudius, who charges them with the task of diverting Hamlet from avenging the murder of his father. At the end of the play, they are sent as messengers to the King of England, carrying with them the instructions for their own executions. Stoppard used 250 lines from *Hamlet* to provide the framework for *Rosencrantz and Guildenstern are Dead*, which focuses on the lives of the two courtiers Instead of developing their personalities, however, he leaves Rosencrantz and Guildenstern as vaguely drawn as they were in the original play. They

TOM STOPPARD

are shown as adjuncts without individual identity who are swept along by events and personalities that they cannot comprehend. In their confusion about the meaning of their lives and their identities, they even mix up their own names. When they discover that they carry their own death warrants, they resolve to deliver them, hoping that the successful completion of their mission will give meaning to their existences.

Some critics viewed Stoppard's play as an "existential" work and compared it to Samuel Beckett's *Waiting for Godot*. Stoppard, however, rejects all classifications of his work. "My play was not written as a response to anything about alienation in our times," he explained to Tom Prideaux in an interview for a *Look* (February 9, 1968) profile. "One writes about human beings under stress—whether it is about losing one's trousers or being nailed to the cross."

Rosencrantz and Guildenstern are Dead was first performed by Oxford University students at the Edinburgh Festival in 1966. The rave reviews of that production prompted the National Theatre's Kenneth Tynan, Sir Laurence Olivier, and director Derek Goldby to stage the play in London. *Rosencrantz and Guildenstern are Dead* opened at the Old Vic in London on April 12, 1967 to unanimously enthusiastic reviews, with one ecstatic British critic praising the "erudite comedy" as "the most brilliant debut by a young playwright since John Arden's." When the play opened in New York City on October 16, 1967, it was an immediate critical and commercial success. A reviewer for *Time* (October 27, 1967) magazine commented that *Rosencrantz and Guildenstern are Dead* was "one of those rare plays able to open worlds of art, life, and death. . . . Broadway may not see a more auspicious playwriting debut this season." In recognition of his talent, the London *Evening Standard* named Stoppard the most promising playwright of 1968. He also received the Antoinette Perry (Tony) Award and the New York Drama Critics Circle Award for the best play of 1968.

When Tom Stoppard's novel, *Lord Malquist and Mr. Moon,* was published in England in 1965, it received little attention from critics and was virtually ignored by British readers. (It sold almost as many copies in Venezuela as in England.) Although it was not a best seller, the American edition, published by Knopf in 1968, was hospitably reviewed. Commenting on the novel for the Washington *Post* (April 16, 1968), Geoffrey Wolff found it to be "a remarkable entertainment, remarkably funny." In his review for the *New Republic* (June 15, 1968) Thomas Rogers compared the young writer to Kingsley Amis, Evelyn Waugh, and P. G. Wodehouse. "Farce, intellectual fantasy, and moments of genuine feeling succeed one another without apparent incongruity. Parody, as Stoppard uses it, is a way of looking with exuberant high spirits at a potentially dismaying reality."

Stoppard's winning streak in the theatre continued with the London production of *The Real Inspector Hound,* a one-act comedy, in 1968. In the play two fiercely competitive drama critics attend the opening performance of a new play, a parody of an Agatha Christie murder mystery. Birdboot, the senior critic, is a philanderer who lusts after the actresses on stage. He is accompanied by Moon, an ambitious second-string critic, who fantasizes the murder of Higgs, his immediate superior. Unwittingly, both men are inextricably drawn into the action of the stage thriller. Stoppard drew on his own experiences as a drama critic to create the stereotyped characters who muddle their way through a devilishly complicated play. When the play opened on Broadway on April 23, 1972, veteran critic Clive Barnes, in his New York *Times* (April 24, 1972) review, applauded the "extravagantly funny and inordinately clever" comedy. He noted that the "portraits of [the] two critics are moderately slanderous and highly amusing. . . . [Stoppard] is perhaps here at his best when he has his critical victims ponder out loud what they are going to write, for here his parodies are delicious and deadly." *After Magritte,* a diverting forty-minute play first produced in London in 1970, toured as a companion piece to *The Real Inspector Hound* in the United States.

Jumpers, Stoddard's second full-length play, had its première at the Old Vic in London early in 1972, and with Michael Hordern and Diana Rigg in the leading roles, it received considerable critical attention. *Jumpers* is an absurdist play that evolved from Stoppard's fascination with the idea of men landing on the moon. In an interview with Kathleen Halton for *Vogue* (October 15, 1967), he said, "You can't just land on the moon. It's much more than a location, it's a whole heritage of associations, poetic and religious. There are probably quite a few people around who'll go mad when the first man starts chumping around this symbol in size-ten boots." Working from that premise, he set *Jumpers* in a future time when the earthly system of moral order has begun to disintegrate, perhaps as a direct consequence of a British moon landing. After discovering that there is not enough fuel for both men to make

the return trip, one astronaut assaults the other and blasts off for earth on his own.

For the principal characters in the play, that event signals the beginning of a pervasive spiritual and ethical decline. A retired *chanteuse,* aptly named Dotty Moore, goes mad when she can no longer remember the lyrics to the "moonie-Junie" songs that comprised her repertoire. Her husband, George, an addlepated philosophy professor, inadvertently kills his two pets, a tortoise and a hare, while attempting to illustrate a lecture on moral standards. When the faculty members—the mental gymnasts or "jumpers," all portrayed by acrobats—form a pyramid, one of them is shot dead. Although that murder gives *Jumpers* the appearance of a mystery, it is, rather, an intellectual exercise. The main strength of *Jumpers,* a three-hour extravaganza of one and one-half million words, is its witty dialogue. Throughout the play, the focus is on George Moore's agonizing quest for a moral absolute. "I don't claim to know that God exists," George says at one point. "I only claim that he does without my knowing it."

Jumpers opened in the United States at the John F. Kennedy Center for the Performing Arts in Washington, D.C. on February 18, 1974, starring Brian Bedford as George and Jill Clayburgh as Dotty. Critical reception was mixed. Although the majority of the critics praised the play, several found fault with the casting and production. Stoppard, who customarily attends the rehearsals of all his plays, made additional script changes and staging suggestions before the New York opening of the play at the Billy Rose Theater on April 22, 1974. Reviewing the play for the New York *Times* (April 23, 1974), Clive Barnes noted that Stoppard "plays with ideas like a juggler, and the ideas he is playing with are sharp, clear, and dazzling." Adopting the "jumpers" metaphor, he added, "Mr. Stoppard sees the theatre as a kind of trampoline for the intellect, a sauna bath for the mind. It is all very refreshing." Other critics were not as enthusiastic. Clifford A. Ridley, for one, commenting on *Jumpers* for the *National Observer* (March 9, 1974), complained about the play's "length," its "incessant circularity," and its theatrical construction: "The play doesn't build to a conclusion; it sort of aimlessly shoots off half-baked hypotheses like an orbiting planet divesting itself of moons."

A compulsive worker, Stoppard adapted Federico García Lorca's *The House of Bernarda Alba* for the Greenwich (England) Theatre company and completed a screenplay for Paramount Pictures based on Bert Brecht's drama *Galileo.* For a change of pace, he directed a recent British production of Garson Kanin's farcical *Born Yesterday.* Meanwhile, he has continued to write plays for radio and television. "I would like ultimately before being carried out feet first to have done a bit of absolutely everything," he told Janet Watts in an interview for the *Guardian* weekly airmail edition (April 7, 1973). "I find it very hard to turn down offers to write an underwater ballet for dolphins or a play for a motorcyclist on the wall of death." *Travesties,* his most recent play, which had its première on June 10, 1974 as the season's final production of the Royal Shakespeare Company, presents an unusual view of the beginning of Dadaism in Switzerland in 1916. In outlining his idea to Jerry Tallmer in an interview for the New York *Post* (August 26, 1972), Stoppard perceived a "hilarious polarity" in the juxtaposition of the Dadaist headquarters in the Cabaret Voltaire and Lenin's Zurich residence. "I think it's fertile," he continued. "In a funny way, the Dadaists have come out on top, haven't they? What with the Cult of Personality. De-Stalinization. Re-Stalinization. This year this poet is the hero. Next year. . . . It proceeds on the Dadaist theory: Not to trust the statement." A reviewer for *Newsweek* (June 24, 1974) wrote of the Royal Shakespeare Company's production, "Performed with mind-spinning precision, . . . the clash of superstars becomes the intellectual donnybrook of the century."

Tom Stoppard, who once described himself as 'thin . . . nervous, [and] lazy," is a tall, gaunt man with long brown hair and large, expressive brown eyes. Despite his financial success and celebrity status, he prefers a relatively simple lifestyle. "I'm a very domestic person," he told Janet Watts. "The idea of doing glam things just fills me with deep depression. I absolutely prefer being at home." In 1972 Stoppard divorced his first wife, Jose Ingle Stoppard, and was awarded custody of his two sons, Oliver and Barnaby. He subsequently married Dr. Miriam Moore-Robinson, a dermatologist and birth control specialist who conducts research for Syntex Pharmaceuticals in Maidenhead. Their son William was born in 1972.

Unlike some of his contemporary playwrights, Stoppard writes purely theatrical plays. He does not subscribe to the "large claims" occasionally made by the authors of social or political protest plays. "I'm an English middle-class bourgeois who prefers to read a book to almost anything else," he told Mel Gussow in an interview for the New York *Times* (April 23, 1974). "It would be an insane pretension for me to write 'Poems of a Petrol Bomber.'" Although Stoppard once insisted to a reporter that writing came "about forty-third" in his personal list of priorities, he remains convinced that the artist is a "lucky man." One of the characters in his *Artist Descending a Staircase* (1972) remarks that in any given community of 1,000 people, 900 of them will be doing the work, ninety "doing well," nine "doing good," and "one lucky bastard [will be] writing about the other 999."

References

N Y Post p15 Ag 26 '72 por
N Y Times p54 Ap 26 '72 por
New Yorker 44:40+ My 4 '68
Time 103:85 My 6 '74 por
Washington Post pP1+ F 17 '74 pors
Taylor, John Russell. The Second Wave (1971)
Who's Who, 1973-74

STRAUSS, ROBERT S(CHWARZ)

Oct. 19, 1918- Chairman of the Democratic National Committee; lawyer; businessman
Address: b. Democratic National Committee, 1625 Massachusetts Ave., N.W., Washington, D.C. 20036; h. 6223 De Loache, Dallas, Tex. 75225

On December 9, 1972 the millionaire Texas lawyer and businessman Robert S. Strauss succeeded Jean Westwood as chairman of the Democratic National Committee after an intraparty power struggle that followed in the wake of the defeat of Senator George S. McGovern in the November 1972 Presidential election. Strauss, who served with distinction as the party's treasurer from 1970 to 1972, had long been identified with the conservative elements of the Texas Democratic organization, and in his campaign for the chairmanship he was backed by the old guard of the Democratic party. But since taking office as party chief, Strauss has acted as a compromiser and conciliator, in his determination to restore the Democratic party to the status of a broadly based organization representing "middle America," the South, and organized labor as well as the liberal McGovern forces.

Robert Schwarz Strauss was born on October 19, 1918 in Lockhart, in south central Texas, the older of the two sons of Charles H. and Edith V. (Schwarz) Strauss, and grew up in Stamford, Texas. Both of his parents were Jewish; his father emigrated from Germany as a young man; his mother's family had lived in Texas since the 1850's. As a boy, Robert Strauss, who with his brother Ted grew up in modest circumstances, helped out behind the counter in his parents' dry goods store. In an interview with Judith Michaelson of the New York *Post* (December 16, 1972), Strauss recalled that it was his mother who encouraged him to seek a career in politics. He remembered his father as "a misplaced merchant with very little business acumen, who never accumulated anything" and as "a gentle man who listened to music."

As a student at the University of Texas, where he was a member of a Jewish fraternity, Strauss worked as a clerk at the state capitol in Austin to meet his expenses. Among his classmates at the university was John B. Connally, with whom he formed an enduring friendship. During his student years Strauss entered politics, and in 1937 he volunteered his services in the first Congressional election campaign of Lyndon B. Johnson, who was then an advocate of the New Deal policies of President Franklin D. Roosevelt. "I came out of college at an impressionable time," Strauss recalled in the New York *Post* interview. "F.D.R. captured my imagination. And that was probably because of Lyndon Johnson."

After graduating from the University of Texas law school with an LL.B. degree in 1941, Strauss joined the Federal Bureau of Investigation, in lieu of entering military service, and worked as

ROBERT S. STRAUSS

a special agent, first in Des Moines, Iowa, then in Columbus, Ohio, and finally in Dallas, Texas. In 1945 he left the FBI and helped found a law firm—now known as Akin, Gump, Strauss, Hauer & Feld—which became one of the most prominent in Dallas, and which now also maintains an office in Washington, D.C. While engaged in the practice of law, Strauss amassed a small fortune by investing in real estate and radio stations. In 1964 he became president of the Strauss Broadcasting company, which operates station KCEE in Tucson, Arizona and formerly owned stations in Dallas and Atlanta that were later sold. Strauss also became board chairman of the Valley View State Bank in Dallas.

When his friend John B. Connally ran for his first term as governor of Texas in 1962, Strauss was one of the chief fund raisers for his campaign. After his inauguration Connally appointed Strauss to the state banking board, where he served for six years. In 1968 he was named by Connally to the Democratic National Committee. As manager of the 1968 Humphrey-Muskie campaign in Texas, Strauss demonstrated his financial wizardry by winding up the campaign with money to spare. He also achieved what has been described as a "small miracle of statesmanship" by persuading Connally and his political archenemy, liberal Senator Ralph Yarborough, to campaign together in behalf of the national ticket.

Elected treasurer of the Democratic National Committee in March 1970, Strauss was charged with the Herculean task of removing the staggering deficit incurred by the party in the 1968 election campaign. "I know this is the world champion debt," Strauss remarked, as quoted in Newsday (March 14, 1970). "But if this job were going to be a cinch, they wouldn't have turned to me. They would have gotten some nice, fashionable, easy-going fellow from somewhere else." As treasurer, Strauss tried to unify the party's various ideological factions in fund-raising efforts. In the fall of 1971, he was urged by party stalwarts in Texas to enter the 1972 race for the

Senate seat occupied by the ultra-conservative Republican John G. Tower, but he was reportedly talked out of it by Democratic national chairman Lawrence F. O'Brien, who felt that he was more needed as a party fund-raiser.

By soliciting private contributions, arranging lucrative fund-raising dinners, and staging a nationwide nineteen-hour telethon shortly before he resigned as treasurer in July 1972, Strauss raised enough money to place the Democratic National Committee's finances on a cash-and-carry basis and to reduce its $9,300,000 debt of 1968 by about one-half. He also obtained the $2,000,000 needed to finance the 1972 Democratic National Convention at Miami Beach. Commenting on his dazzling performance as treasurer, Rowland Evans and Robert Novak wrote in their syndicated column (Washington Post, March 18, 1971) that "seldom has the committee had so aggressive a money-raiser as Strauss." On July 14, 1972, following the nomination of Senator George S. McGovern as the Democratic Presidential candidate, Strauss resigned as party treasurer in favor of McGovern's choice, Donald Petrie. During the election campaign Strauss, while remaining loyal to the Democratic national ticket, devoted his energies to his new post as chairman of the National Committee to Re-elect a Democratic Congress and raised over $1,000,000 for Congressional candidates.

After the landslide defeat of Senator McGovern by President Richard Nixon in the election of November 7, 1972, the "old-guard" of the Democratic establishment, disaffected by the "new politics" of the McGovern forces, tried to regain control of the party and to replace Mrs. Jean Westwood, who had served as chairman since McGovern's nomination in July. In the month-long campaign for the party chairmanship, Strauss had the backing of AFL-CIO president George Meany, Senator Henry M. Jackson of Washington, and others of the old guard. Early in the campaign Mrs. Westwood offered to step aside in favor of a compromise candidate but refused to relinquish the chairmanship to Strauss, who, she felt, symbolized the conservative Democratic establishment. Strauss's campaign took on a new impetus when the Democratic Governors' Conference, meeting at St. Louis on December 3, endorsed him by a vote of eighteen to eight, with six abstentions, and when, a few days later, Senate Majority Leader Mike Mansfield pledged to support him. Meanwhile, Strauss assured liberal Democrats that he would not reverse the recently adopted party reforms that had given a greater voice in party affairs to women, blacks, and youth, and he said that he intended to "create a climate where all sides begin talking to each other again."

At a showdown meeting of the Democratic National Committee on December 9, 1972, Mrs. Westwood voluntarily resigned the party chairmanship, having won a token victory by defeating, with a vote of 105 to 100, an attempt by Strauss supporters to remove her from office. Nominated by Florida Governor Reuben Askew, Strauss was elected on the first ballot with 106½ votes, while his liberal opponents, national committeeman George Mitchell of Maine and California party chairman Charles Manatt, received 71¼ and 26 votes, respectively. Calling his election "a small step forward" in resolving the problems facing the party and the nation, Strauss pledged himself to reconcile divergent factions within the party. "I belong to no man; I am owned by no organization," he told the committee. "I am a centrist, a worker, a doer, a putter-together, and those talents belong to you."

Because of his bond with John Connally—which led one Texas wit to remark that "when Connally eats watermelon, Strauss spits seeds"—Strauss had been widely regarded as a die-hard member of the conservative Texas Democratic establishment. But he has insisted that while he valued Connally's friendship, he was in no way beholden to him. When asked what he would do if Connally—then Secretary of the Treasury in the Nixon Cabinet—were to run for the Vice-Presidency as Nixon's running-mate, Strauss was reported to have said, as quoted in the *National Observer* (December 23, 1972), "I'll do my damndest to whip his ass." After his election as party chairman, Strauss criticized Connally's recent role as head of Democrats for Nixon and declared that no one who supported any other candidate than McGovern during the 1972 campaign should hold any titular office in the Democratic party.

Determined to make the Democratic party "a place where you can have a laugh and a drink again," Strauss embarked on his mission of reconciliation immediately after becoming party chairman. During his first forty-eight hours in office he held friendly meetings with Senators George McGovern and Edward M. Kennedy, who assured him of their support and cooperation. He retained the services of the black ex-state senator Basil A. Patterson of New York as vice-chairman of the national committee and, in keeping with a new rule requiring the party's chairman and vice-chairman to be of opposite sexes, created a new vice-chairmanship to which he appointed the party's Oregon state chairman, Mrs. Caroline Wilkins. He named Jean Westwood to the 107-member commission, headed by Terry Sanford, that she had created to draft a new party charter by 1974. Strauss also retained United Auto Workers President Leonard Woodcock, a McGovern supporter and an adversary of AFL-CIO president George Meany, as chairman of a reform commission to consider the revision of rules for the selection of convention delegates. He assured black caucus spokesmen that blacks would be substantially represented among the twenty-five at-large members to be added to the 278-member Democratic National Committee in early 1973 to increase the influence of under-represented groups within the party.

In the weeks that followed, Strauss continued to try to forge unity in Democratic ranks, by meeting with such divergent representatives of the party as black Congresswoman Shirley Chisholm of New York, Governor George Wallace of Alabama, and Chicago Mayor Richard Daley. From Alexander J. Barkin, head of the AFL-CIO Committee on Political Education, Strauss received assurances that George Meany, who had withheld support from McGovern in 1972 would "come back in and participate" in Democratic party affairs. He persuaded McGovern to make his private list of some 750,000 contributors to his Presidential campaign available to the party for fund-raising purposes. At a news conference on January 8, 1973 Strauss declared his intention to "restructure in a very positive way the whole area of finance." Convinced that the best way to return the control of the party to the people was through increased participation of elected officials, Strauss announced a few weeks later the formation of a new forty-member Democratic advisory council, consisting of mayors, governors, and members of the House and the Senate.

Strauss demonstrated his flair for compromise and conciliation when his slate of twenty-five new at-large members, increasing the membership of the Democratic National Committee to 303, was approved by the party on March 23, 1973. Although at the insistence of AFL-CIO officials he included eight labor members who had followed Meany's policy of neutrality in 1972, he placated McGovern supporters by dropping two of his own non-labor candidates and naming two additional labor representatives who had supported the national ticket. He also mollified the black caucus by including two of its choices among the eight blacks on the slate. Strauss called the almost unanimous acceptance of the list of candidates—who also included eight women, two persons of Hispanic background, and three Southerners, one of them an aide of George Wallace—the first step on the "long road back to party unity."

In the fall of 1973 Strauss faced the problem of renewed friction between party regulars and "new politics" forces over the formulation of new rules for delegate selection. That task was being undertaken by the reform commission under the chairmanship of Baltimore councilwoman Barbara Mikulski, who had replaced Leonard Woodcock in the post earlier in the year. In October the commission unanimously adopted compromise guidelines for 1976 that squared with Strauss's views, abolishing the rigid quotas for women, youth, and minorities that had been introduced in 1972. In their place they adopted a rule requiring "affirmative action" by state parties to involve "all Democrats . . . in the delegate selection process." The commission also approved two provisions that Strauss had insisted on, abolishing the ban on slate-making that had kept such party spokesmen as Richard Daley on the sidelines in 1972, and guaranteeing delegate seats to elected officials.

As for the Watergate affair, Strauss had been pressing the Democratic National Committee's $6,400,000 suit against the Committee to Reelect the President (CREEP). In April 1973 he rejected a $525,000 offer for an out-of-court settlement, on the grounds that the offer amounted to an "admission of guilt" on the part of the Republican committee. But by February 1974 Strauss was willing to agree to an out-of-court settlement of $775,000. The agreement included a promise by the Republicans not to engage in countersuits against the Democrats. Strauss's own home had been burglarized shortly after the Watergate break-in in 1972, although there was no conclusive evidence linking the two events.

In an interview in *Nation's Business* (December 1973) he said that "this crowd around the White House and CREEP . . . is the most lawless band of men and women . . . since the days of Clyde Barrow and Bonnie Parker." Nevertheless, he has warned against inflating the political implications of Watergate. "We're not going to win any congressional, senatorial, or gubernatorial races on Watergate," he told newsmen, as quoted in *U.S. News & World Report* (September 10, 1973). "We've got to win on the issues." When asked by the *Nation's Business* interviewer what message he had for the nation's youth, Strauss replied: "We gave you a bum legacy. We gave you . . . a highly unpopular war, presented you with a number of issues with which you totally disagree, and now . . . Watergate. . . . But we have also given you something far broader, something that makes up for all this. We have shown you in a positive way that this 200-year-old system can withstand almost anything."

Robert S. Strauss was married on May 27, 1941 to Helen Jacobs, the daughter of a publisher of several small Texas newspapers. They have two sons: Robert A. Strauss, who manages the family-owned radio station in Tucson, and Richard Strauss, who is in the construction and real estate business in Dallas; a daughter, Susan (Mrs. Philip Robertson); and five grandchildren. A solidly built man, Strauss is of medium height, with thinning gray hair and bushy eyebrows. He enjoys playing poker and golf and attending horse races, and likes to relax beside the swimming pool of his Dallas home with a martini after a hard day's work. Strauss is president of the board of trustees of Temple Emanu-el, the leading Reform synagogue in Dallas. While serving in his unpaid post as party chairman, Strauss has continued to practise with his law firm and has dismissed allegations of a possible conflict of interest.

One acquaintance, quoted in the New York *Post* (December 16, 1972) credits Strauss with the ability to "charm the pants off a snake"; others, cited in *Newsday* (March 14, 1970), describe him as a man with "guts and nerve" who is "tough as nails," and as an "adroit operator who will compromise on tactics but not on principle." To his brother, as quoted in the *National Observer* (December 23, 1972), Bob Strauss is "as close to Will Rogers in character as anyone I've ever seen" and a man "who has a great faculty for understanding the other man's view."

References

N Y Post p24 D 16 '72 por
N Y Times p28 D 11 '72 por
Martindale-Hubbell Law Directory, 1973
Who's Who in American Politics, 1973-74

STRUTHERS, SALLY (ANN)

July 28, 1948- Actress
Address: b. c/o Columbia Broadcasting System, 4024 Radford Ave., North Hollywood, Calif. 91604; c/o William Morris Agency, 151 El Camino Dr., Beverly Hills, Calif. 90212

For her portrayal in *All in the Family* of Gloria, the vivacious, scatterbrained daughter of the working-class bigot Archie Bunker, Sally Struthers was given an Emmy as the best supporting actress in a comedy series during the 1971-72 television season. Personally selected by the award-winning series' producer Norman Lear, the young comedienne joined a cast of veteran actors to collaborate on one of television's most popular programs, which regularly attracts more than 50 percent of the American viewing audience. Aware that a starring role in a long-running television series poses a problem for a young actress, Miss Struthers chooses unsavory roles in motion pictures, to avoid the type-casting trap. "I am not an All-American sweetie-pie," she insisted to Aljean Harmetz in an interview for *Good Housekeeping* magazine (October 1972). Miss Struthers who compares acting to "cheap group therapy," prefers to change roles occasionally. Acting, she explained to Arthur Bell for a New York *Times* profile (October 29, 1972), "is being different people, like being a schizo fifty different ways. And we're paid . . . terrific amounts of money to play what we did in grandma's attic with old clothes from the trunk."

Of Scottish and Norwegian ancestry, Sally Ann Struthers was born in Portland, Oregon on July 28, 1948. When her father, a surgeon, and her mother became divorced, seven-year-old Sally and an older sister remained with Mrs. Struthers. A chubby child, Sally was teased unmercifully by her sister, who nicknamed her "Packy"—short for "pachyderm." Corrective shoes and a shiny silver front tooth added to her insecurity. "In the seventh grade class play, the coach told me to keep my mouth shut. The reflection was blinding the audience," Miss Struthers recalled in an interview with Dick Hobson published in the July 10, 1971 issue of *TV Guide*. "I was really unattractive." At Portland's U. S. Grant High School, she was an honor student, president of the 1,500-member girls' league, and the head cheerleader in charge of devising unique yells for all school-sponsored athletic events, including wrestling meets. While dating a track star she formed the school's first girls' track team, which became so successful that the school entered some of the girls in the Junior Olympics. A skilled and imaginative graphic artist, she directed advertising and promotion for school games and dances. Despite her heavy academic and extracurricular schedule, Miss Struthers worked as a waitress after school and as a drugstore clerk on Saturdays. "I've always overdone," she once conceded to a magazine writer. "The busier you get, the less time you have to spend alone."

Greatly encouraged by a high school art award that she received for her paintings, Miss Struthers originally planned to enroll at a liberal arts college, with the intent of becoming "a doctor to please her father or an artist to please her mother." Instead she applied to the Pasadena Playhouse. There she received onstage training as well as classroom instruction in dialects, dance, play direction, body movement, and voice. She described her training to Edwin Miller in an interview for *Seventeen* (February 1973): "The first year . . . , I played only ten-year-old children or under, flattened down with Ace bandages, wearing short, tight dresses and little patent leather shoes. My second year I played a ninety-year-old woman. The main thing the Playhouse taught me in two years was that you don't have to go to a school to learn how to act."

After graduating from the Pasadena Playhouse in June 1967, Miss Struthers moved to Los Angeles in search of a career in television or motion pictures. Installed by her mother in the Hollywood Studio Club for women, the quondam home of Marilyn Monroe and Kim Novak, she made the rounds of talent agencies and cast calls. To support herself, she worked as a receptionist, a telephone solicitor, a popcorn seller, and a cleaning woman in a movie theatre. "I kept hoping I'd run into some producer's wife while cleaning the ladies' room," she has recalled. She toured briefly, but unsuccessfully, with the Spike Jones Jr. band, singing "Chloe" and "Cocktails For Two" and "all those songs people don't want to hear any more" to nightclubbers in Palm Springs and Las Vegas. Her talent as a mimic, perfected by the zany Spike Jones routines, landed her a job as a dancer on a Herb Alpert television special. Later, she understudied Margaret O'Brien in the Los Angeles production of *Barefoot in the Park* and appeared in several television commercials that promoted the merits of lima beans and a hamburger mix. In one commercial she allowed herself to be enclosed in a huge, yellow styrofoam ball, to portray a talking lemon.

Miss Struthers stumbled into comedy when her four roommates, trying to cheer her up following her father's death, cut her long blond hair. Because the short curly ringlets made her look like Shirley Temple, she began adapting her personality to the hair style and acted "insane" during job interviews. She was not always hired, but the interviewers did remember her. Signed by a talent agent in May 1970, she joined the cast of the *Smothers Brothers Summer Show*, a summer replacement, and the *Tim Conway Comedy Hour*, a 1970-71 season entry. On the Conway show she appeared in the regular "car pool" segment and enacted the awkward "Tim Conway dancer." Writing in the Washington *Post's* TV *Channels* supplement (April 15, 1973), Lawrence Laurent remembered her performance as the "mindless bit of fluff . . . the curly-topped moppet doing Shirley Temple imitations."

Breaking into motion pictures, Miss Struthers appeared in *Charlotte*, which has never been released, and *The Phynx* (Warner Brothers, 1970),

SALLY STRUTHERS

a box office flop that attempted to cash in on the popularity of rock movies. Her first screen success came with *Five Easy Pieces* (Columbia, 1970), which was directed by Bob Rafelson and starred Jack Nicholson. For the role of Betty, the giggly bowling-alley pick-up who willingly accompanies Nicholson to a motel, Miss Struthers appeared in a brief nude scene. "I couldn't drop that towel in front of six or seven men," she told Earl Wilson for his syndicated column of October 14, 1972. "When I got to Jack, I stayed glued to him . . . I finally went home and bit my nails for six months hoping they'd cut the scene out but they didn't." Although she was onscreen for a mere five minutes, her perceptive portrayal caught the eye of television producer Norman Lear.

Lear, who was casting the pilot film for a proposed television series based on the unconventional BBC-TV comedy hit *Till Death Do Us Part*, had already selected three of its four leading players: Carroll O'Connor as Archie, the intolerant patriarch of the Bunker household; Jean Stapleton as Edith, his long-suffering "dingbat" wife; and Rob Reiner as Mike Stivic, the Bunkers' liberal "Polack" son-in-law. Impressed by her performances in *Five Easy Pieces* and on the Smothers Brothers and Tim Conway television shows, Lear asked Miss Struthers to audition for the part of Gloria Bunker Stivic, Archie's dutiful, featherbrained daughter. "They handed me a yelling scene to do," she remembers. "I had laryngitis, and I didn't do too well, but Norman Lear . . . got hysterical at the sound I made trying." After acting out a series of improvisations with Rob Reiner, Miss Struthers was hired.

With some trepidation, CBS scheduled the controversial series as a midseason replacement beginning January 12, 1971. Hailed by one critic as "the first major social departure" in situation comedy, *All in the Family*, after getting off to a slow start, climbed steadily up the ratings chart and won three Emmy awards for its first half-season, including one for Miss Struthers as best supporting actress in a comedy series. "No one knew it was going to be a hit show which would become the prey of every analyst, psychiatrist, writer, and philosopher," she remarked to Edwin Miller. "It gives people food for thought, but if I ever felt that the show hurt anyone or was teaching anyone something bad, I couldn't do it. . . . It opened up a lot of family discussions, taking the dirt out from under the carpet for everyone to see. Even bigots need heroes; better an innocent hero like Archie Bunker than some others."

At first, Miss Struthers mugged and clowned on the set, breaking into song-and-dance routines at the slightest provocation. "I thought that was the way to get people to like me," she has explained. As she gained confidence, she made dialogue and plot suggestions and modified her characterization of Gloria. Outwardly, Gloria's tousled mop of little-girl curls gave way to a longer, softer style. Her personality changed, too, along with her hair-do. She became more demanding, more outspoken, particularly in the area of women's rights, and perhaps most importantly, she took a job, partly to support her student-husband. Gloria, however, remains a subordinate role. "Rob Reiner and I are . . . straight people for the comedy act," she told Edwin Miller. Acknowledging that Reiner often has better lines because of his frequent arguments with Archie, she described her lines as "winners, like 'I'll help you set the table, Ma!' . . . One out of every two of my lines is '. . . and then what happened?' or 'But, Ma, how come?' to further the story."

During the summer of 1972, Miss Struthers performed in summer stock in *A Girl Could Get Lucky* at the Pheasant Run Playhouse in St. Charles, Illinois, a Chicago suburb. To offset her image as a "rosy-cheeked young kook," she accepted a part in Sam Peckinpah's *The Getaway* (National General, 1972). "In this film I say words and carry attitudes that'll hit people differently, depending on how close-minded they are," she remarked in her New York *Times* interview. In *The Getaway*, a "contemporary western" starring Steve McQueen and Ali MacGraw, Sally Struthers played Fran Clinton, a mindless, sex-starved woman who eagerly succumbs to the advances of a professional killer while her husband watches helplessly. Commenting on the film for *Time* magazine (January 8, 1973), Jay Cocks thought Miss Struthers, like others in the cast, tended to "overact," but *Cue* magazine's William Wolf in his review for the December 23, 1972 issue, praised her "colorful character performance." In her favorable *New York* magazine critique (December 12, 1972), Judith Crist wrote that Miss Struthers was "delicious as a dumb lecherous lady." The young actress enjoys the variety of her film roles. "There are so many ways to represent a woman," she has said. "I would like to play a murderess and an unwed mother, and a nun, and an old Jewish mother. At the end of my career, I'd like to have people say that I am as funny as Judy Holliday and to be as revered as Ruth Gordon."

Standing five feet one inch tall, Sally Struthers has thick, shoulder-length blond hair, large blue eyes, and a "light-up-the-room" smile. "I always wanted to be six feet tall with lovely long legs," she has lamented, "but look at me—a giant midget! . . . Men think of me as a funny little girl only to be patted on the head." To compensate for her small stature, she favors four-inch platform shoes—an affectation which, according to Arthur Bell, causes her to resemble "a cuddle doll on a pull-toy wagon, all blonde and golden and a trifle wobbly." She also indulges in brightly colored, "funky" clothes. Despite her success, she remains, as she admitted in the New York *Times* interview, insecure about her personal appearance. Her busy schedule of ten hours a day, five days a week leaves her little time for relaxation. Although she enjoys cooking exotic dishes for guests, she avoids rich foods to keep her weight at 110 pounds. Miss Struthers, whose only self-indulgence is chain-smoking, shares the upper floor of an old Spanish-style house in Westwood, California with her black cat Baba, whom she named after her grandfather. Her apartment is furnished with odds and ends collected at local "swap meets," such as Coca-Cola crates recycled into end tables and an old-fashioned icebox transformed into a closet.

Already contemplating her post-*Family* career, Miss Struthers is considering a movie musical and a nightclub act. "Show business is feast or famine," she has explained. "All of a sudden, you're a new can of Campbell's soup everybody wants to try, and then you're scheduled for TV game shows like *Password* and *Hollywood Squares* every weekend. . . . Actors turn to drugs or alcohol or uppers or downers or whatever they need to make it through. . . . I want to stay the nice, normal, healthy, bouncy girl I was when I came from Oregon."

References

Good H 175:97+ O '72 por
N Y Times II p15 O 29 '72 por
Seventeen 32:106+ F '73 por
TV Guide 19:31+ Jl 10 '71
Washington Post N p1 S 3 '72 por

TERKEL, STUDS

May 16, 1912- Writer; interviewer
Address: b. 500 N. Michigan, Chicago, Ill. 60611; h. 3152 N. Pine Grove Ave., Chicago, Ill. 60657

Studs Terkel, the radio and television personality and author of three best-selling oral histories, has had a variegated career. The gifted interviewer has been a radio and stage actor, sports columnist, disc jockey, playwright, journalist, lecturer, and host of music festivals. In the 1940's Terkel launched the first of his many talk shows, managing to attract a mass audience without making concessions to commercialism.

Like the late social anthropologist Oscar Lewis, Terkel has shown that the tape recorder can be an enormous asset to social research, dramatizing the thoughts and emotions of those anonymous and faceless Americans who might otherwise be known only as mere statistics. He has used that instrument with consummate skill to compile three penetrating studies of American life that were commissioned by the publishing house of Pantheon Books, in New York City. The first, *Division Street: America* (1966) tapped the sources of conflict that savaged urban America in the 1960's. It was followed in 1970 by *Hard Times: An Oral History of the Great Depression*, which consisted of personal memories of the 1930's and enriched our understanding of that era. Terkel's most recent contribution to what he calls "guerrilla journalism," *Working* (1974), transcribes with immediacy and power the frustrations that trouble contemporary attitudes towards work in the United States.

The third son of working-class parents, Studs Terkel was born Louis Terkel in the Bronx in New York City on May 16, 1912. At about eleven he moved with his family to Chicago, where he has lived most of his life. Like Nelson Algren, Terkel developed indissoluble ties with that city and with its vast industrial population whose problems impinged on his consciousness even as a boy. His father, Samuel Terkel, a tailor and superb craftsman, eventually was invalided by a heart ailment, but his mother, Anna (Finkel) Terkel, whom he remembers as a "tough little sparrow" of a woman, whose pince nez glasses were always slipping down her nose, helped to support the family by taking over the Wells-Grand Hotel on the North Side near Chicago's Loop in 1926 for blue-collar workers, skilled mechanics, and craftsmen. He has affectionate memories of that establishment and of his talks with the roistering workers who got drunk there on Saturday nights until the Great Depression transformed their paychecks to welfare checks. From 1925 through 1928, when he attended McKinley High School on Chicago's West Side, he also became acquainted with another aspect of the city—its gangster element, which flourished in the Prohibition era.

Until 1934 Terkel's parents were not too badly hit by the Depression. By then they had managed to put him through two years at Crane Junior College, another two at the University of Chicago, where he received a Ph.B. in 1932, and three "traumatic" years at the University of Chicago Law School which, he says, he entered "dreaming of Clarence Darrow—and woke up to see Julius Hoffman." Disenchanted with law when he obtained his J.D. degree in 1934, and having failed his first bar examination, Terkel accepted a $94-a-month job with the government, doing statistical research on unemployment in Omaha, Nebraska. After that he moved on to Washington, D.C., where he literally "counted" the baby bonds that veterans of World War I received as bonuses. To relieve the tedium, he acted in the Washington Civic Theatre and earned rave reviews for his performance as Shad Larue, the villain in a dramatized version of Sinclair Lewis' novel about American fascism, *It Can't Happen Here.*

STUDS TERKEL

In 1935 Terkel returned to Chicago, where he joined the Federal Writers Project and, along with such associates as Richard Wright and Nelson Algren, turned out weekly radio shows on WGN, Colonel Robert R. McCormick's station. Those led to assignments as an actor in such radio soap operas of that era as *Ma Perkins* and *Road of Life,* in which he usually played a gangster who came to a sudden and violent end. "With script in hand, I read lines of stunning banality," Terkel recalled in his preface to *Working.* During the late 1930's he returned to the stage with the Chicago Repertory Theater, and around that time rechristened himself "Studs," after Studs Lonigan, the protagonist of James T. Farrell's lumbering and elephantine novels about the Chicago proletarian Irish in the years before and during the Depression era.

In the early 1940's Terkel became an established voice on Chicago radio, first as a news commentator and sportscaster, then as a disc jockey who, in addition to knowing his way around folk music, jazz, and opera, promoted such new talents as the great gospel singer Mahalia Jackson. In 1945 he established *Wax Museum,* the first of the diversified radio programs he has since conducted on station WFMT, Chicago. In that, as in *Studs Terkel Almanac,* launched in 1958, he exhibited an uncanny flair for engaging people in spontaneous interviews, thanks to his warmth, curiosity, and empathy. Those same traits marked his first venture into television, a program called *Studs Place,* which, using a barbecue joint as its setting, featured banter between the bartending Terkel, his waitress, his house jazz pianist or folk singer, and any distinguished guest who might drop in. The basic idea behind *Studs Place,* which lasted from 1949 to 1953, was that "honest human relationships can make for good televiewing." The same conviction accounts for the success of all his radio programs, including his current *Studs Terkel Show,* which is heard daily over WFMT in Chicago.

The 1950's and the 1960's were kaleidoscopic decades for Terkel. He wrote a jazz column for the Chicago *Sun-Times* and managed to find time to continue his stage career, with appearances both in Chicago and in summer stock in *Detective Story* (1950); *Of Mice and Men* and *Time of Your Life* (1952); *A View from the Bridge* (1958); *Light Up the Sky* (1959); and *The Cave Dwellers* (1960). His introduction to American jazz for young fans and neophytes, *Giants of Jazz* (Crowell, 1957), contained brief biographies of such titans as Bessie Smith and Louis Armstrong. He moderated panel discussions, lectured, narrated documentary films, and hosted the 1959 and 1960 Newport Folk Festivals, the 1959 Ravinia (Illinois) Music Festival, and the 1961 University of Chicago Folk Festival. Terkel's work in the mass media has brought him several coveted awards, including first award from Ohio State University in 1959 for *Wax Museum,* which was rated the finest cultural program in the regional radio category; the UNESCO East-West Values award in 1962 for best radio program; the Prix Italiana; and the Communicator of the Year award from the University of Chicago Alumni Association in 1969.

Intent on exploring new genres, in 1959 Terkel wrote a play entitled *Amazing Grace,* about a troubled family operating a sleazy urban hotel. It was not performed, however, until 1967, when the University of Michigan's Professional Theatre selected it for production out of one hundred plays by new playwrights that had been submitted to it. But Terkel's debut as a playwright was none too promising. Despite a generous budget, skilled directing, and an able cast headed by Cathleen Nesbitt and Victor Buono, *Amazing Grace* drew sharply divided reviews. Although the critics of the Detroit *Daily Express* and the Toledo *Blade* acclaimed it as sterling drama, reviewers for *Variety* and the New York *Times* found it a "tasteless work" whose "earnest message" failed to deliver.

Given his extraordinary ability to strike up rapport with "the man of inchoate thought" and his exceptional talent for in-depth interviews, it is not surprising that the literary form to which Terkel ultimately gravitated was oral history. In 1967 he published the first of his triptych of best-selling, tape-recorded works, *Division Street: America,* consisting of transcripts of seventy conversations he had with people living in or near Chicago, including racketeers, landladies, steelworkers, bar owners, John Birchers, window washers, slum dwellers, executives, religious leaders, and social workers. He set out not with a thesis but with a desire to listen, to elicit the spontaneous feelings and opinions of representative Americans.

"The portable tape recorder . . . is for better or for worse," Terkel wrote in his introduction to *Working.* "It can be . . . a means of blackmail, an instrument of the police state or, as is most often the case, a transmitter of the banal. Yet a tape recorder, with microphone in hand, on the table or the arm of the chair or on the grass, can transform both the visitor and the host. . . . It can be used to capture the voice of a celebrity, whose answers are ever ready and flow through all the expected straits. I have yet to be astonished by one. It can be used to capture the thoughts of the non-celebrated—on the steps of a public housing project, in a frame bungalow, in a furnished apartment, in a parked car—and these 'statistics' become persons, each one unique. I am constantly astonished."

To Terkel, Division Street in Chicago was merely a metaphor for the divisiveness that he thought typified every major American city in the 1960's. The interviews themselves seemed to confirm that, since they not only revealed character in a remarkable way but also dramatized the antipathies of rich and poor, old and young, black and white, along with their common despair at the dehumanization of city life. In his long review of *Division Street: America* in the New York *Times* (February 5, 1967), Peter Lyon observed that it resembled "a modern morality play, a drama with as many conflicts as life itself, and as many remorseless, kindless villains." Many critics concurred, although a few detected a sentimental and populist bias in Terkel—a tendency to bypass some of the more ruthless Chicago inhabitants and focus on essentially decent people whose flaws can be attributed to corruption by society.

As if to refute that minority of critics, Terkel's next book, *Hard Times: An Oral History of the Great Depression* (1970), adopted a broader range of inquiry and a wider perspective. From interviews with 100 Americans, both famous and unknown, who had lived through the Great Depression or its peripheral years, he put together a "memory book" that, he said, has less to do with "hard facts" than the "small triumphs" of those who weathered that protracted ordeal. Thus the present generation of students and workers could rediscover a past they knew only in general terms, through academic history books. Terkel concentrated exclusively on personal memories and, in so doing, discovered a significant aspect of the Depression that no historian had observed before—a prevailing sense of guilt and failure on the part of those who had survived it. Among those interviewed were millionaires and prominent New Dealers along with the down-and-out.

Hard Times also revealed that the fear of loss fostered one of two reactions: either an obsession with money and property or a contempt for the entire system and its values. Those insights, coupled with the recollections of such disadvantaged groups as the blue-collar workers and blacks who were hit by hard times long before the stock market crash of 1929, resulted in a history of the Great Depression unlike any other. In the *New York Review of Books* (August 13, 1970) Murray Kempton joined in the chorus of praise for Terkel by noting that his book revises our notion of "Who-Deserves-To-Be-Taken-Seriously" because he found "our instructors in the most unexpected places." *Hard Times* was a best seller for five months and, like *Division Street: America,* was translated into every major Western language as well as into Hungarian and Japanese.

Terkel's most ambitious contribution to guerrilla journalism so far is his latest book, *Working:*

People Talk About What They Do All Day and How They Feel About What They Do (1974). It is, according to Terkel, about "a search . . . for daily meaning as well as daily bread, for recognition as well as cash, for astonishment rather than torpor; in short, for a sort of life rather than a Monday through Friday sort of dying." For three years he used his trusty cassette tape recorder to interview 133 Americans from almost as many occupations, omitting professionals (the movie critic Pauline Kael and the actress Geraldine Page are among the few exceptions), and concentrating on the inarticulate workers whose attitudes towards their jobs have seldom been studied except by social scientists.

The result is a book as profound in its revelation of personal longings and fears as it is in its insights into the collective American attitude towards work today. Most workers Terkel interviewed, whether white collar or blue, assembly line or executive, ventilated their dissatisfaction with the narrow monotony of jobs that offer scant chance for personal fulfillment and for what Freud called a "secure place in the human community." They see themselves as robots, machines, and objects, the inevitable consequence of a runaway technology that is rendering workers and their products more and more obsolete.

Although Terkel discovered that a few workers are still valued for their skills and can take delight in a job well done, an overwhelming number are more often singled out for censure than for praise. Those findings help to explain the disturbing American trends of absenteeism, shoddy work, and a disdain for craftsmanship. The longings that "ordinary people" harbor for work that affords some measure of dignity and individuality suggest, according to Terkel, that it is high time that we redefine the old work ethic and concentrate on "human matters."

A best seller for seventeen weeks, *Working* has been almost unanimously hailed as a documentary that abounds in provocative and arresting insights into the troubled texture of contemporary American life. After reading it, Lewis Mumford went on record as saying: "No one can pretend to know our countrymen and the things that beautify or bedevil their workdays who has not taken in all that Terkel's collaborators say." The majority of critics agreed with Mumford. Only a dissenting minority felt that he had skewed his sample; that he had defined problems without proposing solutions; that it was difficult to generalize from his findings; and that his tendency to sentimentalize and mythicize the common man had resulted in a range of opinion that did not accurately represent the country as a whole. But Loren Baritz argued in the *New Republic* (April 6, 1974) that whatever Terkel's bias may have been, his taste, intuition, and involvement are such that "most available statistics, reified as they are, will not contradict the many voices of working."

Unlike most of his respondents, Studs Terkel is one of the lucky few who thoroughly enjoys his work. Since July 2, 1939 he has been married to the former Ida Goldberg, a social worker from Ashland, Wisconsin, whom he met when they were both members of the Chicago Repertory Theatre. They have one son, Paul. Interviewers have repeatedly commented on his restlessness, buoyant vitality, and youthful attitude, and John Hall of the Manchester *Guardian* (September 26, 1970) saw him as "Spencer Tracy out of John Dewey with Schnozzle Durante up." His office, a rather antiseptic room furnished in formica and steel, contrasts sharply with his own warm and outgoing nature. He fancies such little luxuries as Havana cigars and Jack Daniels Tennessee sour mash "sippin'" whiskey.

As for his acknowledged ease with total strangers, Terkel insists that he has no conscious technique but simply engages them in conversation with much the same kinds of questions he might ask over a drink. His empathy, sensitivity, and the impression he radiates of his own vulnerability to time and circumstance are so compelling that most interviewees are eager to confide in him. Once they have, his real job begins—that of carefully editing the tapes to see that "the person is retained, the essence of the man, with nothing of me in it." He feels that the crucial test of his guerrilla journalism is yet to come, for he is preparing an oral history on the achievement and loss of power, the most complex and exacting subject he has tackled so far. He anticipates that the book will be the "tough" one—his "Everest."

References

Terkel, Studs. Working (1974)
Who's Who in America, 1974-75
Who's Who in the Midwest, 1974-75

THEKAEKARA, MATTHEW P(OTHEN) (the-kā'kə-rə)

Mar. 21, 1914- Roman Catholic cleric; physicist
Address: b. National Aeronautics and Space Administration, Goddard Space Flight Center, Greenbelt, Md. 20771; h. 3 Lakeview Circle, Greenbelt, Md. 20770

The life of Father Matthew Thekaekara, the India-born Jesuit priest, physicist, and inventor, represents a remarkably successful interweaving of two divergent intellectual disciplines—theology and science. Out of that reconciliation has come such notable inventions as the mercury pool and the cone radiometer and a spate of books and articles on subjects ranging from space physics and planning for his native country to religious exposition for children. But perhaps his most important contribution during a long career that has spanned two continents and deepened scientific inquiry into space exploration has been his recalculation of the solar constant—the measurable amount of life-giving energy that travels from the sun to the earth. Father Thekaekara, who formerly belonged to the faculties of Georgetown University and Johns Hopkins University, has since 1964 been research physicist at the Goddard

REV. MATTHEW P. THEKAEKARA

Space Flight Center of the National Aeronautics and Space Administration, in Greenbelt, Maryland.

Matthew Pothen Thekaekara was born on March 21, 1914 in Changanachery, India, a town in the southwestern Indian state of Kerala, bordering on the Arabian Sea. His father, Pothen Chacko Thekaekara, was a schoolteacher, proud of his family's ancient heritage, which can be traced back to the time of St. Thomas, the apostle of India. A man of modest means, he had a house and some acres of paddy land, but supported his wife and two sons on his teaching salary. Mariam, his wife, was a religious woman of another ancient family, the Kannampuzha, timber merchants by trade.

When Matthew Thekaekara was six and his brother, George, was four, their twenty-six-year-old mother died. A few years later their father remarried. Rosamma Thekaekara proved to be a devoted stepmother to her husband's two sons, and she bore four surviving children—Jose Francis, Mary Thankamma, James Ignatius, and Lucyamma. In a break with family tradition Matthew was sent from 1920 to 1922 to the nonparochial government elementary school. His exceptional intellectual ability became apparent soon after he entered St. Berchmans' High School in 1922. Throughout his high school years he was first in his class or near the top. He graduated early, in 1929, after being granted a special underage exemption by the Department of Education.

At the age of fifteen Thekaekara entered St. Berchmans' College to study mathematics, physics, and logic. His growing absorption in science, however, did not diminish his interest in religion or his conviction that God intended him to be a priest. He has attributed his vocation in part to the fact that he was named after an uncle of dynamic personality who was vicar of the cathedral of Changanachery and mayor of the town and who himself had a priest uncle named Matthew. In 1931 Thekaekara applied for admission to Sacred Heart College in Shembaganur, India as a Jesuit novice, beginning several years of rigorous religious training that he carried out in addition to his regular academic work.

After taking his minor religious vows, Thekaekara studied at St. Joseph's College, Madras University from 1935 to 1937, when he graduated with a B.A. degree in physics and mathematics. During his undergraduate years he established a university record for his overall marks that remains unsurpassed. In 1939 he obtained his M.Sc. degree first class with distinction in physics and mathematics from Madras and then began his teaching career, at St. Aloysius College in Mangalore as assistant professor of physics. On the faculty of St. Joseph's College from 1941 to 1944, he taught courses in physics for which he wrote a two-volume textbook. Meanwhile, having continued his studies for the priesthood, he received his licentiate in philosophy in 1942 from Sacred Heart College, where he also taught Sanskrit. He claims only a reading knowledge of Sanskrit, along with Hindi, Hebrew, Aramaic, and Russian; and while he considers his grasp of Greek and German to be just fair, he is fluent in English, French, Latin, Malayalam, and Tamil.

On November 21, 1946 Thekaekara was ordained a priest in the Society of Jesus at St. Mary's in Kurseong, the Jesuit seminary in the foothills of the Himalayas. He continued to devote considerable time, as he had for several years, to writing articles for religious magazines, such as *Eucharistic Congress*, the *Morning Star*, and *Our Lady of Mercy's Message*, and to contribute to magazines in the United States and France. From 1945 to 1948 he wrote weekly editorials for the *Herald*, the major Catholic weekly published in Calcutta, and served as assistant editor of *Modern Student*, another Calcutta periodical. He was also the author of *The Story of Jesus* (Little Flower Press, Calcutta, 1947) and *Planning for India* (Saran Jivan Press, Calcutta, 1947).

Father Matthew, as he came to be called, followed his ordination with a year's lecture tour of France. On his return to India in 1948 he became associate professor and chairman of the physics department at Loyola College, a dual post that he held for about four years. In 1952 he left for the United States and settled in Baltimore, where he served as chaplain of Maryvale Convent while studying and teaching at Johns Hopkins University. During five years as instructor and research assistant in physics he fulfilled requirements for his Ph.D. degree, awarded by Johns Hopkins in 1956, and then completed a year of postdoctoral work. Since the publication of his dissertation in the difficult field of atomic spectroscopy, *The Spectrum of Xenon I*, he has been the author or coauthor of some ninety technical papers, reports, and reviews. His findings in connection with his work on spectrum charts and tables later became integrated into the graduate course in spectroscopy offered at Johns Hopkins University.

Moving to Georgetown University in 1957 as assistant professor of physics and astronomy, Thekaekara advanced to associate professor of physics in 1960 and about the same time took over the position of acting chairman of the department of physics. Also beginning in 1960 he directed a series of summer conferences, sponsored in part by the National Science Foundation, for college professors on recent advances in astro-geophysics. Through those meetings his work in space physics came to the attention of scientists at the National Aeronautics and Space Administration. For about two years he served as a part-time consultant at NASA's Goddard Space Flight Center before leaving the faculty of Georgetown, in 1964, for the post of research physicist at Goddard. He invented the mercury pool as a precision tool for the alignment of instruments for orbiting solar observatories in 1964 and the cone radiometer in the following year.

In his initial experiments for the NASA research center Thekaekara attempted to recreate sunlight in a test chamber as part of an effort to duplicate conditions in space that man-made satellites would be likely to encounter. He and his colleagues sought to measure the amount of the sun's energy reaching the earth—the solar constant—to a degree of accuracy higher than ever before attempted. The results of their studies led Dr. Thekaekara to suspect the validity of the internationally accepted standards regarding the solar constant. NASA agreed to back experiments he proposed for calculating a new value.

As head of a team of about thirty scientists and engineers, Thekaekara first supervised the elaborately technical outfitting of a Convair-990 jet, *Galileo*, to serve as a flying laboratory to check out his theories. They worked at altitudes up to 38,000 feet and also used balloons, since the experiments involved making delicate observations at high altitudes, where some of the errors occurring in earlier, ground-based measurements could be prevented. Measuring the solar constant was also the purpose of a joint undertaking by teams at the Jet Propulsion Laboratory of the California Institute of Technology and at the Eppley Laboratory in Newport, Rhode Island, of which Dr. Andrew J. Drummond was chief scientist. A committee of scientists, under Thekaekara's chairmanship, evaluated the combined findings as well as those of other observers, in the United States, the Soviet Union, and Western Europe.

At the first International Solar Energy Society Conference, in Melbourne, Australia in March 1970, Thekaekara and Drummond made a joint announcement that reverberated throughout the world's scientific community. From their independent research the two scientists concluded that they had sufficient data to prove that the solar constant was 1.940 calories per square centimeter per minute rather than the previously accepted figure of 2 calories per square centimeter per minute. The new estimate, approximately 3 percent lower than the preceding figure, meant that the intensity of visible sunlight reaching the earth was 8 percent less than had been previously calculated. The scientists also proposed a revised curve for the solar spectrum.

Because the solar constant is among the most important constants in physics, the disclosures of Thekaekara and Drummond necessarily had significant implications not only in astrophysics, but in other branches of the physical sciences. It was expected that the new knowledge would increase man's ability to forecast the weather and to discover the causes of the Ice Ages and other major climatic changes. Thekaekara and others predicted that in space exploration the adjusted calculation would affect such diverse problems as the design of protective coatings for spacecraft and solar-driven power packs in satellites. The fine shade of difference in measurement would also make it possible for scientists to determine the temperature at which satellites could operate in space. When a satellite leaves the shield of the earth's atmosphere, the highly sensitive instruments within are exposed to the sun's full radiation, and they run the risk of malfunction because of their exposure to temperatures that may be either too high or too low. Exact calculation based on corrected values may enable NASA spacecraft to withstand hazards of deep space probes.

Besides working at the Goddard Space Flight Center, Thekaekara taught at Pace College as visiting professor from 1965 to 1970. He is a founding member of the Optical Society of America's National Capital Section, of which he has served as both president and vice-president. Among the other professional organizations to which he belongs are the American Institute of Physics, the Albertus Magnus Guild, the American Association of Physics Teachers, the International Solar Energy Society, and the Institute of Environmental Sciences. He is also a member of Phi Beta Kappa, and Sigma Xi and served as president of the Georgetown University chapter of the latter society from 1962 to 1964. His honors include three tributes from NASA: the Quality Performance Award in 1969, the Superior Achievement Award in 1970, and the Exceptional Performance Award in 1970. The Institute of Environmental Sciences bestowed on him its Space Environment Award in 1971.

Father Matthew P. Thekaekara became a naturalized citizen of the United States in 1962. He saves a part of his income to pay for a visit to India every two or three years, but he reportedly contributed most of his government salary to Catholic charities. In 1955 he established the American branch of the All-India Catholic University Federation for Catholic Students from India studying in the United States. National chaplain of that organization from 1955 to 1964, he edited a monthly newsletter as part of his duties. His most important nonscientific work published in the United States is *Meditations for All Seasons and the Mass* (Pageant Press, 1964), a collection of poems written in English but in the Indian idiom.

As resident priest of the Ascension Church in Halethorpe, near Baltimore, from 1964 to 1970, Rev. Thekaekara customarily said Mass for the Sisters of Providence at 6:30 each weekday morning before driving some twenty-five miles to the

Goddard Space Flight Center. Apparently undisturbed by the differences in thinking required by metaphysical speculation and scientific research, he has observed, "Man's searching mind is the same and God is the author of all truth. A scientist who is all science is hardly human. And the priest is not to be confined to the sacristy and sanctuary, less so today than ever before." Man's very nature, according to Thekaekara, who himself has an abundance of vitality and energy, compels him to be dissatisfied, to overreach, "to grope for the infinite," and therefore to journey into space.

References

Arbutus (Md.) Times Ap 16 '70 por
Baltimore Evening Sun B p28+ Ja 25 '66 por
Washington Post A p18 Ag 21 '60 por
American Men and Women of Science 12th ed (1973)
Who's Who in the East, 1970-71
World Who's Who in Science (1968)

THORPE, (JOHN) JEREMY

Apr. 29, 1929- British political leader
Address: b. House of Commons, London SW1 OAA, England; h. 2 Orme Square, London W24RS, England; Upper Chuggaton, Cobbaton, near Chittlehampton, Devon, England

Jeremy Thorpe, the Parliamentary leader of the British Liberal party, is a member of a staunchly Conservative family with a tradition of public service going back several centuries. Attracted by Liberal ideals of social reform as a schoolboy, he began to demonstrate his political talents during his student years at Oxford. After practising for some years as a barrister, he was first elected to Parliament in 1959. Thorpe succeeded Jo Grimond as leader of the Parliamentary Liberal party in 1967. Over the next few years, he built it into a substantial political force, which in the general election of February 1974 won almost 20 percent of the votes cast. Because of inequities in the British electoral system, the Liberals obtained only fourteen Parliamentary seats in that election —enough, however, to give them the balance of power between the Labour and Conservative parties, which were then almost evenly matched. But in the October 1974 elections the Liberals lost their chance to break up the nation's two-party system when the Labour party gained a substantial lead over the Conservatives.

John Jeremy Thorpe was born in London on April 29, 1929, the youngest of the three children, and only son, of John Henry Thorpe, a barrister and King's Counsel who from 1919 to 1923 was Conservative Member of Parliament for the Rusholme division of Manchester. His mother, Ursula, was the daughter of Conservative M.P. Sir John Norton-Griffiths, known as "Empire Jack." Thorpe's ancestors include Sir Robert de Thorpe, Chief Justice of the Common Pleas in 1356 and Chancellor in 1371; Baron John de Thorpe, judge and M.P. under Edward II; and Baron Thomas Thorpe, speaker in Henry IV's Parliament, who was beheaded by a mob in 1461.

Stricken by tuberculosis at the age of six, Jeremy Thorpe was installed in a cottage of his own, with two servants to tend him. There he spent seven months in a spinal carriage. He has not yet completely overcome the physical effects of that ordeal. After the outbreak of World War II in 1939, the Thorpes moved from London to Limpsfield, in Surrey, where Jeremy attended the Hazelwood School. His father's lucrative legal practice declined during the war, and he eventually abandoned it to devote himself to government work, as chairman of the Central Price Regulation Committee and in other posts. Mrs. Thorpe, deprived of servants for the first time in her life, took over the running of her household, at the same time devoting herself to the war effort.

In 1940 Jeremy Thorpe and the younger of his two sisters were sent for safety to the United States. They stayed in West Newton, Massachusetts, with an aunt, Lady Norton-Griffiths, and Thorpe attended the Rectory School at Pomfret, Connecticut. He became an ardent admirer of President Franklin D. Roosevelt—partly in reaction against the equally ardent Republicanism of his American cousins. His political education continued when he returned home in 1943 to enter Eton College. Accustomed to the relative mobility of American society, he was shocked by the stringency of the British class system, of which Eton is a bulwark and a symbol.

Shortly after Thorpe's return to England his father, to whom he was deeply devoted, suffered a massive stroke. He died on October 31, 1944, after he had attained the satisfaction of seeing his son, a talented violinist, win the Boyle Cup for Strings at Eton. It was at this time that Thorpe began to define his political beliefs, largely through the influence of his godmother, Lady Megan Lloyd George, daughter of the great Liberal Prime Minister, David Lloyd George. As a small boy, Thorpe had met the old man himself, and during his years at Eton he became a frequent visitor to the Lloyd George household.

Called up for National Service in 1948, but invalided out of the Rifle Brigade after a few months, Thorpe went to Trinity College, Oxford, in September of that year to read law. Although younger than most of his contemporaries there, he made an impression. Writing in the London *Sunday Times Magazine* (March 3, 1974), Susan Barnes described him, as he appeared at that time, as a "brash, slightly built schoolboy, orating radical views while dressed in posh suits with cuffs on the jacket. He played the violin, collected Chinese vases, took around with him his monocled mother and titled grandmother, and was a *figure*—described by his enemies as a two-dimensional figure. He attracted a lot of jealousy."

At Oxford, Thorpe won the presidency of the Liberal Club, the Law Society, and the Russell and Palmerston Club. In 1951 he became president of the Oxford Union, the debating society that is an acknowledged stepping stone to a career in British politics. It became evident during his Oxford years that Thorpe was a born politician, a devoted student of the masters of the political arts, a powerful and witty orator, and a brilliant organizer with a passion for detail. He demonstrated boundless nervous energy and an unflagging zest for what he called the "Machiavellian aspect" of political maneuver.

Some of Thorpe's Oxford contemporaries found his elegant dinner parties and extravagant clothes at odds with the sober reforming zeal of the Liberal party. Moreover, they found it strange that an ambitious young man of solidly Tory antecedents should throw in his lot with a party that had not enjoyed power since the 1920's. Thorpe, in fact, never concealed his distaste for the kind of dynastic Toryism in which he was reared. He chose the Liberals because they best represented his own ideals of social justice, and he seems never to have doubted that they would in due course return to power.

Because his social life and politicking at Oxford curtailed his studies, Thorpe graduated in 1952 with only a third-class honors degree in jurisprudence. He read for the bar, was called to the Inner Temple in 1954, and over the next six years built up a small practice as a barrister. In 1958 he became a founder of and partner in a firm of economic consultants, External Development Services Ltd. In addition, he began in 1953 to act as moderator on radio programs. Beginning in 1956, he also appeared on television, first as chairman of a scientific Brains Trust program, and later as an interviewer and commentator on the news program This Week.

Meanwhile, making his first bid for political office, in the 1955 general election Thorpe stood as the Liberal candidate for the House of Commons in the agricultural constituency of North Devon, then regarded as a safe Conservative seat. Although he lost, his campaign resulted in an increase in the district's Liberal vote. Over the next four years he made himself thoroughly familiar with his constituency. When he campaigned in the market town of Barnstable in the 1959 general election—wearing the jaunty brown derby that was then his political trademark—he reportedly could address by name almost everyone he met on the street. This time he won the election, taking the seat from the Tory incumbent with a margin of 362 votes.

In Parliament, Thorpe took a position on the left wing of his moderately progressive party, especially on the issues of civil liberties and colonialism. The unpopularity of such views in Thorpe's North Devon constituency seemed to have no effect on his personal standing there, and in the 1964 election his majority soared to 5,136. Although his margin of victory was reduced to 1,166 in the 1966 elections, he continued to maintain a firm hold on his constituency. At the same time he worked diligently for the Liberal party and in 1965 began a successful two-year stint as its treasurer and fund raiser. When Jo

JEREMY THORPE

Grimond retired on January 17, 1967 after ten years as leader of the Parliamentary Liberal party, Thorpe was chosen to succeed him.

The Liberals were one of the two principal British political parties from 1868 until 1922, when Labour supplanted them as the major party of the left. By 1967 they held only twelve of the 630 seats in the House of Commons. The party policies that Thorpe inherited included strong support for Britain's entry into the European Common Market, worker participation in the management of industries, a fairer distribution of the nation's wealth, separate parliamentary assemblies for Scotland and Wales, and a general devolution of government, returning "power to the people."

The Liberal party platform also called for a form of proportional representation. The existing British electoral system—a two-party system with elections based on a single-vote franchise—operates on a "winner-take-all" basis that militates against the minority parties. The Liberals, who during the 1960's commanded around 10 percent of the total British vote, thus often held no more than 5 percent of the Parliamentary seats.

To preserve their standing as a viable "third party," the dozen Liberal M.P.'s had to make themselves heard on every major issue debated in the House of Commons. They had to struggle for the loyalty of a disparate body of supporters, including traditionalists nostalgic for Lloyd George, community activists, fashionable intellectuals, and the Young Liberals, an intensely idealistic, lively, but intransigent group whose policies were often far to the left of the party as a whole.

At the Liberal assembly in September 1967, Jeremy Thorpe launched a "Liberal Crusade" that aimed at welding the party into a cohesive force, adding a million pounds to its treasury, and allowing it to field over 500 candidates in the next election. Two months later, the Liberal Parliamentary leadership was rebuked by the party's national executive for its failure "to make an impact on the electorate as an alternative to the two discredited major parties." Criticism of Thorpe mounted, and many of his party colleagues considered him too young and "too lightweight" for the post he occupied.

Married in May 1968, Thorpe was on his honeymoon on Elba when he learned of a move to oust him from the leadership. Back in London, he faced a meeting of the party executive on June 28 and defended himself with such skill that he emerged with an endorsement of his leadership by a majority of forty-eight to two. Thorpe did not escape criticism in the years that followed, but there were no more serious threats to his leadership, not even when, in the disastrous general election of 1970, six of the twelve Liberal M.P.'s lost their seats and his own North Devon majority fell to 369 votes.

The tragic death of his wife in an automobile accident in June 1970 left Thorpe in a state of shock for more than a year. During his bereavement, the only thing that occupied him intensely was the memorial to his wife that he erected on a prehistoric burial mound behind their Devon cottage. Eventually, however, Thorpe regained his equanimity. According to one of his colleagues, David Steel, Thorpe's recovery "showed a tremendous inner strength that I hadn't known was there. He emerged a much larger person." Partly because of a surer hand at the helm, and partly as a result of widespread disillusionment with the two major parties, the Liberals began to emerge for the first time in forty years as a force to be reckoned with. At a by-election in October 1971 they took Rochdale from the Labour party. A few months later they won Sutton and Cheam from the Tories. Two more "safe" Conservative seats fell to the Liberals in July 1973.

Most of those Parliamentary victories, and accompanying successes in local government elections, were attributed to the Liberals' concern with local issues and community politics. In early 1974 the Liberals proposed several measures to alleviate Britain's critical economic situation, including a penalty tax for those employers and employees contributing to inflation, a permanent prices and incomes policy, and a national minimum wage. Thorpe sharply criticized the Conservative government of Edward Heath for complacency in the face of an economic "crisis of immense proportions."

A general election was called for February 28, 1974 by Prime Minister Heath, who sought a mandate for his controversial handling of several interrelated crises. The Conservatives won 38.1 percent of the vote, and 296 of the 635 seats in the newly enlarged House of Commons. Although Labour received only 37.2 percent of the vote, its 301 seats gave it a plurality in the House. The Liberals scored a triumph in terms of votes— about 20 percent of those cast—but came out of the election with only fourteen Parliamentary seats. That result, which Thorpe called "intolerable," was a dramatic demonstration of the incongruities of the electoral system.

After consulting with other leaders of the Liberal party, Thorpe rejected Heath's offer of a senior Cabinet post within a projected Conservative-Liberal coalition government. Thorpe's subsequent proposal for a "government of national unity," composed of Conservatives, Labour, and Liberals, was rejected by both major parties. After Heath's resignation, on March 4, 1974, Harold Wilson was named Prime Minister and instructed to form a minority Labour government. Although the Liberals thus remained outside of the Cabinet, it appeared, nevertheless, that Thorpe and his colleagues had achieved something of a political miracle. They had emerged as the most important of the assorted minority parties that held the balance of power after a totally inconclusive election. That became very clear in June 1974, when the Conservative opposition, with Liberal help, rejected a series of measures devised by the Labour government to deal with the country's urgent economic problems, thus making another general election inevitable. When the election was held in October 1974, the Labour party retained its control of the government.

According to Bernard D. Nossiter (*International Herald Tribune*, March 2-3, 1974), Thorpe "holds a view of the world closer to the official Washington outlook" than most London politicians. Although he had little admiration for Richard Nixon, he thinks highly of Henry Kissinger. "I believe we behaved like bastards over the Middle East," Nossiter quotes Thorpe as saying, with reference to the Heath government's pro-Arab position at the time of the October 1973 Israeli-Arab war. Thorpe has also criticized the Labour party's efforts to bring about sharp reductions in defense expenditures. A champion of Western European unity, he favors giving genuine power to the European Parliament in Strasbourg and strengthening the Common Market. Thorpe believes that for its long-range defense needs Western Europe should continue to rely on United States nuclear weapons.

Jeremy Thorpe retired from legal practice in 1960, when he entered Parliament. In 1974 he resigned his directorships in broadcasting, financial, and other companies, including the controversial London and County Securities. He has served as a member of the national advisory committee of the British Broadcasting Corporation, as honorary treasurer of the United Nations Parliamentary Group, and as secretary of the World Campaign for the Release of South African Political Prisoners. Thorpe is a vice-president of the Anti-Apartheid Movement, vice-chairman of the Electoral Reform Society, and a founder-member of the National Benevolent Fund for the Aged. In March 1967 Thorpe became a Privy Councillor. He is a Fellow of the Royal Society of Arts and an honorary fellow of Trinity College, Oxford. With Allan Batham he wrote *To All Who Are Interested in Democracy*, a short study of voting methods, issued by the Liberal Party in 1953. He is a contributor to the symposium *Europe: The Case for Going In* (Harrap, 1971).

Jeremy Thorpe's first wife, the former Caroline Allpass, whom he married in May 1968, was killed in a traffic accident in June 1970. Their son, Rupert, was born in 1969. In March 1973 Thorpe married Marion, Countess of Hare-

wood, born Marion Stein in Vienna. She is a
former concert pianist who had been divorced
from the Earl of Harewood in 1967. Thorpe still
plays the violin and collects Chinese ceramics. A
friend, Lady Gladwyn, says that Jeremy Thorpe,
"the scintillating jester, masks a complicated personality, sensitive, deeply serious, even somber."
He does not suffer fools gladly, and it is said
that he can be brusque and even brutal in his
dealings with subordinates. On television he gives
a strong impression of warmth and directness, and
during the February 1974 campaign he outshone
both Edward Heath and Harold Wilson in the
popularity polls. In Barnstable, where he once
gained distinction by knowing most of his constituents by name, he now appears to know their
family histories and circumstances as well. He is
idolized in his constituency, which in February
1974 gave him an unassailable majority of 11,072.
Shortly before that election, Thorpe said: "Jo
Grimond's great achievement was to give the
Liberal Party *intellectual* credibility. I think my
task has been to try to give it *political* credibility."

References

Life 62:37+ Je 2 '67 pors
London Sunday Times Mag p27+ Mr 3 '74
N Y Times p12 Mr 4 '74 por
New Statesm 86:375+ S 21 '73 por
Burke's Peerage, Baronetage and Knight-
age, 1970
International Who's Who, 1973-74
Roth, Andrew, and Kerbey, Janice. The
Business Background of Members of
Parliament (1972)
Who's Who, 1974

TIPPETT, SIR MICHAEL (KEMP)

Jan. 2, 1905- British composer; conductor;
educator
Address: b. c/o Schott & Co., 48 Great Marlborough St., London W1V 2BN, England

Along with Benjamin Britten and Sir William
Walton, Sir Michael Tippett belongs to a world-
famous triumvirate of contemporary British composers, notwithstanding the fact that until 1974
few of his works were performed in the United
States. Tippett is a cerebral and highly individual
composer who shuns the fashionable abstractions of
avant-garde music because he feels they are
divorced from humanistic concerns. In so doing,
he has forged a style marked by utter integrity
and adopted an independent approach to his
craft. Fascinated by language, especially that of
Yeats, Shaw, and Eliot, he has served as his
own librettist on several occasions, even at the
risk of delaying acceptance of his compositions.
More than those of any other English composer,
Tippett's ideas serve as an index to his complex
creative personality. Still youthful as he approaches
seventy, Tippett no longer teaches and limits his
appearances as a conductor to devote more time
to composition.

SIR MICHAEL TIPPETT

The son of a Cornish lawyer named Henry
William Tippett and his wife, Isabel (Kemp)
Tippett, Michael Kemp Tippett was born in a
London nursing home on January 2, 1905. The
Celtic strain that has inspired much of his work
also endowed him with what has been called the
hardy and weatherbeaten look of a Breton sailor.
He spent the first fifteen years of his life in Suf-
folk and was educated at the Stamford Grammar
School in Lincolnshire. At eighteen he entered
the Royal College of Music in London as a Foley
Scholar, knowing, he has said, "absolutely nothing
about music," since that discipline had been drop-
ped from the curricula of British schools during
World War I. There he studied composition under
R.O. Morris and Charles Wood. His teachers in
conducting were Sir Malcolm Sargent and Sir
Adrian Boult.

After directing a choral and orchestral society
in Oxted, Surrey for a time, Tippett taught French
at the Hazelwood School until 1931. Later he
became involved in adult education in the London
County Council and the Royal Arsenal Cooperative
Society. In 1940 he was appointed musical director
of Morley College, a working-class institution in
South London, where he remained through 1951.
One of his famous predecessors was Gustav Holst,
who developed many of the activities at the school.
To devote himself more fully to composition, Tippett resigned his position at Morley College in
1952.

Michael Tippett came of age during the period
when men were returning home from the carnage
of World War I, and their tales of trench warfare
may have been a decisive factor in making him a
confirmed pacifist. He flirted with left-wing politics
for a time as a youth ("reading Marx knocked me
for six," he has said), but as a Trotskyist he was
never admitted to the Communist party. His refusal to surrender his freedom as an artist to the
rigid aesthetic canons of Socialist Realism led to
the inevitable rupture. His pacifist convictions
made him declare himself a conscientious objector
during World War II, and he was sent to prison
in June 1943 for three months.

It was not until he was almost thirty that Tippett wrote his first appreciable work, his Symphony in B-flat major, which owed much to the influence of Sibelius. He later discarded it, along with many of the compositions that he wrote up until 1935. His first choral work, *A Song of Liberty*, which he set to words of William Blake, appeared in 1937. That same year brought the *Fantasy Sonata* for piano, a romantic work that Tippett considers a product of his apprenticeship and therefore no longer suited for inclusion in concerts—the case with virtually all of his prewar compositions except his first string quartet. His first mature work, the contrapuntal and experimental *Concerto for Double String Orchestra*, came in 1939. When Tippett first conducted it in April of 1940, it attracted widespread attention and established him as a major composer.

Outraged by the general apathy to the plight of stranded Jewish refugees and by the Nazi pogrom in 1938 that was set off by a young Jew's assassination in Paris of the German Embassy secretary Ernst vom Rath, Tippett conceived of an oratorio that would embrace a universal ethic. He asked T. S. Eliot, a close friend who became a kind of father figure to him, to collaborate on the libretto of what later became known as *A Child of Our Time*, but the poet, after looking at the musician's rough draft, urged him to write his own words—advice that Tippett has followed ever since. By using Handel's *Messiah* and Bach's Passions as a foundation, Tippett took a specific event and transformed it into an image of reality, and by substituting Negro spirituals for the traditional Lutheran chorales, he gave the oratorio a quality of both timeliness and timelessness. Because of its relevance to today as well as to yesterday, Hubert Saal of *Newsweek* (February 25, 1974) wrote that *A Child of Our Time* "sounds like something Handel might have written had he lived in the age of Auschwitz."

Although Tippett began work on *A Child of Our Time* only a few days after the outbreak of World War II and completed it in 1943, the oratorio was not given its first hearing until March 1944, and the première symphony performance was given by the Philharmonic Society of Liverpool in November 1945. In reviewing a performance of *A Child of Our Time* that was given many years later at the Bath Festival and conducted by the composer, Gerald Larner wrote in the *Guardian* (June 27, 1968): "True, it is a naïve work, awkward at time in its language and its word setting, eclectic in its harmonies, impure in style, not free from banalities. And yet, in the composer's unsensational but totally convincing interpretation, it is plainly also an inspired and often beautiful work." The same subjectivity that colors so many passages of *A Child of Our Time* is evident in *Boyhood's End*, a cantata that Tippett set to words by W. H. Auden. It was given its première in London by Benjamin Britten and Peter Pears in 1943 and successfully revived there in 1962.

After the immediate success of *A Child of Our Time*, Tippett withdrew into a period of semi-retirement and meditation that lasted ten years. During that period of quietude he nonetheless composed a number of works, including a string quartet (his two earlier ones date from 1935 and 1942); a composition called *The Weeping Babe* for soprano and unaccompanied chorus set to a poem by Edith Sitwell; two *Partsongs* based on poems by Gerard Manley Hopkins; an orchestral suite; *Little Music* for string orchestra; and his tonal, though dissonant, First Symphony (1945).

In spite of all that diversified productivity, it was with his first opera, *The Midsummer Marriage*, on which he began to work in 1948, that Tippett made his first really decisive musical move. *The Midsummer Marriage* has been described by critics as a kind of twentieth-century *The Magic Flute* because of its thicket of dense symbolism and its concern with the mating of two radically different couples. Like Mozart's opera, *The Midsummer Marriage* is about the spiritual and physical relationships of two pairs of lovers: Jennifer and Mark (the Pamina and Tamino figures) and Bella and Jack (Papagena and Papageno). Most critics and audiences have found its libretto highly allusive and difficult, but Tippett contends that its perplexities are overcome by growing familiarity with the opera, in whose merits and ultimate success he seemed quite confident from the start.

Neither an inadequately produced presentation at its première at Covent Garden in 1955 nor a fleeting revival there of the same production in 1957 did much to evoke enthusiasm for *The Midsummer Marriage*, although some critics praised its expressive lyricism and the now famous ritual dances of the second act. In 1963 a BBC studio performance under the baton of Norman Del Mar aroused new interest in the opera, and although a second new production of *The Midsummer Marriage* at Covent Garden, in 1968, proved almost as disastrous as the first, its music made a genuine impact. Among those impressed was Colin Davis, the dynamic British conductor who has since become closely identified with much of Tippett's later music. Convinced that the opera deserved another chance, he persuaded the officials of Philips Records to record the opera with its original cast and the Covent Garden Orchestra and Chorus under his direction. With the exception of several works by Benjamin Britten, no other contemporary full-length British opera had until then been recorded. Critical acclaim for the recording was unanimous, with reviewers ransacking their vocabularies for such superlatives as "great," "masterpiece," and "extraordinary."

With his second opera, *King Priam*, Tippett deliberately turned away from the lyrical impulse that had been the prime mover behind *The Midsummer Marriage* and entered the stark and tragic world of the Trojan legend. An austere, spare, and dramatic departure from lyrical expansiveness, *King Priam* was accorded an enthusiastic reception when it had its première at Coventry by the Covent Garden Opera on May 29, 1962. One critic, Peter Heyworth, pointed out in the New York *Times* (June 24, 1962) after *King Priam* reached London a month later, that its well-shaped, coherent, and dramatic libretto had benefited considerably from Tippett's early consultations with Peter Brook and Günther Rennert. According to Heyworth, its "often memorable passages" marked *King Priam* as "the fruit of genius," and proved the power of Tippett's inspiration when he finds adequate means for expressing it.

Several years before the première of *King Priam*, Tippett had completed his Second Symphony, a relatively brief work that makes excessive and difficult demands on the string sections of the orchestra during its half hour of playing time. When it was first performed, by the BBC Symphony under the direction of Sir Adrian Boult in February 1958, it was dismissed out of hand by the critics as weird and unplayable. On that occasion the orchestra broke down in the scherzo movement and had to begin all over again. But later performances of the Second Symphony have vindicated it, and when Colin Davis conducted its Manhattan première in February 1970 Harold C. Schonberg of the New York *Times* (February 26, 1970) called it "a logical, bustling, well-written orthodox work, with well-defined tonal centers, which for all the world reminds one of a British Hindemith." When a recording of the Second Symphony appeared on the Argo label in 1968 under the baton of Colin Davis, Edward Greenfield noted in the *Guardian* (January 18, 1968) that it stood "at the very watershed point between [Tippett's] old, comparatively relaxed style and his new, sharper, less comfortable style." According to Greenfield, even a first hearing proved the argument of the Second Symphony to be taut and meaningful, not just difficult.

Not until 1965, when he was sixty, did Michael Tippett get to visit the United States for the first time, as composer-in-residence at the Aspen Music Festival in Colorado. He immediately fell in love with the country, especially with the West, and before that year was out he returned to the United States twice. In spite of his trans-Atlantic commitments in 1965, Tippett managed to complete his mystical choral work, *The Vision of St. Augustine*, perhaps the least accessible of his works in its thorny baroque complexity, even though it contains some of his most rapt and jubilant music. With Dietrich Fischer-Dieskau negotiating its taxing baritone solo part, Tippett himself conducted the first performance of *The Vision of St. Augustine* with the BBC Orchestra and Chorus at the Royal Festival Hall in London on January 19, 1966. A 1972 recording by RCA, with John Shirley-Quirk singing the Latin text from St. Augustine's *Confessions* to the accompaniment of the London Symphony Orchestra and Chorus under the composer, was warmly received by British critics, who welcomed the opportunity to fathom the profundities of the score at their leisure.

Always a slow worker, Tippett spent seven years on the composition of his third opera, *The Knot Garden*, which had its première at Covent Garden on December 2, 1970. Inspired by Shakespeare's late romantic comedies and the element of forgiveness that resolves them, Tippett wrote a libretto that has as its theme the redemptive power

of mercy and love to lead us out of the labyrinths in which we lose ourselves. *The Knot Garden,* in which Tippett achieved a concision and speed not to be found in his other operas, refers to the Elizabethan formal "love garden" or classical maze. Its action consists of a series of encounters among six tormented characters who finally act out scenes from *The Tempest* as a group therapy experiment under the direction of a Prospero-like psychoanalyst. As Tippett explains its message, "We are offered a new lease on life, if for a timid moment we can submit to love, which is all we have left."

Although London critics differed in their reactions to *The Knot Garden*, all of them agreed that it was the most important opera opening in London in years. *The Knot Garden* was revived at Covent Garden two years after its première and was later recorded by Philips Records. When it received its first American production by Robert Gay's Opera Workshop at Northwestern University on February 22, 1974, with Tippett present in the audience, the event marked the first performance of a Tippett opera in the United States.

That February 1974 had brought such a flurry of performances of Tippett's music in the United States, coincident with the composer's presence in the country, that Hubert Saal observed that Tippett might well be the most popular contemporary composer in America at the moment. His apocalyptic Third Symphony (1972) had its American première in Boston with Colin Davis and the Boston Symphony in late February, with soprano Heather Harper singing the concluding blues sequence, and was repeated a week later by the same artists at Lincoln Center's Avery Fisher Hall. With its deliberate quotations from the choral movement of Beethoven's Ninth and its combination of "arrest" and "movement," the Third Symphony represents the composer's attempt "to resolve all over again what is the nature of symphonic music in our modern times." Finally resigned to the warring elements of what William Blake called the "Tyger" and the "Lamb" in human nature, with one or the other constantly in the ascendant, Tippett ended his Third Symphony with the words, "We sense a huge compassionate power to heal, to love."

Sir Michael Tippett is a tall, spare, and angular man, with piercing blue eyes and a thick shock of raven-black hair that has only recently started to turn gray. All interviewers have commented on the extraordinary youthfulness of his appearance, and he himself has said, "I feel physiologically so much younger than my age." He makes his home in a partly Elizabethan, partly Victorian house in the quiet old Wiltshire village of Corsham not far from Bath, whose music festival he directed from 1969 through 1974. His favorite recreations in the past included games of Monopoly with T. S. Eliot or of croquet, and he remains an omnivorous reader. Something of a specialist in music of the English Restoration, he served as coeditor of the *Voices & Keyboard* series, containing works by Henry Purcell and others, and his book *Moving into Aquarius* was published in 1959. He was made a Commander of the British Empire in 1959 and knighted by the Queen in 1966. The American Academy of Arts and Letters elected him an honorary member in 1973.

As much of a dedicated humanist as ever Tippett continues to believe that "art is concerned with man; man is art's sole measure," and to examine in his work the meaning of the world and of man's life in it. "The only truth I shall ever say," he once told Alan Blyth, "was expressed in *A Child of Our Time*: 'I would know my shadow and my light/So shall I at last be whole.' Anybody who can go down that very difficult road, and learn to know his darker side—his shadow—as his light, is approaching the truth."

References

Christian Sci Mon p8+ My 27 '68 por
Guardian p6 Ap 6 '68 por
Newsweek 83:101 F 25 '74 por
Time 85:57 F 12 '65 por
Ewen, David. Composers Since 1900 (1969)
Grove's Dictionary of Music & Musicians (1954)
International Who's Who, 1969-70
Sternfeld, F. W. Music in the Modern Age (1973)
Who's Who, 1973
Who's Who in the World, 1971-72

TOLBERT, WILLIAM R(ICHARD), JR.

May 13, 1913- President of Liberia
Address: Executive Mansion, Monrovia, Liberia

When William R. Tolbert Jr. became President of the Republic of Liberia on July 23, 1971, succeeding the late William V. S. Tubman, he was virtually unknown as a leader, having served for twenty years in the largely ceremonial post of Vice-President. He is the nineteenth chief of state of the small West African nation, which was founded as a settlement for liberated American slaves in 1822 and established as Africa's first independent republic in 1847. President Tolbert's policies are generally in accord with those of his predecessor, whose twenty-seven years of paternalism had brought economic growth and social reform to Liberia, but his administration differs in style and emphasis from that which had prevailed under the "old man." Since taking office, Tolbert has abolished much of the ceremoniousness of the Tubman era and has conducted the government of Liberia on a more businesslike basis. At the same time, he has made rapid strides in weeding out corruption and promoting economic self-sufficiency, democratization, and a more independent foreign policy.

William Richard Tolbert Jr., who is of "Americo-Liberian" stock—a descendant of former American slaves—was born on May 13, 1913 in Bensonville, Montserrado County, Liberia, the older of the two sons of William R. and Charlotte A. (Hoff) Tolbert. In contrast to the impoverished tribal Africans who make up the majority of Liberia's 1,650,000 people, the Americo-Liberians, although comprising only about 3 percent of the population, possess virtually all the wealth and political power. The senior Tolbert, who immigrated to Liberia from South Carolina about 1880, became a prosperous coffee grower and rice farmer. As was customary among Liberia's elite, he had a number of tribal wives. William R. Tolbert Jr. and his brother, Stephen A. Tolbert—who became Liberia's leading entrepreneur and is now Minister of Finance—have an estimated seventy half-brothers and sisters through their father's tribal marriages.

Tolbert received his early education at an elementary school in Bensonville and then went on to Crummell Hall, a high school run by Episcopalians in Clay Ashland, Liberia. That experience seems to have confirmed Tolbert's religiosity and aroused his interest in the various Christian denominations. He completed his education at Liberia College (now the University of Liberia), where he obtained his B.A. degree *summa cum laude* in 1934.

In 1935 Tolbert began his career in government service as a typist with the national treasury. He became government disbursing officer in 1936 and held that position until 1943, while concurrently fulfilling other official duties. A member of the True Whig party—the only political party of any significant power in Liberia—he was elected to the national House of Representatives in 1943, representing his native county of Montserrado. In May 1951 Tolbert became the youngest man in Liberia's history to be elected Vice-President. He was reelected in 1955, 1959, 1963, 1967, and 1971.

Tolbert became Vice-President during a period of virtual one-man rule by President William Vacanarat Shadrach Tubman. An immensely popular President, "Shad" Tubman counted among the achievements of his twenty-seven years in office the fostering of intertribal unity, the granting of the vote to tribesmen and to women, an "open-door" policy that offered investment incentives to foreign businessmen, and a rapid development of natural resources resulting in substantial growth of the Liberian economy. Tubman ruled with an aura of benevolent autocracy that was enhanced by an emphasis on a court-like formality at government functions. As a result of Tubman's authority as President, Tolbert's position as Vice-President was essentially honorary and devoid of power. Although he was ex-officio president of the Senate and potentially Tubman's successor, and occasionally represented him in meetings with foreign statesmen, including United States Vice-President Hubert H. Humphrey and Secretary of State Dean Rusk, he was not authorized under the Constitution to take the President's place as long as the latter held office. Apparently resigned to his subordinate role, Tolbert was praised by Tubman as "a man with a singleness of purpose and deep conviction for justice and fair play and a man of guarded ambition."

About a year before his death, Tubman said of his Vice-President, as quoted in *Ebony* (October 1971): "With a man of such sterling worth and qualities, . . . any man as President would have great contentment of mind, body and spirit that in case of his death, resignation or retirement, the Vice-President could befittingly take on the toga of presidency, and that the nation and its people would be ensured, assured, and in safe and dependable hands." There was never any hint of conflict between the two men, and when Tubman's eldest son, Senator William V. S. Tubman Jr., married one of Tolbert's daughters, the union served to cement the alliance between the two families. Apart from his role in the government, Tolbert had also become owner and operator of a profitable rubber plantation as well as chairman of the board of directors of the Mesurado Group Companies Inc., a large fishing and refrigeration enterprise established by his brother.

When Tubman died on July 23, 1971, Tolbert became acting President. He signaled the change in style that marked his coming to power at his official inauguration into the Presidency, on January 3, 1972 when, defying the formality that had marked the Tubman era, he appeared in an open-necked blue cotton safari shirt. At the inauguration ceremony, at which Mrs. Richard M. Nixon was among the guests, Tolbert reaffirmed his country's friendship with the United States, with which it shared "the pursuit of liberty, dignity, order, and justice," and asserted that his administration would be characterized by "an accent on youth and speed, and on competence and effectiveness."

Exhorting his people to "total involvement in our sustained upward thrust for higher heights," Tolbert launched with flights of rhetoric what was described in the news magazine *Africa* (April 1973) as a "quiet revolution." He dismissed Cabinet members for their corrupt practices, revamped Tubman's cumbersome security apparatus, freed political prisoners, encouraged greater freedom of the press, lowered the voting age to eighteen, sold the luxurious Presidential yacht that had been maintained at a cost of $250,000 a year, and replaced the Presidential Cadillac limousine with a Volkswagen. To ensure that civil servants were earning their salaries, he made early morning surprise visits to government offices. At the same time, he abolished the practice of requiring civil servants to contribute a month's salary each year to the coffers of the True Whig party.

Concerned with the grinding poverty that afflicts much of Liberia's population, Tolbert told residents of a Monrovia slum he visited in December 1971: "I identify myself with your poverty, and together we should work to better our conditions." Following the visit, he launched a campaign to elevate the masses "from mats on the floors to mattresses on every bed." He has introduced a social security fund to expend some $8,000,000 a year for such benefits as unemployment compensation and the construction of schools and medical facilities; launched a campaign to raise funds for the development of Liberia's badly

WILLIAM R. TOLBERT JR.

neglected interior; and, after visiting a penal institution, ordered improved prison conditions. "We don't want a classless society," he has said, as quoted in *Time* (April 23, 1973), "but we must narrow the gulf between the too few who are high and the too many who are low."

Tolbert has expanded on Tubman's policy of promoting greater unity among the tribal and cultural groups of Liberia, and under his program for integrating tribal groups into the national economy and political system, persons of tribal ancestry have made some headway in attaining higher education, political office, and even positions of wealth. Tolbert himself speaks Kpelle, one of the more common of Liberia's twenty-eight tribal languages, and he occasionally gives portions of his speeches in that tongue. He has encouraged tribesmen to purchase lands and to farm privately rather than communally, as had been the custom, in order to reduce the power of chiefs and to stimulate market-oriented farm production, and he has proposed a more democratic process in the election of tribal chiefs.

In trying to further their country's economic growth, President Tolbert and his brother, whom he appointed Finance Minister in 1972, have promoted greater self-sufficiency while continuing to encourage foreign investment under the "open door" policy. Liberia depends for a major part of its revenue on the export of rubber, much of it grown on the 90,000 acres of plantation land leased since 1925 by the Firestone Tire and Rubber Company, and on more recently developed iron mines, which by 1973 had made Liberia the world's third-largest exporter of iron ore. Another major source of Liberia's income derives from the practice of foreign ship owners of registering their vessels under the Liberian "flag of convenience," which according to official records has made Liberia the world's leading maritime power despite the fact that Liberians own only two merchant ships.

Concerned with the preponderance of foreign control of the Liberian economy, and determined to have his countrymen "make an economic life for themselves in their own country," Tolbert has put pressure on foreign companies to hire and train more Africans and has imposed higher income taxes on foreign exporters of iron and rubber. One problem has been the domination of Liberia's retail trade by Lebanese who, in the absence of restraints on the export of dollars, often send their profits back to their home country, rather than invest in Liberian enterprise. But Tolbert does not appear to anticipate taking any drastic measures against foreigners, since their investments have been responsible for Liberia's high rate of economic growth. Instead, President Tolbert is encouraging more Africans to enter business through education and loan programs.

Since Liberia's reliance on food imports has been a constant drain on its economy, Tolbert has been concerned with making the country self-sufficient in agricultural production. A large-scale program to increase yields of rice, palm oil, and other agricultural products was begun in early 1973 under the auspices of Agrimeco, an Israeli-managed government project, and an exploitation of Liberian lumber resources is also under way. Tolbert has emphasized that his government opposes nationalization and is totally committed to the free enterprise system.

In keeping with his promise that Liberia would "waltz to no foreign rhythm of flirtatious expedience" but would "dance instead, with steadfast grace, to the African drums of age-long passion," Tolbert has tried to divest his country of its image as an American "colony." Although he stressed Liberia's "special relationship" with the United States during his state visit to Washington, D.C. in June 1973, he has maintained an independent foreign policy. Unlike Tubman, who generally steered clear of the Communist bloc, Tolbert has established diplomatic relations with the Soviet Union and Czechoslovakia. On his own continent, Tolbert has largely eliminated frictions with the neighboring states of Guinea, Sierra Leone, and the Ivory Coast, and he has become an influential voice in the Organization of African Unity.

An important aspect of Tolbert's public life is his continuing commitment to the Christian religion in Africa and the world. An ordained minister in the Baptist Church, he has served as president of the Liberia Baptist Missionary and Educational Convention. From 1965 to 1970 he was president of the Baptist World Alliance. When asked, after his election at Miami Beach, how it felt to be the first Negro in that position, he remarked: "I haven't given it much thought. You see, we are not really racially conscious in Liberia." In September 1973 he became chief advisor of the All-African Missionaries Evangelistic Union.

In 1936 William R. Tolbert Jr. married Victoria David, the daughter of an associate justice of Liberia's Supreme Court, and they have two sons and six daughters. One of the sons is adopted. Tolbert found the congenitally armless child during an official visit to the interior of Liberia.

Brought into the Tolbert family, he overcame his handicap to the extent that he now holds a position as a clerk. Tolbert's daughter Wokie Rose, a fashion designer, was married to Senator William V. S. Tubman Jr. in 1961. Another daughter, Dr. Wilhelmina Tolbert, is a graduate of McGill University medical school in Canada, while still another, Willy Mae Tolbert, attends the Wharton School of Business at the University of Pennsylvania. Members of his family have accompanied President Tolbert on state visits abroad.

Described as "affable, bespectacled, and scholarly looking," Tolbert is a short, round-faced, stocky and somewhat bald man who looks younger than his sixty years. Nicknamed "Speedy," because of the pace he has set in bringing about governmental reforms, Tolbert has remarked, as quoted in *Time* (April 23, 1973), "If we can manage to speed things up in this country, I don't care what they call me." Tolbert has served as secretary of the board of trustees of the University of Liberia and as board chairman of the Bank of Liberia. He holds a number of decorations. The University of Liberia presented him with an honorary doctor of civil laws degree in 1952 and a doctor of divinity degree in 1966. Tolbert is grand master emeritus of the Masons of Liberia.

References

Atlan 231:14+ Mr '73
Ebony 26:46+O '71 pors
N Y Times p4 Ja 5 '72 por
Time 101:31+ Ap 23 '73 por
Washington Post A p1+ S 20 '71 por
International Who's Who, 1973-74
Reuters News Agency. The New Africans (1967)
Who's Who in the World, 1971-72

TURCOTTE, RON

July 22, 1941- Jockey
Address: b. c/o Aqueduct Race Track, Rockaway Blvd. and 110th Ave., Ozone Park, Queens, New York 11417

Ranking with Manuel Ycaza among top American thoroughbred jockeys is the French-Canadian equestrian Ron Turcotte, who moved to the United States in 1964 and hit the big time by winning the Preakness aboard Tom Rolfe in 1965. Since then Turcotte has guided thousands of mounts to victories worth a total of $1,000,000 annually in purses. Although he is a freelancer on the flats, under contract to no one owner, he is best known for his association with Meadow Stable and its owner, Helen ("Penny") Tweedy, and trainer, Lucien Laurin. From that stable came Riva Ridge, which Turcotte rode to victory in the Kentucky Derby and the Belmont Stakes in 1972, and Secretariat, the celebrated "superhorse" who won the Triple Crown (the Derby, the Preakness and Belmont) with Turcotte aboard in 1973. A self-

effacing, unostentatious man, Turcotte has a
rather low public profile, considering his achievements, but his dedication to hard work, his physical strength, and his ability to come from behind, to stay out in front, and to win close
finishes do not escape the notice of owners, trainers, and other turf insiders.

One of twelve children (nine boys and three
girls) of Mr. and Mrs. Alfred Turcotte, Ron
Turcotte was born in the village of Drummond,
near Grand Falls in the lumber country of New
Brunswick, Canada on July 22, 1941. Several of
his younger brothers are also jockeys: Rudy and
Noel have already begun to make their mark
professionally; Gaetan is on the way up; and
others are expected to follow.

At thirteen Turcotte dropped out of school to
help his father, a logger, provide for the family.
His father had a log-hauling mare named Bess.
"I got to love old Bess . . . ," Turcotte told
Louis Cauz of the Toronto *Globe and Mail* (June
9, 1973). "[With her] I could lumberjack three
cords a day at six dollars a cord. She helped make
a tough job easier, and I would ride her bareback. She was mainly responsible for my going on the racetracks."

When working as a lumberjack Turcotte ate
enormous breakfasts, consisting, typically, of eggs,
pancakes, beans, a variety of meats, and a slab
of dried fatback. "I blew up to 128 pounds,"
Turcotte, who is only five feet one inch tall, has
recalled. "But when I decided to become a rider,
it wasn't too hard to take off." In 1959, when
the lumber camps of New Brunswick were snowbound, Turcotte, tired of cutting lumber anyway,
went to Toronto expecting to find work in construction. What he found instead was the construction industry tied up by a strike. Following
the advice of his Toronto landlady, he set his
sights on becoming a jockey. At Woodbine Racetrack, eighteen miles outside of Toronto, he got
a job walking horses for E. P. Taylor's stable.
Within a year he was doing workout riding, and
in 1961 he became an apprentice jockey.

In 1962 Turcotte posted 180 victories, and the
following year his wins at Fort Erie, Woodbine,
and Old Greenback Downs in Ontario earned him
the Canadian riding championship. In September
1963 he was the top jockey at Laurel Race Track
in Maryland, and in August 1964 he was among
the top jocks at Saratoga in New York State. His
total of 248 victories placed him third among
all jockeys in North America in 1964. Among his
favorite mounts at that time were Northern
Dancer, whom he rode in four of the Dancer's
two-year-old races in Canada, and Tom Rolfe,
whom he guided to victory in the Preakness, to
second place in the Belmont Stakes, and to third
place in the Kentucky Derby in 1965. His other
favorites in the 1960's included Damascus, One
For All, Fanfreluche, Vent du Nord, Gladwin,
and Shuvee.

In the early 1970's Turcotte was the regular
jockey for Rokeby Stable's Summer Guest, the
champion filly of 1971, and for Meadow Stable's
Riva Ridge and Secretariat. At the start of the

RON TURCOTTE

1972 Preakness, Summer Guest, with Turcotte
aboard, hit the gate and was thrown behind
the field. The average jockey might have despaired of winning at that point, or whipped his
horse mercilessly in an effort to make him catch
up with the pack. But not Turcotte. Riding high
off the saddle, he caught up slowly, found an
opening, went through, and zoomed through to
win by four lengths.

Turcotte first rode Riva Ridge on August 2,
1971, when the horse was a two-year-old. Between that date and the end of the year Riva
Ridge won more than half a million dollars in
purses and in 1972, with Turcotte aboard, the
colt won the Kentucky Derby and the Belmont
Stakes. In *Maclean's* (September 1972) Jack
Ludwig described the Derby race at Churchill
Downs: "Turcotte broke from the gate on top
of the field, beat the rail horses to the first turn,
in front by a length and a half, moving easy with
Hold Your Peace close up behind, the space
between them a solid fixed barrier. Once Hold
Your Peace feinted at Riva Ridge, but Turcotte
wasn't having it. Then again. On the third try,
as Hold Your Peace started its move, Turcotte
looked back over his shoulder, gave a tug, and
Riva Ridge took off."

Ludwig went on to observe: "Anybody who
saw Ron Turcotte win the Derby, the Wood
Memorial on Riva Ridge's stablemate, Upper
Case, the Belmont, the Coaching Club or any of
the dozens of stakes races he has already won,
knows that on any given day any owner or trainer
who wants to give his horse a winning chance
must consider the availability of Ron Turcotte.
He has made it to the top with no gimmicks, no
public relations push."

Turcotte first rode Secretariat in that colt's
third start at Saratoga in 1972, when Secretariat
won the Horse of the Year title. With Turcotte
aboard, Secretariat won the Triple Crown the
following year by finishing first in the Kentucky
Derby, the Preakness at Baltimore, and the Belmont Stakes. At Churchill Downs he came from
behind to win in record time, and clockers at

Baltimore insisted that he established a new mark there. (The mark was not official because of a malfunctioning of the electronic timer.) After the win at Belmont, Louis Cauz wrote in the Toronto Globe and Mail (June 11, 1973): "Citation was the last triple Crown winner, in 1948, and it may be another twenty-five years before a horse of Secretariat's majestic prowess and intelligence emerges. Man O' War and Citation are generally considered the greatest thoroughbreds to step on a North American racetrack. Those two horses will now have to share this honor with Secretariat."

Regarding Turcotte's performance in the Belmont Stakes, Cauz wrote: "Turcotte looked over his left shoulder in the stretch to see if anything was coming up on the inside. Nothing. He then peeked at the mutuels board and the teletimer. The fractions were unbelievably fast . . . two-fifths faster than his Derby time. . . . He got down to riding. Secretariat responded. It was the first time that Turcotte had asked him to run. But he did it without showing the colt the whip."

When he failed to win first place in the voting for the Eclipse Award at the end of 1973—the honor went to Laffit Pincay—Turcotte told William H. Rudy of the New York Post (December 28, 1973): "If I live to be 100, there's no way I can duplicate this year. I rode three Eclipse Award champions, I won the Triple Crown, I won the Marlboro, I won the Travers on another three-year-old. It was a good year—but apparently not good enough. . . . But I had three champions—Secretariat, Riva Ridge, and Talking Picture. I won five of the last six classic [Triple Crown] races."

Secretariat was retired to stud in November 1973. At last report, Turcotte was riding some good horses, including Rube the Great and Capital Asset (owned by Mrs. Tweedy), but he missed Secretariat. "In racing," he told Leonard Lewin of the New York Post (July 29, 1974), "you always hope you find another. Horses are like humans, in a sense. Some great ones come along all the time but a horse like Secretariat comes along once in a lifetime, I guess." Lewin commented: "He knows there always is tomorrow and . . . every day manages to take care of itself."

In his Maclean's magazine article Jack Ludwig said of Turcotte: "In the press rooms the turf writers are full of jockey stories, but Turcotte's name almost never comes up. They don't look for him in a race. Several of them call him Turcotty. . . . Ron Turcotte isn't the first Canadian jockey to make it in the big time. Ted Atkinson, Georgie Woolf and the great Johnny Longden were there before him. But Turcotte is different because he hasn't played the Big-time Jock game. 'We're farm people,' he says simply. And he means it." However low his public profile, Turcotte is held in high esteem by trainers, owners, and racing's executives. Chick Lang, who is general manager of the Pimlico Race Track in Maryland where the Preakness is run, has said of him: "There's the most underrated jock in the

business. He's the most dedicated friend the two-dollar bettor has."

Ron and Gaetane Turcotte, who have been married for nine years, live with their four daughters in a home they own on Long Island. Mrs. Turcotte seldom goes to the track to see her husband at work, preferring to stay at home and watch the races on television with her children. According to Turcotte, she regards the racetrack as his "office." Rhetorically, with his typical shy smile on his face, he asked a reporter for the New York Times (June 9, 1973), "If I was a plumber she wouldn't be following me to work, would she?" Turcotte's agent, Joe Schiavone, has called his client "one of the nicest kids around," and others have described Turcotte as "a real family man" who goes to Mass on Sundays and remains always the simple "Canadian farm boy."

A muscular, wiry man, Turcotte maintains his weight at approximately 110 pounds. His normal routine is to rise at 6:00 A.M., breakfast on eggs, bacon, toast, and coffee, and spend the morning exercising horses at Aqueduct before returning home for a light lunch at noon. (His wife plans his meals with calories in mind.) Not interested in night life or, for that matter, socializing in general, he retires between 10:30 and 11:00 P.M. For recreation, the Turcottes periodically go to Canada in their motor camper, to visit relatives and enjoy the wilderness. Ronnie (as his friends call him), who reportedly earns more than $200,000 a year, keeps most of his money in banks. Distrustful of the stock market, he does not invest, except occasionally in real estate.

References

Maclean's 85:78+ S '72
N Y Daily News p99 Mr 28 '73 por
N Y Herald Tribune p29 N 9 '64 por
N Y Post p78 Ap 3 '74 por
Sport 56:91+ S '73
Toronto Globe and Mail p27 My 1 '65 por; p45 Je 9 '73 por
Washington Post D p9 N 5 '71 por

VILLEMURE, GILLES (vil'e-mür zhēl)

May 30, 1940- Hockey player
Address: b. New York Rangers, Madison Square Garden, 4 Pennsylvania Plaza, New York 10001

After a decade-long apprenticeship in hockey's minor leagues, French-Canadian goalie Gilles Villemure in 1970 joined the New York Rangers, for whom he shares goaltending duties with Ed Giacomin. The placid Villemure is among the least colorful of the men currently in the National Hockey League nets, but he is also among the most consistent, and it would be difficult to find a better angle player. His NHL career record as of the beginning of March 1974 was 369 goals allowed in 170 games, for an average of less than two and one-third per game, and fourteen shutouts. Villemure is a two-sport professional: when he is not playing hockey he raises, trains, and races standardbred horses.

Gilles Villemure was born on May 30, 1940 in Three Rivers (Trois-Rivières), an industrial, river-port city located in southern Quebec, Canada at the point where the St. Maurice River empties into the St. Lawrence. Both of his careers germinated in childhood, as he recalled in an interview with Larry Millson of the Toronto *Globe and Mail* (January 20, 1972): "The hockey rink in Trois-Rivières was right across from the race track. I always wanted to drive. It seemed just a question of time."

When he was twenty Villemure obtained his Canadian Trotting Association license and began driving at the track in Trois-Rivières. Meanwhile, having quit high school to pursue a career in hockey, he was playing with the Long Island Ducks of the Eastern Hockey League in Commack, Long Island, New York. A timid young man whose morale was not helped by the moribund spirit of the Long Island team, he played far below his potential with the Ducks. "He was scoffed at by rivals as 'a little boy' and . . . by teammates as 'not much at all . . . ,'" Dick Sorkin recounted in *Newsday* (November 21, 1963). "'The day I make the NHL will be a cold day in hell,' Villemure said during his last season with the Ducks. They were bitter words spoken more out of a disbelief that a man could rise out of Commack than from a disbelief in his own ability."

Watching Villemure play a game with the Ducks, Ranger player-coach Doug Harvey spotted his professional potential. The Rangers signed Villemure and sent him to Vancouver (British Columbia), their farm team in the Western Hockey League, where he won Rookie of the Year honors in 1962-63. The following season he was called up to New York for five games, as a replacement for injured Jacques Plante, and then sent to Baltimore, in the American Hockey League.

Villemure was again in the Vancouver lineup from 1964 until 1966, when he went back to Baltimore for one season. For three years he was with the American Hockey League club in Buffalo, where he won the league's Most Valuable Player award in 1968-69 and 1969-70. In the latter season he registered eight shutouts, just one short of the AHL record. His best goals-against average in minor-league play was 2.25, compiled in 1968-69. His career record in the minors was 1,447 goals allowed in 442 games, for an average of three per game.

During his tenure in Buffalo, Villemure was summoned to New York as a substitute twice, for a total of eight games. In 1970 the Rangers called him up permanently, as alternate for Ed Giacomin, who had been asking for relief. Manager-coach Emile Francis explained the long delay in moving Villemure into the New York lineup: "We were trying to give one guy [Giacomin] experience, and we didn't want Gilles sitting on the bench. I know it was frustrating for him, but we tried to make amends by making him a well-paid hockey player. I discussed it with him, of course. He preferred

GILLES VILLEMURE

to play and get experience. And he kept getting better and better." Villemure told the press that Francis had been right in his procrastination, that he, Villemure, "wasn't ready until this year." He added: "No matter how well you do in the minors, you never really know whether you're good enough to play up here until you've tried it. Naturally I wondered, and I wanted to find out. But I never got discouraged. I never asked to be traded or anything like that. I just bided my time."

Quickly, Villemure became Giacomin's equal. In his first full season in New York, he played in thirty-four games; allowed seventy-eight goals, for an average of 2.29 per game; had four shutouts; and shared the coveted Vezina Trophy, for best goalie in the NHL, with Giacomin. In 1971-72 he and Giacomin each contributed twenty-four victories to the Rangers' most successful season in two decades. Villemure had the best goals-allowed average of his career, 2.08, as New York came within two games of winning the Stanley Cup.

In the Stanley Cup playoffs Villemure played in three games and surrendered only seven goals to the Boston Bruins, the highest scoring team in professional hockey. For the second time he was named to the East All-Star team, and in the 1971-72 All-Star game, as in the 1970-71 encounter between the Eastern and Western divisions of the NHL, no goals were scored against him. His shot blocking was the major factor in the East's coming from behind to defeat the West, 3-2.

"People think Eddie [Giacomin] and I are rivals," Villemure told Nick Seitz of the *Christian Science Monitor* (February 15, 1972). "Actually, we look on our jobs as a cooperative thing. . . . We room together on the road and perk each other up. Ed has been a great help to me." Giacomin taught him how to handle the various shooters and how to clear the puck away from the goal and wrap it around the boards to any Ranger winger shouting for it. Soon the student surpassed the master in many ways, according to Seitz: "Villemure has become better than Giacomin at not leaving his feet and giving the other team a rebound opportunity. . . . A Villemure strong suit is his equanimity of temperament under pressure. Unlike a lot of goalies, he is not deflated by a bad first period. . . . A number of NHL goalies are brilliant as backup men but less effective as number one. Villemure plays the same whatever he does. . . . Whereas a Giacomin believes he must play regularly to be good, Villemure is able to perform irregularly with no apparent loss of ability."

In 1972-73 Villemure allowed seventy-eight goals in thirty-four games, for an average of 2.29. Three of the games were shutouts. The following season two long bouts with influenza and a knee injury limited his play to fifteen games as of early March. At that point his win-loss record for the season was 6-2-3 and his average was 2.68. He had no shutouts. Gilles Villemure is a sandy-haired man five feet eight inches tall and weighing 180 pounds. His habit of standing "tall" in the nets was in large measure developed to compensate for his short stature. According to Emile Francis, Villemure gives opponents as little of the net as possible to shoot at: "Villemure is quick, very quick. He may look nonchalant sometimes. . . . But he does know what he's doing out there all the time and he gives the shooters so little room to shoot at that he makes it look routine. He plays the angles perfectly."

Francis also observes that Villemure has the perfect disposition for the always difficult and sometimes hazardous profession of goaltending: "He's always cool, calm and collected before and after games." Villemure himself told Hugh Delano of the New York Post (May 11, 1972): "Nothing surprises me. I'm the same whether I play or sit on the bench. I'm always relaxed. I'm always ready. I get myself up for games the same way all the time. I have my steak in the afternoon. I take a little walk, then I take a nap."

Villemure lives with his wife and two children in Westbury, Long Island, near Roosevelt Raceway. He drives his standardbreds at Roosevelt as well as in Three Rivers and Montreal. In 1969 alone he earned purse money of $38,058. "It's a helpful activity for a goalie," Villemure has said of his second career. "You have to be thinking all the time, studying the horses and knowing when to make your move. Winning races is a matter of timing, like playing goal. It keeps my reflexes quick. You use your hands a lot. I'm better with my glove hand in goal as a result." Villemure is five feet eight inches tall and weighs 180 pounds. He is that rarity among goalies, a righthanded shooter.

References

Christian Sci Mon p13 D 21 '72
N Y Post p80 My 11 '72; p81 O 1 '74; p68 O 3 '74
N Y Times p52 Ap 25 '72 por
Newsweek p48 O 1 '74
Sports Illus 34:40+ Ja 11 '71 por
White Plains Reporter Dispatch p31 F 11 '74
New York Rangers Yearbook, 1973-74

VOIGHT, JON (voit)

Dec. 29, 1938- Actor
Address: c/o Warner Brothers, Inc., 666 5th Ave., New York 10019

As the Candide-like Texan who becomes a Times Square hustler in Midnight Cowboy, Jon Voight attained stardom in 1969 with his first major film role. Despite his conventionally handsome looks, he has since then sustained his reputation with character roles, including a maniacally capitalistic lieutenant in Catch-22 (1970), an eccentric young anarchist in The Revolutionary (1970), a drab businessman-turned-killer in Deliverance (1972), a gone-to-seed boxer in The All-American Boy (1973), and a liberal white schoolteacher in a backward black community in Conrack (1974). Before appearing in films, Voight was a stage and television actor in New York City.

Jon Voight was born on December 29, 1938 in Yonkers, New York, the second son of Elmer and Barbara (Camp) Voight. Voight is a Czech name, and the actor's grandfather, who lived with the family for many years, was a coal miner both in Czechoslovakia and in Pennsylvania. Elmer Voight, who for many years was a professional golfer at the Sunningdale Golf Club in Westchester County, died in 1973. Voight's older brother, Barry, is a geologist. His younger brother, James Wesley, who has adopted the professional name of Chip Taylor, writes songs, has had his own rock group, and has worked as a record producer. John Voight grew up in Yonkers, attending parochial schools there and in nearby White Plains, where he was a student at Archbishop Stepinac High. As a child, he showed a flair for entertaining people by imitating accents and creating comic characters. He has recalled for interviewers that he inherited his sense of fun and his picaresque imagination from his father, who "used to do routines, Dr. Jekyll and Mr. Hyde, espionage, fairy tales."

At Stepinac High School, Voight was encouraged to try out for school plays by Father Bernard McMahon, the director of dramatics. One of his first roles was that of an eighty-year-old German roué, foreshadowing his later penchant for character roles. After graduating from high school, around 1956, Voight attended Catholic University in Washington, D.C. Intending to be a painter or a scenic designer, he majored in fine arts, but he was again encouraged, this time by Father Gilbert Hartke, head of the drama department, to concentrate on developing his acting abilities. By the time he graduated from college in 1960 he had decided on an acting career.

In 1960 Voight went to New York City, where he studied acting for four years under the well-known teacher Stanford Meisner at the Neighborhood Playhouse, and in private classes. His parents, who had once wanted him to become a professional golfer like his father and who later hoped he would choose a career with "status" like the law, gradually became reconciled to the idea of his being an actor. When he could not find acting jobs they subsidized his income so that he never had to work at odd jobs. Voight made his Broadway debut in the early 1960's when he took over the role of Rolf, the boy who sings "You Are Sixteen" to one of the Von Trapp daughters, in the long-running Rodgers and Hammerstein musical *The Sound of Music*. He serenaded her for six months.

The first New York stage production in which Voight had a major role was the Off-Broadway revival of Arthur Miller's *A View from the Bridge*, which opened at the Sheridan Square Playhouse on January 28, 1965 and ran for 141 performances. Voight played Rodolpho, the Sicilian immigrant who is loved by the niece of the incestuously inclined hero. In March 1967 he costarred with the Greek actress Irene Pappas on Broadway in the role of Steve in Frank Gilroy's adaptation of *Phèdre*, in which the Greek tragedy was transplanted to a modern Italian family. Entitled *That Summer—That Fall*, the play folded after only twelve performances at the Helen Hayes Theatre, but the role of Steve earned some complimentary reviews for Voight and a Theatre World award for him that year.

In between his New York stage assignments Voight worked in summer stock, including two seasons in Winooski, Vermont and one at the San Diego Shakespeare Festival (1965), where he played Romeo in *Romeo and Juliet* and Ariel in *The Tempest*. In 1966 he worked at the innovative Arena Theatre in Washington, D.C. The young actor also appeared on seven television shows, among them the westerns *Cimarron Strip* and *Gunsmoke*. In January 1968 he appeared on educational television in a Public Broadcast Laboratory presentation of a meandering early work by Harold Pinter entitled *The Dwarfs*. "*The Dwarfs* would have dwindled into incoherent babbling save for the contribution of Mr. Voight, who brought to the part of Len a poetic mysticism that sustained the work as a viewing experience," wrote New York *Times* television critic Jack Gould (January 29, 1968). "The virtuosity of his emotional range and his sensitivity to the Pinter lines gave a lyricism to the composition that compensated for the work's discordant construction."

When, in 1966, Voight read James Leo Herlihy's novel, *The Midnight Cowboy*, he knew that when a film was made of it he wanted to play the title role. At first he was rejected by the film's producer Jerome Hellman, but he eventually persuaded the director John Schlesinger that he should have the part. (According to one version, he was helped to get a screen test by Dustin Hoffman, who had been his friend since they met while Hoffman was assistant stage manager of *A View from the Bridge*.) Voight groomed himself for the film meticulously, gaining eighteen pounds and lifting weights to get the proper "chunky, farm boy look," and perfecting a Texas twang with the help of an actor friend from Texas.

A haunting film about two misfits crawling along the sleazy underbelly of New York City, *Midnight Cowboy* (United Artists, 1969) turned

JON VOIGHT

out to be one of the biggest commercial and critical successes of 1969. Voight gathered rave notices for his portrayal of Joe Buck, a naïve young Texas dishwasher who, fancying himself a stud, dresses himself up in a cowboy suit and comes to New York City to offer his services to lonely women. But homosexuals come to make up most of his clientele, and the garish world of Forty-second Street becomes his night kitchen. "Jon Voight . . . draws a remarkable portrait of Joe Buck," wrote Judith Crist (*New York, June 2, 1969*) in a typical accolade. "His achievement is his making Joe, with all his stupidity and silence, a crystal-clear character as well as a replica of all the 42nd Street cowboys; in all his nothingness, the Texan emerges as a presence, vital and individual." The only redeeming factor in Joe's life is the friendship that he forms with Ratso Rizzo, a crippled, tubercular thief played by Dustin Hoffman. "It is a mark of Voight's intelligence that he works against his role's melodramatic tendencies and toward a central human truth," wrote a reviewer for *Time* (May 30, 1969). "In the process, he and Hoffman bring to life one of the least likely and most melancholy love stories in the history of the American film."

Midnight Cowboy brought to Jon Voight the kind of instant stardom that *The Graduate* had conferred on Hoffman only the year before. Both actors were nominated for Academy Awards for their performances in *Midnight Cowboy*, and Voight was also named best actor of the year by the New York Film Critics and the National Society of Film Critics.

Voight had acted in several low-budget films before his star in *Midnight Cowboy*, but only one, *Hour of the Gun* (United Artists, 1967), which starred James Garner and Jason Robards Jr., had been released before 1969. With his reputation made by the Schlesinger film, his previous movies were released. They included *Fearless Frank* (American International, 1969); *Madigan's Millions* (1970); and *Out of It* (United Artists, 1969), an indictment of the emptiness of American suburban life. The last named was the first film by a young director named Paul Williams.

Voight's next assignment after *Midnight Cowboy*, and a complete change of pace, was a supporting role in Mike Nichols' *Catch-22* (Paramount, 1970), which was based on the World War II satiric masterpiece by novelist Joseph Heller. On the screen Voight played the endlessly enterprising Milo Minderbinder, an evil genius whose passion for profit leads him to contract with the Germans to bomb his own base. Critics tended to be polarized into opposite camps in evaluating *Catch-22*, but Voight came in for his fair share of commendation in the somewhat mixed reviews.

Working with Paul Williams once more, Voight portrayed an idealistic young student who becomes radicalized in *The Revolutionary* (United Artists, 1970). The movie failed to get much attention from audiences, who mostly ignored it, but it drew an admiring review from the New York *Times*'s influential Vincent Canby, who wrote on July 16, 1970: " 'A' as played by Jon Voight mostly in granny specs and a greasy raincoat, with a crooked walk that he may have borrowed from one of Laurence Olivier's more outrageous roles, is absolutely marvelous. Like Voight, *The Revolutionary* . . . is full of character, decency, humor, and tact, a very friendly movie about the evolution of an anarchist."

Based on James Dickey's best-selling novel, *Deliverance* (Warner Brothers, 1972) follows the harrowing weekend of four Atlanta businessmen, who go on a canoe trip through the wilds of northern Georgia and end up fighting the treacherous waters and two sinister, rifle-armed mountain men. In the film Voight played the pivotal role of Ed Gentry, a decent, mild-mannered man who is forced to kill so that he and his companions may survive. Voight performed nearly all of his own stunts for the film, which required his learning how to ride a canoe in white waters, shoot a bow and arrow, and scale a sheer cliff. Some critics felt that Voight, perhaps because of John Boorman's direction, failed to give a performance that went beyond what one called "popeyed, cartoonlike facial contortions in response to the murders and rape he witnesses." Others were more admiring. Judith Crist, for example, wrote in *New York* (July 31, 1972), "As in *Midnight Cowboy*, Voight proves himself an internal performer, his squareness, his secret yearning for machismo, his self-horror at his acceptance of instinctual self-preservation—all come in emanations, by implication and suggestion."

Late in 1973 Warner Brothers released *The All-American Boy*, the first directorial effort of screenwriter Charles Eastman. Made in 1970, the film was judged unsuitable for release for three years, until Voight reportedly sank several thousand dollars into it for new editing. In the film Voight plays a smalltown boxer who fails to measure up to the hopes that others have invested in him. Few critics praised the film, but Voight told one reviewer who was enthusiastic about it, Bernard Drew of the White Plains *Reporter Dispatch*

(November 6, 1973), "I'm very proud of it. . . . I don't think I've ever been prouder of anything I've ever worked in. What people will think of it is something else. . . . Up until three months ago, the film had no chance. . . . Now, at least, it will be seen and Charles [Eastman] will have his chance, and that's the important thing. Me, I kept on working, but he didn't."

Directed by Martin Ritt of *Sounder* fame, and based on Pat Conroy's book, *The Water is Wide*, Voight's later film, *Conrack*, was released early in 1974. A *Variety* (February 20, 1974) previewer found it to be a sentimental and somewhat condescending but well-constructed story about an idealistic young Southern schoolteacher trying to cope with his deprived and retarded black charges on an island off the coast of South Carolina. "At the outset he [Voight] seems strained in a role demanding charm as much as talent, but he soon compensates for this lack through graceful delivery of baroque dialogue and clear empathy with the astonishingly talented group of black students guided by Ritt," wrote the *Variety* critic. In *The Odessa File* (Columbia, 1974), based on Frederick Forsythe's best-selling novel with the same title, Voight was cast as a German journalist who doggedly pursues a World War II war criminal. Critical reviews of the suspense thriller were mixed. While developing his film career, Voight has not completely neglected the theatre, and in 1973 he played Stanley Kowalski to Faye Dunaway's Blanche DuBois in a Los Angeles Center Theatre Group production of *A Streetcar Named Desire*. Comparing his interpretation with that of Marlon Brando, the critics were disappointed. "I saw different things in the role," Voight explained, as quoted in the *National Observer* (May 25, 1974). "Brando saw it as more narcissistic than I did. For me, Stanley's violence was born out of fear."

Jon Voight has been described by interviewers as a decent, serious-minded, and well-liked actor, with a diffident, self-questioning manner. Blond and blue-eyed, he has a baby face that makes him look younger than his years. Six feet three inches tall, he normally weighs a lean and muscular 190 pounds, although he has gained weight for several of his film roles. During the early 1960's he married Lauri Peters, whom he met while they both were in the cast of *The Sound of Music*. Since December 12, 1971 he has been married to Marcheline Bertrand, a former model, and the couple lives in a Tudor style house in the Brentwood section of Los Angeles with their son James Haven. A pacifist, Voight is a member of Jane Fonda's Entertainment People for Peace and Freedom. Although he was brought up a Roman Catholic, he no longer considers himself a member of any organized religion. A fan of the comedies of Laurel and Hardy, W. C. Fields, and the Marx Brothers, Voight has expressed the longing to make an old-fashioned comedy. In the meantime he contents himself with the comic and fantastic characters that he has created in a series of unpublished fables for children that he has written and illustrated.

References

Esquire 77:117+ Ja '72 por
Life 73:44+ S 15 '72 pors
N Y Post p15 Ag 19 '72 pors; p44 N 4 '72
    por
Newsday A p48 Je 6 '69 por
White Plains Reporter Dispatch p11 N 6
    '73 por
International Motion Picture Almanac
    (1973)
Reed, Rex. Conversations in the Raw
    (1969)

VON FRISCH, KARL *See* Frisch, Karl von

WEICKER, LOWELL P(ALMER), JR. (wĭ-ker)

May 16, 1931- United States Senator from
Connecticut
Address: b. 342 Old Senate Office Building,
Washington, D.C.; h. Round Hill Road, Green-
wich, Conn. 06830

LOWELL P. WEICKER JR.

Once an unknown freshman legislator, the junior
member of the former Senate Select Committee on Presidential Campaign Activities, Senator
Lowell P. Weicker Jr., quickly established a reputation as one of the ablest and toughest ques-
tioners on the investigative panel looking into
Watergate. Considered a predictable Republican
voter, the senator surprised party leaders by maintaining a defiantly independent course during the
committee hearings.

After listening to several weeks of testimony,
an outraged Weicker read into the record of the
nationally televised hearings a list of seventeen
"acts proven or admitted" by the executive branch,
including burglary, breaking and entering, perjury, and obstruction of a criminal investigation.
A maverick idealist with absolute faith in "America as advertised," Weicker refuses to accept the
"barroom myth" that politics is, by its nature, a
dirty business. "Political espionage, surveillance
and disruption . . . doesn't go on all the time
or even one-hundredth of the time," Weicker
wrote in an opinion piece for the April 16, 1973
edition of the New York *Times.* He warned, however, that if the Senate hearings failed "to arouse
America's basic honesty and idealism, then the
odious tactics . . . will *de facto* become the rules
for American elections."

The second son of Lowell P. Weicker and the
former Mary Bickford Hastings, Lowell Palmer
Weicker, Jr. was born on May 16, 1931 in Paris,
France. His father was manager of foreign operations and later president of the pharmaceutical
house of E. R. Squibb & Sons. His German-born
paternal grandfather, Theodore, was a manufacturing chemist who acquired a controlling interest
in the Squibb firm in 1904 and served as its
executive vice-president and board chairman until
his death in 1940. The Weicker children grew up
on Park Avenue in New York City, and spent
their summers in Oyster Bay, Long Island. Ac-

customed to affluence, Lowell P. Weicker Jr., according to one Washington observer, developed
"that utter confidence that seems to come with
absolute economic self-sufficiency." Introduced to
campaigning by his politically active mother, five-
year-old Lowell Weicker distributed Alf Landon
buttons during the Presidential campaign of 1936.
A few years later he enacted the role of Franklin Delano Roosevelt in a mock election at the
private Buckley School in Manhattan. "I looked
upon politicians as I looked upon baseball and
hockey players," Weicker recalled to James M.
Perry in an interview for the *National Observer*
(April 7, 1973). "They were my idols."

After graduating from exclusive Lawrenceville
School in 1949, Weicker enrolled at Yale University where he majored in political science. He
obtained a B.A. degree in 1953. At Yale, he
played polo and rowed on the junior varsity crew.
An active member of the local Republican youth
organization, he joined the Political Union, the
campus debating society. "I belonged to the Bull
Moosers," Weicker recalled for the New York *Post* (October
2, 1970). "In my first or second debate I got
involved with [William F.] Buckley. I broke in
pretty fast." Interrupting his academic career,
Weicker served as a first lieutenant in the United
States Army from 1953 to 1955. Returning to
civilian life, he entered the University of Virginia
School of Law, which granted him an LL.B. degree in 1958.

Admitted to the Connecticut bar in 1960, Weicker became a founding member of a Greenwich
law firm and practised for several years before
turning his attention to a political career. In his
first campaign, in 1962, he was elected to the
Connecticut state assembly by a comfortable margin. He was reelected in 1964 and 1966. Representing Greenwich, Weicker led the legislative
defense of residential zoning and acted as legislative consultant to the Connecticut Transportation Authority and as secretary to the Connecticut Tax Study Commission. At the same time he
served as Greenwich's First Selectman, the equiv-

alent of mayor. One of the reasons for Weicker's popularity as a city official was the fact that he managed to keep the local tax rate among the lowest in the state.

In 1967, nearly a year before the election, Weicker announced his intention to challenge incumbent Congressman Donald J. Irwin, a Democrat who had represented Connecticut's Fourth Congressional District since 1964. So tireless and enthusiastic a campaigner that he lost thirty-five pounds during the campaign, Weicker blanketed the district and individually contacted as many voters as possible. Responding to the public's growing dissatisfaction with the Johnson administration's military policy in Southeast Asia, Weicker condemned Irwin's hawkish position and urged an immediate bombing halt in Vietnam. With 52 percent of the vote, the largest plurality in twelve years, Weicker defeated Irwin and a third peace party contender, Morris Earle, by 9,026 votes.

In his first year in Congress, Weicker won an almost unprecedented victory for a freshman legislator. He drafted an amendment to the Housing and Urban Development Act of 1969 stipulating that urban renewal plans must include provisions for the replacement of demolished housing units on a one-for-one basis. With bipartisan support, the bill passed the House 116 to 92 and was signed into law by President Richard Nixon on December 24, 1969. During his term in the House, Weicker also submitted legislation to increase Social Security benefits, to require full financial accounting from high governmental officials, to provide federal funds for a National College of Ecological and Environmental Studies, and to safeguard the health of animals during airplane flights.

Named to the House GOP task force on transportation shortly after the Ninety-first Congress convened in January 1969, Weicker chaired the subcommittee on ground transportation and sponsored the emergency Connecticut Transportation Act that kept the New Haven Railroad running until it merged with the Penn Central. The following year he introduced a bill authorizing a governmental study to determine the feasibility of establishing a nationally coordinated transportation system. On other domestic issues, he approved the right of eighteen-year-olds to vote, the equal rights amendment prohibiting sex discrimination, and the omnibus "D.C. crime bill" that included the controversial "no-knock" entry provision. A vocal advocate of President Nixon's "Vietnamization" program, Weicker supported the American invasion of Cambodia during an angry floor debate and insisted that "the policy of this administration is a policy of withdrawal." Reflecting his unpredictable voting behavior, the liberal Americans for Democratic Action rated him at 40 percent and the conservative Americans for Constitutional Action at 41 percent.

Having served only one term in the House, Weicker decided to run for the Senate seat held by retiring Senator Thomas J. Dodd, even though it meant facing his eighth election in eight years. "I either wanted to make it or get out," he explained to an interviewer for the Ralph Nader Congress Project. Weicker was opposed in the first statewide primary in Connecticut history by state senator John Lupton, a conservative Republican. In reply to Lupton's charges that he voted more like a "liberal Democrat" than a Republican, Weicker defended his record and assured the crowds at political rallies that although he "always believed we had a great President . . . ," he was "not a rubber stamp." Endorsed by 70 percent of the Republican state convention delegates, Weicker defeated Lupton by more than 25,000 votes. In the three-way general election in November, Weicker received 41.7 percent of the votes cast, defeating the Democratic contender Joseph D. Duffey, and the independent challenger, former Senator Dodd.

By his own estimation, during his first two years in office Weicker spent most of his time "representing Connecticut." To maintain close contact with his constituents, the Senator established regular weekend hours at his Connecticut office, arranged consultations with local civic leaders, and wrote a weekly column that appeared in newspapers throughout the state. On the Senate floor he continued to push for more generous federal funding of public transportation systems. As a stopgap solution to the nation's "creeping" transportation problems, Weicker proposed increased funds for AMTRAK and the diversion of moneys from the highway trust fund to mass transit construction projects. A member of the Aeronautical and Space Sciences Committee, he vigorously defended NASA's budget requests and cited the beneficial by-products of the space program. Although a party loyalist who has generally supported Nixon's "enormously adventuresome and innovative" foreign policy, he disagreed with Nixon's decision to mine Haiphong Harbor in May 1972, contending that "this reaction cares not a whit for either North . . . or South Vietnamese." Furthermore, he approved the Case-Church amendment cutting off funds for the war and in October 1973 voted with the majority to limit the President's war-making powers.

Noting that "every major scandal in public office over the past twenty years was uncovered by the press," Weicker introduced legislation to safeguard journalists' sources. In a Senate speech on January 11, 1973 he maintained that the bill, designed "to protect a constitutional right we all have in the free flow of news," was "not for newsmen" but "for the American public." The proposed law guaranteed absolute immunity from forced disclosure before grand juries and other investigative bodies and limited immunity before open courts trying criminal cases. To explain the importance of such a bill to the public, Weicker is writing an examination of recent governmental threats to press freedom, in collaboration with Bernie Yudian, an editorial writer for the Greenwich, Connecticut daily newspaper, *Time*. Commissioned by Doubleday, the book is tentatively titled "The Chilling Effect."

As a member of the Republican Senatorial Campaign Committee, Weicker was appalled by the rampant political corruption of the 1972 Presidential campaign. He was particularly exercised by the apparent misuse of enormous sums of money extorted from corporations by the Committee to Reelect the President, in violation of federal election laws. On a campaign swing through Connecticut in October 1972, Weicker told the Enfield Teachers Association, "It's the Democrats who are the most intellectually dishonest, and . . . the Republicans who in their actual deeds are the most dishonest." Anxious to restore honesty to the political process, Weicker submitted a federal election reform act to the Senate on March 13, 1973. The bill restricted campaign contributions and expenditures to the election year, limited each candidate to one political committee, eliminated the collection of "laundered" funds, and required complete disclosure of campaign costs before the election. Fines levied as penalties for violations of the campaign law would be used to publicize the infractions.

When the Senate voted unanimously to establish a bipartisan seven-member Select Committee on Presidential Campaign Activities, Weicker volunteered his services. "I'm a professional politician," he explained at a news conference in late March 1973. "Because of things like Watergate, people have lost faith in politicians, and I want to see that changed. The only thing that will convince them to respect politicians is to bring dirty business like the Watergate out in the open." One of the few Republicans to denounce White House chief of staff H. R. Haldeman publicly before the Senate committee investigations began, Weicker was determined to pursue a nonpartisan course. In a statement at the opening session of the hearings, chaired by Senator Sam J. Ervin, Weicker told a nationwide television audience that the "gut question" before the committee was "not one of individual guilt or innocence" but "how much truth do we want. . . . The story to come has its significance not in the acts of men breaking, entering and bugging the Watergate, but in the acts of men who almost stole America."

Relying on an indefatigable team of independent legal researchers, Weicker conducted a separate investigation of the Watergate break-in along with related political scandals and released the results of his inquiry to the full Senate committee. His staff uncovered dozens of incriminating documents, including evidence that United States military agents had spied on politically active Americans in Europe; proof that one phase of the Nixon domestic intelligence plan, originally vetoed by J. Edgar Hoover, the director of the Federal Bureau of Investigation, had been put into effect; and several damning Haldeman memoranda suggesting that the White House not only approved but also encouraged staged anti-Nixon demonstrations to elicit underdog sympathy from the voters. "This type of business," Weicker charged, "is a disgrace."

In an emotional speech at the June 28, 1973 meeting of the Ervin committee, an angry Senator Weicker, the victim of an attempted White House "smear" campaign, warned: "There are going to be no more threats, no intimidation, no innuendo, no working through the press to . . . destroy the credibility of individuals." Apologizing to his colleagues for his "partisan moment," Weicker assured the public that "Republicans do not cover up . . . , do not . . . threaten, do not commit illegal acts. And, God knows, Republicans don't view their opponents as enemies to be harassed." Spectators in the gallery responded with a long and loud ovation.

Although his outspokenness antagonized some Republican regulars, Weicker enjoyed rapidly increasing popularity among the voters. According to a Louis Harris poll taken in August 1973, 45 percent of those questioned rated Weicker's conduct of the Watergate investigations as "good" or "excellent," while 18 percent evaluated his performance as "only fair" or "poor." His widespread popularity and telegenic appearance prompted speculation of a possible 1976 Presidential bid, but Weicker denied rumors of Presidential ambitions to Ralph Blumenfeld in an interview for a New York *Post* (July 7, 1973) profile. "They'll have to find someone who's willing to give 100 percent of his time," Weicker explained. "I like playing tennis and softball with my sons, and hockey with my family. The President . . . has to give 100 percent of himself."

Senator Weicker had repeatedly urged the Nixon administration to formulate a national policy that is "pro-democracy"—one that emphasizes the positive aspects of a representative form of government rather than military might. "If democracy is to be a champion, then we have to have more than superiority of arms," Weicker reasoned, as quoted by George Douth in his *Leaders in Profile* (1972). "We have to have superiority of morals." One of the most important effects of the Watergate revelations, in Weicker's judgment, was the "shift of power" from the executive to the legislative branch of government. Appearing on the August 12, 1973 edition of CBS-TV's *Face the Nation*, the Senator predicted that the return to a constitutional participatory democracy would have "a profound effect on the laws that are passed. It's going to be a long time before anybody tries these kinds of stunts again."

The tallest of all the Senators, Lowell Weicker Jr. stands six feet six inches tall. A hefty, broad-shouldered man with graying brown hair, he keeps fit and maintains his weight at 218 pounds by following a daily regimen of early morning exercises and by playing tennis, polo, and baseball. Since his election to the House, he has played in the annual Congressional baseball game as a member of the Republican team. Shunning the Washington cocktail party circuit, Weicker often invites members of his staff for dinner and an evening of bridge or Monopoly at his Arlington, Virginia apartment. An accomplished cook, he usually prepares the food himself. "I think I make the best crepe suzettes in Washington, D.C.," he once boasted in a press interview.

On June 13, 1953 Lowell Weicker Jr. married
the former Marie Louise Godfrey. They have two
sons, Scot Bickford and Gray Godfrey. They are
legal guardians of Bryan Bianchi, a boy whom
the Weickers have been caring for since the death
of his parents. The family lives in a weathered
stone farmhouse set on a ten-acre estate in Greenwich, Connecticut, with their horses, chickens,
donkey, and several dogs.

The Senator has declined several invitations to
White House social functions and, shortly before
the Watergate hearings began, refused to attend
President Nixon's "peace with honor" reception
for legislators who had supported the administration's war policy. "[The invitation] carried with
it the implication that those who weren't invited
were not for peace, or were for peace with dis-
honor," Weicker explained to Ralph Blumenfeld.
"I damn near climbed the wall. I felt deeply offended. I didn't go."

References

N Y Post p20 Jl 7 '73 por; p39 O 2 '73 por
N Y Times p23 Ag 13 '70 por; p44 Ap 29
    '73 por
Nat Observer p5 Ap 7 '73 por
Washington Post H p1 Ap 12 '73 por
Douth, George. Leaders in Profile (1972)
Who's Who in America, 1972-73
Who's Who in American Politics, 1973-
    1974

WELD, TUESDAY

Aug. 27, 1943- Film actress
Address: c/o William Morris Agency, 151 El
Camino, Beverly Hills, Calif. 90212

Long dismissed as a teen-age sex kitten who
purred and pouted her way through films like
Rock, Rock, Rock and *Sex Kittens Go to College*,
Tuesday Weld has in recent years emerged as
a serious actress and a genuine cult figure. Although none of her films has scored commercially,
critics have acclaimed her portrayal of teen-age
Lolitas and troubled child-women in such movies
as *Soldier in the Rain*, *Pretty Poison*, *I Walk the
Line*, and *Play It as It Lays*. A professional model
at the age of three and later a child actress on
New York City television, Miss Weld has been
acting in Hollywood films since 1958, when she
was fifteen.

The youngest child of Lathrop Motley Weld,
a former investment broker, and Aileen (Ker)
Weld, an artists' model, Tuesday Weld was born
Susan Ker Weld on August 27, 1943 at 1:20 A.M.
in a New York City Salvation Army hospital. Her
father, who had been something of a playboy, was
the black sheep of a wealthy and socially prominent New England family. Her mother, the
daughter of British illustrator Balfour Ker, was
his fourth wife. Tuesday has a sister, Sally (Mrs.
Howard Cooper), eight years her senior, and a
brother, David, who is six years older.

There are several stories about how Tuesday
came by her unusual first name. It was not because she was born on that day of the week; she
was in fact born on Friday. The most prevalent
version is that Tuesday was an outgrowth of her
childhood nickname, "Too-too" or "Tu-tu." In
any case, she was called Tuesday from early
childhood, and on October 19, 1959 she had her
first name legally changed from Susan to Tuesday
in a Los Angeles court.

When Tuesday was three years old her father
died of a heart ailment, leaving the family de-
stitute. "My father's family . . . offered to take us
kids and pay for our education, on the condition
that Mama never see us again," Miss Weld told
Guy Flatley of the New York *Times* (November
7, 1971). "Mama was an orphan who had come
here from London, but so far as my father's family was concerned, she was strictly from the gut-
ter. I have to give Mama credit—she refused to
give us up."

Following the father's death, Tuesday's family
lived in a $20-a-month cold water flat in a slum
tenement on Manhattan's East Side. Mrs. Weld
worked sporadically as a sales clerk, all the while
encouraging her three children to become child
models. Her brother and sister resisted, but Tuesday succumbed to her mother's pressures and, at
the age of three, began her childhood career as
a fashion and catalogue model.

Miss Weld's memories of her early years are
bitter. The pressure of auditions, the hot lights,
and the fear of failure drove the child into a shell
of shyness. In her interviews of recent years she
has blamed her mother for her childhood unhappiness. "I became the supporter of the family,
and I had to take my father's place in many,
many ways," she told Guy Flatley of the New
York *Times*. "I was expected to make up for
everything that had ever gone wrong in Mama's
life. She became obsessed with me, pouring out
all her pent-up love—her *alleged* love—on me, and
it's been heavy on my shoulders ever since."

When Tuesday was around nine she had what
she has described as a nervous breakdown, and
her mother moved the family to Fort Lauderdale,
Florida. During the two years they lived there,
Tuesday attended public school. When their
money ran out, Tuesday and her mother returned
to New York, leaving the two older children behind with friends. In New York she resumed
modeling, and began taking drama and dance lessons. By the time she was twelve she was appearing regularly on the covers of magazines and performing child roles on a dozen different television
programs, including *Playhouse 90*, *Kraft Theatre*,
Alcoa Theatre, and *Climax*. She was rejected,
however, when she tried out for the lead in the
Broadway play *A Certain Smile* on the grounds
that she was too young.

Although she succeeded in her new acting
career, Tuesday Weld continued to be emotionally troubled. She has said that she began drinking heavily at the age of ten and at twelve made
the first of several attempts at suicide. "A bottle

of aspirin, a bottle of sleeping pills, and a bottle of gin. I was sure that would do the trick," she told Guy Flatley, "but Mama came in and found me. I was in a coma for a long time and I lost my hearing, my vision and several other things."

Because she began working at such an early age, Tuesday Weld obtained only a haphazard education. Apart from the schooling that she received in Florida, it consisted of nominal enrollment at several New York schools, including the Professional Children's School. When she was working on jobs, she was excused from school attendance, and when she was not working, according to what she has told reporters, she would tell her mother she was going to school and then head for Greenwich Village to get drunk. She maintains that she never learned to read until she was thirteen.

In 1956 the Huntington Hartford Agency arranged for her to audition for the lead role in a low-budget, teen-age rock 'n' roll film entitled Rock, Rock, Rock (Vanguard, 1956). Then thirteen, Tuesday Weld was chosen from among 300 girls to play what a Time reporter (May 15, 1972) described as "the archetypal nymphet, Shirley Temple with a leer." She was paid $400 for the film, which was shot in nine days in the Bronx. The following year she was hired by Elia Kazan to understudy two leading roles in William Inge's The Dark At the Top of the Stairs, and she appeared in the Broadway production for one week when one of the principals became ill. Shortly afterward she was almost admitted to the Actors' Studio, but was turned away when it was discovered she was not eighteen.

After Tuesday's failure to get into the Actors' Studio, her mother brought her to Hollywood, where she appeared on the Matinee Theatre television program in April 1958. When she had finished her stint on the TV program her agent took her to Twentieth Century-Fox to meet Leo McCarey, who was producing and directing Rally Round the Flag, Boys! (1958), which was based on Max Shulman's novel and starred Paul Newman and Joanne Woodward. Without even bothering to go through the formalities of a screen test McCarey signed Tuesday on the spot for the part of the sexy young babysitter, Comfort Goodpasture.

On the strength of her role in the McCarey film, Tuesday Weld was signed by Paramount to play Danny Kaye's crippled daughter in The Five Pennies (1959), a film based on the life of band leader Red Nichols. Next Fox cast her in a featured role in its television series, The Many Loves of Dobie Gillis, which starred Dwayne Hickman. As Thalia Menninger, a teen-age golddigger, she played one of Dobie's girl friends. A few months after the show premièred on CBS in September 1959, however, she was dropped because a sponsor thought that she was too sexy for a family-oriented show.

Although it may have spelled her doom on family television, Tuesday Weld's special brand of pubescent sex appeal brought her a string of

TUESDAY WELD

teeny-bopper roles in Because They're Young (Columbia, 1960), a musical starring Dick Clark as a high school teacher; High Time (Twentieth Century-Fox, 1960), in which Bing Crosby went back to college; Sex Kittens Go to College (Allied Artists, 1960); and The Private Lives of Adam and Eve (Universal, 1961). In Return to Peyton Place (Twentieth Century-Fox, 1961), Miss Weld portrayed Selena, the girl who was raped by her brutal stepfather. She played another troubled teen-ager, this time an unwed mother, in Wild in the Country (Twentieth Century-Fox, 1961), starring Elvis Presley. Her next film was Bachelor Flat (Twentieth Century-Fox, 1962), a mindless romp in which she played Terry-Thomas' luscious stepdaughter.

By late 1963 Miss Weld, nineteen years old and under contract to Twentieth Century-Fox for $35,000 a film, had appeared in ten movies and more than a hundred television programs. Ballyhooed as the successor to Marilyn Monroe, she had been subjected to media exploitation ever since she had arrived in Hollywood at the age of fourteen. Her response had been to shock the film capital's reporters and gossip columnists by showing up barefoot for interviews, making no secret of her drinking, moving out of her mother's home at sixteen, and flaunting her affairs with men often many years older than she. (Among the men whose names were linked romantically with hers were John Ireland, Frank Sinatra, Raymond Burr, Tab Hunter, Elvis Presley, Albert Finney, John Barrymore Jr., Terence Stamp, and George Hamilton.) As a Time reporter (May 15, 1972) commented years later, "Actually, Tuesday's sins—odd clothing, bare feet and open love affairs—would have seemed quite normal a decade later. Her chief offense was to be hip too soon."

In contrast to the precocious worldliness of her private life, Tuesday Weld found herself strictly supervised during her working hours by the Los Angeles Welfare Department. Unlike New York, where she had been largely left alone, California had strict child labor laws and required both that she attend school and be chaperoned on the movie set by a welfare worker until she reached eighteen. She has recalled that the worker on the set guarded her zealously, forbidding her to smoke and chasing off any male who so much as put his arm around her. When she was not working, she attended the Hollywood Professional School. At work she was provided with a tutor and a tiny cardboard booth in which to study between takes. "While they were setting up for the next shot, everyone else would be goofing off, but not little Tuesday," the actress recalled to Margaret Ronan of *Senior Scholastic* (December 13, 1971). "That was cram time with the books, and just when a cohesive thought might get together, the director would call for another take. The only way I kept from really coming apart was to pretend my schoolwork was another role I had to learn—another film I was in."

In 1963 Tuesday Weld appeared in *Soldier in the Rain* (Allied Artists) with Steve McQueen and Jackie Gleason. It was in that bittersweet comedy about two Army buddies that she first attracted the serious attention of critics, who praised her sensitive portrayal of Jackie Gleason's slow-witted girl friend. Judith Crist of the New York *Herald Tribune* (November 28, 1963), for example, called her "a lovely blonde who portrays a teen-age submoron to perfection." In the gambling story, *The Cincinnati Kid* (MGM, 1965), Miss Weld was cast as Steve McQueen's hillbilly girlfriend, and despite the relatively minor nature of the part she attracted generally good reviews. The critics, however, were less taken with both Miss Weld and her next film, *I'll Take Sweden* (United Artists, 1965), a light-weight comedy in which she costarred as Bob Hope's boy-crazy daughter.

The following year Miss Weld starred in George Axelrod's spoof of the beach-party genre, *Lord Love a Duck* (United Artists, 1966), portraying a shallow and ambitious high school beauty who finds herself in the improbable position of having her every wish granted by a youthful Svengali played by Roddy McDowall. "The best thing about the movie is its display of Tuesday Weld not only as a teen-age Lolita of unsurpassed loveliness but also as an actress of unexpected range," wrote Judith Crist in her New York *Herald Tribune* review (February 22, 1966). In 1967 Miss Weld won more critical acclaim when she played Abigail in David Susskind's CBS-TV production of Arthur Miller's *The Crucible*.

In *Pretty Poison* (Twentieth Century-Fox, 1968), a taut chiller about two small-town young people egging each other on to progressively more lethal acts of corruption, Tuesday Weld starred opposite Anthony Perkins. "Tuesday Weld again demonstrates that, with good material and good directing, she has an uncommon flair for roles of curdled innocence," wrote the reviewer for *Time* (November 22, 1968). For her portrayal she was voted first runner-up for the New York Film Critics Circle Award as best actress of the year.

I Walk the Line (Columbia, 1970) presented Miss Weld as a Southern mountain girl who seduces the local sheriff (Gregory Peck) so that he will not shut down her father's illegal whiskey still. "Miss Weld is striking as the moonshiner's daughter, capturing just the right accent and qualities of late teen-age sensuality, amorality and dumb innocence to make her a fatal attraction for an older married man," wrote the reviewer for *Variety* (October 14, 1970).

In *A Safe Place* (Columbia, 1971) Tuesday Weld starred as a disturbed young woman who retreats emotionally into her past. She has told reporters that the part was "written for me and about me" by her friend Henry Jaglom, who also directed. When the film, which had supporting roles by Orson Welles and Jack Nicholson, was screened at the 1971 New York Film Festival, it drew a wildly emotional response of boos and scattered fervent applause from the audience. Miss Weld, in the audience, reportedly became so incensed that she threw something at one of her more vocal critics. Most reviewers found *A Safe Place* self-consciously pretentious and arty, and virtually incoherent. Vincent Canby of the New York *Times* (October 16, 1971), for example, wrote that although Miss Weld was "enchanting to watch," when she opened her mouth what came out sounded like "an amalgam of Chinese fortune cookie and Sir James M. Barrie."

Based on a novel by Joan Didion and directed by Frank Perry, *Play It As It Lays* (Universal, 1972), Miss Weld's latest film, brought her the Best Actress Award at the Venice Film Festival. With a vacuous Hollywood wasteland as its background, the film features Miss Weld as a former model and actress nearing thirty who ends up in a sanitarium after the breakup of her marriage, an abortion, and the suicide of her best friend. Critics were sharply divided in their reaction to the film and its star. "Weld is not only sexy but eloquent in what she doesn't say with words," wrote Joseph Gelmis in *Newsday* (Ocotber 30, 1972). "She reminds me of a less verbal Jane Fonda, more like early Brando—implying experiences and knowledge that can't be conveyed by speech." But Pauline Kael of the *New Yorker* (November 11, 1972) found Tuesday Weld's performance "limited" and "mannered" and went on to complain, "She doesn't use her body anymore . . . she does everything with her face, mainly with her mouth—there are a lot of puckers. With her Alice in Wonderland forehead and her calm, wide eyes, she's like a great pumpkin-headed doll, and she doesn't express pain—just a beautiful blobby numbness that suggests childlike abstraction as much as suffering."

Despite the critical praise that Tuesday Weld has received in recent years, none of her films has been a box office success. She acknowledges that this is at least partly her own fault, for she has turned down starring roles in such major films as *Lolita*, *Bonnie and Clyde*, *Bob & Carol & Ted & Alice*, *Cactus Flower*, and *True Grit*. "I may be self-destructive, but I like taking chances with movies," she told Guy Flatley. "I like challenges, and I also like the particular position I've been in all these years, with people wanting to save me from the awful films I've been in. I'm happy being a legend. I think the Tuesday Weld cult is a very nice thing." In 1971 the cultists held a Tuesday Weld Film Festival at the Eighth Street Playhouse in New York City.

In October 1965 Tuesday Weld married Claude Harz, a writer. By that marriage, which ended in divorce in 1971, she has one daughter, Natasha. Blonde and with eyes that seem to vary in color from green to blue to brown to gray, the actress is about five feet five inches tall and weighs 118 pounds. During the 1960's she granted few interviews, because the lurid publicity she received during her early Hollywood years had undoubtedly damaged her career. Recently, however, she has been more accessible to the press and has talked openly about her miserable childhood and adolescence; her drinking problem, which she claims to have overcome; and her former marriage, which she calls "disastrous." "I don't know where I want to live, who I want to be, or what I want to do," she told Rex Reed of the New York *Sunday News* (October 31, 1971). ". . . I know something's wrong. I'm a displaced person. But I know I'll get it all together in my own way. I really feel like I'm starting everything all over again." As of early 1972 she was living in New York City with her daughter.

References

N Y Post p13 O 16 '71 por
N Y Sunday News II pS9 O 31 '71 pors
N Y Times II p13+ D 13 '70 por; II p9 N 7 '71 por
Parade p8 O 14 '62 pors
Who's Who of American Women, 1974-75

WHITE, KEVIN H(AGAN)

Sept. 25, 1929- Mayor of Boston; lawyer
Address: b. City Hall, Boston, Mass. 02291; h. 158 Mt. Vernon St., Boston, Mass. 02108

Kevin H. White, the dynamic Democratic mayor of Boston, Massachusetts, has demonstrated a considerable political clout that cuts across ethnic, economic, and racial lines. His progressive program of urban renewal, social welfare, tax reform, and citizens' participation in local government has won him the support of both blacks and whites in the ethnically divided city. A lawyer and a public servant since his election to the office of secretary of state of Massachusetts in 1960, White first came to national political attention in 1972 when Senator George S. McGovern seriously considered giving the Bostonian the Vice-Presidential spot on the Democratic Presidential ticket. (He was eventually dropped from the list of potential nominees because of objections from Senator Edward M. Kennedy and from John Kenneth Galbraith, the head of the Massachusetts delegation.)

The son of Joseph C. and Patricia (Hagan) White, Kevin Hagan White was born into a family of Irish-Catholic politicians on September 25, 1929

KEVIN H. WHITE

in West Roxbury, then an affluent district of Boston, Massachusetts. Over the years, Joseph White was a state representative and senator, a member of Boston's School Committee, a city councillor, and president of the Boston City Council. A shoe dealer turned politician, Henry E. Hagan, Kevin White's maternal grandfather, served as president of the Boston City Council and was an active member of the reformist Good Government Association that opposed such powerful Boston mayors as James M. Curley and John F. Fitzgerald.

After graduating from Tabor Academy, a preparatory boarding school in Marion, Massachusetts, White enrolled at Williams College in Williamstown, Massachusetts, where he majored in political science. There he was voted the third best politician in his class. He earned his A.B. degree in 1952 and obtained an LL.B. degree from Boston College Law School three years later. Admitted to the Massachusetts bar in 1955, he worked briefly for Cameron and White, a Boston law firm, and then became corporation counsel for Standard Oil of California. From 1956 to 1958 he was a legal aide to the district attorney of Middlesex County, Massachusetts. In 1958 he became the assistant district attorney for Suffolk County, a post he held until 1960.

In 1960 White began his political career by defeating his Republican opponent, Edward W. Brooke, now a United States Senator from Massachusetts, in the election for secretary of state. Although he was elected to four consecutive terms, he remained politically unfulfilled by a job that has been aptly described as "largely ceremonial." After his election to a fourth term in 1966, White remarked, as quoted in the New York *Post* (November 9, 1967), "Permanence in office tends to stagnation. An office like this should be a training ground. You should move along and let younger people come in. I'd like to move along."

White announced his candidacy for mayor of Boston in early 1967. When the ten-candidate, nonpartisan field was reduced to two in the preliminary election on September 26, he ran second to the formidable Louise Day Hicks. A member of Boston's School Committee for six years and an outspoken foe of busing, Mrs. Hicks vigorously fought all attempts to break down the city's *de facto* school segregation. In contrast to Mrs. Hicks's emotionally charged appeals, White ran an issue-oriented campaign that stressed decentralization of the city government and increased appropriations for neighborhood improvement projects. He called Mrs. Hicks's pledge to raise the salaries of law enforcement officers by more than 30 percent a "fiscal fantasy" and belittled her platform of "Boston for Bostonians." Speaking to a campaign crowd in late October, he promised, "If I am elected mayor, no man or woman is going to tear this city apart with hate or bigotry or false promises." With the endorsements of the influential Boston *Globe*, Senator Edward M. Kennedy, and Republican Governor John A. Volpe, White garnered 53 percent of the votes cast on November 7 to defeat Mrs. Hicks by slightly more than 10,000 votes. In the black districts of the city, he outpolled Mrs. Hicks, the symbol of "white backlash" to many Negroes, by more than ten to one.

As part of his platform, White promised to honor many of the commitments of his progressive predecessor, John F. Collins. Shocked by the long neglected decay of downtown Boston, Collins and Edward J. Logue, the director of the Boston Redevelopment Agency, poured federal funds into urban renewal projects. When residents of designated urban renewal areas complained that they had not been consulted by the Collins administration, White shifted the emphasis from big downtown building projects to public housing and neighborhood rehabilitation programs. On May 13, 1968 he unveiled a new $56,000,000 self-development program to expand home and business ownership among the city's poor and to construct low-income housing units. To finance the plan, the mayor established the Boston Urban Federation, which solicited funds from banks and insurance companies in the city as well as from large local industries.

In an effort to improve communication between the city government and the people, White set up several "little City Halls" around Boston. Housed in trailers, those offices provided ombudsman services and a twenty-four-hour complaint center. In addition, they fought for more frequent garbage pickups, backed citizen opposition to an expressway extension in South Boston, secured rent control for Brighton residents, and joined White's fight against a proposed expansion of Logan International Airport that threatened an East Boston neighborhood. To give Boston's black citizens a voice in their city's government, Mayor White chose Paul Parks, a former educational director of the NAACP, to head the model cities program. He named another local black leader superintendent of police and appointed an outspoken welfare recipient to the public welfare board. Because of those appointments, some detractors labeled him "Mayor Black."

In November 1969 White submitted twenty-six bills for consideration by the 1970 session of the state legislature. Among them were proposals for improved mass transit facilities, governmental reorganization, and tax reform, including an amendment to the state constitution providing for "municipal fiscal home rule." (Under Massachusetts law, cities are prohibited from imposing a local sales tax or income tax.) One of the most controversial bills called for the establishment of an eastern Massachusetts council of municipal governments to deal with regional problems, such as water supply, sewage treatment, and transportation. While local leaders recognized the need for increased cooperation between municipalities, many feared that White's plan would result in increased domination of the region by Boston.

At a City Hall news conference on May 12, 1970, White announced his decision to run for governor. Although public opinion polls gave the mayor a strong lead over his chief Democratic rival in the primary, State Senator Maurice A. Donahue, his candidacy badly split the Democratic party. Taking advantage of the Democrats' poor organization, Republican office seekers accused White of cronyism and of using the mayor's office as a springboard for higher political aspirations. In the November election incumbent Governor Francis W. Sargent, an independent Republican with widespread nonpartisan support, trounced White, 1,044,022 votes to 790,111.

As the incumbent in the 1971 mayoral campaign, White soon found himself on the defensive. "I'm the target this year," he admitted, as quoted in the Washington *Post* (September 12, 1971). "I've built more schools, built more fire stations, built more police stations, built more roads than any mayor in the history of Boston, whether he served two years or ten, but I'm still the target." One of five candidates in the September primary, White was attacked for failing to deal effectively with a rising crime rate and for imposing the biggest property tax increase in the city's history.

Although some observers maintained that the mayoral race was basically a personality contest between White and Louise Day Hicks, who had been elected to the United States House of Representatives in 1970, race became a dominant issue in the campaign. In 1965 the state legislature had passed the Racial Imbalance Act prohibiting any school with greater than 50 percent nonwhite enrollment from receiving state funds. Because of local resistance to the law, it was not enforced and by 1971, 68 percent of Boston's black children attended predominantly black schools. Mrs. Hicks had consistently been associated with the anti-busing position, but in 1971 none of the major candidates, including White and Thomas I. Atkins, a black city councilman, spoke in favor of the Racial Imbalance Act. "I supported the Racial Imbalance Act," White told Robert Reinhold in an interview for a New York *Times Magazine* (September 30, 1973) analysis of Boston's desegregation problems. "But from the very beginning, I felt strongly that the law was not working and that it should be amended. I never have been and never will be for forced busing. The education is poor all over this city. If that is true, then what is the academic value of busing?"

Although White continued to rely heavily on mass rallies, fund-raising dinners, and broadcast interviews and debates to drum up grassroots support, he discarded the expensive and, in his opinion, "inefficient" mass media advertising blitz in favor of a computerized, direct mail campaign. In the summer of 1970 volunteers under the direction of John P. Martilla, White's campaign manager, canvassed neighborhoods and identified about 130,000 Bostonians as possible supporters of White's candidacy. That pool of voters was then showered with "personalized" campaign literature designed to convince them to vote for the incumbent. The strategy paid off in the November elections when White polled 62.8 percent of the votes cast, defeating Mrs. Hicks by a plurality of 42,000. At a post-election celebration, a jubilant Mayor White told a group of campaign workers and journalists, "Maybe I'm the greatest public servant the city has ever seen, or maybe I'm the luckiest. Either way, I'll take it."

Undeterred by substantial cutbacks in federal spending in 1972 and 1973, White went ahead with a number of urban renewal projects. One relatively inexpensive but enormously successful plan was to turn the public schools into community-run activities centers. Encouraged and assisted by the Mayor's office, local schools sponsored after-hours athletic meets, physical fitness classes, adult education courses, and art and crafts workshops. To curb rising property taxes, he proposed an austerity budget for fiscal 1973 and eliminated 1,600 city jobs. "I may fall flat on my face with this budget," he told Bill Kovich in an interview for the New York Times (January 4, 1973) shortly before the public announcement of his financial plan. "But then again, I may just be able to prove that cities can stop this upward spiral of spending and hold the line."

The biggest challenge of White's second term, however, was the court-ordered racial desegregation of the schools. Anticipating a court ruling, the mayor appointed a ten-man task force to investigate the ramifications of the order in March 1973. To insure peaceful compliance with the court's decision, he organized neighborhood teams to promote a spirit of cooperation, conferred with officials from cities that had survived forced busing, set up rumor control centers, and attended morning coffee klatches and evening "sunset hours" with opponents of busing. In a long position paper released in April 1973, White argued that the racial imbalance law was "seriously flawed." The real issue, he contended, was the failure of "schools in all parts of Boston" to teach "the children they are supposed to serve."

As an alternative to forced busing, White suggested a state-funded voluntary busing program similar to the one operated by the Metropolitan Council for Educational Opportunity (METCO). (METCO buses about 1,900 black students to schools in Boston's white suburbs.) In his view, effective integration requires the abolition of class lines as well as neighborhood boundaries. "If you cross-bus within the same class, it doesn't change anything," he remarked in a recent interview. To foster cooperation with the more affluent suburbs, White favored substituting a municipal school department for the independently elected School Committee.

On June 21, 1974 Federal District Judge W. Arthur Garrity, ruling on a suit brought by a group of black parents who accused the School Committee of maintaining a deliberately segregated system, ordered Boston to comply with the state's racial imbalance law. Under the busing plan scheduled for September 1974, about 10,000 students were to be bused, the blacks to primarily white schools in Dorchester and South Boston, the whites to schools in all-black Mattapan and Roxbury. The forced busing reduced the number of racially imbalanced public schools from sixty-seven to forty-four. Although White repeatedly insisted he was "against busing," he urged Bostonians to obey the law. "It's a lousy, rotten law," he told anxious parents, as quoted by Time (September 23, 1974) magazine. "We fought the thing. We lost. Now we have to go along with it."

Angry and defiant, white parents in "Southie" boycotted the schools and staged a number of increasingly violent demonstrations against busing. To calm his constituents, White arranged several meetings between black leaders and antibusing activists and invited Senators Brooke and Kennedy, Governor Sargent, and Lieutenant Governor Donald Dwight to an emergency conference to discuss contingency plans. He refused Sargent's offer to call up the National Guard, citing the Guard's "ill-advised and reckless actions" in previous civil disturbances. The National Guard, White said, "may well be an inept, undisciplined, and untrained militia." After several blacks were injured in sporadic street fights, a black delegation requested federal protection. In a letter to Judge Garrity, made public on October 8, White requested federal marshals to supplement police protection "immediately" and to prevent "an explosive confrontation throughout the city." At a news briefing that day, he asked, "Do we have to have a body on the altar before we get the state police? . . . And a holocaust to move in federal troops?" Patrolled by three companies of the National Guard, the city became comparatively quiet in mid-October of 1974. Phase 2 of the integration program ordered by Judge Garrity was scheduled for implementation when schools opened in September 1975.

Of medium height and build, Kevin H. White has telegenic features and thinning gray hair. To keep trim, he exercises daily at a local YMCA, plays tennis, and skis. Admittedly a finicky eater, he is inordinately fond of ice cream cones. White and the former Kathryn Galvin were married on June 7, 1956. Mrs. White is the daughter of William J. ("Mother") Galvin, a fixture in Boston politics for many years. The couple and their five children Mark, Caitlin, Elizabeth, Christopher, and Patricia Hagan—live in a five-story house at the foot of Boston's Beacon Hill.

References

N Y Post p55 N 9 '67 por
N Y Times Mag p34+ S 30 '73
Who's Who in America, 1974-75
Who's Who in American Politics, 1973-74

WHITE, PATRICK (VICTOR MARTINDALE)

May 28, 1912- Australian writer
Address: b. c/o Viking Press, 625 Madison
Ave., New York 10022; h. 20 Martin Rd., Centennial Park, Sydney, New South Wales, 2021,
Australia

In awarding the 1973 Nobel Prize in Literature
to Patrick White as the writer who "for the
first time, has given the continent of Australia
an authentic voice that carries across the world,"
the Royal Swedish Academy acknowledged the
discovery of Australia in literature and precipitated another discovery—that of White himself
for many English-language readers, especially in
the United States. Although one of White's epic
narratives, *Voss*, had been a 1957 Book-of-the-
Month Club selection, only *The Eye of the Storm*,
published in 1974, enjoyed in the American press
and bookstores the reception owed an author of
international renown.

The best of White's novels, written with bold
and sometimes forbidding virtuosity, reflect his
confrontation with a land that with characteristic
lack of sentimentality he once called "the great
Australian emptiness, in which the mind of man
is the least of possessions." By no means a regionalist, White writes little that is restricted to Australia. His novels, which may be read on more
than one level, abound in allegorical themes. A
character exists not merely as himself, but as
an archetype of a farmer, an explorer, or an artist,
and as the universal man. All of White's novels,
as well as his collections of short stories and plays,
have been published in the United States by
the Viking Press. His chief British publishers have
been Routledge & Kegan Paul, Jonathan Cape,
and Eyre Methuen.

Patrick Victor Martindale White is a fourth-
generation Australian whose great grandfather had
settled on a sheep station in Australia's Hunter
Valley in 1826. His parents, Victor Martindale
and Ruth (Withycombe) White, of Muswellbrook,
New South Wales, happened to be vacationing in
England at the time of his birth, in London on
May 28, 1912. He had a sister, Suzanne, three
years younger. When the boy was six months old,
he was taken to Australia, where he spent the next
twelve or thirteen years, sometimes on New South
Wales sheep and cattle ranches of his well-to-do
father. "Whatever has come since," he wrote in an
autobiographical sketch for *Twentieth Century
Authors* (1942), "I feel that the influences and
impressions of this strange, dead landscape
predominate."

Among the less dominant influences were four
detestable years at Cheltenham College, England.

During the following three years, home again in
Australia, he jackerooned at sheep stations in
Monaro and Walgett, and, in isolated surroundings, wrote what he has called "immature" novels.
White has also said that he made "human contacts" for the first time at King's College, Cambridge, where he studied modern languages from
1932 to 1935. Continuing his apprenticeship as
a writer, he had two comedies, or humorous
dramatic sketches, produced at a small playhouse
in Sydney and some poems and a short story
published in the *London Mercury*.

Then, with London as his temporary base,
White spent some years traveling in the United
States and Europe and writing, mainly about
people and places not related to his homeland.
It was, eventually, his treatment of an entirely
Australian theme that launched his literary career.
The ironically titled *Happy Valley*, the fourth
novel that he wrote and the first that he succeeded in having published, appeared in England
in 1939 and in New York the following year. In
his mordant story of the solitariness in social relationships of a small community in the isolated
Australian outback, White demonstrated his particular gift of creating a group of diverse characters fully rounded in all their complex encounters with each other.

A similar bitter outlook prevails in *The Living
and the Dead* (1941), an unsparing study of
degradation and desperation in the unfulfilled
lives of three prewar Bloomsbury Londoners. Like
its predecessor, White's second novel taxes its
readers with the perplexities and obscurities of
an avant-garde style. Perhaps too often the author
vitiates his personal vibrancy in succumbing to
the influence of the stream-of-consciousness techniques of James Joyce and Virginia Woolf, but
gains ground in his ultimate achievement of Jamesian subtlety and precision.

By the time of the publication of *The Living
and the Dead*, White was serving in the Middle
East, mainly in the Sudanese and Egyptian deserts, as an intelligence officer in the Royal Air
Force. He was also stationed for a time during
World War II in Greece. After the war, in 1946,
he saw his play *Return to Abyssinia* produced in
London. While writing his next novel, *The Aunt's
Story* (1948), he traveled in the United States,
as does his protagonist, a drab Australian spinster
who, unlike the seekers in White's two preceding
novels, manages to reach in some degree an "intenser form of living." Theodora Goodman's story
is a venture in transcendent release from self and
from a sense of aloneness through illusion, or
madness. In telling it, White leavened his stinging views on the values of social conformity
with a witty perspective more often delightful
than scathing.

"Within the narrow limits of [*The Aunt's Story*]
White presents the themes and situations that
have remained central to his work," Rupert
Schieder pointed out in the Toronto *Globe and
Mail* (December 1, 1973). Some reviewers were
partial to the sections of the novel dealing with
Australia. After completing *The Aunt's Story*,

White decided to settle in New South Wales, on six acres of a former duck farm in Castle Hill, some twenty-five miles from Sydney. There he lived largely off the produce of the land, flowers and vegetables that he grew for market. He also cultivated an olive grove and citrus orchard and bred Saanen goats and Schnauzer dogs.

Whenever White went to Sydney, he was likely to attend a concert. He once said that symphonic music helped him with the structure of his novels. The fiction that he wrote in Castle Hill, slowly and at length, shows an indebtedness not only to Beethoven and Mahler, but also to Jane Austen, Dickens, D. H. Lawrence, Faulkner, Balzac, and Proust and to many playwrights as well as other masters of the novel. He turned away from the fashionable in style toward his own smooth amalgam of realism and symbolism.

The first novel to emerge from White's reunion with Australia, *The Tree of Man* (1955), is a long, slow-moving narrative of the lonely struggle of a pioneering husband and wife for survival on a farm in the Australian wilderness at the turn of the century. An even earlier Australia, the still unexplored continent of the mid-nineteenth century, becomes the vast panoramic background of *Voss* (1957), an epic account of an ill-fated expedition led by a megalomaniac explorer, whom White modeled in part on the German explorer of Australia, Ludwig Leichhardt. Character, rather than action or plot, remains White's forte even in this saga of an adventurous and fateful mission that proves his extraordinary narrative power. The realm explored turns into one of religion. A man of overweening pride and ambition, Voss eventually approaches a sense of divinity only when humbled through suffering, somewhat as a Christlike simplicity and humility had led the way to illumination for Stan Parker in *The Tree of Man*.

Similarly, "lovingkindness" is a key word in *Riders in the Chariot* (1961), White's more probing study of mystical experience. The chariot represents moments of beatitude, elusive glimpses of blinding luminosity. Its improbable riders are an epileptic spinster living in a decrepit mansion called Xanadu, a Jewish refugee from Nazism, a half-caste aboriginal artist, and, potentially, a compassionate washerwoman married to a brutal alcoholic. All are outcasts from bourgeois society, united by the intensity of their intimations of immortal glory. With its esoteric theme and technically challenging structure, *Riders in the Chariot* baffled some American and British critics, several of whom found it turgid, abstruse, and confused. But it delighted Jeremy Brooks, who wrote in the *Guardian* (October 27, 1961), "The symbolism is nowhere obtrusive, and is so completely integrated in character that from each new angle the pattern changes, new meanings appear." To Whitney Balliett of the *New Yorker* (December 9, 1961), the novel was "at once infuriating and brilliant."

The concept that the rare flashes of illumination, achieved at the price of loneliness and suffering, expose for an instant only what is unattainable in life suggests that White's view of the

PATRICK WHITE

human state is tragic. But the mere possibility of the vision is an affirmation. It is experienced not through longing or searching or any act of will but by an integrity of character, or authenticity, that isolates a man or woman from a society that demands conformity to values that are often banal and evil. White pursued his theme in *The Solid Mandala* (1966), which shares with *Riders in the Chariot* the locale of Sarsaparilla, an Australian town of vapidity and malice. The mandala, the Oriental circle that represents the universe, serves a purpose similar to the chariot's. It is the "defective" one of two contrasting twin brothers who is vouchsafed insight into the totality symbolized by the mandala and, for him, embodied in a cherished marble.

Of the aboriginal self-taught painter in *Riders in the Chariot*, White had written, "Neither the actor, nor the spectator, he was that most miserable of human beings, the artist." In *The Vivisector* (1970) White—whose work is said to have been influenced by Picasso, Klee, Goya, and El Greco—dealt minutely with the life of the artist, as exemplified by Hurtle Duffield, his struggle in the process of creation, his maladjustment and aloneness in society, and his destructiveness in his relationships with others.

The central character of the many that White created in *The Eye of the Storm* (1974) is also an overpowering, egotistical figure. The wealthy, aged Elizabeth Hunter, once fabulously beautiful remains predatory even on her deathbed. Man's separateness and the transience of his mystical vision are the author's persistent preoccupations here as in his other novels, but the focus is rather on human frailty and Australian society, which he satirized with an abrasive and sardonic wit. His fundamental search continued to be "to discover the extraordinary behind the ordinary," his avowed purpose in *The Tree of Man*. Because *The Eye of the Storm* was published in the United States after the announcement of White's having won the Nobel Prize in Literature, that novel was reviewed in the American press far more widely and thoroughly than any of his earlier books. Judging, at least, from that sample of his work, critics were far apart in their opinion as to whether White deserved the world's most prestigious literary award.

In addition to his eight novels, White wrote *The Ploughman, and Other Poems* (Beacon Press, Sydney, 1935) and a collection of short stories with settings in either Australia or Greece, *The Burnt Ones* (1964). One of the most successful of his short stories, "A Cheery Soul," is a portrait, devastating in its irony, of a Christian do-gooder who eventually alienates even the neighborhood dog. *A Cheery Soul* is also the title of one of White's plays published in *Four Plays* (1966). The other titles are *The Ham Funeral, The Season at Sarsaparilla,* and *Night on Bald Mountain.* All four plays have been performed in Australia.

In paying tribute to White's novels, the Royal Swedish Academy called attention particularly to the recent ones, "which show White's unbroken creative power, an ever deeper restlessness and seeking urge, an onslaught against vital problems that have never ceased to engage him and a wrestling with the language in order to extract all its power and all its nuances, to the verge of the unattainable." Appraising the earlier novels, Peter Thomson wrote in *Penguin Companion to World Literature* (1971), "White has supported his achievement on a prose style able to bear stresses more common to poetry." His style is, in fact, so rich in imagery and cadence, so deliberate in its craftsmanship, that some readers find it self-serving. White's frequent comparison with Dickens for colorful depiction of persons and places is especially valid in his gift for suggestive names, such as suburban Barranugli of *Riders in the Chariot* and Sister Badgery, one of the nurses of *The Eye of the Storm.*

Among the honors bestowed on White before the Nobel Prize were the Australian Literary Society's Gold Medal for *Happy Valley* and *The Tree of Man,* the Miles Franklin Award for *Voss* and *Riders in the Chariot,* and the W. H. Smith Prize for *Voss.* As reported in the *New York Times Book Review* (January 6, 1974), White donated his Nobel Prize money of $121,000 to the establishment of a fund for Australian writers. Because he is an asthmatic, a winter visit to Stockholm would have involved a risk, and he asked the Australian painter Sidney Nolan to accept the Nobel Prize for him at the ceremony in December 1973.

A collector of both modern Australian painting and aboriginal art, White has many friends working in art, as well as in literature. Nolan is among them, and it was from a painting of his that the striking cover of the Penguin edition of *Riders in the Chariot* was taken. Although White has listed friendship first among his recreations, he is known to be a withdrawn, reticent man. Years ago he gave a rare press interview to Ian Moffitt of the Sydney *Morning Herald,* who described him in the New York *Times Book Review* (August 18, 1957) as a "gentle-eyed, strong-jawed giant," slow, quiet, and cultured in speech. Hav-

ing moved from his farm, White now shares a house with a friend of more than thirty years in a residential section of Sydney, across from Centennial Park. Besides listening to music, he spends his time away from his desk in doing his own cooking and housekeeping, which he has said keeps him in close contact with reality, and in gardening and looking after his numerous dogs and cats.

References

London Times Lit Sup p1+ D 15 '61
N Y Times p19 O 19 '73 por
N Y Times Bk R p18 Ag 18 '57 por
Nat Observer p21 Ja 26 '74 por
Toronto Globe and Mail p36 D 1 '73 por
Washington Post A p27 O 19 '73

Encyclopedia of World Literature in the Twentieth Century (1971)
Twentieth Century Authors (1942; First Supplement, 1955)
Who's Who, 1973-74
Who's Who in Australia, 1965

WHITLAM, (EDWARD) GOUGH (gof)

July 11, 1916- Prime Minister of the Commonwealth of Australia
Address: b. Parliament House, Canberra, A.C.T. 2600, Australia; h. 32 Albert St., Cabramatta, N.S.W., Australia

Gough Whitlam, the leader of the Australian Labor party, became the twenty-first Prime Minister of the Commonwealth of Australia in December 1972, succeeding William McMahon, whose conservative coalition of the Liberal and Country parties had dominated the national government for more than two decades. Determined to shake Australia out of its traditional complacency and dependence on a foreign "big brother," Whitlam moved "like a whirlwind" during his first 100 hours in office, trying to fulfill promises to transform Australia's social, economic, and foreign policies. His mission, as he sees it, is to free Australia from its almost slavish adherence to Great Britain and the United States, to assume a leadership role for his country in the South Pacific and Southeast Asia, and to promote greater social benefits for his people, especially the much neglected Aborigines.

A member of the House of Representatives—the lower house of the Australian Parliament—since 1952, Whitlam became leader of the Australian Labor party (ALP) in 1967 and set out to broaden the party's popular appeal and reverse its defeatist attitude. As Cameron Hazlehurst noted in the *New Statesman* (January 19, 1973), Whitlam "has wrought a near miracle in reforming, reorganizing, and leading to electoral victory a party whose personal feuds, ideological rifts and machine warfare have helped to keep it out of office for twenty-three years."

Edward Gough Whitlam was born on July 11, 1916 in Kew, a prosperous suburb of Melbourne, to Harry Frederick Ernest and Martha (Maddocks) Whitlam. His father, a lawyer, served as Commonwealth Crown solicitor general from 1936 to 1948 and was a delegate to the U.N. Human Rights Commission. According to Colin Chapman, writing in the Washington *Post* (December 3, 1972), unlike most Labor party officials, Whitlam did not have a working class background but was "brought up on Dryden, Pope, and Beethoven in lush garden suburbs." His sister, Freda Leslie Whitlam, now the headmistress of a girls' school in Sydney, remembers that as a boy, Gough was known for his phenomenal memory and encyclopedic knowledge. As a student at the Knox Grammar School in Sydney, the Telopea Park High School in Canberra, and the Canberra Grammar School, he did well in English and Latin but not in mathematics, and was classed as an industrious but not a brilliant student. According to *Time* (March 26, 1973), he left one school after a teacher complained of his impudence.

After graduating from Canberra Grammar School, Whitlam entered St. Paul's College at Sydney University, where he took a B.A. degree in the liberal arts in 1938. He remained at Sydney to study law until the war intervened. From 1941 to 1945 he was a bomber-navigator for the Royal Australian Air Force. Following his discharge with the rank of flight lieutenant, he returned to Sydney, took his LL.B. in 1946, and was admitted to the New South Wales and federal bars in 1947. Established in a law practice in the Sydney suburb of Darlinghurst, Whitlam was a member of the New South Wales Bar Council from 1949 to 1953. He served in 1951-52 as junior counsel, assisting a royal commission in its investigation of the liquor trade.

Although Whitlam had shown little previous interest in politics, he joined the Labor party while still in the military service because of his admiration for the policies of John Curtin, Australia's first postwar Prime Minister. His first bids for elective office were failures. In 1947 he was defeated in an effort to become a member of the Sydney council, and in 1950 he lost an election for a seat in the New South Wales state parliament. But in November 1952, in a by-election in Werriwa, an industrial suburb of Sydney, he won a seat in the federal House of Representatives that he has held ever since. Establishing his residence in a modest house in Werriwa, Whitlam became one of the few Australian city politicians who live among their constituents. As a member of Parliament, he served on the Joint Committee on Constitutional Review from 1956 to 1959 and became a member of the Standing Orders Committee in March 1960. He was appointed a Queen's Counsel in 1962.

During his first years in Parliament, Whitlam was distrusted by his ALP colleagues. As Colin Chapman wrote in the Washington *Post*, "To rough-edged Labor parliamentarians, reared in the Australian shearing sheds or at the work benches and nurtured by the trade unions, Whitlam was a city slicker. His well-cut suits, his impressive manner, his command of language, his intellec-

GOUGH WHITLAM

tualism earned him not respect or envy, but scorn." Eventually, however, Whitlam did gain the backing of his party. In 1959 he became a member of the federal parliamentary executive of the ALP, and in March 1960 he was named deputy leader of the party. "When he finally won support," continues Colin Chapman, "it was because of hard work on the hustings and his independence as demonstrated by his forthright and opinionated stands."

Always ready for a political tussle, Whitlam found himself at odds with his fellow Laborites as much as with their opponents in the Liberal and Country parties. The 1950's and early 1960's were difficult years for Labor. Since 1949 a Liberal-Country party coalition under Prime Minister Robert Menzies had held power in Australia. Labor suffered a disastrous split in 1955, when a largely Roman Catholic group separated from it to form the right-wing Democratic Labor party. The powerful ALP machine, controlled by old-line left-wing unionists, held to narrowly doctrinaire and antiquated principles and strategies that in Whitlam's view accounted for the party's election losses.

During the early 1960's Labor policy was still determined by the federal conference of the party, consisting of thirty-six state-level party bosses. On the night of March 20, 1963 Whitlam and Arthur A. Calwell, the ALP leader, were kept waiting outside a hotel, while inside the building the federal conference debated a crucial issue. The next day, the Australian press published photos of the two men standing forlornly in the street, and elections in November of that year were largely fought on the issue of Labor's control by the "thirty-six faceless men." Labor lost ten seats, and Whitlam's disaffection with the party setup was complete.

Although during the early 1960's Whitlam had been a fairly loyal lieutenant of Calwell, he became increasingly critical of his leadership. Convinced that he himself was destined to be the leader of the ALP, Whitlam began to garner support for that eventuality. In a 1964 report he proposed the replacement of the existing confederation of state party organizations by a single body; the upgrading of parliamentarians within party officialdom; a de-emphasis of local politics; and a greater effort to recruit nonunionists into the party's ranks.

After the ALP lost an additional nine parliamentary seats in the November 1966 elections, Calwell resigned as party leader. On February 8, 1967 Whitlam was elected to succeed him, receiving thirty-nine votes out of sixty-eight in a five-way contest. He immediately began to reorganize the party and scored his first major triumph at the Labor federal conference in 1967 when he succeeded in adding several parliamentary leaders to the "thirty-six faceless men" who decided policy. A major battle ensued when Whitlam tried to increase federal control over some state Labor organizations and in April 1968 he was forced to resign as party leader. He was reelected shortly thereafter, but by a narrower majority.

To broaden Labor's constituency, Whitlam directed his efforts toward making ALP policies more palatable to the middle class, a goal that some old-line Laborites regarded as heretical. Determined to end Labor's defeatism, he declared in 1967, as quoted by Alan Reid in *The Gorton Experiment* (Shakespeare Head Press, Sydney, 1972): "The men who formed the ALP in the 1890's knew all about power. They were not ashamed to seek it, and they were not embarrassed when they won it. . . . This party was not conceived in failure, brought forth by failure or consecrated to failure."

By 1969, despite ferocious internal battles, the Labor party under Whitlam had already made much progress. In elections of October of that year for the 125-seat House of Representatives the ALP increased its representation from forty-two to fifty-nine, while the Liberal-County party coalition maintained only a narrow majority of seven. Campaigning against Prime Minister John G. Gorton, Whitlam emphasized domestic problems, playing down the defense and foreign policy issues that had divided Labor in the past. While Calwell and others in the party favored massive demonstrations to protest the Vietnam war, Whitlam felt that foreign policy "should be decided in the Parliament . . . and not in the streets."

Between 1969 and 1972 Whitlam continued his work of reforming the Labor party and purging its leadership of the doctrinaire elements that had weakened it in past elections. While generally taking positions that would draw votes to the party, he did not shy away from controversial issues. For example, he came out in favor of state aid to parochial schools, and he took the initiative in advocating self-government and eventual independence for the trust territory of Papua and New Guinea. In July 1971 he led a Labor delegation to Peking, thus dramatically pointing up his conviction that Australia should establish relations with Communist China. The Liberals, who had won votes by playing on Australian

fears of Communism, attacked the China visit as a threat to the country's security and to the alliance with the United States. But just before Whitlam's return, President Richard Nixon announced his forthcoming trip to China, embarrassing the Liberals and adding to Whitlam's prestige. Meanwhile, the Liberal party was having additional difficulties as a result of a flagging economy and a leadership struggle that led to the replacement of Gorton as Prime Minister by William McMahon in March 1971.

In his fourteen-month campaign for the 1972 general election Whitlam used the services of the McCann-Erickson advertising agency and made many personal appearances throughout the country, attacking McMahon—whom he called "silly Billy"—in his acerbic, mocking style. He promised cheaper housing loans, better schools, higher pensions, revitalization of the federal system, land rights for Aborigines, and improved community centers and public transport. He struck a nationalistic note, declaring that he would end Australia's blind subservience to the United States and pledging to "buy back Australia" from foreign corporations. While foreign policy and defense were played down, Whitlam promised to end the draft, withdraw Australian troops from Vietnam, and recognize the government of Communist China.

In practice, the difference between the Labor and Liberal party programs was more one of emphasis than of substance. The Liberals also promised substantial domestic reforms and greater independence for Australia but planned to move more slowly, maintaining that Labor's "instant utopia" would result in economic chaos. The election centered mainly on the personalities of Whitlam and McMahon, to the former's advantage. Labor's sophisticated campaign, based on the slogan "It's Time," seemed to appeal to many Australians, who felt ready for a change.

The election, on December 2, 1972, gave Labor sixty-seven of the 125 seats in the House. Because of the complexities of the Australian electoral system, Whitlam was able to rule almost dictatorially, unhampered by a Cabinet, the Parliament, or his party colleagues, during the first two weeks following his inauguration as Prime Minister on December 5. Pending appointment of a Cabinet by a party caucus, he temporarily assumed thirteen Cabinet offices, while giving fourteen to his deputy leader, Lance Barnard. A full twenty-seven-member Cabinet was sworn in on December 19, 1972, with Whitlam retaining the portfolio of Foreign Affairs.

With a speed of action not typical of Australians, during his first weeks in office Whitlam broke with Taiwan and began negotiations that led to recognition of Communist China; ended conscription and freed men imprisoned for draft evasion; put a freeze on applications for leases on certain lands to enable Aborigines to advance their claims; barred racially segregated South African athletic teams from Australia; ordered all Australian troops home from Vietnam; petitioned the International Court of Justice to stop French nuclear tests in the Pacific; and initiated action to give the vote to eighteen-year-olds, establish equal pay for women, facilitate divorce, place oral contraceptives among government-subsidized items, and relax censorship of the arts. Rejecting appointment to the Privy Council, to which he would have been entitled, Whitlam made several moves to modify Australia's ties with Great Britain, including suspension of the Australian government's practice of recommending citizens for royal honors. In a surprise move, in late December, he announced the upward valuation of the Australian dollar by 7.05 percent.

Although Australian-American relations became somewhat strained after Whitlam condemned the Nixon administration's Christmas 1972 bombing of Vietnam, Whitlam pledged to maintain a close alliance with the United States during his visit to Washington in July 1973. In his view, his country's relations with the United States, like those with Great Britain, "are of the highest importance but . . . are only one aspect of our interests and obligations . . . around the world." Determined to "help free the Asia-Pacific area from great-power intervention and rivalries," Whitlam proposed a new regional grouping of Asian and Pacific nations during a visit to Indonesia in February 1973. When he returned from a trip to China and Japan a few months later, he suggested that Australia might take on the role of "honest broker" among the nations involved in the Pacific region.

On the home front, Whitlam continued in 1973 to be faced with inflation, industrial unrest, intra-party friction, and resistance on the part of the Australian state governments to any moves that would give greater power to the federal government. The Australian Senate, still controlled by the Liberals, blocked several legislative measures sponsored by Whitlam. In state elections in Victoria and New South Wales in the fall, the ALP suffered severe setbacks. In October, Whitlam announced that he was relinquishing his secondary post of Minister of Foreign Affairs to Senator Donald R. Willesee in order to deal more fully with vital domestic issues. Whitlam retained his post as Prime Minister after a national election was held on May 18, 1974.

An imposing, outspoken, eloquent, and handsome man, Whitlam stands at six feet four inches and is usually impeccably tailored. On April 22, 1942 he married Margaret Elaine Dovey, the daughter of a New South Wales Supreme Court justice, and they have four children: Anthony Philip, Nicholas Richard, Stephen Charles, and Katherine Julia. Although Whitlam has been known to curse fellow parliamentarians and once threw a glass of water on Paul Hasluck—now Australia's governor general—during an angry debate, he is said to have learned to control his acid tongue and testy temper in recent years. Before becoming Prime Minister, Whitlam read about six or seven books a week, mainly in the fields of history and politics. His own writings include *The Constitution vs. Labor* (1957), *Australian Foreign Policy* (1963), *Beyond Vietnam;*

Australia's Regional Responsibility (1968), and *The New Federalism* (1971). Within the Labor party, Whitlam considers his role as that of an innovator. "My style is evolutionary, my substance the most revolutionary they ever had," he told Colin Chapman of the Washington *Post* (December 3, 1972). "No subject is taboo as far as I am concerned."

References
Guardian p3 D 4 '72 por
London Observer p10+ Mr 18 '73 por
N Y Times p28 D 4 '72 por
Toronto Globe and Mail p7 Ap 3 '73 por
Americana Annual, 1973
Britannica Book of the Year, 1973
International Who's Who, 1973-74
Who's Who, 1972-73
Who's Who in Australia, 1971

WILSON, (CHARLES) MALCOLM

Feb. 26, 1914- Governor of New York; lawyer
Address: b. State of New York, Executive Chamber, Albany, N.Y. 12224; h. 24 Windsor Rd., Yonkers, N.Y. 10706

After more than three decades of public service, Malcolm Wilson realized his ambition to become Governor of New York when Nelson A. Rockefeller resigned the post to pursue his own political goals in December of 1973. First elected to the New York State Assembly in 1938, Wilson had held elective office for thirty-five consecutive years—a record in the state—and had never lost an election. As Rockefeller's Lieutenant Governor, he presided over the State Senate, where he proved himself to be a superb parliamentarian, and served as acting Governor during the chief executive's frequent absences from the state. Because of his long years of experience at the grassroots level, Wilson was personally acquainted with the Republican party leaders and committeemen who comprised his solid political base. He was totally committed to state government. "We deal with all matters that are of human interest and concern—the professions and business, the relations of people to other people, indeed, the relationships within the family itself," he once said. "I regard the basic purpose of government as transforming people's problems into people's opportunities." Wilson suffered his first political defeat in the gubernatorial election that was held on November 5, 1974.

Of Irish and Scottish ancestry, Charles Malcolm Wilson, the second of four children born to Charles H. Wilson, a patent attorney, and Agnes (Egan) Wilson, was born in New York City on February 26, 1914. His first name was eventually dropped to distinguish him from his father. In 1920 the family moved to Yonkers, New York. Throughout his youth, Wilson spent his summers in upstate New York where he worked on his uncle's dairy farm in Oneida County and guided tourists visiting Fort Niagara. Both parents were

MALCOLM WILSON

active in politics. Charles Wilson ran unsuccessfully for the New York State Assembly in 1912 and Agnes Wilson, a member of several national Republican women's organizations, served as a party district leader in Yonkers' Eighth Ward. Encouraged by his parents, Wilson began campaigning for Republican candidates at an early age. "I've been in politics all my life," he recalled to Edward O'Neill in an interview for the New York *Sunday News* (December 19, 1971). "As a youngster I can remember spending every election day at the polls, handing out pamphlets."

Wilson attended several parochial elementary and secondary schools, including St. Thomas Academy and Elizabeth Seton Academy. After graduating from Fordham Preparatory School in 1929, Wilson enrolled at Fordham University, where he was an above average student who excelled in history, classical languages, and public speaking. As a member of the college debating team, he took part in victorious debating meets with Oxford University and Cambridge University. After receiving his B.A. degree in 1934, Wilson registered for the night school program at Fordham School of Law. To pay his educational expenses, he clerked for Kent, Hazzard & Jagger, a White Plains, New York law firm, and taught parliamentary procedure to union members at a local General Motors plant. He obtained his LL.B. degree in 1936, was admitted to the New York State Bar, and joined Kent, Hazzard & Jagger as an associate attorney. In 1946 he was made a partner in the firm, which is now known as Kent, Hazzard, Wilson, Freeman & Greer.

In 1938, at the age of twenty-four, Wilson ran for a seat in the New York State Assembly and narrowly defeated his Democratic opponent, an incumbent Assemblyman, by 238 votes. Regularly returned to the state house by the traditionally Democratic voters of Yonkers, the young Republican legislator compiled an enviable vote-getting record by winning ten consecutive elections with an increasing margin of votes. In 1956 he was elected to his last term in the Assembly

by a 16,000-vote landslide. During his third term Wilson interrupted his political career to volunteer for military service in World War II. Commissioned an ensign in the United States Naval Reserve in 1943, he commanded the gun crew on an ammunition ship that supplied the Allied Forces in Europe and took part in the D-day invasion of France. Although overseas duty prevented him from campaigning personally in 1944, his hometown newspaper publicized his war efforts and helped him to win the election.

Wilson quickly gained a reputation in Albany as a budget expert, a brilliant debater, and a skilled parliamentarian. As a member of the state legislature, he sponsored some 432 bills which were signed into law by Governors Herbert H. Lehman, Thomas E. Dewey, and W. Averell Harriman. Of those bills, nearly one-third dealt with court revision, penal reform, or the administration of justice. For example, he submitted legislation to augment rehabilitation programs for parolees, to revise the "impractical" criminal code, and to restructure the juvenile court system. Speaking at a New York University law conference in the summer of 1954, he warned that the excessive penalties mandated for certain crimes could result in fewer convictions. An advocate of state aid to schools, libraries, and other educational institutions, he proposed the establishment of the Higher Education Assistance Corporation to provide loans to needy college students. On other social issues, he drafted legislation to extend social security coverage to municipal and state employees, to expand workmen's compensation programs to include the victims of dust diseases, and to provide tax relief for disabled veterans. Although he supported a number of civil rights bills, Wilson opposed the Metcalf-Baker bill barring discrimination in public housing. "My view is that this is an area in which we must proceed very cautiously," he explained, as quoted in the New York *Post* (September 28, 1958). "There are many people who feel that they may do with their property what they wish to do."

As chairman of the Assembly's powerful Codes Committee, a position he held for twelve years, he prevented certain measures from reaching the floor. In 1952, for instance, he effectively stopped a Democratic move to increase unemployment insurance. His opposition to that bill and to other legislation raising workmen's compensation payments and disability benefits provoked the wrath of organized labor. In addition, he headed a number of joint legislative committees that investigated such matters as the state's economy, retirement plans for public employees, and the continuation of blue laws. In 1957 Westchester County Executive James D. Hopkins appointed Wilson chairman of the so-called "Little Hoover Commission" to reorganize and update that county's government.

Despite several opportunities to run for the United States Senate and the tempting offer of a judgeship, Wilson remained in state politics. "I have never really wanted to be on the bench," he explained to Jim Klurfeld in an interview for

Newsday (December 12, 1973). "As for the Senate, I don't want to start a new field of endeavor. The state has been the beginning and end of my interest." He was, however, admittedly disillusioned after his unsuccessful bids for the majority leadership of the Assembly and for the Republican nomination for state attorney general. According to some observers, he seemed doomed to political obscurity until multimillionaire Nelson A. Rockefeller picked him as pre-convention campaign manager in 1958. "I told [Rockefeller] I knew how to get him the nomination, and it wasn't by just meeting the GOP leaders," Wilson told Klurfeld. "We went across the state in my car to meet Republicans—the club members, the committeemen. No high-pressure campaign, just him and me in a car." Although both men were from Westchester County, Rockefeller insisted that Wilson be his running mate. The Assemblyman's political contacts, conservatism, and quiet manner complemented Rockefeller's wealth, liberalism, and charisma. Wilson's conservative voting record, however, invited criticism from his more liberal opponents, who denounced him for being, in their opinion, indifferent to social welfare, the plight of minority groups, and civil rights. As an example of his "reactionary" legislation, the Democratic opposition cited his proposed state constitutional amendment making it more difficult for a married couple to obtain a divorce or an annulment.

On November 4, 1958 the Rockefeller ticket defeated incumbent Governor Harriman and his running mate, Lieutenant Governor George B. DeLuca by a comfortable margin of 573,334 votes. Two months later, Wilson was sworn in to the first of four consecutive terms as Lieutenant Governor. In subsequent elections, the Rockefeller-Wilson team won over their Democratic opponents by solid majorities. In 1970 the pair trounced former Supreme Court Justice Arthur J. Goldberg and Basil A. Patterson, winning by 730,006 votes. "Frankly, if it weren't for Malcolm, I wouldn't be here," Governor Rockefeller often told Republican gatherings. "And if I weren't here, Malcolm would be."

Upstaged by the flamboyant Rockefeller, Wilson worked tirelessly behind the scenes, as the principal liaison between the Governor's office and the Assembly. In his official capacity as president of the State Senate, he skillfully maneuvered floor debate. Commenting on his political acumen for the New York *Times* (December 12, 1973), one analyst noted: "Mr. Wilson . . . presided over the State Senate as if it were as manageable as an amusing desk-top ant farm. He regularly . . . settled rules conflicts against the Senate minority with such artful legalese that on one occasion the Democrats had to applaud even as they complained that he was changing the shape of the bat and ball in mid-game."

An active member of the gubernatorial policy-making team, Wilson persuaded Rockefeller to support federal revenue sharing. Although the two men often disagreed privately, Wilson clashed publicly with Rockefeller only twice. A devout Roman Catholic, he opposed New York's liberalized abortion law and, according to some observers, quietly prepared legislation to repeal the controversial law. In a statement released in late October 1967 the Lieutenant Governor announced his opposition to the proposed new state constitution. Criticizing the "single package" approach, he called upon each voter to make his own evaluation of the plan. In addition to his regular duties, he headed a special committee that recommended a vested benefit plan to members of the state retirement system and chaired the Capitol City Commission and the New York State Commission on the 1964 World's Fair.

On December 18, 1973, one week after Rockefeller announced his resignation amid speculation of a renewed Presidential drive, Wilson was sworn in as the fiftieth Governor of New York. Flanked by Rockefeller and by members of the Wilson family, he gave a short, simple speech promising "vigorous action in serving the people." Pledging to "pursue the moderate, middle way—where most Americans place their convictions and their confidence," Governor Wilson assured his constituents that his administration would be "progressive in meeting human needs and conservative in handling the people's dollars."

In his first State of the State message, broadcast January 9, 1974, he reiterated his commitment to moderation. His detailed legislative program recommended, among other things, an increase in unemployment benefits and welfare payments to keep pace with inflation, equal protection for women in credit transactions, liberalization of health insurance policies, and a far-reaching consumer protection package. To insure against "extravagant ventures," he established legislative committees to study politically sensitive issues such as election reform and rent control. He lightened the taxpayer's burden by repealing the 2.5 percent state income tax surcharge. At the same time, he retained the "hot dog tax," an unpopular tax on meals costing less than one dollar. Wilson's 1974 budget request of $9.38 billion, a 9 percent increase over the 1973 budget, was widely criticized by Democratic Assemblymen as being "unrealistic in its revenue estimates and unacceptable in its proposed expenditures."

An immediate problem facing the Wilson administration was the energy crisis. New York State was particularly affected by the fuel shortage and, on February 7, 1974, the Governor instituted a voluntary gasoline rationing plan. "I have a visceral reaction against government . . . directing people under criminal penalty or civil fine to do something or to refrain from doing something," he told the Albany press corps at a news conference on February 20, 1974. "I just don't like to push the citizens of this state around with an *ipse dixit* from their Governor." Under the broad emergency powers granted by the Assembly on February 21, 1974, Wilson cracked down on gasoline price gouging, released gas reserves to hard-hit areas of the state, and imposed compulsory rationing. As one viable solution to the energy problem, the Governor suggested an improved mass transit system. He signed a bill to maintain New York City's threatened thirty-five-cent fare, endorsed governmental subsidies of metropolitan transportation systems, and devised a three-point transportation package guaranteeing financial aid to rural railroads as well as to urban transit.

While recognizing that he had strong support on both local and state levels, most political analysts believed that to win a full term in the 1974 elections, he would have had to compensate for his "number two" image, Rockefeller's departure, and a Republican party ravaged by the Watergate scandals. Appearing on the WCBS-TV program *Newsmakers* in February 1974, the Governor indicated that Watergate would "not be an issue" in New York state elections. Although he had supported campaign reform legislation, he told his television audience that "disclosure of income or taxes" was not "relevant" to a political campaign. In 1974 he signed a bill postponing the state primary from June to September, a move some observers interpreted as an attempt to divide his Democratic opposition. Despite his efforts to woo the public, Wilson was defeated in the governor's race by Democrat Hugh J. Carey on November 5, 1974.

Malcolm Wilson stands slightly under six feet tall and is lean and youthful in appearance. He maintains his weight at 160 pounds by carefully watching his diet. He chain-smokes low-tar cigarettes and is a teetotaler. His narrow ties, white shirts, and conservatively tailored suits have become his trademarks. An eloquent speaker, he punctuates his measured and deliberate speech with apt Latin phrases and humorous anecdotes. Wilson and the former Katharine McCloskey were married September 6, 1941. They have two daughters, Kathy (Mrs. John M. Conroy) and Anne (Mrs. Lester G. Mathews), and five grandchildren. The Wilsons divide their time between the executive mansion in Albany and their rambling, ten-room Tudor-style home in Yonkers.

Governor Wilson is fond of quoting Swiss historian Jacob Burckhardt's maxim that "the essence of tyranny is the denial of complexity." He explained his political philosophy to a group of New York businessmen at a luncheon in 1972: "We have to beware of people who have simple solutions to things that sound good to the voters. . . . Oversimplification is the great corrupter of our times, and I suggest that what we need are more complexities." One admiring colleague has described Wilson as "a politician's politician," but he has classified himself perhaps even more accurately as "an economic conservative and a human rights liberal."

References

N Y Post p22 D 15 '73 pors
N Y Sunday News p83 D 19 '71 por
N Y Times p20 Ag 27 '58; p1+ D 12 '73
New York Redbook, 1973
Who's Who in America, 1973-74
Who's Who in American Politics, 1973-74

WISEMAN, FREDERICK

Jan. 1, 1930- Documentary film maker; lawyer; educator
Address: b. Zipporah Films, 54 Lewis Wharf, Boston, Mass. 02110

"I've been responsible for four of the most depressing movies ever made," Frederick Wiseman once observed. A lawyer and professor turned film maker, Wiseman has trained his unblinking camera eye on America's tax-supported institutions since the mid-1960's. Motivated by his conviction that the American public has a right to know about its institutions, he has become "a sort of cinematic Ralph Nader," to quote the epithet bestowed upon him by a *New York* magazine contributing writer, Christopher Byron. His controversial, award-winning films, which one legal scholar has described as the celluloid equivalent to a law review article on public institutions, have elicited official condemnation and legal sanctions as well as virtually unanimous critical acclaim.

Because he refuses to compromise his films for broadcast by commercial television networks or release by major motion picture distribution companies, Wiseman relies heavily on public broadcasting stations, college film societies, and film festivals for public exposure. In May 1972 he signed a five-year contract with WNET-TV to produce one documentary per year for the 219-station public broadcasting network. With the exception of *Titicut Follies*, Wiseman's documentaries are distributed by Zipporah Films.

Frederick Wiseman was born on January 1, 1930 in Boston, Massachusetts. After graduating from high school, which he "hated," he enrolled at Williams College in Williamstown, Massachusetts. He earned his B.A. degree in 1951 and entered Yale Law School. "I never really liked studying law," he recalled to Beatrice Berg in an interview for the New York *Times* (February 1, 1970), "but Yale Law School was a very exciting place intellectually. There were lots of people interested in movies and writing." Despite his apparent indifference to the study of law, he completed the three-year program and received his LL.B. degree in 1954.

After a two-year tour of duty in the United States Army, Wiseman went to Paris in 1956. There he studied law at the University of Paris and maintained a small private practice. "The Paris job financed some time in Europe, seeing things and looking at a lot of movies," he told Gary Arnold in an interview for a Washington *Post* (November 23, 1969) profile. "I didn't intend to practice law even while I was supposedly practicing it." He returned to the United States in 1958 to take a position as an instructor at the Boston University Law-Medicine Institute. In 1959 he joined the faculty of Boston University Law School and taught courses in family law and criminal law for two years. To make his students familiar with conditions in the state's correctional and rehabilitative facilities, he took them to such institutions as the Bridgewater (Massachusetts)

Hospital for the Criminally Insane. From 1961 to 1962 he held a Russell Sage Foundation fellowship to Harvard University's Graduate School of Arts and Sciences and in 1963 he was named a research associate in the department of sociology at Brandeis University. In 1966 he and a partner founded the Organization for Social and Technical Innovations (OSTI) to analyze health service systems and legal assistance to the poor.

Impressed by Warren Miller's *Cool World* (1959), a joltingly realistic novel about a black youth growing up in Harlem, Wiseman convinced award-winning film maker Shirley Clarke to direct a cinematic adaptation. Miss Clarke, whose previous screen credits included the much praised *The Connection,* used amateur actors recruited from the city streets to trace several days in the life of Duke Custis, a fourteen-year-old gang leader. With a small, hand-held camera, she peered into ghetto alleys and tenements to photograph dope pushers, pimps, whores, and back street con artists. Released in 1964 by Zipporah Films, Wiseman's production and distribution company, *The Cool World* quietly gained a reputation as an underground classic despite critics' objections to its "scatter-gun camera technique," its disconcerting "looseness" in style, and its "one-sided picture" of Harlem.

On the basis of his experiences as the producer of *The Cool World,* Wiseman decided to exert closer control over subsequent films. "I decided there isn't any special mystique to directing and that I'd never make a movie I didn't direct and edit myself," he explained to Beatrice Berg. "Producers have all the financial responsibility and no creative opportunity." His first venture as a producer-director was *Titicut Follies* (1967), an eighty-seven minute, 16mm. documentary photographed by John Marshall and distributed by Grove Press. An unflinching examination of the deplorable conditions inside the Bridgewater Hospital for the Criminally Insane, the film was, in Wiseman's view, an "extension" of his teaching. The public "hears about the horrors of Bridgewater," he told a reporter for *Newsweek* (December 4, 1967), "but it can't make any decisions about what to do about it until it tastes something of the life there."

To illustrate the "people-processing" aspects of Bridgewater, Wiseman alternated between excerpts from a musical show staged by the inmates—the "follies" of the title—and self-contained incidents in the day-to-day life of the prisoners, their guards, and their doctors. The filmed episodes include a brutal psychiatric interview of a young man accused of molesting a child; a lone inmate tonelessly singing "The Ballad of the Green Berets"; the stripping and searching of patients recently committed to the hospital; and the intranasal force-feeding of an old man under the supervision of an unconcerned physician. The force-feeding sequences are intercut with flash-forward shots of the man's body being carefully prepared for burial. According to some critics, this cross-cutting technique amounted to "editorial editing" and "over-control." Others, among them film historian and

FREDERICK WISEMAN

critic Richard Schickel, argued that the motion picture's "repulsive reality" forced the audience to confront its "capacity for callousness" and indifference. "When a work achieves that kind of power," Schickel wrote in his review for *Life* (December 1, 1967) magazine, "it must be regarded as art, however artlessly, or even crudely, it generates it."

Contending that Wiseman had deliberately violated his verbal agreement to restrict his filming to the alcoholic wards of the hospital, the Commonwealth of Massachusetts, acting in behalf of the inmates, sued the film maker for invasion of privacy. On November 16, 1967 the state obtained a temporary injunction barring all showings of *Titicut Follies* in Massachusetts. (The injunction became permanent in January 1968.) Additional suits were filed against Wiseman and against Grove Press to prevent the film from being exhibited in other states. In defense of *Titicut Follies* Wiseman maintained that, in this instance, the public's right to know outweighed the individual's right to privacy. "The right to take pictures of Bridgewater is as clear as the right to take pictures of a traffic accident in Scollay Square," he argued, as quoted in *Time* (December 1, 1967). On June 24, 1969 the Massachusetts Supreme Court ruled that the documentary could be shown only to specialized "professional" audiences. Over the dissents of Justices John M. Harlan and William J. Brennan Jr., who argued in favor of a full court review of the *Titicut Follies* case to resolve the issue of the balance between an individual's privacy and "the public's right to know about conditions in public institutions," the Supreme Court, on June 15, 1970, let stand the Massachusetts court's ruling.

High School, Wiseman's second film study of an American institution, was released in 1968. Photographed by Richard Leiterman, the seventy-five-minute documentary, reduced from more than forty hours of film, focused on a predominantly white suburban high school in northeastern Philadelphia. Wiseman had deliberately selected a "good" school to question the goals and policies of a "successful" institution. In twenty-two days

Wiseman filmed student assemblies, pep rallies, classroom sessions, science projects, segregated sex education classes, extracurricular activities, and meetings between teachers and parents. He was particularly impressed by the "enormous passivity" of the students, by the "repression of sexuality," and by the emphasis on conformity. Although they had been at first cooperative, school officials complained about the film's alleged lack of objectivity after film critics and educators commended Wiseman for his "stinging indictment" of the "obvious flaws" of a system that "humiliates" and "insults" students. As a result, under a court order, *High School* cannot be shown in Philadelphia.

Commissioned by National Educational Television's Public Broadcasting Laboratory, *Law and Order* is an examination of a metropolitan police force. It was filmed in Kansas City over a six-week period in 1968, shortly after the bloody confrontation between antiwar demonstrators and Chicago police that took place during the Democratic National Convention. "I thought [it was] a golden opportunity to 'get' the cops!" Wiseman recalled, as quoted in the Washington *Post* (March 7, 1970). "After riding around in prowl cars for a few days, I no longer felt that way. I watched the cops doing some rotten things and some decent things but what struck me wasn't so much 'police brutality' as the brutalities that people in the street were committing against one another."

With his cameraman, William Brayne, Wiseman concentrated on routine situations: lost children, family disputes, purse snatchings, and car thefts. Because only one brief episode—the arrest of a young prostitute—could be interpreted as an example of police brutality, skeptical reviewers concluded that Wiseman had intentionally selected footage to create a favorable image of the police. For example, Stephen Mamber, in his book *Cinéma Vérité in America* (1974), especially criticized one scene, in which an officer bought candy to comfort a lost child, and another, in which two policemen discuss job opportunities in California. The first episode, he wrote, came "closest to a deliberate attempt to upset preconceived notions about the police" and the second sequence seemed "uncomfortably staged." In rebuttal, Wiseman maintained that *Law and Order* was not meant to be "*the* statement about cops." The film was "about Kansas City cops during the time that I was with them," he told G. Roy Levin, in an interview for the book *Documentary Explorations* (1971). *Law and Order* was awarded an Emmy as the best television news documentary in 1969.

In *Hospital* (1970), Wiseman turned his attention to the medical services offered by a large inner-city hospital. Photographed by William Brayne in the emergency ward of New York City's Metropolitan Hospital, the film is not for the squeamish, since it includes shots of accident victims and hysterical, nauseated drug addicts, close-ups of emergency operations, and medically explicit interviews between doctors and patients. "Wiseman's camera seems to miss nothing," Richard Schickel observed in his *Life* (February 6, 1970) column, "but his tact is unique among the *cinéma*

vérité people. One never feels the voyeur, no matter how intimate or revealing the scene." Because of the film's content, however, many educational television stations, at the request of the Corporation for Public Broadcasting, which financed the film, elected to broadcast the documentary at a late hour. "I've gotten used to this kind of thing," Wiseman remarked, as quoted in *New York* magazine (January 26, 1970). "It's just a way for them to ease their consciences without a lot of huffing and puffing." *Hospital* won a number of prestigious awards, including Emmys for the best documentary and best director of the 1969-70 television season and the Alfred I. duPont-Columbia University Award in Broadcast Journalism.

Produced for National Educational Television and telecast on October 4, 1971 as part of PBS's *Special of the Week* series, Wiseman's *Basic Training* follows a group of United States Army recruits from their arrival in boot camp to their graduation nine weeks later. Using a single camera, Wiseman and Brayne filmed calisthenics and military drills, lectures on such mundane subjects as dental hygiene, and "search and destroy" maneuvers in a simulated Vietnamese village. Several critics saw *Basic Training* as the "natural sequel" to *High School*. Wiseman attributes the apparent similarities among his films to the fact that the relationship between the anonymous individual and society's institutions is one of the organizing factors in all his films.

Essene (1972) is the first of Wiseman's documentaries to spotlight a nonpublic institution and the first to feature individual personalities. Its central figures are the middle-aged, contemplative abbot of St. George's Abbey, an Anglican monastery in rural Michigan, and two troubled, questioning monks. In a series of emotionally revealing episodes, the brothers explore the complex interrelationships of an isolated communal life. Although several critics condemned *Essene* as "emotional voyeurism," most agreed with the "pop" evangelist Malcolm Boyd's contention that it ranked as one of the best religious films ever made. According to Boyd, *Essene* is "an ecclesiastical *Who's Afraid of Virginia Woolf?*"

Like *Titicut Follies*, *Juvenile Court* (1973) set off considerable debate about the legal rights of the adolescent offenders, among them a teen-aged drug pusher, a "Jesus freak," and a thirteen-year-old prostitute. Filmed at the Juvenile Court in Memphis, Tennessee, the two-and-one-half-hour documentary traces the disposition of several cases from arraignment to sentencing. When the film was screened by the National Council of Juvenile Court Judges, it was unanimously held "in contempt" by the jurists, who charged Wiseman with invasion of privacy. Critics, on the other hand, unanimously praised *Juvenile Court* as a "demanding" and "rewarding" film which deserved "close and intelligent attention."

Although he is often described as one of the leading practitioners of *cinéma vérité*, Wiseman discounts the term as "a pompous, overly worked" phrase used to classify "all kinds of dreck." He eschews expensive equipment and high-priced technical experts in favor of natural light, fast film, and a dedicated two- or three-man crew, but he maintains that his problems are no different from those of the major motion picture producer. Like a dramatic film, a documentary needs characterization and structure. The "reductive process," or editing, imposes "a form on an experience that had no form," he explained to journalists at [MORE]'s Third A. J. Liebling Counter Convention in May 1974. In spite of mounting psychological evidence to the contrary, he remains convinced that people's behavior is unaffected by the presence of the camera. On the advice of his lawyers, who contend that his films are protected by the First Amendment, he has not obtained written releases from his subjects since he made *Titicut Follies*.

Frederick Wiseman is a short, trimly built man with brown hair. He met his wife, Zipporah, while both were students at Yale Law School. They live in Cambridge, Massachusetts with their two sons, David and Eric. A reticent man, he prefers not to outline future projects for the press. At one point in his career, he intended to use a grant from the American Film Institute to make a fictional film incorporating his documentary techniques. Despite his unquestioned critical success, Wiseman sees no connection between his films and social change. "My feeling is that if the films do anything, they may contribute information that people might not otherwise have," he told G. Roy Levin. "The premise is the simple one that the more information you have, the more informed decision you can make. . . . I really have no particular propagandistic or social change solutions to offer, and I'm wary of them generally."

References

N Y Times II p25 F 1 '70 por
New York 3:60+ Ja 26 '70 por
Newsweek 78:99 O 4 '71 por

Levin, G. Roy. Documentary Explorations (1971)
Mamber, Stephen. Cinéma Vérité in America (1974)

WOOD, ROBERT D(ENNIS)

Apr. 17, 1925- Television executive
Address: b. CBS Television Network, 51 W. 52d St., New York 10019; h. 20 Church St., Greenwich, Conn. 06830

A veteran television executive with twenty years experience at CBS, Inc., Robert D. Wood was named president of its television network in February 1969. Before succeeding to that position, Wood had worked in sales, station management, and network administration. Under his leadership CBS dropped all but four regularly scheduled series in five seasons, substituting such precedent-shattering and Emmy-award-winning programs as *All in the Family*, *M*A*S*H*, *The Mary Tyler Moore Show*, and *The Waltons* for the cornfed situation comedies of the late 1960's. "Society's

ROBERT D. WOOD

impact on TV is much bigger than television's impact on society," he once said to explain CBS's shift to socially relevant programming. "What we in network TV want to do is respond to the mores and social influences."

The only child of Raymond Dennis Wood, a pharmacist, and Euphrosyne (Planck) Wood, a teacher, Robert Dennis Wood was born in Boise, Idaho on April 17, 1925. A short time later, the Woods moved to one of the "poorer" sections of Beverly Hills, California, as Wood recalled to Les Brown, the broadcasting correspondent for the New York *Times*, in an interview for Brown's book *Television: the Business Behind the Box* (1971). He attended the local public schools, where he was active in athletics, particularly football and track. Following his graduation from Beverly Hills High School in 1943, Wood enlisted in the United States Naval Reserve as a seaman third class. After serving in the South Pacific, he was discharged in April 1946, with the rank of pharmacist's mate, second class.

Returning to civilian life, Wood enrolled in the School of Business Administration at the University of Southern California in Los Angeles. At USC he was a member of the Trojan Knights, an upper division honorary society for men, and president of the campus chapter of Sigma Alpha Epsilon, the social fraternity. He graduated in June 1949 with a B.S. degree in advertising.

In 1949 Wood joined the staff of KNX, a CBS-owned radio station in Hollywood, California and within a few months became its sales service manager. After serving for a year as an account executive for KTTV-TV, Wood became an account executive of KNXT-TV, the CBS owned-and-operated television outlet in Los Angeles, in 1952. Two years later he was transferred to New York City as an account executive for CBS television stations division's national sales department. He returned to the West Coast in 1955 to become general sales manager of KNXT-TV and in 1960 was appointed its vice-president and general manager. Scaling the network's corporate ladder, Wood was named an executive vice-president of the CBS television stations division in 1966, responsible for daily operations of the network's five owned-and-operated VHF television stations in New York City, Chicago, Los Angeles, St. Louis, and Philadelphia, and for national sales to the affiliated stations. He became president of the television stations division on October 30, 1967.

Bedeviled by slipping ratings, temperamental stars, and the more adventurous counter-programming of NBC and ABC, CBS had five network presidents in five years. (The average tenure of a network president is about three years.) To restore the network to its former eminence, Dr. Frank Stanton, the president of CBS, Inc., named Robert Wood president of the CBS television network on February 17, 1969. He had been handpicked by Jack Schneider, the influential network executive vice-president whom many insiders considered the logical successor to William S. Paley, board chairman of CBS, Inc. Wood inherited an unimaginative "blocked-in" schedule for the 1970-71 television season as well as the moribund 1969-70 roster from his predecessor, Thomas H. Dawson. "It's my turn to bite the bullet," he remarked during a discussion of programming with other senior corporate officers, as quoted by Les Brown. "I can either reverse back to our old 'I' formation, which our opponents are onto by now, or I can send out a split end. I think we'll opt for the split end."

Unlike Dawson, who left the programming decisions up to Michael H. Dann, the network's senior vice-president for programming, Wood took an active part in program development. One of his first and most controversial decisions was to fire the Smothers Brothers, stars of the *Smothers Brothers Comedy Hour*, the first successful competitor to NBC's long-running *Bonanza*. Tom and Dick Smothers, who had recently signed a $4,500,000 contract with CBS, had survived several censorship battles with network brass since the première of their show in 1967. But when the comedy team allegedly refused to excise comedian David Steinberg's "offensive" religious monologue from the scheduled Easter Sunday broadcast, Wood immediately fired the pair for failing to comply with CBS's "criteria of taste." Determined to fight the decision, the Smothers Brothers argued that they were dismissed for presenting incisive political satire, a position in which they were supported by the New York *Times*, which accused CBS of capitulating to the Nixon administration's campaign against the electronic media. The *Times* editorialized on April 7, 1969 that the cancellation of *The Smothers Brothers Comedy Hour* was the "latest example of how the networks profess their right to freedom of expression but fail to exercise it in defense of their own programs."

Replying to the *Times*'s charges, Wood insisted that the Smothers Brothers had been fired for repeatedly submitting material that "breached . . . standards as to taste" and for issuing "ultimatums" for the "blind clearance" of comedy routines. "The central issue involved here is whether a broadcast organization has some responsibility to the public with respect to questions of taste, and if so, whether it is entitled to establish reasonable procedures in order to exercise that responsibility," he wrote in an open letter to the New York *Times* (April 12, 1969). In May 1969, at the fifteenth annual conference of CBS-TV affiliates in New York City, Wood and two colleagues, Richard S. Salant, the president of CBS News, and Richard W. Jencks, the president of CBS/Broadcast Group, reaffirmed the rights and responsibilities of broadcasters to control their programming. A few weeks later, in an interview with Kay Gardella for a New York *Daily News* profile (August 7, 1969), he said bluntly, "I was not going to turn CBS over to Tommy Smothers."

Convinced that the network's future depended on its ability to attract and hold the eighteen-to-forty-nine-year-old viewers, the prime marketing targets of the major television advertisers, Wood embarked on a campaign to revitalize CBS's staid image. He purchased a package of first-run theatrical motion pictures, encouraged original made-for-television films, and promoted Merv Griffin as a talk show host to compete with NBC's redoubtable Johnny Carson and ABC's affable Dick Cavett. With the support of Jencks and Schneider, Wood suggested that CBS "deruralize" its roster. Long-running hit shows, such as *Petticoat Junction*, *The Jackie Gleason Show*, and *The Red Skelton Show*, while popular with the older, rural audience, were shunned by the younger, better educated, more affluent urban viewers. "CBS is falling behind the times, and we have to get back in step," Wood told Paley, as recounted by Les Brown. "What we need to begin the rebuilding are programs that are relevant to what is happening today, instead of make-believe." Paley agreed and, in the spring of 1970 CBS axed *Red Skelton*, *Jackie Gleason*, *Petticoat Junction*, *Lancer*, *Get Smart*, and *The Tim Conway Show*. "The most compelling reason . . . for revising our program schedule was that we are starting down a new decade," Wood told officials from the CBS-affiliated stations at a meeting in May 1970. "The days are gone when we can afford to be imitative rather than innovative. . . . We have to attract new viewers [from all segments of] American society."

To replace the cancelled shows, Wood selected six new series for the 1970-71 season. In the summer of 1970 he brought the producers of such new programs as *The Interns*, *Arnie*, and *The Mary Tyler Moore Show* to New York City to explain their shows to the press. A summer-long barrage of promotional spots, based on the theme "CBS is putting it all together," introduced the shows to the viewers. Assisted by Fred Silverman, his new programming executive, Wood continued to revise his fall schedule for more effective counter-programming. *Green Acres*, a rural situation comedy sandwiched between two crime shows, and *The Beverly Hillbillies*, a top-rated comedy slotted between *The Storefront Lawyers* and *Medical Center*, were rescheduled opposite ABC's *Mod*

Squad and NBC's *The Don Knotts Show* "to give the viewer something totally dissimilar."

The most provocative of CBS's new shows was *All in the Family,* an American adaptation of the BBC-TV hit comedy series *Till Death Do Us Part.* Intrigued by the similarities between *All in the Family* and *Man in the Middle,* a less promising pilot production then in development for a possible midseason replacement slot in January 1971, Wood purchased the series from Norman Lear and Alan (Bud) Yorkin's Tandem Productions in the spring of 1970. With Wood's unqualified support, *All in the Family,* which premièred on January 12, 1971, weathered the protests of William Tankersley, the director of the network's program practices who objected to its "irreverence" and "vulgarity," to become the nation's most popular program.

Wood was so bolstered by the success of *All in the Family* and its equally popular spin-offs, *Maude* and *Good Times,* that he approved plot outlines that broached such controversial topics as alcoholism, menopause, impotence, childbirth, breast cancer, and premarital sex. Ignoring vocal opposition from antiabortion groups, CBS televised and reran a two-part episode of *Maude* in which the pregnant forty-seven-year-old Maude decides to have an abortion. In a speech to the Better Business Bureau in Nashville, Tennessee on October 16, 1973, Wood said that the network was "facing up to [its] obligations" as a purveyor of entertainment and enlightenment for millions of Americans. "Instead of playing it safe," he continued, "we are meeting the challenges that come from the awareness that our society's standards and tastes are undergoing enormous change, and that television must reflect the growing maturity of the audience."

Despite his liberal stance, Wood occasionally killed questionable episodes if the subject matter seemed "out of keeping" with the show's image. During the 1973-74 season he turned down a script for *The Waltons* that described Mary Ellen Walton's confused reactions to her first menstrual period. He also vetoed a taped segment of *The New Dick Van Dyke Show* in which a bewildered child surprises her parents while they are having sexual intercourse. "There is a certain level of expectancy that each viewer brings to each television show," Wood remarked, as quoted in the New York *Daily News* (February 12, 1974). "I don't like to present a subject that would collide with their level of expectancy. . . . To break the mood the viewer brings to a show . . . is wrong."

For similar reasons Wood postponed the telecast of David Rabe's Tony-award-winning antiwar play, *Sticks and Bones.* The previously scheduled broadcast date of the play, which describes the homecoming of a blind and alienated Vietnam veteran, coincided with the return of several hundred American prisoners of war. In a telegram sent to all CBS affiliates, Wood explained that presenting the play "at this time might be unnecessarily abrasive." Joseph Papp, the producer of *Sticks and Bones,* angrily denounced Wood's decision as "a cowardly cop-out" and "a rotten affront to freedom of speech." Over the objections of nearly sixty affiliates, which refused to carry the program, Wood rescheduled the two-hour production for broadcast on August 17, 1973. Of the more than 1,000 letters received about the play, over half congratulated the network.

Shortly after becoming president of the network, Wood promised its affiliate station managers and owners that CBS would "resist being sucked into the annual ratings rat race." Nevertheless, he readily admits that ratings play an important part in the determination of future programming. The ratings come "closest to reaching what the American public indeed wants from television," Wood observed on the ABC News *Close-up* investigation of prime time television that was broadcast on September 2, 1974. Programs are "voted on . . . 365 days a year," he added. In addition to the ratings, Wood and his staff rely on mail from viewers, press criticism, and the reactions of affiliate stations to make certain a particular program or series is "responsive to the interests, needs and appetites" of the public. In January 1974 Wood told a group of television editors meeting in Hollywood, California that CBS would continue to concentrate on comedy. The 1974-75 season includes nine comedy shows, two of them newcomers, fifteen ninety-minute daytime dramas, and more than eighty hours of special programming. To provide time for additional children's programming, he recommended that the courts rescind the prime time access rule, an FCC ruling that returned the 7:30 to 8:00 P.M. (EST) time slot to the local stations to encourage local programming. (The United States Court of Appeals recently postponed the implementation of new rules for network programs until September 1975.)

Like his counterparts at NBC and ABC, Wood defends the network's policy of scheduling reruns during the summer months. In a speech to the Hollywood Radio and Television Society on September 12, 1972 he argued that television "forces a viewer to make only one program choice at one particular time." Because 131,000,000 people, or approximately 85 percent of the potential viewing audience, do not see a program when it is first telecast, "the only possible way to give the viewer a chance to see his next best choice is to schedule repeat performances," the CBS executive reasoned. Commenting on the FCC's proposed thirteen-week limitation on annual reruns, he cited prohibitive production costs. The introduction of twelve more weeks of first-run programs, each costing about $95,000, would seriously jeopardize the daily news operations, news documentaries, on-location coverage of special events, and the number and quality of entertainment specials, Wood explained. "Only by averaging the high cost of a first-run—with low-cost repeats—[can] programming expenditures be kept under some measure of control," he said. "Tamper with this fine line of balance and the entire broadcast economy is in big trouble."

A vigorous and energetic man, Robert D. Wood stands five feet ten inches tall and weighs 165 pounds. He has brown eyes and retreating gray hair. His favorite recreation is golf. Outgoing and candid, Wood makes himself accessible to his colleagues and to the press. After one interview, Les Brown noted in *Television* that the broadcast executive "gave the impression of someone not above settling an argument with his fists." Wood and his wife, the former Nancy Harwell, whom he married in October 1949, were divorced in March 1972. They have two children, Virginia Lucile and Dennis Harwell. A trustee of the University of Southern California, Wood has also served as the director of the General Alumni Association and as the honorary past president of the Trojan Club. He is the recipient of the School of Business Administration's Distinguished Alumni Award and holds an honorary doctor of laws degree from his alma mater.

References

Broadcasting 58:143 My 1 '61; 76:10 F 17 '69

Brown, Les. Television: The Business Behind the Box (1971)

Who's Who in America, 1974-75

WYNDER, ERNEST L(UDWIG)

Apr. 30, 1922- Physician; foundation executive
Address: b. American Health Foundation, 1370 Ave. of the Americas, New York 10019; "Twin Chimneys," Revolutionary Rd., Scarborough, N.Y. 10510

Some twenty-five years ago, when he was still in medical school, Ernest L. Wynder began the pioneering research that eventually resulted in the identification of cigarette smoking as a principal cause of lung cancer. In his later laboratory and epidemiological investigation of cancer in human beings, much of it conducted at the Sloan-Kettering Institute for Cancer Research in New York, Dr. Wynder grew increasingly concerned with environmental influences on the development of cancer and with means of controlling risk factors. His interest in preventive medicine led in 1969 to his becoming the founding president of the American Health Foundation. The only national organization devoted entirely to the prevention of disease, his crusading foundation has as its motto "To help people die young—as late as possible."

Ernest Ludwig Wynder was born on April 30, 1922 in Herford, Westphalia, Germany, the son of Dr. Alfred and Therese (Godfrey) Wynder. Nazi pogroms forced his father, a well-to-do physician, to flee with his family to the United States in 1938, shortly before the outbreak of World War II. In considerably reduced financial circumstances Ernest Wynder worked his way through New York University by selling newspapers, waiting on table, and doing other odd jobs. During

1943 he obtained both his B.A. degree and American citizenship and also entered the United States Army as a private. His native language gave him an advantage in securing an assignment as chief monitor of German newscasts for a psychological warfare unit.

On his release from military service at the end of the war Wynder enrolled in Washington University School of Medicine in St. Louis, where he earned his B.S. and M.D. degrees in 1950. He then served a one-year internship at Georgetown University Hospital in Washington, D.C. Later moving to New York City, he began his long association with the Memorial Hospital for Cancer & Allied Diseases in 1951 as a junior assistant resident and with the Sloan-Kettering Institute for Cancer Research in 1952 as an assistant in the environmental cancerigenesis division. During his early years in New York he often visited St. Louis to continue work on long-range collaborative research projects.

While a medical student at Washington University, Wynder had found his interest in problems of cancer stimulated by two prominent physicians on the faculty—his professor of anatomy, Dr. Edmund V. Cowdry, former director of the Wernse Cancer Research Laboratory, and the chest surgeon Dr. Evarts A. Graham, who in 1933 performed the first successful removal of an entire lung in treatment of cancer. Graham's observation of an increase in the number of lung cancer patients led Wynder to speculate on a possible link between cancer and smoking. Although skeptical of that relationship, Graham approved his student's ambitious statistical investigation of cancer patients in selected hospitals, including Washington University's Barnes Hospital, of which Graham was surgeon in chief. Published in the May 1950 issue of the *Journal of the American Medical Association*, the Wynder-Graham findings established the first firm statistical connection between tobacco and cancer, with data showing that some 95 percent of the patients studied had a long history of cigarette smoking. Wynder's work on the report won him the university's Borden Undergraduate Research Award in Medicine.

Cancer experts throughout the world began both to reevaluate their data and to conduct their own surveys of lung cancer patients, generally confirming the conclusions of Wynder and Graham. As yet, however, no cancer-causing agent was known in tobacco smoke. To check out the causal relationship implied in their statistical studies, the two doctors, together with Graham's research assistant, Dr. Adele Croninger, undertook ground-breaking laboratory research in cancer etiology. By November 1953 they were able to report that tar obtained from the smoke of thousands of machine-smoked cigarettes and painted on the shaved backs of mice had produced cancers of the epidermoid type that appears in the human lung.

Dr. Wynder's next step after having proved the existence of a carcinogen in the tar of tobacco smoke was to separate and analyze the various chemical fractions of the tar. By 1956 he had determined that cigarette tars were composed of acid, basic, and neutral elements and had located the carcinogenic fractions mainly in the neutral portion. Collaborating with Dr. Dietrich Hoffmann, also of the Sloan-Kettering Institute, he announced in 1959 that eight separate carcinogenic tobacco tar fractions had been identified. They had also made some progress toward identifying chemicals in the tar that trigger and strengthen the cancer-causing agents.

Meanwhile, Dr. Wynder continued through epidemiological evidence to bolster his case against heavy cigarette smoking as a major cause of lung cancer. In a 1957 study he and Dr. Frank Lemon, of the College of Medical Evangelists in Loma Linda, California, compared the hospital records of Seventh-Day Adventists, who neither smoke nor drink alcohol, with data on non-Adventists for incidence of cancer and coronary artery disease. The incidence of cancer in Adventists was the same as that for the non-Adventist group—except for forms of cancer associated with smoking and drinking. Among the abstaining Adventists there were 90 percent fewer lung cancers and 40 percent fewer heart attacks. Adventists who lived in smoggy Los Angeles had the same low incidence of lung cancer as Adventists elsewhere, a discovery that reinforced the conclusions of Wynder and his associate Hoffmann that smoking, and not air pollution alone, was the primary factor in development of lung cancer.

In response to the tobacco industry's concerted attempts to discredit his findings, Wynder challenged cigarette manufacturers to unite in producing a less harmful cigarette. At Sloan-Kettering he carried out research to identify the most carcinogenic parts of the tobacco plant, to find ways to reduce the burning temperature of the cigarette tip, and to develop effective cigarette filters. Outside his laboratory he joined government, scientific, and other groups in promoting measures to prevent lung cancer. In 1957 he was a member of the Study Group on Smoking and Health, a panel of medical experts organized under the auspices of the American Cancer Society, National Cancer Institute, American Heart Association, and National Heart Association to settle the cigarette controversy. Later that year testifying before a House subcommittee, he urged that the government require manufacturers to use more effective filters in order to remove at least 40 percent of tar and nicotine from the smoke. In 1959 he recommended that the tar and nicotine content of various brands of cigarettes be published by a group independent of the tobacco industry.

Three years after the United States Surgeon General's 1964 report, which stated that cigarette smoking is dangerous to health, Dr. Wynder appeared before a Senate subcommittee investigating the progress of subsequent research. He urged the reduction of tar by use of selected tobacco strains or of reconstituted tobaccos, along with filters. As spokesman for participants in a workshop discussion called "A Less Harmful Cigarette," Wynder told delegates to the September 1967 World Conference on Smoking and Health

DR. ERNEST L. WYNDER

of his group's concern over undocumented claims being made for filter cigarettes. The Surgeon General appointed him in November of that year to an eleven-member committee charged with recommending action on protecting the public from the hazards of cigarette smoking. He was also named a member of the tobacco working group of the task force on lung cancer of the National Cancer Institute in 1967, the epidemiological advisory committee for the Third National Cancer Survey in 1968, and the National Cancer Planning Conference in 1971.

About half of all Wynder's research papers have dealt with lung cancer. Other studies have concerned cancer of the respiratory tract, upper alimentary tract, stomach, breast, cervix, endometrium, ovary, bladder, prostate, pancreas, and head and neck. He has investigated the relation of smoking and of cancer to coronary artery disease, the correlation of appendectomy and cancer risk, and the effects of nutritional deficiencies on certain types of cancer.

Through his research over the years Wynder became convinced that diseases of the heart and blood vessels, as well as the majority of cancers, could be related to environmental factors. "We invite major chronic diseases—by what we eat, drink and smoke, and by our inactivity," he once asserted. "But the stubborn combination of human nature together with the legal barriers and industrial and governmental inertia make it difficult to revolutionize medical goals away from crisis-oriented medicine and toward preventive medicine." During the 1960's he felt with increasing concern that action should be taken against medically known hazardous influences. Since 1954 he had been teaching preventive medicine at the Sloan-Kettering division of Cornell University Medical College, with the rank of associate professor since 1956. He gave up that post in 1969 along with an associate membership that he had held since 1960 in the Sloan-Kettering Institute, to devote himself more fully to preventive medicine as president of the American Health Foundation, which he had founded in 1968.

"The major killers are due to lifestyle," Dr. Wynder explained in discussing the purpose of the American Health Foundation, as quoted in *Vogue* (April 1974). "Any disease that is man-made is man-preventable, and we want to be on the first line of defense, to focus public attention on preventive medicine as a way to offset the inroads of disease." To prove the value of periodic examinations, he persuaded six large companies to finance the Health Maintenance Center as an enterprise of the American Health Corporation. The center, which opened in Manhattan in July 1972 and operates in cooperation with the American Health Foundation, provides comprehensive physical examinations utilizing computers in a multiphasic testing program. When doctors detect a health risk factor, they may refer the examinee to one or more of the four foundation-supervised special clinics—smoking withdrawal, nutrition, hypertension, and physical fitness—designed to help people gain control over their health by improving their living habits. Wynder is especially interested in educating children in disease prevention.

Under the auspices of the American Health Foundation Dr. Wynder has also continued his laboratory and statistical research projects. His goal of developing a less harmful cigarette, for example, is regarded as one important means of disease prevention. Wynder and his colleagues have been studying links between diet and colon cancer in experiments that analyze types of bacteria in the colon as well as in continuing epidemiological studies of Seventh-Day Adventists, who avoid eating meat, and comparative data on Japanese Americans and Japanese living in Japan. Reporting on his recent work before the American College of Nutrition in June 1974, he suggested that about half of all cancers in women and about 30 percent of all cancers in men may be related to deficiencies and excesses in diet.

In 1972 the American Health Foundation launched its official journal, *Preventive Medicine*, with Ernest L. Wynder as editor in chief. That international periodical publishes new studies dealing with all aspects of prevention of the leading causes of death, and in his regular column, "A Corner of History," Wynder reprints the originals of medical documents of historic interest. Since 1970 he has also been a member of the editorial advisory board of the journal *Cancer Research*. He is the editor of the book *The Biologic Effects of Tobacco, with Emphasis on the Clinical and Experimental Aspects* (Little, Brown, 1955); the coauthor, with Dietrich Hoffmann, of *Tobacco and Tobacco Smoke; Studies in Experimental Carcinogenesis* (Academic Press, 1967); and the coeditor with Hoffmann of *Towards a Less Harm-*

ful Cigarette (National Cancer Institute Monograph, 1968).

Since 1969 Dr. Wynder has been adjunct professor of public health practice at Columbia University and since 1970 a lecturer in the department of community medicine at Mt. Sinai School of Medicine of the City University of New York. Formerly clinical assistant physician, from 1956 to 1964, and assistant attending physician, from 1964 to 1969, of Memorial Hospital, he retains his affiliation with that institution as a consulting epidemiologist. He was also formerly a visiting physician of James Ewing Hospital of the City of New York, now a pavilion of Memorial.

Dr. Wynder served as a member of the research and development advisory committee for the National Center for Health Services Research and Development in 1968, the task force on atherosclerosis of the National Heart and Lung Institute in 1970, and the White House Conference on Children in 1970. Among the professional organizations to which he belongs are the Industrial Medical Association, the American Cancer Research Association, the American Medical Association, the Air Pollution Control Association, the New York Public Health Association, the New York Academy of Sciences, and the Max Planck Society in Germany. His club is the Lotus in New York City. In 1972 he was appointed to the advisory group of the American Revolution Bicentennial Commission.

Dr. Ernest L. Wynder is a bachelor who does not smoke, seldom takes an alcoholic drink, and follows his own precepts about exercise and nutrition. "Physically," Margaret Kaufman wrote in the *Washington University Magazine* (Fall, 1971), "he is an impressive advertisement for the rewards of good health habits: swarthily handsome and trim, he looks ten to fifteen years younger than his [actual] years." She went on to say that he retains a slight German accent, "which adds to his considerable flair as a public speaker. He has the uncanny ability to captivate and convince any audience." To Rosemary Blackmon of *Vogue* (April 1974), he seemed "a stern man, both rousing and granite-y, brilliant and grinding." His recreations are travel, the theatre, music, playing tennis, and, especially, spending time with his friends.

References

N Y Post p43 Ap 19 '72 por
Washington University Mag Fall '71 pors
American Men and Women of Science 12th ed (1973)
Who's Who in America, 1974-75
World Who's Who in Science (1968)

PHOTO CREDITS

AP Newsfeatures, Wayne Hays; *Australian News & Information Bureau,* Gough Whitlam; *BMI Archives,* Sir Michael Tippett; *Fabian Bachrach,* J. K. Jamieson; *Jerry Bauer,* Jean Genet; *Don Bender,* John R. Coleman; *British Information Services,* Jeremy Thorpe; *Chase, Ltd., Washington,* Yitzhak Rabin; *Floyd Clark, Cal Tech,* William A. Fowler; *Courtesy, The Cleveland Museum of Art,* Sherman E. Lee; *Department of Commerce, Office of Public Affairs,* Frederick B. Dent; *Niki Ekstrom,* Stephen Birmingham; *Ann Elmo Agency, Inc., New York City,* Wole Soyinka; *Elliott Erwitt,* V. S. Pritchett; *Sara Facio-Alicia D'Amico,* Julio Cortázar; *Food & Agricultural Organization,* Addeke H. Boerma; *Madison Geddes, Cleveland,* Semon E. Knudsen; *German Information Center,* Helmut Schmidt; *Mark Gerson, London,* Lady Antonia Fraser; *Kenneth P. Green,* Maya Angelou; *Harvard University News Office,* José Luis Sert; *Andreas Heumann,* John le Carré; *Gina James,* Pauline Kael; *Thomas C. Kelsey,* Garrett Hardin; *A. Kondo,* Takeo Fukuda; *Jill Krementz,* William P. Blatty, Desmond Morris; *Robert Lansdale, Etobicoke, Ontario,* Omond M. Solandt; *Fred W. McDarrah,* Robert C. Scull; *Rollie McKenna,* William Jay Smith; *Nadine Markova,* Octavio Paz; *Miami Dolphins,* Don Shula; *NASA,* Matthew P. Thekaekara; *National Institutes of Health,* Makio Murayama; *New York Rangers,* Gilles Villemure; *Newsweek—Jack Nisberg,* André Masson; *John Olson,* Alistair Cooke; *Pach Bros., New York,* Alan Greenspan; *Dr. Pfeiffer, Graz, Austria,* Karl von Frisch; *Photo Imagery, Washington, D.C.,* David Selden; *Donald L. Pier,* Pat Loud; *Axel Poignant,* Patrick White; *Princeton University,* Melvin B. Gottlieb; *Rocke-feller University—Eugene H. Kone,* Neal E. Miller; *Dave Scherman,* Jessica Mitford; *Iris Schneider,* Lee Krasner; *Scientia,* Jerzy Kosinski; *James C. Smith,* John Reardon; *Gertrud Stahel, Interlaken, Switzerland,* Norman Vincent Peale; *Christian Steiner,* Schuyler G. Chapin; *Studio—Lipnitzki, Paris,* Olivier Messiaen; *United Press International,* Donald C. Alexander, Giorgio Almirante, Robert Altman, Carlos Arias Navarro, William Ball, Abraham D. Beame, Bernardo Bertolucci, Eubie Blake, Sonny Bono, Björn Borg, Edgar M. Bronfman, Joel T. Broyhill, Brendan T. Byrne, Sammy Cahn, Rosemary Casals, Cher, Francis Ford Coppola, Edward E. David, Charles O. Finley, George Foreman, Harold S. Geneen, Valéry Giscard d'Estaing, Lee Grant, Louise Day Hicks, Reggie Jackson, Leon Jaworski, Barbara Jordan, Clarence M. Kelley, Jomo Kenyatta, Carole King, Lubos Kohoutek, Kris Kristofferson, Kathryn Kuhlman, Norman Lear, Edwin Link, Lon Nol, Tom McCall, Guru Maharaj Ji, Gene Mauch, Thomas J. Meskill, Jason Miller, Johnny Miller, Ilie Nastase, Jack Nicholson, Al Pacino, Valery Panov, Merle Park, Juan Perón, Augusto Pinochet Ugarte, Bertram Powers, Diana Rigg, Samuel Rosen, William B. Saxbe, Harrison H. Schmitt, William E. Simon, John J. Sirica, António de Spínola, Adlai E. Stevenson 3d, Tom Stoppard, Robert S. Strauss, William R. Tolbert Jr., Ron Turcotte, Jon Voight, Tuesday Weld, Kevin H. White; *U. S. Army—William Rosenmund,* Frederick E. Davison; *Warner Bros.,* Mel Brooks; *L. Arnold Weissberger,* Anita Loos; *Wide World,* Andrei Amalrik, Matthew Guinan, Rebekah Harkness, Stanley Hiller Jr., Teddy Kollek; *Wooten—Moulton, Chapel Hill, N.C.,* Edward G. Holley.

NECROLOGY

ABBOTT, BUD Oct. 2, 1895-Apr. 24, 1974
Radio, stage, and film comedian; as partner in
popular Abbott and Costello team, played straight
man to Lou Costello in many movies, including
In the Navy (1941). See *Current Biography*
(October) 1941.

Obituary

N Y Times p42 Ap 25 '74

ABRAMS, CREIGHTON W(ILLIAMS, JR.) Sept.
15, 1914-Sept. 4, 1974 General of the United
States Army; World War II commander of 37th
Tank Battalion, which played key role in relief
of Bastogne during Battle of the Bulge; commanded federal troops assigned to allay racial
conflict in South during early 1960's; vice-chief
of staff of Army (1964-67); as commander of
United States Military Assistance Command in
Vietnam (1968-72) implemented "Vietnamization" policy and supervised gradual disengagement of American forces from Indochina; Army
chief of staff (1972-74). See *Current Biography*
(October) 1968.

Obituary

N Y Times p1+ S 4 '74

AICHI, KIICHI Oct. 10, 1907-Nov. 23, 1973
Japanese government official; as Minister of Foreign Affairs (1968-71), negotiated treaty with
United States restoring Okinawa to Japan; also
served as chief Cabinet secretary (1957-58; 1966-
68), and as Minister of International Trade and
Industry (1954-55), Justice (1958-59), Education
(1964-66), and Finance (1972-73). See *Current
Biography* (July) 1971.

Obituary

N Y Times p34 N 24 '73

ALDRICH, WINTHROP W(ILLIAMS) Nov. 2,
1885-Feb. 25, 1974 Lawyer; financier; diplomat;
conducted New York law practice specializing in
finance and banking cases (1919-29); president
(1930-33) and board chairman (1933-53) of
Chase National Bank (now Chase Manhattan
Bank); Ambassador to Great Britain (1953-57).
See *Current Biography* (March) 1953.

Obituary

N Y Times p10 F 26 '74

ALSOP, STEWART (JOHONNOT OLIVER)
May 17, 1914-May 26, 1974 Political columnist;
with *Newsweek* since 1968; previously on staff
of *Saturday Evening Post* (1958-68); with

brother Joseph, wrote syndicated New York
Herald Tribune column (1946-58); a progressive voice of old "WASP" establishment, described himself as "very square New Deal liberal" with moderate "interest in the New Left";
among other books, wrote *Stay of Execution*
(1973), a brave memoir written while he was
dying of acute myeloblastic leukemia. See *Current Biography* (October) 1952.

Obituary

N Y Times p20 My 27 '74

APGAR, VIRGINIA June 7, 1909-Aug. 7, 1974
Physician; medical researcher; developed the Apgar Score System to evaluate the health of a
newborn infant; served the National Foundation-
March of Dimes as head of the division on congenital malformations (1959-67), director of basic
research (1969-72), and senior vice-president for
medical affairs (1973-74); coauthored *Is My
Baby All Right?* (1972). See *Current Biography*
(February) 1968.

Obituary

N Y Times p36 Ag 8 '74

ARQUETTE, CLIFF Dec. 28, 1905-Sept. 23,
1974 Entertainer; musician; comedian and character actor; created the homespun, sly-witted old
bumpkin, Charley Weaver, a role in which he appeared regularly for several years on NBC-TV
Tonight (later the *Jack Paar Show*), beginning in
1957, and on the NBC-TV game show *Hollywood
Squares,* beginning in 1966. See *Current Biography* (June) 1961.

Obituary

N Y Times p44 S 24 '74

ASTURIAS, MIGUEL ANGEL Oct. 19, 1899-June
9, 1974 Guatemalan author, journalist and diplomat; published ten novels, including *El Señor
Presidente* (1964) and *Mulata* (1967), and the
trilogy *Viento Fuerte* (1950), *El Papa Verde*
(1953), and *Los Ojos de los Enterrados* (1960),
as well as stories, poems, and plays reflecting
concern with Indian tradition, national identity,
and compassion for underdog; won Lenin Peace
Prize (1966) and Nobel Prize in Literature
(1967); served in diplomatic posts in 1940's
and 1950's; Ambassador to France (1966-70).
See *Current Biography* (October) 1968.

Obituary

N Y Times p25 Je 10 '74

AYUB KHAN, MOHAMMAD May 14, 1907-Apr. 19, 1974 Pakistani statesman; army officer with rank of field marshal; Minister of Defense (1954-55); chief administrator of martial law and supreme commander of all armed forces (1958); assumed Presidency by proclamation in 1958; resigned under pressure in 1969. See *Current Biography* (April) 1959.

Obituary

N Y Times p53 Ap 21 '74

BATES, H(ERBERT) E(RNEST) May 16, 1905-Jan. 29, 1974 British writer; author of fifty books, including novels, short stories, and autobiography; beginning with *The Two Sisters* (1926), wrote mainly about the English countryside; during World War II was commissioned by the Royal Air Force to write fiction about the war. See *Current Biography* (September) 1944.

Obituary

N Y Times p38 Ja 30 '74

BATES, MARSTON July 23, 1906-Apr. 3, 1974 Zoologist; university professor; author; conducted research in tropical diseases and in mosquito biology for the Rockefeller Foundation (1937-50); professor of zoology at the University of Michigan (1952-71); author of several scientific books for laymen, including *The Prevalence of People* (1955), *The Forest and the Sea* (1960), and *A Jungle in the House* (1970). See *Current Biography* (April) 1956.

Obituary

N Y Times p35 Ap 5 '74

BAYNE, STEPHEN F(IELDING) JR. May 21, 1908-Jan. 18, 1974 Protestant Episcopal clergyman; bishop of Olympia, Washington (1947-59); first vice-president of executive council of Protestant Episcopal Church in the United States (1968-70); professor (1970-73) and dean (1972-73) of General Theological Seminary in New York. See *Current Biography* (January) 1964.

Obituary

N Y Times p34 Ja 19 '74

BEIRNE, J(OSEPH) A(NTHONY) Feb. 16, 1911-Sept. 2, 1974 Labor union official; president of National Federation of Telephone Workers (1943-47) and its successor, Communications Workers of America (1947-74); vice-president of CIO (1949-55) and AFL-CIO (1955-74); played leading role in fight against Communist influence and corruption in labor movement during 1950's; early advocate of equal pay for women; secretary-treasurer of national labor committee supporting George McGovern for President (1972). See *Current Biography* (March) 1946.

Obituary

N Y Times p38 S 3 '74

BEN-GURION, DAVID Oct. 16, 1886-Dec. 1, 1973 Premier and Defense Minister of Israel (1949-53; 1955-63) and one of its principal founders; helped organize labor federation Histadruth and labor party Mapai; secretary general of Histadruth (1921-35); chairman of Jewish Agency for Palestine (1935-48); proclaimed independence of Israel in 1948; provoked worldwide controversy by equating Judaism with Israeli nationality; promoted policy of swift retaliation to Arab attacks, culminating in Suez expedition (1956), but counseled withdrawal from most of Arab territory occupied by Israel in 1967 war; retired from Knesset (parliament) in 1970. See *Current Biography* (January) 1957.

Obituary

N Y Times p1+ D 2 '73

BEST, EDNA Mar. 3, 1900-Sept. 18, 1974 Actress; won acclaim on the London stage for her portrayal of Tessa in *The Constant Nymph* (1926); starred on Broadway in Shaw's *Captain Brassbound's Conversion*, S. N. Behrman's *Jane*, and other plays during the 1940's and 1950's; appeared in many films, beginning in 1923, and on radio programs. See *Current Biography* (July) 1954.

Obituary

N Y Times p46 S 19 '74

BIDDLE, GEORGE Jan. 24, 1885-Nov. 6, 1973 Painter; member of prominent Biddle family of Philadelphia; a leader in organization of Federal Arts Project during Depression; best known for portraits and murals, especially socially oriented frescoes in the Department of Justice building in Washington expressing his belief that concern generated by "the sweatshop and tenement of yesterday" can lead to "the life planned with justice for tomorrow." See *Current Biography* (February) 1942.

Obituary

N Y Times p50 N 8 '73

BIGGERS, JOHN D(AVID) Dec. 19, 1888-Dec. 31, 1973 Business executive; president (1930-53) and board chairman (1953-60) of the Libbey-Owens-Ford Company, a now diversified corporation that originally specialized in the manufacture of glass for automobile windows; in government, was supervisor of the first federal unemployment census (1937-38) and director of production in the United States Office of Production Management during World War II. See *Current Biography* (September) 1941.

Obituary

N Y Times p22 Ja 1 '74

BLACKETT, P(ATRICK) M(AYNARD) S(TUART), BARON BLACKETT Nov. 18, 1897-July 13, 1974 British nuclear physicist; pioneer in development of operations research; on faculty of University of London (1933-53) and Victoria University of Manchester (1937-53); ranged in work from pure research into nature of matter to military advice, especially regarding radar, that helped Britain survive World War II; won 1948 Nobel Prize in physics for studies in cosmic radiation by the "Wilson cloud chamber" method; was created life peer in 1969. See Current Biography (February) 1949.

Obituary

N Y Times p41 Jl 14 '74

BOHLEN, CHARLES E(USTIS) Aug. 30, 1904-Jan. 1, 1974 United States career diplomat; fluent in Russian and steeped in all aspects of Soviet affairs, was leading Sovietologist in United States foreign service during four decades preceding Nixon regime; played key role in every major Soviet-American development, beginning with the opening of the United States Embassy in Moscow in 1934; Ambassador to Kremlin (1953-57), Manila (1957-59), and Paris (1962-68). See Current Biography (May) 1960.

Obituary

N Y Times p1+ Ja 2 '74

BOONE, J(OEL) T(HOMPSON) Aug. 29, 1889-Apr. 2, 1974 Physician; served in United States Navy (1914-50); held rank of vice-admiral for eight years; medical director of Veterans' Administration (1951-55); physician to Presidents Harding, Coolidge, and Hoover. See Current Biography (March) 1951.

Obituary

Washington Post C p22 Ap 4 '74

BOYLE, HAL Feb. 21, 1911-Apr. 1, 1974 Journalist; joined the Associated Press as copy boy in 1928; worked in several Mid-West offices of the AP before being assigned to its New York bureau in 1937; as AP war correspondent covered fighting in Europe and Pacific area during World War II and later in Korea and Vietnam; winner of 1945 Pulitzer Prize for distinguished correspondence. See Current Biography (June) 1945.

Obituary

N Y Times p42 Ap 2 '74

BRENNAN, WALTER July 25, 1894-Sept. 21, 1974 Actor; appeared in over 100 films, often portraying colorful old-timers in westerns; won three Oscars for best supporting actor, in Come and Get It (1936), Kentucky (1938), The Westerner (1940); created the role of Grandpa McCoy in the TV series The Real McCoys. See Current Biography (May) 1941.

Obituary

N Y Times p38 S 23 '74

BRODE, WALLACE (REED) June 12, 1900-Aug. 10, 1974 Chemist; United States government official; associate director of the National Bureau of Standards (1947-57); special scientific adviser to Secretary of State John Foster Dulles (1958-60); specialist in spectroscopy, applied optics, and synthetic chemistry; winner of Priestly Medal of the American Chemical Society (1960). See Current Biography (June) 1958.

Obituary

N Y Times p38 Ag 13 '74

BROGAN, D(ENNIS) W(ILLIAM) Aug. 11, 1900-Jan. 5, 1974 British political scientist; professor emeritus at Cambridge University, where he taught from 1939 to 1968; reached wider audience through his lecture tours and, above all, his books, including The American Political System (1933), The American Character (1944), and numerous other lucid, witty, and highly readable works on the United States, France, and England. See Current Biography (Yearbook) 1947.

Obituary

N Y Times p34 Ja 7 '74

BRONOWSKI, J(ACOB) Jan. 18, 1908-Aug. 22, 1974 British mathematician; tried to establish philosophical basis for scientific research; as member of British mission to Japan (1945), reported on effects of atomic bombings; headed research for British National Coal Board (1950-63); resident fellow at Salk Institute since 1964; filmed thirteen-part Ascent of Man series, shown on BBC television in 1973; author of Science and Human Values (1958) and other books. See Current Biography (September) 1958.

Obituary

N Y Times p32 Ag 23 '74

BROWN, PRENTISS M(ARSH) June 18, 1889-Dec. 19, 1973 Public servant; chairman of Mackinac Bridge Authority; Democratic United States Representative (1932-36) and Senator (1936-43) from Michigan; administrator of Office of Price Administration (1943-44); board chairman of Detroit Edison (1944-54); was proudest of his success in raising funds for building of Mackinac Bridge. See Current Biography (January) 1943.

Obituary

N Y Times p42 D 20 '73

BRUNNER, EDMUND DE S(CHWEINITZ) Nov. 4, 1889-Dec. 21, 1973 Social scientist; Moravian church minister; specialist in rural sociology and the relationship between religion and culture; taught at Columbia University from 1926 to 1963; wrote or coauthored twenty-eight books, including Rural Social Trends (1933), with J. H. Kolb, and The Growth of a Science (1957). See Current Biography (September) 1958.

Obituary

N Y Times p25 D 23 '73

BUSH, VANNEVAR Mar. 11, 1890-June 28, 1974 Electrical engineer; chairman of Massachusetts Institute of Technology Corporation; taught at M.I.T. for two decades and was dean of engineering there from 1932 until 1939, when he began sixteen-year term as president of Carnegie Institution; invented differential analyzer, prototype of analog computer, and codeveloped Smith power-transmission tube, among other devices; cofounded several prosperous enterprises, including American Appliance Company (now Raytheon), electronics manufacturer; planned and headed Office of Scientific Research and Development and the National Defense Research Committee, which mobilized American science and technology in World War II; wrote, among other books, *Modern Arms and Free Men* (1949). See *Current Biography* (May) 1947.

Obituary

N Y Times p1+ Je 30 '74

CAFFERY, JEFFERSON Dec. 1, 1886-Apr. 13, 1974 Diplomat; spent forty-four years in Foreign Service posts in South America, Europe, and Middle East; served as United States delegate to numerous international conferences; was Ambassador to Brazil (1937-43), France (1944-49), and Egypt (1949-55). See *Current Biography* (November) 1943.

Obituary

N Y Times p34 Ap 15 '74

CARRERO BLANCO, LUIS Mar. 4, 1903-Dec. 20, 1973 Premier of Spain since June 1973; most trusted confidant and adviser of Generalíssimo Francisco Franco; pillar of ultraconservatism in the regime of President Franco ever since Civil War; wrote books on sea warfare, among others; assassinated, apparently by Basque separatists, in cleverly engineered automobile explosion. See *Current Biography* (October) 1973.

Obituary

N Y Times p15 D 21 '73

CARTWRIGHT, MORSE A(DAMS) Nov. 3, 1890-Apr. 21, 1974 Professor of education at Teachers College of Columbia University (1940-49); founder (1926) and director (1926-49) of American Association for Adult Education. See *Current Biography* (September) 1947.

Obituary

N Y Times p38 Ap 22 '74

CHADWICK, SIR JAMES Oct. 10, 1891-July 24, 1974 British physicist; discoverer of the neutron; leading member of "Tube Alloys," the British atomic bomb project during World War II; chief scientific adviser to British delegation on joint American-British-Canadian atomic bomb policy committee; winner of Nobel Prize for physics (1935). See *Current Biography* (November) 1945.

Obituary

N Y Times p36 Jl 25 '74; Guardian p6 Jl 26 '74

CHARLESWORTH, JAMES C(LYDE) May 21, 1900-Jan. 21, 1974 Political scientist; authority on public administration; retired professor of University of Pennsylvania; secretary of administration and director of reorganization commission of Pennsylvania (1955-56); president of American Academy of Political and Social Science (1953-71); author of *Government Administration* (1951) and other books. See *Current Biography* (September) 1954.

Obituary

N Y Times p40 Ja 24 '74

CICOGNANI, AMLETO GIOVANNI CARDINAL Feb. 24, 1883-Dec. 17, 1973 Roman Catholic prelate; dean of the College of Cardinals since 1972; after filling various posts in the Roman Curia, served as Apostolic Delegate to the United States for twenty-five years, beginning in 1933; in later years served again in Vatican government, finally as Secretary of State (1961-69). See *Current Biography* (July) 1951.

Obituary

N Y Times p44 D 18 '73

CLAPP, MARGARET (ANTOINETTE) Apr. 11, 1910-May 3, 1974 Author; educator; awarded Pulitzer Prize for biography for *Forgotten First Citizen: John Bigelow* (1947); was president of Wellesley College (1949-66); served as cultural attaché (1968-70) and counselor for cultural affairs (1970-71) at United States Embassy in New Delhi, India. See *Current Biography* (June) 1948.

Obituary

N Y Times p44 My 4 '74

CLINE, JOHN WESLEY July 2, 1898-July 10, 1974 Surgeon professor emeritus of surgery, Stanford University; president of American Medical Association (1951-53) and American Cancer Society (1961-62); staunch opponent of socialized medicine and compulsory health insurance. See *Current Biography* (June) 1951.

Obituary

N Y Times p33 Jl 12 '74

COLDWELL, M(ICHAEL) J. Dec. 2, 1888-Aug. 25, 1974 Member of the Canadian House of Commons (1935-58); principal founder and later president and Parliamentary leader of the socialist-oriented Cooperative Commonwealth Federation (1942-60); delegate to the United Nations General Assembly (1946; 1950; 1952; 1953); author of *Left Turn, Canada* (1945). See *Current Biography* (September) 1943.

Obituary

N Y Times p32 Ag 26 '74

CONDON, E(DWARD) U(HLER) Mar. 2, 1902-Mar. 26, 1974 Physicist; associate director of research at Westinghouse Electric Company (1937-45); made important contributions to World War II atomic bomb and radar programs; director of the National Bureau of Standards (1945-51); professor of physics at Washington University (1956-63) and University of Colorado (since 1963). See *Current Biography* (April) 1946.

Obituary

N Y Times p46 Mr 27 '74

COOLEY, HAROLD D(UNBAR) July 26, 1897-Jan. 15, 1974 United States Democratic Representative from North Carolina (1935-67); chairman of House Agriculture Committee (1949-67); a moderate liberal and internationalist; favored foreign aid, reciprocal trade, and legislation benefiting farmers; refused to go along with Southern manifesto against racial integration in 1956. See *Current Biography* (March) 1951.

Obituary

N Y Times p4 Ja 16 '74

CORDINER, RALPH J(ARRON) Mar. 20, 1900-Dec. 5, 1973 Former industrialist; management and merchandising expert; began career as corporate executive with General Electric Company; became president of Schick Inc., in 1939; was vice-chairman of federal War Production Board during World War II, until 1943, when he returned to General Electric; served as president of G.E. from 1950 and as board chairman from 1958 until retirement in 1963. See *Current Biography* (January) 1951.

Obituary

N Y Times p50 D 6 '73

CORNELL, KATHARINE Feb. 16, 1893-June 9, 1974 Actress; the "gorgeous dark lady"—as George Bernard Shaw called her—of the American theatre; with Helen Hayes and Lynn Fontanne, was reigning female figure on Broadway during second quarter of twentieth century; brought disciplined fire to such romantic roles

as Elizabeth in *The Barretts of Wimpole Street,* a staple in the repertory of her road troupe, along with *Candida* and *Romeo and Juliet;* retired when her husband and director, Guthrie McClintic, died, in 1961. See *Current Biography* (March) 1952.

Obituary

N Y Times p1+ Je 10 '74

CRAIG, LYMAN C(REIGHTON) June 12, 1906-July 7, 1974 Chemist; on faculty of Rockefeller University since 1933; by his research made possible many recent advances in biochemistry, especially in area of refined drug purification; received 1963 Lasker Award in basic medical research for his "creation and continued development of the now widely used countercurrent distribution technique as an effective method for the separation in pure state of biologically and clinically significant compounds." See *Current Biography* (April) 1964.

Obituary

N Y Times p40 Jl 9 '74

CROSSMAN, R(ICHARD) H(OWARD) S(TAFFORD) Dec. 15, 1907-Apr. 5, 1974 British statesman; writer; Member of Parliament (1945-74); Minister of Housing and Local Government (1964-66); theoretician of left wing of Labour party; assistant editor (1938-55) and editor (1970-72) of *New Statesman;* author of *Palestine Mission* (1947) and other books. See *Current Biography* (May) 1947.

Obituary

N Y Times p34 Ap 6 '74

DALEY, ARTHUR (JOHN) July 31, 1904-Jan. 3, 1974 Sportswriter; on staff of New York *Times* since 1926; wrote column "Sports of the Times," beginning in 1942; won Pulitzer Prize in 1956, one of the very few sportswriters thus honored. See *Current Biography* (September) 1956.

Obituary

N Y Times p32 Ja 4 '74

DARIN, BOBBY May 14, 1936-Dec. 20, 1973 Singer; songwriter; motion picture actor; nightclub and television entertainer; rose from impoverished Bronx boyhood to become teen-age idol with his original rock 'n' roll hit "Splish Splash" (1958); won two Grammys for his pulsating pop rendition of "Mack the Knife" (1960), which sold 2,000,000 records, and an Oscar nomination for his supporting role in *Captain Newman M.D.* (1963). See *Current Biography* (March) 1963.

Obituary

N Y Times p38 D 21 '73

DAUGHERTY, JAMES HENRY June 1, 1889-Feb. 21, 1974 Artist; writer; wrote and illustrated American history books for children, including *Abraham Lincoln* (1943), *The Landing of the Pilgrims* (1950), and *Trappers and Traders of the Far West* (1952); won 1939 John Newbery Medal for *Daniel Boone;* painted historical murals in public buildings for Federal Arts Project during Depression; had retrospective exhibition in New York in 1971. See *Current Biography* (July) 1940.

Obituary
N Y Times p36 F 22 '74

DAVIS, ADELLE Feb. 25, 1904-May 31, 1974 Nutritionist; natural food crusader; expert on vitamin supplements; wrote *Let's Cook It Right* (1947) and *Let's Eat Right to Keep Fit* (1954), among other best-selling dietary primers accepted as scripture by a legion of health-conscious Americans. See *Current Biography* (January) 1973.

Obituary
N Y Times p32 Je 1 '74

DAVIS, EDWARD W(ILSON) May 8, 1888-Dec. 4, 1973 Metallurgical engineer; inventor; director of mine research at the University of Minnesota until 1952 and later at Reserve Mining Company, which named E. W. Davis Works at Silver Bay, Minnesota in his honor; developed commercially feasible process of extracting iron-ore pellets from taconite rock, thus giving new lease on life to "depleted" Mesabi Range and making possible today's billion-dollar taconite industry. See *Current Biography* (September) 1955.

Obituary
Washington Post C p14 D 7 '73

DEAN, DIZZY Jan. 16, 1911-July 17, 1974 Former baseball pitcher; reached height of brief, brilliant career as blazing fastballer in 1934, when he (with 30 victories) and brother Paul (with 19) pitched St. Louis Cardinals to National League pennant and then (with 2 wins each in the World Series) to world championship; declined precipitously after injury in 1937; traded to the Chicago Cubs in 1938; after nine years in majors, retired in 1941, at age twenty-nine, with 150-83 career win-loss record; later, as baseball announcer, was known for his "Okie" diction, broken syntax, and outrageous malapropisms. See *Current Biography* (September) 1951.

Obituary
N Y Times p38 Jl 18 '74

DEANE, MARTHA *See* Young, M.

DE SEVERSKY, ALEXANDER P(ROCOFIEFF) June 7, 1894-Aug 24, 1974 Russian-born American aviator and aeronautical engineer; advocated use of strategic air power as "single deterrent force," in Congressional testimony and in such books as the best-selling *Victory Through Air Power* (1942); World War I ace in Czarist naval air force; founder and president of Seversky Aviation Corporation and other firms; made major contributions to commercial and military aviation through inventions and aircraft designs. See *Current Biography* (February) 1941.

Obituary
N Y Times p32 Ag 26 '74

DEUPREE, RICHARD R(EDWOOD) May 7, 1885-Mar. 14, 1974 Manufacturer; president (1930-48), board chairman (1948-59), and honorary chairman (since 1959) of Procter & Gamble; contributed to the human relations program of the company as well as its industrial growth. See *Current Biography* (April) 1946.

Obituary
N Y Times p34 Mr 16 '74

DOAN, LELAND I(RA) Nov. 4, 1894-Apr. 4, 1974 Corporation executive; joined Dow Chemical Company in 1918 and rose through the ranks to become general sales manager in 1929 and director of sales in 1945; served as president during period of company's greatest diversification and expansion (1949-62); chaired company's executive committee from 1962 to 1970. See *Current Biography* (October) 1952.

Obituary
N Y Times p40 Ap 5 '74

DOUGLAS, LEWIS W(ILLIAMS) July 2, 1894-Mar. 7, 1974 United States Democratic Representative from Arizona (1927-33); Ambassador to the Court of St. James's (1947-50); businessman; educator; was New Deal budget director (1933-34); served as first American principal of McGill University (1938-39); as deputy director of War Shipping Board, controlled all American merchant tonnage (1942-44); held high executive offices in several major American corporations. See *Current Biography* (March) 1947.

Obituary
N Y Times p36 Mr 8 '74

DURHAM, CARL (THOMAS) Aug. 28, 1892-Apr. 29, 1974 United States Democratic Representative from North Carolina (1939-61); pharmacist; sponsored legislation creating independent Federal Civil Defense Administration; as member and two-term chairman of Joint Committee on Atomic Energy (1946-71), encouraged development of atomic energy for peaceful purposes. See *Current Biography* (July) 1957.

Obituary
Washington Post C p7 My 1 '74

DUTRA, EURICO GASPAR May 18, 1885-June 11, 1974 Brazilian army marshal; government official; served in Cabinet of dictator Getulio Vargas as Minister of War (1936-45); in move toward democracy, led military overthrow of Vargas; elected president in 1945; headed moderate regime until 1951, when Vargas was returned to power legally, by popular election. See *Current Biography* (March) 1946.

Obituary

N Y Times p48 Je 12 '74

EISENDRATH, MAURICE N(ATHAN) July 10, 1902-Nov. 9, 1973 Rabbi; leader of Reform Judaism in the United States; executive director (1943-46) and president (1946-73) of Union of American Hebrew Congregations; promoted social activist role for the Jewish synagogue, especially in areas of civil rights and alleviation of poverty; outspoken critic of Vietnam war policies of Johnson and Nixon administrations. See *Current Biography* (May) 1950.

Obituary

N Y Times p1+ N 10 '73

ELLINGTON, DUKE Apr. 29, 1899-May 24, 1974 Composer; band leader; pianist; one of outstanding personalities in history of jazz; attained great popularity as leader of own band, particularly during engagement at Harlem's Cotton Club (1927-32); composed over 900 works, including sacred music, compositions for motion pictures, plays, musical comedies, and ballets, symphonic works such as *Harlem Suite* (1950), and many popular song hits, including "In My Solitude" and "Sophisticated Lady"; received Presidential Medal of Freedom (1970) and Légion d'honneur (1973), among other honors. See *Current Biography* (January) 1970.

Obituary

N Y Times p1+ My 25 '74

EWING, (WILLIAM) MAURICE May 12, 1906-May 4, 1974 Geophysicist; university professor; as research associate at Woods Hole Oceanographic Institution (1940-45), perfected underwater communication techniques and pioneered exploration of ocean floors by seismic waves; directed Columbia University's Lamont Doherty Geological Observatory (1949-74); discovered evidence supporting theory of continental drift. See *Current Biography* (January) 1953.

Obituary

N Y Times p77 My 5 '74

FIELDS, DOROTHY July 15, 1905-Mar. 28, 1974 Librettist; lyricist; versatile and prolific lyricist for more than a dozen composers, including Jerome Kern, Jimmy McHugh, Sigmund Romberg, and Cy Coleman; collaborated with brother Herbert Fields on librettos for such Broadway hits as *Mexican Hayride* (1944), *Annie Get Your Gun* (1946), and *Redhead* (1959); awarded "best song" Oscar for "The Way You Look Tonight" in 1936; named to Songwriters' Hall of Fame in 1971. See *Current Biography* (February) 1958.

Obituary

N Y Times p38 Mr 29 '74

FULLER, ALFRED C(ARL) Jan. 13, 1885-Dec. 4, 1973 Manufacturer; self-made millionaire; founder (1906), president (until 1943), and board chairman (until 1968) of Fuller Brush Company; invented comprehensive line of brushes and related products and developed method of retailing them door-to-door through independent salesmen. See *Current Biography* (October) 1960.

Obituary

N Y Times p50 D 5 '73

FURTSEVA, EKATERINA A(LEXEYEVNA) Dec. 7, 1910-Oct. 25, 1974 Soviet politician; government official; Minister of Culture since 1960; was previously secretary of Moscow Communist organization and member of party's ruling national Presidium; helped Khrushchev win post-Stalin power struggle; as Minister of Culture, promoted cultural exchanges with United States and other Western countries. See *Current Biography* (June) 1956.

Obituary

N Y Times p34 O 26 '74

GARAND, JOHN C(ANTIUS) Jan. 1, 1888-Feb. 16, 1974 Design engineer; inventor of semiautomatic World War II M-1 rifle; ordnance engineer at United States Armory in Springfield, Mass. (1919-53); awarded Medal of Merit for outstanding civilian war service in 1944. See *Current Biography* (August) 1945.

Obituary

N Y Times p67 F 17 '74

GERARD, RALPH W(ALDO) Oct. 7, 1900-Feb. 17, 1974 Behavioral scientist; neurophysiologist; noted for experiments in cerebral and nervous functions; discovered causal relationship between schizophrenia and inherited body chemistry; at University of Michigan's Mental Health Research Institute (1955-64), distinguished six types of schizophrenia; professor of biological sciences at University of California since 1964; wrote *Unresting Cells* (1940), among other books. See *Current Biography* (May) 1965.

Obituary

N Y Times p36 F 19 '74

GIEGENGACK, A(UGUSTUS) E(DWARD) Apr. 19, 1890-June 21, 1974 Government official; graphic arts expert; with title of Public Printer, headed United States Government Printing Office from 1934 to 1948; later served as executive vice-president of the Army Times Publishing Company (1954-56) and worked as private consultant. See *Current Biography* (November) 1944.

Obituary

N Y Times p40 Je 25 '74

GOLDWYN, SAMUEL Aug. 27, 1882-Jan. 31, 1974 Motion picture producer; helped to organize several film companies before becoming an independent producer in 1922; pioneered in engaging prominent writers to work on motion pictures; introduced Vilma Banky, Gary Cooper, Danny Kaye, and many other stars; produced some seventy films, including *The Squaw Man* (1913), *Wuthering Heights* (1939), and the Oscar-winning *The Best Years of Our Lives* (1946). See *Current Biography* (January) 1944.

Obituary

N Y Times p1+ F 1 '74

GOTTLIEB, ADOLPH Mar. 14, 1903-Mar. 4, 1974 Artist; a founder of abstract expressionist New York School of painting; noted for distinctive "pictograph" style; during Depression exhibited with influential group of expressionists known as "The Ten"; designed stylized interior and exterior decorations derived from traditional religious iconography for synagogues in and around New York City; in later years concentrated on his "Burst" series, typified by explosive reds and blacks and solar orbs. See *Current Biography* (January) 1959.

Obituary

N Y Times p36 Mr 5 '74

GRIFFIS, STANTON May 2, 1887-Aug 29, 1974 Investment banker; diplomat; partner in Wall Street firm of Hemphill, Noyes & Company from 1919; held top executive posts in Brentano's, Paramount Pictures, and Madison Square Garden; chief of Office of War Information motion picture bureau (1943-44); American Red Cross commissioner for Pacific area (1944-45); Ambassador to Poland (1947), Egypt (1948), and Argentina (1949); as Ambassador to Spain (1951-52), helped to end isolation of Franco regime. See *Current Biography* (October) 1944.

Obituary

N Y Times p32 Ag 30 '74

GRIVAS, GEORGE (THEODORUS) Mar. 23, 1898-Jan. 27, 1974 Greek-Cypriot military leader and politician; as retired Greek army officer led the underground National Organization for the Cyprus Struggle (EOKA) from 1955 to 1959 to win independence from British rule; later opposed Archbishop Makarios, President of Cyprus, in advocating union of Cyprus with Greece. See *Current Biography* (October) 1964.

Obituary

N Y Times p30 Ja 28 '74

GRUENBERG, SIDONIE MATSNER June 10, 1881-Mar. 11, 1974 Educator; author; specialized in child guidance, parent education, and family relationships; directed Child Study Association of America (1923-1950); editor in chief of *The Encyclopedia of Child Care and Guidance* (1954); author of several books, including *The Wonderful Story of How You Were Born* (1952) and *Guiding Your Child From Five to Twelve* (1958). See *Current Biography* (May) 1940.

Obituary

N Y Times p44 Mr 13 '74

GRUENING, ERNEST (HENRY) Feb. 6, 1887-June 26, 1974 Former United States Senator from Alaska; neo-New Deal Democratic "dove"; after taking M.D. degree, abandoned medicine for journalism; between 1912 and 1934 edited *Nation,* Boston *Traveler* and *Journal,* and New York *Tribune* and *Evening Post,* among other publications; was director of territories and island possessions in Department of Interior for five years, until 1939, when he was appointed territorial governor of Alaska; took his Senate seat in 1959, when Alaska was admitted into the Union; reelected in 1962 but lost election in 1970; with one other Senator (Wayne Morse), voted against Gulf of Tonkin resolution, President Johnson's carte blanche for American escalation of Vietnam war. See *Current Biography* (July) 1966.

Obituary

N Y Times p48 Je 27 '74

GUTTMACHER, ALAN F(RANK) May 19, 1898-Mar. 18, 1974 Physician; chief of obstetrics and gynecology at Mt. Sinai Hospital in New York (1952-62); president of the Planned Parenthood Federation of America (since 1962); in books and lectures advocated unlimited access to contraceptive information and liberal abortion regulations. See *Current Biography* (October) 1965.

Obituary

N Y Times p40 Mr 19 '74

HARRIS, SEYMOUR E(DWIN) Sept. 8, 1897-Oct. 27, 1974 Economist; emeritus professor of economics at University of California at La Jolla since 1963; previously taught at Harvard University for forty-one years; brought Keynesian theory to bear on current problems in more than a score of books, including *The Economics of Mobilization and Inflation* (1951) and *Economics of the Kennedy Years and a Look Ahead* (1964); was a chief economic consultant in the administrations of Presidents John F. Kennedy and Lyndon B. Johnson. See *Current Biography* (February) 1965.

Obituary

N Y Times p40 O 29 '74

HARVEY, LAURENCE Oct. 1, 1928-Nov. 25, 1973 Actor; received Academy Award nomination for performance as the haughty, self-serving young opportunist in *Room at the Top* (1958); appeared in many other films, including *Butterfield 8* (1960) and *The Manchurian Candidate* (1962); also performed on London and New York stages, with Old Vic and Royal Shakespeare companies, and on television. See *Current Biography* (May) 1961.

Obituary

N Y Times p47 N 27 '73

HAYAKAWA, SESSUE June 10, 1890-Nov. 23, 1973 Japanese-born actor; Zen Buddhist priest; established himself in Hollywood with starring role in *The Cheat* (1916); played more than 120 silent film roles, from lovers to villains; after advent of talkies, made only rare motion picture appearances, usually as heavy in French productions; in magnificent comeback, earned Academy Award nomination as prison camp commandant in *The Bridge on the River Kwai* (1957); later taught acting in Japan. See *Current Biography* (September) 1962.

Obituary

N Y Times p85 N 25 '73

HEROD, WILLIAM ROGERS Feb. 13, 1898-July 19, 1974 Former business executive; rose through ranks to become, in 1945, president of International General Electric Company, the General Electric subsidiary responsible for all GE business outside United States and Canada; long a backer of world trade, took leave of absence in 1950-51 to coordinate defense production for North Atlantic Treaty Organization; retired in 1960. See *Current Biography* (March) 1951.

Obituary

N Y Times p34 Jl 20 '74

HILLEBOE, HERMAN E(RTRESVAAG) Jan. 8, 1906-Apr. 11, 1974 Physician; specialized in tuberculosis control; Assistant United States Surgeon General (1946-47); New York State Commissioner of Health (1947-62). See *Current Biography* (June) 1955.

Obituary

N Y Times p34 Ap 12 '74

HODGES, LUTHER H(ARTWELL) Mar. 9, 1898-Oct. 6, 1974 Business executive; Democratic Governor of North Carolina (1954-60); as United States Secretary of Commerce (1961-64) promoted an expansion of foreign trade and increase in exports. See *Current Biography* (July) 1956.

Obituary

N Y Times p38 O 7 '74

HOFFMAN, PAUL G(RAY) Apr. 26, 1891-Oct. 8, 1974 Government official; industrialist; president of the Studebaker-Packard Corporation (1954-56); administrator of the Economic Cooperation Administration under the Marshall Plan (1948-50); president of the Ford Foundation (1951-53); administrator of the U.N. Development Program (1966-72). See *Current Biography* (February) 1946.

Obituary

N Y Times p1+ O 9 '74

HOGAN, FRANK S(MITHWICK) Jan. 17, 1902-Apr. 2, 1974 District Attorney of New York County; lawyer; served as assistant to New York special prosecutor Thomas E. Dewey (1937-41); with unanimous support of all political parties, elected on Democratic ticket to nine consecutive four-year terms as District Attorney (1941-73); under his aggressive, nonpartisan administration, the "Hogan office" became national model for metropolitan district attorneys. See *Current Biography* (September) 1953.

Obituary

N Y Times p1+ Ap 3 '74

HUNTLEY, CHET Dec. 10, 1911-Mar. 20, 1974 Radio and television journalist; as newscaster and correspondent for CBS (1939-51), ABC (1951-55) and NBC (1955-70), raised standards of broadcast journalism with thoughtful, reasoned analyses of controversial issues; paired with David Brinkley for *Huntley-Brinkley Report*, NBC-TV's long-running, award-winning nightly newscast (1956-70); helped to develop Big Sky, Montana recreational complex. See *Current Biography* (October) 1956.

Obituary

N Y Times p44 Mr 21 '74

HUROK, S(OLOMON) Apr. 9, 1888-Mar. 5, 1974 Impresario; presented some of the world's most distinguished concert artists, orchestras, theatre troupes, ballet companies, and folk ensembles in bravura style; arranged first American appearances of Bolshoi Ballet and Moiseyev Dance Company, among other Soviet groups; as consultant to NBC-TV's *Producer's Showcase* in the 1950's, was instrumental in introducing "high brow" performers to national television audience. See *Current Biography* (April) 1956.

Obituary

N Y Times p1+ Mr 6 '74

INÖNÜ, ISMET Sept. 24, 1884-Dec. 25, 1973 Turkish political and government leader; helped Kemal Ataturk found Turkish Republic in 1923; served as Premier (1923-37 and 1961-65) and president (1938-50) of the republic; remained chairman of the Republican People's party until 1972; with and after Ataturk, introduced and administered reforms, from cultural to economic, that modernized Turkey and brought it into rapport with Western Europe. See *Current Biography* (October) 1964.

Obituary

N Y Times p42 D 26 '73

JOHNSON, HOWARD A(LBERT) Oct. 8, 1915-June 12, 1974 Episcopal clergyman; canon theologian, Cathedral Church of St. John the Divine, New York City (1954 to 1966); authority on nineteenth-century Danish philosopher Sören Kierkegaard; wrote, among other books, *Global Odyssey* (1963), account of two-year tour of Anglican communions in eighty countries. See *Current Biography* (April) 1964.

Obituary

N Y Times p34 Je 17 '74

JORDAN, B(ENJAMIN) EVERETT Sept. 8, 1896-Mar. 15, 1974 Textile-manufacturing executive; Democratic politician; United States Senator from North Carolina (1958-72); as chairman of the Senate Rules Committee led the 1964 investigation into the activities of Senate aide Bobby Baker. See *Current Biography* (November) 1959.

Obituary

N Y Times p34 Mr 16 '74

KAHN, LOUIS I. Feb. 20, 1901-Mar. 17, 1974 Architect; unorthodox and innovative in his concept that design must follow the "will" of space and construction materials to exist in a certain way; exerted wide influence on modern architecture through the grace and power of his work, such as the Richards Research Building at the University of Pennsylvania. See *Current Biography* (October) 1964.

Obituary

N Y Times p1+ Mr 20 '74

KALLEN, HORACE M(EYER) Aug. 11, 1882-Feb. 16, 1974 Philosopher; educator; prominent in Zionism and various liberal movements; helped found New School for Social Research in New York (1919); author of some thirty books, including *Art and Freedom* (1942) and *The Education of Free Men* (1949). See *Current Biography* (October) 1953.

Obituary

N Y Times p66 F 17 '74

KÄSTNER, ERICH Feb. 23, 1899-July 29, 1974 Writer; editor; one of the most popular German literary figures during Weimar Republic and after World War II; was forbidden to publish in Germany under Hitler regime because of anti-Nazi views; best known internationally for his humorous children's books, including the widely translated *Emil and the Detectives, The 35th of May, Lisa and Lottie,* and *The Animals' Conference;* also wrote poems, adult novels, plays, essays, satirical prose, and the autobiographical *When I Was a Boy.* See *Current Biography* (July) 1964.

Obituary

N Y Times p36 Jl 30 '74

KING, CECIL R(HODES) Jan. 13, 1898-Mar. 17, 1974 Former Democratic Congressman; United States Representative from California (1942-68); member of the Ways and Means Committee and coauthor of the Medicare Act (1965). See *Current Biography* (February) 1952.

Obituary

Washington Post C p14 Mr 22 '74

KIRK, WILLIAM T(ALBOT) Mar. 24, 1908-Jan. 7, 1974 Social worker; international director of International Social Service (1952-61) and general director of its American branch (1951-61); executive director of Motion Picture and Television Fund (1961-71); directed relief and repatriation operations for Allied military government in Europe during World War II. See *Current Biography* (February) 1960.

Obituary

N Y Times p36 Ja 12 '74

KNOWLAND, WILLIAM F(IFE) June 26, 1908-Feb. 23, 1974 Newspaper publisher; former government official; Republican United States Senator from California (1945-58); member of Senate Appropriations and Foreign Relations committees; Senate majority leader (1953-54); minority leader (1955-58); publisher of Oakland (California) *Tribune* since 1965; according to sheriff's report, apparently died "of self-inflicted gunshot wound." See *Current Biography* (April) 1947.

Obituary

N Y Times p30 Feb 25 '74

KOWALSKI, FRANK JR. Oct. 18, 1907-Oct. 11, 1974 Former Democratic Representative-at-Large from Connecticut (1952-62); as career Army officer, served on General Dwight D. Eisenhower's World War II staff; retired with rank of colonel in 1958; in Congress, voted prolabor and profederal programming and brought effective pressure against "improper utilization of services of enlisted men" in armed forces; after leaving Congress, served on Subversive Activities Control Board for five years. See *Current Biography* (July) 1960.

Obituary

N Y Times p46 O 16 '74

KRIPS, JOSEF Apr. 8, 1902-Oct. 12, 1974 Conductor emeritus, San Francisco Symphony Orchestra; regarded as perhaps last representative of great Viennese school of "mellow" conducting that included Gustav Mahler and Bruno Walter; began career conducting Vienna Volksoper in 1921; later conducted Vienna Staatsoper, which he rebuilt following World War II; after three years with London Symphony and ten with Buffalo Philharmonic, moved in 1963 to San Francisco Symphony, which rose to top rank under his leadership; was widely traveled guest conductor. See *Current Biography* (June) 1965.

Obituary

N Y Times p36 O 14 '74

KRISHNA MENON, V(ENGALIL) K(RISH-NAN) May 3, 1897-Oct. 6, 1974 Indian lawyer; government official; active in his country's nationalist movement; served under Jawaharlal Nehru in several diplomatic posts, including chairman of Indian delegation to the U.N. (1953-62) and as Minister of Defense (1957-62); a controversial, pro-Soviet statesman who lost power in government and the Congress party when the India-China war broke out in 1962. See *Current Biography* (March) 1953.

Obituary

N Y Times p64 O 6 '74

KROCK, ARTHUR Nov. 16, 1886-Apr. 12, 1974 Journalist; reporter (1927-32), Washington bureau chief (1932-53) and editorial commentator (1953-67) for the New York *Times*; winner of two Pulitzer Prizes (1935, 1937) and two special Pulitzer awards (1950, 1955); author of several books, including *In the Nation* (1966), *Memoirs: Sixty Years on the Firing Line* (1968), and *The Consent of the Governed and Other Deceits* (1971). See *Current Biography* (February) 1943.

Obituary

N Y Times p1+ Ap 13 '74

KROLL, LEON Dec. 6, 1884-Oct. 25, 1974 Artist; chairman of the art committee of Academy of Arts and Letters; as academic painter and lithographer, did carefully crafted, representational nudes and still-lifes; muralist, did mosaic dome of United States Military Cemetery at "Omaha Beach," France and murals for Worcester (Massachusetts) War Memorial, Department of Justice Building in Washington, and Johns Hopkins University auditorium. See *Current Biography* (March) 1943.

Obituary

N Y Times p34 O 26 '74

KUIPER, GERARD P(ETER) Dec. 7, 1905-Dec. 23, 1973 Dutch-born American astronomer; directed succession of observatories, including University of Arizona's lunar and planetary labora-

tory, which he founded in 1960; upset old hypotheses with discoveries and calculations extending even to measurement of furthest planet in our galaxy, Pluto; correctly described in advance moon's surface ("like crunchy snow") while helping to pinpoint landing sites for Apollo astronauts. See *Current Biography* (February) 1959.

Obituary

N Y Times p24 D 25 '73

KUUSINEN, HERTTA (ELINA) Feb. 14, 1904-Mar. 19, 1974 Finnish government official; journalist; Communist member of the national legislature (1945-72); leader of the parliamentary contingent of the People's Democratic League, formed in 1945; considered one of the most important Communists in Finland. See *Current Biography* (May) 1949.

Obituary

N Y Times p34 Mr 23 '74

LAGERKVIST, PÄR (FABIAN) May 23, 1891-July 11, 1974 Swedish author; foremost Swedish literary figure of his time; in drama, poetry, and fiction expressed enigmatic, paradoxical point of view of "religious atheist," as he described himself; best known in United States for two of his novels, *The Dwarf* and *Barabbas;* received 1951 Nobel Prize in literature "for the artistic power and deep-rooted independence he demonstrates . . . in seeking an answer to the eternal questions of humanity." See *Current Biography* (January) 1952.

Obituary

N Y Times p38 Jl 12 '74

LARSON, LEONARD W(INFIELD) May 22, 1898-Sept. 30, 1974 Physician; helped to develop a cancer program for North Dakota; specialized in devising voluntary prepayment plans for medical care; served as president of the American Medical Association (1961-62). See *Current Biography* (May) 1962.

Obituary

N Y Times p50 O 2 '74

LATHAM, DANA July 7, 1898-Feb. 6, 1974 Government official; United States Commissioner of Internal Revenue (1958-61); founder and partner of Latham & Watkins, tax law specialists (1934-58 and 1961-74); special adviser to Under Secretary of State Herbert Hoover, Jr. (1954-55); simplified income tax filing procedures and methods of equitable tax collection to improve "taxpayer morale." See *Current Biography* (March) 1959.

Obituary

N Y Times p32 F 9 '74

LEECH, MARGARET Nov. 7, 1893-Feb. 24, 1974 Author; won Pulitzer Prize twice, for her lively historical accounts *Reveille in Washington, 1860-1865*, in 1942, and *In the Days of McKinley*, in 1960; wrote several novels, including *Tin Wedding* (1926) and *The Feathered Nest* (1928); coauthored play *Divided by Three* (1934). See *Current Biography* (November) 1960.

Obituary

N Y Times p30 F 25 '74

LESCOT, ÉLIE Dec. 9, 1883-Oct. 22, 1974 Haitian statesman; President of Haiti from 1941 until his oppressive regime was overthrown in 1946; previously filled various government posts, including that of Ambassador to United States. See *Current Biography* (June) 1941.

Obituary

N Y Times p48 O 23 '74

LINDBERGH, CHARLES A(UGUSTUS, JR.) Feb. 4, 1902-Aug. 26, 1974 Aviator; as pilot of monoplane "Spirit of St. Louis," made first solo nonstop trans-Atlantic flight, from New York to Paris (1927); won Congressional Medal of Honor and other distinctions, including Service Cross of the German Eagle, conferred on him by Hermann Goering in 1938; provoked controversy by opposing United States entry into World War II; consultant to aircraft companies, airlines, and United States government; brigadier general in Air Force reserve; author of Pulitzer Prize-winning *The Spirit of St. Louis* (1953) and other books; devoted his later years to conservation. See *Current Biography* (January) 1954.

Obituary

N Y Times p1+ Ag 27 '74

LIU SHAO-CHI 1898-1973 (?) Former Chairman of People's Republic of China; joined Mao Tse-tung's Communist revolutionary movement as student; as his associate, helped muster peasant Red Army and was leading organizer of urban labor force; emerged as a major Communist party theorist in late 1930's; when Communists took power in 1949, became general secretary of party; succeeded Mao as chief of state in 1959; denounced as "revisionist" by young Red Guards in Cultural Revolution of 1966; formally purged in 1968; was rumored dead for months before Communist Chinese publication confirmed rumors, without giving details, on October 31, 1974. See *Current Biography* (October) 1957.

Obituary

N Y Times p1+ N 1 '74

LOWDERMILK, W(ALTER) C(LAY) July 1, 1888-May 6, 1974 Agronomist; authority on land, water, and forest conservation; helped to found the Soil Conservation Service of the United States Agriculture Department and was its associate chief (1933-39) and assistant chief (1939-47); worked as consultant on conservation projects in China, Israel, Yugoslavia, Japan, and other countries; president of American Geophysical Union (1941-44); author of *Palestine—Land of Promise* (1944) and other books. See *Current Biography* (February) 1949.

Obituary

N Y Times p46 My 9 '74

McGEE, (DOCTOR) FRANK Sept. 12, 1921-Apr. 17, 1974 News commentator; anchorman of NBC radio's weekend *Monitor*, WNBC-TV's nightly *Sixth Hour News*, and coanchorman of *NBC Evening News*; popular cohost of NBC-TV's daily *Today* show (1971-74); as adroit moderator of unscheduled documentaries, noted for his flawless delivery and perceptive analyses of such fast-breaking news events as space shots. See *Current Biography* (June) 1964.

Obituary

N Y Times p44 Ap 18 '74

McGUIGAN, JAMES (CHARLES), CARDINAL Nov. 26, 1894-Apr. 8, 1974 Roman Catholic prelate; Archbishop of Toronto (1934-71); first English-speaking Canadian to be named a Cardinal, in 1946. See *Current Biography* (September) 1950.

Obituary

N Y Times p44 Ap 9 '74

McKELDIN, THEODORE R(OOSEVELT) Nov. 20, 1900-Aug. 10, 1974 Republican Governor of Maryland (1951-59); mayor of Baltimore (1943-47, 1963-67); outspoken advocate of racial integration and civil rights. See *Current Biography* (October) 1952.

Obituary

N Y Times p53 Ag 11 '74

McKINNEY, FRANK E(DWARD) June 16, 1904-Jan. 9, 1974 Chairman of Democratic National Committee (1951-53); board chairman of American Fletcher National Bank and Trust Company (from 1959); executive committee chairman of American Fletcher Corporation at time of death; former chairman of board of trustees of Indiana University; named Ambassador to Spain in 1968. See *Current Biography* (January) 1952.

Obituary

N Y Times p34 Ja 11 '74

McNEELY, EUGENE J(OHNSON) Nov. 1, 1900-Dec. 27, 1973 Business executive; entered Bell System as engineer in 1922; rose through ranks to presidency of American Telephone and Telegraph Company, in which he served from 1961 until his retirement in 1964. See *Current Biography* (November) 1962.

Obituary

N Y Times p32 D 28 '73

MALONE, ROSS(ER) L(YNN, JR.) Sept. 9, 1910-Aug. 13, 1974 President of American Bar Association (1958-59) and of American Bar Foundation (1966-69); deputy attorney general of the United States (1952-53); vice-president and general counsel for General Motors Corporation (1967-74); principal drafter of the Twenty-fifth Amendment to the United States Constitution. See *Current Biography* (March) 1959.

Obituary

N Y Times p36 Ag 14 '74

MANGRUM, LLOYD Aug. 1, 1914-Nov. 17, 1973 Former professional golfer; won 1946 United States Open, among other championships; was golf's leading money-maker in 1948 and 1951; retired in 1960. See *Current Biography* (September) 1951.

Obituary

N Y Times p77 N 18 '73

MANNING, HARRY Feb. 3, 1897-Aug. 1, 1974 United States merchant marine officer; vice-admiral in United States Navy; aviator; joined United States Lines in 1921; commanded superliner S.S. *United States* on its record-breaking trans-Atlantic maiden voyage (1952). See *Current Biography* (May) 1952.

Obituary

N Y Times p30 Ag 2 '74

MARIE, ANDRÉ Dec. 3, 1897- June 12, 1974 Former Premier of France (July-September 1948); first elected to Chamber of Deputies in 1928; held various Cabinet posts from 1933 on; as captured Resistance fighter in World War II, was imprisoned in Buchenwald concentration camp; despite impaired health after the war, served in National Assembly until 1962; began to lose political strength when he left the Radical Socialist party to form die-hard group dedicated to keeping Algeria French. See *Current Biography* (September) 1948.

Obituary

N Y Times p36 Je 14 '74

MEHTA, G(AGANVIHARI) L(ALLUBHAI) Apr. 15, 1900-Apr. 28, 1974 Indian diplomat; economist; directed industrial and trade division of India's National Planning Commission (1950-52); was Ambassador to the United States and Mexico (1952-58) and to Cuba (1956-58); headed Indian Investment Center and Industrial Credit Investment Corporation (1958-71). See *Current Biography* (November) 1952.

Obituary

N Y Times p36 Ap 29 '74

MEYER, K(ARL) F(RIEDRICH) May 19, 1884-Apr. 27, 1974 Pathologist; veterinary scientist; university professor; perfected flash sterilization method of canning food; isolated viruses causing ornithosis and encephalitis and developed serums for their cure and control; was director of University of California Medical Center's Hooper Foundation (1916-54); winner of 1951 Lasker Award for contributions to public health. See *Current Biography* (March) 1952.

Obituary

N Y Times p36 Ap 29 '74

MICHIE, ALLAN A(NDREW) July 4, 1915-Nov. 11, 1973 Writer; foreign correspondent for Time-Life publications during World War II; contributing editor of *Reader's Digest* until 1952; on staff of Radio Free Europe from 1952 to 1956; vice-president for public affairs of Academy of Natural Sciences since 1971; coauthored *Their Finest Hour* (1941) and wrote *Retreat to Victory* (1942) and *The Invasion of Europe* (1964), among other books. See *Current Biography* (November) 1942.

Obituary

N Y Times p48 N 13 '73

MILHAUD, DARIUS Sept. 4, 1892-June 22, 1974 French composer; one of major figures on modern musical scene; as member of avant-garde Groupe des Six in 1920's was a pioneer of polytonality; composed over 400 works, including symphonies, operas, ballets, concertos, string quartets, and film scores, in virtually every style and idiom, drawing inspiration from such diverse elements as Jewish liturgical music, Brazilian folk tunes, New Orleans jazz, and the poetry of Paul Claudel; taught composition alternately at Mills College in Oakland, California and Conservatoire Nationale de Musique in Paris, from 1940's to 1972. See *Current Biography* (May) 1961.

Obituary

N Y Times p40 Je 25 '74

MIRÓ CARDONA, JOSÉ 1902(?)-Aug. 10, 1974 Cuban political leader; lawyer; university professor; helped to overthrow dictatorship of Fulgencio Batista; first Premier in revolutionary government of Fidel Castro (1959); Ambassador to Spain (1960); after breaking with Castro, served as president (1961-63) of Miami-based Cuban Revolutionary Council, which helped to prepare the abortive Bay of Pigs invasion under United States sponsorship in 1961. See *Current Biography* (November) 1961.

Obituary

N Y Times p53 Ag 11 '74

MITCHELL, STEPHEN A(RNOLD) Mar. 3, 1903-Apr. 23, 1974 Lawyer; former political party official; chief counsel of a House Judiciary subcommittee to investigate the Justice Department (1952); chairman of the Democratic National Committee (1952-56). See *Current Biography* (October) 1952.

Obituary

N Y Times p47 Ap 24 '74

MOLYNEUX, EDWARD H. Sept. 5, 1894-Mar. 22, 1974 British couturier; operated his own fashion salons in both England and France; was noted for clothes of aristocratic simplicity and prim smartness often designed for the nobility and well-known actresses. See *Current Biography* (June) 1942.

Obituary

N Y Times p34 Mr 23 '74

MOOREHEAD, AGNES Dec. 6, 1906-Apr. 30, 1974 Distinguished character actress of stage, screen, radio and television; charter member of Mercury Players; earned five Academy Award nominations; appeared in more than 100 films, including *The Magnificent Ambersons* (1942), *Johnny Belinda* (1948), and *Hush . . . Hush, Sweet Charlotte* (1965); starred in many Broadway plays, including *Don Juan in Hell* (1951, 1973) and *Gigi* (1973); portrayed Endora on long-running TV series *Bewitched*. See *Current Biography* (June) 1952.

Obituary

N Y Times p48 My 1 '74

MORAES, FRANK (ROBERT) Nov. 12, 1907-May 2, 1974 Indian journalist; noted for pro-Western views; joined staff of British-owned *Times of India* in 1938 and was its first Indian editor (1950-57); editor in chief of *Indian Express* (1957-73); European representative of Indian Express group of newspapers (1973-74); author of *Jawaharlal Nehru: A Biography* (1956) and six other books on national and international affairs. See *Current Biography* (November) 1957.

Obituary

N Y Times p44 My 4 '74

MORSE, WAYNE (LYMAN) Oct. 20, 1900-July 22, 1974 United States Senator from Oregon (1945-69); entered politics as liberal Republican in Populist tradition but became independent in 1953 and Democrat in 1956; champion of organized labor, farmers, and civil rights; one of earliest and most consistent opponents of United States military involvement in Vietnam; narrowly defeated for reelection in 1968, but won 1974 primary in new bid for Senate seat. See *Current Biography* (November) 1954.

Obituary

N Y Times p1+ Jl 23 '74

MUNDT, KARL E(ARL) June 3, 1900-Aug. 16, 1974 United States Republican Senator (1949-72) and Representative (1939-48) from South Dakota; sponsored tough anti-Communist legislation; chaired House Un-American Activities Committee's disputatious investigation of Communist infiltration into government (1948) and Senate's Army-McCarthy hearings (1954); relieved of seniority and key committee assignments in 1972 after debilitating stroke in 1969. See *Current Biography* (July) 1948.

Obituary

N Y Times p26 Ag 17 '74

MUNRO, LESLIE KNOX Feb 26, 1901-Feb. 13, 1974 New Zealand government official and diplomat; Ambassador to the United States (1952-58); United Nations delegate (1952-58); National party M. P. (1963-69); editor of influential *New Zealand Herald* (1942-51); president of U.N. General Assembly (1957-58); U.N. special representative to negotiate political settlement of 1956 anti-Communist revolt in Hungary; author of *United Nations: Hope For a Divided World* (1960). See *Current Biography* (November) 1953.

Obituary

N Y Times p44 F 14 '74

MURRAY, DWIGHT H(ARRISON) May 16, 1888-Oct. 7, 1974 Physician; president of the American Medical Association (1956-57); an outspoken opponent of "socialized" medicine. See *Current Biography* (May) 1957.

Obituary

N Y Times p46 O 9 '74

NABARRO, SIR GERALD (DAVID NUNES) June 29, 1913-Nov. 18, 1973 Conservative member of British House of Commons from 1950 to 1964 and since 1966; as flamboyant maverick M.P., was an effective nettle to both Conservative and Labour governments; before entering politics, managed engineering, sawmilling, and box manufacturing companies. See *Current Biography* (November) 1963.

Obituary

N Y Times p38 N 19 '73

NOURSE, EDWIN G(RISWOLD) May 20, 1883-Apr. 7, 1974 Economist; former United States government official; associated with Brookings Institution in several posts, including vice-president (1942-46); first chairman of the President's Council of Economic Advisers (1946-49); author of *Economics in the Public Service* (1953) and many other books. See *Current Biography* (October) 1946.

Obituary

N Y Times p44 Ap 10 '74

ODRIA (AMORETTI), MANUEL A(POLINARIO)
Nov. 26, 1897-Feb. 18, 1974 Peruvian statesman; served as army chief of staff (1946) and Minister of Interior (1947) before assuming Presidency in bloodless coup (1948); later, as constitutional President (1950-56), used "strong man" techniques to carry out social and economic reforms. See *Current Biography* (November) 1954.

Obituary
N Y Times p36 F 19 '74

OISTRAKH, DAVID (FYODOROVICH) Oct. 30, 1908-Oct. 24, 1974 Soviet violinist; professor at Moscow Conservatory; included United States in his international concert tour itinerary beginning in 1955; curtailed recital schedule after 1964, when his health began to fail, but maintained to the end the sweet lyric power of his bow, which he wielded in unique giant arching lines; was, in words of Yehudi Menuhin, "one of the two or three greatest . . . fiddlers of our age"; left for posterity large legacy of solo and chamber music recordings. See *Current Biography* (March) 1956.

Obituary
N Y Times p1+ O 25 '74

OZBIRN, MRS. E. LEE Nov. 24, 1900(?)-Jan. 24, 1974 Former organization official; president of the General Federation of Women's Clubs (1960-62), the largest women's organization in the world; held advisory posts in federal government on aging and child welfare. See *Current Biography* (January) 1962.

Obituary
N Y Times p36 Ja 25 '74

PAGNOL, MARCEL (PAUL) Feb. 25, 1895-Apr. 18, 1974 French motion picture producer and director; playwright; author of celebrated Marseilles trilogy *Marius* (1929), *Fanny* (1931), and *César* (1936); directed several critically acclaimed and commercially successful films, including *The Baker's Wife* (1938), *The Well-Digger's Daughter* (1940), and *Topaze* (1950); winner of New York Film Critics' awards for *Harvest* (1939) and *Ways of Love* (1950). See *Current Biography* (March) 1956.

Obituary
N Y Times p40 Ap 19 '74

PARTCH, HARRY June 24, 1901-Sept. 3, 1974 Avant-garde composer; originated forty-three-interval microtonal scale, which he used in his unique dramatic-musical composition, including *Oedipus* (1952) and *Water, Water* (1962); invented such bizarre musical instruments as the "kithara" and the "bloboys"; received National Institute of Arts and Letters award, among other distinctions. See *Current Biography* (September) 1965.

Obituary
N Y Times p36 S 6 '74

PATE, WALTER L(ACEY) Sept. 10, 1878-Apr. 27, 1974 Lawyer; non-playing captain of victorious United States Davis Cup tennis team (1937, 1938, 1947); chaired supplies committee of United States Lawn Tennis Association for more than thirty years; partner in Wall Street law firm Cooke, Brown & Pate. See *Current Biography* (March) 1947.

Obituary
N Y Times p44 Ap 30 '74

PERÓN (SOSA), JUAN (DOMINGO) Oct. 8, 1895-July 1, 1974 President of Argentina (1946-55; 1973-74); transformed it from predominantly rural to industrial nation; won devoted following among working masses through major social and economic reforms and public works but also instituted dictatorial repressions and restricted civil liberties; after his overthrow by military, went into exile (1955-73), but retained loyalty of large segment of Argentine people; reassumed Presidency of Argentina in October 1973 after landslide election victory. See *Current Biography* (February) 1974.

Obituary
N Y Times p16 Jl 2 '74

PHILLIPS, IRNA July 1, 1903-Dec 23, 1973 Radio script writer; called "Queen of the Soap Opera" because of her prodigious output of daily daytime serials; was creator or coauthor of *As the World Turns, The Guiding Light, Right to Happiness,* and *Young Doctor Malone,* among other open-ended radio melodramas. See *Current Biography* (April) 1943.

Obituary
N Y Times p31 D 30 '73

POMPIDOU, GEORGES (JEAN RAYMOND) July 5, 1911-Apr. 2, 1974 President of France; confidant of and adviser to General Charles de Gaulle during World War II; director of Rothschild Frères investment bank; member of the Council of State (1946-54); negotiated truce with Algerian Nationalist rebels in 1961; at President de Gaulle's request, formed government in 1962 and served as Premier until resignation in July 1968; with Gaullist support, elected President in June 1969. See *Current Biography* (November) 1962.

Obituary
N Y Times p1+ Ap 3 '74

POPE, LISTON Sept. 6, 1909-Apr. 15, 1974 Congregational clergyman; educator; sociologist; member of the faculty of Yale University Divinity School for thirty-five years (1938-73), thirteen of them as dean (1949-62); member of the executive committee of the World Council of Churches; advocate of ecumenism and racial equality. See *Current Biography* (April) 1956.

Obituary

N Y Times p42 Ap 16 '74

POWERS, MARIE 1913(?)-Dec. 27, 1973 American opera singer; first gained recognition in Europe, where she developed repertoire of fifty roles; in the United States was "discovered" in 1946 by Gian-Carlo Menotti, who was struck as much by her acting and "electrifying vitality" as by her rich contralto; became identified with her creation of characters in Menotti operas, beginning with the title persona in *The Medium* (1947). See *Current Biography* (January) 1951.

Obituary

N Y Times p20 D 31 '73

RANCE, SIR HUBERT ELVIN July 17, 1898-Jan. 24, 1974 British statesman; retired army officer; expert on colonial affairs; served as last British Governor of Burma (1946-48) before it gained independence and as Governor of Trinidad and Tobago (1950-55). See *Current Biography* (December) 1953.

Obituary

N Y Times p34 Ja 26 '74

RANSOM, JOHN CROWE Apr. 30, 1888-July 3, 1974 Poet; critic; professor emeritus of poetry at Kenyon College; known for classical style in which emotion was expressed eloquently but with restraint and ironic detachment; was dominant force in the "Fugitive" and "Agrarian" movements among Southern poets—including Robert Penn Warren and Allen Tate—who rejected sentimentality of machine-age Dixie and sought return to rural, close-to-nature values of Old South; published much of his "new criticism" (his coinage) in enormously influential *Kenyon Review,* which he founded in 1939 and edited for nineteen years. See *Current Biography* (July) 1964.

Obituary

N Y Times p22 Jl 4 '74

RIEFLER, WINFIELD W(ILLIAM) Feb. 9, 1897-Apr. 5, 1974 Economist; monetary expert; educator; former United States government official; professor of School of Economics and Politics of the Institute for Advanced Study (1935-48); assistant to chairman of the Federal Reserve Board (1947-59). See *Current Biography* (May) 1948.

Obituary

N Y Times p44 Ap 10 '74

RITTER, THELMA Feb. 14, 1905-Feb. 5, 1969 Actress; one of few character players to attain star billing; won Emmy award for her performance as Bronx housewife in teleplay *The Catered Affair* (1955), written for her by Paddy Chayevsky; received Tony for her portrayal of alcoholic Marthy in Broadway musical *New Girl in Town* (1957); played memorable roles in *A Letter to Three Wives* (1949), *All About Eve* (1950), and *The Misfits,* among other films; was nominated for Oscar four times. See *Current Biography* (December) 1957.

Obituary

N Y Times p45 F 5 '69

ROBERTSON, SIR BRIAN (HUBERT) July 22, 1896-Apr. 29, 1974 British Army officer; served as quartermaster-general for Allied Forces in Eastern and North African campaigns (1941-43); as military governor of Allied Control Commission in Germany (1947-49), directed Berlin airlift; was commander-in-chief, Middle East Land Forces (1950-53); chaired British Transport Commission (1953-61). See *Current Biography* (September) 1948.

Obituary

Washington Post D p49 My 4 '74

ROMNES, H(AAKON) I(NGOLF) Mar. 2, 1907-Nov. 19, 1973 Corporation executive; vice-chairman (1964-67), chairman and chief executive officer (1967-72), and president (1970-72) of American Telephone and Telegraph Company; joined Bell System as circuit designer in 1928; as president of AT&T subsidiary Western Electric Company (1959-63), made it one of first major defense contractors to pledge equal employment opportunity; held several patents. See *Current Biography* (February) 1968.

Obituary

N Y Times p38 N 19 '73

RUIZ CORTINES, ADOLFO Dec. 30, 1890-Dec. 3, 1973 President of Mexico (1952-58); Governor of state of Veracruz (1944-47); Secretary of Interior in government of President Miguel Alemán (1947-52); noted for skill as conciliator; conducted campaigns against corruption in public service and monopolistic business practices. See *Current Biography* (September) 1952.

Obituary

N Y Times p48 D 4 '73

SAUNDERS, CARL M(AXON) Oct. 26, 1890-Oct. 2, 1974 Journalist; editor of the Jackson (Michigan) *Citizen Patriot* (1934-61); won the 1949 Pulitzer Prize in editorial writing for his "Prayer for Peace" editorial, which led Congress to dedicate Memorial Day as a national day of prayer. See *Current Biography* (June) 1950.

Obituary

N Y Times p42 O 4 '74

SCHIAPARELLI, ELSA 1890(?)-Nov. 13, 1973 Italian-French couturière; beginning in 1920's in Paris, created color revolution in *haute couture* with her "shocking pink" and other dramatic tones; also marketed perfumes to complement her fashions; after several prolonged visits to the United States, opened a New York branch of her salon in 1949. See *Current Biography* (November) 1951.

Obituary

N Y Times p1 + N 15 '73

SEATON, FRED(ERICK) A(NDREW) Dec. 11, 1909-Jan. 16, 1974 United States Republican Senator from Nebraska (1951-52); as United States Secretary of the Interior (1956-61), promoted wildlife conservation, improvements in national parks system, benefits for American Indians, and statehood for Alaska and Hawaii; publisher of Hastings (Nebraska) *Tribune* and other newspapers; radio and television executive; adviser to Nixon administration on environment. See *Current Biography* (November) 1956.

Obituary

N Y Times p36 Ja 18 '74

SENIOR, CLARENCE (OLLSON) June 9, 1903-Sept. 8, 1974 Sociologist; educator; economist; specialized in Puerto Rican migration and Latin American land reform; taught at Brooklyn College during the 1960's and later at the Inter-American University in Puerto Rico; author of *Strangers—Then Neighbors: From Pilgrims to Puerto Ricans* and other books. See *Current Biography* (December) 1961.

Obituary

N Y Times p44 S 10 '74

SHAZAR, (SHNEOR) ZALMAN Oct. 6, 1889-Oct. 5, 1974 Israeli statesman; writer; a leader for many years in the Zionist movement; Israel's first Minister of Education (1949-50); President of Israel (1963-73). See *Current Biography* (February) 1964.

Obituary

N Y Times p65 O 6 '74

SHERMAN, ALLAN Nov. 30, 1924-Nov. 20, 1973 Television producer; writer; comedian; wrote material for radio and early television entertainers; cocreated such television game shows as *I've Got a Secret;* turned performer in 1962 with hit recording *My Son the Folksinger,* an album of folktune travesties written in Jewish "delicatessen" style; perhaps best known for song "Hello Muddah, Hello Faddah" on later parody LP *My Son the Nut* (1963). See *Current Biography* (September) 1966.

Obituary

N Y Times p40 N 22 '73

SIMONDS, G(UY) G(RANVILLE) 1903-May 15, 1974 Canadian Army officer; as a field commander in the Mediterranean theatre of operations in World War II, introduced use of armored troop carriers to move infantry into battle to keep pace with tanks; was Chief of Staff from 1951 until his retirement, in the rank of lieutenant general, in 1955; after retirement assumed several high business posts, including presidency of Toronto Brick Company. See *Current Biography* (October) 1943.

Obituary

N Y Times p42 My 17 '74

SIQUEIROS, (JOSÉ) DAVID ALFARO Dec. 29, 1896-Jan. 6, 1974 Mexican painter; last of the giants of the Mexican Renaissance, in which art became a public educational tool in the service of the indigenous proletarian revolution; with bold strokes, gave his social realism a fantastic touch; painted easel oils for a living but was committed to executing murals that the masses could enjoy gratis; did much of his work while imprisoned for Marxist activism; created masterpiece of his "sculpted painting" style in "The March of Humanity," a "plastic-box" building made of murals. See *Current Biography* (June) 1959.

Obituary

N Y Times p27 Ja 7 '74

SMALLWOOD, ROBERT B(ARTLY) Sept. 26, 1893-June 12, 1974 Former business executive; began career as sales executive with Borden Company; as president from 1939 to 1956, built Thomas J. Lipton Inc. into largest tea company in the United States; remained chairman of board at Lipton until 1960; was president of Tea Association for three terms beginning in 1948; later headed Tea Council of U.S.A. See *Current Biography* (March) 1956.

Obituary

N Y Times p34 Je 15 '74

SOYER, MOSES Dec. 25, 1899-Sept. 2, 1974 Russian-born American painter; noted for sturdy, objective quality of his precise, naturalistic portraits and scenes from everyday life, including *Spanish Refugees* and *Mother and Children;* represented in Metropolitan Museum of Art, Whitney Museum, and other leading collections. See *Current Biography* (March) 1941.

Obituary

N Y Times p38 S 3 '74

SPAATZ, CARL June 28, 1891-July 14, 1974 United States Air Force general; earned "wings" in World War I; during World War II commanded American strategic bombing forces, first in Europe and later in Pacific; after war, was Air Force chief of staff; following retirement, in 1948, was chairman of Civil Air Patrol and military affairs columnist for *Newsweek*. See *Current Biography* (September) 1942.

Obituary

N Y Times p1+ Jl 15 '74

STEINKRAUS, HERMAN W(ILLIAM) Dec. 16, 1890-May 9, 1974 Industrialist; president (1942-58) and board chairman (1946-59) of Bridgeport Brass Company; president of United States Chamber of Commerce (1949-50); president of American Association for the United Nations in early 1960's; helped establish United Nations Association (1964). See *Current Biography* (November) 1949.

Obituary

N Y Times p34 My 11 '74

STRASSER, OTTO (JOHANN MAXIMILIAN) Sept. 10, 1897-Aug. 27, 1974 German political leader; writer; editor; early theoretician of National Socialist party; formulated its Bamberg Program (1925), emphasizing socialist aspects; after expulsion from Nazi party by Hitler in 1930, founded rival Black Front; continued to fight Nazi regime from exile (1933-55); returned to West Germany in 1955 and founded short-lived German Social Union; author of *Hitler and I* (1940), *History in My Time* (1941), and other books. See *Current Biography* (September) 1940.

Obituary

N Y Times p34 Ag 28 '74

STRAUSS, LEWIS L(ICHTENSTEIN) Jan. 31, 1896-Jan 21, 1974 Retired rear admiral of United States Navy; partner in investment banking firm Kuhn, Loeb & Company (1929-47); member (1946-50) and chairman (1953-58) of Atomic Energy Commission; strong advocate of United States development of hydrogen bomb, provoked controversy with involvement in Dixon-Yates affair and role in blocking security clearance for

Dr. Robert J. Oppenheimer (1954); acted as United States Secretary of Commerce (1958-59) but was denied Senate confirmation in the post. See *Current Biography* (February) 1947.

Obituary

N Y Times p1+ Ja 22 '74

SULLIVAN, ED(WARD VINCENT) Sept. 28, 1902-Oct. 13, 1974 Newspaper columnist; television and banquet circuit personality; covered sports for New York newspapers in 1920's; author of syndicated *Daily News* Broadway gossip column "Little Old New York" since 1932; as stone-faced impresario and MC of popular Sunday night variety program the *Ed Sullivan Show* (originally *Toast of the Town*) on CBS-TV from 1948 to 1971, introduced wide range of talent, from the Beatles to Rudolf Nureyev, to American television audience. See *Current Biography* (September) 1952.

Obituary

N Y Times p36 O 14 '74   .

SUSANN, JACQUELINE Aug. 20, 1921-Sept. 21, 1974 Author; actress; wrote several popular, sexy *romans à clef*, including *Valley of the Dolls* (1966), the world's best-selling novel of all time, and *Once Is Not Enough* (1973); was noted for considerable narrative skill and promotional ability. See *Current Biography* (May) 1972.

Obituary

N Y Times p38 S 23 '74

TEAD, ORDWAY Sept. 10, 1891-Nov. 15, 1973 Educator; industrial consultant; chairman, New York City Board of Higher Education, (1938-53); worked, taught, and wrote (twenty-one books) widely in management, personnel relations, and related fields; director of business publications for McGraw Hill (1920-25); economics editor at Harper (1925-62). See *Current Biography* (May) 1942.

Obituary

N Y Times p38 N 17 '73

TORRES BODET, JAIME Apr. 17, 1902-May 13, 1974 Mexican statesman; educator; author; professor of French literature at University of Mexico (1924-29); in 1930's and early 1940's filled positions in Mexican embassies around the world; as Minister of Education (1943-46), modernized Mexico's school and library systems; Foreign Minister (1946-48); director general of the United Nations Educational, Scientific, and Cultural Organization (1948-52); wrote some forty books, including novels, memoirs, and collections of poetry and essays. See *Current Biography* (February) 1948.

Obituary

N Y Times p40 My 14 '74

TOUREL, JENNIE June 22, 1910-Nov. 23, 1973 Opera and concert mezzo-soprano; in 1930's was most prominent interpreter of the roles of Carmen and Mignon in France; made American debut with New York Philharmonic under Arturo Toscanini in 1942; joined Metropolitan Opera in 1944; since 1957, when she became member of faculty of Juilliard School of Music, gave recitals on rare occasions, including a well-received Town Hall appearance in April 1973. See *Current Biography* (February) 1947.

Obituary

N Y Times p84 N 25 '73

UNDEN, BO OSTEN Aug. 25, 1886-Jan. 15, 1974 Swedish government official; Minister of Foreign Affairs (1924-26 and 1945-62); Minister of Justice (1920); Minister Without Portfolio (1917-20 and 1932-36); delegate to League of Nations and United Nations; rector of Uppsala University (1929-32); noted legal scholar and advocate of enforcement of world peace through international law. See *Current Biography* (February) 1947.

Obituary

N Y Times p42 Ja 17 '74

VAN WATERS, MIRIAM Oct. 4, 1887-Jan. 17, 1974 Penologist; pioneering prison reformer; as superintendent of Massachusetts State Reformatory for Women (1932-57), transformed that institution into one of most progressive detention facilities in United States; previously headed detention homes in Portland, Oregon (1914-17) and Los Angeles, California (1917-20); author of *Youth in Conflict* (1925) and *Parents on Probation* (1927). See *Current Biography* (March) 1963.

Obituary

N Y Times p36 Ja 18 '74

VOORHEES, TRACY S(TEBBINS) June 30, 1890-Sept. 25, 1974 Government official; lawyer; Assistant Secretary of the Army (1948-49); Under Secretary of the Army (1949-53); personal representative of President Dwight D. Eisenhower for Hungarian Refugee Affairs and chairman of the President's Committee for Hungarian Refugee Relief (1956-57). See *Current Biography* (February) 1957.

Obituary

N Y Times p32 S 26 '74

WARREN, EARL Mar. 19, 1891-July 9, 1974 Chief Justice of United States Supreme Court (1953-69); attorney general (1939-43) and Governor (1943-53) of California; Republican candidate for Vice-President in 1948 election; presided over Supreme Court during period of its greatest influence as agency of social change; wrote or took part in landmark decisions remov-

ing legal basis for racial segregation of schools, extending rights of defendants in criminal cases, mandating legislative apportionment according to "one man, one vote" principle, and outlawing religious exercises in public schools; chairman of commission investigating assassination of President John F. Kennedy (1963-64). See *Current Biography* (January) 1954.

Obituary

N Y Times p1+ Jl 10 '74

WATSON, ARTHUR K(ITTREDGE) Apr. 23, 1919-July 26, 1974 Corporation executive; diplomat; vice-president (1949-53), president (1954-63), and board chairman (1963-70) of IBM World Trade Corporation; built it from a new subsidiary of International Business Machines Corporation into a multibillion dollar world enterprise; as American Ambassador to France (1970-72), helped establish first official contacts between United States and People's Republic of China. See *Current Biography* (September) 1971.

Obituary

N Y Times p32 Jl 27 '74

WATSON-WATT, SIR ROBERT (ALEXANDER) Apr. 13, 1892-Dec. 5, 1973 British physicist; developed first practical radar system, which helped British forces resist German Luftwaffe during Battle of Britain (1940); served in succession of scientific posts with British government (1917-45); later helped develop radar for civilian use in sea and land navigation; knighted in 1942. See *Current Biography* (September) 1945.

Obituary

N Y Times p44 D 7 '73

WATTS, ALAN (WILSON) Jan. 6, 1915-Nov. 16, 1973 British-born American mystic; writer; lecturer; through his lucid, pithy explanations, at once literate and idiomatic ("no fuss"), helped to popularize Zen Buddhism in the West; became a cult figure in the Beat Generation of the late 1950's and early 1960's and later, as a pioneer experimenter in consciousness expansion, an influence on the hippie movement; wrote a score of books, including *The Spirit of Zen* (1936) and *Psychotherapy East and West* (1961). See *Current Biography* (March) 1962.

Obituary

N Y Times p38 N 17 '73

WENDT, GERALD LOUIS Mar. 3, 1891-Dec. 21, 1973 Educator; scientist; head of UNESCO's publication center (1954-67); after teaching chemistry at Rice and Chicago universities, served as director of science and education at New York World's Fair (1939-40); was science editor of *Time* from 1942 to 1945, when he went to *Science Illustrated* as editorial director; joined United Nations Educational, Scientific, and Cultural Organization as director of natural science teaching and dissemination in 1950; edited *The Humanist* (1959-64); wrote *You and the Atom* (1956), among other books. See *Current Biography* (March) 1940.

Obituary

N Y Times p16 D 24 '73

WHEELER, RAYMOND A(LBERT) July 31, 1885-Feb. 8, 1974 Engineer; retired United States Army officer; as Chief of Army Corps of Engineers (1945-49), promoted St. Lawrence Seaway and Missouri Valley Development projects; assisted in construction of Panama Canal; principal administrative officer of Allied Southeast Asia Command during World War II; directed salvage operations of blocked Suez Canal in 1956. See *Current Biography* (April) 1957.

Obituary

N Y Times p51 F 10 '74

WHITMAN, WALTER G(ORDON) Nov. 30, 1895-Apr. 6, 1974 Chemical engineer; former United States government official; head of chemical engineering department of Massachusetts Institute of Technology (1934-61); chairman of the research and development board of Department of Defense (1951-53). See *Current Biography* (February) 1952.

Obituary

N Y Times p44 Ap 9 '74

WHITTAKER, CHARLES EVANS Feb. 22, 1901-Nov. 26, 1973 Retired Associate Justice of United States Supreme Court; began career as trial lawyer in Missouri; served as federal district court (1954-56) and circuit appeals court (1956-57) judge; as an Eisenhower appointee on the Warren Court from 1957 to 1962 was generally a staunch upholder of law-and-order, but voted against depriving wartime military deserters of citizenship. See *Current Biography* (December) 1957.

Obituary

N Y Times p44 N 27 '73

WOODS, BILL M(ILTON) May 26, 1924-May 1, 1974 Librarian; organization official; executive director of Engineering Index Inc. (1968-73); executive director and secretary of Special Libraries Association (1959-67); head of processing section in Library of Congress' map division (1958-59); assistant professor of library science and map and geography librarian at University of Illinois (1949-58). See *Current Biography* (May) 1966.

Obituary

Library of Congress Information Bulletin p209 Je 21 '74

WOODS, TIGHE E(DWARD) Aug. 2, 1910-July 9, 1974 Housing and real estate expert; former government official; examiner in the rent division of Office of Price Administration (1942-47); as housing expediter in Office of Rent Control (1947-52), successfully fought for extension of wartime controls; chief of Office of Price Stabilization (1952-53); later, as private realtor, real estate appraiser, and land developer, continued to champion fair housing and related liberal causes, such as Urban League and Neighbors Inc. See *Current Biography* (October) 1948.

Obituary

Washington Post B p6 Jl 11 '74

YOUNG, MARIAN Nov. 21, 1909-Dec. 9, 1973 Radio broadcaster; as "Martha Deane," conducted daily interview program over station WOR in New York City since 1941; previously worked as correspondent and editor with NEA news service and as writer for Scripps-Howard newspapers; in private life was Mrs. William Bolling Taylor. See *Current Biography* (June) 1952.

Obituary

N Y Times p40 D 10 '73

ZHUKOV, GEORGI K(ONSTANTINOVICH) Dec. 1896-June 18, 1974 Soviet marshal; known as "the Eisenhower of Russia"; as army chief of staff in World War II, was chiefly responsible for strategy and tactics of the defense of Moscow, the winning of the battle of Stalingrad, the raising of the siege of Leningrad, the liberation of the Ukraine and the Crimea, and the capture of Berlin; hailed as "savior" by the common people of the U.S.S.R., was sent into virtual exile by a jealous Stalin after the war; in 1950's, following Stalin's death, became Defense Minister and member of Presidium. See *Current Biography* (April) 1955.

Obituary

N Y Times p46 Je 20 '74

ZWICKY, FRITZ Feb. 14, 1898-Feb. 8, 1974 Astronomer; physicist; astrophysicist; as director of research for Aerojet-General Corporation, invented jet engine and developed rocket propellants; conducted astronomical research on novae and supernovae; introduced theory that universe may be a million billion years old; author of *Morphological Astronomy* (1957) and *Discovery, Invention, Research* (1969). See *Current Biography* (April) 1953.

Obituary

N Y Times p38 F 11 '74

BIOGRAPHICAL REFERENCES

American Architects Directory, 1970

American Bar, 1965

American Catholic Who's Who, 1972-73

American Medical Directory, 1965

American Men and Women of Science 12th ed (1973)

Annuario Pontificio, 1965

Asia Who's Who (1960)

Author's & Writer's Who's Who (1971)

Baseball Register, 1973

Biographical Directory of Librarians in the United States and Canada (1970)

Biographical Directory of the American Congress, 1774-1961 (1962)

Biographical Encyclopaedia & Who's Who of the American Theatre (1966)

Biographical Encyclopedia of Pakistan, 1969-70

Biographic Directory of the USSR (1958)

Burke's Peerage, Baronetage, and Knightage, 1970

Canadian Parliamentary Guide, 1967

Canadian Who's Who, 1970-72

Catholic Who's Who, 1952

Celebrity Register (1973)

Chemical Who's Who, 1956

Chi è? (1961)

China Yearbook, 1963-64

Chujoy, A., and Manchester, P. W., eds. Dance Encyclopedia (1967)

Clerical Directory of the Protestant Episcopal Church in the U.S.A., 1965

Concise Biographical Dictionary of Singers (1969)

Congressional Directory, 1974

Congressional Quarterly Almanac, 1973

Contemporary Authors (1962-74)

Contemporary Dramatists (1973)

Contemporary Novelists (1972)

Contemporary Poets (1971)

Contemporary Poets of the English Language (1970)

Debrett's Peerage, 1964

Department of State Biographic Register, 1972

Dictionary of Latin American and Carribean Biography (1971)

Dictionnaire de biographie française (1964)

Directory of American Judges (1955)

Directory of American Scholars (1969)

Directory of British Scientists, 1966-67

Directory of Medical Specialists, 1972-73

Ewen, D., ed. Composers of Today (1936); Living Musicians (1940), First Supplement (1957); Men and Women Who Make Music (1949); American Composers Today (1949); European Composers Today (1954); The New Book of Modern Composers (1961); Popular American Composers (1962); Composers Since 1900 (1969)

Feather, Leonard. Encyclopedia of Jazz (1960); Encyclopedia of Jazz in the Sixties (1966)

Filmgoer's Companion (1974)

Foremost Women in Communication (1970)

Grove's Dictionary of Music and Musicians (1955)

Hindustan Year Book and Who's Who, 1963

Hoehn, M. A., ed. Catholic Authors (1957)

Hvem er Hvem? 1968

International Motion Picture Almanac, 1973

International Television Almanac, 1973

International Who's Who, 1973-74

International Who's Who in Poetry (1970-71)

International Year Book and Statesmen's Who's Who, 1974

Japan Biographical Encyclopedia & Who's Who, 1964-65

Jews in the World of Science (1956)

Junior Book of Authors (1956)

Kelly's Handbook to the Titled, Landed and Official Classes, 1964

Kleine Slavische Biographie (1958)

Kraks Blå Bog, 1964

Kürschners Biographisches Theater-Handbuch (1956)

Kürschners Deutscher Gelehrten-Kalender, 1970

Leaders in Education (1971)

McGraw-Hill Modern Men of Science (1966-68)

Martindale-Hubbell Law Directory, 1973

Middle East and North Africa, 1972-73

More Junior Authors (1963)

Nalanda Year-Book and Who's Who in India and Pakistan, 1958

National Cyclopaedia of American Biography current vols A-L (1926-72)

New Century Cyclopedia of Names (1954)

Nordness, Lee, ed. Art USA Now (1963)

Nouveau Dictionnaire National des Contemporains (1961-63)

Official Catholic Directory, 1968

Panorama Biografico degli Italiani d'Oggi (1956)

Poor's Register of Directors and Executives, 1964

Prominent Personalities in the USSR (1968)

Quién es Quién en la Argentina, 1958-59

Quién es Quién en Venezuela, Panama, Ecuador, Colombia, 1956

Robinson, Donald. 100 Most Important People in the World Today (1972)

Slonimsky, Nicholas. Baker's Biographical Dictionary of Musicians (1958)

Thomas, S. Men of Space (1960-68)

Thompson, K. A Dictionary of Twentieth-Century Composers (1973)

Thompson, O., ed. International Cyclopedia of Music and Musicians, 1964

Turkin, H., and Thompson, S. C. Official Encyclopedia of Baseball (1959)

Twentieth Century Authors (1942; First Supplement, 1955)

Two Hundred Contemporary Authors (1969)

Vem är Det, 1973

Webster's Biographical Dictionary (1971)

Wer ist Wer? (1971-73)

Who is Who in Music (1951)

Who's Who, 1973-74

Who's Who in Advertising (1963)

Who's Who in America, 1973-74

Who's Who in American Art (1973)

Who's Who in American Education, 1967-68

Who's Who in American Politics, 1973-74

Who's Who in Art (1972)

Who's Who in Australia, 1971

Who's Who in Austria, 1959-60

Who's Who in Baseball, 1971

Who's Who in Belgium (1962)

Who's Who in Boxing (1974)

Who's Who in California, 1965

Who's Who in Canada, 1969-70

Who's Who in Chicago and Illinois (1950)

Who's Who in Colored America, 1950

Who's Who in Communist China (1969)

Who's Who in Engineering, 1964

Who's Who in Finance and Industry (1974-75)

Who's Who in Foreign Correspondence, 1956-57

Who's Who in France, 1971-72

Who's Who in France (Paris), 1953-54

Who's Who in Germany (1964)

Who's Who in Insurance, 1972

Who's Who in Israel, 1973-74

Who's Who in Italy, 1957-58

Who's Who in Latin America Pts 1-7 (1946-51)

Who's Who in Library Service (1966)

Who's Who in Malaysia, 1967

Who's Who in Music, 1969

Who's Who in New York, 1960

Who's Who in New Zealand (1965)

Who's Who in Philosophy (1969)

Who's Who in Professional Baseball (1972)

Who's Who in Publishing (1971)

Who's Who in Railroading in North America (1959)

Who's Who in Space, 1966-67

Who's Who in Spain, 1965

Who's Who in Switzerland, 1970-71

Who's Who in the Arab World, 1971-72

Who's Who in the East, 1974-75

Who's Who in the Midwest, 1974-75

Who's Who in the Netherlands, 1962-63

Who's Who in the South and Southwest, 1973-74

Who's Who in the Theatre (1972)

Who's Who in the United Nations (1951)

Who's Who in the USSR, 1972

Who's Who in the West, 1974-75

Who's Who in the World, 1971-72

Who's Who in World Aviation and Astronautics (1958)

Who's Who in World Jewry (1972)

Who's Who of American Women, 1974-75

Who's Who of British Engineers, 1970-71

Who's Who of British Scientists, 1971-72

Who's Who of Jazz (1972)

Who's Who of Rhodesia, Mauritius, Central and East Africa, 1965

Who's Who of Southern Africa, 1970

Wie is Dat? (1956)

Women Lawyers in the United States (1957)

Wood, C. TV Personalities vols 1-3 (1955-57)

World Biography (1954)

World Who's Who in Commerce and Industry, 1968-69

World Who's Who in Science (1968)

World Who's Who of Women (1973)

PERIODICALS AND NEWSPAPERS CONSULTED

ALA Bul—American Library Association Bulletin
After Dark—After Dark
Am Artist—American Artist
Am Assn Univ Women J—Journal of the American Association of University Women
Am Bar Assn J—American Bar Association Journal
Am Hist R—American Historical Review
Am Pol Sci R—American Political Science Review
Am Scholar—American Scholar
Am Sociol R—American Sociological Review
Am W—American Weekly (discontinued)
America—America
Américas—Américas (incorporating Bul Pan Am Union)
Ann Am Acad—Annals of the American Academy of Political and Social Science
Arch Forum—Architectural Forum, The Magazine of Building
Arch Rec—Architectural Record
Archaeology—Archaeology: A Magazine Dealing with the Antiquity of the World
Art N—Art News
Arts—Arts
Arts & Arch—Arts & Architecture
Atlan—Atlantic Monthly
Aviation W—Aviation Week and Space Technology

Barrons—Barron's
Bet Hom & Gard—Better Homes and Gardens
Biog N—Biography News
Book-of-the-Month Club N—Book-of-the-Month Club News
Book W—Book Week (discontinued)
Broadcasting—Broadcasting
Bsns W—Business Week
Bul Atomic Sci—Bulletin of the Atomic Scientists

Can Hist R—Canadian Historical Review
Cath World—Catholic World
Chem & Eng N—Chemical and Engineering News
Christian Sci Mon—Christian Science Monitor
Colliers—Collier's (discontinued)
Commonweal—Commonweal
Cong Digest—Congressional Digest
Cong Q—Congressional Quarterly Weekly Report
Coronet—Coronet
Cosmop—Cosmopolitan
Cue—Cue
Cur Hist—Current History

Dance Mag—Dance Magazine

Ebony—Ebony
Ed—Education
Ed & Pub—Editor & Publisher
Ed Res Reports—Editorial Research Reports

Encounter—Encounter
Esquire—Esquire
Etude—Etude (discontinued)

Facts on File—Facts on File
For Affairs—Foreign Affairs
For Policy Bul—Foreign Policy Bulletin
Forbes—Forbes
Fortune—Fortune

Good H—Good Housekeeping
Guardian—Guardian (formerly Manchester Guardian)

Harpers—Harper's Magazine
Hi Fi—High Fidelity; The Magazine for Music Listeners
Hi-Fi/Stereo R—Hi-Fi/Stereo Review
Holiday—Holiday
House & Gard—House & Garden

Illus Lond N—Illustrated London News
Intellectual Digest—Intellectual Digest

J Am Med Assn—Journal of the American Medical Association

Ladies Home J—Ladies' Home Journal
Lib J—Library Journal
Life—Life (discontinued)
London Observer—London Observer
Look—Look (discontinued)

McCalls—McCall's
Macleans Mag—Maclean's Magazine
Mag Wall St—Magazine of Wall Street and Business Analyst
Mlle—Mademoiselle
Mus Am—Musical America (incorporated in High Fidelity)
Mus Courier—Musical Courier (discontinued)
Mus Mod Art—Museum of Modern Art Bulletin

NEA J—Journal of the National Education Association
N Y Herald Tribune—New York Herald Tribune (discontinued)
N Y Herald Tribune Bk R—New York Herald Tribune Book Review (discontinued)
N Y Post—New York Post
N Y Rev of Books—New York Review of Books

N Y Sunday News—New York Sunday News
N Y Times—New York Times
N Y Times Bk R—New York Times Book Review
N Y Times Mag—New York Times Magazine
N Y World-Telegram—New York World-Telegram and Sun (discontinued)
N Y World Journal Tribune—New York World Journal Tribune (discontinued)
Nat Geog Mag—National Geographic Magazine

Nat Observer—National Observer
Nation—The Nation
Nations Bsns—Nation's Business
Nature—Nature
New Engl Q—New England Quarterly
New Repub—New Republic
New Statesm—New Statesman
New Times—New Times
New York—New York Magazine
New Yorker—New Yorker
Newsday—Newsday
Newsweek—Newsweek

Opera N—Opera News

People—People
Philadelphia Inquirer—Philadelphia Inquirer
Playboy—Playboy
Pol Sci Q—Political Science Quarterly
Pop Sci—Popular Science Monthly
Ptr Ink—Printers' Ink (discontinued)
Pub W—Publishers' Weekly

Read Digest—Reader's Digest
Reporter—The Reporter (discontinued)

Sat Eve Post—Saturday Evening Post
Sat Night—Saturday Night
Sat R—Saturday Review

Sch & Soc—School and Society
Sci Am—Scientific American
Sci Mo—Scientific Monthly (combined with Science)
Sci N L—Science News Letter
Science—Science (incorporating Sci Mo)
Show—Show (discontinued)
Show Bus Illus—Show Business Illustrated (discontinued)
Spec—Spectator
Sport—Sport
Sports Illus—Sports Illustrated
Sr School—Senior Scholastic

Theatre Arts—Theatre Arts (discontinued)
This Week—This Week Magazine (discontinued)
Time—Time
Times Lit Sup—London Times Literary Supplement
Toronto Globe and Mail—Toronto Globe and Mail
Travel—Travel
TV Guide—TV Guide

U N Rev—United Nations Review
U S Dept State Bul—United States Department of State Bulletin
U S News—U.S. News & World Report

Variety—Variety
Village Voice—Village Voice
Vision—Visión
Vital Speeches—Vital Speeches of the Day
Vogue—Vogue

Wall St J—Wall Street Journal
Washington Post—Washington Post
White Plains Reporter Dispatch—White Plains Reporter Dispatch
Wilson Lib Bul—Wilson Library Bulletin

Yale R—Yale Review

CLASSIFICATION BY PROFESSION—1974

AGRICULTURE
Boerma, Addeke H.

ARCHITECTURE
Sert, José Luis

ART
Krasner, Lee
Lee, Sherman E.
Masson, André
Morris, Desmond
Scull, Robert C.

ASTRONAUTICS
Link, Edwin
Schmitt, Harrison H.

AVIATION
Hiller, Stanley, Jr.
Link, Edwin
Scott, Sheila

BUSINESS
Bronfman, Edgar M.
Broyhill, Joel T.
Dent, Frederick B.
Finley, Charles O.
Geneen, Harold S.
Greenspan, Alan
Haughton, Daniel J.
Hiller, Stanley, Jr.
Jamieson, J. K.
Knudsen, Semon E.
Link, Edwin
Scull, Robert C.
Wood, Robert D.

DANCE
Harkness, Rebekah
Hawkins, Erick
Panov, Valery
Park, Merle

DIPLOMACY
Porter, William J.
Rabin, Yitzhak

EDUCATION
Coleman, John R.
Crumb, George
De Pauw, Gommar A.

Fowler, William A.
Hardin, Garrett
Holley, Edward G.
Kristol, Irving
Lee, Sherman E.
Messiaen, Olivier
Miller, Neal E.
Morris, Desmond
Paz, Octavio
Rosen, Samuel
Selden, David
Sert, José Luis
Smith, William Jay
Solandt, Omond M.
Soyinka, Wole
Wiseman, Frederick
Wynder, Ernest L.

ENGINEERING
David, Edward E.
Link, Edwin

FINANCE
Alexander, Donald C.
Beame, Abraham D.
Bronfman, Edgar M.
Fukuda, Takeo
Geneen, Harold S.
Simon, William E.

GOVERNMENT, Foreign
Almirante, Giorgio
Arias Navarro, Carlos
Carl XVI Gustaf, King of
  Sweden
Fukuda, Takeo
Giscard d'Estaing, Valéry
Kenyatta, Jomo
Kollek, Teddy
Lon Nol
Perón, Juan
Pinochet Ugarte, Augusto
Rabin, Yitzhak
Schmidt, Helmut
Solandt, Omond M.
Spínola, António de
Thorpe, Jeremy
Tolbert, William R., Jr.
Whitlam, Gough

GOVERNMENT, U.S.
Alexander, Donald C.
Baker, Howard

Beame, Abraham D.
Broyhill, Joel T.
Byrne, Brendan T.
David, Edward E.
Dent, Frederick B.
Greenspan, Alan
Hays, Wayne L.
Hicks, Louise Day
Jaworski, Leon
Jordan, Barbara
Kelley, Clarence M.
McCall, Tom
Meskill, Thomas J.
O'Neill, Thomas P., Jr.
Porter, William J.
Saxbe, William B.
Simon, William E.
Sirica, John J.
Steinfeld, Jesse L.
Stevenson, Adlai E., 3d
Weicker, Lowell P., Jr.
White, Kevin H.
Wilson, Malcolm

INDUSTRY
Bronfman, Edgar M.
David, Edward E.
Dent, Frederick B.
Geneen, Harold S.
Hiller, Stanley, Jr.
Jamieson, J. K.
Knudsen, Semon E.
Link, Edwin
Solandt, Omond M.

INTERNATIONAL RELA-
TIONS
Fukuda, Takeo
Geneen, Harold S.
Paz, Octavio
Porter, William J.

JOURNALISM
Angelou, Maya
Cooke, Alistair
Kael, Pauline
Kristol, Irving
Loeb, William
McCall, Tom
Powers, Bertram
Stoppard, Tom

LABOR
Guinan, Matthew
Miller, Arnold
Powers, Bertram
Selden, David

LAW
Alexander, Donald C.
Baker, Howard
Byrne, Brendan T.
Deloria, Vine, Jr.
Hicks, Louise Day
Jaworski, Leon
Jordan, Barbara
Meskill, Thomas J.
Saxbe, William B.
Sirica, John J.
Smith, Chesterfield H.
Stevenson, Adlai E., 3d
Strauss, Robert S.
Thorpe, Jeremy
Weicker, Lowell P., Jr.
White, Kevin H.
Whitlam, Gough
Wilson, Malcolm
Wiseman, Frederick

LIBRARY SERVICE
Holley, Edward G.

LITERATURE
Amalrik, Andrei
Angelou, Maya
Birmingham, Stephen
Blatty, William Peter
Comfort, Alex
Cortázar, Julio
Friel, Brian
Genet, Jean
Kosinski, Jerzy
Le Carré, John
Loos, Anita
Miller, Jason
Paz, Octavio
Pritchett, V. S.
Robbe-Grillet, Alain
Smith, William Jay
Soyinka, Wole
Stoppard, Tom
White, Patrick

MEDICINE
Comfort, Alex
Cooper, Irving S.
Murayama, Makio
Rosen, Samuel

Solandt, Omond M.
Steinfeld, Jesse L.
Wynder, Ernest L.

MILITARY
Davison, Frederic E.
Perón, Juan
Pinochet Ugarte, Augusto
Rabin, Yitzhak
Spínola, António de

MOTION PICTURES
Altman, Robert
Angelou, Maya
Bertolucci, Bernardo
Blatty, William Peter
Bono, Sonny
Brando, Marlon
Brooks, Mel
Cahn, Sammy
Cher
Coco, James
Coppola, Francis Ford
Dewhurst, Colleen
Fonda, Henry
Garfunkel, Art
Grant, Lee
Hampshire, Susan
Kael, Pauline
Kristofferson, Kris
Lear, Norman
Loos, Anita
Nicholson, Jack
Pacino, Al
Powell, Jane
Rigg, Diana
Robbe-Grillet, Alain
Struthers, Sally
Voight, Jon
Weld, Tuesday
Wiseman, Frederick

MUSIC
Angelou, Maya
Blake, Eubie
Bono, Sonny
Cahn, Sammy
Chapin, Schuyler G.
Cher
Crumb, George
Garfunkel, Art
King, Carole
Kristofferson, Kris
Messiaen, Olivier
Powell, Jane
Reardon, John
Stewart, Thomas
Tippett, Sir Michael

NONFICTION
Angelou, Maya
Birmingham, Stephen
Coggan, F. Donald
Coleman, John R.
Comfort, Alex
Cooke, Alistair
Deloria, Vine, Jr.
Fraser, Lady Antonia
Frisch, Karl von
Hardin, Garrett
Holley, Edward G.
Kael, Pauline
Kosinski, Jerzy
Krishnamurti, Jiddu
Kristol, Irving
Lee, Sherman E.
Mitford, Jessica
Morris, Desmond
Paz, Octavio
Peale, Norman Vincent
Pomeroy, Wardell B.
Pritchett, V. S.
Robbe-Grillet, Alain
Rosen, Samuel
Schmidt, Helmut
Scott, Sheila
Sert, José Luis
Terkel, Studs
Thekaekara, Matthew P.
Whitlam, Gough

ORGANIZATIONS
Boerma, Addeke H.
Deloria, Vine, Jr.
Smith, Chesterfield H.
Strauss, Robert S.

PHILOSOPHY
Krishnamurti, Jiddu
Maharaj Ji, Guru

POLITICS, Foreign
Almirante, Giorgio
Arias Navarro, Carlos
Fukuda, Takeo
Giscard d Estaing, Valéry
Kenyatta, Jomo
Kollek, Teddy
Lon Nol
Perón, Juan
Pinochet Ugarte, Augusto
Rabin, Yitzhak
Schmidt, Helmut
Spínola, António de
Thorpe, Jeremy
Tolbert, William R., Jr.
Whitlam, Gough

POLITICS, U.S.
Baker, Howard
Beame, Abraham D.
Broyhill, Joel T.
Byrne, Brendan T.
Hays, Wayne L.
Hicks, Louise Day
Jordan, Barbara
McCall, Tom
Meskill, Thomas J.
O'Neill, Thomas P., Jr.
Saxbe, William B.
Stevenson, Adlai E., 3d
Strauss, Robert S.
Weicker, Lowell P., Jr.
White, Kevin H.
Wilson, Malcolm

PSYCHOLOGY
Miller, Neal E.
Pomeroy, Wardell B.

PUBLISHING
Kristol, Irving
Loeb, William
Powers, Bertram

RADIO
Comfort, Alex
Cooke, Alistair
Stoppard, Tom
Terkel, Studs

RELIGION
Coggan, F. Donald
De Pauw, Gommar A.
Krishnamurti, Jiddu
Kuhlman, Kathryn
Maharaj Ji, Guru
Peale, Norman Vincent
Tolbert, William R., Jr.

SCIENCE
Boerma, Addeke H.
Comfort, Alex
Cooper, Irving S.
David, Edward E.

Fowler, William A.
Frisch, Karl von
Gottlieb, Melvin B.
Hardin, Garrett
Kohoutek, Lubos
Link, Edwin
Miller, Neal E.
Morris, Desmond
Murayama, Makio
Schmitt, Harrison H.
Solandt, Omond M.
Thekaekara, Matthew P.

SOCIAL ACTIVISM
Comfort, Alex
Deloria, Vine, Jr.

SOCIAL SCIENCE
Amalrik, Andrei
Coleman, John R.
Deloria, Vine, Jr.
Greenspan, Alan
Kristol, Irving
Morris, Desmond
Pomeroy, Wardell B.

SPORTS
Borg, Björn
Casals, Rosemary
Finley, Charles O.
Foreman, George
Jackson, Reggie
Mauch, Gene
Miller, Johnny
Nastase, Ilie
Seagren, Bob
Shula, Don
Turcotte, Ron
Villemure, Gilles

TECHNOLOGY
Gottlieb, Melvin B.
Haughton, Daniel J.
Knudsen, Semon E.
Solandt, Omond M.
Thekaekara, Matthew P.

TELEVISION
Angelou, Maya
Bertolucci, Bernardo
Bono, Sonny
Brooks, Mel
Cahn, Sammy
Cher
Coco, James
Comfort, Alex
Cooke, Alistair
Dewhurst, Colleen
Fonda, Henry
Grant, Lee
Hampshire, Susan
Lear, Norman
Loud, Pat
Reardon, John
Rigg, Diana
Stoppard, Tom
Struthers, Sally
Terkel, Studs
Weld, Tuesday
Wiseman, Frederick
Wood, Robert D.

THEATRE
Angelou, Maya
Ball, William
Blake, Eubie
Brando, Marlon
Cahn, Sammy
Coco, James
Coppola, Francis Ford
Dewhurst, Colleen
Fonda, Henry
Friel, Brian
Genet, Jean
Grant, Lee
Hampshire, Susan
Loos, Anita
Miller, Jason
Pacino, Al
Reardon, John
Rigg, Diana
Soyinka, Wole
Stoppard, Tom
Struthers, Sally
Voight, Jon

OTHER CLASSIFICATIONS
Harkness, Rebekah

CUMULATED INDEX—1971-1974

For the index to 1940-1970 biographies, see
Current Biography Cumulated Index 1940-1970

Abbado, Claudio May 73
Abbott, Bud obit Jun 74
Abrams, Creighton W(illiams, Jr.) obit Oct 74
Abzug, Bella (Savitsky) Jul 71
Acheson, Dean (Gooderham) obit Nov 71
Adams, Sir Grantley H(erbert) obit Jan 72
Adams, Roger obit Sep 71
Adamson, Joy(-Friederike Victoria) Oct 72
Adolfo Nov 72
Agar, William (Macdonough) obit Jul 72
Agnelli, Giovanni Jan 72
Aichi, Kiichi Jul 71 obit Jan 74
Aiken, Conrad (Potter) obit Oct 73
Aiken, Howard (Hathaway) obit May 73
Aldrich, Winthrop W(illiams) obit Apr 74
Alexander, Donald C(richton) Dec 74
Alinsky, Saul (David) obit Jul 72
Allen, Dick May 73
Allen, George E(dward) obit Jun 73
Allen, James E(dward), Jr. obit Dec 71
Allen, Jay (Cooke, Jr.) obit Feb 73
Allen, Leo E(lwood) obit Mar 73
Allende (Gossens), Salvador Sep 71 obit Nov 73
Allman, David B(acharach) obit May 71
Almirante, Giorgio Jan 74
Altmeyer, Arthur J(oseph) obit Dec 72
Alsop, Stewart (Johonnot Oliver) obit Jul 74
Altman, Robert Feb 74
Amalrik, Andrei (Alekseyevich) Apr 74
Ames, Amyas Apr 72
Amin, Idi Feb 73
Anderson, Jack(son Northman) Jun 72
Angelou, Maya Jun 74
Anne, Princess Oct 73
Apgar, Virginia obit Oct 74
Arafat, Yasir Mar 71
Arbenz Guzman, Jacobo obit Mar 71

Ardrey, Robert Jul 73
Arias Navarro, Carlos Oct 74
Armand, Louis obit Oct 71
Armstrong, (Daniel) Louis obit Sep 71
Armstrong, Hamilton Fish obit Jun 73
Arness, James Nov 73
Arquette, Cliff obit Nov 74
Arrabal (Terán), Fernando Sep 72
Arroyo, Martina Feb 71
Arthur, Beatrice Dec 73
Ashbrook, John M(ilan) Oct 73
Askew, Reubin (O'Donovan) Apr 73
Astor, John Jacob, 1st Baron of Hever obit Sep 71
Asturias, Miguel Angel obit Jul 74
Athenagoras I, Patriarch obit Sep 72
Aubrey, James T(homas), Jr. Mar 72
Auden, W(ystan) H(ugh) Sep 71 obit Nov 73
Ayub Khan, Mohammad obit Jun 74

Bach, Richard (David) Oct 73
Badillo, Herman May 71
Baker, Howard (Henry, Jr.) Mar 74
Baker, Janet Jun 71
Bakke, E(dward) Wight obit Jan 72
Bakshi, Ghulam Mohammad obit Sep 72
Balaban, Barney obit Apr 71
Balchen, Bernt obit Dec 73
Balenciaga, (Cristóbal) obit May 72
Ball, William May 74
Banfield, Edward C(hristie) May 72
Banzer Suárez, Hugo Sep 73
Banzhaf, John F(rancis), 3d Dec 73
Barber, Anthony (Perrinott Lysberg) Jan 71
Baring, George Rowland Stanley See Cromer, 3d Earl of May 71
Barlow, Howard obit Mar 72
Barnes, Clive (Alexander) Mar 72

Barry, Rick Mar 71
Barzini, Luigi (Giorgio, Jr.) Jul 72
Bates, H(erbert) E(rnest) obit Mar 74
Bates, Marston obit May 74
Bates, Sanford obit Nov 72
Batista (y Zaldívar), Fulgencio obit Oct 73
Battle, John S(tewart) obit Jun 72
Baxter, Anne May 72
Bayne, Stephen F(ielding) Jr. obit Mar 74
Bazelon, David L(ionel) Jan 71
Beall, J(ames) Glenn obit Mar 71
Beame, Abraham D(avid) Jul 74
Bearden, Romare Jan 72
Beauvoir, Simone (Bertrand) de Jan 73
Behrman, S(amuel) N(athaniel) obit Nov 73
Beirne, J(oseph) A(nthony) obit Oct 74
Beitz, Berthold Feb 73
Béjart, Maurice Mar 71
Békésy, Georg von obit Sep 72
Bell, Daniel Dec 73
Bell, Daniel W(afena) obit Nov 71
Bemis, Samuel Flagg obit Nov 73
Ben-Gurion, David obit Jan 74
Bench, Johnny Oct 71
Benson, Sally obit Sep 72
Bentley, Helen Delich Dec 71
Benton, William (Burnett) obit May 73
Bentsen, Lloyd (Millard, Jr.) Sep 73
Berendsen, Sir Carl August obit Dec 73
Berio, Luciano Mar 71
Berkeley, Busby Apr 71
Berle, Adolf A(ugustus) obit Apr 71
Berman, Emile Zola Jun 72
Berman, Eugene obit Feb 73
Berryman, James Thomas obit Oct 71
Berryman, John obit Feb 72
Bertolucci, Bernardo Jul 74
Best, Edna obit Nov 74
Betjeman, Sir John Mar 73
Bhutto, Zulfikar Ali Apr 72
Biddle, George obit Jan 74

Biggers, John D(avid) obit Feb 74

Birmingham, Stephen May 74

Black, Hugo L(a Fayette) obit **Nov 71**

Blackett, P(atrick) M(aynard) S(tuart), Baron Blackett obit Sep 74

Blake, Eubie Apr 74

Blanchfield, Florence A. obit Jun 71

Blanda, George (Frederick) Sep 72

Blandford, John B(ennett), Jr. obit Mar 72

Blank, Theodor obit Jul 72

Blatchford, Joseph H(offer) Mar 71

Blattenberger, Raymond obit Jun 71

Blatty, William Peter Jun 74

Blaustein, Jacob obit Jan 71

Blue, Vida Mar 72

Bobst, Elmer H(olmes) Dec 73

Boerma, Addeke H(endrik) Dec 74

Boeschenstein, Harold obit Dec 72

Bogdanovich, Peter Jun 72

Boggs, Hale See Boggs, (Thomas) H. obit Mar 73

Boggs, (Thomas) Hale obit Mar 73

Bohlen, Charles E(ustis) obit Feb 74

Bok, Derek C(urtis) Jul 71

Böll, Heinrich (Theodor) Jul 72

Bono, Cher See Cher Jan 74

Bono, Sonny Feb 74

Bontemps, Arna (Wendell) obit Jul 73

Boone, J(oel) T(hompson) obit Jun 74

Borch, Fred J. Oct 71

Borg, Björn Dec 74

Borlaug, Norman E(rnest) Jul 71

Boumedienne, Houari Jan 71

Bourke-White, Margaret obit Oct 71

Bouton, Jim Oct 71

Bowen, Catherine (Shober) Drinker obit Dec 73

Bowen, Ira Sprague obit Apr 73

Bowen, William G(ordon) May 73

Boyce, Westray Battle obit Mar 72

Boyd, Bill obit Nov 72

Boyd, Louise A(rner) obit Nov 72

Boyd Orr, John Boyd Orr, 1st Baron obit Sep 71

Boyd, William See Boyd, B. obit Nov 72

Boyle, Hal obit May 74

Braddock, Bessie See Braddock, E. M. obit Jan 71

Braddock, E(lizabeth) M(argaret Bamber) obit Jan 71

Bradley, Thomas Nov 73

Brando, Marlon Mar 74

Brandt, Willy Dec 73

Braun, (Joachim) Werner obit Jan 73

Brel, Jacques Mar 71

Brennan, Peter J(oseph) Apr 73

Brennan, Walter obit Nov 74

Breslin, Jimmy Dec 73

Bresson, Robert Jan 71

Brick, John obit Dec 73

Brock, William Emerson, 3d May 71

Brode, Wallace (Reed) obit Oct 74

Brogan, D(ennis) W(illiam) obit Feb 74

Bronfman, Edgar M(iles) Jul 74

Bronowski, J(acob) obit Oct 74

Brooke, Sir Basil (Stanlake) See Brookeborough, Lord obit Oct 73

Brookeborough, Lord obit Oct 73

Brooks, Donald (Marc) Mar 72

Brooks, Mel Sep 74

Brothers, Joyce Apr 71

Browder, Earl (Russell) obit Sep 73

Brower, David (Ross) Jun 73

Brown, George H(ay) Jan 71

Brown, Joe E(van) obit Sep 73

Brown, Larry Mar 73

Brown, Prentiss M(arsh) obit Feb 74

Broyhill, Joel T(homas) May 74

Bruce, Louis R(ooks, Jr.) May 72

Brunner, Edmund de S(chweinitz) obit Feb 74

Buck, Pearl (Sydenstricker) obit Apr 73

Buckley, James L(ane) Oct 71

Budd, Edward G(owen), Jr. obit Jul 71

Budenny, Semyon M(ikhailovich) obit Dec 73

Budenz, Louis F(rancis) obit Jun 72

Buetow, Herbert P(aul) obit Mar 72

Bultmann, Rudolf (Karl) Jan 72

Bunche, Ralph J(ohnson) obit Jan 72

Burgess, Anthony May 72

Burke, Michael Apr 72

Burke, Thomas A(loysius) obit Jan 72

Burnett, Whit obit Jun 73

Burns, H(enry) S(tuart) M(ackenzie) obit Dec 71

Burns, John A(nthony) Feb 72

Burroughs, William S(eward) Nov 71

Busch, August A(dolphus), Jr. Jul 73

Bush, George (Herbert Walker) Jan 72

Bush, Prescott S(heldon) obit Dec 72

Bush, Vannevar obit Sep 74

Butz, Earl L(auer) Jul 72

Byington, Spring obit Oct 71

Byrne, Brendan T(homas) May 74

Byrnes, James F(rancis) obit Jun 72

Caffery, Jefferson obit Jun 74

Cahn, Sammy Nov 74

Caldwell, Sarah Oct 73

Calisher, Hortense Nov 73

Câmara, Helder Pessoa Jul 71

Campbell, E. Simms obit Mar 71

Cámpora, Héctor José Oct 73

Carey, James B(arron) obit Nov 73

Carington, Peter Alexander Rupert, 6th Baron Carrington See Carrington, 6th Baron Jun 71

Carl XVI Gustaf, King of Sweden Feb 74

Carmines, Al(vin Allison Jr.) Sep 72

Carr, (Leonard) Robert Jan 73

Carrero Blanco, Luis Oct 73 obit Feb **74**

Carrington, 6th Baron Jun 71

Carter, James Earl, Jr. See Carter, Jimmy Sep 71

Carter, Jimmy Sep 71

Carter, (William) Hodding, Jr. obit May 72

Cartwright, Morse A(dams) obit Jun 74

Casadesus, Robert (Marcel) obit Nov 72

Casals, Pablo obit Dec 73

Casals, Rosemary Feb 74

Casey, William J(oseph) Mar 72

Cecil of Essendon, Robert Arthur James Cecil, 1st Baron See Salisbury, Robert Arthur Cecil, 5th Marquis obit Apr 72

Ceram, C. W. See Marek, K. W. obit Jun 72

Cerf, Bennett (Alfred) obit Oct 71

Cernan, Eugene A(ndrew) May 73

Chadwick, Sir James obit Oct 74

Chalk, O(scar) Roy Nov 71

Chandler, Norman obit Dec 73

Chandos, Oliver Lyttelton, 1st Viscount obit Mar 72

Chanel, Gabrielle (Bonheur) obit Feb 71

Chapin, Schuyler G(arrison) Feb 74

Charlesworth, James C(lyde) obit Mar 74

Chase, Mary Ellen obit Oct 73

Chen Yi obit Feb 72

Cher Jan 74

Chevalier, Maurice obit Feb 72

Chichester, Sir Francis (Charles) obit Oct 72

Chiles, Lawton (Mainor, Jr.) Sep 71

Chiperfield, Robert B(ruce) obit May 71

Chirico, Giorgio de Jun 72

Chisholm, (George) Brock obit Mar 71

Christenberry, Robert K(eaton) obit Jun 73

Christofilos, Nicholas C(onstantine) obit Nov 72

Cicognani, Amleto Giovanni, Cardinal obit Feb 74

Clapp, Margaret (Antoinette) obit Jun 74

Clapp, Verner W(arren) obit Sep 72

Clark, J(oseph) J(ames) obit Sep 71

Clark, Paul F(oster) obit Mar 73

Clarke, Ron May 71

Clayton, P(hilip Thomas) B(yard) obit Mar 73

Clemente, Roberto (Walker) Feb 72 obit Feb 73

Clifford, John Nov 72

Clift, David H(orace) obit Dec 73

Cline, John Wesley obit Sep 74

Clyde, George D(ewey) obit May 72

Coanda, Henri (-Marie) obit Feb 73

Cochran, H(orace) Merle obit Nov 73

Coco, James May 74

Coggan, F(rederick) Donald Jul 74

Coldwell, M(ichael) J. obit Oct 74

Cole, Edward N(icholas) Jul 72

Coleman, John R(oyston) Oct 74

Colombo, Emilio Apr 71

Comfort, Alex(ander) Sep 74

Condon, Eddie obit Oct 73

Condon, E(dward) U(hler) obit May 74

Conigliaro, Tony Feb 71

Cook, Marlow W(ebster) Jan 72

Cooke, (Alfred) Alistair May 74

Cooley, Harold D(unbar) obit Mar 74

Cooper, Dame Gladys obit Jan 72

Cooper, Irving S(pencer) Apr 74

Coppola, Francis Ford May 74

Cordiner, Ralph J(arron) obit Jan 74

Cornell, Katharine obit Jul 74

Correll, Charles J. obit Nov 72

Cortázar, Julio Feb 74

Cortney, Philip obit Jul 71

Cosell, Howard Nov 72

Cost, March obit Apr 73

Costa-Gavras, (Henri) Sep 72

Coudenhove-Kalergi, Richard N(icolaus), Count obit Oct 72

Coudert, Frederic René, Jr. obit Jul 72

Courant, Richard obit Mar 72

Court, Margaret (Smith) Sep 73

Coward, Sir Noel (Pierce) obit May 73

Cox, Wally obit Apr 73

Craig, Lyman C(reighton) obit Sep 74

Cranko, John obit Sep 73

Creasey, John obit Jul 73

Cromer, 3d Earl of May 71

Crossman, R(ichard) H(oward) S(tafford) obit Jun 74

Crowley, Leo T(homas) obit Jun 72

Crown, Henry Jan 72

Crumb, George (Henry) Dec 74

Cullman, Howard S(tix) obit Sep 72

Cushman, Robert E(verton), Jr. Nov 72

Daley, Arthur (John) obit Feb 74

Dancer, Stanley Jun 73

Daniels, Farrington obit Sep 72

Darin, Bobby obit Feb 74

Dassin, Jules Mar 71

Daugherty, James Henry obit Apr 74

David, Edward E(mil, Jr.) May 74

Davis, Adelle Jan 73 obit Jul 74

Davis, Angela (Yvonne) Nov 72

Davis, Benjamin O(liver), Sr. obit Jan 71

Davis, Edward W(ilson) obit Feb 74

Davis, William (Grenville) May 73

Davison, Frederic E(llis) Feb 74

Dawson, William obit Sep 72

Day-Lewis, C(ecil) obit Jul 72

Dean, Dizzy obit Sep 74

Dean, Vera Micheles obit Dec 72

Deane, Martha See Young, M. obit Jan 74

Debus, Kurt H(einrich) Nov 73

DeBusschere, Dave Oct 73

De Kruif, Paul (Henry) obit Apr 71

Dellums, Ronald V. Sep 72

Deloria, Vine (Victor), Jr. Sep 74

Denenberg, Herbert S(idney) Dec 72

Denfeld, Louis E(mil) obit May 72

Dent, Frederick B(aily) Apr 74

De Pauw, Gommar A(lbert) May 74

DeSeversky, Alexander P(rocofieff) obit Oct 74

Deupree, Richard R(edwood) obit May 74

Dewey, Thomas E(dmund) obit Apr 71

Dewhurst, Colleen Jul 74

Diebenkorn, Richard (Clifford, Jr.) Dec 71

Dies, Martin obit Jan 73

Dieterle, William obit Feb 73

Dixon, Jeane (L.) Feb 73

Doan, Leland I(ra) obit May 74

Dodd, Thomas J(oseph) obit Jul 71

Dodge, Bayard obit Jul 72

Dole, Robert J(oseph) Apr 72

Domingo, Placido Mar 72

Dominguín, Luis Miguel Mar 72

Doms, Keith Jun 71

Donnelly, Walter J(oseph) obit Jan 71

Douglas, Lewis W(illiams) obit May 74

Dowell, Anthony May 71

Dowling, Robert W(hittle) obit Nov 73

Dreyfuss, Henry obit Dec 72
Drinan, Robert F(rederick) Jun 71
Dubos, René J(ules) Jan 73
Duerk, Alene (Bertha) Sep 73
Duffey, Joseph D(aniel) Mar 71
Duffy, Bernard C(ornelius) obit Nov 72
Dunaway, Faye Feb 72
Durham, Carl (Thomas) obit Jun 74
Dutra, Eurico Gaspar obit Sep 74
Duvalier, François obit Jun 71
Duvalier, Jean-Claude Jun 72
Dykstra, John obit May 72

Eagleton, Thomas (Francis) Nov 73
Eastwood, Clint Oct 71
Eccles, Sir John (Carew) Oct 72
Echeverría, Álvarez, Luis Nov 72
Edwards, Charles C(ornell) Oct 73
Eisendrath, Maurice N(athan) obit Jan 74
Eliot, George Fielding obit Jun 71
Elisofon, Eliot Jan 72 obit May 73
Ellender, Allen J(oseph) obit Oct 72
Ellington, Duke obit Jul 74
Ellington, (E.) Buford obit May 72
Ellsberg, Daniel Dec 73
Enrique Tarancón, Vincente Cardinal Oct 72
Erdman, Jean Sep 71
Erikson, Erik H(omburger) May 71
Erskine, G(raves) B(lanchard) obit Jul 73
Ervin, Sam(uel) J(ames), Jr. Oct 73
Esposito, Phil May 73
Ettinger, Richard P(rentice) obit Apr 71
Evans, Herbert M(cLean) obit Apr 71
Evans, Walker Sep 71
Evergood, Philip (Howard Francis Dixon) obit Apr 73
Evert, Chris(tine Marie) Apr 73
Ewing, (William) Maurice obit Jun 74
Eysenck, Hans J(ürgen) Nov 72

Fairchild, John B(urr) Jun 71
Falk, Peter Jul 72
Farber, Sidney obit May 73

Faulkner, (Arthur) Brian (Deane) Feb 72
Fawcett, Sherwood L(uther) Dec 72
Feather, Vic(tor) Grayson Hardie) Mar 73
Feis, Herbert obit May 72
Feld, Eliot Oct 71
Fernandel obit Apr 71
Field, Betty obit Nov 73
Fields, Dorothy obit May 74
Finch, Peter Sep 72
Finley, Charles O(scar) Jun 74
Firestone, Harvey S(amuel), Jr. obit Jul 73
Fisher of Lambeth, Geoffrey Francis Fisher, Baron obit Nov 72
Fitzsimmons, Frank E(dward) May 71
Flack, Roberta Nov 73
Fleisher, Leon Jan 71
Fleming, Lady Amalia Nov 72
Fletcher, Arthur A(llen) Nov 71
Fletcher, James C(hipman) May 72
Fonda, Henry Nov 74
Fonteyn, Margot Mar 72
Forand, Aime J(oseph) obit Mar 72
Ford, Eileen (Otte) Oct 71
Ford, John obit Nov 73
Foreman, George May 74
Forman, Milos Dec 71
Forsythe, John May 73
Fosdick, Raymond B(laine) obit Sep 72
Fosse, Bob Jun 72
Foster, John S(tuart), Jr. Dec 71
Fowler, William A(lfred) Sep 74
Foxx, Redd Dec 72
Foyle, Gilbert (Samuel) obit Jan 72
Francis, Sam(uel Lewis) Oct 73
Frank, Reuven Jun 73
Franklin, Walter S(imonds) obit Oct 72
Frasconi, Antonio Mar 72
Fraser, Lady Antonia Oct 74
Frazer, Joseph W(ashington) obit Sep 71
Frazier, Joe Apr 71
Frazier, Walt Feb 73
Frederik IX, King of Denmark obit Mar 72
Friedman, Bruce Jay Jun 72
Friel, Brian Jun 74
Frisch, Karl von Feb 74
Frost, Leslie M(iscampbell) obit Jul 73
Frowick, Roy Halston See Halston Dec 72

Fuentes, Carlos Oct 72
Fukuda, Takeo Jun 74
Fuller, Alfred C(arl) obit Jan 74
Furtseva, Ekaterina A(lexeyevna) obit Dec 74

Gabo, Naum Apr 72
Gabor, Dennis Oct 72
Gaddafi, Moamar al- See Qaddafi, M. Sep 73
Gades, Antonio Feb 73
Garand, John C(antius) obit Apr 74
Garcia, Carlos P. obit 71
García Márquez, Gabriel José Jul 73
Garfunkel, Art Jun 74
Gebel-Williams, Gunther Dec 71
Geneen, Harold S(ydney) Feb 74
Genet, Jean Apr 74
Gentele, Goeran Sep 72 obit Sep 72
Gerard, Ralph W(aldo) obit Apr 74
Gerow, Leonard Townsend obit Dec 72
Getz, Stan Apr 71
Gibson, Kenneth A(llen) May 71
Giegengack, A(ugustus) E(dward) obit Sep 74
Gierek, Edward May 71
Gilbreth, Lillian (Evelyn) M(oller) obit Feb 72
Gillette, Guy M(ark) obit Apr 73
Gilligan, John J(oyce) May 72
Ginastera, Alberto (Evaristo) Jan 71
Ginsberg, Mitchell I(rving) Jun 71
Giovanni, Nikki Apr 73
Gipson, Lawrence Henry obit Nov 71
Giscard d'Estaing, Valéry Oct 74
Givens, Willard E(arl) obit Jul 71
Glueck, Eleanor T(ouroff) obit Nov 72
Glueck, Nelson obit Mar 71
Goldberg, Rube(n Lucius) obit Jan 71
Goldwyn, Samuel obit Mar 74
Golschmann, Vladimir obit May 72
Gonzalez, Efren W(illiam) Jun 71
Good, Robert A(lan) Mar 72
Goodman, Paul obit Oct 72
Goolagong, Evonne Nov 71

Gorbach, Alfons obit Oct 72
Gordon, Ruth Apr 72
Gottlieb, Adolph obit Apr 74
Gottlieb, Melvin B(urt) Jan 74
Gould, Chester Sep 71
Gould, Elliott Feb 71
Gove, Philip B(abcock) obit Jan 73
Grace, Alonzo G(askell) obit Dec 71
Graf, Herbert obit May 73
Graham, Billy Jan 73
Graham, Frank P(orter) obit Apr 72
Graham, Katharine (Meyer) Jan 71
Graham, William Franklin See Graham, B. Jan 73
Grant, Lee Mar 74
Gravel, Maurice Robert See Gravel, Mike Jan 72
Gravel, Mike Jan 72
Gray, L(ouis) Patrick, 3d Sep 72
Grayson, C(harles) Jackson, Jr. Sep 72
Greeley, Andrew M(oran) Dec 72
Greenspan, Alan Dec 74
Greer, Germaine Nov 71
Grey, Joel Jan 73
Griffis, Stanton obit Oct 74
Grimes, W(illiam) H(enry) obit Mar 72
Grivas, George (Theodorus) obit Mar 74
Grofé, Ferde obit May 72
Grooms, Charles Roger See Grooms, R. Dec 72
Grooms, Red Dec 72
Grossinger, Jennie obit Jan 73
Gruenberg, Sidonie Matsner obit May 74
Gruening, Ernest (Henry) obit Sep 74
Grzimek, Bernhard Mar 73
Guggenheim, Harry F(rank) obit Mar 71
Guinan, Matthew Sep 74
Gustaf VI, King of Sweden obit Nov 73
Guston, Philip Feb 71
Guthrie, Sir (William) Tyrone obit Jul 71
Guttmacher, Alan F(rank) obit May 74

Hackman, Gene Jul 72
Hackworth, Green H(aywood) obit Sep 73
Haig, Alexander Meigs, Jr. Jan 73
Hailey, Arthur Feb 72
Halberstam, David Apr 73

Hall, Gus May 73
Halston Dec 72
Hammer, Armand Jun 73
Hampshire, Susan Jan 74
Hampton, Lionel (Leo) Oct 71
Handke, Peter Apr 73
Handley, Harold W(illis) obit Nov 72
Hanks, Nancy Sep 71
Hardin, Garrett (James) Sep 74
Hargis, Billy James Mar 72
Harkness, Rebekah (West) Apr 74
Harlan, John Marshall obit Feb 72
Harridge, Will(iam) obit Jun 71
Harrington, Russell C(hase) obit Oct 71
Harris, Seymour E(dwin) obit Dec 74
Hart, Thomas C(harles) obit Sep 71
Hartman, Paul (William) obit Dec 73
Harvey, Laurence obit Jan 74
Hatcher, Richard G(ordon) Feb 72
Haughton, Daniel J(eremiah) Sep 74
Hawkins, Erick Jan 74
Hawkins, Jack obit Oct 73
Hawks, Howard May 72
Hawn, Goldie Dec 71
Hayakawa, Sessue obit Jan 74
Hayden, Carl T(rumbull) obit Mar 72
Hayes, Isaac Oct 72
Hays, Wayne L(evere) Nov 74
Hayward, Leland obit Apr 71
Healey, Denis (Winston) Dec 71
Heatter, Gabriel obit May 72
Heflin, Van obit Sep 71
Heidegger, Martin Jun 72
Height, Dorothy I(rene) Sep 72
Heiser, Victor G(eorge) obit May 72
Heller, Joseph Jan 73
Helpern, Milton May 73
Henderson, Florence Apr 71
Herman, Woody Apr 73
Hernandez, Aileen C(larke) Jul 71
Hernández Colón, Rafael May 73
Herod, William Rogers obit Sep 74
Herzberg, Gerhard Feb 73
Heschel, Abraham Joshua obit Mar 73
Hewitt, Henry K(ent) obit Nov 72

Heyerdahl, Thor Sep 72
Hickenlooper, Bourke B(lakemore) obit Oct 71
Hicks, Louise Day Mar 74
Hill, Arthur M(iddleton) obit Nov 72
Hill, Graham Jul 73
Hill, Harry W(ilbur) obit Sep 71
Hill, William S(ilas) obit Nov 72
Hilleboe, Herman E(rtresvaag) obit Jun 74
Hiller, Stanley, Jr. Nov 74
Hirschfeld, Albert Jan 71
Hockney, David Jul 72
Hodges, Gil(bert Ray) obit May 72
Hodges, Luther H(artwell) obit Nov 74
Hoffa, James R(iddle) May 72
Hoffman, Paul G(ray) obit Nov 74
Hogan, Frank S(mithwick) obit May 74
Holland, Spessard L(indsey) obit Dec 71
Holley, Edward G(ailon) Jun 74
Holton, (Abner) Linwood, (Jr.) Feb 71
Holtzman, Elizabeth Nov 73
Homer, Arthur B(artlett) obit Sep 72
Honecker, Erich Apr 72
Hoo (Chi-Tsai), Victor obit Jul 72
Hoover, J(ohn) Edgar obit Jun 72
Horgan, Paul Feb 71
Horner, Matina Souretis Jul 73
Horsfall, Frank L(appin), Jr. obit Apr 71
Houssay, Bernardo Alberto obit Nov 71
Hoveyda, Amir Abbas Oct 71
Howard, Frank (Oliver) Jan 72
Howell, Charles R(obert) obit Sep 73
Huck, Arthur obit Mar 73
Huebner, Clarence R(alph) obit Nov 72
Hull, Helen R(ose) obit Sep 71
Humbard, (Alpha) Rex (Emmanuel) Sep 72
Huntington, Anna Hyatt obit Dec 73
Huntley, Chet obit May 74
Hurley, Roy T. obit Dec 71
Hurok, S(olomon) obit Apr 74
Husak, Gustav Oct 71
Hussein, Taha obit Dec 73
Huxtable, Ada Louise (Landman) Mar 73

Iacocca, Lee A(nthony) Oct 71
Indiana, Robert Mar 73
Inge, William (Motter) obit Jul 73
Inönü, Ismet obit Feb 74
Iselin, Columbus O'D(onnell) obit Feb 71
Isherwood, Christopher (William) Oct 72
Ishibashi, Tanzan obit Jun 73

Jackson, Glenda Dec 71
Jackson, Mahalia obit Mar 72
Jackson, Reggie Jan 74
Jackson, William H(arding) obit Nov 71
Jagger, Mick Dec 72
James, Arthur Horace obit Jun 73
Jamieson, J(ohn) K(enneth) Jun 74
Jamison, Judith Jan 73
Jarvis, Lucy (Howard) Apr 72
Jastrow, Robert Jan 73
Jaworski, Leon Jun 74
Jencks, Christopher (Sandys) Apr 73
Jensen, Arthur R(obert) Jan 73
Johns, Glynis Sep 73
Johnson, Alvin (Saunders) obit Jul 71
Johnson, Howard A(lbert) obit Sep 74
Johnson, Lyndon B(aines) obit Mar 73
Jones, E(li) Stanley obit Mar 73
Jones, Howard P(alfrey) obit Nov 73
Jordan, Barbara (Charline) Sep 74
Jordan, B(enjamin) Everett obit May 74
Jordan, Vernon E(ulion), Jr. Feb 72

Kael, Pauline Mar 74
Kahane, Meir (David) Oct 72
Kahn, Ely Jacques obit Nov 72
Kahn, Louis I. obit May 74
Kallen, Horace M(eyer) obit Apr 74
Karinska, Barbara Jan 71
Kästner, Erich obit Oct 74
Katz-Suchy, Juliusz obit Dec 71
Kawabata, Yasunari obit Jun 72
Kazan, Elia Oct 72
Keach, Stacy Nov 71
Keeler, Ruby Dec 71
Kelley, Clarence M(arion) May 74

Kelly, John B(renden), Jr. Jun 71
Kelly, Marvin J(oe) obit May 71
Kelly, Walt(er Crawford) obit Dec 73
Kelsen, Hans obit Jun 73
Kemeny, John G(eorge) Feb 71
Kempton, (James) Murray Jun 73
Kendall, Edward C(alvin) obit Jun 72
Kent, Rockwell obit Apr 71
Kenyatta, Jomo Apr 74
Kenyon, Dorothy obit Apr 72
Kepes, György Mar 73
Khadafy, Muammar See Qaddafi, M. Sep 73
Khrushchev, Nikita S(ergeyevich) obit Oct 71
Kiley, Richard Apr 73
Killanin, Michael Morris, 3d Baron Apr 73
Kincaid, Thomas C(assin) obit Jan 73
King, Carole Jan 74
King, Cecil R(hodes) obit May 74
Kingdon, Frank obit Apr 72
Kirk, William T(albot) obit Mar 74
Kirkpatrick, Miles W(ells) Feb 72
Kirkpatrick, Ralph Sep 71
Kissinger, Henry A(lfred) Jun 72
Klassen, Elmer T(heodore) May 73
Klein, Herbert G(eorge) Feb 71
Kleindienst, Richard G(ordon) Oct 72
Klemperer, Otto obit Sep 73
Knatchbull-Hugessen, Sir Hughe (Montgomery) obit May 71
Knaths, (Otto) Karl obit Apr 71
Knievel, Evel Feb 72
Knowland, William F(ife) obit Apr 74
Knudsen, Semon E(mil) Jan 74
Kohoutek, Lubos Jun 74
Kollek, Teddy Oct 74
Kollmar, Richard obit Feb 71
Konev, Ivan S(tepanovich) obit Jul 73
Kopit, Arthur L(ee) Dec 72
Korbut, Olga Jul 73
Kosinski, Jerzy (Nikodem) Mar 74
Kowalski, Frank, Jr. obit Dec 74
Krasner, Lee Mar 74

Krips, Josef obit Dec 74
Krishna Menon, V(engalil) K(rishnan) obit Nov 74
Krishnamurti, Jiddu Oct 74
Kristofferson, Kris Nov 74
Kristol, Irving (William) Sep 74
Kroc, Ray(mond) A. Mar 73
Krock, Arthur obit Jun 74
Kroll, Jack obit Jul 71
Kroll, Leon obit Dec 74
Krupa, Gene obit Dec 73
Kuhlman, Kathryn Jul 74
Kuiper, Gerard P(eter) obit Feb 74
Kunstler, William M(oses) Apr 71
Kuper, Gerard P(eter) obit Feb 74
Kusner, Kathy Apr 73
Kuusinen, Hertta (Elina) obit May 74
Kuznets, Simon May 72

Lagerkvist, Pär (Fabian) obit Sep 74
Laich, Katherine (Wilhelmina Schlegel) June 72
Laing, R(onald) D(avid) Mar 73
Land, Emory S(cott) obit Jan 72
Landry, Tom Jun 72
Langlois, Henri Jan 73
Lanusse, Alejandro Augustín Apr 73
Larkin, Oliver W(aterman) obit Feb 71
Larson, Leonard W(infield) obit Nov 74
Lash, Joseph P. Dec 72
Latham, Dana obit Apr 74
Lawrence, David obit Apr 73
Lazareff, Pierre obit Jun 72
Leahy, Frank (William) obit Sep 73
Leakey, Louis S(eymour) B(azett) obit Dec 72
Lear, Evelyn Apr 73
Lear, Norman (Milton) Feb 74
Le Carré, John Dec 74
Lee, Sherman E(mery) Jun 74
Leech, Margaret obit Apr 74
Lefèvre, Théo(dore Joseph Albéric Marie) obit Nov 73
Lemass, Seán F(rancis) obit Jun 71
Leone, Giovanni May 72
Leoni, Raúl obit Sep 72
Lescot, Élie obit Dec 74
Levant, Oscar obit Oct 72
Lévi-Strauss, Claude Mar 72
Levin, Yehuda Leib (Ilyich) obit Jan 72

Levine, David Feb 73
Lewis, Henry Feb 73
Lewis, Oscar obit Feb 71
Lewis, Roger Dec 73
Lewis, Wilmarth Sheldon Jul 73
Liebermann, Rolf Sep 73
Liebes, Dorothy (Wright) obit Dec 72
Lifton, Robert Jay Nov 73
Limón, José (Arcadio) obit Jan 73
Lin, Piao obit Oct 72
Lindbergh, Charles A(ugustus, Jr.) obit Oct 74
Link, Edwin (Albert) Jan 74
Lipchitz, Jacques obit Jul 73
Little, Clarence C(ook) obit Feb 72
Liu Shao-chi obit Dec 74
Lloyd, Harold (Clayton) obit Apr 71
Loeb, William Mar 74
Lon Nol Feb 74
Lonergan, Bernard J(oseph) F(rancis) Jan 72
Long, Edward V(aughan) obit Jan 73
Long, Westray See Boyce, W. B. obit Mar 72
Loos, Anita Feb 74
López Bravo, Gregorio Jul 71
López Rodó, Laureano Feb 72
Lord, John Wesley May 71
Lord, Walter Oct 72
Loring, Eugene Mar 72
Loud, Pat Jul 74
Lowdermilk, W(alter) C(lay) obit Jul 74
Lowell, Robert (Traill Spence, Jr.) Jan 72
Lowenstein, Allard K(enneth) Sep 71
Lowrie, Jean E(lizabeth) Jun 73
Lozowick, Louis obit Nov 73
Lübke, Heinrich obit May 72
Lucas, Jerry Jun 72
Ludwig, Christa Mar 71
Lukas, Paul obit Oct 71
Lusk, Georgia L(ee) obit Feb 71
Lynde, Paul (Edward) Nov 72
Lynn, Diana obit Feb 72
Lynn, James T(homas) Dec 73
Lynn, Loretta Oct 73
Lyttelton, Oliver See Chandos, O. L., 1st Viscount obit Mar 72

McCall, Tom (Lawson) Jun 74
McCleery, Albert (Kenny) obit Jul 72
McCloskey, Paul N(orton), Jr. Nov 71

McCormick, Fowler obit Feb 73
McCracken, Robert James obit Apr 73
McDowell, Malcolm Dec 73
McElroy, Neil H(osler) obit Jan 73
McGannon, Donald H(enry) Feb 71
McGee, (Doctor) Frank obit Jun 74
McGill, William J(ames) Jun 71
McGinnis, Patrick B(enedict) obit Apr 73
McGregor, G(ordon) R(oy) obit Apr 71
McGuigan, James (Charles), Cardinal obit Jun 74
McIntire, Carl Oct 71
McKay, Jim Oct 73
McKayle, Donald (Cohen) Jun 71
McKeldin, Theodore R(oosevelt) obit Oct 74
McKenney, Ruth obit Oct 72
McKinney, Frank E(dward) obit Mar 74
McLean, Don May 73
McMahon, William Sep 71
MacMillan, Sir Ernest (Campbell) obit Jun 73
McNair, Barbara Nov 71
McNarney, Joseph T(aggart) obit Mar 72
McNeely, Eugene J(ohnson) obit Feb 74
MacVeagh, Lincoln obit Mar 72
Maddox, William P(ercy) obit Dec 72
Madeira, Jean (Browning) obit Sep 72
Magnani, Anna obit Nov 73
Magruder, William M(arshall) Mar 72
Maharaj Ji, Guru Dec 74
Mahendra, King of Nepal obit Mar 72
Mahesh Yogi, Maharishi Dec 72
Makarova, Natalia Feb 72
Malone, Ross(er) L(ynn, Jr.) obit Oct 74
Malvern Godfrey (Martin) Huggins, 1st Viscount obit Jun 71
Mangrum, Lloyd obit Jan 74
Manna, Charlie obit Dec 71
Manning, Harry obit Oct 74
Manstein, Fritz Erich Von obit Sep 73
Marek, Kurt W. obit Jun 72
Margrethe II, Queen of Denmark Nov 72
Marías, Julián (Aguilera) Feb 72

Marie, André obit Sep 74
Maritain, Jacques obit Jun 73
Marland, Sidney P(ercy), Jr. Apr 72
Marriott, J(ohn) Willard Jun 72
Marshak, Robert E(ugene) Jul 73
Martin, Thomas E(llsworth) obit Sep 71
Marx, Groucho Feb 73
Masson, André Nov 74
Mathias, Charles McC(urdy) Dec 72
Mattson, Henry (Elis) obit Nov 71
Mauch, Gene (William) Dec 74
Maurer, Ion Gheorghe Sep 71
Max, Peter May 71
Maxon, Lou R(ussell) obit Jul 71
May, Rollo (Reece) Jun 73
Mayer, Maria Goeppert obit Apr 72
Mayer, René obit Feb 73
Mazzo, Kay Jul 71
Mead, Sylvia (Alice) Earle May 71
Medeiros, Humberto S(ousa) Nov 71
Médici, Emilio Garrastazú Oct 71
Medina-Sidonia, Duchess of Apr 72
Medvedev, Zhores A(leksandrovich) Nov 73
Mehta, G(aganvihari) L(allubhai) obit Jun 74
Melchior, Lauritz (Lebrecht Hommel) obit May 73
Menuhin, Yehudi May 73
Mercer, Mabel Feb 73
Meskill, Thomas J. Mar 74
Messiaen, Oliver (Eugène Prosper Charles) Feb 74
Meyer, K(arl) F(riedrich) obit Jun 74
Michie, Allan A(ndrew) obit Jan 74
Midler, Bette Jun 73
Miers, Earl Schenck obit Jan 73
Milhaud, Darius obit Sep 74
Miller, Arnold (Ray) Nov 74
Miller, Arthur Feb 73
Miller, Frieda S(egelke) obit Oct 73
Miller, Jason Jan 74
Miller, Johnny Sep 74
Miller, Justin obit Mar 73
Miller, Marvin (Julian) May 73
Miller, Neal (Elgar) Jul 74
Millett, Kate Jan 71
Mingus, Charles Feb 71
Miró, Joan Nov 73

Miró Cardona, José obit Oct 74
Mitchell, Stephen A(rnold) obit Jun 74
Mitford, Jessica (Lucy) Sep 74
Molyneux, Edward H. obit May 74
Monod, Jacques Jul 71
Monroe, Vaughn (Wilton) obit Jul 73
Moore, Marianne (Craig) obit Mar 72
Moore, Mary Tyler Feb 71
Moore, Melba Jan 73
Moorehead, Agnes obit Jun 74
Moorer, Thomas H(inman) Apr 71
Moraes, Frank (Robert) obit Jul 74
Morin, Relman (George) obit Oct 73
Morita, Akio Feb 72
Morón, Alonzo G(raseano) obit Dec 71
Morris, Desmond (John) Nov 74
Morris, Robert Apr 71
Morsch, Lucile M. obit Nov 72
Morse, Wayne (Lyman) obit Sep 74
Morton, Rogers C(lark) B(allard) Nov 71
Moss, Frank E(dward) Dec 71
Mott, C(harles) S(tewart) obit Apr 73
Mowery, Edward J(oseph) obit Feb 71
Muhammad, Elijah Jan 71
Mujibur Rahman, Sheik See Rahman, Sheik Mujibur Jan 73
Mundt, Karl E(arl) obit Oct 74
Munro, Leslie Knox obit Apr 74
Murayama, Makio Oct 74
Murphy, Franklin D(avid) Mar 71
Murphy, Patrick V(incent) Nov 72
Murray, Dwight H(arrison) obit Nov 74
Murray, T(h)om(as Jefferson) obit Jan 72

Nabarro, Sir Gerald obit Jan 74
Naish, J. Carrol obit Mar 73
Nash, Ogden obit Jul 71
Nastase, Ilie Oct 74
Nearing, Scott Oct 71
Neill, A(lexander) S(utherland) obit Nov 73
Neruda, Pablo obit Nov 73
Nevins, Allan obit Apr 71
Ne Win Apr 71
Newton, Huey P(ercy) Feb 73

Nichols, Roy Franklin obit Mar 73
Nicholson, Jack Oct 74
Nidetch, Jean Dec 73
Niebuhr, Reinhold obit Jul 71
Nkrumah, Kwame obit Jun 72
Noguès, Auguste (Paul) obit Jun 71
Noland, Kenneth (Clifton) Sep 72
Nolde, O(tto) Frederick obit Sep 72
Norell, Norman obit Dec 72
Nourse, Edwin G(riswold) obit Jun 74
Nye, Gerald P(rentice) obit Sep 71

O'Boyle, Patrick (Aloysius) Cardinal Jul 73
O'Connor, Basil obit May 72
O'Connor, Carroll Jul 72
Odishaw, Hugh Feb 71
O'Donnell, Emmett, Jr. obit Feb 71
Odria (Amoretti), Manuel A(polinario) obit Apr 74
Oistrakh, David (Fyodorovich) obit Dec 74
Oliver, Lyttelton See Chando, O. L., 1st Viscount Mar 72
O'Neal, Ryan Feb 73
O'Neill, Thomas P(hilip), Jr. Apr 74
Ono, Yoko Nov 72
Orr, John Boyd See Boyd Orr, John Boyd Orr, 1st Baron obit Sep 71
Otto, Frei (Paul) Oct 71
Owings, Nathaniel A(lexander) May 71
Ozbirn, Mrs. E. Lee obit Mar 74

Pacino, Al(fred) Jul 74
Packard, Eleanor obit Jun 72
Padilla, Ezequial obit Oct 71
Pagnol, Marcel (Paul) obit Jun 74
Paisley, Ian (Richard Kyle) Jan 71
Panov, Valery Oct 74
Park, Merle Sep 74
Parks, Bert Feb 73
Parsons, Louella obit Jan 73
Partch, Harry obit Oct 74
Pastrana Borrero, Misael Jul 71
Pate, Walter L(acey) obit Jun 74
Paul-Boncour, Joseph obit May 72
Pavarotti, Luciano Jun 73
Paxinou, Katina obit Apr 73
Payson, Joan Whitney Jul 72
Paz, Octavio Jun 74

Peale, Mundy I(ngalls) obit Jan 73
Peale, Norman Vincent Oct 74
Pearlstein, Philip Feb 73
Pearson, Lester Bowles obit Feb 73
Peckinpah, Sam May 73
Pell, Claiborne (deBorda) Mar 72
Penderecki, Krzysztof Jun 71
Penn, Arthur (Hiller) Jan 72
Penney, J(ames) C(ash) obit Mar 71
Pepitone, Joe Jan 73
Pereira, I(rene) Rice obit Feb 71
Perelman, S(idney) J(oseph) Mar 71
Perón (Sosa), Juan (Domingo) Feb 74 obit Sep 74
Perot, H(enry) Ross Jul 71
Perry, Frank Oct 72
Peterson, Peter G(eorge) Jun 72
Phillips, Irna obit Feb 74
Picasso, Pablo obit May 73
Pinochet Ugarte, Augusto Dec 74
Plunkett, Jim Sep 71
Polyansky, Dmitry S(tepanovich) Mar 71
Pomeroy, Wardell B(axter) Jul 74
Pompidou, Georges (Jean Raymond) obit May 74
Poor, Henry Varnum obit Jan 71
Pope, Liston obit Jun 74
Popovic, Vladimir obit May 72
Portal of Hungerford, Charles Frederick Algernon Portal, 1st Viscount obit Jun 71
Porter, William J(ames) Mar 74
Porter, William N(ichols) obit Apr 73
Pound, Ezra (Loomis) obit Dec 72
Poussaint, Alvin F(rancis) Jul 73
Powell, Adam Clayton, Jr. obit May 72
Powell, Jane Dec 74
Power, Thomas S(arsfield) obit Jan 71
Powers, Bertram (Anthony) Jan 74
Powers, Marie obit Feb 74
Prescott, Robert W(illiam) Jul 71
Previn, André (George) May 72
Prince, Harold Apr 71
Pritchett, V(ictor) S(awdon) Jan 74
Prouty, Winston L(ewis) obit Oct 71

Qaddafi, Muammar el- Sep 73
Quayle, Anthony Dec 71
Queler, Eve Jul 72

Rabe, David Jul 73
Rabin, Yitzhak Sep 74
Radford, Arthur W(illiam) obit Oct 73
Rahman, Sheik Mujibur Jan 73
Rajagopalachari, Chakravarti obit Feb 73
Rakosi, Matyas obit Mar 71
Raman, Sir (Chandrasekhara) Venkata obit Jan 71
Ramspeck, Robert (C. Word) obit Dec 72
Rance, Sir Hubert Elvin obit Mar 74
Ranganathan, S(hiyali) R(am-amrita) obit Dec 72
Rank, Joseph Arthur Rank, 1st Baron obit May 72
Ransom, John Crowe obit Sep 74
Ravdin, I(sidor) S(chwaner) obit Oct 72
Ray, Dixy Lee Jun 73
Reading, Stella (Charnaud Isaacs), Marchioness of obit Jul 71
Reardon, John (Robert) Nov 74
Reber, Samuel obit Feb 72
Redford, Robert Apr 71
Reed, Rex Jan 72
Reed, Willis Jan 73
Reese, Della Sep 71
Rehnquist, William H(ubbs) Apr 72
Reich, Charles A(lan) Jun 72
Reith, John Charles Walsham, 1st Baron obit Jul 71
Reynolds, Burt Oct 73
Rhys, Jean Dec 72
Riad, Mahmoud Nov 71
Rich, Buddy Jun 73
Richards, Dickinson W(oodruff) obit Apr 73
Richards, I(vor) A(rmstrong) Dec 72
Richardson, Elliot L(ee) Mar 71
Rickenbacker, Edward Vernon obit Oct 73
Riefler, Winfield W(illiam) obit Jun 74
Rigg, Diana Oct 74
Righter, Carroll Oct 72
Riklis, Meshulam Dec 71
Riles, Wilson (Camanza) Dec 71
Rinfret, Pierre A(ndré) Jul 72
Ritter, Thelma obit Feb 74 (died Feb 69)

Rivers, L(ucius) Mendel obit Feb 71
Rizzo, Frank L(azarro) Mar 73
Roa(y García), Raúl Nov 73
Robbe-Grillet, Alain Dec 74
Robertson, A. Willis obit Dec 71
Robertson, Sir Brian (Hubert) obit Jun 74
Robey, Ralph W(est) obit Sep 72
Robinson, Brooks Sep 73
Robinson, Edward G. obit Mar 73
Robinson, Frank Jun 71
Robinson, Jackie obit Dec 72
Rockefeller, Winthrop obit Apr 73
Rogers, Fred M(cFeely) Jul 71
Romnes, H(aakon) I(ngolf) obit Jan 74
Rooth, Ivar obit Apr 72
Roper, Elmo (Burns, Jr.) obit Jun 71
Rosen, Samuel Feb 74
Rosenman, Samuel I(rving) obit Sep 73
Ross, Diana Mar 73
Rosset, Barnet (Lee, Jr.) Apr 72
Rothschild, Guy (Edouard Alphonse Paul), Baron de Mar 73
Royall, Kenneth C(laiborne) obit Sep 71
Ruckelshaus, William D(oyle) Jul 71
Rudolph, Paul (Marvin) Feb 72
Ruiz Cortines, Adolfo obit Jan 74
Russell, Richard B(revard, Jr.) obit Mar 71
Rutherford, Dame Margaret obit Jul 72
Ryan, Robert (Bushnell) obit Sep 73
Ryan, William F(itts) obit Dec 72
Ryle, Sir Martin Sep 73

Saarinen, Aline B(ernstein Louchheim) obit Sep 72
Sadat, Anwar (el-) Mar 71
Safire, William (L.) Dec 73
St. Laurent, Louis S(tephen) obit Oct 73
Sakharov, Andrei D(mitriyevich) Jul 71
Salisbury, Robert Arthur Cecil, 5th Marquis obit Apr 72
Samaras, Lucas Nov 72
Sanders, George obit Jun 72
Sanders, Harland Apr 73

Santos, Rufino J(iao), Cardinal obit Nov 73
Sardiña, Adolfo See Adolfo Nov 72
Sargent, Francis W(illiams) Jun 71
Sarnoff, David obit Feb 72
Saroyan, William Nov 72
Sartre, Jean-Paul May 71
Saul, Ralph S(outhy) Feb 71
Saund, Dalip S(ingh) obit Jun 73
Saunders, Carl M(axon) obit Nov 74
Saxbe, William B(art) Jul 74
Sayre, Francis B(owes) obit May 72
Scali, John (Alfred) Sep 73
Scammon, Richard M(ontgomery) Mar 71
Scheel, Walter Feb 71
Schiaparelli, Elsa obit Jan 74
Schiller, Karl (August Fritz) Dec 71
Schiotz, Fredrik A(xel) Apr 72
Schlesinger, James R(odney) Oct 73
Schmidt, Helmut (Heinrich Waldemar) Oct 74
Schmitt, Gladys (Leonore) obit Dec 72
Schmitt, Harrison H(agan) Jul 74
Schneiderman, Rose obit Oct 72
Schranz, Karl Jan 71
Schuster, M(ax) Lincoln obit Feb 71
Scott, David R(andolph) Oct 71
Scott, George C(ampbell) Apr 71
Scott, Sheila Nov 74
Scull, Robert C. Apr 74
Seagren, Bob Jun 74
Seaton, Fred(erick) A(ndrew) obit Mar 74
Seferis, George See Sepheriades, G. S. obit Nov 71
Segal, Erich (Wolf) Apr 71
Segal, George Jan 72
Segni, Antonio obit Jan 73
Selden, David (Seeley) Jul 74
Senanayake, Dudley (Shelton) obit Jun 73
Senior, Clarence (Ollson) obit Nov 74
Sepheriades, Georgios S(tylianou) obit Nov 71
Serlin, Oscar obit Apr 71
Sert, José Luis Apr 74
Shapley, Harlow obit Dec 72
Shapp, Milton J(errold) Jul 73
Shaw, Ralph R(obert) obit Dec 72

Shawn, Ted obit Feb 72
Shazar, (Shenor) Zalman obit Nov 74
Shea, Andrew B(ernard) obit Jan 73
Shelepin, Aleksandr (Nikolaevich) Feb 71
Sherman, Allan obit Jan 74
Shikler, Aaron (A.) Dec 71
Short, Bobby Jul 72
Shula, Don Mar 74
Shumway, Norman E(dward) Apr 71
Shvernik, Nikolai (Mikhailovich) obit Feb 71
Sikorsky, Igor I(van) obit Dec 72
Simon, William E(dward) Apr 74
Simonds, G(uy) G(ranville) obit Jul 74
Simons, Hans obit May 72
Singh, (Sardar) Swaran Mar 71
Siqueiros, (José) David Alfaro obit Feb 74
Sirica, John J(oseph) May 74
Siroky, Viliam obit Nov 71
Sisco, Joseph J(ohn) Jan 72
Skouras, Spyros P(anagiotes) obit Nov 71
Slim, William Joseph Slim, Viscount obit Feb 71
Sloane, Eric Sep 72
Smallens, Alexander obit Jan 73
Smallwood, Robert B(artly) obit Sep 74
Smith, Betty obit Mar 72
Smith, Chesterfield H(arvey) Nov 74
Smith, Hazel Brannon Sep 73
Smith, (Oliver) Harrison obit Feb 71
Smith, William Jay Mar 74
Snow, Edgar (Parks) obit Apr 72
Sobeloff, Simon E(rnest) obit Sep 73
Solandt, Omond M(cKillop) Mar 74
Soleri, Paolo Feb 72
Sondheim, Stephen (Joshua) Nov 73
Soong, T. V. obit Jun 71
Souers, Sidney W(illiam) obit Mar 73
Soyer, Moses obit Oct 74
Soyinka, Wole Dec 74
Spaak, Paul-Henri obit Oct 72
Spaatz, Carl obit Sep 74
Spassky, Boris (Vasilyevich) Nov 72
Spectorsky, A(uguste) C(omte) obit Mar 72

Spingarn, Arthur B(arnett) obit Jan 72
Spínola, António (Sebastião Ribeiro) de Sep 74
Spitz, Mark (Andrew) Oct 72
Staggers, Harley O(rrin) Mar 71
Stanley, W(endell) M(eredith) obit Sep 71
Stapleton, Jean Dec 72
Stark, Harold Raynsford obit Oct 72
Staubach, Roger (Thomas) Apr 72
Steichen, Edward obit May 73
Stein, Herbert Mar 73
Steinem, Gloria Mar 72
Steiner, Max(imilian Raoul) obit Feb 72
Steinfeld, Jesse L(eonard) Apr 74
Steinkraus, Herman W(illiam) obit Jul 74
Stella, Frank (Philip) Apr 71
Stern, Bill obit Jan 72
Stevenson, Adlai E(wing), 3d Apr 74
Stewart, Ellen Jun 73
Stewart, Thomas (James) May 74
Still, Clyfford Sep 71
Stockhausen, Karlheinz Dec 71
Stone, I(sidor) F(einstein) Sep 72
Stone, W. Clement Feb 72
Stoppard, Tom Jul 74
Storey, David Sep 73
Stout, Wesley Winans obit Jan 72
Strang, Ruth (May) obit Feb 71
Strasser, Otto (Johann Maximilian) obit Oct 74
Strauss, Lewis L(ichtenstein) obit Mar 74
Strauss, Robert S(chwarz) Mar 74
Stravinsky, Igor (Fëdorovich) obit May 71
Strong, Maurice, F(rederick) Dec 73
Struthers, Sally (Ann) Jan 74
Stump, Felix B(udwell) obit Sep 72
Sullivan, Ed(ward Vincent) obit Nov 74
Summerfield, Arthur E(llsworth) obit Jun 72
Sun Fo obit Dec 73
Susann, Jacqueline May 72 obit Nov 74
Sutton, Percy (Ellis) Mar 73
Switzer, Mary E(lizabeth) obit Dec 71
Szigeti, Joseph obit Apr 73

Talal obit Sep 72
Talese, Gay Jul 72
Tamm, Igor (Evgenyevich) obit Jun 71
Tanaka, Kakuei Dec 72
Taylor, George W(illiam) obit Feb 73
Taylor, James Jun 72
Tead, Ordway obit Jan 74
Tello (Baurraud), Manuel obit Jan 72
Teresa, Mother Sep 73
Terkel, Studs Nov 74
Tetley, Glen Jun 73
Theiler, Max obit Oct 72
Thekaekara, Matthew P(othen) May 74
Theodorakis, Mikis Jul 73
Thomas, J(ohn) Parnell obit Jan 71
Thomas, Michael Tilson May 71
Thompson, Llewellyn, E., Jr. obit Mar 72
Thompson, Sada Mar 73
Thorpe, (John) Jeremy Oct 74
Tijerina, Reies Lopez Jul 71
Tippett, Sir Michael (Kemp) Sep 74
Tiselius, Arne (Wilhelm Kaurin) obit Dec 71
Tisserant, Eugène, Cardinal obit Apr 72
Tolbert, William R(ichard), Jr. Mar 74
Tolkien, J(ohn) R(onald) R(euel) obit Nov 73
Tomlin, Lily Sep 73
Tong, Hollington K(ong) obit Feb 71
Torre, Joe May 72
Torres Bodet, Jaime obit Jul 74
Torrijos Herrera, Omar Jul 73
Tourel, Jennie obit Jan 74
Trammell, Niles obit May 73
Trampler, Walter Nov 71
Traubel, Helen obit Oct 72
Tregaskis, Richard obit Oct 73
Trenkler, Freddie Jun 71
Trevino, Lee (Buck) Nov 71
Truex, Ernest obit Sep 73
Truman, David B(icknell) Jan 72
Truman, Harry S. obit Feb 73
Trussell, Ray E(lbert) Jan 71
Tsaldaris, Constantin obit Jan 71
Tubman, William V(acanarat) S(hadrach) obit Sep 71
Tunney, John V(arick) Jun 71
Turcotte, Ron Nov 74
Tvardovsky, Alexandr T(rifonovich) May 71 obit Feb 72

Ulbricht, Walter obit Oct 73
Ullman, James R(amsey) obit Sep 71
Ullmann, Liv Dec 73
Unden, Bo Osten obit Apr 74

Valentino Nov 73
Vandegrift, Alexander Archer obit Jun 73
Vanderbilt, Gloria Jul 72
Van Doren, Mark obit Feb 73
Van Slyke, Donald D(exter) obit Jul 71
Van Waters, Miriam obit Apr 74
Vasarely, Victor Feb 71
Vilar, Jean (Louis Côme) obit Sep 71
Villemure, Gilles Apr 74
Voight, Jon Apr 74
Volcker, Paul A(dolph) Jul 73
Von Békésy, George See Békésy, George von obit Sep 72
Von Frisch, Karl Feb 74 See Frisch, Karl von
Voorhees, Tracy S(tebbins) obit Nov 74

Waksman, Selman A(braham) obit Oct 73
Waldheim, Kurt May 72
Walker, Ralph (Thomas) obit Mar 73
Walters, Barbara Feb 71
Wangchuk, Jigme Dorji, Druk Gyalpo of Bhutan obit Sep 72
Warren, Earl obit Sep 74
Watkins, Arthur V(ivian) obit Dec 73
Watson, Arthur K(ittredge) Sep 71 obit Oct 74
Watson-Watt, Sir Robert (Alexander) obit Jan 74
Watts, Alan obit Jan 74
Wayne, John Jul 72

Webster, Margaret obit Jan 73
Webster, William obit Jul 72
Weede, Robert obit Sep 72
Weeks, Sinclair obit Mar 72
Weicker, Lowell P(almer) Jr. Jan 74
Weinberger, Caspar W(illard) Jun 73
Weisgal, Meyer W(olf) Oct 72
Weiskopf, Tom Nov 73
Welch, Raquel May 71
Weld, Tuesday Jul 74
Wendt, Gerald Louis obit Feb 74
Wheeler, Raymond A(lbert) obit Apr 74
Whitaker, Douglas (Merritt) obit Dec 73
White, Kevin H(agan) Dec 74
White, Margaret Bourke See Bourke-White, M. obit Oct 71
White, Patrick (Victor Martindale) Jun 74
White, Paul Dudley obit Dec 73
White, William L(indsay) obit Oct 73
Whitlam, (Edward) Gough Jan 74
Whitman, Marina von Neumann Oct 73
Whitman, Walter G(ordon) obit Jun 74
Whittaker, Charles Evans obit Jan 74
Wicker, Tom Nov 73
Wigman, Mary obit Nov 73
Wilder, Thornton (Niven) Nov 71
Wilhelm, (James) Hoyt Jul 71
Williams, Dick Dec 73
Williams, Tennessee Apr 72
Wilson, Charles E(dward) obit Feb 72
Wilson, (Charles) Kemmons Sep 73
Wilson, (Charles) Malcolm May 74

Wilson, Edmund obit Jul 72
Wilson, J(ohn) Tuzo Apr 73
Wilson, Joseph C(hamberlain) obit Jan 72
Wilson, O(rlando) W(infield) obit Dec 72
Winchell, Walter obit Apr 72
Windsor, Duke of obit Jul 72
Wiseman, Frederick Dec 74
Wodehouse, P(elham) G(renville) Nov 71
Wolfe, Tom Jan 71
Wood, Robert D(ennis) Dec 74
Woods, Bill M(ilton) obit Sep 74
Woods, Tighe E(dward) obit Sep 74
Wuorinen, Charles (Peter) Apr 72
Wurster, William Wilson obit Nov 73
Wynder, Ernest L(udwig) Nov 74

Yahya Khan A(gha) M(uhammad) Jan 71
Youlou, Fulbert obit Jun 72
Young, Marian obit Jan 74
Young, Whitney M(oore), Jr. obit Apr 71

Zabaleta, Nicanor Jun 71
Zerbe, Karl obit Jan 73
Zhukov, Georgi K(onstantinovich) obit Sep 74
Ziegler, Ronald L(ewis) Nov 71
Zindel, Paul Jun 73
Zirato, Bruno obit Jan 73
Zuckerman, Lord Jul 72
Zuckerman, Sir Solly See Zuckerman, Lord Jul 72
Zumwalt, E(lmo) R(ussell), Jr. Jun 71
Zwicky, Fritz obit Apr 74